Common Abbreviations Used in the Text

Greek Letters	η	(eta)	Elasticity
	Δ	(delta)	Change in

Abbreviations

Microeconomics

ATC	Average Total Cost
AVC	Average Variable Cost
D	Demand
i	Interest Rate
$LRAC$	Long-Run Average Cost
MC	Marginal Cost
MP	Marginal Product
MR	Marginal Revenue
MRP	Marginal Revenue Product
S	Supply
TC	Total Cost
TR	Total Revenue

Macroeconomics

AD	Aggregate Demand
AS	Aggregate Supply
AE	(Desired) Aggregate Expenditure
C	Aggregate Consumption Expenditure
CPI	Consumer Price Index
G	Government Purchases
GDP	Gross Domestic Product
GNP	Gross National Product
I	Aggregate Investment Expenditure
i	Nominal Interest Rate
IM	Imports of Goods and Services
M_S, M_D	Money Supply/Money Demand
$M1, M2, M2+$	Measures of Money Supply
P	Price Level
r	Real Interest Rate
S	Private Saving
T	Government Tax Revenue (Net of Transfers)
U	Unemployment Rate
U^*	Natural Rate of Unemployment (NAIRU)
X	Exports of Goods and Services
$X\text{-}IM$ or NX	Net Exports of Goods and Services
Y	Real GDP
Y^*	Potential GDP
Y_D	Disposable Income

ECONOMICS

FOURTEENTH CANADIAN EDITION

CHRISTOPHER T.S. RAGAN

McGILL UNIVERSITY

PEARSON

Toronto

Vice-President, Editorial Director: Gary Bennett
Editor-in-Chief: Nicole Lukach
Acquisitions Editor: Claudine O'Donnell
Marketing Manager: Leigh-Anne Graham
Developmental Editor: Suzanne Schaan
Project Manager: Andrea Falkenberg
Production Editor: Melinda Durham
Project Coordination and Editorial Services: Electronic Publishing Services Inc., NYC
Art Rendering and Electronic Page Makeup: Jouve
Copy Editor: Linda Jenkins
Proofreader: Megan Smith-Creed
Photo Researcher: Marta Johnson
Permissions Researcher: Marnie Lamb
Art Director: Julia Hall
Interior Designer: Opushouse Inc./Sonya Thursby
Cover Designer: Miriam Blier
Cover Image: Steve McDonald

---

10 9 8 7 6 5 4 3 2 1 [CKV]

Library and Archives Canada Cataloguing in Publication

Ragan, Christopher
  Economics / Christopher T.S. Ragan. — 14th Canadian ed.

Includes index.
ISBN 978-0-321-72878-4

1. Economics—Textbooks. 2. Economics—Canada—Textbooks. I. Title.

HB171.5.R35 2013   330   C2012-906725-3

ISBN 978-0321-72878-4

Brief Contents

Contents

List of Boxes

Extensions in Theory

Additional Topics on MyEconLab (www.myeconlab.com)

To the Instructor

Economics is a living discipline, changing and evolving in response to developments in the world economy and in response to the research of many thousands of economists throughout the world. Through fourteen editions, *Economics* has evolved with the discipline. Our purpose in this edition, as in the previous thirteen, is to provide students with an introduction to the major issues facing the world's economies, to the methods that economists use to study those issues, and to the policy problems that those issues create. Our treatment is everywhere guided by three important principles:

1. Economics is *scientific*, in the sense that it progresses through the systematic confrontation of theory by evidence. Neither theory nor data alone can tell us much about the world, but combined they tell us a great deal.

2. Economics is *useful*, and it should be seen by students to be so. An understanding of economic theory combined with knowledge about the economy produces many important insights about economic policy. Although we stress these insights, we are also careful to point out cases in which too little is known to support strong statements about public policy. Appreciating what is not known is as important as learning what is known.

3. We strive always to be *honest* with our readers. Although we know that economics is not always easy, we do not approve of glossing over difficult bits of analysis without letting readers see what is happening and what has been assumed. We take whatever space is needed to explain why economists draw their conclusions, rather than just asserting the conclusions. We also take pains to avoid simplifying matters so much that students would have to unlearn what they have been taught if they continue their study beyond the introductory course. In short, we have tried to follow Albert Einstein's advice:

Everything should be made as simple as possible, but not simpler.

Current Economic Issues

In writing the fourteenth edition of *Economics*, we have tried to reflect the major economic issues that we face in the early twenty-first century.

Living Standards and Economic Growth

One of the most fundamental economic issues is the determination of overall living standards. Adam Smith wondered why some countries become wealthy while others remain poor. Though we have learned much about this topic in the past 240 years since Adam Smith's landmark work, economists recognize that there is still much we do not know.

The importance of technological change in determining increases in overall living standards is a theme that permeates both the microeconomics and macroeconomics halves of this book. Chapter 8 explores how firms deal with technological change at the micro level, and how changes in their economic environment lead them to create new products and new production processes. Chapters 11 and 12 discuss how imperfectly competitive firms often compete through their innovative practices, and the importance for policymakers of designing competition policy to keep these practices as energetic as possible.

Technological change also plays a central role in our discussions of long-run economic growth in Chapters 25 and 26. We explore not only the traditional channels of saving, investment, and population growth, but also the more recent economic theories that emphasize the importance of increasing returns and endogenous growth.

We are convinced that no other introductory economics textbook places as much emphasis on technological change and economic growth as we do in this book. Given the importance of continuing growth in living standards and understanding where that growth comes from, we believe this emphasis is appropriate. We hope you agree.

Financial Crisis, Recession, and Recovery

The collapse of U.S. housing prices in 2007 led to a global financial crisis the likes of which had not been witnessed in a century, and perhaps longer. A deep recession, experienced in many countries, followed quickly on its heels. These dramatic events re-awakened many people to two essential facts about economics. First, modern economies *can and do* go into recession. This essential fact had perhaps been forgotten by many who had become complacent after more than two decades of economic prosperity. Second, financial markets are crucial to the operation of modern economies. Like an electricity system, the details of financial markets are a mystery to most people, and the system itself is often ignored when it is functioning properly. But when financial markets cease to work smoothly and interest rates rise while credit flows decline, we are all reminded of their importance. In this sense, the financial crisis of 2007–2008 was like a global power failure for the world economy.

The financial crisis had micro causes and macro consequences. The challenges of appropriate regulation for financial and nonfinancial firms are explored in Chapters 12 and 16. The market for financial capital and the determination of interest rates are examined in Chapter 15. And debates regarding the appropriate role of the government in a market economy occur throughout the book, including in Chapters 1, 5, 16, and 18.

On the macro side, the financial crisis affected the Canadian banking system, as discussed in Chapter 27, and led to some aggressive actions by the Bank of Canada, as discussed in Chapter 29. Moreover, as the global financial crisis led to a deep recession worldwide, Canadian fiscal policy was forced to respond, as we review in Chapters 24 and 32. Finally, as has happened several times throughout history, the recession raised the threat of protectionist policies, as we examine in Chapter 34.

Globalization

Enormous changes have occurred throughout the world over the last few decades. Flows of trade and investment between countries have risen so dramatically that it is now common to speak of the "globalization" of the world economy. Today it is no longer possible to study any economy without taking into account developments in the rest of the world.

Throughout its history, Canada has been a trading nation, and our policies relating to international trade have often been at the centre of political debates. International trade shows up in many parts of this textbook, but it is the exclusive focus of two chapters. Chapter 33 discusses the theory of the gains from trade; Chapter 34 explores trade policy, with an emphasis on NAFTA and the WTO.

With globalization and the international trade of goods and assets come fluctuations in exchange rates. In recent years there have been substantial changes in the Canada–U.S. exchange rate—a 15-percent depreciation followed the Asian economic crisis in 1997–1998, and an even greater appreciation occurred in the 2002–2008 period. Such volatility in exchange rates complicates the conduct of economic policy. In Chapters 28 and 29 we explore how the exchange rate fits into the design and operation of Canada's monetary policy. In Chapter 35 we examine the debate between fixed and flexible exchange rates.

The forces of globalization are with us to stay. In this fourteenth edition of *Economics*, we have done our best to ensure that students are made aware of the world outside Canada and how events elsewhere in the world affect the Canadian economy.

The Role of Government

Between 1980 and 2008, the political winds shifted in Canada, the United States, and many other countries. Political parties that previously advocated a greater role for government in the economy argued the benefits of limited government. But the political winds shifted again with the arrival of the financial crisis and global recession in 2008, which led governments the world over to take some unprecedented actions. Many soon argued that we were observing the "end of laissez-faire" and witnessing the return of "big government." But was that really true?

Has the *fundamental* role of government changed significantly over the past 35 years? In order to understand the role of government in the economy, students must understand the benefits of free markets as well as the situations that cause markets to fail. They must also understand that governments often intervene in the economy for reasons related more to equity than to efficiency.

In this fourteenth edition of *Economics*, we continue to incorporate the discussion of government policy as often as possible. Here are but a few of the many examples that we explore:

- tax incidence (in Chapter 4)
- the effects of minimum wages and rent controls (in Chapter 5)

- economic regulation and competition policy (in Chapter 12)
- pay equity policy (in Chapter 13)
- environmental policies (in Chapter 17)
- the disincentive effects of income taxes (in Chapter 18)
- fiscal policy (in Chapters 22 and 24)
- policies related to the economy's long-run growth rate (in Chapter 26)
- monetary policy (in Chapters 28, 29, and 30)
- policies that affect the economy's long-run unemployment rate (in Chapter 31)
- the importance of debt and deficits (in Chapter 32)
- trade policies (in Chapter 34)
- policies related to the exchange rate (in Chapter 35)

The Book

Economic growth, financial crisis and recession, globalization, and the role of government are pressing issues of the day. Much of our study of economic principles and the Canadian economy has been shaped by these issues. In addition to specific coverage of growth and internationally oriented topics, growth and globalization appear naturally throughout the book in the treatment of many topics once thought to be entirely "domestic."

Most chapters of *Economics* contain some discussion of economic policy. We have two main goals in mind when we present these discussions:

1. We aim to give students practice in using economic theory, because applying theory is both a wonderfully effective teaching method and a reliable test of students' grasp of theory.

2. We want to introduce students to the major policy issues of the day and to let them discover that few policy debates are as "black and white" as they often appear in the press.

Both goals reflect our view that students should see economics as useful in helping us to understand and deal with the world around us.

The choice of whether to study macro first or micro first is partly a personal one that cannot be decided solely by objective criteria. We believe that there are excellent reasons for preferring the micro–macro order, and we have organized the book accordingly. For those who prefer the macro–micro order, we have attempted to make reversibility easy. The first three chapters provide a solid foundation whether you choose to first introduce microeconomics (Chapters 4–18) or macroeconomics (Chapters 19–35).

Microeconomics: Structure and Coverage

To open Part 1, Chapter 1 begins with an informal presentation of six major issues of the day. We then introduce scarcity and choice, and this leads to a discussion of the market as a coordinating device. Finally, we turn to alternative economic systems. Comparisons with command economies help to establish what a market economy is *by showing what it is not*. The Appendix to Chapter 1 provides a useful refresher on graphing. Chapter 2 makes the important distinction between positive and normative inquiries and goes on to an introductory discussion of the construction and testing of economic theories.

Part 2 deals with demand and supply. After introducing price determination and elasticity in Chapters 3 and 4, we apply these tools in Chapter 5. The case studies are designed to provide practice in applying the tools rather than to give full coverage of each case presented. Chapter 5 also has an intuitive and thorough treatment of economic value and market efficiency.

Part 3 presents the foundations of demand and supply. The theory of consumer behaviour is developed via marginal utility theory in Chapter 6, which also provides an introduction to consumer surplus and an intuitive discussion of income and substitution effects. The Appendix to Chapter 6 covers indifference curves, budget lines, and the derivation of demand curves using indifference theory. Chapter 7 introduces the firm as an institution and develops short-run costs. Chapter 8 covers long-run costs and the principle of substitution and goes on to consider shifts in cost curves due to technological change. The latter topic is seldom if ever covered in the micro part of elementary textbooks, yet applied work on firms' responses to changing economic signals shows it to be extremely important.

The first two chapters of Part 4, Chapters 9 and 10, present the standard theories of perfect competition and monopoly with a thorough discussion of price discrimination and some treatment of international cartels. Chapter 11 deals with monopolistic competition and oligopoly, which are the market structures most commonly found in Canadian industries. Strategic behaviour plays a central part in the analysis of this chapter. The first half of Chapter 12 deals with the efficiency of competition and the in-efficiency of monopoly. The last half of the chapter deals with regulation and competition policy.

Part 5 begins with Chapter 13, which discusses the general principles of factor pricing and how factor prices are influenced by factor mobility. Chapter 14 then examines the operation of labour markets, addressing issues such as wage differentials, discrimination, labour unions, and the "good jobs–bad jobs" debate. Chapter 15 discusses investment in physical capital, the role of the interest rate, and the overall functioning of capital markets.

The first chapter of Part 6 (Chapter 16) provides a general discussion of market success and market failure and outlines the arguments for and against government intervention in a market economy. Chapter 17 deals with environmental regulation, with a detailed discussion of market-based policies and an introduction to the issue of global climate change. Chapter 18 analyzes taxes, public expenditure, and the main elements of Canadian social policy. These three chapters expand on the basics of microeconomic analysis by providing current illustrations of the relevance of economic theory to contemporary policy situations.

Macroeconomics: Structure and Coverage

Our treatment of macroeconomics is divided into six parts. We make a clear distinction between the economy in the short run and the economy in the long run, and we get quickly to the material on long-run economic growth. Students are confronted with issues of long-run economic growth *before* they are introduced to issues of money and banking. Given the importance of economic growth in driving overall living standards, we believe that this is an appropriate ordering of the material, but for those who prefer to discuss money before thinking about economic growth, the order can be easily switched without any loss of continuity.

The first macro chapter, Chapter 19, introduces readers to the central macro variables, what they mean, and why they are important. The discussion of national income accounting in Chapter 20 provides a thorough treatment of the distinction between real and nominal GDP, the distinction between GDP and GNP, and a discussion of what measures of national income *do not measure* and whether these omissions really matter.

Part 8 develops the core short-run model of the macro economy, beginning with the fixed-price

(Keynesian Cross) model in Chapters 21 and 22 and then moving on to the *AD/AS* model in Chapter 23. Chapter 21 uses a closed economy model with no government to explain the process of national-income determination and the nature of the multiplier. Chapter 22 extends the setting to include international trade and government spending and taxation. Chapter 23 rounds out our discussion of the short run with the *AD/AS* framework, discussing the importance of both aggregate demand and aggregate supply shocks. We place the Keynesian Cross before the *AD/AS* model to show that there is no mystery about where the *AD* curve comes from and why it is downward sloping; the *AD* curve is derived directly from the Keynesian Cross model. In contrast, books that begin their analysis with the *AD/AS* model are inevitably less clear about where the model comes from. We lament the growing tendency to omit the Keynesian Cross from introductory macroeconomics textbooks; we believe the model has much to offer students in terms of economic insights.

Part 9 begins in Chapter 24 by showing how the short-run model evolves toward the long run through the adjustment of factor prices—what we often call the Phillips curve. We introduce potential output as an "anchor" to which real GDP returns following *AD* or *AS* shocks. This chapter also addresses issues in fiscal policy, including the important distinction between automatic stabilizers and discretionary fiscal stabilization policy. Chapter 25 is a short chapter that contrasts short-run with long-run macroeconomics, emphasizing the different typical causes of output changes over the two time spans. Using Canadian data, we show that long-run changes in GDP have their root causes in changes in factor supplies and productivity, whereas short-run changes in GDP are more closely associated with changes in the factor utilization rate. With this short-run/long-run distinction firmly in place, we are well positioned for the detailed discussion of long-run economic growth that appears in Chapter 26. Our treatment of long-run growth, which we regard as one of the most important issues facing Canada and the world today, goes well beyond the treatment in most introductory texts.

Part 10 focuses on the role of money and financial systems. Chapter 27 discusses the nature of money, various components of the money supply, the commercial banking system, and the Bank of Canada. In Chapter 28 we offer a detailed discussion of the link between the money market and other economic variables such as interest rates, the exchange rate, national income, and the price level. In Chapter 29 we discuss the Bank of Canada's monetary policy, including a detailed discussion of inflation targeting. The chapter ends with a review of Canadian monetary policy over the past 30 years.

Part 11 deals with some of today's most pressing macroeconomic policy issues. It contains separate chapters on inflation, unemployment, and government budget deficits. Chapter 30 on inflation examines the central role of expectations in determining inflation and the importance of credibility on the part of the central bank. Chapter 31 on unemployment examines the determinants of frictional and structural unemployment and discusses likely reasons for increases in the NAIRU over the past few decades. Chapter 32 on budget deficits stresses the effect of deficits on long-term economic growth.

Virtually every macroeconomic chapter contains at least some discussion of international issues. However, the final part of *Economics* focuses primarily on international economics. Chapter 33 gives the basic treatment of international trade, developing both the traditional theory of static comparative advantage and newer theories based on imperfect competition and dynamic comparative advantage. Chapter 34 discusses both the positive and normative aspects of trade policy, as well as the WTO and NAFTA. Chapter 35 introduces the balance of payments and examines exchange-rate determination. Here we also discuss three important policy issues: the desirability of current-account deficits or surpluses, whether there is a "right" value for the Canadian exchange rate, and the costs and benefits of Canada's adopting a fixed exchange rate.

We hope you find this menu both attractive and challenging; we hope students find the material stimulating and enlightening. Many of the messages of economics are complex—if economic understanding were only a matter of common sense and simple observation, there would be no need for professional economists and no need for textbooks like this one. To understand economics, one must work hard. Working at this book should help readers gain a better understanding of the world around them and of the policy problems faced by all levels of government. Furthermore, in today's globalized world, the return to education is large. We like to think that we have contributed in some small part to the understanding that increased investment in human capital by the next generation is necessary to restore incomes to the rapid growth paths that so benefited our parents and our peers. Perhaps we may even contribute to some income-enhancing accumulation of human capital by some of our readers.

Substantive Changes to This Edition

We have revised and updated the entire text with guidance from an extensive series of formal reviews and other feedback from both users and nonusers of the previous editions of this book. As always, we have striven very hard to improve the teachability and readability of the book. We have focused the discussions so that each major point is emphasized as clearly as possible, without distracting the reader with nonessential points. *Additional Topics*, available on MyEconLab (www.myeconlab.com), address theoretical, empirical, and policy discussions that are interesting but optional. (A complete listing of the *Additional Topics* is provided following the Contents after the List of Boxes.) As in recent editions, we have kept all core material in the main part of the text. Three types of boxes (Applying Economic Concepts, Lessons from History, and Extensions in Theory) are used to show examples or extensions that can be skipped without fear of missing an essential concept. But we think it would be a shame to skip too many of them, as there are many interesting examples and policy discussions in these boxes.

What follows is a brief listing of the main changes that we have made to the textbook.

Microeconomics

Part 1: What Is Economics?

Chapter 1 has been significantly rewritten and rearranged. We now begin with a brief discussion of six key issues in the Canadian and world economies, and then turn to examine resources and scarcity, coordination in markets, and alternative economic systems. We have added a discussion of the role of economic policy. In Chapter 2, we have improved our discussion of the nature of theories, causation, and predictions, and we have added a new box discussing where economists get jobs and what kinds of work they do.

Part 2: An Introduction to Demand and Supply

In Chapter 3 on the basics of demand and supply, we have added a new box explaining why the model works well for commodities (like apples) but not so well for differentiated products (like iPhones). Chapter 4 on elasticity begins with the example of the effect of the 2011 Libyan war on the price of oil. We have also streamlined the discussion of supply elasticity.

Part 3: Consumers and Producers

In Chapter 6, we have clarified the discussion of the condition for utility maximization, and the material on individual and market demand curves is now in the main text rather than in an optional box. Chapter 7 examines the short-run theory of the firm; we say more about the role of bank lending, have better explanations for diminishing returns, and the box on flat cost curves has been improved. We have expanded and clarified our discussion in Chapter 8 of the principle of substitution and have added a new discussion on the importance of productivity growth in driving long-run living standards.

Part 4: Market Structure and Efficiency

In Chapter 9 on perfect competition, we have improved our discussion of whether firms should produce at all, the concept of the shut-down price, and the meaning of loss minimization. In Chapter 10, we have clarified the comparison of price and marginal cost for determining efficiency. We have added Potash and Canpotex as examples of an active cartel, and car prices between Canada and the United States as an example of price discrimination. In Chapter 11, we have streamlined the discussion of monopolistic competition, including an improved discussion of short-run profits and losses. We have also added a new discussion about how profit maximization among oligopolists involves perceptions of rivals' responses and have included a new discussion about extensions beyond simple game theory. In Chapter 12, we have clarified the discussion about regulation of natural monopolies, and we have added a new box on the regulation of Canadian banks motivated by the need to reduce risks and enhance stability. We have updated the discussion of Canadian competition policy, including the recent example of the proposed joint venture between Air Canada and United Continental.

Part 5: Factor Markets

Chapter 13 begins with a section on income distribution, and we have added a new box on rising income inequality in Canada and the other OECD economies, and why it matters. We have also entirely rewritten and shortened the discussion of a firm's demand for a factor of production and what determines the elasticity of factor demand. In Chapter 15, we have improved our discussion of what events change a firm's demand for capital, and why household saving is related to the interest rate.

Part 6: Government in the Market Economy

In Chapter 16, we have improved our discussion and diagram explaining the meaning of positive and negative externalities. We have improved the box on the market for lemons and also our explanation of rent seeking. We have also deleted the old material on inefficient public choices and the box on the Arrow Impossibility Theorem, which many reviewers thought was too advanced. In Chapter 17 on environmental regulation, we have improved our discussion of direct controls, including a passage about when they are effective. We also have several changes in the section on climate change, including a new discussion of the state of play after the Kyoto Protocol. In Chapter 18, we have improved our discussions of the GST, the disincentive effects of taxation, the funding paths for CST and CHT, and the details surrounding the OAS and the Child Tax Benefits.

Macroeconomics

Part 7: An Introduction to Macroeconomics

We motivate Chapter 19 with a new discussion of the onset and effects of the global financial crisis, as well as the associated debates over the role of government intervention. We have improved our discussion of output gaps and the meaning of full employment. In Chapter 20, we have expanded our discussion of whether and why the omissions from GDP matter.

Part 8: The Economy in the Short Run

In Chapter 21, we have clarified the key assumptions used in the short-run macro model. In Chapter 22, we have sharpened the discussion about fiscal policy in the final section. In Chapter 23, we have streamlined and improved our discussion of the slope of the AS curve, and we have simplified our discussion of how technological changes shift the curve. We have also clarified the existing box on the Keynesian AS curve.

Part 9: The Economy in the Long Run

In Chapter 24, we have clarified what we mean by the short run, the adjustment process, and the long run. We clarify the assumption that AD and AS shocks do not change the value of Y^*, but state that this assumption is debated (and addressed in later chapters). We have improved our discussion of the paradox of thrift and the motivation for fiscal stabilization policy. When examining the connection between fiscal policy and growth, we now address the possibility that fiscal policy may have a direct effect on Y^* and thereby reduce the extent of crowding out. In Chapter 25, we have streamlined the opening discussions about inflation and Japanese growth. We have also added a new box explaining what productivity growth "really looks like" in some easy-to-imagine occupational settings. Chapter 26 on long-run economic growth now has a substantially improved introduction. We have deleted the old boxes on "growth is good" and "growth is bad" but have added a new box outlining the modern and respectable arguments against continued growth in the developed economies. We have shortened the discussion of the opportunity cost of growth, and we have improved our discussion of the limits to growth.

Part 10: Money, Banking, and Monetary Policy

In Chapter 27 we have rewritten and modernized the discussion of deposit money and have streamlined the discussion of commercial banks. In Chapter 28, we have added more on riskiness to our existing discussion of bonds, including reference to some European countries today. We have completely rewritten our section on the neutrality and nonneutrality of money and have added new discussions on hysteresis effects—two reasons why Y^* may be affected by changes in the money supply. We have also added a new box on money neutrality as it applies to monetary reform and a new discussion of the connection between inflation and money growth across countries. In Chapter 29, we have clarified our discussion of how the Bank achieves its target for the overnight rate. We have entirely rewritten our discussion about the motivation for the adoption of inflation targeting and also about the role of the output gap, although the central messages are unchanged.

Part 11: Macroeconomic Problems and Policies

In Chapter 30, we have streamlined the discussion of accelerating inflation and have substantially shortened the discussion of the three phases of a disinflation. In Chapter 31 on unemployment, we have added a new discussion of discouraged workers and underemployment. We have also entirely rewritten our discussion of competing theories of the labour market—now posed as market-clearing versus non-market-clearing theories. We have deleted the old box on RBC models but have added a new box on

additional reasons for wage stickiness. Chapter 32 examines debt and deficits. We have deleted the old box on the algebra of debt dynamics (which now occurs in a math note) and have added a new box that applies the debt-dynamics equation to the situation of Greece in 2011. We have reworked the section on crowding out and make the point that if the fiscal expansion increases the value of Y^*, then the extent of crowding out will fall. We have deleted the old box on foreign-held debt and also deleted the repetitive section on the effect of budget surpluses. We have improved the discussion of fiscal rules, especially regarding the emphasis on a relatively stable debt-to-GDP ratio.

Part 12: Canada in the Global Economy

Chapter 33 on the gains from international trade has been updated and revised, but there is no substantial change to its structure or messages. In Chapter 34, we have reworked and clarified our discussion of the case for protection. We have shortened the discussion of countervailing duties but expanded the discussion and examples of national treatment in NAFTA. We have also streamlined our discussion of the ongoing WTO Doha round. Our mention of the new Trans Pacific Partnership now leads us to a new box on the ongoing drive to diversify Canada's trade. In Chapter 35, we have clarified our explanation for why the balance of payments must balance, and we have simplified our discussion of why changes in export prices lead to exchange-rate fluctuations.

* * *

If you are moved to write to us (and we hope that you will be!), please do. You can send any comments or questions regarding the text (or any of the supplementary material, such as the *Instructor's Manual*, the *Study Guide*, the *TestGen*, or the web-based *Additional Topics*) to:

Christopher Ragan
Department of Economics
McGill University
855 Sherbrooke St. West
Montreal, Quebec H3A 2T7
e-mail: christopher.ragan@mcgill.ca

To the Student

Welcome to what is most likely your first book about economics! You are about to encounter what is for most people a new way of thinking, which often causes people to see things differently than they did before. But learning a new way of thinking is not always easy, and you should expect some hard work ahead. We do our best to be as clear and logical as possible and to illustrate our arguments whenever possible with current and interesting examples.

You must develop your own technique for studying, but the following suggestions may prove helpful. Begin by carefully considering the Learning Objectives at the beginning of a chapter. Read the chapter itself relatively quickly in order to get the general idea of the argument. At this first reading, you may want to skip the boxes and any footnotes. Then, after reading the Summary and the Key Concepts (at the end of each chapter), reread the chapter more slowly, making sure that you understand each step of the argument.

With respect to the figures and tables, be sure you understand how the conclusions that are stated in boldface at the beginning of each caption have been reached. You should be prepared to spend time on difficult sections; occasionally, you may spend an hour on only a few pages. Paper and pencil are indispensable equipment in your reading. It is best to follow a difficult argument by building your own diagram while the argument unfolds rather than by relying on the finished diagram as it appears in the book.

The end-of-chapter Study Exercises require you to practise using some of the concepts that you learned in the chapter. These will be excellent preparation for your exams. To provide you with immediate feedback, we have posted Solutions to Selected Study Exercises on MyEconLab (www.myeconlab.com). We strongly advise that you should seek to understand economics, not to memorize it.

The red numbers in square brackets in the text refer to a series of mathematical notes that are found starting on page M-1 at the end of the book. For those of you who like mathematics or prefer mathematical argument to verbal or geometric exposition, these may prove useful. Others may disregard them.

In this edition of the book, we have incorporated many elements to help you review material and prepare for examinations. A brief description of all the features in this book is given in the separate section that follows.

We encourage you to make use of MyEconLab that accompanies this book (www.myeconlab.com) at the outset of your studies. MyEconLab contains a wealth of valuable resources to help you. MyEconLab provides Solutions to Selected Study Exercises. It also includes many additional practice questions, some of which are modelled on Study Exercises in the book. MyEconLab also contains many *Additional Topics*—these represent material written especially for this textbook and include many interesting theoretical, empirical, and policy discussions. You can also find animations of some of the key figures in the text, marked with the symbol ☀ below the figure number, as well as an electronic version of the textbook. For more details about MyEconLab, please see the description on the inside front cover of your text.

We strongly suggest you make use of the excellent *Study Guide* written expressly for this text. The *Study Guide* is closely integrated with the book; it offers practice questions and exercises that will test and reinforce your understanding of the concepts and analytical techniques stressed in each chapter of the text and will help you prepare for your examinations. Explanations are provided for the answers to many of the Multiple-Choice Questions to facilitate your independent study. Being able to solve problems and to communicate and interpret your results are important goals in an introductory course in economics. The *Study Guide* can play a crucial role in your acquisition of these skills.

Over the years, the book has benefited greatly from comments and suggestions we have received from students. Please feel free to send your comments to christopher.ragan@mcgill.ca. Good luck, and we hope you enjoy your course in economics!

Features of This Edition

We have made a careful effort with this edition to incorporate features that will facilitate the teaching and learning of economics.

- A set of **Learning Objectives** at the beginning of each chapter, correlated to the **Chapter Outline**, clarifies the skills and knowledge to be learned in each chapter. These same learning objectives are used in the chapter summaries, as well as in the *Study Guide*.

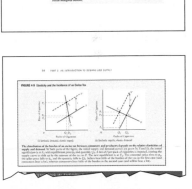

- **Major ideas** are highlighted with a yellow background in the text.
- **Key terms** are boldfaced where they are defined in the body of the text, and they are restated with their definitions in the margins. In the index at the back of the book, each key term and the page reference to its definition are boldfaced.
- **Weblinks** to useful Internet addresses are given in the margins. Each weblink presents a URL address, along with a brief description of the material available there. Some links are to government home pages where you can obtain much additional data. Other links are to organizations such as OPEC, the UN, and the WTO.

- The **colour scheme for figures** consistently uses the same colour for each type of curve. For example, all demand curves are blue and all supply curves are red.
- **A caption for each figure and table** summarizes the underlying economic reasoning. Each caption begins with a boldfaced statement of the relevant economic conclusion.

- **Applying Economic Concepts** boxes demonstrate economics in action, providing examples of how theoretical material relates to issues of current interest.
- **Extensions in Theory** boxes provide a deeper treatment of a theoretical topic that is discussed in the text.
- **Lessons from History** boxes contain discussions of a particular policy debate or empirical finding that takes place in a historical context.
- **Photographs with short captions** are interspersed throughout the chapters to illustrate some of the arguments.

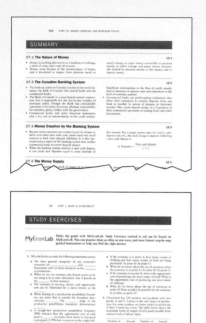

- **Chapter Summaries** are organized using the same numbered heading as found in the body of the chapter. The relevant Learning Objective (LO) numbers are given in red next to each heading in the summary.
- **Key Concepts** are listed near the end of each chapter.

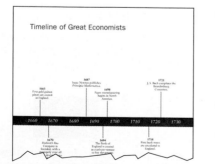

- A set of **Study Exercises** is provided for each chapter. These often quantitative exercises require the student to analyze problems by means of computations, graphs, or explanations.

- A set of **Mathematical Notes** is presented in a separate section near the end of the book. Because mathematical notation and derivations are not necessary to understand the principles of economics but are more helpful in advanced work, this seems to be a sensible arrangement. References in the text to these mathematical notes are given by means of red numbers in square brackets.

- A **Timeline of Great Economists,** extending from the mid-seventeenth century to the late twentieth century, is presented near the end of the book. Along this timeline we have placed brief descriptions of the life and works of some great economists, most of whom the reader will encounter in the textbook. The timeline also includes some major world events in order to give readers an appreciation of when these economists did their work.
- **Economists on Record,** on the inside of the back cover, provides some classic quotations that are relevant to the study and practice of economics.
- For convenience, a list of the **Common Abbreviations Used in the Text** is given inside the front cover.

Supplements

A comprehensive set of supplements has been carefully prepared to assist students and instructors in using this new edition.

MyEconLab

The moment you know.

Educators know it. Students know it. It's that inspired moment when something that was difficult to understand suddenly makes perfect sense. Our MyLab products have been designed and refined with a single purpose in mind—to help educators create that moment of understanding with their students.

MyEconLab delivers proven results in helping individual students succeed. It provides engaging experiences that personalize, stimulate, and measure learning for each student. And, it comes from a trusted partner with educational expertise and an eye on the future.

MyEconLab can be used by itself or linked to any learning management system. Visit MyEconLab to learn more about how it combines proven learning applications with powerful assessment.

MyEconLab—the moment you know.

MyEconLab provides students with personalized Study Plans and the opportunity for unlimited practice. It also provides instructors with ready-to-use assignments that can be graded electronically. For more information on MyEconLab, please visit www.myeconlab.com.

Pearson eText gives students access to the text whenever and wherever they have access to the Internet. eText pages look exactly like the printed text, offering powerful new functionality for students and instructors. Users can create notes, highlight text in different colours, create bookmarks, zoom, click hyperlinked words and phrases to view definitions, and view in single-page or two-page view. Pearson eText allows for quick navigation to key parts of the eText using a table of contents and provides full-text search. The eText may also offer links to associated media files, enabling users to access videos, animations, or other activities as they read the text.

Study Guide

A robust Study Guide, written by Paul T. Dickinson and Gustavo Indart, is available as split volumes for microeconomics (978-0-321-82840-8) and macroeconomics (978-0-321-82839-2). It is designed for use either in the classroom or by students on their own. The *Study Guide* offers additional study support and reinforcement for each text chapter. It is closely integrated with the textbook, offering relevant practice exercises for each chapter. To facilitate independent study, explanations are provided for about 70 percent of the answers to the Additional Multiple-Choice Questions. For each chapter, the *Study Guide* provides the following helpful material:

- Learning Objectives matching those in the textbook
- Chapter Overview
- Hints and Tips
- Chapter Review consisting of Multiple-Choice Questions, organized into sections matching the numbered sections in the textbook
- Short-Answer Questions
- Exercises
- Extension Exercises
- Additional Multiple-Choice Questions
- Solutions to all of the Questions and Exercises above
- Explanations for the answers to at least 70 percent of the Additional Multiple-Choice Questions

CourseSmart for Students

CourseSmart goes beyond traditional expectations—providing instant, online access to the textbooks and course materials you need at an average savings of 60 percent. With instant access from any computer and the ability to search your text, you'll find the content you need quickly, no matter where you are. And with online tools like highlighting and note-taking, you can save time and study efficiently. See all the benefits at www.coursesmart.com/students.

Instructor's Resource CD-ROM

The *Instructor's Resource CD-ROM* (978-0-321-88969-0) for this new edition contains the following items:

- An **Instructor's Manual** (in both Word and PDF format) written by Christopher Ragan. It includes full solutions to all the Study Exercises.
- A **Computerized Testbank** (**Pearson TestGen**) prepared by Ingrid Kristjanson and Christopher Ragan. The testbank consists of 4000 multiple-choice questions, with an emphasis on applied questions (as opposed to recall questions) and quantitative questions (as opposed to qualitative questions). Approximately 60 percent of the questions test applied skills, about 20 percent of the questions are quantitative, and about 20 percent of the questions have a graph or table. All the questions have been carefully checked for accuracy. For each question, the authors have provided the correct answer, identified the relevant section number in the textbook chapter, specified the concept being tested, assigned a level of difficulty (easy, moderate, or challenging), identified the skill tested (recall or applied), noted whether the question is qualitative or quantitative, and noted whether the question involves a graph or table. *TestGen* enables instructors to search for questions according to any of these attributes and to sort questions into any order desired. With *TestGen*, instructors can easily edit existing questions, add questions, generate tests, and print the tests in a variety of formats. *TestGen* also allows instructors to administer tests on a local area network, have the tests graded electronically, and have the results prepared in electronic or printed reports.
- **PowerPoint® Slides**, covering the key concepts of each chapter, that can be adapted for lecture presentations.
- An **Image Library**, consisting of all the figures and tables from the textbook in gif format. These files can easily be imported into PowerPoint slides for class presentation.
- **Additional Topics**, written by Christopher Ragan, offering optional topics on a wide variety of economic subjects. A list of these topics is included in the text; students can access them on MyEconLab (www.myeconlab.com).

These instructor supplements are also available for download from a password-protected section of Pearson Education Canada's online catalogue (www.pearsoncanada.ca/highered). Navigate to your book's catalogue page to view a list of those supplements that are available. See your local Pearson representative for details and access.

CourseSmart for Instructors

CourseSmart goes beyond traditional expectations—providing instant, online access to the textbooks and course materials you need at a lower cost for students. And even as students save money, you can save time and hassle with a digital eTextbook that allows you to search for the most relevant content at the very moment you need it. Whether it's evaluating textbooks or creating lecture notes to help students with difficult concepts, CourseSmart can make life a little easier. See how when you visit www.coursesmart.com/instructors.

Technology Specialists

Pearson's **Technology Specialists** work with faculty and campus course designers to ensure that Pearson technology products, assessment tools, and online course materials are tailored to meet your specific needs. This highly qualified team is dedicated to helping students take full advantage of a wide range of educational resources by assisting in the integration of a variety of instructional materials and media formats. Your local Pearson Canada sales representative can provide you with more details about this service program.

Pearson Custom Library

For enrollments of at least 25 students, you can create your own textbook by choosing the chapters that best suit your own course needs. To begin building your custom text, visit www.pearsoncustomlibrary.com. You may also work with a dedicated Pearson Custom editor to create your ideal text—publishing your own original content or mixing and matching Pearson content. Contact your local Pearson representative to get started.

Acknowledgements

It would be impossible to acknowledge here by name all the teachers, colleagues, and students who contributed to the development and improvement of this book over its previous thirteen editions. Hundreds of users have written to us with specific suggestions, and much of the credit for the improvement of the book over the years belongs to them. We can no longer list them individually but we thank them all sincerely.

For the development of this fourteenth edition, we are grateful to the many people who offered informal suggestions. We would also like to thank the following instructors who provided us with formal reviews of the textbook. Their observations and recommendations were extremely helpful.

- Benjamin Atkinson (Mount Royal University)
- Iris Au (University of Toronto Scarborough)
- Lee Bailey (University of Toronto Mississauga)
- Natalya Brown (Nipissing University)
- Marilyn Cottrell (Brock University)
- Ajit Dayanandan (University of Northern British Columbia)
- Paul Dickinson (McGill University)
- Michael Doyle (Memorial University of Newfoundland)
- Byron Eastman (Laurentian University)
- Oliver Franke (Concordia University of Alberta)
- Bruno Fullone (George Brown College)
- David Gray (University of Ottawa)
- Narine Grigoryan (Camosun College)
- Gustavo Indart (University of Toronto)
- Byron Lew (Trent University)
- Junjie Liu (Simon Fraser University)
- M. A. McGregor (Mount Royal University)
- Manish Pandey (University of Winnipeg)
- Amy Peng (Ryerson University)
- Kevin Richter (Douglas College)
- Gary Riser (Memorial University of Newfoundland)
- Rob Scharff (Kwantlen Polytechnic University)
- Jim Sentance (University of PEI)
- Fulton Tom (Langara College)
- and others, who choose to remain anonymous

We would like to express our thanks to the many people at Pearson Canada involved in the development and production of this textbook. We would especially like to thank three individuals with whom we worked closely. Claudine O'Donnell (Acquisitions Editor), Suzanne Schaan (Supervising Developmental Editor), and Leigh-Anne Graham (Senior Marketing Manager) all showed their professionalism, dedication, and enthusiasm in guiding this book through the publication and marketing processes. We would also like to thank the many sales representatives who work to bring this book to professors across the country. These individuals have been a pleasure to work with each step along the way, and we are deeply grateful for their presence and their participation and delighted to consider them friends as well as professional colleagues.

Our thanks also to the many people at Pearson with whom we work less closely but who nonetheless toil behind the scenes to produce this book, including Andrea Falkenberg, Melinda Durham, Julia Hall, Marta Johnson, Sonya Thursby, and Miriam Blier.

Thanks also to Linda Jenkins for copyediting, Kevin Richter for the technical review, and to Megan Smith-Creed for proofreading, all of whom provided an invaluable service with their attention to detail.

In short, we realize that there is a great deal more involved in producing a book than *just* the writing. Without the efforts of all of these dedicated professionals, this textbook simply would not exist. Our sincere thanks to all of you.

For this fourteenth edition, we enjoyed the help of several students and we would like to thank them all. David Meredith assembled much of the data for the necessary updates in the text; Justine Gagnepain and Katherine Ragan reviewed the solutions to all of the Study Exercises and also helped us to compile a list of websites, and Hannah Herman closely reviewed all of the questions in the Testbank. We thank all of them for their diligence and hard work.

Finally, Ingrid Kristjanson is deeply involved in the revision of this textbook and has been for several years. Without her participation, the quality and efficiency of this project would suffer greatly. In addition, for the past three editions she has played a leading role in the improvement, rewriting, and expansion of the electronic Testbank. With her active involvement, the lengthy revision of the textbook and its supplements continues to be an enriching and pleasant experience.

Christopher Ragan

About the Author

Chris Ragan received his B.A. in economics from the University of Victoria, his M.A. from Queen's University, and his Ph.D. from the Massachusetts Institute of Technology in Cambridge, Massachusetts in 1990. He then joined the Department of Economics at McGill University in Montreal, where he has taught graduate courses in macroeconomics and international finance and undergraduate courses in macroeconomic theory and policy, current economic issues, and financial crises. Over the years he has taught principles of economics (micro and macro) to thousands of students at McGill and maintains a reputation on campus as being "super-excited" about economics. In 2007, Chris Ragan was awarded the Noel Fieldhouse Teaching Award from McGill for teaching excellence.

Professor Ragan's research focuses mainly on the design and implementation of macroeconomic policy in Canada. He has been privileged to serve the federal government in Ottawa as Special Advisor to the Governor of the Bank of Canada and as the Clifford Clark Visiting Economist at the Department of Finance. He currently serves on the Monetary Policy Council of the C.D. Howe Institute, where he also holds the David Dodge Chair in Monetary Policy.

Chris Ragan used the third edition of this textbook as an undergraduate student in 1981 and joined Richard Lipsey as a co-author in 1997 for the book's ninth edition. For several editions, Lipsey and Ragan worked diligently to maintain the book's reputation as the clearest and most comprehensive introductory economics textbook in Canada. Although Professor Ragan is now the sole listed author, this fourteenth edition of *Economics* still owes much to the dedication of previous authors, including Richard Lipsey, Douglas Purvis, and Gordon Sparks.

About the Cover

The cover image of this edition is an aerial drawing of the bustling port of Collingwood, Ontario, by artist Steve McDonald. Steve is an established Canadian artist and founding member of the acclaimed collective Drawnonward. The collective has been the subject of award-winning documentaries shown on CBC, Bravo, and TVO, profiled for the artists' unique bond with Canada's landscape. For more information, visit www.steviemcd.com.

Economic Issues and Concepts

CHAPTER OUTLINE	LEARNING OBJECTIVES (LO)
	After studying this chapter you will be able to
1.1 WHAT IS ECONOMICS?	1 explain the importance of scarcity, choice, and opportunity cost, and how all three concepts are illustrated by the production possibilities boundary.
1.2 THE COMPLEXITY OF MODERN ECONOMIES	2 view the market economy as self-organizing in the sense that order emerges from a large number of decentralized decisions.
	3 explain how specialization gives rise to the need for trade, and that trade is greatly facilitated by money.
	4 identify the economy's decision makers and see how their actions create a circular flow of income and expenditure.
1.3 IS THERE AN ALTERNATIVE TO THE MARKET ECONOMY?	5 see that all actual economies are mixed economies, having elements of free markets, tradition, and government intervention.

MANY of the challenges we face in Canada and around the world are primarily economic. Some are mostly environmental, social, or political, but with many issues there is also a significant economic dimension. Wars and civil unrest throughout history have often had economic roots, with antagonists competing for control over vital resources; global climate change is a phenomenon that engages the attention of the scientific and environmental communities, but the economic implications of both the problem and its solutions will be tremendous; population aging in Canada and other developed countries will have consequences for the structure of our societies, but it will also have significant economic effects; and the existence of poverty, whether in Canada or in the much poorer nations of the world, most certainly has economic causes and consequences. We begin by discussing several issues that are currently of pressing concern, both inside and outside of Canada.

Productivity Growth Productivity growth lies at the heart of the long-term increase in Canadians' average living standards. Productivity is a measure of how much output (or income) is produced by one hour of work effort, and it has been rising gradually over the past century. In recent years, however, productivity growth has been slowing in Canada, and economists in universities and governments have been examining the cause of the slowdown and also examining what policies, if any, might reverse this trend. If your living standards are to improve over your lifetime as much as your grandparents' did over theirs, Canada's rate of productivity growth will need to increase significantly.

Population Aging The average age of the Canadian population is steadily rising, due both to a long-term decline in fertility and to an increase in average life-expectancy. This population aging has several effects. First, since people eventually retire as they approach their "golden years," there will be a decline in the growth rate of Canada's labour force. As a result, some firms and industries will find it more difficult to find workers, and wages are likely to rise as a result. Second, since our publicly funded health-care system tends to spend much more on seniors than it does on Canadians under the age of 55, there will be a significant increase in public health-care spending as a share of the total size of the economy. This will put new and difficult demands on governments' fiscal positions, and force them either to increase tax rates or reduce spending in order to balance their budgets. This same demographic problem is being encountered in most developed countries.

Climate Change Climate change is a global phenomenon that will have important implications for most nations on Earth. The long-term increase in the emission of greenhouse gases—caused largely from the burning of fossil fuels such as oil, coal, and natural gas—has led to an accumulation of these gases in the atmosphere and is contributing to a long-term increase in Earth's average temperature. The rise in temperature is leading to the melting of polar ice caps, a slow increase in sea level, a creeping expansion of the world's great deserts, and reductions in agricultural productivity. Particularly troubling is that much of the burden of climate change appears to be falling on developing countries that are least able to bear the burden. Global climate change presents a challenge for the design of better economic policy, aimed at reducing greenhouse-gas emissions without unduly slowing the growth of material living standards. It also presents a challenge for global diplomacy, aimed at getting all countries—rich and poor—involved in a collective effort of reducing their emissions.

Global Financial Stability The collapse of the U.S. housing market in 2007–2008 led to the failure of several major financial institutions and caused a global financial crisis. The largest and most synchronized worldwide recession in over 70 years followed in its wake. Many elements came together to cause these events, including new mortgage practices, innovative financial instruments, expansionary monetary policy, regulation in the financial sector, and many others. The crisis led most of the world's major governments to intervene considerably in their economies—by providing assistance to their financial institutions, by directly expanding expenditures on goods and services, and by providing liquidity to their financial markets. By 2010 most of these economies had emerged from recession and were on their way to healthy economic recoveries. However, it was then clear that governments needed to play a role in redesigning their financial systems to reduce the likelihood that similar events would occur in the future. The quest for "financial stability" has become a policy imperative in many countries.

Rising Government Debt The aggressive government response to the global financial crisis led to massive new public spending in an effort to dampen the effects of the recession. These increases in government spending, however, took place when the recession was causing a decline in government tax revenues. As a result, governments' budget deficits increased for several years, and government debt in most countries increased significantly between 2008 and 2012. Even by 2010 it had become clear that government debt in some European countries (especially Greece, Portugal, Ireland, Italy, and Spain) was so high that bondholders were no longer prepared to purchase new government bonds or renew their existing holdings of bonds. The resulting upward spike in interest rates made it almost impossible for these countries to carry out their regular business without special financial assistance from other governments or from the International Monetary Fund. The political tensions created among European governments threatened to spell the end of Europe's common currency, the euro. The European "sovereign debt crisis" is still largely unresolved.

Globalization Canada is a small nation that relies significantly on trade with the rest of the world for its prosperity. We sell our lumber and oil and beef to the world, as we do our engineering and legal and financial services. As consumers we buy a wide variety of products from the rest of the world, including coffee, leather shoes, and fine wine; our firms also buy many inputs from abroad, including machine tools, software, and some specialized raw materials. In short, international trade and the ongoing process of globalization are crucial to Canada's economic prosperity. Yet globalization also presents some challenges. A decision to reduce tariffs on imported goods generates overall benefits for Canada, but it also generates temporary costs for those Canadians who are displaced from their previously protected occupations. And greater competition for Canadian firms from those in developing countries leads to overall increases in domestic living standards, as Canadians now have access to cheaper goods. However, it may also lead to a decline in some middle-level jobs in Canada that get replaced slowly with jobs in expanding sectors.

These six issues are only a small sample of the many economic issues that confront Canada and other countries. To understand any of them it is necessary to have a basic understanding of economics—how markets work, how prices are determined, in what sense markets sometimes fail to work well, and how government policy can be used to improve outcomes. These are the main topics of this book. There is a lot to learn, and not many weeks in your college or university course. So, let's get started at the very beginning.

1.1 What Is Economics?

These issues would not matter much if we lived in an economy of such plenty that there was always enough to fully satisfy everyone's wants. If we could always get all the goods we wanted, it wouldn't be so important to be more productive in our work. Rapid growth in health-care spending would not be such a problem if governments had no limits on what they could spend, or if there were not problems associated with high levels of government debt. And there would be no need to trade with other countries if Canada could easily and cheaply produce coffee, clothing, electronic components, and all those other things that we currently import from foreign lands. But such an economy with unlimited products is impossible. Why?

The short answer is because we live in a world of *scarcity*. Compared with the desires of individuals for products such as better food, clothing, housing, education, holidays, health care, and entertainment, the existing supplies of resources are clearly inadequate. They are sufficient to produce only a small fraction of the goods and services that we desire. This scarcity gives rise to the basic economic problem of choice. If we cannot have everything we want, we must choose what we will and will not have.

One definition of *economics* comes from the great economist Alfred Marshall (1842–1924), who we will encounter at several points in this book: "Economics is a study of mankind in the ordinary business of life." A more informative definition is

> **Economics is the study of the use of scarce resources to satisfy unlimited human wants.**

Scarcity is inevitable and is central to economic problems. What are society's resources? Why is scarcity inevitable? What are the consequences of scarcity?

Resources

A society's resources are often divided into the three broad categories of land, labour, and capital. *Land* includes all natural endowments, such as arable land, forests, lakes, crude oil, and minerals. *Labour* includes all mental and physical human resources, including entrepreneurial capacity and management skills. *Capital* includes all manufactured aids to production, such as tools, machinery, and buildings. Economists call such resources **factors of production** because they are used to produce the things that people desire. We divide what is produced into goods and services. **Goods** are tangible (e.g., cars and shoes), and **services** are intangible (e.g., haircuts and education).

People use goods and services to satisfy many of their wants. The act of making them is called **production**, and the act of using them to satisfy wants is called **consumption**. Goods are valued for the services they provide. For example, a car helps to satisfy its owner's desires for transportation, mobility, and possibly status.

Scarcity and Choice

For almost all of the world's 7 billion people, scarcity is real and ever-present. As we said earlier, relative to our desires, existing resources are inadequate; there are enough to produce only a fraction of the goods and services that we want.

factors of production Resources used to produce goods and services; frequently divided into the basic categories of land, labour, and capital.

goods Tangible commodities, such as cars or shoes.

services Intangible commodities, such as haircuts or medical care.

production The act of making goods or services.

consumption The act of using goods or services to satisfy wants.

But aren't the advanced industrialized nations rich enough that scarcity is nearly banished? After all, they are "affluent" societies. Whatever affluence may mean, however, it does not mean the end of the problem of scarcity. Canadian families that earn $75 000 per year, the average after-tax income for a Canadian family in 2013 but a princely amount by *world* standards, have no trouble spending it on things that seem useful to them, and they would certainly have no trouble convincing you that their resources are scarce relative to their desires.

Because resources are scarce, all societies face the problem of deciding what to produce and how much each person will consume. Societies differ in who makes the choices and how they are made, but the need to choose is common to all. Just as scarcity implies the need for choice, so choice implies the existence of cost. A decision to have more of one thing requires a decision to have less of something else. The less of "something else" can be thought of as the cost of having more of that "one thing."

> Scarcity implies that choices must be made, and making choices implies the existence of costs.

Opportunity Cost To see how choice implies cost, we look first at a trivial example and then at one that affects all of us; both examples involve precisely the same fundamental principles.

Consider the choice David faces when he goes out for pizza and beer with his friends. Suppose that he has only $16 for the night and that each beer costs $4 and each slice of pizza costs $2. Since David is both hungry and thirsty, he would like to have 4 slices of pizza and 3 beers, but this would cost $20 and is therefore unattainable given David's scarce resources of $16. There are several combinations, however, that are attainable: 8 slices of pizza and 0 beers; 6 slices of pizza and 1 beer; 4 slices of pizza and 2 beers; 2 slices of pizza and 3 beers; and 0 slices of pizza and 4 beers.

David's choices are illustrated in Figure 1-1, which graphs the combinations of beers and slices of pizza that David considers buying. The numbers of slices of pizza are shown on the horizontal axis; the numbers of beers are shown on the vertical axis. The downward-sloping line connects the five possible combinations of beer and pizza that use up all of David's resources—$16. This is David's *budget line*. Notice that point A shows a combination—4 slices of pizza and 3 beers—that lies outside the line because its total cost is more than $16. Point A is *unattainable* to David. If David could buy fractions of a beer and of a slice of pizza, *all* points that lie on or inside the line would be *attainable* combinations.

In this setting David can ask himself, "What is the cost of one beer?" One answer is that the cost is $4. An equivalent answer, assuming that he wanted to spend all of this $16 on these two items, is that the cost of one beer is the two slices

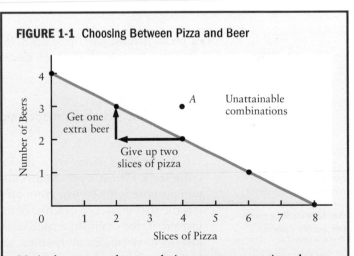

FIGURE 1-1 Choosing Between Pizza and Beer

Limited resources force a choice among competing alternatives. Given a total of $16 to spend on $2 slices of pizza and $4 beers, some choices are unattainable, such as point A. The five points on the green line show *all* combinations that are attainable by spending the $16. If it were possible to buy parts of a beer and parts of a slice of *pizza*, then all combinations on the line and in the green area would be attainable. If the entire $16 is to be spent, the choice between more pizza and more beer involves an opportunity cost. The *slope* of the green line reflects opportunity costs. The opportunity cost of one extra slice of pizza is half of a beer; the opportunity cost of one extra beer is two slices of pizza.

APPLYING ECONOMIC CONCEPTS 1-1

The Opportunity Cost of Your University Degree

The opportunity cost of choosing one thing is what must be given up as the best alternative. Computing the opportunity cost of a college or university education is a good example to illustrate which factors are included in the computation of opportunity cost. You may also be surprised to learn how expensive your university degree really is!*

Suppose that a bachelor's degree requires four years of study and that each year you spend $6000 for tuition fees—approximately the average at Canadian universities in 2013—and a further $1500 per year for books and materials. Does this mean that the cost of a university education is only $30 000? Unfortunately not; the true cost of a university degree to a student is much higher.

The key point is that the opportunity cost of a university education does not include just the out-of-pocket expenses on tuition and books. You must also take into consideration *what you are forced to give up* by choosing to attend university. Of course, if you were not studying you could have done any one of a number of things, but the relevant one is *the one you would have*

chosen instead—your best alternative to attending university.

Suppose that your best alternative to attending university was to get a job. In this case, the opportunity cost of your university degree must include the earnings that you would have received had you taken that job. Suppose that your (after-tax) annual earnings would have been $25 000 per year, for a total of $100 000 if you had stayed at that job for four years. To the direct expenses of $30 000, we must therefore add $100 000 for the earnings that you gave up by not taking a job. This brings the true cost of your university degree—the opportunity cost—up to $130 000!

Notice that the cost of food, lodging, clothing, and other living expenses did not enter the calculation of the opportunity cost in this example. The living expenses must be incurred in either case—whether you attend university or get a job.

If the opportunity cost of a degree is so high, why do students choose to go to university? Maybe students

---

of pizza he must give up to get it. In fact, we say in this case that two slices of pizza is the *opportunity cost* of one beer, since they are the opportunity David must give up to get one extra beer.

> **Every time a choice is made, opportunity costs are incurred.**

opportunity cost The cost of using resources for a certain purpose, measured by the benefit given up by not using them in their best alternative use.

As simple as it may seem, the idea of opportunity cost is one of the central insights of economics. Here is a precise definition: The **opportunity cost** of using resources for a certain purpose is *the benefit given up by not using them in the best alternative way*. That is, it is the cost measured in terms of other goods and services that could have been obtained instead. If, for example, resources that could have produced 20 km of road are best used instead to produce one hospital, the opportunity cost of a hospital is 20 km of road; looked at the other way round, the opportunity cost of 20 km of road is one hospital.

See *Applying Economic Concepts 1-1* for an example of opportunity cost that should seem quite familiar to you: the opportunity cost of getting a university degree.

Production Possibilities Boundary Although David's choice between pizza and beer may seem to be a trivial consumption decision, the nature of the decision is the same whatever the choice being made. Consider, for example, the choice that any country must face between producing military goods (such as ships, tanks, and guns) and civilian goods (such as food, clothing, and housing).

If resources are fully and efficiently employed, it is not possible to have more of both. However, as the government cuts defence expenditures, resources needed to produce civilian goods will be freed up. The opportunity cost of increased civilian goods is therefore

The opportunity cost to an individual completing a university degree in Canada is large. It includes the direct cost of tuition and books as well as the earnings forgone while attending university.

simply enjoy learning and thus are prepared to incur the high cost to be in the university environment. Or maybe they believe that a university degree will significantly increase their future earning potential. In Chapter 14 we will see that this is true. In this case, they are giving up four years of earnings at one salary so that they can invest in building their skills in the hope of enjoying many more years in the future at a considerably higher salary.

Whatever the reason for attending college or university, the recognition that a post-secondary degree is very expensive should convince students to make the best use of their time while they are there. Read on!

---

*This box considers only the cost *to the student* of a university degree. For reasons that will be discussed in detail in Part Six of this book, provincial governments heavily subsidize post-secondary education in Canada. Because of this subsidy, the cost *to society* of a university degree is generally much higher than the cost to an individual student.

the forgone military output. Or, if we were considering an increase in military output, the opportunity cost of increased military output would be the forgone civilian goods.

The choice is illustrated in Figure 1-2. Because resources are scarce, some combinations—those that would require more than the total available supply of resources for their production—cannot be attained. The negatively sloped curve on the graph divides the combinations that can be attained from those that cannot. Points above and to the right of this curve cannot be attained because there are not enough resources, points below and to the left of the curve can be attained without using all of the available resources, and points on the curve can just be attained if all the available resources are used efficiently. The curve is called the **production possibilities boundary**. (Sometimes "boundary" is replaced with "curve" or "frontier.") It has a negative slope because when all resources are being used efficiently, producing more of one good requires producing less of others.

> **A production possibilities boundary illustrates three concepts: scarcity, choice, and opportunity cost. Scarcity is indicated by the unattainable combinations outside the boundary; choice, by the need to choose among the alternative attainable points along the boundary; and opportunity cost, by the negative slope of the boundary.**

The shape of the production possibilities boundary in Figure 1-2 implies that an increasing amount of civilian production must be given up to achieve equal successive increases in military production. This shape, referred to as *concave* to the origin, indicates that the opportunity cost of either good increases as we increase the amount of it that is produced. A straight-line boundary, as in Figure 1-1, indicates that the opportunity cost of one good stays constant, no matter how much of it is produced.

production possibilities boundary
A curve showing which alternative combinations of commodities can just be attained if all available resources are used efficiently; it is the boundary between attainable and unattainable output combinations.

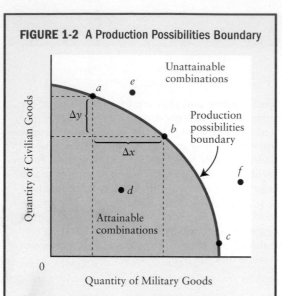

FIGURE 1-2 A Production Possibilities Boundary

Quantity of Civilian Goods

Unattainable
combinations

Production
possibilities
boundary

Δy

Δx

Attainable
combinations

0

Quantity of Military Goods

The negatively sloped boundary shows the combinations that are attainable when all resources are used efficiently. The production possibilities boundary separates the attainable combinations of goods, such as *a, b, c,* and *d,* from unattainable combinations, such as *e* and *f.* Points *a, b,* and *c* represent full and efficient use of society's resources. Point *d* represents either inefficient use of resources or failure to use all the available resources. If production changes from point *a* to point *b,* an opportunity cost is involved. The opportunity cost of producing Δx more military goods is the necessary reduction in the production of civilian goods equal to Δy.

The concave shape in Figure 1-2 is the way economists usually draw a country's production possibilities boundary. The shape occurs because each factor of production is not equally useful in producing all goods. To see why differences among factors of production are so important, suppose we begin at point *c* in Figure 1-2, where most resources are devoted to the production of military goods, and then consider gradually shifting more and more resources toward the production of civilian goods. We might begin by shifting nutrient-rich land that is particularly well suited to growing wheat. This land may not be very useful for making military equipment, but it is very useful for making certain civilian goods (like bread). This shift of resources will therefore lead to a small reduction in military output but a substantial increase in civilian output. Thus, the opportunity cost of producing a few more units of civilian goods, which is equal to the forgone military output, is small. But as we shift more and more resources toward the production of civilian goods, and therefore move along the production possibilities boundary toward point *a,* we must shift more and more resources that are actually quite well suited to the production of military output, like aerospace engineers or the minerals needed to make gunpowder. As we produce more and more civilian goods (by devoting more and more resources to producing them), the amount of military output that must be forgone to produce one *extra* unit of civilian goods rises. That is, the opportunity cost of producing one good rises as more of that good is produced.

Four Key Economic Problems

Modern economies involve millions of complex production and consumption activities. Despite this complexity, however, the basic decisions that must be made are not very different from those that were made in ancient and primitive economies in which people worked with few tools and bartered with their neighbours. Nor is the essence of the decisions in modern, complex economies different from those in current-day developing economies, where many people struggle for their daily survival. In all cases, scarcity, opportunity cost, and the need for choice play crucial roles. Whatever the economic system, whether modern or ancient or complex or primitive, there are four key economic problems.

1. What Is Produced and How? This question concerns the *allocation* of scarce resources among alternative uses. This **resource allocation** determines the quantities of various goods that are produced. Choosing to produce a particular combination of goods means choosing a particular allocation of resources among the industries or regions producing the goods. What determines which goods are produced and which ones are not?

Furthermore, because resources are scarce, it is desirable that they be used efficiently. Hence, it matters which of the available methods of production is used to produce each of the goods. What determines which methods of production get used and which ones do not? Any economy must have some mechanism by which these decisions about resource allocation are made.

resource allocation The allocation of an economy's scarce resources among alternative uses.

Is there some combination of the production of goods that is "better" than others? If so, should governments try to alter the pattern of production in this direction? Could they achieve this if they tried?

2. What Is Consumed and by Whom? Economists seek to understand what determines the distribution of a nation's total output among its people. Who gets a lot, who gets a little, and why? Should governments care about this *distribution* of consumption and, if so, what tools do they have to alter it?

If production takes place on the production possibilities boundary, then how about consumption? Will the economy consume exactly the same goods that it produces? Or will the country's ability to trade with other countries permit the economy to consume a different combination of goods?

3. Why Are Resources Sometimes Idle? Sometimes large numbers of workers who would like to have jobs are unable to find employers to hire them. At the same time, the managers and owners of offices and factories could operate at a higher level of activity—that is, they could produce more goods and services. For some reason, however, these resources—land, labour, and factories—lie idle. Thus, in terms of Figure 1-2, the economy sometimes operates inside its production possibilities boundary.

Why are resources sometimes idle? Should governments worry about such idle resources, or is there some reason to believe that such occasional idleness is necessary for a well-functioning economy? Is there anything governments can do to reduce such idleness?

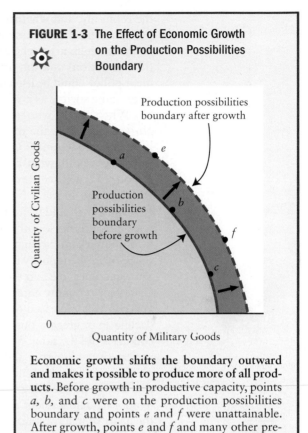

FIGURE 1-3 The Effect of Economic Growth on the Production Possibilities Boundary

Economic growth shifts the boundary outward and makes it possible to produce more of all products. Before growth in productive capacity, points *a*, *b*, and *c* were on the production possibilities boundary and points *e* and *f* were unattainable. After growth, points *e* and *f* and many other previously unattainable combinations are attainable.

4. Is Productive Capacity Growing? The capacity to produce goods and services grows rapidly in some countries, grows slowly in others, and actually declines in others. Growth in productive capacity can be represented by an outward shift of the production possibilities boundary, as shown in Figure 1-3. If an economy's capacity to produce goods and services is growing, some combinations that are unattainable today will become attainable in the future. What are the determinants of such growth? Are there some undesirable side effects of growth? Can governments do anything to influence economic growth?

Economics and Government Policy

Questions relating to what is produced and how, and what is consumed and by whom, fall within the realm of microeconomics. **Microeconomics** is the study of the causes and consequences of the allocation of resources as it is affected by the workings of the price system and government policies that seek to influence it. Questions relating to the idleness of resources and the growth of the economy's productive capacity fall within the realm of macroeconomics. **Macroeconomics** is the study of the determination of economic aggregates, such as total output, total employment, interest rates, the price level, and the rate of economic growth.

The design and effectiveness of government policy is relevant to discussing all four economic problems. When asking what combination of goods and services is produced in

microeconomics The study of the causes and consequences of the allocation of resources as it is affected by the workings of the price system.

macroeconomics The study of the determination of economic aggregates such as total output, the price level, employment, and growth.

the economy, and whether some combinations might be better than others, government policy enters the discussion. In later chapters we will examine situations called *market failures,* which arise when free markets lead to too much of some goods being produced (like pollution) and too little of others (like national parks). In such situations, government policy could be used to alter the allocation of the economy's resources in such a way as to make society as a whole better off.

When asking who gets to consume the economy's output, it is natural to discuss the *fairness* regarding the distribution of consumption across individuals. Do free markets lead to fair outcomes? Can we even decide objectively what is fair and what is unfair? And if we could, what kind of government policies could be used to improve the distribution? We will see throughout this book that many government policies are designed with fairness in mind. We will also encounter an ongoing debate about how much the government should try to improve the fairness of market outcomes. Some argue that it is reasonable to do so; others argue that attempts to improve fairness often lead to reductions in market efficiency that impose large costs on society.

Government policy is also part of the discussion of why a nation's economic resources are sometimes idle and what can be done to reduce such idleness. For example, when the Canadian economy entered a major global recession in 2009, the federal and provincial governments increased their planned spending significantly in an attempt to dampen the decline in aggregate output and rise in unemployment that was then occurring. Other countries did the same. Some critics argued that such "fiscal stimulus" packages could not increase overall output and income, since the increase in government spending would simply displace private spending. Others argued that recessions are caused largely by a reduction in private spending, and that an increase in government spending can be an effective temporary replacement to help sustain the level of economic activity. Such debates lie at the heart of macroeconomic policy, and we have much to say about them in this book.

1.2 The Complexity of Modern Economies

If you want a litre of milk, you go to your local grocery store and buy it. When the grocer needs more milk, he orders it from the wholesaler, who in turn gets it from the dairy, which in turn gets it from the dairy farmer. The dairy farmer buys cattle feed and electric milking machines, and he gets power to run all his equipment by putting a plug into a wall outlet where the electricity is supplied as he needs it. The milking machines are made from parts manufactured in several different places in Canada, the United States, and overseas. The parts themselves are made from materials mined and smelted in a dozen or more countries.

As it is with the milk you drink, so it is with everything else that you buy. When you go to the appropriate store, what you want is normally on the shelf. Those who make these products find that all the required components and materials are available when they need them—even though these things typically come from many different parts of the world and are made by many people who have no direct dealings with one another.

Your own transactions are only a small part of the remarkably complex set of transactions that takes place every day in a modern economy. Shipments arrive daily at our ports, railway terminals, and airports. These shipments include raw materials, such as iron ore, logs, and oil; parts, such as automobile engines, transistors, and circuit boards; tools, such as screwdrivers, lathes, and digging equipment; perishables, such as fresh flowers, coffee beans, and fruit; and all kinds of manufactured goods, such as washing machines, computers, and cell phones. Railways and trucking lines move these goods among thousands of different destinations within Canada. Some go directly to consumers. Others are used by local firms to manufacture their products—some of which will be sold domestically and others exported to other countries.

The Nature of Market Economies

An *economy* is a system in which scarce resources—such as labour, land, and capital— are allocated among competing uses. Decisions must be made about which goods are produced and which are not; who works where and at what wage; and who consumes which goods at what times. Although each of these individual decisions may seem simple, the entire combination is remarkably complex, especially in modern societies.

Self-Organizing Early in the development of modern economics, thoughtful observers wondered how such a complex set of dealings gets organized. Who coordinates the whole set of efforts? Who makes sure that all the activities fit together, providing jobs to produce the things that people want and delivering those things to where they are wanted? The answer is, surprisingly, no one!

A great insight of early economists was that an economy based on free-market transactions is *self-organizing*.

A market economy is self-organizing in the sense that when individual consumers and producers act independently to pursue their own self-interests, responding to prices determined in open markets, the collective outcome is coordinated—there is a "spontaneous economic order." In that order, literally thousands of millions of transactions and activities fit together to produce the things that people want within the constraints set by the resources that are available to the nation.

The great Scottish economist and political philosopher Adam Smith (1723–1790),[1] who was the first to develop this insight fully, put it this way:

> *It is not from the benevolence of the butcher, the brewer, or the baker, that we expect our dinner, but from their regard to their own interest. We address ourselves, not to their humanity but to their self-love, and never talk to them of our own necessities but of their advantages.*

Smith is not saying that benevolence is unimportant. Indeed, he praises it in many other passages of his book. He is saying, however, that the massive number of economic interactions that characterize

Adam Smith wrote An Inquiry into the Nature and Causes of the Wealth of Nations *in 1776. Now referred to by most people simply as* The Wealth of Nations, *it is considered to be the beginning of modern economics.*

---

[1] Throughout this book, we encounter many great economists from the past whose ideas shaped the discipline of economics. At the back of the book you will find a timeline that begins in the 1600s. It contains brief discussions of many of these thinkers and places them in their historical context.

a modern economy cannot all be motivated by benevolence. Although benevolence does motivate some of our actions, often the very dramatic ones, the vast majority of our everyday actions are motivated by self-interest. Self-interest, not benevolence, is therefore the foundation of economic order.

Efficiency Another great insight, which was hinted at by Smith and fully developed over the next century and a half, was that this spontaneously generated economic order is relatively *efficient*. Loosely speaking, efficiency means that the resources available to the nation are organized so as to produce the various goods and services that people want to purchase and to produce them with the least possible amount of resources.

An economy organized by free markets behaves almost as if it were guided by "an invisible hand," in Smith's now-famous words. This does not literally mean that a supernatural presence runs a market economy. Instead it refers to the relatively efficient order that emerges spontaneously out of the many independent decisions made by those who produce, sell, and buy goods and services. The key to explaining this market behaviour is that these decision makers all respond to the same set of prices, which are determined in markets that respond to overall conditions of national scarcity or plenty. Much of this book is devoted to a detailed elaboration of how this market order is generated and how efficiently that job is done.

That free markets usually generate relatively efficient outcomes does not mean that they are *always* efficient or that everyone views the outcomes as desirable or even *fair*. Free markets sometimes fail to produce efficient outcomes, and these failures often provide a motivation for government intervention. In addition, many market outcomes may be efficient but perceived by many to be quite unfair. For example, we will see that an efficient labour market may nonetheless lead to large differentials in wages, with some individuals receiving low incomes while others receive enormous incomes. So, while a central aspect of economics is the study of how markets allocate resources efficiently, much emphasis is also placed on what happens when markets fail in various ways.

Incentives and Self-Interest Lying at the heart of modern economies are *incentives* and *self-interest*. Individuals generally pursue their own self-interest, buying and selling what seems best for them and their families. They purchase products that they want rather than those they dislike, and they buy them when it makes sense given their time and financial constraints. Similarly, they sell products, including their own labour services, in an attempt to improve their own economic situation. When making such decisions about what to buy or sell and at what prices, people respond to *incentives*. Sellers usually want to sell more when prices are high because by doing so they have command over more resources that can be used to purchase the things they want. Similarly, buyers usually want to buy more when prices are low because by doing so they are better able to use their scarce resources to acquire the many things they desire.

With self-interested buyers and sellers responding to incentives when determining what they want to buy and sell, the overall market prices and quantities are determined by their collective interactions. Changes in their preferences or productive abilities lead to changes in their desired transactions and thus to fluctuations in market prices and quantities.

The millions of market transactions occurring on a daily basis in a modern economy are governed by a set of institutions largely created by government. Most often these institutions are so much a part of the fabric of our society that we barely notice their existence, but their importance should not be ignored. The most important of these institutions are private property, the freedom to enter into contracts, and the rule of law. The natures of private property and contractual obligations are defined by laws passed by legislatures and enforced by the police and the courts.

The Decision Makers and Their Choices

Three broad groups of decision makers operate in any economy. The first group is *consumers*. Sometimes we think of consumers as being individuals and sometimes we think in terms of families or households. Consumers purchase various kinds of goods and services with their income; they usually earn their income by selling their labour services to their employers. Sometimes their income is earned by renting out the land or buildings or machines that they own.

The second group of decision makers is *producers*. Producers may be firms that are interested in earning profits or they may be non-profit or charitable organizations. In any case, producers hire workers, purchase or rent various kinds of material inputs and supplies, and then produce and sell their products. In the cases of charitable organizations, their products are often distributed for free.

The third group of decision makers is *government*. In Canada, this group includes the federal, provincial, territorial, and municipal governments. Like producers, governments hire workers, purchase or rent material and supplies, and produce goods and services. Unlike most producers, however, governments usually provide their goods and services at no direct cost to the final user; their operations are financed not by revenue from the sale of their products but instead by the taxes they collect from individual consumers and producers. In addition to producing and providing many goods and services, governments create and enforce laws, and design and implement regulations that must be followed by consumers and producers.

How Are Decisions Made? How do consumers, producers, and governments make decisions? Thinking about how governments make decisions is not straightforward. Indeed, it is not uncommon to hear Canadians say something like "How could the government possibly do something so stupid?" As we will see in later chapters, however, there is usually a sensible explanation for why a government makes the decisions that it does, though it is often not clear until you think carefully about what the government's objectives really are. We will examine government policies in detail at many points throughout this book.

For now, let's focus on how consumers and producers make their decisions. Economists usually assume that consumers' and producers' decisions are both "maximizing" and "marginal." What does this mean?

Maximizing Decisions. The important assumption that economists usually make about how these two groups make their decisions is that everyone tries to do as well as possible for himself or herself. In the jargon of economics, people are assumed to be *maximizers*. When individuals decide how many factor services to sell to producers and how many products to buy from them, they are assumed to make choices designed to maximize their well-being, or *utility*. When producers decide how many factor services to buy from individuals and how many goods to produce and sell to them, they are assumed to make choices designed to maximize their *profits*. We explore the details of utility and profit maximization in later chapters.

Marginal Decisions. Firms and consumers who are trying to maximize usually need to weigh the costs and benefits of their decisions *at the margin*. For example, when you consider buying an additional pair of shoes, you know the *marginal cost* of the shoes—that is, how much you must pay to get them—and you need to compare that cost to the *marginal benefit* that you will receive—the *extra* satisfaction you get from having those shoes. If you are trying to maximize your utility, you will buy the new pair of shoes only if you think that the benefit to you in terms of extra utility exceeds the marginal cost.

Similarly, a producer attempting to maximize its profits and considering whether to hire an extra worker must determine the *marginal cost* of the worker—the extra wages and benefits that must be paid—and compare it to the *marginal benefit* of the worker—the increase in sales revenues the extra worker will generate. A producer interested in maximizing its profit will hire the extra worker only if the benefit in terms of extra revenue exceeds the cost in terms of extra wages.

> In order to achieve their objectives, maximizing consumers and producers make marginal decisions; they decide whether they will be made better off by buying or selling a little more or a little less of any given product.

Voting in an election is an example in which decisions are *not* made on a marginal basis. When you vote in a Canadian federal election, you have only one vote and you must support one party over the others. When you do, you vote for everything that party stands for, even though you may prefer to pick and choose elements from each party's political platform. You cannot say "I vote for the Liberals on issue A and for the Conservatives on issue B." You must make a total, rather than a marginal, decision.

The Flow of Income and Expenditure Figure 1-4 shows the basic decision makers and the flows of income and expenditure that they set up. Individuals own factors of production. They sell the services of these factors to producers and receive payments in return. These are their incomes. Producers use the factor services that they buy to make goods and services. They sell these to individuals, receiving payments in return. These are the incomes of producers. These basic flows of income and expenditure pass through markets. Individuals sell the services of the factor that they own in what are collectively called *factor markets*. When you get a part-time job during university, you are participating in the factor market. Producers sell their outputs of goods and services in what are collectively called *goods markets*. When you purchase a haircut, an airplane ticket, or a new pair of shoes, for example, you are participating in the goods market.

The prices that are determined in these markets determine the incomes that are earned. People who get high prices for their factor services earn high incomes; those who get low prices earn low incomes. The *distribution of income* refers to how the nation's total income is distributed among its citizens. This is largely determined by the price that each type of factor service receives in factor markets.

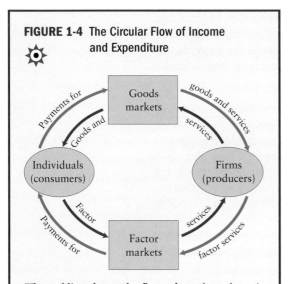

FIGURE 1-4 The Circular Flow of Income and Expenditure

The red line shows the flow of goods and services; the blue line shows the payments made to purchase these. Factor services flow from individuals who own the factors (including their own labour) through factor markets to firms that use them to make goods and services. These goods and services then flow through goods markets to those who consume them. Money payments flow from firms to individuals through factor markets. These payments become the income of individuals. When they spend this income buying goods and services, money flows through goods markets back to producers.

Production and Trade

Individual producers decide which goods to produce and how to produce them. Production is a very complex process in any modern economy. For example, a typical car manufacturer assembles a product out of thousands of individual parts. It makes some of these parts itself. Most are subcontracted to parts manufacturers, and many of the major parts manufacturers subcontract some of their work to smaller firms. The same is true for producing consumer electronics, clothing, home appliances, furniture, fashion accessories, cleaning products, restaurant meals, and most other products you can imagine purchasing. Such complex production displays two characteristics noted long ago by Adam Smith—*specialization* and the *division of labour*.

Specialization In ancient hunter–gatherer societies and in modern subsistence economies, most people make most of the things they need for themselves. However, from the time that people first engaged in settled agriculture and some of them began to live in towns, people have specialized in doing particular jobs. Artisan, soldier, priest, and government official were some of the earliest specialized occupations. Economists call this allocation of different jobs to different people the **specialization of labour**. There are two fundamental reasons why specialization is extraordinarily efficient compared with universal self-sufficiency.

> **specialization of labour** The specialization of individual workers in the production of particular goods or services.

First, individual abilities differ, and specialization allows individuals to do what they can do relatively well while leaving everything else to be done by others. Even when people's abilities are unaffected by the act of specializing, the economy's total production is greater when people specialize than when they all try to be self-sufficient. This is true for individuals, but it is also true for entire countries, and it is one of the most fundamental principles in economics: the principle of *comparative advantage*. A much fuller discussion of comparative advantage is found in Chapter 33, where we discuss the gains from international trade.

The second reason why specialization is more efficient than self-sufficiency concerns changes in people's abilities that occur *because* they specialize. A person who concentrates on one activity becomes better at it than could a jack-of-all-trades. This is called *learning by doing*, and it was a factor much stressed by early economists; research shows that it is important in many modern industries.

The Division of Labour Throughout most of history each artisan who specialized in making some product made the whole of that product. But over the last several hundred years, many technical advances have made it efficient to organize production methods into large-scale firms organized around what is called the **division of labour**. This term refers to specialization *within* the production process of a particular product.

> **division of labour** The breaking up of a production process into a series of specialized tasks, each done by a different worker.

Mass Production. In a mass-production factory, work is divided into highly specialized tasks by using specialized machinery. Each individual repeatedly does one or a few small tasks that represent only a small fraction of those necessary to produce any one product.

Flexible Manufacturing. Two recent changes have significantly altered the degree of specialization found in many modern production processes. First, individual artisans have recently reappeared in some lines of production. They are responding to a revival in the demand for individually crafted, rather than mass-produced, products. Second, many manufacturing operations are being reorganized along new lines called *flexible manufacturing*, which was pioneered by Japanese car manufacturers in the mid-1950s. It has led back to a more craft-based form of organization within the factory. In this technique, employees work as a team; each employee is able to do every team member's job rather than only one very specialized task at one point on the assembly line. However, even these workers are practising the division of labour—but the division is not as fine as it is in mass production.

Money and Trade   People who specialize in doing only one thing must satisfy most of their wants by consuming things made by other people. In early societies the exchange of goods and services took place by simple mutual agreement among neighbours. In the course of time, however, trading became centred on particular gathering places called markets. For example, the French markets or trade fairs of Champagne were known throughout Europe as early as the eleventh century. Even now, many small towns in Canada have regular market days. Today, however, the term "market" has a much broader meaning, referring to any institutions that allow buyers and sellers to transact with each other, which could be by meeting physically or by trading over the Internet. Also, we use the term "market economy" to refer to a society in which people specialize in productive activities and meet most of their material wants through voluntary market transactions with other people.

> **Specialization must be accompanied by trade. People who produce only one thing must trade most of it to obtain all the other things they want.**

barter An economic system in which goods and services are traded directly for other goods and services.

Early trading was by means of **barter**, the trading of goods directly for other goods. But barter is costly in terms of time spent searching out satisfactory exchanges. If a farmer has wheat but wants a hammer, he must find someone who has a hammer and wants wheat. A successful barter transaction thus requires what is called a *double coincidence of wants*.

Money eliminates the cumbersome system of barter by separating the transactions involved in the exchange of products. If a farmer has wheat and wants a hammer, she merely has to find someone who wants wheat. The farmer takes money in exchange. Then she finds a person who wants to sell a hammer and gives up the money for the hammer.

> **Money greatly facilitates trade, which itself facilitates specialization.**

Globalization   Market economies constantly change, largely as a result of the development of new technologies and the new patterns of production and trade that result. Many of the recent changes are referred to as *globalization,* a term often used loosely to mean the increased importance of international trade. International trade is, however, a very old phenomenon. The usual pattern over most of the last 200 years was manufactured goods being sent from Europe and North America to the rest of the world, with raw materials and primary products being sent in return. What is new in the last few decades is the globalization of manufacturing. Assembly of a product may take place in the most industrialized countries, but the hundreds of component parts are manufactured in dozens of different countries and delivered to the assembly plant "just in time" for assembly.

Two major causes of globalization are the rapid reduction in transportation costs and the revolution in information technology that have occurred in the past 50 years. The cost of moving products around the world fell greatly over the last half of the twentieth century because of containerization and the increasing size of ships. Our ability to transmit and analyze data increased even more dramatically, while the costs of doing so decreased equally dramatically. For example, today $1000 buys an ultra-slim tablet or laptop computer that has the same computing power as a "main-frame" computer that in 1970 cost $10 million and filled a large room. This revolution in information and communication technology has made it possible to coordinate economic transactions around the world in ways that were difficult and costly 50 years ago and quite impossible 100 years ago.

Globalization is as important for consumers as it is for producers. For example, as some tastes become universal to young people, spread by ever-increasing access to foreign television stations and global social networks, we can see the same clothes and hear the same music in virtually all big cities. McDonald's restaurants are as visible in Moscow or Beijing as in London, New York, Vancouver, or Montreal. Many other brands are also known around the world, such as Louis Vuitton, Hilfiger, Gucci, Rolex, Nike, Coca-Cola, Kellogg's, Heinz, Nestlé, Molson, Toyota, Rolls-Royce, Sony, and Mitsubishi.

The revolution in shipping and in computer technology has drastically reduced communication and transportation costs. This reduction in costs lies at the heart of globalization.

> Through the ongoing process of globalization, national economies are ever more linked to the global economy, in which an increasing share of jobs and incomes is created.

Globalization comes with challenges, however. As Canadian firms relocate production facilities to countries where costs are lower, domestic workers are laid off and must search for new jobs, perhaps needing retraining in the process. The location of production facilities in countries with lower environmental or human-rights records raises difficult questions about the standards that should be followed by Canadian-owned firms in foreign lands. And firms often use the threat of relocation in an attempt to extract financial assistance from governments, placing those governments in difficult positions. These concerns have led in recent years to "anti-globalization protests" that have raised awareness of some of the costs associated with the process of globalization. We have more to say about these issues in Chapters 33 and 34.

1.3 Is There an Alternative to the Market Economy?

In this chapter we have discussed the elements of an economy based on free-market transactions—what we call a *market economy*. Are there any alternatives to this type of economy? The answer is no in one sense and yes in another. We answer no because the modern economy has no *practical* alternative to reliance on market determination for many of its transactions. We answer yes because not all transactions take place in free markets even in the most market-oriented society. To go further we need to identify various types of economic systems.

Types of Economic Systems

It is helpful to distinguish three pure types of economies, called *traditional, command,* and *free-market economies.* These economies differ in the way in which economic decisions are coordinated. But no actual economy fits neatly into one of these three categories—all real economies contain some elements of each type.

Traditional Economies A **traditional economy** is one in which behaviour is based primarily on tradition, custom, and habit. Young men follow their fathers' occupations. Women do what their mothers did. There is little change in the pattern of goods produced from year to year, other than those imposed by the vagaries of nature. The techniques of production also follow traditional patterns, except when the effects of an occasional new invention are felt. Finally, production is allocated among the members according to long-established traditions.

Such a system works best in an unchanging environment. Under such static conditions, a system that does not continually require people to make choices can prove effective in meeting economic and social needs.

Traditional systems were common in earlier times. The feudal system, under which most people in medieval Europe lived, was a largely traditional society. Peasants, artisans, and most others living in villages inherited their positions in that society. They also usually inherited their specific jobs, which they handled in traditional ways.

Some elements of traditional economies persist today. In some cases, the traditional behaviour is natural and probably desirable, as when a child with considerable expertise takes over a successful family business. In other situations, the traditional behaviour is the result of a resistance to change and fear of less familiar and more risky career paths. In these cases, the traditions may clash with the change that is a hallmark of a modern and dynamic economy.

Command Economies In command economies, economic behaviour is determined by some central authority, usually the government, which makes most of the necessary decisions on what to produce, how to produce it, and who gets to consume which products and in what quantities. Such economies are characterized by the *centralization* of decision making. Because centralized decision makers usually create elaborate and complex plans for the behaviour that they want to impose, the terms **command economy** and *centrally planned economy* are usually used synonymously.

The sheer quantity of data required for the central planning of an entire modern economy is enormous, and the task of analyzing it to produce a fully integrated plan can hardly be exaggerated. Moreover, the plan must be continually modified to take account not only of current data but also of future trends in labour supplies, technological developments, and people's tastes for various goods and services. This is a notoriously difficult exercise, not least because of the unavailability of all essential, accurate, and up-to-date information.

Thirty years ago, more than one-third of the world's population lived in countries that relied heavily on central planning. Today, after the fall of the Berlin Wall and the collapse of the Soviet Union, the number of such countries is small. Even in countries in which central planning is the proclaimed system, as in Cuba, increasing amounts of market determination are gradually being permitted.

Free-Market Economies In the third type of economic system, the decisions about resource allocation are made without any central direction. Instead, they result from innumerable independent decisions made by individual producers and consumers. Such a system is known as a **free-market economy** or, more simply, a *market economy*. In such an economy, decisions relating to the basic economic issues are *decentralized*.

traditional economy An economy in which behaviour is based mostly on tradition.

command economy An economy in which most economic decisions are made by a central planning authority.

free-market economy An economy in which most economic decisions are made by private households and firms.

Despite the absence of a central plan, these many decentralized decisions are nonetheless coordinated. The main coordinating device is the set of market-determined prices—which is why free-market systems are often called *price systems*.

In a pure market economy, all these decisions are made by buyers and sellers acting through unhindered markets. The government provides the background of defining property rights and protecting citizens against foreign and domestic enemies but, beyond that, markets determine all resource allocation and income distribution.

Mixed Economies Economies that are fully traditional or fully centrally planned or wholly free-market are pure types that are useful for studying basic principles. When we look in detail at any actual economy, however, we discover that its economic behaviour is the result of some mixture of central control and market determination, with a certain amount of traditional behaviour as well.

> In practice, every economy is a mixed economy in the sense that it combines significant elements of all three systems in determining economic behaviour.

mixed economy An economy in which some economic decisions are made by firms and households and some by the government.

Furthermore, within any economy, the degree of the mix varies from sector to sector. For example, in some planned economies, the command principle was used more often to determine behaviour in heavy-goods industries, such as steel, than in agriculture. Farmers were often given substantial freedom to produce and sell what they wanted in response to varying market prices.

When economists speak of a particular economy as being centrally planned, we mean only that the degree of the mix is weighted heavily toward the command principle. When we speak of one as being a market economy, we mean only that the degree of the mix is weighted heavily toward decentralized decision making.

Although no country offers an example of either system working alone, some economies, such as those of Canada, the United States, France, and Hong Kong, rely much more heavily on market decisions than others, such as the economies of China, North Korea, and Cuba. Yet even in Canada, the command principle has some sway. Crown corporations, legislated minimum wages, rules and regulations for environmental protection, quotas on some agricultural outputs, and restrictions on the import of some items are just a few examples.

The Great Debate

As we saw earlier, in 1776 Adam Smith was one of the first people to analyze the operation of markets, and he stressed the relative efficiency of free-market economies. A century later, another great economist and political philosopher, Karl Marx (1818–1883), argued that although free-market economies would indeed be successful in producing high levels of output, they could not be relied on to ensure that this output would be fairly distributed among citizens. He argued the benefits of a centrally planned system in which the government could ensure a more equitable distribution of output.

Beginning with the Soviet Union in the early 1920s, many nations adopted systems in which conscious government central planning

Karl Marx argued that free-market economies could not be relied on to ensure an equitable distribution of income. He advocated a system of central planning in which government owns most of the means of production.

replaced the operation of the free market. For almost a century, a great debate then raged on the relative merits of command economies versus market economies. Along with the Soviet Union, the countries of Eastern Europe and China were command economies for much of the twentieth century. Canada, the United States, and most of the countries of Western Europe were, and still are, primarily market economies. The apparent successes of the Soviet Union and China in the 1950s and 1960s, including the ability to mobilize considerable resources into heavy industries, suggested to many observers that the command principle was at least as good for organizing economic behaviour as the market principle. Over the long run, however, planned economies proved to be a failure of such disastrous proportions that they seriously depressed the living standards of their citizens.

During the last decade of the twentieth century, most of the world's centrally planned economies began the difficult transition back toward freer markets. These transitions occurred at different paces in different countries, but in most cases the initial few years were characterized by significant declines in output and employment. Twenty years later, however, most of the "transition" economies are experiencing growth rates above the ones they had in their final years as centrally planned economies. Living standards are on the rise.

Lessons from History 1-1 discusses in more detail why the centrally planned economies failed. This failure suggests the superiority of decentralized markets over centrally

LESSONS FROM HISTORY 1-1

The Failure of Central Planning

The fall of the Berlin Wall in November 1989 was the beginning of the end of the Soviet system of central planning.

The Bolshevik Revolution in 1917 in Russia brought the world its first example of a large-scale communist society. With the rise to power of Joseph Stalin and the creation of the Soviet Union in 1922, communism and central economic planning began their spread throughout Eastern and Central Europe. This spread of central planning was accelerated by the Soviet Union's role following the Second World War in "liberating" several countries from Nazi domination, thus creating the group of countries that became known as the Eastern Bloc or the Soviet Bloc.

Despite the successful geographic spread of communism, the Soviet system of central economic planning had many difficulties. By 1989, communism had collapsed throughout Central and Eastern Europe, and the economic systems of formerly communist countries began the difficult transition from centrally planned to market economies. Although political issues played an enormous role in these events, the economic changes generally confirmed the superiority of a market-oriented price system over central planning as a method of organizing economic activity. The failure of central planning had many causes, but four were particularly significant.

Failure of Coordination

In the centrally planned economies, a body of planners attempted to coordinate all the economic decisions about production, investment, trade, and consumption that were likely to be made by producers and consumers throughout the country. Without the use of prices to signal relative scarcity and abundance, central planning generally proved impossible to do with any reasonable degree of success. Bottlenecks in production, shortages of some goods, and gluts of others plagued the Soviet economy for decades.

planned ones as mechanisms for allocating an economy's scarce resources. Put another way, it demonstrates the superiority of mixed economies with substantial elements of market determination over fully planned command economies. However, it does *not* demonstrate, as some observers have asserted, the superiority of completely free-market economies over mixed economies.

There is no guarantee that completely free markets will, on their own, handle such urgent matters as controlling pollution, providing public goods (like national defence), or preventing financial crises, such as occurred in 2008–2009 in most of the developed countries. Indeed, as we will see in later chapters, much economic theory is devoted to explaining why free markets often *fail* to do these things. Mixed economies, with significant elements of government intervention, are needed to do these jobs.

Furthermore, acceptance of the free market over central planning does not provide an excuse to ignore a country's pressing social issues. Acceptance of the benefits of the free market still leaves plenty of scope to debate the most appropriate levels and types of government policies directed at achieving specific social goals. It follows that there is still considerable room for disagreement about the degree of the mix of market and government determination in any modern mixed economy—room enough to accommodate such divergent views as could be expressed by conservative, liberal, and modern social democratic parties.

Failure of Quality Control

Central planners could monitor the number of units produced by any factory, reward plants that exceeded their production targets, and punish those that fell short. Factory managers operating under these conditions would meet their quotas by whatever means were available, and once the goods passed out of their factory, what happened to them was someone else's headache.

In market economies, poor quality is punished by low sales, and retailers soon give a signal to factory managers by shifting their purchases to other suppliers. The incentives that obviously flow from such private-sector purchasing discretion were generally absent from centrally planned economies, where purchases and sales were organized by the body of planners, and prices and profits were not used to signal customer satisfaction or dissatisfaction.

Misplaced Incentives

In market economies, relative wages and salaries provide incentives for labour to move from place to place, and the possibility of losing one's job provides an incentive to work diligently. This is a harsh mechanism that punishes job losers with loss of income (although social programs provide floors to the amount of economic punishment that can be suffered). In centrally planned economies, workers usually had complete job security. Industrial unemployment was rare,

and even when it did occur, new jobs were usually found for all who lost theirs. Although the high level of security was attractive to many people, it proved impossible to provide sufficient incentives for reasonably hard and efficient work under such conditions.

Environmental Degradation

Fulfilling production plans became the all-embracing goal in centrally planned economies, to the exclusion of most other considerations, including the environment. As a result, environmental degradation occurred in the Soviet Union and the countries of Eastern Europe on a scale unknown in advanced Western nations. A particularly disturbing example (only one of many) occurred in Central Asia, where high quotas for cotton output led to indiscriminate use of pesticides and irrigation. Birth defects became very common, and the vast Aral Sea was more than three-quarters drained, causing major environmental effects.

This failure to protect the environment stemmed from the pressure to fulfill production plans and the absence of a "political marketplace" where citizens could express their preferences for the environment. Imperfect though the system may be in democratic market economies—and in some particular cases it has been quite poor—their record of environmental protection has been vastly better than that of the centrally planned economies.

So, the first answer to the question about the existence of an alternative to the market economy is no: There is no practical alternative to a mixed system with major reliance on markets but some government presence in most aspects of the economy. The second answer is yes: Within the framework of a mixed economy there are substantial alternatives among many different and complex mixes of free-market and government determination of economic life.

Government in the Modern Mixed Economy

Market economies in today's advanced industrial countries are based primarily on voluntary transactions between individual buyers and sellers. Private individuals have the right to buy and sell what they want, to accept or refuse work that is offered to them, and to move where they want when they want.

> Key institutions are private property and freedom of contract, both of which must be maintained by active government policies. The government creates laws of ownership and contract and then provides the institutions, such as police and courts, to enforce these laws.

In modern mixed economies, governments go well beyond these important basic functions. They intervene in market transactions to correct what economists call *market failures*. These are well-defined situations in which free markets do not work well. Some products, called *public goods*, are usually not provided at all by markets because their use cannot usually be restricted to those who pay for them. Defence and police protection are examples of public goods. In other cases, private producers or consumers impose costs called *externalities* on those who have no say in the transaction. This is the case when factories pollute the air and rivers. The public is harmed but plays no part in the transaction. In yet other cases, financial institutions, such as banks, mortgage companies, and investment houses, may indulge in risky activities that threaten the health of the entire economic system. These market failures explain why governments sometimes intervene to alter the allocation of resources.

Also, important issues of *equity* arise from letting free markets determine people's incomes. Some people lose their jobs because firms are reorganizing to become more efficient in the face of new technologies. Others keep their jobs, but the market places so little value on their services that they face economic deprivation. The old and the chronically ill may suffer if their past circumstances did not allow them to save enough to support themselves. For many reasons of this sort, almost everyone accepts some government intervention to redistribute income. Care must be taken, however, not to kill the goose that lays the golden egg. By taking too much from higher-income people, we risk eliminating their incentives to work hard and produce income, some of which is to be redistributed to those in need.

These are some of the reasons that all modern economies are mixed economies. Throughout most of the twentieth century in advanced industrial societies, the mix had been shifting toward more and more government participation in decisions about the allocation of resources and the distribution of income. Starting in the early 1980s, a worldwide movement began to reduce the degree of government participation in economies. With the onset of the global financial crisis of 2008–2009, however, there has been some movement back toward a greater involvement of government in the economy. These shifts in the market/government mix, and the reasons for them, are some of the major issues that will be studied in this book.

SUMMARY

1.1 What Is Economics?   LO 1

- Scarcity is a fundamental problem faced by all economies. Not enough resources are available to produce all the goods and services that people would like to consume.
- Scarcity makes it necessary to choose. All societies must have a mechanism for choosing what goods and services will be produced and in what quantities.
- The concept of opportunity cost emphasizes the problem of scarcity and choice by measuring the cost of obtaining a unit of one product in terms of the number of units of other products that could have been obtained instead.

- A production possibilities boundary shows all the combinations of goods that can be produced by an economy whose resources are fully and efficiently employed. Movement from one point to another along the boundary requires a reallocation of resources.
- Four basic questions must be answered in all economies: What is produced and how? What is consumed and by whom? Why are resources sometimes idle? Is productive capacity growing?
- Issues of government policy enter into discussions of all four questions.

1.2 The Complexity of Modern Economies   LO 2, 3, 4

- A market economy is self-organizing in the sense that when individual consumers and producers act independently to pursue their own self-interest, responding to prices determined in open markets, the collective outcome is coordinated.
- Incentives and self-interest play a central role for all groups of decision makers: consumers, producers, and governments.
- Individual consumers are assumed to make their decisions in an effort to maximize their well-being or utility. Producers' decisions are assumed to be designed to maximize their profits.

- The interaction of consumers and producers through goods and factor markets is illustrated by the circular flow of income and expenditure. Individual consumers sell factor services to producers and thereby earn their income. Similarly, producers earn their income by selling goods and services to individual consumers.
- Modern economies are based on the specialization and division of labour, which necessitate the exchange (trading) of goods and services. Exchange takes place in markets and is facilitated by the use of money.
- Driven by the ongoing revolution in transportation and communications technology, the world economy is rapidly globalizing.

1.3 Is There an Alternative to the Market Economy?   LO 5

- We can distinguish three pure types of economies: traditional, command, and free-market. In practice, all economies are mixed economies in that their economic behaviour responds to mixes of tradition, government command, and price incentives.
- In the late 1980s, events in Eastern Europe and the Soviet Union led to the general acceptance that the system of fully centrally planned economies had failed to produce minimally acceptable living standards for

its citizens. All these countries are now moving toward greater market determination and less state command in their economies.
- Governments play an important role in modern mixed economies. They create and enforce important background institutions such as private property and freedom of contract. They intervene to correct market failures. They also redistribute income in the interests of equity.

KEY CONCEPTS

Resources
Scarcity and the need for choice
Choice and opportunity cost
Production possibilities boundary
The self-organizing economy

Incentives and self-interest
Specialization
The division of labour
Trade and money
Globalization

Traditional economies
Command economies
Free-market economies
Mixed economies

STUDY EXERCISES

MyEconLab Make the grade with MyEconLab: Study Exercises marked in red can be found on MyEconLab. You can practise them as often as you want, and most feature step-by-step guided instructions to help you find the right answer.

1. Fill in the blanks to make the following statements correct.

   a. The three general categories of any economy's resources are _____, _____, and _____. Economists refer to these resources as the _____ of production.

   b. When we use any resource, the benefit given up by not using it in its best alternative way is known as the _____ of that resource.

   c. The concepts of scarcity, choice, and opportunity cost can be illustrated by a curve known as the _____.

   d. When looking at a production possibilities boundary, any point that is outside the boundary demonstrates _____. The _____ slope of the production possibilities boundary demonstrates _____.

   e. A straight-line production possibilities boundary (PPB) indicates that the opportunity cost of each good is _____, no matter how much of that good is produced. A PPB that is concave to the origin indicates that a(n) _____ amount of one good must be given up to produce more of the other good.

   f. Consider an economy producing two goods, A and B, with a PPB that is concave to the origin. As the economy produces more of good A and less of good B, its opportunity cost of producing A _____.

2. Explain the three economic concepts illustrated by the production possibilities boundary.

3. Consider an economy that produces only food and clothing. Its production possibilities boundary is shown below.

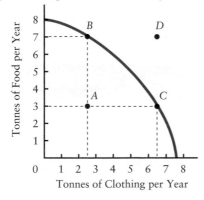

a. If the economy is at point A, how many tonnes of clothing and how many tonnes of food are being produced? At point B? At point C?

b. What do we know about the use of resources when the economy is at point A? At point B? At point C?

c. If the economy is at point B, what is the opportunity cost of producing one more tonne of food? What is the opportunity cost of producing one more tonne of clothing?

d. What do we know about the use of resources at point D? How would it be possible for the economy to produce at point D?

4. Choiceland has 250 workers and produces only two goods, X and Y. Labour is the only factor of production, but some workers are better suited to producing X than Y (and vice versa). The table below shows the maximum levels of output of each good possible from various levels of labour input.

Number of Workers Producing X	Annual Production of X	Number of Workers Producing Y	Annual Production of Y
0	0	250	1300
50	20	200	1200
100	45	150	900
150	60	100	600
200	70	50	350
250	75	0	0

a. Draw the production possibilities boundary for Choiceland on a scale diagram, with the production of X on the horizontal axis and the production of Y on the vertical axis.

b. Compute the opportunity cost of producing an extra 15 units of X if the economy is initially producing 45 units of X and 900 units of Y. How does this compare to the opportunity cost if the economy were initially producing 60 units of X and 600 units of Y?

c. If the economy is producing 40 units of X and 600 units of Y, what is the opportunity cost of producing an extra 20 units of X?

d. Suppose now that the technology associated with producing good Y improves, so that the maximum level of Y that can be produced from any given level of labour input increases by 10 percent. Explain (or show in a diagram) what happens to the production possibilities curve.

5. Explain why a technological improvement in the production of one good means that a country can now produce more of *other* goods than it did previously. Hint: Draw a country's production possibilities boundary to help answer this question.

6. Consider your decision whether to go skiing for the weekend. Suppose transportation, lift tickets, and accommodation for the weekend cost $300. Suppose also that restaurant food for the weekend will cost $75. Finally, suppose you have a weekend job that you will have to miss if you go skiing, which pays you $120 (after tax) for the one weekend day that you work. What is the opportunity cost of going skiing? Do you need any other information before computing the opportunity cost?

7. Suppose you and a friend are stranded on an island and must gather firewood and catch fish to survive. Through experience, you know that if each of you spends an entire day on either activity, the result is given in the following table:

	Fish	Firewood (bundles)
You	6	3
Your friend	8	2

You and your friend decide that you should each specialize so that one person catches fish while the other gathers firewood. But who should do which task?

a. What is the opportunity cost for you to gather an additional bundle of firewood? What is your friend's opportunity cost of gathering an extra bundle of firewood?

b. Assuming that you and your friend specialize, what allocation of tasks maximizes total output for your one day of joint effort?

c. Suppose you both decide to work for two days according to the allocation in part (b). What is the total amount of output? What would it have been had you chosen the reverse allocation of tasks?

8. In this chapter we used a simple idea of a production possibilities boundary to illustrate the concepts of scarcity, choice, and opportunity cost. We assumed there were only two goods—call them X and Y. But we all know that any economy produces many more than just two goods. Explain why the insights illustrated in Figure 1-2 on page 8 are more general, and why the assumption of only two goods is a useful one.

9. What is the difference between microeconomics and macroeconomics?

10. For each of the following situations, explain how a change in the stated "price" is likely to affect your incentives regarding the stated decision.

a. the price of ski-lift tickets; your decision to purchase a ski-lift ticket

b. the hourly wage for your weekend job; the decision to not work and go skiing on the weekend instead

c. the value of a speeding ticket; your decision to speed on the highway

d. the weight of your course grade attached to an assignment; your decision to work hard on that assignment

e. the level of tuition fees at your college or university; your decision to attend that college or university

11. State and explain two reasons why the specialization of labour is more efficient than universal self-sufficiency.

12. Consider the market for doctors' services. In what way has this market taken advantage of the specialization of labour?

13. List the four main types of economic systems and their main attributes.

14. As we said in the text, the average family income in Canada is about $75 000 per year. Imagine a hypothetical world in which *all* Canadian families had this income.

a. In such a world, would poverty exist in Canada?

b. In such a world, would scarcity exist in Canada?

c. Explain the difference between poverty and scarcity.

15. Comment on the following statement: "One of the mysteries of semantics is why the government-managed economies ever came to be called planned and the market economies unplanned. It is the former that are in chronic chaos, in which buyers stand in line hoping to buy some toilet paper or soap. It is the latter that are in reasonable equilibrium—where if you want a bar of soap or a steak or a shirt or a car, you can go to the store and find that the item is magically there for you to buy. It is the liberal economies that reflect a highly sophisticated planning system, and the government-managed economies that are primitive and unplanned."

A Refresher on Graphing

This appendix is a refresher on the basic graphing techniques you saw in high school mathematics. Economists use graphs to illustrate theories and show data, and you will see many graphs throughout this course. Here, we review the most basic concepts for those who need review.

Displaying Points on a Graph

Coordinate Space A graph begins with two number lines, one horizontal and one vertical. We call the horizontal number line the x axis because we often label the variable displayed along this axis x. We call the vertical number line the y axis because we often label the variable displayed along this axis y. In Figure 1 the x axis displays the number line horizontally from –5 to 5 with intervals of 1. The y axis displays the number line vertically from –3 to 3, also with intervals of 1. We have now created a two-dimensional space that is called a *coordinate space*.

Now look at point A in the figure. Point A represents two numbers: 3 on the horizontal, or x, axis and 2 on the vertical, or y, axis. We write point A as (3, 2)

and we call the 3 and the 2 the *coordinates* of point A. The usual practice in graphing is to list the x-axis coordinate first and the y-axis coordinate second. In the same way, we can read point B(2, –2), point C(–1, –2), and point D(–4, 3).

Any point on a graph is simply a visual representation of two numbers. For example, point A represents the numbers 3 and 2. For the graph to be meaningful to us, however, the numbers must tell us something. Let's take an example from economics and plot a graph with the information from the table in Figure 2 that shows how much Katie saves at various levels of income (both measured in dollars). Each point on the graph now represents a particular level of income and the associated level of saving, or an income-saving combination. For example, point C shows that at an income of $30 000, Katie saves $5000. It is also easy to see when looking at this graph that when Katie's level of income goes up, her level of saving goes up.

Notice that each increment indicated on the x axis is 10 000 and the increment on the y axis is only 5 000. We adjust the scales on the axes to fit the information we want to graph. In Figure 1 we called each interval 1 on both axes, and in Figure 2 we called each interval on the x axis 10 000 and each interval on the y axis 5 000. Imagine trying to graph Canadian national income, which is in the range of $1.7 trillion, on a graph using intervals of $1 or even $10 000. The resulting graph would have to be enormous, and would not be helpful in displaying the information. Therefore, we choose the scales on each axis to best display the specific data we are considering.

Variables Our graph in Figure 2 now visually represents the relationship between the two variables, income and saving. *Variable* is the word we use to describe the items on the axes to which we are giving numeric values; in this case, income and saving. The *independent* variable, in this case income, is represented on the

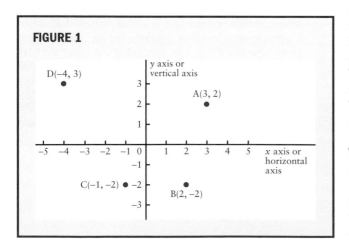

FIGURE 1

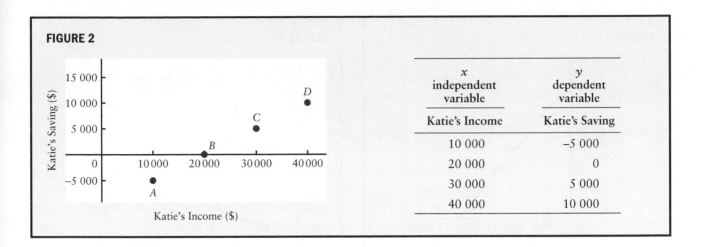

FIGURE 2

x independent variable	y dependent variable
Katie's Income	Katie's Saving
10 000	–5 000
20 000	0
30 000	5 000
40 000	10 000

horizontal axis (the x axis) and the *dependent* variable, in this case saving, is represented on the vertical axis (the y axis). (Though this is the usual way to draw a graph, you will later see that economists are sometimes accused of doing it backward—see footnote 3 on page 71 in Chapter 3.)

Linear Curves

When two variables move, either in the same or in opposite directions, we can plot the data points on a graph and join their points to form a curve. If joining the points gives us a straight line we call it a linear curve and we say that x and y have a linear *relationship*. A relationship in which the two variables move in the same direction is called a *positive,* or *direct,* relationship—when one variable goes up, the other goes up. A relationship in which the two variables move in opposite directions is called a *negative,* or *inverse,* relationship—when one variable goes up, the other goes down.

A Positive Relationship Figure 3 shows two variables, the number of pizza toppings and the total price of a pizza. A cheese pizza has zero toppings and costs $5; each additional topping costs $1.50. The two variables, number of toppings and price of pizza, move in the same direction—as the number of toppings (the x variable) goes up, the price of the pizza (the y variable) goes up—so this is a positive or direct

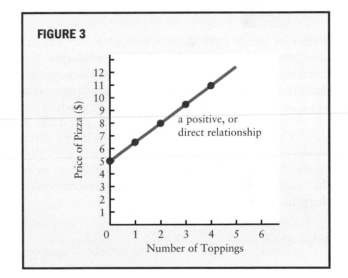

FIGURE 3

a positive, or direct relationship

relationship. Joining the points gives us an upward-sloping straight line, so we call this a positive, linear relationship.

A Negative Relationship Figure 4 shows two variables, the price of tickets for a university basketball game and the number of people who choose to purchase tickets and attend the game. (In Chapter 3 we describe such a relationship as a *demand curve* for basketball tickets.) The two variables move in opposite directions—this is a negative, or inverse, relationship. Joining the points gives us a downward-sloping straight line, so we call this a negative linear relationship.

FIGURE 4

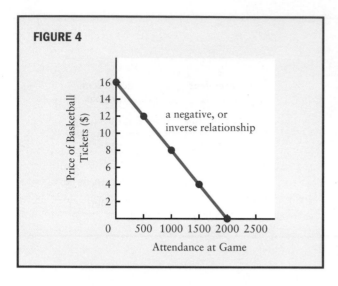

a negative, or inverse relationship

FIGURE 5

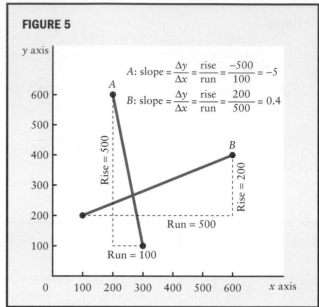

Slopes of Linear Curves The slope of a line tells us how much the y variable changes whenever the x variable changes. For example, the slope of the straight line in Figure 3 tells us how much the price of pizza changes (the change on the y axis) when the number of toppings changes (the change on the x axis). The slope is defined as the change in the value on the vertical axis divided by the change in the value on the horizontal axis. It is commonly referred to as the "rise over the run." We can write a description of slope in a few ways:

$$\text{Slope} = \frac{\text{rise}}{\text{run}} = \frac{\text{change in value on vertical axis}}{\text{change in value on horizontal axis}}$$

$$= \frac{\Delta y}{\Delta x}$$

The last term uses the Greek letter delta, Δ, which means "the change in." For Figure 3, the slope of the curve is $1.50 per topping, indicating that each extra topping increases the price of the pizza by $1.50.

Figure 5 shows the calculation of slopes for two linear curves. (Work through each of these calculations and then draw various linear curves of your own and practise calculating their slopes. Try using different units and intervals on the axes and see if this affects the slope.) Notice that the upward-sloping curve has a positive slope and the downward-sloping curve has a negative slope. Also notice that the steeper the line, upward- or downward-sloping, the higher the absolute number value of the slope.

A linear curve has the same slope over the entire length of the curve.

Infinite and Zero Slopes Figure 6 shows two extreme cases that we see often in economics. For the horizontal line, we calculate the slope as rise/run = $\Delta y/\Delta x = 0/\infty$. We say that the run, or Δx, is ∞ because the linear curve extends to infinity. Zero divided by infinity is zero. Remember that the flatter is the curve, the smaller is the slope. Here is the extreme case of a flat curve; the slope is zero. For the vertical line, we calculate the slope as rise/run = $\Delta y/\Delta x = \infty/0$. Infinity divided by zero is infinity. Remember that the

FIGURE 6

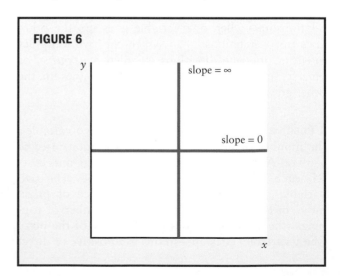

steeper is the curve, the higher is the slope. This is the extreme case of a steep curve; the slope is infinite.

Understanding the concept of the slope of a line is crucial when studying economics. Economists are interested in how much one variable changes in response to a change in another variable, and it is the slope of the curve that tells them this.

Equation of a Linear Curve A linear curve is a visual representation of the linear relationship between two variables. The same relationship can also be described in an equation. The general equation for a linear curve is

$$y = a + bx,$$

where y is the dependent variable and x is the independent variable. The letter a represents the y *intercept,* or the point at which the line intersects the y axis. The letter b represents the slope of the line.

In Figure 7 we plot the linear curve, A, given by the relationship between the x and y variables in Table A of Figure 7. The equation for this linear curve is

$$y = 2 + 0.5x$$

Prove this to yourself by calculating y for any value of x. For example, when $x = 3$, $y - 2 + 0.5(3) = 3.5$. When $x = 7$, $y = 2 + 0.5(7) = 5.5$. The y intercept of this line is 2, and thus the line intersects the y axis at 2.

The slope of the line is 0.5. Verify this by calculating $\Delta y/\Delta x$ between any two points on the line. Between points C and D, for example, the Δy (or the rise) is 1 and the Δx (or the run) is 2. So the slope of the linear curve is $\Delta y/\Delta x = 1/2 = 0.5$.

The equation for a downward-sloping linear curve works the same way. In Figure 7 we plot the linear curve, B, given by the relationship between the x and y variables in Table B of Figure 7. The equation for this linear curve is $y = 8 - 4x$. Once again, prove this to yourself by calculating y for various levels of x. The y intercept for this line is 8 and the slope is -4. Notice, of course, that the slope of the downward-sloping linear curve is negative.

Non-Linear Curves

All the curves we have looked at so far have been straight lines—they have been linear curves. (So they haven't really been "curves" at all!) However, not all relations between two economic variables can be graphed as a straight line. More often, the relation is *non-linear*. In a non-linear relationship between x and y, each unit change in x does not always bring about the same change in the y variable. Figure 8 shows four curves, two with positive slopes and two with negative slopes.

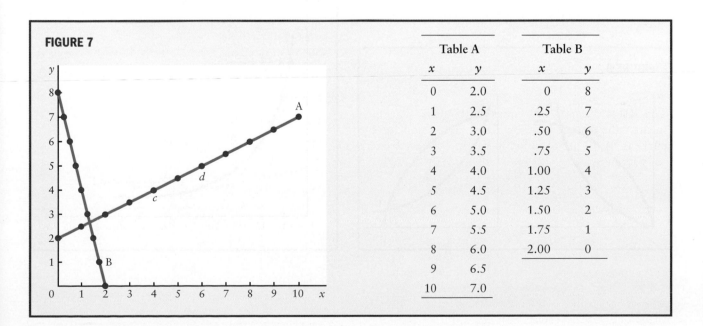

FIGURE 7

Table A		Table B	
x	y	x	y
0	2.0	0	8
1	2.5	.25	7
2	3.0	.50	6
3	3.5	.75	5
4	4.0	1.00	4
5	4.5	1.25	3
6	5.0	1.50	2
7	5.5	1.75	1
8	6.0	2.00	0
9	6.5		
10	7.0		

Curves A and B both show positive relationships between x and y—the slopes are both positive. As x increases, so does y. Curve A, however, becomes flatter as x increases, and curve B becomes steeper as x increases. Similarly, curves C and D both show negative relationships between x and y—both slopes are negative because in each case, as x increases, y decreases. Curve C becomes flatter as x increases and curve D becomes steeper as x increases.

Slopes of Non-Linear Curves Examine curves A, B, C, and D in Figure 8 to see how y changes in response to a one-unit change in x, at various levels of x. You will see that for curves A and C, the change in y becomes smaller as we move along the x axis. We can describe the slopes of curves A and C as starting out steep and becoming flatter as x increases. For curves B and D, however, the change in y becomes larger as we move along the x axis. We can describe the slopes of curves B and D as starting out flat and becoming steeper as x increases. The slopes of these non-linear curves are changing as we move along the curve. How do we measure the slope of a curve when the slope is different at each point along the curve?

Remember that we measured the slope of a straight line by choosing two points on the line and dividing the change in y by the change in x. Doing the same thing to measure the slope of a non-linear curve, however, would give us the slope of the line connecting the two specific points that we chose on the curve but would not give us the slope of the curve itself.

Since the slope of the curve is continuously changing, we must measure the slope *at specific points* along the curve. To do so, we simply draw a straight line *tangent* to the curve at the point at which we want to measure the slope. A line is tangent to a curve if it touches *but does not intersect* the curve at that point. The slope of this tangent line then tells us the slope of the curve *at the point of tangency*. Figure 9 shows the calculation of the slope at three points along a downward-sloping curve like our curve C in Figure 8.

Consider the slope of the curve at point A. The tangent to the curve at point A has a y intercept at 50 and an x intercept at 10. Thus the slope of the tangent line is $\Delta y/\Delta x = -50/10 = -5$. Thus the slope of the curve at point A is −5. Now consider the slope of the curve at point C. The tangent line to point C has an x intercept of 50 and a y intercept of 10. The slope of the tangent line is $\Delta y/\Delta x = -10/50 = -0.2$. Therefore the slope of the curve at point C is −0.2. Thus, although the slope of the curve is always negative, its slope falls (in absolute value) from 5 at point A to 0.2 at point C.

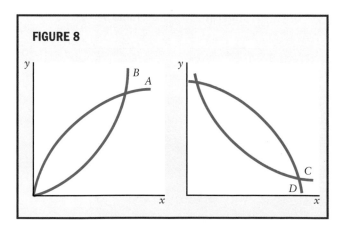

FIGURE 8

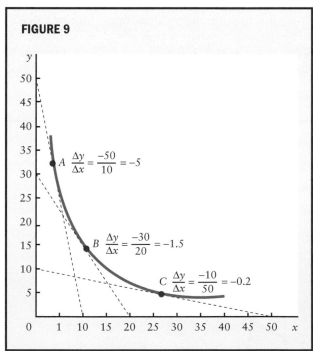

FIGURE 9

We leave it to you to draw more non-linear curves (like curves A, B, and D in Figure 8) and compute the slopes at various points along each curve. For each computation, simply draw a straight line tangent to the curve, and then compute the slope of the tangent line. This will give you the slope of the non-linear curve *at the point of tangency*.

A Final Word

Graphing can be intimidating, but a little practice goes a long way. By working your way carefully through the various parts of this section, plus the graphing questions in the Study Exercises at the end of Chapter 2, you will soon be comfortable with the basics of graphing.

Economic Theories, Data, and Graphs

LEARNING OBJECTIVES (LO)

After studying this chapter, you will be able to

1 distinguish between positive and normative statements.

2 explain why and how economists use theories to help them understand the economy.

3 understand the interaction between economic theories and empirical observation.

4 identify several types of economic data, including index numbers, time-series and cross-sectional data, and scatter diagrams.

5 see that the slope of a line on a graph relating two variables shows how one responds to a small change in the other.

IF you follow the news, whether online, TV, newspaper, or radio, you are likely to hear the views of economists being discussed—about debt crises, unemployment, attempts to reform the health-care system, environmental policy, changes to corporate income-tax rates, or a myriad of other issues. Where do economists' opinions come from? Are they supported by hard evidence, and if so, why do economists sometimes disagree with each other over important issues?

Economics is a social science, and in this chapter we explore what it means to be "scientific" in the study of economics. Along the way we will learn much about theories, predictions, data, testing, and graphing—economists use all of these tools and techniques in their attempt to understand the economic world. We begin with the important distinction between positive and normative statements.

2.1 Positive and Normative Statements

Economists give two broad types of advice, called *normative* and *positive*. For example, they sometimes advise that the government ought to try harder to reduce unemployment. When they say such things, they are giving normative advice; in this case, they are making judgements about the value of the various things that the government could do with its limited resources and about the costs and benefits of reducing unemployment. Advice that depends on a value judgement is normative—it tells others what they *ought* to do.

Another type of advice is illustrated by the statement "If the government wants to reduce unemployment, reducing unemployment insurance benefits is an effective way of doing so." This is positive advice. It does not rely on a judgement about the value of reducing unemployment. Instead, the expert is saying, "If this is what you want to do, here is a way to do it."

Normative statements depend on value judgements and cannot be evaluated solely by a recourse to facts. In contrast, **positive statements** do not involve value judgements. They are statements about matters of fact, and so disagreements about them are appropriately dealt with by an appeal to evidence. The distinction between positive and normative is fundamental to scientific progress. Much of the success of modern science depends on the ability of scientists to separate their views on *what does happen* in the world from their views on *what they would like to happen*. For example, until the eighteenth century almost everyone believed that Earth was only a few thousand years old. Evidence then began to accumulate that Earth was billions of years old. This evidence was hard for most people to accept, since it ran counter to a literal reading of many religious texts. Many did not want to believe the evidence. Nevertheless, scientists, many of whom were religious, continued their research because they refused to allow their feelings about what they wanted to believe to affect their scientific search for the truth. Eventually, all scientists and most members of the public came to accept that Earth is about 4 billion years old.

normative statement A statement about what ought to be as opposed to what actually is.

positive statement A statement about what actually is (was, or will be), as opposed to what ought to be.

> Distinguishing what is actually true from what we would like to be true requires distinguishing between positive and normative statements.

Examples of both types of statements are given in Table 2-1. All five positive statements in the table are assertions about the nature of the world in which we live. In contrast, the five normative statements involve value judgements. Notice two things about the positive/normative distinction. First, positive statements need not be true. Statement C is almost certainly false, and yet it is positive, not normative. Second, the inclusion of a value judgement in a statement does not necessarily make the statement itself normative. Statement D is a positive statement about the value judgements that people hold. We could conduct a survey to check if people really do prefer low unemployment to low inflation. We could ask them and we could observe how they voted. There is no need for the economist to rely on a value judgement to check the validity of the statement itself.

We leave you to analyze the remaining eight statements to decide precisely why each is either positive or normative. Remember to apply the two tests. First, is the statement only about actual or alleged facts? If so, it is a positive one. Second, are value judgements necessary to assess the truth of the statement? If so, it is normative.

TABLE 2-1   Positive and Normative Statements

Positive	Normative
A Raising interest rates encourages people to save.	F People should be encouraged to save.
B High rates of income tax encourage people to evade paying taxes.	G Governments should arrange taxes so that people cannot avoid paying them.
C Lowering the price of cigarettes leads people to smoke less.	H The government should raise the tax on cigarettes to discourage people from smoking.
D The majority of the population would prefer a policy that reduced unemployment to one that reduced inflation.	I Unemployment is a more important social problem than inflation.
E Government financial assistance to commercial banks is ineffective at preventing job losses.	J Government should not spend taxpayers' money on supporting commercial banks.

Disagreements Among Economists

Economists often disagree with one another in public discussions, frequently because of poor communication. The adversaries fail to define their terms or their points of reference clearly, and so they end up "arguing past" each other, with the only certain result being that the audience is left confused.

Economists often disagree with one another in the media or at conferences, but their debates are more often about normative issues than positive ones.

Another source of disagreement stems from some economists' failure to acknowledge the full state of their ignorance. There are many points on which the evidence is far from conclusive. Informed judgements are required to take a position on even a purely positive question. In such cases, a responsible economist makes clear the extent to which his or her view is based on judgements about the relevant facts.

Many other public disagreements are based on the positive/normative distinction. Different economists have different values, and these normative views play a large part in most discussions of public policy. Many economists stress the importance of individual responsibility and argue, for example, that lower employment insurance benefits would be desirable because people would have a greater incentive to search for a job. Other economists stress the need for a generous "social safety net" and argue that higher employment insurance benefits are desirable because human hardship would be reduced. In such debates, and there are many in economics, it is the responsibility of the economist to state clearly what part of the proffered advice is normative and what part is positive.

Because the world is complex and because no issue can be settled beyond any doubt, economists rarely agree unanimously on an issue. Nevertheless, there is an impressive amount of agreement on many aspects of how the economy works and what happens when governments intervene to alter its workings. A survey published in the *American*

Economic Review, perhaps the most influential economics journal, showed strong agreement among economists on many propositions, including "Rent control leads to a housing shortage" (85 percent yes), "Tariffs usually reduce economic welfare" (93 percent yes), "Large government budget deficits have adverse effects on the economy" (83 percent yes), and "A minimum wage increases unemployment among young workers" (79 percent yes). Notice that all these are positive rather than normative statements. Other examples of these areas of agreement will be found in many places throughout this book.

Whether they agree or disagree with one another, economists are in demand in many sectors of the economy. See *Applying Economic Concepts 2-1* for a discussion of the many organizations that employ economists.

APPLYING ECONOMIC CONCEPTS 2-1

Where Economists Work

This chapter discusses the theoretical and empirical tools that economists use. After reading this material, you might wonder where economists find jobs and what kind of work they actually do. The skills of economists are demanded in many parts of the economy by governments, private and crown corporations, non-profit organizations, and universities.

In Ottawa and the provincial and territorial capitals, economists are hired in most government departments to analyze the effects of government policies and to design ways to improve those policies. At Finance Canada, economists design and analyze the income-tax system and the effects of current spending programs. At Environment Canada, they help design and evaluate policies aimed at reducing water and air pollution. At Industry Canada, they study the sources of productivity growth and design policies to encourage innovation in the private sector. At the Bank of Canada, economists research the link between interest rates, the aggregate demand for goods and services, and the rate of increase in prices. They also monitor developments in the global economy and their effects on the Canadian economy. Statistics Canada employs many economists to design methods of collecting and analyzing data covering all aspects of Canadian society.

The analysis of economic policies also takes place in independent research organizations, often called "think tanks." The C.D. Howe Institute in Toronto is one of Canada's best-known think tanks, and it regularly publishes papers on topics ranging from monetary policy and the state of public pensions to the effects of immigration and the challenges in reforming Canada's policies for foreign development assistance. Other think tanks include the Institute for Research on Public Policy, the Canadian Centre for Policy Alternatives, the Fraser Institute, the Centre for the Study of Living Standards, and the Conference Board of Canada. All of these independent and non-profit organizations hire economists to study economic issues and then write and edit the economic publications that address them.

Private and public (crown) corporations in many sectors of the economy also hire economists in a variety of positions. Economists at Canadian Pacific Railway monitor how changes in world commodity prices will lead to changes in Canadian resource production and thus to changes in the demand for their rail transport services. Economists at Manitoba Hydro study the link between economic growth and electricity demand to help the firm with its long-run investment decisions. Those at Export Development Canada examine how economic and political risks in various countries influence the demand for the products of Canadian exporters. Economists at Bombardier are hired to determine how ongoing negotiations within the World Trade Organization will affect tariff levels in various countries and how these changes will affect the demand for Bombardier jets.

Finally, many economists are hired by universities all over the world to teach students like you and to conduct research on a wide variety of economic topics. Some of this research is theoretical and some is empirical, using data to test economic theories. Other academic economists focus their research on the design and implementation of better economic policy, and often spend considerable time interacting with the economists employed by government departments.

Training in economics provides useful analytical skills that are valuable for learning about the workings of a complex economic world. There is no shortage of demand for people who can think clearly and analytically about economic issues. This course could well be the start of a great career for you. Study hard!

2.2 Building and Testing Economic Theories

The economic world is complex. Many things are changing at the same time, and it is difficult to distinguish cause from effect. Economists who are observing the world carefully, however, see regularities in the data—for example, that unemployment tends to rise when national income slows, or that periods of higher inflation often follow periods of very low interest rates. In order to better understand such regularities in the data, and to identify the likely causes and effects, economists develop *theories*, which they sometimes call *models*. Theories are used to both explain events that have already happened and to help predict events that might happen in the future.

What Are Theories?

Theories are constructed to explain things. For example, economists may seek to explain what determines the quantity of eggs bought and sold in a particular month in Manitoba and the price at which they are sold. Or they may seek to explain what determines the quantity of oil bought and sold around the world on a particular day and the price at which it is traded. As part of the answer to such questions, economists have developed theories of demand and supply—theories that we will study in detail in the next three chapters. These and all other theories are distinguished by their *variables, assumptions,* and *predictions*.

variable Any well-defined item, such as the price or quantity of a commodity, that can take on various specific values.

Variables The basic elements of any theory are its variables. A **variable** is a well-defined item, such as a price or a quantity, that can take on different possible values.

In a theory of the egg market, the variable *quantity of eggs* might be defined as the number of cartons of 12 Grade A large eggs. The variable *price of eggs* is the amount of money that must be given up to purchase each carton of eggs. The particular values taken by those two variables might be 20 000 cartons per week at a price of $2.60 in July 2011, 18 000 cartons per week at a price of $2.75 in July 2012, and 19 500 cartons per week at a price of $2.95 in July 2013.

There are two broad categories of variables that are important in any theory. An **endogenous variable** is one whose value is determined within the theory. An **exogenous variable** influences the endogenous variables but is itself determined outside the theory. To illustrate the difference, the price of eggs and the quantity of eggs are endogenous variables in our theory of the egg market—our theory is designed to explain them. The state of the weather, however, is an exogenous variable. It may well affect the number of eggs consumers demand or producers supply, but we can safely assume that the state of the weather is not influenced by the market for eggs.

endogenous variable A variable that is explained within a theory. Sometimes called an *induced variable* or a *dependent variable.*

exogenous variable A variable that is determined outside the theory. Sometimes called an *autonomous variable* or an *independent variable.*

Assumptions A theory's assumptions concern motives, directions of causation, and the conditions under which the theory is meant to apply.

Motives. The theories we study in this book make the fundamental assumption that everyone pursues his or her own self-interest when making economic decisions. Individuals are assumed to strive to maximize their *utility,* while firms are assumed to try to maximize their *profits*. Not only are they assumed to know what they want, but we also assume that they know how to go about getting it within the constraints they face.

Direction Of Causation. When economists assume that one variable is related to another, they are usually assuming some causal link between the two. For example, when the amount of wheat that producers want to supply is assumed to increase when the quality of their fertilizer improves, the causation runs from the quality of fertilizer to the supply of wheat. Producers supply more wheat because they now have access to better fertilizer; they are not assumed to get access to better fertilizers as a result of their increased supply of wheat.

Conditions Of Application. Assumptions are often used to specify the conditions under which a theory is meant to hold. For example, a theory that assumes there is "no government" usually does not mean literally the absence of government but only that the theory is meant to apply when governments are not significantly affecting the situation being studied.

Although assumptions are an essential part of all theories, students are often concerned about those that seem unrealistic. An example will illustrate some of the issues involved. Much of the theory that we are going to study in this book uses the assumption that owners of firms attempt to make as much money as they can—that is, to maximize their profits. The assumption of profit maximization allows economists to make predictions about the behaviour of firms, such as "firms will supply more output if the market price increases."

Profit maximization may seem like a rather crude assumption. Surely, for example, the managers of firms sometimes choose to protect the environment rather than pursue certain highly polluting but profitable opportunities. Does this not discredit the assumption of profit maximization by showing it to be unrealistic?

The answer is no; to make successful predictions, the theory does not require that managers be solely and unwaveringly motivated by the desire to maximize profits at all times. All that is required is that profits be a sufficiently important consideration that a theory based on the assumption of profit maximization will lead to explanations and predictions that are substantially correct. It is not always appropriate to criticize a theory because its assumptions seem unrealistic. A good theory abstracts in a useful way; a poor theory does not. If a theory has ignored some genuinely important factors, its predictions will usually be contradicted by the evidence.

> **All theory is an abstraction from reality. If it were not, it would merely duplicate the world in all its complexity and would add little to our understanding of it.**

Predictions A theory's predictions are the propositions that can be deduced from it. They are often called *hypotheses*. For example, a prediction from a theory of the oil market is that a rise in the world price for oil will lead Canadian oil producers to produce and supply more oil. Another prediction in the same market is that a decision by the members of the OPEC cartel to reduce their annual output of oil will lead to an increase in the world price. The economic logic behind such predictions will be explained in several chapters of this book; for now we can proceed to see how economists *test* such predictions or hypotheses.

Testing Theories

A theory is tested by confronting its predictions with evidence. For example, is an increase in the world price of oil *actually* followed by an increase in oil production by Canadian producers? A theory ceases to be useful when it cannot predict better than an alternative theory. When a theory consistently fails to predict better than an available alternative, it is either modified or replaced.

The old question "Which came first: the chicken or the egg?" is often raised when discussing economic theories. In the first instance, it was observation that preceded economic theories; people were not born with economic theories embedded in their minds. However, once economics was established as a scientific line of inquiry, theories and evidence interacted with each other. It has now become impossible to say that one precedes the other. In some cases, empirical evidence may suggest inadequacies that require the development of better theories. In other cases, an inspired guess may lead to a theory that has little current empirical support but is subsequently found to explain many observations. This interaction between theory and empirical observation is illustrated in Figure 2-1.

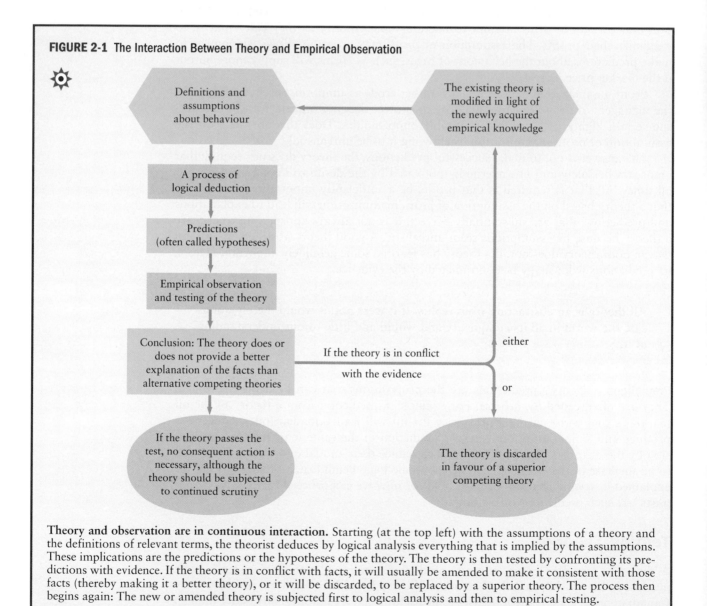

FIGURE 2-1 The Interaction Between Theory and Empirical Observation

Theory and observation are in continuous interaction. Starting (at the top left) with the assumptions of a theory and the definitions of relevant terms, the theorist deduces by logical analysis everything that is implied by the assumptions. These implications are the predictions or the hypotheses of the theory. The theory is then tested by confronting its predictions with evidence. If the theory is in conflict with facts, it will usually be amended to make it consistent with those facts (thereby making it a better theory), or it will be discarded, to be replaced by a superior theory. The process then begins again: The new or amended theory is subjected first to logical analysis and then to empirical testing.

The scientific approach is central to the study of economics: Empirical observation leads to the construction of theories, theories generate specific predictions, and the predictions are tested by more detailed empirical observation.

Rejection Versus Confirmation An important part of the scientific approach consists of creating a theory that will explain some observation. A theory designed to explain observation X will typically generate a prediction about some other observable variables, Y and Z. The prediction about Y and Z can be tested and may be *rejected* by the data. If the prediction is rejected, the value of the theory is brought into question.

The alternative to this approach is to create a theory and then look for *confirming* evidence. Such an approach is hazardous because the world is sufficiently complex that some confirming evidence can be found for any theory, no matter how unlikely the theory may be. For example, flying saucers, the Loch Ness monster, fortune telling, and astrology all have their devotees who can quote confirming evidence in spite of the failure of many attempts to discover systematic, objective evidence of these things.

Statistical Analysis Most theories generate a prediction of the form "If X increases, then Y will also increase." A specific example is "If national income rises, the level of employment will rise." Statistical analysis can be used to test such predictions and to estimate the numerical values of the function that describes the relationship. In practice, the same data can be used simultaneously to test whether a relationship exists and, if it does exist, to provide an estimate of the magnitude of that relationship.

Because economics is primarily a non-laboratory science, it lacks the controlled experiments central to such sciences as physics and chemistry. Economics must therefore use millions of uncontrolled "experiments" that are going on every day in the marketplace. Households are deciding what to purchase given changing prices and incomes, firms are deciding what to produce and how, and governments are involved in the economy through their various taxes, subsidies, and regulations. Because all these activities can be observed and recorded, a mass of data is continually being produced by the economy.

The variables that interest economists—such as the level of employment, the price of a DVD, and the output of automobiles—are generally influenced by many forces that vary simultaneously. If economists are to test their theories about relations among specific variables, they must use statistical techniques designed for situations in which other things *cannot* be held constant. Fortunately, such techniques exist, although their application is usually neither simple nor straightforward.

Later in this chapter we provide a discussion of some graphical techniques for describing data and displaying some of the more obvious relationships. Further examination of data involves techniques studied in elementary statistics courses. More advanced courses in econometrics deal with the array of techniques designed to test economic hypotheses and to measure economic relations in the complex circumstances in which economic evidence is often generated.

Correlation Versus Causation Suppose you want to test your theory's prediction that "If X increases, Y will also increase." You are looking for a *causal* relationship from X to Y, because a change in X is predicted to *cause* a change in Y. When you look at the data, suppose you find that X and Y are positively correlated—that is, when X rises, Y also tends to rise. Is your theory supported? It might appear that way, but there is a potential problem.

A finding that X and Y are positively correlated means only that X and Y tend to move together. This correlation is *consistent* with the theory that X causes Y, but it is *not* direct evidence of this causal relationship. The causality may be in the opposite direction—from *Y* to *X*. Or *X* and *Y* may have no direct causal connection; they may instead be jointly caused by some third variable, *Z*.

Here is an example. Suppose your theory predicts that individuals who get more education will earn higher incomes as a result—the causality in this theory runs from education to income. In the data, suppose we find that education and income are positively correlated (as they are). This should not, however, be taken as direct evidence for the causal prediction. The data are certainly consistent with that theory, but they are also consistent with others. For example, individuals who grow up in higher-income households may "buy" more education, just as they buy more clothes or entertainment. In this case, income causes education, rather than the other way around. Another possibility is that education and income are positively correlated because the personal characteristics that lead people to become more educated—ability and motivation—are the same characteristics that lead to high incomes. In this case, the *causal* relationship runs from personal characteristics to both income and education.

> Most economic predictions involve causality. Economists must take care when testing predictions to distinguish between correlation and causality. Correlation can establish that the data are consistent with the theory; establishing the likelihood of causality usually requires advanced statistical techniques.

| 2.3 Economic Data

For data on the Canadian economy and many other quantifiable aspects of Canadian life, see Statistics Canada's website: www.statcan.gc.ca

Economists use real-world observations to test their theories. For example, did the amount that people saved last year rise—as the theory predicts it should have—when a large tax cut increased their after-tax incomes? To test this prediction we need reliable data for people's incomes and their savings.

Political scientists, sociologists, anthropologists, and psychologists often collect for themselves the data they use to formulate and test their theories. Economists are unusual among social scientists in mainly using data collected by others, often government statisticians. In economics there is a division of labour between collecting data and using them to test theories. The advantage is that economists do not need to spend much of their scarce research time collecting the data they use. The disadvantage is that they are often not as well informed about the limitations of the data collected by others as they would be if they had collected the data themselves.

After data are collected, they can be displayed in various ways, many of which we will see later in this chapter. They can be laid out in tables. They can be displayed in various types of graphs. And when we are interested in relative movements rather than absolute ones, the data can be expressed in *index numbers*. We begin with a discussion of index numbers.

Index Numbers

Economists frequently look at data on prices or quantities and explore how specific variables change over time. For example, they may be interested in comparing the time paths of output in two industries: steel and newsprint. The problem is that it may be difficult to compare the time paths of the two different variables if we just look at the "raw" data.

Table 2-2 shows some hypothetical data for the volume of output in the steel and newsprint industries. Because the two variables are measured in different units, it is not immediately clear which of the two variables is more volatile or which, if either, has an upward or a downward trend.

It is easier to compare the two paths if we focus on *relative* rather than *absolute* changes. One way to do this is to construct some **index numbers**.

How to Build an Index Number We start by taking the value of the variable at some point in time as the "base" with which the values in other periods will be compared. We call this the *base period*. In the present example, we choose 2004 as the base year for both series. We then take the output in each subsequent year, called the "given year," divide it by the output in the base year, and then multiply the result by 100. This gives us an index number for the output of steel and a separate index number for the output of newsprint. For each index number, the value of output in the base year is equal to 100. The details of the calculations are shown in Table 2-3.

An index number simply expresses the value of some series in any given year as a percentage of its value in the base year. For example, the 2014 index of steel output of 122.5 tells us that steel output in 2014 was 22.5 percent greater than in 2004. In contrast, the 2014 index for newsprint output of 93.8 tells us that newsprint output in 2014 was only 93.8 percent of the output in 2004—that is, output was 6.2 percent

TABLE 2-2 Volume of Steel and Newsprint Output

Year	Volume of Steel (thousands of tonnes)	Volume of Newsprint (thousands of rolls)
2004	200	3200
2005	210	3100
2006	225	3000
2007	215	3200
2008	250	3100
2009	220	3300
2010	265	3100
2011	225	3300
2012	255	3100
2013	230	3200
2014	245	3000

Comparing the time paths of two data series is difficult when absolute numbers are used. Since steel output and newsprint output have quite different absolute numbers, it is difficult to detect which time series is more volatile.

index number A measure of some variable, conventionally expressed relative to a base period, which is assigned the value 100.

TABLE 2-3 Constructing Index Numbers

Year	Steel Procedure		Index	Newsprint Procedure		Index
2004	(200/200) × 100	=	100.0	(3200/3200) × 100	=	100.0
2005	(210/200) × 100	=	105.0	(3100/3200) × 100	=	96.9
2006	(225/200) × 100	=	112.5	(3000/3200) × 100	=	93.8
2007	(215/200) × 100	=	107.5	(3200/3200) × 100	=	100.0
2008	(250/200) × 100	=	125.0	(3100/3200) × 100	=	96.9
2009	(220/200) × 100	=	110.0	(3300/3200) × 100	=	103.1
2010	(265/200) × 100	=	132.5	(3100/3200) × 100	=	96.9
2011	(225/200) × 100	=	112.5	(3300/3200) × 100	=	103.1
2012	(255/200) × 100	=	127.5	(3100/3200) × 100	=	96.9
2013	(230/200) × 100	=	115.0	(3200/3200) × 100	=	100.0
2014	(245/200) × 100	=	122.5	(3000/3200) × 100	=	93.8

Index numbers are calculated by dividing the value in the given year by the value in the base year and multiplying the result by 100. The 2014 index number for steel tells us that steel output in 2014 was 22.5 percent greater than in the base year, 2004. The 2014 index number for newsprint tells us that newsprint output in 2014 was 93.8 percent of the output in the base year, 2004.

lower in 2014 than in 2004. The results in Table 2-3 allow us to compare the relative fluctuations in the two series. It is apparent from the values in the table that the output of steel has shown significantly more percentage variability than has the output of newsprint. This is also clear in Figure 2-2.

The formula of any index number is

$$\text{Value of index in any given period} = \frac{\text{Absolute value in given period}}{\text{Absolute value in base period}} \times 100$$

Care must be taken, however, when using index numbers. The index number always tells you the percentage change compared with the base year, but when comparing an index number across non-base years, the percentage change in the index number is *not* given by the absolute difference in the values of the index number. For example, if you want to know how much steel output changed from 2008 to 2010, we know from Table 2-3 that the index number for steel output increased from 125.0 to 132.5. But this is not an increase of 7.5 percent. The *percentage* increase in steel output is computed as $(132.5 - 125.0)/125.0 = 7.5/125.0 = 0.06$, or 6 percent.

More Complex Index Numbers Perhaps the most famous index number used by economists is the index of average prices—the Consumer Price Index (CPI). This is a price index of the *average* price paid by consumers for the typical basket of goods that they buy. The inclusion of the word "average," however, makes the CPI a more complex index number than the ones we have constructed here.

With what you have just learned, you could construct separate index numbers for the price of beef, the price of coffee, and the price of orange juice. But to get the

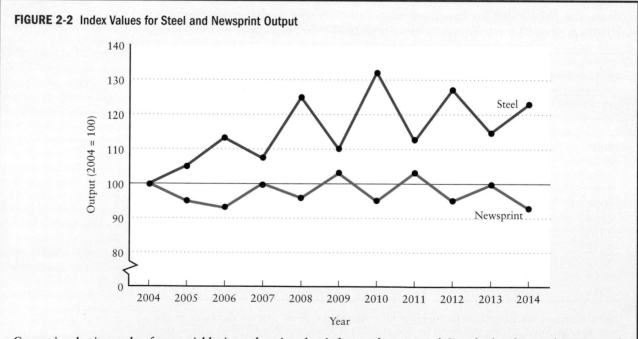

FIGURE 2-2 Index Values for Steel and Newsprint Output

Comparing the time paths of two variables is much easier when index numbers are used. Since both index numbers are equal to 100 in the base year, relative volatility and trends become clear. Steel output is clearly more volatile in percentage terms than newsprint output. Steel output also has an upward trend, whereas newsprint output appears to have little or no trend.

Consumer Price Index, we need to take the *average* of these separate price indexes (plus thousands of others for the goods and services we have ignored here). But it cannot be a simple average. Instead, it must be a *weighted* average, in which the weight assigned to each price index reflects the relative importance of that good in the typical consumer's basket of goods and services. For example, since the typical consumer spends a tiny fraction of income on sardines but a much larger fraction of income on housing, the weight on the "sardines" price index in the CPI is very small and the weight on the "housing" price index is very large. The result is that even huge swings in the price of sardines have negligible effects on the CPI, whereas much more modest changes in the price of housing have noticeable effects on the CPI.

We will spend much more time discussing the Consumer Price Index when we study macroeconomics beginning in Chapter 19. For now, keep in mind the usefulness of the simple index numbers we have constructed here. They allow us to compare the time paths of different variables.

Graphing Economic Data

A single economic variable, such as unemployment, national income, or the average price of a house, can come in two basic forms.

Cross-Sectional and Time-Series Data The first is called **cross-sectional data**, which means a number of different observations on one variable all taken in different places at the same point in time. Figure 2-3 shows an example. The variable in the figure is the average selling price of a house. It is shown for each of the ten Canadian provinces in April 2012.

The second type of data is called **time-series data**. It refers to observations of one variable at successive points in time. The data in Figure 2-4 show the unemployment rate for Canada from 1978 to 2012. (Note that the Canadian unemployment rate is simply a weighted average of the 13 provincial and territorial unemployment rates, where the weight for each region is that region's labour force as a fraction of the total Canadian labour force.) Time-series graphs are quite useful in economics because we often want to know how specific economic numbers are changing over time. As is clear in Figure 2-4, the Canadian unemployment rate is relatively volatile over long periods of time, but in recent years it has been low by historical standards.

Scatter Diagrams Another way data can be presented is in a **scatter diagram**. It is designed to show the relation between two different variables. To plot a scatter

cross-sectional data A set of observations made at the same time across several different units (such as households, firms, or countries).

time-series data A set of observations made at successive periods of time.

scatter diagram A graph showing two variables, one measured on the horizontal and the other on the vertical axis. Each point represents the values of the variables for a particular unit of observation.

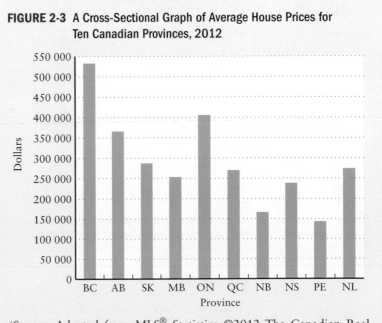

FIGURE 2-3 A Cross-Sectional Graph of Average House Prices for Ten Canadian Provinces, 2012

(*Source*: Adapted from MLS® Statistics ©2012 The Canadian Real Estate Association; www.crea.ca/content/national-average-price-map)

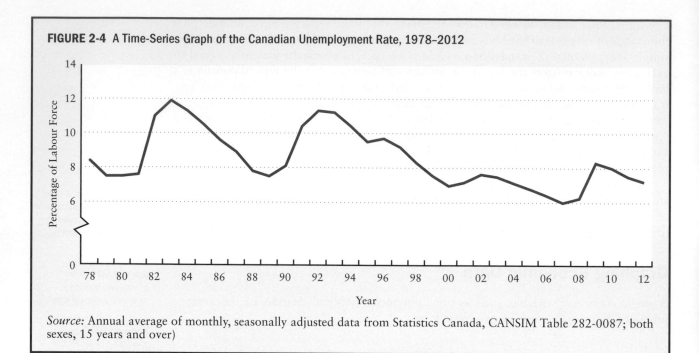

FIGURE 2-4 A Time-Series Graph of the Canadian Unemployment Rate, 1978–2012

Source: Annual average of monthly, seasonally adjusted data from Statistics Canada, CANSIM Table 282-0087; both sexes, 15 years and over)

FIGURE 2-5 A Scatter Diagram of Household Income and Saving

Household	Annual Income	Annual Saving
1	$ 70 000	$10 000
2	30 000	2 500
3	100 000	12 000
4	60 000	3 000
5	80 000	8 000
6	10 000	500
7	20 000	2 000
8	50 000	2 000
9	40 000	4 200
10	90 000	8 000

Saving tends to rise as income rises. The table shows the amount of income earned by ten selected households together with the amount they saved during the same year. The scatter diagram plots the income and saving for the ten households listed in the table. The number on each dot refers to the household in the corresponding row of the table.

diagram, values of one variable are measured on the horizontal axis and values of the second variable are measured on the vertical axis. Any point on the diagram relates a specific value of one variable to a corresponding specific value of the other.

The data plotted on a scatter diagram may be either cross-sectional data or time-series data. An example of the former is shown in Figure 2-5. The table in the figure shows data for the income and saving of ten households in one particular year, and these data are plotted on a scatter diagram. Each point in the figure represents one household, showing its income and its saving. The positive relation between the two stands out. The higher the household's income, the higher its saving tends to be.

2.4 Graphing Economic Theories

Theories are built on assumptions about relationships between variables. For example, the quantity of eggs demanded is assumed to fall as the price of eggs rises, and the total amount an individual saves is assumed to rise as his or her income rises. How can such relations be expressed?

Functions

When one variable, X, is related to another variable, Y, in such a way that to every value of X there is only one possible value of Y, we say that Y is a *function* of X. When we write this relation down, we are expressing a *functional relation* between the two variables.

Here is a specific but hypothetical example. Consider the relation between an individual's annual income, which we denote by the symbol Y, and the amount that person spends on goods and services during the year, which we denote by the symbol C (for consumption). Any particular example of the relation between C and Y can be expressed several ways: in words, in a table or schedule, in a mathematical equation, or in a graph.

Verbal Statement. When income is zero, the person will spend $800 a year (either by borrowing the money or by consuming past savings), and for every extra $1 of income the person will increase expenditure by 80 cents.

Schedule. This table shows selected values of the person's income and consumption.

Annual Income	Consumption	Reference Letter
$ 0	$ 800	p
2 500	2 800	q
5 000	4 800	r
7 500	6 800	s
10 000	8 800	t

Mathematical Equation. $C = \$800 + 0.8\,Y$ is the equation of the relation just described in words and displayed in the table. As a check, you can first see that when Y is zero, C is $800. Further, you can see that every time Y increases by $1, the level of C increases by $0.8(\$1)$, which is 80 cents.

Graph. Figure 2-6 shows the points from the preceding schedule and the line representing the equation given in the previous paragraph.

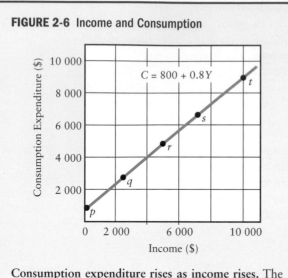

FIGURE 2-6 Income and Consumption

Consumption expenditure rises as income rises. The figure graphs the schedule and the equation for the hypothetical functional relation discussed in the text.

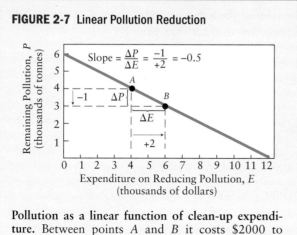

FIGURE 2-7 Linear Pollution Reduction

Pollution as a linear function of clean-up expenditure. Between points A and B it costs $2000 to reduce pollution by 1000 tonnes. The cost of pollution reduction is the same elsewhere on the line. The slope of the line, -0.5, indicates that any $1 expenditure on pollution clean-up reduces the amount of pollution by 0.5 tonnes.

Comparison of the values on the graph with the values in the schedule, and with the values derived from the equation just stated, shows that these are alternative expressions of the same relation between C and Y. All four of these modes of expression refer to the same relation between the person's consumption expenditure and income.

Graphing Functions

Different functions have different graphs, and we will meet many of these in subsequent chapters. Figure 2-6 is an example of a relation in which the two variables move together. When income goes up, consumption goes up. In such a relation the two variables are *positively related* to each other.

Figure 2-7 gives an example of variables that move in opposite directions. As the amount spent on reducing pollution goes up, the amount of remaining pollution goes down. In such a relation the two variables are *negatively related* to each other.

Both of these graphs are straight lines. In such cases the variables are *linearly related* to each other (either positively or negatively).

The Slope of a Straight Line Slopes are important in economics. They show you how much one variable changes as the other changes. The slope is defined as the amount of change in the variable measured on the vertical axis per unit change in the variable measured on the horizontal axis. In the case of Figure 2-7 it tells us how many tonnes of pollution, symbolized by P, are removed per dollar spent on reducing pollution, symbolized by E. Consider moving from point A to point B in the figure. If we spend $2000 more on clean-up, we reduce pollution by 1000 tonnes. This is 0.5 tonnes per dollar spent. On the graph the extra $2000 is indicated by ΔE, the arrow indicating that E rises by 2000. The 1000 tonnes of pollution reduction is indicated by ΔP, the arrow showing that pollution falls by 1000. (The Greek uppercase letter delta, Δ, stands for "the change in.") To get the amount of pollution reduction per dollar of expenditure, we merely divide one by the other. In symbols this is $\Delta P / \Delta E$.

If we let X stand for whatever variable is measured on the horizontal axis and Y for whatever variable is measured on the vertical axis, the slope of a straight line is $\Delta Y / \Delta X$. [1]

---

[1] Red numbers in square brackets indicate mathematical notes that are found in a separate section at the back of the book.

The equation of the line in Figure 2-7 can be computed in two steps. First, note that when $E = 0$, the amount of remaining pollution, P, is equal to 6 (thousand tonnes). Thus, the line meets the vertical axis ($E = 0$) when P equals 6. Second, we have already seen that the slope of the line, $\Delta P / \Delta E$, is equal to -0.5, which means that for every one-unit increase in E, P falls by 0.5 unit. We can thus state the equation of the line as

$$P = 6 - (0.5)E$$

where both P and E are expressed as thousands of units (tonnes and dollars, respectively).

Non-linear Functions Although it is sometimes convenient to simplify a real relation between two variables by assuming them to be linearly related, this is seldom the case over their whole range. Non-linear relations are much more common than linear ones. In the case of reducing pollution, it is usually quite cheap to eliminate the first units of pollution. Then, as the environment gets cleaner and cleaner, the cost of further clean-up tends to increase because more and more sophisticated and expensive methods need to be used. As a result, Figure 2-8 is more realistic than Figure 2-7. Inspection of Figure 2-8 shows that as more and more is spent, the amount of pollution reduction for an additional $1 of clean-up expenditure gets smaller and smaller. This is shown by the diminishing slope of the curve as we move rightward along it. For example, as we move from point A to point B, an increase in expenditure of $1000 is required to reduce pollution by 1000 tonnes. Thus, each tonne of pollution reduction costs $1. But as we move from point C (where we have already reduced pollution considerably) to point D, an extra $6000 must be spent in order to reduce pollution by 1000 tonnes. Each tonne of pollution reduction therefore costs $6.

Economists call the change in pollution when a bit more or a bit less is spent on clean-up the *marginal* change. The figure shows that the slope of the curve at each point measures

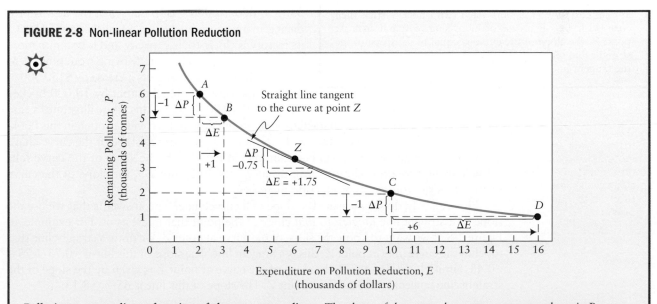

FIGURE 2-8 Non-linear Pollution Reduction

Pollution as a non-linear function of clean-up expenditure. The slope of the curve changes as we move along it. Between points A and B, it costs $1000 to reduce pollution by 1000 tonnes. Between points C and D, it costs $6000 to reduce pollution by 1000 tonnes. At point Z, the slope of the curve is equal to the slope of the straight line tangent to the curve at point Z. The slope of the tangent line is $-0.75/1.75 = -0.43$.

this marginal change. It also shows that in the type of curve illustrated, the marginal change per dollar spent is diminishing as we spend more on reducing pollution. There is always a payoff to more expenditure over the range shown in the figure, but the payoff diminishes as more is spent. This relation can be described as *diminishing marginal response*. We will meet such relations many times in what follows, so we emphasize now that diminishing marginal response does not mean that the *total* response is diminishing. In Figure 2-8, the total amount of pollution continues to fall as more and more is spent on clean-up. But diminishing marginal response does mean that the amount of pollution reduced per dollar of expenditure gets less and less as the total expenditure rises.

Figure 2-9 shows a graph in which the marginal response is increasing. The graph shows the relationship between annual production costs and annual output for a firm that makes hockey sticks. Notice that the more sticks produced annually, the higher the firm's costs. This is shown by the positive slope of the line. Notice also that as more and more hockey sticks are produced, the extra amount that the firm must pay to produce each extra stick rises. For example, as the firm moves from point A to point B, annual costs rise by $30 000 in order to increase its annual output by 10 000 hockey sticks. Each extra stick costs $3 ($30 000/10 000 = $3). But when the firm is producing many more hockey sticks, such as at point C, its factory is closer to its capacity and it becomes more costly to increase production. Moving from point C to point D, the firm's annual costs increase by $150 000 in order to increase its annual output by 10 000 hockey sticks. Each extra stick then costs $15 ($150 000/10 000 = $15). This figure illustrates a case of *increasing marginal cost*, a characteristic of production that we will see often in this book.

Figures 2-8 and 2-9 show that with non-linear functions the slope of the curve changes as we move along the curve. For example, in Figure 2-8, the slope of the curve falls as the expenditure on pollution clean-up increases. In Figure 2-9, the slope of the curve increases as the volume of production increases.

How, exactly, do we measure the slope of a curved line? The answer is that we use the slope of a straight line *tangent to that curve* at the point that interests us. For example, in Figure 2-8, if we want to know the slope of the curve at point Z, we draw a straight line that touches the curve *only* at point Z; this is a tangent line. The slope of this line is −0.75/1.75 = −0.43. Similarly, in Figure 2-9, the slope of the curve at point Z is given by the slope of the straight line tangent to the curve at point Z. The slope of this line is 65/8 = 8.13.

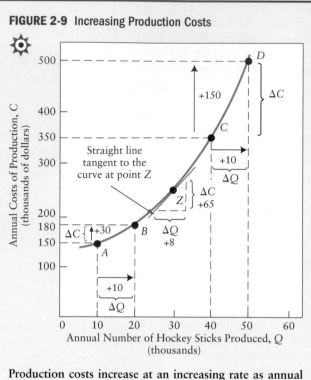

FIGURE 2-9 Increasing Production Costs

Production costs increase at an increasing rate as annual output rises. From point A to point B, an extra annual output of 10 000 hockey sticks increases annual costs by $30 000. Each extra stick costs $3. From point C to point D, an extra output of 10 000 hockey sticks increases annual costs by $150 000. Each extra hockey stick then costs $15. This is a case of increasing marginal cost. At point Z, the slope of the curve is equal to the slope of the straight line tangent to the curve at point Z. The slope of the tangent line is 65/8 = 8.13.

For non-linear functions, the slope of the curve changes as X changes. Therefore, the marginal response of Y to a change in X depends on the value of X.

Functions with a Minimum or a Maximum So far, all the graphs we have shown have had either a positive or a negative slope over their entire range. But many relations change directions as the independent variable increases. For example, consider a firm that is attempting to maximize its profits and is trying to determine how much output to produce. The firm may find that its unit production costs are lower than the market price of the good, and so it can increase its profit by producing more. But as it increases its level of production, the firm's unit costs may be driven up because the capacity of the factory is being approached. Eventually, the firm may find that extra output will actually cost so much that its profits are *reduced*. This is a relationship that we will study in detail in later chapters, and it is illustrated in Figure 2-10. Notice that when profits are maximized at point *A*, the slope of the curve is zero (because a tangent to the curve at point *A* is horizontal), and so the *marginal response* of profits to output is zero.

Now consider an example of a function with a minimum. You probably know that when you drive a car, the fuel consumption per kilometre depends on your speed. Driving very slowly uses a lot of fuel per kilometre travelled. Driving very fast also uses a lot of fuel per kilometre travelled. The best fuel efficiency—the lowest fuel consumption per kilometre travelled—occurs at a speed of approximately 95 kilometres per hour. The relationship between speed and fuel consumption is shown in Figure 2-11 and illustrates

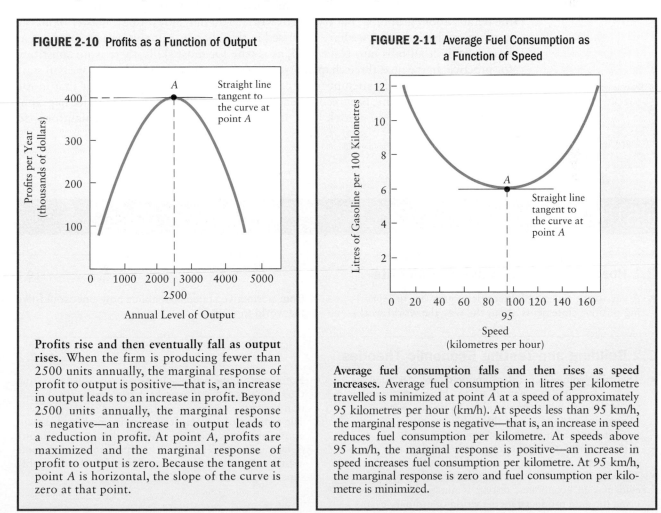

FIGURE 2-10 Profits as a Function of Output

Profits rise and then eventually fall as output rises. When the firm is producing fewer than 2500 units annually, the marginal response of profit to output is positive—that is, an increase in output leads to an increase in profit. Beyond 2500 units annually, the marginal response is negative—an increase in output leads to a reduction in profit. At point *A*, profits are maximized and the marginal response of profit to output is zero. Because the tangent at point *A* is horizontal, the slope of the curve is zero at that point.

FIGURE 2-11 Average Fuel Consumption as a Function of Speed

Average fuel consumption falls and then rises as speed increases. Average fuel consumption in litres per kilometre travelled is minimized at point *A* at a speed of approximately 95 kilometres per hour (km/h). At speeds less than 95 km/h, the marginal response is negative—that is, an increase in speed reduces fuel consumption per kilometre. At speeds above 95 km/h, the marginal response is positive—an increase in speed increases fuel consumption per kilometre. At 95 km/h, the marginal response is zero and fuel consumption per kilometre is minimized.

a function with a minimum. Note that at point *A* the slope of the curve is zero (because a tangent to the curve at point *A* is horizontal), and so the *marginal response* of fuel consumption to speed is zero.

> At either a minimum or a maximum of a function, the slope of the curve is zero. Therefore, at the minimum or maximum, the marginal response of *Y* to a change in *X* is zero.

A Final Word

We have done much in this chapter. We have discussed why economists develop theories (or models) to help them understand the world. We have also discussed how they test their theories and how there is a continual back-and-forth process between empirical testing of predictions and refining the theory. Finally, we have devoted considerable time and space to exploring the many ways that data can be displayed in graphs and how economists use graphs to illustrate their theories.

Many students find themselves intimidated when they are first confronted with all the details about graphing. But try not to worry. You may not yet be a master of all the graphing techniques that we have discussed in this chapter, but you will be surprised at how quickly it all falls into place. And, as is true for most skills, there is no substitute for practice. In the next three chapters we will encounter many graphs. But we will start simply and then slowly attempt more complicated cases. We are confident that in the process of learning some basic economic theories you will get enough practice in graphing that you will very soon look back at this chapter and realize how straightforward it all is.

SUMMARY

2.1 Positive and Normative Statements

LO 1

- A key to the success of scientific inquiry lies in separating positive statements about the way the world works from normative statements about how one would like the world to work.

2.2 Building and Testing Economic Theories

LO 2, 3

- Theories (sometimes called models) are designed to explain and predict what we see. A theory consists of a set of definitions of the variables to be discussed, a set of assumptions about how things behave, and the conditions under which the theory is meant to apply.
- A theory provides predictions of the type "If one event occurs, then another event will also occur."
- Theories are tested by checking their predictions against evidence. In economics, testing is almost always done using the data produced by the world of ordinary events.

- Economists make use of statistical analysis when testing their theories. They must take care to make the distinction between correlation and causation.
- The progress of any science lies in finding better explanations of events than are now available. Thus, in any developing science, one must expect to discard some existing theories and replace them with demonstrably superior alternatives.

2.3 Economic Data

- Index numbers express economic series in relative form. Values in each period are expressed in relation to the value in the base period, which is given a value of 100.
- Economic data can be graphed in three different ways. Cross-sectional graphs show observations taken at the same time. Time-series graphs show observations on one variable taken over time. Scatter diagrams show many points, each of which refers to specific observations on two different variables.

2.4 Graphing Economic Theories

- A functional relation can be expressed in words, in a schedule giving specific values, in a mathematical equation, or in a graph.
- A graph of two variables has a positive slope when they both increase or decrease together and a negative slope when they move in opposite directions.
- The marginal response of a variable gives the amount it changes in response to a change in a second variable. When the variable is measured on the vertical axis of a diagram, its marginal response at a specific point on the curve is measured by the slope of the line at that point.
- Some functions have a maximum or minimum point. At such points, the marginal response is zero.

KEY CONCEPTS

Positive and normative statements
Endogenous and exogenous variables
Theories and models
Variables, assumptions, and predictions

Correlation versus causation
Functional relations
Positive and negative relations between variables

Positively and negatively sloped curves
Marginal responses
Maximum and minimum values

STUDY EXERCISES

MyEconLab Make the grade with MyEconLab: Study Exercises marked in red can be found on MyEconLab. You can practise them as often as you want, and most feature step-by-step guided instructions to help you find the right answer.

1. Determine whether each of the following statements is positive or normative.

   a. The government should impose stricter regulations on the banking sector to avoid future financial crises.
   b. Financial aid to developing countries has no impact on per capita GDP in those countries.
   c. Tuition fee increases at Canadian universities lead to reduced access for low-income students.
   d. It is unfair that Canadians have universal access to health care but not to dental care.
   e. Canadians currently have too much personal debt.

2. What are some of the positive and normative issues that lie behind the disagreements in the following cases?

   a. Economists disagree on whether the government of Canada should try to stimulate the economy in the next six months.
   b. European and North American negotiators disagree over the desirability of reducing European farm subsidies.
   c. Economists argue about the merits of a voucher system that allows parents to choose the schools their children will attend.

d. Economists debate the use of a two-tier medical system in Canada (whereby health care continues to be publicly provided, but individuals are permitted to be treated by doctors who bill the patient directly—an approach known as "extra billing").

e. Economists debate the costs of global climate change and the relative merits of carbon taxes and other policies to reduce greenhouse gas emissions.

f. Policymakers disagree about the extent to which financial markets need to be regulated.

3. In the following examples, identify the exogenous (or independent) variable and the endogenous (or dependent) variable.

a. The amount of rainfall on the Canadian prairies determines the amount of wheat produced in Canada.

b. When the world price of coffee increases, there is a change in the price of your cup of coffee at Tim Hortons.

c. If student loans were no longer available, there would be fewer students attending university.

d. An increase in the tax on gasoline leads people to drive more fuel-efficient vehicles.

4. Economists sometimes make each of the following assumptions when they construct models. Discuss some situations in which each of these assumptions might be a useful simplification in order to think about some aspect of the real world.

a. Earth is flat.

b. There are no differences between men and women.

c. There is no tomorrow.

d. There are only two periods: this year and next year.

e. A country produces only two types of goods.

f. People are wholly selfish.

5. Fill in the blanks to make the following statements correct.

a. Economists have designed _____ to better explain and predict the behaviour we observe in the world around us.

b. A variable, such as price or quantity, that is determined within a theory is known as a(n) _____ variable. A variable that is determined outside the theory is known as a(n) _____ variable.

c. When, based on a theory, we claim that "If A occurs, then B will follow," we are making a _____ that can then be tested by _____ observation.

d. If we observe that when variable A decreases, variable B also decreases, we can say that the two variables are _____. We cannot necessarily say

that there is a _____ relationship between A and B.

6. Use the appropriate graph—time-series, cross-sectional, or scatter diagram—to illustrate the economic data provided in each part below.

a. The Canadian-dollar price of one U.S. dollar (the "exchange rate") in 2011:

January	0.994
February	0.988
March	0.977
April	0.958
May	0.968
June	0.977
July	0.956
August	0.982
September	1.003
October	1.019
November	1.026
December	1.024

b. A comparison of average household expenditures across provinces in 2010:

British Columbia	$72 486
Alberta	84 087
Saskatchewan	69 237
Manitoba	66 330
Ontario	74 521
Quebec	61 536
New Brunswick	59 943
Nova Scotia	61 907
Prince Edward Island	58 194
Newfoundland and Labrador	60 139

c. Per capita growth rates of real GDP and investment rates for various countries, averaged over the period 1950–2009:

Country	Average Growth Rate (% per year)	Average Investment Rate (% of GDP)
Canada	2.0	18.2
Austria	3.1	22.0
Japan	4.0	26.6
United States	1.9	18.1
United Kingdom	2.0	14.5
Spain	3.4	23.0
Norway	2.8	27.4
South Korea	5.1	27.2
Iceland	2.7	28.0

7. Use the following figure to answer the questions below.

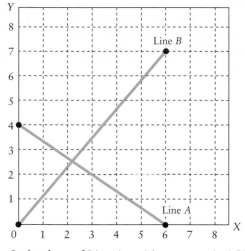

a. Is the slope of Line *A* positive or negative? Line *B*?
b. Calculate the slope of Line *A*. Write the equation describing the line in the form $Y = mX + b$, where m is the slope of the line and b is a constant term.
c. Calculate the slope of Line *B*. Write the equation describing the line in the form $Y = mX + b$, where m is the slope of the line and b is a constant term.

8. Suppose the relationship between the government's tax revenue (T) and national income (Y) is represented by the following equation: $T = 10 + 0.25Y$. Plot this relationship on a scale diagram, with Y on the horizontal axis and T on the vertical axis. Interpret the equation.

9. Consider the following three specific functions for a functional relation between X and Y:
   i) $Y = 50 + 2X$
   ii) $Y = 50 + 2X + 0.05X^2$
   iii) $Y = 50 + 2X - 0.05X^2$
   a. For the values of X of 0, 10, 20, 30, 40, and 50, plot X and Y on a scale diagram for each specific function. Connect these points with a smooth line.
   b. For each function, state whether the slope of the line is constant, increasing, or decreasing as the value of X increases.
   c. Describe for each function how the marginal change in Y depends on the value of X.

10. Suppose you want to create a price index for the price of a particular physics textbook over ten years in your university bookstore. The price of the book on September 1 of each year is as follows:

Year	Price ($)	Year	Price ($)
2000	85	2006	120
2001	87	2007	125
2002	94	2008	127
2003	104	2009	127
2004	110	2010	130
2005	112		

a. The base year is 2000. Construct a physics textbook price index.
b. What is the percentage increase in the price of the book between the base year and 2005?
c. What is the percentage increase in the price of the book from 2007 to 2010?
d. Are the data listed above time-series or cross-sectional data? Explain why.

11. Suppose you want to create a price index for the price of pizza across several Canadian university campuses, as of March 1, 2013. The data are as follows:

University	Price per Pizza
Dalhousie	$6.50
Laval	5.95
McGill	6.00
Queen's	8.00
Waterloo	7.50
Manitoba	5.50
Saskatchewan	5.75
Calgary	6.25
UBC	7.25
Victoria	7.00

a. Using Calgary as the "base university," construct the Canadian university pizza price index.
b. At which university is pizza the most expensive, and by what percentage is the price higher than in Calgary?
c. At which university is pizza the least expensive, and by what percentage is the price lower than in Calgary?
d. Are the data listed above time-series or cross-sectional data? Explain why.

12. For each of the functional relations listed below, plot the relations on a scale diagram (with X on the horizontal axis and Y on the vertical axis) and compute the slope of the line.
   a. $Y = 10 + 3X$
   b. $Y = 20 + 4X$
   c. $Y = 30 + 5X$
   d. $Y = 10 + 5X$

13. Suppose we divide Canada into three regions: the West, the Centre, and the East. Each region has an unemployment rate, defined as the number of people unemployed, expressed as a fraction of that region's labour force. The table that follows shows each region's unemployment rate and the size of its labour force.

Region	Unemployment Rate	Labour Force
West	5.5%	5.3 million
Centre	7.2%	8.4 million
East	12.5%	3.5 million

a. Compute an unemployment rate for Canada using a simple average of the rates in the three regions. Is this the "right" unemployment rate for Canada as a whole? Explain why or why not.

b. Now compute an unemployment rate for Canada using weights that reflect the size of that region's labour force as a proportion of the overall Canadian labour force. Explain the difference in this unemployment rate from the one in part (a). Is this a "better" measure of Canadian unemployment? Explain why.

14. Draw three graphs in which the dependent variable increases at an increasing rate, at a constant rate, and at a diminishing rate. Then draw three graphs in which it decreases at an increasing, constant, and diminishing rate. State a real relation that each of these graphs might describe, other than the ones given in the text of this chapter.

Demand, Supply, and Price

CHAPTER OUTLINE

LEARNING OBJECTIVES (LO)

After studying this chapter, you will be able to

3.1 DEMAND

1 list the factors that determine the quantity demanded of a good.
2 distinguish between a shift of the demand curve and a movement along the demand curve.

3.2 SUPPLY

3 list the factors that determine the quantity supplied of a good.
4 distinguish between a shift of the supply curve and a movement along the supply curve.

3.3 THE DETERMINATION OF PRICE

5 explain the forces that drive market price to equilibrium, and how equilibrium price is affected by changes in demand and supply.

WE are now ready to study the important question of how markets work. The answer leads us to develop a simple model of supply and demand. And though there is much more to economics than just demand and supply (as many following chapters will illustrate), this is an essential starting point for understanding how a market economy functions.

As a first step, we need to understand what determines the demand for and the supply of particular products. Then we can see how demand and supply together determine the prices of products and the quantities that are bought and sold. Finally, we examine how the price system allows the economy to respond to changes in demand and supply. The concepts of demand and supply help us to understand the price system's successes and failures, and the consequences of many government policies.

This chapter deals with the basic elements of demand, supply, and price. In the next two chapters we use the theory of demand and supply to discuss such issues as cigarette taxes, legislated minimum wages, rent controls, and the burden of payroll taxes.

3.1 Demand

What determines the demand for any given product? How have Canadian consumers responded to the recent declines in the prices of smartphones and laptop computers? How will they respond to the next sudden change in the price of gasoline or coffee? We start by developing a theory designed to explain the demand for some typical product.

Quantity Demanded

quantity demanded The amount of a good or service that consumers want to purchase during some time period.

The total amount of any particular good or service that consumers want to purchase in some time period is called the **quantity demanded** of that product. It is important to notice two things about this concept.

First, quantity demanded is a *desired* quantity. It is the amount that consumers want to purchase when faced with a particular price of the product, other products' prices, their incomes, their tastes, and everything else that might matter. It may be different from the amount that consumers actually succeed in purchasing. If sufficient quantities are not available, the amount that consumers want to purchase may exceed the amount that they actually purchase. (For example, think of standing in line to purchase tickets to a show, only to find out that the show is sold out before you get to the head of the line.) To distinguish these two concepts, the term *quantity demanded* is used to refer to desired purchases, and such phrases as *quantity bought* or *quantity exchanged* are used to refer to actual purchases.

Second, quantity demanded refers to a *flow* of purchases, expressed as so much per period of time: 1 million units per day, 7 million per week, or 365 million per year. For example, being told that the quantity of new cars demanded (at current prices) in Canada is 50 000 means nothing unless you are also told the period of time involved. For a country as large as Canada, 50 000 cars demanded per day would be an enormous rate of demand, whereas 50 000 per year would be a very small rate of demand. The important distinction between *stocks* and *flows* is discussed in *Extensions in Theory 3-1*.

The total amount of some product that consumers in the relevant market want to buy in a given time period is influenced by the following important variables: [2]

- Product's own price
- Consumers' income
- Prices of other products
- Tastes
- Population
- Expectations about the future

We will discuss the separate effects of each of these variables later in the chapter. For now, we focus on the effects of changes in the product's own price. But how do we analyze the distinct effect of changes in one variable when all are likely to be changing at once? Since this is difficult to do, we consider the influence of the variables one at a time. To do this, we hold all but one of them constant. Then we let the selected variable

EXTENSIONS IN THEORY 3-1

The Distinction Between Stocks and Flows

An important conceptual issue that arises frequently in economics is the distinction between *stock* and *flow* variables. Economic theories use both, and it takes a little practice to keep them straight.

As noted in the text, a flow variable has a time dimension—it is so much *per unit of time*. For example, the quantity of Grade A large eggs purchased in Edmonton is a flow variable. No useful information is conveyed if we are told that the number purchased was 2000 dozen eggs unless we are also told the period of time over which these purchases occurred. Two thousand dozen eggs per hour would indicate a much more active market in eggs than would 2000 dozen eggs per month.

In contrast, a stock variable is a variable whose value has meaning *at a point in time*. Thus, the number of eggs in the egg producer's warehouse on a particular day—for example, 10 000 dozen eggs on September 3, 2013—is a stock variable. All those eggs are there at one time, and they remain there until something happens to change the stock held in the warehouse. The stock variable is just a number at a point in time, not a rate of flow of so much per unit of time.

The terminology of stocks and flows can be understood using an analogy to a bathtub. At any moment, the tub holds so much water. This is the *stock,* and it can be measured in terms of the volume of water, say, 100 litres. There might also be water flowing into the tub from the tap; this *flow* is measured as so much water per unit time, say, 10 litres per minute.

The distinction between stocks and flows is important. Failure to keep them straight is a common source of confusion and even error. Note, for example, that a stock variable and a flow variable cannot be added together without specifying some time period for which the flow persists. We cannot add the stock of 100 litres of water in the tub to the flow of 10 litres per minute to get 110 litres. The new stock of water will depend on how long the flow persists; if it lasts for 20 minutes, the new stock will be 300 litres; if the flow persists for 60 minutes, the new stock will be 700 litres (or the tub will overflow!).

The amount of income earned is a flow; it is so much per year or per month or per hour. The amount of a consumer's expenditure is also a flow—so much spent per week or per month or per year. The amount of money in a bank account (earned, perhaps, in the past but unspent) is a stock—just so many thousands of dollars. The key test is always whether a time dimension is required to give the variable meaning.

The amount of water behind the dam at any time is the stock of water; the amount moving through the gate is the flow, which is measured per unit of time.

vary and study how its change affects quantity demanded. We can do the same for each of the other variables in turn, and in this way we can come to understand the importance of each variable.

Holding all other variables constant is often described by the expressions "other things being equal," "other things given," or the equivalent Latin phrase, *ceteris paribus.* When economists speak of the influence of the price of gasoline on the quantity of gasoline demanded, *ceteris paribus,* they refer to what a change in the price of gasoline would do to the quantity of gasoline demanded *if all other variables that influence the demand for gasoline did not change.*

Quantity Demanded and Price[1]

We are interested in studying the relationship between the quantity demanded of a product and that product's price. This requires that we hold all other influences constant and ask, "How will the quantity demanded of a product change as its price changes?"

A basic economic hypothesis is that the price of a product and the quantity demanded are related *negatively,* other things being equal. That is, the lower the price, the higher the quantity demanded; the higher the price, the lower the quantity demanded.

The great British economist Alfred Marshall (1842–1924) called this fundamental relation the "law of demand." In Chapter 6, we will derive the law of demand as a prediction that follows from more basic assumptions about the behaviour of individual consumers. For now, let's simply explore why this relationship seems reasonable. Products are used to satisfy desires and needs, and there is almost always more than one product that will satisfy any desire or need. Hunger may be alleviated by eating meat or vegetables; a desire for green vegetables can be satisfied by broccoli or spinach. The desire for a vacation may be satisfied by a trip to the ocean or to the mountains; the need to get there may be satisfied by different airlines, a bus, a car, or a train. For any general desire or need, there are almost always many different products that will satisfy it.

Now consider what happens if income, tastes, population, and the prices of all other products remain constant and the price of only one product changes. As the price goes up, that product becomes an increasingly expensive means of satisfying a desire. Many consumers will decide to switch wholly or partly to other products. Some consumers will stop buying it altogether, others will buy smaller amounts, and still others may continue to buy the same quantity. But the overall effect is that less will be demanded of the product whose price has risen. As meat becomes more expensive, for example, some consumers will switch to meat substitutes; others may forgo meat at some meals and eat less meat at others. Taken together as a group, consumers will want to buy less meat when its price rises.

Conversely, as the price goes down, the product becomes a cheaper way of satisfying a desire. Households will demand more of it. At the same time they will buy less of similar products whose prices have not fallen and as a result have become expensive *relative* to the product in question. For example, when the price of tomatoes falls, many shoppers will switch to tomatoes and cut their purchases of other vegetables that are now relatively more expensive.

Changes in prices lead most consumers to alter their choices. For example, as prices for hotel rooms fall, vacationers may be more likely to take weekend trips.

---

[1] In this chapter we explore a product's demand curve for the market as a whole—what we often call the *market demand curve.* In Chapter 6 we discuss how this market demand curve is derived by adding up, or *aggregating,* the demands of different individuals.

Demand Schedules and Demand Curves

A **demand schedule** is one way of showing the relationship between quantity demanded and the price of a product, other things being equal. It is a table showing the quantity demanded at various prices.

The table in Figure 3-1 shows a hypothetical demand schedule for apples.[2] It lists the quantity of apples that would be demanded at various prices, given the assumption that all other variables are held constant. We should note in particular that average household income is assumed to be $50 000 per year because later we will want to see what happens when income changes. The table gives the quantities demanded for five selected prices, but in fact a separate quantity would be demanded at every possible price.

A second method of showing the relationship between quantity demanded and price is to draw a graph. The five price–quantity combinations shown in the table are plotted in Figure 3-1. Price is plotted on the vertical axis, and the quantity demanded is plotted on the horizontal axis.

The curve drawn through these points is called a **demand curve**. It shows the quantity that consumers would like to buy at each price. The negative slope of the curve indicates that the quantity demanded increases as the price falls. Each point on the demand curve indicates a single price–quantity combination. The demand curve as a whole shows something more.

demand schedule A table showing the relationship between quantity demanded and the price of a commodity, other things being equal.

demand curve The graphical representation of the relationship between quantity demanded and the price of a commodity, other things being equal.

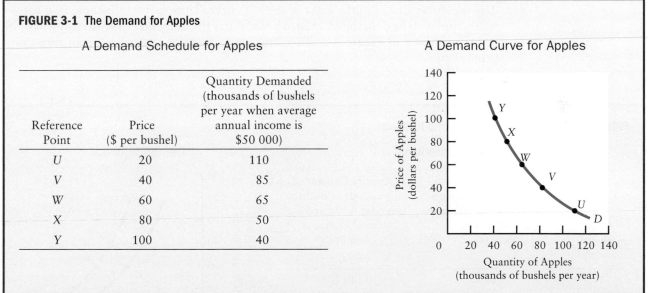

FIGURE 3-1 The Demand for Apples

A Demand Schedule for Apples

Reference Point	Price ($ per bushel)	Quantity Demanded (thousands of bushels per year when average annual income is $50 000)
U	20	110
V	40	85
W	60	65
X	80	50
Y	100	40

A Demand Curve for Apples

Both the table and the graph show the total quantity of apples that would be demanded at various prices, *ceteris paribus.* For example, row *W* indicates that if the price of apples were $60 per bushel, consumers would desire to purchase 65 000 bushels of apples per year, holding constant the values of the other variables that affect quantity demanded. The demand curve, labelled *D*, relates quantity of apples demanded to the price of apples; its negative slope indicates that quantity demanded increases as price falls.

---

[2] We realize that apples are not a very exciting product to discuss, and many students wonder why we do not instead use cell phones, restaurant meals, or cars as our hypothetical example. The model of demand and supply, however, best applies to products that are demanded by many consumers and supplied by many producers, each of which offers for sale a virtually identical ("homogeneous") version of the product. For this reason, we have chosen a simple agricultural product, but we could have illustrated the same principles with beef, wheat, copper, newsprint, oil, and a whole host of what economists call "commodities."

The demand curve represents the relationship between quantity demanded and price, other things being equal.

When economists speak of demand in a particular market, they are referring not just to the particular quantity being demanded at the moment (i.e., not just to one point on the demand curve) but to the entire demand curve—to the relationship between desired purchases and all the possible prices of the product.

The term **demand** therefore refers to the entire relationship between the quantity demanded of a product and the price of that product. In contrast, a single point on a demand schedule or curve is the quantity demanded at that point. This distinction between "demand" and "quantity demanded" is an extremely important one and we will examine it more closely later in this chapter.

demand The entire relationship between the quantity of a commodity that buyers want to purchase and the price of that commodity, other things being equal.

Shifts in the Demand Curve The demand curve is drawn with the assumption that everything except the product's own price is being held constant. But what if other things change, as they often do? For example, consider an increase in average household income while the price of apples remains constant. If consumers spend some of their extra income on apples, the new quantity demanded cannot be represented by a point on the original demand curve. It must be represented on a new demand curve that is to the right of the old curve. Thus, a rise in income that causes more apples to be demanded *at each price* shifts the demand curve for apples to the right, as shown in Figure 3-2. This shift illustrates the operation of an important general rule.

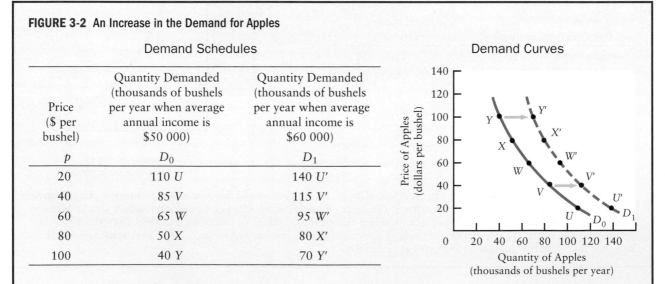

FIGURE 3-2 An Increase in the Demand for Apples

Demand Schedules

Price ($ per bushel)	Quantity Demanded (thousands of bushels per year when average annual income is $50 000)	Quantity Demanded (thousands of bushels per year when average annual income is $60 000)
p	D_0	D_1
20	110 U	140 U'
40	85 V	115 V'
60	65 W	95 W'
80	50 X	80 X'
100	40 Y	70 Y'

An increase in annual household income increases the quantity demanded at each price (for all normal goods). This is shown by the rightward shift in the demand curve, from D_0 to D_1. When average income rises from $50 000 to $60 000 per year, quantity demanded at a price of $60 per bushel rises from 65 000 bushels per year to 95 000 bushels per year. A similar rise occurs at every other price.

A demand curve is drawn with the assumption that everything except the product's own price is held constant. A change in any of the variables previously held constant will shift the demand curve to a new position.

A demand curve can shift in two important ways. In the first case, more is desired at each price—the demand curve shifts rightward so that each price corresponds to a higher quantity than it did before. In the second case, less is desired at each price—the demand curve shifts leftward so that each price corresponds to a lower quantity than it did before.

Let's now consider five important causes of shifts in the demand curve.

1. Consumers' Income. If *average* income rises, consumers as a group can be expected to desire more of most products, other things being equal. Goods for which the quantity demanded increases when income rises are called *normal goods*; goods for which the quantity demanded falls when income rises are called *inferior goods*. The term *normal goods* reflects economists' empirical finding that the demand for most goods rises when income rises. We therefore expect that a rise in average consumer income shifts the demand curve for most products to the right, indicating that more will be demanded at any given price. Such a shift is illustrated in Figure 3-2.

A change in the *distribution* of income can also lead to changes in demand. In particular, a change in the distribution of income will cause an increase in the demand for products bought most by consumers whose incomes increase and a decrease in the demand for products bought most by consumers whose incomes decrease. If, for example, the government increases the child tax credit and at the same time raises basic tax rates, income will be transferred from households without children to households with children. Demands for products more heavily bought by persons without children will decline, while demands for products more heavily bought by households with children will increase.

2. Prices of Other Goods. We saw that the negative slope of a product's demand curve occurs because the lower its price, the cheaper the product becomes relative to other products that can satisfy the same needs or desires. These other products are called **substitutes in consumption.** Another way for the same change to come about is that the price of the substitute product rises. For example, apples can become cheap relative to oranges either because the price of apples falls or because the price of oranges rises. Either change will increase the amount of apples that consumers want to buy as some consumers substitute away from oranges and toward apples. Thus, a rise in the price of a substitute for a product shifts the demand curve for the product to the right. More will be demanded at each price.

substitutes in consumption
Goods that can be used in place of another good to satisfy similar needs or desires.

Complements in consumption are products that tend to be used jointly. Cars and gasoline are complements; so are golf clubs and golf balls, and airplane flights to Calgary and ski-lift tickets in Banff. Because complements tend to be consumed together, a fall in the price of one will increase the quantity demanded of *both* products. Thus, a fall in the price of a complement for a product will shift that product's demand curve to the right. More will be demanded at each price. For example, a fall in the price of airplane trips to Calgary will lead to a rise in the demand for ski-lift tickets in Banff, even though the price of those lift tickets is unchanged. (The demand curve for ski-lift tickets will shift to the right.)

complements in consumption
Goods that tend to be consumed together.

3. Tastes. Tastes have a powerful effect on people's desired purchases. A change in tastes may be long-lasting, such as the shift from typewriters to computers, or it may be a

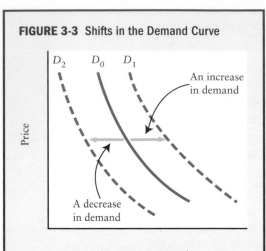

FIGURE 3-3 Shifts in the Demand Curve

An increase
in demand

A decrease
in demand

Quantity per Period

A rightward shift in the demand curve from D_0 to D_1 indicates an increase in demand; a leftward shift from D_0 to D_2 indicates a decrease in demand. An increase in demand means that more is demanded at each price. Such a rightward shift can be caused by a rise in income, a rise in the price of a substitute, a fall in the price of a complement, a change in tastes that favours that product, an increase in population, or the anticipation of a future event that will increase the price.

A decrease in demand means that less is demanded at each price. Such a leftward shift can be caused by a fall in income, a fall in the price of a substitute, a rise in the price of a complement, a change in tastes that disfavours the product, a decrease in population, or the anticipation of a future event that will decrease the price.

short-lived fad as is common with many electronic games, such as the latest versions of Need for Speed or Just Dance. In either case, a change in tastes in favour of a product shifts the demand curve to the right. More will be demanded at each price. Of course, a change in tastes against some product has the opposite effect and shifts the demand curve to the left.

4. Population. If there is an increase in population with purchasing power, the demands for all the products purchased by the new people will rise. Thus, we expect that an increase in population will shift the demand curves for most products to the right, indicating that more will be demanded at each price.

5. Expectations about the Future. Our discussion has so far focused on how changes in the current value of variables may change demand. But it is also true that changes in people's *expectations about future values* of variables may change demand. For example, suppose you are thinking about buying a vacation property in a small town in Nova Scotia, and you have learned that in the near future a large high-tech firm will be moving its head office and several hundred employees to this same small town. Since their future movement into your town will probably increase the demand for housing and drive up the *future* price of houses, this expectation will lead you (and others like you) to increase your demand *today* so as to make the purchase before the price rises. Thus, the demand curve for houses will shift to the right today in anticipation of a future event.

Figure 3-3 summarizes the changes that cause demand curves to shift.

Movements Along the Curve Versus Shifts of the Whole Curve
Suppose you read in today's newspaper that a sharp increase in the world price of coffee beans has been caused by an increased worldwide demand for coffee. Then tomorrow you read that the rising price of coffee is reducing the typical consumer's purchases of coffee, as shoppers switch to other beverages. The two stories appear to contradict each other. The first associates a rising price with rising demand; the second associates a rising price with declining demand. Can both statements be true? The answer is yes—because the two statements actually refer to different things. The first describes a shift in the demand curve; the second describes a movement along the demand curve in response to a change in price.

Consider first the statement that the increase in the price of coffee has been caused by an increased demand for coffee. This statement refers to a shift in the demand curve for coffee—in this case, a shift to the right, indicating more coffee demanded at each price. This shift, as we will see later in this chapter, will increase the price of coffee.

Now consider the second statement—that less coffee is being bought because of its rise in price. This refers to a movement along the *new* demand curve and reflects a change between two specific quantities demanded, one before the price increased and one afterward.

Possible explanations for the two stories are as follows:

1. A rise in population and income in coffee-drinking countries shifts the demand curve for coffee to the right. This, in turn, raises the price of coffee (for reasons we will soon study in detail). This was the first newspaper story.

2. The rising price of coffee is causing each individual household to cut back on its coffee purchases. The cutback is represented by an upward movement to the left along the new demand curve for coffee. This was the second newspaper story.

To prevent the type of confusion caused by our two newspaper stories, economists use a specialized vocabulary to distinguish between shifts of demand curves and movements along demand curves.

We have seen that "demand" refers to the *entire* demand curve, whereas "quantity demanded" refers to a particular *point* on the demand curve. Economists reserve the term **change in demand** to describe a change in the quantity demanded at *every* price. That is, a change in demand refers to a shift of the entire demand curve. The term **change in quantity demanded** refers to a movement from one point on a demand curve to another point, either on the same demand curve or on a new one.

change in demand A change in the quantity demanded at each possible price of the commodity, represented by a shift in the whole demand curve.

change in quantity demanded A change in the specific quantity of the good demanded, represented by a change from one point on a demand curve to another point, either on the original demand curve or on a new one.

> A change in quantity demanded can result from a shift in the demand curve with the price constant, from a movement along a given demand curve due to a change in the price, or from a combination of the two. [3]

We consider these three possibilities in turn.

An increase in demand means that the whole demand curve shifts to the right; at any given price, an increase in demand causes an increase in quantity demanded. For example, in Figure 3-2 on page 60, the shift in the demand curve for apples from D_0 to D_1 represents an increase in demand, and at a price of $40 per bushel, quantity demanded increases from 85 000 bushels to 115 000 bushels, as indicated by the move from V to V'.

A movement down and to the right along a demand curve represents an increase in quantity demanded. For example, in Figure 3-2, with the demand for apples given by the curve D_1, an increase in price from $40 to $60 per bushel causes a movement along D_1 from V' to W', and quantity demanded decreases from 115 000 bushels to 95 000 bushels.

When there is a change in demand *and* a change in the price, the overall change in quantity demanded is the net effect of the shift in the demand curve and the movement along the new demand curve. Figure 3-4 shows the combined effect of an increase in demand, shown by a rightward shift in the whole demand curve, and an upward movement to the left along the new demand curve caused

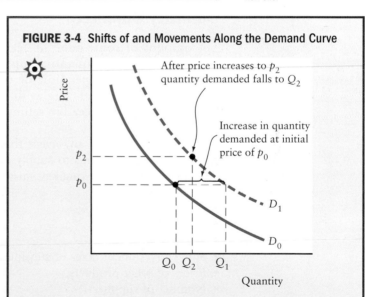

FIGURE 3-4 Shifts of and Movements Along the Demand Curve

An increase in demand means that the demand curve shifts to the right, and hence quantity demanded will be higher at each price. A rise in price causes a movement upward and to the left along the demand curve, and hence quantity demanded will fall. The demand curve is originally D_0 and price is p_0, which means that quantity demanded is Q_0. Suppose demand increases to D_1, which means that at any particular price, there is a larger quantity demanded; for example, at p_0, quantity demanded is now Q_1. Now suppose the price rises above p_0. This causes a movement up and to the left along D_1, and quantity demanded falls below Q_1. As the figure is drawn, the quantity demanded at the new price p_2 is less than Q_1 but greater than Q_0. So in this case the combined effect of the increase in demand and the rise in price is an increase in quantity demanded from Q_0 to Q_2.

A rise in the price of wheat, other things being equal, will lead farmers to plant less of other crops and plant more wheat.

by an increase in price. The increase in demand causes an increase in quantity demanded at the initial price, whereas the movement along the new demand curve causes a decrease in the quantity demanded. Whether quantity demanded rises or falls overall depends on the relative magnitudes of these two changes.

3.2 Supply

What determines the supply of any given product? Why do Canadian oil producers extract and sell more oil when the price of oil is high? Why do Canadian cattle ranchers raise and sell more beef when the price of cattle-feed falls? We start by developing a theory designed to explain the supply of some typical product.

Quantity Supplied

quantity supplied The amount of a commodity that producers want to sell during some time period.

The amount of some good or service that producers want to sell in some time period is called the **quantity supplied** of that product. Quantity supplied is a flow; it is so much per unit of time. Note also that quantity supplied is the amount that producers are willing to offer for sale; it is not necessarily the amount that they succeed in selling, which is expressed by *quantity sold* or *quantity exchanged*.

As a general rule, any event that makes production of a specific product more profitable will lead firms to supply more of it. The quantity supplied of a product is influenced by the following key variables: [4]

- Product's own price
- Prices of inputs
- Technology
- Some government taxes or subsidies
- Prices of other products
- Number of suppliers

The situation with supply is the same as that with demand: There are several influencing variables, and we will not get far if we try to discover what happens when they all change at the same time. Again, we use the convenient *ceteris paribus* assumption to study the influence of the variables one at a time.

Quantity Supplied and Price

We begin by holding all other influences constant and ask, "How do we expect the total quantity of a product supplied to vary with its own price?"

A basic economic hypothesis is that the price of the product and the quantity supplied are related *positively*, other things being equal. That is, the higher the product's own price, the more its producers will supply; the lower the price, the less its producers will supply.

In later chapters we will derive this hypothesis as a prediction from more basic assumptions about the behaviour of individual profit-maximizing firms. For now we simply note that as the product's price rises, producing and selling this product becomes a more profitable activity. Firms interested in increasing their profit will therefore choose to increase their production.

Supply Schedules and Supply Curves

The general relationship just discussed can be illustrated by a **supply schedule**, which shows the relationship between quantity supplied of a product and the price of the product, other things being equal. The table in Figure 3-5 presents a hypothetical supply schedule for apples.

A **supply curve**, the graphical representation of the supply schedule, is illustrated in Figure 3-5. Each point on the supply curve represents a specific price–quantity combination; however, the whole curve shows something more.

When economists make statements about the conditions of supply, they are not referring just to the particular quantity being supplied at the moment—that is, not to just one point on the supply curve. Instead, they are referring to the entire supply

supply schedule A table showing the relationship between quantity supplied and the price of a commodity, other things being equal.

supply curve The graphical representation of the relationship between quantity supplied and the price of a commodity, other things being equal.

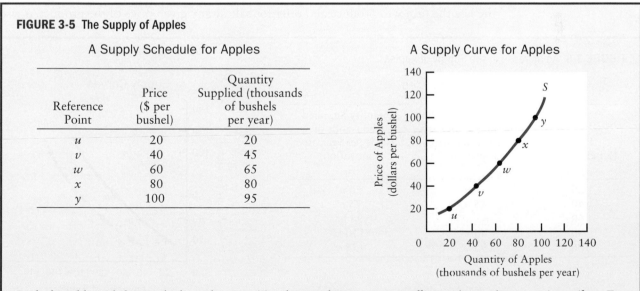

FIGURE 3-5 The Supply of Apples

A Supply Schedule for Apples

Reference Point	Price ($ per bushel)	Quantity Supplied (thousands of bushels per year)
u	20	20
v	40	45
w	60	65
x	80	80
y	100	95

A Supply Curve for Apples

Both the table and the graph show the quantities that producers want to sell at various prices, *ceteris paribus*. For example, row *w* indicates that if the price of apples were $60 per bushel, producers would want to sell 65 000 bushels per year. The supply curve, labelled *S*, relates quantity of apples supplied to the price of apples; its positive slope indicates that quantity supplied increases as price increases.

> The supply curve represents the relationship between quantity supplied and price, other things being equal; its positive slope indicates that quantity supplied increases when price increases.

supply The entire relationship between the quantity of some commodity that producers wish to sell and the price of that commodity, other things being equal.

curve, to the complete relationship between desired sales and all possible prices of the product.

Supply refers to the entire relationship between the quantity supplied of a product and the price of that product, other things being equal. A single point on the supply curve refers to the *quantity supplied* at that price.

Shifts in the Supply Curve A shift in the supply curve means that at each price there is a change in the quantity supplied. An increase in the quantity supplied at each price is shown in Figure 3-6. This change appears as a rightward shift in the supply curve. In contrast, a decrease in the quantity supplied at each price would appear as a leftward shift. For supply, as for demand, there is an important general rule:

> A change in any of the variables (other than the product's own price) that affects the quantity supplied will shift the supply curve to a new position.

Let's now consider the possible causes of shifts in supply curves.

1. Prices of Inputs. All things that a firm uses to produce its outputs, such as materials, labour, and machines, are called the firm's *inputs*. Other things being equal, the higher the price of any input used to make a product, the less profit there will be from making that product. We expect, therefore, that the higher the price of any input used by a firm, the less the firm will produce and offer for sale at any given price of the product. A rise

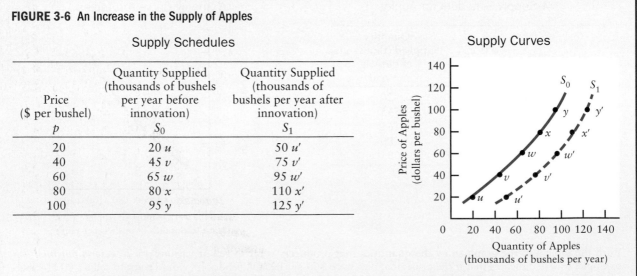

FIGURE 3-6 An Increase in the Supply of Apples

Supply Schedules

Price ($ per bushel) p	Quantity Supplied (thousands of bushels per year before innovation) S_0	Quantity Supplied (thousands of bushels per year after innovation) S_1
20	20 u	50 u'
40	45 v	75 v'
60	65 w	95 w'
80	80 x	110 x'
100	95 y	125 y'

A **cost-saving innovation increases the quantity supplied at each price.** This is shown by the rightward shift in the supply curve, from S_0 to S_1. As a result of a cost-saving innovation, the quantity that is supplied at a price of $100 per bushel rises from 95 000 to 125 000 bushels per year. A similar rise occurs at every price.

in the price of inputs therefore shifts the supply curve to the left, indicating that less will be supplied at any given price; a fall in the price of inputs makes production more profitable and therefore shifts the supply curve to the right.

2. Technology. At any time, what is produced and how it is produced depend on what is known. Over time, knowledge changes. The enormous increase in production per worker that has been going on in industrial societies for about 200 years is due largely to improved methods of production. The Industrial Revolution is more than a historical event; it is a present reality. Discoveries in chemistry have led to lower costs of production for well-established products, such as paints, and to a large variety of new products made of plastics and synthetic fibres. Such inventions as silicon chips and fibre optics have radically changed products, such as cell phones, computers, and surgical devices, and the consequent development of smaller computers has revolutionized the production and lowered the costs of countless other non-electronic products.

Any technological innovation that decreases the amount of inputs needed per unit of output reduces production costs and hence increases the profits that can be earned at any given price of the product. Because increased profitability leads to increased willingness to produce, this change shifts the supply curve to the right.

For producers of agricultural products, extreme weather events are similar to a deterioration in technology because they reduce the amount of output that can be produced with a given amount of land, labour, and other inputs. Agricultural production generally depends on specific weather conditions, and extreme deviations from normal can lead to dramatic reductions in output. Droughts, floods, hurricanes, tornados, and early frosts are a few examples of extreme weather events that usually reduce the supply of agricultural products.

3. Government Taxes or Subsidies. We have just seen that anything increasing firms' costs will shift the supply curve to the left, and anything decreasing firms' costs will shift the supply curve to the right. As we will see in later chapters, governments often levy special taxes on the production of specific goods, such as gasoline, cigarettes, and alcohol. These taxes make the production and sale of these goods less profitable. The result is that the supply curve shifts to the left.

For other goods, governments often subsidize producers—that is, they pay producers a specific amount for each unit of the good produced. This often occurs for agricultural products, especially in the United States and the European Union. In such situations, the subsidy increases the profitability of production and shifts the supply curve to the right. For example, environmental concerns have led the U.S. and Canadian governments in recent years to provide subsidies for the production of biofuels. These subsidies have caused the supply curve for biofuels to shift to the right.

4. Prices of Other Products. Changes in the price of one product may lead to changes in the supply of some other product because the two products are either *substitutes* or *complements* in the production process.

A prairie farmer, for example, can plant his field in wheat or oats. If the market price of oats falls, thus making oat production less profitable, the farmer will be more inclined to plant wheat. In this case, wheat and oats are said to be *substitutes* in production—for every extra hectare planted in one crop, one fewer hectare can be planted in the other. In this example, a reduction in the price of oats leads to an increase in the supply of wheat.

An excellent example in which two products are *complements* in production is oil and natural gas, which are often found together below Earth's surface. If the market price of oil rises, producers will do more drilling and increase their production of oil. But as more oil wells are drilled, the usual outcome is that more of *both* natural gas and oil are discovered and then produced. Thus, the rise in the price of oil leads to an increase in the supply of the complementary product—natural gas.

5. Number of Suppliers. For given prices and technology, the total amount of any product supplied depends on the number of firms producing that product and offering it for sale. If profits are being earned by current firms, then more firms will choose to enter this industry and begin producing. The effect of this increase in the number of suppliers is to shift the supply curve to the right. Similarly, if the existing firms are losing money, they will eventually leave the industry; such a reduction in the number of suppliers shifts the supply curve to the left.

Movements Along the Curve Versus Shifts of the Whole Curve As with demand, it is important to distinguish movements along supply curves from shifts of the whole curve. Economists reserve the term **change in supply** to describe a shift of the whole supply curve—that is, a change in the quantity that will be supplied at every price. The term **change in quantity supplied** refers to a movement from one point on a supply curve to another point, either on the same supply curve or on a new one. In other words, an increase in supply means that the whole supply curve has shifted to the right, so that the quantity supplied at any given price has increased; a movement up and to the right along a supply curve indicates an increase in the quantity supplied in response to an increase in the price of the product.

> **A change in quantity supplied can result from a change in supply with the price constant, a movement along a given supply curve because of a change in the price, or a combination of the two.**

An exercise you might find useful is to construct a diagram similar to Figure 3-4 (see page 63), emphasizing the difference between a shift of the supply curve and a movement along the supply curve.

change in supply A change in the quantity supplied at each possible price of the commodity, represented by a shift in the whole supply curve.

change in quantity supplied A change in the specific quantity supplied, represented by a change from one point on a supply curve to another point, either on the original supply curve or on a new one.

3.3 The Determination of Price

So far we have considered demand and supply separately. We now come to a key question: How do the two forces of demand and supply interact to determine price? Before considering this question, you should know that the demand-and-supply model does *not* apply to all markets. See *Applying Economic Concepts 3-1* for a discussion of why the model in this chapter applies well to apples but not to more interesting products, such as iPhones.

The Concept of a Market

Originally, the term *market* designated a physical place where products were bought and sold. We still use the term this way to describe such places as Granville Island Market in Vancouver, Kensington Market in Toronto, or Jean Talon Market in Montreal.

APPLYING ECONOMIC CONCEPTS 3-1

Why Apples But Not iPhones?

The demand-and-supply model that we have developed in this chapter does *not* apply to the markets for all goods and services, and there is a good reason why our example throughout the chapter has been apples and not, for example, iPhones, cars, brand-name clothing, or even textbooks. Three conditions must be satisfied in order for price determination in a market to be well described by the demand-and-supply model.

1. There must be a large number of consumers of the product, each one small relative to the size of the market.

2. There must be a large number of producers of the product, each one small relative to the size of the market.

3. Producers must be selling identical or "homogeneous" versions of the product.

The first assumption ensures that no single consumer is large enough to influence the market price through their buying actions. This is satisfied in most markets, although there are important exceptions. For example, Canadian provincial governments are dominant purchasers of prescription drugs in Canada, and their *market power* tends to keep prices below what they would otherwise be.

The second assumption ensures that no single producer is large enough to influence the market price through their selling actions. There are many markets in which this is not true. For example, DeBeers controls the sale of a large fraction of the world's rough diamonds, and thus it can alter the market price through its sales

restrictions. Hydro Quebec is the sole producer of electricity in the province of Quebec and sets the price that consumers pay. In contrast, most producers of fruits and vegetables are very small relative to the size of the market and have no ability to influence the market price.

The third assumption ensures that there will be a single price in the market because producers have no ability to *differentiate* their product from those of other producers. This condition is satisfied in many markets for commodities—steel, aluminum, copper, wheat, oil, natural gas, lumber, newsprint, beef, pork, etc. But it is *not* satisfied in the markets for many consumer products such as smartphones and other electronic devices, cars and motorcycles, clothing, and fast food and other restaurant meals. In these cases, each producer sells a different version of the product and spends considerable advertising resources trying to convince consumers to purchase their version. In these markets, differentiated products sell at different prices.

When all three conditions are satisfied, economists use the demand-and-supply model to explain the determination of market price and quantity. This model has proven to be very successful in explaining outcomes in markets such as oil, steel, copper, wheat, soybeans, beef, pork, newsprint, lumber, foreign currencies, financial assets like stocks and bonds—and apples!

So be careful when you try to apply the demand-and-supply model. It works very well in describing the events in many markets, but not so well for others. Later chapters in this book will examine the more complex markets for which we need a more advanced model.

Once developed, however, theories of market behaviour were easily extended to cover products, such as wheat or oil, that can be purchased anywhere in the world at a price that tends to be uniform the world over. Today we can also buy and sell items in markets that exist online—consider the auction services provided by eBay or the almost limitless list of products available from Amazon (including a wedding chapel and a UFO detector!). The idea that a *market* must be a single geographic location where consumers can go to buy something became obsolete long ago.

For present purposes, a **market** may be defined as existing in any situation (such as a physical place or an electronic medium) in which buyers and sellers negotiate the exchange of goods or services.

Individual markets differ in the degree of *competition* among the various buyers and sellers. In the next few chapters we will examine markets in which the number of buyers and sellers is sufficiently large that no one of them has any appreciable influence on the market price. This is a rough definition of what economists call *perfectly competitive*

market Any situation in which buyers and sellers can negotiate the exchange of goods or services.

markets. Starting in Chapter 10, we will consider the behaviour of markets in which there are small numbers of either sellers or buyers. But our initial theory of markets, based on the interaction of demand and supply, will be a very good description of the markets for such things as wheat, pork, newsprint, coffee, copper, oil, and many other commodities.

Market Equilibrium

The table in Figure 3-7 brings together the demand and supply schedules from Figures 3-1 and 3-5. The quantities of apples demanded and supplied at each price can now be compared.

excess demand A situation in which, at the given price, quantity demanded exceeds quantity supplied.

excess supply A situation in which, at the given price, quantity supplied exceeds quantity demanded.

There is only one price, $60 per bushel, at which the quantity of apples demanded equals the quantity supplied. At prices less than $60 per bushel, there is a shortage of apples because the quantity demanded exceeds the quantity supplied. This is a situation of **excess demand**. At prices greater than $60 per bushel, there is a surplus of apples because the quantity supplied exceeds the quantity demanded. This is a situation of **excess supply**. This same story can also be told in graphical terms. The quantities demanded and supplied at any price can be read off the two curves; the excess supply or excess demand is shown by the horizontal distance between the curves at each price.

To examine the determination of market price, let's suppose first that the price is $100 per bushel. At this price, 95 000 bushels are offered for sale, but only 40 000 bushels are demanded. There is an excess supply of 55 000 bushels per year. Apple sellers are then likely to cut their prices to get rid of this surplus. And purchasers, observing the stock of unsold apples, will begin to offer less money for the product. In other words, *excess supply causes downward pressure on price*.

Now consider the price of $20 per bushel. At this price, there is excess demand. The 20 000 bushels produced each year are snapped up quickly, and 90 000 bushels of desired purchases cannot be made. Rivalry between would-be purchasers may lead them to offer more than the prevailing price to outbid other purchasers. Also, sellers may begin to ask a higher price for the quantities that they do have to sell. In other words, *excess demand causes upward pressure on price*.

Finally, consider the price of $60. At this price, producers want to sell 65 000 bushels per year, and purchasers want to buy that same quantity. There is neither a shortage nor a surplus of apples. There are no unsatisfied buyers to bid the price up, nor are there unsatisfied sellers to force the price down. Once the price of $60 has been reached, therefore, there will be no tendency for it to change.

equilibrium price The price at which quantity demanded equals quantity supplied. Also called the *market-clearing price*.

Equilibrium implies a state of rest, or balance, between opposing forces. The **equilibrium price** is the one toward which the actual market price will tend. Once established, it will persist until it is disturbed by some change in market conditions that shifts the demand curve, the supply curve, or both.

> **The price at which the quantity demanded equals the quantity supplied is called the equilibrium price, or the market-clearing price. [5]**

disequilibrium price A price at which quantity demanded does not equal quantity supplied.

disequilibrium A situation in a market in which there is excess demand or excess supply.

Any price at which the market does not "clear"—that is, quantity demanded does not equal quantity supplied—is called a **disequilibrium price**. Whenever there is either excess demand or excess supply in a market, that market is said to be in a state of **disequilibrium**, and the market price will be changing.

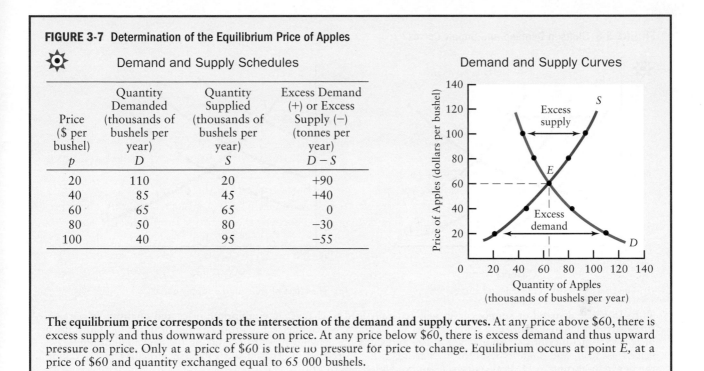

FIGURE 3-7 Determination of the Equilibrium Price of Apples

Demand and Supply Schedules

Price ($ per bushel) p	Quantity Demanded (thousands of bushels per year) D	Quantity Supplied (thousands of bushels per year) S	Excess Demand (+) or Excess Supply (−) (tonnes per year) D − S
20	110	20	+90
40	85	45	+40
60	65	65	0
80	50	80	−30
100	40	95	−55

Demand and Supply Curves

The equilibrium price corresponds to the intersection of the demand and supply curves. At any price above $60, there is excess supply and thus downward pressure on price. At any price below $60, there is excess demand and thus upward pressure on price. Only at a price of $60 is there no pressure for price to change. Equilibrium occurs at point E, at a price of $60 and quantity exchanged equal to 65 000 bushels.

Figure 3-7 makes it clear that the equilibrium price occurs where the demand and supply curves intersect. Below that price, there is excess demand and hence upward pressure on the existing price. Above that price, there is excess supply and hence downward pressure on the existing price.[3]

Changes in Market Equilibrium

Changes in any of the variables, other than price, that influence quantity demanded or supplied will cause a shift in the demand curve, the supply curve, or both. There are four possible shifts: an increase in demand (a rightward shift in the demand curve), a decrease in demand (a leftward shift in the demand curve), an increase in supply (a rightward shift in the supply curve), and a decrease in supply (a leftward shift in the supply curve).

Commodities & Futures	Price (US$)	Chg		Price (US$)	Chg
Crude Oil	96.57	−0.27	Lumber	292.50	−4.40
Natural Gas	2.816	0.041	Cocoa	2400.00	−33.00
Heating Oil	3.1244	−0.0073	Corn	829.25	−2.00
Gold	1642.70	−0.20	Soybeans	1727.50	−5.00
Silver	29.48	−0.034	Oat	393.25	−3.75
Copper	3.4565	−0.0045	Live Cattle	124.775	0.15
Platinum	1524.10	16.30	Wood Pulp	865.00	3.50
Palladium	629.75	5.55	Lean Hogs	75.175	−0.625

Many commodities like those listed here are actively traded in international markets and their equilibrium prices fluctuate daily.

Source: "Commodities & Futures," *TMX Money*, tmx.quotemedia.com/futures.php. Accessed August 22, 2012.

---

[3] When economists graph a demand (or supply) curve, they put the variable to be explained (the dependent variable) on the horizontal axis and the explanatory variable (the independent variable) on the vertical axis. This is "backward" to what is usually done in mathematics. The rational explanation of what is now economists' odd practice is buried in the history of economics and dates back to Alfred Marshall's *Principles of Economics* (1890) [6]. For better or worse, Marshall's scheme is now used by all economists, although mathematicians never fail to wonder at this example of the odd ways of economists.

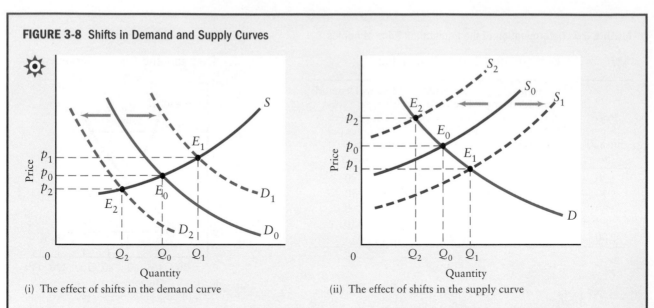

FIGURE 3-8 Shifts in Demand and Supply Curves

(i) The effect of shifts in the demand curve

(ii) The effect of shifts in the supply curve

Shifts in either demand or supply curves will generally lead to changes in equilibrium price and quantity. In part (i), suppose the original demand and supply curves are D_0 and S, which intersect to produce equilibrium at E_0, with a price of p_0 and a quantity of Q_0. An increase in demand shifts the demand curve to D_1, taking the new equilibrium to E_1. Price rises to p_1 and quantity rises to Q_1. Starting at E_0, a decrease in demand shifts the demand curve to D_2, taking the new equilibrium to E_2. Price falls to p_2 and quantity falls to Q_2.

In part (ii), the original demand and supply curves are D and S_0, which intersect to produce equilibrium at E_0, with a price of p_0 and a quantity of Q_0. An increase in supply shifts the supply curve to S_1, taking the new equilibrium to E_1. Price falls to p_1 and quantity rises to Q_1. Starting at E_0, a decrease in supply shifts the supply curve from S_0 to S_2, taking the new equilibrium to E_2. Price rises to p_2 and quantity falls to Q_2.

comparative statics The derivation of predictions by analyzing the effect of a change in some exogenous variable on the equilibrium.

To discover the effects of each of the possible curve shifts, we use the method known as **comparative statics**.[4] With this method, we derive predictions about how the *endogenous* variables (equilibrium price and quantity) will change following a change in some *exogenous* variable (the variables whose changes cause shifts in the demand and supply curves). We start from a position of equilibrium and then introduce the change to be studied. We then determine the new equilibrium position and compare it with the original one. The difference between the two positions of equilibrium must result from the change that was introduced, because everything else has been held constant.

The changes caused by each of the four possible curve shifts are shown in Figure 3-8. Study the figure carefully. Previously, we had given the axes specific labels, but because it is now intended to apply to any product, the horizontal axis is simply labelled "Quantity." This means quantity per period in whatever units output is measured. "Price," the vertical axis, means the price measured as dollars per unit of quantity for the same product.

The effects of the four possible curve shifts are as follows:

1. An increase in demand causes an increase in both the equilibrium price and the equilibrium quantity exchanged.

---

[4] The term *static* is used because we are not concerned with the actual path by which the market goes from the first equilibrium position to the second, or with the time taken to reach the second equilibrium. Analysis of these movements would be described as *dynamic analysis*.

2. A decrease in demand causes a decrease in both the equilibrium price and the equilibrium quantity exchanged.

3. An increase in supply causes a decrease in the equilibrium price and an increase in the equilibrium quantity exchanged.

4. A decrease in supply causes an increase in the equilibrium price and a decrease in the equilibrium quantity exchanged.

Demonstrations of these effects are given in the caption to Figure 3-8. The intuitive reasoning behind each is as follows:

1. **An increase in demand (the demand curve shifts to the right).** An increase in demand creates a shortage at the initial equilibrium price, and the unsatisfied buyers bid up the price. This rise in price causes a larger quantity to be supplied, with the result that at the new equilibrium more is exchanged at a higher price.

2. **A decrease in demand (the demand curve shifts to the left).** A decrease in demand creates a surplus at the initial equilibrium price, and the unsuccessful sellers bid the price down. As a result, less of the product is supplied and offered for sale. At the new equilibrium, both price and quantity exchanged are lower than they were originally.

3. **An increase in supply (the supply curve shifts to the right).** An increase in supply creates a surplus at the initial equilibrium price, and the unsuccessful suppliers force the price down. This drop in price increases the quantity demanded, and the new equilibrium is at a lower price and a higher quantity exchanged.

4. **A decrease in supply (the supply curve shifts to the left).** A decrease in supply creates a shortage at the initial equilibrium price that causes the price to be bid up. This rise in price reduces the quantity demanded, and the new equilibrium is at a higher price and a lower quantity exchanged.

By using the tools we have learned in this chapter, we can link many real-world events that cause demand or supply curves to shift and thus lead to changes in market prices and quantities. *Lessons from History 3-1* shows how we can use demand-and-supply analysis to examine the effects of two major weather shocks: Quebec's 1998 ice storm and Hurricane Katrina in 2005.

Our discussion of demand, supply, and market equilibrium has explained why equilibrium price and quantity are found at the intersection of the demand and supply curves. We have shown diagrams (Figures 3-7 and 3-8) illustrating this in the general case. But we have not presented a specific algebraic example of demand and supply and "solved" precisely for the equilibrium price and quantity. See *Extensions in Theory 3-2* for an algebraic solution to a specific model of demand and supply.

Relative Prices and Inflation

The theory we have developed explains how individual prices are determined by the forces of demand and supply. To facilitate matters, we have made *ceteris paribus* assumptions. Specifically, we have assumed the constancy of all prices except the one we are studying. Does this mean that our theory is inapplicable to an inflationary world in which all prices are rising at the same time? Fortunately, the answer is no.

LESSONS FROM HISTORY 3-1

Ice Storms, Hurricanes, and Economics

Here are two simple examples of the demand-and-supply model in action. Both examples show how the weather—something that changes in unpredictable and often dramatic ways—can have significant effects on either the demand or the supply of various products, with obvious implications for the observed market price.

The Weather and a Demand Shock

In January 1998, Quebec, Eastern Ontario, and parts of the northeastern United States were hit by a massive ice storm. So unprecedented was this storm in its magnitude that many electric power systems were devastated. Homes and businesses in the Montreal area went without power for as long as four weeks.

This electric power shortage had many economic effects, including lost factory production, damage to many businesses, the death of farm livestock, and the displacement of thousands of people into shelters. Another effect of the power shortage, as soon as it became clear that it would last for more than just a few hours, was a sudden and substantial increase in the demand for portable gas-powered generators. Within just a few days,

all stores in the greater Montreal area were sold out of such generators, and the prices for newly ordered units increased sharply.

Furthermore, the shortages and price increases for generators were not confined to the area directly hit by the ice storm. As it became clear that there was an excess demand for generators in Quebec, sellers in other parts of the country began to divert their supply toward Quebec. This reduction in supply caused shortages, and thus price increases, in other parts of the country, as far away as Edmonton.

The Weather and a Supply Shock

In late August 2005, Hurricane Katrina emerged from the Caribbean, gathered strength as it crossed the Gulf of Mexico, and unleashed its fury on New Orleans, Louisiana. The damage to New Orleans was massive, especially after the levee holding back Lake Pontchartrain broke and much of the city was flooded. Katrina was then the worst natural disaster in U.S. history; the cost of the damage to buildings, bridges, houses, and other infrastructure was estimated to be close to U.S.$125 billion.

---

absolute price The amount of money that must be spent to acquire one unit of a commodity. Also called *money price.*

relative price The ratio of the money price of one commodity to the money price of another commodity; that is, a ratio of two absolute prices.

The price of a product is the amount of money that must be spent to acquire one unit of that product. This is called the **absolute price** or *money price*. A **relative price** is the ratio of two absolute prices; it expresses the price of one good in terms of (relative to) another.

We have been reminded several times that what matters for demand and supply is the price of the product in question *relative to the prices of other products*; that is, what matters is the relative price. For example, if the price of carrots rises while the prices of other vegetables are constant, we expect consumers to reduce their quantity demanded of carrots as they substitute toward the consumption of other vegetables. In this case, the *relative* price of carrots has increased. But if the prices of carrots and all other vegetables are rising at the same rate, the relative price of carrots is constant. In this case we expect no substitution to take place between carrots and other vegetables.

In an inflationary world, we are often interested in the price of a given product as it relates to the average price of all other products. If, during a period when all prices were increasing by an average of 5 percent, the price of coffee increased by 30 percent, then the price of coffee increased relative to the prices of other goods as a whole. Coffee became *relatively* expensive. However, if coffee had increased in price by

Hurricane Katrina had an instant effect on the world market for oil. Over short periods of time, the world demand curve for oil is relatively steep, reflecting the fact that users of oil initially reduce their purchases only slightly when the price rises.

Hurricane Katrina interrupted the local production and distribution of oil, thereby causing a temporary reduction in world supply. Several large oil rigs in the Gulf of Mexico were damaged and were shut down or operating well below their capacity for several weeks. In addition, the major pipelines that transport this oil from the Gulf ports to the inland refineries were also seriously damaged. For both reasons, the supply curve for oil shifted to the left. And given the relatively steep demand curve, this reduction in supply caused a sharp increase in the equilibrium price. The price per barrel of oil, which had averaged roughly U.S.$40 earlier that year, reached U.S.$70 on August 29, and stayed above U.S.$65 for about a month. As the rigs and pipelines were repaired, and Gulf-area oil production began to approach its pre-Katrina levels, the supply curve shifted back to the right and the price returned to levels between U.S.$55 and U.S.$60 per barrel.

Hurricane Katrina in August 2005 damaged several oil platforms operating in the Gulf of Mexico, causing a temporary reduction in the supply of oil.

30 percent when other prices increased by 40 percent, then the relative price of coffee would have fallen. Although the money price of coffee increased substantially, coffee became *relatively* cheap.

In this chapter we have been assuming that changes in a particular price occur when all other prices are constant. We can easily extend the analysis to an inflationary setting by remembering that any force that raises the price of one product when other prices remain constant will, given general inflation, raise the price of that product faster than the price level is rising. For example, consider a change in tastes in favour of coffee that raises its price by 5 percent when other prices are constant. The same change would raise its price by 8 percent if, at the same time, the general price level were rising by 3 percent. In each case, the price of coffee rises 5 percent *relative to the average of all prices*.

> In microeconomics, whenever we refer to a change in the price of one product, we mean a change in that product's relative price, that is, a change in the price of that product relative to the prices of all other goods.

EXTENSIONS IN THEORY 3-2

The Algebra of Market Equilibrium

This box presents an algebraic model of demand and supply and the method for determining the equilibrium price and quantity. For simplicity, we assume that the demand and supply curves are linear relationships between price and quantity.

Consider the following demand and supply curves:

Demand: $Q^D = a - bp$

Supply: $Q^S = c + dp$

where p is the price, Q^D is quantity demanded, Q^S is quantity supplied, and $a, b, c,$ and d are positive constants. Both relationships are plotted in the accompanying figure.

What is the interpretation of the demand curve and how do we plot it? First, at a price of zero, consumers will buy a units—this is the horizontal intercept of the demand curve. Second, at a price of a/b, consumers will buy zero units, so a/b is the vertical intercept of the demand curve. Finally, the slope of the demand curve is $-1/b$; the quantity demanded increases by b units for every \$1 that price falls.

What is the interpretation of the supply curve, and how do we plot it? First, if the price is zero, suppliers will sell c units—this is the horizontal intercept of the supply curve. Second, for every \$1 increase in price, the quantity supplied increases by d units. Thus, the slope of the supply curve is $1/d$.

Given these demand and supply curves, the market equilibrium can be determined in two ways. The first is to construct a scale diagram and plot the two curves accurately. If you do this carefully, you will be able to read the equilibrium price and quantity off the diagram. But your diagram will have to be very accurate for this to work!

A more precise method is to use algebra to solve for the equilibrium price and quantity. Here is how we do

it. We know that in equilibrium quantity demanded equals quantity supplied, or $Q^D = Q^S$. We call the equilibrium quantity Q^*. But we also know that in equilibrium the price paid by the consumers will equal the price received by the producers—that is, there is only one equilibrium price, which we call p^*. Putting these two facts together, we know that in equilibrium

Demand: $Q^* = a - bp^*$

Supply: $Q^* = c + dp^*$

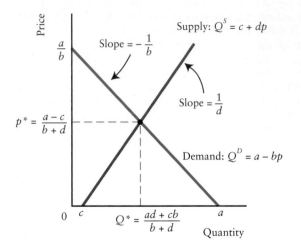

We now have two equations and two unknown variables (p^* and Q^*) and can proceed to solve the system of equations. Since Q^* from the demand curve equals Q^* from the supply curve, it follows that

$$a - bp^* = c + dp^*$$

SUMMARY

3.1 Demand

LO 1, 2

- The amount of a product that consumers want to purchase is called *quantity demanded*. It is a flow expressed as so much per period of time. It is determined by tastes, income, the product's own price, the prices of other products, the size of the population, and expectations about the future.

- The relationship between quantity demanded and price is represented graphically by a demand curve that shows how much will be demanded at each market price. Quantity demanded is assumed to increase as the price of the product falls, other things held constant. Thus, demand curves are negatively sloped.

This implies

$$a - c = (b + d)p^*$$

which can be solved for p^* to get

$$p^* = \frac{a - c}{b + d}$$

This is the solution for the equilibrium market price. By substituting this value of p^* back into *either* the demand curve or the supply curve (it doesn't matter which), we get the solution for Q^*:

$$Q^* = a - bp^* = a - \frac{b(a - c)}{(b + d)}$$

which can be simplified to

$$Q^* = \frac{a(b + d)}{(b + d)} - \frac{b(a - c)}{(b + d)}$$

which can be further simplified to

$$Q^* = \frac{(ad + bc)}{b + d}$$

We now have the precise solutions for the equilibrium price and quantity in this market. Notice that the solutions for p^* and Q^* naturally depend on those (exogenous) variables that shift the demand and supply curves. For example, an increase in demand for the product would be reflected by an increase in a. This would shift the demand curve to the right, increasing both p^* and Q^*. A decrease in supply would have a different effect. It would be reflected by a decrease in c that would shift the supply curve to the left, leading to an increase in p^* and a reduction in Q^*.

Now let's do the same thing but with even more specific demand and supply curves. Suppose we have the following relationships:

$$Q^D = 18 - 3p$$
$$Q^S = 2 + 5p$$

The equilibrium condition is that $Q^D = Q^S = Q^*$. And when quantity is equal to Q^*, price will be equal to p^*. Thus, in equilibrium we will have

$$Q^* = 18 - 3p^*$$
$$Q^* = 2 + 5p^*$$

Since Q^* from the demand curve obviously equals Q^* from the supply curve, we have

$$18 - 3p^* = 2 + 5p^*$$

which can be solved for p^* to get

$$8p^* = 16$$
$$p^* = 2$$

Putting this value of p^* back into the demand curve we get

$$Q^* = 18 - 3(2)$$
$$Q^* = 12$$

We have therefore solved for the equilibrium price and quantity in this specific numerical model of demand and supply.

Mastering the algebra of demand and supply takes a little practice, but is worth the effort. If you would like to practise, try the Study Exercises at the end of the chapter (and Chapters 4 and 5) that deal with the algebra of demand and supply.

- A shift in a demand curve represents a change in the quantity demanded at each price and is referred to as a *change in demand*.
- An increase in demand means the demand curve shifts to the right; a decrease in demand means the demand curve shifts to the left.

- It is important to make the distinction between a movement along a demand curve (caused by a change in the product's price) and a shift of a demand curve (caused by a change in any of the other determinants of demand).

3.2 Supply   LO 3, 4

- The amount of a good that producers wish to sell is called *quantity supplied*. It is a flow expressed as so much per period of time. It depends on the product's own price, the costs of inputs, the number of suppliers, government taxes or subsidies, the state of technology, and prices of other products.

- The relationship between quantity supplied and price is represented graphically by a supply curve that shows how much will be supplied at each market price. Quantity supplied is assumed to increase as the price of the product increases, other things held constant. Thus, supply curves are positively sloped.
- A shift in the supply curve indicates a change in the quantity supplied at each price and is referred to as a *change in supply*.

- An increase in supply means the supply curve shifts to the right; a decrease in supply means the supply curve shifts to the left.
- It is important to make the distinction between a movement along a supply curve (caused by a change in the product's price) and a shift of a supply curve (caused by a change in any of the other determinants of supply).

3.3 The Determination of Price   LO 5

- The *equilibrium price* is the price at which the quantity demanded equals the quantity supplied. At any price below equilibrium, there will be excess demand; at any price above equilibrium, there will be excess supply. Graphically, equilibrium occurs where the demand and supply curves intersect.
- Price rises when there is excess demand and falls when there is excess supply. Thus, the actual market price will be pushed toward the equilibrium price. When it is reached, there will be neither excess demand nor excess supply, and the price will not change until either the supply curve or the demand curve shifts.
- By using the method of *comparative statics,* we can determine the effects of a shift in either demand or

supply. An increase in demand raises both equilibrium price and equilibrium quantity; a decrease in demand lowers both. An increase in supply raises equilibrium quantity but lowers equilibrium price; a decrease in supply lowers equilibrium quantity but raises equilibrium price.
- The absolute price of a product is its price in terms of money; its relative price is its price in relation to other products. In an inflationary period, a rise in the *relative price* of one product means that its absolute price rises by more than the average of all prices; a fall in its relative price means that its absolute price rises by less than the average of all prices.

KEY CONCEPTS

Stock and flow variables
Ceteris paribus or "other things being equal"
Quantity demanded
Demand schedule and demand curve

Change in quantity demanded versus change in demand
Quantity supplied
Supply schedule and supply curve
Change in quantity supplied versus change in supply

Equilibrium, equilibrium price, and disequilibrium
Comparative statics
Relative price

STUDY EXERCISES

MyEconLab   Make the grade with MyEconLab: Study Exercises marked in red can be found on MyEconLab. You can practise them as often as you want, and most feature step-by-step guided instructions to help you find the right answer.

1. Fill in the blanks to complete the statements about a supply-and-demand model, as applied in the following situations.

   a. Consider the market for cement in Toronto. If, *ceteris paribus,* half the producers in this market shut down, the _____ curve for cement will shift to the _____, indicating a(n) _____ in _____.

   b. Consider the market for Canadian softwood lumber (a normal good). If, *ceteris paribus,* average incomes in both Canada and the United States rise over several years, the _____ curve for lumber will shift to the _____, indicating a(n) _____ in _____.

c. Consider the market for Quebec artisanal cheeses. If, *ceteris paribus,* the price of imported cheeses from France rises significantly, the _____ curve for Quebec cheeses will shift to the _____, indicating a(n) _____ in _____.

d. Consider the market for milk in the United States. If *ceteris paribus,* the U.S. government decreases subsidies to dairy farmers, the _____ curve for milk will shift to the _____, indicating a(n) _____ in _____.

e. Consider the world market for shipping containers. If, *ceteris paribus,* the price of steel (a major input) rises, the _____ curve for shipping containers will shift to the _____, indicating a(n) _____ in _____.

f. Consider the market for hot dog buns. If, *ceteris paribus,* the price of wieners doubles, the _____ curve for hot dog buns will shift to the _____, indicating a(n) _____ in _____.

2. The following table shows hypothetical demand schedules for sugar for three separate months. To help make the distinction between changes in demand and changes in quantity demanded, choose the wording to make each of the following statements correct.

Price/kg	Quantity Demanded for Sugar (in kilograms)		
	October	November	December
$1.50	11 000	10 500	13 000
1.75	10 000	9 500	12 000
2.00	9 000	8 500	11 000
2.25	8 000	7 500	10 000
2.50	7 000	6 500	9 000
2.75	6 000	5 500	8 000
3.00	5 000	4 500	7 000
3.25	4 000	3 500	6 000
3.50	3 000	2 500	5 000

a. When the price of sugar rises from $2.50 to $3.00 in the month of October there is a(n) (*increase/ decrease*) in (*demand for/quantity demanded of*) sugar of 2000 kg.

b. We can say that the demand curve for sugar in December shifted (*to the right/to the left*) of November's demand curve. This represents a(n) (*increase/ decrease*) in demand for sugar.

c. An increase in the demand for sugar means that quantity demanded at each price has (*increased/ decreased*), while a decrease in demand for sugar means that quantity demanded at each price has (*increased/decreased*).

d. In the month of December, a price change for sugar from $3.50 to $2.75 per kilogram would mean a change in (*demand for/quantity demanded of*) sugar of 3000 kg.

e. Plot the three demand schedules on a graph and label each demand curve to indicate whether it is the demand for October, November, or December.

3. Classify the effect of each of the following as (i) a decrease in the demand for fish or (ii) a decrease in the quantity of fish demanded. Illustrate each diagrammatically.

a. The government of Canada closes the Atlantic cod fishery.

b. People buy less fish because of a rise in fish prices.

c. The Catholic Church relaxes its ban on eating meat on Fridays.

d. The price of beef falls and, as a result, consumers buy more beef and less fish.

e. Fears of mercury poisoning lead locals to shun fish caught in nearby lakes.

f. It is generally alleged that eating fish is better for one's health than eating meat.

4. Are the following two observations inconsistent?

a. Rising demand for housing causes prices of new homes to soar.

b. Many families refuse to buy homes as prices become prohibitive for them.

5. For each of the following statements, determine whether there has been a change in supply or a change in quantity supplied. Draw a demand-and-supply diagram for each situation to show either a movement along the supply curve or a shift of the supply curve.

a. The price of Canadian-grown peaches skyrockets during an unusually cold summer that reduces the size of the peach harvest.

b. An increase in income leads to an increase in the price of family-restaurant meals, and to an increase in their sales.

c. Technological improvements in electronic publishing lead to price reductions for e-books and an increase in e-book sales.

d. A low-carb diet becomes popular and leads to a reduction in the price of bread and less bread being sold.

6. The following diagram describes the hypothetical demand and supply for canned tuna in Canada in 2013.

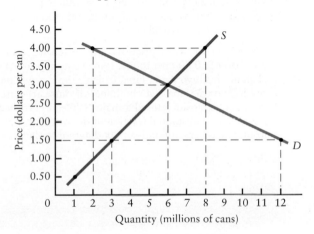

a. Suppose the price of a can of tuna is $4.00. What is the quantity demanded? What is the quantity supplied? At this price, is there a shortage or a surplus? By what amount?

b. Suppose the price of a can of tuna is $1.50. What is the quantity demanded? What is the quantity supplied? At this price, is there a shortage or a surplus? By what amount?

c. What is the equilibrium price and quantity in this market?

7. Consider households' demand for chicken meat. For each of the events listed below, state and explain the likely effect on the demand for chicken. How would each event be illustrated in a diagram?

a. A medical study reports that eating chicken reduces the likelihood of suffering from particular types of heart problems.

b. A widespread bovine disease leads to an increase in the price of beef.

c. Average household income increases.

8. Consider the world market for a particular quality of coffee beans. The following table shows the demand and supply schedules for this market.

Price (per kilogram)	Quantity Demanded	Quantity Supplied
	(millions of kilograms per year)	
$2.00	28	10
$2.40	26	12
$3.10	22	13.5
$3.50	19.5	19.5
$3.90	17	22
$4.30	14.5	23.5

a. Plot the demand and supply schedules on a diagram.

b. Identify the amount of excess demand or supply associated with each price.

c. Identify the equilibrium price in this market.

d. Suppose that a collection of national governments were somehow able to set a minimum price for coffee equal to $3.90 per kilogram. Explain the outcome in the world coffee market.

9. Early in 2011, the world price of copper reached a record high of over $10 000 per tonne. Two events appeared to lie behind this high price. First, China's rapid economic growth and the massive building of infrastructure. Second, an explosion closed a major Chilean port used for shipping a substantial fraction of the world's copper output. Use a demand-and-supply diagram to illustrate these events in the copper market, and explain how each event shifts either the demand curve or the supply curve.

10. Consider the world market for wheat. Suppose there is a major failure in Russia's wheat crop because of a severe drought. Explain the likely effect on the equilibrium price and quantity in the world wheat market. Also explain why Canadian wheat farmers certainly benefit from Russia's drought. The following diagrams provide a starting point for your analysis.

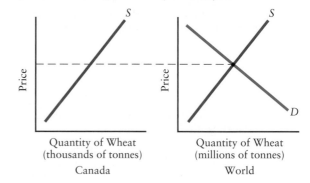

Quantity of Wheat (thousands of tonnes)
Canada

Quantity of Wheat (millions of tonnes)
World

11. This question requires you to solve a supply-and-demand model algebraically. Letting p be the price of the product, suppose the demand and supply functions for some product are given by

$$Q^D = 100 - 3p$$
$$Q^S = 10 + 2p$$

a. Plot both the demand curve and the supply curve.

b. What is the condition for equilibrium in this market?

c. By imposing the condition for equilibrium, solve for the equilibrium price.

d. Substitute the equilibrium price into either the demand or the supply function to solve for the equilibrium quantity. Check to make sure you get the same answer whether you use the demand function or the supply function.

e. Now suppose there is an increase in demand so that the new demand function is given by

$$Q^D = 180 - 3p$$

Compute the new equilibrium price and quantity. Is your result consistent with the "law" of demand?

f. Now suppose that with the new demand curve in place, there is an increase in supply so that the new supply function is given by $Q^S = 90 + 2p$. Compute the new equilibrium price and quantity. Is your result consistent with the "law" of supply?

Elasticity

THE laws of demand and supply predict the direction of changes in equilibrium price and quantity in response to various shifts in demand and supply curves. For many purposes, however, it is not enough to know merely whether price and quantity rise or fall; it is also important to know by how much each changes.

For example, during the 2011 civil war in Libya, that country's oil production was sharply reduced for over six months. As a result, global oil production fell by over 1.5 million barrels per day, a decline of just under 2 percent. This drop in the world supply of oil led to an immediate increase in the world price, from $100 to $120 per barrel, which persisted until Libya's production returned to more normal levels after the end of the civil war. How can we explain why the increase in the price of oil in this situation was 20 percent rather than 50 percent or only 5 percent? As we will see in this chapter, the shapes of the demand and supply curves determine the sensitivity of prices and quantities to various economic shocks. Precise measures of these sensitivities are provided by what are called the elasticity of demand and supply.

4.1 Price Elasticity of Demand

Suppose there is a decrease in the supply of some farm crop—that is, a leftward shift in the supply curve. We saw in Figure 3-8 (see page 72) when we examined the laws of supply and demand that such a decrease in supply will cause the equilibrium price to rise and the equilibrium quantity to fall. But by how much will each change? The answer depends on what is called the *price elasticity of demand*.

Loosely speaking, demand is said to be *elastic* when quantity demanded is quite responsive to changes in price. When quantity demanded is relatively unresponsive to changes in price, demand is said to be *inelastic*.

The importance of elasticity is illustrated in Figure 4-1. The two parts of the figure have the same initial equilibrium, and that equilibrium is disturbed by the same leftward shift in the supply curve. But the demand curves are different in the two parts of the figure, and so the sizes of the changes in equilibrium price and quantity are also different.

Part (i) of Figure 4-1 illustrates a case in which the quantity that consumers demand is quite responsive to price changes—that is, demand is relatively *elastic*. The reduction in supply pushes up the price, but because the quantity demanded is quite responsive to changes in price (demand is elastic), only a small change in price is necessary to restore equilibrium.

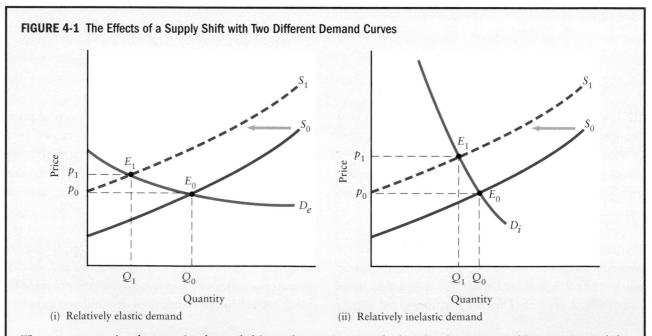

FIGURE 4-1 The Effects of a Supply Shift with Two Different Demand Curves

(i) Relatively elastic demand

(ii) Relatively inelastic demand

The more responsive the quantity demanded is to changes in price, the less the change in equilibrium price and the greater the change in equilibrium quantity resulting from any given shift in the supply curve. Both parts of the figure are drawn to the same scale. They show the same initial equilibrium, E_0, and the same shift in the supply curve, from S_0 to S_1. In each part, initial equilibrium is at price p_0 and output Q_0 and the new equilibrium, E_1, is at p_1 and Q_1. In part (i), the effect of the reduction in supply is a slight rise in the price and a large decrease in quantity. In part (ii), the effect of the identical reduction in supply is a large increase in the price and a relatively small decrease in quantity.

Part (ii) of Figure 4-1 shows a case in which the quantity demanded is quite unresponsive to price changes—that is, demand is relatively *inelastic*. As in part (i), the decrease in supply at the original price causes a shortage that increases the price. However, in this case the quantity demanded by consumers does not fall much in response to the rise in price (demand is inelastic). The result is that equilibrium price rises more, and equilibrium quantity falls less, than in the first case.

In both cases shown in Figure 4-1, the shifts of the supply curve are identical. The sizes of the effects on the equilibrium price and quantity are different only because of the different elasticities of demand.

The Measurement of Price Elasticity

In Figure 4-1, we were able to say that the demand curve in part (i) showed more responsiveness to price changes than the demand curve in part (ii) because two conditions were fulfilled. First, both curves were drawn on the same scale. Second, the initial equilibrium prices and quantities were the same in both parts of the figure. Let's see why these conditions matter.

First, by drawing both figures on the same scale, we saw that the demand curve that *looked* steeper actually did have the larger absolute slope. (The slope of a demand curve tells us the amount by which price must change to cause a unit change in quantity demanded.) If we had drawn the two curves on different scales, we could have concluded nothing about which demand curve actually had the greater slope.

Second, because we started from the same price–quantity equilibrium in both parts of the figure, we did not need to distinguish between *percentage* changes and *absolute* changes. If the initial prices and quantities are the same in both cases, the larger absolute change is also the larger percentage change. However, when we want to deal with different initial price–quantity equilibria, we need to decide whether we are interested in absolute or percentage changes.

To see why the difference between absolute and percentage change matters, consider the changes in price and quantity demanded for three different products: cheese, T-shirts, and coffee machines. The information is shown in Table 4-1. Should we conclude that the demand for coffee machines is not as responsive to price changes as the demand for cheese? After all, price cuts of $2 cause quite a large increase in the quantity of cheese demanded, but only a small increase in the quantity demanded of coffee machines. It should be obvious that a $2 price reduction is a large price cut for a low-priced product and an insignificant price cut for a high-priced product. In Table 4-1, each price reduction is $2, but they are clearly different proportions of the respective prices. It is usually more revealing to know the *percentage* change in the prices of the various products.

For similar reasons, knowing the quantity by which demand changes is not very revealing unless the initial level of demand is also known. An increase of 7500 kilograms is quite a significant change if the quantity formerly bought was 15 000 kilograms, but it is insignificant if the quantity formerly bought was 10 million kilograms.

TABLE 4-1 Price Reductions and Corresponding Increases in Quantity Demanded for Three Products

Commodity	Reduction in Price	Increase in Quantity Demanded (per month)
Cheese	$2 per kilogram	7500 kilograms
T-shirts	$2 per shirt	25 000 shirts
Coffee machines	$2 per machine	500 machines

For each of the three products, the data show the change in quantity demanded resulting from the same absolute fall in price. The data are fairly uninformative about the responsiveness of quantity demanded to price because they do not tell us either the original price or the original quantity demanded.

TABLE 4-2 Price and Quantity Information Underlying Data of Table 4-1

Product	Unit	Original Price ($)	New Price ($)	Average Price ($)	Original Quantity	New Quantity	Average Quantity
Cheese	kilogram	5.00	3.00	4.00	116 250	123 750	120 000
T-shirts	shirt	17.00	15.00	16.00	187 500	212 500	200 000
Coffee machines	machine	81.00	79.00	80.00	9 750	10 250	10 000

These data provide the appropriate context for the data given in Table 4-1. The table relates the $2-per-unit price reduction of each product to the actual prices and quantities demanded.

Table 4-2 shows the original and new levels of price and quantity. Note that it also shows the *average* price and *average* quantity. These averages will be necessary for our computation of elasticity.

The **price elasticity of demand,** the measure of responsiveness of the quantity of a product demanded to a change in that product's price, is symbolized by the Greek letter eta, η. It is defined as follows:

price elasticity of demand (η)
A measure of the responsiveness of quantity demanded to a change in the commodity's own price.

$$\eta = \frac{\text{Percentage change in quantity demanded}}{\text{Percentage change in price}}$$

This measure is called the price elasticity of demand, or simply demand elasticity. Because the variable causing the change in quantity demanded is the product's own price, the term *own-price elasticity of demand* is also used.

The Use of Average Price and Quantity in Computing Elasticity Table 4-3 shows the percentage changes for price and quantity using the data from Table 4-2. The caption in Table 4-3 stresses that the demand elasticities are computed by using changes in price and quantity measured in terms of the *average* values of each. Averages are used to avoid the ambiguity caused by the fact that when a price or quantity changes, the change is a different percentage of the original value than it is of the new value. For example, the $2.00 change in the price of cheese shown in Table 4-2 represents a 40 percent change in the original price of $5.00 but a 66.7 percent change in the new price of $3.00.

Using average values for price and quantity means that the measured elasticity of demand between any two points on the demand curve, call them *A* and *B,* is independent of whether the movement is from *A* to *B* or from *B* to *A*. In the example of cheese in Table 4-2 and 4-3, the $2.00 change in the price of cheese is unambiguously 50 percent of the average price of $4.00, and that percentage applies to a price increase from $3.00 to $5.00 or to a price decrease from $5.00 to $3.00.

TABLE 4-3 Calculation of Demand Elasticities

Product	(1) Percentage Decrease in Price	(2) Percentage Increase in Quantity	(3) Elasticity of Demand (2) ÷ (1)
Cheese	50.0	6.25	0.125
T-shirts	12.5	12.5	1.0
Coffee machines	2.5	5.0	2.0

Elasticity of demand is the percentage change in quantity demanded divided by the percentage change in price. The percentage changes are based on average prices and quantities shown in Table 4-2. For example, the $2.00-per-kilogram decrease in the price of cheese is 50 percent of the average price $4.00. A $2.00 change in the price of coffee machines is only 2.5 percent of the average price per machine of $80.00.

Once we have computed the average prices and quantities as in Table 4-2, the algebraic formula for price elasticity is straightforward. Suppose we have an initial price of p_0 and an initial quantity of Q_0. We then consider a new price of p_1 and a new quantity of Q_1 (both price–quantity combinations lie on the demand curve for the product). The formula for price elasticity is then

$$\eta = \frac{\dfrac{\Delta Q}{\overline{Q}}}{\dfrac{\Delta p}{\overline{p}}} = \frac{\dfrac{Q_1 - Q_0}{\overline{Q}}}{\dfrac{p_1 - p_0}{\overline{p}}}$$

where $\overline{p}$ is the average price and $\overline{Q}$ is the average quantity. In the case of cheese from Table 4-2, we have

$$\eta = \frac{7500/120\,000}{2.0/4.0} = \frac{0.0625}{0.5} = 0.125$$

as shown in Table 4-3. Notice that elasticity is *unit free*—even though prices are measured in dollars and quantity of cheese is measured in kilograms, the elasticity of demand has no units.

We leave it to you to use this formula to confirm the price elasticities for T-shirts and coffee machines shown in Table 4-3. [7]

Interpreting Numerical Elasticities Because demand curves have negative slopes, an increase in price is associated with a decrease in quantity demanded, and vice versa. Because the percentage changes in price and quantity have opposite signs, demand elasticity is a negative number. However, here we will ignore the negative sign and speak of the measure as a positive number, as we have done in the illustrative calculations in Table 4-3. Thus, the more responsive the quantity demanded to a change in price, the greater the elasticity and the larger is η.

The numerical value of demand elasticity can vary from zero to infinity. First consider the extreme cases. Elasticity is zero when a change in price leads to *no change* in quantity demanded. This is the case of a vertical demand curve, and it is quite rare because it indicates that consumers do not alter their consumption at all when price changes. At the other extreme, elasticity is very large when even a very small change in price leads to an enormous change in quantity demanded. In these situations, the demand curve is very flat, almost horizontal. (In the rare limiting case, the demand curve is perfectly horizontal and elasticity is infinite.) Most of reality lies between the extremes of vertical and horizontal demand curves. We divide this "realistic" range of elasticities into two regions.

When the percentage change in quantity demanded is less than the percentage change in price (elasticity less than 1), there is said to be **inelastic demand**. When the percentage change in quantity is greater than the percentage change in price (elasticity greater than 1), there is said to be **elastic demand**. The dividing line between these two cases occurs when the percentage change in quantity demanded is exactly equal to the percentage change in price, and so elasticity is equal to 1. Here we say that demand is *unit elastic*. This important terminology is summarized in part A of *Extensions in Theory 4-2*, which is found on page 96.

inelastic demand Following a given percentage change in price, there is a smaller percentage change in quantity demanded; elasticity less than 1.

elastic demand Following a given percentage change in price, there is a greater percentage change in quantity demanded; elasticity greater than 1.

FIGURE 4-2 Elasticity Along a Linear Demand Curve

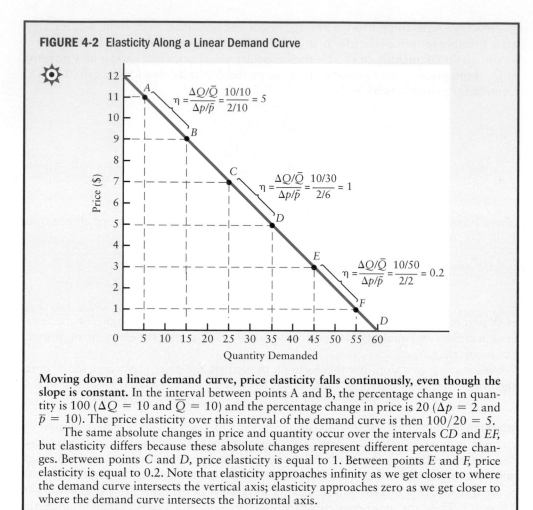

Moving down a linear demand curve, price elasticity falls continuously, even though the slope is constant. In the interval between points A and B, the percentage change in quantity is 100 ($\Delta Q = 10$ and $\overline{Q} = 10$) and the percentage change in price is 20 ($\Delta p = 2$ and $\overline{p} = 10$). The price elasticity over this interval of the demand curve is then $100/20 = 5$.

The same absolute changes in price and quantity occur over the intervals *CD* and *EF*, but elasticity differs because these absolute changes represent different percentage changes. Between points *C* and *D*, price elasticity is equal to 1. Between points *E* and *F*, price elasticity is equal to 0.2. Note that elasticity approaches infinity as we get closer to where the demand curve intersects the vertical axis; elasticity approaches zero as we get closer to where the demand curve intersects the horizontal axis.

A demand curve need not, and usually does not, have the same elasticity over its whole length. Figure 4-2 shows that a negatively sloped linear demand curve does not have a constant elasticity, even though it does have a constant slope. A linear demand curve has constant elasticity only when it is vertical or horizontal. Figure 4-3 illustrates these two cases, in addition to a third case of a particular *non-linear* demand curve that also has a constant elasticity.

What Determines Elasticity of Demand?

Elasticity of demand is mostly determined by the *availability of substitutes* and the *time period* under consideration.

Availability of Substitutes Some products, such as margarine, broccoli, Dell PCs, and Toyota cars, have quite close substitutes—butter, other green vegetables, Toshiba PCs, and Mazda cars. A change in the price of these products, *with the prices of the substitutes remaining constant,* can be expected to cause much substitution. A fall in price leads consumers to buy more of the product and less of the substitutes, and a rise in price leads consumers to buy less of the product and more of the substitutes.

A related point concerns *product definition*. Products defined more broadly, such as *all* foods or *all* clothing or *all* methods of transportation, have many fewer satisfactory substitutes than do products defined much more narrowly. A rise in their prices can be expected to cause a smaller fall in quantities demanded than would be the case if close substitutes were available. For example, there are far more substitutes for Diet Pepsi than there are for the broader categories of diet colas, soft drinks, or all beverages. As a result, the demand elasticity for Diet Pepsi is significantly higher than for beverages overall.

> Products with close substitutes tend to have elastic demands; products with no close substitutes tend to have inelastic demands. Narrowly defined products have more elastic demands than do more broadly defined products.

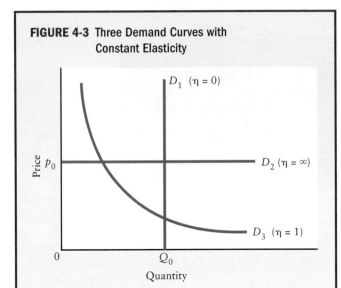

FIGURE 4-3 Three Demand Curves with Constant Elasticity

Each of these demand curves has a constant elasticity. D_1 has zero elasticity: The quantity demanded is equal to Q_0, independent of the price. D_2 has infinite elasticity at the price p_0: A small price increase from p_0 decreases quantity demanded from an indefinitely large amount to zero. D_3 has unit elasticity: A given percentage increase in price brings an equal percentage decrease in quantity demanded at all points on the curve; it is a rectangular hyperbola for which price times quantity demanded is a constant.

Short Run and Long Run Demand elasticity also depends to a great extent on the time period being considered. Because it takes time to develop satisfactory substitutes, a demand that is inelastic in the short run may prove to be elastic when enough time has passed. A dramatic example of this principle occurred in 1973 when the Organization of the Petroleum Exporting Countries (OPEC) shocked the world with its sudden and large increase in the price of oil. At that time, the short-run demand for oil proved to be highly inelastic. Large price increases were met in the short run by very small reductions in quantity demanded. In this case, the short run lasted for several years. Gradually, however, the high price of oil led to such adjustments as the development of smaller, more fuel-efficient cars, economizing on heating oil by installing more efficient insulation, and replacing fuel oil in many industrial processes with other power sources, such as coal and hydroelectricity. The long-run elasticity of demand, relating the change in price to the change in quantity demanded after all adjustments were made, turned out to have an elasticity of much more than 1, although the long-run adjustments took as much as a decade to work out.[1]

---

[1] Note that the dramatic increase in the world price of oil that occurred between 2002 and 2008, as well as the even more dramatic decline from 2008 to 2009, does not illustrate the same points about the elasticity of demand for oil as the OPEC-related events from the 1970s. In the earlier period, the dominant economic shocks were (OPEC-induced) shifts in the supply of oil which led to movement along a more-or-less stable demand curve. From 2002 to 2009, in contrast, the dominant shocks were changes in the world demand for oil and thus movements along a more-or-less stable supply curve.

Because most people cannot easily or quickly change the size of car they drive or their method of transportation, the demand for gasoline is much less elastic in the short run than in the long run.

> The response to a price change, and thus the measured price elasticity of demand, will tend to be greater the longer the time span.

For products for which substitutes only develop over time, it is helpful to identify two kinds of demand curves. A *short-run demand curve* shows the immediate response of quantity demanded to a change in price. The *long-run demand curve* shows the response of quantity demanded to a change in price after enough time has passed to develop or switch to substitute products.

Figure 4-4 shows the short-run and long-run effects of an increase in supply. In the short run, the supply increase leads to a movement down the relatively inelastic short-run demand curve; it thus causes a large fall in price but only a small increase in quantity. In the long run, demand is more elastic; thus long-run equilibrium has price and quantity above those that prevailed in short-run equilibrium.

FIGURE 4-4 Short-Run and Long-Run Equilibrium Following an Increase in Supply

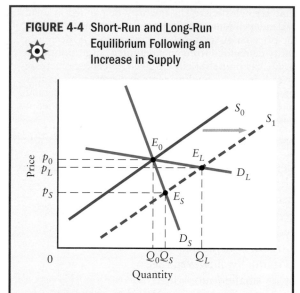

The magnitude of the changes in the equilibrium price and quantity following a shift in supply depends on the time allowed for demand to adjust. The initial equilibrium is at E_0, with price p_0 and quantity Q_0. Supply then increases and the supply curve shifts from S_0 to S_1.

Immediately following the increase in supply, the relevant demand curve is the short-run curve D_S, and the new equilibrium immediately following the supply shock is E_S. Price falls sharply to p_S, and quantity rises only to Q_S. In the long run, the demand curve is the more elastic one given by D_L, and equilibrium is at E_L. The long-run equilibrium price is p_L (greater than p_S), and quantity is Q_L (greater than Q_S).

Elasticity and Total Expenditure

We know that quantity demanded increases as price falls, but what happens to the total expenditure on that product? It turns out that the response of total expenditure depends on the price elasticity of demand.

To see the relationship between the elasticity of demand and total expenditure, we begin by noting that total expenditure at any point on the demand curve is equal to price times quantity:

$$\text{Total expenditure} = \text{Price} \times \text{Quantity}$$

Because price and quantity move in opposite directions along a demand curve, the change in total expenditure is ambiguous if all we know about the demand curve is that it has a negative slope. The change in total expenditure depends on the *relative* changes in the price and quantity. As an example, consider a price decline of 10 percent. If quantity demanded rises by more than 10 percent (elastic demand), then the quantity change will dominate and total expenditure will rise. In contrast, if quantity demanded increases by less than 10 percent (inelastic demand), then the price change will dominate and total expenditure will fall. If quantity demanded increases by exactly 10 percent (unit elastic demand), then the two percentage changes exactly offset each other and total expenditure will remain unchanged.

Figure 4-5 illustrates the relationship between elasticity and total expenditure; it is based on the linear demand curve in Figure 4-2. Total expenditure at each of a number

FIGURE 4-5 Total Expenditure and Quantity Demanded

Price ($)	Quantity Demanded	Expenditure ($)
12	0	0
10	10	100
8	20	160
6	30	180
4	40	160
2	50	100
0	60	0

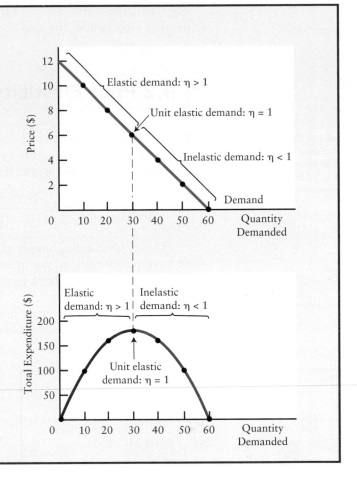

The change in total expenditure on a product in response to a change in price depends on the elasticity of demand. The table and graph are based on the demand curve shown in Figure 4-2. For quantities demanded that are less than 30, elasticity of demand is greater than 1, and hence any increase in quantity demanded will be proportionately larger than the fall in price that caused it. In that range, total expenditure increases as price falls. For quantities greater than 30, elasticity of demand is less than 1, and hence any increase in quantity demanded will be proportionately smaller than the fall in price that caused it. In that range, total expenditure decreases as price falls. The maximum of total expenditure occurs where the elasticity of demand equals 1.

of points on the demand curve is calculated in the table, and the general relationship between total expenditure and quantity demanded is shown by the plotted curve. In the figure we see that expenditure reaches its maximum when elasticity is equal to 1. [8]

Our earlier example of the 1973 OPEC-induced increase in the world price of oil can be used to illustrate this relationship between elasticity, price, and total expenditure. As the OPEC countries acted together to restrict supply and push up the world price of oil, quantity demanded fell, but only by a small percentage—much smaller than the percentage increase in price. World demand for oil (at least in the short run) was very inelastic, and the result was that total expenditure on oil *increased* dramatically. The OPEC oil producers, therefore, experienced an enormous increase in income.

The world wheat market provides another example. This market is strongly influenced by weather conditions in the major wheat-producing countries. If one major wheat-producing country, like Russia, suffers a significant failure in its wheat crop, the world supply curve for wheat shifts to the left and the equilibrium world price rises. Because the world demand for wheat is inelastic, the world's total expenditure on wheat will rise. In this case, even though many individual Russian wheat producers will be worse off because their crop failed, the total income of the *world's* wheat producers will increase. One other observation is relevant: Wheat producers in other countries, like Canada, benefit by selling their (unchanged) crop at a higher world price. And the

For information on OPEC and its activities, see www.opec.org.

less elastic the world demand for wheat, the more the price will rise as a result of the Russian crop failure, and thus the *more* Canadian wheat farmers will benefit.

4.2 Price Elasticity of Supply

price elasticity of supply (η_S)
A measure of the responsiveness of quantity supplied to a change in the product's own price.

The concept of elasticity can be applied to supply as well as to demand. **Price elasticity of supply** measures the responsiveness of the quantity supplied to a change in the product's price. It is denoted η_S and defined as follows:

$$\eta_S = \frac{\text{Percentage change in quantity supplied}}{\text{Percentage change in price}}$$

This is often called *supply elasticity.* The supply curves considered in this chapter all have positive slopes: An increase in price causes an increase in quantity supplied. Such supply curves all have positive elasticities because price and quantity change in the same direction.

Figure 4-6 shows a simple linear supply curve to illustrate the measurement of supply elasticity. Between points *A* and *B,* the change in price is $1.50 and the average price is $4.25. Between the same two points, the change in quantity supplied is 20 units and the average quantity is 40 units. The value of supply elasticity between points *A* and *B* is therefore

$$\eta_S = \frac{\Delta Q / \overline{Q}}{\Delta p / \overline{p}} = \frac{20/40}{1.50/4.25} = \frac{0.5}{0.353} = 1.42$$

As was the case with demand, care must be taken when computing supply elasticity. Keep in mind that even though the supply curve may have a constant slope, the measure of supply elasticity may be different at different places on the curve. When $\eta_S > 1$, supply is said to be elastic; when $\eta_S < 1$, supply is said to be inelastic.

Some important special cases need to be noted. If the supply curve is vertical—the quantity supplied does not change as price changes—then elasticity of supply is zero. A horizontal supply curve has an infinite elasticity of supply: There is one critical price at which output is supplied but where a small drop in price will reduce the quantity that producers are willing to supply from an indefinitely large amount to zero. Between these two extremes, elasticity of supply varies with the shape of the supply curve.[2]

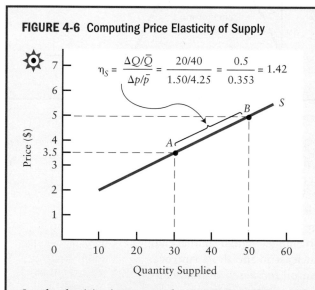

FIGURE 4-6 Computing Price Elasticity of Supply

$$\eta_S = \frac{\Delta Q / \overline{Q}}{\Delta p / \overline{p}} = \frac{20/40}{1.50/4.25} = \frac{0.5}{0.353} = 1.42$$

Price ($) / Quantity Supplied

Supply elasticity is computed using average price and average quantity supplied. Between points *A* and *B,* the elasticity of supply is 1.42. The same approach shown here can be used to compute elasticity between any two points on the supply curve.

---

[2] Here is another special case that is often puzzling at first glance. Consider a linear supply curve that begins at the origin. It is easy to show that the elasticity of supply along such a curve is always 1—no matter how steep the supply curve is! See Study Exercise #10 on page 101 to explore this further.

Determinants of Supply Elasticity

Because much of the treatment of demand elasticity carries over to supply elasticity, we can cover the main points quickly.

Substitution and Production Costs The ease of substitution can vary in production as well as in consumption. If the price of a product rises, how much more can be produced profitably? This depends in part on how easy it is for producers to shift from the production of other products to the one whose price has risen. If agricultural land and labour can be readily shifted from wheat to canola, for example, the supply of each crop will be more elastic than if they cannot. Or if a factory that produces snowmobiles can easily be refitted to produce Jet Skis, then the supply of each product will be more elastic than if the factory and equipment could not be easily modified.

Supply elasticity also depends on how costs behave as output is varied. If the costs of producing a unit of output rise rapidly as output rises, then the stimulus to expand production in response to a rise in price will quickly be choked off by increases in costs. In this case, supply will tend to be rather inelastic. If, however, the costs of producing a unit of output rise only slowly as production increases, a rise in price that raises profits will elicit a large increase in quantity supplied before the rise in costs puts a halt to the expansion in output. In this case, supply will tend to be rather elastic.

Short Run and Long Run As with demand, length of time for response is important. It may be difficult to change quantity supplied in response to a price increase in a matter of weeks or months but easy to do so over years. An obvious example relates to oil production. New oil fields can be discovered, wells drilled, and pipelines built over years but not in a few months. Thus, the elasticity of oil supply is much greater over five years than over one year.

As with demand, it is useful to make the distinction between the short-run and the long-run supply curves. The *short-run supply curve* shows the immediate response of quantity supplied to a change in price given producers' current capacity to produce the good. The *long-run supply curve* shows the response of quantity supplied to a change in price after enough time has passed to allow producers to adjust their productive capacity.

> The long-run supply for a product is more elastic than the short-run supply.

Figure 4-7 illustrates the short-run and long-run effects of an increase in demand. The immediate effect of the shift in demand is a sharp increase in price (p_0 to p_S) and only a modest increase in quantity (Q_0 to Q_S). The inability of firms to change their productive capacity in the short run in response to the increase in demand means that the market-clearing response is

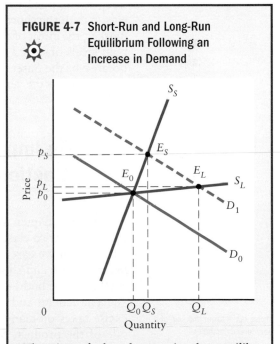

FIGURE 4-7 Short-Run and Long-Run Equilibrium Following an Increase in Demand

The size of the changes in the equilibrium price and quantity following a shift in demand depends on the time frame of the analysis. The initial equilibrium is at E_0, with price p_0 and quantity Q_0. Demand then increases such that the demand curve shifts from D_0 to D_1.

Immediately following the demand shift, the relevant supply curve is the short-run curve S_S, so that the new equilibrium immediately following the demand shock is at E_S. Price rises sharply to p_S, and quantity rises only to Q_S. In the long run, the supply curve is the more elastic one given by S_L. The long-run equilibrium is at E_L; price is p_L (less than p_S) and quantity is Q_L (greater than Q_S).

mostly an increase in price. Over time, however, as firms are more able to increase their capacity, the consequences of the demand shift fall more on quantity and less on price.

A recent example of this price and quantity behaviour is found in the world oil market in the years between 1998 and 2008. Because of relatively rapid rates of economic growth in many countries, and especially in the large emerging markets of China and India, the world demand for oil was growing significantly. During this period, however, most oil producers were at or close to their production limits: The number of oil-producing wells could increase only with costly new exploration and drilling, and each active well delivered a daily flow of oil that was difficult to increase. Producers' inability to easily expand oil production in the short term means that the short-run supply of oil is quite inelastic. As a result, the increase in demand led to sharp price increases—from about U.S.$15 per barrel in 1998 to just under U.S.$150 per barrel in mid-2008.

Over time, however, to the extent that oil producers are able to increase their exploration and drilling activities, the high price should induce a larger increase in quantity supplied. In other words, the long-run supply of oil can be expected to be more elastic than the short-run supply. If no other significant changes occur in the world oil market, the effect of this new oil production should be to reduce oil prices from the very high levels observed in 2008. (As it turned out, the price dropped sharply in late 2008 because of the onset of a major world recession, but since then prices have risen again, though not to the very high levels observed in 2008.)

4.3 An Important Example Where Elasticity Matters

So far, this chapter may have seemed fairly tough going. We have spent much time examining price elasticity (of both demand and supply) and how to measure it. But why should we care about this? In this section, we explore the important concept of *tax incidence* and show that elasticity is crucial to determining whether consumers or producers (or both) end up bearing the burden of excise taxes.

excise tax A tax on the sale of a particular commodity.

The federal and provincial governments in Canada levy special sales taxes called **excise taxes** on many goods, such as cigarettes, alcohol, and gasoline. At the point of sale of the product, the sellers collect the tax on behalf of the government and then remit the tax collections. When the sellers write their cheques to the government, these firms feel that they are the ones paying the whole tax. Consumers, however, argue that *they* are the ones who are shouldering the burden of the tax because the tax causes the price of the product to rise. Who actually bears the burden of the tax?

tax incidence The location of the burden of a tax—that is, the identity of the ultimate bearer of the tax.

The question of who *bears the burden* of a tax is called the question of **tax incidence**. A straightforward application of demand-and-supply analysis will show that tax incidence has nothing to do with whether the government collects the tax directly from consumers or from firms.

> The burden of an excise tax is distributed between consumers and sellers in a manner that depends on the relative elasticities of supply and demand.

Let's consider a case where the government imposes an excise tax on cigarettes. The analysis begins in Figure 4-8. To simplify the problem, we analyze the case where there is initially no tax. The equilibrium without taxes is illustrated by the solid supply and demand curves. What happens when a tax of *t* dollars per pack of cigarettes is introduced? With an excise tax, the price paid by the consumer, called the *consumer price,* and the price ultimately received by the seller, called the *seller price*, must differ by the amount of the tax, *t*.

In terms of the figure, we can analyze the effect of the tax by considering a new supply curve S' that is above the original supply curve S by the amount of the tax, *t*. This reduction in supply, caused by the imposition of the excise tax, will cause a movement *along* the demand curve, reducing the equilibrium quantity. At this new equilibrium, E_1, the consumer price rises to p_c (greater than p_0), the seller price falls to p_s (less than p_0), and the equilibrium quantity falls to Q_1. Notice that the difference between the consumer price and the seller price is exactly the amount of the excise tax, *t*.

Note also that the quantity demanded *at the consumer price* is equal to the quantity supplied *at the seller price,* a condition that is required for equilibrium. As shown in the figure, compared with the original equilibrium, the consumer price is higher and the seller price is lower, although in each case the change in price is less than the full extent of the excise tax. The difference between p_0 and p_c is the amount of the tax that the consumer ends up paying; the difference between p_0 and p_s is the amount of the tax the seller ends up paying. The burden of the excise tax is shared between consumers and sellers in proportion to the rise in price to consumers relative to the fall in price received by sellers.

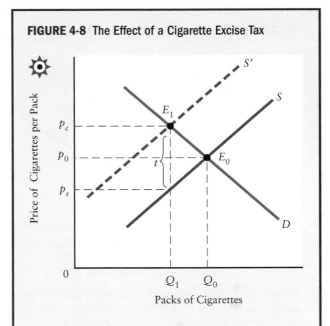

FIGURE 4-8 The Effect of a Cigarette Excise Tax

The burden of an excise tax is shared by consumers and producers. The original supply and demand curves for cigarettes are given by the solid lines S and D; equilibrium is at E_0 with price p_0 and quantity Q_0. When an excise tax of *t* per pack is imposed, the supply curve shifts up to the dashed line S', which lies above the original supply curve by the amount of the tax, *t*. The new equilibrium is at E_1. The tax increases the consumer price but by less than the full amount of the tax, and reduces the seller price, also by less than the full amount of the tax. The tax also reduces the equilibrium quantity exchanged.

After the imposition of an excise tax, the difference between the consumer and seller prices is equal to the tax. In the new equilibrium, the quantity exchanged is less than that exchanged before the imposition of the tax.

The role of the relative elasticities of supply and demand in determining the incidence of the excise tax is illustrated in Figure 4-9. In part (i), demand is inelastic relative to supply; as a result, the fall in quantity is quite small, whereas the price paid by consumers rises by almost the full extent of the tax. Because neither the price received by sellers nor the quantity sold changes very much, sellers bear little of the burden of the tax. In part (ii), supply is inelastic relative to demand; in this case, consumers can more easily substitute away from cigarettes. There is little change in the price, and hence they bear little of the burden of the tax, which falls mostly on suppliers. Notice in Figure 4-9 that the size of the upward shift in supply is the same in the two cases, indicating the same tax in both cases.

When demand is inelastic relative to supply, consumers bear most of the burden of excise taxes. When supply is inelastic relative to demand, producers bear most of the burden.

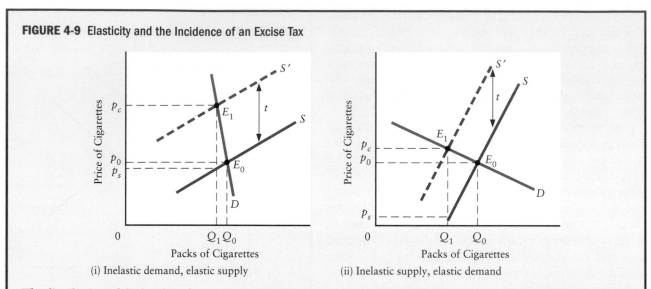

FIGURE 4-9 Elasticity and the Incidence of an Excise Tax

(i) Inelastic demand, elastic supply

(ii) Inelastic supply, elastic demand

The distribution of the burden of an excise tax between consumers and producers depends on the relative elasticities of supply and demand. In both parts of the figure, the initial supply and demand curves are given by S and D; the initial equilibrium is at E_0 with equilibrium price p_0 and quantity Q_0. A tax of t per pack of cigarettes is imposed, causing the supply curve to shift up by the amount of the tax to S'. The new equilibrium is at E_1. The consumer price rises to p_c, the seller price falls to p_s, and the quantity falls to Q_1. Sellers bear little of the burden of the tax in the first case (and consumers bear a lot), whereas consumers bear little of the burden in the second case (and sellers bear a lot).

EXTENSIONS IN THEORY 4-1

The Algebra of Tax Incidence

It is straightforward to show precisely the burden of an excise tax by using algebra to solve for the equilibrium price and quantity. Suppose the demand-and-supply model of the market is given by the following two linear equations.

(1) $Q^D = a - bp_c$ Demand curve
(2) $Q^S = c + dp_s$ Supply curve

Where Q^D is quantity demanded at the consumer price, p_c, and Q^S is quantity supplied at the seller price, p_s. The presence of an excise tax of t dollars per unit implies that the price received by the seller, p_s, must be t dollars less than the price paid by the consumer, p_c:

(3) $P_s = p_c - t$

We can substitute equation (3) into (2) to express the supply curve in terms of the consumer price:

(4) $Q^S = c + d(p_c - t)$

or

(5) $Q^S = c - dt + dp_c$

When the market is in equilibrium, $Q^D = Q^S$, and so we can equate Q^D from equation (1) with Q^S from equation (5). This gives us

$$a - bp_c = c - dt + dp_c$$

This equation allows us to solve for the equilibrium consumer price, p_c^*.

$$p_c^* = \frac{a - c}{b + d} + \frac{d}{b + d}t$$

This solution for p_c^* can now be substituted back into the demand curve, equation (1), to solve for the equilibrium quantity, Q^*.

$$Q^* = a - bp_c^* = a - \frac{b(a - c + dt)}{b + d}$$

$$= \frac{ad + bc}{b + d} - \frac{bd}{b + d}t$$

Now we can examine who really pays for cigarette tax increases (or tax increases on gasoline and alcohol). The demand for cigarettes is inelastic both overall and relative to supply, suggesting that the burden of a cigarette tax is borne more by consumers than by producers. The demand for gasoline is also inelastic, but much more so in the short run than in the long run. (In the long run, drivers can change their driving habits and improve the efficiency of their vehicles, but in the short run such changes are very costly.) The supply of gasoline, given world trade in petroleum and petroleum products, is elastic relative to demand. The relatively inelastic demand and elastic supply imply that the burden of gasoline taxes falls mostly on consumers.

Extensions in Theory 4-1 shows how to work through the algebra of demand and supply in the presence of an excise tax.

4.4 Other Demand Elasticities

The price of the product is not the only important variable determining the quantity demanded for that product. Changes in income and changes in the prices of other products also lead to changes in quantity demanded, and elasticity is a useful concept in measuring their effects.

Now compare these solutions for p_c^* and Q^* to the case where there is no tax, $t = 0$. This exercise reveals what we already know from Figures 4-8 and 4-9—that the excise tax increases the equilibrium consumer price and reduces the equilibrium quantity from the levels that we would observe in the absence of the excise tax.

Who bears the burden of the excise tax? To answer this question, we must examine both the equilibrium consumer and seller prices, p_c^* and p_s^*. We just saw that

$$(6) \quad p_c^* = \frac{a - c}{b + d} + \frac{d}{b + d}t$$

and we also know that $p_c^* - t = p_s^*$. It follows that

$$(7) \quad p_s^* = \frac{a - c}{b + d} + \frac{d}{b + d}t - t$$

$$= \frac{a - c}{b + d} - \frac{b}{b + d}t$$

Note that when $t = 0$, the equilibrium price in this model, for both consumers and sellers, is

$$p^* = \frac{a - c}{b + d}$$

We can therefore express the equilibrium consumer and seller prices in the presence of an excise tax in terms of p^*:

$$(8) \quad p_c^* = p^* + \frac{d}{b + d}t$$

$$(9) \quad p_s^* = p^* - \frac{b}{b + d}t$$

These solutions for p_c^* and p_s^* show precisely how the burden of the excise tax depends on the slopes of the demand and supply curves. For example, consider a small value of d, which reflects a relatively steep supply curve. The small value of d means that p_c^* is only a little above p^*, whereas p_s^* is considerably below p^*; thus, when the supply curve is relatively steep, sellers bear more of the burden of the tax. In contrast, consider a small value of b, which reflects a relatively steep demand curve. The small value of b means that p_s^* is only a little below p^*; but p_c^* is considerably above p^*; thus, consumers bear more of the burden of the tax when the demand curve is relatively steep.

Income Elasticity of Demand

income elasticity of demand
(η_Y) A measure of the
responsiveness of quantity
demanded to a change in
income.

An important determinant of demand is the income of the customers. The responsiveness of demand to changes in income is termed the **income elasticity of demand** and is symbolized η_Y.

$$\eta_Y = \frac{\text{Percentage change in quantity demanded}}{\text{Percentage change in income}}$$

normal good A good for which
quantity demanded rises
as income rises—its income
elasticity is positive.

inferior good A good for which
quantity demanded falls as
income rises—its income
elasticity is negative.

For most goods, increases in income lead to increases in demand—their income elasticity is positive. These are called **normal goods**. Goods for which demand decreases in response to a rise in income have negative income elasticities and are called **inferior goods**.

The income elasticity of normal goods can be greater than 1 (elastic) or less than 1 (inelastic), depending on whether the percentage change in quantity demanded is greater or less than the percentage change in income that brought it about. It is also common to use the terms *income-elastic* and *income-inelastic* to refer to income elasticities of greater or less than 1. (See *Extensions in Theory 4-2* for a summary of the different elasticity concepts.)

EXTENSIONS IN THEORY 4-2

The Terminology of Elasticity

Term	Numerical Measure of Elasticity	Verbal Description
A. Price elasticity of demand (supply)		
Perfectly or completely inelastic	0	Quantity demanded (supplied) does not change as price changes.
Inelastic	Between 0 and 1	Quantity demanded (supplied) changes by a smaller percentage than does price.
Unit elastic	1	Quantity demanded (supplied) changes by exactly the same percentage as does price.
Elastic	Greater than 1 but less than infinity	Quantity demanded (supplied) changes by a larger percentage than does price.
Perfectly, completely, or infinitely elastic	Infinity	Purchasers (sellers) are prepared to buy (sell) all they can at some price and none at all at a higher (lower) price.
B. Income elasticity of demand		
Inferior good	Negative	Quantity demanded decreases as income increases.
Normal good	Positive	Quantity demanded increases as income increases:
Income-inelastic	Less than 1	Less than in proportion to income increase
Income-elastic	Greater than 1	More than in proportion to income increase
C. Cross elasticity of demand		
Substitute	Positive	Price increase of a substitute leads to an increase in quantity demanded of this good.
Complement	Negative	Price increase of a complement leads to a decrease in quantity demanded of this good.

How the demand for goods and services reacts to changes in income has important economic effects. In most Western countries during the twentieth century, economic growth caused the level of income to double every 20 to 30 years. This rise in income was shared to some extent by almost all citizens. As they found their incomes increasing, they increased their demands for most products. In the first part of that century, however, the demands for some products (such as food and basic clothing) were income-inelastic, whereas the demands for durable goods (such as cars and TVs) were income-elastic. As a result, the demand for food and clothing grew less rapidly than did the demand for cars and TVs. Later in the century, as incomes rose still further, the income elasticity of demand for manufactured durables fell while that for services (such as restaurant meals and entertainment) increased. During this period the ongoing income growth led the demand for services to grow more rapidly than the demand for durable goods.

In some developing countries, where per capita incomes today are close to those of the Western nations at the beginning of the twentieth century, it is the demands for durable manufactured goods that are increasing most rapidly as income rises. In future years (assuming that the current growth of income continues), these same countries will likely experience the same shift in demand toward services that was experienced by the Western countries in the last part of the twentieth century.

The uneven impact of the growth of income on the demands for different products has important effects on the pattern of employment. For example, in Western countries, employment in agriculture fell during the first part of the twentieth century, while employment in manufacturing rose. In the last half of the century, employment in manufacturing fell gradually whereas employment in services increased rapidly (and employment in agriculture continued its gradual decline). We will see many other consequences of these demand shifts later in this book.

Luxuries Versus Necessities Different products typically have different income elasticities of demand. For example, empirical studies find that basic food items—such as vegetables, bread, and cereals—usually have positive income elasticities less than 1 (so an increase in income of 10 percent leads to an increase in quantity demanded of less than 10 percent). Such goods are often called **necessities**. In contrast, more expensive foods—such as prime cuts of meat, prepared meals, and wine—usually have positive income elasticities greater than 1 (so an increase in income of 10 percent leads to an increase in quantity demanded of more than 10 percent). These products are often called **luxuries**.

necessities Products for which the income elasticity of demand is positive but less than 1.

luxuries Products for which the income elasticity of demand is positive and greater than 1.

> The more necessary an item is in the consumption pattern of consumers, the lower is its income elasticity.

Income elasticities for any one product also vary with the level of a consumer's income. When incomes are low, consumers may eat almost no green vegetables and consume lots of starchy foods, such as bread and pasta; when incomes are higher, they may eat cheap cuts of meat and more green vegetables along with their bread and pasta; when incomes are higher still, they are likely to eat higher-quality and prepared foods of a wide variety.

The distinction between luxuries and necessities helps to explain differences in income elasticities. The case of restaurant meals is one example. Such meals are almost always more expensive, calorie for calorie, than meals prepared at home. It would

Substitute products have a positive cross elasticity; an increase in the price of one leads to an increase in demand for the other.

thus be expected that at lower incomes, restaurant meals would be regarded as an expensive luxury but that the demand for them would expand substantially as consumers became richer. This is actually what happens.

Notice that both necessities and luxuries have positive income elasticities and thus are *normal* goods. In contrast, *inferior* goods have a negative income elasticity because an increase in income actually leads to a *reduction* in quantity demanded. An example of an inferior good for some consumers might be ground beef or packages of instant noodles; as consumers' incomes rise, they reduce their demand for these products and consume more of higher-quality items.

Cross Elasticity of Demand

cross elasticity of demand
(η_{XY}) A measure of the responsiveness of the quantity of one commodity demanded to changes in the price of another commodity.

The responsiveness of quantity demanded to changes in the price of *another* product is called the **cross elasticity of demand**. It is denoted η_{XY} and defined as follows:

$$\eta_{XY} = \frac{\text{Percentage change in quantity demanded of good } X}{\text{Percentage change in price of good } Y}$$

The change in the price of good Y causes the *demand curve* for good X to shift. If X and Y are substitutes, an increase in the price of Y leads to an increase in the demand for X. If X and Y are complements, an increase in the price of Y leads to a reduction in demand for X. In either case, we are holding the price of X constant. We therefore measure the change in the quantity demanded of X (at its unchanged price) by measuring the shift of the demand curve for X.

Cross elasticity can vary from minus infinity to plus infinity. Complementary products, such as cars and gasoline, have negative cross elasticities. A rise in the price of gasoline will lead to a decline in the demand for cars, as some people decide to do without a car and others decide not to buy an additional car. Substitute products, such as cars and public transport, have positive cross elasticities. A rise in the price of cars (relative to public transport) will lead to a rise in the demand for public transport as some people shift from cars to public transport.

> The positive or negative signs of cross elasticities tell us whether goods are substitutes or complements.

Measures of cross elasticity sometimes prove helpful in defining whether producers of similar products are in competition with each other. For example, glass bottles and aluminum cans have a high cross elasticity of demand. The producer of bottles is thus in competition with the producer of cans. If the bottle company raises its price, it will lose substantial sales to the can producer. In contrast, men's shoes and women's shoes have a low cross elasticity, and thus a producer of men's shoes is not in close competition with a producer of women's shoes. If the former raises its price, it will not lose many sales to the latter. Knowledge of cross elasticity can be important in matters of *competition policy*, in which the issue is whether a firm in one industry is or is not competing with firms in another industry. We discuss competition policy in more detail in Chapter 12.

SUMMARY

4.1 Price Elasticity of Demand
LO 1, 2

- Price elasticity of demand is a measure of the extent to which the quantity demanded of a product responds to a change in its price. Represented by the symbol η, it is defined as

$$\eta = \frac{\text{Percentage change in quantity demanded}}{\text{Percentage change in price}}$$

- The percentage changes are usually calculated as the change divided by the average value. Elasticity is defined to be a positive number, and it can vary from zero to infinity.
- When elasticity is less than 1, demand is inelastic—the percentage change in quantity demanded is less than the percentage change in price. When elasticity exceeds 1,

demand is elastic—the percentage change in quantity demanded is greater than the percentage change in price.
- The main determinant of demand elasticity is the availability of substitutes for the product. Any one of a group of close substitutes will have a more elastic demand than will the group as a whole.
- Items that have few substitutes in the short run tend to develop many substitutes when consumers and producers have time to adapt. Therefore, demand is more elastic in the long run than in the short run.
- Elasticity and total expenditure are related. If elasticity is less than 1, total expenditure is positively related with price. If elasticity is greater than 1, total expenditure is negatively related with price. If elasticity is 1, total expenditure does not change as price changes.

4.2 Price Elasticity of Supply
LO 3

- Elasticity of supply measures the extent to which the quantity supplied of some product changes when the price of that product changes. Represented by the symbol η_s, it is defined as

$$\eta_S = \frac{\text{Percentage change in quantity supplied}}{\text{Percentage change in price}}$$

- Supply tends to be more elastic in the long run than in the short run because it usually takes time for producers to alter their output in response to price changes.

4.3 An Important Example Where Elasticity Matters
LO 4

- The distribution of the burden of an excise tax between consumers and producers depends on the relative elasticities of supply and demand for the product.
- The less elastic demand is relative to supply, the more of the burden of an excise tax falls on the consumers. The

more elastic demand is relative to supply, the more of the burden of an excise tax falls on producers.

4.4 Other Demand Elasticities
LO 5, 6

- Income elasticity of demand is a measure of the extent to which the quantity demanded of some product changes as income changes. Represented by the symbol η_Y, it is defined as

$$\eta_Y = \frac{\text{Percentage change in quantity demanded}}{\text{Percentage change in income}}$$

- The income elasticity of demand for a product will usually change as income varies. A product that has a high income elasticity at a low income may have a low or negative income elasticity at higher incomes.

- Cross elasticity of demand is a measure of the extent to which the quantity demanded of one product changes when the price of a different product changes. Represented by the symbol η_{XY}, it is defined as

$$\eta_{XY} = \frac{\text{Percentage change in quantity demanded of good } X}{\text{Percentage change in price of good } Y}$$

- It is used to define products that are substitutes for one another (positive cross elasticity) and products that are complements for one another (negative cross elasticity).

KEY CONCEPTS

Price elasticity of demand
Inelastic and perfectly inelastic
  demand
Elastic and infinitely elastic demand
Relationship between demand elasti-
  city and total expenditure

Elasticity of supply
Short-run and long-run responses to
  shifts in demand and supply
The burden of an excise tax
Consumer price and seller price
Income elasticity of demand

Normal goods and inferior goods
Luxuries and necessities
Cross elasticity of demand
Substitutes and complements

STUDY EXERCISES

MyEconLab **Make the grade with MyEconLab: Study Exercises marked in red can be found on MyEconLab. You can practise them as often as you want, and most feature step-by-step guided instructions to help you find the right answer.**

1. Fill in the blanks to make the following statements correct.

   a. When a 10 percent change in the price of a good brings about a 20 percent change in its quantity demanded, the price elasticity of demand is _____. We can say that demand for this good is _____.

   b. When a 10 percent change in the price of a good brings about a 4 percent change in its quantity demanded, the price elasticity of demand is _____. We can say that demand for this good is _____.

   c. When a 10 percent change in the price of a good brings about a 10 percent change in its quantity demanded, the price elasticity of demand is _____. We can say that demand for this good is _____.

2. A hypothetical demand schedule for comic books in a small town is provided below.

Price	Quantity Demanded	Total Expen- diture	Percent Change in Price	Percent Change in Quantity Demanded	Elasticity of Demand
$11	1	_____			
9	3	_____	_____	_____	_____
7	5	_____	_____	_____	_____
5	7	_____	_____	_____	_____
3	9	_____	_____	_____	_____
1	11	_____	_____	_____	_____

   a. Fill in the table and calculate the price elasticity of demand over each price range. Be sure to use average prices and quantities when computing the percentage changes.

   b. Plot the demand curve and show the elasticities over the different ranges of the curve.

   c. Explain why demand is more elastic at the higher prices.

3. Suppose the market for frozen orange juice is in equilibrium at a price of $2.00 per can and a quantity of 4200 cans per month. Now suppose that at a price of $3.00 per can, quantity demanded falls to 3000 cans per month and quantity supplied increases to 4500 cans per month.

   a. Draw the appropriate diagram for this market.

   b. Calculate the price elasticity of demand for frozen orange juice between the prices of $2.00 and $3.00. Is the demand elastic or inelastic?

   c. Calculate the elasticity of supply for frozen orange juice between the prices of $2.00 and $3.00. Is the supply elastic or inelastic?

   d. Explain in general what factors would affect the elasticity of demand for frozen orange juice.

   e. Explain in general what factors would affect the elasticity of supply of frozen orange juice.

4. From the following quotations, what, if anything, can you conclude about elasticity of demand?

   a. "Good weather resulted in record wheat harvests and sent wheat prices tumbling. The result has been disastrous for many wheat farmers."

b. "Ridership always went up when bus fares came down, but the increased patronage never was enough to prevent a decrease in overall revenue."

c. "As the price of cell phones fell, producers found their revenues soaring."

d. "Coffee to me is an essential good—I've just gotta have it no matter what the price."

e. "The soaring price of condominiums does little to curb the strong demand in Vancouver."

5. Interpret the following statements in terms of the relevant elasticity concept.

a. "As fuel for tractors has become more expensive, many farmers have shifted from plowing their fields to no-till farming. No-till acreage increased dramatically in the past 20 years."

b. "Fertilizer makers brace for a dismal year as fertilizer prices soar."

c. "When farmers are hurting, small towns feel the pain."

d. "The development of the Alberta oil sands may bring prosperity to many northern Alberta merchants."

6. What would you predict about the relative price elasticity of demand for each of the following items? Explain your reasoning.

a. food
b. vegetables
c. leafy vegetables
d. leafy vegetables sold at your local supermarket
e. leafy vegetables sold at your local supermarket on Wednesdays

7. Suppose a stamp dealer buys the only two existing copies of a stamp at an auction. After the purchase, the dealer goes to the front of the room and burns one of the stamps in front of the shocked audience. What must the dealer believe in order for this to be a wealth-maximizing action? Explain with a demand-and-supply diagram.

8. For each of the following events, state the relevant elasticity concept. Then compute the measure of elasticity, using average prices and quantities in your calculations. In all cases, assume that these are *ceteris paribus* changes.

a. When the price of movie tickets is reduced from $14.00 to $11.00, ticket sales increase from 1200 to 1350.

b. As average household income in Canada increases by 10 percent, annual sales of BMWs increase from 56 000 to 67 000.

c. After a major failure of Brazil's coffee crop sent coffee prices up from $3.00 per kilogram to $4.80

per kilogram, sales of tea in Canada increased from 7500 kg per month to 8000 kg per month.

d. An increase in the world demand for pulp (used in producing newsprint) increases the price by 14 percent. Annual Canadian production increases from 8 million tonnes to 11 million tonnes.

9. The following table shows the demand schedule for PlayStation video games.

	Price (per unit)	Quantity Demanded (per year)	Total Expenditure
A	$30	400 000	_____
B	35	380 000	_____
C	40	350 000	_____
D	45	320 000	_____
E	50	300 000	_____
F	55	260 000	_____
G	60	230 000	_____
H	65	190 000	_____

a. Compute total expenditure for each row in the table.

b. Plot the demand curve and the total expenditure curve.

c. Compute the price elasticities of demand between points A and B, B and C, C and D, and so on.

d. Over what range of prices is the demand for video games elastic? Explain.

e. Over what range of prices is the demand for video games inelastic? Explain.

10. Consider the following straight-line supply curves. In each case, p is the price (measured in dollars per unit) and Q^S is the quantity supplied of the product (measured in thousands of units per month).

i) $p = 2Q^S$
ii) $p = 4Q^S$
iii) $p = 5Q^S$
iv) $p = 10Q^S$

a. Plot each supply curve on a scale diagram. In each case, plot point A (which corresponds to price equal to $20) and point B (which corresponds to price equal to $40).

b. For each supply curve, compute the price elasticity of supply between points A and B.

c. Explain why the slope of a supply curve is not the same as the elasticity of supply.

11. This is a challenging question intended for those students who like mathematics. It will help you work through the issue of tax incidence. (See *Extensions in Theory 4-1* on pages 94–95 if you get stuck!)

Consider the market for gasoline. Suppose the market demand and supply curves are as given below. In each case, quantity refers to millions of litres of gasoline per month; price is the price per litre (in cents).

$$\text{Demand: } p = 80 - 5Q^D$$
$$\text{Supply: } p = 24 + 2Q^S$$

a. Plot the demand and supply curves on a scale diagram.

b. Compute the equilibrium price and quantity.

c. Now suppose the government imposes a tax of 14 cents per litre. Show how this affects the market equilibrium. What is the new "consumer price" and what is the new "producer price"?

d. Compute the total revenue raised by the gasoline tax. What share of this tax revenue is "paid" by consumers, and what share is "paid" by producers? (Hint: If the consumer price were unchanged from the pre-tax equilibrium, we would say that consumers pay none of the tax.)

Markets in Action

LEARNING OBJECTIVES (LO)

After studying this chapter, you will be able to

1 explain why individual markets are not isolated from the rest of the economy and how changes in one market typically have repercussions in other markets.

2 describe how the presence of legislated price ceilings and price floors affect equilibrium price and quantity.

3 compare the short-run and long-run effects of legislated rent controls.

4 explain why government interventions that cause prices to deviate from their market-clearing levels tend to be inefficient for society as a whole.

OVER the past two chapters, we have developed the model of demand and supply that you can now use to analyze individual markets. A full understanding of the basic theory, however, comes only with practice. This chapter will provide some practice by analyzing several examples, including minimum wages, rent controls, and output quotas.

Before examining these cases, however, we begin the chapter by discussing how various markets are related to one another. In Chapters 3 and 4, we used the simple demand-and-supply model to describe a single market, ignoring what was going on in other markets. For example, when we examined the market for apples, we made no mention of the markets for milk, TVs, or labour services. In other words, we viewed the market for apples in isolation from all other markets. But this was only a simplification. In this chapter's opening section we note that the economy should not be viewed as a series of isolated markets. Rather, the economy is a complex system of inter-related markets. The implication of this complex structure is that events leading to changes in one market typically lead to changes in other markets as well.

| 5.1 The Interaction Among Markets

Suppose an advance is made that reduces the cost of extracting natural gas. This technological improvement would be represented as a rightward shift in the supply curve for natural gas. The equilibrium price of natural gas would fall and there would be an increase in the equilibrium quantity exchanged.

How would other markets be affected? As natural-gas firms expanded their production, they would increase their demand for the entire range of goods and services used for the extraction, processing, pumping, and distribution of natural gas. This increase in demand would tend to raise the prices of those items and lead the producers of those goods to devote more resources to their production. The natural-gas firms would also increase their demand for labour, since more workers would be required to drill for and extract more natural gas. The increase in demand for labour would tend to push wages up. Firms that hire similar workers in other industries would have to pay higher wages to retain their workers. As a result, profits of those firms would fall and they would employ fewer workers, thus freeing up the extra workers needed in the natural-gas industry.

There would also be a direct effect on consumers. The reduction in the equilibrium price of natural gas would generate some substitution away from other fuels, such as oil and propane, and toward the now-lower-priced natural gas. Such reductions in demand would tend to push down the price of oil and propane, and producers of those fuels would devote fewer resources to their production.

In short, a technological improvement in the natural-gas industry would have effects in many other markets. But there is nothing special about the natural-gas industry. The same would be true about a change in almost any market you can think of.

No market or industry exists in isolation from the economy's many other markets.

A change in one market will lead to changes in many other markets. The induced changes in these other markets will, in turn, lead to changes in the first market. This is what economists call *feedback*. In the example of the natural-gas industry, the reduction in the price of natural gas leads consumers to reduce their demand for oil and propane, thus driving down the prices of these other fuels. But when we draw any given demand and supply curves for natural gas, we assume that the *prices of all other goods are constant*. So, when the prices of oil and propane fall, the feedback effect on the natural-gas market is to shift the demand curve for natural gas to the left (because natural gas is a substitute for both oil and propane).

Predicting the precise size of this feedback effect is difficult, and the analysis of the natural-gas industry—or any other industry—would certainly be much easier if we could simply ignore it. But we cannot always ignore such feedback effects. Economists make a distinction between cases in which the feedback effects are small enough that they can safely be ignored, and cases in which the feedback effects are large enough that ignoring them would significantly change the analysis.

Partial-equilibrium analysis is the analysis of a single market in situations in which the feedback effects from other markets are ignored. This is the type of analysis that we have used so far in this book, and it is the most common type of analysis in microeconomics. For example, when we examined the market for cigarettes at

partial-equilibrium analysis The analysis of a single market in isolation, ignoring any feedbacks that may come from induced changes in other markets.

the end of Chapter 4, we ignored any potential feedback effects that could have come from the market for alcohol, coffee, or many other goods or services. In this case, we used partial-equilibrium analysis, focusing only on the market for cigarettes, because we assumed that the changes in the cigarette market would produce small enough changes on the other markets that the feedback effects from the other markets would, in turn, be sufficiently diffused that we could safely ignore them. This suggests a general rule telling us when partial-equilibrium analysis is a legitimate method of analysis:

> If a specific market is quite small relative to the entire economy, changes in the market will have relatively small effects on other markets. The feedback effects on the original market will, in turn, be even smaller. In such cases, partial-equilibrium analysis can successfully be used to analyze the original market.

When economists study all markets together, rather than a single market in isolation, they use what is called **general-equilibrium analysis**. This is more complicated than partial-equilibrium analysis because the economist not only must consider what is happening in each individual market but also must take into account how events in each market affect all the other markets.

general-equilibrium analysis The analysis of all the economy's markets simultaneously, recognizing the interactions among the various markets.

> General-equilibrium analysis is the study of how all markets function together, taking into account the various relationships and feedback effects among individual markets.

As you go on to learn more microeconomics in this and later chapters, you will encounter mostly partial-equilibrium analysis. The book is written this way intentionally—it is easier to learn about the basic ideas of monopoly, competition policy, labour unions, and environmental policy (as well as many other topics) by restricting our attention to single markets. But keep in mind that many other markets are "behind the scenes," linked to the individual markets we choose to study.

We now go on to examine the effects of government-controlled prices. These appear prominently in labour markets and rental housing markets.

5.2 Government-Controlled Prices

In a number of important cases, governments fix the price at which a product must be bought and sold in the domestic market. Here we examine the general consequences of such policies. Later, we look at some specific examples.

In a free market the equilibrium price equates the quantity demanded with the quantity supplied. Government *price controls* are policies that attempt to hold the price at some *disequilibrium* value. Some controls hold the market price below its equilibrium value, thus creating a shortage at the controlled price. Other controls hold price above its equilibrium value, thus creating a surplus at the controlled price.

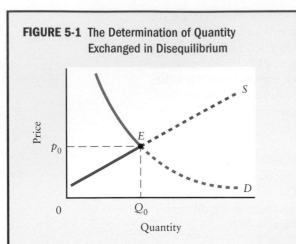

FIGURE 5-1 The Determination of Quantity Exchanged in Disequilibrium

In disequilibrium, quantity exchanged is determined by the lesser of quantity demanded and quantity supplied. At E, the market is in equilibrium, with quantity demanded equal to quantity supplied. For any price below p_0, the quantity exchanged will be determined by the supply curve. For any price above p_0, the quantity exchanged will be determined by the demand curve. Thus, the solid portions of the S and D curves show the actual quantities exchanged at different disequilibrium prices.

Disequilibrium Prices

When controls hold the price at some disequilibrium value, what determines the quantity *actually traded* on the market? This is not a question we have to ask when examining a free market because the price adjusts to equate quantity demanded with quantity supplied. But this adjustment cannot take place if the government is controlling the price. So, in this case, what determines the quantity actually exchanged?

The key to the answer is the fact that any *voluntary* market transaction requires both a willing buyer and a willing seller. So, if quantity demanded is less than quantity supplied, demand will determine the amount actually exchanged, while the rest of the quantity supplied will remain in the hands of the unsuccessful sellers. Conversely, if quantity demanded exceeds quantity supplied, supply will determine the amount actually exchanged, while the rest of the quantity demanded will represent unsatisfied demand of would-be buyers. Figure 5-1 illustrates the general conclusion:

> **At any disequilibrium price, quantity exchanged is determined by the *lesser* of quantity demanded or quantity supplied.**

Price Floors

Governments sometimes establish a *price floor,* which is the minimum permissible price that can be charged for a particular good or service. A price floor that is set at or below the equilibrium price has no effect because the free-market equilibrium remains attainable. If, however, the price floor is set above the equilibrium, it will raise the price, in which case it is said to be *binding*.

Price floors may be established by rules that make it illegal to sell the product below the prescribed price, as in the case of a legislated minimum wage. Or the government may establish a price floor by announcing that it will guarantee a certain price by buying any excess supply. Such guarantees are a feature of many agricultural support policies.

The effects of a binding price floor are illustrated in Figure 5-2, which establishes the following key result:

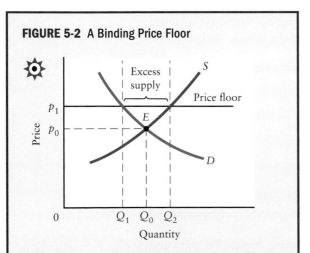

FIGURE 5-2 A Binding Price Floor

A binding price floor leads to excess supply. The free-market equilibrium is at E, with price p_0 and quantity Q_0. The government now establishes a binding price floor at p_1. The result is excess supply equal to Q_1Q_2.

> **Binding price floors lead to excess supply. Either an unsold surplus will exist, or someone (usually the government) must enter the market and buy the excess supply.**

The consequences of excess supply differ from product to product. If the product is labour, subject to a minimum wage, excess supply translates into people without jobs (unemployment). If the product is wheat, and more is produced than can be sold to consumers, the surplus wheat will accumulate in grain elevators or government warehouses. These consequences may or may not be worthwhile in terms of the other goals achieved. But worthwhile or not, these consequences are inevitable in a competitive market whenever a price floor is set above the market-clearing equilibrium price.

Why might the government want to incur these consequences? One reason is that the people who succeed in selling their products at the price floor are better off than if they had to accept the lower equilibrium price. Workers and farmers are among the politically active, organized groups who have gained much by persuading the government to establish price floors that enable them to sell their goods or services at prices above free-market levels. If the demand is inelastic, as it often is for agricultural products, producers earn more income in total (even though they sell fewer units of the product). The losses are spread across the large and diverse set of consumers, each of whom suffers only a small loss.

Applying Economic Concepts 5-1 examines the case of a legislated minimum wage in more detail, and explains the basis of the often-heard claim that minimum wages increase unemployment. We discuss the effects of minimum wages in greater detail in Chapter 14 when we examine various labour-market issues.

For information on various labour-market policies in Canada, see HRSDC's website: www.hrsdc.gc.ca. Then click on "Programs and Policies."

Price Ceilings

A *price ceiling* is the maximum price at which certain goods and services may be exchanged. Price ceilings on oil, natural gas, and rental housing have been frequently imposed by federal and provincial governments. If the price ceiling is set above the equilibrium price, it has no effect because the free-market equilibrium remains attainable. If, however, the price ceiling is set below the free-market equilibrium price, the price ceiling lowers the price and is said to be *binding*. The effects of binding price ceilings are shown in Figure 5-3, which establishes the following conclusion:

> **Binding price ceilings lead to excess demand, with the quantity exchanged being less than in the free-market equilibrium.**

Allocating a Product in Excess Demand Free markets eliminate excess demand by allowing prices to rise, thereby allocating the available supply among would-be purchasers. Because this adjustment cannot happen in the presence of a binding price ceiling, some other method of allocation must be adopted. Experience suggests what we can expect.

If stores sell their available supplies on a *first-come, first-served* basis, people will rush to stores that are said to have stocks of the product. Buyers may wait hours to get into the store, only to find that supplies are exhausted before they can be served. This is why standing in lines

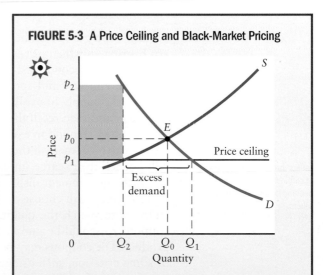

FIGURE 5-3 A Price Ceiling and Black-Market Pricing

A binding price ceiling causes excess demand and invites a black market. The equilibrium point, E, is at a price of p_0 and a quantity of Q_0. If a price ceiling is set at p_1, the quantity demanded will rise to Q_1 and the quantity supplied will fall to Q_2. Quantity actually exchanged will be Q_2. But if all the available supply of Q_2 were sold on a black market, the price to consumers would rise to p_2. Because black marketeers buy at the ceiling price of p_1 and sell at the black-market price of p_2, their profits are represented by the shaded area.

APPLYING ECONOMIC CONCEPTS 5-1

Minimum Wages and Unemployment

All Canadian governments, provincial, territorial, and federal, have legislated minimum wages. For those industries covered by provincial or territorial legislation (which includes most industries except banking, airlines, trucking, and railways), the minimum wage in 2012 ranged from a low of $9.50 per hour in Saskatchewan to a high of $11.00 per hour in Nunavut. This box examines the effects of implementing a minimum wage in a competitive labour market and provides a basis for understanding the often-heard claim that minimum wages lead to an increase in unemployment.

The accompanying figure shows the demand and supply curves for labour services in a fully competitive market with Employment on the horizontal axis and Hourly Wage Rate on the vertical axis. In the absence of any legislated minimum wage, the equilibrium in the labour market would be a wage equal to w_0 and a level of employment equal to E_0.

Now suppose the government introduces a minimum wage equal to w_{min} that is greater than w_0. The

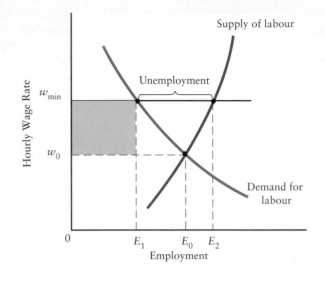

became a way of life in the centrally planned economies of the Soviet Union and Eastern Europe, in which price controls and product shortages were pervasive.

In market economies, "first-come, first-served" is often the basis for allocating tickets to concerts and sporting events when promoters set a price at which demand exceeds the supply of available seats. In these cases, ticket "scalpers" often buy blocks of tickets and then resell them at market-clearing prices. Storekeepers (and some ticket sellers) often respond to excess demand by keeping goods "under the counter" and selling only to customers of their own choosing. When sellers decide to whom they will and will not sell their scarce supplies, allocation is said to be by **sellers' preferences**.

sellers' preferences Allocation of commodities in excess demand by decisions of the sellers.

If the government dislikes the allocation of products by long line-ups or by sellers' preferences, it can choose to *ration* the product. To do so, it prints only enough ration coupons to match the quantity supplied at the price ceiling and then distributes the coupons to would-be purchasers, who then need both money and coupons to buy the product. The coupons may be distributed equally among the population or on the basis of some criterion, such as age, family status, or occupation. Rationing of this sort was used by Canada and many other countries during both the First and Second World Wars.

black market A situation in which goods are sold at prices that violate a legal price control.

Black Markets Price ceilings usually give rise to black markets. A **black market** is any market in which transactions (which are themselves legal) take place at prices that violate a legal price control.

> Binding price ceilings always create the potential for a black market because a profit can be made by buying at the controlled price and selling at the (illegal) black-market price.

increased wage has two effects. First, by increasing the cost of labour services to firms, the minimum wage reduces the level of employment to E_1. The second effect is to increase the quantity supplied of labour services to E_2. Thus, the clear effect of the binding minimum wage, as seen in the figure, is to generate unemployment—workers that want a job in this market but are unable to get one—equal to the amount E_1E_2.

Whom does this policy benefit? And whom does it harm? The owners of firms are clearly made worse off since they are now required to pay a higher wage than before the minimum wage was imposed. They respond to this increase in costs by reducing their use of labour. Some (but not all) workers are made better off. The workers who are lucky enough to keep their jobs—E_1 workers in the figure—get a higher wage than before. The shaded area shows the redistribution of income away from firms and toward these fortunate workers. Some workers are harmed by the policy—the ones who lose their jobs as

a result of the wage increase, shown in the figure as the quantity E_1E_0.

These are the effects of minimum wages in a competitive labour market—one in which there are many firms and many workers, none of whom have the power to influence the market wage. In Chapter 14 we will examine non-competitive labour markets, and we will then see that minimum wages may have a different effect on the market. This different behaviour of competitive and non-competitive markets in the presence of minimum wages probably accounts for the disagreements among economists and policymakers regarding the effects of minimum-wage legislation. Until we proceed to that more advanced discussion, however, the analysis of a competitive labour market in this box provides an excellent example of the economic effects of a binding price floor in specific circumstances.

Figure 5-3 illustrates the extreme case, in which all the available supply is sold on a black market. We say this case is extreme because there are law-abiding people in every society and because governments ordinarily have at least *some* power to enforce their price ceilings. Although some units of a product subject to a binding price ceiling will be sold on the black market, it is unlikely that all of that product will be.

Does the existence of a black market mean that the goals sought by imposing price ceilings have been thwarted? The answer depends on what the goals are. Three of the goals that governments often have when imposing a price ceiling are as follows:

1. To restrict production (perhaps to release resources for other uses, such as wartime military production)

2. To keep specific prices down

3. To satisfy notions of equity in the consumption of a product that is temporarily in short supply (such as building supplies immediately following a natural disaster)

When price ceilings are accompanied by a significant black market, it is not clear that any of these objectives are achieved. First, if producers are willing to sell (illegally) at prices above the price ceiling, nothing restricts them to the level of output of Q_2 in Figure 5-3. As long as they can receive more than a price of p_1, they have an incentive to increase their production. Second, black markets clearly frustrate the second objective since the *actual* prices are not kept down; if quantity supplied remains below Q_0, then the black-market price will be *higher* than the free-market equilibrium price, p_0. The third objective may also be thwarted, since with an active black market it is likely that much of the product will be sold only to those who can afford the black-market price, which will often be well above the free-market equilibrium price.

> To the extent that binding price ceilings give rise to a black market, it is likely that the government's objectives motivating the imposition of the price ceiling will be thwarted.

The market for health care in Canada is an important example in which market-clearing prices are not charged; instead, the price is controlled at zero and the services are rationed by customers having to wait their turn to be served. No black market has arisen, although when some Canadians travel to the United States and pay cash for health-care services that they cannot get quickly enough in Canada, or when they pay cash for the limited services provided by Canadian private clinics, the effects are similar to those that occur in a black market. Even though there is not enough of the product available in the public system to satisfy all demand at the controlled price of zero, many people's sense of social justice is satisfied because health care, at least in principle, is freely and equally available to everyone. In recent years, there has been a great deal of debate regarding potential reforms to Canada's health-care system; we discuss this debate in more detail in Chapter 18.

5.3 Rent Controls: A Case Study of Price Ceilings

For long periods over the past hundred years, rent controls existed in London, Paris, New York, and many other large cities. In Sweden and Britain, where rent controls on apartments existed for decades, shortages of rental accommodations were chronic. When rent controls were initiated in Toronto and Rome, severe housing shortages developed, especially in those areas where demand was rising.

Rent controls provide a vivid illustration of the short- and long-term effects of this type of market intervention. Note, however, that the specifics of rent-control laws vary greatly and have changed significantly since they were first imposed many decades ago. In particular, current laws often permit exemptions for new buildings and allowances for maintenance costs and inflation. Moreover, in many countries rent controls have evolved into a "second generation" of legislation that focuses on *regulating* the rental housing market rather than simply controlling the price of rental accommodation.

In this section, we confine ourselves to an analysis of rent controls that are aimed primarily at holding the price of rental housing below the free-market equilibrium value. It is this "first generation" of rent controls that produced dramatic results in such cities as London, Paris, New York, and Toronto.

The Predicted Effects of Rent Controls

Binding rent controls are a specific case of price ceilings, and therefore Figure 5-3 can be used to predict some of their effects:

1. There will be a shortage of rental housing in the sense that quantity demanded will exceed quantity supplied. Since rents are held below their free-market levels, the

available quantity of rental housing will be less than if free-market rents had been charged.

2. The shortage will lead to alternative allocation schemes. Landlords may allocate by sellers' preferences, or the government may intervene, often through security-of-tenure laws, which protect tenants from eviction and thereby give them priority over prospective new tenants.

3. Black markets will appear. For example, landlords may (illegally) require tenants to pay "key money" equal to the difference in value between the free-market and the controlled rents. In the absence of security-of-tenure laws, landlords may force tenants out when their leases expire in order to extract a large entrance fee from new tenants.

The unique feature of rent controls, however, as compared with price controls in general, is that they are applied to a highly *durable good* that provides services to consumers for long periods. Once built, an apartment can be used for decades. As a result, the immediate effects of rent control are typically quite different from the long-term effects.

The short-run supply response to the imposition of rent controls is usually quite limited. Some conversions of apartment units to condominiums (that are not covered by the rent-control legislation) may occur, but the quantity of apartments does not change much. The short-run supply curve for rental housing is quite *inelastic*.

In the long run, however, the supply response to rent controls can be quite dramatic. If the expected rate of return from building new rental housing falls significantly below what can be earned on other investments, funds will go elsewhere. New construction will be halted, and old buildings will be converted to other uses or will simply be left to deteriorate. The long-run supply curve of rental accommodations is highly *elastic*.

Figure 5-4 illustrates the housing shortage that worsens as time passes under rent control. Because the short-run supply of housing is inelastic, the controlled rent causes only a moderate housing shortage in the short run. Indeed, most of the shortage comes from an increase in the quantity demanded rather than from a reduction in quantity supplied. As time passes, however, fewer new apartments are built, more conversions take place, and older buildings are not replaced (and not repaired) as they wear out. As a result, the quantity supplied shrinks steadily and the extent of the housing shortage worsens.

Along with the growing housing shortage comes an increasingly inefficient use of rental accommodation space. Existing tenants will have an incentive to stay where they are even though their family size, location of employment, or economic circumstances may change. Since they cannot move without giving up their low-rent accommodation, some may accept lower-paying jobs

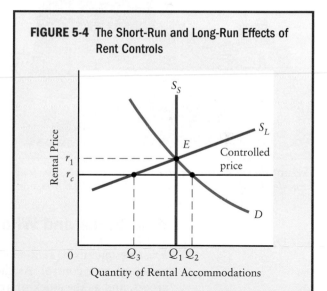

FIGURE 5-4 The Short-Run and Long-Run Effects of Rent Controls

Rental Price (vertical axis)

Quantity of Rental Accommodations (horizontal axis)

S_S, S_L, E, Controlled price, r_1, r_c, D, Q_3, Q_1 Q_2

Rent control causes housing shortages that worsen as time passes. The free-market equilibrium is at point E. The controlled rent of r_c forces rents below their free-market equilibrium value of r_1. The short-run supply of housing is shown by the perfectly inelastic curve S_S. Thus, quantity supplied remains at Q_1 in the short run, and the housing shortage is Q_1Q_2. Over time, the quantity supplied shrinks, as shown by the long-run supply curve S_L. In the long run, there are only Q_3 units of rental accommodations supplied, fewer than when controls were instituted. The long-run housing shortage of Q_3Q_2 is larger than the initial shortage of Q_1Q_2.

nearby simply to avoid the necessity of moving. Thus, a situation will arise in which existing tenants will hang on to accommodation even if it is poorly suited to their needs, while individuals and families who are newly entering the housing market will be unable to find any rental accommodation except at black-market prices.

The province of Ontario instituted rent controls in 1975 and tightened them on at least two subsequent occasions. The controls permitted significant increases in rents only where these were needed to pass on cost increases. As a result, the restrictive effects of rent controls were felt mainly in areas where demand was increasing rapidly (as opposed to areas where only costs were increasing rapidly).

During the mid- and late-1990s, the population of Ontario grew substantially but the stock of rental housing did not keep pace. A shortage developed in the rental-housing market, and was especially acute in Metro Toronto. This growing housing shortage led the Conservative Ontario government in 1997 to loosen rent controls, in particular by allowing landlords to increase the rent as much as they saw fit *but only as tenants vacated the apartment.* Not surprisingly, this policy had both critics and supporters. Supporters argued that a loosening of controls would encourage the construction of

apartments and thus help to reduce the housing shortage. Critics argued that landlords would harass existing tenants, forcing them to move out so that rents could be increased for incoming tenants. (Indeed, this behaviour happened in rent-controlled New York City, where a landlord pleaded guilty to hiring a "hit man" to kill some tenants and set fires to the apartments of others to scare them out so that rents could be increased!)

Rent control still exists in many Canadian provinces, and the governments place limits on the annual rate of increase of rents. In Ontario in 2012, for example, the maximum allowable increase was 3.1 percent, although landlords could apply to the regulatory body for permission to have a larger increase.

Perhaps the most striking effect of rent control is the long-term decline in the amount and quality of rental housing.

Who Gains and Who Loses?

Existing tenants in rent-controlled accommodations are the principal gainers from a policy of rent control. As the gap between the controlled and the free-market rents grows, and as the stock of available housing falls, those who are still lucky enough to live in rent-controlled housing gain more and more.

Landlords suffer because they do not get the rate of return they expected on their investments. Some landlords are large companies, and others are wealthy individuals. Neither of these groups attracts great public sympathy, even though the rental companies' shareholders are not all rich. But some landlords are people of modest means who may have put their retirement savings into a small apartment block or a house or two. They find that the value of their savings is diminished, and sometimes they find themselves in the ironic position of subsidizing tenants who are far better off than they are.

The other important group of people who suffer from rent controls are *potential future* tenants. The housing shortage will hurt some of them because the rental housing they will require will not exist in the future. These people, who wind up living farther from their places of employment and study or in apartments otherwise inappropriate to their situations, are invisible in debates over rent control because they cannot obtain housing in the rent-controlled jurisdiction. Thus, rent control is often stable politically even when it causes a long-run housing shortage. The current tenants benefit, and they outnumber the current landlords, while the potential tenants, who are harmed, are nowhere to be seen or heard.

Policy Alternatives

Most rent controls today are meant to protect lower-income tenants, not only against "profiteering" by landlords in the face of severe local shortages but also against the steadily rising cost of housing. The market solution is to let rents rise sufficiently to cover the rising costs. If people decide that they cannot afford the market price of apartments and will not rent them, construction will cease. Given what we know about consumer behaviour, however, it is more likely that people will make agonizing choices, both to economize on housing and to spend a higher proportion of total income on it, which mean consuming less housing and less of other things as well.

If governments do not want to accept this market solution, there are many things they can do, but they cannot avoid the fundamental fact that the opportunity cost of good housing is high. Binding rent controls create housing shortages. The shortages can be removed only if the government, at taxpayer expense, either subsidizes housing production or produces public housing directly.

Alternatively, the government can make housing more affordable to lower-income households by providing income assistance directly to these households, thereby giving them access to higher-quality housing than they could otherwise afford. Whatever policy is adopted, it is important to recognize that providing greater access to rental accommodations has a resource cost. The costs of providing additional housing cannot be voted out of existence; all that can be done is to transfer the costs from one set of persons to another.

5.4 An Introduction to Market Efficiency

In this chapter we have seen the effects of governments intervening in competitive markets by setting price floors and price ceilings. In both cases, we noted that the imposition of a controlled price generates benefits for some individuals and costs for others. For example, in the case of the legislated minimum wage (a price floor), firms are made worse off by the minimum wage, but workers who retain their jobs are made better off. Other workers, those unable to retain their jobs at the higher wage, may be made worse off. In the example of legislated rent controls (a price ceiling), landlords are made worse off by the rent controls, but some tenants are made better off. Those tenants who are no longer able to find an apartment when rents fall are made worse off.

Is it possible to determine the *overall* effects of such policies, rather than just the effects on specific groups? For example, can we say that a policy of legislated minimum wages, while harming firms, nonetheless makes *society as a whole* better off because it helps workers more than it harms firms? Or can we conclude that the imposition of rent controls makes society as a whole better off because it helps tenants more than it harms landlords?

To address such questions, economists use the concept of *market efficiency*. We will explore this concept in more detail in later chapters, but for now we simply introduce the idea and see how it helps us understand the overall effects of price controls. We begin by taking a slightly different look at market demand and supply curves.

Demand as "Value" and Supply as "Cost"

In Chapter 3 we saw that the market demand curve for any product shows, for each possible price, how much of that product consumers want to purchase. Similarly, we saw that the market supply curve shows how much producers want to sell at each possible price. But we can turn things around and view these curves in a slightly different way—by starting with any given quantity and asking about the price. Specifically, we can consider the highest price that consumers are *willing to pay* and the lowest price that producers are *willing to accept* for any given unit of the product. As we will see, viewing demand and supply curves in this manner helps us think about how society as a whole benefits by producing and consuming any given amount of some product.

Let's begin by considering the market demand curve for pizza, as shown in part (i) of Figure 5-5. Each point on the demand curve shows the highest price consumers are willing to pay for a given pizza. (We assume for simplicity that all pizzas are identical.) At point *A* we see that consumers are willing to pay up to $20 for the 100th pizza, and at point *B* consumers are willing to pay up to $15 for the 200th pizza. In both cases, these maximum prices reflect the *value* consumers place on that particular pizza. In general, for each pizza, the price on the demand curve shows the value to consumers from consuming that pizza.

FIGURE 5-5 Reinterpreting the Demand and Supply Curves for Pizza

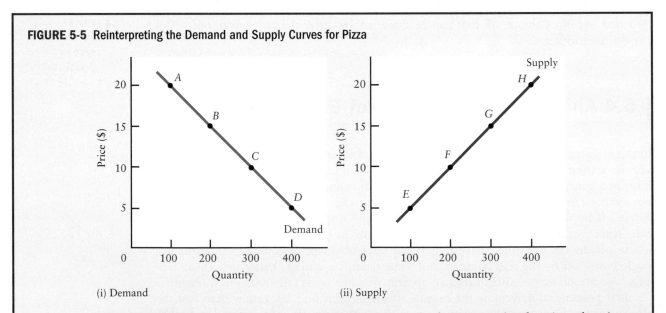

For each pizza, the price on the demand curve shows the value consumers receive from consuming that pizza; the price on the supply curve shows the additional cost to firms of producing that pizza. Each point on the demand curve shows the maximum price consumers are willing to pay to consume that unit. This maximum price reflects the value that consumers get from that unit of the product. Each point on the supply curve shows the minimum price firms are willing to accept for producing and selling that unit. This minimum price reflects the additional costs incurred by producing that unit.

The reason the demand curve is downward sloping is that not all consumers are the same. Some consumers value pizza so highly that they are willing to pay $20 for a pizza; others are prepared to pay only $10, while some value pizza so little that they are prepared to pay only $5. There is nothing special about pizza, however. What is true for the demand for pizza is true for the demand for any other product:

> **For each unit of a product, the price on the market demand curve shows the value to consumers from consuming that unit.**

Now let's consider the market supply curve for pizza, shown in part (ii) of Figure 5-5. Each point on the market supply curve shows the lowest price firms are willing to accept to produce and sell a given pizza. (We maintain our simplifying assumption that all pizzas are identical.) At point *E* firms are willing to accept a price no lower than $5 for the 100th pizza, and at point *F* firms are willing to accept a price no lower than $10 for the 200th pizza. The lowest acceptable price as shown on the supply curve reflects the *additional cost* firms incur to produce each given pizza. To see this, consider the production of the 200th pizza at point *F*. If the firm's total costs increase by $10 when this pizza is produced, the firm will be able to increase its profits as long as it can sell that pizza at a price greater than $10. If it sells the pizza at any price below $10, its profits will decline. If it sells the pizza at a price of exactly $10, its profits will neither rise nor fall. Thus, for a profit-maximizing firm, the *lowest acceptable price* for the 200th pizza is $10.

The reason that the supply curve is upward sloping is that not all producers are the same. Some are so good at producing pizzas (low-cost producers) that they would be willing to accept $5 per pizza; others are less easily able to produce pizzas (high-cost producers) and hence would need to receive $15 in order to produce and sell the identical pizza. What is true for the supply of pizza is true for the supply of other products:

> **For each unit of a product, the price on the market supply curve shows the lowest acceptable price to firms for selling that unit. This lowest acceptable price reflects the additional cost to firms from producing that unit.**

Economic Surplus and Market Efficiency

Once the demand and supply curves are put together, the equilibrium price and quantity can be determined. This brings us to the important concept of *economic surplus*. We continue with our pizza example in Figure 5-6, which shows the demand and supply curves together. Consider a quantity of 100 pizzas. For each one of those 100 pizzas, the value to consumers is given by the height of the demand curve. The additional cost to firms from producing each of these 100 pizzas is shown by the height of the supply curve. For the entire 100 pizzas, the difference between the value to consumers and the additional costs to firms is called *economic surplus* and is shown by the shaded area ① in the figure.

> **For any given quantity of a product, the area below the demand curve and above the supply curve shows the economic surplus associated with the production and consumption of that product.**

What does this economic surplus represent? The economic surplus is the net value that *society as a whole* receives by producing and consuming these 100 pizzas. It arises because firms and consumers have taken resources that have a lower value (as shown by the height of the supply curve) and transformed them into something valued more highly (as shown by the height of the demand curve). To put it differently, the value from consuming the 100 pizzas is greater than the cost of the resources necessary to produce those 100 pizzas—flour, yeast, tomato sauce, cheese, and labour. Thus, the act of producing and consuming those 100 pizzas "adds value" and generates benefits for society as a whole.

We are now ready to introduce the concept of market efficiency. In later chapters, after we have explored consumer and firm behaviour in greater detail, we will have a more detailed discussion of efficiency. For now, we simply introduce the concept and see how it relates to the imposition of government price controls.

Economists say that a market for any specific product is efficient if the quantity of the product produced and consumed is such that the economic surplus in that market is maximized. Note that this refers to the *total* surplus but not its distribution between consumers and producers. For example, as we will see in the next section, the removal of a binding set of rent controls will increase total surplus and thus improve the efficiency of the market. At the same time, however, some tenants will be made worse off while some landlords will be made better off. The fact that total surplus has increased means that, at least in principle, it would be possible for those who gain to compensate those who lose so that everyone ends up being better off. When economists say that "society gains" when market efficiency is enhanced, even though these compensations rarely occur, there is an implicit value judgement being made that the benefits to those who gain outweigh the costs to those who lose.

Let's apply this concept of efficiency to the pizza market shown in Figure 5-6 and ask, What level of pizza production and consumption is efficient? Consider the quantity of 100 pizzas. At this quantity, the shaded area ① shows the total economic surplus that society receives from producing and consuming 100 pizzas. But if output were to increase beyond 100 pizzas, more economic surplus would be generated because the value placed by consumers on additional pizzas is greater than the additional costs associated with their production. Specifically, if production and consumption were to increase to 200 pizzas, additional economic surplus would be generated, as shown by shaded area ②. Continuing this logic, we see that the amount of economic surplus is

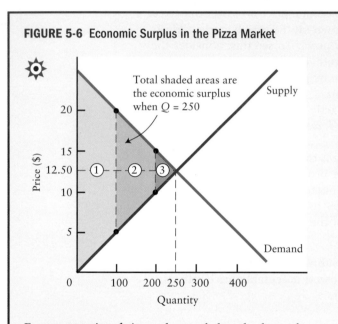

FIGURE 5-6 Economic Surplus in the Pizza Market

For any quantity of pizzas, the area below the demand curve and above the supply curve shows the economic surplus generated by the production and consumption of those pizzas. The demand curve shows the value consumers place on each additional pizza; the supply curve shows the additional cost associated with producing each pizza. For example, consumers value the 100th pizza at $20, whereas the additional cost to firms of producing that 100th pizza is $5. The economic surplus generated by producing and consuming this 100th pizza is therefore $15 ($20 − $5). For any range of quantity, the shaded area between the curves over that range shows the economic surplus generated by producing and consuming those pizzas.

Economic surplus in the pizza market is maximized—and thus market efficiency is achieved—at the free-market equilibrium quantity of 250 pizzas and price of $12.50. At this point, total economic surplus is the sum of the three shaded areas.

maximized when the quantity is 250 units, and at that quantity the total economic surplus is equal to the sum of areas ①, ②, and ③.

What would happen if the quantity of pizzas were to rise further, say to 300 units? For any pizzas beyond 250, the value placed on these pizzas by consumers is *less than* the additional costs associated with their production. In this case, producing the last 50 pizzas would actually *decrease* the amount of economic surplus in this market because society would be taking highly valued resources (flour, cheese, etc.) and transforming them into pizzas, which are valued less.

In our example of the pizza market, as long as the price is free to adjust to excess demands or supplies, the equilibrium price and quantity will be determined where the demand and supply curves for pizza intersect. In Figure 5-6, the equilibrium quantity is 250 pizzas, the quantity that maximizes the amount of economic surplus in the pizza market. In other words, the free interaction of demand and supply will result in market efficiency. This result in the pizza market suggests a more general rule:

> A competitive market will maximize economic surplus and therefore be efficient when price is free to achieve its market-clearing equilibrium level.[1]

Market Efficiency and Price Controls

At the beginning of this section we asked whether we could determine if *society as a whole* is made better off or worse off as a result of the government's imposition of price floors or price ceilings. With an understanding of economic surplus and market efficiency, we are now ready to consider these questions.

Let's begin with the case of a price floor, as shown in part (i) of Figure 5-7. The free-market equilibrium is shown by point E, with price p_0 and quantity Q_0. When the government imposes a price floor at p_1, the quantity exchanged falls to Q_1. In the free-market case, each of the units of output between Q_0 and Q_1 generates some economic surplus. But when the price floor is put in place, these units of the good are no longer produced or consumed, and thus they no longer generate any economic surplus. The purple shaded area is called the *deadweight loss* caused by the binding price floor, and it represents the overall loss of economic surplus to society. The size of the deadweight loss reflects the extent of *market inefficiency*.

The case of a price ceiling is shown in part (ii) of Figure 5-7. The free-market equilibrium is again shown by point E, with price p_0 and quantity Q_0. When the government imposes a price ceiling at p_2, the quantity exchanged falls to Q_2. In the free-market case, each unit of output between Q_0 and Q_2 generates some economic surplus. But when the price ceiling is imposed, these units of the good are no longer produced or consumed, and so they no longer generate any economic surplus. The purple shaded area is the *deadweight loss* and represents the overall loss of surplus to society caused by the policy. The size of the deadweight loss reflects the extent of market inefficiency.

> The imposition of a binding price ceiling or price floor in an otherwise free and competitive market leads to market inefficiency.

---

[1] In Part 6 of this book, we will see some important exceptions to this rule when we discuss "market failures."

FIGURE 5-7 Market Inefficiency with Price Controls

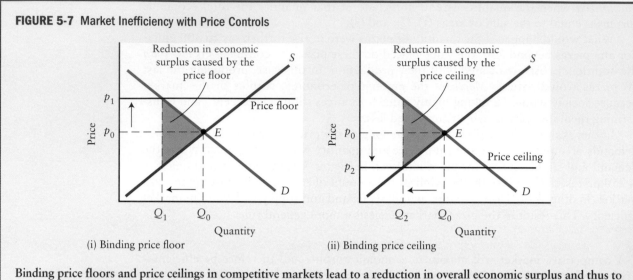

(i) Binding price floor   (ii) Binding price ceiling

Binding price floors and price ceilings in competitive markets lead to a reduction in overall economic surplus and thus to market inefficiency. In both parts of the figure, the free-market equilibrium is at point E with price p_0 and quantity Q_0. In part (i), the introduction of a price floor at p_1 reduces quantity to Q_1. In part (ii), the introduction of a price ceiling at p_2 reduces quantity to Q_2. In both parts, the purple shaded area shows the reduction in overall economic surplus—the deadweight loss—created by the price floor or ceiling. Both outcomes display market inefficiency.

It is worth repeating a central point: binding price floors and price ceilings do more than merely redistribute a given amount of economic surplus between buyers and sellers. They also lead to a reduction in the quantity of the product transacted and a reduction in total economic surplus. Society as a whole receives less economic surplus as compared with the free-market case.

One Final Application: Output Quotas

Before ending this chapter, it is useful to consider one final application of government intervention in a competitive market, and to examine the effects on overall economic surplus and market efficiency. Figure 5-8 illustrates the effects of introducing a system of *output quotas* in a competitive market. Output quotas are commonly used in Canadian agriculture, especially in the markets for milk, butter, and cheese. Output quotas are sometimes used in other industries as well; for example, they are often used in large cities to regulate the number of taxi drivers.

The equilibrium in the free-market case is at point E, with price p_0 and quantity Q_0. When the government introduces an output quota, it restricts total output of this product to Q_1 units and then distributes quotas—"licences to produce"—among the producers. With output restricted to Q_1 units, the market price rises to p_1, the price that consumers are willing to pay for this quantity of the product. The purple shaded area—the deadweight loss of the output quota—shows the overall loss of economic surplus as a result of the quota-induced output restriction.

One interesting consequence of the use of output quotas relates to the market value of the quotas themselves. When quota systems are used, firms initially issued quotas by the government are usually permitted to buy or sell quotas to each other or to new firms interested in entering the industry. The quota itself simply provides the holder permission to produce and sell in that industry, but the market value of the quota reflects the profitability of that production.

As you can see from Figure 5-8, the output restriction created by the quota leads to an increase in the product's price. If demand for the product is inelastic, as is the case in the dairy markets where quotas are commonly used, total income to producers rises as a result of the reduction in output. (Refer back to Figure 4-5 in Chapter 4.) But since their output falls, firms' production costs are also reduced. The introduction of a quota system therefore leads to a rise in revenues and a fall in production costs—a clear benefit for producers! Not surprisingly, individual producers are often prepared to pay a high price to purchase quotas from other producers because having more quotas gives them the ability to produce more output.

There is a catch, however: producers must incur a very high cost in order to purchase the quotas. For example, an average dairy farm in Ontario or Quebec has about 90 cows and produces about 2300 litres of milk per day. The market value of the quota required to produce this amount of milk is approximately $2.2 million. The ownership of a quota therefore represents a considerable asset for those producers who were lucky enough to receive it (for free) when it was initially issued by the government. But for new producers wanting to get into the industry, the need to purchase an expensive quota represents a considerable obstacle. These large costs from purchasing the quota offset the benefits from selling the product at the (quota-induced) high price.

FIGURE 5-8 The Inefficiency of Output Quotas

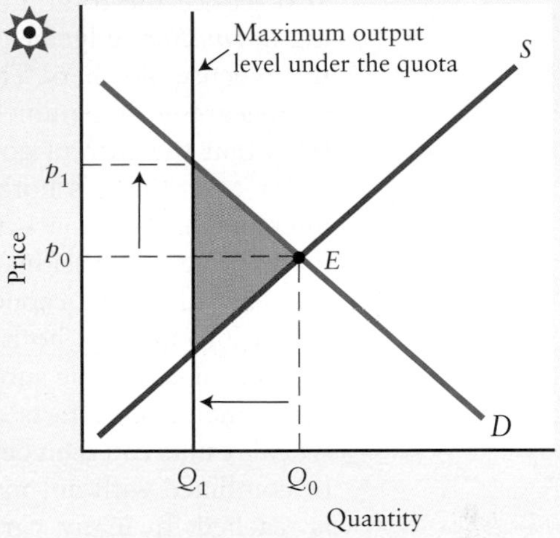

Binding output quotas lead to a reduction in output and a reduction in overall economic surplus. The free-market equilibrium is at point E with price p_0 and quantity Q_0. Suppose the government then restricts total quantity to Q_1 by issuing output quotas to firms. The market price rises to p_1. The purple shaded area shows the reduction in overall economic surplus—the deadweight loss—created by the quota system.

A Cautionary Word

In this chapter we have examined the effects of government policies to control prices in otherwise free and competitive markets, and we have shown that such policies usually have two results. First, there is a redistribution between buyers and sellers; one group is made better off while the other group is made worse off—at least as far as the economic value of production is concerned. Second, there is a reduction in the overall amount of economic surplus generated in the market; the result is that the outcome is inefficient and society as a whole is made worse off.

The finding that government intervention in otherwise free markets leads to inefficiency should lead one to ask why government would ever intervene in such ways. The answer in many situations is that the government policy is motivated by the desire to help a specific group of people and that the overall costs are deemed to be a worthwhile price to pay to achieve the desired effect. For example, legislated minimum wages are often viewed by politicians as an effective means of reducing poverty—by increasing the wages received by low-wage workers. The costs such a policy imposes on firms, and on society overall, may be viewed as costs worth incurring to redistribute economic surplus toward low-wage workers. Similarly, the use of output quotas in certain agricultural markets is sometimes viewed by politicians as an effective means of increasing income to specific farmers. The costs that such quota systems impose on consumers, and on society as a whole, may be viewed by some as acceptable costs in achieving a redistribution of economic surplus toward these farmers.

In advocating these kinds of policies, ones that redistribute economic surplus but also reduce the total amount of economic surplus available, policymakers are making *normative* judgements regarding which groups in society deserve to be helped at the expense of others. These judgements may be informed by a careful study of which groups are most genuinely in need, and they may also be driven by political considerations that the current government deems important to its prospects for re-election. In either case, there is nothing necessarily "wrong" about the government's decision to intervene in these markets, even if these interventions lead to inefficiency. Not surprisingly, however, decisions like this are often controversial and hotly debated.

The job of the economist is to carefully analyze the effects of such policies, taking care to identify both the distributional effects and the implications for the overall amount of economic surplus generated in the market. This is *positive* analysis, emphasizing the *actual* effects of the policy rather than what might be *desirable*. These analytical results can then be used as inputs to the decision-making process, where they will be combined with normative and political considerations before a final policy decision is reached. In many parts of this textbook, we will encounter policies that governments implement (or consider implementing) to alter market outcomes, and we will examine the effects of those policies. A full understanding of why specific policies are implemented requires paying attention to the effects of such policies on both the overall amount of economic surplus and the distribution of that surplus.

SUMMARY

5.1 The Interaction Among Markets   LO 1

- Partial-equilibrium analysis is the study of a single market in isolation, ignoring events in other markets. General-equilibrium analysis is the study of all markets together.

- Partial-equilibrium analysis is appropriate when the market being examined is small relative to the entire economy.

5.2 Government-Controlled Prices   LO 2

- Government price controls are policies that attempt to hold the price of some good or service at some disequilibrium value—a value that could not be maintained in the absence of the government's intervention.
- A binding price floor is set above the equilibrium price; a binding price ceiling is set below the equilibrium price.
- Binding price floors lead to excess supply. Either the potential sellers are left with quantities that cannot

be sold, or the government must step in and buy the surplus.
- Binding price ceilings lead to excess demand and provide a strong incentive for black marketeers to buy at the controlled price and sell at the higher free-market (illegal) price.

5.3 Rent Controls: A Case Study of Price Ceilings   LO 3

- Rent controls are a form of price ceiling. The major consequence of binding rent controls is a shortage of rental accommodations and the allocation of rental housing by sellers' preferences.

- Because the supply of rental housing is much more elastic in the long run than in the short run, the extent of the housing shortage caused by rent controls worsens over time.

5.4 An Introduction to Market Efficiency

- Demand curves show consumers' willingness to pay for each unit of the product. For any given quantity, the area below the demand curve shows the overall value that consumers place on that quantity of the product.
- Supply curves show the lowest price producers are prepared to accept in order to produce and sell each unit of the product. This lowest acceptable price for each additional unit reflects the firm's costs required to produce each additional unit.
- For any given quantity exchanged of a product, the area below the demand curve and above the supply curve (up to that quantity) shows the economic surplus generated by the production and consumption of those units.
- Economic surplus is a common measure of market efficiency. A market's surplus is maximized when the quantity exchanged is determined by the intersection of the demand and supply curves. This outcome is said to be efficient.
- Policies that intervene in otherwise free and competitive markets—such as price floors, price ceilings, and output quotas—generally lead to a reduction in the total amount of economic surplus generated in the market. Such policies are inefficient for society overall.

KEY CONCEPTS

General-equilibrium analysis
Partial-equilibrium analysis
Price controls: floors and ceilings
Allocation by sellers' preferences

Black markets
Rent controls
Short-run and long-run supply curves
   of rental accommodations

Economic surplus
Market efficiency
Inefficiency of price controls and
   output quotas

STUDY EXERCISES

MyEconLab   Make the grade with MyEconLab: Study Exercises marked in red can be found on MyEconLab. You can practise them as often as you want, and most feature step-by-step guided instructions to help you find the right answer.

1. Consider the market for straw hats on a tropical island. The demand and supply schedules are given below.

Price ($)	Quantity Demanded	Quantity Supplied
1	1000	200
2	900	300
3	800	400
4	700	500
5	600	600
6	500	700
7	400	800
8	300	900

  a. The equilibrium price for straw hats is _____.
The equilibrium quantity demanded and quantity supplied is _____.

  b. Suppose the government believes that no islander should have to pay more than $3 for a hat. The government can achieve this by imposing a _____.

  c. At the government-controlled price of $3 there will be a _____ of _____ hats.

  d. Suppose now that the government believes the island's hat makers are not paid enough for their hats and that islanders should pay no less than $6 for a hat. They can achieve this by imposing a _____.

  e. At the new government-controlled price of $6 there will be a _____ of _____ hats.

2. The following questions are about resource allocation in the presence of price ceilings and price floors.

  a. A binding price ceiling leads to excess demand. What are some methods, other than price, of allocating the available supply?

b. A binding price floor leads to excess supply. How might the government deal with this excess supply?

c. Why might the government choose to implement a price ceiling?

d. Why might the government choose to implement a price floor?

3. Consider the market for some product X that is represented in the demand-and-supply diagram.

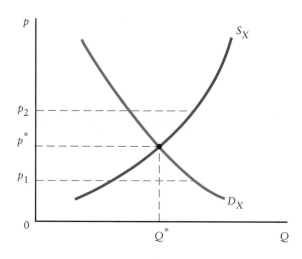

a. Suppose the government decides to impose a price floor at p_1. Describe how this affects price, quantity, and market efficiency.

b. Suppose the government decides to impose a price floor at p_2. Describe how this affects price, quantity, and market efficiency.

c. Suppose the government decides to impose a price ceiling at p_1. Describe how this affects price, quantity, and market efficiency.

d. Suppose the government decides to impose a price ceiling at p_2. Describe how this affects price, quantity, and market efficiency.

4. Consider the market for rental housing in Yourtown. The demand and supply schedules for rental housing are given in the table.

Price ($ per month)	Quantity Demanded (thousands of units)	Quantity Supplied (thousands of units)
1100	40	80
1000	50	77
900	60	73
800	70	70
700	80	67
600	90	65
500	100	60

a. In a free market for rental housing, what is the equilibrium price and quantity?

b. Now suppose the government in Yourtown decides to impose a ceiling on the monthly rental price.

What is the highest level at which such a ceiling could be set in order to have any effect on the market? Explain your answer.

c. Suppose the maximum rental price is set equal to $500 per month. Describe the effect on quantity demanded, supplied, and exchanged in the rental-housing market.

d. Suppose a black market develops in the presence of the rent controls in part (c). What is the black-market price that would exist if all of the quantity supplied were sold on the black market?

5. Explain and show in a diagram why the short-run effects of rent control are likely to be less significant than the long-run effects.

6. In cities experiencing rapid growth, like Calgary and Saskatoon, it is often claimed that the "overheated" real estate market puts housing out of reach of ordinary Canadians. Not surprisingly, governments often debate how best to deal with this issue. Who bears the heaviest cost when rents are kept artificially low by each of the following means?

a. legislated rent controls

b. a subsidy to tenants equal to some fraction of their rent

c. the provision of public housing which is made available at below-market rents

7. Consider the market for burritos in a hypothetical Canadian city, blessed with thousands of students and dozens of small burrito stands. The demand and supply schedules are shown in the table.

Price ($)	Quantity Demanded (thousands of burritos per month)	Quantity Supplied (thousands of burritos per month)
0	500	125
1.00	400	175
1.50	350	200
2.00	300	225
2.50	250	250
3.00	200	275
3.50	150	300
4.00	100	325
5.00	0	375

a. Graph the demand and supply curves. What is the free-market equilibrium in this market?

b. What is the total economic surplus in this market in the free-market equilibrium? What area in your diagram represents this economic surplus?

c. Suppose the local government, out of concern for the students' welfare, enforces a price ceiling on burritos at a price of $1.50. Show in your diagram the effect on price and quantity exchanged.

d. Are students better off as a result of this policy? Explain.

e. What happens to overall economic surplus in this market as a result of the price ceiling? Show this in the diagram.

8. Consider the market for milk in Saskatchewan. If p is the price of milk (cents per litre) and Q is the quantity of litres (in millions per month), suppose that the demand and supply curves for milk are given by

$$\text{Demand: } p = 225 - 15Q^D$$
$$\text{Supply: } p = 25 + 35Q^S$$

a. Assuming there is no government intervention in this market, what is the equilibrium price and quantity?

b. Now suppose the government guarantees milk producers a price of $2 per litre and promises to buy any amount of milk that the producers cannot sell. What are the quantity demanded and quantity supplied at this guaranteed price?

c. How much milk would the government be buying (per month) with this system of price supports?

d. Who pays for the milk that the government buys? Who is helped by this policy and who is harmed?

9. This question is related to the use of output quotas in the milk market in the previous question. Suppose the government used a quota system instead of direct price supports to assist milk producers. In particular, it issued quotas to existing milk producers for 1.67 million litres of milk per month.

a. If milk production is exactly equal to the amount of quotas issued, what price do consumers pay for milk?

b. Compared with the direct price controls in the previous question, whose income is higher under the quota system? Whose is lower?

10. This question relates to the section **Linkages Between Markets** found on the MyEconLab (**www.myeconlab. com**). In 1994, the Quebec and Ontario governments significantly reduced their excise taxes on cigarettes, but Manitoba and Saskatchewan left theirs in place. This led to cigarette smuggling between provinces that linked the provincial markets.

a. Draw a simple demand-and-supply diagram for the "Eastern" market and a separate one for the "Western" market.

b. Suppose that cigarette taxes are reduced in the eastern market. Show the immediate effects.

c. Now suppose that the supply of cigarettes is (illegally) mobile. Explain and show what happens.

d. What limits the extent of smuggling that will take place in this situation?

11. Consider a simple demand-and-supply model of a competitive labour market in a small town. The demand and supply curves for labour are given by

$$\text{Demand: } w = 18 - 3L^D$$
$$\text{Supply: } w = 3 + 2L^S$$

where w is the wage ($ per hour) and L is the number of hours of employment (measured in thousands of hours per month).

a. Plot the demand and supply curves to scale.

b. Solve for the equilibrium level of w and L in the case of no government intervention.

c. Now suppose that the town council imposes a minimum wage equal to $10 per hour. What is the new level of employment?

d. Identify in your diagram the area that is the deadweight loss. Compute its size, measured in thousands of dollars per month.

Consumer Behaviour

CHAPTER OUTLINE

LEARNING OBJECTIVES (LO)

After studying this chapter you will be able to

6.1 MARGINAL UTILITY AND CONSUMER CHOICE

1 describe the difference between marginal and total utility.
2 explain how utility-maximizing consumers adjust their expenditure until the marginal utility per dollar spent is equalized across products.

6.2 INCOME AND SUBSTITUTION EFFECTS OF PRICE CHANGES

3 understand how any change in price generates both an income and a substitution effect on quantity demanded.

6.3 CONSUMER SURPLUS

4 see that consumer surplus is the "bargain" the consumer gets by paying less for the product than the maximum price he or she is willing to pay.
5 explain the "paradox of value."

IMAGINE that you stop at a corner store with a $20 bill in your pocket, looking for late-night snacks to have while you are studying. You must choose how to divide this $20 between frozen burritos and bottles of your favourite fruit juice. How do you make this decision? In this chapter we look at how economists analyze such problems—the theory of consumer behaviour. Not surprisingly, economists think about consumers as caring both about the prices of the goods and the satisfaction they get from the goods.

The first two sections of the chapter explore the underpinnings of consumer behaviour and explain in some detail why demand curves are negatively sloped—and also discuss the rare situations in which demand curves might be positively sloped. The third and final section examines an important implication of having negatively sloped demand curves and introduces the concept of consumer surplus, which is part of the economic surplus that we discussed in Chapter 5. As you will see in later chapters, consumer surplus is useful in showing that free and competitive markets often generate efficient outcomes.

6.1 Marginal Utility and Consumer Choice

Consumers make all kinds of decisions—they choose to drink coffee or tea (or neither), to go to the movies, to go out for dinner, and to buy top-of-the-line (or not so good) computer equipment. As we discussed in Chapter 1, economists assume that in making their choices, consumers are motivated to maximize their **utility**, the total satisfaction that they derive from the goods and services that they consume.

utility The satisfaction that a consumer receives from consuming some good or service.

Although utility cannot be measured directly, it is still a useful concept. You know that you derive satisfaction—or utility—from eating a good meal, listening to music, buying new shoes, or taking a walk through a park. And we need some way to think about how you as a consumer make your decisions. As we will see in this chapter, it is possible to construct a useful theory of consumer behaviour based on the idea of *utility maximization*.

In developing our theory of consumer behaviour, we begin by considering the consumption of a single product. It is useful to distinguish between the consumer's **total utility**, which is the full satisfaction resulting from the consumption of that product by a consumer, and the consumer's **marginal utility**, which is the *additional* satisfaction resulting from consuming one more unit of that product. For example, the total utility of consuming five bottles of fruit juice per day is the total satisfaction that those five juices provide. The marginal utility of the fifth juice consumed is the additional satisfaction provided by the consumption of that fifth juice each day.[1]

total utility The total satisfaction resulting from the consumption of a given commodity by a consumer.

marginal utility The additional satisfaction obtained from consuming one additional unit of a commodity.

Diminishing Marginal Utility

The central hypothesis of utility theory, often called the *law of diminishing marginal utility,* is as follows:

> The utility that any consumer derives from *successive* units of a particular product consumed over some period of time diminishes as total consumption of the product increases (holding constant the consumption of all other products).

Consider your utility from using clean water, for drinking, bathing, washing your dishes or clothes, and all its other purposes. Some minimum quantity is very important and you would, if necessary, give up a considerable sum of money to obtain that quantity of water. Thus, your marginal utility of that basic quantity of water is very high. You will, of course, consume more than this bare minimum, but your marginal utility of successive litres of water used over a period of time will decline steadily.

We will consider evidence for this hypothesis later, but you can convince yourself that it is at least reasonable by asking a few questions. How much money would be needed to induce you to reduce your consumption of water by one litre per week? The answer is *very little*. How much would induce you to reduce it by a second litre? By a third litre? To only one litre consumed per week? The answer to the last question is *quite a lot*. The fewer litres you are already using, the higher the marginal utility of one more litre of water.

---

[1] Technically, incremental utility is measured over a discrete interval, such as from four juices to five juices, whereas marginal utility is a rate of change measured over an infinitesimal interval. However, common usage applies the word *marginal* when the last unit is involved, even if a one-unit change is not infinitesimal.[9]

Utility Schedules and Graphs

In Figure 6-1 we make the assumption that utility can be measured, and thus the different amount of utility received from consuming different units can be compared. This is a helpful assumption in allowing us to see the important difference between total and marginal utility. The figure illustrates the assumptions that have been made about utility, using Alison's daily consumption of fruit juice as an example. The table shows that Alison's total utility rises as she drinks more bottles of juice per day. However, the utility that she gets from each *additional* juice per day is less than that of the previous one—that is, her marginal utility declines as the quantity she consumes rises. [10]

The data are graphed in the two parts of Figure 6-1.

Maximizing Utility

As already noted, economists assume that consumers try to make themselves as well off as they possibly can in the circumstances in which they find themselves. In other words,

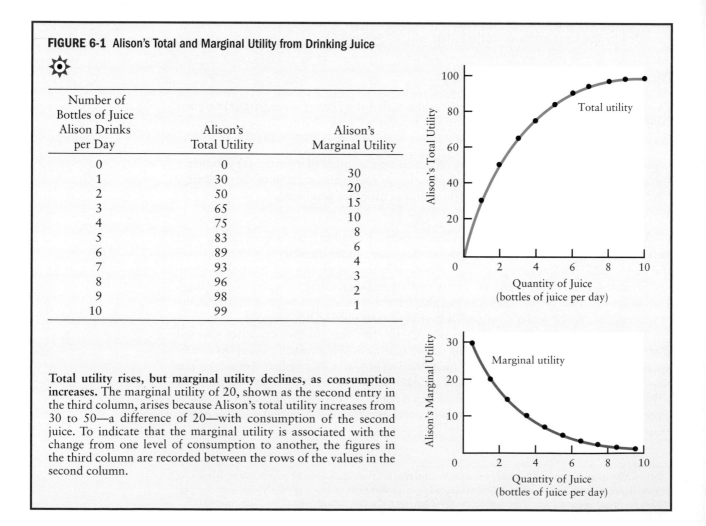

FIGURE 6-1 Alison's Total and Marginal Utility from Drinking Juice

Number of Bottles of Juice Alison Drinks per Day	Alison's Total Utility	Alison's Marginal Utility
0	0	
1	30	30
2	50	20
3	65	15
4	75	10
5	83	8
6	89	6
7	93	4
8	96	3
9	98	2
10	99	1

Total utility rises, but marginal utility declines, as consumption increases. The marginal utility of 20, shown as the second entry in the third column, arises because Alison's total utility increases from 30 to 50—a difference of 20—with consumption of the second juice. To indicate that the marginal utility is associated with the change from one level of consumption to another, the figures in the third column are recorded between the rows of the values in the second column.

consumers seek to maximize their total utility subject to the constraints they face—in particular, their income and the market prices of various products.

The Consumer's Decision Now that we have examined the concepts of total utility and marginal utility, we are ready to answer the question posed at the beginning of the chapter: How can consumers decide to allocate their consumption of juice and burritos in such a way as to maximize their utility? Of course, we could ask the same question about any two goods, or any number of goods, but we will focus on juice and burritos to keep the example simple.

The utility-maximizing consumer should consume juice and burritos to the point at which the marginal utility *per dollar spent* on the last juice is just equal to the marginal utility *per dollar spent* on the last burrito. In this way, the consumer's utility will be maximized.

> **A utility-maximizing consumer allocates expenditures so that the marginal utility obtained from the last dollar spent on each product is equal.**

Let's consider an example. Imagine that Alison's utility from the last dollar spent on juice is three times her utility from the last dollar spent on burritos. In this case, Alison can increase her total utility by spending less on burritos and spending more on juice.

If Alison wants to *maximize* her utility, she will continue to switch her expenditure from burritos to juice as long as her last dollar spent on juice yields more utility than her last dollar spent on burritos. This switching, however, reduces the quantity of burritos consumed and, given the law of diminishing marginal utility, raises the marginal utility of burritos. At the same time, switching increases the quantity of juice consumed and thereby lowers the marginal utility of juice.

Eventually, the marginal utilities will have changed enough so that the utility received from the last dollar spent on juice is just equal to the utility received from the last dollar spent on burritos. At this point, Alison gains nothing from further switches. (In fact, switching further would *reduce* her total utility.)

So much for the specific example. What can we say more generally about utility maximization? Suppose we denote the marginal utility of the last unit of product X by MU_X and its price by p_X. Let MU_Y and p_Y refer, respectively, to the marginal utility of a second product Y and its price. The marginal utility per dollar spent on X will be MU_X/p_X. For example, if the last unit of X increases utility by 30 and costs \$3, its marginal utility per dollar is $30/3 = 10$. If the last unit of Y increases utility by 10 and costs \$1, its marginal utility per dollar is $10/1 = 10$. With these numbers, the marginal utilities from the last dollar spent on X and Y are equal.

The condition required for a consumer to be maximizing utility, for any pair of products, is

$$\frac{MU_X}{p_X} = \frac{MU_Y}{p_Y} \qquad (6\text{-}1)$$

This equation says that a utility-maximizing consumer will allocate expenditure so that the utility gained from the last dollar spent on one product is equal to the marginal utility gained from the last dollar spent on any other product.

This is the fundamental equation of marginal utility theory. With only a given amount of income to spend, a consumer demands each good up to the point at which the marginal utility per dollar spent on it is the same as the marginal utility per dollar spent on every other good. When this condition is met for all goods, the consumer cannot increase utility further by reallocating expenditure. That is, utility will be maximized. (Of course, if she gets more income to spend, she can raise her total utility by buying more of each good.)

An Alternative Interpretation If we rearrange the terms in Equation 6-1, we can gain additional insight into consumer behaviour.

$$\frac{MU_X}{MU_Y} = \frac{p_X}{p_Y}$$

(6-2)

The right side of this equation is the *relative* price of the two goods. It is determined by the market and is beyond Alison's control. She reacts to these market prices but is powerless to change them. The left side is the *relative* ability of the two goods to add to Alison's utility. This is within her control because in determining the quantities of different goods to buy, she also determines their marginal utilities. (If you have difficulty seeing why, look again at Figure 6-1.)

If the two sides of Equation 6-2 are not equal, Alison can increase her total utility by rearranging her purchases of X and Y. Suppose that the price of X is \$4 and the price of Y is \$2. The right-hand side of Equation 6-2 is then $p_X/p_Y = 4/2 = 2$. Remember that Alison can do nothing to change the right-hand side of this equation—the prices are determined in the market and are beyond her control. Suppose also that Alison is currently purchasing X and Y such that the marginal utility for X is 12 and the marginal utility for Y is 4. The left-hand side of Equation 6-2 is then $MU_X/MU_Y = 12/4 = 3$. In this case $MU_X/MU_Y > p_X/p_Y$. Alison can increase her total utility by increasing her purchases of X (which have a high MU) and reducing her purchases of Y (which have a low MU) until the ratio MU_X/MU_Y is equal to 2, the same as the ratio of the prices. At this point Alison cannot increase her total utility any further by rearranging her purchases between the two products.

Consider what Alison is doing. She is faced with a set of prices that she cannot change. She responds to these prices and maximizes her utility by adjusting the things that she *can* change—the quantities of the various goods that she purchases—until Equation 6-2 is satisfied for all pairs of products.

Is This Realistic? It may seem unrealistic to argue that consumers maximize utility in the precise way we have described. After all, not many of us stand in the aisles of a store and compute ratios of marginal utilities and prices. Keep in mind, though, that utility theory is used by economists to predict how consumers will behave when faced with such events as changing prices and incomes. As long as consumers seek to do the best they can for themselves with their limited resources, the consumer's actual thought process does not concern us. The theory is not meant to be a description of *how* they reach their decisions but is rather a convenient way of discovering the *implications* of their maximizing behaviour. Like many theories, utility-maximization theory leads to predictions that can be tested empirically. Economists continue to use the theory of utility maximization because its predictions are rarely rejected by the data. One of the most important of these predictions is that consumers who act as if they are following a rule like Equation 6-2 have negatively sloped demand curves for goods and services. In the next section we derive this result.

The Consumer's Demand Curve

To derive the consumer's demand curve for a product, we need to ask what happens when there is a change in the price of that product. As an example, let us derive Alison's demand curve for fruit juice. Consider Equation 6-2 and let *X* represent juice and *Y* represent *all other products taken together*. In this case, the price of *Y* is interpreted as the average price of all other products. What will Alison do if, with all other prices remaining constant, there is an increase in the price of juice? Alison cannot avoid suffering some loss in utility—whereas her income is unchanged, it costs more to buy each juice and the same to buy each unit of everything else. She might decide to spend less on everything else and increase her spending on juice in order to hold her juice consumption constant. But she can do better than that. To see why, notice that when the price of juice rises, the right side of Equation 6-2 increases. But, until Alison adjusts consumption, the left side is unchanged. Thus, after the price changes but before Alison reacts, the following situation exists:

$$\frac{MU \text{ of juice}}{MU \text{ of } Y} < \frac{\text{Price of juice}}{\text{Price of } Y}$$

What does Alison do to restore the equality? The hypothesis of diminishing marginal utility tells us that as she buys fewer bottles of juice, the *marginal* utility of juice will rise and thereby increase the ratio on the left side. Thus, in response to an increase in the price of juice, with all other prices constant, Alison reduces her consumption of juice until the marginal utility of juice rises sufficiently that Equation 6-2 is restored. (See Study Exercise #5 on page 140 to work through a specific numerical example.)

This analysis leads to the basic prediction of demand theory:

> **A rise in the price of a product (with all other determinants of demand held constant) leads each consumer to reduce the quantity demanded of the product.**

Market Demand Curves

If this is what each consumer does, it is also what all consumers taken together do. Thus, the theory of consumer behaviour that we have considered here predicts a negatively sloped market demand curve in addition to a negatively sloped demand curve for each individual consumer.

As we first saw in Chapter 3, market demand curves show the relationship between the product's price and the amount demanded by all consumers together. The market demand curve is the horizontal sum of the demand curves of individual consumers. It is the horizontal sum because we want to add quantities demanded at a given price, and quantities are measured in the horizontal direction on a conventional demand curve.

Figure 6-2 illustrates a market made up of only two consumers: Arun and Bashira. At a price of $3, Arun purchases 2 units and Bashira purchases 4 units; thus, together they purchase 6 units, yielding one point on the market demand curve. No matter how many consumers are involved, the process is the same: Add the quantities demanded by all consumers at each price, and the result is the market demand curve.

FIGURE 6-2 Market and Individual Demand Curves

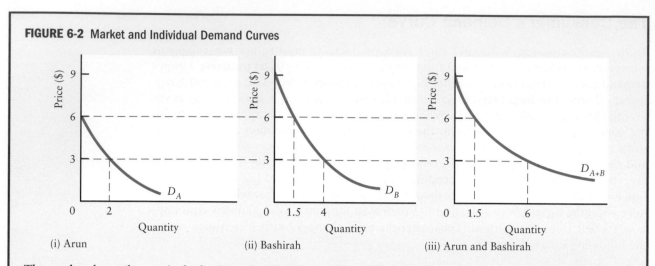

(i) Arun   (ii) Bashirah   (iii) Arun and Bashirah

The market demand curve is the horizontal sum of the individual demand curves. At any given price, the quantity demanded by Arun is added to the quantity demanded by Bashira to yield the total quantity demanded by the market. However large the number of consumers in the market, the derivation of the market demand curve follows the same summation process.

6.2 Income and Substitution Effects of Price Changes

We have just seen the relationship between the *law of diminishing marginal utility* and the slope of the consumer's demand curve for some product. Here we consider an alternative method for thinking about the slope of an individual's demand curve. This alternative method can also be used to think about the slope of a market demand curve.

Let's consider Tristan, a student who loves to eat—and especially loves to eat ice cream. A fall in the price of ice cream affects Tristan in two ways. First, it provides an incentive to buy more ice cream (and less of other things) because eating ice cream is now a cheaper way to satisfy some of his cravings. Thus, a reduction in the price of ice cream—which, with all other prices constant means a fall in the *relative* price of ice cream—leads Tristan to *substitute* away from other products toward ice cream.

Second, because the price of ice cream has fallen, Tristan has more *purchasing power* or **real income** available to spend on all products. Suppose the price of premium ice cream fell from $5 to $4 per litre and Tristan was in the habit of eating half a litre of ice cream a day. In the course of a 30-day month, Tristan could keep his ice cream habit unchanged but save $15, money that would be available for any purpose—more ice cream, blueberry muffins, rounds of mini golf, or photocopies of your economics notes.

Let's now explore these two separate effects in a little more detail.

real income Income expressed in terms of the purchasing power of money income—that is, the quantity of goods and services that can be purchased with the money income.

The Substitution Effect

To isolate the effect of the change in relative price when the price of ice cream falls, we can consider what would happen if we also reduce Tristan's money income to restore the original purchasing power. Suppose Tristan's uncle sends him a monthly allowance for ice cream, and when the price of ice cream falls, the allowance is reduced by $15 so that Tristan can buy just as much ice cream—and everything else—as he could before. Tristan's purchasing power will be unchanged. If his behaviour remains unchanged, however, he will no longer be maximizing his utility. Recall that utility maximization requires that the ratio of marginal utility to price be the same for all goods. In our example, with no change in behaviour, the quantities (and hence marginal utilities) and the prices of all goods other than ice cream are unchanged. The quantity of ice cream is also unchanged, but the price has fallen. To maximize his utility after the price of ice cream falls, Tristan must therefore increase his consumption (reduce his marginal utility) of ice cream and reduce his consumption of other goods. In other words, he must *substitute* away from other goods and toward ice cream.

When purchasing power is held constant, the change in the quantity demanded of a good whose relative price has changed is called the **substitution effect** of the price change.[2]

> **substitution effect** The change in the quantity of a good demanded resulting from a change in its relative price (holding real income constant).

> The substitution effect increases the quantity demanded of a good whose price has fallen and reduces the quantity demanded of a good whose price has risen.

The Income Effect

To examine the substitution effect, we reduced Tristan's *money* income following the price reduction so that we could see the effect of the relative price change, holding purchasing power constant. Now we want to see the effect of the change in purchasing power, *holding relative prices constant at their new value.* To do this, suppose that after Tristan has adjusted his purchases to the new price and his reduced income, he then calls his uncle and pleads to have his allowance restored to its original (higher) amount. Tristan's uncle agrees, and Tristan's money income is returned to its original level. If we assume that ice cream is a normal good, Tristan will increase his consumption of ice cream (even beyond the increase we have already seen as a result of the substitution effect). The change in the quantity of ice cream demanded as a result of Tristan's reaction to increased real income is called the **income effect.**

> **income effect** The change in the quantity of a good demanded resulting from a change in real income (holding relative prices constant).

> The income effect leads consumers to buy more of a product whose price has fallen, provided that the product is a normal good.

Notice that the size of the income effect depends on the amount of income spent on the good whose price changes and on the amount by which the price changes. In our example, if Tristan were initially spending half of his income on ice cream, a reduction

---

[2] This measure, which isolates the substitution effect by holding the consumer's purchasing power constant, is known as the Slutsky effect. A related but slightly different measure that holds the consumer's level of utility constant is discussed in the appendix to this chapter.

in the price of ice cream from \$5 to \$4 would be equivalent to a 10 percent increase in real income (20 percent of 50 percent). Now consider a different case: The price of gasoline falls by 20 percent. For a consumer who was spending 5 percent of income on gas, this is equivalent to a 1 percent increase in real income (20 percent of 5 percent).

The Slope of the Demand Curve

We have now divided Tristan's reaction to a change in the price of ice cream into a substitution effect and an income effect. Of course, when the price changes, Tristan moves directly from the initial consumption pattern to the final one; we do not observe any "halfway" consumption pattern. However, by breaking this movement into two parts for analytical purposes, we are able to study Tristan's total change in quantity demanded as a response to a change in relative prices plus a response to a change in real income.

What is true for Tristan is also true, in general terms, for all consumers. The substitution effect leads consumers to increase their demand for goods whose prices fall. The income effect leads consumers to buy more of all normal goods whose prices fall.

Putting the income and substitution effects together gives the following statement of the law of demand:

> Because of the combined operation of the income and substitution effects, the demand curve for any normal good will be negatively sloped. Thus, a fall in price will increase the quantity demanded.

Figure 6-3 illustrates how the combination of the substitution effect and the income effect determines the slope of any demand curve. In each part of the figure, we begin at point A with the price p_0. We then consider a reduction in the price to p_1. In each case, the substitution effect (shown by the green arrow) increases the quantity demanded. In each case there is also an income effect (the red arrow), but the size and sign of the income effect differs in each case. The sum of the income and substitution effects determines the total effect of the price change and thus how overall quantity demanded responds to the price reduction. Note that all normal goods have negatively sloped demand curves. The same is true for *most* inferior goods. The figure illustrates why in the case of an inferior good the income effect must be very strong in order to generate a positively sloped demand curve. This is a very rare case in economics, but there is some interesting history behind it.

Giffen Goods Great interest was generated by the apparent refutation of the law of demand by the English economist Sir Robert Giffen (1837–1910). He is alleged to have observed that when a rise in the price of imported wheat led to an increase in the price of bread, members of the British working class *increased* their consumption of bread, suggesting that their demand curve for bread was positively sloped.

As is clear in Figure 6-3, two things must be true in order for a good to have a positively sloped demand curve—a so-called **Giffen good**. First, the good must be an inferior good, meaning that a reduction in real income leads households to purchase *more* of that good. Second, the good must take a large proportion of total household expenditure and therefore have a large income effect. Bread was indeed a dietary staple of the British working classes during the nineteenth century. A rise in the price of bread

Giffen good An inferior good for which the income effect outweighs the substitution effect so that the demand curve is positively sloped.

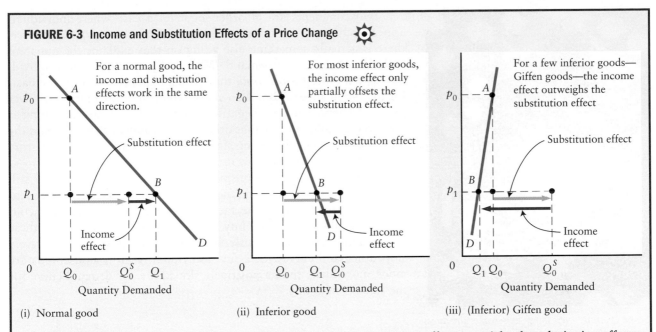

FIGURE 6-3 Income and Substitution Effects of a Price Change

For a normal good, the income and substitution effects work in the same direction.

For most inferior goods, the income effect only partially offsets the substitution effect.

For a few inferior goods—Giffen goods—the income effect outweighs the substitution effect

(i) Normal good

(ii) Inferior good

(iii) (Inferior) Giffen good

Demand curves for inferior goods are negatively sloped unless the income effect outweighs the substitution effect. In each of the diagrams, the initial price is p_0 and the initial quantity demanded is Q_0. Thus, A is a point on all three demand curves. For all three goods, a price reduction to p_1 creates a substitution effect that increases quantity demanded to Q_0^S.

For normal goods in part (i), the reduction in price increases real income and leads to a further increase in quantity demanded. The income effect is shown as the increase from Q_0^S to Q_1. The total effect of the price change is therefore the change from Q_0 to Q_1, and point B is on the negatively sloped demand curve.

For inferior goods, the price reduction causes an increase in real income that leads to a reduction in quantity demanded. If the good makes up a small fraction of the consumer's total expenditure, which is the case for most goods, then this income effect will be small. In part (ii), the income effect reduces quantity demanded from Q_0^S to Q_1, and so the total effect of the price change is the change from Q_0 to Q_1. In this case, the income effect does not fully offset the substitution effect and so the demand curve is still negatively sloped through point B. In part (iii), the income effect is very large, reducing quantity demanded from Q_0^S to Q_1, and the overall change is therefore a reduction in quantity demanded from Q_0 to Q_1. In this case the demand curve is positively sloped through point B. This is the case of a Giffen good.

would therefore cause a large reduction in people's real income. This could lead people to eat more bread (and less meat) in order to consume enough calories to stay alive. Though possible, such cases are all but unknown in the modern world, for in all but the poorest societies, typical households do not spend large proportions of their incomes on any single inferior good.

Conspicuous Consumption Goods Thorstein Veblen (1857–1929), in *The Theory of the Leisure Class*, noted that some products were consumed not for their intrinsic qualities but because they had "snob appeal." He suggested that the more expensive such a commodity became, the greater might be its ability to confer status on its purchaser.

Consumers might value diamonds, for example, precisely because everyone knows they are expensive. Thus, a fall in price might lead them to stop buying diamonds and to switch to a more satisfactory object of conspicuous consumption. They may behave in the same way with respect to luxury cars, buying them *because* they are expensive. Does this sort of behaviour violate our basic theory of utility maximization?

Some people buy very expensive products because their extreme prices confer status on the purchaser. But holding this status constant, people would still probably buy more at lower prices, suggesting a downward-sloping demand curve.

Two comments are in order. First, in a case where individuals appear to buy more goods at a higher price *because of the high price,* there is actually something else going on that explains the apparent violation of the law of demand. What really appeals to such individuals is that *other people think* they paid a high price—this is the basis for the "snob appeal." But such snobs would still buy more at a lower price (and hence still have negatively sloped demand curves) as long as they were absolutely sure that other people *thought* they had paid the high price. As one advertising slogan for a discount department store puts it, "Only you know how little you paid."

Second, even if such conspicuous consumers do exist, it is still unlikely that the *market* demand curve is positively sloped. The reason is easy to discover. The fact that countless lower-income consumers would be glad to buy diamonds or BMWs only if these commodities were sufficiently inexpensive suggests that positively sloped demand curves for a few individual wealthy households are much more likely than a positively sloped *market* demand curve for the same commodity.

6.3 Consumer Surplus

Our discussion of consumer behaviour has led us to a better understanding of demand curves and how they are derived. At the heart of our discussion has been the concept of utility and the law of diminishing marginal utility.

In this section we introduce the important concept of *consumer surplus,* which requires that we make a clear distinction between *marginal* and *total* utility. Understanding this difference will help us to resolve a famous paradox in the history of economic theory.

The Concept

Imagine yourself facing an either/or choice concerning some particular product, say, ice cream: You can have the amount you are now consuming, or you can have none of it. Suppose you would be willing to pay as much as $100 per month for the eight litres of gourmet ice cream that you now consume, rather than do without it. Further, suppose you actually buy those eight litres for only $40 instead of $100. What a bargain! You have paid $60 less than the most you were willing to pay. Actually this sort of bargain occurs every day in the economy. Indeed, it is so common that the $60 "saved" in this example has been given a name: *consumer surplus.* **Consumer surplus** is the difference between the total value that consumers place on all the units consumed of some product and the payment they actually make to purchase that amount of the product.

Consumer surplus is a direct consequence of negatively sloped demand curves. This is easiest to understand if you think of an individual's demand curve as showing his or her willingness to pay for successive units of the product. (You may recall our discussion of this point in Chapter 5.) To illustrate the concept, suppose we have

consumer surplus The difference between the total value that consumers place on all units consumed of a commodity and the payment that they actually make to purchase that amount of the commodity.

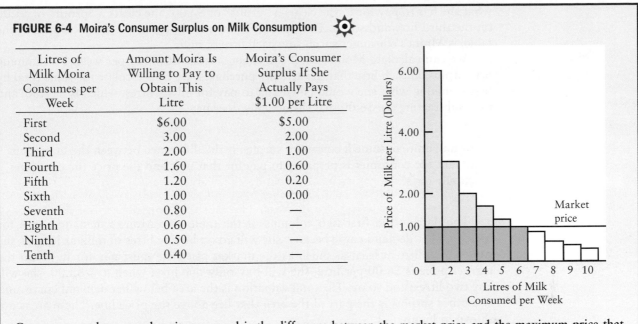

FIGURE 6-4 Moira's Consumer Surplus on Milk Consumption

Litres of Milk Moira Consumes per Week	Amount Moira Is Willing to Pay to Obtain This Litre	Moira's Consumer Surplus If She Actually Pays $1.00 per Litre
First	$6.00	$5.00
Second	3.00	2.00
Third	2.00	1.00
Fourth	1.60	0.60
Fifth	1.20	0.20
Sixth	1.00	0.00
Seventh	0.80	—
Eighth	0.60	—
Ninth	0.50	—
Tenth	0.40	—

Consumer surplus on each unit consumed is the difference between the market price and the maximum price that the consumer is willing to pay to obtain that unit. The table shows the value that Moira puts on successive litres of milk consumed each week. Her negatively sloped demand curve shows that she would be willing to pay progressively smaller amounts for each additional unit consumed. If the market price is $1.00 per litre, Moira will buy six litres of milk per week and pay the amount in the dark shaded area. The total value she places on these six litres is the entire shaded area. Her consumer surplus is the light shaded area.

interviewed your classmate Moira and displayed the information from the interview in the table in Figure 6-4. Our first question to Moira is, "If you were drinking no milk at all, how much would you be willing to pay for one litre per week?" With no hesitation she replies, "$6.00." We then ask, "If you had already consumed that one litre, how much would you be willing to pay for a second litre per week?" After a bit of thought, she answers, "$3.00." Adding one litre per week with each question, we discover that she would be willing to pay $2.00 to get a third litre per week and $1.60, $1.20, $1.00, $0.80, $0.60, $0.50, and $0.40 for successive litres from the fourth to the tenth litre per week.

The sum of the values that she places on each litre of milk gives us the *total value* that she places on all ten litres. In this case, Moira values the 10 litres of milk per week at $17.10. This is the amount that she would be willing to pay if she faced the either/or choice of 10 litres or none. This is also the amount she would be willing to pay if she were offered the milk one litre at a time and charged the maximum she was willing to pay for each litre.

However, Moira does not have to pay a different price for each litre of milk she consumes each week; she can buy all she wants at the prevailing market price. Suppose the price is $1.00 per litre. She will buy six litres per week because she values the sixth litre just at the market price but all earlier litres at higher amounts. She does not buy a seventh litre because she values it at less than the market price.

Because Moira values the first litre at $6.00 but gets it for $1.00, she makes a "profit" of $5.00 on that litre. Between her $3.00 valuation of the second litre and what she has to pay for it, she clears a "profit" of $2.00. She clears a "profit" of $1.00 on the third litre and so on. This "profit," which is shown in the third column of the table, is Moira's consumer surplus on each litre of milk.

We can calculate Moira's total consumer surplus of $8.80 per week by summing her surplus on each litre that she actually purchases; we can calculate the same total by first summing what she would be willing to pay for all six litres, which is $14.80, and then subtracting the $6.00 that she actually does pay.

> **For any unit consumed, consumer surplus is the difference between the maximum amount the consumer is prepared to pay for that unit and the price the consumer actually pays.**

The data in the first two columns of the table give Moira's demand curve for milk. It is her demand curve because she will go on buying litres of milk as long as she values each litre at least as much as the market price she must pay for it. When the market price is $6.00 per litre, she will buy only one litre; when it is $3.00, she will buy two litres; and so on. The total valuation is the area below her demand curve, and consumer surplus is the part of the area that lies above the price line. These areas are shown in Figure 6-4.

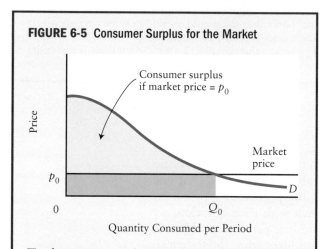

FIGURE 6-5 Consumer Surplus for the Market

Total consumer surplus is the area under the demand curve and above the price line. The area under the demand curve shows the total valuation that consumers place on all units consumed. For example, the total value that consumers place on Q_0 units is the entire shaded area under the demand curve up to Q_0. At a market price of p_0, the amount paid for Q_0 units is the dark shaded area. Hence, consumer surplus is the light shaded area.

Figure 6-5 shows that the same relationship holds for the smooth market demand curve that indicates the total amount that all consumers would buy at each price. Figure 6-4 is a bar chart because we allowed Moira to vary her consumption only in discrete units of one litre at a time. Had we allowed her to vary her consumption of milk one drop at a time, we could have traced out a continuous curve similar to the one shown in Figure 6-5.

> **The market demand curve shows the valuation that consumers place on each unit of the product. For any given quantity, the area under the demand curve and above the price line shows the consumer surplus received from consuming those units.**

The Paradox of Value

Consumer surplus is an important concept. It will prove useful in later chapters when we evaluate the performance of the market system.[3] For now, however, we discuss an example in which the concept of consumer surplus helps us to understand apparently paradoxical market outcomes. The distinction between total value and marginal value is crucial.

Early economists, struggling with the problem of what determines the relative prices of products, encountered what they called the *paradox of value*. Many necessary

[3] Indeed, consumer surplus is part of what, in Chapter 5, we called economic surplus when we discussed market efficiency. We will return to a detailed discussion of market efficiency in Chapter 12.

products, such as water, have prices that are low compared with the prices of luxury products, such as diamonds. Water is necessary to our existence, whereas diamonds are used mostly for luxury purposes and are not in any way essential to life. Isn't it odd, then, that water is so cheap and diamonds are so expensive? As it took a long time to resolve this apparent paradox, it is not surprising that even today, similar confusions cloud many policy discussions.

The first step in resolving this paradox is to use the distinction between the total and marginal values of any product. We have seen already that the area under the demand curve is a measure of the *total value* placed on all the units that the consumer consumes. For example, for all consumers together, the total value of consuming Q_0 units is the entire shaded area (light and dark) under the demand curve in Figure 6-5.

What about the *marginal value* that consumers place on one additional unit? This is given by the product's market price, which is p_0 in Figure 6-5. Facing a market price of p_0, each consumer buys all the units that he or she values at p_0 or greater but does not purchase any units valued at less than p_0. Therefore, each consumer values the last unit consumed of any product at its market price.

The second step in resolving the paradox is to recognize that supply plays just as important a role in determining market price as does demand. Early economists thought the price or "value" of a product depended only on its use by consumers—that is, by demand. But we now know that supply aspects are just as important—including the costs of production, the number of producers, and so on.

Given this joint importance of supply and demand, it is easy to imagine a situation in which two products, such as water and diamonds, have very different market prices (and hence *marginal* values) even if their respective prices do not reflect the *total* value consumers place on the two goods. Figure 6-6 resolves the diamond–water paradox.

The resolution of the paradox of value is that a good that is very plentiful, such as water, will have a low price and will thus be consumed to the point where all consumers place a low value on the last unit consumed, whether or not they place a high value on their *total* consumption of the product. By contrast, a product that is relatively scarce in the marketplace will have a high market price, and consumption will therefore stop at a point where consumers place a high value on the last unit consumed, regardless of the value that they place on their total consumption of the good.

Because the market price of a product depends on both demand and supply, there is nothing paradoxical in there being a product on which consumers place a high *total* value (such as water) selling for a low price and hence having a low *marginal* value.

The same paradox exists in many markets, including labour markets. As we all know, professional hockey players earn many times more than nurses and doctors, even though most consumers probably place more total value on health care than they do on sports entertainment. But top-quality hockey players have a set of skills that are in much shorter supply than even highly skilled medical professionals, and this difference in supply helps to explain their different incomes. We have much more to say about the operation of labour markets in Chapters 13 and 14.

FIGURE 6-6 Resolving the Paradox of Value

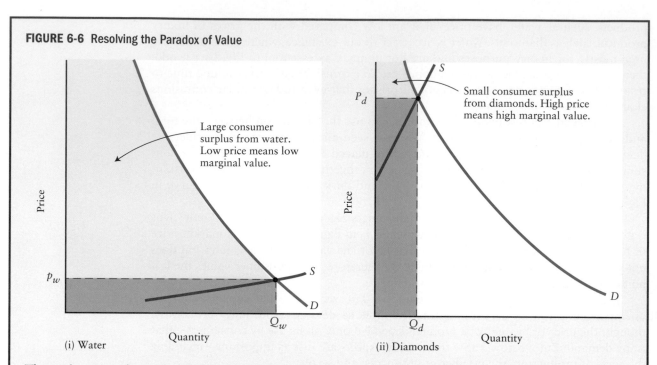

(i) Water

(ii) Diamonds

The market price of a product does not just reflect the total value that consumers place on that product; supply also matters. The graph presents hypothetical demand curves for water and diamonds. The total value that consumers place on Q_w units of water, as shown by the total shaded area under the demand curve, is great. The total value that consumers place on Q_d units of diamonds is shown by the total shaded area under the demand curve for diamonds. This is clearly less than the total value placed on water.

The large supply of water makes water plentiful and makes water low in price, as shown by p_w in part (i) of the figure. The relatively low supply of diamonds makes diamonds scarce and keeps diamonds high in price, as shown by p_d in part (ii) of the figure. The high total value for water, combined with its low price, leads to a large consumer surplus for water. For diamonds, the low total value and high price lead to a small consumer surplus.

SUMMARY

6.1 Marginal Utility and Consumer Choice

LO 1, 2

- Marginal utility theory distinguishes between the total utility from the consumption of all units of some product and the incremental (or marginal) utility derived from consuming one more unit of the product.
- The basic assumption in marginal utility theory is that the utility consumers derive (over some given time period) from the consumption of successive units of a product diminishes as the number of units consumed increases.
- Consumers are assumed to make their decisions in a way that maximizes their utility. Utility-maximizing consumers make their choices such that the utilities derived from the last dollar spent on each product are equal. For two goods X and Y, utility will be maximized when

$$\frac{MU_X}{p_X} = \frac{MU_Y}{p_Y}$$

- Demand curves have negative slopes because when the price of one product falls, each consumer responds by increasing purchases of that product sufficiently to restore the ratio of that product's marginal utility to its now lower price (MU/p) to the same level achieved for all other products.
- Market demand curves for any product are derived by horizontally summing all of the individual demand curves for that product.

6.2 Income and Substitution Effects of Price Changes   LO 3

- A change in the price of a product generates both an income effect and a substitution effect. The substitution effect is the reaction of the consumer to the change in relative prices, with purchasing power (real income) held constant. The substitution effect leads the consumer to increase purchases of the product whose relative price has fallen.
- The income effect is the reaction of the consumer to the change in purchasing power (real income) that is caused by the price change, holding relative prices constant at their new level. A fall in one price will lead to an increase in the consumer's real income and thus to an increase in purchases of all normal goods.
- The combined income and substitution effects ensure that the quantity demanded of any normal good will increase when its price falls, other things being equal. Normal goods, therefore, have negatively sloped demand curves.
- An inferior good will have a negatively sloped demand curve unless the income effect is strong enough to outweigh the substitution effect. This situation is very rare and is called a Giffen good.

6.3 Consumer Surplus   LO 4, 5

- For each unit of a product, consumer surplus is the difference between what consumers would be willing to pay for that unit and what consumers actually pay for that unit.
- Consumer surplus arises because demand curves are negatively sloped and consumers purchase units of a product up to the point where the value of the marginal unit consumed—the marginal value—equals the market price. On all units before the marginal unit, consumers value the product more than the price and hence they earn consumer surplus.
- It is important to distinguish between total and marginal values because choices concerning a bit more and a bit less cannot be predicted from a knowledge of total values. The paradox of value involves confusion between total value and marginal value.
- Price is related to the marginal value that consumers place on having a bit more or a bit less of some product; it bears no necessary relationship to the total value that consumers place on all of the units consumed of that product.

KEY CONCEPTS

Total utility and marginal utility
Utility maximization
Equality of MU/p across different goods

Slope of the demand curve
Market and individual demand curves
Income effect and substitution effect

Giffen goods and conspicuous consumption goods
Consumer surplus
The paradox of value

STUDY EXERCISES

MyEconLab Make the grade with MyEconLab: Study Exercises marked in red can be found on MyEconLab. You can practise them as often as you want, and most feature step-by-step guided instructions to help you find the right answer.

1. Fill in the blanks to make the following statements correct.
   a. Utility theory is based on the hypothesis that the _____ received from each additional unit of the good _____ as total consumption of the good increases.
   b. A utility-maximizing consumer will allocate expenditure such that the _____ per dollar spent on each product is _____ for all products.

c. An equation that represents a utility-maximizing pattern of consumption of two goods, *A* and *B,* is _____.

d. Marginal utility analysis tells us that a rise in the price of a good, *ceteris paribus,* leads each consumer to reduce the _____ of the good. This, in turn, predicts a _____ demand curve.

2. The table below shows how Brett's utility increases as the number of avocados he consumes (per month) increases. Brett's utility is measured in utils, a name that economists invented to describe units of utility.

Avocados	Total Utility (in utils)	Marginal Utility (in utils)
Zero	0	
First	100	____
Second	185	____
Third	245	____
Fourth	285	____
Fifth	315	____
Sixth	335	____
Seventh	345	____
Eighth	350	____

a. Plot Brett's total utility on a scale diagram, with utils on the vertical axis and the number of avocados (per month) on the horizontal axis.

b. Compute the marginal utility for each avocado and fill in the table.

c. Plot the marginal utility on a scale diagram, with utils on the vertical axis and the number of avocados (per month) on the horizontal axis. (Make sure to plot marginal utility at the midpoints between units.)

d. Explain why it is reasonable that Brett's utility increases by smaller and smaller amounts for each successive avocado consumed.

3. In each of the cases listed below, identify whether Claudia's expenditure on each product should rise or fall in order to maximize her utility.

Case	Price of X ($)	Marginal Utility of X (units of utility)	Price of Y ($)	Marginal Utility of Y (units of utility)
A	10	2	5	3
B	12	4	4	2
C	3	1	6	2
D	4	2	4	2
E	8	4	4	3

4. Rupert really loves pizza, but he eventually tires of it. The table below shows the highest price that Rupert is willing to pay for each successive pizza per week.

Pizza	Rupert's Willingness to Pay
First	$18
Second	$16
Third	$13
Fourth	$9
Fifth	$4
Sixth	$0

a. Suppose Rupert were to eat five pizzas per week. What is the total value Rupert would place on his five weekly pizzas?

b. If the market price is $10 per pizza, how many pizzas will Rupert buy and eat per week?

c. If the market price is $10 per pizza, what is the weekly consumer surplus that Rupert gets from eating pizza?

5. Sally consumes only two goods, shoes and "everything else." For five different shopping trips (each with different prices), the prices and Sally's marginal utilities are shown below.

	Shoes		Everything Else	
	MU	Price ($)	MU	Price ($)
Trip 1	125	250	50	100
Trip 2	100	200	50	100
Trip 3	75	150	50	100
Trip 4	50	100	50	100
Trip 5	25	50	50	100

a. Is Sally maximizing her total utility on each shopping trip? Explain why or why not.

b. Using what you have learned in this chapter about marginal utility, explain how the number of shoes consumed is changing as their price changes.

c. Can you detect the shape of Sally's demand curve for shoes from the data shown in the table?

6. Suppose there is a 10 percent increase in the prices of the following products. Keeping in mind how large a fraction of a typical consumer's budget these items are, explain whether you think the income effect in each case would be small or large, and why.

a. salt
b. jeans
c. canned vegetables
d. gasoline
e. mini-vans
f. rental apartments
g. luxury cars
h. cell phones
i. vacations to Cuba
j. fee for one-day car rentals

7. Use the following diagram of a market for potted plants to answer the questions below about consumer surplus.

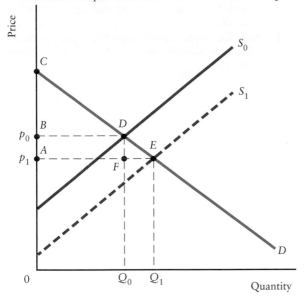

a. With demand curve D and supply curve S_0, the equilibrium price and quantity in this market are p_0 and Q_0. At the price p_0, what is the area that represents total consumer surplus in this market? (Use the letter point labels to describe the area.)

b. Now suppose supply increases to S_1. Determine the new equilibrium price and quantity. What is the area that now represents total consumer surplus?

c. At the new lower price, what is the area that represents the increased consumer surplus earned on the original units purchased?

d. At the new lower price, what is the area that represents consumer surplus earned on the new units purchased?

8. In what situations do the substitution effect and the income effect work in the same direction to produce a downward-sloping demand curve? In what situations do they have opposing effects?

9. See the diagrams at the bottom of the page. Consider the supply-and-demand diagrams depicting the markets for X and Y, respectively. In the market for good X, supply is perfectly elastic, indicating that producers are prepared to supply any amount of X at price p_0.

a. In the market for X, demand increases from D_0 to D_1. Explain what happens to the total value that consumers place on X.

b. Explain how the increase in demand for X alters the marginal value that consumers place on X.

c. In the market for Y, a technological improvement causes supply to increase from S_0 to S_1, causing price to fall from p_0 to p_1. Explain what happens to the total value that consumers place on a given quantity of Y.

d. Explain why the increase in supply leads consumers to reduce their marginal value of Y even though there has been no change in their preferences regarding Y (and thus no shift in the demand curve).

10. Consider the market for some product. The demand and supply curves are given by:

$$\text{Demand: } p = 30 - 4Q^D$$
$$\text{Supply: } p = 6 + 2Q^S$$

a. Plot the demand and supply curves on a scale diagram. Compute the equilibrium price (p^*) and quantity (Q^*).

b. Show in the diagram the total value that consumers place on Q^* units of the good.

c. What is the value that consumers place on an additional unit of the good?

d. Now suppose that production costs fall, and thus the market supply curve shifts to a new position given by $p = 2 + 2Q^S$. How do consumers now value an additional unit of the good?

e. Explain why consumers' marginal value has fallen even though there has been no change in their preferences (and thus no change in the demand curve).

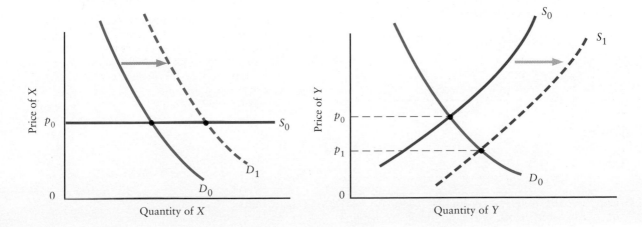

11. Using marginal utility theory, discuss why newspaper publishers are prepared to use vending machines that allow customers to pay for one newspaper and remove several, whereas candy and soft-drink producers use vending machines that allow customers to remove only the single product that is purchased.

12. Many medical and hospital services in Canada are provided at zero direct cost to all Canadians and are financed out of general government revenues.

a. What would be the marginal value of such services consumed by each Canadian if the government provided the necessary resources to satisfy all demand?

b. How does your answer to part (a) relate to the total value that Canadians probably place on medical services?

Indifference Curves

In Chapter 6, we covered some basic material concerning the theory of demand; here we extend the treatment of demand theory by considering in more detail the assumptions about consumer behaviour that underlie the theory of demand.

The history of demand theory has seen two major breakthroughs. The first was marginal utility theory, which we used in Chapter 6. By distinguishing total and marginal values, this theory helped to explain the so-called paradox of value. The second breakthrough came with indifference theory, which showed that the stringent assumption of measurable utility (required for marginal utility theory) could be dispensed with. Indifference theory is based on the much weaker assumption that consumers can always say which of two consumption bundles they prefer without having to say by how much they prefer it.

6A.1 Indifference Curves

Suppose Hugh currently has available some specific bundle of goods, say, 18 units of clothing and 10 units of food. Now offer him an alternative bundle of, say, 13 units of clothing and 15 units of food. This alternative combination of goods has 5 fewer units of clothing and 5 more units of food than the first one. Whether Hugh prefers this new bundle depends on the relative valuation that he places on 5 more units of food and 5 fewer units of clothing. If he values the extra food more than the forgone clothing, he will prefer the new bundle to the original one. If he values the extra food less than the forgone clothing, he will prefer the original bundle. If Hugh values the extra food the same as the forgone clothing, he is said to be indifferent between the two bundles.

Suppose that after much trial and error, we have identified several bundles between which Hugh is indifferent. In other words, all bundles give him equal satisfaction or utility. They are shown in the table in Figure 6A-1.

Of course, there are combinations of the two products other than those enumerated in the table that will give Hugh the same level of utility. All of these combinations are shown in Figure 6A-1 by the smooth curve that passes through the points plotted from the table. This curve, called an indifference curve, shows all combinations of products that yield Hugh the same utility.

> The consumer is indifferent between the combinations indicated by any two points on one indifference curve.

Any points above the curve show combinations of food and clothing that Hugh prefers to points on the curve. Consider, for example, the combination of 20 units of food and 18 units of clothing, represented by point g in Figure 6A-1. Although it may not be obvious that this bundle must be preferred to bundle a (which has more clothing but less food), it is obvious that it will be preferred to bundle c because both less clothing and less food are represented at c than at g. Inspection of the graph shows that any point above the curve will be superior to some points on the curve in the sense that it will contain both more food and more clothing than those points on the curve. However, because all points on the curve are equal in Hugh's eyes, any point above the curve must be superior to all points on the curve. By a similar argument, all points below and to the left of the curve represent bundles that are inferior to bundles represented by points on the curve.

> Any point above an indifference curve is preferred to any point along that same indifference curve; any point on the curve is preferred to any point below it.

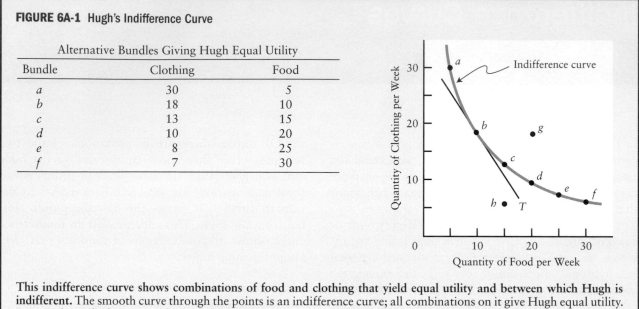

FIGURE 6A-1 Hugh's Indifference Curve

Alternative Bundles Giving Hugh Equal Utility

Bundle	Clothing	Food
a	30	5
b	18	10
c	13	15
d	10	20
e	8	25
f	7	30

This indifference curve shows combinations of food and clothing that yield equal utility and between which Hugh is indifferent. The smooth curve through the points is an indifference curve; all combinations on it give Hugh equal utility. Point *g* above the line is a preferred combination to any point on the line; point *h* below the line is an inferior combination to any point on the line. The slope of the line *T* gives the marginal rate of substitution at point *b*. Moving down the indifference curve from *b* to *f*, the slope flattens, showing that the more food and the less clothing Hugh has, the less willing he is to sacrifice further clothing to get more food.

Diminishing Marginal Rate of Substitution

How much clothing would Hugh be willing to give up to get one more unit of food but to keep his utility unchanged? The answer to this question measures what is called Hugh's marginal rate of substitution of clothing for food. The marginal rate of substitution (MRS) is the amount of one product that a consumer is willing to give up to get one more unit of another product.

> The first basic assumption of indifference theory is that the algebraic value of the MRS between two goods is always negative.

A negative MRS means that to increase consumption of one product, Hugh is prepared to decrease consumption of a second product. The negative value of the marginal rate of substitution is indicated graphically by the negative slope of indifference curves.

Consider a case in which Hugh has a lot of clothing and only a little food. Common sense suggests that he might be willing to give up quite a bit of plentiful clothing to get one more unit of scarce food. It suggests as well that if Hugh had little clothing and a lot of food he would be willing to give up only a little scarce clothing to get one more unit of already plentiful food.

This example illustrates the hypothesis of diminishing marginal rate of substitution. The less of one product, *A*, and the more of a second product, *B*, that the consumer has already, the smaller the amount of *A* that the consumer will be willing to give up to get one additional unit of *B*. The hypothesis says that the marginal rate of substitution changes when the amounts of two products consumed change. The graphical expression of this hypothesis is that any indifference curve becomes flatter as the consumer moves downward and to the right along the curve. In Figure Figure 6A-1, a movement downward and to the right means that Hugh is consuming less clothing and more food. The decreasing steepness of the curve means that

Hugh is willing to sacrifice less and less clothing to get each additional unit of food. [11]

> **Diminishing MRS is the second basic assumption of indifference theory.**

The hypothesis of diminishing marginal rate of substitution is illustrated in Table 6A-1, which is based on the example in Figure 6A-1. The last column of the table shows the rate at which Hugh is prepared to sacrifice units of clothing per unit of food obtained. At first, Hugh will sacrifice 2.4 units of clothing to get 1 unit more of food, but as his consumption of clothing diminishes and his consumption of food increases, Hugh becomes less and less willing to sacrifice further clothing for more food.

The Indifference Map

So far, we have constructed only a single indifference curve for Hugh. However, starting at any other point in Figure 6A-1, such as g, there will be other combinations that will give Hugh equal utility. If the points indicating all of these combinations are connected, they will form another indifference curve. This exercise can be repeated many times, and we can thereby generate many indifference curves for Hugh. The farther any indifference curve is from the origin, the higher will be the level of Hugh's utility given by any of the points on the curve.

A set of indifference curves is called an indifference map, an example of which is shown in Figure 6A-2. It specifies the consumer's tastes by showing his rate of substitution between the two products for every possible level of current consumption of these products.

> **When economists say that a consumer's tastes are given, they do not mean that the consumer's current consumption pattern is given; rather, they mean that the consumer's entire indifference map is given.**

TABLE 6A-1	Hugh's Marginal Rate of Substitution Between Clothing and Food		
Movement	(1) Change in Clothing	(2) Change in Food	(3) Marginal Rate of Substitution (1) ÷ (2)
From a to b	12	5	2.4
From b to c	5	5	1.0
From c to d	3	5	0.6
From d to e	2	5	0.4
From e to f	1	5	0.2

The marginal rate of substitution of clothing for food declines (in absolute value) as the quantity of food increases. This table is based on Figure 6A-1. When Hugh moves from a to b, he gives up 12 units of clothing and gains 5 units of food; he remains at the same level of overall utility. At point a, Hugh is prepared to sacrifice 12 units of clothing for 5 units of food (i.e., 12/5 = 2.4 units of clothing per unit of food obtained). When he moves from b to c, he sacrifices 5 units of clothing for 5 units of food (a rate of substitution of 1 unit of clothing for each unit of food).

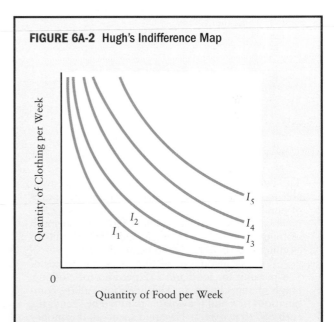

FIGURE 6A-2 Hugh's Indifference Map

An indifference map consists of a set of indifference curves. All points on a particular curve indicate alternative combinations of food and clothing that give Hugh equal utility. The farther the curve is from the origin, the higher is the level of utility it represents. For example, I_5 is a higher indifference curve than I_4, which means that all the points on I_5 give Hugh a higher level of utility than do the points on I_4.

6A.2 The Budget Line

Indifference curves illustrate consumers' tastes. To develop a complete theory of their choices, we must also illustrate the available alternatives. These are shown as the solid line *ab* in Figure 6A-3. That line, called a budget line, shows all the combinations of food and clothing that Hugh can buy if he spends a fixed amount of money, in this case his entire money income of $720 per week, at fixed prices of the products (in this case, $12 per unit for clothing and $24 per unit for food).

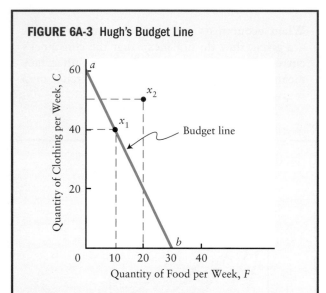

FIGURE 6A-3 Hugh's Budget Line

The budget line shows the quantities of goods available to a consumer given money income and the prices of goods. Any point in this diagram indicates a combination (or bundle) of so much food and so much clothing. Point x_1, for example, indicates 40 units of clothing and 10 units of food per week.

With an income of $720 a week and prices of $24 per unit for food and $12 per unit for clothing, Hugh's budget line is *ab*. This line shows all the combinations of *F* and *C* available to him if he spends the entire $720 per week. He could spend all this money income on clothing and obtain 60 units of clothing and zero food each week. Or he could go to the other extreme and purchase only food, buying 30 units of *F* and zero units of *C*. Hugh could also choose an intermediate position and consume some of both goods—for example, spending $240 to buy 10 units of *F* and $480 to buy 40 units of *C* (point x_1). Points above the budget line, such as x_2, are not attainable.

Properties of the Budget Line

The budget line has several important properties:

1. Points on the budget line indicate bundles of products that use up the consumer's entire income. (Try, for example, the point 20*C*, 20*F*.)

2. Points between the budget line and the origin indicate bundles of products that cost less than the consumer's income. (Try, for example, the point 20*C*, 10*F*.)

3. Points above the budget line indicate combinations of products that cost more than the consumer's income. (Try, for example, the point 30*C*, 40*F*.)

> The budget line shows all combinations of products that are available to the consumer given his money income and the prices of the goods that he purchases.

We can also show Hugh's alternatives with an equation that uses symbols to express the information contained in the budget line. Let *E* stand for Hugh's money income, which must be equal to his total expenditure on food and clothing. If p_F and p_C represent the money prices of food and clothing, respectively, and *F* and *C* represent the quantities of food and clothing that Hugh chooses, then his spending on food is equal to p_F times *F*, and his spending on clothing is equal to p_C times *C*. Thus the equation for the budget line is

$$E = p_F \times F + p_C \times C$$

The Slope of the Budget Line

Look again at Hugh's budget line in Figure 6A-3. The vertical intercept is 60 units of clothing, and the horizontal intercept is 30 units of food. Thus the slope is equal to 2. The minus sign means that increases in Hugh's purchases of one of the goods must be accompanied by decreases in his purchases of the other. The numerical value of the slope indicates how much of one good must be given up to obtain an additional unit of the other; in our example, the slope of 2 means that Hugh must forgo the purchase of 2 units of clothing to acquire 1 extra unit of food.

Recall that in Chapter 3 we contrasted the absolute, or money, price of a product with its relative price, which is the ratio of its absolute price to that of some other product or group of products. One important point is that the relative price determines the slope of the budget line. In terms of our example of food and clothing, the slope of the budget line is determined by the relative price of food in terms of clothing, p_F/p_C; with the price of food (p_F) at \$24 per unit and the price of clothing (p_C) at \$12 per unit, the slope of the budget line (in absolute value) is 2. [12]

The significance of the slope of Hugh's budget line for food and clothing is that it reflects his opportunity cost of food in terms of clothing. To increase food consumption while maintaining expenditure constant, Hugh must move along the budget line and therefore consume less clothing; the slope of the budget line determines how much clothing he must give up to obtain an additional unit of food.

> The opportunity cost of food in terms of clothing is measured by the (absolute value of the) slope of the budget line, which is equal to the relative price ratio, p_F/p_C.

In the example, with fixed income and with the relative price of food in terms of clothing (p_F/p_C) equal to 2, Hugh must forgo the purchase of 2 units of clothing to acquire 1 extra unit of food. The opportunity cost of a unit of food is thus 2 units of clothing. Notice that the relative price (in our example, $p_F/p_C = 2$) is consistent with an infinite number of absolute prices. If $p_F = \$40$ and $p_C = \$20$, it is still necessary to sacrifice 2 units of clothing to acquire 1 unit of food.[4] Thus relative, not absolute, prices determine opportunity cost.

6A.3 The Consumer's Utility-Maximizing Choices

An indifference map describes the preferences of a consumer, and a budget line describes the possibilities available to a consumer. To predict what a consumer will actually do, both sets of information must be combined, as is done in Figure 6A-4. Hugh's budget line is shown

---

[4] Of course, with a given income, Hugh can afford much less of each at these higher money prices, but the opportunity cost of food in terms of clothing remains unchanged.

by the straight line, and the curves from the indifference map are also shown. Any point on the budget line is attainable, but which point will Hugh actually choose?

Because Hugh wants to maximize utility, he wants to reach the highest attainable indifference curve. Inspection of Figure 6A-4 shows that if Hugh purchases any bundle on the budget line at a point cut by an indifference curve, he can reach a higher indifference curve. Only when the bundle purchased is such that the indifference curve is tangent to the budget line is it impossible for Hugh to reach a higher curve by altering his purchases.

> The consumer's utility is maximized at the point where an indifference curve is tangent to the budget line. At that point, the consumer's marginal rate of substitution for the two goods is equal to the relative prices of the two goods.

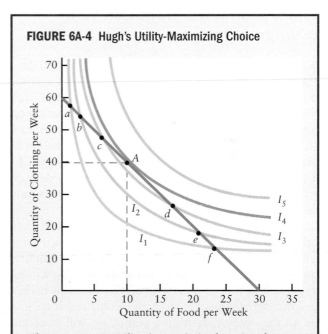

FIGURE 6A-4 Hugh's Utility-Maximizing Choice

The consumer's utility is maximized at A, where an indifference curve is tangent to the budget line. Hugh has a money income of \$720 per week and faces money prices of \$12 per unit for clothing and \$24 per unit for food. A combination of units of clothing and food indicated by point a on I_1 is attainable but, by moving along the budget line, Hugh can reach higher indifference curves. The same is true at b on I_2 and at c on I_3. At A, however, where an indifference curve (I_4) is tangent to the budget line, Hugh cannot reach a higher curve by moving along the budget line.

The intuitive explanation for this result is that if Hugh values goods differently from the way the market does, there is room for profitable exchange. Hugh can give up some of the good that he values relatively less than the market does and take in return some of the good that he values relatively more than the market does. When he is prepared to exchange goods at the same rate as they can be traded on the market, there is no further opportunity for him to raise utility by substituting one product for the other.

The theory thus proceeds by supposing that Hugh is presented with market prices that he cannot change and then by analyzing how he adjusts to these prices by choosing a bundle of goods such that, at the margin, his own subjective valuation of the goods coincides with the valuations given by market prices.

We will now use this theory to predict the typical consumer's response to a change in income and in prices.

The Consumer's Reaction to a Change in Income

A change in Hugh's money income will, *ceteris paribus*, shift his budget line. For example, if Hugh's income doubles, he will be able to buy twice as much of both food and clothing compared with any combination on his previous budget line. His budget line will therefore shift out parallel to itself to indicate this expansion in his consumption possibilities. (The fact that it will be a parallel shift is established by the previous demonstration that the slope of the budget line depends only on the relative prices of the two products.)

For each level of Hugh's income, there will be a utility-maximizing point at which an indifference curve is tangent to the relevant budget line. Each such utility-maximizing position means that Hugh is doing as well as possible at that level of income. If we move the budget line through all possible levels of income and if we join up all the utility-maximizing points, we will trace out what is called an income–consumption line, an example of which is shown in Figure 6A-5. This line shows how Hugh's consumption bundle changes as his income changes, with relative prices being held constant.

The Consumer's Reaction to a Change in Price

We already know that a change in the relative prices of the two goods changes the slope of the budget line. Given the price of clothing, for each possible price of

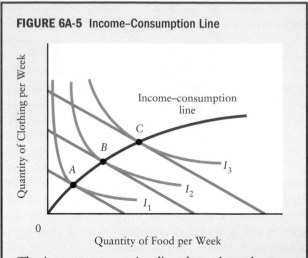

FIGURE 6A-5 Income–Consumption Line

The income–consumption line shows how the consumer's purchases react to a change in money income with relative prices being held constant. Increases in Hugh's money income cause a parallel outward shift of his budget line, moving his utility-maximizing point from A to B to C. By joining all the utility-maximizing points, Hugh's income–consumption line is traced out.

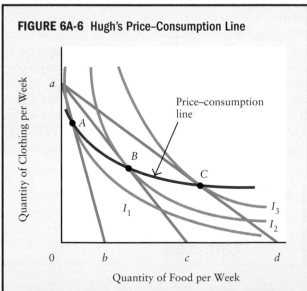

FIGURE 6A-6 Hugh's Price-Consumption Line

The price–consumption line shows how the consumer's purchases react to a change in one price with money income and other prices being held constant. Decreases in the price of food (with money income and the price of clothing held constant) pivot Hugh's budget line from *ab* to *ac* to *ad*. Hugh's utility-maximizing bundle moves from A to B to C. By joining all the utility-maximizing points, a price–consumption line is traced out, showing that Hugh purchases more food and less clothing as the price of food falls.

food there is a different utility-maximizing consumption bundle for Hugh. If we connect these bundles, at a given money income, we will trace out a price–consumption line, as shown in Figure 6A-6. Notice that in this example, as the relative prices of food and clothing change, the quantities of food and clothing that Hugh purchases also change. In particular, as the price of food falls, Hugh buys more food and less clothing.

6A.4 Deriving the Demand Curve

What happens to the consumer's demand for some product, say, gasoline, as the price of that product changes, holding constant the prices of all other goods?

If there were only two products purchased by consumers, we could derive a demand curve for one of the products from the price–consumption line like the one we showed for Hugh in Figure 6A-6. When there are many products, however, a change in the price of one product generally causes substitution toward (or away from) all other goods. Thus, we would like to have a simple way of representing the individual's tastes in a world of many products.

In part (i) of Figure 6A-7, a new type of indifference map is plotted in which litres of gasoline per month are measured on the horizontal axis and the value of all other goods consumed per month is plotted on the vertical axis. We have in effect used "everything but gasoline" as the second product. The indifference curves in this figure then show the rate at which the consumer is prepared to substitute gasoline for money (which allows him to buy all other goods) at each level of consumption of gasoline and of all other goods.

To illustrate the derivation of demand curves, we use the numerical example shown in Figure 6A-7. The consumer is assumed to have an after-tax money income of $4000 per month. This level of money income is plotted on the vertical axis, showing that if the consumer consumes no gasoline, he can consume $4000 worth of other goods each month. When gasoline costs $1.50 per litre, the consumer could buy a maximum of 2667 litres per month. This set of choices gives rise to the innermost budget line. Given the consumer's tastes, utility is maximized at point *A*, consuming 600 litres of gasoline and $3100 worth of other products.

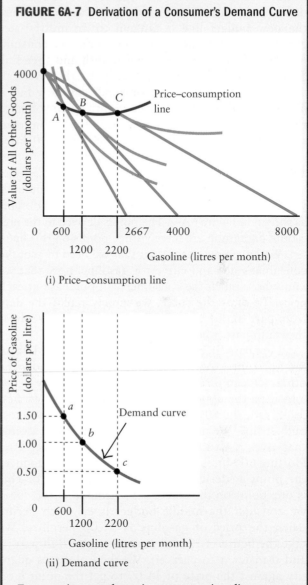

FIGURE 6A-7 Derivation of a Consumer's Demand Curve

(i) Price–consumption line

(ii) Demand curve

Every point on the price–consumption line corresponds to both a price of the product and a quantity demanded; this is the information required for a demand curve. In part (i), the consumer has a money income of $4000 and alternatively faces prices of $1.50, $1.00, and $0.50 per litre of gasoline, choosing positions *A*, *B*, and *C* at each price. The information for litres of gasoline demanded at each price is then plotted in part (ii) to yield the consumer's demand curve. The three points *a*, *b*, and *c* in part (ii) correspond to the points *A*, *B*, and *C* in part (i).

Next, let the price of gasoline fall to $1.00 per litre. Now the maximum possible consumption of gasoline is 4000 litres per month, giving rise to the middle budget line in the figure. The consumer's utility is maximized, as always, at the point where the new budget line is tangent to an indifference curve. At this point, B, the consumer is consuming 1200 litres of gasoline per month and spending $2800 on all other goods. Finally, let the price fall to 50 cents per litre. The consumer can now buy a maximum of 8000 litres per month, giving rise to the outermost of the three budget lines. The consumer maximizes utility by consuming 2200 litres of gasoline per month and spending $2900 on other products.

If we let the price vary over all possible amounts, we will trace out a complete price–consumption line, as shown in Figure 6A-7. The points derived in the preceding paragraph are merely three points on this line.

We have now derived all that we need to plot the consumer's demand curve for gasoline, now that we know how much the consumer will purchase at each price. To draw the curve, we merely replot the data from part (i) of Figure 6A-7 onto a demand graph, as shown in part (ii) of Figure 6A-7.

Like part (i), part (ii) has quantity of gasoline on the horizontal axis. By placing one graph under the other, we can directly transcribe the quantity determined on the upper graph to the lower one. We first do this for the 600 litres consumed on the innermost budget line. We now note that the price of gasoline that gives rise to that budget line is $1.50 per litre. Plotting 600 litres against $1.50 in part (ii) produces the point a, derived from point A in part (i). This is one point on the consumer's demand curve. Next we consider the middle budget line, which occurs when the price of gasoline is $1.00 per litre. We take the figure of 1200 litres from point B in part (i) and transfer it to part (ii). We then plot this quantity against the price of $1.00 to get the point b on the demand curve. Doing the same thing for point C yields the point c in part (ii): price 50 cents, quantity 2200 litres.

Repeating the operation for all prices yields the demand curve in part (ii). Note that the two parts of Figure 6A-7 describe the same behaviour. Both parts measure the quantity of gasoline on the horizontal axes; the only difference is that in part (i) the price of gasoline determines the slope of the budget line, whereas in part (ii) the price of gasoline is plotted explicitly on the vertical axis.

Income and Substitution Effects

The price–consumption line in part (i) of Figure 6A-7 indicates that as price decreases, the quantity of gasoline demanded increases, thus giving rise to the negatively sloped demand curve in part (ii). As we saw in Chapter 6, the key to understanding the negative slope of the demand curve is to distinguish between the income effect and the substitution effect of a change in price. We can make this distinction more precisely, and somewhat differently, by using indifference curves.

In Chapter 6, we examined the substitution effect of a reduction in price by eliminating the income effect. We did this by reducing money income until the consumer could just purchase the original bundle of goods. We then examined how the change in relative prices affected the consumer's choices. In indifference theory, however, the income effect is removed by changing money income until the original level of utility—the original indifference curve—can just be achieved. This method results in a slightly different measure of the income effect, but the principle involved in separating the total change into an income effect and a substitution effect is exactly the same as in Chapter 6.

The separation of the two effects according to indifference theory is shown in Figure 6A-8. The figure shows in greater detail part of the price–consumption line first drawn in Figure 6A-7. Points A_0 and A_2 are on the price–consumption line for gasoline; A_0 is the consumer's utility-maximizing point at the initial price, whereas A_2 is the consumer's utility-maximizing point at the new price.

We can think of the separation of the income and substitution effects as occurring in the following way. After the price of the good has fallen, we reduce money income until the original indifference curve can just be obtained. The consumer moves from point A_0 to an intermediate point A_1, and this response is defined as the substitution effect. Then, to measure the income effect, we restore money income. The consumer moves from the point A_1 to the final point A_2, and this response is defined as the income effect.

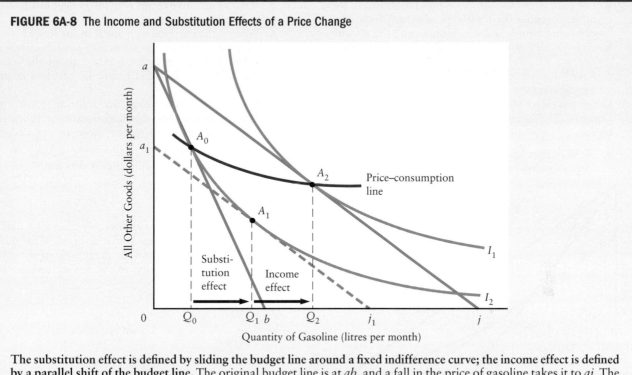

FIGURE 6A-8 The Income and Substitution Effects of a Price Change

The substitution effect is defined by sliding the budget line around a fixed indifference curve; the income effect is defined by a parallel shift of the budget line. The original budget line is at ab, and a fall in the price of gasoline takes it to aj. The original utility-maximizing point is at A_0 with Q_0 of gasoline being consumed, and the new utility-maximizing point is at A_2 with Q_2 of gasoline being consumed. To remove the income effect, imagine reducing the consumer's money income until the original indifference curve is just attainable. We do this by shifting the line aj to a parallel line nearer the origin $a_1 j_1$ that just touches the indifference curve that passes through A_0. The intermediate point A_1 divides the quantity change into a substitution effect $Q_0 Q_1$ and an income effect $Q_1 Q_2$.

STUDY EXERCISES

1. Consider Katie's preferences for magazines and ice cream cones. Several "consumption bundles" are shown in the table below.

Bundle	Ice Cream Cones	Magazines
a	9	0
b	7	2
c	6	2
d	5	3
e	4	4
f	4	3
g	3	4
h	2	6
i	0	6

a. On a scale diagram with the quantity of ice cream cones on the vertical axis and the quantity of magazines on the horizontal axis, plot the various bundles.

b. Suppose that Katie is indifferent between bundles c and i. She is also indifferent between bundles d, g, and h, but all three of these are preferred to c or i. Finally, suppose that, of the bundles shown in the table, bundle e is Katie's favourite. Draw three indifference curves showing this information.

c. Consider bundles e, f, and g. What can you conclude about how Katie would rank these bundles?

2. Continue with Katie from the previous question. Katie has a monthly allowance of $36 that she chooses to divide between magazines and ice cream cones. Magazines cost $6 each and ice cream cones cost $4 each.

a. For each of the consumption bundles shown in the table, compute the total expenditure. Which ones can Katie afford, and which ones can't she afford?

b. Draw Katie's budget line. What is the slope of the line?

c. Given Katie's monthly budget constraint, which bundle does she choose to maximize her utility?

3. Debra travels to Mexico and enjoys both burritos and Coronas. The diagram shows her utility-maximizing choices.

a. If the budget line is line 1, describe why point A is Debra's utility-maximizing choice.

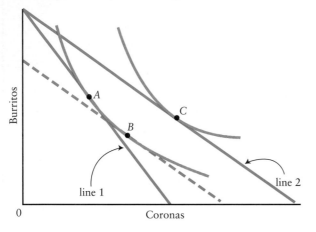

b. What event can explain why the budget line moves to line 2?

c. What is the meaning of point B in the figure?

d. Suppose Coronas are a normal good for Debra. What does this restriction imply about the location of point C? Is this restriction satisfied in the diagram?

e. Suppose Coronas were an inferior good for Debra. How would this information be reflected in her choice following the move of the budget line to line 2?

4. Consider your sets of indifference curves for

   i. Coke and chips
   ii. Coke and Pepsi

Explain why these sets of indifference curves are likely to look different. Illustrate with a diagram. What does this difference imply about the magnitude of the substitution effects in response to changes in the price of Coke?

Producers in the Short Run

LEARNING OBJECTIVES (LO)

After studying this chapter, you will be able to

1 identify the various forms of business organization and discuss the different ways that firms can be financed.

2 distinguish between accounting profits and economic profits.

3 understand the relationships among total product, average product, and marginal product; and the law of diminishing marginal returns.

4 explain the difference between fixed and variable costs, and the relationships among total costs, average costs, and marginal costs.

IN Chapter 6, we went behind the demand curve to understand how it is determined by the behaviour of consumers. In this chapter and the next, we go behind the supply curve to understand how it is determined by the behaviour of firms.

We begin by comparing the firms that we see in the real world with those that appear in economic theory. Next we introduce the concepts of costs, revenues, and profits, and we outline the key role that profits play in determining the allocation of the nation's resources. To determine the most profitable quantity for a firm to produce and supply to the market, we need to see how its costs vary with its output.

When examining the relationship between output and cost, *time* plays an important role. In this chapter, we focus on the short run, where a firm can change only some of its inputs, and output is governed by the famous "law of diminishing returns." In the next chapter we examine the firm's behaviour in the long run—when all the firm's inputs are variable—and in the very long run—when the state of technology changes. There we encounter "scale economies" and firms' incentives for research and development.

7.1 What Are Firms?

We start by taking a brief look at the concept of a firm. How are firms organized? How are they financed? What are their goals?

Organization of Firms

A firm can be organized in any one of six different ways.

single proprietorship A firm that has one owner who is personally responsible for the firm's actions and debts.

ordinary partnership A firm that has two or more joint owners, each of whom is personally responsible for the firm's actions and debts.

limited partnership A firm that has two classes of owners: general partners, who take part in managing the firm and are personally liable for the firm's actions and debts, and limited partners, who take no part in the management of the firm and risk only the money that they have invested.

corporation A firm that has a legal existence separate from that of the owners.

state-owned enterprise A firm that is owned by the government. In Canada, these are called *Crown corporations*.

non-profit organizations Firms that provide goods and services with the objective of just covering their costs. These are often called NGOs, for non-governmental organizations.

multinational enterprises (MNEs) Firms that have operations in more than one country.

1. A **single proprietorship** has one owner–manager who is personally responsible for all aspects of the business, including its debts.

2. An **ordinary partnership** has two or more joint owners, each of whom is personally responsible for all the partnership's debts.

3. The **limited partnership**, which is less common than an ordinary partnership, provides for two types of partners. *General partners* take part in the running of the business and are liable for all the firm's debts. *Limited partners* take no part in the running of the business, and their liability is limited to the amount they actually invest in the enterprise.

4. A **corporation** is a firm regarded in law as having an identity of its own; its owners are not personally responsible for anything that is done in the name of the firm, though its directors may be. The shares of a *private* corporation are not traded on any stock exchange (such as the Toronto or New York Stock Exchanges), whereas the shares of a *public* corporation are.

5. A **state-owned enterprise** is owned by the government but is usually under the direction of a more or less independent, state-appointed board. Although its ownership differs, the organization and legal status of a state-owned enterprise are similar to those of a corporation. In Canada, such state-owned enterprises are called *Crown corporations*.

6. **Non-profit organizations** are established with the explicit objective of providing goods or services to customers but having any profits that are generated remain with the organization and not claimed by individuals. In many cases, some goods or services are sold to consumers while others are provided free of charge. Non-profit firms therefore earn their revenues from a combination of sales and donations. An example is your local YMCA—it sells memberships to consumers for use of the health facilities, but it also provides free services to needy individuals in the community.

Firms that have locations in more than one country are often called **multinational enterprises (MNEs)**. Having locations in several countries is very unusual for single proprietorships and ordinary partnerships, but is common for limited partnerships (such as large law and accounting firms) and very common for large corporations. The number and importance of MNEs have increased greatly over the last few decades. A large amount of international trade represents business transactions of MNEs—between different corporations, as well as between different regional operations of the same corporation. MNEs thus play an increasing role in the ongoing process of globalization.

Finally, note that not all production in the economy takes place within firms. Many government agencies provide goods and services, such as defence, roads, primary and secondary education, and health-care services. In most of these cases, goods and services are provided to citizens without charging directly for their use; costs are financed through the government's general tax revenues.

Financing of Firms

The money a firm raises for carrying on its business is sometimes called its financial capital, as distinct from its real capital, which is the firm's physical assets, such as factories, machinery, offices, fleets of vehicles, and stocks of materials and finished goods. Although the use of the term *capital* to refer to both an amount of money and a quantity of goods can be confusing, it will usually be clear from the context which sense is being used.

The basic types of financial capital used by firms are *equity* and *debt*. Equity is the funds provided by the owners of the firm. Debt is the funds borrowed from creditors (individuals or institutions) outside the firm.

Equity In individual proprietorships and partnerships, one or more owners provide much of the required funds. A corporation acquires funds from its owners in return for stocks, shares, or equities (as they are variously called). These are basically ownership certificates. The money goes to the company and the shareholders become owners of the firm, risking the loss of their money and gaining the right to share in the firm's profits. Profits that are paid out to shareholders are called **dividends**.

> **dividends** Profits paid out to shareholders of a corporation.

One easy way for an established firm to raise money is to retain current profits rather than paying them out to shareholders. Financing investment from such *retained earnings* adds to the value of the firm and hence raises the market value of existing shares.

Debt The firm's creditors are not owners; they have lent money in return for some form of loan agreement, or IOU. Firms often borrow from commercial banks or other financial institutions, who channel money from their depositors to interested borrowers. Firms can also choose to borrow money directly from non-bank lenders, with whom there are many possible types of loan agreements, which are collectively called *debt instruments* in the business world and **bonds** in economic theory. Each has its own set of characteristics and its own name. Two characteristics are, however, common to all loan agreements. First, they carry an obligation to repay the amount borrowed, called the *principal* of the loan. Second, they carry an obligation to make some form of payment to the lender called *interest*. The time at which the principal is to be repaid is called the *redemption date* of the debt. The amount of time between the issue of the debt and its redemption date is called its *term*.

> **bond** A debt instrument carrying a specified amount, a schedule of interest payments, and (usually) a date for redemption of its face value.

Many firms raise money by issuing shares and selling them to interested investors. For example, in 1928 the Canadian Pacific Railway Company (which still exists today) raised funds by issuing this share certificate and selling it to Westminster Bank, Ltd.

Goals of Firms

The theory of the firm that we study in this book is based on two key assumptions about firm behaviour. First, all firms are assumed to be profit-maximizers, seeking to

APPLYING ECONOMIC CONCEPTS 7-1

Is It Socially Responsible to Maximize Profits?

In recent years there has been growing public discussion of the need for firms, especially large ones, to behave in a socially responsible manner. Advocates of this view start from the position that unadorned capitalism, and the associated goal of profit maximization, does not serve the broader public interest: corporate profits clearly help firms' shareholders, but the public interest is not being served. In this view, corporate social responsibility must involve more than simply maximizing profits.

Others argue that firms should indeed focus on the goal of maximizing profits and that, by doing so, they are providing significant benefits to their customers and their employees, not just their shareholders. In addition, it is the pursuit of profits that leads firms to develop new products and production methods, innovations that lie at the heart of ongoing improvements in overall living standards. This opposing view is grounded in the same insight of Adam Smith's that we saw in Chapter 1—that the pursuit of private gain creates benefits for society as a whole.

What about corporate profits generated through a production process that damages the environment? Surely there are costs imposed on society when firms, through their profit-maximizing decisions, are led to emit poisonous effluents into the air or into local waterways. Or how about firms—such as investment banks or mortgage brokers—making unethical business decisions and thereby earning profits at the expense of other parties? Isn't simple profit maximization in these cases socially irresponsible?

One response is that it is the duty of governments to set rules in the public interest and then leave firms free to maximize their profits within the constraints set by those rules. For example, the government can design and enforce environmental, labour, banking, accounting, and tax regulations deemed to be in the public interest. Faced with these laws and regulations, private firms are then free to take whatever action is expected to maximize their profits; violations of the established laws or regulations will be met with appropriate penalties. Such a division of responsibilities—the government setting the rules and the firms maximizing profits within the implied constraints—recognizes that although private firms are usually not good judges of the public interest, they are quite good at making decisions about how best to use scarce resources in order to satisfy consumers' desires. Government policymakers, through a process that involves consultation with various groups in society, and the trading off of competing demands, are usually better placed to judge what is and is not in the overall public interest.

This position still recognizes two methods for modifying corporate behaviour. Those who believe that certain corporate actions are not in the public interest can try to convince policymakers to design new rules that will make it costly for firms to continue such actions. Various non-governmental organizations (NGOs), ranging from environmental organizations to consumer-advocacy groups, can play an important role in identifying and publicizing poor corporate behaviour, and also in lobbying the government

---

To see what the Canadian Council of Chief Executives thinks about "corporate citizenship," go to www. ceocouncil.ca *and click on "Issues" and then "Corporate and Public Governance."*

One Canadian magazine is devoted entirely to discussing and identifying socially responsible corporate behaviour. See www. corporateknights.ca.

make as much profit for their owners as possible. Second, each firm is assumed to be a single, consistent decision-making unit.

Recall from Chapter 2 that assumptions are used to simplify a theory so that economists can focus on the essential aspects of the issue. These two specific assumptions allow the theory to ignore both the firm's internal organization and its financial structure. Using these assumptions, economists can predict the behaviour of firms. To do this, they first study the choices open to the firm, establishing the effect that each choice would have on the firm's profits. They then predict that the firm will select the alternative that produces the largest profits.

Is maximizing profit the only thing firms care about? In recent years there has been much public discussion of the need for firms to be "socially responsible" in addition to being motivated by the pursuit of profits. Some people argue that every firm has a responsibility to society that goes well beyond the responsibility to its shareholders. Others disagree and argue that by maximizing profits, firms are providing a valuable service to society. For a discussion of both sides of this interesting debate, see *Applying Economic Concepts 7-1*.

for change. If the case is persuasive, and sufficient public pressure can be brought to bear on the policymakers, policies will eventually be changed. An example is the relatively recent design of environmental protection policies. Many years ago, Canadian firms could pollute the environment with impunity, whereas today many types of pollution are illegal and some emissions are closely monitored by government agencies. Another more recent example is the push by governments for improved financial-market regulation following the global financial crisis of 2008–2009 that caused a major world-wide recession.

A second way that firms can be encouraged to change their behaviour is through the expression of consumers' preferences in the marketplace. If enough consumers dislike a certain activity by a specific firm, and these views can be expressed clearly enough in terms of consumers' demand for the firm's products, the firm may be convinced to change its behaviour. In this case, new laws or regulations may not be required; the firm decides, on the basis of the possible decline in sales it will suffer if it continues its unpopular activities, that a change in its behaviour is required for profit maximization. An example occurred in the mid-1990s when Nike was heavily criticized for contracting its production to Asian "sweatshops," where workers were treated very poorly. A widespread boycott of Nike products began and Nike eventually responded by improving working conditions and allowing independent monitors into its factories. The threat of a loss of sales was so powerful that competing companies Reebok and Adidas, who had not yet attracted

There is considerable debate about whether profit-maximizing firms can be "socially responsible."

any negative publicity, began making improvements in their factories just to prevent being tarred by the Nike brush.

What is the bottom line? Corporations *do* change their behaviour over time—in response to changes in laws and regulations, and in response to changes in consumer attitudes. If governments can be relied upon to establish and enforce rules and regulations in the public interest, and consumers continue to actively express their preferences through their decisions in the marketplace, then firms may be able to be socially responsible and profit seeking at the same time.

7.2 Production, Costs, and Profits

We must now specify a little more precisely the concepts of production, costs, and profits that are used by economists.

Production

In order to produce the goods or services that it sells, each firm needs inputs. Hundreds of inputs enter into the production of any specific output. Among the many inputs entering into car production, for example, are steel, rubber, spark plugs, electricity, the site of the factory, machinists, accountants, spray-painting machines, forklift trucks, lawyers, and managers. These inputs can be grouped into four broad categories:

- inputs that are outputs from some other firm, such as spark plugs, electricity, and steel

- inputs that are provided directly by nature, such as the land owned or rented by the firm

- inputs that are the services of workers and managers employed by the firm

- inputs that are the services of physical capital, such as the facilities and machines used by the firm

intermediate products All outputs that are used as inputs by other producers in a further stage of production.

The items that make up the first group of inputs are called **intermediate products** because they are the output of one firm but the input for another. If these intermediate products are traced back to their sources, all production can be accounted for by the services of the other three kinds of input, which we first discussed in Chapter 1 and which are called *factors of production*. These are the gifts of nature, such as soil and raw materials, called *land*; physical and mental efforts provided by people, called *labour*; and factories, machines, and other human-made aids to production, called *capital*.

production function A functional relation showing the maximum output that can be produced by any given combination of inputs.

The **production function** describes the technological relationship between the inputs that a firm uses and the output that it produces. In terms of functional notation, a simplified production function (in which we ignore the role of land) is written as

$$Q = f(L, K)$$

where Q is the flow of output, K is the flow of capital services, and L is the flow of labour services.[1] f is the production function itself. Changes in the firm's technology, which alter the relationship between inputs and output, are reflected by changes in the function f.

The robotic equipment used inside an auto assembly plant is an example of capital. These machines deliver a flow of capital services to the firm that uses them.

Costs and Profits

The production function specifies the *maximum* amount of output that can be obtained from any given amounts of inputs. Firms arrive at what they call *profits* by taking the revenues they obtain from selling their output and subtracting all the costs associated with their inputs. When all costs have been correctly deducted, the resulting profits are the return to the owners' financial investment in the firm.

Economic Versus Accounting Profits Compared with accountants, economists use somewhat different concepts of costs and profits. When accountants measure profits, they begin with the firm's revenues and then subtract all of the *explicit* costs incurred by the firm. By explicit costs, we mean the costs that actually involve a purchase of goods or services by the firm. The obvious explicit costs include the hiring of workers, the rental of equipment, interest payments on debt, and the purchase of intermediate inputs.[2]

Accounting profits = Revenues − Explicit costs

---

[1] Remember that production is a flow: it is so many units per period of time. For example, when we say that production rises from 100 to 101 units, we mean that the rate of production has risen from 100 units each period to 101 units each period.

[2] *Depreciation* is also among the firm's explicit costs, even though it does not involve a market transaction. Depreciation is a cost to the firm that arises because of the wearing out of its physical capital.

Like accountants, economists subtract from revenues all explicit costs, but they also subtract some *implicit* costs that accountants ignore. These are items for which there is no market transaction but for which there is still an opportunity cost for the firm that should be included in the complete measure of costs. The two most important implicit costs are the opportunity cost of the owner's time (over and above his or her salary) and the opportunity cost of the owner's capital (including a possible risk premium). When this more complete set of costs is subtracted from the firm's revenues, the result is called **economic profit** and is sometimes called *pure profit*.

$$\text{Economic profits} = \text{Revenues} - (\text{Explicit costs} + \text{Implicit costs})$$
$$= \text{Accounting profits} - \text{Implicit costs}$$

economic profits The difference between the revenues received from the sale of output and the opportunity cost of the inputs used to make the output. Negative economic profits are called economic losses.

Opportunity Cost Of Time. Especially in small and relatively new firms, owners spend a tremendous amount of their time developing the business. Often they pay themselves far less than they could earn if they were instead to offer their labour services to other firms. For example, an entrepreneur who opens a restaurant may pay herself only $1000 per month while she is building her business, even though she could earn $4000 per month in her next best alternative job. In this case, there is an *implicit* cost to her firm of $3000 per month that would be missed by the accountant who measures only the explicit cost of her wage at $1000 per month.[3]

Opportunity Cost Of Financial Capital. What is the opportunity cost of the financial capital that owners have tied up in a firm? This question applies equally to small, owner-operated businesses and to large corporations. The answer is best broken into two parts. First, ask what could be earned by lending this amount to someone else in a riskless loan. The owners could have purchased a government bond, which has no significant risk of default. Suppose the return on this is 4 percent per year. This amount is the risk-free rate of return on capital. It is clearly an opportunity cost, since the firm could close down operations, lend out its money, and earn a 4 percent return. Next, ask what the firm could earn in addition to this amount by lending its money to another firm where risk of default was equal to the firm's own risk of loss. Suppose this is an additional 3 percent. This is the risk premium, and it is clearly also a cost. If the firm does not expect to earn this much in its own operations, it could close down and lend its money out to some equally risky firm and earn 7 percent (4 percent pure return plus 3 percent risk premium).

Economists include both implicit and explicit costs in their measurement of profits, whereas accounting profits include only explicit costs. Economic profits are therefore less than accounting profits.

Table 7-1 compares economic and accounting profits for a hypothetical owner-operated firm that produces gourmet soups. In that example, both accounting profits and economic profits are positive (though accounting profits are larger). Another possibility, however, is that a firm has positive *accounting* profits even though it has zero *economic* profits. If a firm's *accounting* profits represent a return just equal to what is available if the owner's capital and time were used elsewhere, then opportunity costs

---

[3] For larger firms that are not operated by their owners, this element of implicit costs is not relevant because the owners usually do not work at the firm. In these cases, the salaries to the firm's managers appear in the firm's accounts as explicit costs.

TABLE 7-1 Accounting Versus Economic Profit for Ruth's Gourmet Soup Company

Total Revenues ($)		2000
Explicit Costs ($)		
Wages and Salaries	500	
Intermediate Inputs	400	
Rent	80	
Interest on Loan	100	
Depreciation	80	
Total Explicit Costs	1160	
Accounting Profit		840
Implicit Costs ($)		
Opportunity Cost of Owner's Time	160	
Opportunity Cost of Owner's $1500 Capital		
(a) risk-free return of 4%	60	
(b) risk premium of 3%	45	
Total Implicit Costs	265	
Economic Profit		575

Economic profits are less than accounting profits because of implicit costs. The table shows a simplified version of a real profit-and-loss statement. Accounting profits are computed as revenues minus explicit costs (including depreciation), and in the table are equal to $840 for the period being examined. When the correct opportunity cost of the owner's time (in excess of what is recorded in wages and salaries) and capital are recognized as implicit costs, the firm appears less profitable. Economic profits are still positive but equal only $575.

are just being covered. In this case, there are zero *economic* profits, even though the firm's accountant will record positive profits.

Is one of these concepts better than the other? No. Firms are interested in the return to their owners, which is what they call *profits*. They must also conform with tax laws, which define profits in the same way. In contrast, economists are interested in how profits affect resource allocation; their definition is best for that purpose and is the definition used throughout this book. Let's see why economic profit is a useful concept when thinking about resource allocation.

Profits and Resource Allocation When resources are valued by the opportunity-cost principle, their costs show how much these resources would earn if used in their best alternative uses. If the revenues of all the firms in some industry exceed opportunity cost, the firms in that industry will be earning pure or economic profits. Hence, the owners of factors of production will want to move resources into the industry, because the earnings available to them are greater there than in alternative uses. If, in some other industry, firms are incurring economic losses, some or all of this industry's resources are more highly valued in other uses, and owners of the resources will want to move them to those other uses.

> Economic profits and losses play a crucial signalling role in the workings of a free-market system.

Economic profits in an industry are the signal that resources can profitably be moved into that industry. Losses are the signal that the resources can profitably be moved elsewhere. Only if there are zero economic profits is there no incentive for resources to move into or out of an industry. We will examine the role of profits and losses in determining industry entry and exit in Chapters 9 and 10.

Profit-Maximizing Output

To develop a theory of supply, we need to determine the level of output that will maximize a firm's profit, to which we give the symbol π (the lowercase Greek letter pi). This is the difference between the total revenue (TR) each firm derives from the sale of its output and the total cost (TC) of producing that output:

$$\pi = TR - TC$$

Thus, what happens to profits as output varies depends on what happens to both revenues and costs.[4] In the rest of this chapter, we develop a theory of how costs vary with output when the firm has some inputs that are fixed. In the next chapter, we allow all inputs to be fully variable. The theory that we develop about costs and output is common to all firms. In the chapters that follow, we consider how revenue varies with output. Costs and revenues are then combined to determine the profit-maximizing choices for firms in various market situations. The resulting theory can then be used to predict the outcome of changes in such things as demand, costs, taxes, and subsidies. This may seem like quite a long route to get to a theory of supply, and it is, but the payoff when we get there is in being able to understand and evaluate a great deal of economic behaviour.

Time Horizons for Decision Making

Economists classify the decisions that firms make into three types: (1) how best to use existing plant and equipment—the *short run*; (2) what new plant and equipment and production processes to select, given known technical possibilities—the *long run*; and (3) how to encourage, or adapt to, the development of new techniques—the *very long run*.

The Short Run The **short run** is a time period in which the quantity of some inputs, called **fixed factors**, cannot be changed. A fixed factor is usually an element of capital (such as plant and equipment), but it might be land, the services of management, or even the supply of skilled labour. Inputs that are not fixed but instead can be varied in the short run are called **variable factors**.

The short run does not correspond to a specific number of months or years. In some industries, it may extend over many years; in others, it may be a matter of months or even weeks. In the electric power industry, for example, it takes three or more years to acquire and install a steam turbine generator. An unforeseen increase in demand will involve a long period during which the extra demand must be met with the existing capital equipment. In contrast, a car mechanic's shop may be able to acquire new equipment in a few weeks. An increase in demand will have to be met with the existing stock of capital for only a brief time, after which it can be adjusted to the level made desirable by the higher demand.

short run A period of time in which the quantity of some inputs cannot be increased beyond the fixed amount that is available.

fixed factor An input whose quantity cannot be changed in the short run.

variable factor An input whose quantity can be changed over the time period under consideration.

> The short run is the length of time over which some of the firm's factors of production are fixed.

The Long Run The **long run** is a time period in which all inputs may be varied but in which the basic technology of production cannot be changed. Like the short run, the long run does not correspond to a specific length of time.

The long run corresponds to the situation the firm faces when it is planning to go into business, to expand the scale of its operations, to branch out into new products or new areas, or to change its method of production. The firm's *planning decisions* are

long run A period of time in which all inputs may be varied, but the existing technology of production cannot be changed.

---

[4] From this point on in this book, all costs include both explicit and implicit costs, and thus profits are economic rather than accounting profits.

long-run decisions because they are made from given technological possibilities but with freedom to choose from a variety of production processes that will use factor inputs in different proportions.

> The long run is the length of time over which all of the firm's factors of production can be varied, but its technology is fixed.

very long run A period of time that is long enough for the technological possibilities available to a firm to change.

The Very Long Run Unlike the short run and the long run, the **very long run** is a period of time in which the technological possibilities available to a firm will change. Modern industrial societies are characterized by continually changing technologies that lead to new and improved products and production methods.

> The very long run is the length of time over which all the firm's factors of production and its technology can be varied.

For the remainder of this chapter, we consider costs and production in the short run. We continue with our simplified situation in which there are only two factors of production—labour and capital. We will assume that capital is the fixed factor whereas labour is the variable factor. In the next chapter, we explore the firm's decisions in the long run and the very long run.

7.3 Production in the Short Run

Consider a Regina-based company producing specialty wooden skateboards. The firm owns a small factory with the necessary machinery and equipment—this is the firm's stock of capital, and we will assume that it is fixed in quantity. We call these the *fixed* factors of production. The firm also purchases intermediate inputs, such as wood, glue, and electricity, and, of course, hires workers. The intermediate inputs and the labour services are the firm's *variable* inputs.

In the following discussion, we will focus on the relationship between the firm's use of labour and the firm's production of skateboards. In particular, we want to know—with a fixed amount of capital—how output changes as the firm varies its amount of labour. To simplify the discussion at the outset, we will assume that all of the firm's capital is used all of the time. Thus, when output is varied, more or less labour is applied to a constant amount of capital. (The case in which the firm can "idle" some of its capital by letting it sit unused is considered later in *Extensions in Theory 7-1* on page 171.) The table in Figure 7-1 shows three different ways of looking at how output varies with the quantity of labour services.

Total, Average, and Marginal Products

total product (TP) Total amount produced by a firm during some time period.

Total product (*TP*) is the total amount that is produced during a given period of time. Total product will change as more or less of the variable factor is used in conjunction with the given amount of the fixed factor. This variation is shown in columns 1 and 2

FIGURE 7-1 Total, Average, and Marginal Products in the Short Run

Quantity of Labour (L)	Total Product (TP)	Average Product $\left(AP = \dfrac{TP}{L}\right)$	Marginal Product $\left(MP = \dfrac{\Delta TP}{\Delta L}\right)$
(1)	(2)	(3)	(4)
0	0		
			3
1	3	3	
			4
2	7	3.5	
			6
3	13	4.3	
			9
4	22	5.5	
			13
5	35	7.0	
			20
6	55	9.2	
			25
7	80	11.4	
			18
8	98	12.3	
			9
9	107	11.9	
			6
10	113	11.3	
			4
11	117	10.6	
			2
12	119	9.9	

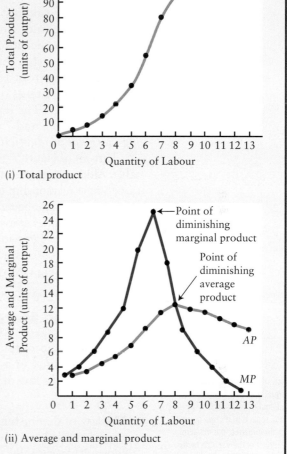

(i) Total product

(ii) Average and marginal product

The relation of output to changes in the quantity of the variable factor (labour) can be looked at in three different ways. As the quantity of labour increases, total output increases, as shown in column 2. The average product in column 3 is found by dividing the total product in column 2 by the quantity of labour shown in the corresponding row of column 1. The marginal product is shown between the rows because it refers to the change in output from one level of labour input to another. The curves are plotted from the data in the table. In part (i), the *TP* curve shows the total product steadily rising, first at an increasing rate, then at a decreasing rate. This causes both the average and the marginal product curves in part (ii) to rise at first and then decline. Where *AP* reaches its maximum, *MP* = *AP*.

of the table in Figure 7-1. Part (i) of Figure 7-1 plots the schedule from the table. (The shape of the curve will be discussed shortly.)

   Average product (*AP*) is the total product divided by the number of units of the variable factor used to produce it. If we let the number of units of labour be denoted by *L*, the average product is given by

$$AP = \frac{TP}{L}$$

   Notice in column 3 of the table that as more labour is used, average product first rises and then falls. The level of labour input at which average product reaches a maximum (8 units of labour in the example) is called the *point of diminishing average productivity.* Up to that point, average product is increasing; beyond that point, average product is decreasing.

average product (*AP*) Total product divided by the number of units of the variable factor used in its production.

marginal product (MP) The change in total output that results from using one more unit of a variable factor.

Marginal product *(MP)* is the *change* in total product resulting from the use of one additional unit of labour. [13] Recalling that the Greek letter Δ (delta) means "the change in," marginal product is given by

$$MP = \frac{\Delta TP}{\Delta L}$$

Computed values of marginal product are shown in column 4 of the table in Figure 7-1. The values in this column are placed between the other rows of the table to stress that the concept refers to the *change* in output caused by the *change* in quantity of the variable factor. For example, the increase in labour from 3 to 4 units ($\Delta L = 1$) increases output from 13 to 22 ($\Delta TP = 9$). Thus, the *MP* equals 9, and it is recorded between 3 and 4 units of labour. Note that *MP* in the table first rises and then falls as output increases. The level of labour input at which marginal product reaches a maximum (between 6 and 7 units of labour in this example) is called the *point of diminishing marginal productivity.*

Part (ii) of Figure 7-1 plots the average product and marginal product curves from the table. Although three different curves are shown in Figure 7-1, they are all aspects of the same single relationship described by the production function. As we vary the quantity of labour, with capital being fixed, output changes. Sometimes it is interesting to look at total product, sometimes at average product, and sometimes at the marginal product.

We will see later in this chapter that understanding firms' costs requires understanding how total, average, and marginal products are related to one another. We now turn to examining two aspects of this relationship.

Diminishing Marginal Product

The variations in output that result from applying more or less of a variable factor to a given quantity of a fixed factor are the subject of a famous economic hypothesis, referred to as the **law of diminishing returns**.

law of diminishing returns The hypothesis that if increasing quantities of a variable factor are applied to a given quantity of fixed factors, the marginal product of the variable factor will eventually decrease.

> **The law of diminishing returns states that if increasing amounts of a variable factor are applied to a given quantity of a fixed factor (holding the level of technology constant), eventually a situation will be reached in which the marginal product of the variable factor declines.**

Notice in Figure 7-1 that the marginal product curve rises at first and then begins to fall with each successive increase in the quantity of labour.

The common sense explanation of the law of diminishing returns is that in order to increase output in the short run, more and more of the variable factor is combined with a given amount of the fixed factor. As a result, each unit of the variable factor has less and less of the fixed factor to work with. When the fixed factor is capital and the variable factor is labour, each worker (or worker hour) gets a declining amount of capital to assist it in producing more output. It is not surprising, therefore, that sooner or later, equal increases in work effort eventually begin to add less and less to total output.

To illustrate the concept, consider the number of workers in our skateboard manufacturing firm, which has only a given amount of factory space and machinery. If there is only one worker, that worker must do all the tasks, shifting from one to another and becoming competent at each. As a second, third, and subsequent workers are added, each can specialize in one task, becoming expert at it. One can cut the wood into the required pieces, the second can glue the pieces together, a third worker can do the necessary planing and sanding, while a fourth worker attaches the wheels. This process, as we noted in Chapter 1, is called the *division of labour*. If additional workers allow more efficient divisions of labour, marginal product will rise: each newly hired worker will add more to total output than each previous worker did. However, according to the law of diminishing returns, when there is only an unchanging amount of physical capital the scope for such increases must eventually disappear, and sooner or later the marginal products of additional workers must decline. When the decline takes place, each additional worker will increase the total output of skateboards by less than did the previous worker.

Eventually, as more and more workers are employed, marginal product may reach zero and even become negative. It is not hard to see why if you consider the extreme case, in which there would be so many workers in a limited space that additional workers would simply get in the way, thus reducing the total output of skateboards (a negative marginal product).

Empirical confirmation of diminishing marginal returns occurs frequently. Some examples are illustrated in *Applying Economic Concepts 7-2*. But one might wish that it were not so. There would then be no reason to fear a food crisis caused by the population explosion in developing countries. If the marginal product of additional workers applied to a fixed quantity of land were constant, food production could be expanded in proportion to population growth merely by keeping a constant fraction of

---

APPLYING ECONOMIC CONCEPTS 7-2

Three Examples of Diminishing Returns

Sport Fishing

British Columbia's Campbell River, a noted sport-fishing area, has long been the centre of a thriving, well-promoted tourist trade. As sport fishing has increased over the years, the total number of fish caught has steadily increased, but the number of fish *per person fishing* has decreased and the average hours fished for each fish caught has increased.*

Pollution Control

When Southern California Edison was required to modify its Mojave power plant to reduce the amount of pollutants emitted into the atmosphere, it discovered that a series of filters applied to the smokestacks could do the job. A single filter eliminated one-half of the discharge. Five filters in series reduced the discharge to the 3 percent allowed by law. When a state senator proposed a new standard that would permit no more than 1 percent of the pollutant to be emitted, the company brought in experts who testified that this would require at least 15 filters per stack and would triple the cost. In other words, increasing the number of filters leads to diminishing marginal returns in pollution reduction.

Portfolio Diversification

Most people have heard the expression "don't put all your eggs in one basket." This advice definitely applies when you invest in the stock market because the risk level of your stock portfolio—typically measured with a statistical concept called the *standard deviation*—can be reduced by purchasing the stocks of several different companies rather than just one or two. However, the mathematics of finance shows that the greatest reduction in risk is achieved when you increase the number of individual stocks from one to two. After this point, adding more stocks still reduces risk but at a decreasing rate. These diminishing returns to reducing risk have led many investment advisers to suggest that a sensible portfolio should contain stocks from no more than 15 to 20 well-chosen companies.

---

*For a *given stock of fish* and increasing numbers of boats, this example is a good illustration of the law of diminishing returns. But in recent years the story has become more complicated as overfishing has depleted the stock of fish. We examine the reasons for overfishing in Chapter 16.

the population on farms. With fixed techniques, however, diminishing returns dictate an inexorable decline in the marginal product of each additional worker because an expanding population must work with a fixed supply of agricultural land.

Thus, except where it is offset by sufficiently powerful improvements in the techniques of production, continuous population growth would bring with it, according to the law of diminishing returns, declining living standards and eventually widespread famine. Because he did not appreciate the extent to which agricultural technologies would be improved over time, the English economist Thomas Malthus (1766–1834) predicted that the increase in the world's population would be accompanied by such a fall in living standards. His gloomy (and incorrect) forecast is discussed further in the next chapter.

The Average–Marginal Relationship

We have so far examined the concept of diminishing *marginal* returns; but *average* returns are also expected to diminish. If increasing quantities of a variable factor are applied to a given quantity of fixed factors, the average product of the variable factor will eventually decrease. [14]

Notice that in part (ii) of Figure 7-1, the *MP* curve cuts the *AP* curve at the *AP*'s maximum point. This is not a matter of luck or the way the artist just happened to draw the figure. Rather, it illustrates a fundamental property of the relationship between average and marginal product curves, one that is important to understand.

The average product curve slopes upward as long as the marginal product curve is *above* it; whether the marginal product curve is itself sloping upward or downward is irrelevant. For example, if an additional worker is to raise the average product of all workers, that additional worker's output must be greater than the average output of the other workers. In other words, in order for the average product to rise when a new worker is added, the marginal product (the output of the new worker) must exceed the average product. [15]

The relationship between marginal and average measures is very general. If the marginal is greater than the average, the average must be rising; if the marginal is less than the average, the average must be falling. For example, if you had a 3.6 cumulative grade point average (GPA) last semester and in this (marginal) semester you get only a 3.0 GPA, your cumulative GPA will fall. To increase your cumulative GPA, you must score better in this (marginal) semester than you have on average in the past—that is, to increase the average, the marginal must be greater than the average.

| 7.4 Costs in the Short Run

We now shift our attention from production to costs. The majority of firms cannot influence the prices of the inputs that they use; instead, they must pay the going market price for their inputs. For example, an electronic game maker in Montreal, a petrochemicals producer in Sarnia, a rancher in Red Deer, and a boat builder in Prince Rupert are each too small a part of the total demand for the factors that they use to be able to influence their prices significantly. The firms must pay the going rent for the land that they need, the going wage rate for the labour that they employ, and the going interest rate that banks charge for loans; so it is with most other firms. Given these prices and the physical returns summarized by the product curves, the costs of producing different levels of output can be calculated.

Defining Short-Run Costs

Several different types of costs are relevant in the short run, and we must be careful to get them straight. They are all related to the product concepts that we have just discussed.

Total Cost (TC). **Total cost** is the sum of all costs that the firm incurs to produce a given level of output. Total cost is divided into two parts: *total fixed cost* and *total variable cost*.

$$TC = TFC + TVC$$

total cost (*TC*) The total cost of producing any given level of output; it can be divided into total fixed cost and total variable cost.

Total Fixed Cost (TFC). **Total fixed cost** is the cost of the fixed factor(s). This does not vary with the level of output; it is the same whether output is 1 unit or 1000 units. Total fixed cost is also referred to as *overhead cost*. An example of a fixed cost is the annual cost associated with renting a factory (or servicing the debt incurred to build a factory). Whether the level of output increases or decreases, this annual fixed cost does not change.

total fixed cost (*TFC*) All costs of production that do not vary with the level of output.

Total Variable Cost (TVC). **Total variable cost** is the cost of the variable factors. It varies directly with the level of output—that is, it rises when output rises and it falls when output falls. Examples of variable costs are the cost of labour and intermediate inputs that are used to produce output. As the level of output increases or decreases, the amount of labour and intermediate inputs required for production changes in the same direction.

total variable cost (*TVC*) Total costs of production that vary directly with the level of output.

Average Total Cost (ATC). The total cost of producing any given number of units of output divided by that number of units tells us the **average total cost** per unit of output. We let Q be the total units of output (what we earlier referred to as total product, TP). Since total cost is split into fixed and variable costs, we can also divide average total cost into its fixed and variable components:

$$ATC = TC/Q$$
$$ATC = AFC + AVC$$

average total cost (*ATC*) Total cost of producing a given output divided by the number of units of output; it can also be calculated as the sum of average fixed costs and average variable costs. Also called *unit cost* or *average cost*.

Average Fixed Cost (AFC). Total fixed cost divided by the number of units of output tells us the average fixed cost per unit of output. **Average fixed cost** declines continually as output increases because the amount of the fixed cost attributed to each unit of output falls. This is known as *spreading overhead*.

average fixed cost (*AFC*) Total fixed cost divided by the number of units of output.

$$AFC = TFC/Q$$

Average Variable Cost (AVC). Total variable cost divided by the number of units of output tells us the average variable cost per unit of output. For reasons that we will soon see, **average variable cost** first declines as output rises, reaches a minimum, and then increases as output continues to rise.

average variable cost (*AVC*) Total variable cost divided by the number of units of output.

$$AVC = TVC/Q$$

Marginal Cost (MC). The increase in total cost resulting from a one-unit increase in the level of output is called **marginal cost**. (Marginal costs are always marginal *variable* costs because fixed costs do not change as output varies.) Marginal cost is calculated as the change in total cost divided by the change in output that brought it about: [16]

marginal cost (*MC*) The increase in total cost resulting from increasing output by one unit.

$$MC = \Delta TC/\Delta Q$$

Short-Run Cost Curves

Using the firm's production relationships from Figure 7-1 on page 163, suppose the price of labour is $20 per unit and the price of capital is $10 per unit. Also suppose the firm has 10 units of capital (the fixed factor). The firm's resulting costs are shown in Table 7-2.

Columns 4 through 6 in Table 7-2 show the firm's total costs. *TFC* is simply $10 per unit of capital times 10 units of capital. *TVC* is $20 per unit of labour times the increasing amount of labour shown in column 2. *TC* is the sum of *TFC* and *TVC*. Columns 7 through 9 show the average costs. For each average cost concept, the number is computed as the total cost from columns 4, 5, or 6 divided by the number of units of output shown in column 3.

Column 10 shows the marginal cost. For each change in the level of output, *MC* is equal to the change in *TC* divided by the change in output. For example, as output increases from 22 to 35 units (which occurs when *L* rises from 4 to 5), total costs rise from $180 to $200. Thus, marginal cost over this range of output is equal to $20/13 = $1.54.

The graphs in Figure 7-2 plot the cost curves from the data in Table 7-2. Part (i) plots the various total cost curves and shows that *TVC* rises at a decreasing rate until output is approximately 60 units. For output levels above 60, *TVC* rises at an increasing rate. Total fixed costs (*TFC*), of course, do not vary as the level of output changes. Since *TFC* is horizontal, the shape of *TC* comes from the shape of *TVC*.

Part (ii) of Figure 7-2 plots the average cost curves and the marginal cost curve. Notice that the *MC* curve cuts the *ATC* curve and the *AVC* curve at their lowest points. This is another example of the relationship between a marginal and an average curve. The *ATC* and *AVC* curves slope downward whenever the *MC* curve is below them; they slope upward whenever the *MC* curve is above them. Now let's consider the various curves in a little more detail.

TABLE 7-2 Short-Run Costs: Fixed Capital and Variable Labour

Inputs		Output	Total Costs			Average Costs			Marginal Cost
Capital (K) (1)	Labour (L) (2)	(Q) (3)	Fixed (TFC) (4)	Variable (TVC) (5)	Total (TC) (6)	Fixed (AFC) (7)	Variable (AVC) (8)	Total (ATC) (9)	(MC) (10)
10	0	0	$100	$0	$100	—	—	—	
10	1	3	100	20	120	$33.33	$6.67	$40.00	$6.67
10	2	7	100	40	140	14.29	5.71	20.00	5.00
10	3	13	100	60	160	7.69	4.62	12.31	3.33
10	4	22	100	80	180	4.55	3.64	8.18	2.22
10	5	35	100	100	200	2.86	2.86	5.71	1.54
10	6	55	100	120	220	1.82	2.18	4.00	1.00
10	7	80	100	140	240	1.25	1.75	3.00	0.80
10	8	98	100	160	260	1.02	1.63	2.65	1.11
10	9	107	100	180	280	0.93	1.68	2.62	2.22
10	10	113	100	200	300	0.88	1.77	2.65	3.33
10	11	117	100	220	320	0.85	1.88	2.74	5.00
10	12	119	100	240	340	0.84	2.02	2.86	10.00
10	13	120	100	260	360	0.83	2.17	3.00	20.00

These cost schedules are computed from the product curves of Figure 7-1, given the price of capital of $10 per unit and the price of labour of $20 per unit.

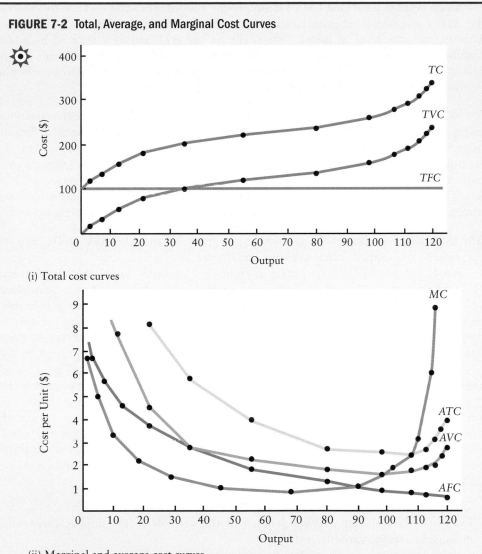

FIGURE 7-2 Total, Average, and Marginal Cost Curves

(i) Total cost curves

(ii) Marginal and average cost curves

These curves are plotted from the data in Table 7-2. In part (i), total fixed cost does not vary with output. Total variable cost and total cost ($TC = TVC + TFC$) rise with output, first at a decreasing rate, then at an increasing rate. The total cost curves in (i) give rise to the average and marginal curves in (ii). Average fixed cost (AFC) declines as output increases. Average variable cost (AVC) and average total cost (ATC) fall and then rise as output increases. Marginal cost (MC) does the same, intersecting the ATC and AVC curves at their minimum points. Capacity output is at the minimum point of the ATC curve, which is an output of about 105 in this example.

The AFC, AVC, and ATC Curves In part (ii) of Figure 7-2, the average fixed cost (AFC) curve is steadily declining as output rises. Since there is a given amount of capital with a total fixed cost of $100, increases in the level of output lead to a steadily declining fixed cost per unit of output. This is the phenomenon of *spreading overhead*.

The average variable cost (AVC) curve shows the variable cost per unit of output. It declines as output rises, reaching a minimum at approximately 100 units of output. As output increases above this level, AVC rises.

Since average total cost (*ATC*) is simply the sum of *AFC* and *AVC*, it follows that the *ATC* curve is derived geometrically by vertically adding the *AFC* and *AVC* curves. That is, for each level of output, the point on the *ATC* curve is derived by adding together the values of *AFC* and *AVC*. The result is an *ATC* curve that declines initially as output increases, reaches a minimum, and then rises as output increases further. Economists usually refer to this as a "U-shaped" *ATC* curve.

The MC Curve Figure 7-2 also shows the marginal cost (*MC*) curve. Notice that the points on the curve are plotted at the *midpoint* of the output interval shown in the table (because marginal cost refers to the *change* in cost as output rises from one level to another). For example, when we plot the marginal cost of $1.54 as output increases from 22 to 35 units, the point is plotted at an output level of 28.5 units (the midpoint between 22 and 35). The *MC* curve declines steadily as output initially increases, reaches a minimum somewhere near 70 units of output, and then rises as output increases further.

Why U-Shaped Cost Curves? It is clear from Figure 7-2 that the *AVC*, *ATC*, and *MC* curves are all U-shaped. What explains this shape?

Recall that the *MP* and *AP* curves in Figure 7-1 are both "hill-shaped" (an inverted "U") whereas the *AVC* and *MC* curves are both U-shaped. Is this just a coincidence, or is there some relationship between the two sets of curves? The answer is that this is no coincidence. Since labour input adds directly to cost, it should not surprise you that the relationship between labour input and output—the *AP* and *MP* curves—is closely linked to the relationship between output and cost—the *AVC* and *MC* curves.

Consider first the relationship between the *AP* and *AVC* curves. The *AP* curve shows that as the amount of labour input increases, the average product of labour rises, reaches a maximum, and then eventually falls. But each unit of labour adds the same amount to total variable cost ($20 in this example). Thus, each additional worker adds the same amount to cost but a different amount to output. When output per worker (*AP*) is rising, the variable cost per unit of output (*AVC*) is falling, and when output per worker (*AP*) is falling, average variable cost (*AVC*) is rising. *AVC* is at its minimum when *AP* reaches its maximum. [17]

> **Eventually diminishing average product of the variable factor implies eventually increasing average variable cost.**

Exactly the same logic applies to the relationship between the *MP* and *MC* curves. Since each unit of labour adds the same amount to cost but has a different marginal product, it follows that when *MP* is rising *MC* is falling, and when *MP* is falling *MC* is rising. The *MC* curve reaches its minimum when the *MP* curve reaches its maximum. [18]

> **Eventually diminishing marginal product of the variable factor implies eventually increasing marginal costs.**

Finally, we can return to the *ATC* curve to consider its shape. Since *ATC* = *AFC* + *AVC*, the *ATC* curve gets its shape from both the *AFC* and the *AVC* curves. The *AFC* curve is steadily declining as a given amount of overhead (fixed factor) is spread over an increasing number of units of output. And the *AVC* curve is U-shaped for the reasons we have just seen regarding the relationship between *AP* and *AVC*. It follows that the *ATC* curve begins to rise (after reaching its minimum) only when the effect of the increasing *AVC* dominates the effect of the declining *AFC*. We therefore see the *ATC* curve reaching its minimum at a level of output above where *AVC* reaches its minimum.

In the short-run theory we have developed in this chapter, we have assumed that the firm has and uses an unchangeable amount of the fixed factor, usually physical capital. However, in some settings it is more realistic to assume that the firm has a given amount of capital but can choose to use less of it in situations where less is needed. For example, if demand for the firm's product declines, the firm could decide to lay off some workers and also "lay off" some of its machines, letting them sit idle until some point in the future when demand picks up again. *Extensions in Theory 7-1* discusses this case and explains why marginal and variable cost curves that are flat over some range of output eventually rise as output rises.

EXTENSIONS IN THEORY 7-1

Idle Capital Equipment and Flat Cost Curves

Statistical studies have shown that the short-run *MC* and *AVC* curves for some manufacturing and service firms are flat over a wide range of output. Flat curves imply that output can be varied without causing a change in marginal and average costs. Then, beyond some critical level of output, marginal and average variable costs begin to rise as output rises.

To see why firms often have such flat cost curves, consider again the law of diminishing returns. As we have seen, the U-shaped short-run cost curve arises when a variable amount of one factor (labour) is applied to a fixed amount of a second factor (capital). However, even though the firm's plant and equipment is fixed in the short run, so that no more than what exists can be used, it is often possible to use *less* than this amount.

For example, consider a factory that contains ten sewing machines, each of which has a productive capacity of 20 jackets per day when operated by one operator during a normal shift. If 200 jackets per day are required, then all ten machines would be operated by ten workers on a normal shift. If demand falls to 160, then two operators could be laid off. There is no need, however, to have the eight remaining operators dashing about trying to work all ten sewing machines. Two machines can also be "laid off," leaving constant the ratio of employed labour to "employed" machines.

Production could be adjusted between 20 and 200 jackets per day without any change in the proportions in which the employed factors are used. In this case, we would expect the factory to have constant marginal and average variable costs between 20 and 200 jackets per day.

Only for output levels beyond 200 jackets per day would it begin to encounter rising costs, because production would then have to be extended by overtime and other means of combining more labour with the maximum available number of ten sewing machines.

More generally, whenever some capital can be left idle, there is no need to depart from the most efficient ratio of employed labour to employed capital as production is decreased. Thus, the law of diminishing returns may not apply over a wide range because variations in output below full capacity are accomplished by reducing the input of *both* labour and capital. Average variable costs can be constant over a wide range, up to the point at which all of the fixed factor is fully used.

For example, when increases in demand lead car assembly plants to run "an extra shift," or when demand slumps and they cut one of their shifts, they are changing the amount of labour employed and they are also adjusting the amount of time their machines are idle. When such changes in the number of shifts take place, the car firms' average variable costs and marginal costs will remain constant, even though output clearly changes. The central ideas discussed in the text are not affected by the existence of these constant costs because the important results in the text require only that costs *eventually* rise as output rises. This must always happen if there is some maximum amount of the fixed factor that can be used. What the flat cost curves explain well, however, is the observed fact in many manufacturing industries that firms' costs do not always rise and fall precisely as output rises and falls in response to seasonal and cyclical variations in demand.

Capacity

The level of output that corresponds to the minimum short-run average total cost is often called the *capacity* of the firm. When used in this sense, capacity is the largest output that can be produced without encountering rising average costs per unit. In part (ii) of Figure 7-2, capacity output is about 105 units, but higher outputs can be achieved, provided that the firm is willing to accept the higher per-unit costs that accompany any level of output that is "above capacity." A firm that is producing at an output less than the point of minimum average total cost is said to have *excess capacity*.

This technical definition gives the word *capacity* a meaning that is different from the one used in everyday speech, in which it often means an upper limit that cannot be exceeded. The technical definition is, however, a useful concept in economic and business discussions.

Shifts in Short-Run Cost Curves

Remember that a firm's short-run cost curves are drawn holding two things constant. First, the amount of the fixed factor used by the firm is held constant (indeed, it is the existence of such a fixed factor that ensures we are in the short run). Second, factor prices—the price per unit of labour and the price per unit of capital—are held constant. How would changes in factor prices and in the amount of the fixed factor affect the firm's short-run cost curves?

Changes in Factor Prices Factor prices change frequently, sometimes dramatically, and such changes naturally affect firms' costs. Consider a change in the wage, the price of a unit of labour services. An increase in the wage increases variable costs, leaves fixed costs unaffected, and therefore increases the firm's total costs. Since marginal costs are always marginal *variable* costs, such a change will also increase the firm's marginal costs. An increase in the price of the variable factor will therefore cause an upward shift in the firm's ATC and MC curves, as shown in Figure 7-3.

Now consider an increase in the price of a unit of the fixed factor. The firm's total *fixed* costs will rise, but its variable costs will be unaffected. Thus, in a diagram like Figure 7-3, the ATC curve will shift up but the MC curve will not move.

Changes in the Amount of the Fixed Factor In the short run, the firm has a fixed amount of some factor of production. Economists usually think of physical capital as the fixed factor in the short run, especially the physical capital embodied in a plant or factory. What happens to the firm's production costs if it increases the size of its factory?

There are two effects from such a change. First, once the larger factory is in place, the firm's total fixed costs have increased. Second, the increase in the size

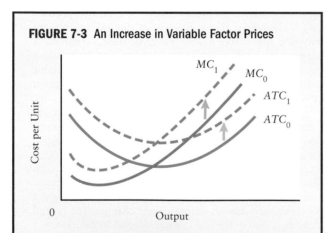

FIGURE 7-3 An Increase in Variable Factor Prices

A change in the price of a variable factor shifts the average total cost curve and the marginal cost curve. The original average total cost and marginal cost curves are shown by ATC_0 and MC_0. A rise in the price of a variable input—for example, the wage rate—raises the cost of producing each level of output. As a result, the average total cost curve and the marginal cost curve shift upward to ATC_1 and MC_1.

of the factory means that labour and other variable factors now have more physical capital with which to work, and this generally increases their average and marginal product, and thus reduces marginal and average costs (at any given level of output). What is the combined effect of these two forces?

The overall effect on the *ATC* curve is difficult to predict without having more information about the firm's technology. It depends on how much the firm's output rises when it increases its use of *all* factors. In other words, we need to have more detailed information about the firm's production function before we know how a change in the firm's plant size will affect its *ATC* curve.

Changing from one plant size to another is considered by economists to be a long-run decision by the firm. This brings us to the next chapter, in which we explore how firms make decisions in a setting in which all factors of production are variable.

SUMMARY

7.1 What Are Firms?

LO 1

- Production is organized either by private-sector firms, which take four main forms—single proprietorships, ordinary partnerships, limited partnerships, and corporations—or by state-owned enterprises and non-profit organizations.
- Modern firms finance themselves by selling shares, using their retained earnings, or borrowing from lenders, such as banks.

- A firm's profit is the difference between its total revenue and its total costs.
- Economists usually assume that firms attempt to maximize profits.

7.2 Production, Costs, and Profits

LO 2

- The production function relates inputs of factor services to output.
- Accounting profit is the difference between the firm's revenues and its explicit costs, including labour costs, capital costs, the costs of intermediate inputs, and depreciation.
- Economic profit is the difference between the firm's revenues and total costs, including both explicit and implicit costs. Implicit costs include the opportunity cost of the owner's time (for owner-managed firms) and capital.

- Economic profits play a key role in resource allocation. Positive economic profits attract resources into an industry; negative economic profits induce resources to move elsewhere.
- Economists divide the firm's production decisions into three time frames. The short run involves decisions in which one or more factors of production are fixed. The long run involves decisions in which all factors are variable but technology is unchanging. The very long run involves decisions in which technology can change.

7.3 Production in the Short Run

LO 3

- The theory of short-run costs is concerned with how output varies as different amounts of the variable factors are combined with given amounts of the fixed factors. Total, average, and marginal product describe relationships between output and the quantity of the variable factors of production.

- The law of diminishing returns asserts that if increasing quantities of a variable factor are combined with given quantities of fixed factors, the marginal and the average products of the variable factor will eventually decrease. For given factor prices, this hypothesis implies that marginal and average costs will eventually rise.

7.4 Costs in the Short Run

- Short-run average total cost curves are often U-shaped because average productivity increases at low levels of outputs but eventually declines sufficiently to offset advantages of spreading overheads. The output corresponding to the minimum point of a short-run average total cost curve is called the plant's capacity.
- Changes in factor prices shift the short-run cost curves—upward when prices rise and downward when prices fall.

KEY CONCEPTS

Forms of business organization
Methods of financing firms
Profit maximization
Inputs and factors of production
Accounting versus economic profits

Economic profits and resource allocation
Short run, long run, and very long run
Total product, average product, and marginal product

The law of diminishing returns
Total cost, marginal cost, and average cost
Short-run cost curves
Capacity

STUDY EXERCISES

MyEconLab Make the grade with MyEconLab: Study Exercises marked in red can be found on MyEconLab. You can practise them as often as you want, and most feature step-by-step guided instructions to help you find the right answer.

1. Fill in the blanks to make the following statements correct.

   a. The relationship between the inputs of factor services and output is called the _____

   b. A firm earning positive accounting profits could have zero _____ if the owner's capital is earning exactly its _____.

   c. A firm's planning decisions made when some inputs are variable but others are fixed are made in the time period known as the _____. The time period over which all factors are variable but technology is fixed is known as the _____.

2. Fill in the blanks to make the following statements correct.

   a. The _____ tells us that as more of a variable factor is used in combination with given quantities of fixed factors, the marginal product of the variable factor will eventually decrease.

   b. The _____ is the change in total output resulting from the use of one additional unit of the variable factor.

   c. If average product and marginal product curves are plotted on a graph, the *AP* curve is rising as long as the *MP* curve lies _____ the *AP* curve.

   The *AP* curve is falling when the *MP* curve lies _____ the *AP* curve.

3. Fill in the blanks to make the following statements correct.

   a. For given factor prices, when average product per worker is at a maximum, average variable cost is at a _____.

   b. If marginal costs are above average costs, then producing one more unit of output will _____ the average cost.

   c. The level of output that corresponds to a firm's minimum short-run average total cost is called the _____ of the firm.

4. Which concept of profits—accounting or economic—is implied in the following quotations?

   a. "Profits are necessary if firms are to stay in business."

   b. "Profits are signals for firms to expand production and investment."

   c. "Accelerated depreciation allowances reduce profits and thus benefit the company's owners."

   d. "A firm is profitable as long as the amount of money flowing in exceeds the amount of money flowing out."

5. Wacky Wintersports Inc. can produce snowboards according to the following schedule.

Inputs of Labour (per week)	Number of Snowboards (per week)	Average Product	Marginal Product
0	0	—	
1	2	—	—
2	5	—	—
3	9	—	—
4	14	—	—
5	18	—	—
6	21	—	—
7	23	—	—
8	24	—	

a. Complete the table by calculating the marginal and average products.
b. Plot the *AP* and *MP* curves on a single graph, and identify the point of diminishing marginal product.

6. Consider the revenues and costs in 2013 for Spruce Decor Inc., an Alberta-based furniture company entirely owned by Mr. Harold Buford.

Furniture Sales	$ 645 000
Catalogue Sales	$ 12 000
Labour Costs	$ 325 000
Materials Costs	$ 157 000
Advertising Costs	$ 28 000
Debt-Service Costs	$ 32 000

a. What would accountants determine Spruce Decor's profits to be in 2013?
b. Suppose Mr. Buford has $400 000 of capital invested in Spruce Decor. Also suppose that equally risky enterprises earn a 16 percent rate of return on capital. What is the opportunity cost for Mr. Buford's capital?
c. What are the *economic* profits for Spruce Decor in 2013?
d. If Spruce Decor's economic profits were typical of furniture makers in 2013, what would you expect to happen in this industry? Explain.

7. A carpenter quits his job at a furniture factory to open his own cabinetmaking business. In his first two years of operation, his sales average $100 000 per year and his operating costs for wood, workshop and tool rental, utilities, and miscellaneous expenses average $70 000 per year. Now his old job at the furniture factory is again available. What is the lowest wage at which he should decide to return to his old job? Why?

8. Consider an example of a production function that relates the monthly production of widgets to the monthly use of capital and labour services. Suppose

the production function takes the following specific algebraic form:

$$Q = KL - (0.1) L^2$$

where Q is the output of widgets, K is the input of capital services, and L is the input of labour services.

a. Suppose that, in the short run, K is constant and equal to 10. Fill in the following table.

K	L	Q
10	5	—
10	10	—
10	15	—
10	20	—
10	25	—
10	30	—
10	40	—
10	50	—

b. Using the values from the table, plot the values of Q and L on a scale diagram, with Q on the vertical axis and L on the horizontal axis. (This is analogous to the *TP* curve in Figure 7-1.)
c. Now suppose that K increases to 20 because the firm increases the size of its widget factory. Re-compute the value of Q for each of the alternative values of L. Plot the values of Q and L on the same diagram as in part (b).
d. Explain why an increase in K increases the level of Q (for any given level of L).

9. The following table shows how the total output of skates (per month) changes when the quantity of the variable input (labour) changes. The firm's amount of capital is fixed.

Hours of Labour (per month)	Pairs of Skates (per month)	Average Product	Marginal Product
100	200	—	
120	260	—	—
140	350	—	—
160	580	—	—
180	720	—	—
200	780	—	—
220	800	—	—
240	810	—	

a. Compute the average product of labour for each level of output and fill in the table. Plot the *AP* curve on a scale diagram.
b. Compute the marginal product of labour for each interval (that is, between 100 and 120 hours, between 120 and 140 hours, and so on). Fill in the table and plot the *MP* curve on the same diagram.

Remember to plot the value for *MP* at the midpoint of the output intervals.

c. Is the "law of diminishing marginal returns" satisfied?

d. Explain the relationship between the marginal product of labour and the average product of labour.

10. Consider the table below, which shows the total fixed costs (*TFC*) and total variable costs (*TVC*) for producing specialty bicycles in a small factory with a fixed amount of capital.

Output Per Year (thousands of bicycles)	TFC	TVC	AFC	AVC	ATC
	(thousands of dollars)				
1	200	40	—	—	—
2	200	70	—	—	—
3	200	105	—	—	—
4	200	120	—	—	—
5	200	135	—	—	—
6	200	155	—	—	—
7	200	185	—	—	—
8	200	230	—	—	—
9	200	290	—	—	—
10	200	350	—	—	—
11	200	425	—	—	—

a. Compute average fixed costs (*AFC*) for each level of output.

b. Compute average variable costs (*AVC*) for each level of output.

c. Compute average total cost (*ATC*) for each level of output. What level of output (per year) is the firm's "capacity"?

d. Plot the *AFC, AVC,* and *ATC* curves on a scale diagram with dollars on the vertical axis and the level of output on the horizontal axis.

11. This question requires you to understand the relationship between total product, average product, and marginal product. Each of the diagrams below shows how total product (*TP*) changes as the quantity of the variable input (which we call *L*) changes. These reflect four *different* production functions.

a. In each case, describe in words how total output depends on the amount of variable input.

b. For each production function, draw a diagram showing the average product (*AP*) curve. (Recall that *AP* is given by total output divided by total variable input. The value of *AP* is also equal to the slope of a straight line from the origin to the *TP* curve.)

c. On the same diagram, draw the marginal product (*MP*) curve. (Recall that *MP* is given by the *change* in total output divided by the *change* in the variable input. The value of *MP* is also equal to the slope of a tangent line to the *TP* curve.)

d. Is the relationship between *AP* and *MP* discussed in the text satisfied by each of the production functions?

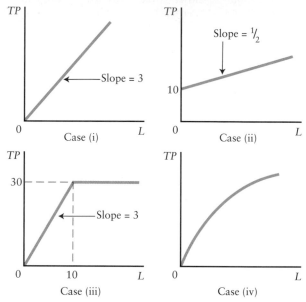

Case (i)

Case (ii)

Case (iii)

Case (iv)

12. In 1921, a classic set of experiments with chemical fertilizers was performed at the Rothampsted Experimental Station, an agricultural research institute in Hertfordshire, England. Researchers applied different amounts of a particular fertilizer to ten apparently identical plots of land. The results for one test, using identical seed grain, are listed in the following table. Create a graph with the fertilizer dose on the horizontal axis and output on the vertical axis. (With no fertilizer, output = 100.) Compute the average and marginal product of fertilizer, and identify the (approximate) points of diminishing average and marginal productivity.

Plot	Fertilizer Dose	Output Index*
1	15	104.2
2	30	110.4
3	45	118.0
4	60	125.3
5	75	130.2
6	90	131.4
7	105	131.9
8	120	132.3
9	135	132.5
10	150	132.8

*Output without fertilizer = 100.

Producers in the Long Run

LEARNING OBJECTIVES (LO)

After studying this chapter you will be able to

1 explain why profit maximization requires firms to equate marginal product per dollar spent for all factors.
2 explain why profit-maximizing firms substitute away from factors whose prices have risen and toward factors whose prices have fallen.
3 understand the relationship between short-run and long-run cost curves.

4 discuss the importance of technological change and why firms are motivated to innovate.

IN the first part of this chapter we look at the long run, in which firms are free to vary all factors of production. Recall from the end of the previous chapter that different amounts of the fixed factor lead to different short-run cost curves. The choice faced by a firm in the long run is to determine how much of the fixed factor to install—that is, to decide *which* of the several short-run cost curves to use. Some firms use a great deal of capital and only a small amount of labour. Others use less capital and more labour. Here we examine the effects these choices have on firms' costs, and we look at the conditions that influence these choices.

In the second part of the chapter, we examine the *very* long run, a period of analysis over which technology changes. The discussion concerns the improvements in technology and productivity that have dramatically increased output and incomes in all industrial countries over centuries. Firms are among the most important economic actors that cause technological advances to take place. Evidence shows that the hypothesis of profit maximization can help us to understand technological change. Here, as in the short and long run, firms respond to events, such as changes in factor prices. But in the very long run, firms often respond by innovating—that is, by developing *new* technologies.

Throughout this chapter, we should remember that the lengths of the various "runs" under consideration are defined by the kinds of changes that can take place, not by calendar time. Thus, we would expect actual firms in any given time period to be on their short-run cost curves, as described in Chapter 7; to choose among alternative short-run cost curves in the long run, as described in the first part of this chapter; and to change technologies in the very long run as described in the latter part of this chapter.

8.1 The Long Run: No Fixed Factors

In the short run, when at least one factor is fixed, the only way to produce a given output is to adjust the input of the variable factors. In the long run, when all factors can be varied, there are numerous ways to produce any given output. For example, the firm could use complex automated machines and few workers, or simple machines and many workers. Thus, firms in the long run must choose the type and amount of plant and equipment and the size of their labour force.

technical efficiency When a given number of inputs are combined in such a way as to maximize the level of output.

In making these choices, the profit-maximizing firm will try to be **technically efficient**, which means using no more of all inputs than necessary—that is, the firm does not want to waste any of its valuable inputs. For example, consider the situation faced by a crate-manufacturing firm. If the firm is *able* to produce 100 crates per day by using two machines and eight workers, the firm would be technically *inefficient* if it decided instead to produce only 90 crates per day while still employing the same amount of (expensive) labour and capital. If the firm decides that it wants to produce only 90 crates per day, technical efficiency requires that it use fewer workers, fewer machines, or both.

Technical efficiency is not enough for profits to be maximized, however. In order to maximize its profit, the firm must choose from among the many technically efficient options the one that produces a given level of output at the lowest cost. For example, if the firm decides to produce 100 crates per day, it still must decide whether to use two simple machines and eight workers, or perhaps four automated machines and six workers. If it wants to maximize its profits, it should choose the lowest-cost combination of labour and capital.

Such choices about how much capital and labour to use are *long-run* choices because all factors of production are assumed to be variable. These long-run planning decisions are important. A firm that decides to build a new steel mill and invest in the required machinery can choose among many alternatives. Once installed, that equipment is fixed for a long time. If the firm makes a poor choice, its survival may be threatened; if it chooses well, it may be rewarded with large profits.

Profit Maximization and Cost Minimization

Any firm that seeks to maximize its profits in the long run should select the production method that produces its output at the lowest possible cost. This implication of the hypothesis of profit maximization is called **cost minimization**: From among the many technically efficient methods of production available to it, the profit-maximizing firm will choose the least costly means of producing whatever level of output it chooses.

cost minimization An implication of profit maximization that firms choose the production method that produces any given level of output at the lowest possible cost.

Long-Run Cost Minimization If it is possible to substitute one factor for another to keep output constant while reducing total cost, the firm is currently not minimizing its costs. In such a situation, the firm should substitute one factor for another factor as long as the marginal product of the one factor *per dollar spent on it* is greater than the marginal product of the other factor *per dollar spent on it*. The firm is not minimizing its costs whenever these two magnitudes are unequal. For example, if an extra dollar spent on labour produces more output than an extra dollar spent on capital, the firm can reduce costs by spending less on capital and more on labour.

Suppose we use K to represent capital, L to represent labour, and p_L and p_K to represent the prices per unit of the two factors. The necessary condition for cost minimization is then

$$\frac{MP_K}{p_K} = \frac{MP_L}{p_L} \tag{8-1}$$

> **Whenever the ratio of the marginal product of each factor to its price is not equal for all factors, there are possibilities for factor substitutions that will reduce costs (for a given level of output).**

To see why Equation 8-1 must be satisfied when costs are being minimized, consider an example in which the equation is *not* satisfied. Suppose the marginal product of capital is 40 units of output and the price of 1 unit of capital is $10. Also suppose the marginal product of labour is 20 units of output and the price of one unit of labour is $2. Then we have

$$\frac{MP_K}{p_K} = \frac{40}{10} = 4 < \frac{MP_L}{p_L} = \frac{20}{2} = 10$$

Thus, the last dollar spent on capital adds only 4 units to output, whereas the last dollar spent on labour adds 10 units to output. In this case, the firm can reduce the cost of producing its current level of output by using more labour and less capital. Specifically, suppose the firm used 2 more units of labour and 1 fewer unit of capital. The 2 more units of labour would cause output to rise by 40 units and costs to increase by $4; the 1 fewer unit of capital would cause output to fall back by 40 units and costs to decline by $10. After this substitution of labour for capital, output would be unchanged but costs would be lower by $6. Thus, the original combination of factors was not a cost-minimizing one.

Of course, as the firm substitutes between labour and capital, the marginal products of both factors, MP_L and MP_K, will change. Specifically, the law of diminishing marginal returns says that with other inputs held constant, an increase in the amount of one factor used will decrease that factor's marginal product. As the firm in the previous example reduces its use of K and increases its use of L, MP_K will rise and MP_L will fall. These changes help to restore the equality in Equation 8-1.

By rearranging the terms in Equation 8-1, we can look at the cost-minimizing condition a bit differently.

$$\frac{MP_K}{MP_L} = \frac{p_K}{p_L} \tag{8-2}$$

The ratio of the marginal products on the left side compares the contribution to output of the last unit of capital and the last unit of labour. The right side shows how the cost of an additional unit of capital compares to the cost of an additional unit of labour. If the two sides of Equation 8-2 are the same, then the firm cannot make any substitutions between labour and capital to reduce costs (if output is held constant). However, with the marginal products

Oil is a very important input in many industries. Increases in the price of oil will lead profit-maximizing firms to substitute away from oil toward other factors of production, whenever that is technically possible.

and factor prices used in the example above, the left side of the equation equals 2 but the right side equals 5; the last unit of capital is twice as productive as the last unit of labour but it is five times more expensive. It will thus pay the firm to switch to a method of production that uses less capital and more labour. If, however, the ratio on the right side were less than the ratio on the left, then it would pay the firm to switch to a method of production that uses less labour and more capital. Only when the ratio of marginal products is exactly equal to the ratio of factor prices is the firm using the cost-minimizing production method.[1]

> **Profit-maximizing firms adjust the quantities of factors they use to the prices of the factors given by the market.**

The Principle of Substitution The preceding discussion suggests that profit-maximizing (and therefore cost-minimizing) firms will react to changes in factor prices by changing their methods of production. This is referred to as the **principle of substitution**.

principle of substitution The principle that methods of production will change if relative prices of inputs change, with relatively more of the cheaper input and relatively less of the more expensive input being used.

Suppose the firm's use of capital and labour currently satisfies Equation 8-1. Then consider a decrease in the price of capital while the price of labour remains unchanged. The least-cost method of producing any output will now use less labour and more capital than was required to produce the same output before the factor prices changed.

> **Methods of production will change if the relative prices of factors change. Relatively more of the cheaper factor and relatively less of the more expensive factor will be used.**

The principle of substitution plays a central role in resource allocation because it relates to the way in which individual firms respond to changes in relative factor prices that are caused by the changing relative scarcities of factors in the economy as a whole. Individual firms are motivated to use less of factors that become scarcer to the economy and more of factors that become more plentiful. Here are four examples of the principle of substitution in action.

Over the past three decades, the improvements in computing equipment have led to many changes in everyday life. One change involves customers' transactions with their commercial banks—especially cash deposits and withdrawals. Banks used to employ large numbers of tellers to deal with the hundreds of customers that needed to be serviced each day. Now most retail banking transactions are facilitated with computers and are dealt with either by automated teller machines (ATMs), automated telephone banking, or Internet banking that can be done using a computer or smartphone. The dramatic reduction in the price of computers over the past three decades (and also the more modest increase in wages) has encouraged banks to make this substitution of capital for labour.

The principle of substitution can also explain why methods of producing the same product often differ across countries. In Canada, where labour is generally highly skilled and expensive, farmers use elaborate machinery to economize on labour. In many developing countries, however, where labour is abundant and capital is scarce,

---

[1] The appendix to this chapter provides a graphical analysis of this condition, which is similar to the analysis of consumer behaviour that we developed in the appendix to Chapter 6.

a much less mechanized method of production is appropriate. The Western engineer who believes that these countries are inefficient because they are using methods long ago discarded in the West is missing the truth about efficiency in the use of resources: Where factor scarcities differ across nations, so will the cost-minimizing methods of production.

The principle of substitution also shows that firms can be induced to substitute between capital and material inputs, such as fuel. In the past few years, with the dramatic increases in the world price of oil, airlines have reduced their reliance on expensive jet fuel (derived from oil) by substituting toward planes that are constructed with lighter materials and have more fuel-efficient jet engines. In these situations, the increase in the price of fuel leads the airlines to change their *type* of capital equipment—to substitute away from jets that use a lot of fuel toward ones that are more fuel efficient.

In many developing countries, labour is used much more intensively in agriculture than is the case in richer, developed countries. This does not mean methods are somehow "backward" in the developing countries; the intensive use of labour reflects a cost-minimizing response to low wages.

Our final example involves a cross-country comparison of how firms substitute between capital and electricity. In North America, the price of electricity is quite low, and hotels usually do not worry about the extra expense when customers leave lights and air conditioning on when they leave their rooms during the day. In Europe and Central America, however, where electricity is far more expensive, many hotels are built so that all lights and air conditioning inside the room automatically turn off when you leave the room. The high price of electricity leads these firms to substitute toward a different kind of capital—one that uses less electricity.

Long-Run Cost Curves

We have been discussing a typical firm's cost-minimizing choices between various factors of production. Remember that these are *long-run* decisions because we are assuming that the firm is free to alter the amounts of all factors of production. As we have seen, when all factors can be varied, there exists a least-cost method of producing any given level of output. Thus, with given factor prices, there is a minimum achievable cost for each level of output; if this cost is expressed in terms of dollars per unit of output, we obtain the long-run average cost of producing each level of output. When this minimum cost of producing each level of output is plotted on a graph, the result is called a **long-run average cost (*LRAC*) curve**. Figure 8-1 shows one such curve.

The *LRAC* curve is determined by the firm's current technology and by the prices of the factors of production. It is a "boundary" in the sense that points below it are unattainable; points on the curve, however, are attainable if sufficient time elapses for all inputs to be adjusted. To move from one point on the *LRAC* curve to another requires an adjustment in *all* factor inputs, which may, for example, require building a larger, more elaborate factory.

long-run average cost (*LRAC*) curve The curve showing the lowest possible cost of producing each level of output when all inputs can be varied.

The *LRAC* curve is the boundary between cost levels that are attainable, with known technology and given factor prices, and those that are unattainable.

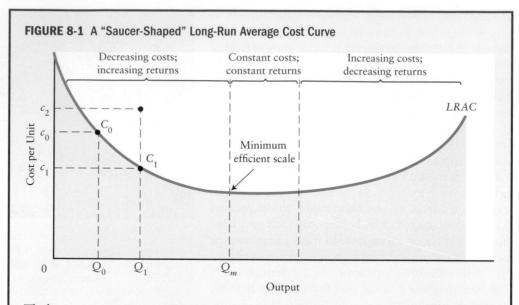

FIGURE 8-1 A "Saucer-Shaped" Long-Run Average Cost Curve

The long-run average cost ($LRAC$) curve is the boundary between attainable and unattainable levels of costs. If the firm wants to produce output Q_0, the lowest attainable cost is c_0 per unit. Thus, point C_0 is on the $LRAC$ curve. At point C_1, the firm has achieved the lowest possible average cost of producing Q_1. Suppose a firm is producing at Q_0 and desires to increase output to Q_1. In the long run, a larger plant can be built and the average cost of c_1 can be attained. However, in the short run, it will not be able to vary all factors, and thus costs per unit will be above c_1—say, c_2. For a range of output beginning at Q_m, the firm attains its lowest possible average cost of production for the given technology and factor prices.

Just as the short-run cost curves discussed in Chapter 7 relate to the production function describing the physical relationship between factor inputs and output, so does the $LRAC$ curve. The difference is that in deriving the $LRAC$ curve, there are no fixed factors of production. Thus, since all costs are variable in the long run, we do not need to distinguish among AVC, AFC, and ATC, as we did in the short run; in the long run, there is only one $LRAC$ for any given set of input prices.

The Shape of the Long-Run Average Cost Curve The $LRAC$ curve shown in Figure 8-1 first falls and then rises. Like the short-run cost curves we saw in Chapter 7, this curve is often described as U-shaped, although empirical studies suggest it is often "saucer-shaped." Consider the three portions of any such saucer-shaped $LRAC$ curve.

Decreasing Costs. Over the range of output from zero to Q_m, the firm has falling long-run average costs: An expansion of output permits a reduction of average costs. When long-run average costs fall as output rises, the firm is said to have **economies of scale**. Because the $LRAC$ curve is drawn under the assumption of constant factor prices, the decline in long-run average cost occurs because output is increasing *more than* in proportion to inputs as the scale of the firm's production expands. Over this range of output, the decreasing-cost firm is often said to enjoy long-run **increasing returns**.[2]

Increasing returns may occur as a result of increased opportunities for specialization of tasks made possible by the division of labour. Even the most casual observation of the

economies of scale Reduction of long-run average costs resulting from an expansion in the scale of a firm's operations so that more of all inputs is being used.

increasing returns (to scale) A situation in which output increases more than in proportion to inputs as the scale of a firm's production increases. A firm in this situation is a decreasing-cost firm.

---

[2] Economists shift back and forth between speaking in physical terms ("increasing returns") and cost terms ("decreasing costs"). As the text explains, the same relationship can be expressed either way.

differences in production techniques used in large and small plants shows that larger plants use greater specialization. These differences arise because large, specialized equipment is useful only when the volume of output that the firm can sell justifies using that equipment. For example, assembly lines which intensively use expensive robotics are cost-minimizing techniques for producing cars and trucks only when individual operations are repeated thousands of times. Use of elaborate and very expensive harvesting equipment provides the least-cost method of production on a big farm but not on one of only a few hectares.

Constant Costs. In Figure 8-1, the firm's long-run average costs fall until output reaches Q_m, which is known as the firm's **minimum efficient scale**. It is the smallest level of output at which *LRAC* reaches its minimum. The *LRAC* curve is then flat over some range of output. With such a flat portion, the firm encounters constant costs over the relevant range of output, meaning that the firm's long-run average costs do not change as its output rises. Because factor prices are assumed to be fixed, the firm's output must be increasing *exactly in proportion to* the increase in inputs. When this happens, the constant-cost firm is said to have **constant returns**.

Increasing Costs. When the *LRAC* curve is rising, a long-run expansion in production is accompanied by a rise in average costs. If factor prices are constant, the firm's output must be increasing *less than* in proportion to the increase in inputs. When this happens, the increasing-cost firm is said to encounter long-run **decreasing returns**. Decreasing returns imply that the firm suffers some *diseconomies of scale.*

Such diseconomies may be associated with the difficulties of managing and controlling an enterprise as its size increases. At first, there may be scale economies as the firm grows and benefits from greater specialization. But sooner or later, planning and coordination problems may multiply more than in proportion to the growth in size. If so, management costs per unit of output will rise.

Other diseconomies are the possible alienation of the labour force as size increases; it becomes more difficult to provide appropriate supervision as more layers of supervisors and middle managers come between the person at the top and the workers on the shop floor. Control of middle-range managers may also become more difficult. As the firm becomes larger, managers may begin to pursue their own goals rather than devote all of their efforts to making profits for the firm. Much recent "re-engineering" of large firms has been aimed at reducing the extent to which management difficulties increase with firm size, but the problem has not been, and probably cannot be, eliminated entirely.

Note that long-run decreasing returns differ from short-run diminishing returns. In the short run, at least one factor is fixed, and the law of diminishing returns ensures that returns to the variable factor will eventually diminish. In the long run, all factors are variable, and it is possible that physically diminishing returns will never be encountered—at least as long as it is genuinely possible to increase inputs of all factors.

The Relationship Between Long-Run and Short-Run Costs The short-run cost curves from the previous chapter and the long-run cost curve studied in this chapter are all derived from the same production function. Each curve assumes given prices for all factor inputs. The *LRAC* curve shows the lowest cost of producing any output when all factors are variable. Each short-run average total cost (*SRATC*) curve shows the lowest cost of producing any output when one or more factors are fixed.

minimum efficient scale (MES) The smallest output at which *LRAC* reaches its minimum. All available economies of scale have been realized at this point.

constant returns (to scale) A situation in which output increases in proportion to inputs as the scale of production is increased. A firm in this situation is a constant-cost firm.

decreasing returns (to scale) A situation in which output increases less than in proportion to inputs as the scale of a firm's production increases. A firm in this situation is an increasing-cost firm.

> No short-run cost curve can fall below the long-run cost curve because the *LRAC* curve represents the lowest attainable cost for each possible output.

FIGURE 8-2 *LRAC* and *SRATC* Curves

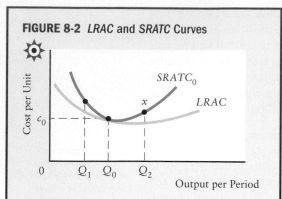

Each *SRATC* curve is tangent at some point to the *LRAC* curve. With given technology, each plant size gives rise to a different *SRATC* curve. The *SRATC* curve shown corresponds to the optimal plant size for producing Q_0 units of output because the average cost, c_0, is the lowest attainable. For output levels less than or greater than Q_0, such as Q_1 or Q_2, the plant size embodied in $SRATC_0$ is not optimal because the cost given by the $SRATC_0$ curve is greater than the minimum possible cost, given by the *LRAC* curve.

For example, if the firm wants to increase production from Q_0 to Q_2 in the short run, its average total costs will rise above the *LRAC* curve to point x. To achieve the minimum possible cost of producing output Q_2 in the long run, the firm must increase its plant size. By doing so the firm moves to a different *SRATC* curve, one that is tangent to the *LRAC* curve at output Q_2.

As the level of output is changed, a different-size plant is normally required to achieve the lowest attainable cost. Figure 8-2 shows that the *SRATC* curve lies above the *LRAC* curve at all levels of output except Q_0.

Note that any individual *SRATC* curve is just one of many such curves, each one corresponding to a different plant size. The single *SRATC* curve in Figure 8-2 shows how costs vary as output is varied, holding the plant size constant. Figure 8-3 shows a family of *SRATC* curves, along with a single *LRAC* curve. The *LRAC* curve is sometimes called an *envelope curve* because it encloses (or envelops) a series of *SRATC* cost curves by being tangent to them.

> Each *SRATC* curve is tangent to the *LRAC* curve at the level of output for which the quantity of the fixed factor is optimal, and lies above it for all other levels of output.

The relationship between the *LRAC* curve and the many different *SRATC* curves has a famous history in economics. The economist who is credited with first working out this relationship, Jacob Viner, initially made a serious mistake that ended up being published; *Lessons From History 8-1* explains his mistake and shows how it illustrates an important difference between short-run and long-run costs. Study Exercise #7 at the end of the chapter requires you to think through and explain the relationship between the *SRATC* and *LRAC* curves.

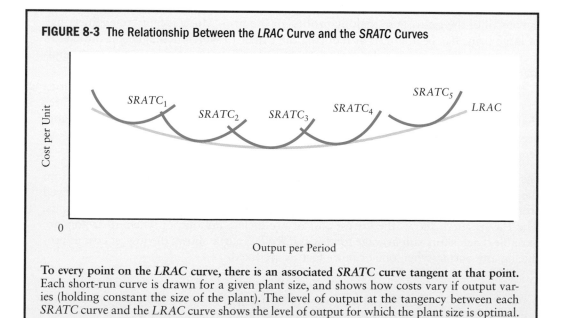

FIGURE 8-3 The Relationship Between the *LRAC* Curve and the *SRATC* Curves

To every point on the *LRAC* curve, there is an associated *SRATC* curve tangent at that point. Each short-run curve is drawn for a given plant size, and shows how costs vary if output varies (holding constant the size of the plant). The level of output at the tangency between each *SRATC* curve and the *LRAC* curve shows the level of output for which the plant size is optimal.

LESSONS FROM HISTORY 8-1

Jacob Viner and the Clever Draftsman

Jacob Viner (1892–1970) was born in Montreal and studied economics at McGill University under Stephen Leacock (1869–1944). Viner was clearly an outstanding student and, according to some of his McGill classmates, knew much more about economics than did Leacock, who was actually better known as a humorist than an economist. Viner was such a good economist that he was the first person to work out the relationship between a firm's long-run average costs and its short-run average costs. He went on to teach economics at the University of Chicago and at Princeton University and became one of the world's leading economic theorists.

If you find the relationship between *SRATC* and *LRAC* hard to understand you may take some comfort from the fact that when Jacob Viner first worked out this relationship, and published it in 1931, he made a crucial mistake. In preparing a diagram like Figure 8-3, he instructed his draftsman to draw the *LRAC* curve through the *minimum points* of all the *SRATC* curves, "but so as to never lie above" the *SRATC* curves. Viner later said of the draftsman: "He is a mathematician, however, not an economist, and he saw some mathematical objection to this procedure which I could not succeed in understanding. I could not persuade him to disregard his scruples as a craftsman and to follow my instructions, absurd though they might be."

Viner's mistake was to require that the draftsman connect all the *minimum* points of the *SRATC* curves

rather than to construct the curve that would be the *lower envelope* of all the *SRATC* curves. The former curve can, of course, be drawn, but it is not the *LRAC* curve. The latter curve is the *LRAC* curve and is tangent to each *SRATC* curve.

Since Viner's article was published in 1931, generations of economics students have experienced great satisfaction when they finally figured out his crucial mistake. Viner's famous article was often reprinted, for its fame was justly deserved, despite the importance of the mistake. But Viner always rejected suggestions that he correct the error because he did not want to deprive other students of the pleasure of feeling one up on him.

The economic sense of the fact that tangency is not at the minimum points of *SRATC* rests on the subtle distinction between the least-cost method of utilizing a *given plant* and the least-cost method of producing a *given level of output*. The first concept defines the minimum of any given *SRATC* curve, whereas the second defines a point on the *LRAC* curve for any given level of output. It is the second concept that interests us in the long run. If bigger plants can achieve lower average costs, there will be a gain in building a bigger plant *and underutilizing it* whenever the gains from using the bigger plant are enough to offset the costs of underutilizing the plant. If there are gains from building bigger plants (i.e., if *LRAC* is declining), some underutilization is always justified.

Shifts in *LRAC* Curves

We saw in Chapter 7 how changes in either technological knowledge or factor prices will cause the entire family of short-run cost curves to shift. The same is true for long-run cost curves. Because loss of existing technological knowledge is rare, we focus on the effects of technological improvement. Improved ways of producing existing products make lower-cost methods of production available, thereby shifting *LRAC* curves downward.

Changes in factor prices can exert an influence in either direction. If a firm has to pay more for any factor that it uses, the cost of producing each level of output will rise; if the firm has to pay less for any factor that it uses, the cost of producing each level of output will fall.

A rise in factor prices shifts *LRAC* curves upward. A fall in factor prices or a technological improvement shifts *LRAC* curves downward.

8.2 The Very Long Run: Changes in Technology

In the long run, profit-maximizing firms faced with given technologies choose the cost-minimizing mix of factors to produce their desired level of output. Firms are therefore on, rather than above, their long-run cost curves. In the very long run, however, there are changes in the available techniques and resources. Such changes cause *shifts* in long-run cost curves.

The decrease in costs that can be achieved by choosing from among available factors of production, known techniques, and alternative levels of output is necessarily limited by the existing state of knowledge. In contrast, improvements by invention and innovation are potentially limitless.

technological change Any change in the available techniques of production.

Technological change refers to all changes in the available techniques of production. There are countless examples, including the invention of the assembly line, the development of robotics, the invention of fuel-efficient jet engines, the creation of new medical and drug treatments, the creation of the Internet, and the development of wireless communication devices. To measure the extent of technological change, economists usually use the notion of **productivity**, defined as a measure of output produced per unit of input used. Two widely used measures of productivity are output per worker and output per hour of work. The rate of increase in productivity provides one measure of technological change.

productivity Output produced per unit of some input; frequently used to refer to labour productivity, measured by total output divided by the amount of labour used.

Most economists believe that productivity growth driven by technological change is the primary cause of rising material living standards over decades and centuries. If you want to know why your real income (purchasing power) is likely to be several times that enjoyed by your great-grandparents 75 or 100 years ago, the reason is that you are likely to be much more productive than they were. Your greater productivity is due to better health, better skills, and the fact that you work with much better equipment than did workers back then.

In recent years, however, the rate of productivity growth in Canada has been slowing, and it has also become clear that it is below the rate of growth in other developed countries like the United States and the United Kingdom. The importance of productivity growth in sustaining our rising path of living standards has led economists in universities and government to spend a great deal of effort researching the causes of the slowdown as well as policies that might encourage faster productivity growth. See *Applying Economic Concepts 8-1* for more on this important issue.

Technological Change

Technological change was once thought to be mainly a random process, brought about by inventions made by crackpots and eccentric scientists working in garages and scientific laboratories. As a result of recent research by historians and economists, we now know better.

Many changes in technology are based on scientific discoveries made in such non-profit organizations as universities and government research laboratories; others come out of laboratories run by private firms. Whatever their origin, most technological advances are put into practice by firms in search of profits. A firm that first develops a new product, a new wrinkle on an old product, or a new process that lowers production costs gets a temporary advantage over its competitors. This advantage creates profits that persist until others can copy what the original firm has done. So in the very

APPLYING ECONOMIC CONCEPTS 8-1

The Significance of Productivity Growth

Long ago, economics was known as the "dismal science" because some of its predictions were grim. Thomas Malthus (1766–1834) and other Classical economists predicted that the pressure of more and more people on the world's limited resources would cause a decline in output per person because of the law of diminishing returns. Human history would see more and more people living less and less well and the surplus population, which could not be supported, dying off from hunger and disease.

This prediction has proven wrong for industrialized countries for two main reasons. First, their populations have not expanded as rapidly as predicted by early economists, who were writing before birth-control techniques were widely used. Second, technological advances have been so important during the past 150 years that output has increased much faster than the population. We have experienced sustained growth in productivity that has permitted significant increases in output per person—often referred to as material living standards. As the accompanying figure shows, real output per worker in Canada increased by 300 percent between 1926 and 2011, an average annually compounded growth rate of 1.65 percent.

Even such small annual productivity increases are a powerful force for increasing material living standards over many years. Our great-grandparents would have regarded today's standard of living in most industrialized countries as unattainable. An apparently modest rate of increase in productivity of 2 percent per year leads to a doubling of per capita output every 36 years.[3]

Because of the importance of productivity growth in raising long-run material living standards, it is not surprising that explaining the sources of technological progress has become a very active area of research among both academic and government economists.

---

[3] The mathematical "rule of 72" says that for any variable growing at X percent per year, 72/X gives the approximate number of years required for the variable to double.

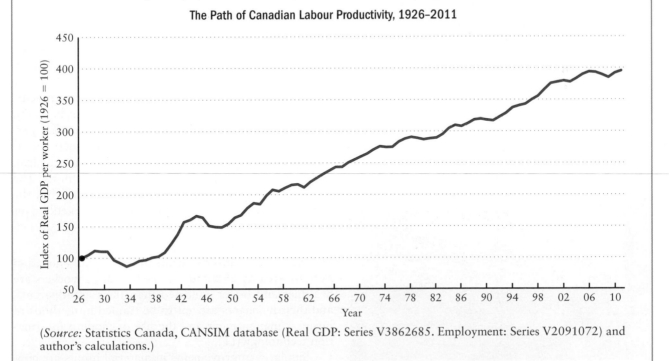

The Path of Canadian Labour Productivity, 1926–2011

(*Source:* Statistics Canada, CANSIM database (Real GDP: Series V3862685. Employment: Series V2091072) and author's calculations.)

long run, the search for profit takes the form not just of choosing the most efficient technique among known alternatives but also of inventing and innovating new products and processes. Since firms do this in search of profits, we say that the technological change is *endogenous* to the economic system rather than something that just occurs for unknown reasons.

Sometimes innovations come from new ideas that are the next extension of existing knowledge, where the motivation is to raise profits by developing these opportunities. Examples include new features in Facebook or on cell phones, or the developments of new apps for smartphones. At other times innovations are a response to some obvious challenge. For example, in our discussion of long-run demand curves in Chapter 4, we looked at technological changes that came in response to rising relative prices when we spoke of the developments in the 1970s of smaller, more fuel-efficient cars in the wake of dramatic increases in the price of gasoline. From the mid-1980s to the mid-1990s, declines in the price of gasoline led to the re-emergence of large cars and the development of fuel-inefficient sport utility vehicles, or SUVs. More recently, however, we have once again seen consumers respond to higher gasoline prices by reducing their demand for such large vehicles, returning to smaller, more fuel-efficient cars, and the combination of high fuel prices and environmental changes are driving the development of electric cars.

Consider three kinds of change that influence production and cost in the very long run: *new techniques, improved inputs,* and *new products.*

New Techniques Throughout the nineteenth and twentieth centuries, changes in the techniques available for producing existing products have been dramatic; this is called *process innovation.* A century ago, roads and railways were built by gangs of workers who used buckets, shovels, and draft horses. Today, bulldozers, giant trucks, and other specialized equipment have banished the workhorse completely from construction sites and to a great extent have displaced the pick-and-shovel worker. Before the Second World War, electricity was generated either by burning fossil fuels or by harnessing the power of flowing water. With the rise of the atomic age immediately following the war, many countries developed large-scale nuclear generating capacity. Economies of scale in electricity production were significant. In recent years, however, the development of small-scale, gas-combustion and wind-powered turbines has permitted inexpensive construction of small generating stations that can produce electricity at a lower average cost than the much larger nuclear, hydro, or fossil fuel–burning generating stations. The product—electricity—is absolutely unchanged, but the techniques of production have changed markedly over the past several decades.

Environmental concerns combined with increases in the world price of oil have led to the development of hybrid and fully electric cars.

Improved Inputs Improvements in health and education raise the quality of labour services. Today's workers are healthier and better educated than their grandparents, and their managers are apt to be trained in methods of business management and the use of modern information technology (IT).

Similarly, improvements in material inputs are constantly occurring. For example, the type and quality of metals have changed. Steel has replaced iron, and aluminum substitutes for steel in a process of change that makes a statistical category such as "primary metals" seem unsatisfactory. Even for a given category, say, steel, today's product is lighter, stronger, and more flexible than the "same" product manufactured only 20 years ago. Furthermore, the modern "materials revolution" allows new materials to be tailor-made for the specific purposes for which they are required.

> The invention of new production techniques and the development of new and better inputs are important aspects of technological improvement. They lead to reductions in firms' costs and a downward shift in *LRAC* curves.

New Products New goods and services are constantly being invented and marketed; this is called *product innovation*. CD players, DVDs, cell phones, BlackBerries, MP3 players, MRIs, CAT scans, DNA tests, hybrid cars, personal GPS devices, and many other products did not exist 30 years ago. Other products have changed so dramatically that the only connection they have with the "same" product from the past is the name. Today's Ford car is very different from a 1920 Ford, and it is even different from a 1990 Ford in size, safety, and gasoline consumption. Modern jet aircraft are revolutionary compared with the first passenger jet aircraft, which were in turn many times larger and faster than the DC-3, the workhorse of the airlines during the 1930s and 1940s. Beyond having wings and engines, the DC-3 itself bore little resemblance to the Wright brothers' original flying machine.

> The development of new products is a crucial part of the steady increase in living standards.

Applying Economic Concepts 8-2 discusses an everyday example of technological change in banking: the creation and adoption of the automated teller machine (ATM) and the more recent development of online banking. This evolution in personal banking involves both long-run decisions—substitutions between capital and labour—and very long-run decisions involving innovation and the creation of new products.

Firms' Choices in the Very Long Run

Firms respond to signals that indicate changes in the economic environment. For example, consider the situation faced by Dofasco—a major steel producer located in Hamilton, Ontario—when the price of coal (a major input) increases and is expected to remain at the higher level for some time. How can Dofasco respond to this change in the economic environment?

One option for Dofasco is to make a long-run response by substituting away from the use of coal by changing its production techniques within the confines of existing technology. This might involve switching to other fuels (whose prices have not increased) to operate Dofasco's enormous blast furnaces. Another option is to invest in research in order to develop new production techniques that innovate away from coal (and other fuels as well), such as the design of blast furnaces that require less fuel to process each unit of iron ore.

APPLYING ECONOMIC CONCEPTS 8-2

The Remarkable Evolution in Personal Banking

Until the early 1980s, all personal banking required a visit to the bank. For many working individuals, banking could take place only on the lunch hour, with the result that long line-ups were commonplace. Banks were then faced with a difficult choice: Have unhappy customers in long line-ups, or hire more tellers.

The development of automatic teller machines (ATMs), made possible by the declining cost and increasing efficiency of computing equipment, revolutionized banking and presented banks with a new set of choices. As you know, ATMs are now located on street corners, in shopping malls and universities, and inside many large stores and even some small ones. As a result, individuals do not have to go to a bank to gain access to their money. And ATMs are very efficient: They take no time at all to "learn" their job and they can handle thousands of transactions per week—all with no direct labour cost per transaction. There is, of course, a significant capital cost for each ATM, as well as some labour cost for servicing the equipment.

Since the early 1980s, the use of ATMs has skyrocketed in Canada. Whereas in 1982 there were only a handful in the downtown core of even the major Canadian cities, today it is virtually impossible to walk even a few blocks anywhere in any Canadian city without seeing one. Over the same period, there has been a decline in the number of bank tellers (although because of ATMs we typically go inside the bank so seldom that we don't notice this!). In the language of this chapter, the rise of ATMs and decline of bank tellers has been a long-run substitution of capital for labour.

There have also been some very long-run changes in personal banking. Beginning in the late 1990s, the development of telephone banking and, more recently, online banking, vastly improved services received by customers, who can now pay bills and make transfers between their accounts without leaving the comfort of their homes or offices. Not only are traditional types of transactions made easier, but new banking services have also been created. One example is the creation of online accounts for buying and selling stocks and bonds in the global financial markets. Whereas even a few years ago individuals could make such transactions only by employing the services of a registered stock broker (at considerable expense), it is now very simple to create a trading account at your bank—linked to your other accounts and accessible by the ATMs—and make trades whenever you want and at a much lower cost per transaction. In the language of this chapter, such creation of new banking services is an example of very long-run innovation.

Faced with increases in the price of an input, firms may either *substitute away* or *innovate away* from the input—or do both over different time horizons.

It is important to recognize that the two options can involve quite different actions and can ultimately have quite different implications for productivity.

For example, consider three different responses to an increase in Canadian labour costs. One firm reallocates its production activities to Mexico or India, where labour costs are relatively low and hence labour-intensive production techniques remain quite profitable. A second firm chooses to reduce its use of labour but increase its use of capital equipment. These two firms have, in different ways, chosen to *substitute away* from the higher-priced Canadian labour. A third firm devotes resources to developing new production techniques, perhaps by using robotics or other new equipment. This firm has *innovated away* from higher-priced Canadian labour.

All three are possible reactions to the changed circumstances. The first two are largely well understood in advance and will lead to reduced costs relative to continued reliance on the original production methods. The third response, depending on the often unpredictable results of the innovation, may fail completely or it may succeed and so reduce costs sufficiently to warrant the investment in research and development and may even lead to substantially more effective production techniques that allow the firm to maintain an advantage over its competitors for a number of years. Invention and innovation are subject to great uncertainties that are hard to estimate in advance. For this reason, they must produce large profits when they do succeed in order to induce inventing firms to incur the costs of pushing into the unknown.

SUMMARY

8.1 The Long Run: No Fixed Factors

LO 1, 2, 3

- There are no fixed factors in the long run. Profit maximizing firms choose from the available alternatives the least-cost method of producing any specific output.
- Profit-maximizing firms must minimize the cost of producing any given level of output. The condition for cost minimization is

$$\frac{MP_K}{MP_L} = \frac{p_K}{p_L}$$

- The principle of substitution states that, in response to changes in factor prices, profit-maximizing firms will substitute toward the cheaper factors and substitute away from the more expensive factors.
- A long-run cost curve represents the boundary between attainable and unattainable costs for the given technology and given factor prices.

- The shape of the *LRAC* curve depends on the relationship of inputs to outputs as the whole scale of a firm's operations changes. Increasing, constant, and decreasing returns lead, respectively, to decreasing, constant, and increasing long-run average costs.
- The *LRAC* and *SRATC* curves are related. Each *SRATC* curve represents a specific plant size and is tangent to the *LRAC* curve at the level of output for which that plant size is optimal.
- *LRAC* curves shift upward or downward in response to changes in the prices of factors or changes in technology. Increases in factor prices shift *LRAC* curves upward. Decreases in factor prices and technological advances shift *LRAC* curves downward.

8.2 The Very Long Run: Changes in Technology

LO 4

- Over the very long run, the most important influence on costs of production and on material standards of living has been increases in output made possible by technological improvements.
- Changes in technology are often *endogenous responses* to changing economic signals; that is, they result from the firms' responses to changes in the economic environment.
- There are three important kinds of technological change: developments of new production techniques, improved

inputs, and new products. All three play an important role in increasing material living standards.
- To understand any industry's response to changes in its operating environment, it is important to consider the effects of endogenous innovations in technology as well as substitution based on changes in the use of existing technologies.

KEY CONCEPTS

The implication of cost minimization
The interpretation of $MP_K/MP_L = p_K/p_L$
The principle of substitution
Increasing, constant, and decreasing returns

Economies and diseconomies
  of scale
LRAC curve as an envelope of
  SRATC curves

Technological change and productivity
  growth
Changes in technology as endogenous
  responses

STUDY EXERCISES

MyEconLab Make the grade with MyEconLab: Study Exercises marked in red can be found on MyEconLab. You can practise them as often as you want, and most feature step-by-step guided instructions to help you find the right answer.

1. Fill in the blanks to make the following statements correct.

   a. In the long run, if a firm is maximizing its profits while producing a given level of output, then this firm is also _____ its costs.

   b. In the long run, all factors of production are _____. There are no _____ factors.

   c. Profit-maximizing firms employ factors of production such that the marginal products per dollar spent on each factor are _____.

   d. Firms adjust their methods of production in response to changes in relative prices. This is known as the _____.

2. The long-run average cost curve is often saucer-shaped. Fill in the blanks to make the following statements about the $LRAC$ curve correct.

   a. Over the range of output where the $LRAC$ curve is falling, the firm is experiencing _____ or _____. As output increases, average costs are _____.

   b. When the $LRAC$ curve reaches its minimum, the firm has reached its _____. If the curve is flat over some range of output, we say the firm is exhibiting _____.

   c. Over the range of output in which the $LRAC$ curve is rising, the firm is experiencing _____ or _____. As output increases, average costs are _____.

   d. The $LRAC$ curve represents the _____ for each level of output.

   e. Each short-run average total cost curve is _____ at some point to the $LRAC$ curve. The $LRAC$ curve shows the lowest possible cost of producing any output when all factors are _____. The $SRATC$ curve shows the lowest possible cost of producing any output when one or more factors are _____.

3. Explain why a profit-maximizing firm must also minimize costs.

4. Industrial Footwear Inc. uses capital and labour to produce workboots. Suppose this firm is using capital and labour such that the MP_K is equal to 80 and the MP_L is equal to 20. For each set of per-unit prices of capital and labour given below, determine whether Industrial Footwear Inc. is minimizing its costs. If it is not, determine the direction of factor substitution the firm should make in order to do so.

   a. $P_K = \$2$ $P_L = \$10$
   b. $P_K = \$20$ $P_L = \$5$
   c. $P_K = \$40$ $P_L = \$5$

5. Use the principle of substitution to predict the effect in each of the following situations.

   a. During the past 30 years, technological advances in the computer industry have led to dramatic reductions in the prices of personal and business computers. At the same time, real wages have increased slowly.

   b. The ratio of land costs to building costs is much higher in big cities than in small cities.

   c. Wages of textile workers and shoe machinery operators are higher in Canada than in the Southern United States, but the price of capital equipment is approximately the same.

   d. A new collective agreement results in a significant increase in wages for pulp and paper workers.

6. The following table shows the marginal product of capital and labour for each of several methods of producing 1000 kilograms of flour per day.

Production Method	MP_K	MP_L
A	14	3
B	12	6
C	10	9
D	8	12
E	6	15
F	4	18
G	2	21

   a. As we move from A to G, are the production methods becoming more or less *capital intensive*? Explain.

   b. If capital costs \$8 per unit and labour costs \$4 per unit, which production method minimizes the cost of producing 1000 kg of flour?

   c. For each of the methods that are not cost minimizing (with the factor prices from part (b)), describe how the firm would have to adjust its use of capital and labour to minimize costs.

d. Now suppose the price of capital falls to $4 per unit and the price of labour rises to $6 per unit. Which method now minimizes costs?

7. Consider the following diagram of *SRATC* and *LRAC* curves.

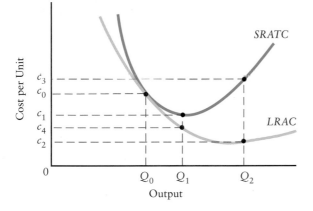

a. The *SRATC* curve is drawn for a given plant size. Given this plant size, what is the level of output that minimizes short-run average costs? What are unit costs in the short run at this level of output?

b. What is the level of output for which this plant size is optimal in the long run? What are unit costs in the short run at this level of output?

c. Explain the economics of why c_1 is greater than c_4.

d. Suppose the firm wants to increase output to Q_2 in the short run. How is this accomplished, and what would unit costs be?

e. Suppose the firm wants to increase output to Q_2 in the long run. How is this accomplished, and what would unit costs be?

8. The following diagram shows three possible *SRATC* curves and an *LRAC* curve for a single firm producing light bulbs, where each *SRATC* curve is associated with a different-sized plant.

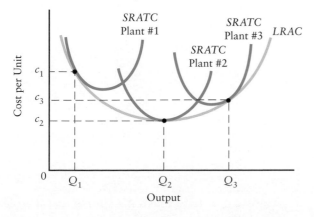

a. If the firm is producing Q_1 light bulbs with Plant #1, what are the firm's average costs?

b. At Q_1, does the firm display decreasing, constant, or increasing costs?

c. How does your answer in part (b) relate to the concept of *economies of scale*?

d. Repeat parts (a), (b), and (c) for output level Q_2 with Plant #2 and output level Q_3 with Plant #3.

9. In the text, we stated that the *LRAC* curve eventually slopes upward because of *diseconomies of scale*. In the previous chapter we saw that the *SRATC* curve eventually slopes upward because of *diminishing marginal product of the variable factor*.

a. Explain the difference between *diseconomies of scale* and *diminishing marginal product of the variable factor*. Why is one a short-run concept and the other a long-run concept?

b. Draw a diagram with short-run and long-run average cost curves that illustrates *for the same level of output* both diseconomies of scale and diminishing marginal product of the variable factor.

10. In the text, we stated that the *LRAC* curve initially slopes downward because of *economies of scale*. In the previous chapter we saw that the *SRATC* curve can initially slope downward because of spreading overhead.

a. Explain the difference between *economies of scale* and *spreading overhead*. Why is one a short-run concept and the other a long-run concept?

b. Draw a diagram with short-run and long-run average cost curves that illustrates *for the same level of output* both economies of scale and spreading overhead.

11. This question combines the various concepts from Questions 9 and 10.

a. Draw a diagram with short-run and long-run average cost curves that illustrates *for the same level of output* economies of scale in the long run but diminishing marginal product for the variable factor in the short run.

b. Draw a diagram with short-run and long-run average cost curves that illustrates *for the same level of output* diseconomies of scale in the long run but falling average total costs in the short run.

12. Each of the following is a means of increasing productivity. Discuss which groups in a society might oppose each one.

a. A labour-saving invention that permits all goods to be manufactured with less labour than before

b. The removal of all government production safety rules

c. A reduction in corporate income taxes

d. A reduction in the stringency of environmental standards for new factories

13. In the fall of 2008, after the collapse of the U.S. housing market and the onset of a major global recession, a Canadian newspaper headline claimed "Drastic Cost Reductions Needed to Save 13 B.C. Sawmills."

    a. Does the headline suggest that the B.C. lumber companies are not profit maximizers?
    b. If long-run unit costs are "too high," what is stopping the lumber companies from simply moving down their *LRAC* curves?

14. This question relates to the material in the Appendix. The following table shows several methods of producing 500 rubber tires per day. There are two factors, labour and capital, with prices per unit of $3 and $6, respectively.

Production Method	Units of Labour	Units of Capital	Total Cost
A	110	20	—
B	90	25	—
C	70	33	—
D	50	43	—
E	30	55	—
F	10	70	—

a. Compute the total cost for each production method and fill in the table.
b. Which production method minimizes costs for producing 500 tires?
c. Plot the isoquant for 500 tires, with units of capital on the vertical axis and units of labour on the horizontal axis.
d. Given the factor prices, draw the isocost line that corresponds to the cost-minimizing production method.
e. Now suppose the price of labour rises to $5 per unit but the firm still wants to produce 500 tires per day. Explain how a cost-minimizing firm adjusts to this change (with no change in technology).

Isoquant Analysis

The production function gives the relationship between the factor inputs that the firm uses and the output that it obtains. In the long run, the firm can choose among many different combinations of inputs that yield the same output. The production function and the long-run choices open to the firm can be represented graphically by using *isoquants*.

8A.1 Isoquants

The table in Figure 8A-1 illustrates a hypothetical example in which several combinations of two inputs, labour and capital, can produce a given quantity of output. The data from the table are plotted graphically in Figure 8A-1. A smooth curve is drawn through the points to indicate that there are additional ways, which are not listed in the table, of producing the same output.

This curve is called an *isoquant*. It shows the whole set of technically efficient factor combinations for producing a given level of output. This is an example of graphing a relationship among three variables in two dimensions. It is analogous to the contour line on a map, which shows all points of equal altitude, and to an indifference curve (discussed in the Appendix to Chapter 6), which shows all combinations of products that yield the consumer equal utility.

As we move from one point on an isoquant to another, we are *substituting one factor for another* while holding output constant. If we move from point *b* to point *c*, we are substituting 1 unit of labour for 3 units of capital.

> The marginal rate of substitution measures the rate at which one factor is substituted for another with output being held constant.

Sometimes the term *marginal rate of technical substitution* is used to distinguish this concept from the analogous one for consumer theory (the marginal rate of substitution) that we examined in Chapter 6.

Graphically, the marginal rate of substitution is measured by the slope of the isoquant at a particular point. We adopt the standard practice of defining the marginal rate of substitution as the negative of the slope of the isoquant so that it is a positive number. The table in Figure 8A-1 shows the calculation of some marginal rates of substitution between various points on an isoquant. [19]

The marginal rate of substitution is related to the marginal products of the factors of production. To see how, consider an example. Suppose at the present level of inputs of labour and capital, the marginal product of labour is 2 units of output and the marginal product of capital is 1 unit of output. If the firm reduces its use of capital and increases its use of labour to keep output constant, it needs to add only one-half unit of labour for 1 unit of capital given up. If, at another point on the isoquant with more labour and less capital, the marginal products are 2 for capital and 1 for labour, the firm will have to add 2 units of labour for every unit of capital it gives up. The general proposition is this:

> The marginal rate of (technical) substitution between two factors of production is equal to the ratio of their marginal products.

Economists assume that isoquants satisfy two important conditions: they are downward sloping, and they are convex when viewed from the origin. What is the economic meaning of these conditions?

The downward slope indicates that each factor input has a positive marginal product. If the input of one factor is reduced and that of the other is held constant, output will be reduced. Thus, if one input is decreased, production can be held constant only if the other factor input is increased.

To understand the convexity of the isoquant, consider what happens as the firm moves along the isoquant of Figure 8A-1 downward and to the right. Labour is being added and capital reduced to keep output constant. If labour is added in increments of

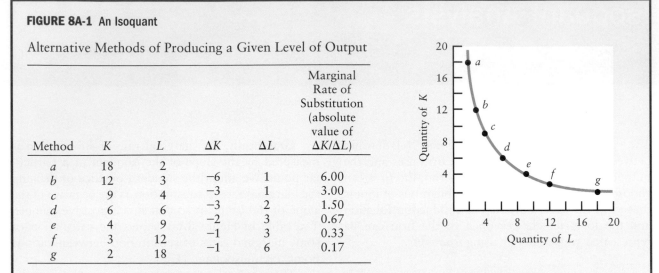

FIGURE 8A-1 An Isoquant

Alternative Methods of Producing a Given Level of Output

Method	K	L	ΔK	ΔL	Marginal Rate of Substitution (absolute value of ΔK/ΔL)
a	18	2			
b	12	3	−6	1	6.00
c	9	4	−3	1	3.00
d	6	6	−3	2	1.50
e	4	9	−2	3	0.67
f	3	12	−1	3	0.33
g	2	18	−1	6	0.17

An isoquant describes the firm's alternative methods for producing a given level of output. Method *a* uses a great deal of capital (*K*) and very little labour (*L*). As we move down the table, labour is substituted for capital in such a way as to keep output constant. Finally, at the bottom, most of the capital has been replaced by labour. The marginal rate of substitution between the two factors is calculated in the last three columns of the table. Note that as we move down the table, the marginal rate of substitution declines.

When the isoquant is plotted, it is downward sloping and convex. The downward slope reflects the requirement of technical efficiency: Keeping the level of output constant, a reduction in the use of one factor requires an increase in the use of the other factor. The convex shape of the isoquant reflects a diminishing marginal rate of (technical) substitution.

exactly 1 unit, how much capital can be dispensed with each time? The key to the answer is that both factors are assumed to be subject to the law of diminishing returns. Thus, the gain in output associated with each additional unit of labour added is *diminishing*, whereas the loss of output associated with each additional unit of capital forgone is *increasing*. Therefore, it takes ever-smaller reductions in capital to compensate for equal increases in labour. Viewed from the origin, therefore, the isoquant is convex.

An Isoquant Map

The isoquant of Figure 8A-1 is for a given level of output. Suppose it is for 6 units. In this case, there is another isoquant for 7 units, another for 7000 units, and a different one for every other level of output. Each isoquant refers to a specific level of output and connects combinations of factors that are technically efficient methods of producing that output. If we plot a representative set of these isoquants from the same production function on a single graph, we get an *isoquant map* like that in Figure 8A-2. The higher the

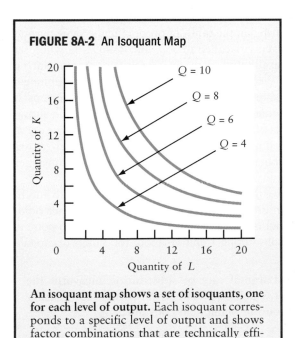

FIGURE 8A-2 An Isoquant Map

An isoquant map shows a set of isoquants, one for each level of output. Each isoquant corresponds to a specific level of output and shows factor combinations that are technically efficient methods of producing that output.

level of output along a particular isoquant, the farther the isoquant is from the origin.

8A.2 Cost Minimization

Finding the cost-minimizing method of producing any output requires knowledge of the factor prices. Suppose capital is priced at $4 per unit and labour at $1 per unit. An *isocost line* shows alternative combinations of factors that a firm can buy for a given total cost. Four different isocost lines appear in Figure 8A-3. The slope of each isocost line reflects *relative* factor prices. For given factor prices, a series of parallel isocost lines will reflect the alternative levels of expenditure on factor purchases that are available to the firm. The higher the level of expenditure, the farther the isocost line is from the origin.

In Figure 8A-4, the isoquant and isocost maps are brought together. The cost-minimizing method of production must be a point on an isoquant that just touches (is tangent to) an isocost line. If the isoquant cuts the isocost line, it is possible to move along the isoquant and reach a lower level of cost. Only at a point of tangency is a movement in either direction along the isoquant a movement to a higher cost level.

As shown in Figure 8A-4, the lowest attainable cost of producing 6 units is $24, and this requires using 12 units of labour and 3 units of capital.

> The least-cost position is given graphically by the tangency point between the isoquant and the isocost lines.

The slope of the isocost line is given by the ratio of the prices of the two factors of production. The slope of the isoquant is given by the ratio of their marginal products. When the firm reaches its cost-minimizing position, it has equated the price ratio (which is given to it by the market) with the ratio of the marginal products (which it can adjust by changing its usage of the factors). In symbols,

$$\frac{MP_L}{MP_K} = \frac{p_L}{p_K}$$

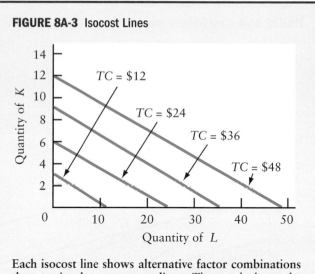

FIGURE 8A-3 Isocost Lines

Each isocost line shows alternative factor combinations that require the same expenditure. The graph shows the four isocost lines that result when labour costs $1 per unit and capital $4 per unit and when expenditure (total cost, *TC*) is held constant at $12, $24, $36, and $48, respectively.

This is the same condition that we derived in the text (see Equation 8-2 on page 179), but here we have derived it by using the isoquant analysis of the firm's decisions. [20]

Note the similarity of this condition for a cost-minimizing firm to Equation 6-2 (page 128), where we saw how utility maximization for a consumer requires that the ratio of marginal utilities of consuming two products must equal the ratio of the two product prices. Both conditions reveal the basic principle that the decision makers (consumers or producers) face market prices beyond their control and so adjust quantities (consumption or factor inputs) until they are achieving their objective (utility maximization or cost minimization).

The Principle of Substitution

Suppose with technology unchanged (that is, for a given isoquant map), the price of one factor changes. In particular, suppose with the price of capital unchanged at $4 per unit, the price of labour rises from $1 to $4 per unit. Originally, the cost-minimizing factor combination for producing 6 units of output was 12 units of labour and 3 units of capital. Total cost was $24. To produce that same output in the same way would now cost $60 at the new factor prices. Figure 8A-5 shows why this production method is no

FIGURE 8A-4 Cost Minimization

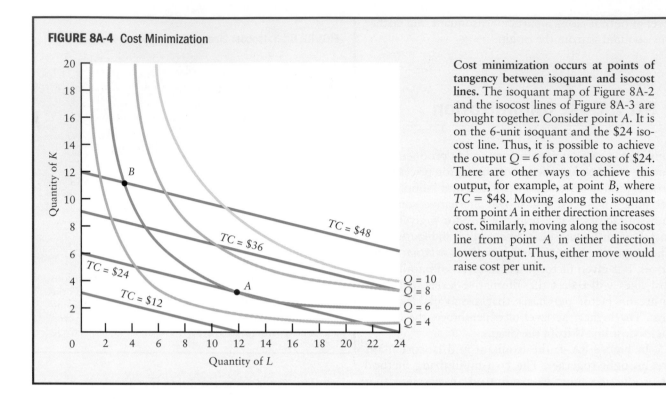

Cost minimization occurs at points of tangency between isoquant and isocost lines. The isoquant map of Figure 8A-2 and the isocost lines of Figure 8A-3 are brought together. Consider point *A*. It is on the 6-unit isoquant and the $24 isocost line. Thus, it is possible to achieve the output *Q* = 6 for a total cost of $24. There are other ways to achieve this output, for example, at point *B*, where *TC* = $48. Moving along the isoquant from point *A* in either direction increases cost. Similarly, moving along the isocost line from point *A* in either direction lowers output. Thus, either move would raise cost per unit.

FIGURE 8A-5 The Effects of a Change in Factor Prices on Costs and Factor Proportions

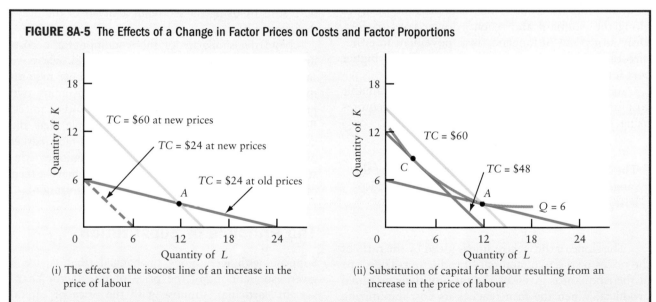

(i) The effect on the isocost line of an increase in the price of labour

(ii) Substitution of capital for labour resulting from an increase in the price of labour

An increase in the price of labour pivots the isocost line inward, increasing its slope. This changes the cost-minimizing method of producing any level of output. In part (i), the rise in the price of *L* from $1 to $4 per unit (with the price of *K* being held constant at $4) pivots the $24 isocost line inward to the dashed line. Any output previously produced for $24 will cost more at the new prices if it uses any labour. The new cost of using the factor combination at *A* rises from $24 to $60. In part (ii), the steeper isocost line is tangent to the *Q* = 6 isoquant at *C*, not *A*, so that more capital and less labour is used. Costs at *C* are $48, higher than they were before the price increase but not as high as they would be if the factor substitution had not occurred.

longer the cost-minimizing one. The slope of the isocost line has changed, which makes it efficient to substitute the now relatively cheaper capital for the relatively more expensive labour. The change in slope of the isocost line illustrates the principle of substitution.

> **Changes in relative factor prices will cause a partial replacement of factors that have become relatively more expensive by factors that have become relatively cheaper.**

Of course, substitution of capital for labour cannot fully offset the effects of a rise in the cost of labour, as Figure 8A-5(i) shows. Consider the output attainable for $24. In the figure, there are two isocost lines representing $24 of outlay—at the old and new prices of labour. The new isocost line for $24 lies inside the old one (except where no labour is used). The $24 isocost line must therefore be tangent to a lower isoquant. Thus, if production is to be held constant, higher costs must be accepted. However, because of substitution, it is not necessary to accept costs as high as those that would accompany an unchanged factor proportion. In the example, 6 units can be produced for $48 rather than the $60 that would be required if no change in factor proportions were made.

This analysis leads to the following predictions:

> **A rise in the price of one factor with all other factor prices held constant will (1) shift the cost curves of products that use that factor upward and (2) lead to a substitution of factors that are now relatively cheaper for the factor whose price has risen.**

Both of these predictions were stated in Chapter 8; now they have been derived formally by the use of isoquants and isocost lines.

Competitive Markets

DOES MasterCard compete with Visa? Does a wheat farmer from Biggar, Saskatchewan, compete with a wheat farmer from Brandon, Manitoba? If we use the ordinary meaning of the word *compete*, the answer to the first question is plainly yes, and the answer to the second question is no.

MasterCard and Visa both advertise extensively to persuade consumers to use their credit cards. We are told that some of life's pleasures are priceless, and "for everything else, there's MasterCard," while other happy customers assure us that only with a Visa card can their pleasures be ours.

When we shift our attention to wheat farmers, however, we see the Saskatchewan farmer can do nothing to affect either the sales or the profits of the Manitoba farmer. Even if the Saskatchewan farmer could do something to influence the profits of the Manitoba farmer, there would be no point in doing so, since changes in the profits of the Manitoba farmer would not affect the Saskatchewan farmer.

To sort out the questions of who is competing with whom and in what sense, it is useful to distinguish between the behaviour of individual firms and the type of market in which they operate. Economists are interested in two different concepts—*competitive market structure* and *competitive behaviour*.

9.1 Market Structure and Firm Behaviour

The term **market structure** refers to all the features that may affect the behaviour and performance of the firms in a market, such as the number of firms in the market or the type of product that they sell. In this chapter, we focus on a *competitive* market structure.

market structure All features of a market that affect the behaviour and performance of firms in that market, such as the number and size of sellers, the extent of knowledge about one another's actions, the degree of freedom of entry, and the degree of product differentiation.

Competitive Market Structure

Economists say that firms have **market power** when they can influence the price of their product. The *competitiveness* of the market is the degree to which individual firms *lack* such market power.

market power The ability of a firm to influence the price of its product.

> A market is said to have a competitive structure when its firms have little or no market power. The more market power the firms have, the less competitive is the market structure.

The extreme form of competitive market structure occurs when each firm has zero market power. In such a case, there are so many firms in the market that each must accept the price set by the forces of market demand and supply. The firms perceive themselves as being able to sell as much as they choose at the prevailing market price and as having no power to influence that price. If the firm charged a higher price, it would make no sales; so many other firms would be selling at the market price that buyers would take their business elsewhere.

This extreme is called a *perfectly competitive market structure* or, more simply, a *perfectly competitive market*. In such a market there is no need for individual firms to compete actively with one another because none has any power over the market. One firm's ability to sell its product does not depend on the behaviour of any other firm. For example, the Saskatchewan and Manitoba wheat farmers operate in a perfectly competitive market over which they have no power. Neither can change the market price for wheat by altering their own behaviour.

Visa "competes" very actively in the credit-card market against Mastercard and American Express, but economists nonetheless refer to the structure of this market as non-competitive.

Competitive Behaviour

In everyday language, the term *competitive behaviour* refers to the degree to which individual firms actively vie with one another for business. For example, MasterCard and Visa clearly engage in competitive behaviour. It is also true, however, that both companies have some real power over their market. Each has the power to decide the fees that people will pay for the use of their credit cards, within limits set by buyers' tastes, the fees of competing cards, and some government regulations. Either firm could raise its fees and still continue to attract some customers. Even though they actively compete with each other, they do so in a market that does not have a perfectly competitive structure.

A wheat farmer in Saskatchewan does not "compete" in any real way with a wheat farmer elsewhere in the world. However, both exist in what economists call a perfectly competitive market.

In contrast, the Saskatchewan and Manitoba wheat farmers do not engage in competitive behaviour because the only way they can affect their profits is by changing their own outputs of wheat or their own production costs.

The distinction that we have just made between behaviour and structure explains why firms in perfectly competitive markets (e.g., the Saskatchewan and Manitoba wheat producers) do not compete actively with each other, whereas firms that do compete actively with each other (e.g., MasterCard and Visa) do not operate in perfectly competitive markets.

The Significance of Market Structure

When a firm decides how much output to produce in order to maximize its profit, it needs to know the demand for its product and also its costs of production. We examined the various costs in detail in Chapters 7 and 8. Now we need to think about the demand for the firm's product. This is where market structure enters our analysis because the details of market structure determine how we get from the *industry* demand curve to the demand curve facing any individual *firm* in that industry.

We will see in the next few chapters that market structure plays a central role in determining the behaviour of individual firms and also in the overall *efficiency* of the market outcomes. In this chapter, we focus only on *competitive* market structures. In later chapters, we explore non-competitive market structures.

| 9.2 The Theory of Perfect Competition

perfect competition A market structure in which all firms in an industry are price takers, and in which there is freedom of entry into and exit from the industry.

The perfectly competitive market structure—usually referred to simply as **perfect competition**—applies directly to a number of markets, especially many agricultural and raw-materials markets. It also provides an important benchmark for comparison with other market structures.

The Assumptions of Perfect Competition

In addition to the fundamental assumption that firms seek to maximize their profits, the theory of perfect competition is built on a number of assumptions relating to each firm and to the industry as a whole.

1. All the firms in the industry sell an identical product. Economists say that the firms sell a **homogeneous product**.

2. Consumers know the nature of the product being sold and the prices charged by each firm.

homogeneous product In the eyes of purchasers, every unit of the product is identical to every other unit.

3. The level of each firm's output at which its long-run average cost reaches a minimum is small relative to the *industry's* total output. (This is a precise way of saying that each firm is small relative to the size of the industry.)

4. The industry is characterized by *freedom of entry and exit*; that is, any new firm is free to enter the industry and start producing if it so wishes, and any existing firm is free to cease production and leave the industry. Existing firms cannot block the entry of new firms, and there are no legal prohibitions or other barriers to entering or exiting the industry.

The first three assumptions imply that each firm in a perfectly competitive industry is a **price taker**, meaning that the firm can alter its output and sales without affecting the market price of its product. Thus, a firm operating in a perfectly competitive market has no market power. It must passively accept whatever happens to be the market price, but it can sell as much as it wants at that price.

Our Saskatchewan and Manitoba wheat farmers provide us with good illustrations of firms that are operating in a perfectly competitive market. Because each individual wheat farmer is just one of a very large number of producers who are all growing the same product, one firm's contribution to the industry's total production is a tiny drop in an extremely large bucket. Each firm will correctly assume that variations in its output have no effect on the price of wheat. Thus, each firm, knowing that it can sell as much or as little as it chooses at that price, adapts its behaviour to a given market price of wheat. Furthermore, there is nothing that any one farmer can do to stop another farmer from growing wheat, and there are no legal deterrents to becoming a wheat farmer. Anyone who has enough money to buy or rent the necessary land, labour, and equipment can become a wheat farmer.

The difference between the wheat farmers and MasterCard or Visa is the *degree of market power*. Each firm that is producing wheat is an insignificant part of the whole market and thus has no power to influence the price of wheat. MasterCard and Visa have power to influence the credit-card market because each firm's sales represent a significant part of the total sales of credit-card services.

price taker A firm that can alter its output and sales without affecting the market price of its product.

The Demand Curve for a Perfectly Competitive Firm

A major distinction between firms in perfectly competitive markets and firms in any other type of market is the shape of the demand curve facing the firm.

> Even though the demand curve for the entire industry is negatively sloped, each firm in a perfectly competitive market faces a horizontal demand curve because variations in the firm's output have no significant effect on market price.

The horizontal (perfectly elastic) demand curve does not indicate that the firm could actually sell an infinite amount at the going price. It indicates, rather, that any feasible variations in that firm's production will leave price unchanged because the effect on total industry output will be negligible.

Figure 9-1 contrasts the market demand curve for the product of a competitive industry with the demand curve that a single firm in that industry faces. *Applying Economic Concepts 9-1* provides an example of the important difference between the firm's demand curve and the market demand curve. It uses a numerical example to show why the demand curve facing any individual wheat farmer is very nearly perfectly elastic, even though the *market* demand for wheat is quite inelastic.

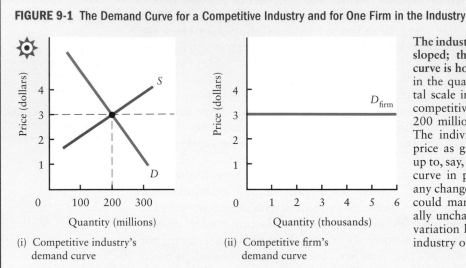

FIGURE 9-1 The Demand Curve for a Competitive Industry and for One Firm in the Industry

(i) Competitive industry's demand curve

(ii) Competitive firm's demand curve

The industry's demand curve is negatively sloped; the competitive firm's demand curve is horizontal. Notice the difference in the quantities shown on the horizontal scale in each part of the figure. The competitive industry has an output of 200 million units when the price is $3. The individual firm takes that market price as given and considers producing up to, say, 6000 units. The firm's demand curve in part (ii) is horizontal because any change in output that this single firm could manage would leave price virtually unchanged at $3. The firm's output variation has an imperceptible effect on industry output and thus market price.

APPLYING ECONOMIC CONCEPTS 9-1

Why Small Firms Are Price Takers

Consider an individual wheat farmer and the world market for wheat. Since products have negatively sloped market demand curves, any increase in the industry's output (caused by a shift in supply) will cause some fall in the market price. However, as the calculations here show, any conceivable increase that one wheat farm could make in its output has such a negligible effect on the industry's price that the farmer correctly ignores it—the individual wheat farmer is thus a price taker.

The *market* elasticity of demand for wheat is approximately 0.25. (Recall from Chapter 4 that an elasticity of 0.25 means that a 10 percent decline in market price is associated with only a 2.5 percent increase in quantity demanded.) Thus, if the quantity of wheat supplied in the world were to increase by 1 percent, the price of wheat would have to fall by roughly 4 percent to induce the world's wheat buyers to purchase the extra wheat.

The total world production of wheat in 2012 was approximately 650 million tonnes, of which 24 million tonnes were produced in Canada. In that year there were approximately 20 000 wheat farms in Canada. Thus, the average crop size for a Canadian wheat farmer in 2012 was about 1200 tonnes (= 24 million/20 000), only 0.0002 percent of the world wheat crop.

As a result of being such a small fraction of the overall market, individual wheat farmers face a horizontal demand curve. To see this, suppose an individual farmer on an average-sized farm decided in one year to produce nothing and in another year managed to produce twice the average output of 1200 tonnes. This is an extremely large variation in one farm's output. The increase in output from 0 to 2400 tonnes represents a 200 percent variation measured around the farm's average output. Yet the percentage increase in world output is only (2400/650 million) × 100 = 0.0004 percent. Given that the world's demand for wheat has a price elasticity of about 0.25, this increase in output would lead to a decrease in the world price of 0.0016 percent.

This very small decline in price, together with the 200 percent increase in the farm's own output, implies that the farm's own demand curve has an elasticity of 125 000 (= 200/0.0016). This enormous elasticity of demand means that the farm would have to increase its output by 125 000 percent to bring about a 1 percent decrease in the world price of wheat. Because the farm's output cannot be varied this much, it is not surprising that the farmer regards the price of wheat as unaffected by any change in output that he or she could conceivably make. For all intents and purposes, the individual farmer faces a perfectly elastic—horizontal—demand curve for the product and is thus a *price taker*.

Total, Average, and Marginal Revenue

To study the revenues that firms receive from the sale of their products, economists define three concepts called *total, average,* and *marginal revenue.*

Total revenue (*TR*) is the total amount received by the firm from the sale of a product. If *Q* units are sold at *p* dollars each,

$$TR = P \times Q$$

Average revenue (*AR*) is the amount of revenue per unit sold. It is equal to total revenue divided by the number of units sold and is thus equal to the price at which the product is sold:

$$AR = \frac{TR}{Q} = \frac{(p \times Q)}{Q} = p$$

Marginal revenue (*MR*) is the *change* in a firm's total revenue resulting from a *change* in its sales by 1 unit. Whenever output changes by more than 1 unit, the change in revenue must be divided by the change in output to calculate the approximate marginal revenue. For example, if an increase in output of 3 units is accompanied by an increase in revenue of $1500, the marginal revenue is $1500/3, or $500. [21]

$$MR = \frac{\Delta TR}{\Delta Q}$$

To illustrate each of these revenue concepts, consider a farmer who is selling barley in a perfectly competitive market at a price of $3 per bushel. Total revenue rises by $3 for every bushel sold. Because every bushel brings in $3, the average revenue per bushel sold is clearly $3. Furthermore, because each *additional* bushel sold brings in $3, the marginal revenue of an extra bushel sold is also $3. The table in Figure 9-2 shows calculations of these revenue concepts for a range of outputs between 10 and 13 bushels. The figure plots the various revenue curves.

The important point illustrated in the table is that as long as the firm's own level of output cannot affect the price of the product it sells, then the firm's marginal revenue is equal to its average revenue. Thus, for a price-taking firm, *AR* = *MR* = price. Graphically, as shown in part (i) of Figure 9-2, average revenue and marginal revenue are the same horizontal line drawn at the level of market price. Because the firm can sell any quantity it chooses at this price, the horizontal line is also the firm's demand curve; it shows that any quantity the firm chooses to sell will be associated with this same market price.

total revenue (*TR*) Total receipts from the sale of a product; price times quantity.

average revenue (*AR*) Total revenue divided by quantity sold; this is the market price when all units are sold at the same price.

marginal revenue (*MR*) The change in a firm's total revenue resulting from a change in its sales by one unit.

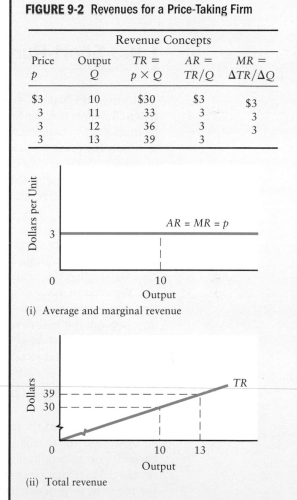

FIGURE 9-2 Revenues for a Price-Taking Firm

Revenue Concepts				
Price p	Output Q	$TR = p \times Q$	$AR = TR/Q$	$MR = \Delta TR/\Delta Q$
$3	10	$30	$3	
3	11	33	3	$3
3	12	36	3	3
3	13	39	3	3

(i) Average and marginal revenue

(ii) Total revenue

When the firm is a price taker, *AR* = *MR* = *p*. Because price does not change as a result of the firm changing its output, neither marginal revenue nor average revenue varies with output. In the table, marginal revenue is shown between the rows because it represents the *change* in total revenues in response to a *change* in quantity. When price is constant, total revenue (which is price times quantity) is an upward-sloping straight line starting from the origin.

> If the market price is unaffected by variations in the firm's output, the firm's demand curve, its average revenue curve, and its marginal revenue curve all coincide in the same horizontal line.

This result can be stated in a slightly different way that turns out to be important for our later study:

> For a firm in perfect competition, price equals marginal revenue.

9.3 Short-Run Decisions

We learned in Chapter 7 how each firm's costs vary with its output in the short run. Recall that in the short run, the firm has one or more fixed factors, and the only way it can change its output is by changing the amount of its variable factor inputs. In this chapter, we have seen how the firm's total, average, and marginal revenues vary as the firm changes its level of output. The next step is to put the cost and revenue information together to determine the level of output that will maximize the firm's economic profits. Recall also from Chapter 7 that economic profit is the difference between total revenue and total cost,

$$\pi = TR - TC$$

where all costs are measured as economic (as opposed to accounting) costs. If total revenues are not enough to cover total costs, economic profits will be negative—in this case we say that the firm is making *losses*.

We need to ask and answer two questions for a competitive firm. First, should the firm produce any output at all, or would it be better to shut down and produce nothing? Second, if it makes economic sense for the firm to remain in business and produce some output, *what level* of output should it produce? To answer both questions, we assume the firm's objective is to maximize its profits.

Should the Firm Produce At All?

The firm always has the option of producing nothing. If it produces nothing, it will have an operating loss that is equal to its fixed costs. If it decides to produce, it will add the variable cost of production to its costs and the receipts from the sale of its product to its revenue. Therefore, since it must pay its fixed costs in any event, it will be worthwhile for the firm to produce as long as it can find some level of output for which revenue exceeds *variable* cost. However, if its revenue is less than its variable cost at every level of output, the firm will actually lose more by producing than by not producing at all.

Table 9-1 shows an example of a firm that decides to minimize its losses by producing no output when it faces a low market price. The table shows the firm's variable and fixed costs for each level of output. (If you were to graph the *TVC*, *TFC*, and *TC* curves from this table, you would find that they look like the curves we studied in Chapter 7.) The table also shows the firm's total revenues and profits at each level of output. When the market price is $2 per unit, the firm's profits are negative *at any level of output*—the

TABLE 9-1 Negative Profits and the Firm's Shut-Down Decision

Q	TVC	TFC	TC	Low Price ($2)		High Price ($5)	
				TR	Profit (TR − TC)	TR	Profit (TR − TC)
0	0	200	200	0	−200	0	−200
10	50	200	250	20	−230	50	−200
20	80	200	280	40	−240	100	−180
30	100	200	300	60	−240	150	−150
40	110	200	310	80	−230	200	−110
50	130	200	330	100	−230	250	−80
60	160	200	360	120	−240	300	−60
70	200	200	400	140	−260	350	−50
80	260	200	460	160	−300	400	−60
90	320	200	520	180	−340	450	−70
100	380	200	580	200	−380	500	−80

A competitive firm may maximize its profits (or minimize its losses) by shutting down and producing zero output. The data in the table show costs and revenues at various levels of output. The firm must pay its fixed costs even if it shuts down and earns no revenue. At a price of $2, there is no level of output at which the firm's revenues cover its variable costs. In this situation, the firm can minimize its losses by shutting down and producing zero output.

At a higher price of $5, the profit-maximizing firm should choose to produce 70 units of output even though its profits are negative. At this level of output, the firm's revenues more than cover its variable costs and help to pay some portion of the fixed costs. Since the firm must pay its fixed costs no matter what level of output is produced, its profits would be even lower if it chose to produce zero output.

firm's revenues *never* cover its costs. At this low market price, the firm's revenues don't even cover its variable costs and, in fact, the negative profits (losses) only grow larger as output increases. In this situation, the firm is better off to shut down and produce no output at all. In this case, the firm is maximizing its profits by *minimizing its losses*. (The table also presents a situation in which the price is $5 per unit; for reasons that we will soon see, the firm's best option in this case is to produce output even though its profits are negative.)

> **Rule 1: A firm should not produce at all if, for all levels of output, total revenue (TR) is less than total variable cost (TVC). Equivalently, the firm should not produce at all if, for all levels of output, the market price (p) is less than average variable cost (AVC). [22]**

We have been looking at the firm's decision about whether to produce at all by comparing total revenues with total variable costs. Equivalently, we can examine this decision by comparing the market price with average variable cost.

The price at which the firm can just cover its average variable cost, and so is indifferent between producing and not producing, is called the **shut-down price**. Such a price is shown in Figure 9-3. At a price of p_0, the firm can just cover its variable cost

shut-down price The price that is equal to the minimum of a firm's average variable costs. At prices below this, a profit-maximizing firm will shut down and produce no output.

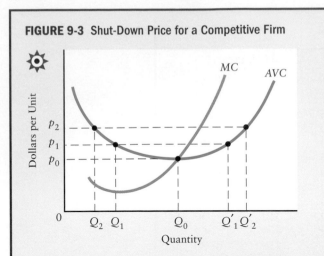

FIGURE 9-3 Shut-Down Price for a Competitive Firm

When the market price is less than the minimum average variable cost, the competitive firm will shut down. If the price is exactly p_0, the firm can just cover its variable costs by producing Q_0 units of output (and so is indifferent between shutting down and continuing its operations). At any price below p_0, the firm is better off shutting down and producing no output. At any price above p_0, there are many output levels that cover variable costs. For example, at price p_1, any level of output between Q_1 and Q_1' will cover variable costs (but only one will maximize profits).

by producing Q_0 units. For any price *below* p_0, there is no level of output at which variable costs can be covered, and thus the firm will shut down. The price p_0 is therefore the firm's shut-down price. At any price above p_0, there are many levels of output that cover average variable costs (but for each price above p_0 there is only a single level of output that *maximizes* the firm's profit).

How Much Should the Firm Produce?

If a firm decides that, according to Rule 1, production is worth undertaking, it must then decide *how much* to produce. The key to understanding how much a profit-maximizing firm should produce is to think about it on a unit-by-unit basis. If any unit of production adds more to revenue than it does to cost, producing and selling that unit will increase profits. According to the terminology introduced earlier, a unit of production raises profits if the *marginal* revenue obtained from selling it exceeds the *marginal* cost of producing it. By the same logic, an extra unit of production will reduce profits if the marginal revenue is less than the marginal cost.

Now let's consider a firm already producing some level of output and see what happens if it increases or decreases its output. If an extra unit of output will increase the firm's revenues by more than it increases costs ($MR > MC$), the firm should expand its output. However, if the last unit produced increases revenues by less than it increases costs ($MR < MC$), the profit-maximizing firm should reduce its output. From this it follows that the only time the firm should leave its output unaltered is when the last unit produced adds the same amount to revenues as it does to costs ($MR = MC$).[1]

> **Rule 2: If it is worthwhile for the firm to produce at all, the firm should produce the output at which marginal revenue equals marginal cost. [23]**

The two rules that we have stated refer to each firm's own costs and revenues, and they apply to all profit-maximizing firms, whatever the market structure in which they operate. However, we have already seen that for price-taking firms, marginal revenue

---

[1] The equality of *MR* and *MC* is a *necessary* condition for profit maximization, but it is not *sufficient*. If the *MC* curve cuts the *MR* curve from above, as it might if *MC* were *falling* as output increased, then the level of output where *MR* equals *MC* would actually *minimize* profits. Here, we restrict ourselves to the more realistic settings in which the *MC* curve is upward sloping over the relevant range of output. In such cases, the equality of *MR* and *MC* is both necessary and sufficient for profit maximization.

is equal to the market price. Combining these two results gives us an important conclusion:

> **A profit-maximizing firm that is operating in a perfectly competitive market will produce the output that equates its marginal cost of production with the market price of its product (as long as price exceeds average variable cost).**

If you look back to Table 9-1, when the market price is $5 the application of this rule is evident after doing a few calculations. Since price is $5, and the firm is a price taker, the firm's MR is also $5. If you compute the firm's MC between output levels $Q = 60$ and $Q = 80$, you see that the firm's $MC = \Delta TC/\Delta Q = \$100/20 = \$5$. Thus, the highlighted row which indicates the firm's maximum profits (or minimum losses) also shows the level of output where $MR = MC$.

In a perfectly competitive industry, the market determines the price at which the firm sells its product. The firm then picks the quantity of output that maximizes its profits. We have seen that this is the output for which price equals marginal cost. When the firm has reached a position in which its profits are maximized, it has no incentive to change its output. Therefore, unless prices or costs change, the firm will continue to produce this output because it is doing as well as it can do, given the market situation. This profit-maximizing behaviour is illustrated in Figure 9-4.

> **The perfectly competitive firm adjusts its level of output in response to changes in the market-determined price.**

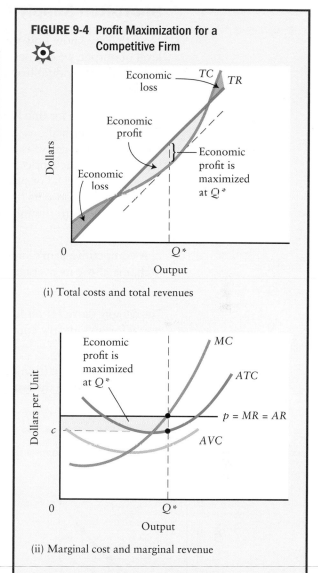

FIGURE 9-4 Profit Maximization for a Competitive Firm

(i) Total costs and total revenues

(ii) Marginal cost and marginal revenue

The firm chooses the level of output at which profits are maximized. If it is profitable to produce at all (that is, if $p >$ minimum of AVC), the firm chooses the level of output where marginal revenue equals marginal cost. In part (i), this is shown as the level of output where the vertical distance between TR and TC is largest (and thus where the slopes of the TR and TC curves are the same). In part (ii), price is equal to marginal revenue since the firm is a price taker, and so the profit-maximizing level of output is the point at which price (marginal revenue) equals marginal cost. For each of the Q^* units sold, the firm earns revenue of p and the average total cost is c; therefore, total profit is $(p - c)Q^*$, which is the shaded area.

Figure 9-4 shows the profit-maximizing choice of the firm in two different ways. In part (i), the firm's total cost and total revenue curves are shown, and the profit-maximizing level of output, Q^*, is the level that shows the largest positive gap between total revenues and total costs. In part (ii), the firm's average and marginal cost curves are shown together with the market price (which for a price-taking firm equals average and marginal revenue) and the profit-maximizing level of output, Q^*, is the level at which price equals marginal cost. These are two different ways of viewing the same profit-maximization problem; the value of Q^* in part (i) must be the same as the value of Q^* in part (ii).

Short-Run Supply Curves

Now that we know how the perfectly competitive firm determines its profit-maximizing level of output, we can derive its supply curve that reflects these decisions. Once we have derived the individual firm's supply curve, we can derive the supply curve for the entire market.

The Supply Curve for One Firm The competitive firm's supply curve is derived in part (i) of Figure 9-5, which shows a firm's marginal cost curve and four alternative prices. What we are trying to derive is a supply curve that shows the quantity of output that the firm will supply at each price. For prices below average variable cost, the firm will supply zero units (Rule 1). For prices above the minimum of average variable cost, the competitive firm will choose its level of output to equate price and marginal cost (Rule 2). This behaviour leads to the following conclusion:

> **A competitive firm's supply curve is given by the portion of its marginal cost curve that is above its average variable cost curve.**

The Supply Curve for an Industry Figure 9-6 shows the derivation of an industry supply curve for an industry containing only two firms. The general result is as follows:

> **In perfect competition, the industry supply curve is the horizontal sum of the marginal cost curves (above the level of average variable cost) of all firms in the industry.**

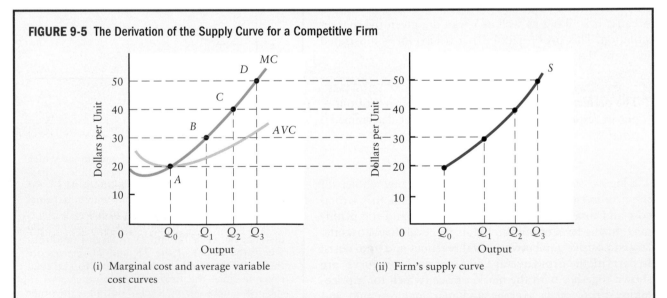

FIGURE 9-5 The Derivation of the Supply Curve for a Competitive Firm

(i) Marginal cost and average variable cost curves

(ii) Firm's supply curve

The supply curve of the competitive firm is the portion of its *MC* curve above the *AVC* curve. For prices below $20, output is zero because there is no output at which variable costs can be covered. The point *A*, at which the price of $20 is just equal to the minimum of *AVC,* is the point at which the firm will shut down. As price rises to $30, $40, and $50, the profit-maximizing point changes to *B, C,* and *D,* taking output to Q_1, Q_2, and Q_3. At any of these prices, the firm's revenue exceeds its variable costs of production and thus can help to cover some part of its fixed costs.

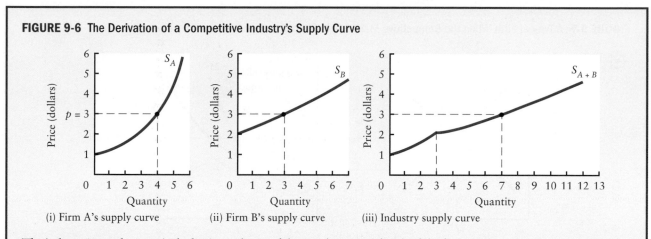

FIGURE 9-6 The Derivation of a Competitive Industry's Supply Curve

(i) Firm A's supply curve

(ii) Firm B's supply curve

(iii) Industry supply curve

The industry's supply curve is the horizontal sum of the supply curves of each of the firms in the industry. At a price of $3, Firm A would supply 4 units and Firm B would supply 3 units. Together, as shown in part (iii), they would supply 7 units. If there are hundreds of firms, the process is the same. In this example, because Firm B does not enter the market at prices below $2, the supply curve S_{A+B} is identical to S_A up to the price $2 and is the horizontal sum of S_A and S_B above $2.

Each firm's marginal cost curve shows how much that firm will supply at each given market price, and the industry supply curve is the sum of what each firm will supply. Notice in Figure 9-6 the "kink" in the industry supply curve, which occurs at the price of $2; at any lower price the second firm chooses not to produce any output.

This supply curve, based on the short-run marginal cost curves of all the firms in the industry, is the industry's supply curve that we first encountered in Chapter 3. We have now established the profit-maximizing behaviour of individual firms that lies behind that curve. It is sometimes called a *short-run supply curve* because it is based on the short-run, profit-maximizing behaviour of all the firms in the industry.

Short-Run Equilibrium in a Competitive Market

The price of a product sold in a perfectly competitive market is determined by the inter-action of the market supply curve and demand curve. Although no single firm can influ-ence the market price significantly, the collective actions of all firms in the industry (as shown by the market supply curve) and the collective actions of households (as shown by the market demand curve) together determine the equilibrium price. This occurs at the point at which the market demand and supply curves intersect.

When a perfectly competitive industry is in **short-run equilibrium**, each firm is produ-cing and selling a quantity for which its marginal cost equals the market price. No firm is motivated to change its output in the short run. Because total quantity demanded equals total quantity supplied, there is no reason for market price to change in the short run.

short-run equilibrium For a competitive industry, the price and output at which industry demand equals short-run industry supply, and all firms are maximizing their profits. Either profits or losses for individual firms are possible.

> When an industry is in short-run equilibrium, quantity demanded equals quantity supplied, and each firm is maximizing its profits given the market price.

Figure 9-7 shows the relationship between the market equilibrium, determined by the intersection of demand and supply, and a typical profit-maximizing firm within

FIGURE 9-7 A Typical Firm When the Competitive Market Is in Short-Run Equilibrium

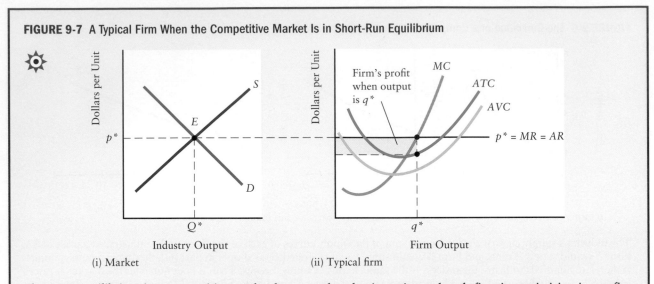

(i) Market   (ii) Typical firm

Short-run equilibrium in a competitive market has a market-clearing price and each firm is maximizing its profits. Part (i) shows the overall market. The equilibrium price and quantity (p^*, Q^*) are determined at the intersection of the market demand and supply curves at point E. Part (ii) shows a typical firm in the market. Notice that the horizontal scales are different in the two parts of the figure—total market output is designated by Q, whereas firm-level output is designated by q. The equilibrium price in part (i) becomes the MR curve for each firm in the market. Given its MC curve, the firm's profit-maximizing level of output is q^*. In the case shown, the firm is making positive profits equal to the shaded area.

that market.[2] The individual firm is shown to have positive (economic) profits in the short-run equilibrium. We can see that the firm's profits are positive because the market price exceeds average total costs when the firm is producing its profit-maximizing level of output, q^*. But such positive profits need not always occur in the short run. In general, we do not know whether firms in the short-run competitive equilibrium will be earning positive, zero, or negative profits. We *do* know that each firm is maximizing its profits; we just don't know how large those profits are.

Figure 9-8 shows three possible positions for a firm when the industry is in short-run equilibrium. In all cases, the firm is maximizing its profits by producing where price equals marginal cost, but in part (i) the firm is suffering losses, in part (ii) it is just covering all of its costs (breaking even), and in part (iii) it is making profits because price exceeds average total cost. In all three cases, the firm is doing as well as it can, given its costs and the market price.

Note that the competitive firm's profit per unit is shown by the difference between price and average total cost. To see this algebraically, note that the firm's total profits are

$$\text{Profits} = TR - TC$$
$$= (p \times Q) - (ATC \times Q)$$
$$= (p - ATC) \times Q$$

---

[2] In diagrams with both firm-level and industry-level output, we use q for the firm's output and Q for total industry output.

FIGURE 9-8 Alternative Short-Run Profits of a Competitive Firm

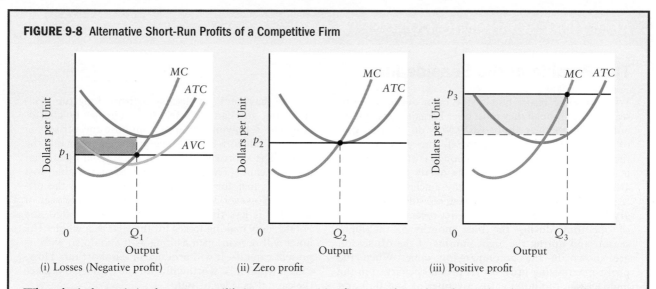

(i) Losses (Negative profit)   (ii) Zero profit   (iii) Positive profit

When the industry is in short-run equilibrium, a competitive firm may be making losses, breaking even, or making profits. The diagrams show a firm with given costs that faces three alternative short-run equilibrium market prices: p_1, p_2, and p_3. In each part of the figure, $MC = MR =$ price. Because in all three cases price exceeds AVC, the firm produces positive output in each case.

In part (i), price is p_1 and the firm is making losses, shown by the red shaded area, because price is below average total cost. Because price exceeds average variable cost, it is worthwhile for the firm to keep producing, but it is not worthwhile for it to replace its capital equipment as it wears out. In part (ii), price is p_2 and the firm is just covering its total costs. It is worthwhile for the firm to replace its capital as it wears out, since it is covering the full opportunity cost of its capital. In part (iii), price is p_3 and the firm is earning profits, shown by the green shaded area.

So, profit *per unit* is given by $p - ATC$, whereas the firm's *total* profit (or loss) associated with the production of all Q units is $(p - ATC) \times Q$, and is illustrated by the shaded rectangles in Figure 9-8.

It is worth emphasizing that some firms will continue producing even though they are making losses. The firm shown in part (i) of Figure 9-8 is incurring losses every period that it remains in business, but it is still better for it to carry on producing than to temporarily halt production. If the firm produces nothing this period, it still must pay its fixed costs, so it makes sense to continue producing as long as its revenues more than cover its variable costs or, equivalently, as long as price exceeds AVC. Any amount of money left over after the variable costs have been paid can then go toward paying some of the fixed costs. This is more than the firm would have if it simply produced nothing and hence earned no revenue whatsoever. (Look back to Table 9-1 on page 207 to see an example of this situation, in the case where market price is $5 per unit.) *Applying Economic Concepts 9-2* discusses an interesting example of a firm that remains in operation even though it is making losses. You would probably see many firms like this one if you drove through small towns in any part of Canada.

APPLYING ECONOMIC CONCEPTS 9-2

The Parable of the Seaside Inn

Why do some resort hotels stay open during the off-season, even though they must offer bargain rates that do not even cover their "full costs"? Why do the managers of other hotels allow them to fall into disrepair even though they are able to attract enough customers to stay in business? Are the former being overly generous, and are the latter being irrational penny-pinchers?

To illustrate what is involved, consider an imaginary hotel called the Seaside Inn. Its revenues and costs of operating during the four months of the high-season and during the eight months of the off-season are shown in the accompanying table. When the profit-maximizing price for its rooms is charged in the high-season, the hotel earns revenues of $58 000 and incurs variable costs equal to $36 000. Thus, there is an "operating profit" of $22 000 during the high-season. This surplus goes toward meeting the hotel's annual fixed costs of $24 000. Thus, $2000 of the fixed costs are not yet paid.

The Seaside Inn: Total Costs and Revenues ($)

Season	Total Revenue (TR)	Total Variable Cost (TVC)	Contribution to Fixed Costs (TR − TVC)	Total Fixed Costs
High-Season	58 000	36 000	22 000	
Off-Season	20 000	18 000	2 000	
Total	78 000	54 000	24 000	24 000

If the Seaside Inn were to charge the same rates during the off-season, it could not attract enough customers even to cover its costs of maids, receptionists, and managers. However, the hotel discovers that by charging lower rates during the off-season, it can rent some of its rooms and earn revenues of $20 000. Its costs of operating (variable costs) during the off-season are $18 000. So, by operating at reduced rates in the off-season, the hotel is able to contribute another $2000 toward its annual fixed costs, thereby eliminating the shortfall.

Therefore, the hotel stays open during the whole year by offering off-season bargain rates to grateful guests. Indeed, if it were to close during the off-season, it would not be able to cover its total fixed and variable costs solely through its high-season operations.

We have not yet discussed firms' long-run decisions, but you can get a feel for the issues by considering the following situation. Suppose the off-season revenues fall to $19 000 (everything else remains the same). The short-run condition for staying open, that total revenue (TR) must exceed total variable cost (TVC), is met for both the high-season and the off-season. However, since the TR over the whole year of $77 000 is less than the total costs of $78 000, the hotel is now making losses for the year as a whole. The hotel will remain open as long as it can do so with its present capital—it will produce in the short run. However, it will not be worthwhile for the owners to replace the capital as it wears out.

If the reduction in revenues persists, the hotel will become one of those run-down hotels about which guests ask, "Why don't they do something about this place?" But the owners are behaving quite sensibly. They are operating the hotel as long as it covers its variable costs, but they are not putting any more investment into it because it cannot cover its fixed costs. Sooner or later, the fixed capital will become too old to be run, or at least to attract customers, and the hotel will be closed.

Hotels and other resorts often charge low prices in the off-season, low enough that they do not cover their total costs. But as long as the price more than covers the variable costs, it is better than shutting down during the off-season.

9.4 Long-Run Decisions

In Chapter 7 and 8, we described the short run as the span of time for which individual firms have a fixed factor of production (typically capital), and the long run as the span of time for which all of the firm's factors are variable. When we look at the entire industry, the distinction is very similar. In the short run, there is a given number of firms and each has a given plant size. In the long run, both the number of firms and the size of each firm's plant are variable.

We begin our discussion of the long run by assuming that all firms in the industry have the same technology and therefore have the same set of cost curves. Thus, the short-run equilibrium in the industry will have *all* firms in the industry being equally profitable (or making equal losses). Toward the end of the chapter we relax this assumption when we allow new firms to have better technologies and thus lower costs than older firms already in the industry.

Entry and Exit

The key difference between a perfectly competitive industry in the short run and in the long run is the entry or exit of firms. We have seen that all the firms in the industry may be making profits, suffering losses, or just breaking even when the industry is in short-run equilibrium. Because economic costs include the opportunity cost of capital, if the firms are just breaking even they are doing as well as they could do by investing their capital elsewhere. Hence, there will be no incentive for firms to leave the industry if economic profits are zero. Similarly, if new entrants expect just to break even, there will be no incentive for firms to enter the industry because capital can earn the same return elsewhere in the economy. If, however, the existing firms are earning revenues in excess of all costs, including the opportunity cost of capital, new capital will eventually enter the industry to share in these profits. Conversely, if the existing firms are suffering economic losses, capital will eventually leave the industry because a better return can be obtained elsewhere in the economy. Let us now consider this process in a little more detail.

An Entry-Attracting Price First, suppose there are 100 firms in a competitive industry, all making positive profits like the firm shown in part (iii) of Figure 9-8. New firms, attracted by the profitability of existing firms, will enter the industry. Suppose that in response to the high profits, 20 new firms enter. The market supply curve that formerly added up the outputs of 100 firms must now add up the outputs of 120 firms. At any price, more will be supplied because there are more producers. This entry of new firms into the industry causes a rightward shift in the industry supply curve.

With an unchanged market demand curve, this rightward shift in the industry supply curve will reduce the equilibrium price. In order to maximize profits, both new and old firms will have to adjust their output to this new price. New firms will continue to enter, and the equilibrium price will continue to fall, until all firms in the industry are just covering their total costs. The industry has now reached what is called a *zero-profit equilibrium*. The entry of new firms then ceases. The effect of entry is shown in Figure 9-9.

> **Profits in a competitive industry are a signal for the entry of new firms; the industry will expand, pushing price down until economic profits fall to zero.**

FIGURE 9-9 The Effect of New Entrants Attracted by Positive Profits

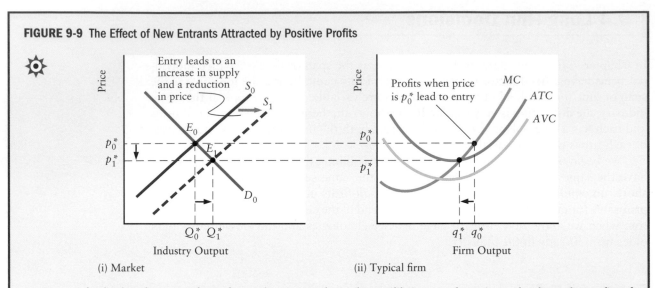

(i) Market   (ii) Typical firm

Positive profits lead to the entry of new firms; this entry reduces the equilibrium market price and reduces the profits of all firms. The initial short-run equilibrium is E_0 in part (i) with equilibrium price p_0^*. At this price, a typical firm in the industry is producing q_0^* units of output and is earning positive profits (since $p_0^* > ATC$ at q_0^*). These positive profits attract other firms who then enter the industry, causing the supply curve to shift to the right and reducing the market price. The process of entry will continue until profits are driven to zero. S_1 is the final supply curve and the equilibrium market price has fallen to p_1^*. At the new market price, firms have each reduced their output to q_1^* and are now just covering their total costs. Notice that each of the original firms is producing less than before, but because of the new entrants total industry output has increased from Q_0^* to Q_1^*.

An Exit-Inducing Price We saw in Figure 9-5 (see page 210) that the firm's supply curve is the section of its marginal cost curve above the average variable cost curve. If the market price falls below the minimum of average variable cost, the firm will simply shut down its production and exit the industry.

If firms are making losses but the market price is *above* the shut-down point, there will still be exit from the industry, but it will be gradual. Suppose the firms in a competitive industry are making losses, like the firm shown in part (i) of Figure 9-8 on page 213. Although the firms are covering their variable costs, the return on their capital is less than the opportunity cost of capital. They are not covering their total costs. This is a signal for the gradual exit of firms. Old plants and equipment will not be replaced as they wear out. As a result, the industry's supply curve eventually shifts leftward, and the market price rises. Firms will continue to exit, and the market price will continue to rise, until the remaining firms can cover their total costs. Once again the market reaches a zero-profit equilibrium. The exit of firms then ceases. This gradual process of exit is shown in Figure 9-10.

> **Losses in a competitive industry are a signal for the exit of firms; the industry will contract, driving the market price up until the remaining firms are just covering their total costs.**

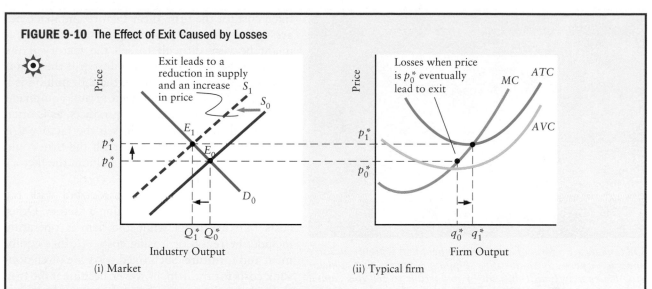

FIGURE 9-10 The Effect of Exit Caused by Losses

(i) Market

(ii) Typical firm

Negative profits lead to the eventual exit of some firms as their capital becomes obsolete or becomes too costly to operate; this exit increases the equilibrium price and increases profits for those firms remaining in the market. The initial market equilibrium is E_0 in part (i), with equilibrium price p_0^*. At this market price, a typical firm is producing q_0^* units and is making negative profits but, because price exceeds AVC, the firm remains in business. Since firms are earning less than the opportunity cost on their capital, they do not replace their capital as it becomes obsolete. Eventually, some firms close down. As firms exit the industry, the industry supply curve shifts to the left and the market price increases to p_1^*. For the remaining firms, this price increase leads them to increase their output from q_0^* to q_1^*, the level of output at which they are just covering their total costs. Notice that the remaining firms are producing more than before, but because of the exit of firms total industry output has fallen from Q_0^* to Q_1^*.

Sunk Costs and the Speed of Exit The process of exit is not always quick and is sometimes painfully slow for the loss-making firms in the industry. The rate at which firms leave unprofitable industries depends on how quickly their capital becomes obsolete or becomes too costly to operate because of rising maintenance costs as it ages. In many professional service industries, such as graphic design or consulting, the physical capital is mostly office equipment, such as computers, printers, and so on. This equipment becomes obsolete in just a few years, and thus loss-making firms will tend to exit the industry very quickly. In other industries, such as railways or shipping, the physical capital takes much longer to wear out or become obsolete. The result is that loss-making firms in these industries will remain in operation for many years.

> The longer it takes for firms' capital to become obsolete or too costly to operate, the longer firms will remain in the industry while they are earning economic losses.

Another important factor in the speed of exit from an industry is the nature of firms' fixed costs. Economists divide a firm's fixed costs into *sunk costs*—costs that could never be recovered—and *non-sunk costs*—costs that could be recovered by the firm by such means as selling its capital or terminating its rental agreement for its factory.

As an example, consider a competitive firm in the machine-tools industry. It builds a factory and equips it for a total cost of $30 million. This $30 million is an important

Oil tankers are a form of capital equipment that is highly industry specific. A perfectly competitive shipping company that is incurring losses may find it difficult or impossible to sell this capital equipment and to exit the industry. In this case, the capital is mostly a sunk cost, and the firm will remain in business as long as it can cover its variable costs.

fixed cost for the firm. If the factory and machines are useful only for producing in this industry, it might be very difficult to sell the factory if the firm ever wanted to exit the industry. If the firm is unable to sell the plant at all, the $30 million is a sunk cost. However, if the factory and equipment can be used to produce other products, as is often the case, then the firm could sell the factory if it ever wanted to exit the industry. If the firm could sell its factory for the full $30 million, the factory would be a fixed, but non-sunk, cost.

Not all fixed costs are associated with the capital cost of building or renting a factory. Other costs that are fixed while the firm is operating include the rental or leasing costs of office equipment and furniture. Such fixed costs are often non-sunk costs for the firm, however, because if the firm shuts down, it can terminate these rental or lease agreements, thus avoiding the costs altogether.

This distinction between sunk and non-sunk costs affects the speed of exit for loss-making firms. To see why, suppose our machine-tools firm is making losses in the short-run market equilibrium (as in Figure 9-10). If the $30 million factory is a sunk cost, then the firm cannot recover the cost by selling the factory. In this case, the firm will remain in business as long as the market price of its product exceeds its *AVC*; the alternative of closing down and earning no revenue is less profitable. If all firms are like this, the adjustment shown in Figure 9-10 will be slow and gradual. Conversely, if the firm is able to sell the factory at a price equal to its full fixed costs, it can shut down its production and *avoid* paying the fixed costs. In this case, it makes no sense to remain in business making losses just because price is greater than average variable cost. It would be better to sell the factory, recover the fixed costs, and exit the industry. If all firms are like this, the adjustment shown in Figure 9-10 will be relatively quick. (In practice the sale price is likely to be less than the full fixed costs and the firm will stay in business as long as its losses are less than the difference between its fixed costs and the sale price of its fixed asset.)

> If firms' fixed costs are mostly sunk costs, the process of exit in loss-making industries will be slow. If firms' fixed costs are mostly non-sunk costs, the process of exit will be faster.

Long-Run Equilibrium

Because sooner or later firms exit when they are making losses, and enter in pursuit of profits, we get the following conclusion:

> The long-run equilibrium of a competitive industry occurs when firms are earning zero profits.

When a perfectly competitive industry is in long-run equilibrium, each firm will be like the firm in part (ii) of Figure 9-8 on page 213, earning zero economic profit. For such firms, the price p_2 is sometimes called the **break-even price**. It is the price at which all economic costs, including the opportunity cost of capital, are being covered. Any firm that is just breaking even is willing to stay in the industry. It has no incentive to leave, nor do other firms have an incentive to enter.

break-even price The price at which a firm is just able to cover all of its costs, including the opportunity cost of capital.

Conditions for Long-Run Equilibrium The previous discussion suggests four conditions for a competitive industry to be in long-run equilibrium.

1. Existing firms must be maximizing their profits, given their existing capital. Thus, short-run marginal costs of production must be equal to market price.

2. Existing firms must not be suffering losses. If they are suffering losses, they will not replace their capital and the size of the industry will decline over time.

3. Existing firms must not be earning profits. If they are earning profits, then new firms will enter the industry and the size of the industry will increase over time.

4. Existing firms must not be able to increase their profits by changing the size of their production facilities. Thus, each existing firm must be at the minimum point of its *long-run* average cost (*LRAC*) curve.

This last condition is new to our discussion. Figure 9-11 shows that if the condition does not hold—that is, if the firm is *not* at the minimum of its *LRAC* curve—a firm can increase its profits. In the case shown, although the firm is maximizing its profits with its existing production facilities, there are unexploited economies of scale. By building a larger plant, the firm can move down its *LRAC* curve and reduce its average cost. Alternatively, if the firm were producing at an output that put it beyond the lowest point on its *LRAC* curve, it could raise its profits by reducing its plant size. Because in either situation average cost is just equal to the market price, any reduction in average cost must yield profits.

> For a competitive firm to be maximizing its long-run profits, it must be producing at the minimum point on its *LRAC* curve.

As we saw in Chapter 8, the level of output at which *LRAC* reaches a minimum is known as the firm's *minimum efficient scale* (*MES*). When each firm in the industry is producing at the minimum point of its long-run average cost curve and just covering its costs, as in Figure 9-12, the industry is in long-run equilibrium. Because

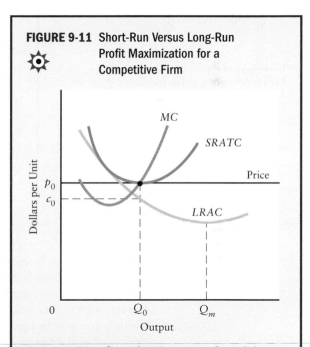

FIGURE 9-11 Short-Run Versus Long-Run Profit Maximization for a Competitive Firm

A competitive firm that is not at the minimum point on its *LRAC* curve is not maximizing its long-run profits. A competitive firm with short-run cost curves *SRATC* and *MC* faces a market price of p_0. The firm produces Q_0, where *MC* equals price and total costs are just being covered. However, the firm's long-run average cost curve lies below its short-run curve at output Q_0. The firm could produce output Q_0 at cost c_0 by building a larger plant so as to take advantage of economies of scale. Profits would rise, because average total costs of c_0 would then be less than price p_0. The firm cannot be maximizing its long-run profits at any output below Q_m because, with any such output, average total costs can be reduced by building a larger plant. The output Q_m is the minimum efficient scale of the firm.

FIGURE 9-12 A Typical Competitive Firm When the Industry Is in Long-Run Equilibrium

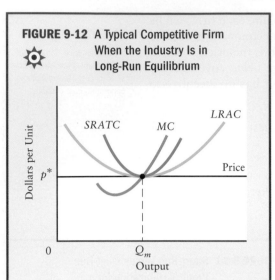

In long-run competitive equilibrium, each firm is operating at the minimum point on its *LRAC* curve. In long-run equilibrium, each firm must be (1) maximizing short-run profits, $MC = p$; (2) earning profits of zero on its existing plant, $SRATC = p$; and (3) unable to increase its profits by altering the scale of its operations. These three conditions can be met only when the firm is at the minimum point on its *LRAC* curve, with price p^* and output Q_m.

marginal cost equals price, no firm can improve its profits by varying its output in the short run. Because each firm is at the minimum point on its *LRAC* curve, there is no incentive for any existing firm to alter the scale of its operations. Because there are neither profits nor losses, there is no incentive for entry into or exit from the industry.

> In long-run competitive equilibrium, each firm's average cost of production is the lowest attainable, given the limits of known technology and factor prices.

Changes in Technology

Our discussion of firms' long-run decisions has assumed that all firms in the industry have the same technology and thus the same cost curves. We now relax that assumption and consider how a competitive industry responds to technological improvements *by new firms*.

Consider a competitive industry in long-run equilibrium. Because the industry is in long-run equilibrium, each firm must be earning zero profits. Now suppose that some technological development lowers the cost curves of *newly built plants* but no further advances are anticipated. Because price is just equal to the average total cost for the *existing plants*, new plants will be able to earn profits, and some of them will now be built. The resulting expansion in capacity shifts the short-run supply curve to the right and drives price down.

The expansion in industry output and the fall in price will continue until price is equal to the short-run average total cost of the *new* plants. At this price, old plants will not be covering their long-run costs. As long as price exceeds their average variable cost, however, such plants will continue in production. As the outmoded plants wear out or become too costly to operate, they will gradually be closed. Eventually, a new long-run equilibrium will be established in which all plants will use the new technology; market price will be lower and output higher than under the old technology.

What happens in a competitive industry in which technological change does not occur as a single isolated event but instead happens more or less continuously? Plants built in any one year will tend to have lower costs than plants built in any previous year. This common occurrence is illustrated in Figure 9-13.

Industries that are subject to continuous technological change have three common characteristics. The first is that plants of different ages and with different costs exist side by side. In the steel and newsprint industries, for example, there are ongoing and gradual technological improvements, and thus it is common for new plants to have considerably lower costs than the plants built several years earlier. Most of us do not see these differences, however, because we rarely if ever visit production facilities in these industries. But the same characteristic is dramatically displayed in an industry that most of us observe casually through our car windows—agriculture. You will probably have noticed different farms with different vintages of agricultural machinery; some farms

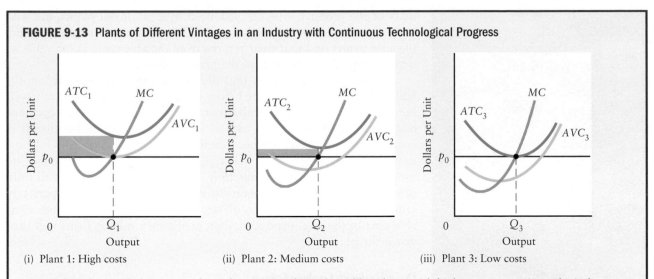

FIGURE 9-13 Plants of Different Vintages in an Industry with Continuous Technological Progress

(i) Plant 1: High costs   (ii) Plant 2: Medium costs   (iii) Plant 3: Low costs

Entry of progressively lower-cost firms forces price down, but older plants with higher costs remain in the industry as long as price covers their average variable costs. Plant 3 is the newest plant with the lowest costs. Long-run equilibrium price will be determined by the average total costs of plants of this type because entry will continue as long as the owners of the newest plants expect to earn profits from them. Plant 1 is the oldest plant in operation. It is just covering its *AVC*, and if the price falls any further, it will be closed down. Plant 2 is a plant of intermediate age. It is covering its variable costs and earning some contribution toward its fixed costs. Losses at all but the newest plants, in parts (i) and (ii), are shown by the shaded areas.

have much newer and better equipment than others. Indeed, even any individual farm that has been in operation for a long time will have various vintages of equipment, all of which are in use. Older models are not discarded as soon as a better model comes on the market.

Critics who observe the continued use of older, higher-cost plants and equipment often urge that something be done to "eliminate these wasteful practices." These critics miss an important aspect of profit maximization. If the plant or piece of equipment is already there and has little or no resale value, it can be profitably operated as long as its revenues more than cover its *variable* costs. As long as a plant or some equipment can produce goods that are valued by consumers at an amount above the value of the resources currently used up for their production (variable costs), the value of society's total output is increased by using it.

> **In industries with continuous technological improvement, low-cost firms will exist side by side with older high-cost firms. The older firms will continue operating as long as their revenues cover their variable costs.**

A second characteristic of a competitive industry that is subject to continuous technological improvement is that price is eventually governed by the minimum *ATC* of the *lowest-cost* (i.e., the newest) plants. New firms using the latest technologies will enter the industry until their plants are just expected to earn normal profits over their lifetimes. The benefits of the new technology are passed on to consumers because all the

New plants are usually built with the latest technology. This often results in new plants having lower unit costs (and thus higher profits) than the existing plants built with older technology.

units of the product, whether produced by new or old plants, are sold at a price that is related solely to the *ATCs* of the new plants. Owners of older plants find that their returns over variable costs fall steadily as newer plants drive the price of the product down.

A third characteristic is that old plants are discarded (or "mothballed") when the price falls below their *AVCs*. This may occur well before the plants are physically worn out. In industries with continuous technological progress, capital is usually discarded because it is *economically obsolete*, not because it is physically worn out. Old capital is obsolete when the market price of output does not cover its average variable cost of production. Thus, a steel mill that is still fully capable of producing top-quality steel may be shut down for perfectly sensible reasons; if the price of steel cannot cover the average variable cost of the steel produced, then profit-maximizing firms will shut down the plant.

Declining Industries

What happens when a competitive industry in long-run equilibrium experiences a continual decrease in the demand for its product? One example of this might be a long-term reduction in demand for in-store video rentals driven by the availability of online movies. Another example is the ongoing substitution away from glass soft-drink bottles to plastic ones. As market demand for these products declines, market price falls, and firms that were previously covering average total costs are no longer able to do so. They find themselves suffering losses instead of breaking even; the signal for the exit of capital is given, but exit takes time.

The Response of Firms The profit-maximizing response to a steadily declining demand is to continue to operate with existing equipment as long as revenues can cover the variable costs of production. As equipment becomes obsolete because the firm cannot cover even its variable cost, it will not be replaced unless the new equipment can cover its total cost. As a result, the capacity of the industry will shrink. If demand keeps declining, capacity will continue shrinking.

Declining industries typically present a sorry sight to the observer. Revenues are below long-run total costs and, as a result, new equipment is not brought in to replace old equipment as it wears out. The average age of equipment in use rises steadily. The untrained observer, seeing the industry's plight, is likely to blame it on the old equipment.

> The antiquated equipment in a declining industry is typically the effect rather than the cause of the industry's decline.

The Response of Governments Governments are often tempted to support declining industries because they are worried about the resulting job losses. Experience suggests, however, that propping up genuinely declining industries only delays their demise—at significant cost to the taxpayers. When the government finally withdraws its support, the decline is usually more abrupt and, hence, the required adjustment is more difficult than it would have been had the industry been allowed to decline gradually under the natural market forces.

Once governments recognize that the decay of certain industries and the collapse of certain firms are an inevitable part of a changing and evolving economy, a more effective response is to provide retraining and temporary income-support schemes that cushion the impacts of change. These can moderate the effects on the incomes of workers who lose their jobs and make it easier for them to transfer to expanding industries. Intervention that is intended to increase mobility while reducing the social and personal costs of mobility is a viable long-run policy; trying to freeze the existing industrial structure by shoring up an inevitably declining industry is not.

SUMMARY

9.1 Market Structure and Firm Behaviour

LO 1

- A competitive market structure is one in which individual firms have no market power—that is, they have no power to influence the price at which they sell their product.
- Competitive behaviour exists when firms actively compete against one another, responding directly to other firms' actions.

- Perfectly competitive firms *do not* have competitive behaviour because the actions of any one firm would have no effect on any other firm.

9.2 The Theory of Perfect Competition

LO 2

- Four key assumptions of the theory of perfect competition are as follows:

  1. All firms produce a homogeneous product.
  2. Consumers know the nature of the product and the price charged for it.
  3. Each firm's minimum efficient scale occurs at a level of output that is small relative to the industry's total output.

  4. The industry displays freedom of entry and exit.

- Each firm in perfect competition is a price taker. It follows that each firm faces a horizontal demand curve at the market price (even though the market demand curve is downward sloping).

9.3 Short-Run Decisions

LO 3, 4

- Any profit-maximizing firm will produce at a level of output at which (a) price is at least as great as average variable cost and (b) marginal cost equals marginal revenue.
- In perfect competition, firms are price takers, so marginal revenue is equal to price. Thus, a profit-maximizing competitive firm chooses its output so that its marginal cost equals the market price.
- Under perfect competition, each firm's short-run supply curve is identical to its marginal cost curve above

average variable cost. The perfectly competitive industry's short-run supply curve is the horizontal sum of the supply curves of the individual firms.

- In short-run equilibrium, each firm is maximizing its profits. However, any firm may be making losses (price is less than average total cost), making profits (price is greater than average total cost), or just breaking even (price is equal to average total cost).

9.4 Long-Run Decisions

LO 5

- In the long run, profits or losses will lead to firms' entry into or exit out of the industry. This pushes any competitive industry to a long-run, zero-profit equilibrium and moves production to the level that minimizes average cost.
- The long-run response of an industry to steadily changing technology is the gradual replacement of less efficient

plants by more efficient ones. Older plants will be discarded and replaced by more modern ones only when price falls below average variable cost.

- The long-run response of a declining industry will be to continue to satisfy demand by employing its existing plants as long as price exceeds short run average variable cost.

KEY CONCEPTS

Competitive behaviour and competitive market structure

Perfect competition

Price taking and a horizontal demand curve

Average revenue, marginal revenue, and price under perfect competition

Rules for maximizing profits

The relationship of supply curves to marginal cost curves

Short-run and long-run equilibrium of competitive industries

Entry and exit in achieving long-run equilibrium

STUDY EXERCISES

MyEconLab Make the grade with MyEconLab: Study Exercises marked in red can be found on MyEconLab. You can practise them as often as you want, and most feature step-by-step guided instructions to help you find the right answer.

1. Fill in the blanks to make the following statements correct.

   a. The demand curve faced by a single firm in a perfectly competitive market is _____.

   b. The demand curve faced by a single firm in a perfectly competitive industry coincides with the firm's _____ curve and its _____ curve.

   c. Total revenue is calculated by multiplying _____ and _____. Average revenue is calculated by dividing _____ by _____. Marginal revenue is calculated by dividing _____ by _____.

   d. A firm's loss when it produces *no* output is equal to its _____.

2. Fill in the blanks to make the following statements correct.

   a. The shut-down price is the price at which the firm can just cover its _____.

   b. If the average variable cost of producing any given level of output exceeds the price at which it can be sold, then the firm should _____.

   c. If a firm is producing a level of output such that $MC > MR$, that firm should _____ output.

   d. The profit-maximizing level of output for a price-taking firm is the output at which MR and MC are _____ and the gap between TR and TC is _____.

   e. If a perfectly competitive firm is producing its profit-maximizing level of output and the price of its output rises, then MR will be _____ MC and the firm should _____ output.

3. Fill in the blanks to make the following statements correct.

   a. The short-run supply curve for a perfectly competitive firm is that firm's marginal cost curve for levels of output where marginal cost exceeds _____.

   b. If a firm is producing a level of output where $MR = MC$ but is suffering losses, we know that price is below _____. This firm should continue to produce as long as price exceeds _____.

   c. If a firm is earning profits, we know that price is above its _____. There is an incentive for other firms to _____ this industry.

4. In Figure 9-1 on page 204, we explain the difference between the demand curve for a competitive industry and the demand curve facing an individual firm in that industry. Review that figure and answer the following questions.

   a. Explain what would happen if the individual firm tried to charge a higher price for its product.

   b. Explain why the individual firm has no incentive to charge a lower price for its product.

   c. Explain why the demand curve for an individual firm is horizontal at the current market price.

5. Consider the following table showing the various revenue concepts for DairyTreat Inc., a perfectly

competitive firm that sells milk by the litre. Suppose the firm faces a constant market price of $2 per litre.

Price (p)	Quantity	Total Revenue (TR)	Average Revenue (AR)	Marginal Revenue (MR)
$2	150	—	—	
2	175	—	—	—
2	200	—	—	—
2	225	—	—	—
2	250	—	—	—

a. Compute total revenue for each level of output. Fill in the table.
b. Compute average and marginal revenue for each level of output. Fill in the table. (Remember to compute marginal revenue *between* successive levels of output.)
c. Explain why for a perfectly competitive firm, $AR = MR = p$.
d. Plot the TR, MR, and AR curves on a scale diagram. What is the slope of the TR curve?

6. The diagram below shows the various short-run cost curves for a perfectly competitive firm.

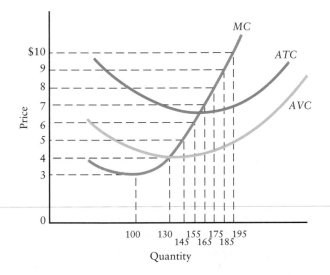

Market Price ($)	Firm's Output	Is Price > ATC?	Is Price > AVC?	Are Profits Positive?
$3	—	—	—	—
4	—	—	—	—
5	—	—	—	—
6	—	—	—	—
7	—	—	—	—
8	—	—	—	—
9	—	—	—	—
10	—	—	—	—

a. Based on the diagram, and the assumption that the firm is maximizing its profit, fill in the table. The last three columns require only a "yes" or "no."
b. What is this firm's shut-down price? Explain.
c. What is this firm's supply curve? Explain.

7. Consider the table below showing the supply schedules for three competitive firms, each producing honey. These three firms make up the entire industry.

Market Price ($/kg)	Output (kg)			
	Firm A	Firm B	Firm C	Industry
2.50	100	0	0	—
3.00	125	0	0	—
3.50	150	100	0	—
4.00	175	150	0	—
4.50	200	200	100	—
5.00	225	250	175	—
5.50	250	300	250	—
6.00	275	350	325	—

a. Compute the total industry supply at each price and fill in the table.
b. On a scale diagram similar to Figure 9-6 on page 211, plot the supply curve for each firm and for the industry as a whole.
c. Can you provide a likely explanation for why Firm B produces no output at prices $3 and lower, and why Firm C produces no output at prices $4 and lower?

8. Consider the perfectly competitive barley industry. It is initially in long-run equilibrium at quantity Q_0 and price p_0.

a. Draw a supply-and-demand diagram for the barley market, showing the initial long-run equilibrium.
b. Draw a diagram for a typical firm when the industry is in its initial long-run equilibrium, showing its MC, ATC, and $LRAC$ curves. Are any profits being earned by the typical barley farmer?
c. Now suppose there is an increase in demand (caused by an increase in demand for beer, which uses barley as an input). Price for barley rises to p_1. In your diagram, show the typical firm's short-run response to the increase in market price from p_0 to p_1. Show the area that represents the typical firm's profits at this new price.
d. Explain how this industry adjusts to its new long-run equilibrium. Illustrate this adjustment both in the demand-and-supply diagram and in the diagram of the typical firm. (You may assume that the cost curves for barley firms are unaffected by this change.)

9. The diagrams below show short-run cost curves for four perfectly competitive firms. Assume that each firm faces a market price of p_0.

a. Which firms could earn positive profits at some level of output?

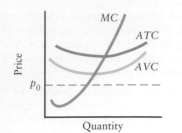

(i) Firm 1

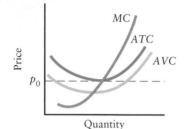

(ii) Firm 2

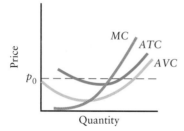

(iii) Firm 3

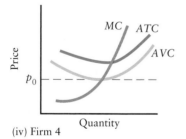

(iv) Firm 4

b. Which firms would be incurring losses at their profit-maximizing level of output, but will continue producing in the short run?

c. Which firms will choose not to produce at price p_0?

10. Which of the following observed facts about an industry are inconsistent with its being a perfectly competitive industry?

a. Different firms use different methods of production.

b. The industry's product is extensively advertised by a trade association.

c. Individual firms devote a large fraction of their sales receipts to advertising their own product brands.

d. There are 24 firms in the industry.

e. The largest firm in the industry makes 40 percent of the sales, and the next largest firm makes 20 percent of the sales, but the products are identical, and there are 61 other firms.

f. All firms made large profits last year.

11. What, if anything, does each one of the following tell you about ease of entry into or exit from an industry?

a. Profits have been very high for two decades.

b. No new firms have entered the industry for 20 years.

c. The average age of the firms in the 40-year-old industry is less than 7 years.

d. Most existing firms are using old-technology equipment alongside newer, more modern equipment.

e. Profits are low or negative; many firms are still producing, but from steadily aging equipment.

12. This question is based on the section **The Long-Run Industry Supply Curve** found on this book's MyEconLab (**www.myeconlab.com**). A major theme of this chapter is the role that *free entry and exit* play in determining a competitive industry's long-run equilibrium. Keeping this theme in mind, consider the following statement:

> *In Industry X, demand and supply do determine price in the short run, but in the long run, only supply matters.*

a. Assuming that Industry X is a constant-cost industry, use a demand-and-supply diagram to illustrate why the statement is exactly correct.

b. Now, assuming that Industry X is an increasing-cost industry, show in a demand-and-supply diagram why the statement is not quite correct.

Monopoly, Cartels, and Price Discrimination

LEARNING OBJECTIVES (LO)

After studying this chapter you will be able to

1 explain why marginal revenue is less than price for a profit-maximizing monopolist.
2 understand how entry barriers can allow monopolists to maintain positive profits in the long run.

3 describe why firms would form a cartel to restrict industry output and how this would increase their profits.

4 explain how some firms can increase their profits through price discrimination.

PERFECT competition is at one end of the spectrum of market structures. At the other end is monopoly. Economists say that a **monopoly** occurs when the output of an entire industry is produced by a single firm, called a **monopolist** or a *monopoly firm*. Examples of monopoly are rare at the national level but are more common for smaller geographical areas, but even there technological changes are eroding once-powerful monopolies. The company that supplies electric power to your home is almost certainly a monopoly, and until very recently so were the firms that provided local land-line telephone service and cable television.

Since monopoly is the market structure that allows for the maximum possible exercise of market power on the part of the firm, monopoly markets and perfectly competitive markets provide two extremes of behaviour that are useful for economists in their study of market structure. And even though monopolies are rare, the key price–output tradeoff that they face extends to other market structures that we study in later chapters.

In this chapter we examine how a profit-maximizing monopolist determines its price and quantity. We begin by considering a monopolist that sells all its output at a single price. We then consider *cartels* that are formed when several firms band together in order to behave more like a monopolist. We end the chapter by examining situations in which monopolists and other firms with market power are able to charge different prices to different customers—something you have probably observed with airline tickets, subway and bus passes, movie tickets, and even some products at your local grocery store.

10.1 A Single-Price Monopolist

monopoly A market containing a single firm.

monopolist A firm that is the only seller in a market.

We look first at a monopolist that charges a single price for its product. This firm's profits, like those of all firms, will depend on the relationship between its costs and its revenues.

Revenue Concepts for a Monopolist

We saw in Chapter 7 that the shape of a firm's short-run cost curves arises from the conditions of production rather than from the market structure in which the firm operates. As a result, the same forces that lead perfectly competitive firms to have U-shaped cost curves apply equally to monopolists. Therefore we do not need to introduce any new cost concepts to analyze a monopoly firm—everything that we saw in Chapter 7 applies equally to firms in *all* market structures. We can therefore focus our attention on a monopolist's revenues.

Because a monopolist is the sole producer of the product that it sells, the demand curve it faces is simply the market demand curve for that product. The market demand curve, which shows the total quantity that buyers want to purchase at each price, also shows the quantity that the monopolist will be able to sell at each price.

Unlike a perfectly competitive firm, a monopolist faces a negatively sloped demand curve.

A monopolist therefore faces a tradeoff between the price it charges and the quantity it sells. For a monopolist, sales can be increased only if price is reduced, and price can be increased only if sales are reduced.

Average Revenue Starting with the market demand curve, we can readily derive the monopolist's average and marginal revenue curves. When the monopolist charges the same price for all units sold, its total revenue (*TR*) is simply equal to the single price times the quantity sold:

$$TR = p \times Q$$

Since average revenue is total revenue divided by quantity, it follows that average revenue is equal to the price:

$$AR = \frac{TR}{Q} = \frac{p \times Q}{Q} = p$$

And since the demand curve shows the price of the product, it follows that the demand curve is also the monopolist's average revenue curve.

Marginal Revenue Now let's consider the monopolist's *marginal revenue*—the revenue resulting from the sale of one more unit of the product. Because its demand curve is negatively sloped, the monopolist must reduce the price that it charges on *all* units in order to sell an extra unit. But this implies that the price received for the extra unit sold is *not* the firm's marginal revenue because, by reducing the price on all previous units, the firm loses some revenue. Marginal revenue is therefore equal to the price *minus* this lost revenue. It follows that the marginal revenue resulting from the sale of an extra unit is less than the price that the monopolist receives for that unit.

The monopolist's marginal revenue is less than the price at which it sells its output. Thus the monopolist's *MR* curve is below its demand curve. [24]

The relationship between marginal revenue and price for a numerical example is shown in detail in Figure 10-1. Consider the table first. Notice that the numbers in columns 4 and 5 are plotted between the rows that refer to specific prices, because the numbers refer to what happens when the price changes from one row to the next. As price declines and quantity sold increases, marginal revenue is calculated as the change in total revenue divided by the change in quantity:

$$MR = \frac{\Delta TR}{\Delta Q}$$

FIGURE 10-1 A Monopolist's Average and Marginal Revenue

Computing Average and Marginal Revenue

Price (Average Revenue) (1)	Quantity Sold Q (2)	Total Revenue $(p \times Q)$ (3)	Change in Total Revenue (ΔTR) (4)	Marginal Revenue $(\Delta TR/\Delta Q)$ (5)
10	0	0		
			90	9
9	10	90		
			70	7
8	20	160		
			50	5
7	30	210		
			30	3
6	40	240		
			10	1
5	50	250		
			−10	−1
4	60	240		
			−30	−3
3	70	210		
			−50	−5
2	80	160		
			−70	−7
1	90	90		
			−90	−9
0	100	0		

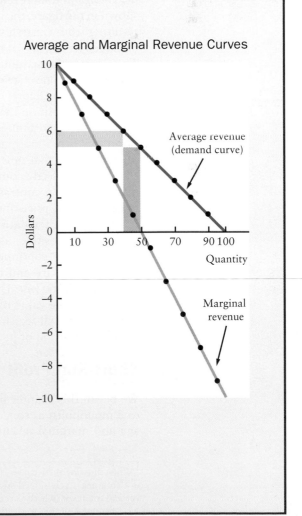

Average and Marginal Revenue Curves

Average revenue (demand curve)

Marginal revenue

Marginal revenue is less than price because the price must be reduced on all units in order to sell an additional unit. Our example shows that every time the firm lowers its price by $1, its sales increase by 10 units. At a price of $6, the firm sells 40 units for a total revenue of $240. If it lowers its price to $5 *on all units*, total sales rise to 50 units and total revenue rises to $250. The purple rectangle shows the $50 gain in revenue associated with the 10 extra units sold at $5 each. The green rectangle shows the $40 *loss* in revenue associated with reducing the price by $1 on the original 40 units. Thus, the firm's marginal revenue when it reduces its price from $6 to $5 is the change in total revenue ($250 − $240 = $10) divided by the change in quantity (50 − 40 = 10). *MR* = $10/10 = $1.

Now look at the figure. It plots the demand curve described by the price and quantity values shown in the first two columns of the table. It also plots the marginal revenue curve and locates the specific points on it that were calculated in the table. For purposes of illustration, a straight-line demand curve has been chosen.[1]

Notice that marginal revenue is positive up to 50 units of sales, indicating that reductions in price between $10 and $5 increase total revenue. Notice also that marginal revenue is *negative* for sales greater than 50 units, indicating that reductions in price below $5 cause total revenue to fall even though total sales increase.

The figure also illustrates the two opposing forces that are present whenever the monopolist considers changing its price. As an example, consider the reduction in price from $6 to $5. First, the 40 units that the firm was already selling bring in less money at the new lower price than at the original higher price. This loss in revenue is the amount of the price reduction multiplied by the number of units already being sold (40 units × $1 per unit = $40). This is shown as the green shaded area in the figure. The second force, operating in the opposite direction, is that new units are sold, which adds to revenue. This gain in revenue is given by the number of new units sold multiplied by the price at which they are sold (10 units × $5 = $50). This is shown as the purple shaded area. The *net change* in total revenue is the *difference* between these two amounts. In the example shown in the figure, the increase resulting from the sale of new units exceeds the decrease resulting from existing sales now being made at a lower price. Since total revenue has increased as a result of the price reduction, we know that marginal revenue is positive. To calculate the marginal revenue, remember that $MR = \Delta TR/\Delta Q$. In this example the change in total revenue is $10 and the change in quantity is 10 units, so $\Delta TR/\Delta Q = \$1$, as plotted in the figure at a quantity of 45 units (halfway between $Q = 40$ and $Q = 50$).

The proposition that marginal revenue is always less than price for a monopolist provides an important contrast with perfect competition. Recall that in perfect competition, the firm's marginal revenue from selling an extra unit of output is equal to the price at which that unit is sold. The reason for the difference is not difficult to understand. The perfectly competitive firm is a price taker; it can sell all it wants at the given market price. In contrast, the monopolist faces a negatively sloped demand curve; it must reduce its price in order to increase its sales.

If you plot the data on *TR* from the table in Figure 10-1, you will notice that *TR* rises (*MR* is positive) as price falls, reaching a maximum where $p = \$5$ and $MR = 0$. Then, as price continues to fall, *TR* falls (*MR* is negative). Using the relationship between elasticity and total revenue that we first saw in Chapter 4, it follows that demand is elastic ($\eta > 1$) when *MR* is positive and demand is inelastic ($\eta < 1$) when *MR* is negative. The value of elasticity (η) declines steadily as we move down the demand curve. As we will see shortly, a profit-maximizing monopolist will always produce on the *elastic* portion of its demand curve (that is, where *MR* is positive).

Short-Run Profit Maximization

We began this chapter by noting that the cost concepts from Chapter 7 apply equally to a monopolist as to a competitive firm. We have now examined a monopolist's average and marginal revenues and are therefore ready to combine the cost and revenue

---

[1] When drawing these curves, note that if the demand curve is a negatively sloped straight line, the *MR* curve is also a negatively sloped straight line but is exactly twice as steep as the demand curve. The *MR* curve's vertical intercept (where $Q = 0$) is the same as that of the demand curve, and its horizontal intercept (where $p = 0$) is one-half that of the demand curve. [25]

information to determine the monopolist's profit-maximizing price and level of output.

Recall the two general rules about profit maximization from Chapter 9:

Rule 1: The firm should not produce at all unless price (average revenue) exceeds average variable cost.

Rule 2: If the firm does produce, it should produce a level of output such that marginal revenue equals marginal cost.

Figure 10-2 illustrates a monopolist's choice of output to equate its marginal cost with its marginal revenue. Recall that it is the intersection of the *MR* and *MC* curves that determines the firm's profit-maximizing *quantity*, but the price charged to consumers is then determined by the demand curve. With the firm's costs given by the *ATC* curve shown in the figure, the monopolist is making positive profits, as shown by the red shaded area.

In general, however, a profit-maximizing monopolist need not be making *positive* profits. Even when the firm is choosing its quantity to maximize its profits, the *size* of those profits depends on the position of the *ATC* curve. In Figure 10-2

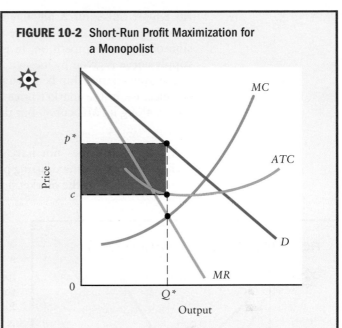

FIGURE 10-2 Short-Run Profit Maximization for a Monopolist

The profit-maximizing output is Q^*, where $MR = MC$; price is p^*. The rules for profit maximization require $MR = MC$ and $p > AVC$. (*AVC* is not shown in the graph, but it must be below *ATC*.) With average costs given by *ATC*, unit costs at Q^* are given by c and the monopolist makes positive profits shown by the red shaded area.

the monopolist is earning positive profits. But you can easily imagine other possibilities. If the firm's *ATC* curve was higher (perhaps because of higher fixed costs), the firm with the same level of output and charging the same price could be breaking even (zero profits) or even making negative profits (losses). (You can create your own diagrams like Figure 10-2 and draw in the appropriate *ATC* curves to illustrate these two possibilities.)

Nothing guarantees that a monopolist will make positive profits in the short run, but if it suffers persistent losses, it will eventually go out of business.

If you look again at Figure 10-2, you will see an important aspect of monopoly. The profit-maximizing level of output is determined where $MR = MC$ (Rule 2). But since MR is less than price for a monopolist, it must follow that price exceeds marginal cost.

For a profit-maximizing monopolist, price is greater than marginal cost.

We come back to this important point shortly when we address the *efficiency* of monopoly and compare the monopoly outcome to that in a perfectly competitive market.

No Supply Curve for a Monopolist In describing the monopolist's profit-maximizing behaviour, we did not introduce the concept of a supply curve, as we did in the discussion of perfect competition. In perfect competition, each firm is a price taker and its supply curve is given by its own *MC* curve. It follows that in perfect competition there is a unique relationship between market price and quantity supplied by any single firm: An increase in the market price leads to an increase in quantity supplied as the firm moves along its *MC* curve. But there is no such relationship in monopoly.

A monopolist does not have a supply curve because it is not a price taker; it chooses its profit-maximizing price–quantity combination from among the possible combinations on the market demand curve.

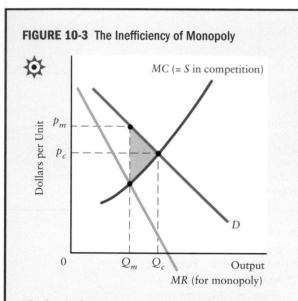

FIGURE 10-3 The Inefficiency of Monopoly

The level of output in a monopolized industry is less than the level of output that would be produced if the industry were perfectly competitive. If the industry is made up of many price-taking firms, the industry supply curve *S* is the horizontal sum of the many individual marginal cost curves. Given the market demand curve *D*, the competitive equilibrium quantity is Q_c and the price is p_c. Now suppose the industry has a monopolist with marginal costs given by the *MC* curve shown. In this case, *MR* is the monopolist's marginal revenue curve. The profit-maximizing monopolist produces Q_m units of output and charges a price of p_m.

Notice in the monopoly outcome that for the units of output between Q_m and Q_c, the marginal value to society of extra units of the good (as shown by the demand curve) exceeds the marginal cost of producing extra units, and thus society would benefit from having these units produced. The monopolist's restriction of output below Q_c creates a deadweight loss for society shown by the purple area. The monopoly outcome is *inefficient*.

Like a perfectly competitive firm, a monopolist has a marginal cost curve. But unlike a competitive firm, a monopolist does not face a given market price. The monopolist *chooses* the price-quantity combination on the market demand curve that maximizes its profits. Following Rule 2, the profit-maximizing level of output is determined where the *MC* and *MR* curves intersect.

Firm and Industry Because the monopolist is the only producer in an industry, there is no need for a separate discussion about the firm and the industry, as is necessary with perfect competition. The monopolist *is* the industry. Thus, the short-run, profit-maximizing position of the firm, as shown in Figure 10-2, is also the short-run equilibrium of the industry.

Competition and Monopoly Compared The comparison of monopoly with perfect competition is important. For a perfectly competitive industry, the equilibrium is determined by the intersection of the industry demand and supply curves. Since the industry supply curve is simply the sum of the individual firms' marginal cost curves, the equilibrium output in a perfectly competitive industry is such that price equals marginal cost. As shown in Figures 10-2 and 10-3, however, the monopolist produces a *lower* level of output and, at that output level, price is greater than marginal cost.

In Chapter 5 we briefly discussed the meaning of *market efficiency* and how it relates to the amount of *economic surplus* generated in the market. We will examine these concepts in more detail in Chapter 12. For now we can observe why the decisions of the monopolist—though perhaps very profitable for the firm—lead to an inefficient outcome for society as a whole.

Since price exceeds marginal cost for a monopolist, society as a whole would benefit if more units of the good were produced—because the marginal value to society of extra units, as reflected by the price, exceeds the marginal cost of producing the extra units. In the terminology we introduced in Chapter 5, more *economic surplus* would be generated for society if the monopolist increased its level of output. The monopolist's profit-maximizing decision to restrict output below the competitive level creates a loss of economic surplus for society—a deadweight loss. In other words, it leads to market *inefficiency*.

> A monopolist restricts output below the competitive level and thus reduces the amount of economic surplus generated in the market. The monopolist therefore creates an inefficient market outcome.

Entry Barriers and Long-Run Equilibrium

In a monopolized industry, as in a perfectly competitive one, losses and profits provide incentives for exit and entry. If the monopoly is making losses in the short run, it will continue to operate as long as it can cover its variable costs. In the long run, however, it will leave the industry unless it can find a scale of operations at which its full opportunity costs can be covered.

If the monopoly is making profits, other firms will want to enter the industry in order to earn more than the opportunity cost of their capital. If such entry occurs, the firm will cease to be a monopoly. Instead of facing the entire market demand curve, the (former) monopolist will have to compete with the new firms and thus will capture only part of the overall market demand.

> If monopoly profits are to persist in the long run, the entry of new firms into the industry must be prevented.

Anything that prevents the entry of new firms is called an **entry barrier**. Such barriers may be natural or created.

entry barrier Any barrier to the entry of new firms into an industry. An entry barrier may be natural or created.

Natural Entry Barriers Natural barriers most commonly arise as a result of economies of scale. When the long-run average cost curve is negatively sloped over a large range of output, big firms have significantly lower average total costs than small firms. Recall from Chapter 8 that the *minimum efficient scale* (*MES*) is the smallest-size firm that can reap all the economies of large-scale production. It occurs at the level of output at which the firm's long-run average cost curve reaches a minimum.

To see how economies of scale can act as an entry barrier, consider the production of newsprint. Suppose the technology of newsprint production is such that a firm's *MES* is 10 000 tonnes per year at an average total cost of $500 per tonne. Further suppose that at a price of $600, the quantity demanded in the entire market is 11 000 tonnes per year. Under these circumstances, only one firm could operate at or near its *MES*. Any potential entrant would have unit costs higher than those of the existing firm and so could not compete successfully.

A **natural monopoly** occurs when the industry's demand conditions allow no more than one firm to cover its costs while producing at its minimum efficient scale. Electrical power transmission is a natural monopoly—with current technology it is cheaper to have only one set of power lines (rather than two or more) serving a given region.

natural monopoly An industry characterized by economies of scale sufficiently large that only one firm can cover its costs while producing at its minimum efficient scale.

Another type of natural entry barrier is *setup cost*. If a firm could be catapulted fully grown into the market, it might be able to compete effectively with the existing monopolist. However, the cost to the new firm of entering the market, developing its products and establishing such things as its brand image and its dealer network, may be so large that entry would be unprofitable.

Created Entry Barriers Many entry barriers are created by conscious government action. Patent laws, for instance, prevent entry by conferring on the patent holder the sole legal right to produce a particular product for a specific period of time. A firm may also be granted a charter or a franchise that prohibits competition by law. Canada Post, for example, has a government-sanctioned monopoly on the delivery of first-class mail. In other cases the regulation and/or licensing of firms severely restricts entry. Professional organizations for dentists or engineers, for example, often restrict the number of places in accredited dental or engineering schools and thus restrict entry into those industries.

The six large Canadian banks have extensive country-wide networks of retail branches. In order to compete effectively in this market, any new entrant would need to build a similar network, at enormous cost. The established network of retail branches is therefore an effective entry barrier.

Other barriers can be created by the firm or firms already in the market. In extreme cases, the threat of force or sabotage can deter entry. The most obvious entry barriers of this type are encountered in organized crime, where operation outside the law makes available an array of illegal but potent barriers to new entrants. But law-abiding firms must use legal tactics in an attempt to increase a new entrant's setup costs. Such tactics range from the threat of price cutting—designed to impose unsustainable losses on a new entrant—to heavy brand-name advertising. (These and other created entry barriers will be discussed in more detail in Chapter 11.)

Applying Economic Concepts 10-1 discusses an interesting example from Ireland in the 1990s in which government regulations, by restricting entry, led local pubs to have considerable monopoly power. At a time when Irish pubs are becoming a popular trend in many countries, it is ironic to see how a booming Irish economy combined with government regulation caused a shortage of Irish pubs in Ireland itself!

The Very Long Run and Creative Destruction

In the very long run, technology changes. New ways of producing old products are invented, and new products are created to satisfy both familiar and new wants. These are related to the concept of entry barriers; a monopoly that succeeds in preventing the entry of new firms capable of producing its product will sooner or later find its barriers circumvented by innovations.

A firm may be able to develop a new production process that circumvents a patent upon which a monopolist relies to bar the entry of competing firms.

A firm may compete by producing a somewhat different product satisfying the same need as the monopolist's product. An example is the courier services provided by United Parcel Service or Federal Express that compete with the package delivery of Canada Post. Canada Post still has a government-granted monopoly on the delivery of first-class mail, but it has no monopoly on the delivery of packages, whatever their size.

APPLYING ECONOMIC CONCEPTS 10-1

Entry Barriers for Irish Pubs During the Booming 1990s

During the 1990s the Irish economy was booming—so much so that many economists referred to it as the "Celtic Tiger," putting it in the same category as the Asian tigers of Taiwan, Singapore, Hong Kong, and South Korea. As the Irish economy boomed, however, line-ups and prices in many Irish pubs skyrocketed. The shortage of pubs was so severe that some pub operators implemented their own rationing schemes by turning away young people, bachelor parties, and sloppy dressers. In some cases, pub owners even threatened to expel anyone who started to sing, a long-standing tradition in Irish pubs.

So what was going on in the pub industry in Ireland? Ordinarily, as demand increases and profits rise, new pubs would be established. This entry of new pubs would keep the existing pubs from earning high profits.

The problem in Ireland was that the issuance of pub licences was governed by a 1902 law that froze the number of licences at the level in place at that time. As incomes grew over time and the demand for pubs increased, the entry of new pubs was prevented. It is therefore no surprise that prices in pubs were rising and that existing pubs were extremely profitable. This profitability was reflected in the high purchase prices of the pub licences, which were tradable (although in fixed total supply). If pubs earned zero economic profit, these licences would have had no market value. The Irish Competition Authority estimated the total value of existing licences at between 1 billion and 2 billion euros. The market value of these licences was a rough measure of the deadweight loss imposed on society by the regulations limiting the entry of new pubs.

Another aspect of the 1902 legislation that caused local pub shortages is that pub owners were prevented from transferring licences across county lines. As the population increasingly moved from small towns to larger cities over the past several decades, small towns were left with too many pubs while neighbourhoods in the larger cities had far too few. This distortion was seen clearly in Dublin, where approximately 35 percent of the Irish population was served by only 12 percent of the country's pubs.

Though new pubs could not be built in urban areas, the legislation allowed existing urban pubs to expand. This enabled more consumers to be served, but many complained that it led to the rise of the "super pubs"— larger establishments that lacked the social atmosphere that made Irish pubs famous the world over.

Who gained from this legislation, and who lost? The clear losers were the pubs' customers (especially in growing towns and cities) who were faced with higher prices and longer line-ups. The clear gainers were the owners of the pubs in areas where demand was strong. It is no surprise, therefore, that Ireland's powerful pub lobby continued to fight efforts by the government to review pub legislation.

Government legislation in Ireland restricted the entry of new pubs and therefore permitted existing pubs to earn high profits without the threat of competition.

Finally, a firm may get around a natural monopoly by inventing a technology that produces at a low minimum efficient scale (*MES*) and allows it to enter the industry and still cover its full costs. Cell-phone technology, for example, allows the provider of cell-phone services to compete with the provider of local land-line telephone services without having to establish an expensive network of wires, thus allowing successful competition at a much smaller scale of operations. In addition, Skype, Facetime, and other Internet-based substitutes to land-line telephone services are further eroding the market power of the traditional phone companies.

LESSONS FROM HISTORY 10-1

Creative Destruction Through History

Creative destruction, the elimination of one product by a superior product, is a major characteristic of all advanced countries. It eliminates the strong market position of the firms and workers who make the threatened product.

Steel-nibbed pens eliminated the quill pen with its sharpened bird's feather nib. Fountain pens eliminated the steel pen and its accompanying inkwell. Ballpoint pens virtually eliminated the fountain pen. Who knows what will come next in writing implements?

Silent films eliminated vaudeville. The talkies eliminated silent films and colour films have all but eliminated black and white. Television seriously reduced the demand for films (and radio) while not eliminating either of them. Cable greatly reduced the demand for direct TV reception by offering a better picture and a more varied selection. Satellite TV threatened to eliminate cable by offering much more selection, and access to movies and programs that can be live-streamed on the Internet is now challenging the dominance of conventional TV, cable, and satellite services.

Joseph Schumpeter argued that entry barriers could be circumvented in the very long run by technological change and the process of "creative destruction."

A monopolist's entry barriers are often circumvented by the innovation of production processes and the development of new goods and services. Such innovation explains why monopolies rarely persist over long periods, except those that are protected through government charter or regulation.

The distinguished economist Joseph Schumpeter (1883–1950) took the view that entry barriers were not a serious obstacle in the very long run. He argued that the short-run profits of a monopoly provide a strong incentive for others, through their own innovations and product development, to try to usurp some of these profits for themselves. If a frontal attack on the monopolist's entry barriers is not possible, the barriers will be circumvented by such means as the development of similar products against which the monopolist will not have entry protection. Schumpeter called the replacement of one product by another the process of *creative destruction*. "Creative" referred to the rise of new products; "destruction" referred to the demise of the existing products and perhaps the firms that produced them. Some examples of creative destruction are presented in *Lessons From History 10-1*.

Schumpeter argued that this process of creative destruction reflects new firms' abilities to circumvent entry barriers that would otherwise permit monopolists to earn profits in the long run. He also argued that because creative destruction thrives on innovation, the existence of monopoly profits is a major incentive to economic growth.

For long-distance passenger travel by sea, the steamship eliminated the sailing vessel around the beginning of the twentieth century. In the 1960s the airplane eliminated the ocean liner as a means of long-distance travel (but not for holiday cruises). For passenger travel on land, the train eliminated the stagecoach, while the bus competed with the train without eliminating it. The airplane wiped out the passenger train in most of North America while leaving the bus still in a low-cost niche used mainly for short and medium distances.

These examples all involve the elimination of a product by the development of a new, preferred product. But creative destruction also occurs with the development of better *processes*. The laborious hand-setting of metal type for printing was replaced by linotype that allowed the type to be set by a keyboard operator, but it still involved a costly procedure for making corrections. The linotype was swept away by computer typesetting and much of the established printing shop operations have now been replaced by low-cost laser or laserjet printing.

A century ago, automobiles were produced with skilled craftsmen operating relatively unsophisticated equipment. When Henry Ford perfected the techniques of mass production in the early 1920s, masses of less-skilled workers operated specialized and inflexible equipment. Then Toyota revolutionized the industry with its techniques of lean production, which did away with much of the repetitive tasks of mass production. Today, relatively few highly skilled workers operate very sophisticated robotics equipment to produce today's vehicles.

These cases all illustrate the same general message. Technological change transforms the products we consume, how we make those products, and how we work. It continually sweeps away positions of high income and economic power established by firms that were in the previous wave of technological change and by those who work for them. It is an agent of dynamism in our economy, an agent of change and economic growth, but it is not without its dark side in terms of the periodic loss of privileged positions on the part of the replaced firms and their workers.

Schumpeter was writing at a time when the two dominant market structures studied by economists were perfect competition and monopoly. His argument easily extends, however, to any market structure that allows profits to exist in the long run. Today, pure monopolies are few, but there are many industries in which profits can be earned for long periods of time. Such industries, which are called oligopolies, are conducive to the process of creative destruction. We study these industries in detail in Chapter 11.

10.2 Cartels as Monopolies

So far in our discussion, a monopoly has meant that there is only one firm in an industry. A second way a monopoly can arise is for many firms in an industry to agree to cooperate with one another, eliminating competition among themselves. In this case, they would band together and behave as if they were a single seller with the objective of maximizing their joint profits. Such a group of firms is called a **cartel**. The firms can agree among themselves to restrict their total output to the level that maximizes their joint profits.

Some of the best examples of cartels come from history. In the United States in the last half of the nineteenth century, cartels existed in the steel and oil industries. These cartels were so successful in restricting output and elevating prices that much of current U.S. anti-trust policy dates from that time. As we will see in Chapter 12, U.S. and

cartel An organization of producers who agree to act as a single seller in order to maximize joint profits.

DeBeers controls approximately 40 percent of the world's supply of diamonds through its Diamond Trading Company.

Canadian policy has been quite effective at preventing the creation of large cartels that would otherwise possess considerable market power.

As a result of successful policies aimed at preventing the creation of *domestic* cartels, the best current examples of cartels are ones that operate in global markets and are supported by national governments. The Organization of the Petroleum Exporting Countries (OPEC) is perhaps the best-known cartel in the world. This cartel first came to prominence when, in 1973, its members collectively agreed to restrict their output of crude oil and thereby increased the world price of oil by nearly 300 percent. In 1979, further output restrictions led the price to increase by another 120 percent. During the 1980s and 1990s, as oil production by non-OPEC countries increased significantly, OPEC found it difficult to maintain such a controlling influence on the oil market. OPEC also ran into problems enforcing the agreements among its members. As we will see in this section, these are typical challenges that all cartels face.

Another well-known example of a cartel that was successful over many years is the diamond cartel controlled by the South African company DeBeers. DeBeers produces a significant share of the world's annual output of rough diamonds but also purchases diamonds from smaller producers worldwide. The result is that about 40 percent of the world's annual diamond supply is marketed through the DeBeers-controlled Diamond Trading Company (DTC). In years when demand is slack, DeBeers restricts the output of diamonds through the DTC to keep prices from falling.

A third, less familiar example has recently gained prominence. In 1970, three Canadian companies that produce potash in Saskatchewan—a mineral used to produce fertilizer—created a special company to sell their product in world markets. Canpotex (named for *Can*adian *pot*ash *ex*ports) now sells about 40 percent of the world's potash, and the three companies restrict their combined annual production in an attempt to influence the world price. In recent years, Canpotex has also devised special grades of potash designed to suit specific crops, and in doing so the company has secured a much larger market share in countries such as South Korea, Japan, and Taiwan.

Notice in all three examples that there are firms *outside* the cartel. There are many oil producers (including all those in Canada and the United States) that are not part of OPEC; there are many diamond mines that are not owned or controlled by DeBeers (two of which are the Ekati and Diavik mines in the Northwest Territories that together make up approximately nine percent of total world diamond production); and there are other large potash producers in Belarus, Russia, Germany, and Israel that do not sell their potash through Canpotex. Indeed, this type of cartel is much more common than one in which *all* firms in the industry successfully band together.

In this chapter, however, we simplify the analysis by considering the case in which *all* firms in the industry form a cartel. This is the easiest setting in which to see the central point—that cartels are inherently unstable.

To learn more about OPEC, see its website at www.opec.org.

The Effects of Cartelization

If all firms in a competitive industry come together to form a cartel, they must recognize the effect their *joint* output has on price. That is, like a monopolist they must recognize that an increase in the total volume of their sales requires a reduction in price. They can agree to restrict industry output to the level that maximizes their joint profits (where the industry's marginal cost is equal to the industry's marginal revenue). The incentive for firms to form a cartel lies in the cartel's ability to restrict output, thereby raising price and increasing profits. This is shown in Figure 10-4.

> The profit-maximizing cartelization of a competitive industry will reduce output and raise price from the perfectly competitive levels.

Problems That Cartels Face

Cartels encounter two characteristic problems. The first is ensuring that members follow the behaviour that will maximize the cartel members' *joint* profits. The second is preventing these profits from being eroded by the entry of new firms.

Enforcement of Output Restrictions The managers of any cartel want the industry to produce its profit-maximizing output. Their job is made more difficult if individual firms either stay out of the cartel or join the cartel and then "cheat" by producing too much output. Any one firm, however, has an incentive to do just this—to be either the one that stays out of the organization or the one that enters and then cheats. For the sake of simplicity, assume that all firms enter the cartel; thus enforcement problems are concerned strictly with cheating by its members.

If Firm X is the only firm to cheat, it is then in the best of all possible situations. All other firms restrict output and hold the industry price up near its monopoly level. They earn profits but only by restricting output. Firm X can then reap the full benefit of the other firms' output restraint and sell some additional output at the high price that has been set by the cartel's actions. However, if all the firms cheat, the price will be pushed back to the competitive level, and all the firms will return to their competitive position.

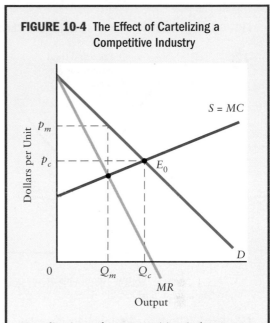

FIGURE 10-4 The Effect of Cartelizing a Competitive Industry

Cartelization of a competitive industry can always increase that industry's profits. Equilibrium for a competitive industry occurs at E_0. Equilibrium price and output are p_c and Q_c.

If the industry is cartelized, profits can be increased by reducing output. All units between Q_m and Q_c add less to revenue than to cost—the MR curve lies below the MC curve—and therefore will not be produced by a profit-maximizing cartel. The cartel maximizes its joint profits by producing output of Q_m and setting price equal to p_m (the same as the monopoly outcome).

This conflict between the interests of the group as a whole and the interests of each individual firm is the cartel's main dilemma and is illustrated in Figure 10-5. Provided that enough firms cooperate in restricting output, all firms are better off than they would be if the industry remained perfectly competitive. Any one firm, however, is even better off if it remains outside or if it enters and cheats. However, if all firms act on this incentive, all will be worse off than if they had joined the cartel and restricted output.

> Cartels tend to be unstable because of the incentives for individual firms to violate the output restrictions needed to sustain the joint-profit-maximizing (monopoly) price.

To learn more about Canpotex and the marketing of potash, see www.canpotex.com.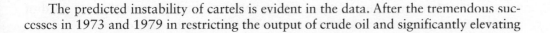

The predicted instability of cartels is evident in the data. After the tremendous successes in 1973 and 1979 in restricting the output of crude oil and significantly elevating

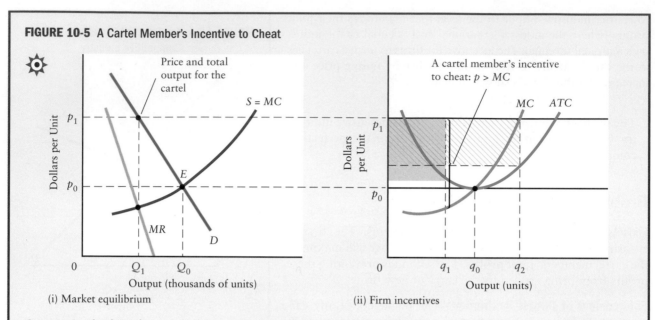

FIGURE 10-5 A Cartel Member's Incentive to Cheat

(i) Market equilibrium

(ii) Firm incentives

Cooperation leads to the monopoly price, but individual self-interest can lead to production in excess of the monopoly output. Market conditions are shown in part (i), and the situation of a typical firm is shown in part (ii). (The change of scale between the two graphs is reflected by the upper case Q in part (i) and the lower case q in part (ii).) Initially, the market is in competitive equilibrium with price p_0 and quantity Q_0. The individual firm is producing output q_0 and is just covering its total costs.

A successful cartel reduces total output to Q_1 and elevates price to p_1. Q_1 is the joint-profit-maximizing level of output because industry MR equals industry MC. A typical firm in the cartel bound to the output restriction is then producing output q_1 in part (ii). The firm's profits rise from zero to the amount shown by the grey shaded area in part (ii). Once price is raised to p_1, however, the individual firm would like to increase output to q_2, where its marginal cost is equal to the price set by the cartel. This would allow the firm to earn much larger profits, shown by the diagonally striped area. However, if all firms increase their output in such a manner, industry output will increase far beyond Q_1, and the resulting fall in price will reduce the joint profits of the cartel.

its world price, the members of the OPEC cartel began to encounter difficulties in enforcing their agreements. After several years of sluggish world demand for oil, the cartel almost collapsed in 1986 as several OPEC members increased their output in efforts to generate more income. Throughout the 1990s, however, OPEC members learned the important lesson that their attempts to push oil prices very high attract entry, encourage the development of alternative oil supplies, and undermine their output restrictions. As a result, OPEC members avoided the large output restrictions and price increases of the 1970s, instead trying to keep oil prices relatively stable at more moderate levels.

In recent years, however, OPEC's market power has increased, despite its relatively small share of the world market. The world price of oil increased from about U.S.$15 per barrel in 1998 to approximately U.S.$100 per barrel in 2012. These price changes were caused mostly by changes in the world demand for oil in a market in which most producers did not have significant excess capacity, which would allow them to increase their output. In other words, the world demand curve was shifting to the right from 1998 to 2012 (and to the left during the major global recession of 2009), while the world supply curve was stable and quite steep. In this environment, a decision by OPEC to considerably restrict output, even though OPEC represents only about a third of total world production, would have a noticeable effect on the market price.

Another example of a cartel's instability involves the world coffee market. In 2000, the Association of Coffee Producing Countries (ACPC), a cartel of 15 countries that produced approximately 75 percent of the world's coffee, agreed to restrict coffee output to keep coffee prices between U.S.\$0.95 and U.S.\$1.05 per pound. Within two years, however, a bumper crop in Brazil, the world's largest coffee producer, led to the inevitable pressure to cheat. Brazil had the incentive to sell its new production rather than incur storage costs. Other countries, facing low prices, had the incentive to increase their sales to bolster their incomes. By 2003, the ACPC had closed down its operations. Perhaps the cartel will be re-established at some point in the future when it has improved its ability to enforce its members' behaviour.

For interesting information about coffee and the world coffee market, go to www.ico.org.

Restricting Entry A successful cartel not only must police the behaviour of its members but also be able to prevent the entry of new producers. An industry that is able to support a number of individual firms presumably has no overriding natural entry barriers. Thus, if it is to maintain its profits in the long run, a cartel of many separate firms must create barriers that prevent the entry of new firms that are attracted by the cartel's profits. Successful cartels are often able to license the firms in the industry and to control entry by restricting the number of licences. This practice is often used by doctors, lawyers, dentists, and engineers, whose professional organizations restrict entry to those individuals who meet certain qualifications. At other times, the government has operated a quota system and has given it the force of law. If no one can produce without a quota and the quotas are allocated among existing producers, entry is successfully prevented. This approach is used to limit the number of taxicabs in many cities as well as the quantity of milk produced by Canada's dairy farmers. Governments also directly own some firms and prohibit competition from the private sector. In most Canadian provinces, for example, retail liquor sales are permitted only by government-owned establishments.

As we mentioned earlier, for many years DeBeers was successful at preventing the entry of new diamond producers and was able to control a large fraction of the world's annual sales of rough diamonds. But restricting entry into the diamond industry has become more challenging. In the diamond industry, of course, "entry" means the development of new diamond mines. In 2004, two new mines in the Northwest Territories reached full-scale production. The combined annual output of rough diamonds from the Ekati and Diavik mines is about nine percent of total world production. The owners of the Ekati and Diavik mines, however, market their diamonds independently rather than going through DeBeers. With entries such as this, combined with some Russian and Australian producers also choosing to sell their diamonds independently, DeBeers is faced with the challenge of keeping diamond prices supported above competitive levels. The challenges faced by cartels—both for enforcing output restrictions and for restricting entry—involve conflicting incentives between individual firms. To analyze these sorts of problems more completely, economists use *game theory*, a tool that we introduce and discuss in detail in Chapter 11.

For more information on the diamond industry in the Northwest Territories, see www. iti.gov.nt.ca/diamonds.

10.3 Price Discrimination

So far in this chapter, we have assumed that the monopolist charges the same price for every unit of its product, no matter where or to whom it sells that product. But as we will soon see, a monopolist always finds it profitable to sell different units of the same product at different prices whenever it gets the opportunity. In principle, the same is true for *any* firm that faces a negatively sloped demand curve. Because this practice is prevalent both for monopoly and for markets in which there are a few large sellers, the range of examples we will discuss covers both types of market structure.

Airlines often charge less to people who stay over a Saturday night than to those who come and go within the week. In countries in which medical services are provided by the market, physicians in private practice often charge for their services according to the incomes of their patients. Movie theatres often have lower admission prices for seniors and children (and for everyone on Tuesdays). Bus and transit passes are usually cheaper for students than for others. Electric companies typically sell electricity at one rate to homes and at a different rate to firms.

price discrimination The sale by one firm of different units of a product at two or more different prices for reasons not associated with differences in cost.

Price discrimination occurs when a producer charges different prices for different units of the same product *for reasons not associated with differences in cost*. Not all price differences represent price discrimination. Quantity discounts, differences between wholesale and retail prices, and prices that vary with the time of day or the season of the year may not represent price discrimination because the same product sold at a different time, in a different place, or in different quantities may have different costs. An excellent example is electricity. If an electric power company has unused capacity at certain times of the day, it may cost less for the company to provide service at those hours than at peak demand hours.

> **If price differences reflect cost differences, they are not discriminatory. When price differences are based on different buyers' valuations of the same product, they are discriminatory.**

It does not cost a movie-theatre operator less to fill seats with senior citizens than with non-seniors, but it is worthwhile for the movie theatre to let the seniors in at a discriminatory low price if few of them would attend at the full adult fare and if they take up seats that would otherwise be empty. Similarly, it does not cost VIA Rail any less to sell a ticket to a student than to a non-student. But since few students may be inclined to buy tickets at the full price, it is profitable for VIA Rail to attract more students with a lower price and, in that manner, fill up seats that would otherwise be empty.

Why do firms price discriminate? It may seem odd that they sell some units of output at a low price and other units at a high price. The simple answer is that firms price discriminate because they find it profitable to do so. As we will see shortly, price discrimination is profitable for two reasons. First, even if firms do not alter their level of sales, price discrimination allows them to "capture" some consumer surplus that would otherwise go to the buyer. Second, price discrimination allows firms to sell extra units of output without reducing the price on their existing sales.

> **Any firm that faces a downward-sloping demand curve can increase its profits if it is able to charge different prices for different units of its product.**

Note two important points. First, only firms facing negatively sloped demand curves—that is, firms with market power—are able to price discriminate. Perfectly competitive firms are price takers and therefore have no ability to set one price, let alone multiple prices. Second, firms will price discriminate *if they are able to*. Before we explore the various types of price discrimination, let's lay out the conditions under which it is possible.

When Is Price Discrimination Possible?

Three conditions must be satisfied before a firm can successfully price discriminate.

1. Market Power As we have just said, any firm that is a price taker cannot discriminate because it has no power to influence the price at which it sells its product. Our entire discussion about price discrimination therefore applies only to firms with some amount of market power. For simplicity, we will consider the case of a monopoly firm, although *any* firm with market power will, in general, be interested in the greater profits that are possible through price discrimination.

2. Identification of Consumers' Different Valuations Price discrimination is possible only when consumers value different units of the product differently. This could occur in two situations. First, the same consumer might be prepared to pay a different price for different units of the good. Second, consumers of one particular type (or in one geographic region) may be prepared to pay more for the good than consumers of a different type (or in a different region). We will see some examples shortly.

In the situation where price discrimination occurs between groups of consumers, the firm must somehow be able to determine which group of consumers is prepared to pay a high price and which group is prepared to pay only a low price. This is referred to as *segmenting* the market. Sometimes this market segmentation is relatively easy, as when the market is divided into geographic regions. Other times the firm must create innovative pricing strategies that will lead consumers to segment themselves. We will see examples of both shortly.

3. Prevent Arbitrage Whenever the same product is being sold at different prices, there is an incentive for buyers to purchase the product at the lower price and re-sell it at the higher price, thereby making a profit on the transaction. This is called *arbitrage*. A price-discriminating firm must be able to

In markets like this in which bargaining takes place, the sellers tend to be very good at determining each consumer's genuine willingness to pay. As a result, different consumers end up paying different prices for the same products. This is effective price discrimination.

prevent people from conducting such transactions. Otherwise the firm will end up selling only at the low price and all the profits that the strategy of price discrimination was designed to produce will accrue to those who do the arbitrage. As we will soon see, the successful prevention of this arbitrage depends crucially on the nature of the product being sold.

Different Forms of Price Discrimination

Now that we have seen the conditions that make price discrimination possible, let's examine the two general forms that it can take: price discrimination among *units of output* and price discrimination among *market segments*.

Price Discrimination Among Units of Output Recall our discussion in Chapter 6 where we noted that the demand curve can be viewed as a *willingness to pay* curve. We also discussed the concept of *consumer surplus*, the difference between the price the consumer is *willing* to pay and the price that the consumer *actually* pays.

A firm that charges different prices for different units of a product is trying to capture some of this consumer surplus. Figure 10-6 shows a monopolist's profits in two situations. In the first, the monopolist is only able to charge a single price per unit. In the second, the monopolist is able to charge different prices on different units of output and it increases its profits by doing so. Notice that even in the case where the firm charges several prices, consumers still earn some consumer surplus. In principle, however, a firm could charge a different price for each different unit of the product and thereby extract all of the consumer surplus. This situation is referred to as *perfect price discrimination* and is rare because it is very difficult for the firm to ascertain the consumers' willingness to pay for each individual unit. However, in some countries where local doctors know their patients very well and thus can make informed judgements about the consumers' willingness to pay, this type of price discrimination is observed.

Price discrimination among units of output sold to the *same* consumer requires that the firm be able to keep track of the units that a buyer consumes in each period. Thus, the tenth unit purchased by a given consumer in a given month can be sold at a price that is different from the fifth unit *only* if the firm can keep track of that consumer's purchases. This can be done, for example, by an electric company through its meter readings or by a coffee shop by using a "loyalty card," whereby after paying for seven coffees the customer gets the eighth for free. Another way in which some sellers keep track of consumers' purchases is to offer quantity discounts that take the form "buy two and get the third at half-price."

FIGURE 10-6 Price Discrimination Among Units of Output

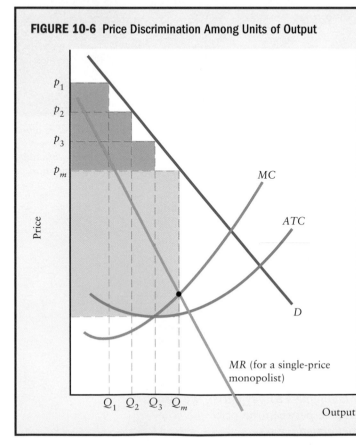

Profits can be increased by price discriminating. A single-price monopolist produces where $MR = MC$, output is Q_m, and price is p_m. In this case, profits are the light shaded area, and consumers receive consumer surplus given by the entire area above p_m and below the demand curve.

Price discrimination is designed to transfer some of this consumer surplus to the firm. Suppose the firm keeps output constant at Q_m but is able to charge different prices for different blocks of units. For example, it might charge p_1 for the first Q_1 units, p_2 for the next block of units up to Q_2, p_3 for the next block of units up to Q_3, and p_m for the remaining units up to Q_m. (The firm would expand output beyond Q_m if it could offer even more prices, but we simplify here to focus on the transfer of surplus with unchanged output.) In this case, the firm's costs have not changed but its revenues have increased by the dark shaded area. Since costs have not changed, the increase in revenue earned by price discrimination also represents an increase in profits for the firm. Consumer surplus has been reduced to the unshaded triangles just below the demand curve.

Price Discrimination Among Market Segments It is usually much easier for firms to distinguish between different groups of consumers of a product—different market segments—than it is to detect an individual consumer's willingness to pay for different units of that product. As a result, price discrimination among market segments is more common than price discrimination among units.

Suppose a monopolist faces a market demand curve that is made up of distinct market segments. These market segments may correspond to the age of consumers, such as children, adults, and seniors. Or the segments may correspond to different regions in which the consumers live, such as the North American automobile market being segmented into the Canadian and U.S. market segments. Whatever the nature of the market segmentation, suppose the monopolist recognizes the distinct market segments and is able to prevent any purchase-and-resale between them. What is the firm's profit-maximizing pricing policy?

The answer is for the firm to charge a higher price in the market segment with the *less elastic demand,* as shown in the numerical example in Figure 10-7. To understand this result, recall our discussion from Chapter 4 regarding elasticity. The elasticity of demand reflects consumers' ability or willingness to substitute between this product and other products. The market segment with less elastic demand therefore contains consumers that are more "committed" to this product than are the consumers in the market segment with more elastic demand. To put it differently, the consumers with less elastic demand represent a more "captive" market for the firm. It should not be surprising, therefore, that the profit-maximizing firm will charge a higher price to the more captive consumers and a lower price to those consumers who can more easily substitute away to other products.

> A firm with market power that can identify distinct market segments will maximize its profits by charging higher prices in those segments with less elastic demand.

Price discrimination among market segments is very common. When the different segments occur in different regions or countries, distance and transportation costs keep the markets separate, but sometimes those impediments are not enough. For example, new cars in the United States typically sell at a tax-inclusive price between 10 percent and 20 percent below the price for the same car in Canada. For several years it was common to hear of Canadians crossing the border to purchase their cars, paying the necessary Canadian sales taxes when they returned to Canada, and still saving several thousand dollars on the purchase. When such behaviour became widespread enough to present a serious problem to the Canadian dealers who were losing sales to those enterprising customers, the car companies effectively put an end to the practice by requiring their Canadian dealers to not honour service warranties for cars purchased in the United States. In this way, the car companies successfully maintain their strategy of market segmentation and price discrimination.

A more local example of price discrimination among market segments is the different prices charged by movie theatres for adults and seniors. The cost to the theatre of providing a seat to any customer is independent of the customer's age. But the two market segments contain consumers who are thought to have different elasticities of demand, the adults with the less elastic demand than seniors. The profit-maximizing pricing policy by the theatre is therefore to charge a higher price to adults than to seniors. This same logic applies to many goods and services for which there are "seniors' discounts."

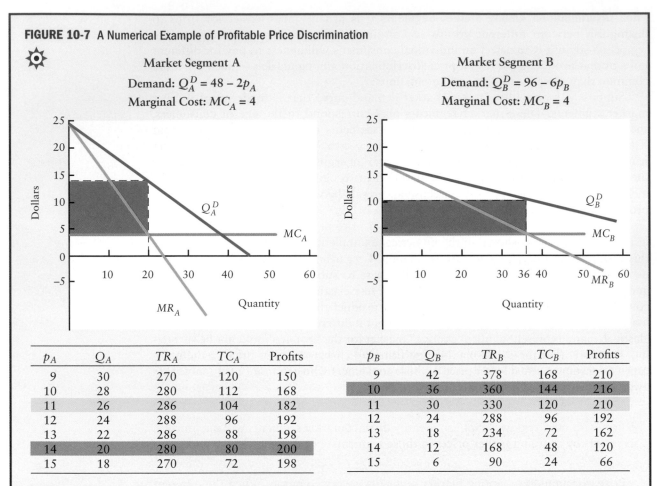

FIGURE 10-7 A Numerical Example of Profitable Price Discrimination

Market Segment A

Demand: $Q_A^D = 48 - 2p_A$

Marginal Cost: $MC_A = 4$

Market Segment B

Demand: $Q_B^D = 96 - 6p_B$

Marginal Cost: $MC_B = 4$

p_A	Q_A	TR_A	TC_A	Profits
9	30	270	120	150
10	28	280	112	168
11	26	286	104	182
12	24	288	96	192
13	22	286	88	198
14	20	280	80	200
15	18	270	72	198

p_B	Q_B	TR_B	TC_B	Profits
9	42	378	168	210
10	36	360	144	216
11	30	330	120	210
12	24	288	96	192
13	18	234	72	162
14	12	168	48	120
15	6	90	24	66

Profit-maximizing price discrimination results in higher prices in those market segments with less elastic demand. The figure shows two market segments, each with a different demand curve. At any given price, demand in segment A is less elastic than demand in segment B. Profit-maximizing price discrimination requires that $MC = MR$ in each market segment.

For each market segment, the table shows different possible prices, and the associated quantities, revenues, costs, and profits. Marginal costs are assumed to be $4 for each unit produced. Suppose first that the firm is unable to price discriminate and thus charges the same price in each segment. By comparing the total profit in the two segments *along any single row of the table,* it is apparent that the single profit-maximizing price is $11, total output is 56 units, and the resulting total profit is $392, as shown by the green shaded row. The firm can increase its profits, however, if it can charge different prices in the two market segments. By charging $14 in segment A and only $10 in segment B, the firm's total output is unchanged at 56 units, but the allocation of that output across the market segments is changed, and the firm's total profit increases to $416, as shown by the two red shaded rows.

The example of seniors' discounts at theatres also illustrates an important point about how the firm prevents arbitrage when price discriminating. When you buy a ticket to see a movie, you are buying a service rather than a tangible good. You don't take anything away with you after the movie—you are really just paying for the right to see the movie. This aspect of the product makes price discrimination easier to enforce. A young adult trying to circumvent the price discrimination could buy a senior's ticket, but upon entry to the theatre that person would be stopped and easily recognized as ineligible for the seniors' discount.

Price discrimination is easier for services than for tangible goods because for most services the firms transact directly with the final customer and thus can more easily prevent arbitrage.

One example of price discrimination is seniors' discounts at grocery stores or pharmacies. These typically place limits on the number of units that can be purchased at the discounted price.

That price discrimination is often difficult to sustain with tangible goods explains another familiar observation. Grocery stores and drugstores often have promotions with widely used products (toilet paper and paper towels, for example) on sale at heavily discounted prices. What prevents entrepreneurial shoppers in these situations from buying a large number of units at the special price and re-selling them to others at a higher price? The answer is that firms usually place quantity limits on special deals, thus preventing any large-scale arbitrage that would undermine their pricing policy.

Hurdle Pricing Market segments are often well defined but very difficult for the firm to detect. For example, we all know people who are sufficiently impatient that they *must* buy the latest Hollywood movie released on DVD, whereas many other people are prepared to wait several months until it is available at a considerably lower price. This pricing strategy is intentional and is referred to as *hurdle pricing*. The firms producing these goods know that some people are patient and others are impatient. By setting a high initial price and a lower price only after several months, the firms are setting a "hurdle" that consumers must "jump over" in order to get the low price. In this case, the hurdle is that consumers must wait a few months. This same type of hurdle exists in the pricing of high-priced hardcover books and lower-priced paperback books that are released a few months later. In this case, the slightly altered products do have different costs, although the cost differences are considerably smaller than the differences in prices.

Hurdle pricing exists when firms create an obstacle that consumers must overcome in order to get a lower price. Consumers then assign themselves to the various market segments—those who don't want to jump the hurdle and are willing to pay the high price, and those who choose to jump the hurdle in order to benefit from the low price.

Another familiar example of hurdle pricing involves coupons for discounts at grocery stores. Most of us receive grocery-store flyers in the mail every week. Many people ignore grocery store coupons because they can't be bothered to look through them and clip out their chosen ones, while others do so studiously. In this case, the price discrimination is between those people who can't be bothered to deal with the coupons (less elastic demand) and those people who care enough about the discounts to clip the coupons (more elastic demand). Everyone is presented with the option between higher prices and lower prices, and the hurdle of clipping coupons is designed to have people assign themselves to the two market segments.

The Consequences of Price Discrimination

What are the consequences of price discrimination? We can examine the consequences for firm profits, output, and consumer surplus.

Price Discrimination and Firm Profits Our first proposition is about the consequences of price discrimination for firm profits:

> **For any given level of output, the most profitable system of discriminatory prices will always provide higher profits to the firm than the profit-maximizing single price.**

This proposition, which was illustrated in Figure 10-6 on page 244, requires only that the demand curve have a negative slope. To see that the proposition is correct, remember that a monopolist with the power to discriminate could produce exactly the same quantity as a single-price monopolist and charge everyone the same price. Therefore, it need never receive less revenue, and it can do better if it can raise the price on even one unit sold, so long as the price need not be reduced on any other. This proposition is also illustrated in Figure 10-7 (page 246) in which the firm faces two market segments. When charging a single price, the monopolist produces 56 units, charges a price of $11, and earns profits of $392. By price discriminating across the two market segments, however, its profits rise to $416 even though its total output is unchanged.

Price Discrimination and Output Our second proposition relates to how price discrimination affects the level of output.

> **A monopolist that price discriminates among units will produce more output than will a single-price monopolist.**

To understand this second proposition, remember that a single-price monopolist will produce less than would all the firms in a perfectly competitive industry (recall Figure 10-3 on page 232). It produces less because it knows that selling more depresses the price. Price discrimination allows it to reduce this disincentive. To the extent that the firm can sell its output in separate blocks, it can sell another block without spoiling the market for blocks that are already sold. In the case of perfect price discrimination, in which every unit of output is sold at a different price, the profit-maximizing monopolist will produce every unit for which the price charged is greater than or equal to its marginal cost. A perfect-price-discriminating monopolist will therefore produce the same quantity of output as would all firms combined in a perfectly competitive industry (assuming that costs are the same in both situations).

This second proposition has implications for *market efficiency,* a concept we introduced in Chapter 5 and reviewed earlier in this chapter. Recall that a single-price monopolist produces at a level of output at which price exceeds marginal cost. Thus, society would benefit from having more of the good produced because the marginal value of the good to society (as reflected by its price) exceeds the marginal cost of the good. Put differently, a higher level of output would lead to more economic surplus being generated in the market and thus a more efficient outcome for society as a whole.

For a monopolist that price discriminates among units, however, there are several prices rather than just a single price. As you can see in Figure 10-6 on page 244, if the firm sold another block of output beyond Q_m at a price below p_m it would increase its profits further (because the new price would still be above MC). And the more output it produces, the more economic surplus is generated in the market.

> **If price discrimination leads the firm to increase total output, the total economic surplus generated in the market will increase, and the outcome will be more efficient.**

Price Discrimination and Consumer Surplus The final aspect of price discrimination is its effect on consumers, and this is where we often witness strong emotional reactions to price discrimination. But one's view will depend on who benefits and who loses.

For instance, when railways discriminate against small farmers, the results arouse public anger. It seems acceptable to many people, however, that doctors practise price discrimination in countries where medical services are provided by the market, charging lower prices to poor patients than to wealthy ones. And few people disapprove when airlines discriminate by giving senior citizens and vacationers lower fares than business travellers.

By increasing the seller's profits, price discrimination transfers income from buyers to sellers. When buyers are poor and sellers are rich, this transfer may seem undesirable. However, as in the case of doctors' fees and senior citizens' discounts, discrimination sometimes allows lower-income people to buy a product that they would otherwise be unable to afford if it were sold at the single price that maximized the producer's profits. In this case some consumers are made better off by the firm's decision to price discriminate.

> **There is no general relationship between price discrimination and consumer welfare. Price discrimination usually makes some consumers better off and other consumers worse off.**

SUMMARY

10.1 A Single-Price Monopolist

LO 1, 2

- Monopoly is a market structure in which an entire industry is supplied by a single firm. The monopolist's own demand curve is identical to the market demand curve for the product. The market demand curve is the monopolist's average revenue curve, and its marginal revenue curve always lies below its demand curve.

- A single-price monopolist is maximizing its profits when its marginal revenue is equal to marginal costs. Since marginal costs are positive, profit maximization means that marginal revenue is positive. Thus, in turn, elasticity of demand is greater than 1 at the monopolist's profit-maximizing level of output.

- A monopolist produces such that price exceeds marginal cost, whereas in a perfectly competitive industry,

price equals marginal cost. By restricting output below the competitive level, the monopolist imposes a deadweight loss on society; this is the inefficiency of monopoly.

- The profits that a monopoly earns may be positive, zero, or negative in the short run, depending on the relationship between demand and cost.

- For monopoly profits to persist in the long run, there must be effective barriers to the entry of other firms. Entry barriers can be natural or created.

- In the very long run, it is difficult to maintain entry barriers in the face of the process of creative destruction—the invention of new processes and new products to attack the entrenched position of existing firms.

10.2 Cartels as Monopolies

- A group of firms may form a cartel by agreeing to restrict their joint output to the monopoly level. Total profits at this reduced level of output exceed total profits in the competitive equilibrium.

- Cartels tend to be unstable because of the strong incentives for each individual firm to cheat by producing more than its agreed-upon level of output.

10.3 Price Discrimination

- Any firm that faces a downward-sloping demand curve can increase its profits if it can price discriminate.
- Successful price discrimination requires that the firm be able to control the supply of the product offered to particular buyers and to prevent the resale of the product.
- A firm that price discriminates among units will produce more output than if it sets only a single price. Price discrimination of this type is possible only if it can monitor use of the product by consumers.
- A firm that discriminates between different market segments will equate *MC* and *MR* in each market. The

market with the less elastic demand will have the higher price.
- Hurdle pricing is a common form of price discrimination that requires customers to overcome some obstacle in order to benefit from a lower price. This method of price discrimination leads customers to reveal through their actions which market segment they are in.
- If price discrimination leads the firm to increase output, market efficiency is improved. In general, some consumers will benefit and others will be made worse off by the firm's ability to price discriminate.

KEY CONCEPTS

The relationship between price and
   marginal revenue for a monopolist
Short-run monopoly profits
Natural and created entry barriers
The process of creative destruction

Cartels as monopolies
The instability of cartels
Arbitrage
Price discrimination among units

Perfect price discrimination
Price discrimination among market
   segments
Hurdle pricing

STUDY EXERCISES

MyEconLab   Make the grade with MyEconLab: Study Exercises marked in red can be found on MyEconLab. You can practise them as often as you want, and most feature step-by-step guided instructions to help you find the right answer.

1. Fill in the blanks to make the following statements correct.

   a. A perfectly competitive firm faces a _____ demand curve, whereas a single-price monopolist faces a _____ demand curve.
   b. A single-price monopolist that maximizes profits will produce at the output where _____ equals _____. A perfectly competitive firm (and industry)

   produces a level of output such that price _____ marginal cost. The monopolist produces a level of output such that price _____ marginal cost.
   c. A monopolist will be earning profits as long as price is _____ average total cost.
   d. At its profit-maximizing level of output, marginal cost for a single-price monopolist is always _____ the price it charges for its output.

2. The following table shows data for a monopolist. The first two columns provide all the data necessary to plot the monopolist's demand curve.

Price	Quantity Demanded	Total Revenue (TR)	Average Revenue (AR)	Marginal Revenue (MR)
$20	100	—	—	—
18	125	—	—	—
16	150	—	—	—
14	175	—	—	—
12	200	—	—	—
10	225	—	—	—
8	250	—	—	—
6	275	—	—	—
4	300	—	—	—

a. Compute total and average revenue for each level of output and fill in the third and fourth columns in the table. Explain why average revenue is equal to price.

b. Compute marginal revenue for each successive change in output and fill in the last column. Explain why MR is less than price.

c. On a scale diagram, plot the demand (average revenue) curve and the marginal revenue curve.

d. On a second scale diagram, with dollars on the vertical axis and output on the horizontal axis, plot the TR curve. What is the value of MR when TR reaches its maximum?

3. The diagram below shows the demand curve, marginal revenue curve, and cost curves for a monopolist that owns the only golf course on Eagle Island. The monopolist's product is 18-hole golf games.

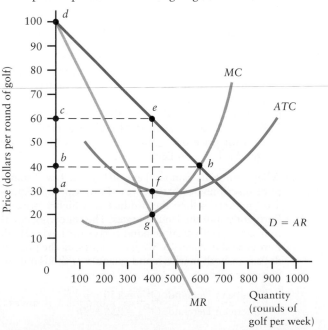

a. What is the profit-maximizing price and output (number of rounds of golf per week) for the monopolist on Eagle Island?

b. What is the average total cost per round of golf at the profit-maximizing level of output?

c. Calculate the profit, in dollars per week, to this monopolist.

4. The diagram below shows a monopolist's MC and ATC curves as well as the industry demand and MR curves.

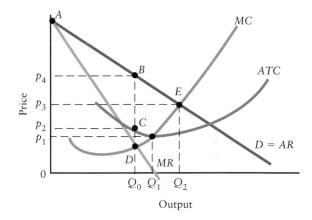

a. What is the profit-maximizing price and level of output for the monopolist?

b. What area in the figure shows the level of profits for the monopolist? Are profits positive or negative?

c. What area shows the deadweight loss to society resulting from the monopolist's output decision?

d. Now suppose the industry is made up of many small, price-taking firms (with the same technology). What are the equilibrium price and level of output in this case?

5. Imagine a monopolist that has fixed costs but no variable costs (thus there are no marginal costs, so $MC = 0$). For example, consider a firm that owns a spring of water that can produce indefinitely once it installs certain pipes, in an area where no other source of water is available.

a. Draw a downward-sloping demand curve for water, its associated MR curve, and the monopolist's MC curve.

b. On your diagram, show the monopolist's profit-maximizing price and level of output.

c. At the monopolist's profit-maximizing level of output, what is the marginal value of this good to society, and how does it compare with the marginal cost?

6. Consider the market for corn. Suppose this is a competitive industry, made up of many price-taking farmers. We begin in a situation where market price is p_0,

industry output is Q_0, and the typical farm is earning zero profit.

a. Draw the two diagrams below.

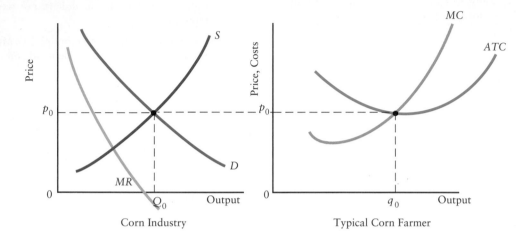

Corn Industry   Typical Corn Farmer

b. Now suppose that the farmers in this industry form a cartel and collectively agree to restrict the industry output of corn to the level that a monopolist would produce. Call this level of output Q^M and call the new price p^M. Each firm now produces output of $q^M < q_0$. Show this outcome in the two diagrams.

c. Show how the cartel raises the profits for the typical farmer.

d. Now consider the incentives for an individual farm to cheat on its fellow cartel members. Would it be profitable to produce an extra unit and sell it at the cartel price? How is this incentive illustrated in your diagram?

e. Show how the typical farm's profits would rise if it were the only farm to cheat. What level of output would the cheating farm produce?

f. Explain what would happen if *all* farms tried to cheat in this way.

7. Consider each of the following examples in which a firm sells the same product to different customers at different prices. Identify in each case whether price discrimination is likely to be taking place. If there is unlikely to be price discrimination occurring, what explains the different prices?

a. Weekend airline fares that are less than weekday fares

b. Business-class airline fares that are 50 percent higher than economy-class fares. (Recognize that two business-class seats take the same space inside the plane as three economy-class seats.)

c. Discounts on furniture negotiated from the "suggested retail price" for which sales personnel are authorized to bargain and to get as much in each transaction as the customer is prepared to pay.

d. Higher tuition for law students than for graduate students in economics.

8. Look back to the diagram of the monopolist on Eagle Island in Question 3.

a. Suppose the monopolist is able to practise *perfect* price discrimination. What would be the total number of rounds of golf sold per week? What would be the price on the last round sold?

b. What is the area representing consumer surplus in the absence of any price discrimination?

c. What is the area representing consumer surplus when the monopolist is practising perfect price discrimination?

d. Could this monopolist realistically engage in perfect price discrimination? Describe a more likely form of price discrimination that this monopolist could achieve on Eagle Island.

9. When selling its famous Levi 501 jeans, Levi Strauss price discriminates between the European and American markets, selling the product at a higher price in Europe than in the United States. The following equations are hypothetical demand curves for Levi 501s in Europe and in America. We have expressed the price in dollars in both markets, and quantity is thousands of units per year.

European Demand: $Q^D{}_E = 150 - p$
American Demand: $Q^D{}_A = 250 - 4p$

a. On separate scale diagrams, one for Europe and one for America, plot the two demand curves.

b. Recalling that a straight-line demand curve has an associated *MR* curve that has twice its slope, plot the two *MR* curves.

c. Suppose Levi Strauss has a constant marginal cost of $15 per unit. Plot the *MC* curve in both diagrams.

d. What is the profit-maximizing price in each market? Explain why profit maximization requires that *MC* be equated to *MR* *in each market segment.*

e. Compute the price elasticity of demand (at the profit-maximizing points) in each market segment. (You may want to review Chapter 4 on elasticity at this point.) Does the market segment with less elastic demand have the higher price?

10. Consider each of the following examples of price discrimination. For each case, explain how the price discrimination works. Also explain which consumers would be worse off and which consumers would be better off if the firm were *unable* to price discriminate in this way.

a. Seniors pay lower prices for theatre tickets than do other adults.

b. Consumers pay less for paperback books than for hardcover books, but must wait 6 to 12 months before the paperbacks are made available.

c. Customers at garage sales often pay a lower price if they ask for one—that is, if they reveal that they are prepared to haggle.

d. Airline customers get a discount fare if they are prepared to stay over a Saturday night at their destination.

11. Consider the following industries:

- chocolate bars
- copper wire
- outboard motors
- coal
- local newspaper

a. Which of these industries would it be most profitable to monopolize, and why?

b. Does your answer to part (a) depend on several factors or just one or two?

c. As a consumer, which of these industries would you least like to have monopolized by someone else?

d. If your answers to parts (a) and (c) are different, explain why.

12. Acme Department Store has a sale on luggage. It is offering $30 off any new set of luggage to customers who trade in an old suitcase. Acme has no use for the old luggage and throws it away at the end of each day. Is this price discrimination? Why or why not? Which of the conditions necessary for price discrimination are or are not met?

Imperfect Competition and Strategic Behaviour

THE two market structures that we have studied so far—perfect competition and monopoly—are polar cases; they define the two extremes of a firm's market power within an industry. Under perfect competition, firms are price takers, price is equal to marginal cost, and economic profits in the long run are zero. Under monopoly, the firm is a price setter, it sets price above marginal cost, and it can earn positive profits in the long run if there are sufficient entry barriers.

Although they provide important insights, these two polar cases are insufficient for understanding the behaviour of *all* firms. Indeed, most of the products that we easily recognize—swimsuits, cell phones, jeans, cameras, hamburgers, sunglasses, perfume, running shoes, computers, breakfast cereals, and cars, to name just a few—are produced by firms that have market power yet are not monopolists.

This chapter discusses market structures that lie between these two polar cases of perfect competition and monopoly. Before discussing the theory, however, we turn to a brief discussion of the prevalence of these "intermediate" market structures in the Canadian economy.

11.1 The Structure of the Canadian Economy

We can divide Canadian industries into two broad groups: those with a large number of relatively small firms and those with a small number of relatively large firms.

Industries with Many Small Firms

About two-thirds of Canada's total annual output is produced by industries made up of firms that are small relative to the size of the market in which they sell.

The perfectly competitive model does quite well in explaining the behaviour of some of these industries. These are the ones in which individual firms produce more-or-less identical products and so are price takers. Forest and fish products are two broad examples. Agriculture also fits fairly well in most ways since individual farmers are clearly price takers. Many basic raw materials, such as iron ore, tin, copper, oil, and paper, are sold on world markets where most individual firms lack significant market power.

Other industries, however, are not well described by the perfectly competitive model, even though they contain many small firms. In retail trade and in services, for example, most firms have some influence over prices. Your local grocery stores, clothing shops, nightclubs, and restaurants may spend a good deal of money advertising—something they would not have to do if they were price takers. Moreover, each store in these industries has differentiated products and also has a unique location, both of which give it some market power over its customers.

The theory of *monopolistic competition,* which we will examine in this chapter, was originally developed to help explain economic behaviour and outcomes in industries in which there are many small firms, each with some market power.

Industries with a Few Large Firms

About one-third of Canada's total annual output is produced by industries that are dominated by either a single firm or a few large ones.

The most striking cases of monopolies in today's economy are the electric utilities which are typically owned by provincial governments. The firms that provide local telephone, cable or digital TV, and Internet services are not strictly monopolies, although in some situations they may have local monopoly power—but in all cases they are subject to considerable government regulation. Other than these and a few other similar cases in which government ownership or regulation play an important role, cases of monopoly are rare in Canada today. However, there are some notable examples of monopoly (or near monopoly) from many years ago. For example, the Eddy Match Company was virtually the sole producer of wooden matches in Canada between 1927 and 1940, and Canada Cement Limited produced nearly all of the output of cement until the 1950s.

Sun Life is one of only a few large firms serving the Canadian life-insurance market. This is an oligopolistic industry.

For data on many aspects of Canadian industries, see Industry Canada's website: www.ic.gc.ca.

concentration ratio The fraction of total market sales (or some other measure of market activity) controlled by a specified number of the industry's largest firms.

This type of market dominance by a single large firm is now a thing of the past. Today, most modern industries that are dominated by large firms contain several firms. Their names are part of the average Canadian's vocabulary: Canadian National and Canadian Pacific railways; Bank of Montreal, Royal Bank, and Scotiabank; Imperial Oil, Encana, and Irving; Bell, Telus, and Rogers; Loblaws, Safeway, and Sobeys; Ford, Toyota, and GM; Sony, Mitsubishi, and Toshiba; Great-West Life, Sun Life, and Manulife; and General Foods, Nabisco, and Kellogg. Many service industries that used to be dominated by small independent firms have in recent decades seen the development of large firms operating on a worldwide basis. SNC-Lavalin and Acres are two examples of very large engineering firms that have business contracts all over the world. In management consulting, McKinsey & Co., Boston Consulting Group, and Monitor are also very large firms with market power.

The theory of *oligopoly*, which we will examine later in this chapter, helps us understand industries in which there are small numbers of large firms, each with market power, that compete actively with each other.

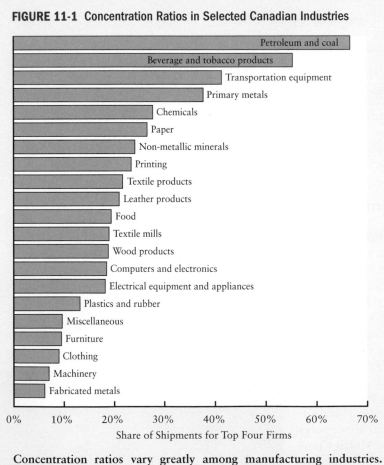

FIGURE 11-1 Concentration Ratios in Selected Canadian Industries

Share of Shipments for Top Four Firms (0% to 70%)

- Petroleum and coal
- Beverage and tobacco products
- Transportation equipment
- Primary metals
- Chemicals
- Paper
- Non-metallic minerals
- Printing
- Textile products
- Leather products
- Food
- Textile mills
- Wood products
- Computers and electronics
- Electrical equipment and appliances
- Plastics and rubber
- Miscellaneous
- Furniture
- Clothing
- Machinery
- Fabricated metals

Concentration ratios vary greatly among manufacturing industries. These data show the share of total annual shipments (in dollar terms) accounted for by the four largest firms in the industry.

(*Source*: Author's calculations based on data provided by Statistics Canada.)

Industrial Concentration

An industry with a small number of relatively large firms is said to be highly *concentrated*. A formal measure of such industrial concentration is given by the *concentration ratio*.

Concentration Ratios When we measure whether an industry has power concentrated in the hands of only a few firms or dispersed over many, it is not sufficient to count the firms. For example, an industry with one enormous firm and 29 very small ones is more concentrated in any meaningful sense than an industry with only five equal-sized firms. One approach to this problem is to calculate what is called a **concentration ratio**, which shows the fraction of total market sales (or shipments) controlled by the largest sellers, often taken as the largest four or eight firms.

Figure 11-1 shows the four-firm concentration ratios in several Canadian manufacturing industries. As is clear, the degree of concentration is quite varied across these industries. In the petroleum industry, for example, the largest four firms account for about 65 percent of total sales. At the other extreme, the largest four firms in the fabricated metals industry account for less than 10 percent of sales. These largest firms may be large in some absolute sense, but the low concentration ratios suggest that they have quite limited market power.

Defining the Market The main problem associated with using concentration ratios is to *define the market* with reasonable accuracy. On the one hand, the market may be much smaller than the whole country. For example, concentration ratios in national cement sales are low, but they understate the market power of cement companies because high transportation costs divide the cement *industry* into a series of *regional markets,* with each having relatively few firms. On the other hand, the market may be larger than one country, as is the case for most internationally traded commodities. This is particularly important for Canada.

The globalization of competition brought about by the falling costs of transportation and communication has been one of the most significant developments in the world economy in recent decades. As the world has "become smaller" through the advances in transportation and communication technologies, the nature of domestic markets has changed dramatically. For example, the presence of only a single firm in one industry in Canada in no way implies monopoly power when it is in competition with several foreign firms that can easily sell in the Canadian market. This is the situation faced by many Canadian companies producing raw materials, such as Cameco, Encana, Suncor, Canfor, Rio Tinto Alcan, and Barrick. These companies may be large relative to the *Canadian* market, but the relevant market in each case (uranium, natural gas, oil, forest products, aluminum, and gold) is the *global* one in which these firms have no significant market power.

In the cases of markets for internationally traded products, concentration ratios (appropriately adjusted to define the relevant market correctly) can still be used to provide valuable information about the degree to which production in a given market is concentrated in the hands of a few firms.

11.2 What Is Imperfect Competition?

We have identified two types of industries that are not well described by the theories of perfect competition or monopoly. In one type, there is a large number of small firms, but the theory of perfect competition is not appropriate because each of the many firms has some market power. In the other type, there is a small number of large firms, each with considerable market power. That these industries have more than a single firm makes the theory of monopoly inappropriate. We need theories to understand these market structures *between* the polar cases of perfect competition and monopoly.

The market structures that we are now going to study are called *imperfectly competitive*. The word *competitive* emphasizes that we are not dealing with monopoly, and the word *imperfect* emphasizes that we are not dealing with perfect competition (in which firms are price takers). Let's begin by noting a number of characteristics that are typical of imperfectly competitive firms. To help organize our thoughts, we classify these under two main headings. First, firms choose the *variety* of the product that they produce and sell. Second, firms choose the *price* at which they will sell that product.

Firms Choose Their Products

If a new farmer enters the wheat industry, the full range of products that the farmer can produce is already in existence. In contrast, if a new firm enters the smartphone or tablet industry, that firm must decide on the characteristics of the new products it is to design and sell. It will not produce smartphones that are identical to those already in production. Rather, it will develop variations on existing products or even a product with a whole new capability. Each of these will have its own distinctive characteristics including colour, size, shape, screen quality, video capability, and so on. As a result, firms in the smartphone and tablet industries sell an array of differentiated products, no two of which are identical.

differentiated product A group of commodities that are similar enough to be called the same product but dissimilar enough that all of them do not have to be sold at the same price.

The term **differentiated product** refers to a group of commodities that are similar enough to be called the same product but dissimilar enough that they can be sold at different prices. For example, although one brand of shampoo is similar to most others, shampoos differ from each other in chemical composition, colour, smell, brand name, packaging, and reputation. All shampoos taken together can be regarded as one differentiated product.

> Most firms in imperfectly competitive markets sell differentiated products. In such industries, the firm itself must choose which characteristics to give the products that it will sell.

Firms Choose Their Prices

Whenever different firms' products are not identical, each firm must decide on a price to set. For example, no market sets a single price for cars or TVs or jeans by equating overall demand with overall supply. What is true for cars and TVs is true for virtually all consumer goods. Any one manufacturer will typically have several product lines that differ from each other and from the competing product lines of other firms. Each product has a price that must be set by its producer.

price setter A firm that faces a downward-sloping demand curve for its product. It chooses which price to set.

Firms that choose their prices are said to be **price setters**. Each firm has expectations about the quantity it can sell at each price that it might set. Unexpected demand fluctuations then cause unexpected variations in the quantities that are sold at these prices.

> In market structures other than perfect competition, firms set their prices and then let demand determine sales. Changes in market conditions are signalled to the firm by changes in the firm's sales.

One striking contrast between perfectly competitive markets and markets for differentiated products concerns the behaviour of prices. In perfect competition, prices change continually in response to changes in demand and supply. In markets where differentiated products are sold, prices change less frequently.

Modern firms that sell differentiated products typically have hundreds of distinct products on their price lists. Changing such a long list of prices is often costly enough that it is done only infrequently. The costs of changing the prices include the costs of printing new list prices and notifying all customers, the difficulty of keeping track of frequently changing prices for purposes of accounting and billing, and the loss of customer and retailer goodwill because of the uncertainty caused by frequent changes in prices. As a result, imperfectly competitive firms often respond to fluctuations in demand by changing output and holding prices constant. Only after changes in demand are expected to persist will firms incur the expense of adjusting their entire list of prices.

Since the advent of the Internet, however, some firms find it much easier to change prices almost continuously, just as would happen in perfect competition. For example, airlines have websites on which they post their prices, which change very frequently, even hourly. And for retailers who use the Internet or social networking to contact their customers, "flash sales" are now common, whereby the store advertises special sale prices that last for one day or even one hour.

These breakfast cereals are different enough that each can have its own price, but they are similar enough to be called the same product—they are a differentiated product.

Non-Price Competition

Firms in imperfect competition behave in other ways that are not observed under either perfect competition or monopoly.

First, many firms spend large sums of money on advertising. They do so in an attempt both to shift the demand curves for the industry's products and to attract customers from competing firms. A firm in a perfectly competitive market would not engage in advertising because the firm faces a perfectly elastic (horizontal) demand curve at the market price and so advertising would involve costs but would not increase the firm's revenues. A monopolist has no competitors in the industry and so will not advertise to attract customers away from other brands. However, in some cases a monopolist will still advertise in an attempt to convince consumers to shift their spending away from other types of products and toward the monopolist's product.

Second, many firms engage in a variety of other forms of non-price competition, such as offering competing standards of quality and product guarantees. In the car industry, for example, Toyota and GM compete actively in terms of the duration of their "bumper-to-bumper" warranties. Many firms also compete through the services they offer along with their products. The car industry is again a good example, with manufacturers and dealers competing in their "after-sales" services provided to the customer, ranging from oil changes and car washes to emergency on-road assistance.

Third, firms in many industries engage in activities that appear to be designed to hinder the entry of new firms, thereby preventing the erosion of existing profits by entry. For example, a retailer's public commitment to match any price offered by a competing retailer may convince potential entrants not to enter the industry.

Two Market Structures

Our discussion in this section has been a general one concerning firms in imperfectly competitive market structures. We now go into a little more detail and make a distinction between industries with a large number of small firms and industries with a small number of large firms.

Behaviour in the first group of industries can be understood with the theory of *monopolistic competition*. To understand behaviour in the second group we use the theory of *oligopoly*, in which *game theory* plays a central role. As you will see in the remainder of this chapter, a key difference between these two market structures is the amount of *strategic behaviour* displayed by firms.

11.3 Monopolistic Competition

monopolistic competition Market structure of an industry in which there are many firms and freedom of entry and exit but in which each firm has a product somewhat differentiated from the others, giving it some control over its price.

The theory of **monopolistic competition** was originally developed to deal with the phenomenon of product differentiation. This theory was first developed by U.S. economist Edward Chamberlin in his pioneering 1933 book *The Theory of Monopolistic Competition*.

This market structure is similar to perfect competition in that the industry contains many firms and exhibits freedom of entry and exit. It differs, however, in one important respect: Whereas firms in perfect competition sell an identical product and are price takers, firms in monopolistic competition sell a differentiated product and thus have some power over setting price.

Product differentiation leads to the establishment of brand names and advertising, and it gives each firm a degree of market power over its own product. Each firm can raise its price, even if its competitors do not, without losing all its sales. This is the *monopolistic* part of the theory. However, each firm's market power is severely restricted in both the short run and the long run. The short-run restriction comes from the presence of similar products sold by many competing firms; this causes the demand curve faced by each firm to be very elastic. The long-run restriction comes from free entry into the industry, which permits new firms to compete away the profits being earned by existing firms. These restrictions comprise the *competition* part of the theory.

Many of the small, service-based businesses located in your neighbourhood are monopolistic competitors—corner stores, dry cleaners, hair stylists, restaurants, auto mechanics, shoe-repair shops, grass-cutting and snow-removal services, home-renovation firms, and plumbers, electricians, and painters. In each case, the firm tries to differentiate its product by offering more convenient hours, better workmanship, guarantees of some kind, or perhaps just nicer people. And in each case the firm has some ability to set its own price—but its market power is limited by the nearby presence of other firms selling similar products.

The Assumptions of Monopolistic Competition

The theory of monopolistic competition is based on four key simplifying assumptions.

1. Each firm produces its own version of the industry's differentiated product. Each firm thus faces a demand curve that, although negatively sloped, is highly elastic because competing firms produce many close substitutes.

2. All firms have access to the same technological knowledge and so have the same cost curves.

3. The industry contains so many firms that each one ignores the possible reactions of its many competitors when it makes its own price and output decisions. In this

respect, firms in monopolistic competition are similar to firms in perfect competition.

4. There is freedom of entry and exit in the industry. If profits are being earned by existing firms, new firms have an incentive to enter. When they do, the demand for the industry's product must be shared among the increased number of firms.

Predictions of the Theory

Product differentiation, which is the *only* thing that makes monopolistic competition different from perfect competition, has important consequences for behaviour in both the short and the long run.

Most of the service-based businesses in your neighbourhood, such as hair salons, exist in monopolistically competitive markets.

The Short-Run Decision of the Firm In the short run, a firm that is operating in a monopolistically competitive market structure is similar to a monopoly. It faces a negatively sloped demand curve and maximizes its profits by choosing its level of output such that marginal costs equal marginal revenue. The firm shown in part (i) of Figure 11-2 makes positive profits, although in the short run it is possible for a monopolistically competitive firm to break even or even to make losses.

The Long-Run Equilibrium of the Industry Profits, as shown in part (i) of Figure 11-2, provide an incentive for new firms to enter the industry. As they do so, the total demand for the industry's product must be shared among this larger number of firms; thus, each firm gets a smaller share of the total market. Such entry shifts to the left the demand curve faced by each existing firm. Entry continues until profits are eliminated. When this has occurred, each firm is in the position shown in part (ii) of Figure 11-2. Its demand curve has shifted to the left until the curve is *tangent* to the long-run average cost (*LRAC*) curve. Each firm is still maximizing its profit, but its profit is now equal to zero.[1]

To see why this "tangency solution" provides the only possible long-run equilibrium for an industry that fulfills all of the theory's assumptions, consider the two possible alternatives. First, suppose the demand curve for each firm lies below and never touches its *LRAC* curve. There would then be no output at which costs could be covered, and firms would leave the industry. With fewer firms to share the industry's demand, the demand curve for each *remaining* firm shifts to the right. Exit will continue until the demand curve for each remaining firm touches and is tangent to its *LRAC* curve. Second, suppose the demand curve for each firm *cuts* its *LRAC* curve. There would then be a range of output over which positive profits could be earned. Such profits would lead firms to enter the industry, and this entry would shift the demand curve for each existing firm to the left until it is just tangent to the *LRAC* curve, where each firm earns zero profit.

---

[1] A standard assumption in this theory is that the industry is symmetric in the sense that when a new firm enters the industry, it takes demand away equally from all existing firms, thus ensuring that all industry profits are eliminated in the long run. The asymmetric case, in which the industry's differentiated products have varying degrees of substitutability for each other, making long-run profits possible for some of the firms, is discussed in advanced courses in industrial organization.

FIGURE 11-2 Profit Maximization for a Firm in Monopolistic Competition

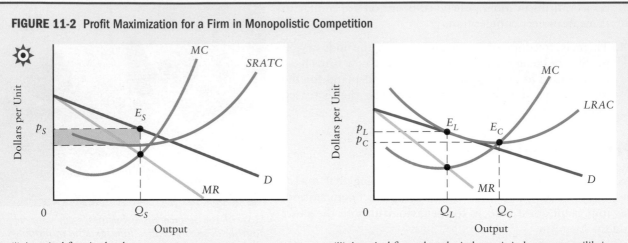

(i) A typical firm in the short run

(ii) A typical firm when the industry is in long-run equilibrium

The short-run position for a monopolistically competitive firm is similar to that of a monopolist—profits can be positive, zero, or negative. In the long run, firms in a monopolistically competitive industry have zero profits and excess capacity. Note the very elastic demand curve—this reflects the fact that each firm produces a good for which there are many close (but not perfect) substitutes. Short-run profit maximization occurs in part (i) at E_S, the output for which $MR = MC$. Price is p_S and quantity is Q_S. Profits or losses may exist in the short run; in this example profits are positive and are shown by the shaded area. Starting from the short-run position shown in part (i), entry of new firms shifts each firm's demand curve to the left until profits are eliminated. In part (ii), point E_L, where demand is tangent to $LRAC$, is the position of each firm when the industry is in long-run equilibrium. Price is p_L and quantity is Q_L. In such a long-run equilibrium, each monopolistically competitive firm has zero profits and excess capacity of $Q_L Q_C$.

The Excess-Capacity Theorem Part (ii) of Figure 11-2 makes it clear that monopolistic competition results in a long-run equilibrium of zero profits, even though each individual firm faces a negatively sloped demand curve. It does this by forcing each firm into a position in which it has *excess capacity*; that is, each firm is producing an output less than that corresponding to the lowest point on its *LRAC* curve. If the firm were to increase its output, it would reduce its cost per unit, but it does not do so because selling more would reduce revenue by more than it would reduce cost. This result is often called the **excess-capacity theorem**.

excess-capacity theorem The property of long-run equilibrium in monopolistic competition that firms produce on the falling portion of their long-run average cost curves. This results in excess capacity, measured by the gap between present output and the output that coincides with minimum average cost.

> **In long-run equilibrium in monopolistic competition, goods are produced at a point where average total costs are not at their minimum.**

In contrast, the long-run equilibrium under perfect competition has price equal to the minimum of long-run average costs. In part (ii) of Figure 11-2, this is shown as point E_C, with price p_C and output Q_C. (Recall that with perfect competition, each firm faces a horizontal demand curve at the market price, so at price p_C each firm would be on its *MC* curve at point E_C.)

The excess-capacity theorem once aroused passionate debate among economists because it seemed to show that all industries selling differentiated products would produce them at a higher cost than was necessary. Because product differentiation is a characteristic of virtually all modern consumer goods and many service industries, this theorem seemed to suggest that modern market economies were systematically inefficient.

Subsequent analysis by economists has shown that the charge of inefficiency has not been proven. The excess capacity of monopolistic competition does not necessarily indicate a waste of resources because some benefits accrue to consumers who can choose among the variety of products.

Saying that consumers value variety is not saying that *each* consumer necessarily values variety. You might like only one of the many brands of toothpaste and be better off if only that one brand were sold at a lower price. But other consumers would prefer one of the other brands. Thus, it is the differences in tastes *across many consumers* that give rise to the social value of variety, and the cost of achieving that greater variety is the higher price per unit that consumers must pay.

The Canadian wine-making industry contains many firms producing similar but differentiated products. It is a monopolistically competitive industry.

From society's point of view, there is a tradeoff between producing more brands to satisfy diverse tastes and producing fewer brands at a lower cost per unit.

Monopolistic competition produces a wider range of products but at a somewhat higher cost per unit than perfect competition (which produces only one type of each generic product). As consumers clearly value variety, the benefits of variety must be matched against the extra cost that variety imposes. Product differentiation is wasteful only if the costs of providing variety exceed the benefits of the variety itself.

11.4 Oligopoly and Game Theory

Industries that are made up of a small number of large firms have a market structure called *oligopoly*, from the Greek words *oligos polein*, meaning "few to sell." An **oligopoly** is an industry that contains two or more firms, at least one of which produces a significant portion of the industry's total output. Whenever there is a high concentration ratio for the firms that are serving one particular market, that market is oligopolistic. The market structures of oligopoly, monopoly, and monopolistic competition are similar in that firms in all these markets face negatively sloped demand curves.

oligopoly An industry that contains two or more firms, at least one of which produces a significant portion of the industry's total output.

Profit Maximization Is Complicated

Like firms in other market structures, an oligopolist that wants to maximize its profits produces the level of output where its marginal revenue equals its marginal cost. But determining this level of output is more complicated for an oligopolist than it is for any other kind of firm because the firm's marginal revenue depends importantly on what its rivals do. For example, if Toyota decides to increase its production of compact cars in an attempt to equate its *MR* with its *MC*, Ford and Nissan may respond by aggressively increasing their output of compacts—thus reducing Toyota's marginal revenue. Alternatively, Ford and Nissan might *reduce* their output of compacts and instead focus their attention on market niches in which Toyota plays a smaller role. Or they might leave their output levels unchanged and introduce new options on their compact cars in an attempt to attract consumers to their products.

The general point is that determining the level of output that maximizes profits is complicated for an oligopolistic firm because it must consider its rivals' likely responses to its actions. Economists say that oligopolists exhibit **strategic behaviour**, which means that they take explicit account of the impact of their decisions on competing firms and of the reactions they expect competing firms to make. In the remainder of this section we examine the strategic behaviour practised by oligopolistic firms.

strategic behaviour Behaviour designed to take account of the reactions of one's rivals to one's own behaviour.

> Oligopolistic firms often make strategic choices; they consider how their rivals are likely to respond to their own actions.

The Basic Dilemma of Oligopoly

The basic dilemma faced by oligopolistic firms is very similar to the dilemma faced by the members of a cartel, which we studied in Chapter 10. There we saw that the cartel as a whole had an incentive to form an agreement to restrict total output, but each individual member of the cartel had the incentive to cheat on the agreement and increase its own level of output.

For the small number of firms in an oligopoly, the incentives are the same. We say that firms can either *cooperate* (or *collude*) in an attempt to maximize joint profits, or they can *compete* in an effort to maximize their individual profits. Not surprisingly, the decision by one firm to cooperate or to compete will depend on how it thinks its rivals will respond to its decision.

When thinking about how firm behaviour leads to market outcomes, we distinguish between *cooperative* and *non-cooperative* behaviour. If the firms cooperate to produce among themselves the monopoly output, they can maximize their joint profits. If they do this, they will reach what is called a **cooperative** (or **collusive**) **outcome**, which is the position that a single monopoly firm would reach if it owned all the firms in the industry.

cooperative (collusive) outcome A situation in which existing firms cooperate to maximize their joint profits.

If the firms are at the cooperative outcome, it will usually be worthwhile for any one of them to cut its price or to raise its output, so long as the others do not do so. However, if every firm does the same thing, they will be worse off as a group and may all be worse off individually. An industry outcome that is reached when firms proceed by calculating only their own gains without cooperating with other firms is called a **non-cooperative outcome**.

non-cooperative outcome An industry outcome reached when firms maximize their own profit without cooperating with other firms.

The behaviour of firms in an oligopoly is complex, and studying it requires much attention to detail. As in other market structures, it is necessary to think about how individual firm behaviour affects the overall market outcome. Unlike other market structures, however, in oligopoly each firm typically thinks about how the other firms in the industry will react to its own decisions. Then, of course, the other firms may respond to what the first firm does, and so on. To help us keep our thoughts organized, we will use *game theory*.

Some Simple Game Theory

Game theory is used to study decision making in situations in which there are a number of players, each knowing that others may react to their actions and each taking account of others' expected reactions when making moves. For example, suppose a firm is deciding whether to raise, lower, or maintain its price. Before arriving at an answer, it asks, "What will the other firms do in each of these cases, and how will their actions affect the profitability of whatever decision I make?"

> **game theory** The theory that studies decision making in situations in which one player anticipates the reactions of other players to its own actions.

> When game theory is applied to oligopoly, the players are firms, their game is played in the market, their strategies are their price or output decisions, and the payoffs are their profits.

An illustration of the basic dilemma of oligopolists, to cooperate or to compete, is shown in Figure 11-3 for the case of a two-firm oligopoly, called a *duopoly*. In this simplified game, we assume that both firms are producing the same product, and so there is a single market price. The only choice for each firm is how much output to produce. If the two firms "cooperate" to jointly act as a monopolist, each firm produces one-half of the monopoly output and each earns large profits. If the two firms "compete," they each produce more than half (say two-thirds) of the monopoly output, and in this case both firms earn low profits. As we will see, even this very simple example is sufficient to illustrate several key ideas in the modern theory of oligopoly.

A Payoff Matrix Figure 11-3 shows a *payoff matrix* for this simple game. It shows the profits that each firm earns in each possible combination of the two firms' actions. The upper-left cell in this example shows that if each firm produces one-half of the monopoly output, each firm will earn profits of 20. The lower-right cell shows that if each firm produces two-thirds of the monopoly output, each firm will earn a profit of 17. Since *joint* profits must be maximized at the monopoly output, the total profit in the upper-left cell (40) is greater than the total profit in the lower-right cell (34).

The upper-right and lower-left cells show the profits in the case where one firm produces one-half of the monopoly output and the other firm produces two-thirds of the monopoly output. Note that in these cells, the firm that produces more earns the greater profit. The firm that produces one-half of the monopoly output is helping to restrict output and keep prices high. The firm that produces two-thirds of the monopoly output then benefits from the first firm's output restrictions.

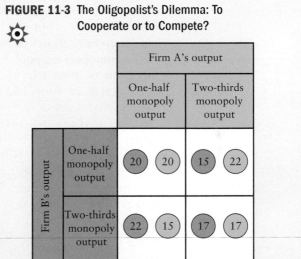

FIGURE 11-3 The Oligopolist's Dilemma: To Cooperate or to Compete?

		Firm A's output	
		One-half monopoly output	Two-thirds monopoly output
Firm B's output	One-half monopoly output	20 20	15 22
	Two-thirds monopoly output	22 15	17 17

Cooperation to determine the overall level of output can maximize joint profits, but it leaves each firm with an incentive to cheat. The figure shows a payoff matrix for a two-firm game. Firm A's production is indicated across the top, and its payoffs are shown in the green circles within each cell. Firm B's production is indicated down the left side, and its payoffs are shown in the red circles within each cell.

If A and B cooperate, each produces one-half the monopoly output and receives a payoff of 20. If A and B do not cooperate, they each end up producing two-thirds of the monopoly output and receiving a payoff of 17. In this example, this non-cooperative outcome is a Nash equilibrium.

Strategic Behaviour The payoff matrix shows the profit each player earns with each combination of the two players' moves. But what will actually happen? To answer this question, we must first know what type of game is being played. Specifically, can the players *cooperate* or is the game a *non-cooperative* one?

Cooperative Outcome. If the two firms in this duopoly can cooperate, the payoff matrix shows that their highest *joint* profits will be earned if each firm produces one-half of the monopoly output. This is the cooperative outcome. The payoff matrix also shows, however, that if each firm thinks the other will cooperate (by producing half of the monopoly output), then it has an incentive to cheat and produce two-thirds of the monopoly output. Thus, the cooperative outcome can only be achieved if the firms have some effective way to enforce their output-restricting agreement. As we will see in Chapter 12, explicit output-restricting agreements are usually illegal.

Non-Cooperative Outcome. Now suppose that firms believe cooperation to be impossible because they have no legal way of enforcing an agreement. What will be the non-cooperative outcome in this duopoly game? To answer this question, we must examine each player's incentives, given the possible actions of the other player.

Firm A reasons as follows: "If B produces one-half of the monopoly output (upper row of the matrix), then my profit will be higher if I produce two-thirds of the monopoly output. Moreover, if B produces two-thirds of the monopoly output (bottom row of the matrix), my profit will be higher if I also produce two-thirds of the monopoly output. Therefore, no matter what B does, I will earn more profit if I produce two-thirds of the monopoly output." A quick look at the payoff matrix in Figure 11-3 reveals that this game is *symmetric,* and so Firm B's reasoning will be identical to A's: It will conclude that its profit will be higher if it produces two-thirds of the monopoly output no matter what A does.

The final result is therefore clear. Each firm will end up producing two-thirds of the monopoly output and each firm will receive a profit of 17. This is the non-cooperative outcome. Note that each firm will be worse off than it would have been had they been able to enforce an output-restricting agreement and thus achieve the cooperative outcome. This type of game, in which the non-cooperative outcome makes *both* players worse off than if they had been able to cooperate, is called a *prisoners' dilemma.* The reason for this curious name is discussed in *Extensions in Theory 11-1.*

Nash Equilibrium. The non-cooperative outcome shown in Figure 11-3 on page 265 is called a **Nash equilibrium**, after the U.S. mathematician John Nash, who developed the concept in the 1950s and received the Nobel Prize in economics in 1994 for this work. (The 2002 movie *A Beautiful Mind* is about John Nash's life and contains a few fascinating bits of game theory!) In a Nash equilibrium, each player's best strategy is to maintain its current behaviour *given the current behaviour of the other players.*

It is easy to see that there is only one Nash equilibrium in Figure 11-3.[2] In the bottom-right cell, the best decision for each firm, given that the other firm is producing two-thirds of the monopoly output, is to produce two-thirds of the monopoly output

Nash equilibrium An equilibrium that results when each player is currently doing the best that it can, given the current behaviour of the other players.

---

[2] In general, an economic "game" may have zero, one, or more Nash equilibria. For an example of an economic setting in which there are two Nash equilibria, see Study Exercise #12 on page 279.

EXTENSIONS IN THEORY 11-1

The Prisoners' Dilemma

The game shown in Figure 11-3 on page 265 is often known as a prisoners' dilemma game. This is the story behind the name:

Two men, John and William, are arrested on suspicion of jointly committing a crime and, in the absence of witnesses, are interrogated separately. They know that if they both plead innocence, they will get only a light sentence, and if they both admit guilt they will both receive a medium sentence. Each is told, however, that if either protests innocence while the other admits guilt, the one who claims innocence will get a severe sentence while the other will be released with no sentence at all.

Here is the payoff matrix for that game:

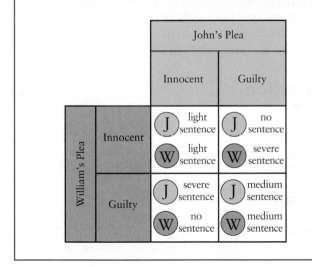

John reasons as follows: "William will plead either guilty or innocent. If he pleads innocent, I will get a light sentence if I also plead innocent but no sentence at all if I plead guilty, so guilty is my better plea. If he pleads guilty, I will get a severe sentence if I plead innocent and a medium sentence if I plead guilty. So once again guilty is my preferred plea."

William reasons in the same way and, as a result, they both plead guilty and get a medium sentence. Note, however, that if they had been able to communicate and coordinate their pleas, they could both have agreed to plead innocent and get off with a light sentence.

The prisoners' dilemma arises in many economic situations. We have already seen an example of a two-firm oligopoly. Economists use the basic structure of this simple game to think about how firms compete in their decisions to build new factories, launch advertising campaigns, and adjust the prices of their differentiated products.

Simple game theory and the prisoners' dilemma also figure prominently in the study of political science. Robert Axelrod's 1984 book *The Evolution of Cooperation* discusses how the key insights from the prisoners' dilemma have been used in the analysis of elections (where candidates' choices are their electoral platforms) and the nuclear arms race (in which national governments' choices are their decisions to build and stockpile weapons).*

---

*For those interested in a very readable treatment of game theory applied to many aspects of life, see *Thinking Strategically* (Norton, 1993) by Avinash Dixit and Barry Nalebuff, two leading economists.

---

itself. Between them, they produce a joint output of 1.33 times the monopoly output. Neither firm has an incentive to depart from this position (except through enforceable cooperation with the other). In any other cell, each firm has an incentive to change its output *given the output of the other firm*.

The basis of a Nash equilibrium is rational decision making in the absence of cooperation. Its particular importance in oligopoly theory is that it is a self-policing equilibrium. It is self-policing in the sense that there is no need for group behaviour to enforce it. Each firm has a self-interest to maintain it because no move will improve its profits, given what other firms are currently doing.

If a Nash equilibrium is established by any means whatsoever, no firm has an incentive to depart from it by altering its own behaviour.

Extensions in Game Theory

The simple game that we have just described helps us understand the dilemma faced by oligopolists producing identical products, such as steel, aluminum, cement, newsprint, and copper pipe. But game theory can also be used in other settings, such as

- examining how oligopolists interact when they charge different prices for their differentiated products, such as Nike and Reebok for running shoes, Coke and Pepsi for soft drinks, or Toshiba and Dell for personal computers

- examining how oligopolists interact when the decision is not about how much to produce or what price to charge, but rather whether to develop a new product, such as GM's and Toyota's decisions to introduce an electric car, or Research in Motion's and Apple's decisions to introduce a new wireless device

For almost any oligopolistic business decision you can imagine, it is possible to describe and analyze the firms' decisions by using game theory. Sometimes the game and the solution are relatively simple, as in Figure 11-3. Often, however, the game and solution are much more complicated. If you take an advanced course in industrial organization you will encounter some of these situations. Until then the straightforward intuition developed in our simple game can help explain a great deal of real-world behaviour.

| 11.5 Oligopoly in Practice

We have examined the incentives for firms in an oligopoly to cooperate and the incentives for firms to cheat on any cooperative agreement. We can now look at the behaviour that we actually observe among oligopolists. How do they cooperate? How do they compete?

Types of Cooperative Behaviour

collusion An agreement among sellers to act jointly in their common interest. Collusion may be overt or covert, explicit or tacit.

When firms agree to cooperate in order to restrict output and raise prices, their behaviour is called **collusion**. Collusive behaviour may occur with or without an explicit agreement to collude. Where explicit agreement occurs, economists speak of *overt* or *covert collusion*, depending on whether the agreement is open or secret. Where no explicit agreement actually occurs, economists speak of *tacit collusion*. In this case, all firms behave cooperatively without an explicit agreement to do so. They merely understand that it is in their mutual interest to restrict output and to raise prices.

Explicit Collusion The easiest way for firms to ensure that they will all maintain their joint profit-maximizing output is to make an explicit agreement to do so. Such collusive agreements have occurred in the past, although they have been illegal among privately owned firms in Canada for a long time (with some exceptions made for firms exporting their product). When they are discovered today, they are rigorously prosecuted. We will see, however, that such agreements are not illegal everywhere in the world, particularly when they are supported by national governments.

We saw in Chapter 10 that when several firms get together to act in this way, they create a *cartel*. Cartels show in stark form the basic conflict between cooperation and competition that we just discussed. Cooperation among cartel members allows them to restrict output and raise prices, thereby increasing the cartel members' profits. But it also presents each cartel member with the incentive to cheat. The larger the number of firms, the greater the temptation for any one of them to cheat. After all, cheating by one small firm may not be noticed because it will have a small effect on price. Conversely, a cartel made up of a small number of firms is more likely to persist because cheating by any one member is more difficult to conceal from the other members.

As we mentioned in Chapter 10, DeBeers is an example of a firm that has been able to assemble a cartel in the world's diamond industry. Through its own Diamond Trading Company (DTC), DeBeers markets approximately 40 percent of the world's annual diamond production. With such influence over the market, it is able to manage the flow of output, in response to changes in world demand, to keep prices high. In recent years, however, the discovery of large diamond mines by firms that wanted to remain independent of DeBeers has led to a reduction in DeBeers' ability to set the market price. In fact, the independent producers—in particular, Canadian producers—have been successful at establishing their own "brand" of diamonds. This has led DeBeers to reduce its efforts through the DTC to manage market prices and instead focus more of its efforts on creating its own brand of diamonds and other luxury products.

The most famous example of a cartel—and the one that has had the most dramatic effect on the world economy—is the Organization of the Petroleum Exporting Countries (OPEC). OPEC's explicit cooperation over the past four decades, as well as its failure to always sustain such cooperation, is discussed in *Lessons From History 11-1*.

For more information on OPEC, check out its website: www. opec.org.

Tacit Collusion Although collusive behaviour that affects prices is illegal, a small group of firms that recognizes the influence that each has on the others may act without any explicit agreement to achieve the cooperative outcome. In such tacit agreements, the two forces that push toward cooperation and competition are still evident. First, firms have a common interest in cooperating to maximize their joint profits at the cooperative solution. Second, each firm is interested in its own profits, and any one of them can usually increase its profits by behaving competitively.

In many industries there is suggestive evidence of tacit collusion, although it is very difficult to prove rigorously. For example, when one large steel company announces that it is raising its price for a specific quality of steel, other steel producers will often announce similar price increases within a day or two. Or when one Canadian bank announces an increase in its interest rate for five-year mortgages, other banks usually increase their rates within a few days. These seemingly coordinated actions may be the result of a secret explicit agreement or of tacit collusion. However, the firms that followed the first firm's price or interest-rate increase could easily argue (and usually do in such cases) that with their competitor raising prices, and thereby driving some customers toward them, the natural response is to raise their own prices.

Types of Competitive Behaviour

Although the most obvious way for a firm to violate the cooperative solution is to produce more than its share of the joint profit-maximizing output, there are other ways in which rivalrous behaviour can occur.

Competition for Market Share Even if *joint* profits are maximized, there is still a question of how the profit-maximizing level of sales is to be divided among the colluding firms. Competition for market share may upset the tacit agreement to hold to joint profit-maximizing behaviour. Firms often compete for market share through various forms of non-price competition, such as advertising and variations in the quality of their product. Such costly competition may increase one firm's profits only by decreasing profits for other firms, but since the activities are costly, total industry profits would be reduced.

LESSONS FROM HISTORY 11-1

Explicit Cooperation in OPEC

The experience of the Organization of the Petroleum Exporting Countries (OPEC) in the 1970s and 1980s illustrates the power of cooperative behaviour to create short-run profits, as well as the problems of trying to exercise long-run market power in an industry without substantial entry barriers.

OPEC did not attract worldwide attention until 1973, when its members voluntarily restricted their output by negotiating quotas among themselves. In that year, OPEC countries accounted for about 70 percent of the world's supply of crude oil. Although it was not a complete monopoly, the cartel came close to being one. By reducing output, the OPEC countries were able to reduce the world supply of oil and thereby increase its world price by almost 300 percent. Their actions resulted in massive profits both for themselves and for non-OPEC producers, who obtained the high prices without having to limit their output. After several years of success, however, OPEC began to experience the typical problems of cartels.

High Prices Lead to Entry

Entry became a problem for the OPEC countries. The high price of oil encouraged the development of new supplies, and within a few years, new productive capacity was coming into use at a rapid rate in non-OPEC countries. The development of North Sea oil by the United Kingdom, the oil sands in Alberta, and the Hibernia oil field in Newfoundland and Labrador are three examples of this new productive capacity.

Long-Run Adjustment of Demand

The short-run demand for oil proved to be highly inelastic. Over the long run, however, adaptations to reduce the demand for oil were made within the confines of existing technology. Homes and offices were insulated more efficiently, and smaller, more fuel-efficient cars became popular. This is an example of the distinction between the short-run and long-run demand for a commodity first introduced in Chapter 4.

Innovation further reduced the demand for oil in the very long run. Over time, technologies that were more efficient in their use of oil were developed, as were alternative energy sources.

This experience in both the long run and the very long run shows the price system at work, signalling the need for adaptation and providing the incentives for that adaptation. It also provides an illustration of Joseph Schumpeter's concept of creative destruction, which we first discussed in Chapter 10. To share in the profits generated by high oil prices, new technologies and new substitute products were developed, and these reduced much of the market power of the original cartel.

Cheating in the Early 1980s

At first, there was little incentive for OPEC countries to violate their production quotas. Member countries found themselves with such undreamed-of increases in incomes that they found it difficult to use all of their money productively. As the output of non-OPEC oil grew, however, OPEC's output had to be reduced to maintain the high prices. Furthermore, as the long-run adjustments in demand occurred, even larger output restrictions by OPEC were required to prop up the price of oil. Incomes in OPEC countries declined as a result.

Many OPEC countries had become used to their enormous incomes, and their attempts to maintain them in the face of falling output quotas brought to the surface the instabilities inherent in all cartels. In 1981, oil prices reached U.S.$35 per barrel. In real terms, this was about six times as high as the 1972 price, but production quotas were less than one-half of OPEC's capacity. Eager to increase their oil revenues, many individual OPEC members gave in to the pressure to cheat and produced in excess of their production quotas. In 1984, Saudi Arabia indicated that it would not tolerate further cheating by its OPEC partners and demanded that others share equally in reducing their quotas yet further. However, agreement proved impossible. In December 1985, OPEC decided to eliminate production quotas altogether and let each member make its own decisions about output. The end of the production quotas effectively meant the end of the cartel.

After the Collapse

OPEC's collapse as an output-restricting cartel led to a major reduction in world oil prices. Early in 1986, the downward slide took the price to U.S.$20 per barrel, and it fell to U.S.$11 per barrel later in the year. In real terms, this was still double the price that had prevailed just before OPEC introduced its output restrictions in 1973. Following the 1986 collapse, and for the next decade or so, the world price of oil fluctuated between U.S.$15 per barrel and U.S.$25 per barrel. With the continuing expansion of output from non-OPEC producers, OPEC's share of world output steadily fell, reaching approximately 35 percent by the mid-1990s, where it remains today.

Beginning in the late 1990s, the world price of oil began to rise again, as the accompanying figure shows. Measured in 2001 U.S. dollars, the price increased from below U.S.$20 per barrel in 1998 to just under U.S.$80 in 2008 (although it was almost U.S.$150 per barrel briefly during that year). The main cause of this significant price increase was a booming world economy that increased the world's demand for oil. The sharp price increase reflected an increase in demand at a time when the world supply curve was relatively inelastic. This supply inelasticity, in turn, reflected the fact that most oil producers—both inside and outside OPEC—were producing at or close to their capacity and thus were unable to easily respond to higher prices by increasing their output. In this setting of low global excess capacity, OPEC's ability to increase prices through output restrictions was partially restored, even though their share of world output was much less than in the 1970s.

With the arrival of a major global recession in 2008–2009, the world price fell sharply to U.S. $50 per barrel. By 2012, however, after two years of a modest economic recovery and renewed growth in world demand, the price had recovered to over U.S.$80 per barrel (in 2001 U.S. dollars), where it remains today.

OPEC members continue to negotiate output-restricting agreements in an attempt to raise (and stabilize) the world price of oil. With a global market share of only 35 percent, however, and both economic and political volatility affecting the world oil market, cartel members have a difficult task. As we have seen in this chapter, maintaining an effective cartel is quite a challenge.

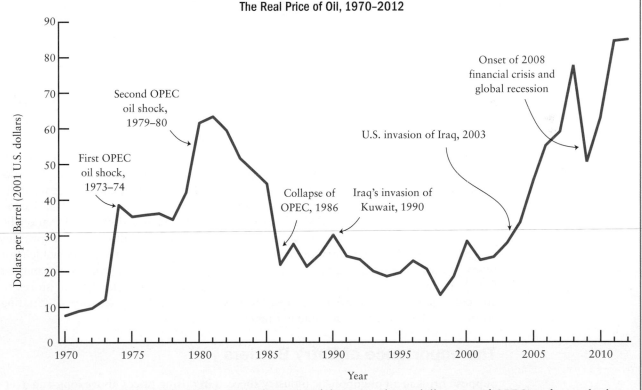

The Real Price of Oil, 1970–2012

(Source: Based on author's calculations. Annual average of the nominal U.S.-dollar price of OPEC's reference basket: www.opec.org. U.S. CPI [all items]: www.bls.gov.)

Oligopolistic firms producing differentiated products often compete very little through prices. Sometimes the most aggressive competition takes place through their continual processes of innovation, as well as the introduction of new products.

In an industry with many differentiated products and in which sales are often by contract between buyers and sellers, covert rather than overt cheating may seem attractive. Secret discounts and rebates can allow a firm to increase its sales at the expense of its competitors while appearing to hold to the tacitly agreed price.

Innovation A firm may find that by innovating it can behave competitively, keeping ahead of its rivals, and thereby maintain a larger market share. In this way, it will earn larger profits than it would if it cooperated with the other firms in the industry, even though all the firms' joint profits are lower. The great Austrian economist Joseph Schumpeter called the process by which one firm attacks another's monopolistic position by developing new products "creative destruction." Such competition through innovation contributes to the long-run growth of living standards and may provide social benefits over time that outweigh any losses caused by the restriction of output at any one point in time.

Oligopolistic firms typically compete by innovating. A firm can rectify a mistake in its price-setting decisions easily, but falling behind its competitors in developing new products and new production processes can spell disaster. A reading of the business pages of any newspaper shows firms in continuous competition to outdo each other in innovations.

> **There are strong incentives for oligopolistic firms to compete rather than to maintain the cooperative outcome, even when they understand the inherent risks to their joint profits.**

An obvious example of oligopolistic competition through innovation is Apple's ongoing development of new products. In the last decade, Apple has been highly successful with its iPod, iPhone, and iPad and is currently developing an iTV. In each case, the features and remarkable consumer appeal of the products not only took sales away from Apple's rivals (such as RIM and Nokia) but also expanded the total market by attracting consumers who previously owned no such products. But Apple's enormous success has attracted the entry of rivals, as is so often the case. Microsoft, which for many years focused only on the development of software, has now entered the market for electronic devices and is in the process of opening a network of retail stores to compete against the iconic Apple stores. The next few years should see some fascinating rivalry between these two technology titans.

The Importance of Entry Barriers

Suppose firms in an oligopolistic industry succeed in raising prices above long-run average costs and earn substantial profits that are not completely eliminated by competition among them. In the absence of significant entry barriers, new firms will enter the industry and erode the profits of existing firms, as they do in monopolistic competition. Natural barriers to entry were discussed in Chapter 10. They are an important part of the explanation of the persistence of profits in many oligopolistic industries.

Where such natural entry barriers do not exist, however, oligopolistic firms can earn profits in the long run only if they can *create* entry barriers. To the extent this is done, existing firms can move toward joint profit maximization without fear that new firms will enter the industry. We now discuss some types of *firm-created* entry barriers.

Brand Proliferation as an Entry Barrier By altering the characteristics of a differentiated product, it is possible to produce a vast array of variations on the general theme of that product, each with its unique identifying brand. Think, for example, of the many different brands of soap or shampoo, breakfast cereals or cookies, and even cars or motorcycles. In these cases, each firm in the industry produces *several* brands of the differentiated product.

Although such brand proliferation is no doubt partly a response to consumers' tastes, it can also have the effect of discouraging the entry of new firms. To see why, suppose the product is the type for which there is a substantial amount of brand switching by consumers. In this case, the larger the number of brands sold by existing firms, the smaller the expected sales of a new entrant.

Suppose, for example, that an industry contains three large firms, each selling one brand of beer, and say that 30 percent of all beer drinkers change brands in a random fashion each year. If a new firm enters the industry, it can expect to pick up one-third of the customers who change brands (a customer who switches brands now has three *other* brands among which to choose). The new firm would get 10 percent (one-third of 30 percent) of the total market the first year merely as a result of picking up its share of the random switchers, and it would keep increasing its share for some time thereafter. If, however, the existing three firms have five brands each, there would be 15 brands already available, and a new firm selling one new brand could expect to pick up only one-fifteenth of the brand switchers, giving it only 2 percent of the total market the first year, with smaller gains also in subsequent years. This is an extreme case, but it illustrates a general result.

The larger the number of differentiated products that are sold by existing oligopolists, the smaller the market share available to a new firm that is entering with a single new product. Brand proliferation therefore can be an effective entry barrier.

Advertising as an Entry Barrier In addition to producing useful information about existing products, advertising can operate as a potent entry barrier by increasing the costs of new entrants. Where heavy advertising has established strong brand images for existing products, a new firm may have to spend heavily on advertising to create its own brand images in consumers' minds. If the firm's sales are small, advertising costs *per unit* will be large, and price will have to be correspondingly high to cover those costs. Consider Nike, Reebok, and their competitors. They advertise not so much the quality of their athletic shoes as images that they want consumers to associate with the shoes. The same is true for cosmetics, beer, cars, hamburgers, and many more consumer goods. The ads are lavishly produced and photographed. They constitute a formidable entry barrier for a new producer.

A new entrant with small sales but large required advertising costs finds itself at a substantial cost disadvantage relative to its established rivals.

Advertising can be very informative for consumers. But by raising the costs of new entrants, advertising can also act as a potent entry barrier.

The combined use of brand proliferation and advertising as an entry barrier helps to explain one apparent paradox of everyday life—that one firm often sells multiple brands of the same product, which compete actively against one another as well as against the products of other firms. The soap and beer industries provide classic examples of this behaviour. Because all available scale economies can be realized by quite small plants, both industries have few natural barriers to entry. Both contain a few large firms, each of which produces an array of heavily advertised products. The proliferation of brands makes it harder for a new entrant to obtain a large market niche with a single new product. The heavy advertising, although directed against existing products, creates an entry barrier by increasing the average costs of a new product that seeks to gain the attention of consumers and to establish its own brand image.

Predatory Pricing as an Entry Barrier A firm will not enter a market if it expects continued losses after entry. An existing firm can create such an expectation by cutting prices below costs whenever entry occurs and keeping them there until the entrant goes bankrupt. The existing firm sacrifices profits while doing this, but it sends a discouraging message to potential future rivals, as well as to present ones. Even if this strategy is costly in terms of lost profits in the short run, it may pay for itself in the long run by creating *reputation effects* that deter the entry of new firms at other times or in other markets that the firm controls.

Predatory pricing is controversial. Some economists argue that pricing policies that appear to be predatory can be explained by other motives and that existing firms only hurt themselves when they engage in such practices instead of accommodating new entrants. Others argue that predatory pricing has been observed and that it is in the long-run interests of existing firms to punish the occasional new entrant even when it is costly to do so in the short run.

See Industry Canada's website at www.ic.gc.ca for a discussion of predatory pricing in Canada.

Canadian courts have taken the position that predatory pricing does indeed occur and a number of firms have been convicted of using it as a method of restricting entry.

Oligopoly and the Economy

Oligopoly is found in many industries and in all advanced economies. It typically occurs in industries in which both perfect and monopolistic competition are made impossible by the existence of major economies of scale. In such industries, there is simply not enough room for a large number of firms all operating at or near their minimum efficient scales.

Two questions are important for the evaluation of oligopoly. First, in their short-run and long-run outcomes, where do oligopolistic firms typically settle between the extreme outcomes of earning zero profits and earning monopoly profits? Second, how much do oligopolists contribute to economic growth by encouraging innovative activity in the very long run?

Profits Under Oligopoly Some firms in some oligopolistic industries succeed in coming close to joint profit maximization in the short run. In other oligopolistic industries, firms compete so intensely among themselves that they come close to achieving competitive prices and outputs.

In the long run, those profits that do survive competitive behaviour among existing firms will tend to attract entry. Profits will persist only insofar as entry is restricted either by natural barriers, such as large minimum efficient scales for potential entrants, or by barriers created, and successfully defended, by the existing firms or, perhaps, created by government regulations.

Innovation Which market structure—oligopoly or perfect competition—is most conducive to innovation? As we discussed in Chapter 8, innovation and productivity improvements are the driving force of the economic growth that has so greatly raised living standards over the past two centuries. They are intimately related to Schumpeter's concept of creative destruction, which we first encountered in our discussion of entry barriers in Chapter 10.

Examples of creative destruction abound. In the nineteenth century, railways began to compete with wagons and barges for the carriage of freight. In the twentieth century, trucks operating on newly constructed highways began competing with trains. During the 1950s and 1960s, airplanes began to compete seriously with both trucks and trains. In recent years, the development of Internet banking has allowed many payments to be made online, thereby undermining the monopoly power of the postal service. Cell phones have significantly weakened the monopoly power that telephone companies had for the provision of local phone service. And the Internet has allowed consumers to download music easily (though often in violation of copyright laws), and has dramatically reduced the market power of the music production companies that sell CDs.

An important defence of oligopoly is based on Schumpeter's idea of creative destruction. Some economists argue that oligopoly leads to more innovation than would occur in either perfect competition or monopoly. They argue that the oligopolist faces strong competition from existing rivals and cannot afford the more relaxed life of the monopolist. Moreover, oligopolistic firms expect to keep a good share of the profits that they earn from their innovative activity and thus have considerable incentive to innovate.

Everyday observation provides support for this view. Leading North American firms that operate in highly concentrated industries, such as Alcoa, Apple, Canfor, Bombardier, DuPont, General Electric, Canadian National, Xerox, Research In Motion, and Boeing, have been highly innovative over many years.

This observation is not meant to suggest that *only* oligopolistic industries are innovative. Much innovation is also done by very small, new firms. If today's small firms are successful in their innovation, they may become tomorrow's corporate giants. For example, Microsoft, Research In Motion, Apple, and Intel, which are enormous firms today, barely existed 40 years ago; their rise from new start-up firms to corporate giants reflects their powers of innovation.

Oligopoly is an important market structure in modern economies because there are many industries in which the minimum efficient scale is simply too large to support many competing firms. The challenge to public policy is to keep oligopolists competing, rather than colluding, and using their competitive energies to improve products and to reduce costs, rather than merely to erect entry barriers.

SUMMARY

11.1 The Structure of the Canadian Economy

- Most industries in the Canadian economy lie between the two extremes of monopoly and perfect competition. Within this spectrum of market structure we can divide Canadian industries into two broad groups: those with a large number of relatively small firms and those with a small number of relatively large firms. Such intermediate market structures are called imperfectly competitive.
- When measuring whether an industry has power concentrated in the hands of only a few firms or dispersed over many, it is not sufficient to count the firms. Instead,

economists consider the concentration ratio, which shows the fraction of total market sales controlled by a group of the largest sellers.
- One important problem associated with using concentration ratios is to define the market with reasonable accuracy. Since many goods produced in Canada compete in foreign markets with foreign-produced goods, the national concentration ratios overstate the degree of industrial concentration.

11.2 What Is Imperfect Competition?

- Most firms operating in imperfectly competitive market structures sell differentiated products whose characteristics they choose themselves.

- Imperfectly competitive firms usually choose their prices and engage in non-price competition.

11.3 Monopolistic Competition

- Monopolistic competition is a market structure that has the same characteristics as perfect competition except that the many firms each sell a differentiated product rather than all selling a single homogeneous product. Firms face negatively sloped demand curves and may earn profits in the short run.
- As in a perfectly competitive industry, the long run in the theory of monopolistic competition sees new firms enter the industry whenever profits can be made. Long-run equilibrium in the industry requires that each firm earn zero profits.

- In long-run equilibrium in the theory of monopolistic competition, each firm produces less than its minimum-cost level of output. This is the excess-capacity theorem associated with monopolistic competition.
- Even though each firm produces at a cost that is higher than the minimum attainable cost, the resulting product variety is valued by consumers and so may be worth the extra cost.

11.4 Oligopoly and Game Theory

- Oligopolies are dominated by a few large firms that have significant market power. They can maximize their joint profits if they cooperate to produce the monopoly output. By acting individually, each firm has an incentive to depart from this cooperative outcome.
- Oligopolists have difficulty cooperating to maximize joint profits unless they have a way of enforcing their output-restricting agreement.

- Economists use game theory to think about the strategic behaviour of oligopolists—that is, how each firm will behave when it recognizes that other firms may respond to its actions.
- A possible non-cooperative outcome is a Nash equilibrium in which each player is doing the best it can, given the actions of all other players.

11.5 Oligopoly in Practice

- Explicit collusion between oligopolists is illegal in domestic markets. But it can take place in situations where firms in global markets are supported by national governments, as is the case for OPEC.

- Tacit collusion is possible but may break down as firms struggle for market share, indulge in non-price competition, and seek advantages through the introduction of new technology.

- Oligopolistic industries will exhibit profits in the long run only if there are significant barriers to entry. Natural barriers relate to the economies of scale in production, finance, and marketing, and also to large entry costs. Firm-created barriers can be formed by proliferation of competing brands, heavy brand-image advertising, and the threat of predatory pricing when new entry occurs.

- In the presence of major scale economies, oligopoly may be the best of the feasible alternative market structures. Evaluation of oligopoly depends on how much interfirm competition (a) drives the firms away from the cooperative, profit-maximizing solution and (b) leads to innovations in the very long run.

KEY CONCEPTS

Concentration ratios
Product differentiation
Monopolistic competition
The excess-capacity theorem
Oligopoly

Strategic behaviour
Game theory
Cooperative and non-cooperative
  outcomes
Nash equilibrium

Explicit and tacit collusion
Natural and firm-created entry
  barriers
Oligopoly and creative destruction

STUDY EXERCISES

MyEconLab   Make the grade with MyEconLab: Study Exercises marked in red can be found on MyEconLab. You can practise them as often as you want, and most feature step-by-step guided instructions to help you find the right answer.

1. Fill in the blanks to make the following statements correct.

   a. Suppose the four largest steel producers in Canada among them control 85 percent of total market sales. We would say that this industry is highly _____. We say that 85 percent is the _____ in this industry.

   b. A firm that has the ability to set prices faces a _____ demand curve.

   c. The theory of monopolistic competition helps explain industries with a _____ number of _____ firms. The theory of oligopoly helps explain industries with a _____ number of _____ firms.

   d. A firm operating in a monopolistically competitive market structure maximizes profits by equating _____ and _____. A firm that is operating in an oligopolistic market structure maximizes profit by equating _____ and _____ although its rivals' responses to its actions will affect its _____.

   e. In long-run equilibrium, and in comparison to perfect competition, monopolistic competition produces a _____ range of products but at a _____ cost per unit.

2. Fill in the blanks to make the following statements correct.

   a. Economists say that oligopolistic firms exhibit _____ behaviour. These firms are aware of and take account of the decisions of _____.

   b. The firms in an oligopoly have a collective incentive to _____ in order to maximize joint _____; individually, each firm has an incentive to _____ in order to maximize individual _____.

   c. Oligopolistic firms exhibit profits in the long run only if there are significant _____.

   d. Three examples of non-competitive behaviour practised by firms with market power are _____, _____, and _____.

   e. An important defence of oligopoly is the idea that it leads to more _____ than would occur in either perfect competition or monopoly. The oligopolistic firm has an incentive to _____ because it can expect to keep a good share of the resulting profit.

3. Each of the statements below describes a characteristic of the following market structures: perfect competition, monopolistic competition, oligopoly, and monopoly.

Identify which market structure displays each of the characteristics. (There may be more than one.)

a. Each firm faces a downward-sloping demand curve.
b. Price is greater than marginal revenue.
c. Each firm produces at *MES* in long-run equilibrium.
d. Firms earn profit in long-run equilibrium.
e. Firms produce a homogeneous product.
f. Firms advertise their product.
g. Each firm produces output where $MC = MR$.
h. Each firm produces output where $P = MC$.
i. There is free entry to the industry.
j. Firms produce a differentiated product.

4. Do you think any of the following industries might be monopolistically competitive? Why or why not?

   a. Textbook publishing (approximately 10 introductory economics textbooks are in use on campuses in Canada this year)
   b. Post-secondary education

   c. Cigarette manufacturing
   d. Restaurant operation
   e. Automobile retailing
   f. Landscaping services
   g. Home renovation firms

5. The following table provides annual sales for the four largest firms in four industries in Canada. Also provided are total Canadian and total world sales for the industry. (All figures are hypothetical and are in millions of dollars.)

   a. Suppose Canada does not trade internationally any of the goods produced in these industries. Compute the four-firm Canadian concentration ratio for each industry.
   b. Rank the industries in order from the most concentrated to the least concentrated.
   c. Now suppose goods in these industries are freely traded around the world. Are the concentration ratios from part (a) still relevant? Explain.

	Firm 1	Firm 2	Firm 3	Firm 4	Total Sales (Canada)	Total Sales (World)
Forestry products	185	167	98	47	550	1368
Chemicals	27	24	9	4	172	2452
Women's clothing	6	5	4	2	94	3688
Pharmaceuticals	44	37	22	19	297	2135

6. The table below provides price, revenue, and cost information for a monopolistically competitive firm selling drive-through car washes in a large city.

   a. Complete the table.
   b. Plot the demand, marginal revenue, marginal cost, and average cost curves for the firm. (Be sure to plot *MR* and *MC* at the midpoint of the output intervals.)

   c. What is the profit-maximizing number of car washes (per month)?
   d. What is the profit-maximizing price?
   e. Calculate the total maximum profit (per month).
   f. How can this firm differentiate its product from other car washes?

Quantity (number of car washes per month)	Price	Total Revenue	Marginal Revenue	Total Cost	Average Total Cost	Marginal Cost	Total Profit
1000	30	____		25 000	____		____
1100	29	____	____	26 000	____	____	____
1200	28	____	____	27 200	____	____	____
1300	27	____	____	28 500	____	____	____
1400	26	____	____	30 000	____	____	____
1500	25	____	____	32 200	____	____	____
1600	24	____	____	35 000	____	____	____
1700	23	____	____	38 500	____	____	____
1800	22	____	____	43 000	____	____	____

7. Draw two diagrams of a monopolistically competitive firm. In the first, show the firm earning profits in the short run. In the second, show the firm in long-run equilibrium earning zero profits. What changed for this firm between the short run and the long run?

8. The following figure shows the revenue and cost curves for a typical monopolistically competitive firm in the short run.

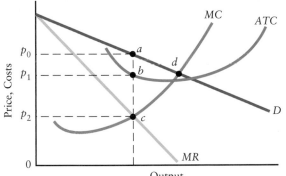

a. Note that the firm's demand curve is shown to be quite flat. Explain which assumption of monopolistic competition suggests a relatively elastic demand curve for each firm.
b. Show the profit-maximizing level of output for the firm on the diagram.
c. At the profit-maximizing level of output, are profits positive or negative? What area in the diagram represents the firm's profits?
d. Will firms enter or exit the industry? Explain.

9. The diagram below shows a typical monopolistically competitive firm when the industry is in long-run equilibrium.

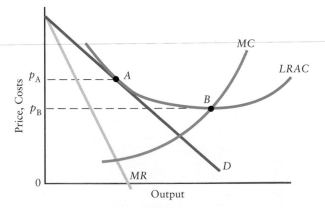

a. Explain why free entry and exit implies that the long-run equilibrium is at point A.
b. What is the significance of point B and price p_B?
c. Explain the sense in which long-run equilibrium in monopolistic competition is less efficient than in perfect competition.

10. In the text we argued that a key difference between monopolistic competition and oligopoly is that in the former firms do not behave *strategically* whereas in the latter they do. For each of the goods or services listed below, state whether the industries are likely to be best described by monopolistic competition or oligopoly. Explain your reasoning.

   a. Car repair
   b. Haircuts
   c. Dry cleaning
   d. Soft drinks
   e. Breakfast cereals
   f. Restaurant meals
   g. Automobiles

11. Consider the following industries in Canada that have traditionally been oligopolistic.

   • Brewing
   • Airlines
   • Railways
   • Banking
   • Internet service providers
   • Grocery stores

   a. What are the barriers to entry in each of these industries that might explain persistently high profits?
   b. Explain in each case how technology is changing in ways that circumvent these entry barriers.

12. The table below is the payoff matrix for a simple two-firm game. Firms A and B are bidding on a government contract, and each firm's bid is not known by the other firm. Each firm can bid either $10 000 or $5000. The cost of completing the project for each firm is $4000. The low-bid firm will win the contract at its stated price; the high-bid firm will get nothing. If the two bids are equal, the two firms will split the price and costs evenly. The payoffs for each firm under each situation are shown in the matrix.

	A bids $10 000	A bids $5000
B bids $10 000	Firms share the contract	A wins the contract
	Payoff to A = $3000 Payoff to B = $3000	Payoff to A = $1000 Payoff to B = $0
B bids $5000	B wins the contract	Firms share the contract
	Payoff to A = $0 Payoff to B = $1000	Payoff to A = $500 Payoff to B = $500

a. Recall from the text that a Nash equilibrium is an outcome in which each player is maximizing his or her own payoff *given the actions of the other players*. Is there a Nash equilibrium in this game?
b. Is there more than one Nash equilibrium? Explain.
c. If the two firms could cooperate, what outcome would you predict in this game? Explain.

13. The table below shows the payoff matrix for a game between Toyota and Honda, each of which is contemplating building a factory in a new market. Each firm can either build a small factory (and produce a small number of cars) or build a large factory (and produce a large number of cars). Suppose no other car manufacturers are selling in this market.

		Toyota's Decision	
		Small Factory	Large Factory
Honda's Decision	Small Factory	*High Industry Price* Honda profits: $20 million Toyota profits: $20 million	*Medium Industry Price* Honda profits: $12 million Toyota profits: $25 million
	Large Factory	*Medium Industry Price* Honda profits: $25 million Toyota profits: $12 million	*Low Industry Price* Honda profits: $14 million Toyota profits: $14 million

a. Assuming that the demand curve for cars in this new market is negatively sloped and unchanging, explain the economic reasoning behind the prices and profits shown in each cell in the payoff matrix.

b. What is the cooperative outcome in this game? Is it likely to be achievable? Explain.

c. What is Honda's best action? Does it depend on Toyota's action?

d. What is Toyota's best action? Does it depend on Honda's action?

e. What is the non-cooperative outcome in this game? Is it a Nash equilibrium?

Economic Efficiency and Public Policy

IN the previous three chapters we examined various market structures, from perfect competition at one end of the spectrum to monopoly at the other end. In the middle were two forms of imperfect competition: monopolistic competition and oligopoly. We have considered how firms behave in these various market structures, and we are now able to evaluate the *efficiency* of the market structures. Then we will see why economists are suspicious of monopolistic practices and seek to encourage competitive behaviour. Table 12-1 provides a review of the four market structures and the industry characteristics relevant to each.

We begin our discussion in this chapter by examining the various concepts of efficiency used by economists. This discussion will develop more fully the concept of efficiency we first saw at the end of Chapter 5. We then discuss how public policy deals with the challenges of monopoly and oligopoly in an effort to improve the efficiency of the economy.

12.1 Productive and Allocative Efficiency

Efficiency requires that factors of production are fully employed. However, full employment of resources is not enough to prevent the *waste* of resources. Even when resources are fully employed, they may be used inefficiently. Here are three examples of inefficiency in the use of fully employed resources.

TABLE 12-1 Review of Four Market Structures

Market Structure	Industry Characteristics
Perfect competition	• Many small firms • Firms sell identical products • All firms are price takers • Free entry and exit • Zero profits in long-run equilibrium • Price $= MC$
Monopolistic competition	• Many small firms • Firms sell differentiated products • Each firm has some power to set price • Free entry and exit • Zero profits in long-run equilibrium • Price $> MC$; less output than in perfect competition; excess capacity
Oligopoly	• Few firms, usually large • Strategic behaviour among firms • Firms often sell differentiated products and are price setters • Often significant entry barriers • Usually economies of scale • Profits depend on the nature of firm rivalry and on entry barriers • Price usually $> MC$; output usually less than in perfect competition
Monopoly	• Single firm faces the entire market demand • Firm is a price setter • Profits persist if sufficient entry barriers • Price $> MC$; less output than in perfect competition

1. If firms do not use the least-cost method of producing their chosen outputs, they are being inefficient. For example, a firm that produces 30 000 pairs of shoes at a resource cost of $400 000 when it could have been done at a cost of only $350 000 is using resources inefficiently. The lower-cost method would allow $50 000 worth of resources to be transferred to other productive uses.

2. If the marginal cost of production is not the same for every firm in an industry, the industry is being inefficient. For example, if the cost of producing the last tonne of steel is higher for some firms than for others, the industry's overall cost of producing a given amount of steel is higher than necessary. The same amount of steel could be produced at lower total cost if the total output were distributed differently among the various producers.

3. If too much of one product and too little of another product are produced, the economy's resources are being used inefficiently. To take an extreme example, suppose so many shoes are produced that every consumer has all the shoes he or she could possibly want and thus places a zero value on obtaining an additional pair of shoes. Suppose also that so few coats are produced that consumers place a high value on obtaining an additional coat. In these circumstances, consumers can be made better off if resources are reallocated from shoe production, where the last shoe produced has a low value in the eyes of each consumer, to coat production, where one more coat produced would have a higher value to each consumer.

These three examples illustrate inefficiency in the use of resources. But the *type* of inefficiency is different in each case. The first example considers the cost for a single firm producing some level of output. The second example is related, but the focus is on the total cost for all the firms in an industry. The third example relates to the level of output of one product compared with another. Let's explore these three types of inefficiency in more detail.

Productive Efficiency

Productive efficiency has two aspects, one concerning production within each firm and one concerning the allocation of production among the firms in an industry. The first two examples above relate to these two different aspects of productive efficiency.

Productive efficiency for the firm requires that the firm produce any given level of output at the lowest possible cost. In the short run, with at least one fixed factor, the firm merely uses enough of the variable factors to produce the desired level of output. In the long run, however, more methods of production are available. Productive efficiency requires that the firm use the least costly of the available methods of producing any given output—that is, firms are located on, rather than above, their long-run average cost curves.

> Productive efficiency for the firm requires the firm to be producing its output at the lowest possible cost.

Any firm that is not being productively efficient is producing at a higher cost than is necessary and thus will have lower profits than it could have. It follows that any profit-maximizing firm will seek to be productively efficient no matter the market structure within which it operates—perfect competition, monopoly, oligopoly, or monopolistic competition.

Productive efficiency for the industry requires that the industry's total output be allocated among its individual firms in such a way that the total cost in the industry is minimized. If an industry is productively *inefficient*, it is possible to reduce the industry's total cost of producing any given output by reallocating production among the industry's firms.

> Productive efficiency for the industry requires that the marginal cost of production be the same for each firm.

To see why marginal costs must be equated across firms, consider a simple example that is illustrated in Figure 12-1. Aslan Widget Company has a marginal cost of $80 for the last widget of some standard type it produces. Digory Enterprises has a marginal cost of only $40 for its last widget of the same type. If Aslan were to produce one fewer widget and Digory were to produce one more widget, total production would be unchanged. Total industry costs, however, would be lower by $40.

Clearly, this cost saving can go on as long as the two firms have different marginal costs. However, as Aslan produces fewer widgets, its marginal cost falls, and as Digory produces more widgets, its marginal cost rises. Once marginal cost is equated across the two firms, at a marginal cost of $60 in the figure, there are no further cost savings to be obtained by reallocating production. Only at this point is the industry productively efficient.

Over the next few pages we will see how such an efficient allocation of output across firms is achieved, but for now the point is simply that if marginal costs are not equated across firms, then a reallocation of output is necessary in order for the industry to become productively efficient.

Productive Efficiency and the Production Possibilities Boundary If firms are productively efficient, they are minimizing their costs; there is no way for them to increase output without using more resources. If an industry is productively efficient, the industry as a whole is producing its output at the lowest possible cost; the industry could not increase its output without using more resources.

productive efficiency for the firm When the firm chooses among all available production methods to produce a given level of output at the lowest possible cost.

productive efficiency for the industry When the industry is producing a given level of output at the lowest possible cost. This requires that marginal cost be equated across all firms in the industry.

FIGURE 12-1 Productive Efficiency for the Industry

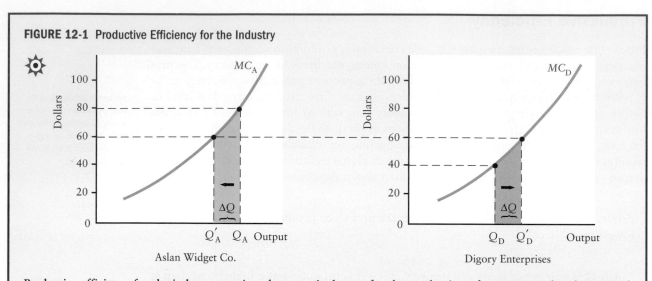

Aslan Widget Co.   Digory Enterprises

Productive efficiency for the industry requires that marginal costs for the production of any one product be equated across firms. At the initial levels of output, Q_A and Q_D, marginal costs are \$80 for Aslan and \$40 for Digory. If Digory increases output by ΔQ to Q'_D and Aslan reduces output by the same amount ΔQ to Q'_A, total output is unchanged. Aslan's total costs have fallen by the green shaded area, whereas Digory's total costs have increased by the smaller purple shaded area. Total industry costs are therefore reduced when output is reallocated between the firms. When marginal costs are equalized, at \$60 in this example, no further reallocation of output can reduce costs—productive efficiency will have been achieved.

Now think about the economy's production possibilities boundary (PPB), which we first saw in Chapter 1 and which is shown again in Figure 12-2. The PPB shows the combinations of output of two products that are possible when the economy is using its resources *efficiently*. An economy that is producing at a point inside the PPB is being productively inefficient—it could produce more of one good without producing less of the other. This inefficiency may occur because individual firms are not minimizing their costs or because, within an industry, marginal costs are not equalized across the various firms. Either situation would lead the economy to be inside its production possibilities boundary.

> **If firms and industries are productively efficient, the economy will be on, rather than inside, the production possibilities boundary.**

In Figure 12-2, every point on the PPB is productively efficient. Is there one point on the PPB that is "better" in some way than the others? The answer is yes, and this brings us to the concept of *allocative efficiency*.

Allocative Efficiency

allocative efficiency A situation in which the output of each good is such that its market price and marginal cost are equal.

Allocative efficiency concerns the quantities of the various products to be produced. When the combination of goods produced is allocatively efficient, economists say that the economy is *Pareto efficient,* in honour of nineteenth-century Italian economist Vilfredo Pareto (1843–1923), who developed this concept of efficiency.

How do we find the allocatively efficient point on the production possibilities boundary? The answer is as follows:

> The economy is allocatively efficient when, for each good produced, its marginal cost of production is equal to its price.

To understand this answer, recall our discussion in Chapters 5 and 6 about the marginal value that consumers place on the next unit of some good. When utility-maximizing consumers face the market price for some good, they adjust their consumption of the good until their marginal value is just equal to the price. Since price then reflects the marginal value of the good to consumers, we can restate the condition for allocative efficiency to be that for each good produced, marginal cost must equal marginal value.[1]

If the level of output of some product is such that marginal cost to producers exceeds marginal value to consumers, too much of that product is being produced, because the cost to society of the last unit produced exceeds the benefits of consuming it. Conversely, if the level of output of some good is such that the marginal cost is less than the marginal value, too little of that good is being produced, because the cost to society of producing the next unit is less than the benefits that would be gained from consuming it.

Allocative Efficiency and the Production Possibilities Boundary

Figure 12-3 shows a production possibilities boundary in an economy that can produce wheat and steel, and also shows the individual supply-and-demand diagrams for the two markets. Notice that the vertical axis in each of the supply-and-demand diagrams shows the *relative* price of the appropriate good. For example, in the market for wheat, the relevant price is the price of wheat *relative to the price of steel*. This is consistent with our initial treatment of supply and demand in Chapter 3, in which we held constant all other prices and then examined how the price of any specific product was determined.

Figure 12-3 illustrates how the allocation of resources in the economy changes as we move along the production possibilities boundary. For example, as the economy moves from point A to point B to point C along the PPB, resources are being transferred from the steel sector to the wheat sector, so steel output is falling and wheat output is rising.

What is the allocatively efficient combination of steel and wheat output in this economy? Allocative efficiency will be achieved when in each market the marginal cost of producing the good equals the marginal value of consuming the good. In Figure 12-3, allocative efficiency is achieved at point B, with S_B steel being produced and W_B wheat being produced.[2]

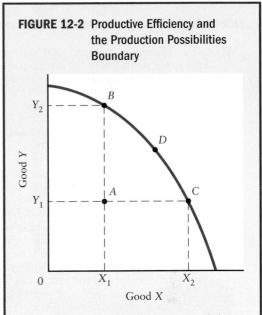

FIGURE 12-2 Productive Efficiency and the Production Possibilities Boundary

Any point on the production possibilities boundary is productively efficient. The boundary shows all combinations of two goods X and Y that can be produced when the economy's resources are fully employed and productively efficient.

Any point inside the curve, such as A, is productively inefficient. If the inefficiency exists in industry X, then either some producer of X is productively inefficient or industry X as a whole is productively inefficient. In either case, it is possible to increase total production of X without using more resources, and thus without reducing the output of Y. This would take the economy from point A to point C. Similarly, if the inefficiency exists in industry Y, production of Y could be increased, moving the economy from point A to point B.

---

[1] Allocative efficiency is exactly the same concept as market efficiency that we discussed in Chapter 5. Now that we have introduced the distinction between productive and allocative efficiency, we will continue to use these two terms only.

[2] Note that allocative efficiency requires that price equal marginal cost in all industries simultaneously. Based on what economists call the "theory of the second best," there is no guarantee that achieving $p = MC$ in one industry will improve overall welfare when price does not equal marginal cost in all other industries.

FIGURE 12-3 Allocative Efficiency and the Production Possibilities Boundary ☼

Allocative efficiency requires that all goods be produced to the point where the marginal cost to producers equals the marginal value to consumers. The production possibilities boundary shows the combinations of wheat and steel that are possible if firms and industries are productively efficient. The lower diagrams show the marginal cost (supply) and marginal value (demand) curves in each industry.

At point A, steel output is S_A and wheat output is W_A. As the lower figures show, however, at W_A the marginal value of wheat consumption exceeds its marginal cost of production. Thus, society would be better off if more wheat were produced. Similarly, at S_A the marginal cost of steel production exceeds its marginal value to consumers, and thus society would be better off with less steel being produced.

Point A is therefore not allocatively efficient; there is too little wheat and too much steel being produced. The argument is similar at point C, at which there is too much wheat and too little steel being produced. Only at point B is each good produced to the point where the marginal cost to producers is equal to the marginal value to consumers. Only point B is allocatively efficient.

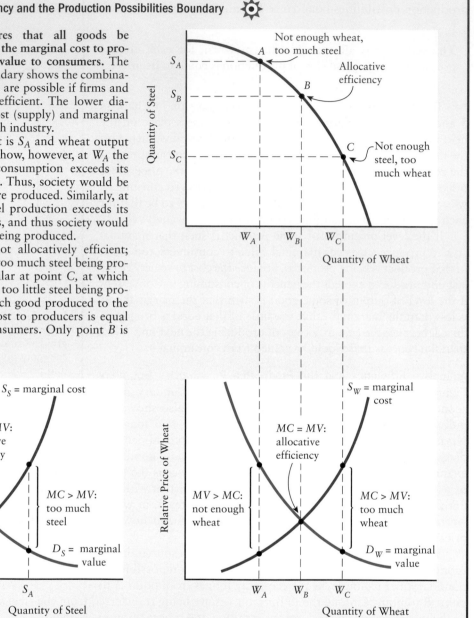

Which Market Structures Are Efficient?

We now know that for productive efficiency, all firms must be minimizing their costs and marginal cost should be the same for all firms in any one industry. For allocative efficiency, marginal cost should be equal to price in each industry. Do the market structures that we have studied in earlier chapters lead to productive and allocative efficiency?

Perfect Competition We saw in Chapter 9 that in the long run under perfect competition, each firm produces at the lowest point on its long-run average cost curve. Therefore, no one firm could reduce its costs by altering its own production. Every firm in perfect competition is therefore productively efficient.

We also know that in perfect competition, all firms in an industry face the same price of their product and they equate marginal cost to that price. It follows immediately that marginal cost will be the same for all firms. (Suppose, for example, that Aslan and Digory each face the same market price, p, in a figure like Figure 12-1 on page 284. Aslan will produce where $MC_A = p$ and Digory will produce where $MC_D = p$. It follows that $MC_A = MC_D$.) Thus, in perfectly competitive industries with profit-maximizing firms, the industry as a whole is productively efficient.

We have already seen that perfectly competitive firms maximize their profits by choosing an output level such that marginal cost equals market price. Thus, when perfect competition is the market structure for the whole economy, price is equal to marginal cost in each industry, resulting in allocative efficiency.

> Perfectly competitive industries are productively efficient. If an economy were made up entirely of perfectly competitive industries, the economy would be allocatively efficient.

Note, however, that perfect competition exists only in some industries in modern economies. So, while specific industries may be perfectly competitive and therefore allocatively efficient, entire modern economies are neither perfectly competitive nor allocatively efficient. *Extensions in Theory 12-1* explains why, even in an economy made up entirely of perfectly competitive industries, the point on the production possibilities boundary that is allocatively efficient depends on the economy's distribution of income.

Monopoly Monopolists have an incentive to be productively efficient because their profits will be maximized when they adopt the lowest-cost production method. Hence, profit-maximizing monopolists will operate on their *LRAC* curves and thus be productively efficient.

Although a monopolist will be productively efficient, it will choose a level of output that is too low to achieve allocative efficiency. This result follows from what we saw in Chapter 10—that the monopolist chooses an output at which the price charged is *greater than* marginal cost. Such a choice violates the conditions for allocative efficiency because the price, and hence the marginal value to consumers, exceeds the marginal cost of production. From this result follows the classic efficiency-based preference for competition over monopoly:

> Monopoly is not allocatively efficient because the monopolist's price always exceeds its marginal cost.[3]

This result has important policy implications for economists and for policymakers, as we will see later in this chapter.

---

[3] A perfect price discriminating monopoly that maximizes its profits (see Chapter 10) is actually allocatively efficient. With a single price or even several prices, however, price exceeds marginal cost and the outcome is allocatively inefficient.

EXTENSIONS IN THEORY 12-1

Allocative Efficiency and the Distribution of Income

We have said in the text that economy-wide perfect competition would lead to an efficient allocation of resources, with production and consumption at a point like *B* on the production possibilities boundary in Figure 12-3. But even for an economy with widespread perfect competition and a given production possibilities boundary, there is not a unique allocation of resources that is efficient or "optimal." Specifically, changes in the distribution of income, which naturally change the relative demands for various products, will also change the allocatively efficient point.

By means of a simple example, consider a country in which there are only two income classes: the *rich* consume a lot of steel but little wheat, whereas the *poor* consume a lot of wheat but little steel. (In a more general mathematical model, we could have three or more products and three or more income groups, each with different expenditure patterns.) Further, suppose that the demand curves shown in Figure 12-3 are based on the existing distribution of income between these two income classes. Point *B* is then the allocatively efficient point of consumption and production.

But now suppose that a new, more egalitarian government is elected. The new government alters the structure of taxes and transfers so as to leave less income in the hands of the rich and more income in the hands of the poor. In other words, it alters the distribution of income in favour of the poor. In our example, the demand curve for wheat shifts to the right because the poor are relatively intensive wheat consumers; at the same time, the demand curve for steel shifts to the left because the rich are intensive steel consumers. The relative price of wheat therefore rises, as does its production and consumption, whereas the relative price and quantity of steel both fall. The whole society then moves to a new allocatively efficient point on the production possibilities boundary, away from point *B* and toward point *C*. It should now be clear that point *B* is an optimal allocation of resources for the initial distribution of income, whereas point *C* could be the optimal allocation for a *different* distribution.

The moral of this story is very general. There is no unique efficient (or "optimal") allocation of resources for any one society. The efficient point on the production possibilities boundary depends on the distribution of income. So, unless we are willing to make value judgements between various distributions of income, we cannot say that one efficient point on the production possibilities boundary is "better" than any other.

Monopolistic Competition and Oligopoly Like all other firms, monopolistic competitors and oligopolists have the incentive to maximize their profits, and thus to choose the lowest-cost method of producing their output. If they act on this incentive, they will be productively efficient.

It is difficult to say, however, whether the overall *industry* in these cases will be productively efficient. Monopolistic competitors and many oligopolists sell differentiated products and thus there is no single industry-wide price. As a result, even though all firms may equate their marginal costs and marginal revenues (and thus maximize their profits), we cannot conclude that marginal cost will be equated across all firms.

As for allocative efficiency in these market structures, the theory of monopolistic competition clearly predicts that price will exceed marginal cost and so allocative efficiency will not occur. For oligopoly, allocative efficiency will only exist in those rare situations where the nature of interfirm rivalry drives price to marginal cost; in most situations, however, price will exceed marginal cost and so the outcome will be allocatively inefficient.

Oligopoly is an important market structure in today's economy because in many industries the minimum efficient scale is simply too high to support a large number of competing firms. Monopolistic competition is also important, especially in many service industries in which economies of scale are not so extreme but product differentiation is an important market characteristic. Although neither oligopoly nor monopolistic competition achieves the conditions for allocative efficiency, they may nevertheless produce more satisfactory results than monopoly.

We observed one reason why oligopoly may be preferable to monopoly in Chapter 11: Competition among oligopolists encourages innovations that result in both new products and cost-reducing methods of producing old ones. An important defence of oligopoly as an acceptable market structure is that it may be the best of the available alternatives when minimum efficient scale is large. As we observed at the end of Chapter 11, the challenge to public policy is to keep oligopolists competing and using their competitive energies to improve products and to reduce costs rather than to restrict interfirm competition and to erect entry barriers. As we will see later in this chapter, much public policy has just this purpose. What economic policymakers call *monopolistic practices* include not only output restrictions operated by firms with complete monopoly power but also anticompetitive behaviour among firms that are operating in oligopolistic industries.

Allocative Efficiency and Total Surplus

By using the concepts of marginal value to consumers and the marginal cost of production, we have established the basic points of productive and allocative efficiency. A different way of thinking about allocative efficiency—though completely consistent with the first approach—is to use the concepts of consumer and producer surplus, both of which are part of the economic surplus that we first introduced in Chapter 5.

producer surplus The price of a good minus the marginal cost of producing it, summed over the quantity produced.

Consumer and Producer Surplus Recall from Chapter 6 that consumer surplus is the difference between the value that consumers place on a product and the payment that they actually make to buy that product. In Figure 12-4, if the competitive market price is p_0 and consumers buy Q_0 units of the product, consumer surplus is the blue shaded area.

Producer surplus is an analogous concept to consumer surplus. **Producer surplus** is the difference between the actual price that the producer receives for a product and the lowest price that the producer would be willing to accept for the sale of that product. By producing one more unit, the producer's costs increase by the marginal cost, and this is the lowest amount that the producer will accept for the product. To accept any amount less than the marginal cost would *reduce* the firm's profits.

> **For each unit sold, producer surplus is the difference between price and marginal cost.**

For a producer that sells many units of the product, total producer surplus is the difference between price and marginal cost summed over all the units sold. So, for an individual producer, total producer surplus is the area above the marginal cost curve and below the price line.

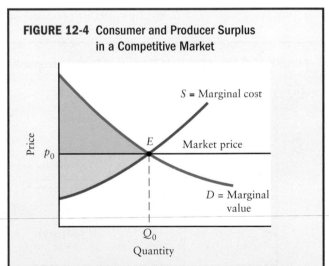

FIGURE 12-4 Consumer and Producer Surplus in a Competitive Market

Consumer surplus is the area under the demand curve and above the market price line. Producer surplus is the area above the supply curve and below the market price line. The total value that consumers place on Q_0 of the commodity is given by the area under the demand curve up to Q_0. The amount they pay is the rectangle p_0Q_0. The difference, shown as the blue shaded area, is consumer surplus.

The revenue to producers from the sale of Q_0 units is p_0Q_0. The area under the supply curve is the minimum amount producers require to supply the output. The difference, shown as the red shaded area, is producer surplus.

For the industry as a whole, we need to know the industry supply curve in order to compute overall producer surplus. Since in perfect competition the industry supply curve is simply the horizontal sum of all firms' *MC* curves, producer surplus in a perfectly competitive market is the area above the market supply curve and below the price line, as shown in Figure 12-4.

The Allocative Efficiency of Perfect Competition Revisited
In Chapter 5 we said that (allocative) efficiency exists in a market if the total economic surplus is maximized. At that point, we did not make the distinction between the component parts of total surplus—consumer surplus and producer surplus. Now that we have identified these different parts of total surplus, we can restate the conditions for allocative efficiency in a slightly different way.

Allocative efficiency occurs at the level of output where the sum of consumer and producer surplus is maximized.

The allocatively efficient output occurs under perfect competition where the demand curve intersects the supply curve—that is, the point of equilibrium in a competitive market. This is shown as the output Q^* in Figure 12-5. For any level of output below Q^*, such as Q_1, the demand curve lies above the supply curve, showing that consumers value the product more than it costs to produce it. Thus, society would be better off if more than Q_1 units were produced. Notice that if output is only Q_1 there is no consumer or producer surplus earned on the units between Q_1 and Q^*. Thus, the areas 1 and 2 in Figure 12-5 represent a loss to the economy. Total surplus—consumer plus producer surplus—is lower at Q_1 than at Q^*.

For any level of output above Q^*, such as Q_2, the demand curve lies below the supply curve, showing that consumers value the product less than the cost of producing it. Society would be better off if less than Q_2 units were produced. If output is Q_2, total surplus is less than it is at Q^*. To see this, suppose that the price is p^*. Producers would earn *negative* producer surplus on the units above Q^* because the marginal cost on those units exceeds p^*. Similarly, consumers would earn *negative* consumer surplus on the units above Q^* because their marginal value of the product is less than p^*. (You should be able to convince yourself that for any price, the total surplus earned on the units above Q^* is negative.) From the figure, we conclude that at any level of output above Q^*, total surplus is less than it is at Q^*.

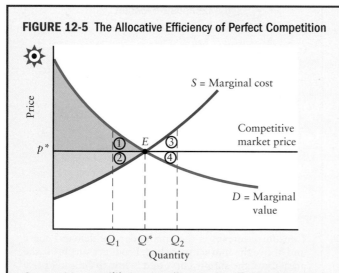

FIGURE 12-5 The Allocative Efficiency of Perfect Competition

Competitive equilibrium is allocatively efficient because it maximizes the sum of consumer and producer surplus. The competitive equilibrium occurs at the price–output combination of p^* and Q^*. At this equilibrium, consumer surplus is the blue area above the price line, while producer surplus is the red area below the price line.

For any output that is less than Q^*, the sum of the two surpluses is less than at Q^*. For any output that is greater than Q^*, the sum of the surpluses is also less than at Q^*. Thus, total surplus is maximized when output is Q^*.

The sum of producer and consumer surplus is maximized only at the perfectly competitive level of output. This is the only level of output that is allocatively efficient.

The Allocative Inefficiency of Monopoly Revisited We have just seen in Figure 12-5 that the output in perfectly competitive equilibrium maximizes the sum of consumer and producer surplus. It follows that the lower monopoly output must result in a smaller total of consumer and producer surplus.

The monopoly equilibrium is not the outcome of a voluntary agreement between the one producer and the many consumers. Instead, it is imposed by the monopolist by virtue of the power it has over the market. When the monopolist chooses an output below the competitive level, market price is higher than it would be under perfect competition. As a result, consumer surplus is diminished, and producer surplus is increased. In this way, the monopolist gains at the expense of consumers. This is not the whole story, however.

When output is below the competitive level, there is always a *net loss* of total surplus: More surplus is lost by consumers than is gained by the monopolist. Some surplus is lost because output between the monopolistic and the competitive levels is not produced. This loss of surplus is called the *deadweight loss of monopoly*. It is illustrated in Figure 12-6.

It follows that there is a conflict between the private interest of the monopolist and the public interest of all the nation's consumers. This creates grounds for government intervention to prevent the formation of monopolies or at least to control their behaviour. *Extensions in Theory 12-2* presents an alternative view of monopoly, one that emphasizes the incentives for innovation that come from the monopolist's temporary ability to earn large profits by setting price above marginal cost.

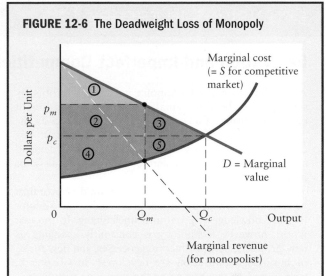

FIGURE 12-6 The Deadweight Loss of Monopoly

Monopoly restricts output and reduces total surplus, thereby imposing a deadweight loss on society. If this market were perfectly competitive, output would be Q_c and price would be p_c. Total surplus would be the total shaded area. Consumer surplus would be the sum of areas 1, 2, and 3. Producer surplus would be the sum of areas 4 and 5.

When the industry is monopolized, and the monopolist has the same marginal costs as the competitive industry, output is restricted to Q_m and price rises to p_m. Consumer surplus is reduced to the blue area. Producer surplus rises by area 2 but falls by area 5. (Since p_m must maximize the producer's profit, we know that area 2 is larger than area 5.) Total producer surplus for the monopolist is therefore the red area.

The deadweight loss of monopoly is the purple area. This area represents the additional surplus that would be earned if the market were competitive. Since the monopolist restricts output to Q_m, the units between Q_m and Q_c are not produced and therefore they generate neither consumer nor producer surplus.

Allocative Efficiency and Market Failure

We have seen that perfect competition is allocatively efficient and that monopoly, in general, is not. Most of the remainder of this chapter presents ways in which public policy has attempted to deal with problems raised by monopoly. Before we go on, however, it is important to re-emphasize that perfect competition is a theoretical ideal that exists in a small number of industries, is at best only approximated in some others, and is not even closely resembled in most. Hence, to say that perfect competition is allocatively efficient is not to say that real-world market economies are ever allocatively efficient.

In Chapter 16, we discuss the most important ways (other than monopoly) in which market economies may fail to produce efficient outcomes. In Chapters 17 and 18, we discuss and evaluate the most important public policies that have been used to try to correct for these *market failures*. One of the most important problems arises when market transactions—production and consumption—impose costs or confer benefits

EXTENSIONS IN THEORY 12-2

Innovation and Imperfect Competition

As we have seen, a monopolist who earns profits by setting price above marginal cost also creates a loss of economic surplus for society, a loss referred to as the *deadweight loss* of monopoly. This same kind of loss occurs whenever firms face negatively sloped demand curves, whether they are monopolists, oligopolists, or monopolistic competitors.

This result follows from the long-run theory of firm behaviour in which all inputs are variable but technological knowledge is given and unchanging. In the real world, however, technology is constantly changing as new products, new production processes, and new forms of business organization are developed. In Chapter 8, we referred to this setting as the *very long run*. Economists who stress the importance of such very long-run changes question whether deadweight losses should be condemned. Although they regard the special case of an entrenched monopoly that does not innovate as undesirable, most imperfectly competitive situations are seen as providing the climate that drives economic growth. For example, the U.S. economist William Baumol devotes his entire book *The Free-Market Innovation Machine: Analyzing the Growth Miracle of Capitalism* to arguing that it is the profits in imperfect competition that drive the "technological arms race," which ultimately ends up generating the long-term growth that has been the source of steadily rising average living standards in the industrialized countries over the last three centuries.

These economists follow in the footsteps of the great Austrian economist Joseph Schumpeter, whose concept of "creative destruction" we first encountered in Chapter 10. Like Schumpeter, they point out that innovation rarely occurs in perfectly competitive industries. The main innovators are rather oligopolies and small start-up firms that produce new products or develop new production processes. One need only consider firms like Google, Research in Motion, Facebook, and Twitter to see current examples of such innovation. None of these companies existed prior to 1990 and two of them were created in the past decade. All have been innovative in the creation of new products, most of which could barely be imagined back in 1990.

Successful innovators know how to do something that their rivals have not yet learned how to do; innovators thus have market power and can earn large profits—but only until their rivals learn what the innovators know. The opportunity for profit drives the system in the very long run. Large profits are the incentive that induces inventing firms to attempt leaps into the unknown. They also provide most of the funds that allow such firms to engage in the costly research and development that is necessary for further invention and innovation.

The long-run gains from cost-reducing innovation can be seen in the accompanying standard monopoly diagram. The initial monopoly outcome is output of Q_m and price of p_m. If the innovations undertaken by the firm reduce its marginal costs, the MC curve shifts over time to the right. Even if the firm retains its complete monopoly situation—a very unlikely outcome—the change in costs will lead the firm to increase output and lower its price, as shown. The monopoly outcome involves a deadweight loss at any point in time, but over time the firm's innovation generates benefits to consumers through better products and lower prices.

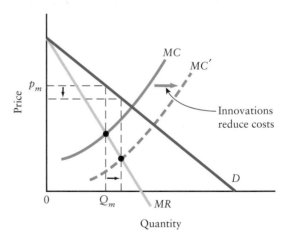

In sum, before condemning monopolists and other imperfect competitors for the deadweight losses that result from their business decisions, we must assess their positive contributions to the development of better technologies and the raising of average living standards.

on economic agents who are not involved in the transaction. Cases like these, which are called *externalities* because they involve economic costs or benefits for parties that are "external" to the transaction, generally raise the possibility that market outcomes will be allocatively inefficient.

A simple example illustrates the problem. We know that markets for most agricultural commodities are highly competitive, with many small producers who are unable to affect the price of the goods they are producing. At the same time, the technology of agricultural production involves the extensive use of fertilizers that pollute nearby streams and rivers. This pollution imposes costs on downstream households who use the water for drinking. Because these costs are not taken into account in the market for the agricultural products, they will be external to transactions in those markets. Generally, when production of a good or service causes pollution, the quantity produced in a perfectly competitive industry will exceed the efficient amount.

> One of the most important issues in public policy is whether, and under what circumstances, government action can increase the allocative efficiency of market outcomes.

As we will see later in this book, there are many circumstances in which there is room to increase the efficiency of market outcomes, but there are also many cases in which the cure is worse than the disease. In the remainder of this chapter we examine economic regulation and competition policy, both of which are designed to promote allocative efficiency.

12.2 Economic Regulation to Promote Efficiency

Monopolies, cartels, and price-fixing agreements among oligopolists, whether explicit or tacit, have met with public suspicion and official hostility for more than a century. These and other non-competitive practices are collectively referred to as *monopoly practices*. The laws and other instruments that are used to encourage competitive behaviour and discourage monopoly practices make up *competition policy* (referred to as *anit-trust* policy in the United States). By and large, Canadian competition policy has sought to create more competitive market structures where possible, to discourage monopolistic practices, and to encourage competitive behaviour where competitive market structures cannot be established.

Federal, provincial, and local governments also employ *economic regulations,* which prescribe the rules under which firms can do business and in some cases determine the prices that businesses can charge for their output. For example, the Canadian Radio-television and Telecommunications Commission (CRTC) is a federal agency that regulates many aspects of the radio, television, and telecommunications industries, including the price you pay for cell phone and cable TV services. Another federal agency is the Office of the Superintendent of Financial Institutions Canada (OSFI), which oversees the regulation of Canada's banks and insurance companies. Provincial governments regulate the extraction of fossil fuels and the harvesting of forests within their provincial boundaries. Local governments regulate the zoning of land and thus have an important influence on where firms can and cannot operate their businesses.

The quest for allocative efficiency provides rationales both for competition policy and for economic regulation. Competition policy is used to promote allocative efficiency by increasing competition in the marketplace. Where competitive behaviour is not possible (as in the case of natural monopolies, such as natural gas or electricity

To learn about the Canadian Radio-television and Telecommunications Commission (CRTC), see its website: www.crtc.gc.ca.

Visit the website for the Office of the Superintendent of Financial Institutions Canada at www.osfi-bsif.gc.ca.

distribution companies), public ownership or economic regulation of privately owned firms can be used as a substitute for competition. Consumers can then be protected from the high prices and restricted output that would likely result from the unregulated use of monopoly power.[4]

In the remainder of this chapter, we look at a variety of ways in which policymakers have chosen to intervene in the workings of the market economy using economic regulation and competition policy.

Regulation of Natural Monopolies

natural monopoly An industry characterized by economies of scale sufficiently large that one firm can most efficiently supply the entire market demand.

The clearest case for public intervention arises with a **natural monopoly**—an industry in which economies of scale are so dominant that there is room for *at most* one firm to operate at the minimum efficient scale. (In other words, the firm's *LRAC* curve is declining over the entire range of the market demand curve.) Natural monopolies are found mainly in public utilities, such as electricity transmission and natural gas distribution. These industries require the establishment of large and expensive distribution networks (transmission lines and pipelines) and the size of the market is such that only a single firm can achieve its minimum efficient scale while still covering these fixed costs. Local telephone service and cable TV were also natural monopolies for many years. Recent technological change, however, has now allowed other firms to compete effectively in these markets.

Crown corporations In Canada, business concerns owned by the federal or provincial government.

One response to natural monopoly is for government to assume ownership of the single firm. In Canada, such government-owned firms are called **Crown corporations**. In these cases, the government appoints managers and directors who are supposed to set prices in the public interest. Another response to the problem of natural monopoly is to allow private ownership but to *regulate* the monopolist's behaviour. In Canada, both government ownership (e.g., Canada Post and most of the provincial hydro authorities) and regulation (e.g., cable television and local Internet service providers) are used actively. In the United States, with a few notable exceptions, private ownership with regulation has been the preferred alternative.

Whether the government owns or merely regulates natural monopolies, the industry's pricing policy is determined by the government. The industry is typically required to follow some pricing policy that *conflicts* with the goal of profit maximization. We will see that such government intervention must deal with problems that arise in the short run, the long run, and the very long run.

Short-Run Price and Output Three general types of pricing policies exist for regulated natural monopolies: *marginal-cost pricing, two-part tariffs,* and *average-cost pricing.* We discuss each in turn.

Marginal-Cost Pricing. Sometimes the government dictates that the natural monopoly set a price where the market demand curve and the firm's marginal cost curve intersect. This policy, called *marginal-cost pricing,* leads to the allocatively efficient level of output. This is not, however, the profit-maximizing output, which is where marginal cost equals marginal revenue. Thus, marginal-cost pricing sets up a tension between the regulator's desire to achieve the allocatively efficient level of output and the monopolist's desire to maximize profits.

---

[4] A second kind of regulation involves the legislated rules that require firms to consider the environmental and other consequences of their behaviour. Environmental regulation is discussed in Chapter 17.

Figure 12-7 illustrates a natural monopoly and shows that the firm's *LRAC* curve is declining over the entire range of the market demand curve. Since *LRAC* is declining, *MC* is less than long-run average cost. It follows that when price is set equal to marginal cost, price will be less than average cost, and marginal-cost pricing will lead to losses.

> When a natural monopoly with falling average costs sets price equal to marginal cost, it will suffer losses.

If regulations impose marginal-cost pricing, and the firm ends up incurring economic losses, this situation cannot be sustained for long. This problem provides the motivation for two alternative pricing policies.

Two-Part Tariff. One pricing policy that permits the natural monopoly to cover its costs is to allow it to charge a *two-part tariff* in which customers pay one price to gain access to the product and a second price for each unit consumed. Consider the case of a regulated cable TV company or Internet service provider (ISP). In principle, the hook-up fee covers fixed costs, and then each unit of output can be priced at marginal cost. Indeed, many new subscribers to cable TV or Internet service are surprised at how high the hook-up fee is—clearly much higher than the cost of the cable guy's half-hour to complete the job! Yet if this fee also includes that household's share of the firm's fixed costs (spread over many thousands of households), then the large hook-up fee is more understandable.

Average-Cost Pricing. Another method of regulating a natural monopoly is to set prices just high enough to cover total costs, thus generating neither profits nor losses. This is called *average-cost pricing.* The firm produces the level of output at which the demand curve cuts the *LRAC* curve. Figure 12-7 shows that for a firm with declining long-run average costs, this pricing policy requires producing at less than the allocatively efficient output. The firm's financial losses that would occur under marginal-cost pricing are avoided by producing less output than what is socially optimal.

> For a natural monopoly with falling average costs, a policy of average-cost pricing will not result in allocative efficiency because price will not equal marginal cost.

On what basis do we choose between marginal-cost pricing and average-cost pricing? Marginal-cost pricing generates allocative efficiency, but the firm incurs losses. In this case, the firm will eventually go out of business unless someone is prepared to cover the firm's losses. If the

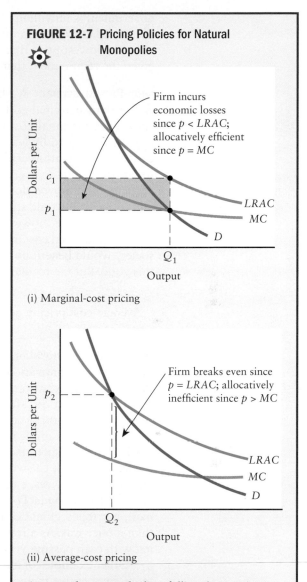

FIGURE 12-7 Pricing Policies for Natural Monopolies

Firm incurs economic losses since $p < LRAC$; allocatively efficient since $p = MC$

(i) Marginal-cost pricing

Firm breaks even since $p = LRAC$; allocatively inefficient since $p > MC$

(ii) Average-cost pricing

A natural monopoly has falling long-run average costs; marginal-cost pricing leads to losses, whereas average-cost pricing leads to allocative inefficiency. In both parts, average costs are falling as output rises, and thus the *MC* curve is below the *LRAC* curve.

In part (i), a policy that requires setting price equal to *MC* leads to output Q_1 and price p_1. This outcome is allocatively efficient but the firm cannot cover its full unit costs of c_1. In part (ii), a policy that requires setting price equal to average cost results in output Q_2 and price p_2. The firm can cover its full costs but the outcome is allocatively inefficient because price exceeds marginal cost.

government is unwilling to do so, seeing no reason why taxpayers should subsidize the users of the product in question, then average-cost pricing may be preferable. It provides the lowest price that can be charged and the largest output that can be produced, given the requirement that revenue must cover the total cost of producing the product.

Long-Run Investment We have seen why regulators may choose average-cost pricing rather than marginal-cost pricing. What is the implication of this choice in the long run? Since marginal cost for a natural monopoly is below average cost, average-cost pricing will generally lead to inefficient patterns of long-run investment. For example, consider the situation depicted in part (ii) of Figure 12-7—a natural monopoly required to set price equal to average cost. The firm will be just breaking even. If it expanded its capacity (and moved downward along its *LRAC* curve) the regulated price would fall and so the firm would still be breaking even. Thus, it has no incentive to undertake such investment. Note, however, that the price in this case must exceed the marginal cost (because marginal cost must be below average cost if average cost is falling). As a result, society would benefit by having a larger amount of fixed capital allocated to producing this good. But the regulated utility will not undertake this socially desirable investment.

> Average-cost pricing generally leads to inefficient long-run investment decisions.

Very Long-Run Innovation In many places in the last few chapters we have discussed the importance of innovation and technological change. In particular, we mentioned how innovation can lead to the erosion of market power through Schumpeter's process of "creative destruction." Technological changes have led to the evolution of many natural monopolies into more competitive industries.

A striking example is found in the telecommunications industry. Thirty years ago, hard-copy message transmission in Canada was close to a natural monopoly belonging to Canada Post, a Crown corporation. Today, technological developments, such as efficient courier services, e-mail, scanners, and the Internet, have made this activity highly competitive. Canada Post still has a legislated monopoly over delivery of first-class mail, but this segment of the overall "package delivery" market is now much smaller than it once was. As a result, the demand for Canada Post's services is gradually shrinking with each passing year.

Other examples of industries that used to be natural monopolies but are now much more competitive include airlines, long-distance telephone service, and the generation of electricity (the *distribution* of electricity continues to be a natural monopoly).

The case of electricity is particularly interesting. The combined production and distribution of electricity was once viewed as a natural monopoly, and the policy response was either to establish publicly owned power authorities (as happened in Canadian provinces) or to regulate privately owned power companies (as occurred in the United States). The source of the natural monopoly was twofold. First, the generation of electricity at low unit cost required large and expensive generating stations. Second, the transmission of power required the establishment of power grids, with networks of wires running from the generating stations to the users.

In recent years, however, the technology of electricity *generation* has changed. Though nuclear and hydro stations are still very expensive to build, it is now possible to build small and relatively inexpensive natural gas–powered generating stations that produce electricity at low unit costs. These technological changes have led to the realization that the generation of electricity is no longer a natural monopoly even though the distribution of electricity still is. This realization has led several jurisdictions in Canada and the United States to embark on a path of privatization or deregulation of electricity markets. Although this path has been rough in some areas—especially in California and Alberta, both of which experienced severe brownouts and price escalations on a temporary basis—the underlying technological change continues to suggest that the generation of electricity is no longer a natural monopoly.

Practical Problems Many practical problems arise with regulations designed to prevent natural monopolies from charging profit-maximizing prices. These problems begin with the fact that regulators usually do not have enough data to determine demand and cost curves precisely. In the absence of accurate data, regulators have tended to judge prices according to the level of the regulated firm's profits. Regulatory agencies tend to permit price increases only when profits fall below "fair" levels and require price reductions if profits exceed such levels. What started as price regulation becomes instead profit regulation, which is often called *rate-of-return regulation*. Concepts of marginal cost and allocative efficiency are typically ignored in such regulatory decisions.

If average-cost regulation is successful, only a normal rate of return will be earned; that is, economic profits will be zero. Unfortunately, the reverse is not necessarily true. Profits can be zero for any of a number of reasons, including inefficient operation, excessive salaries or employee benefits, and misleading accounting. Thus, regulatory commissions that rely on rate of return as their guide to pricing must monitor a number of other aspects of the regulated firm's behaviour in order to limit the possibility of wasting resources. This monitoring itself requires a considerable expenditure of resources.

Canada Post has long held a legislated monopoly for the delivery of first-class mail, but technological change has provided an expanding set of alternatives to its services, thereby eroding its monopoly power.

Regulation of Oligopolies

Governments have from time to time intervened in industries that were oligopolies (rather than natural monopolies), seeking to enforce the type of price and entry behaviour that was thought to be in the public interest. Such intervention has typically taken two distinct forms. In the period following the Second World War, many European countries, including Britain, primarily used nationalization of whole oligopolistic industries, such as railways, steel, and coal mining, which were then to be run by government-appointed boards. In the United States, such firms as airlines and railways were left in private hands, but their decisions were regulated by government-appointed bodies that set prices and regulated entry. As often happens, Canada followed a mixture of British and American practices. Many Canadian Crown corporations were established, and many firms that remained in private hands were regulated. For example, Canadian Pacific Railway was privately owned and regulated while Canadian National Railway, until it was privatized in 1995, was a Crown corporation.

Skepticism About Direct Control Policymakers have become increasingly skeptical of their ability to improve the behaviour of oligopolistic industries by having governments control the details of their behaviour through either ownership or regulation. Two main experiences have been important in developing this skepticism.

Oligopolies And Innovation. During the twentieth century and into the present, new products and production methods have followed each other in rapid succession, leading to higher living standards and higher productivity. Many of these innovations have been provided by firms in oligopolistic industries, such as cars, agricultural machinery, petroleum refining, chemicals, electronics, computing, and telecommunications. As long as oligopolists continue to compete with one another, rather than cooperating to produce monopoly profits, most economists see no need to regulate such things as the prices at which oligopolists sell their products and the conditions of entry into oligopolistic industries.

Protection From Competition. The record of postwar government intervention into regulated industries seemed poorer in practice than its supporters had predicted. Research by the University of Chicago Nobel Laureate George Stigler (1911–1991) and others established that in many industries, regulatory bodies were "captured" by the very firms that they were supposed to be regulating. As a result, the regulatory bodies that were meant to ensure competition often acted to enforce monopoly practices that would have been illegal if instituted by the firms themselves.

Why did regulatory bodies shift from protecting consumers to protecting firms? One reason is that the regulatory commissions were gradually captured by the firms they were supposed to regulate. In part, this capture was natural enough. When regulatory bodies were hiring staff, they needed people who were knowledgeable about the industries they were regulating. Where better to go than to people who had worked in these industries? Naturally, these people tended to be sympathetic to firms in their own industries. Also, because many of them aspired to go back to those industries once they had gained experience within the regulatory bodies, they were not inclined to arouse the wrath of industry officials by imposing policies that were against the firms' interests.

Deregulation and Privatization The 1980s witnessed the beginning of a movement in many advanced industrial nations to reduce the level of government control over industry. Various experiences in these countries were pushing in this direction:

- The realization that regulatory bodies often sought to reduce, rather than increase, competition

- The dashing of the hopes that publicly owned firms would work better than privately owned firms in the areas of efficiency, productivity growth, and industrial relations

- The awareness that falling transportation costs and revolutions in data processing and communications exposed local industries to much more widespread international competition than they had previously experienced domestically

These revised views led to two policy responses. The first was deregulation—intended to leave prices and entry free to be determined by private decisions. The second was privatization of publicly owned firms.

In the United States, where regulation rather than government ownership had been the adopted policy, many industries were deregulated. In the United Kingdom, virtually all of the formally nationalized industries were privatized. The level of public ownership in that country now compares with that in the United States. In Canada, hundreds of Crown corporations that the government had acquired for a variety of reasons (but were neither natural monopolies nor operating in highly concentrated industries) were sold off. Many large Crown corporations operating in oligopolistic industries, such as Air Canada, Petro-Canada, and Canadian National Railway, were privatized. Also, many industries, such as airlines and gas and oil, were deregulated. Prices were freed, to be set by the firms in the industries, and entry was no longer restricted by government policy.

A Return to Government Control? With the onset of a global financial crisis in 2008 followed immediately by a severe global recession, governments found themselves faced with a tough choice. Many large U.S. financial institutions were threatened with collapse, as were General Motors and Chrysler. Should these companies be allowed to fail, as was likely to happen without government action? Or should the government intervene to support these firms in an attempt to dampen the reduction in output and rise in unemployment that were already occurring? As it happened, the U.S. government intervened aggressively to support the financial institutions and the U.S. and Canadian (and Ontario) governments intervened to support operations of the two major car companies on both sides of the border. In all cases, however, the government support was designed to be temporary. The intervention was not designed to be a return to the government control of private firms, but rather it was seen as a temporary but pragmatic government response to extraordinary problems during extraordinary times.

Applying Economic Concepts 12-1 discusses a different kind of regulation for an important Canadian industry. The Canadian banking industry is oligopolistic, containing a small number of very large banks. Some of the most important regulations in the banking industry, however, are aimed at promoting confidence and reducing risk-taking behaviour rather than at encouraging competition.

12.3 Canadian Competition Policy

The least stringent form of government intervention is designed neither to force firms to sell at particular prices nor to regulate the conditions of entry and exit; it is designed, instead, to create conditions of competition by preventing firms from merging unnecessarily or from engaging in anticompetitive practices, such as colluding to set monopoly prices. This is referred to as **competition policy**.

competition policy Policy designed to prohibit the acquisition and exercise of monopoly power by business firms.

The Evolution of Canadian Policy

Canadian competition policy began in the late 1890s and evolved gradually over the next half-century. By the 1950s, the following three broad classes of activity were illegal:

- Price-fixing agreements that unduly lessen competition

- Mergers or monopolies that operate to the detriment of the public interest

- "Unfair" trade practices

An alleged offence under any of these categories was handled by the criminal justice system, and conviction required the standard level of proof "beyond a reasonable doubt."

APPLYING ECONOMIC CONCEPTS 12-1

Confidence, Risk, and Regulation in Canadian Banking

Credit is crucial for any modern economy. Most consumers borrow to buy a house and car, and many have lines of credit which allow them to finance other purchases. Most firms borrow to expand their facilities, but also to pay their workers on a regular basis when their revenues arrive in a less predictable way. In short, credit is a crucial input, and without a well-functioning credit market it would be difficult if not impossible to maintain our current high level of economic activity.

Banks play a vital role as *intermediaries* in the credit market. They accept deposits from millions of households and firms who want to save, and then channel those funds to other firms and households who want to borrow. The business model for banks is actually quite simple: pay a relatively low interest rate on deposits, charge a higher interest rate on loans, and the bank then earns a profit based on the *spread* in interest rates.

At the core of the banking system lies both *confidence* and *risk*. The banks' depositors require confidence that they can access their funds when they want and that the bank will not collapse. Without such confidence, few would deposit their money in the bank, and without deposits the bank would not be able to make loans. The loans that the bank makes are inherently risky because firms and households may fail to repay what they owe.

Given the role of banks as intermediaries in the credit market and the need to maintain confidence in an industry that is inherently about risk-taking, several government regulations apply to Canadian banks (and those in most other countries as well). Examples of such regulations are:

- All Canadian banks are members of the Canada Deposit Insurance Corporation (CDIC). CDIC is a Crown corporation that uses fees paid by the member banks to provide insurance to depositors against the risk of bank failure. This insurance is central in providing individuals confidence that their deposits are safe (up to a limit of $100 000 per deposit.)

- Banks are limited in the amount of their assets (loans) that can be financed by customer deposits. Some fraction of their assets must be financed by the financial capital provided by the banks' owners. Such restrictions permit the banks' assets to fall in value by a modest amount (as occasionally happens) without leading to bank insolvency and failure.

- Banks that extend home mortgages to customers are required to purchase mortgage insurance if the value of the loan exceeds 80 percent of the value of the home (i.e., if the borrower's down payment is less than 20 percent). With such insurance, the bank is protected from loss in the event that the borrower defaults on the loan. The bank can purchase mortgage insurance from the Canada Mortgage and Housing Corporation (CMHC), a Crown corporation, or from private-sector insurers.

This is just a small sample of the many regulations that apply to Canadian banks. Given the nature of the industry it is not surprising that many regulations are aimed at promoting confidence and limiting the amount and nature of risks to which banks are exposed.

This aspect of Canadian bank regulation came to the attention of international observers during the global financial crisis of 2008–2009. While several large banks in other developed economies collapsed, and many others required significant government assistance in order to avoid collapse, no Canadian banks experienced equivalent strains. Some argue that Canadian bankers have traditionally been more prudent than bankers in other countries; others argue that Canada was just lucky. Most economists agree, however, that Canadian bank regulation prevented some of the extreme risk-taking behaviour that occurred elsewhere and was partly responsible for the better performance of the Canadian banking industry.

Many cases of unfair trade practices were successfully pursued under these laws, but few cases were brought against mergers, and none of those that were brought were successful. The reasons most often cited for this lack of success were the inability of criminal legislation to cope with complex economic issues and the inability to establish proof "beyond a reasonable doubt."

A major review of Canadian legislation was undertaken in the late 1960s and led to changes in policy that were implemented in stages. The revisions were completed with the *Competition Act* of 1986. This Act is currently in force and contains some important modifications to the earlier legislation. Perhaps most important is that the Act allows *civil* actions, rather than *criminal* actions, to be brought against firms for alleged offences in the three categories listed above. This change is important because in civil cases the standard of proof is less strict than in criminal cases.

In order to adjudicate such civil cases, a Competition Tribunal was established. The Commissioner of the Competition Bureau now acts as a "watchdog" for the economy, looking out for mergers or trade practices that are likely to have detrimental effects on overall welfare. In such cases, the Commissioner sends the alleged violations to the Competition Tribunal for adjudication.

In the case of a large merger that might substantially lessen competition, the firms are required to notify the Competition Bureau of their intention to merge. The Bureau then reviews the proposed merger, evaluates its probable effect on the economy, and then allows or disallows it.

Another important aspect of the 1986 legislation is that economic effects are now considered to be directly relevant in judging the acceptability of a proposed merger. When reviewing a merger, the Competition Bureau is obliged to consider such things as effective competition after the merger, the degree of foreign competition, barriers to entry, the availability of substitutes, and the financial state of the merging firms.

The Competition Bureau also considers any reduction in costs that a merger might generate. Even in a situation where there are considerable entry barriers to an industry, a merger may bring benefits to consumers even though it raises the industry's measured concentration. If, by merging, two firms can achieve scale economies that were not achievable separately, reductions in average total costs may get passed on to consumers in the form of lower prices.

This possibility presents a significant challenge to competition policy. The challenge is to prevent those mergers that mostly lead to less competition, producing only small cost reductions, but to allow those mergers that mostly lead to cost reductions, with only small reductions in competition. The practical problem for the authorities is to identify the likely effects of each merger.

To read the Competition Bureau's assessment of various proposed mergers, go to its website: www.competitionbureau.gc.ca. *Go to "Reviewing Mergers."*

Recent Reforms

For many years, Canadian legislation provided substantial protection to consumers against the misuse of market power by large firms. With the 1986 revisions, it also provides substantial protection against the creation, through mergers, of market power that is not justified by gains to efficiency or international competitiveness.

Canadian competition policy continues to evolve. In 2009, the *Competition Act* was amended to

- increase the penalties for deceptive marketing, and empowering the courts to award restitution to victims of false advertising

- create a more effective mechanism for the criminal prosecution of significant cartel agreements

- introduce a two-stage merger review process to improve efficiency and effectiveness

- allow the Competition Tribunal to assign monetary penalties to companies who abuse a dominant position in the marketplace

A recent example illustrates the kind of market developments that attract the attention of the Competition Bureau. In June of 2011 Air Canada and a U.S. airline, United Continental, announced their plans to create a "joint venture" on a number of air routes between major U.S. and Canadian cities. The joint venture would allow the two airlines to share costs and revenues on a total of 19 routes. The Competition Bureau saw this venture as a clear effort to create monopoly power that would raise prices to consumers. Of the 19 routes included in the proposed joint venture, the Competition Bureau estimated that the market share of the joint venture would be 100 percent on 10 of the routes, and would average 68 percent on the remaining 9 routes. The Competition Bureau filed an application with the Competition Tribunal to block the joint venture. After a series of discussions between the two airlines and the Competition Bureau, the airlines agreed to suspend their joint venture, at least temporarily.

Future Challenges

What type of other reforms might we expect in the years ahead? The ongoing process of globalization poses two challenges for Canadian competition policy. First, as the flow of goods and services across national boundaries increases, it becomes more important to define markets on an international rather than a national basis. For example, consider the Canadian banking industry. With the continuing development of the Internet, it becomes possible for foreign-based banks to sell some financial services to Canadians without establishing a costly *physical* presence in Canada—such as a network of branches. In this case, the appropriate definition of the market (for the case of assessing the impact of a merger) is larger than just the one defined by Canada's borders.

The second challenge posed by globalization is the desirability of standardizing competition policy across countries. Firms that are mobile and have considerable market power may tend to locate their firms where competition policy is the most lax, exporting into other countries. To avoid such socially inefficient locational choices, countries have an incentive to standardize their competition policy—in this case, firms would choose their locations on the basis of economic rather than legal forces.

These are challenges for the near future. Time will tell how Canadian competition authorities respond.

SUMMARY

12.1 Productive and Allocative Efficiency   LO 1, 2

- Productive efficiency for the firm requires that the firm be producing its output at the lowest possible cost. Productive efficiency for the industry requires that all firms in the industry have the same marginal cost.
- Allocative efficiency in an individual industry exists when the level of output is such that the marginal cost of production equals the market price. The overall economy is allocatively efficient when price equals marginal cost in all industries simultaneously.
- Productive efficiency and allocative efficiency are both achieved in perfect competition.
- Monopoly is allocatively inefficient because price exceeds marginal cost. Monopoly leads to a deadweight loss for the economy.

12.2 Economic Regulation to Promote Efficiency

LO 3

- Two broad types of policies are designed to promote allocative efficiency in imperfectly competitive markets. These can be divided into *economic regulations* and *competition policy*. Economic regulation is used both in the case of a natural monopoly and in the case of an oligopolistic industry. Competition policy applies more to the latter.
- For a natural monopoly (with a declining *LRAC* curve), marginal-cost pricing is allocatively efficient but will lead the firm to make economic losses.
- Average-cost pricing allows the natural monopoly to break even but leads to allocative inefficiency (because price is not equal to marginal cost).

- Two-part tariffs can allow the firm with falling long-run costs to break even and also be consistent with allocative efficiency.
- The deregulation of oligopolistic industries has been based on the observations that (1) oligopolistic industries are major engines of growth, and (2) direct control of such industries has produced disappointing results in the past.

12.3 Canadian Competition Policy

LO 4

- Canadian competition policy is designed to restrict mergers and trade practices that unduly lessen competition.
- In the past, mergers were criminal offences and difficult to prosecute. The current legislation allows civil cases to be brought against firms, making prosecution less difficult.
- The *Competition Act* of 1986 established a Competition Tribunal to adjudicate cases brought to it by the Competition Bureau.

- In the case of mergers, the Competition Bureau and Tribunal must consider whether the merger will generate cost reductions that will offset the effects of any lessening of competition.

KEY CONCEPTS

Productive and allocative efficiency	The allocative inefficiency of monopoly	Two-part tariffs
Consumer and producer surplus	Regulation of natural monopolies	Regulation of oligopolies
The allocative efficiency of competition	Marginal- and average-cost pricing	Deregulation and privatization
		Canadian competition policy

STUDY EXERCISES

 MyEconLab Make the grade with MyEconLab: Study Exercises marked in red can be found on MyEconLab. You can practise them as often as you want, and most feature step-by-step guided instructions to help you find the right answer.

1. Summer Tees and Fancy Tees make up an industry of two firms producing T-shirts. The table below shows the average cost of producing T-shirts for the two companies.

Summer Tees				Fancy Tees			
Quantity	ATC	TC	MC	Quantity	ATC	TC	MC
5	$8	—	—	5	$9	—	—
10	7	—	—	10	7	—	—
15	6	—	—	15	6	—	—
20	6	—	—	20	5	—	—
25	7	—	—	25	5.50	—	—
30	9	—	—	30	6.50	—	—
35	11	—	—	35	8	—	—

a. Calculate TC and MC for both companies and fill in the table.
b. Draw, in separate diagrams, the ATC and MC curves for each firm.
c. Summer Tees is initially producing 30 shirts; Fancy Tees is initially producing 15 shirts. What is the total industry production cost?
d. Now suppose that Summer Tees produces 10 fewer shirts. By how much do its costs fall?
e. Suppose that Fancy Tees produces 10 more shirts. By how much do its costs rise?
f. If the two firms are to produce 45 shirts in total, what is the cost-minimizing way to allocate production between the two firms? (Assume that production must be changed by increments of five shirts, as shown in the table.)
g. Explain how this question relates to the concept of productive efficiency.

2. Fill in the blanks to make the following statements correct.

a. If the marginal cost of producing the last unit of a product is the same for all firms in an industry, we can say that the industry is _____ efficient, but we do not know enough to say that the industry is _____ efficient.
b. If the marginal cost of some product is $12, and the market price of that product is $15, then to achieve allocative efficiency, the economy should produce _____ of this product and therefore _____ of other products.
c. The market structure that leads to both productive and allocative efficiency is _____.
d. A monopolistic industry may be productively efficient but will not be allocatively efficient because _____.
e. The sum of consumer surplus and producer surplus is _____ at the competitive equilibrium.
f. At the monopolist's profit-maximizing output there is _____ total surplus than at the competitive

output. Some surplus is transferred from _____ to _____. The surplus lost because the output is not produced is called _____.

3. Assume that the market for eggs is perfectly competitive. The diagram shows the demand and supply for eggs.

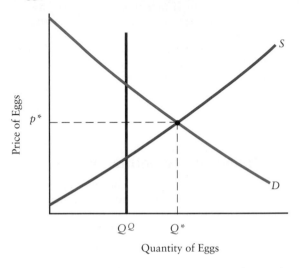

a. At the free-market equilibrium, p^* and Q^*, show what areas represent consumer and producer surplus.
b. Now suppose the egg producers organize themselves and establish a system of quotas. Each farmer's output is restricted by an amount to keep aggregate output at Q^Q. What happens to industry price?
c. In the quota system in part (b), what areas now represent consumer and producer surplus? Is the quota system allocatively efficient? Explain.

4. The diagram below shows supply and demand in the labour market.

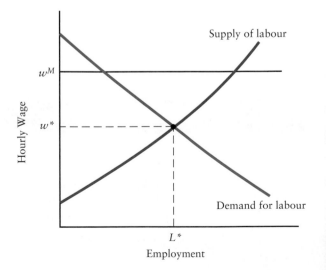

a. At the free-market equilibrium, w^* and L^*, show what areas represent consumer and producer surplus.

b. Now suppose the government establishes a minimum wage at w^M. Show on the diagram and label the new level of employment in this case.

c. In the situation of part (b), what areas now represent consumer and producer surplus? Is the outcome allocatively efficient? Explain.

5. The diagram below shows the demand, marginal cost, and marginal revenue curves for a monopolist. Redraw the diagram for yourself to be able to answer the following questions.

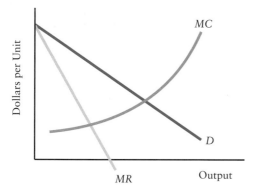

a. If the monopolist charges its single profit-maximizing price, show what areas are consumer surplus and producer surplus.

b. Now suppose the industry is perfectly competitive and the industry supply curve is given by the MC curve. What areas would be consumer and producer surplus in this case?

c. Use the concept of surplus to explain the economic argument against monopoly and in favour of competition.

d. Consider again the situation of monopoly, but now assume the firm can *perfectly* price discriminate—that is, it can charge a different price for every unit of the good. What areas now represent consumer and producer surplus?

e. Does the possibility of perfect price discrimination lead you to change your argument from part (c)? Are there considerations other than allocative efficiency that might be important here?

6. The diagram below shows the production possibilities boundary for a country that produces only two goods: limes and coconuts. Assume that resources are fully employed at points A, B, C, and D.

a. Suppose individual firms in the lime industry are not producing at their minimum possible cost. Which point(s) could represent this situation?

b. Suppose all firms and both industries are productively efficient. Which points could represent this situation?

c. Suppose point B occurs when the lime industry is monopolized but the coconut industry is perfectly competitive. Is point B allocatively efficient? Is it productively efficient?

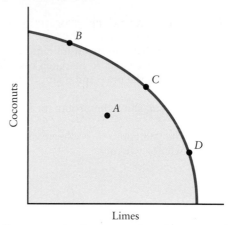

d. Suppose point D occurs when the coconut industry is monopolized but the lime industry is perfectly competitive. Is point D allocatively efficient? Is it productively efficient?

e. Suppose point C is allocatively efficient. What do we know about each industry in this case?

7. Fill in the blanks to make the following statements correct.

a. The term *natural monopoly* refers to an industry in which only a single firm can operate at its _____.

b. A regulated natural monopoly that is forced to set its price equal to marginal cost will earn _____ if its long-run average costs are falling.

c. A regulated natural monopoly that is subject to average-cost pricing and operating on the downward-sloping portion of its *LRAC* curve will earn _____ profits. Since price _____ marginal cost, this outcome will not be allocatively efficient.

d. Marginal-cost pricing for a natural monopoly is an efficient pricing system, but it leads to _____ for the firm if average costs are falling.

8. The following diagram shows the *LRAC* and *MC* curves for a natural monopoly—long-run average costs are falling over the entire range of the demand curve.

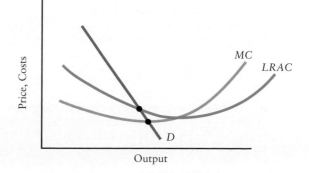

a. Show on the diagram the price and quantity that would exist if the firm were required by regulators to set price equal to average cost.

b. In the diagram, show the profits (or losses) in this case.

c. Would the outcome be allocatively efficient? Explain why or why not.

d. Suppose now that the firm were required by regulators to set price equal to marginal cost. Show on the graph what the price and quantity would be in this case.

e. In the diagram, show the profits (or losses) in this case.

f. Would the outcome be allocatively efficient? Explain why or why not.

9. One important factor that the Canadian Competition Bureau must consider when assessing the likely effects of a merger is the definition of the market. Discuss how geography is likely to affect the definition of the market for the following products:

a. Fresh-baked breads and cakes
b. Cement
c. Gold jewellery
d. Computer hardware

10. "Allocative efficiency is really about whether the economy 'has the quantities right'—it is not really about prices at all. Prices are important only in a discussion about allocative efficiency because *in a free market* changes in prices bring about the efficient allocation of resources." Comment on this statement.

How Factor Markets Work

CHAPTER OUTLINE	LEARNING OBJECTIVES (LO)
	After studying this chapter you will be able to
13.1 INCOME DISTRIBUTION	1 discuss the size and functional distribution of income in Canada.
13.2 THE DEMAND FOR FACTORS	2 determine a profit-maximizing firm's demand for a factor of production.
13.3 THE SUPPLY OF FACTORS	3 examine the role of factor mobility in determining factor supply.
13.4 THE OPERATION OF FACTOR MARKETS	4 distinguish between temporary and equilibrium factor-price differentials.
	5 discuss "economic rent" and how it relates to factor mobility.

WHAT determines the wages that individuals earn? What explains why neurosurgeons usually are paid more than family doctors, or why movie stars are paid more than "extras"? Labour is not the only factor of production, of course. Physical capital and land are also important. What determines the payments that these factors earn? Why does a hectare of farmland in Northern Saskatchewan rent for much less than a hectare of land in downtown Toronto? Not surprisingly, understanding why different factors of production earn different payments requires us to understand both demand-side and supply-side aspects of the relevant factor markets.

In this chapter we examine the issue of factor pricing and the closely related issue of factor mobility. Understanding what determines the payments to different factors of production will help us to understand the overall distribution of income in the economy, which is where we begin.

13.1 Income Distribution

The founders of Classical economics, Adam Smith (1723–1790) and David Ricardo (1772–1823), were concerned with the distribution of income among what were then the three great social classes: workers, capitalists, and landowners. They defined three factors of production as labour, capital, and land. The payment to each factor was treated as the income of the respective social class.

Smith and Ricardo were interested in what determined the share of total income that each class received. Their theories predicted that as society progressed, landlords would become relatively better off and capitalists would become relatively worse off. Karl Marx (1818–1883) had a different theory, which predicted that as growth occurred, capitalists would become relatively better off and workers would become relatively worse off (until the whole capitalist system collapsed).

These nineteenth-century debates focused on what is now called the **functional distribution of income**, defined as the distribution of national income among the major factors of production. Modern economists, however, emphasize the **size distribution of income**. This refers to the distribution of income among different individuals without reference to the source of the income or the "social class" of the individual.

If we want to measure and understand the income inequality between individuals, the size distribution of income is a better indicator than is the functional distribution of income. The reason is that income classes no longer coincide closely with "social" classes. Many capitalists, such as the owners of small retail stores, have relatively low incomes. Conversely, many wage earners, such as professional athletes and corporate executives, have very high incomes. Furthermore, it is becoming increasingly difficult to distinguish "workers" from "capitalists." Through employer-sponsored pension plans, workers now own much more of the country's capital than do the richer "non-working" capitalists.

Figure 13-1 shows that among Canadian families (couples with or without children, and lone-parent families), there was substantial inequality in the distribution of (pre-tax) income in 2009. Another way to show the size distribution of income is found in Figure 13-2. The curves in the figure are **Lorenz curves**, showing how much of total income goes to different proportions of the nation's families. If every family had the same income, 20 percent of total income would go to 20 percent of families, 40 percent of total income would go to 40 percent of families, and so on. In this case, the Lorenz curve would lie exactly along the diagonal. The farther the curve bends away from the diagonal, the less equal the distribution of income.

The orange Lorenz curve in Figure 13-2 shows that in 2010, the bottom 20 percent of all Canadian families received 1.0 percent of all pre-tax income, whereas the top 20 percent of families received 52.6 percent of all pre-tax income. Canada's tax-and-transfer system, however, had a marked effect on the income distribution. The blue Lorenz curve in Figure 13-2 shows the distribution of after-tax family income—that is, income after all taxes have been paid and transfers have been received. The bottom 20 percent of families receive 4.8 percent of after-tax income while the top 20 percent of families receive 44.3 percent. The difference between the orange and blue Lorenz curves shows the extent to which Canada's tax-and-transfer system reduces income inequality.

In the past few years, growing attention has been paid to rising income inequality in Canada and other countries, especially the United States and the United Kingdom. While real average per capita income has been growing gradually over many years, most of the observed income growth in the past few years has accrued to the very

---

functional distribution of income The distribution of national income among the major factors of production: labour, capital, and land.

size distribution of income The distribution of income among individuals, without regard to source of income.

Lorenz curve A graph showing the extent of inequality of income distribution.

FIGURE 13-1 Distribution of Family Income, 2009

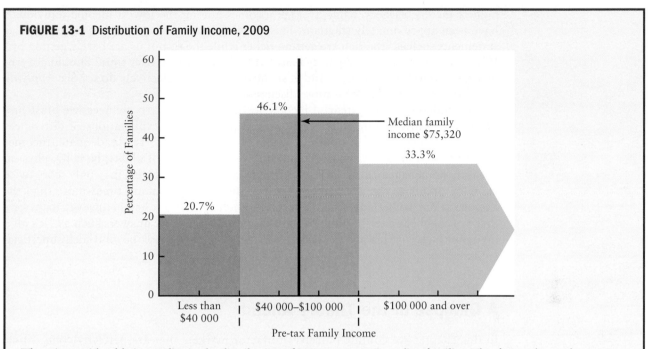

There is considerable inequality in the distribution of income across Canadian families. This figure shows the percentage of Canadian families (couples with or without children and lone-parent families) in each broad income group. More than 20 percent of families had pre-tax income less than $40 000; almost half had total income between $40 000 and $100 000; and one-third of families had total income above $100 000. The median family pre-tax income for 2009 was $75 320.

(*Source:* Author's calculations based on data available on Statistics Canada's website: www.statcan.gc.ca. Go to Summary Tables and search for "Family Income.")

FIGURE 13-2 The Lorenz Curve for Canadian Family Income, 2010

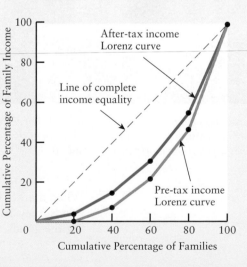

Percentage of Families	Pre-tax Income		After-tax Income	
	Percentage	Cumulative Percentage	Percentage	Cumulative Percentage
Lowest 20	1.0	1.0	4.8	4.8
Second-lowest 20	7.1	8.1	10.7	15.5
Middle 20	14.6	22.7	16.2	31.7
Second-highest 20	24.7	47.4	24.0	55.7
Highest 20	52.6	100.0	44.3	100.0

The size of the area between the Lorenz curve and the diagonal is a measure of the inequality of income distribution. If there were complete income equality, the bottom 20 percent of income receivers would receive 20 percent of total income, and so forth, and the Lorenz curve would coincide with the diagonal line. The orange Lorenz curve shows the distribution of pre-tax income. The blue Lorenz curve shows the distribution of after-tax income—income after taxes have been paid and transfers have been received. The blue curve being closer to the diagonal than the orange curve shows that Canada's tax-and-transfer system reduces the inequality of income.

(*Source:* Adapted from Statistics Canada, CANSIM Table 202-0701.)

highest income earners, while average incomes among the lowest-income individuals have been approximately stagnant. This growing income inequality has led to popular statements such as "the rich are getting richer while the rest of us are barely getting by." Why does such income inequality exist, and why is it rising over time? Should governments try to reverse this trend, and, if so, how could they effectively do so? See *Applying Economic Concepts 13-1* for more discussion on this topic.

To understand the extent of income inequality and why it changes, we must first study how individual incomes are determined. Superficial explanations of differences in income, such as "People earn according to their ability," are inadequate. Incomes are distributed much less equally than any *measured* index of ability, be it IQ, physical strength, or management skill. The best professional sports players may only score twice as many points as the average players, but their salary is many times more than the average salary. Something other than simple ability is at work here. However, if answers that are couched in terms of ability are easily refuted, so are answers such as "It's all a matter of luck" or "It's just the system." In this chapter, we look beyond such superficial explanations.

A Glimpse of the Theory Ahead

In this chapter, we confine ourselves to factor markets that are perfectly competitive. As a result, the firms we study face a given price of each factor that they buy. Similarly, owners of factors face a given price for the factor services that they sell.

Growing income inequality in many developed countries was a key motivation for the 'Occupy' movement that captured headlines around the world in 2011 and 2012.

Dealing first with competitive factor markets allows us to study the principles of factor-price determination in the simplest context. Once these principles are understood, it is relatively easy to extend the theory to more complicated settings. This is done for labour markets in Chapter 14.

Goods markets and factor markets are closely related. Firms' production decisions imply specific demands for the various factors of production. These demands, together with the supplies of the factors of production (which are determined by the owners of the factors), come together in factor markets. Together they determine the quantities of the various factors of production that are employed, their prices, and the incomes earned by their owners. This relationship between goods markets and factor markets leads to one of the great insights about economics:

> When market forces interact to determine the prices and quantities of various goods, they also determine the incomes of the factors that are used in producing the goods.

The rest of this chapter is an elaboration of this important theme. We first study the demand for factors, then their supply, and finally how demand and supply come together to determine equilibrium factor prices and quantities.

13.2 The Demand for Factors

Firms require the services of land, labour, and capital to be used as inputs. Firms also use as inputs the products of other firms, such as steel, legal services, computer software, and electricity.

Firms require inputs not for their own sake but as a means to produce goods and services. For example, the demand for computer programmers and technicians is growing as more and more computers and software are produced. The demand for carpenters and building materials rises and falls as the amount of housing construction rises and falls. The demand for any input is therefore *derived from the demand* for the goods and services that it helps to produce; for this reason, the demand for a factor of production is said to be a **derived demand**.

derived demand The demand for a factor of production that results from the demand for the products that it is used to make.

Marginal Revenue Product

What determines whether an individual firm will choose to hire one extra worker, or whether the same firm will decide to use one extra machine, or an extra kilowatt-hour of electricity? Just as a firm makes a profit-maximizing decision to produce a level of output where the last unit produced adds as much to revenue as to cost (where $MR = MC$), the firm makes a similar decision about the quantity of a factor to employ. A profit-maximizing firm will increase its use of any factor of production until the last unit of the factor adds as much to revenue as it does to costs.

> Profit-maximizing firms will hire units of a variable factor up to the point at which the marginal revenue generated by the factor equals the marginal cost of employing the factor.

This implication of profit-maximizing behaviour is true of all profit-maximizing firms, whether they are selling under conditions of perfect competition, monopolistic competition, oligopoly, or monopoly.

Now we introduce a new term to help us state this profit-maximizing condition more clearly. The **marginal revenue product** (**MRP**) is the extra revenue generated by hiring one more unit of a variable factor. How is it computed? Recall that marginal revenue (*MR*) is the change in revenue resulting from the sale of one additional unit of output. Also recall that the marginal product (*MP*) of a factor is the additional output that results from the use of one additional unit of that factor. By multiplying marginal revenue and marginal product we determine the marginal revenue product of the factor. [26] For example, if the factor's marginal product is 2 units and the firm's marginal revenue is $7.50, the factor's marginal revenue product is $15 ($2 \times \$7.50$).

We can now restate the condition for a firm to be maximizing its profits:

marginal revenue product (**MRP**) The extra revenue that results from using one unit more of a variable factor.

$$\begin{array}{c} \text{Marginal cost} \\ \text{of the factor} \end{array} = \underbrace{\begin{array}{c} \text{Marginal revenue product} \\ \text{of the factor} \end{array}}_{MP \,\times\, MR} \qquad (13\text{-}1)$$

This condition applies to *any* firm and any factor, in any market structure. In the special case of competitive goods and factor markets, however, we can simplify the equation. In competitive factor markets the marginal cost of the factor is simply the factor's price, since the firm can hire any amount of the factor at a given price. Call this factor

APPLYING ECONOMIC CONCEPTS 13-1

Rising Income Inequality in Canada and Other Developed Countries

There are many measures of income inequality. Some are based on the share of total income that accrues to different segments of the population, as shown in Figure 13-2. Others are based on the absolute income gap between high-income and low-income earners. In addition, researchers can choose to examine individual income or household income, and pre-tax income or after-tax income. However, all of these measures show that income inequality has been rising in most of the world's developed economies since the late 1980s.

The first accompanying figure shows one simple measure of income inequality in 2008 for selected members of the Organization for Economic Cooperation and Development (OECD). The measure for each country is the ratio of the 90th percentile income to the 10th percentile income, and it applies to households' disposable (after-tax) incomes. The 90th percentile income is the level of income such that 90 percent of households have incomes below that level, while the 10th percentile income is such that only 10 percent of households have income below it. In Mexico and Chile, for example, the 90th percentile income is roughly 9 times greater than the 10th percentile income. In Canada and Italy the ratio is 4.2, whereas in the Scandinavian countries the ratios are around 3. Though it is not shown in the figure, this measure of income inequality has been increasing for most of the OECD countries over the past 25 years.

A similar measure of income inequality is based on the gap between the *average* income of the richest 10 percent and the poorest 10 percent of individual income earners. In Canada in 2008, the average income of the top 10 percent of earners was $103 500 while the average income of the bottom 10 percent of earners was $10 260. The ratio was therefore just slightly over 10:1. In the early 1990s, the same ratio in Canada was 8:1, a considerable increase in this measure of income inequality.

The second figure shows the time-series paths for two different measures of income inequality in Canada since 1941. The top solid line shows the share of total pre-tax income (excluding capital gains) received by the top 10 percent of all earners; the top dashed line shows a new measure that replaced the old one in 2000. In 1941, 45 percent of all pre-tax income went to the richest 10 percent, but the fraction fell quickly and remained

between 30 and 40 percent until the late 1980s. Since then, however, the fraction has clearly been rising. The bottom solid line in the figure shows the share of total pre-tax income (excluding capital gains) accruing to the richest 1 percent of earners; the bottom dashed line is again a replacement measure beginning in 2000. The richest 1 percent's share of total pre-tax income has also been increasing since the late 1980s, after several decades of relative stability.

Three central questions arise from these data. First, what is the cause of growing income inequality? Second, why does income inequality matter? Third, what policies, if any, could governments use to slow or even reverse the recent trend? Much academic research has been focused on these questions. But since the ideas are both complex and controversial, we offer here no more than a brief outline of some of the possible answers.

Many economists think that the combination of increasing globalization and the continued development of information technology is contributing to rising income inequality. The greater use of information technology in the workplace means that individuals with those skills are in high demand by employers; the result is their growing *wage premium* relative to the earnings of workers who lack those skills. The ongoing process of globalization implies that firms can more easily locate

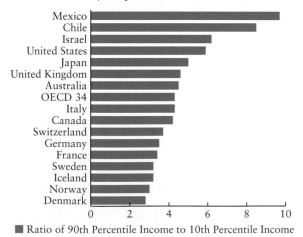

Income Inequality in OECD Countries, 2008

■ Ratio of 90th Percentile Income to 10th Percentile Income

their production facilities in developing countries where costs are low, and this is especially attractive for production that requires primarily unskilled workers. The result of these two forces in the developed countries is that skilled workers are working more hours at relatively high wages while unskilled workers are working less at relatively low wages. This ongoing *polarization* in the labour market tends to increase measured income inequality in the developed countries.

Why does this inequality matter? Recent research emphasizes the negative impact on *social cohesion* that comes from having very large income gaps between society's richest and poorest, and the lack of trust between members of society that develops when rich and poor see themselves as members of different communities. This research also notes the strong connection between income inequality and many social problems, including crime, children's educational performance, obesity, and mental illness. A recent book, *The Spirit Level* by Richard Wilkinson and Kate Pickett, has received considerable attention for showing these relationships across time for a large group of countries.

What can governments do to slow or reverse the trend of rising income inequality? Few economists would suggest that the process of globalization or the use of information technology are themselves undesirable, even though they may be partly responsible for changing market outcomes in ways that generate more income inequality. The policy challenge is to continue reaping their considerable benefits while designing policies that encourage individuals to acquire valuable skills and also ease their transition between regions and sectors in response to the inevitable adjustments that are part of a dynamic market economy. We will encounter some of these kinds of policies in Chapter 18 when we examine the Canadian taxation and expenditure system.

The causes and consequences of rising income equality are complex and not yet fully understood. The same is true of the policies that might be used to address it, and there is even disagreement about *whether* governments should actively try to reduce income inequality. Yet this issue is unlikely to disappear in the near future, so knowing its outlines will help you to assess the various aspects of the debate.

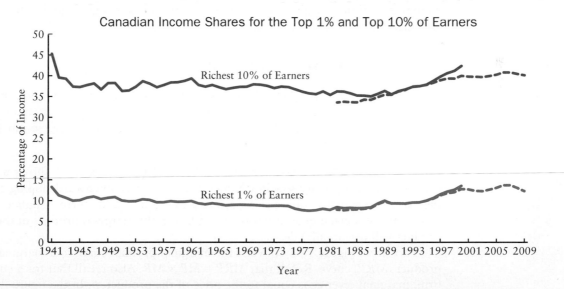

The international data used in this box are drawn from *Divided We Stand: Why Inequality Keeps Rising*, OECD, 2011. The Canadian time-series data are from A. Yalnizyan, "The Rise of Canada's Richest 1%," Canadian Centre for Policy Alternatives, December 2010. For a detailed treatment of the effects of income inequality on a variety of social indicators, see *The Spirit Level: Why Equality Is Better for Everyone*, R. Wilkinson and K. Pickett, Penguin, 2009.

price w. Also, we know that in competitive goods markets, the firm's MR is just the market price of the product, p. It follows that MRP is equal to $MP \times p$. Thus, the condition for profit maximization for a competitive firm is

$$w = MP \times p \qquad (13\text{-}2)$$

To check your understanding of Equation 13-2, consider an example. Suppose labour is available to the firm at a cost of $10 per hour ($w = \$10$). Suppose also that employing another hour of labour adds 3 units to output ($MP = 3$). Suppose further that any amount of output can be sold for $5 per unit ($p = \$5$). Thus, the additional hour of labour adds $15 to the firm's revenue but only $10 to its costs. In this case, the firm will increase profits by hiring more hours of labour.

Now suppose, however, that the last hour of labour hired by the firm has a marginal product of 1 unit of output and so adds only $5 to revenue. In this case, the firm can increase profits by reducing its use of labour.

Finally, suppose another hour of labour adds to revenue by $10. Now the firm cannot increase its profits by altering its use of labour in either direction.

> To maximize its profits, any firm must hire each factor of production to the point where the factor's marginal revenue product just equals the factor's price.

In Chapters 9 and 10, we saw the firm varying its output until the marginal cost of producing another unit was equal to the marginal revenue derived from selling that unit. Now we see the same profit-maximizing behaviour in terms of the firm's varying its inputs until the marginal cost of another unit of input is just equal to the extra revenue derived from selling that unit's marginal product.

The Firm's Demand Curve for a Factor

Now that we have determined the firm's profit-maximizing decision about how much of a factor to employ given a specific factor price (w) and a specific output price (p), we next want to derive the firm's *entire* demand curve for the factor. How much will the firm hire at *each* factor price?

The *MRP* Curve Is the Factor Demand Curve Part (i) of Figure 13-3 shows a marginal product curve, just as we saw in Chapter 7. The curve is downward sloping because of the law of (eventually) diminishing returns; as the firm adds further units of the variable factor to a given quantity of the fixed factor, the marginal product of the variable product will (eventually) decrease.

Part (ii) of Figure 13-3 converts the marginal product curve to a marginal revenue product (MRP) curve. Recall that $MRP = MP \times MR$. Also recall that for a competitive firm, marginal revenue is equal to the price of the product, p. In the figure the market price (and thus the firm's MR) is $5 per unit. The MRP curve, therefore, has the same shape as the MP curve. Notice that on the vertical axis, the MRP is simply the MP from part (i) multiplied by $5.

Equation 13-2 states that a profit-maximizing competitive firm will employ additional units of the factor up to the point at which the MRP equals the price of the factor. For example, in Figure 13-3, if the price of hiring one unit of the factor were $2000 per month, the profit-maximizing firm would employ 60 units of the factor. However, if hiring an extra unit of the factor cost $3000 per month, the firm would only choose to hire 45 units. It should be clear that since the MRP curve shows how many units of

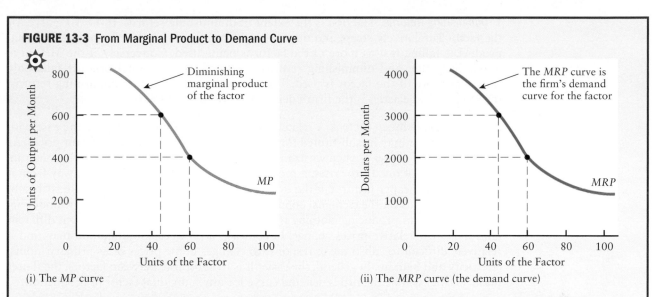

FIGURE 13-3 From Marginal Product to Demand Curve

(i) The *MP* curve

(ii) The *MRP* curve (the demand curve)

The law of diminishing marginal returns implies that firms have a negatively sloped demand curve for factors of production. In part (i), the *MP* curve for a factor is downward sloping because of the law of diminishing marginal returns. If the firm uses 60 units of the factor per month, the factor's *MP* will be 400 units of output per month. In part (ii), it is assumed that each unit of the firm's output can be sold at $5. If the firm uses 60 units of the factor per month, the factor's *MRP* is $2000 (400 units per month × $5 per unit). Since the *MRP* curve shows, for each separate factor price, how many units of the factor will be hired by a profit-maximizing firm, the *MRP* curve is the firm's demand curve for the factor.

Note that if the firm is not perfectly competitive in its product market, each additional unit of output produced leads to a decline in the product's price. In this case, the firm's *MR* decreases as output increases, and so the factor's *MRP* curve is steeper than the one shown here.

the factor will be hired at different factor prices, the factor's *MRP* curve is the firm's demand curve for the factor.

> **A competitive firm's demand curve for a factor is given by that factor's *MRP* curve.**

This logic applies equally to any factor of production. A profit-maximizing farmer will rent land up to the point where the marginal revenue product from an extra acre of land is just equal to the rental price for that acre of land. A profit-maximizing machine-tools manufacturer will use extra machines (capital) until the marginal revenue product from an extra machine just equals the price of using that machine. And a profit-maximizing paper mill will hire workers up to the point where the marginal revenue product of an extra worker is just equal to that worker's wage.

Elasticity of the Firm's Factor Demand Curve The elasticity of demand for a factor measures the *degree* of the response of the quantity demanded to a change in its price. The preceding sections have explained the *direction* of the response; that is, that quantity demanded is negatively related to price. But what determines the magnitude of the response? The answer, in a word, is *technology*. Figure 13-3 shows that a firm's demand curve for a factor of production (the factor's *MRP* curve) is the same shape as that factor's *MP* curve. The shape of the *MP* curve, in turn, is determined by the firm's technology. There are two aspects of the firm's technology that influence the elasticity of the factor demand curve.

1. Diminishing Returns. The first is the extent of diminishing returns. If the *MP* curve for the factor is relatively steep, and diminishing returns are therefore large, the marginal product is falling fast as more of the factor is being used. Conversely, if the *MP* curve is relatively flat, and diminishing returns are small, the marginal product falls only slowly as more of the factor is used. The larger the extent of the diminishing returns, the steeper (less elastic) is the firm's demand curve for that factor.

2. Substitution Between Factors. A related aspect of the firm's technology is the ease with which one factor may be substituted for others in response to changes in factor prices. As we first saw in Chapter 8 when we examined the *principle of substitution* in the long run, when the price of one factor rises, a profit-maximizing firm will substitute away from it and toward a cheaper factor. But the extent to which the firm is able to make such substitutions depends on the technical conditions of production. For example, by modifying its designs, a firm producing clothing may be easily able to substitute between different fabrics as their relative prices change. In contrast, a producer of aluminum may find it relatively difficult to substitute in response to changes in the prices of its primary inputs, electricity and bauxite. In general, the easier it is to substitute between factors, the flatter (more elastic) will be the firm's demand curve for any individual factor of production.

The Market Demand Curve for a Factor

We saw in Chapter 6 that the market demand curve for any good or service is simply the horizontal summation of all the individual consumers' demand curves. With factor demand curves, the same basic logic applies except for one important complication. As all firms hire more of any specific factor of production, the supplies of the goods produced by that factor increase and the prices of these products fall. This decline in product prices leads firms to increase their hiring of the factors by less than would otherwise occur. The result is that the *market* demand curve for any specific factor of production is *less elastic* than would be the case if we took a simple horizontal summation of the individual firms' factor demand curves.

An example will clarify this point. Consider a competitive furniture-building industry and the individual firms' demand for carpenters. Any one firm's production of furniture will have no significant effect on the equilibrium price of furniture, and so its hiring of carpenters similarly has no effect on the market price of furniture. But all furniture-building firms taken together *do* have an effect on the equilibrium price of furniture. As *all* such firms increase their hiring of carpenters, the total supply of furniture increases and the equilibrium price of furniture declines. As the price falls, each firm will reduce its hiring of carpenters, offsetting to some extent the initial increase in hiring.

> The market demand curve for any factor of production is less elastic than what would result from a simple horizontal summation of all the firms' demand curves for that factor.

Shifts of the Market Factor Demand Curve Why might the market demand curve for a factor shift? To answer this question, let's go back and think about what is happening at the level of the individual firms. If we know why individual firms' factor demand curves shift, we will also know why the *market* factor demand curve shifts.

Figure 13-3 on page 315 illustrated a firm's demand curve for a factor of production and showed that the factor's *MRP* curve was also the firm's demand curve for that factor. Since *MRP* is equal to *MP* times *MR,* there are two reasons why the demand curve for a factor can shift—because of a shift in the factor's *MP* curve or because of a change in firms' *MR*.

A Change in the Factor's Marginal Product. Anything that changes the marginal product of a factor will change the *MP* curve and therefore the *MRP* curve in Figure 13-3. Improvements in technology often increase the marginal product of factors of production, and thus lead to a rightward shift of the *MP* curve. For example, if better education increases the marginal product of labour, the *MP* curve for labour will shift to the right, firms' demand for labour will increase, and firms will hire more labour at any given wage.

A second way in which the marginal product of a factor can increase is if there are more units of *other factors* with which to work. An increase in the amount of physical capital, for example, will generally increase the marginal product of any given amount of labour. Suppose that Figure 13-3 shows the marginal product (and *MRP*) for labour under the assumption that the firm has a given stock of capital. If the firm now expands its capital stock by building a larger factory, the marginal product of any given amount of labour will increase, thus shifting the *MP* curve in part (i) to the right. The result will be that the *MRP* curve in part (ii) also shifts to the right, thus increasing the firm's demand for labour.

> Any increase in a factor's marginal product will lead to an increase in demand for that factor. Such an increase can come about through improvements in the quality of the factor or an increase in the amount of other factors of production.

A Change in Firms' Marginal Revenue. Anything that increases firms' marginal revenue will increase the *MRP* of a factor and thus lead to an increase in demand for that factor. For firms that operate in a competitive product market, an increase in marginal revenue is simply an increase in the market price of the product. In Figure 13-3, if the product price rises from $5 to $10, the *MRP* curve shifts to the right (even though the *MP* curve does not move). For imperfectly competitive firms, an increase in *MR* occurs if the demand curve faced by those firms shifts to the right. In both cases, the increase in *MR* leads to an increase in the demand for the factor.

> Anything that leads to an increase in demand for a product will lead to an increase in demand for the factors used to produce that product.

13.3 The Supply of Factors

When we consider the supply of any factor of production, we can consider supply at three different levels of aggregation:

- The amount supplied to the economy as a whole
- The amount supplied to a particular industry
- The amount supplied to a particular firm

To illustrate, consider your decision to seek employment—to supply your labour services to the labour market. You must make three general decisions. First, you must decide whether to supply your labour services at all, the alternative being not to seek employment. Your decision will influence the overall supply of labour to the economy (though only by a tiny amount). Second, once you have decided to supply your labour services, you must choose an industry and occupation. Your decision to seek employment in the telecommunications industry rather than the auto manufacturing industry influences the economy's allocation of labour across industries. Third, once you have decided to seek employment in a particular industry, you must choose which firms in that industry appeal to you. Your decision influences the allocation of labour across firms.

The elasticity of supply of a factor will normally be different at each of these levels of aggregation because the amount of *factor mobility* is different in each case. A given factor of production is often very mobile between firms within a given industry, less mobile between different industries, and even less mobile from the perspective of the entire economy. For example, an electrician may be very mobile between industries within a given city, and reasonably mobile between provinces, but it may be very difficult for that electrician to move to another country to find a job. In this section, we examine the relationship between factor mobility and the supply of factors of production. We start with the highest level of aggregation, the supply of each factor to the economy as a whole.

The Supply of Factors to the Economy

At any one time, the total supply of each factor of production is given. For example, in each country, the labour force is of a certain size, so much arable land is available, and there is a given stock of physical capital. However, these supplies can and do change. Sometimes the change is very gradual, as when climate change slowly turns arable land into desert or when medical advances reduce the rate of infant mortality and increase the rate of population growth, thereby eventually increasing the supply of adult labour. Sometimes the changes can be more rapid, as when a boom in business activity brings retired persons back into the labour force.

Physical Capital The capital stock in a country is the existing machines, factories, and equipment. Capital is a manufactured factor of production, and its total supply changes slowly. Each year, the stock of capital goods is diminished by the amount that becomes physically or economically obsolete and is increased by the amount of new investment by firms. But the stock of capital is so large that even when there is an investment boom the percentage change in the stock of capital will be tiny. On balance, the trend has been for the capital stock to grow from decade to decade over the past few centuries. We will consider the determinants of investment in physical capital in Chapter 15.

Land The total area of dry land in a country is almost completely fixed, but the supply of *arable* land is not. Considerable care and effort are required to sustain the productive power of land. If farmers earn low incomes, they may not provide the necessary care, and the land's suitability for growing crops may be destroyed within a short time. In contrast, high earnings from farming may provide the incentive to increase the supply of arable land by irrigation and other forms of reclamation.

Labour The number of people willing to work is called the labour force; the total number of hours they are willing to work is called the *supply of labour*. The supply of labour depends on three influences: the size of the population, the proportion of the population willing to work, and the number of hours that each individual wants to work. Each of these is partly influenced by economic forces.

Population. The population of a country varies over time, and these variations are influenced to some extent by economic forces. There is some evidence, for example, that the birthrate and the net immigration rate (immigration minus emigration) are higher in good economic times than in bad.

Labour-Force Participation. The proportion of the total population that is willing to work is called the *labour-force participation rate*. Economists also define participation rates for subgroups, such as women or youths. Participation rates vary in response to many influences, including changes in attitudes and tastes. The enormous rise in female participation rates that began in the 1960s, for example, has had a significant effect on the Canadian labour force.

Changes in real wages also play a role in determining the labour-force participation rate. A rise in the demand for labour, and an accompanying rise in the real wage, will lead to an increase in the proportion of the population willing to work. For example, in Alberta in recent years, a booming economy driven by high energy prices increased real wages up to the point that there was a notable increase in high-school dropout rates as some students chose instead to pursue employment in the labour market.

The significant increase in female labour-force participation that occurred between the 1960s and the 1990s had a significant effect on the growth of Canada's aggregate labour supply.

Hours per Person. The wage rate influences not only the number of people who want to work but also the number of hours that each person wants to work. When workers sell their labour services to employers, they are giving up leisure in order to gain income with which to buy goods. They can therefore be thought of as trading leisure for goods. A rise in the wage implies a change in the relative price of goods and leisure. An increase in the wage means that leisure becomes more expensive relative to goods, because each hour of leisure consumed is at the cost of more goods forgone.

It is not necessarily the case, however, that an increase in the wage increases the amount of hours worked. In fact, an increase in the wage generates both income and substitution effects (see Chapter 6). As the wage rises, the substitution effect leads the individual to work more hours (consume less leisure) because leisure is now relatively more expensive. The income effect of a higher wage, however, leads the individual to work fewer hours (consume more leisure). Because the two effects work in the opposite direction we are, in general, unsure how a rise in the wage will affect the number of hours an individual chooses to work.

The economy's total supplies of land, labour, and capital each respond to economic forces, but tend to change only gradually.

The Supply of Factors to a Particular Industry

Most factors have many uses. A given piece of land can be used to grow any one of several crops, or it can be subdivided for a housing development. A computer programmer living in the Ottawa Valley can work for one of many firms, for the government, or for Carleton University. A lathe can be used to make many different products, and it requires no adaptation when it is turned for one use or another.

> One industry can attract a factor away from another industry, even though the economy's total supply of that factor may be fixed. Thus, a factor's elasticity of supply to a particular industry is larger than its elasticity of supply to the entire economy.

factor mobility The ease with which a factor of production can move between firms, industries, occupations, or regions.

When we consider the supply of a factor for a particular use, the most important concept is **factor mobility**. A factor that shifts easily between uses in response to small changes in incentives is said to be *mobile*. Its supply to any one use will be elastic because a small increase in the price offered will attract many units of the factor from other uses. A factor that does not shift easily from one use to another, even in response to large changes in remuneration, is said to be *immobile*. It will be in inelastic supply in any one use because even a large increase in the price offered will attract only a small inflow from other uses. Generally, a factor is less mobile in the short run than in the long run.

> An important determinant of factor mobility is time: The longer the time interval, the easier it is for a factor to convert from one use to another.

Consider the factor mobility among particular uses for each of the three key factors of production.

The Mobility of Capital Some kinds of capital equipment—lathes, trucks, and computers, for example—can be shifted readily among firms, among industries, and even across different regions of the country. These are considered *mobile* capital. Other kinds of capital are quite immobile. For example, some plants and machinery are built for a specific purpose and are difficult, if not impossible, to modify for other purposes. Equipment of this type is immobile across uses, although it might be mobile in the sense that one firm could sell it to another. Factories designed for a specific purpose are immobile both across uses and across regions, though they could still be transferred from one owner to another.

The Mobility of Land Land, which is physically the least mobile of factors, is one of the *most* mobile in an economic sense. Consider agricultural land. In a given year, one crop can be harvested and a totally different crop can be planted. A farm on the outskirts of a growing city can be sold for subdivision and development on short notice. Once land is built on, however, its mobility is much reduced.

Although land is highly mobile among alternative uses, it is completely immobile as far as location is concerned. There is only so much land within a given distance of the centre of any city, and no increase in the price paid can induce further land to be located within that distance. This locational immobility has important consequences, including high prices for desirable locations and the tendency to build tall buildings to economize on the use of scarce land. It is no accident that the downtown cores of New York, Hong Kong, Toronto, Chicago, and many other large cities contain so many tall buildings.

The Mobility of Labour The supply of labour services usually requires the physical presence of the person who supplies it. Absentee landlords, while continuing to live in the place of their choice, can obtain income from land that is located in remote parts of the world. Similarly, investment can be shifted from iron mines in South Africa to mines in Labrador while the mine owners commute between Calgary and Hawaii. The same is true for some workers, such as designers or bookkeepers, who can work in one location and submit their work to clients in other locations. But almost all workers involved in manufacturing and most of those involved in serving the public in stores, restaurants, and so on must actually be present to supply their labour services to an employer. When a worker who is employed by a firm producing men's suits in Montreal decides instead to supply his or her labour services to a firm producing women's shoes in Winnipeg, the worker must physically travel to Winnipeg. This has an important consequence.

The high prices paid for land in the centre of large cities, where demand for land is highest, cannot lead to an increase in the quantity of land supplied because it is an immobile factor. The natural market response is the construction of very tall buildings, increasing the amount of office space supplied per unit of land.

> Because of the need for labour's physical presence when its services are provided for the production of many goods and services, non-monetary considerations are much more important for the supply of labour than for other factors of production.

People may be satisfied with or frustrated by the kind of work that they do, where they do it, the people with whom they do it, and the social status of their occupations. Because these considerations influence their decisions about what they will do with their labour services, they will not always move just because they could earn a higher wage.

Nevertheless, labour is mobile among industries, occupations, and regions in response to changes in the signals provided by wages and opportunities for employment. The ease with which such mobility occurs depends on many forces. For example, it is not difficult for a secretary to shift from one company to another in order to take a job in Edmonton instead of Regina, but it can be difficult for a secretary to become an editor, a model, a machinist, or a doctor within a short period of time. Workers who lack ability, training, or inclination find certain kinds of mobility difficult or impossible.

Some barriers to movement may be virtually insurmountable once a person's training has been completed. For example, it may be impossible for a farmer to become a surgeon or for a truck driver to become a professional athlete, even if the relative wage rates change greatly. However, the children of farmers, doctors, truck drivers, and athletes, when they are deciding how much education or training to obtain, are not nearly as limited in their choices as their parents, who have already completed their education and are settled in their occupations.

A cruise ship like this one is very mobile between firms but almost completely immobile between industries—it is very difficult to convert a cruise ship into any other kind of capital equipment.

The labour force as a whole is mobile, even though many individual members in it are not.

The Supply of Factors to a Particular Firm

Most firms employ only a very small proportion of the economy's total supply of each factor. As a result, they can usually obtain their factors at the going market price. This is true for labour, capital, and land. For example, a commercial bank that is hoping to expand its economics department can hire an extra economist and it will need to pay the going wage (or salary) to attract that economist. A car manufacturer can purchase new robotics equipment and will pay the market price to get it. And a rancher can buy more land at the going market price. In each case the firm's actions will have no effect on the market price for the factors of production.

Individual firms generally face perfectly elastic supply curves for factors, even though the supply for the economy as a whole may be quite inelastic.

| 13.4 The Operation of Factor Markets

Once you have mastered the basic analysis of demand and supply in Chapters 3, 4, and 5, the determination of the price, quantity, and income of a factor in a single market poses no new problems. Figure 13-4 shows a competitive market for a factor. In both parts of the figure, the intersection of the demand and supply curves determines the factor's price and the quantity of the factor employed. The total market income earned by the factor is given by the equilibrium price times the equilibrium quantity.

Changes in factor markets can occur either because of a change in demand for the factor or because of a change in the supply of the factor, or both. Part (i) of Figure 13-4 illustrates a case in which an increase in demand for a factor leads to a rise in that factor's price and an increase in total income earned by that factor. What could cause such a change? Recall that the market demand curve for any factor comes from the many firms' *MRP* curves for that factor. An increase in the productivity of that factor (or an increase in demand for the products using that factor) would lead to a rightward shift in the *MRP* curves and thus to an increase in the market demand for the factor. Indeed, increases in productivity account for a gradual but ongoing increase in the demand for most factors of production.

Part (ii) of Figure 13-4 shows that an increase in the supply of some factor of production leads to a decline in that factor's equilibrium price and an increase in the quantity of the factor employed. (The total income earned by the factor may rise or fall,

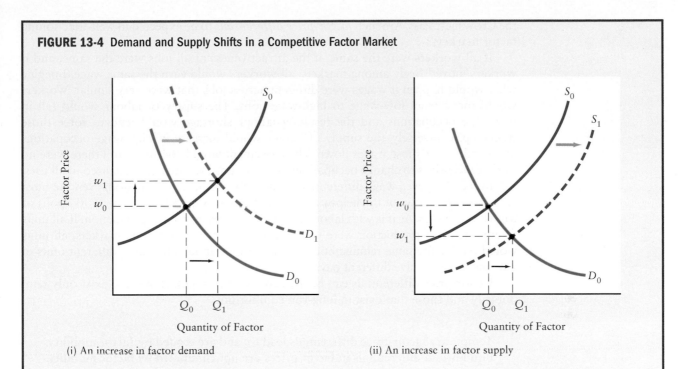

FIGURE 13-4 Demand and Supply Shifts in a Competitive Factor Market

(i) An increase in factor demand   (ii) An increase in factor supply

Equilibrium factor prices and quantities are determined by the demand for and supply of factors. In both parts of the figure, the initial equilibrium is determined by D_0 and S_0. The equilibrium factor price is w_0 and the equilibrium quantity of the factor is Q_0.

In part (i), an increase in demand for the factor shifts the demand curve to D_1. The equilibrium factor price rises to w_1 and quantity increases to Q_1. Since both price and quantity have increased, the total income earned by the factor clearly increases.

In part (ii), an increase in the supply of the factor shifts the supply curve to S_1. The equilibrium factor price falls to w_1 but the quantity increases to Q_1. Since price falls but quantity rises, the effect on total factor income is unclear. If demand for the factor is inelastic, total factor income will fall; if demand is elastic, total factor income will rise.

depending on the elasticity of demand for the factor.) Though the supply of any factor to a specific firm may change suddenly, the supply to the economy as a whole tends to change very gradually. The labour force grows slowly, physical capital accumulates gradually as firms build more capital equipment, and the amount of arable land changes slowly as new land is cleared or reclaimed.

We now go on to explore three issues relating to factor pricing. First, what explains the differences in payments received by different units of the same factor? For example, why do some workers get paid more than others? Second, what is the effectiveness of government policies designed to reduce these differences? Finally, we explore the important concept of *economic rent*.

Differentials in Factor Prices

Airline pilots typically get paid more than auto mechanics, and a hectare of land in downtown Calgary rents for much more than a hectare of land 150 kilometres away in the Crowsnest Pass. Are such *factor-price differentials* to be expected in well-functioning factor markets?

If all workers were the same, if the attractiveness of all jobs were the same, and if workers moved freely among markets, all workers would earn the same wage. Imagine what would happen if wages were different across jobs that were very similar. Workers would move from low-wage to high-wage jobs. The supply of labour would fall in low-wage occupations and the resulting labour shortage would tend to force those wages up. Conversely, the supply of labour would increase in high-wage occupations and would force those wages down. The movement would continue until there were no further incentives to change occupations—that is, until wages were equalized in all uses.

In fact, however, wage differentials commonly occur, as is clear from even the most cursory examination of the help-wanted ads in any newspaper or on the Workopolis or Monster websites. As it is with labour, so it is with other factors of production. If all units of any factor of production were identical and moved freely among markets, all units would receive the same remuneration in equilibrium. In fact, however, different units of any one factor receive different payments.

Factor-price differentials can be divided into two types: those that exist only temporarily and those that exist in long-run equilibrium.

> **Temporary factor-price differentials lead to, and are eroded by, factor mobility. Equilibrium differentials in factor prices are not eliminated by factor mobility.**

Temporary Differentials Some factor-price differentials reflect temporary disturbances, such as the growth of one industry or the decline of another. The differentials themselves lead to the movement of factors, and such movements in turn act to eliminate the differentials.

Consider the effect on factor prices of a rise in the demand for air transport when there is no change in the demand for rail transport. Specifically, consider the wages

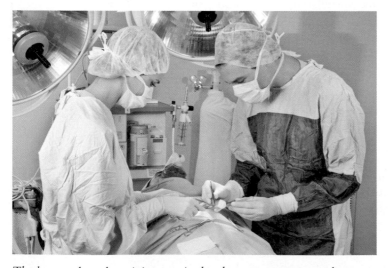

The long and costly training required to become a surgeon reduces the supply of surgeons relative to many other occupations. As a result, surgeons typically earn very high incomes. This is an equilibrium wage differential.

for the individuals who organize and handle freight shipments in the two industries. The airline industry's demand for workers increases while there is no change in demand for workers in the railway industry. Wages will rise in the airline industry and create a factor-price differential. The differential in wages causes a net movement of workers away from the railway industry and toward the airline industry, and this movement causes the wage differentials to lessen and eventually to disappear. This adjustment process is illustrated in Figure 13-5. How long this process takes depends on how easily workers can be reallocated from one industry to the other—that is, on the degree of factor mobility.

The behaviour that causes the erosion of temporary differentials is summarized in the hypothesis of the *maximization of net*

FIGURE 13-5 The Creation and Erosion of Temporary Factor-Price Differentials

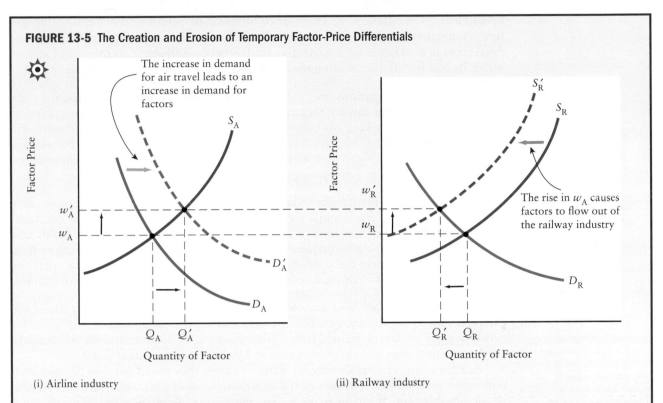

(i) Airline industry

(ii) Railway industry

The mobility of factors leads to the erosion of temporary differentials in factor prices. The two figures show the markets for some factor of production (land, labour, or capital) in the airline and railway industries. Suppose the initial equilibrium has the factor receiving the same price in both industries $(w_A = w_R)$. Q_A units are employed in the airline industry, and Q_R units are employed in the railway industry.

An increase in demand for air travel leads to an increase in demand for factors in the airline industry. The demand curve shifts to D_A' and factor prices in that industry rise to w_A'. As factor prices in the airline industry rise, factors leave the railway industry and enter the airline industry. This flow of factors is a leftward shift of S_R to S_R' and a movement upward along S_A. There is a reduction of factors employed in the railway industry and an increase in factors employed in the airline industry. The flow of factors stops when factor prices are again equalized, $w_A' = w_R'$.

advantage: The owners of factors of production will allocate those factors to uses that maximize the net advantages to themselves, taking both monetary and non-monetary rewards into consideration. If net advantages were higher in occupation *A* than in occupation *B*, factors would move from *B* to *A*. The increased supply in *A* and the reduced supply in *B* would drive factor earnings down in *A* and up in *B* until net advantages would be equalized, after which no further movement would occur. This analysis gives rise to the prediction of *equal net advantage*: In equilibrium, units of each kind of factor of production will be allocated among alternative possible uses in such a way that the net advantages in all uses are equalized.

> A change in the relative price of a factor between two uses will lead to a shift of some units of that factor to the use for which relative price has increased. This factor mobility will, in turn, tend to reduce the differential in relative prices.

Equilibrium Differentials Some factor-price differentials persist without generating any forces that eliminate them. These equilibrium differentials can be explained by intrinsic differences in the factors themselves and, for labour, by differences in the cost of acquiring skills and by different non-monetary advantages of different occupations.

Intrinsic Differences. If various units of a factor have different characteristics, the price that is paid may differ among these units. If a high level of numeracy is required to accomplish a task, workers who are good at arithmetic and other kinds of math will earn more than workers who are not so good with numbers. If land is to be used for agricultural purposes, highly fertile land will earn more than poor land. These differences will persist even in long-run equilibrium.

Acquired Differences. If the fertility of land can be increased only by costly methods, then more fertile land must command a higher price than less fertile land. If it did not, land-owners would not incur the costs of improving fertility. The same principle holds true for labour since it is costly to acquire most skills. For example, an engineer must train for some time, and unless the earnings of engineers remain sufficiently above what can be earned in occupations requiring fewer skills, people will not incur the cost of training.

Compensating Differentials. Whenever working conditions differ across jobs, workers will earn different equilibrium wages. Because such factor-price differentials *compensate* for non-monetary aspects of the job, they are commonly called **compensating differentials**; they were introduced into economics almost 250 years ago by Adam Smith.

Academic researchers commonly earn less than they could earn in the world of commerce and industry because of the substantial non-monetary advantages of academic employment. If chemists were paid the same in both sectors, many chemists would prefer academic to industrial jobs. Excess demand for industrial chemists and excess supply of academic chemists would then force chemists' wages up in industry and down in academia until the two types of jobs seemed equally attractive on balance.

Compensating differentials also exist in the regional earnings of otherwise identical factors. People who work in remote logging or mining areas are paid more than are people who do jobs requiring similar skills in large cities. Without higher pay, not enough people would be willing to work at sometimes dangerous jobs in unattractive or remote locations.

compensating differential A difference in the payment to a factor of production (usually labour) across two jobs to compensate the factor for differences in non-monetary aspects of the two jobs.

Policies to Promote "Pay Equity"

The distinction between temporary and equilibrium factor-price differentials raises an important consideration for policy. Trade unions and governments sometimes have explicit policies about earnings differentials and seek to eliminate them in the name of equity. The success of such policies depends to a great extent on the kind of differential that is being attacked. An important general lesson from this experience is the following: Policies that attempt to eliminate *temporary* differentials may be successful in speeding up what may otherwise be a slow adjustment process. But policies aimed at eliminating *equilibrium* differentials will encounter several difficulties.

Canadian governments in the recent past have introduced legislation to redress male–female wage differentials that appear to exist *only* because of discrimination in the labour market. We will discuss labour-market discrimination in more detail in Chapter 14, but for now think of discrimination between men and women who have the same qualifications and are in the same jobs. As the social norms that sustain these discriminatory forces change, so too will the wage differentials. But the adjustment may be very gradual, as the norms themselves will change only gradually. Canadian *pay-equity* legislation has been designed to speed this adjustment and, in the process, reduce the underlying discriminatory forces. These policies have been successful in reducing male–female wage differentials in situations where the men and women concerned are equally qualified and are in the same jobs.

Other government pay-equity legislation is less successful because it attempts to reduce or eliminate *equilibrium* wage differentials. Some pay-equity legislation is based on the principle of *equal pay for work of equal value*, an idea that is very difficult to implement in practice. Such policy is designed to eliminate the wage differentials that exist between workers *in different jobs* but who are deemed to have approximately the same skills and responsibilities. For example, the policy might require that a nurse with 10 years of experience receive the same salary as a teacher with 10 years of experience. Whatever the social value of such laws, they run into trouble whenever they require equal pay for jobs that have different non-monetary advantages or require different amounts of training.

Jobs with unpleasant working conditions usually pay higher wages than more pleasant jobs requiring the same skills. Such differences in wages are called "compensating differentials." Any policy that attempts to eliminate these differentials is likely to be ineffective.

> **Policies that seek to eliminate equilibrium factor-price differentials without consideration of what causes them or how they affect the supply of the factor often have perverse results.**

To illustrate the nature of the problem encountered by such legislation, consider the example of two types of construction workers—those who work mostly indoors doing home and building renovations, and those who work mostly outdoors on bridges or the exteriors of buildings. Suppose these two jobs demand equal skills, training, and everything else that is taken into account in a decision about what constitutes work of equal value. But in a city with a harsh climate, the outside construction job is less pleasant than the inside construction job. In the absence of pay-equity legislation, the wage for outside workers would exceed that for inside workers, and this would be an equilibrium wage differential. If legislation now requires equal pay for both jobs, there will be a shortage of people who are willing to work outside and an excess of people who want to work inside. Employers will seek ways to attract outside workers. Higher pensions, shorter hours, and longer holidays may be offered. If these are allowed, they will achieve the desired result but will defeat the original purpose of equalizing the monetary benefits of the inside and outside jobs. If the jobs are unionized or if the government prevents such "cheating," the shortage of workers for outside jobs will remain.

Economic Rent

One of the most important concepts in economics is that of *economic rent*.

A mobile factor must earn a certain amount in its present use to prevent it from moving to another use—the great nineteenth-century economist Alfred Marshall called this amount the factor's **transfer earnings**, but most economists today would simply call

transfer earnings The minimum payment required by a factor in order to prevent it from leaving to other uses.

it the factor's opportunity cost. If there were no non-monetary advantages in alternative uses, as is typically the case for land and capital, the factor would have to earn the same payment it could earn elsewhere to keep it in its current use.

For labour, however, the non-monetary advantages of various jobs are important. Labour must earn enough in each use to equate the total advantages—both monetary and non-monetary—among various jobs. For example, in order to remain in a job that is dirty or unsafe, workers will require a higher wage than in other jobs that are otherwise comparable. As a result, the total advantage of the unsafe job equals the total advantage of some alternative job.

A factor's transfer earnings are the amount it needs in order to remain in its current use. Any amount that the factor earns *above* this is called **economic rent**. Economic rent is analogous to economic profit as a surplus over the opportunity cost of capital. Here are three examples:

economic rent The excess of total earnings over the minimum necessary to prevent a factor from moving to another use.

1. Consider a farmer who grows wheat and earns $1000 per hectare. She has calculated that if her earnings fall to $900 per hectare, she will switch to growing barley instead, her next best alternative. In this case, each hectare of land growing wheat is earning $100 of economic rent.

2. A famous actor earns $15 million per year. He decides that his next best alternative to acting is appearing in TV commercials, in which case he would earn $5 million per year. He is earning $10 million per year of economic rent.

3. An individual has invested $300 000 of financial capital into a restaurant and currently earns a 20 percent annual return—investment income of $60 000 annually. The next best alternative investment (with similar risk) can earn a 15 percent return, or $45 000 annually. The $300 000 of capital is thus earning economic rent equal to $15 000 per year. In this case, rent is just another name for profit in the economist's sense of the term.

The concept of economic rent is crucial for predicting the effects that changes in earnings have on the movement of factors among alternative uses. However, the terminology is confusing because economic rent is often simply called rent, which can of course also mean the price paid to hire something, such as a machine, a piece of land, or an apartment. How the same term came to be used for these two different concepts is explained in *Lessons from History 13-1*.

How Much of Factor Earnings Is Rent? In most cases, as in the three previous examples, economic rent makes up part of the factor's total earnings. From the definitions just given, however, note that total earnings for any factor are the sum of its transfer earnings and its economic rent.

> **A factor's transfer earnings plus its economic rent equals its total earnings.**

But *how much* of total earnings is economic rent? A different but related question is, How much would the factor price have to fall before the factor left its current use?

The possibilities are illustrated in Figure 13-6. When supply is perfectly elastic, as in part (i), the factor is extremely mobile between various uses. In this case, all of the factor's income is transfer earnings and so none of it is economic rent. If any lower price is offered, nothing whatsoever will be supplied since all units of the factor will transfer to some other use.

LESSONS FROM HISTORY 13-1

David Ricardo and "Economic Rent"

In the early nineteenth century, there was a public debate about the high price of wheat in England. The high price was causing great hardship because bread was a primary source of food for the working class. Some people argued that wheat had a high price because landlords were charging high rents to tenant farmers. Some of those who held this view advocated restricting the rents that landlords could charge.

David Ricardo (1772–1823), a great British economist who was one of the originators of Classical economics, argued that the situation was exactly the reverse. The price of wheat was high, he said, because there was a shortage, caused by the Napoleonic Wars. Because wheat was profitable to produce, there was keen competition among farmers to obtain land on which to grow wheat. This competition in turn forced up the rental price of wheat land. Ricardo advocated removing the existing tariff on wheat so that plentiful imported wheat could come into the country. The increase in imports would then increase the supply of wheat in England and lower its price. This would then reduce the rent on land.

The essentials of Ricardo's argument were these: The supply of land was fixed. Land was regarded as having only one use, the growing of wheat. Nothing had to be paid to prevent land from transferring to a different use because it had no other use. No landowner would leave land idle as long as some return could be obtained by renting it out. Therefore, all the payment to land—that is, rent in the ordinary sense of the word—was a surplus over and above what was necessary to keep it in its present use.

Given a fixed supply of land, the price of land depended on the demand for land, which depended in turn on the price of wheat. Rent, the term for the payment for the use of land, thus became the term for a surplus payment to a factor over and above what was necessary to keep it in its present use.

Later, two facts were realized. First, land often had alternative uses, and, from the point of view of any one use, part of the payment made to land would necessarily have to be paid to keep it in that use. Second, factors of production other than land also often earned a surplus over and above what was necessary to keep them in their present use. This surplus is now called *economic rent*, whether the factor is land, labour, or a piece of capital equipment.

David Ricardo was the first economist to clarify the connection between factor earnings and economic rent.

When supply is perfectly inelastic, as in part (iii), the same quantity is supplied whatever the price. Evidently, the quantity supplied does not decrease, no matter how low the price goes. This inelasticity indicates that the factor has no alternative use, and thus requires no minimum payment to keep it in its present use. In this case, there are no transfer earnings and so the whole of the payment is economic rent.

The more usual situation is that of an upward-sloping supply curve, as shown in part (ii) of Figure 13-6. A rise in the factor's price serves the allocative function of attracting more units of the factor into the market in question, but the same rise provides additional economic rent to all units of the factor that are *already employed*. We know that the extra pay that is going to the units already employed is economic rent because the owners of these units were willing to supply them at the previous lower price.

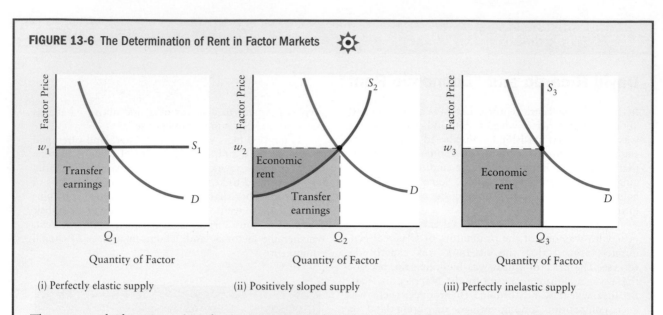

FIGURE 13-6 The Determination of Rent in Factor Markets

(i) Perfectly elastic supply   (ii) Positively sloped supply   (iii) Perfectly inelastic supply

The amount of a factor's earnings that is economic rent depends on the mobility (and thus on the elasticity of supply) of the factor. In each case, the equilibrium is determined by the intersection of the demand and supply curves, and total factor earnings are given by factor price times quantity, wQ.

In part (i), supply is perfectly elastic, indicating that even a slightly lower factor price would cause the factor to leave. None of the earnings are economic rent; all are the factor's transfer earnings.

In part (ii), supply is positively sloped, indicating that more units of the factor will be supplied at a higher price. The area below the supply curve is the amount needed to keep Q_2 units of the factor in its current use—this area is the factor's transfer earnings. The red shaded area above the supply curve is economic rent.

In part (iii), supply is perfectly inelastic, indicating that the factor has no other uses. In this case, transfer earnings are zero and all of the factor's earnings are economic rent.

The production and sale of oil (and natural gas) in Alberta in the past few years provides a good example of the relationship between economic rent and market prices. In Canada, natural resources are owned by the provinces, and oil producers must pay a share of their revenues as *royalties* to the government of the province where the resources are located. Alberta's supply curve for oil is upward sloping, as in part (ii) of Figure 13-6. As the market price for oil rises, production from wells that were not profitable at lower prices comes on-line and producers therefore increase the quantity of barrels supplied. For these *marginal* barrels of oil, the market price is just equal to the transfer earnings; there are no economic rents earned on these units. But the increase in market price does generate pure economic rent for those output levels that were already being produced at lower prices; these units were being produced anyway (at lower prices), and the rise in market price simply increases the rents earned by the producer. These economic rents in Alberta's oil industry account for a considerable fraction of that province's increase in income in recent years.

Various Perspectives on Economic Rent The proportion of a given factor payment that is economic rent varies from situation to situation. We cannot point to a factor of production and assert that some fixed fraction of its income is always its economic rent. The proportion of its earnings that is rent depends on its alternatives.

Consider first a narrowly defined use of a given factor—say, its use by a particular firm. From that firm's point of view, the factor will be highly mobile, as it could readily move to another firm in the same industry. The firm must pay the going wage or risk losing that factor. From the perspective of the single firm, a large proportion of the payment made to a factor is needed to prevent it from transferring to another use. Thus, only a small portion of its payment is rent.

Now consider a more broadly defined use—for example, the factor's use in an entire industry. From the industry's point of view, the factor is less mobile because it would be more difficult for it to gain employment quickly outside the industry. From the perspective of the particular *industry* (rather than the specific *firm* within the industry), a larger proportion of the payment to a factor is economic rent.

From the even more general perspective of a particular *occupation*, mobility is likely to be even less, and the proportion of the factor payment that is economic rent is likely to be more. It may be easier, for example, for a carpenter to move from the construction industry to the furniture industry than to retrain to be a computer programmer.

Increases in the price of oil that are not needed to increase the quantity supplied generate economic rents for producers. For example, if the owner of this well is only willing to operate it when the price of oil is $35 per barrel or higher, then any price above that level generates some economic rent for the producer.

> As the perspective moves from a narrowly defined use of a factor to a more broadly defined use of a factor, the mobility of the factor decreases; as mobility decreases, the share of the factor payment that is economic rent increases.

Consider how this relationship applies to the often controversial large salaries that are received by some highly specialized types of workers, such as movie stars and professional athletes. These performers have a unique style and a talent that cannot be duplicated, whatever the training. The earnings that they receive are mostly economic rent from the viewpoint of the occupation: These performers generally enjoy their occupations and would pursue them for much less than the high remuneration that they actually receive.

For example, Sidney Crosby would probably have chosen hockey over other alternatives even at a much lower salary. However, because of Crosby's amazing skills as a hockey player, most hockey teams would pay handsomely to have him on their rosters, and he is able to command a high salary from the team for which he does play. From the perspective of the individual firm, the Pittsburgh Penguins, most of Crosby's salary is required to keep him from switching to another team and hence is not economic rent. From the point of view of the hockey "industry," however, much of his salary is economic rent.

Notice also that Sidney Crosby's salary is largely determined by the demand for his services. The supply is perfectly inelastic—no one else has his particular combination of skills. So the market-clearing price is determined by the position of the demand curve.

A Final Word

This chapter has examined the operation of factor markets. You should now be able to answer the questions that we posed in the opening paragraph. Here are some of the key points for two of those questions.

What explains why neurosurgeons usually are paid more than family doctors? Part of the answer is that to be a neurosurgeon requires more years of costly specialized training than that needed to be a family doctor. Since that extra training is costly and time-consuming, it is not surprising that fewer people are willing or able to become neurosurgeons than family doctors. This lower supply for neurosurgeons, other things being equal, leads to a higher wage.

Why does a hectare of farmland in Northern Saskatchewan rent for far less than a hectare of land in downtown Toronto? To answer this, just think about the alternative uses for the farm land, and compare them with the alternative uses for the hectare in downtown Toronto. The hectare of farmland has very few alternative uses. Or, more correctly, it has many alternative uses, but there is little demand to use that particular piece of land to build a skyscraper, shopping mall, or baseball stadium. But one hectare of land in downtown Toronto has many alternative uses—there always seems to be demand for additional space for parking garages, office buildings, retail stores, and many other things. Since the piece of farmland in Saskatchewan must stay where it is, its rental price is determined by demand. Since there is little demand for the land, its rental price is low. Similarly, the land in downtown Toronto cannot move anywhere, and so its rental price is determined by demand. And since there is lots of demand for a hectare in downtown Toronto, its rental price is high.

Having learned about factor markets in general, we are now ready to examine some specific factor markets. In Chapter 14, we examine some details about labour markets, such as minimum wages, discrimination, and labour unions. In Chapter 15, we examine capital markets and the interest rate.

SUMMARY

13.1 Income Distribution

LO 1

- The functional distribution of income refers to the shares of total national income going to each of the major factors of production; it focuses on sources of income. The size distribution of income refers to the shares of total national income going to various groups of households; it focuses only on the amount of income, not its source.

- Canada has considerable inequality in the distribution of pre-tax income. The poorest fifth of families currently receives 1.0 percent of aggregate pre-tax income; the richest fifth receives 52.6 percent. Canada's tax-and-transfer system reduces this inequality modestly.

13.2 The Demand for Factors

LO 2

- A firm's decisions on how much to produce and how to produce it imply demands for factors of production, which are said to be derived from the demand for goods they are used to produce.
- A profit-maximizing firm will hire units of a factor until the last unit adds as much to revenue as it does to cost. Thus, the marginal revenue product of the factor will be equated with that factor's marginal cost.

- When the firm is a price taker in factor markets, the marginal cost of the factor is its price per unit. When the firm sells its output in a competitive market, the marginal revenue product is the factor's marginal product multiplied by the market price of the output.

- A price-taking firm's demand for a factor is negatively sloped because the law of diminishing returns implies that the marginal product of a factor declines as more of that factor is employed (with other inputs held constant).

- The demand for a factor will increase if the factor becomes more productive or if the price of the product increases.

13.3 The Supply of Factors

LO 3

- The total supply of each factor is fixed at any moment but varies over time. The supply of labour depends on the size of the population, the participation rate, and the number of hours that people want to work.
- A rise in the wage rate has a substitution effect, which tends to induce more work, and an income effect, which tends to induce less work (more leisure consumed).

- The supply of a factor to a particular industry or occupation is more elastic than its supply to the whole economy because one industry can bid units away from other industries.
- The elasticity of supply to a particular use depends on factor mobility, which tends to be greater the longer the time allowed for a reaction to take place.

13.4 The Operation of Factor Markets

LO 4, 5

- Factor-price differentials often occur in competitive markets. Temporary differentials in the earnings of different units of factors of production induce factor movements that eventually remove the differentials. Equilibrium differentials reflect differences among units of factors as well as non-monetary benefits of different jobs; they can persist indefinitely.
- Factors will be allocated between uses to generate the greatest net advantage to their owners, allowing for both the monetary and non-monetary advantages of a particular employment.

- Some amount must be paid to a factor to prevent it from moving to another use. This amount is the factor's transfer earnings. Economic rent is the difference between that amount and a factor's total earnings.
- Whenever the supply curve is positively sloped, part of the total payment going to a factor is needed to prevent it from moving to another use, and part of it is economic rent. The more narrowly defined the use, the larger the fraction that is transfer earnings and the smaller the fraction that is economic rent.

KEY CONCEPTS

Functional distribution and size distribution of income
Derived demand for a factor
Marginal product (*MP*)
Marginal revenue product (*MRP*)

The determinants of elasticity of factor demand
Factor mobility
Temporary versus equilibrium factor-price differentials

Equal net advantage
Transfer earnings
Economic rent

STUDY EXERCISES

MyEconLab Save Time. Improve Results Make the grade with MyEconLab: Study Exercises marked in red can be found on MyEconLab. You can practise them as often as you want, and most feature step-by-step guided instructions to help you find the right answer.

1. The table below shows the size distribution of income for Fantasyland.

Household Income Rank	Percentage of Aggregate Income	Cumulative Total
Lowest fifth	6.8	—
Second fifth	14.1	—
Third fifth	21.5	—
Fourth fifth	26.2	—
Highest fifth	31.4	—

a. Compute the cumulative percentage of total income. Fill in the table.
b. On a scale diagram, with the percentage of households on the vertical axis and the percentage of aggregate income on the horizontal axis, plot the Lorenz curve for Fantasyland.
c. How does the diagram show the extent of income inequality in Fantasyland?
d. Now suppose Fantasyland introduces a system that redistributes income from higher-income households to lower-income households. How would this affect the Lorenz curve?

2. According to *The Globe and Mail*, the fastest-growing small businesses in Canada in 2011 were

a. specialty clothes manufacturing
b. health practitioners
c. accounting and bookkeeping
d. computer-software design
e. machinery and equipment repair
f. architectural services

In each case, list two derived demands that you predict will be increasing as a result, and explain your reasoning.

3. Fill in the blanks to make the following statements correct.

a. Marginal revenue product is calculated by multiplying _____ and _____.
b. Marginal revenue product represents the addition to a firm's total revenue as a result of _____.
c. To maximize its profits, a firm will hire all units of a factor that have a(n) _____ greater than or equal to its _____.
d. To maximize its profits, any firm will hire each factor of production to the point where the factor's _____ equals the _____.

4. Fill in the blanks to make the following statements correct.

a. The *MRP* curve for a factor is the same as the firm's _____ for that factor.
b. Demand for a factor will be relatively _____ if the marginal product declines rapidly as more of that factor is used.
c. Other things being equal, if the demand for a product that a factor is used to produce is relatively inelastic, the demand for that factor will be relatively _____.
d. An increase in the price at which a competitive firm sells its product leads the firm's demand curve for its factor to _____.
e. If a technological improvement leads every unit of a given factor to produce 10 percent more output than previously, the _____ curve will _____ and thus the firm's demand curve for the factor will _____.

5. Other things being equal, how would you expect each of the following events to affect the size distribution of after-tax income?

a. An increase in unemployment
b. Rapid population growth in an already crowded city
c. An increase in food prices relative to other prices
d. An increase in employment-insurance benefits and premiums
e. Elimination of the personal income-tax exemption for interest earned within an RRSP or TFSA

6. The Apple Pie Factory produces apple pies. The firm sells its product and hires its workers in competitive markets. The market price (p) for a pie is $4 and the wage rate ($w$) is $10 per hour. The table below shows the total hourly production (Q) for varying amounts of workers (L). (Remember that for a price-taking firm, $p = MR$.)

L	Q	w	p	MP	MRP
4	40	—	—		
5	48	—	—		
6	55	—	—		
7	61	—	—		
8	66	—	—		
9	70	—	—		
10	73	—	—		
11	75	—	—		
12	76	—	—		

a. Fill in the p and w columns.
b. Calculate the *MP* and the *MRP* for each amount of labour employed. Put the numbers between the rows.

c. What is the logic of the firm's profit-maximizing condition for hiring labour?

d. How many workers should this profit-maximizing firm hire?

7. Refer back to the production schedule for the Apple Pie Factory in Question 6. In this question we will derive the firm's demand curve for labour.

    a. On a diagram, with *MRP* on the vertical axis and the number of workers on the horizontal axis, plot the *MRP* curve.

    b. If the wage is $10 per hour, how many workers will be hired? Why?

    c. If the wage is $5 per hour, how many workers will be hired? Why?

    d. If the wage is $20 per hour, how many workers will be hired? Why?

    e. Explain why the *MRP* curve is the firm's factor demand curve.

8. The diagram below shows the market for fast-food workers in British Columbia.

    a. The supply curve is upward sloping. If the wage in this industry rises, where do the extra workers come from?

    b. Suppose there is a significant decrease in demand for fast food. How is this likely to affect the earnings of fast-food workers? Show this in the diagram.

    c. Now suppose new legislation bans the assignment of homework to high school students. As a result, more students look for jobs in the fast-food industry. How will this affect the labour market for fast-food workers? Show this in the diagram.

    d. What will be the effect on total earnings in the fast-food industry from the change in part (c)? On what does the answer depend?

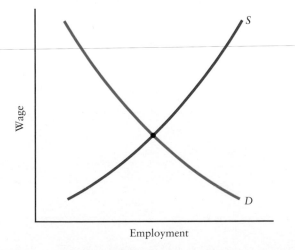

Employment

9. The three following diagrams show the supply of luxury ocean liners at three different levels of aggregation—the entire world, a particular country, and a particular firm.

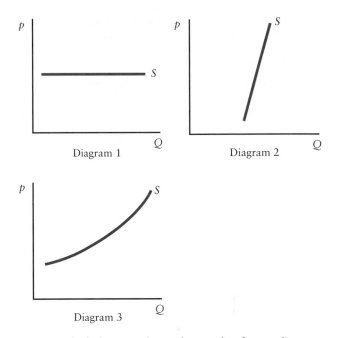

Diagram 1

Diagram 2

Diagram 3

a. Which diagram shows the supply of ocean liners to the world as whole? Explain its elasticity.

b. Which diagram shows the supply of ocean liners to Canada? Explain its elasticity.

c. Which diagram shows the supply of ocean liners to an individual Canadian firm? Explain its elasticity.

d. What is the general relationship between factor mobility and the elasticity of factor supply?

10. In the text we argued that temporary factor-price differentials tend to be eroded by factor mobility. This question requires you to think about this process. Consider the two markets for sheet-iron workers and steel-pipe workers in the same region. Suppose both markets are competitive. We begin in a situation in which both sheet-iron workers and steel-pipe workers earn $20 per hour. Assume that workers can switch easily between the two jobs.

    a. Draw diagrams showing the supply and demand for labour in each market.

    b. Now suppose there is a sharp increase in the demand for steel pipe. Explain what happens in the market for steel-pipe workers.

    c. If the employment of steel-pipe workers increased in part (b), explain where the extra workers came from.

    d. What effect does the event in part (b) have on the market for sheet-iron workers?

    e. What is the long-run effect of the shock on the relative wages in the two types of jobs?

11. How much of the following payments for factor services is likely to be economic rent?

    a. The $750 per month that a landlord receives for an apartment rented to students

    b. The salary of the Canadian prime minister

    c. The annual income of Tiger Woods or Shania Twain

d. The salary of a window cleaner who says, "It's dangerous work, but it beats driving a truck."

e. An engineer at Google headquarters who loves going to work every day

12. It is common to hear comments like "Why do baseball players earn millions of dollars a year for their negligible contribution to society while major contributors—such as schoolteachers, police officers, firefighters, and ambulance drivers—earn barely enough to survive?" Can you offer an answer based on what was discussed in this chapter?

13. Using the concepts of transfer earnings and economic rent, can you derive a form of taxation—of the earnings by oil companies, for example—that would generate tax revenue but not influence the companies' supply decisions? Is your approach consistent with that followed by Canada's provincial governments when they collect royalties on natural-resource revenues?

Labour Markets

LEARNING OBJECTIVES (LO)

After studying this chapter you will be able to

1 explain wage differentials in both competitive and non-competitive labour markets.
2 describe the possible effects of legislated minimum wages.

3 discuss the tradeoff that unions usually face between wages and employment.

4 explain why the trend away from manufacturing jobs and toward service jobs is not necessarily a problem for the economy as a whole.

THE competitive theory of factor-price determination, presented in Chapter 13, tells us a great deal about the determinants of factor incomes and factor movements. In this chapter, we look specifically at labour markets. We begin by discussing why some workers get high wages and others get low wages. We then look beyond our theory of competitive labour markets to examine situations where either firms or workers have some market power. We also discuss the effects of legislated minimum wages, as well as the debate surrounding this contentious policy. The chapter then discusses labour unions, and the tradeoff they face between increasing their membership and increasing their members' wages. Finally, we examine an often-heard claim that Canada and other developed economies are gaining "bad jobs" in the service sector at the expense of "good jobs" in the manufacturing sector.

14.1 Wage Differentials

We argued in the last chapter that if all workers were identical, all jobs had the same working conditions, and labour markets were perfectly competitive, all workers would earn the same wage. In reality, however, wages vary enormously across such dimensions as occupations, skills, amounts of education, and geographical areas. Generally, the more education and experience a worker has, the higher are his or her wages. Given equal education and experience, women on average earn less than men. Workers in highly unionized industries tend to be paid more than workers with similar skills and experience in non-unionized industries. Such differentials arise because workers are not all identical, jobs are not all identical, and important non-competitive forces sometimes operate in labour markets. We now look more systematically at some of the main reasons that different workers earn different wages.

Wage Differentials in Competitive Markets

Where there are many employers (buyers) and many workers (sellers), there is a competitive labour market of the kind discussed in Chapter 13. Under competitive conditions, the wage rate and level of employment are set by supply and demand. No worker or group of workers, and no firm or group of firms, is able to affect the market wage. In practice, however, there are many kinds of workers and many kinds of jobs. We can therefore think of a series of related labour markets rather than a single national market. Among these various labour markets, there are several reasons for wage differentials.

Many jobs involve dangerous or unpleasant working conditions. Wages in such jobs are generally higher than in other jobs requiring comparable skills. These are called compensating wage differentials.

Working Conditions Given identical skills, those working under relatively onerous or risky conditions earn more than those working in pleasant or safe conditions. For example, construction workers who work the "high iron," assembling the frames for skyscrapers, are paid more than workers who do similar work at ground level. The reason is simple: Risk and unpleasantness reduce the supply of labour, thus raising the wage above what it would otherwise be. Different working conditions in different jobs thus lead to *compensating differentials* as we discussed in Chapter 13. These wage differentials are not temporary—they are *equilibrium* wage differentials.

Inherited Skills Large incomes will be earned by people who have scarce skills that cannot be taught and that are in high demand—for example, an NBA basketball player, an opera singer, or a movie star. In these cases, the combination of a small and inelastic supply and a large enough demand of the relevant kind of labour cause the market-clearing wage to be high. Wage differentials of this kind are also equilibrium wage differentials.

> **Working conditions and workers' inherited skills have important effects on wages.**

Human Capital A machine is physical capital. It requires an investment of time and money to create it, and once created, it yields valuable services over a long time. In the same way, labour skills require an investment of time and money to acquire, and once acquired, they may yield an increased income for their owner over a long time. Since investment in labour skills is similar to investment in physical capital, acquired skills are called **human capital**. The more costly it is to acquire the skill required for a particular job, the higher its pay must be to attract people to train for it.

human capital The acquired skills that individuals have, usually from formal education or on-the-job training.

Investment in human capital is costly, and the return is usually in terms of higher future wages.

The two main ways in which human capital is acquired are through formal education and on-the-job training.

Formal Education. Compulsory primary and secondary education provides some minimum human capital for all citizens. People who decide to stay in school beyond the years of compulsory education, such as those of you who are reading this book, are deciding to invest voluntarily in acquiring further human capital. The opportunity cost is measured by the income that you could have earned if you had entered the labour force immediately, in addition to the direct costs for such items as tuition fees and books and equipment. The financial return is measured by the higher income earned when a better job is obtained.

How large is the payoff from higher education? Figure 14-1 shows how average employment income varies with years of schooling. In 2007, the last year these data were made available, the average employment income for Canadians with a university degree was more than $61 400; in contrast, someone who failed to complete high school had an average employment income of less than $21 000.[1]

Evidence suggests that in recent years the demand for workers with more skills and education has been rising relative to the demand for those with less. As we would expect, this change in relative demand raises the relative wages of more-educated people, thereby increasing the payoff to their investment in education. Not surprisingly, students today find that further investment in human capital is even more important than did students a generation ago.

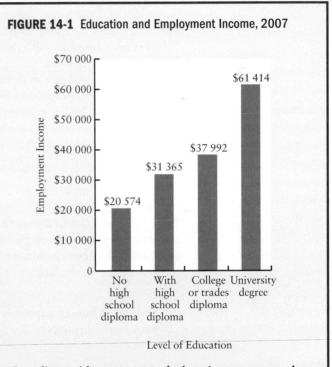

FIGURE 14-1 Education and Employment Income, 2007

Employment Income

- No high school diploma: $20 574
- With high school diploma: $31 365
- College or trades diploma: $37 992
- University degree: $61 414

Level of Education

Canadians with more years of education earn more than those with less education. The increase in employment income that can be expected from extra education is modest for levels of education below a university degree. But the payoff for completing a university degree is very substantial.

(*Source:* These data are available on Statistics Canada's website, www.statcan.gc.ca. See *Income Trends in Canada 1976 to 2007*, publication 13-F0022X.)

---

[1] Figure 14-1 actually shows only the *correlation* between education and earnings; these raw data do not indicate a *causal* relationship. More advanced statistical studies, however, show that there is a clear financial payoff from additional years of education.

Changes in labour-market conditions alter the costs and benefits of acquiring human capital. Individuals respond according to their personal assessment of these costs and benefits.

On-The-Job Training. Wage differentials according to experience are readily observable in most firms and occupations. To a significant extent, these differentials are a response to human capital acquired on the job. For example, a civil engineer with 20 years' experience in bridge design will generally earn more than a newly graduated civil engineer, even though they both have the same formal education.

On-the-job training is important in creating rising wages for employees and for making firms competitive. Evidence suggests that people who miss on-the-job training early in life are handicapped relative to others throughout much of their later working careers.

Temporary or Equilibrium Differentials? As we saw in Chapter 13, wage differentials due to different working conditions are equilibrium differentials. In contrast, wage differentials caused by differences in human capital are partly temporary and partly equilibrium differentials.

Suppose an increase in demand for university graduates increases their wages relative to high-school graduates. In response, more people will decide to attend university in pursuit of the higher earnings. This increase in the supply of university-trained individuals will reduce their wage relative to high-school graduates, thus diminishing the observed differentials, such as those shown in Figure 14-1. However, as long as it is costly to acquire human capital—and as you know, attending university *is* costly—then in equilibrium there will still be wage differentials in favour of university graduates. In equilibrium, the higher wages of university graduates will just compensate them for the higher costs associated with acquiring their greater stock of human capital. Notice that this argument refers to *averages*. Every person who acquires a university education does not earn more than every person who does not—differences in such things as innate skills, attitudes to work, and the subject chosen for a university major matter as well. But on average those who acquire a university education earn more than those who do not.

As long as human capital is costly to acquire, some wage differentials will persist in equilibrium.

Discrimination Wage differentials can also exist due to *discrimination* in the labour market, but care must be taken when interpreting the data. For example, in 2009 the average female full-time worker in Canada earned just under 75 percent of the wage of the average full-time male worker. More detailed studies suggest that a significant part of these differences can be explained by such considerations as the nature of the job and the amount of human capital acquired through both formal education and on-the-job experience. When all such explanations are taken into account, however, there still appears to be a gap between male and female wages that reveals gender-based discrimination.

To understand the effects of labour-market discrimination, we begin by building a simplified model of a non-discriminating labour market and then introduce discrimination between two sets of equally qualified workers. The discussion here is phrased in terms of males and females but the analysis applies equally well to any situation in which workers are distinguished on grounds *other than* their ability, such as race or skin colour, citizenship, religion, sexual orientation, or political beliefs.

Suppose half of the people in the labour force are male and the other half are female. Each group has the same proportion who are educated to various levels, identical distributions of talent, and so on. Suppose also that there are two occupations. Occupation E (*elite*) requires people of above-average education and skills, and occupation O (*ordinary*) can use anyone. Finally, suppose the non-monetary aspects of the two occupations are the same.

In the absence of discrimination, the theory of competitive factor markets that we have developed suggests that the wages in E occupations will be bid up above those in O occupations in order that the E jobs attract the workers of above-average skills. Men and women of above-average skill will take the E jobs, while the others, both men and women, will have no choice but to seek O jobs. Because skills are equally distributed between both sexes, each occupation will employ one-half men and one half women.

Now suppose discrimination enters in an extreme form. All E occupations are hereafter open only to men, but O occupations are open to either men or women. The immediate effect is to reduce by 50 percent the supply of job candidates for E occupations; all previously qualified female candidates are no longer eligible because candidates must now be *both* men and above average. The discrimination also increases the supply of applicants for O jobs because the women who cannot be employed in E jobs move instead to get O jobs. The new group of O-job candidates now includes all women and the below-average men.

As shown in Figure 14-2, wages rise in E occupations and fall in O occupations.

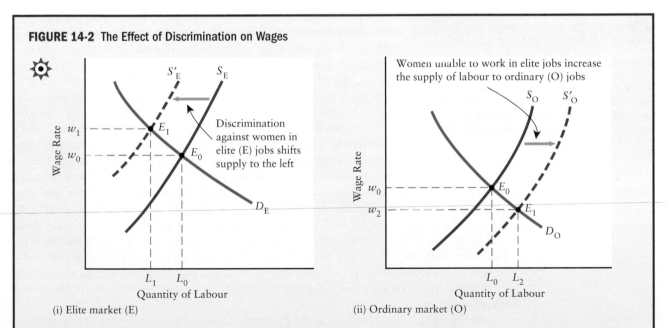

FIGURE 14-2 The Effect of Discrimination on Wages

(i) Elite market (E)

(ii) Ordinary market (O)

If market E discriminates against one group and market O does not, wages will rise in E and fall in O. Market E requires above-average skills, while market O requires only ordinary skills. When there is no discrimination, demand and supply are D_E and S_E in market E and D_O and S_O in market O. Initially, the wage rate is w_0 and employment is L_0 in each market. (w_0 in market E is higher than w_0 in market O because the workers in E have higher skills than those in O. This is an equilibrium wage differential.) When discrimination excludes women from E occupations, the supply curve shifts to S'_E, and the wage earned by the remaining workers, all of whom are men, rises to w_1. Women ineligible for work in the E occupations now seek work in the O occupations. The resulting shift in the supply curve to S'_O reduces the wage to w_2 in the O occupations. Because all women are in O occupations, they have a lower wage rate than many men. The average male wage in the economy is higher than the average female wage.

Labour-market discrimination, by changing equilibrium supply, decreases the wages of a group that is discriminated against and increases the wages of the "favoured" group.

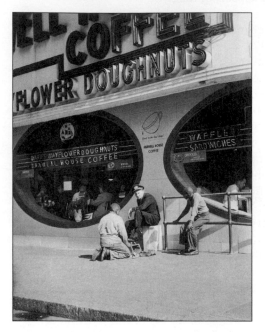

The attitudes of many white customers were responsible for much discrimination against black people in the United States in the first few decades of the twentieth century. As long as these attitudes persist, so will the discrimination, unless legislation forces a change.

In the longer run, further changes may occur. Employers that continue to discriminate against women may find ways to attract the slightly below-average male workers away from the O occupations. Although this will raise O wages slightly, it will also make these occupations increasingly "female occupations." If discrimination has been in place for a sufficient length of time, women will learn that it does not pay to acquire above-average skills because even with such skills they cannot get the best jobs. Regardless of ability, women are forced by discrimination to work in unskilled jobs.

The final point to address regarding labour-market discrimination is whether discriminatory wage differentials are equilibrium or temporary differentials. The simple answer is that the differentials will persist as long as the discrimination itself persists. Consider three general cases.

In the first case, the discrimination is supported by government policy, as in the South African apartheid system in which blacks were prohibited by law from holding prestigious and high-paying jobs. In such cases, as long as the law remains in place, so too will the discriminating wage differentials. If political pressure forces a change in the law, as happened in South Africa in the 1980s and 1990s, the effects of the discrimination will be reversed, but it may take some time. In particular, it will take time for the once-discriminated-against individuals, who had little incentive to invest in their own human capital, to acquire the human capital necessary for them to qualify for the prestigious jobs. The effects of the legislated discrimination are likely to linger long after the policy itself.

In the second case, discrimination is not supported by official government policy but instead reflects the views of the firms' managers. In this case, there are economic pressures opposing the discrimination. For example, if some firms discriminate against even well-qualified women, our analysis in Figure 14-2 suggests there will be well-qualified women who can only find low-wage jobs. There is an incentive for other, non-discriminating firms to hire these well-qualified women and thereby benefit from lower costs. If enough firms see this advantage, there will be an increase in demand for well-qualified women, eventually reversing the effects of the initial discrimination.

In the third case, the cause of the discrimination is the preferences of the *customers*. Unlike the second case where the discrimination reflects the views of the firms' managers, there are no economic forces working to offset this customer-driven discrimination. As long as such discriminatory views persist, the discriminatory wage differentials will be sustained—only legislation or fundamental changes in customers' attitudes will reverse the situation. For many years, this was an important aspect of racial discrimination in the southern U.S. states, where many white customers were not prepared to have some services, such as haircuts, provided to them by blacks.

If discrimination is supported by governments or reflects the views of consumers, the discriminatory wage differentials will persist as long as the discrimination itself persists. If the discrimination only reflects the views of the firms' managers, the pursuit of profits generates economic forces that tend to reduce the discriminatory wage differentials.

Wage Differentials in Non-competitive Markets

We have examined several explanations for why wage differentials exist in competitive labour markets. Another explanation for wage differentials is that many labour markets are not competitive. To study the influence of different labour-market structures on wages, consider the case of an industry that employs identical workers for only one kind of job. In this way, we eliminate the possibility that any wage differentials are caused by differences between workers or differences between jobs—we thus highlight the role of market structure.

Let's examine two general cases. The first is one in which workers form a group and exercise some market power over setting the wage. This is a case in which a labour union acts as a monopoly seller of labour services. The second case is one in which a single firm is the only purchaser of labour—a *monopsony* firm in the labour market.

labour union An association authorized to represent workers in bargaining with employers.

A Union in a Competitive Labour Market For the purposes of our discussion of labour markets, a **labour union** is an association that is authorized to represent workers in negotiations with their employers. We examine labour unions in greater detail later in this chapter. For now we take the simple view that when workers are represented by a labour union, there is only a single supplier of labour.

As the single seller of labour for many buyers, the union is a monopolist, and it can establish a wage below which no one will work, thus changing the supply curve of labour. Firms can hire as many units of labour as are prepared to work at the union wage but no one at a lower wage. Thus, the industry as a whole (and each firm in the industry) faces a supply curve that is horizontal at the level of the union wage up to the maximum quantity of (union) labour that is willing to work at that wage.

If the union uses its monopoly power, it will negotiate a wage above the competitive level. This situation is shown in Figure 14-3, in which the intersection of this horizontal supply curve and the demand curve establishes a higher wage rate and a lower level of employment than the competitive equilibrium. In this case, there will be some workers who would like to work in the unionized industry or occupation but cannot. A conflict of interest has been created between serving the interests of the union's employed members and members who are unemployed or who must seek employment in less preferred jobs.

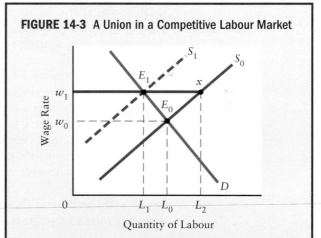

FIGURE 14-3 A Union in a Competitive Labour Market

A union operating in a competitive market can raise the wages of people who continue to be employed but only by reducing the number of people employed. The competitive equilibrium is at E_0, the wage is w_0, and employment is L_0. If a monopoly union enters this market and sets a wage of w_1, a new equilibrium will be established at E_1. The supply curve has become $w_1 x S_0$. At the new wage w_1, employment will be L_1, and there will be $L_1 L_2$ workers who would like to work but whom the industry will not hire.

The wage w_1 can be achieved without generating a pool of unemployed persons. To do so, the union must restrict entry into the occupation and thus shift the supply curve to the left to S_1. Employment will again be L_1.

An alternative way to achieve the higher wage is to shift the supply curve to the left. The union may do this by restricting entry into the occupation by methods such as lengthening the required period of apprenticeship and reducing openings for trainees. The union could also shift the supply curve to the left by persuading the government to impose restrictive licensing or certification requirements on people who wish to work in certain occupations. The union might even lobby the government to implement restrictive immigration policies in an attempt to reduce the supply of labour to specific industries.

By restricting entry into the occupation or industry, unions can drive the wage above the competitive level. As a result, the level of employment will fall.

Raising wages by restricting entry is not limited to unions. It occurs, for example, with many professional groups, including doctors, architects, engineers, and lawyers. By limiting enrollments in professional programs at universities, the restricted supply of labour drives wages in these occupations higher than they would otherwise be.

A Monopsony Firm in the Labour Market A **monopsony** is a market in which there is only one buyer; monopsony is to the buying side of the market what monopoly is to the selling side. Although monopsony is not very common, it sometimes occurs in small towns that contain only one industry and often only one large plant or mine. For example, Iroquois Falls and Dryden in Ontario are small towns in which the principal employer is a single firm that operates a newsprint plant. Although both towns provide alternative sources of employment in retailing and service establishments, the large industrial employer has some monopsony power over the local labour market. Other examples of monopsony include cities in which a single school board is the sole employer of teachers or a regional health authority that is the sole employer of nurses.

monopsony A market structure in which there is a single buyer.

In less extreme cases, local labour markets may contain only a few large industrial employers. Individually, each has substantial market power, and if they act together, either explicitly or tacitly, they can behave as if they were a single monopsonist. Our analysis applies whenever employers have substantial monopsony power, but for concreteness, we consider a case in which the few firms operating in one labour market form an employers' hiring association in order to act as a single buying unit. We therefore refer to a single monopsonist.

Monopsony Without a Union. Suppose there are many potential workers and they are not members of a labour union. The monopsonist can offer any wage rate that it chooses, and the workers must either accept employment at that rate or find a different job.

Suppose the monopsonist decides to hire some specific quantity of labour. The labour supply curve shows the wage that it must offer. To the monopsonist, this wage is the *average cost* of labour. In deciding how much labour to hire, however, the monopsonist trying to maximize its profits is interested in the *marginal cost* of hiring additional workers. The monopsonist wants to know how much its total costs will increase as it takes on additional units of labour.

Whenever the supply curve of labour slopes upward, the marginal cost of employing extra units will exceed the average cost.

The marginal cost exceeds the wage paid (the average cost) because the increased wage rate necessary to attract an extra worker must also be paid to *everyone already employed*. [27] For example, assume that 100 workers are employed at $15.00 per hour and that to attract an extra worker, the wage must be raised to $15.25 per hour. The marginal cost of that 101st worker is not the $15.25 per hour paid to the worker but $40.25 per hour—made up of the extra 25 cents per hour paid to the 100 existing workers and $15.25 paid to the new worker. Thus, the marginal cost is $40.25, whereas the average cost is $15.25.

The profit-maximizing monopsonist will hire labour up to the point at which the marginal cost of labour just equals the amount that the firm is willing to pay for an additional unit of labour. That amount is determined by labour's marginal revenue product and is shown by the *MRP* curve illustrated in Figure 14-4.

> **The full exercise of monopsony power in a labour market will result in a lower level of employment and lower wages than would exist in a competitive labour market.**

The intuitive explanation is that the monopsonistic employer is aware that by trying to purchase more, it is responsible for driving up the wage. If it wants to maximize its profits it will therefore stop short of the point that is reached when workers are hired by many competitive firms, no one of which can exert a significant influence on the wage rate.

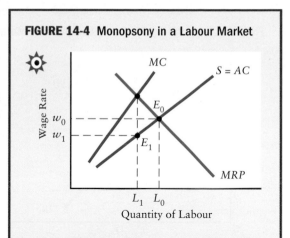

FIGURE 14-4 Monopsony in a Labour Market

A profit-maximizing monopsonist lowers both the wage rate and employment below their competitive levels. *MRP* and *S* are the competitive demand and supply curves, respectively. The competitive equilibrium is E_0. The marginal cost of labour (*MC*) to the monopsonist is above the average cost. The monopsonistic firm maximizes profits at E_1. It hires only L_1 units of labour. At L_1, the marginal cost of the last worker is just equal to the amount that the worker adds to the firm's revenue, as shown by the *MRP* curve. The wage that must be paid to get L_1 workers is only w_1.

Monopsony with a Union: "Bilateral Monopoly." In situations where there is a single large employer in the labour market, workers often create or join a labour union so their collective market power can better match that of the employer. This situation is often referred to as *bilateral monopoly* since both sides of the market have considerable market power. In this case, the two sides will settle the wage through a process known as *collective bargaining*. The outcome of this bargaining process will depend on each side's objective and on the skill that each has in bargaining for its objective. We have seen that, left to itself, the profit-maximizing employer's organization will set the monopsonistic wage shown in Figure 14-4. To understand the possible outcomes for the wage after the monopoly union enters the market, let us ask what the union would do if it had the power to set the wage unilaterally. The result will give us insight into the union's objectives in the actual collective bargaining that does occur.

Suppose the union can set a wage below which its members will not work. Here, just as in the case of a wage-setting union in a competitive market, the union presents the employer with a horizontal supply curve (up to the maximum number of workers who will accept work at the union wage). As shown in Figure 14-5, if the union sets the wage above the monopsony wage but below the competitive wage, the union can raise *both* wages and employment above the monopsonistic level.

However, the union may prefer to raise wages further above the competitive level. If it does, the outcome will be similar to that shown in Figure 14-3. If the wage is raised

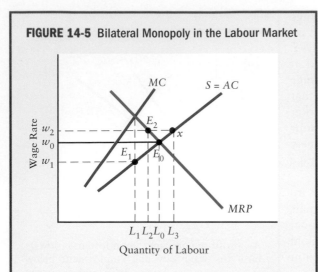

FIGURE 14-5 Bilateral Monopoly in the Labour Market

By presenting a monopsonistic employer with a fixed wage, the union can raise both wages and employment over the monopsonistic level. The monopsony position before the union enters is at E_1 (from Figure 14-4), with a wage rate of w_1 and L_1 workers hired. A union now enters and sets the wage at w_0. The supply curve of labour becomes $w_0 E_0 S$, and wages and employment rise to their competitive levels of w_0 and L_0 without creating a pool of unemployed workers. If the wage is raised further, say, to w_2, the supply curve will become $w_2 x S$, the quantity of employment will fall below the competitive level to L_2, and a pool of unsuccessful job applicants of $L_2 L_3$ will develop.

above the competitive level, the employer will no longer wish to hire all the labour that is offered at that wage; it will choose the level of employment along its labour-demand curve. The amount of employment will fall, and some who would like to work at the union wage will be unemployed or drift off to other, less preferred occupations. These changes are also shown in Figure 14-5.

We now know that the profit-maximizing employer would like to set the monopsonistic wage (w_1) while the union would like a wage *no less than* the competitive wage (w_0). (Any wage below w_0 will reduce *both* wages and employment.) The union may target a still higher wage, depending on how it trades off employment losses against wage gains. If the union is content with an amount of employment as low as would occur at the monopsonistic wage, it could target a wage substantially higher than the competitive wage.

Simple demand and supply analysis can take us no further. The actual outcome will depend on such other things as what target wage the two sides actually set for themselves, their relative bargaining skills, and how each side assesses the costs of concessions. We discuss unions in more detail in the next section of this chapter.

Legislated Minimum Wages

We have examined wage differentials arising in competitive and non-competitive labour markets. Government policy can also affect observed wage differentials by legislating minimum wages. Governments in Canada and many other countries legislate specific **minimum wages**, which define the lowest wage rates that may legally be paid. In 2012, minimum wages ranged from $9.50 per hour in Saskatchewan to $11.00 per hour in Nunavut.

Although legislated minimum wages are now an accepted part of the labour scene in Canada and many other industrialized countries, there is significant debate among economists about the benefits from such a policy. As our analysis in Chapter 5 indicated, a binding price floor in a competitive market leads to a market surplus of the product—in this case, an excess supply of labour, or unemployment. Thus, theory predicts that a policy that legislates minimum wages in an otherwise competitive market will benefit some workers only by hurting others. In the cases of non-competitive labour markets, however, the analysis is a little more complicated.

Predicted Effects of a Minimum Wage Minimum-wage laws usually apply uniformly to almost all occupations, but they will be *binding* only in the lowest-paid occupations and industries, which often involve unskilled or semi-skilled workers. These workers are usually not members of labour unions. Thus, the situations in which minimum wages will affect labour-market outcomes include competitive labour markets and those in which employers exercise some monopsony power. The effects on employment are different in the two cases.

Competitive Labour Markets. The predicted consequences for employment of a binding minimum wage are unambiguous when the labour market is competitive. By raising the wage

minimum wages Legally specified minimum rate of pay for labour.

For interesting information on labour-market policies in Canada, see the website for Human Resources and Skills Development Canada: www.hrsdc.gc.ca. *Click on "Labour Programs."*

that employers must pay, minimum-wage legislation leads to a reduction in the quantity of labour that is demanded and an increase in the quantity of labour that is supplied. As a result, the actual level of employment falls, and unemployment rises. The excess supply of labour at the minimum wage also creates incentives for people to evade the law by working "under the table" at wages below the legal minimum wage. The predicted effect of a minimum wage in a competitive labour market is shown in part (i) of Figure 14-6.

Firms with Monopsony Power. Our theory predicts that the minimum-wage law can simultaneously increase both wages and employment in markets in which firms have monopsony power. In part (ii) of Figure 14-6, the monopsony wage is w_1. If the minimum wage pushes the wage up to w_2, both employment and wages will rise. But beyond the competitive wage (w^*), further increases in the minimum wage will begin to decrease employment and create a pool of unemployed workers.

Evidence on the Effects of Minimum Wages Empirical research on the effects of minimum-wage laws reflects these mixed theoretical predictions. There is some evidence that people who keep their jobs gain when the minimum wage is raised. There is some evidence that some groups suffer a decline in employment consistent with raising the wage in a fairly competitive market. At other times and places, there is evidence that both wages and employment *rise* when the minimum wage rises, consistent with labour markets in which employers have monopsony power.

Some widely discussed research in the United States has produced hotly debated results. David Card, from Berkeley, and Alan Krueger, from Princeton University, traced

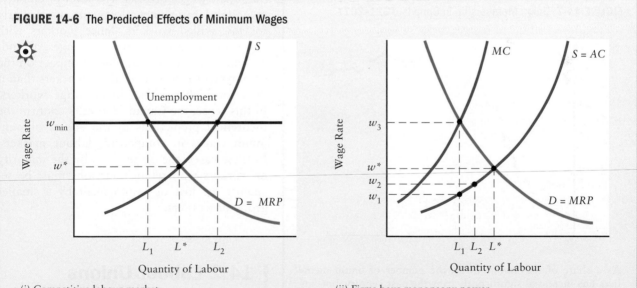

FIGURE 14-6 The Predicted Effects of Minimum Wages

(i) Competitive labour market

(ii) Firms have monopsony power

Minimum wages are predicted to reduce employment in competitive labour markets; the predicted effects on employment in monopsonistic labour markets are less clear. Part (i) shows a competitive labour market with the competitive equilibrium at w^* and L^*. A binding minimum wage raises the wage to w_{min}. Firms respond by reducing employment to L_1. The quantity of labour supplied by workers increases to L_2. Unemployment is equal to L_1L_2 workers.

Part (ii) shows a labour market in which firms behave as a monopsonist. The monopsony equilibrium is w_1 and L_1. If the minimum wage is set at w_2, employment will rise to L_2. If the minimum wage is set as high as the competitive wage w^*, employment rises to the competitive level L^*. But if the minimum wage rises above w^*, employment will fall below L^*. If the minimum wage were set above w_3, employment would fall below the monopsony level, L_1.

the effects of minimum-wage increases in California during 1988 and New Jersey during 1992 and found that substantial rises in these states' minimum wages not only increased wages but also were associated with small employment *gains* for teenagers. Card and Krueger argue that these findings are inconsistent with a competitive labour market and thus take the results as evidence in support of the view that firms have some monopsony power in the labour market.

The Card and Krueger results have been criticized by many economists. One criticism is that some of the data used by Card and Krueger are faulty, and that their conclusions are therefore suspect. However, in a follow-up paper from 2000 that uses different data, Card and Krueger find broadly similar results as in their original study. Another criticism relates to the short span of time covered by their study. The argument is that firms will not immediately reduce the level of employment in response to an increase in the minimum wage—they will instead choose *not to* replace workers who leave their jobs in the natural turnover process that occurs in labour markets. But workers who are receiving the minimum wage may be more reluctant to leave their job after an increase in their wages, thereby reducing this natural turnover. Thus, it is not surprising to see few employment losses (or slight gains) when one examines the labour market immediately before and immediately after the change in legislation. Proponents of this view argue that the total employment effects of minimum wages can be detected only by examining the data over longer periods of time.

Several Canadian studies have examined the relationship between minimum wages and employment (or unemployment). Though the studies differ in their approaches and data used, there is a broad consensus that minimum wages decrease the level of employment (and raise unemployment), particularly for low-skilled workers. Since workers with few skills often earn only low wages, a binding minimum wage has a larger impact on the employment prospects of these workers than it does for higher-skilled, higher-wage workers. In this sense, the Canadian results confirm the theoretical predictions of the effects of minimum wages in competitive labour markets. In these cases, the wage gains by the majority of workers who retain their jobs must be set against the loss of employment by a smaller group of workers.

FIGURE 14-7 Union Membership in Canada, 1921–2011

As a share of the labour force, the number of union members has increased significantly over the past century, but has declined gradually since the mid-1970s. The large increases in Canadian unionization occurred during and after the Second World War, and during the 1960s. (Data are missing for 1950 and 1996.)

(*Source:* Based on author's calculations, using data from Statistics Canada. The most recent labour force data are from Table 282-0001; union membership data are from Table 282-0077.)

14.2 Labour Unions

Unions currently represent about 25 percent of the labour force in Canada. Of those workers employed in the public sector, however, approximately 70 percent are unionized or covered by a union contract. Figure 14-7 shows how union membership has changed in Canada over the past several decades. For various industries,

Table 14-1 shows the percentage of workers whose wages and salaries are covered by a union contract (even though they may not be members of a union). As is clear from the table, unionization is most common in the public, educational, and health-care sectors and least common in agriculture, finance, and trade.

Despite the relatively low degree of unionization among Canada's private-sector workers, unions have a considerable influence in the private sector. One reason is the impact that union wage contracts have on other labour markets. When, for example, the Canadian Auto Workers negotiates a new contract with an automobile producer in Oshawa, its provisions set a pattern that directly or indirectly affects other labour markets, both in Ontario and in other provinces. A second reason is the major leadership role that unions have played in the past 50 years in the development of labour market practices and in lobbying for legislation that applies to all workers.

In this section, we discuss the process of *collective bargaining* and, in particular, examine the inherent conflict that unions face between striving for higher wages and for increasing employment. *Lessons from History 14-1* examines the historical development of labour unions in Canada.

TABLE 14-1 Union Coverage by Industry, 2011

Industry	Percentage of workers covered by unions	
Goods Producing		28.3
Agriculture	3.9	
Mining, Oil & Gas, Forestry, and Fishing	21.2	
Utilities	66.0	
Construction	30.9	
Manufacturing	26.7	
Services Producing		32.0
Trade	14.0	
Transportation and Warehousing	41.1	
Finance, Insurance, and Real Estate	9.7	
Education	71.0	
Health Care and Social Assistance	54.4	
Public Administration	71.9	
Total Employees		31.2

There is considerable variation across Canadian industries in the extent of union coverage. The public sector and the educational services sector are the most unionized; agriculture, finance, and trade are the least unionized.

(*Source:* Adapted from Statistics Canada, Labour Force Survey, Table 282-0077.)

Collective Bargaining

The process by which unions and employers reach an agreement is known as **collective bargaining**. This process has an important difference from the theoretical models that we discussed in the previous section. In those models, we assumed that the union had the power to set the wage unilaterally; the employer then decided how much labour to hire. In actual collective bargaining, however, the firm and union typically bargain over the wage (as well as other aspects of the employment relationship, such as benefits, pensions, working conditions, overtime conditions, and flexibility in scheduling). There is usually a substantial range over which an agreement can be reached, and the actual result in particular cases will depend on the strengths of the two bargaining parties and on the skill of their negotiators. Note that while actual collective bargaining has the firm and union bargaining over the wage, it is typically the case that the firm retains the "right to manage"—meaning that the firm can decide how much labour it wants to employ at the negotiated wage.

collective bargaining
The process by which unions and employers arrive at and enforce agreements.

Wages Versus Employment Unions seek many goals when they bargain with management. They may push for higher wages, more generous benefits, or less onerous working conditions. Many unions in Canada also emphasize the importance of "job security," meaning a commitment by the firm not to lay workers off in the event of a downturn

LESSONS FROM HISTORY 14-1

The Development of Unions in Canada

Early Canadian unionization was strongly dominated by the influence of international unions, which had their headquarters and an overwhelming proportion of their membership outside Canada. The creation of Canadian locals of American unions began in the 1860s. By 1911, 90 percent of Canadian union members belonged to international unions.

During the first half of the twentieth century, there was strong pressure: first, toward a single national federation; and second, to achieve autonomy from American unions. The issues became intertwined when conflicts in the United States arose between craft and industrial unions. Until the 1930s, *craft unions*—which cover persons in a particular occupation—were the characteristic form of collective action in the United States. In Canada, meanwhile, it was more common for trade unionists to be members of *industrial unions* that embraced unskilled workers as well as skilled craftsmen in one industry, such as steel making, forest products, or railways.

Because of the impossibility of establishing bargaining strength by controlling the supply of unskilled workers, the rise of industrial unionism in Canada was associated with political action as an alternative means of improving the lot of the membership. In general, social and political reform were given much more emphasis by Canadian unionists than by their American counterparts. Political action here extended to the support for social democratic political parties: first, the Co-operative Commonwealth Federation (CCF), established in 1932, and later its successor, the New Democratic Party (NDP), formed in 1961.

The unification of the bulk of Canadian unions under the Canadian Labour Congress in 1956 is viewed by many as the beginning of virtual autonomy for Canadian locals from their U.S. head offices. Throughout the postwar period, the percentage of total Canadian union membership represented by international unions fell: in the mid-1950s, it was about 70 percent, and by the mid-1990s, it was just over 30 percent.

One factor in the increased share of national unions was the growth of membership in the two unions representing government workers: the Canadian Union of Public Employees and the Public Service Alliance. Another major component of non-international union membership arose out of the distinct aspirations of French-Canadian workers. In the mid-1980s, the formation of the Canadian Auto Workers, independent of the American Auto Workers, represented a significant further increase in the role of the national (rather than the international) labour unions in Canada.

The Winnipeg General Strike of 1919 began a wave of increased unionism and militancy across Canada.

in business conditions. Firms, however, are understandably reluctant to promise such security since reducing their workforce is an effective way to reduce costs when business conditions deteriorate.

Whatever unions' specific goals, unless they face a monopsonist across the bargaining table, they must deal with a fundamental dilemma.

An inherent conflict exists between the level of wages and the size of the union itself.

The more successful a union is in raising wages, the more management will reduce the size of its workforce, substituting capital for labour. This will lead to lower union membership. However, if the union is unable to offer better wages or benefits to its members, they have little incentive to remain with the union and will eventually seek employment elsewhere.

The Union Wage Premium Despite the costs to unions (i.e., reduced membership) of pushing for higher wages, there is clear evidence in Canada of a *union wage premium*—that is, a higher wage attributed only to the union status of the job. It is not easy to measure this wage premium, however, because it is not appropriate simply to compare the average wage of unionized workers with the average wage of non-unionized workers. After all, unions may occur mainly in industries where workers have higher skills or where working conditions are less pleasant. And we know from the first section of this chapter that differences in skills or working conditions can lead to equilibrium wage differentials. Economists therefore rely on advanced statistical techniques to identify this union wage premium.

For 2012, the raw data show that average hourly wages are about 23 percent greater for union workers than for non-union workers. After controlling for the observable attributes of the workers and jobs, however, the evidence suggests that the union wage premium in Canada is between 10 and 15 percent—that is, unionized workers with a particular set of skills in particular types of jobs get paid 10 to 15 percent more than *otherwise identical workers* who are not members of unions.

> On average, unionized workers earn between 10 and 15 percent higher wages than non-unionized workers with similar characteristics.

There is also evidence that the size of this union wage premium differs across industries. Given that workers in different industries and with different occupations are often represented by different unions, this cross-industry difference in the union wage premium may simply reflect the differences in unions' preferences for higher wages versus higher employment.

For information on the Canadian labour movement, see the website for the Canadian Labour Congress: www.canadianlabour.ca.

Employment Effects of Unions We said earlier that unions face an inherent conflict between the level of wages and the level of employment in their industry. This conflict simply reflects the firm's profit-maximizing behaviour as embodied in its negatively sloped demand curve for labour. As the union pushes for higher wages, the firm naturally chooses to hire fewer workers.

What continues to puzzle economists, however, is how the clear evidence of a 10 to 15 percent union wage premium can be consistent with a second empirical result—the *absence* of any clear effect on employment in unionized industries. One possible explanation for the absence of an employment effect is that unions use the collective bargaining process to pressure firms to hire more workers than they otherwise would. This practice is known as *featherbedding* and for years was infamous in the railways, where union contracts required the railways to hire firemen (whose job was to keep the coal fires burning) long after the widespread adoption of diesel locomotives.

If such featherbedding is pervasive in unionized firms, it may be the explanation for the absence of an observable union effect on employment. The employment reduction caused by the higher wage may be offset by the employment increase due to featherbedding.

Another possible explanation for the absence of a union employment effect is union campaigns to increase the demand for the goods produced by their members. We sometimes see labels on products that proclaim them to be "union made" or "made with union labour." Unions also spend considerably on magazine and television advertising stressing the value of union labour. Some unions also lobby the government to restrict the import of foreign-made products in an attempt to increase Canadian consumers' demand for the

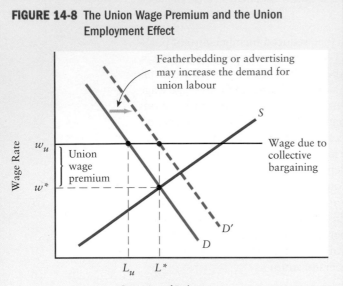

FIGURE 14-8 The Union Wage Premium and the Union Employment Effect

Featherbedding or advertising may increase the demand for union labour

Wage due to collective bargaining

Quantity of Labour

Featherbedding and advertising may explain the absence of a union employment effect even though there is a clear union wage effect. If the labour market is competitive, wages and employment will be given by w^* and L^*. The collective bargaining between firms and unions results in a wage of w_u, showing a clear premium above the competitive wage. If the demand for labour remains at D, employment would fall to L_u and there would be a reduction in employment caused by the higher negotiated wage. If the collective agreement requires firms to use more labour, however, or if the union successfully promotes union-made products, the demand for labour shifts to D'. In this case, the combination of the higher wage and the greater demand for labour may result in the competitive level of employment.

domestic goods made with union labour. To the extent that these campaigns convince consumers to buy more union-made products than they otherwise would, the result will be an increase in demand for union labour.

Figure 14-8 shows how the combination of the union wage premium and the increases in demand for union labour (either through featherbedding or advertising) can explain the *absence* of an observed union employment effect.

Unanswered Questions

Labour unions have played a significant role in the economies of Canada, the United States, and Europe for many years. It is therefore surprising how little economists actually know about how unions influence economic outcomes. One important unanswered question is how unions affect long-run productivity.

Unions may reduce long-run productivity through a process known as the *hold-up* of capital. Much physical capital, once it is installed, is very difficult to move or resell. For this reason, *installed* capital has a very inelastic supply and, following the discussion from Chapter 13, a large part of its factor payment takes the form of economic rent. The union may be able to extract these rents from the firm in the form of higher wages. That is, once the firm has already installed its capital equipment the union may be able to *hold up* the firm by forcing it to pay higher wages; the firm is stuck with its installed capital and thus pays the higher wages and, in turn, receives lower profits. If firms are forward-looking, however, they can anticipate this sort of behaviour from unions *before* making such investments in physical capital. The possibility of being held up by union wage demands reduces the expected profitability of investment and may result in a reduction in investment. This decision to make fewer investments in physical capital would likely have negative implications for productivity growth in the industry.

There is some empirical evidence that the presence of a union does reduce investment by firms. It is not yet clear, however, whether such reduced investment has long-term effects on productivity. This issue is currently unresolved.

14.3 The "Good Jobs–Bad Jobs" Debate

In the 2011 federal election campaign, Conservative Prime Minister Stephen Harper emphasized the solid performance of the Canadian economy, noting especially the large number of new jobs that had been created in the years following the major global recession of 2009. The political opposition parties, however, argued that many of these new jobs were low-paying jobs in the service sector—often referred to as "McJobs"—and thus the large increase in employment was not necessarily an indicator of solid economic performance. This general issue has been debated in Canada and other countries for several years: Is there an ongoing trend away from "good" jobs and toward "bad" jobs?

Figure 14-9 shows how the composition of Canadian employment has changed over the past century. The share of total employment in agriculture fell from 45 percent in 1891 to just under 2 percent today, while the share of total employment in services (including government) increased from 20 percent in 1891 to 78 percent today. The combined share for manufacturing, construction, and natural resources (forestry, mining, oil and gas, etc.) has been more stable over the last century, but has been on a gradual downward trend for the past 50 years, falling from about 35 percent in 1951 to about 20 percent today.

The rise of service-sector employment, and the decline in the relative importance of the agriculture and manufacturing sectors as providers of jobs, is not just a Canadian phenomenon—it has happened in all developed economies. Table 14-2 shows the percentage of total employment provided by the service sector in several developed countries in 2011.

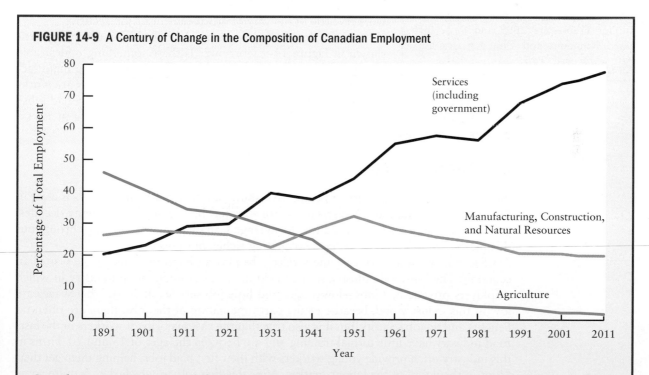

FIGURE 14-9 A Century of Change in the Composition of Canadian Employment

Over the past century, major shifts in employment have taken place between sectors of the economy. In 1891, more than 45 percent of Canadian employment was in agriculture, and only 20 percent in services (including government). By 2011, agriculture accounted for only 1.8 percent of employment, while services had increased to 78 percent. The share of employment in manufacturing increased from 26 percent in 1891 to 32 percent just after the Second World War, and then declined to 20 percent by 2011.

(*Source: Canadian Census*, various years, and author's calculations. The most recent data are available on the Statistics Canada website at www.statcan.gc.ca. Choose "Summary Tables" and then type in "employment by industry.")

TABLE 14-2	The Importance of Service-Sector Employment, 2011

Country	Percentage of Civilian Employment in Services
Australia	76.4
Belgium	75.5
Canada	78.1
France	77.5
Japan	70.2
Sweden	78.1
United Kingdom	79.6
United States	81.2

For most developed economies, about three-quarters of employment is in the service sector.

(*Source*: OECD, ALFS Summary Tables; data for France are 2009 and those for United Kingdom and United States are 2010. www.oecd.org.)

The service sector contains an enormous variety of occupations. Many jobs in the service sector require considerable education and training, and thus the workers in these jobs are highly paid. Obvious examples include lawyers, doctors, architects, design engineers, accountants, management consultants, and professors. On the other hand, the service sector also contains many jobs that require much less training and whose workers therefore receive much lower wages. Examples of these occupations include many restaurant waiters, fast-food employees, store clerks, flight attendants, telephone solicitors, janitors, and hotel maids.

In general, we can divide service-sector employment into two parts—the first part containing highly paid jobs and the second containing mostly low-wage jobs. The concerns sometimes heard about the growing importance of service-sector jobs are really concerns about this low-wage part of the service sector. In these jobs—many of which are in the retail sector—there are fewer possibilities for using more capital per worker and thus fewer possibilities to increase the productivity of labour. Another concern is that many of these low-wage service-sector jobs offer workers little in the way of advancement or job security.

Are the dramatic changes in the composition of employment shown in Figure 14-9 worrying? Is there something undesirable about the fact that fewer workers are now producing manufactured goods than 40 years ago? Or that more workers are working in the service sector than 40 years ago? Are good jobs being replaced by bad jobs? The final section of this chapter provides six observations that are important in assessing this contentious issue.

Six Observations

First, we need to keep a sense of perspective about labour-market changes. As is clear in Figure 14-9, the trend toward service-sector jobs has been going on for many decades, yet real income per hour worked for the average Canadian has been rising throughout this period; as a nation, Canadians are getting richer, not poorer.

Second, even the lowest-paying service jobs play an important role in the Canadian economy. The fast-food industry is often held up as an example of an industry in which employers provide bad jobs—low wages and little job security. It *is* true that wages are low in this industry and, because of the part-time nature of the jobs, there are often no benefits and no job security. But it is also true that the vast majority of workers in the fast-food industry have little formal training and are between the ages of 15 and 20. Firms in this industry often provide young workers with their first paid jobs, helping them get their "foot in the door" of the labour market. After this first job, in which they acquire some skills and demonstrate responsibility, many young workers move on to jobs that are more demanding and for which they would not have qualified before their experience in the fast-food industry. In other words, some low-paying service-sector jobs provide employment to young, untrained individuals who would otherwise find it difficult to find a job at all.

Third, the decrease in the share of manufacturing in total employment is partly a result of that sector's dynamism and dramatic increases in productivity over many years. More and more manufactured goods have been produced by fewer and fewer workers, leaving more workers to produce services. This movement is analogous to the developments in agriculture in the twentieth century. At the turn of the twentieth century, nearly 45 percent of the Canadian labour force worked on farms. Today that number is about 2 percent, yet they produce more total agricultural output than did the 45 percent in 1900. This movement away from agricultural employment freed workers to move into manufacturing, raising our living standards and transforming our way of life. In like manner, the movement away from manufacturing has been freeing workers to move into services, and by replacing many unpleasant blue-collar jobs of the smoke-stack industries with more pleasant white-collar jobs in the service industries, it has once again transformed our way of life.

Fourth, the decrease in the share of manufacturing in total employment also fol-lows from consumers' tastes. Just as consumers in the first half of the twentieth cen-tury did not want to go on consuming more and more food products as their incomes increased, today's consumers do not want to spend all of their additional income on manufactured products. Households have chosen to spend a high proportion of their increases in income on services, thus creating employment opportunities in that sector. This simply reflects the fact that many products of the service sector—like restaurant meals, hotel stays, and airline flights—are products that have a high income elasticity of demand. Thus, as the income of the average Canadian household increases, so too does that household's demand for these products of the service sector.

Fifth, it is easy to underestimate the scope for quality, quantity, and productivity increases in services. But these changes permit us to have a higher standard of living than we would otherwise have. As just one example of productivity increases, consider your ability to make an automatic cash withdrawal, at any time of the day or night, from your bank account in Nova Scotia, while you are on vacation in Brazil. Compare that with the apprehension your parents faced 35 years ago when they had to get to their bank branch before 3:00 p.m. on a Friday afternoon to make sure they had enough cash for the weekend. ATMs did not yet exist and it would have been impossible for them to cash a cheque in Brazil without having made elaborate prior arrangements.

Finally, many quality improvements in services go unrecorded even though they still contribute to our improved living standards. Today's hotel room is vastly more comfortable than a hotel room of 40 years ago, yet this quality improvement does not show up in our national income statistics. Measuring such technological improvements is even more difficult when they take the form of entirely new products. Airline trans-portation, telecommunication, fast-food chains, and financial services are prominent examples. The resulting increase in output is not always properly captured in existing statistics, though the resulting improvements in our living standards are easy for us to acknowledge.

A Mixed Blessing?

It is easy to become concerned when looking at the official statistics, which show low wages earned in some service jobs. Indeed, the shift in employment toward services is, like most changes that hit the economy, a mixed blessing. It entails a significant increase in the number of "bad" service-sector jobs with low pay or low job security. Further, such transitions often generate temporary unemployment as workers get laid off from a shrinking manufacturing sector and only slowly find jobs in the expanding service sector. Such transitions suggest a role for government policy to maintain the income of those workers temporarily unemployed (we will discuss employment insurance and other income-support programs in Chapter 18). However, if we focus on the *overall economy*, and consider the growth in the real living standards of the *average* Canadian household, we are reminded that average real income has continued to rise, not only throughout the shift from agriculture to manufacturing, but also throughout the shift from manufacturing to services. There is little reason to think that the continued growth of the service sector will stand in the way of this slow but steady improvement in Canadians' living standards.

SUMMARY

14.1 Wage Differentials
LO 1, 2

- In a competitive labour market, wages are set by the forces of supply and demand. Differences in wages will arise because some skills are more valued than others, because some jobs are more onerous than others, because of varying amounts of human capital, and because of discrimination based on such factors as gender and race.
- A union entering a competitive market can act as a monopolist and can raise wages but at a predicted cost of reducing employment.
- A profit-maximizing monopsonistic employer entering a competitive labour market will reduce both the wage and the level of employment.
- A union in a monopsonistic labour market—a case of bilateral monopoly—may increase both employment and wages relative to the pure monopsony outcome. If the union sets wages above the competitive level, however, the prediction is that it will create a pool of workers who are unable to get the jobs that they want at the going wage.
- Governments set some wages above their competitive levels by passing minimum-wage laws. In competitive labour markets, a minimum wage is predicted to reduce employment and create some unemployment. In monopsonistic labour markets, a legislated minimum wage (as long as it is not too high) can raise both wages and employment.

14.2 Labour Unions
LO 3

- Labour unions seek many goals when they bargain with management. They may push for higher wages, higher benefits, more stable employment, or less onerous working conditions. Whatever their specific goals, unless they face a monopsonist across the bargaining table, they must recognize the inherent conflict between the level of wages and the size of the union itself.
- There is clear evidence in Canada of a union wage premium: Unionized workers with a particular set of skills in particular types of jobs get paid 10 to 15 percent more than otherwise identical workers who are not union members.

14.3 The "Good Jobs–Bad Jobs" Debate
LO 4

- The past half-century has witnessed an increase in the share of total employment in the service sector and a decline in the share of employment in manufacturing.
- One part of the service sector requires considerable skills and pays high wages, while another part requires few skills and pays low wages. Some people are concerned that some "good" manufacturing jobs are being replaced by "bad" service jobs.
- The service sector provides many young people with their first job, and this prepares them for better, more permanent jobs in the future.
- The decline in manufacturing employment is partly due to the technological improvements in that sector and partly due to shifts in consumers' tastes toward services.
- Though the shift away from manufacturing and toward services involves some costs during the transition period, the ongoing growth in average per capita income (plus the hard-to-measure quality improvements) suggests that the shift is not a problem for the economy as a whole.

KEY CONCEPTS

Wage differentials in competitive
  labour markets
Effects of discrimination on wages and
  employment
Labour unions as monopolists

Single employer as monopsonist
Bilateral monopoly
Effects of legislated minimum wages
Collective bargaining

Union goals: wages versus employment
Union wage premium
"Good jobs" vs. "bad jobs"

STUDY EXERCISES

MyEconLab Make the grade with MyEconLab: Study Exercises marked in red can be found on MyEconLab. You can practise them as often as you want, and most feature step-by-step guided instructions to help you find the right answer.

1. Fill in the blanks to make the following statements correct.

   a. If all workers were identical, all jobs had identical working conditions, and labour markets were perfectly competitive, then all wages would be _____.

   b. In reality there is wide variation in wages. Four reasons for wage differentials are _____, _____, _____, and _____.

   c. A country that invests in its public education and public health systems is improving the _____ of its population.

   d. If there are two groups of workers in a competitive labour market, and one group becomes discriminated against, the labour supply curve for jobs that remain available for that group will shift to the _____ and the wages for these jobs will _____.

2. Suppose there are only two industries in the economy. All workers have the same skills and the same preferences. But the jobs in the two industries are different. In the Pleasant industry, working conditions are desirable (quiet, safe, clean, etc.). In the Grimy industry, working conditions are awful (noisy, unsafe, dirty, etc.).

   a. Draw supply-and-demand diagrams for the labour market in each industry.

   b. In which industry are wages higher? Why?

   c. Now suppose the Grimy industry made its working conditions just as pleasant as in the Pleasant

   industry. Explain what happens in *both* labour markets.

3. Suppose there are two types of basketball players—black and white. Suppose also that, on average, black players are no better and no worse than white players. Furthermore, suppose there are only two types of basketball teams—good and bad. Good teams hire only good players; bad teams will hire both good and bad players. The two diagrams that follow show the initial outcomes in the labour markets for good teams and bad teams. Assume there is *no discrimination based on race*.

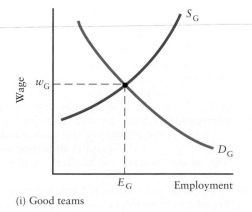

(i) Good teams

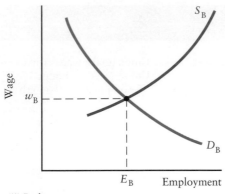

(ii) Bad teams

a. As shown in the figures, the wage paid by good teams is higher than the wage paid by bad teams. What explains this wage differential?

b. Do black players earn more or less than white players, on average? Explain.

c. Now suppose the good teams discriminate against white players—rightly or wrongly they *believe* that black players are better than white players. Show in your diagram what happens in both labour markets.

d. In the situation in part (c), what happens to the wage differential between good and bad teams?

e. In the situation in part (c), what happens to the average black–white wage differential?

4. Suppose *in the real world* you observe that black basketball players get paid more than white basketball players. Do you conclude that discrimination is present? Explain why or why not.

5. Fill in the blanks to make the following statements correct.

a. If workers in a competitive labour market join together to form a union, the effect will be a(n) _____ wage and _____ quantity of labour demanded.

b. If firms in a competitive labour market form an employers' association and become a monopsonist, employment will be _____ and wages will be _____ than in the competitive outcome.

c. A legislated and binding minimum wage in a competitive labour market will lead to a(n) _____ in the quantity of labour demanded and a(n) _____ in the quantity of labour supplied. The actual number of workers employed will _____.

d. A legislated and binding minimum wage in a market where the employer has monopsony power and the wage is initially below the competitive level will lead to a(n) _____ in the number of workers employed.

6. The table below shows how many workers are prepared to work at various hourly wages in the forestry industry. It also shows the workers' marginal revenue product (*MRP*).

Number of Workers	Wage ($)	Marginal Cost of Labour ($)	MRP ($)
50	10		40
100	12	14	30
150	14	18	24
200	16	—	22
250	18	—	20
300	20	—	18
350	22		

a. On a diagram, draw the supply of labour curve and the demand for labour curve.

b. What is the equilibrium wage and level of employment if the labour market is competitive?

c. Now suppose there is only a single buyer for labour—a *monopsonist*. Compute the marginal cost of labour for each level of employment and fill in the table. (Recall that the *MC* of labour is the change in labour cost divided by the change in employment. The first two rows have been completed for you.)

d. What wage and level of employment would the monopsonist choose? Explain.

7. The following diagram shows the market for labour in a particular industry. It shows both the supply of labour (the average cost of labour) and the marginal cost of labour.

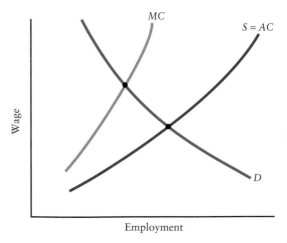

a. Suppose the labour market is competitive. Indicate on the diagram the equilibrium wage and level of employment (call them w^* and L^*).

b. Now suppose the government imposes a minimum wage equal to $w^{min} > w^*$. Show what happens to wages and employment.

c. In the absence of a minimum wage, show the outcome if there is a monopsony buyer of labour services. Call this wage w^p.

d. Beginning with the monopsony outcome, show what happens if the government imposes a minimum wage above w^p but lower than w^*.

e. Do minimum wages always reduce employment? Explain.

8. For each of the cases below, identify whether the observed wage differential is likely to be an *equilibrium* or a *temporary* differential, and explain why.

a. Pilots in one non-unionized airline earn 20 percent more than pilots in a second non-unionized airline.

b. Construction workers employed near Alberta's oil sands earn 30 percent more than similar workers in Manitoba.

c. Dental surgeons earn far more than dental hygienists.

d. Pilots in a non-unionized airline earn more than flight attendants in the same airline.

e. Economists employed by universities earn significantly less than economists of similar skills employed by commercial banks.

9. The following diagram shows the market for labour in a particular industry. It shows both the supply of labour (the average cost of labour) and the marginal cost of labour. If the labour market were competitive, the outcome would be w^* and L^*.

a. Suppose the workers in this industry form a union that is able to raise the wage above w^*. Show the expected outcome in the figure.

b. Now suppose there is no union, but there is a monopsony buyer of labour. Show the expected outcome in this market.

c. Now suppose there is both a union and a monopsony firm. What can you predict about the outcome in this case?

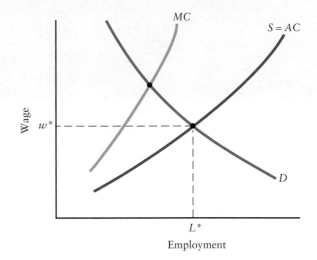

10. In trying to measure the extent to which labour unions are responsible for increasing wages, economists use sophisticated statistical methods to compare the wages of unionized workers with those of non-unionized workers. Explain why it is not legitimate simply to compare the average wage across the two groups and attribute the difference to the effects of unionization.

11. "One can judge the presence or absence of discrimination by looking at the proportion of the population in different occupations." Does such information help? Does it suffice? Consider each of the following examples. Relative to their numbers in the total population, there are

a. Too many blacks and too few Jews among professional athletes

b. Too few male secretaries

c. Too few female judges

d. Too few female prison guards

e. Too few male schoolteachers

f. Too few female graduate students in economics

12. One concern often expressed about the ongoing rise of services and decline of manufacturing is that the production of "things" is somehow better for wealth generation than the production of intangible services. Can you provide an argument in support of this view?

Interest Rates and the Capital Market

ECONOMISTS use the word *capital* in three different ways. *Human capital*, which we discussed in Chapter 14, is the set of skills that workers acquire through education and on-the-job training. *Physical capital* is a produced factor of production, such as a machine, a factory, or a bridge. *Financial capital* refers to financial assets in the form of loans, bonds, or stocks. In this chapter, we focus on what economists call the "capital market," which involves both physical and financial capital. We also examine the role played in this market by the interest rate.

15.1 A Brief Overview of the Capital Market

Firms require physical capital to produce their goods and services. Their purchase of new capital equipment is called *investment* in physical capital. They also require working capital—the funds necessary to purchase material inputs and pay workers while the goods are being made and even while the firm is waiting to be paid for its sales.

We saw in Chapter 7 that firms can finance their activities in one of four ways. First, they can use profits that are not remitted to shareholders—these are called *retained earnings*. Second, they can borrow from commercial banks or other financial intermediaries, such as credit unions and trust companies. Third, they can issue *bonds* (an IOU) and thereby borrow directly from lenders. Fourth, they can issue and sell *stock* (a share of the company) directly to shareholders. However firms choose to finance their activities, their demand for financial capital comes from their demands for physical capital and working capital.

> Firms' demand for financial capital is derived from their demands for physical capital and working capital.

The supply of financial capital comes mostly from households' saving decisions. Every year, millions of households decide how much of their after-tax income to save. These funds are often deposited into various types of accounts at commercial banks, each of which is a loan from a household to the bank. Sometimes the funds are used to buy bonds so that households are lending directly to non-bank borrowers. Households may also decide to purchase stocks, thereby acquiring shares of firms. Finally, some household saving is not done directly by households at all, but rather by employers and the government in the form of employer-sponsored and public pension plans (like the Canada Pension Plan). Whatever the form, households' saving determines their total supply of financial capital.

> Households' supply of financial capital is derived from their supply of saving.

Figure 15-1 illustrates the interaction of firms and households in the market for financial capital. Note that some funds flow directly between firms and households (bond and stock purchases) whereas other funds flow through financial intermediaries (bank deposits and loans). Financial intermediaries play an important role in the economy for two reasons. First, they are specialists in assessing the *riskiness* of potential borrowers and thus are better suited than most households to making loans to firms. Second, they have the ability to *pool* the savings from a large number of households and thereby make large loans to firms. Despite the importance of financial intermediaries to the economy, in this chapter we will focus our attention on households and firms, thus focusing on the fundamental determinants of the demand for and supply of capital.

During normal times, the process of financial intermediation—the flow of funds between households and firms through institutions, such as commercial banks—works so well that we barely notice its presence. In the financial crisis that began in 2008, however, this process was disrupted by the failure of several large financial institutions

FIGURE 15-1 The Interaction of Firms and Households in the Capital Market

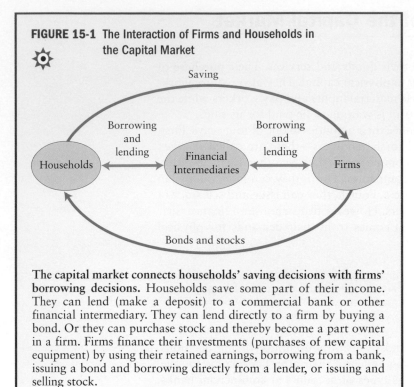

Saving

Borrowing and lending

Borrowing and lending

Households

Financial Intermediaries

Firms

Bonds and stocks

The capital market connects households' saving decisions with firms' borrowing decisions. Households save some part of their income. They can lend (make a deposit) to a commercial bank or other financial intermediary. They can lend directly to a firm by buying a bond. Or they can purchase stock and thereby become a part owner in a firm. Firms finance their investments (purchases of new capital equipment) by using their retained earnings, borrowing from a bank, issuing a bond and borrowing directly from a lender, or issuing and selling stock.

in the United States and Europe. With globally integrated financial markets, the result in Canada and elsewhere was an increase in the perceived risks associated with borrowing and lending, and thus a dramatic decline in the flows depicted in Figure 15-1. By late 2009, however, these financial flows had returned approximately to normal, partly in response to significant policy actions taken by governments and central banks in many countries.

In this chapter, we look first at firms' demand for physical capital, which leads us to an understanding of their demand for financial capital. As we will see, the interest rate plays an important role in determining how much capital is demanded by firms. We then examine households' saving decisions and thus their supply of financial capital. The interest rate also plays an important role in determining how much financial capital households want to supply. Once we understand the demand and supply for financial capital, we will be ready to put the two sides of the capital market together to determine the equilibrium "price" of financial capital—the interest rate. Finally, we will look at how economic events or policies can affect the equilibrium levels of investment, saving, and the interest rate.

Before beginning our analysis of the demand for capital, it is necessary to clarify one important difference between labour and physical capital as factors of production. When economists speak of the demand and supply for labour, they are referring to the *flow* of labour services. For example, a firm considers hiring the services of a worker for a month, after which the firm and the worker go their separate ways. In contrast, when a firm considers its demand for physical capital, it is considering purchasing a new piece of equipment and thereby adding to its *stock* of capital. This piece of capital equipment will usually deliver services to the firm over many years before it is eventually discarded because it has worn out or become obsolete. The durability of physical capital means that we must distinguish between the *stock* of capital and the *flow* of services that it delivers. We need a way to evaluate the flow of services that a piece of capital equipment delivers for many years into the future. Only then can we determine how much a firm would be willing to pay for the piece of capital equipment. This takes us to the concept of *present value*.

15.2 Present Value

Suppose a firm buys a piece of capital equipment and thereby obtains the use of that equipment until it wears out. The capital equipment delivers a flow of benefits over its lifetime—that is, it delivers some benefit every year for many years. The financial benefit to the firm in any given year is the marginal revenue product (*MRP*) of that unit of capital (recall from Chapter 13 that the *MRP* is the extra revenue generated by that unit). A given piece of capital may deliver different *MRP*s in different years—the *MRP* may change because of changes in market conditions or simply because the capital wears out slowly over time. In reality, the stream of future *MRP*s is uncertain. No firm can know with certainty how its market will evolve, how consumers will respond to the product, or even how long the capital equipment will last.

How much would a firm be willing to pay today to purchase a piece of capital equipment that will deliver a stream of benefits into the future? In order to answer this question we introduce the concept of *present value*. The **present value** of a future amount is the most that someone would be prepared to pay today to get that amount in the future. The concept of present value is used extensively in financial analysis as well as in the analysis of economic policies, where costs and benefits occur at different points in time.

In what follows, we simplify our discussion by assuming that the future benefits from a piece of capital equipment are known with certainty. This allows us to develop the central insights about present value and the interest rate without dealing with complications arising from uncertainty.

present value The value today of a future stream of payments discounted using the market interest rate.

The Present Value of a Single Future Payment

To begin our analysis, consider a very simple setting in which the piece of capital equipment produces an *MRP* only in one future period. Since most physical capital is durable and thus generates a *stream* of benefits, this assumption is quite unrealistic, but it is only our starting point. In our first example, the *MRP* occurs one period from now. In the second, the *MRP* occurs several periods from now.

One Period in the Future How much would a firm be prepared to pay now to purchase a capital good that produces an *MRP* of $100 in one year's time, after which time the capital good will be useless? One way to answer this question is to ask a somewhat *opposite* question: How much would the firm have to *lend* now in order to be repaid $100 a year from now? Suppose for the moment that the interest rate is 5 percent per year, which means that $1.00 loaned today will lead to a repayment of $1.05 in one year's time.

If we use *PV* to stand for this unknown amount, we can write $PV \times (1.05) = \$100$. Thus, $PV = \$100/1.05 = \$95.24$. This tells us that the present value of $100 receivable in one year's time is $95.24 when the interest rate is 5 percent. Anyone who lends out $95.24 for one year at 5 percent interest will receive $95.24 back plus $4.76 in interest, or $100 in total. When we calculate this present value, the interest rate is used to *discount* (reduce to its present value) the $100 to be received in one year's time.

The actual present value that we have calculated depended on our assumption that the interest rate was 5 percent. What if the interest rate is 7 percent? At that interest rate, the present value of the $100 receivable in one year's time would be $100/1.07 = \$93.46.

These examples are easy to generalize. In both cases, we have found the present value by dividing the sum that is receivable in the future by 1 plus the rate of interest.[1]

---

[1] In this type of formula, the interest rate *i* is expressed as a decimal fraction where, for example, a 7 percent annual interest rate is expressed as 0.07, so that $1 + i = 1.07$. We also assume throughout our analysis that discounting by the interest rate occurs annually rather than semi-annually, monthly, or continuously.

TABLE 15-1 The Present Value of a Single Sum One Year in the Future

	MRP	Interest Rate per Year	Present Value
1.	$500	4% = 0.04	$500/(1.04) = $480.77
2.	$500	5% = 0.05	$500/(1.05) = $476.19
3.	$500	6% = 0.06	$500/(1.06) = $471.70
4.	$500	7% = 0.07	$500/(1.07) = $467.29
5.	$500	8% = 0.08	$500/(1.08) = $462.96

For any given sum at a given point in the future, the present value of the sum is negatively related to the interest rate. The firm earns an *MRP* of $500 in one year's time. Using the formula developed in the text, it is clear that present value is lower when the interest rate is higher.

In general, if the interest rate is i per year, then the present value of the *MRP* (in dollars) received one year hence is

$$PV = \frac{MRP}{(1 + i)}$$

Table 15-1 computes the present value of an *MRP* of $500, received one year from now, under alternative assumptions of the interest rate. There is a negative relationship between present value and the interest rate.

Several Periods in the Future Now we know how to calculate the present value of a single sum that is receivable one year in the future. The next step is to ask what would happen if the sum were receivable at a later date. For example, what is the present value of $100 to be received *two* years hence when the interest rate is 5 percent? The answer is $100/[(1.05)(1.05)] = $90.70. We can check this by seeing what would happen if $90.70 were lent out for two years. In the first year, the loan would earn interest of $(0.05)($90.70) = 4.54, and hence after one year, the outstanding loan would be worth $95.24. If we assume that interest is compounded annually, then in the second year the interest earned would equal $(0.05)($95.24) = 4.76. Hence, after two years the firm would be repaid $100.

In general, the present value of *MRP* dollars received t years in the future when the interest rate is i per year is

$$PV = \frac{MRP}{(1 + i)^t}$$

This formula simply discounts the *MRP* by the interest rate, repeatedly, once for each of the t periods that must pass until the *MRP* becomes available. If we look at the formula, we see that the higher is i or t, the higher is the whole term $(1 + i)^t$. This term, however, appears in the denominator, so *PV* is *negatively* related to both i and t.

Table 15-2 computes the present value of an *MRP* of $500 received several years in the future. The table has two parts. In Part A, we keep the date of the *MRP* fixed and vary the interest rate. In Part B, we keep the interest rate fixed and vary the date of the *MRP*. This allows us to see the separate effects of varying i and t, and leads to the following conclusion.

> Other things being equal, the present value of a given sum payable in the future will be smaller the more distant the payment date, and it will be smaller the higher the rate of interest.

The Present Value of a Stream of Future Payments

Now consider the present value of a stream of payments that continues for *many* periods into the future. As we said earlier, the future benefits that a firm receives from a piece of capital equipment may not be constant. Changes in market conditions, technology, or the quality of the capital itself may result in different *MRP*s in different periods.

TABLE 15-2 The Present Value of a Single Sum Several Years in the Future

Part A: Date Fixed; Interest Rate Variable

	MRP	Date	Interest Rate per Year	Present Value
1.	$500	3 years	4% = 0.04	$500/(1.04)^3 = $444.50
2.	$500	3 years	5% = 0.05	$500/(1.05)^3 = $431.92
3.	$500	3 years	6% = 0.06	$500/(1.06)^3 = $419.81
4.	$500	3 years	7% = 0.07	$500/(1.07)^3 = $408.15

Part B: Date Variable; Interest Rate Fixed

	MRP	Date	Interest Rate per Year	Present Value
1.	$500	2 years	6% = 0.06	$500/(1.06)^2 = $445.00
2.	$500	3 years	6% = 0.06	$500/(1.06)^3 = $419.81
3.	$500	4 years	6% = 0.06	$500/(1.06)^4 = $396.05
4.	$500	5 years	6% = 0.06	$500/(1.06)^5 = $373.63

The present value of a future sum is negatively related to the interest rate and negatively related to the length of time before the sum occurs. In all the rows in Part A, the firm receives an *MRP* of $500 in three years' time, but the interest rate varies. Using the formula from the text, we see that the higher is the interest rate, the lower is the present value of the future *MRP*. In all the rows in Part B, the interest rate is 6 percent per year, but the future date of the *MRP* varies. The computations show that the more distant in time is the *MRP*, the lower is the present value.

For example, one new lathe may generate a marginal revenue product equal to $200 one year from now, $180 two years from now, and $210 in the third year—before it wears out and ceases to generate any further benefits.

How do we compute the present value of such an uneven stream of *MRP*s? The answer is surprisingly simple. We just treat each future *MRP* as a single *MRP* that occurs at some point in the future. We then apply our earlier formula to each *MRP* and add them up. For example, suppose the interest rate is 6 percent per year and the capital generates *MRP*s equal to $200 in one year, $180 in two years, $210 in three years, and nothing thereafter. The present value of this stream of *MRP*s is

$$PV = \frac{\$200}{1.06} + \frac{\$180}{(1.06)^2} + \frac{\$210}{(1.06)^3}$$
$$= \$188.68 + \$160.20 + \$176.32$$
$$= \$525.20$$

In general, if MRP_t is the *MRP* that occurs t years from now, if i is the interest rate, and if the stream of *MRP*s lasts for N years, the present value of the stream of *MRP*s is

$$PV = \frac{MRP_1}{1+i} + \frac{MRP_2}{(1+i)^2} + \cdots + \frac{MRP_N}{(1+i)^N}$$

Table 15-3 computes the present value of several streams of *MRP*s. It confirms the relationships we observed earlier. First, other things being equal, a higher interest rate leads to a lower present value. Second, for a given interest rate, a larger *MRP* leads to a larger present value. But now that we have a stream of *MRP*s that lasts for several periods, rather than just a single period, we can add a third general result: The longer a stream of *MRP*s lasts into the future, the greater is the present value.

TABLE 15-3 The Present Value of a Stream of Future Payments

Part A: Alternative Interest Rates

	MRP_1	MRP_2	MRP_3	Interest Rate per Year	Present Value
1.	$500	$400	$300	8% = 0.08	$\dfrac{500}{1.08} + \dfrac{400}{(1.08)^2} + \dfrac{300}{(1.08)^3} = \$1044.05$
2.	$500	$400	$300	5% = 0.05	$\dfrac{500}{1.05} + \dfrac{400}{(1.05)^2} + \dfrac{300}{(1.05)^3} = \$1098.15$

Part B: Alternative MRPs

	MRP_1	MRP_2	MRP_3	Interest Rate per Year	Present Value
3.	$300	$300	$300	5% = 0.05	$\dfrac{300}{1.05} + \dfrac{300}{(1.05)^2} + \dfrac{300}{(1.05)^3} = \$816.97$
4.	$400	$400	$400	5% = 0.05	$\dfrac{400}{1.05} + \dfrac{400}{(1.05)^2} + \dfrac{400}{(1.05)^3} = \$1089.30$

Part C: Alternative Lengths of Stream

	MRP_1	MRP_2	MRP_3	Interest Rate per Year	Present Value
5.	$500	$500	$0	5% = 0.05	$\dfrac{500}{1.05} + \dfrac{500}{(1.05)^2} + 0 = \$929.70$
6.	$500	$500	$500	5% = 0.05	$\dfrac{500}{1.05} + \dfrac{500}{(1.05)^2} + \dfrac{500}{(1.05)^3} = \$1361.62$

The present value of a future stream of sums is negatively related to the interest rate, positively related to the size of each payment, and positively related to the length of time the stream continues. Part A presents a given stream of MRPs over three years but considers two different interest rates. The PV of the stream of MRPs is higher when the interest rate is lower.

Part B uses only a single interest rate of 5 percent but considers two different streams of MRPs. One is a stream of $300 that lasts for three years; the other is a higher stream of $400 that also lasts for three years. The stream with the higher MRPs has the higher present value.

Part C uses an interest rate of 5 percent and a constant stream of MRPs of $500 per year. One stream lasts for two years, whereas the other lasts for three years. The longer-lasting stream of MRPs has the higher present value.

Conclusions

The concept of present value can be confusing at first, but you should now see the straightforward way to evaluate a stream of benefits into the distant future. Let's summarize our findings.

1. A piece of capital is valuable because it generates a *stream* of financial benefits into the future. These benefits in each period are the capital's marginal revenue product (MRP). The value to the firm of owning this capital now is what we have called its *present value*.

2. The larger is each future MRP, or the longer the stream of MRPs lasts, the greater is the present value of the capital.

3. For a given stream of future *MRP*s, the present value of the capital is negatively related to the interest rate. That is, when interest rates are higher, a given piece of capital is valued less. When interest rates are lower, the capital is valued more highly.

4. Capital that delivers its *MRP*s in the more distant future has a lower present value than capital that delivers the same stream of *MRP*s sooner.

We now go on to examine an individual firm's demand for capital goods. We will then consider the economy's overall demand for capital. Present value and the interest rate play a central role in our analysis.

15.3 Investment Demand

As we said earlier, a firm's demand for financial capital comes from its demand for physical capital. Economists assume that the amount of physical capital the firm chooses to use comes from its objective of maximizing profit. We now examine this decision in detail.

The Firm's Demand for Capital

An individual firm faces a given interest rate and a given purchase price of capital goods. The firm can vary the quantity of capital that it employs, and as a result, the marginal revenue product of its capital varies. The hypothesis of diminishing marginal returns (see Chapter 7) predicts that the more capital the firm uses, the lower its *MRP*.

The Decision to Purchase a Unit of Capital Consider a profit-maximizing firm that is deciding whether or not to add to its capital stock and is facing an interest rate of *i* at which it can borrow or lend money. The first thing the firm has to do is to estimate the expected stream of *MRP*s from the new piece of capital over its lifetime. Then it discounts this stream at the interest rate of *i* per year to find the present value of the stream of benefits the machine will generate. Having computed the *PV* of the stream of *MRP*s, the firm can then compare this *PV* with the purchase price of the capital good. The decision rule for a profit-maximizing firm is simple: If the *PV* is greater than or equal to the purchase price, the firm should buy the capital good; if the *PV* is less than the purchase price, the firm should not buy it.

Consider the following simple example. Suppose a computer appropriate for high-quality graphic design has an *MRP* of $1000 each year—that is, by buying this computer a graphic-design firm can produce more output and thereby increase its revenues by $1000 each year. Suppose further that the computer delivers benefits this year (now) and for two more years—after that, the computer is completely obsolete

A profit-maximizing firm will purchase units of physical capital up to the point at which the present value of the future stream of output produced by the last unit of capital equals its purchase price.

and worth nothing. Finally, suppose the interest rate is 6 percent per year. The *PV* of this stream of *MRP*s is then equal to

$$PV = \$1000 + \frac{\$1000}{(1.06)} + \frac{\$1000}{(1.06)^2}$$

$$= \$2833.40$$

The present value tells us how much any flow of future receipts is worth now. If the firm can buy the computer for less than its *PV*—that is, for any amount less than $2833.40—then this computer is a good buy. If it must pay more, the computer is not worth its price to this firm.

> If a firm wants to maximize its profits, it is worthwhile to buy another unit of capital whenever the present value of the stream of future *MRP*s generated by that unit equals or exceeds its purchase price.

The Firm's Optimal Capital Stock Because of the law of diminishing marginal returns, the *MRP* of each unit of capital generally declines as the firm buys more capital. The profit-maximizing firm will thus go on adding to its stock of capital until the present value of the stream of *MRP*s generated by the *last unit* added is equal to the purchase price of that unit.

> The profit-maximizing capital stock of the firm is such that the present value of the flow of *MRP*s that is provided by the last unit of capital is equal to its purchase price.

Figure 15-2 continues our earlier example of a graphic-design firm considering the purchase of a specialized computer. In this case, however, the firm is determining *how many* computers it wants to own and so must compare the purchase price and the present value of the stream of *MRP*s produced by each successive computer. Because the *MRP* of each computer declines as the firm uses more of them, Figure 15-2 shows a negative relationship between the purchase price of the computer and the quantity the firm chooses to own.

What economic events, other than a change in the price of capital, might lead the firm to change its optimal capital stock? In terms of the example shown in Figure 15-2, anything that increases the *PV* of the future *MRP*s of computers will increase the height of the bars in the figure and, for a given purchase price of computers, lead the firm to purchase more computers. More generally, anything that increases the *PV* of the future *MRP*s of capital will lead firms to increase their desired capital stock. This can occur in two general ways.

Increase in Future MRPs. If capital becomes more productive so that the stream of future *MRP*s increases, firms will choose to own more capital, even if the purchase price of capital is unchanged. For example, in Figure 15-2, if a technological improvement increases the annual *MRP* for each computer by 20 percent, each computer's *PV* will also increase by 20 percent. The bars in the figure will increase in height and, for any given purchase price, the firm will increase its desired stock of computers.

The future *MRP*s can also increase if the market price for the firm's product increases (or if demand for its product increases and it operates in an imperfectly competitive

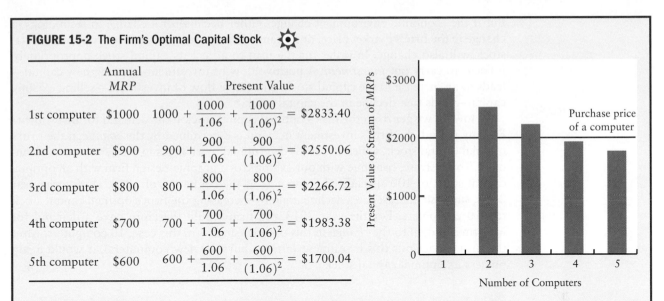

FIGURE 15-2 The Firm's Optimal Capital Stock ☼

	Annual MRP	Present Value
1st computer	$1000	$1000 + \dfrac{1000}{1.06} + \dfrac{1000}{(1.06)^2} = \$2833.40$
2nd computer	$900	$900 + \dfrac{900}{1.06} + \dfrac{900}{(1.06)^2} = \$2550.06$
3rd computer	$800	$800 + \dfrac{800}{1.06} + \dfrac{800}{(1.06)^2} = \$2266.72$
4th computer	$700	$700 + \dfrac{700}{1.06} + \dfrac{700}{(1.06)^2} = \$1983.38$
5th computer	$600	$600 + \dfrac{600}{1.06} + \dfrac{600}{(1.06)^2} = \$1700.04$

The firm's optimal capital stock is chosen so that the present value of the future MRPs on the last unit of capital is just equal to its purchase price. In this example, each computer delivers a stream of MRPs that begins now and lasts for two years, and the interest rate is 6 percent per year. The second column in the table shows the diminishing marginal revenue product of capital—the annual MRP generated by each computer is less than for the previous one. The third column computes the PV of the stream of MRPs for each computer, and these are plotted in the accompanying figure. If the purchase price of a computer is $2000, the firm will choose to own only three computers; any additional computer delivers a PV of MRPs that is less than the purchase price and thus is not profitable to the firm. An increase in the purchase price of a computer to $2400 would lead the firm to reduce its desired stock of computers to two.

market). Even without any technological change, an increase in price leads to an increase in the MRPs and thus to an increase in the height of the bars in Figure 15-2; the firm would buy more capital at any given purchase price.

Reduction in the Interest Rate. The PV of the stream of MRPs will also increase if the interest rate falls. A lower interest rate means that future MRPs get discounted at a lower rate—and therefore have greater present value. Thus, as the interest rate declines, the firm's optimal capital stock increases. In Figure 15-2, imagine that the interest rate is 3 percent per year instead of 6 percent. In this case, the PV of each computer's stream of future MRPs will rise, and each bar in the figure will increase in height. For a given purchase price of computers, the firm will therefore increase its desired stock of computers.

Anything that causes the present value of future MRPs of capital to increase—technological improvement, an increase in the firm's market price, or a reduction in the interest rate—leads firms to increase their desired capital stock.

From Capital Stock to Investment Demand We have just examined how a profit-maximizing firm determines its optimal stock of physical capital. It is important to emphasize again the distinction between *stocks* and *flows*—in this case the distinction between the firm's optimal *stock* of capital and its optimal *flow* of investment. In any given period, a firm can determine its optimal stock of capital as shown in Figure 15-2.

But if the economic environment changes either because of a change in technology, a change in the firm's market price, or a change in interest rates, the firm's optimal capital stock will also change. In order for the firm to adjust its capital stock appropriately, it needs to carry out *investment*. A positive flow of investment—buying new capital— leads to an increase in the capital stock; a negative flow of investment—selling existing capital—leads to a decline in the capital stock.[2]

How do we get from the firm's optimal capital stock to its demand for investment? For any period, the firm's investment demand is determined by the *change* in the firm's optimal capital stock, which in turn is determined by changes in the economic environment. To illustrate, continue with our example of a graphic-design firm with an optimal capital stock of 100 specialized computers at the beginning of 2013. During the year 2013, suppose interest rates decline, thereby increasing the firm's optimal capital stock to 110 computers. For the year 2013, the firm would therefore have a demand for investment equal to the *change* in this optimal stock—in this case, 10 computers. After the firm carries out this investment (after it buys 10 new computers), it would again possess its optimal capital stock.

> In any given period, the profit-maximizing firm's investment demand is given by the *change* in the firm's optimal capital stock.

Emphasis on the Interest Rate In Figure 15-2, there is a negative relationship between the purchase price of a computer and the desired stock of computers the firm wants to own. Firms use many types of physical capital, however, including buildings, factories, furniture, computer equipment, and various types of tools and machines. Each different type of physical capital has a different price and therefore it is impossible to think of any individual firm's desired capital stock in terms of any single price. For this reason, economists instead focus on the negative relationship between the firm's desired capital stock and the interest rate. Indeed, since firms use financial capital to purchase their physical capital, it is natural to think of the interest rate as the "price" of financial capital.

We just saw that when the interest rate falls, the *PV* of the future stream of *MRP*s will rise. This increase in the present value of capital will lead firms to increase their desired capital stock, and thus the quantity of investment demanded. The opposite happens when the interest rate rises. We thus get a general prediction about firms' investment behaviour:

> Other things being equal, firms' desired demand for investment (additions to physical capital) is negatively related to the interest rate.

This negative relationship between the interest rate and the firm's desired investment demand can be given another interpretation. Instead of purchasing physical capital that will generate future benefits, the firm could instead decide to purchase a bond that pays interest in the future. The interest rate on such a bond is the *opportunity cost* the firm faces if it chooses to invest in physical capital. A higher interest rate makes the

---

[2] Positive investment may not add to the firm's capital stock if it is just enough to replace obsolete capital. In this discussion, however, we make the simplifying assumption that all investment is *net* investment and thus increases the firm's capital stock.

bond purchase relatively more attractive and the investment in physical capital relatively less attractive, and thus it leads the firm to reduce its desired investment demand.

This negative relationship is shown in Figure 15-3. The negative relationship between the interest rate and the quantity of investment demanded can be thought of as the firm's demand curve for additional physical capital where the relevant "price" is the interest rate.

What would cause a firm's investment demand curve to shift? First, suppose the firm's expectations about future demand for its product improve. This optimism leads the firm to expect an increase in the future stream of *MRP*s produced by capital. With higher expected *MRP*s, the firm is prepared to purchase more units of capital (at any interest rate). Thus, the firm's investment demand curve shifts to the right. Second, suppose an improvement in technology increases the future stream of *MRP*s. Again, the higher future *MRP*s lead the firm to purchase more units of capital at any interest rate—a rightward shift in the firm's investment demand curve.

> **Any event that increases the expected future stream of *MRP*s leads to an increase in the firm's investment demand.**

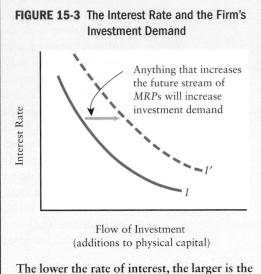

FIGURE 15-3 The Interest Rate and the Firm's Investment Demand

Anything that increases the future stream of *MRP*s will increase investment demand

Interest Rate

I'

I

Flow of Investment
(additions to physical capital)

The lower the rate of interest, the larger is the firm's demand for investment. The lower the interest rate, the higher is the present value of any given stream of *MRP*s and hence the more capital that the firm will wish to use.

Anything that increases the future stream of *MRP*s produced by the capital leads the firm to demand more units of capital at any interest rate—the investment demand curve shifts to *I'*.

The Economy's Demand for Investment

The economy's overall demand for investment is determined from the demands of individual firms. Thus, there is a negative relationship between the interest rate and the desired *aggregate* investment for the same reasons that the negative relationship exists for any individual firm. The economy's demand for investment can therefore be represented by a downward-sloping curve like the one in Figure 15-3.

The economy's investment demand curve shifts for the same reasons that individual firms' demand curves shift. Anything that increases the future stream of *MRP*s of capital leads to a rightward shift in the investment demand curve. Technological improvements are a key reason for such increases in the demand for investment. (We will say more about this later.)

15.4 The Supply of Saving

The supply of financial capital is determined by households' saving decisions. Saving is the difference between income and current spending. At any given time, households have a stock of *assets* that represents the accumulation of their past saving. During any given year, households modify their accumulated stock of assets by either saving or borrowing. (Saving leads to an increase in the accumulated stock of assets; borrowing leads to a reduction in the accumulated stock of assets.) Thus, the annual *flow* of saving by households leads to a change in the total *stock* of assets.

Households save because it allows them to spend in the future some of the income they earned today. They do this for several reasons. First, most people work for only part of their lives and, during their retirement, must live off their accumulated assets (plus whatever income they receive from employer or public pensions). Saving in the current year is a way of building up this retirement "nest egg." A second reason people save is that the future is uncertain. Next year they might become unemployed and thus lose their source of income, or they may have to provide for a relative who has lost a job or become incapacitated. In any case, uncertainty about the future provides a good reason to save. Finally, many households save in anticipation of specific large future expenditures. Young couples, for example, save in order to accumulate enough funds for a down payment on a house. Couples with young children save to help finance their children's university education.

Despite the many and varied reasons why any individual household chooses to save a lot or a little, to understand the economy's overall supply of financial capital, economists focus on three key determinants of saving—current income, expected future income, and the interest rate.

Saving and Current Income

Most people try to *smooth* their spending across time. Instead of spending a lot when income is high and spending only a little when income is low, most people prefer to spend a relatively stable amount from year to year. The result is that in high-income years people tend to save a lot, and in low-income years people tend to save only a little. (In years when income is very low, people may save a negative amount, meaning that they spend partially out of their accumulated assets or go into debt by borrowing to finance their expenditures.) When economists examine statistics across many households in the economy, they find that the positive relationship between total income and total saving is relatively stable.

Household saving is positively related to current income. An increase in current income increases the supply of financial capital.

Saving and Expected Future Income

For any given level of current income, households tend to save less when their expected future income is higher. If people anticipate that their income will be higher in the near future, their desire to smooth their spending (between now and the future) means that they will want to spend some of that higher future income now. An increase in their current spending, however, combined with an unchanged level of *current* income, means that their current saving must fall.

The best example of this behaviour is shown by many of you who are reading this book. Students are busy acquiring human capital and are usually earning little or no income. As we discussed in Chapter 14, people with university degrees earn more on average than people with only a high-school diploma. Thus, students are examples of people whose expected future income is considerably higher than their current income. The result is that many students are spending at levels that would be unaffordable (and quite imprudent!) if they were to earn their current incomes permanently. These students are spending at relatively high levels precisely because they expect to have much higher incomes in the near future. They are borrowing now (from parents or through student loans) because their future income will be high enough to pay back these debts.

> An increase in expected future income leads to a decline in current saving, and thus to a reduction in the supply of financial capital.

Saving and the Interest Rate

How does an increase in the interest rate affect households' desire to save? The interest rate is the "price" of financial capital. Like any price, the interest rate represents an opportunity cost—it is the opportunity cost of spending now rather than in the future. For example, suppose the interest rate is 5 percent per year. Your decision to spend $100 now "costs" you $105 in forgone spending one year from now. An increase in the interest rate increases the "price"—or opportunity cost—of current spending. Households respond to an increase in the interest rate by substituting away from (relatively expensive) current spending and toward (relatively inexpensive) future spending.

> An increase in the interest rate causes households to reduce their spending and increase their saving, thus increasing the quantity of financial capital supplied.[3]

The Economy's Supply of Saving

The economy's supply of saving is shown in Figure 15-4, which shows a positive relationship between the interest rate and the quantity of financial capital supplied by households. An increase in the interest rate leads the economy's households to increase their desired saving. This is a movement upward along the supply curve.

An increase in current income leads to an increase in households' desired saving *at any given interest rate* and thus causes the supply curve to shift to the right. An increase in expected future income (holding current income constant) leads to a decrease in households' desired saving *at any given interest rate* and thus causes the supply curve to shift to the left.

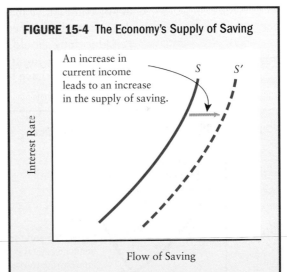

FIGURE 15-4 The Economy's Supply of Saving

An increase in current income leads to an increase in the supply of saving.

Interest Rate

Flow of Saving

There is a positive relationship between the interest rate and the flow of saving supplied by households. An increase in the interest rate increases the opportunity cost of current spending and leads households to increase their desired saving.

---

[3] This is the substitution effect of an increase in the interest rate and it works in the same direction for all individuals. There is also an income effect, which operates in one direction for households with negative net assets (debtors) and in the opposite direction for households with positive net assets (creditors). Economists often assume that, when summed across all households in the economy, some of which are debtors and others creditors, the overall effect of a change in the interest rate is in the direction of the substitution effect.

15.5 Investment, Saving, and the Interest Rate

We have discussed how the economy's demand for financial capital is related to the interest rate; a rise in the interest rate leads firms to reduce their desired capital stock and thus reduce their need for financial capital. We have also discussed how the economy's supply of financial capital is related to the interest rate; a rise in the interest rate leads households to increase their desired saving and thus provide more financial capital. We are now ready to put these two sides of the capital market together to examine market equilibrium.

Equilibrium in the Capital Market

There is an important difference between the analysis of individual firms and households on the one hand, and the analysis of the overall capital market on the other. Individual firms and households take the interest rate as given because they are so small relative to the entire economy that their own actions have no effect on the interest rate. For firms and households, the interest rate is *exogenous*. In the overall capital market, however, the interest rate is determined by the interaction of demand and supply—that is, the interest rate is *endogenous*. This important distinction is analogous to the one that exists in any competitive market; firms face a given market price for the product they sell, but the price is determined in equilibrium through the interaction of demand and supply.

One thing should be mentioned before we go on. In this chapter we have spent much time discussing the role of the interest rate in determining how firms and households behave. But we have ignored an important distinction between the *nominal* interest rate and the *real* interest rate. The *nominal* interest rate is the rate stated in the loan agreement. The *real* interest rate adjusts the nominal interest rate for the effects of inflation, and better represents the true cost of borrowing. (The real interest rate is approximately equal to the nominal interest rate minus the rate of inflation. The quality of this approximation is better the lower are interest and inflation rates.) *Extensions in Theory 15-1* examines this distinction in more detail. In the discussion that follows, we restrict our attention to the real interest rate.

Figure 15-5 shows how the interest rate is determined in the market for financial capital. The intersection of the investment demand curve and the saving supply curve determines the equilibrium interest rate, i^*. If the interest rate were above i^*, there would be an excess supply of capital; households' desired saving would exceed firms' desired borrowing. This excess supply of financial capital would cause the interest rate—the price of financial capital—to fall. Conversely, if the interest rate were below i^*, there would be an excess demand for capital; firms' desired borrowing would exceed households' desired saving. This excess demand for capital would cause the interest rate to rise. Only at i^* is the market in equilibrium—the quantity of investment demanded by firms is just equal to the quantity of saving supplied by households.

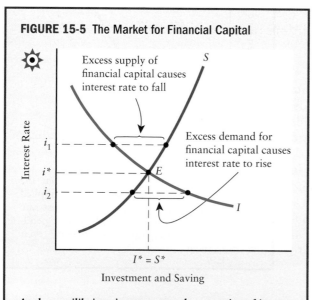

FIGURE 15-5 The Market for Financial Capital

Excess supply of financial capital causes interest rate to fall

Excess demand for financial capital causes interest rate to rise

At the equilibrium interest rate, the quantity of investment demanded equals the quantity of saving supplied. The equilibrium interest rate is i^* where the quantity of investment demanded by firms equals the quantity of saving supplied by households (point E).

EXTENSIONS IN THEORY 15-1

Inflation and Interest Rates

Inflation means the prices of all goods in the economy are rising. More correctly, it means that the prices of goods are rising on *average*—some prices may be rising and others may be falling, but if there is inflation then the average price is rising. Economists refer to the average price of all goods as the *price level*. When the price level is rising, inflation is positive; if prices are rising at a rate of 5 percent per year, the rate of inflation is 5 percent. When the price level is falling, inflation is negative. If prices are falling at a rate of 2 percent per year, the rate of inflation is –2 percent.

Real and Nominal Interest Rates

In the presence of inflation, we need to distinguish between the *real interest rate* and the *nominal interest rate*. The nominal interest rate is measured simply in dollars paid. If you pay me $7 interest for a $100 loan for one year, the nominal interest rate is 7 percent.

Consider further my one-year loan to you of $100 at the nominal rate of 7 percent. The *real* rate that I earn depends on what happens to the price level during the course of the year. If the price level remains constant over the year, then the real rate that I earn is also 7 percent—because I can buy 7 percent more goods and services with the $107 that you repay me than with the $100 that I lent you. However, if the price level were to rise by 7 percent during the year, the real rate would be zero because the $107 you repay me will buy exactly the same quantity of goods as did the $100 I gave up. If I were unlucky enough to have lent money at a nominal rate of 7 percent in a year in which prices rose by 10 percent, the real rate would be –3 percent. The real rate of interest concerns the ratio of the purchasing power of the money repaid to the purchasing power of the money initially borrowed, and it will be different from the nominal rate whenever inflation is not zero. *The real interest rate is the difference between the nominal interest rate and the rate of inflation.*

If lenders and borrowers are concerned with the real costs measured in terms of purchasing power, the nominal interest rate will be set at the real rate they require plus an amount to cover any expected rate of inflation. Consider a one-year loan that is meant to earn a real return to the lender of 3 percent. If the expected rate of inflation is zero, the nominal interest rate for the loan will also be 3 percent. If, however, a 10 percent inflation is expected, the nominal interest rate will have to be set at 13 percent in order for the real return to be 3 percent.

This point is often overlooked, and as a result people are surprised at the high nominal interest rates that exist during periods of high inflation. But it is the real interest rate that matters more to borrowers and lenders. For example, as the accompanying figure shows, in 1981 the nominal interest rate on three-month Treasury bills was almost 18 percent, but the high inflation rate at the time meant that the real interest rate was just over 5 percent. In contrast, a decade later in 1990, nominal rates had fallen to just below 13 percent but inflation had fallen further so that the real interest rate had actually *increased* to almost 8 percent. Thus, the period of lower nominal interest rates was actually a period of higher real interest rates.

Back to Capital

In this chapter we have examined investment demand by firms and the supply of saving by households. In both cases, the interest rate plays an important role. For firms, the interest rate reflects the cost of financial capital required to purchase physical capital. For households, the interest rate reflects the benefit of delaying their spending until the future and thus increasing their current saving. In both cases, though we did not say it, we were referring to the *real* interest rate.

When you go on to study *macroeconomics*, you will learn more about what causes inflation, and thus what forces us to make the distinction between real and nominal interest rates. For now, however, we assume in this chapter that there is no inflation; thus, real and nominal interest rates are the same.

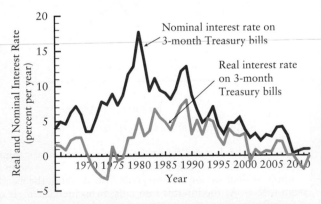

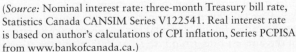

(*Source:* Nominal interest rate: three-month Treasury bill rate, Statistics Canada CANSIM Series V122541. Real interest rate is based on author's calculations of CPI inflation, Series PCPISA from www.bankofcanada.ca.)

Changes in the Capital-Market Equilibrium

We are now ready to examine some of the changes that occur in the market for financial capital and how these changes affect the equilibrium interest rate and levels of investment and saving.

Increases in the Supply of Financial Capital Anything that increases the flow of households' desired saving *at the given interest rate* will shift the supply curve for saving to the right. At the initial interest rate, this increase in desired saving will lead to an excess supply of financial capital and thus to a decline in the equilibrium interest rate. As the equilibrium interest rate falls, firms will find it profitable to expand their capital stock and will therefore increase their quantity of investment demanded. The rightward shift in the saving supply curve will therefore lead to a movement downward along the investment demand curve. The effect of an increase in the supply of saving is illustrated in part (i) of Figure 15-6. Three possible causes of such an increase in the supply of saving are provided.

Income Growth. As income increases, households desire to consume more, both now and in the future. The greater income leads to an increase in households' desired saving and thus to an increase in the supply of financial capital. Gradual but ongoing income growth over a period of many years is an important reason that the economy's supply of saving continues to increase.

FIGURE 15-6 Changes in Demand and Supply in the Market for Financial Capital

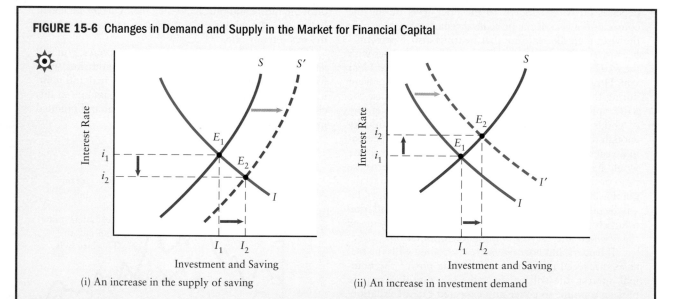

(i) An increase in the supply of saving   (ii) An increase in investment demand

Changes in the demand for or the supply of financial capital lead to changes in the equilibrium interest rate and levels of investment and saving. Part (i) illustrates an increase in the supply of saving. As households decide to increase the amount of their saving (at any given interest rate), the excess supply of capital leads to a reduction in the interest rate, from i_1 to i_2. As the interest rate falls, firms increase their quantity of investment demanded. The equilibrium level of investment (and saving) increases from I_1 to I_2.

Part (ii) illustrates an increase in investment demand. As firms decide to increase their desired investment, they require more financial capital (at any given interest rate). This leads to an excess demand for capital and to an increase in the interest rate, from i_1 to i_2. As the interest rate rises, households decide to increase their desired saving. The equilibrium level of investment (and saving) increases from I_1 to I_2.

Population Growth. An increase in the population—either through higher birth rates or greater immigration—leads to an increase in the supply of financial capital. The simple reason is that most households save, and so an increase in the number of households leads to an increase in the total amount of desired saving. For the effects on the capital market, there is little difference between an increase in the supply of capital caused by an increase in the number of households, and an increase in the supply of capital caused by higher income for an unchanged number of households. Both events will increase the economy's total income and thus total desired saving; both events will increase the economy's supply of financial capital.

Policies to Increase Desired Saving. Some Canadian government policies may increase households' desired saving. Registered Retirement Savings Plans (RRSPs) and Tax-Free Savings Accounts (TFSAs), for example, offer tax benefits to households who contribute to special "registered" savings accounts. For every dollar contributed to an RRSP (up to a limit), the household reduces its taxable income by a dollar and thus benefits by paying less income tax. While the funds remain in the RRSP account, the household does not pay any tax on the interest income earned. When the funds are eventually removed from the RRSP at some point in the future, the full amount of the withdrawal gets added to the household's taxable income at that point. TFSAs allow individuals to contribute up to $5000 per year and pay no taxes on the income generated within the account. Both RRSPs and TFSAs make saving more attractive by offering the household a tax benefit for saving.

There is some debate about whether RRSPs and TFSAs actually increase the *total* amount of household saving. Many households have taken advantage of these plans and have a large stock of accumulated assets inside their special accounts. The debate, however, centres on whether the funds inside these accounts would have been saved anyway through ordinary savings accounts that do not offer special tax treatment.

If RRSPs and TFSAs are successful in increasing the flow of total saving by households, the result is an increase in the economy's supply of financial capital and a reduction in the equilibrium interest rate. As the interest rate falls, firms will increase their planned investment. In the new equilibrium, the levels of both investment and saving will be higher.

Increases in the Demand for Financial Capital Anything that increases firms' desired investment *at the given interest rate* will shift the investment demand curve to the right. At the initial interest rate, this increase in the need for financial capital will lead to an excess demand for capital and thus to a rise in the equilibrium interest rate. As the equilibrium interest rate increases, households will find it desirable to reduce their current spending and increase their saving. The rightward shift in the investment demand curve will therefore lead to a movement upward along the saving supply curve. This case is illustrated in part (ii) of Figure 15-6. Let's briefly review some possible causes of an increase in the demand for financial capital.

Population and Income Growth. As the economy's total income grows, either through growth in population or in per capita income, the demand for goods and services increases. This increase in the demand for firms' products leads to an increase in the marginal revenue product (*MRP*) of capital. As we saw earlier in the chapter, an increase in capital's *MRP* leads to an increase in the economy's investment demand. The gradual but ongoing growth in the economy's total income is an important explanation for the gradual increase in the economy's investment demand.

Technological Improvement. Over time, there are technological improvements in the quality of factors of production. This is especially true for physical capital. Many of these improvements occur when obsolete or worn-out capital is replaced by new and better capital. For example, dramatic improvements in computer and information technology have occurred over the past two decades. New desktop computers are thousands of times faster and more powerful than two decades ago, and access to the Internet makes large quantities of information more readily available than it has ever been. Such improvements in computing power lead to large increases in the marginal product of some types of capital and thus an increase in the economy's investment demand.

Policies to Encourage Investment. Over the years, Canadian federal and provincial governments have designed policies to encourage firms to increase their investment in physical capital. One effect of such policies is to increase firms' demand for financial capital. Reductions in corporate income-tax rates, special investment tax credits, support for specific kinds of research and development, and loans guaranteed by governments are four different policies that increase the profitability of investment to firms and lead to an increase in their demand for financial capital.

Long-Run Trends in the Capital Market

Part (i) of Figure 15-7 shows the annual flow of net non-residential investment from 1965 to 2011. It is quite volatile over time, though always positive. Part (ii) shows how this volatile flow of investment has led to an ever-increasing non-residential capital stock; it grew at an average annual rate of 3.2 percent over the period shown. Even in years when the flow of investment is relatively large, the growth rate of the overall capital stock rises only slightly, reflecting the small size of the investment *flow* relative to the large accumulated capital *stock*. For similar reasons, large declines in the flow of investment—like the one that occurred during the major recession of 2009—led to only a slight slowdown in the growth of the capital stock. Part (iii) of the figure shows the path of the real interest rate, which is quite volatile and displays no clear trend over the 45-year period. How can we use our model of the capital market to understand these data?

Over long periods of time, technological change and population growth can explain both a rising capital stock and an interest rate with no clear long-run trend. We have already stated that population growth leads to an increase in both the demand for and the supply of financial capital. A larger population implies more demand for goods and services, and thus greater investment demand by firms. A larger population, even with an unchanged level of income per person, leads to more income and greater saving by households. With both the demand and the supply curves for financial capital shifting to the right because of population growth, there will be ongoing growth in the flow of investment and an ever-rising capital stock; the effect on the interest rate will depend on the relative size of the demand and supply shifts.

Technological change also affects both sides of the capital market. Improvements in technology that increase capital's *MRP* lead firms to increase their investment demand. As we have said several times already in this book, technological change also lies at the heart of increasing productivity and growing per capita income. As income grows, so too does the supply of saving. Thus, through its effect on income, technological improvements that stimulate investment demand also lead to an increase in the supply of financial capital. With both the demand and the supply curves shifting to the right

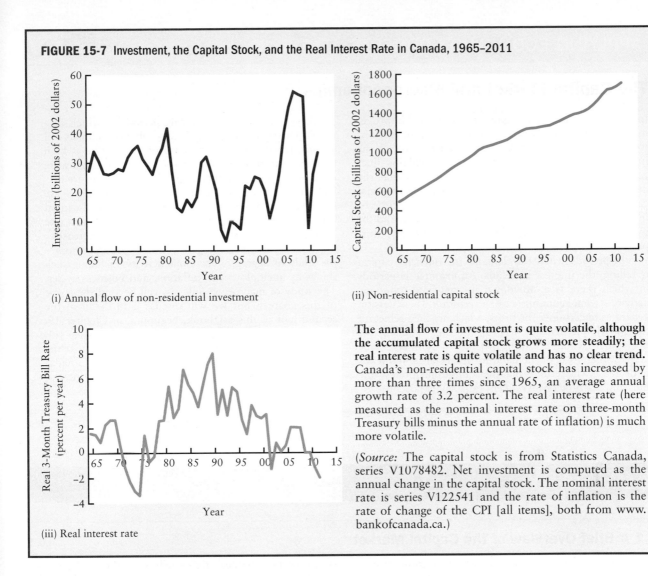

FIGURE 15-7 Investment, the Capital Stock, and the Real Interest Rate in Canada, 1965–2011

(i) Annual flow of non-residential investment

(ii) Non-residential capital stock

(iii) Real interest rate

The annual flow of investment is quite volatile, although the accumulated capital stock grows more steadily; the real interest rate is quite volatile and has no clear trend. Canada's non-residential capital stock has increased by more than three times since 1965, an average annual growth rate of 3.2 percent. The real interest rate (here measured as the nominal interest rate on three-month Treasury bills minus the annual rate of inflation) is much more volatile.

(*Source:* The capital stock is from Statistics Canada, series V1078482. Net investment is computed as the annual change in the capital stock. The nominal interest rate is series V122541 and the rate of inflation is the rate of change of the CPI [all items], both from www.bankofcanada.ca.)

because of technological improvements, there will be growth in the flow of investment and an ever-rising capital stock; the effect on the interest rate will again depend on the relative size of the demand and supply shifts.

Ongoing technological improvement and population growth, by increasing both the demand for and the supply of financial capital, explain a rising capital stock with no clear trend in the interest rate.

Our model of the capital market and the equilibrium interest rate can also be used to shed light on some *macroeconomic* issues—in particular, the nature of aggregate economic fluctuations. *Applying Economic Concepts 15-1* examines why during *recessions* and *booms* the demand for capital and the supply of capital often move in opposite directions, and why this helps to explain the volatility of the equilibrium interest rate.

APPLYING ECONOMIC CONCEPTS 15-1

The Capital Market and Macroeconomics

In the text we said that ongoing technological improvement and population growth can explain an upward trend in the capital stock with no clear trend in the interest rate. If this is the case, what explains fluctuations in the interest rate? The answer is that the demand and supply shifts in the market for financial capital are not happening at exactly the same time or in the same magnitude. In particular, firms' demand for investment can be quite volatile over relatively short periods of time.

In periods when the demand for financial capital is falling, the interest rate falls. An example is periods in which there is a slowdown in aggregate economic activity—what economists call a *recession*. The recession generates uncertainty for firms, which are then reluctant to embark on investment projects, thus reducing the demand for capital. During periods of slow economic activity, therefore, the demand for financial capital tends to decrease. The result is that the equilibrium interest rate falls and the flow of investment (and saving) declines.

The opposite is true during periods in which economic activity is growing quickly—what economists call *booms*. During booms, the level of production is high and growing in many industries, and there is growing demand for many factors of production. Firms are actively engaged in planning investment projects. These are times when the economy's demand for financial capital is growing. The result is that the equilibrium interest rate rises and the flow of investment (and saving) increases.

The topic of this box gets us into *macroeconomics*—the study of aggregate economic activity, including such things as unemployment, inflation, and business cycles. The study of macroeconomics is well beyond the scope of this chapter, but we will discuss it in detail in the second half of this textbook, beginning in Chapter 19. At this point, however, it is worth noting that when you go on to study macroeconomics, you will learn that the central bank (in Canada, it is called the Bank of Canada) also plays an important role in influencing the interest rate, at least over the short run.

SUMMARY

15.1 A Brief Overview of the Capital Market

LO 1

- The demand for financial capital comes from firms' need to finance their investment in new physical capital. The supply of financial capital comes from households' saving decisions.
- The capital market connects households' saving decisions with firms' financing requirements.

- Financial intermediaries—such as commercial banks—play an important role in bringing the two sides of the capital market together.

15.2 Present Value

LO 2

- Since physical capital is durable, it delivers benefits to its owners over many years. As a result, firms need to evaluate the stream of future benefits produced by capital.
- *Present value* is the value today of any stream of future sums; it is computed by discounting the future sums using the rate of interest. The present value of X

receivable in t years' time when the interest rate is i per year is

$$PV = \frac{X}{(1 + i)^t}$$

15.3 Investment Demand
LO 3

- Profit-maximizing firms will purchase capital up to the point at which the present value of the future stream of *MRP*s generated by the last unit of capital equals its purchase price.
- Economists focus on the relationship between the interest rate and firms' desired capital stock; an increase in the interest rate reduces the present value of any given stream of future *MRP*s and thus reduces firms' desired capital stock.
- Since firms require financial capital to finance their investment in additional capital equipment, the economy's demand for financial capital comes from the many individual firms' demand for investment. An increase in the interest rate leads to a decline in firms' quantity of investment demanded.
- An increase in the marginal product of capital increases firms' desired capital stock at any given interest rate and therefore leads to an increase in the economy's demand for financial capital. This is represented by a rightward shift in the economy's investment demand curve.

15.4 The Supply of Saving
LO 4

- The economy's supply of capital comes from households' flow of desired saving.
- An increase in the interest rate increases the opportunity cost of current spending and thus leads households to increase their desired saving. This is a movement upward along the economy's supply of saving curve.
- An increase in aggregate income—either through population growth or growth in per capita income—leads to an increase in total household saving at any given interest rate. The result is a rightward shift in the economy's supply of saving curve.

15.5 Investment, Saving, and the Interest Rate
LO 5

- Equilibrium in the market for financial capital is determined where the quantity of capital supplied by households equals the quantity of capital demanded by firms.
- Changes in the demand for capital or the supply of capital lead to changes in the equilibrium interest rate and equilibrium levels of investment and saving.
- Technological improvement and population growth lead to increases in both the demand for and the supply of capital. Continual technological improvement and population growth can therefore explain the ongoing growth in the capital stock with little or no trend in the interest rate.

KEY CONCEPTS

Physical capital and financial capital
Present value and the interest rate
A firm's optimal capital stock
The economy's demand for financial capital

Households' saving decisions
The economy's supply of financial capital

Equilibrium interest rate
Technological change and a rising capital stock

STUDY EXERCISES

MyEconLab   Make the grade with MyEconLab: Study Exercises marked in red can be found on MyEconLab. You can practise them as often as you want, and most feature step-by-step guided instructions to help you find the right answer.

1. Fill in the blanks to make the following statements correct.

   a. A firm's demand for financial capital is derived from its demand for _____.
   b. A firm that decides to invest in additional machinery will _____ its requirement for financial capital.
   c. An increase in the marginal product of capital will lead firms to _____ their desired capital stock and therefore _____ their demand for financial capital.
   d. An increase in the interest rate will _____ the present value of capital's *MRP* and therefore _____ firms' desired capital stock. The result will be a _____ in the quantity of financial capital demanded by firms.
   e. An increase in capital's *MRP* results in a(n) _____ in the economy's investment demand curve, whereas an increase in the interest rate results in a(n) _____ the economy's investment demand curve.

2. Fill in the blanks to make the following statements correct.

   a. An increase in the interest rate leads households to _____ their current spending and _____ their current saving. The result is an _____ in the quantity of financial capital supplied.
   b. An increase in current income leads to an _____ in household saving at any given interest rate. This results in a _____ in the economy's supply curve for capital.
   c. An increase in expected future income leads to an _____ in current household spending. The result is a _____ in household saving and therefore a _____ in the quantity of capital supplied at any given interest rate. This is represented by a _____ in the economy's supply curve for financial capital.

3. Fill in the blanks to make the following statements correct.

   a. The economy's equilibrium interest rate is determined where _____. At an interest rate above the equilibrium interest rate, the quantity of capital supplied _____ the quantity of capital demanded, and the result is a(n) _____ in the interest rate.
   b. At an interest rate below the equilibrium interest rate, the quantity of capital demanded _____ the quantity of capital supplied, and the result is a(n) _____ in the interest rate.
   c. Beginning in equilibrium in the capital market, an increase in the supply of financial capital leads to a(n) _____ in the equilibrium interest rate, a(n) _____ in borrowing by firms, and a(n) _____ in the equilibrium level of investment and saving.
   d. Beginning in equilibrium in the capital market, an increase in the demand for financial capital leads to a(n) _____ in the equilibrium interest rate, a(n) _____ in desired saving by households, and a(n) _____ in the equilibrium level of investment and saving.
   e. Technological improvements lead to a(n) _____ in both the demand for and the supply of financial capital. As a result, technological improvements can

   explain a(n) _____ capital stock and _____ in the interest rate.

4. The following table shows the stream of income produced by several different assets. In each case, P_1, P_2, and P_3 are the payments made by the asset at the end of years 1, 2, and 3.

Asset	i	P_1	P_2	P_3	Present Value
A	8%	$1000	$0	$0	—
B	7%	0	0	5000	—
C	9%	200	0	200	—
D	10%	50	40	60	—

   a. For each asset, compute the asset's present value. (Note that the market interest rate, i, is not the same in each situation.)
   b. In each case, what is the most a firm would be prepared to pay to acquire the asset?
   c. Suppose the listed purchase price for an asset were less than its present value. What would you expect to observe?

5. How would you go about evaluating the present value of each of the following?

   a. The existing reserves of a relatively small oil company
   b. The total world reserves of an exhaustible natural resource with a known completely fixed supply
   c. A long-term bond, issued by a very unstable third-world government, that promises to pay the bearer $1000 per year forever
   d. A lottery ticket that your neighbour bought for $10, which was one of 1 million tickets sold for a drawing that will be held in one year's time paying $2 million to the single winner

6. The following table shows how the present value of the future *MRP*s produced by each unit of capital changes as the firm's total capital stock increases.

Units of Capital	PV of Future *MRP*s
100	$10 000
101	9 000
102	8 000
103	7 000
104	6 000
105	5 000
106	4 000
107	3 000

   a. Notice that the present value of the *MRP* declines as more capital is used. What economic principle accounts for this?
   b. If a unit of capital can be purchased for $5000, how many will the firm purchase? Explain.
   c. Suppose the market interest rate falls. Explain what happens to the *PV* of the stream of future *MRP*s. What happens to the firm's profit-maximizing level of capital?

7. The diagram below shows an individual firm's investment demand curve. The market interest rate is i_0.

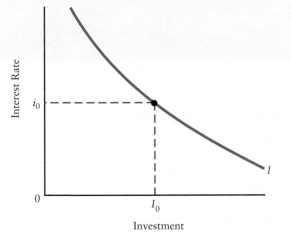

a. Explain why the firm's investment demand curve is downward sloping.
b. Suppose the firm now expects the market for its product to be especially good in the future. Explain what happens to its investment demand curve.
c. Now suppose some technical problem leads to a reduction in the future stream of $MRPs$ produced by capital. How does this affect the firm's investment demand curve?

8. For each interest rate below, compute the opportunity cost (in terms of forgone spending next year) to a household of spending $1000 this year:

a. The interest rate is 5 percent per year.
b. The interest rate is 7 percent per year.
c. The interest rate is 9 percent per year.
d. Explain why, other things being equal, households save more when the interest rate is higher.

9. Since the interest rate is the price of financial capital, a change in the interest rate generates both an income effect and a substitution effect.

a. Explain how the substitution effect of an increase in the interest rate influences households' desired saving.
b. Explain how the income effect of an increase in the interest rate influences households' desired saving. Why does the direction of the income effect depend on whether the household is a net debtor or a net creditor?
c. Explain why, for the economy as a whole, the substitution effect is likely to dominate the income effect.
d. What is the importance of the result in part (c) for the economy's supply of financial capital?

10. The accompanying figure shows the economy's capital market, with the initial equilibrium at point E, with an interest rate of i^* and investment (and saving) equal to I^*.

a. Suppose the government introduces a program of tax credits to firms that increase their desired investment in new physical capital. What is the

effect on the equilibrium interest rate, investment, and saving of this policy? Show the effect of this policy in the diagram.
b. In part (a), the policy has led to a higher interest rate *and* higher investment by firms. Does this contradict our discussion in this chapter about how firms' desired investment is negatively related to the interest rate? Explain.
c. Now suppose the government introduces a program of tax credits to households who save. What is the effect on the equilibrium interest rate, investment, and saving of this policy? Show the effect of this policy in the diagram.

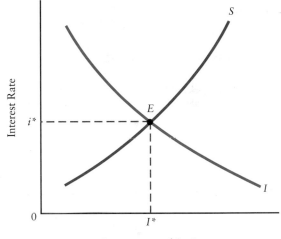

d. In part (c), the policy has led to a lower interest rate and higher saving by households. Does this contradict our discussion in this chapter about how households' desired saving is positively related to the interest rate? Explain.

11. "Profit-maximizing firms will reduce their desired investment when the interest rate rises, other things being equal. As a result, empirical economists should always expect to see a negative correlation between actual investment and the interest rate." Comment.

12. For parts of this question, it is useful to read **Investment and Saving in Globalized Financial Markets** in the *Additional Topics* section of this book's MyEconLab.

a. Suppose Canada were a closed economy, with no trade in financial capital with the rest of the world. In such a world, explain why a government that wanted to encourage domestic saving could achieve this outcome either by designing a policy to increase saving or by designing a policy to increase investment.
b. Now suppose financial capital is easily tradable between countries. What determines the Canadian real interest rate in such a setting?
c. Explain why the government objective to increase saving now requires a policy aimed directly at increasing saving (and not investment).

Market Failures and Government Intervention

CHAPTER OUTLINE	LEARNING OBJECTIVES (LO)
	After studying this chapter you will be able to
16.1 BASIC FUNCTIONS OF GOVERNMENT	1 discuss the importance of the government's "monopoly of violence."
16.2 THE CASE FOR FREE MARKETS	2 describe the "informal" defence of free markets.
16.3 MARKET FAILURES	3 explain what externalities are and why they lead to allocative inefficiency.
	4 explain why public goods are underprovided by private markets.
16.4 BROADER SOCIAL GOALS	5 understand why free markets may not achieve some desirable social goals.
16.5 GOVERNMENT INTERVENTION	6 identify the direct and indirect costs of government intervention, and some of the important causes of government failure.

MANY aspects of Canadian economic life are determined in free markets. Most of the goods and services that you buy are produced by privately owned profit-making firms, and the prices of those goods and services are determined in free markets. The incomes of most Canadian workers are also determined by free-market forces.

But government intervention and regulation are also pervasive even though they are often not easily visible. Canadian governments own and operate the Coast Guard, hundreds of national and provincial parks, and the RCMP as well as provincial and city police forces. Provincial governments own electricity transmission systems and regulate the price of electricity. The federal government owns Export Development Canada, the Business Development Bank of Canada, Canada Post, and dozens of other Crown corporations that sell goods or services to firms and households. Governments also have extensive regulations regarding many aspects of our lives, including waste disposal, workplace safety, building codes, minimum wages, taxi service, and so on. And governments take a substantial portion of our incomes in the form of taxes, with which they finance their provision of services to us.

Which elements of the economy are best left to free markets and which elements require government intervention? Governments are clearly necessary to provide law and order and to define and enforce property rights. But beyond these basic functions—ones that we all too often take for granted—what is the case for government intervention in otherwise free markets?

The general case for some reliance on free markets is that allowing decentralized decision making is more desirable than having all economic decisions made by a centralized planning body. The general case for *some* government intervention is that almost no one wants to let markets decide *everything* about our economic affairs. Most people believe that there are areas in which markets do not function well and in which government intervention can improve the general social good.

> The operative choice is not between an unhampered free-market economy and a fully centralized command economy. It is rather the choice of which mix of markets and government intervention best suits people's hopes and needs.

In this chapter, we discuss the role of the government in market-based economies, identifying why markets sometimes fail and why government policies sometimes fail. We begin by examining the basic functions of government.

16.1 Basic Functions of Government

Governments are very old institutions. They arose shortly after the Neolithic Agricultural Revolution turned people from hunter–gatherers into settled farmers about 10 000 years ago. An institution that has survived that long must be doing something right! Over the intervening 100 centuries, the functions undertaken by governments have varied enormously. But through all that time, the function that has not changed is to provide what is called a *monopoly of violence*. Violent acts can be conducted by the military and the civilian police arms of government, and through its judicial system the government can deprive people of their liberty by incarcerating them or, in extreme cases, by executing them. This is a dangerous monopoly that is easily abused. For this reason, stable and well-functioning societies have systems of checks and balances designed to keep the government's monopoly directed to the general good rather than to the good of a narrow government circle.

The importance of having a monopoly of violence can be seen in those countries whose governments do not have it. Somalia in recent decades and China in the 1920s provide examples of countries in which individual warlords commanded armies that could not vanquish each other. Mexico and Russia provide examples of organized crime having substantial power to commit violence that the government cannot control. In extreme cases where many groups have almost equal ability to exert military violence, power struggles can create havoc with normal economic and social life. Life then becomes "nasty, brutish, and short"—to use the words of the seventeenth-century English political philosopher Thomas Hobbes (1588–1679).

The importance of having checks on the government's arbitrary use of its monopoly is seen in the disasters that ensue in the many dictatorships that misuse their power. The USSR under Stalin, Uganda under Idi Amin, Nigeria under Sanni Abacha,

The provision of national defence, police protection, and a judicial system is a basic function of government, which allows citizens to carry out their ordinary economic and social activities.

Cambodia under Pol Pot, Iraq under Saddam Hussein, Zimbabwe under Robert Mugabe, and Libya under Muammar Gadaffi are a few of many examples from the past 75 years.

> When the government's monopoly of violence is secure and functions with effective restrictions against its arbitrary use, citizens can safely carry out their ordinary economic and social activities.

As the founder of British Classical economics, Adam Smith, wrote over two centuries ago:

> *The first duty of the sovereign [is] that of protecting the society from the violence and invasion of other independent societies . . . The second duty of the sovereign [is] that of protecting, as far as possible, every member of the society from the injustice or oppression of every other member of it.*[1]

A related government activity is to provide security of property. Governments define and enforce property rights that give people a secure claim to the fruits of their own labour. These property rights include clear definition and enforcement of the rights and obligations of institutions, such as corporations, religious organizations, and non-profit enterprises.

In a modern complex economy, providing these "minimal" government services is no simple task. Countries whose governments are not good at doing these things have seldom prospered economically.

The importance of these basic functions of government should not be under-estimated. In recent years, economists and policymakers in rich, developed countries have come to a greater understanding of the challenges in developing countries that stem from their ineffective political structures. Local corruption, powerful warlords, and a lack of basic political infrastructure combine to make official development aid less effective than it would be in countries with more stable and representative political structures. As a result, a growing share of official assistance to developing countries is taking the form of *political* rather than *economic* assistance—a process often referred to as *institution building*. A 2012 best-selling book *Why Nations Fail* by professors Daron Acemoglu and James Robinson argues the importance of institutions in explaining the economic success or failure of countries.

---

[1] Adam Smith, *The Wealth of Nations* (1776; New York: Random House, 1937 ed., pp. 653, 669).

16.2 The Case for Free Markets

Within a secure framework of law and order, and well-defined and enforced property rights, a modern economy can function at least moderately well without further government assistance. In this section we review the case for free markets. In subsequent sections we study government functions that arise when free markets fail to produce acceptable results.

Free markets are impressive institutions. Consumers' preferences and producers' costs help to generate price signals. These signals coordinate separate decisions taken by millions of independent agents, all pursuing their own self-interest. In doing so, they allocate the nation's resources without conscious central direction. Markets also determine the distribution of income by establishing prices of factors of production, which provide incomes for their owners. Furthermore, modern market economies, where firms compete to get ahead of each other by producing better goods more cheaply, generate the technological changes that have raised average living standards fairly steadily over the past two centuries.

In presenting the case for free markets, economists have used two quite different approaches. The first of these may be characterized as the "formal defence," and is based on the concept of allocative efficiency, discussed in Chapters 5 and 12. The essence of the formal defence of free-market economies is that if all markets were perfectly competitive, and if governments allowed all prices to be determined by demand and supply, then price would equal marginal cost for all products and the economy would be allocatively efficient. Allocative efficiency means that resources are used in such a way that total surplus to society—consumer surplus plus producer surplus—is maximized. Since we discussed allocative efficiency extensively in earlier chapters, we will say no more about it at this point.

The other defence of free markets—what might be called the "informal defence"—is at least as old as Adam Smith and applies to market economies whether or not they are perfectly competitive. The informal defence is not laid out in a formal model of an economy, but it does follow from some hard reasoning, and over the years it has been subjected to much intellectual probing. The informal defence of free markets is based on three central arguments:

1. Free markets provide automatic coordination of the actions of decentralized decision makers.

2. The pursuit of profits in free markets provides a stimulus to innovation and rising material living standards.

3. Free markets permit a decentralization of economic power.

Automatic Coordination

Defenders of the market economy argue that compared with the alternatives, the decentralized market system is more flexible and adjusts more quickly to changes.

Suppose, for example, that the world price of oil rises. One household might prefer to respond by maintaining a high temperature in its house and economizing on its driving; another household might do the reverse. A third household might give up air-conditioning instead. This flexibility can be contrasted with centralized control, which

Producers in market economies have the incentive to provide the goods and services that customers value, and the result is that line-ups rarely exist in these economies. In the former Soviet Union, however, the central planning system was very slow to respond, and line-ups like this were very common.

would force the same pattern on everyone, say, by rationing heating oil and gasoline, by regulating permitted temperatures, and by limiting air-conditioning to days when the temperature exceeded 27°C.

Furthermore, as conditions continue to change, prices in a market economy will also change, and decentralized decision makers can react continually. In contrast, government quotas, allocations, and rationing schemes are much more difficult to adjust. As a result, there are likely to be shortages and surpluses before adjustments are made. One great value of the market is that it provides automatic signals *as a situation develops* so that not all of the consequences of an economic change have to be anticipated and allowed for by a group of central planners. Millions of responses to millions of changes in thousands of markets are required every year, and it would be a Herculean task to anticipate and plan for them all.

A market system allows for coordination *without anyone needing to understand how the whole system works*. Professor Thomas Schelling, who was awarded the Nobel Prize in economics in 2005, illustrated this idea:

> *The dairy farmer doesn't need to know how many people eat butter and how far away they are, how many other people raise cows, how many babies drink milk, or whether more money is spent on beer or milk. What he needs to know is the prices of different feeds, the characteristics of different cows, the different prices . . . for milk . . . , the relative cost of hired labor and electrical machinery, and what his net earnings might be if he sold his cows and raised pigs instead.[2]*

It is, of course, an enormous advantage that all the producers and consumers of a country collectively can make the system operate—yet not one of them, much less all of them, has to understand the details of *how* that system works.

Innovation and Growth

Technology, preferences, and resource availability are changing all the time, in all economies. Forty years ago there was no such thing as a hand-held GPS or a digital camera. Hybrid cars did not exist. Manuscripts existed only as hardcopy, not as electronic files in an ultralight, wireless, laptop computer. The Internet did not exist—nor did smartphones, tablets, electronic airline tickets, cost-effective solar panels and wind turbines, income-tax software packages, computer-assisted design (CAD) programs, regional jets, standardized containers for transoceanic shipping, and a whole host of other goods and services that we now take for granted.

Digital cameras, tablet computers, social-networking sites, hybrid cars, and regional jets are all products that were invented or developed by individuals or firms in pursuit of profits. An entrepreneur who correctly "reads" the market and perceives that a demand for some product may exist or be created has a profit incentive to develop it.

---

[2] T.C. Schelling, 1978. *Micro Motives and Macro Behavior*. New York: Norton.

The next 20 years will also surely see changes great and small. Changes in technology may make an idea that is not practical today practical five years from now. New products and techniques will be devised to adapt to shortages, gluts, and changes in consumer demands and to exploit new opportunities made available by new technologies.

In a market economy, individuals risk their time and money in the hope of earning profits. Though many fail, some succeed. New products and processes appear and disappear. Some are fads or have little impact; others become items of major significance. The market system works by trial and error to sort them out and allocates resources to what prove to be successful innovations.

In contrast, planners in more centralized systems have to guess which innovations will be productive and which goods will be strongly demanded. Central planning may achieve wonders by permitting a massive effort in a chosen direction, but central planners also may guess incorrectly about the direction and put too many eggs in the wrong basket or reject as unpromising something that will turn out to be vital. Perhaps the biggest failure of centrally planned economies was their inability to encourage the experimentation and innovation that have proven to be the driving forces behind long-run growth in advanced market economies. It is striking that since the early 1990s most centrally planned economies abandoned their system in favour of a price system in one fell swoop while the only remaining large planned economy, China, is quickly increasing the role of markets in most aspects of its economy.

Decentralization of Power

Another important part of the case for a free-market economy is that it tends to decentralize power and thus requires less coercion of individuals than any other type of economy. Of course, even though markets tend to diffuse power, they do not do so completely; large firms and large labour unions clearly have and exercise substantial economic power. In recent years, especially in the United States, many economists have expressed concern about the concentration of economic power within large financial institutions and, in particular, their ability to influence legislation through lobbying and contributions to political parties and candidates.[3]

Though the market power of large corporations is sometimes quite large, it tends to be constrained both by the competition of other large entities and by the emergence of new products and firms. This is the process of creative destruction that was described by Joseph Schumpeter and that we examined in Chapter 10. In any case, say defenders of the free market, even such concentrations of private power are far less substantial than government power.

Governments must coerce if markets are not allowed to allocate people to jobs and goods to consumers. Not only will such coercion be regarded as arbitrary (especially by those who do not like the results), but the power also creates major opportunities for bribery, corruption, and allocation according to the preferences of the central administrators. If, at the going prices and wages, there are not enough apartments or coveted jobs to go around, the bureaucrats can allocate some to those who pay the largest bribe, some to those with religious beliefs or political views that they like, and only the rest to those whose names come up on the waiting list.

---

[3] For an excellent current discussion of these concerns, see Simon Johnson and James Kwak, *13 Bankers: The Wall Street Takeover and the Next Financial Meltdown*. Pantheon, 2010.

The late Milton Friedman, one of the most influential economists of the twentieth century, argued strongly that free markets were essential to the maintenance of political freedoms.

market failure Failure of the unregulated market system to achieve allocative efficiency.

This line of reasoning was articulated forcefully by the late Nobel laureate Milton Friedman (1912–2006), who was for many years a professor of economics at the University of Chicago. Friedman argued that economic freedom—the ability to allocate resources through private markets—is essential to the maintenance of political freedom.[4] Other economists and social theorists have challenged this extreme position, while not challenging the basic proposition that free-market economies tend to have more diffusion of power than centrally planned ones.

16.3 Market Failures

The term **market failure** describes the failure of the market economy to achieve an efficient allocation of resources. We observed in previous chapters that firms in many industries have market power because they face negatively sloped rather than horizontal demand curves for their products. When firms face such demand curves, price will exceed marginal cost in equilibrium. Thus, no real market economy has ever achieved perfect allocative efficiency. The conditions for efficiency are meant only as a benchmark to help in identifying important market failures. These market failures provide a motivation for government interventions designed to improve allocative efficiency.

> Market failure describes a situation in which the free market, in the absence of government intervention, fails to achieve allocative efficiency.

It is useful at this point to recall the distinction between normative and positive statements that we first encountered in Chapter 2. The statement that the economy is allocatively efficient (or not) is a *positive* statement. We can say that the economy has or has not achieved allocative efficiency without making any value judgement—the statement uses only an observation about the economy and the definition of allocative efficiency. It is important to note, however, that the allocatively efficient outcome may not be the most desirable outcome in a normative sense. For example, an economy may be allocatively efficient even though the distribution of income is judged by some to be undesirable. As we see later in the chapter, such concerns provide another motivation for government intervention.

We now examine four situations in which the free market fails to achieve allocative efficiency—*market power*, *externalities*, *non-rivalrous* and *non-excludable goods*, and *asymmetric information*. Many of these market failures provide a justification for government intervention in markets. We then discuss other reasons for government intervention that are not based on market failure—chief among these is intervention to achieve a more equitable distribution of income.

---

[4] Milton Friedman, *Capitalism and Freedom*. The University of Chicago Press, 1982.

Market Power

Market power is inevitable in any market economy for three reasons. First, in many industries economies of scale are such that there is room for only a few firms to operate at low costs, each having some ability to influence market conditions. Second, in many industries, firms sell differentiated products and thus have some ability to set their prices. Third, firms that innovate with new products or new production processes gain a temporary monopoly until other firms learn what the innovator knows. As we saw in Chapters 10, 11, and 12, firms that have market power will maximize their profit at a level of output at which price exceeds marginal cost. The result is allocatively inefficient, even though it is the inevitable outcome of the kinds of innovation that raise living standards over the long term.

This last reason sets up a conflict between achieving allocative efficiency at any given point in time and encouraging economic growth over time—a conflict that we explored in *Extensions in Theory 12-2* on page 292. Government policymakers clearly take the dynamic view of competition. They do not try to turn imperfectly competitive industries into perfectly competitive ones. Nor do they try to induce such firms to produce where marginal cost is equal to price. Not only would this be impossible, given the pervasiveness of oligopoly and monopolistic competition, but it would also be undesirable since much innovation and productivity growth comes from firms with market power. Instead, as we saw in Chapter 12, governments use competition policy to prevent monopolistic practices that would permit firms to avoid behaving competitively with respect to one another. The challenge of economic policy is then to accept monopolistic and oligopolistic "imperfect" competition for the range of choices and scale advantages they provide, while keeping firms in active competition with one another so as to gain the economic growth that results from their innovative practices.

Externalities

Recall from Chapter 12 that in order for the economy to be allocatively efficient, marginal benefit must equal marginal cost for all products. But whose benefits and costs are relevant? Firms that are maximizing their *own* profits are interested only in their own costs of production—they may not care about any benefits or costs their actions might create for others. Similarly, insofar as individual consumers are interested in the benefits *they* receive from any given product, they ignore any costs or benefits that may accrue to others. An **externality** occurs whenever actions taken by firms or consumers directly impose costs or confer benefits on others. If you smoke a cigarette in a restaurant, you impose costs on others present; when you renovate your home, you confer benefits on your neighbours by improving the general look of the neighbourhood. Externalities are also called *third-party effects* because parties other than the two primary participants in the transaction (the buyer and the seller) are affected.

The foregoing discussion suggests the importance of the distinction between *private cost* and *social cost*. **Private cost** measures the cost faced by the private decision maker, including production costs, advertising costs, and so on. **Social cost** includes the private cost (since the decision maker is a member of society) but also includes any other costs imposed on third parties. There is a similar distinction between *private benefit* and *social benefit*. To simplify things, however, we will discuss all externalities in terms of the distinction between private and social cost. But this does not limit our discussion in any way. If we want to consider a situation in which your listening to

externality An effect on parties not directly involved in the production or use of a commodity. Also called *third-party effects.*

private cost The value of the best alternative use of resources used in production as valued by the producer.

social cost The value of the best alternative use of resources used in production as valued by society.

good music confers benefits to your nearby friends, we can think of your action as either increasing their benefits or, equivalently, as decreasing their costs. Similarly, your smoking of cigarettes can be viewed either as reducing their benefits or, equivalently, as increasing their costs. By expressing everything in terms of costs (rather than benefits), we merely simplify the discussion.

> Discrepancies between private cost and social cost occur when there are externalities. The presence of externalities, even when all markets are perfectly competitive, leads to allocatively inefficient outcomes.

Externalities arise in many different ways, and they may be harmful or beneficial to the third parties. When they are harmful, they are called *negative externalities*; when they are beneficial, they are called *positive externalities*. Figure 16-1 shows why an externality leads to allocative inefficiency, even though the market is perfectly competitive. Here are two examples.

FIGURE 16-1 Externalities Lead to Allocative Inefficiency

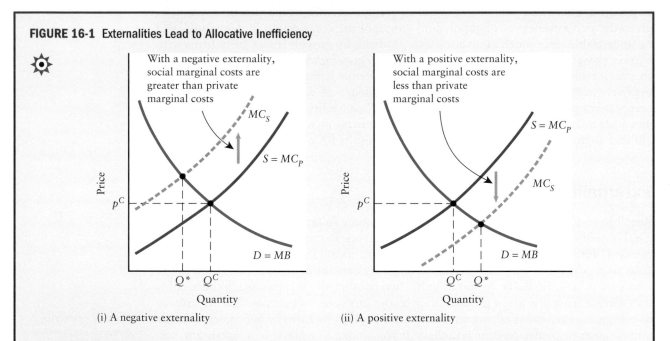

(i) A negative externality

(ii) A positive externality

When there is an externality, either too much or too little of the good is produced. If the market for this good is perfectly competitive and there is no government intervention, the equilibrium is shown by p^C and Q^C in both parts of the figure. If there is no externality, social and private marginal cost are the same and so the outcome is allocatively efficient.

Part (i) shows a situation where the production or the consumption of the good imposes costs on third parties. This is a negative externality—social marginal costs are MC_S, above MC_P. The vertical distance between MC_P and MC_S reflects the per-unit external cost. The allocatively efficient quantity is now Q^*, where MB equals MC_S. But the free market will produce Q^C, too much of the good.

Part (ii) shows a situation where the production or consumption of the good instead confers benefits on third parties. This is a positive externality—social marginal costs are MC_S, below MC_P. The vertical distance between MC_P and MC_S reflects the per-unit external benefit. The allocatively efficient quantity is again Q^* where MB equals MC_S. But the free market will produce Q^C, too little of the good.

Consider the case of a firm whose production process for steel generates harmful smoke as a byproduct. Individuals who live and work near the firm bear real costs as they cope with breathing (or trying to avoid breathing) the harmful smoke. When the profit-maximizing firm makes its decision concerning how much steel to produce, it ignores the costs that it imposes on other people. This is a negative externality. In this case, because the firm ignores those parts of social cost that are not its own private cost, the firm will produce too much steel relative to what is allocatively efficient.

A second example involves an individual who renovates her home and thus improves its external appearance. Such improvements enhance the neighbours' view and the value of their property. Yet the individual renovator ignores the benefits that her actions have on the neighbours. This is a positive externality. In this case, because the renovator ignores those parts of social benefits that are not her own private benefits, there will be too little home renovation done relative to what is allocatively efficient.

> With a positive externality, a competitive free market will produce too little of the good. With a negative externality, a competitive free market will produce too much of the good.

The allocative inefficiency caused by an externality provides a justification for government intervention. In the case of a negative externality, the government may levy a tax on the firms or consumers responsible, as is often done in the case of pollution; we explore specific policies to address pollution externalities in Chapter 17. In the case of positive externalities, the government may provide a subsidy (a negative tax) to the firms or consumers responsible, as is done in the case of publicly provided education; we examine education and other social policies in Chapter 18.

Non-rivalrous and Non-excludable Goods

Economists classify goods and services into four broad categories depending on the *rivalry* for the good and the *excludability* of the good. Table 16-1 shows these four types of goods.

A good or service is said to be **rivalrous** if one person's consumption of one unit of the good means that no one else can also consume that same unit. For example, a chocolate bar is rivalrous because if you eat the entire bar, it cannot also be eaten by your friend. In contrast, a television signal is not rivalrous. You and your friend can sit in your separate living rooms and both receive the same signal, neither of you diminishing the amount available to the other.

A good is said to be **excludable** if people can be prevented from consuming it. A chocolate bar is excludable because you cannot eat it unless you buy it first. A regular TV signal is not excludable, but some speciality channels are because only those who pay for the special receivers can view them. Your use of the light produced by street lights is non-excludable, as is your access to the air you breathe.

rivalrous A good or service is rivalrous if one person's consumption of it reduces the amount available for others.

excludable A good or service is excludable if its owner can prevent others from consuming it.

The airborne emissions from coal-fired power plants are one important example of a negative externality. The social costs associated with these emissions exceed the private costs.

TABLE 16-1 Four Types of Products

	Excludable	Non-Excludable
Rivalrous	*Private Goods* DVDs A seat on an airplane An hour of legal advice	*Common-Property Resources* Fisheries Rivers and streams Wildlife Clean air
Non-rivalrous (up to capacity)	*Club Goods* Art galleries Roads Bridges Cable or satellite TV signal	*Public Goods* National defence Public information Public protection Regular TV signal

Free markets cope best with rivalrous and excludable goods—what we here call "private" goods. The table gives examples of goods in each of four categories, depending on whether consumption of the good or service is rivalrous and whether one can be excluded from consuming it.

private goods Goods or services that are both rivalrous and excludable.

common-property resource A product that is rivalrous but not excludable.

Private Goods Most goods and services that you consume are both rivalrous and excludable. Your consumption of food, clothing, a rental apartment, a car, gasoline, CDs, airline tickets, and textbooks are only possible because you pay the seller for the right to own those goods or services. Furthermore, your consumption of those goods reduces the amount available for others. In Table 16-1 we simply refer to these goods as **private goods**.

> Goods that are both rivalrous and excludable—private goods—pose no particular problem for public policy.

Common-Property Resources Goods that are rivalrous but non-excludable pose an interesting challenge for public policy. Note in Table 16-1 that the examples of these goods include such things as fisheries, common grazing land, wildlife, rivers and streams, and so on. These are called **common-property resources**.

My use of river water reduces the amount available for you, but there is no practical way that my access to the water can be controlled. And since my access to the water cannot be controlled, there is no practical way to make me pay for it. The result is that there is a zero price. The zero price leads to the obvious result that in the absence of government intervention, private users will tend to *overuse* common-property resources, driving their marginal benefit to zero. At the same time, however, there will be some positive marginal cost to society of using the resource. Since the marginal cost will exceed the marginal benefit, society would be better off if *less* of the resource was used. The social costs associated with the overuse of common-property resources is often referred to as the "tragedy of the commons."

> **Common-property resources tend to be overused by private firms and consumers.**

The overuse of common-property resources is especially noticeable in such cases as the Atlantic cod and Pacific salmon fisheries, where individual fishers have a natural incentive to overfish. After all, if they don't catch a particular fish, they will merely be leaving it to be caught by the next fisher who comes along. It is this natural inclination to overuse the fisheries that has led the Canadian government over the years to develop a system of licences and quotas that restrict access to the common-property resource. *Applying Economic Concepts 16-1* examines the depletion of the world's fisheries.

APPLYING ECONOMIC CONCEPTS 16-1

The World's Endangered Fish

Fish in the ocean are a common-property resource, and theory predicts that such a resource will be overexploited if there is a high enough demand for the product and suppliers are able to meet that demand. In the past centuries there were neither enough people eating fish nor efficient enough fishing technologies to endanger stocks. Over the last 50 years, however, the population explosion has added to the demand for fish and advances in technology have vastly increased the ability to catch fish. Large boats, radar detection, and more murderous nets have tipped the balance in favour of the human predator and against the animal prey. As a result, the overfishing prediction of common property theory has been amply borne out. Today, fish are a common-property resource; tomorrow, they could become no one's resource.

Since 1950 the world's annual capture of fish has increased by more than four times, from 20 million tonnes in 1950 to more than 80 million tonnes today (not including the "catch" from farmed fish, which raises the current annual haul to more than 130 million tonnes). The increase was sustained only by substituting smaller, less desirable fish for the diminishing stocks of the more desirable fish and by penetrating ever farther into remote oceans. Today, all available stocks are being exploited, and now even the total tonnage of captured fish is beginning to fall. The UN estimates that the total value of the world's catch could be increased by nearly $30 billion if fish stocks were properly managed by governments interested in the total catch, rather than exploited by individuals interested in their own catch.

The developed countries have so overfished their own stocks that Iceland and the European Union could cut their fleets by 40 percent and catch as much fish as they do today. This is because more fish would survive to spawn, allowing each boat in a smaller fleet to catch about 40 percent more than does each boat in today's large fishing fleet.

The problem became so acute that Canada shut down its entire Atlantic cod fishing industry in 1992. Tens of thousands of Newfoundland and Labrador residents lost their livelihoods in an industry that had flourished for five centuries (although some of the fishers have since turned to catching lobsters and different species of fish and harvesting farmed mussels).

Some developing countries are taking action to conserve their fish stocks, but in many the need for current prosperity is outweighing the desire to conserve for long-term future benefits. As a result, many developing countries are encouraging rapid expansion of their own fishing fleets with the all-too-predictable results that their domestic waters will soon be seriously overfished.

Worldwide action saved most species of whales. It remains to be seen how many types of fish will be caught to extinction and how many will recover as individual nations slowly learn the lesson of economic theory. Common-property resources need central management if they are not to be overexploited to an extent that risks extinction.

Trends in the State of the World's Marine Fish Stocks

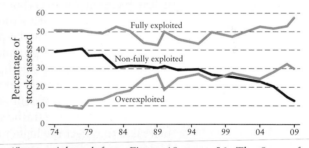

(*Source:* Adapted from Figure 18, page 56, *The State of World Fisheries and Aquaculture 2012*. Food and Agriculture Organization of the United Nations (FAO). www.fao.org.)

Excludable but Non-rivalrous Goods Goods that are excludable but not rivalrous are sometimes called *club goods*. Many of the obvious examples of these—such as art galleries, roads, and bridges—are typically provided by government. The non-rivalry for these goods means that the marginal cost of providing the good to one extra person is zero. As an example, ask yourself what it costs for an extra person to walk through the Canadian Museum of Civilization in Gatineau, given that it is already open but not many people are there. Or what is the social cost for allowing one more person to drive on an uncrowded road? The answer in both cases is zero. But if the marginal cost to society of providing one more unit of the good is zero, then allocative efficiency requires that the price also be zero. Any positive price would prevent some people from using it, but this would be inefficient. As long as their marginal benefit exceeds the social marginal cost of providing the good (zero in this case), it is efficient for these people to use the good.

> **To avoid inefficient exclusion, the government often provides for free non-rivalrous but excludable goods and services.**

For this reason, art galleries, museums, libraries, roads, bridges, and national parks are often provided by various levels of government. In some cases, like libraries and roads, the price to consumers is usually zero. In others, like national parks and art galleries, governments are often led to charge a price to help cover some of the operating costs (even though the marginal cost of use is very close to zero).

The positive price in some of these cases can be explained by another feature of club goods. What happens in the Canadian Museum of Civilization on a summer Saturday morning? What happens on Highway 401 outside Toronto at rush hour? The answer is *congestion*. When congestion occurs on roads and bridges, or in art galleries and museums, it is no longer true that the marginal cost of providing a club good to one more user is zero.

By increasing the amount of congestion, providing the good to one more person imposes costs on those already using the good. If I enter an already-busy highway, I slow down all the existing traffic. If you visit an already-crowded museum, you make it less pleasant for everybody else. In these cases, a good that is non-rivalrous when uncongested becomes rivalrous when congested. At this point it becomes (in economic terms) a private good, and a positive price is efficient.

Governments that provide such goods often charge a price to help ration the good when rivalry becomes significant. An excellent example of this occurs in several U.S. states where special toll highways, with the aid of powerful cameras and computers, charge motorists a different amount per kilometre driven depending on the congestion of the highway. As the traffic slows down because of congestion, the price per kilometre increases to reflect the higher marginal cost. This higher price is indicated on electronic highway signs posted regularly along the highway. Drivers can then choose either to remain on the highway and pay the higher price, or exit the highway and take another (less expensive) route to their destination.

This same principle also applies to city roads in London, England. A daily fee of £10 (roughly $15) is charged to each vehicle entering the city centre. After this road-pricing scheme was first introduced in 2003, there was a 30 percent drop in the volume of downtown traffic and thus a decline in road congestion.

public goods Goods or services that can simultaneously provide benefits to a large group of people. Also called *collective consumption goods.*

Public Goods Finally, some goods are neither excludable nor rivalrous. These are called **public goods** or sometimes *collective consumption goods*. The classic case of a public good is national defence. All residents of Canada are equally protected and defended by the Canadian Forces. It is not possible to provide national defence to some residents and not to others.

Information is also often a public good. Suppose a certain food additive causes cancer. The cost of discovering this fact needs to be borne only once. The information is then of value to everyone, and the cost of making the information available to one more consumer is approximately zero. Furthermore, once the information about the newly discovered carcinogen is available, it is impossible to prevent people from using that information. Other public goods include street lighting, weather forecasts (a type of information), and some forms of environmental protection.

All these examples raise what is called the *free-rider problem*. Since public goods are (by definition) not excludable, it is impossible to prevent anyone from using them once they are provided. If the provider charged a price, non-payers would take a *free ride* at the expense of those individuals with a social conscience who do pay. But the existence of free riders, in turn, implies that the private market will generally not produce efficient amounts of the public good because once the good is produced, it is impractical (or impossible) to make people pay for its use. Indeed, free markets may fail to produce public goods at all. The obvious remedy in these cases is for the government to provide the good, financed from its general tax revenues.

> Because of the free-rider problem, private markets will usually not provide public goods. In such situations, public goods must be provided by government.

How much of a public good should the government provide? It should provide the public good up to the point at which the *sum* of everyone's individual marginal benefit from the good is just equal to the marginal cost of providing the good. We add everyone's individual marginal benefit to get the total marginal benefit because a public good—unlike an ordinary private good—can be used simultaneously by everyone. It therefore generates value to more than one person at a time. Figure 16-2 shows the optimal provision of a public good in the simple case of only two individuals.

> The optimal quantity of a public good is such that the marginal cost of the good equals the *sum* of all users' marginal benefits of the good.

Asymmetric Information

Information is, of course, a valuable commodity, and markets for information and expertise are well developed, as every student is aware. Markets for expertise are conceptually identical to markets for any other valuable service. They can pose special problems, however. One of these we have already

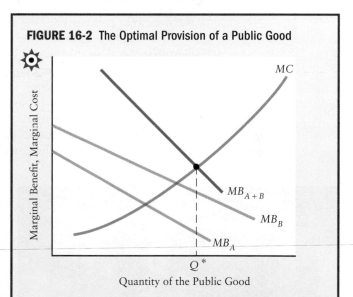

FIGURE 16-2 The Optimal Provision of a Public Good

Determining the optimal provision of a public good requires adding together the marginal benefits for each individual. The figure shows marginal benefit curves for a public good for two individuals, Andrew and Brenda. Since both can consume the good simultaneously, society's marginal benefit of the good is the sum of their own marginal benefits. By adding MB_A and MB_B *vertically*, we derive society's marginal benefit curve, MB_{A+B}. The marginal cost of providing the public good is shown by MC. The allocatively efficient level of the public good is Q^*, where the marginal cost to society is just equal to the marginal benefit to society.

discussed: Information is often a public good and, when it is, it tends to be under-produced by a free market.

Even when information is not a public good, markets for expertise are prone to market failure. The reason is that one party to a transaction can often take advantage of special knowledge in ways that change the nature of the transaction itself. Situations in which one party to a transaction has special knowledge are called situations of **asymmetric information**.

asymmetric information A situation in which one party to a transaction has more or better relevant information about the transaction than the other party.

The importance of asymmetric information to the operation of the economy has received considerable attention in recent years. In 2001, Professors George Akerlof, Michael Spence, and Joseph Stiglitz shared the Nobel Prize in economics for their insights about how asymmetric information can lead to market failures. The two important sources of market failure that arise from situations of asymmetric information are *moral hazard* and *adverse selection*.

moral hazard A situation in which an individual or a firm takes advantage of special knowledge while engaging in socially inefficient behaviour.

Moral Hazard In general, **moral hazard** exists when one party to a transaction has both the *incentive* and the *ability* to shift costs onto the other party. Moral hazard problems often arise from insurance contracts. The classic example is the homeowner who does not bother to shovel snow from his sidewalk because he knows that his insurance will cover the cost if the mail carrier should fall and break a leg. The costs of the homeowner's lax behaviour will be borne largely by others, including the mail carrier and the insurance company.

Individuals and firms who are insured against loss will often take less care to prevent that loss than they would in the absence of insurance. They do so because they do not bear all of the marginal cost imposed by the risk, whereas they do bear all of the marginal cost of taking action to reduce the risk.

With moral hazard, the market failure arises because the action by the insured individual or firm raises total costs for society. In our first example, the decision not to shovel the sidewalk reduces costs for the individual but, in the event of an accident, increases by much more the costs to other individuals and firms.

Insurance is not the only context in which moral hazard problems arise. Another example is professional services. Suppose you ask a dentist whether your teeth are healthy or a lawyer whether you need legal assistance. The dentist and the lawyer both face moral hazard in that they both have a financial interest in giving you answers that will encourage you to buy their services, and it is difficult for you to find out if their advice is good. In both cases, one party to the transaction has special knowledge that he or she could use to change the nature of the transaction in his or her favour. Codes of professional ethics and licensing and certification practices, both governmental and private, are reactions to concerns about this kind of moral hazard.

Moral hazard can also be created by government policies, especially those applying to financial institutions. One argument against deposit insurance, for example, is that the government's guarantee of individuals' bank deposits (as provided by the Canada Deposit Insurance Corporation) may

Your auto mechanic probably knows far more about cars than you do and is therefore able to benefit by convincing you to make unnecessary expenditures. This is an example of moral hazard caused by asymmetric information. One partial solution to this problem is to get a second (or third!) estimate before you spend any money.

lead commercial banks to undertake more risky lending practices than they otherwise would. And in the 2008 financial crisis, when the U.S. government used more than U.S.$700 billion of taxpayers' funds to inject liquidity into several large commercial banks that were on the edge of bankruptcy, many economists argued that the expectation of similar future policies would lead the banks to continue their excessively risky behaviour. The problem of moral hazard in financial markets is an important topic in macroeconomics; we will say more about it in Chapter 27.

Adverse Selection **Adverse selection** refers to the tendency for people who are more at risk than the average to purchase insurance and for those who are less at risk than the average to reject insurance. A person who has a heart condition may seek to increase his life insurance coverage by purchasing as much additional coverage as is available without a medical examination. People who buy insurance almost always know more about themselves as individual insurance risks than do their insurance companies. The company can try to limit the variation in risk by requiring physical examinations (for life or health insurance) and by setting up broad categories based on variables, such as age and occupation, over which actuarial risk is known to vary. The rate charged is then different across categories and is based on the average risk in each category, but there will always be much variability of risk *within* any one category.

> **adverse selection** Self-selection, within a single risk category, of persons of above-average risk.

People who know that they are well above the average risk for their category are offered a bargain and will be led to take out more car, health, life, or fire insurance than they otherwise would. Their insurance premiums will also not cover the full expected cost of the risk against which they are insuring. Once again, their private cost (their insurance premium) is less than the total cost (the expected insurance payout by the insurance company). On the other side, someone who knows that she is at low risk and pays a higher price than the amount warranted by her risk is motivated to take out less insurance than she otherwise would. In this case, her private cost (her insurance premium) is more than the total cost (the expected insurance payout). In both cases, resources are allocated inefficiently because the marginal private benefit of purchasing insurance is not equal to the marginal cost of providing it.

An excellent and familiar example of market failure caused by asymmetric information and adverse selection is the apparent overdiscounting of the prices of used cars because of the buyer's risk of acquiring a "lemon." See the discussion of this problem in *Applying Economic Concepts 16-2*.

Summary

Our discussion about market failures has covered a lot of ground. Before we move on to explore some details of government intervention, it is worthwhile to summarize briefly what we have learned. The following four situations result in market failures and, at least in principle, provide a rationale for government intervention:

1. Firms with market power will charge a price greater than marginal cost. The level of output in these cases is less than the allocatively efficient level.

2. When there are externalities, social and private marginal costs are not equal. If there is a negative externality, output will be greater than the allocatively efficient level. If there is a positive externality, output will be less than the allocatively efficient level.

3. Common-property resources will be overused by private firms and consumers. Public goods will be underprovided by private markets.

4. Situations in which there is asymmetric information—both moral hazard and adverse selection—can lead to allocative inefficiency.

These situations of market failure justify a role for government in a market economy. We now explore some reasons for government intervention that are *not* based on market failures.

APPLYING ECONOMIC CONCEPTS 16-2

Used Cars and the Market for "Lemons"

It is common for people to regard the large loss of value of a new car in the first year of its life as a sign that consumers are overly style conscious and will always pay a big premium for the latest in anything. Professor George Akerlof of the University of California at Berkeley suggests a different explanation. His theory, contained in his now-famous paper "The Market for Lemons," is based on the proposition that the flow of services expected from a one-year-old car that is *purchased on the used-car market* will be lower than that expected from an *average* one-year-old car on the road. Consider his theory.

Any particular model year of car will include a certain proportion of "lemons"—cars that have one or more serious defects. Purchasers of new cars of a certain year and model take a chance on their car turning out to be a lemon. Those who are unlucky and get a lemon are more likely to resell their car than those who are lucky and get a high-quality car. Hence, in the used-car market, there will be a disproportionately large number of lemons for sale. For example, maybe only 1 percent of all 2013 Toyota Corollas have a significant defect and are thus lemons. But in the market for *used* 2013 Toyota Corollas, 20 percent of them may be lemons.

Buyers of used cars are therefore right to be on the lookout for lemons, while salespeople are quick to invent reasons for the high quality of the cars they are selling. Because it is difficult to identify a lemon or a badly treated used car before buying it, the purchaser is prepared to buy a used car only at a price that is low enough to offset the increased probability that it is a lemon.

The market failure in this situation arises because of the asymmetric information between the buyers and the sellers. If there were perfect information, prices would better reflect the quality of the used car. Good used cars would command higher prices than used cars known to be lemons. Buyers and sellers would then conduct more transactions, for two reasons. First, sellers of good used cars would be more likely to sell them since they know they will get a good price. In contrast, when information is poor, owners of good used cars are less inclined

to sell their cars because the prices of used cars reflect the average quality, which of course is diminished by the presence of the lemons. Second, when information is good, consumers know precisely what it is they are buying. Consumers who want to spend more on a good used car can do so; other consumers who want the bargain price on a car known to be a lemon can also be satisfied. A larger number of successful transactions between buyers and sellers means more surplus on both sides of the market—that is, a more efficient outcome.

The now-standard existence of five-year bumper-to-bumper warranties on new cars helps to improve the efficiency of the used-car market. With such warranties, buyers are prepared to pay a higher price for a used car as long as there is still some time remaining on the warranty. Yet even when repairs are covered under warranty, the significant time and inconvenience costs associated with getting a car serviced mean that the unavoidable asymmetric information in the used-car market still leads to inefficient outcomes.

Owners have an incentive to keep good-quality used cars because it is difficult to convince buyers that a used car is not a "lemon." As a result, lemons represent a larger proportion of used-car sales than of the total car population.

16.4 Broader Social Goals

Suppose markets *did* generate allocatively efficient outcomes. That is, suppose all markets were perfectly competitive and there were no problems of market power, externalities, public goods, or asymmetric information. In such an extreme world, does the achievement of allocative efficiency mean that the government would have no reason to intervene in free markets? The answer is no.

> **Even in the absence of market failures, the government may choose to intervene in markets to achieve broader social goals.**

It should not be surprising that even if the free-market system were to generate an allocatively efficient outcome, it would be unlikely to achieve broader social goals. Some of these goals (for example, the desire for an "equitable" income distribution) are basically economic. Some, especially notions that people in a given society should have shared values, such as social responsibility or a belief in basic human rights, are clearly not economic. In either set of cases, however, markets are not very effective, precisely because the "goods" in question are not of the kind that can be exchanged in decentralized transactions.

Income Distribution

As we saw in Chapter 13, an important characteristic of a market economy is the *distribution of income* that it determines. People whose services are in heavy demand relative to supply, such as good television news anchors, wise corporate CEOs, and outstanding hockey players, earn large incomes, whereas people whose services are not in heavy demand relative to supply, such as high-school graduates without work experience, earn much less.

Such differentials in income, as we discussed in Chapter 13, can be either temporary or equilibrium phenomena. The temporary differentials, caused by changes in demand or supply in specific industries or regions, will eventually be eliminated by the mobility of workers. Equilibrium differentials will persist, whether they are created by differences in non-monetary aspects of the job or by differences in human capital or acquired or inherited skills.

Equilibrium differences in income seem unfair to many people. A free-market system rewards certain groups and penalizes others. Because the workings of the market may be stern, even cruel, society often chooses to intervene. Should heads of households be forced to bear the full burden of their misfortune if, through no fault of their own, they lose their jobs? Even if they lose their jobs through their own fault, should they and their families have to bear the whole burden, which may include starvation? Should the ill and the aged be thrown on the mercy of their families? What if they have no families? Both private charities and a great many government policies are concerned with modifying the distribution of income that results from such things as where one starts, how able one is, how lucky one is, and how one fares in the labour market. We discuss many government policies of this kind in Chapter 18.

We might all agree that it is desirable to have a more equal distribution of income than the one generated by the free market. We might also agree that the pursuit of

EXTENSIONS IN THEORY 16-1

Arthur Okun's "Leaky Bucket"

Economists recognize that government actions can affect both the allocation of resources and the distribution of income. Resource allocation is easier to talk about simply because economists have developed precise definitions of *efficient* and *inefficient* allocations. Distribution is more difficult because we cannot talk about *better* or *worse* distributions of income without introducing value judgements. Recall, however, as pointed out in Chapter 12, that an allocation of resources is efficient only with respect to one particular distribution of income. For a different income distribution, there is a different efficient allocation.

To the extent that government policy aims to redistribute income, allocative efficiency will often be reduced. Arthur Okun (1928–1980), who was a noted economist at Yale University, developed the image of a "leaky bucket" to illustrate this problem. Suppose we have a well-supplied reservoir of water and we want to get some water to a household that is not able to come to the reservoir. The only vessel available for transporting the water is a leaky bucket; it works, in that water is deliverable to the intended location, but it works at a cost, in that some of the water is lost on the trip. Thus, to get a litre of water to its destination, more than a litre of water has to be removed from the reservoir. It may be possible to design better or worse buckets, but all of them will leak somewhat.

The analogy to an economy is this: The act of redistribution (carrying the water) reduces the total value of goods and services available to the economy (by the amount of water that leaks on the trip). Getting a dollar to the poor reduces the resources available to everyone else by more than a dollar. Thus, pursuing social goals—like the redistribution of income—conflicts with the goal of allocative efficiency.

Why is the bucket always leaky? Because there is no way to redistribute income without changing the incentives that private households and firms face. For example, a tax-and-transfer system that takes from the rich and gives to the poor will reduce the incentives of both the rich and the poor to produce income. This redistribution of income will often lead to less total income being generated. As another example, a policy of subsidizing goods that are deemed to be important, such as post-secondary education or daycare services, will cause the market prices of those goods to be lower than marginal costs, a result implying that resources used to produce those goods could be used to produce goods of higher value elsewhere in the economy.

Measuring the efficiency costs of redistribution is an important area of economic research. One result from this research is that some methods of redistribution are more efficient than others. For example, most economists agree that programs that directly redistribute income are more efficient (per dollar of resources made available to a given income group) than programs that subsidize the prices of specific goods. One reason for this is that price subsidies apply even when high-income households purchase the goods in question. These high-income households therefore benefit from the subsidy—an unintended (and perhaps undesirable) consequence of the program.

Redistribution often entails some efficiency cost. However, this inefficiency does *not* imply that such programs should not be undertaken. (That buckets leak surely does not imply that they should not be used to transport water, given that we want to transport water and that the buckets we have are the best available tools.) Whatever the social policy regarding redistribution of income, economics has an important role to play in measuring the efficiency costs and distributional consequences of different programs of redistribution. Put another way, it has useful things to say about the design and deployment of buckets.

allocative efficiency is a good thing. It is important to understand, however, that the goal of a more equitable distribution of income often conflicts with the goal of allocative efficiency. To understand why this is so, see *Extensions in Theory 16-1*, which discusses Arthur Okun's famous analogy of the "leaky bucket."

Preferences for Public Provision

Police protection and justice could, in principle, be provided by private-market mechanisms. Security guards, private detectives, and bodyguards all provide police-like protection. Privately hired arbitrators, "hired guns," and vigilantes of the Old West represent private ways of obtaining "justice." Yet the members of society may believe that a public police force is *preferable* to a private one and that public justice is preferable to justice for hire.

The question of the boundary between public and private provision of any number of goods and services became an important topic of debate during the late 1980s and early 1990s. In Canada, the United States, and Western Europe, the issue was expressed in terms of the costs and benefits of *privatization*. These debates are no longer as intense as they were 20 years ago, although for some goods and services—like the provision of health care—the issue is still controversial. Part of the debate is about the magnitude of the efficiency gains that could be realized by private organization, and part is about less tangible issues, such as changes in the nature and distribution of goods and services that may take place when production is shifted from the public sector to the private sector.

A judicial system could be provided privately, with the judges levying charges to plaintiffs and defendants in order to hear their cases. But most people believe that for reasons of fairness and objectivity, it is better for the government to provide the judicial system, financed by money raised through general taxation.

Protecting Individuals from Others

People can use and even abuse other people for economic gain in ways that members of society find offensive. Child labour laws, minimum standards of working conditions, and laws against physical abuse and sexual harassment are responses to such actions. Yet direct abuse is not the only example of this kind of undesirable outcome. In an unhindered free market, the adults in a household would usually decide how much education to buy for their children. Selfish parents might buy no education, while egalitarian parents might buy the same education for all their children, regardless of their abilities. The rest of society may want to interfere in these choices, both to protect the child of the selfish parent and to ensure that some of the scarce educational resources are distributed according to the ability and the willingness to use them rather than according to a family's wealth. The government requires all households to provide a minimum of education for their children, and a number of inducements are offered—through public universities, scholarships, and other means—for talented children to consume more education than they or their parents might choose if they had to pay the entire cost themselves.

Paternalism

Members of society, acting through government, often seek to protect adult (and presumably responsible) individuals, not from others, but from themselves. Laws prohibiting the use of addictive drugs and laws requiring the use of seat belts are intended primarily to protect individuals from their own ignorance or short-sightedness. These kinds of interference in the free choices of individuals are examples of **paternalism**. Whether such actions reflect the wishes of the majority in the society or whether they reflect the actions of overbearing governments, there is no doubt that the market will not provide this kind of protection. Buyers do not buy things they do not want, even if these things are "good for them," and sellers have no motive to provide them.

paternalism Intervention in the free choices of individuals by others (including governments) to protect them against what is presumed to be their own ignorance or folly.

Social Responsibility

In a free-market system, if you can pay another person to do things for you, you may do so. If you persuade someone else to clean your house in return for $75, presumably both parties to the transaction are better off (otherwise neither of you would have voluntarily conducted the transaction). Normally, society does not interfere with people's ability to negotiate mutually advantageous contracts.

Most people do not feel this way, however, about activities that are regarded as social responsibilities. For example, in countries where military service is compulsory, contracts similar to the one between you and a housekeeper could also be negotiated. Some persons faced with the obligation to do military service could no doubt pay enough to persuade others to do their military service for them. Indeed, during the U.S. Civil War, it was common practice for a man to avoid the draft by hiring a substitute to serve in his place. Yet such contracts are usually prohibited by law. They are prohibited because there are values to be considered other than those that can be expressed in a market. In times when it is necessary, military service is usually held to be a duty that is independent of an individual's tastes, wealth, influence, or social position. It is felt that everyone *ought* to do this service, and exchanges between willing traders are prohibited.

Military service is not the only example of a social responsibility. Citizens cannot buy their way out of jury duty or legally sell their voting rights to others, even though in many cases they could find willing trading partners.

Economic Growth

Over the long haul economic growth is the most powerful determinant of material living standards. Whatever their policies concerning efficiency and equity, people who live in economies with rapid rates of growth find their real per capita incomes rising (on average) faster than those of people who live in countries with low rates of growth. Over a few decades these growth-induced changes tend to have much larger effects on living standards than any policy-induced changes in the efficiency of resource allocation or the distribution of income.

For the last half of the twentieth century, most economists viewed growth mainly as a macroeconomic phenomenon related to total saving and total investment. Reflecting this view, many textbooks do not even mention growth in the chapters on microeconomic policy.

More recently there has been a shift back to the perspective of earlier economists, who saw technological change as the engine of growth, with the individual entrepreneurs and firms as the agents of innovation. This is a microeconomic perspective, which is meant to add to, not replace, the macroeconomic emphasis on total saving and total investment.

Over the last decade or so, governments have placed considerable emphasis on this new microeconomic perspective on economic growth. Today few microeconomic policies escape being exposed to the question "Even if this policy achieves its main goal, will it have unfavourable effects on growth?" Answering yes is not a sufficient reason to abandon a specific policy. But it is a sufficient reason to think again. Is it possible to redesign the policy so that it can still achieve its main micro objectives while removing its undesirable side effects on economic growth?

A General Principle

We have discussed how the free market may fail to achieve social goals that members of society deem to be desirable. This discussion suggests the following general principle:

Even if free markets generated allocatively efficient outcomes, they would be unlikely to generate outcomes consistent with most people's social goals. Furthermore, there is often a tradeoff between achieving these social goals and increasing allocative efficiency.

16.5 Government Intervention

Since markets sometimes *do* fail, and since even efficient markets produce some undesirable outcomes, there is scope for governments to intervene in beneficial ways. Whether government intervention is warranted in any particular case depends both on the magnitude of the benefits that the intervention is designed to produce and on the costs of the government action itself.

The benefits of some types of government intervention—such as a publicly provided justice system—are both difficult to quantify and large. Further, government intervention often imposes difficulties of its own. For many types of government activity, however, *cost–benefit analysis* can be helpful in considering the general question of when and to what extent governments can successfully intervene.

The idea behind **cost–benefit analysis** is simple: Add up the total costs associated with a given policy, then add up the benefits, and implement the policy only if the benefits outweigh the costs. In practice, however, cost–benefit analysis is usually quite difficult for three reasons. First, it may be difficult to ascertain what will happen when an action is undertaken. Second, many government actions involve costs and benefits that will occur only in the distant future; thus, they will be more complicated to assess. Third, some benefits and costs—such as the benefits of prohibiting actions that would harm members of an endangered animal species—are difficult to quantify. Indeed, some people argue that they cannot be and should not be quantified, as they involve values that are not commensurate with money. The practice then is to use cost–benefit analysis to measure the things that can be measured and to be sure that the things that cannot be measured are not ignored when collective decisions are made. By narrowing the range of things that must be determined by informal judgement, cost–benefit analysis can still play a useful role.

In this chapter, we have been working toward a cost–benefit analysis of government intervention. We have made a general case *against* government intervention, stressing that free markets are great economizers on information and coordination costs. We have also made a general case *for* government intervention, emphasizing that free markets fail to produce allocative efficiency when there are firms with market power, public goods, externalities, or information asymmetries, and may also fail to achieve broader social goals. We now turn to the more specific issues of how governments intervene, the costs of government intervention, and why government intervention sometimes fails to improve on imperfect market outcomes.

cost-benefit analysis An approach for evaluating the desirability of a given policy, based on comparing total (opportunity) costs with total benefits.

The Tools of Government Intervention

Visit the Government of Canada's web page to see how many federal government departments and Crown corporations exist: www.gc.ca. Go to "About Government" and "Departments and Agencies."

The legal power of Canadian governments to intervene in the workings of the economy is limited by the Charter of Rights (as interpreted by the courts), the willingness of Parliament and provincial legislatures to pass laws, and the willingness and ability of the police and courts to enforce them. There are numerous ways in which one or another level of government can prevent, alter, complement, or replace the workings of the unrestricted market economy.

1. Public Provision National defence, the criminal justice system, public schools, universities, the highway system, and national parks are all examples of goods or services that are provided by governments in Canada. Public provision is the most obvious remedy for market failure to provide public goods, but it is also often used in the interest of redistribution and other social goals (e.g., public schools and health-care services). We will consider public spending in detail in Chapter 18.

2. Redistribution Programs Taxes and government spending are often used to provide a distribution of income that is different from that generated by the free market. Government *transfer* programs affect the distribution of income in this way. We examine the distributive effects of the Canadian tax-and-transfer system in Chapter 18.

3. Regulation Government regulations are public rules that apply to private behaviour. In Chapter 12, we saw that governments regulate private markets to limit the use of monopoly power. In Chapter 17, we will focus on regulations designed to deal with environmental degradation. Among other things, government regulations prohibit minors from consuming alcohol, require that children attend school, penalize racial discrimination in housing and labour markets, and require that all cars have seat belts. Government regulation is used to deal with all of the sources of market failure that we have discussed in this chapter; it applies at some level to virtually all spheres of modern economic life.

Altered Incentives Almost all government actions, including the kinds we have discussed here, change the incentives that consumers and firms face. If the government provides a park, people will have a reduced incentive to own large plots of land of their own. Fixing minimum or maximum prices (as we saw in Chapter 5) affects privately chosen levels of output. If the government taxes income, people may have a reduced incentive to work.

The government can adjust the tax system to provide subsidies for some kinds of behaviour and penalties for others. For example, taxes on gasoline raise the price to consumers and may lead them to reduce the quantity used, especially over the long run. Special tax treatment for saving within Tax-Free Savings Accounts (TFSAs) and Registered Retirement Savings Plans (RRSPs) increase the rate of return to saving and may lead individuals to increase their total amount of saving. In both cases, the government policy alters prices and sends the household signals different from those sent by the free market.

The Costs of Government Intervention

Consider the following argument: The market system produces some particular outcome that is deemed to be undesirable; government has the legal means to improve the situation; therefore, the public interest will be served by government intervention.

At first glance the argument is appealing. But it is deficient because it neglects three important considerations. First, government intervention is itself costly since it uses scarce resources; for this reason alone, not every undesirable free-market outcome is worth correcting, because the cost of doing so may exceed the perceived benefits. Second, government intervention is generally imperfect. Just as markets sometimes succeed and sometimes fail, so government interventions sometimes succeed and sometimes fail. Third, deciding what governments are to do and how they are to do it is also costly and intrinsically imperfect.

> **Large potential benefits do not necessarily justify government intervention; nor do large potential costs necessarily make it unwise. What matters is the balance between actual benefits and actual costs.**

Government intervention involves several different costs. Economists divide these costs into two categories—*direct costs* and *indirect costs*.

Direct Costs Government intervention uses real resources that could be used elsewhere. Civil servants must be paid and computer systems need to be purchased. Paper, photocopying, and other trappings of bureaucracy—the steel in the navy's ships, the fuel for the army's tanks, and the pilot of the prime minister's jet—all have valuable alternative uses. The same is true of the accountants who administer the Canada Pension Plan, the economists who are employed by the Competition Bureau, and the educators who retrain displaced workers.

Similarly, when government inspectors visit plants to monitor compliance with federally imposed standards of health, industrial safety, or environmental protection, they are imposing costs on the public in the form of their salaries and expenses. When regulatory bodies develop rules, hold hearings, write opinions, or have their staff prepare research reports, they are incurring costs. The costs of the judges, clerks, and court reporters who hear, transcribe, and review the evidence are also imposed by government regulation. All these activities use valuable resources that could have been used to produce very different goods and services.

> **All forms of government intervention use real resources and hence impose direct costs.**

The direct costs of government intervention are fairly easy to identify, as they almost always involve well-documented expenditures. In 2010, the total expenditures by all levels of government in Canada were $681 billion, just under 41 percent of total national income.

Indirect Costs Most government interventions in the economy impose costs on firms and households over and above the taxes that must be paid to finance government policies. The nature and the size of the extra costs borne by firms and households vary with the type of intervention. A few examples will illustrate what is involved.

1. Changes in Costs of Production. Government safety and emissions standards for cars raise the costs of both producing and operating cars. Environmental policies that require firms to treat their waste products and emissions increase the overall costs of those firms. In both cases, these costs are much greater than the direct budgetary costs of administering the regulations.

Farmers in Canada often request government assistance to offset the effects of low crop prices or bad weather. This is one example of rent seeking.

2. Costs of Compliance.
Government regulation and supervision generate a flood of reporting and related activities that are often referred to collectively as *red tape*. The number of hours of business time devoted to understanding, reporting, and contesting regulatory provisions is enormous. Regulations dealing with occupational safety and environmental control have all increased the size of non-production payrolls. The legal costs alone of a major corporation sometimes can run into tens or hundreds of millions of dollars per year. While all this provides lots of employment for lawyers and economic experts, it is costly because these professionals could be producing other valuable goods and services.

Households also bear compliance costs directly. The annual exercise of completing income-tax returns requires every taxpayer to spend considerable time or money making sure that the forms are correctly filled out and submitted on time. In addition to costs of compliance, there are costs borne as firms and households try to avoid regulation. There is a substantial incentive to find loopholes in regulations. Resources that could be used elsewhere are devoted to the search for such loopholes and then, in turn, by regulators to counteract such evasion.

3. Rent Seeking.
A different kind of problem arises from the mere existence of government and its potential to use its tools in ways that affect the distribution of economic resources. This phenomenon has been dubbed **rent seeking** by economists because private firms, households, and business groups will use their political influence to seek *economic rents* from the government in ways that impose costs on society as a whole. These economic rents can come in the form of legislated quotas or price controls, favourable regulations or direct subsidies, or even lucrative contracts that do not use public funds in a prudent manner. In all cases the individual or firm involved will be better off and will likely argue that their private interests are aligned with the public interest. Unless there is a market failure to be corrected, however, it is more likely that the government is simply pandering to a vocal and well-organized interest group by redistributing resources in their direction. And these resources do not come for free; they must be provided in some way by the taxpayers who finance government activities.

Rent seeking is endemic to mixed economies. Because of the many things that governments are called on to do, they have the power to act in ways that transfer resources among private entities. Because they are democratic, they are responsive to public pressures of various kinds. If a government's behaviour can be influenced, whether by voting, campaign contributions, lobbying, or bribes, real resources will be used in trying to do so.

rent seeking Behaviour whereby private firms and individuals try to use the powers of the government to enhance their own economic well-being in ways that are not in the social interest.

In the aggregate, the indirect costs of government intervention are substantial. But they are difficult to measure and are usually dispersed across a large number of firms and households.

Government Failure

Even in the cases in which the benefits and costs of government intervention can be easily identified and measured, governments, like private markets, are imperfect. Often they will fail, in the same sense that markets do, to achieve their potential.

The reason for government failure is not that public-sector employees are less able, honest, or virtuous than people who work in the private sector. Rather, the causes of government failure are inherent in government institutions, just as the causes of market failure stem from the nature of markets. Importantly, some government failure is an inescapable cost of democratic decision making.

Decision Makers' Objectives By far the most important cause of government failure arises from the nature of the government's own objectives. Traditionally, economists did not concern themselves greatly with the motivation of government. The theory of economic policy implicitly assumed that governments had no objectives of their own. As a result, economists needed only to identify places where the market functioned well on its own, and places where government intervention could improve the market's functioning. Governments would then stay out of the former markets and intervene as necessary in the latter.

This model of government behaviour never fitted reality, and economists were gradually forced to think more deeply about the motivation of governments. Today economists no longer assume that governments are faceless robots doing whatever economic analysis suggests is in the social interest. Instead they are modelled just as are producers and consumers—as units with their own objectives, which they seek to maximize.

Governments undoubtedly do care about the social good to some extent, but public officials have their own careers, self-interest, and prejudices as well. As a result, public officials' own needs are seldom wholly absent from their consideration of the actions

Public choice theory seeks to explain how public officials make their decisions. They are assumed to act not in the best interests of their constituents but according to their own agendas, which often conflict with the public interest.

they will take. Similarly, their definition of the public interest is likely to be influenced heavily by their personal views of what policies are best. It is therefore often the case that the policies supported by the public are different from the policies advocated by policymakers.

Modelling governments as maximizers of their own welfare, and then incorporating them into theoretical models of the working of the economy, was a major intellectual breakthrough. One of the pioneers of this development was the American economist James Buchanan, who was awarded the 1986 Nobel Prize in economics for his work in this field. The theory that he helped to develop is called *public choice theory*. The key breakthrough was to view the government as just another economic agent engaging in its own maximizing behaviour.

Public Choice Theory Full-blown public choice theory deals with three maximizing groups. Elected officials seek to maximize their votes. Civil servants seek to maximize their salaries and their influence. Voters seek to maximize their own utility. To this end, voters look to the government to provide them with goods and services and income transfers that raise their personal utility. No one cares about the general interest!

On the one hand, this surely is not a completely accurate characterization of motives. Some elected officials have acted in what they perceive to be the public interest, hoping to be vindicated by history even if they know they risk losing the next election. Some civil servants expose inside corruption—so-called whistleblowers—even though it can cost them their jobs. Some high-income individuals vote for the political party that advocates the most, not the least, income redistribution, and some poorer taxpayers vote for a party that advocates lower taxes on the rich and lower transfers to the poor.

On the other hand, the characterization is close to the mark in many cases. Most of us have read of politicians whose only principle appears to be "What will get me the most votes?" And many voters ask only "What is in it for me?" This is why the theory can take us a long way in understanding what we see, even though real behaviour is more complex.

Here is one example relevant to Canada and many other developed economies. Why, in spite of strong advice from economists, have governments persisted in assisting agriculture for decades, until many governments now have major farm crises on their hands? Public choice theory considers the winners and the losers among the voters.

The winners from agricultural supports are farmers. They are a politically powerful group and are aware of what they will lose if farm supports are reduced. They would show their disapproval of such action by voting against any government that even suggests it. The losers are the entire group of consumers or taxpayers. Although they are more numerous than farmers, and although their total loss is large, each individual suffers only a small loss. Citizens have more important things to worry about, and so they do not vote against the government just because it supports farmers. As long as the average voters are unconcerned about, and often unaware of, the losses they suffer, the vote-maximizing government will ignore the interests of the many and support the interests of the few. The vote-maximizing government will consider changing the agricultural policy only when the cost of agricultural support becomes so large that ordinary taxpayers begin to be concerned by the cost. What is required for a policy change, according to this theory, is that those who lose become sufficiently aware of their losses for this awareness to affect their voting behaviour.

Another example, which we will see in Chapter 34, is the use of tariffs. When a tariff is imposed on an imported good, it increases the domestic price of the good. Tariffs therefore provide protection to the domestic firms producing competing products. This protection typically raises prices, profits, and wages in those firms. The costs of such tariffs are borne by a much larger number of consumers, each of whom is hurt a relatively small amount by the higher price. This concentration of benefits and the dispersion of costs explains to a large extent why tariffs, once in place, are so politically difficult to remove.

rational ignorance When agents have no incentive to become informed about some government policy because the costs of becoming informed exceed the benefits of any well-informed action the agent might take.

The ability of elected officials and civil servants to ignore the public interest is strengthened by a phenomenon called **rational ignorance**. Many policy issues are extremely complex. For example, even the experts are divided when assessing the pros and cons of Canada's maintaining a flexible exchange rate rather than pegging the value of the Canadian dollar to the U.S. dollar. Much time and effort is required for a layperson even to attempt to understand the issue. Similar comments apply to the evidence for and against capital punishment or lowering the age of criminal liability. Yet one person's vote has little influence on which party is elected or on what they will really do about the issue in question once elected. So the costs of informing oneself are large, while the benefits of acting on that information are small. Thus, a majority of rational, self-interested voters will choose to remain innocent of the complexities involved in most policy issues.

Who will be the informed minority? The answer is often those who stand to gain or lose a lot from the policy, those with a strong sense of moral obligation, and those policy junkies who just like thinking about these kinds of issues.

Governments as Monopolists Governments face the same problems of cost minimization that private firms do but often operate in an environment in which they are monopoly producers without shareholders. Large governments (provinces, big cities, the federal government) face all of the organizational problems faced by large corporations. They tend to use relatively rigid rules and hence respond slowly to change. Building codes are an example of this type of problem. Most local governments have detailed requirements regarding the materials that must go into a new house, factory, or office building. When technology changes, the codes often lag behind. For example, plastic pipe, which is cheaper and easier to use than copper pipe, was prohibited by building codes for decades after its use became efficient. Changes in technology may make a regulation inefficient, but the regulation may stay in place for a long time.

In the private sector, market forces often push firms into revising their view of the problem at hand, whereas there is ordinarily no market mechanism to force governments to adopt relatively efficient regulations. Put another way, government failure often arises precisely because governments do not have competitors and are not constrained by the "bottom line."

How Much Should Government Intervene?

Do governments intervene too little, or too much, in response to market failure? This question reflects one aspect of the continuing debate over the role of government in the economy. Although many economists might agree on the theoretical principles that should guide government intervention in selected cases, there is more disagreement about the broader role of government in the economy. Unfortunately, the issue is often framed ideologically. Those on the "right wing" tend to compare heavy-handed government with a hypothetical and perfectly operating competitive market. In contrast, those on the "left wing" tend to compare hypothetical and ideal government intervention with a laissez-faire economy rife with market failures. Both perspectives are in danger of missing the more relevant debate.

Evaluating the costs and benefits of government intervention requires a comparison of the private economic system as it actually works (not as it might work ideally) with the pattern of government intervention as it actually performs (not as it might perform ideally).

Over the last three decades in most of the advanced industrial countries, the mix of free-market determination and government ownership and regulation has been shifting toward more market determination. No reasonable person believes that government intervention can, or should, be reduced to zero. Do we still have a long way to go in reversing the tide of big intrusive government that flowed through most of the twentieth century? Or have we gone too far by giving some things to the market that governments could do better?

These questions lie at the heart of one of the great social debates of our time. And in the fall of 2008 it was pushed onto headlines around the world. With the onset of the global financial crisis of 2008—which involved the collapse of the U.S. housing market, the bankruptcy of several large financial institutions, and the discovery that mortgage-backed securities of doubtful value were held on corporate balance sheets all over the world—the appropriate role of government intervention became a central issue. Some argued that government intervention and better regulations were necessary to support the financial system so that it could continue to play its vital economic role. Others argued that troubled banks and other institutions should be allowed to fail and that the health of the overall system would thereby be improved. As it turned out, governments in the United States, Europe, Asia, and Canada intervened on a massive scale in efforts to support their respective financial systems. By the fall of 2009, it appeared that the policy interventions were successful in preventing large-scale collapse of the financial sector and restoring a considerable measure of financial stability.

In general, the cases we have made for the costs and benefits of government intervention are both valid, depending on time, place, and the values that are brought to bear. At this point, we turn to the issue of what government actually does, something that will perhaps illuminate the question of what it could do better. In Chapter 12, we discussed government action that is designed to affect monopoly and competition. In the next two chapters, we discuss in some detail three other important types of intervention in the Canadian economy today: environmental regulation, taxation, and public spending.

SUMMARY

16.1 Basic Functions of Government

LO 1

- The government's monopoly of violence gives it the ability to enforce laws and protect its citizens. But restrictions on the government's power are required to ensure that individuals' rights are not unnecessarily violated.

16.2 The Case for Free Markets

LO 2

- The case for free markets can be made in two different ways. The "formal defence" is based on the concept of allocative efficiency, as seen in Chapter 12.
- The "informal defence" of free markets is not specifically based on the idea of allocative efficiency and thus applies to market structures other than just perfect competition. The informal defence of free markets is based on three central arguments:

1. Free markets provide automatic coordination of the actions of decentralized decision makers.
2. The pursuit of profits, which is central to free markets, provides a stimulus to innovation and economic growth.
3. Free markets permit a decentralization of economic power.

16.3 Market Failures

LO 3, 4

- Market failure refers to situations in which the free market does not achieve allocative efficiency. Four main sources of market failure are
  1. market power
  2. externalities
  3. public goods
  4. information asymmetries

- Pollution is an example of an externality. A producer who pollutes the air or water does not pay the social cost of the pollution and is therefore not motivated to avoid the costs. Private producers will therefore produce too much pollution relative to what is allocatively efficient.
- National defence is an example of a public good. Markets fail to produce public goods because the benefits of

CHAPTER 16: MARKET FAILURES AND GOVERNMENT INTERVENTION

such goods are available to people whether they pay for them or not.

- Information asymmetries cause market failure when one party to a transaction is able to use personal expertise to manipulate the transaction in his or her own favour. Moral hazard and adverse selection are consequences of information asymmetries.

16.4 Broader Social Goals   LO 5

- Changing the distribution of income is one of the roles for government intervention that members of a society may desire. Others include values that are placed on public provision for its own sake, on protection of individuals from themselves or from others, on recognition of social responsibilities, and on the promotion of economic growth.

16.5 Government Intervention   LO 6

- Major tools of microeconomic policy include (a) public provision, (b) redistribution, and (c) regulation.
- Most government actions—especially taxes or subsidies—change incentives that consumers and firms face.
- The costs and benefits of government intervention must be considered in deciding whether, when, and how much intervention is appropriate. Among the costs are the direct costs that are incurred by the government, the costs that are imposed on the parties who are regulated, directly and indirectly, and the costs that are imposed on third parties. These costs are seldom negligible and are often large.
- The possibility of government failure, as well as the costs of successful intervention, must be balanced against the potential benefits of removing market failure. It is neither possible nor efficient to correct all market failure; neither is it always efficient to do nothing.

KEY CONCEPTS

Market failure
Externalities
Private and social cost
Excludable and non-excludable goods
Rivalrous and non-rivalrous goods

Private goods
Common-property resources
Public goods
Information asymmetries
Moral hazard and adverse selection

Cost–benefit analysis
Rent seeking
Government failure
Public choice theory

STUDY EXERCISES

MyEconLab Make the grade with MyEconLab: Study Exercises marked in red can be found on MyEconLab. You can practise them as often as you want, and most feature step-by-step guided instructions to help you find the right answer.

---

1. Fill in the blanks to make the following statements correct.

   a. The "formal defence" of free markets is that, if all markets were perfectly competitive, then prices would equal _____ for all products and the economy would be _____.

   b. The "informal defence" of free markets is based on the following three central arguments:
      - _____
      - _____
      - _____

c. A situation in which the free market, in the absence of government intervention, fails to achieve allocative efficiency is called _____.

d. There are four major market failures that, in principle, justify government intervention in markets. They are as follows:

- _____
- _____
- _____
- _____

2. Fill in the blanks to make the following statements correct.

a. The marginal cost faced by the private decision maker is known as _____. The marginal cost faced by the private decision maker *plus* any other costs imposed on third parties is known as _____. If there is a divergence between these two marginal costs, then we can say that _____ are present.

b. An economic outcome is allocatively efficient when marginal social cost and marginal social benefit are _____.

c. Suppose a potato chip plant is operating beside a residential neighbourhood and produces noise and an unpleasant odour. We can say that there is a _____ externality because the marginal social cost of producing potato chips is _____ the private cost of producing potato chips. As a result, the free market is producing too _____ potato chips.

d. Suppose an apple orchard is operating beside a residential neighbourhood and provides beautiful blossoms and a pleasant fragrance. We can say that there is a _____ externality because the marginal social cost of apples is _____ the marginal private cost of apples. As a result, the free market is producing too _____ apples.

3. Fill in the blanks to make the following statements correct.

a. A good or service that is rivalrous and excludable (e.g., a restaurant meal or a sofa) is known as a _____ good and is most efficiently provided by the _____.

b. A good that is rivalrous and non-excludable (e.g., fish in the ocean, or common grazing land) is known as a(n) _____ and tends to be overused by _____.

c. Goods that are non-rivalrous and excludable (e.g., roads, museums, and parks) are often provided by government because the marginal cost of provision to society is _____ and so the allocatively efficient price is _____.

d. Goods and services that are non-rivalrous and non-excludable (e.g., national defence, a lighthouse)

are known as _____. Private markets will not provide these goods or services because of the _____ problem.

e. If an auto mechanic tells you that your car needs a new transmission, there is the possibility of market failure in the form of _____.

f. If you take up cliff diving as a new hobby and increase your life insurance, just in case, there is a possible market failure in the form of _____.

4. In each case, identify any divergence between social and private costs.

a. Cigarette smoking
b. Getting a university education
c. Private ownership of guns
d. Drilling for offshore oil

5. For each of the situations in the table below, indicate whether there is a positive or a negative externality. Indicate in each case whether social marginal cost (MC_S) is greater than or less than private marginal cost (MC_P).

	Positive or negative externality?	MC_S greater than or less than MC_P?
You smoke a cigarette and blow the smoke into others' faces.		
You cut your lawn early on a Sunday morning.		
A firm conducts R&D and generates useful "basic" knowledge that is freely available.		
A firm produces aluminum, but also produces toxic waste as a by-product.		

6. Consider the following diagram showing the monthly market demand for electricity, where the electricity is generated by burning coal. The mining, processing, and burning of coal have considerable environmental and health costs associated that are not reflected in the market price for the final product—electricity. The diagram below shows the market demand for electricity and private marginal costs of production.

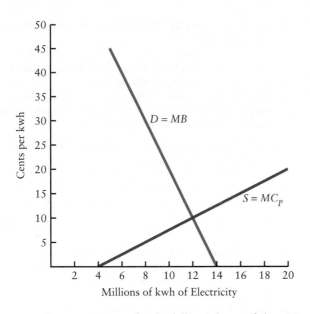

Cents per kwh / Millions of kwh of Electricity

a. Current estimates for the full social cost of electricity generated by burning coal vary greatly but suggest that it could be many times higher than current market prices in Canada and the United States. Supposing the external cost associated with producing one kilowatt hour (kwh) of electricity is $0.25, draw the marginal social cost curve for this market.

b. What quantity of electricity will be produced and consumed in the absence of government intervention in this market? What will be the price?

c. What is the socially optimal price per kwh and quantity consumed of electricity? Explain.

d. Explain how a special tax might be used to get electricity-producing firms to produce the allocatively efficient level of output.

7. Suppose that health care is provided privately in a free market and families are responsible for paying for polio vaccinations for their children. The following supply and demand diagram shows the private marginal costs and private marginal benefits in this market.

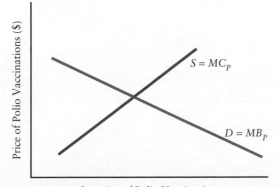

Quantity of Polio Vaccinations

a. Show on the diagram the quantity of polio vaccinations that would be undertaken in the absence of government intervention.

b. Describe the externality associated with having a polio vaccination.

c. Draw a new demand curve that reflects the externalities associated with the vaccinations and show the socially optimal quantity of vaccinations. Explain.

d. Explain why the government might choose to subsidize vaccinations (or perhaps even provide them for free). Are there both efficiency and equity motivations for government involvement in this market?

8. What market failures does public support of higher education seek to remedy? How would you go about evaluating whether the benefits of this support outweigh the costs?

9. For each of the listed goods, indicate whether they are rivalrous or non-rivalrous, and whether the use of them is excludable or non-excludable.

	Rivalrous?	Excludable?
Laptop computer		
Clothing		
Library		
Lighthouse		
Medical services		
Published product safety information		
Pacific salmon		

a. Which of the goods in the table are public goods? Explain.

b. Which are common-property resources? Explain.

10. Art galleries, museums, roads, and bridges are usually provided by the government.

a. Explain why uncrowded goods of this sort should have a price of zero if allocative efficiency is to be achieved.

b. Would allocative efficiency be achieved if private firms provided these goods? Explain.

c. What happens when access to these goods becomes congested? Does efficiency still require a zero price? Explain.

11. In this chapter we discussed common-property resources such as the fisheries. The same basic issues applied to grazing land in the past when small towns would set aside an area, known as the "commons," on which the residents' livestock could graze. Suppose the social

marginal benefits and social marginal costs of using the grazing land are as shown below.

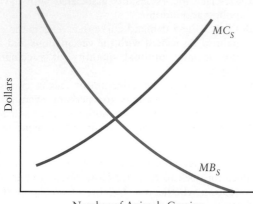

Number of Animals Grazing
on Fixed Quantity of Land

a. If residents are permitted unlimited access to the use of the grazing land at a zero price, what is the *private* marginal cost of grazing? Draw the MC_P curve in the diagram.

b. Given your answer to part (a), what level of grazing will occur if there is unrestricted access to the land?

c. Is the outcome from part (b) efficient? Why or why not?

d. What is the efficient level of grazing, and how is this shown in the diagram? Explain.

e. Explain why charging residents a fee per unit of access would improve allocative efficiency. How would this be shown in the diagram?

f. Explain why selling individual parcels of the grazing land to the town's residents is also likely to improve efficiency.

12. Consider a small town deciding whether to build a public park. The town council conducts a survey of its 100 residents and asks them how much they would each value the park. The survey results are as follows:

Number of people	Value of park per person	Total
10	$1000	$10 000
30	500	15 000
30	200	6 000
20	50	1 000
10	0	0
100		$32 000

a. Suppose it costs $35 000 to build the park. Should the town do it?

b. Suppose the park costs only $20 000 to build. Should the town build the park? If so, how should the town pay for building the park?

c. Suppose the town builds the park but charges people $50 for an annual pass. Does this present a problem for efficiency? Explain.

13. In the text we discussed how rent seeking is one of the costs of government intervention. Consider a group of pig farmers who are lobbying the federal government for some form of financial assistance (as they did in 1998 when the world price of pork declined steeply).

a. Explain why economists call such lobbying "rent seeking."

b. Suppose the farmers spend $500 000 in their lobbying efforts but have no effect on government policy. What is the cost to society of the rent seeking? Explain.

c. Suppose the $500 000 of lobbying *does* lead to a change in government policy. Now what is the social cost of the rent seeking?

14. This question is based on **Externalities and the Coase Theorem** on the book's MyEconLab at www.myeconlab.com. Consider a steel producer that dumps one litre of toxic waste into a river for every tonne of steel produced. A fishing camp located downstream bears the cost of cleaning up this toxic waste: $10 for every litre. Discuss how negotiations between the steel producer and the fishing camp may result in an allocatively efficient level of steel output even without direct government involvement. Does the nature of the negotiations depend on who owns the river?

The Economics of Environmental Protection

IN almost everything we do, we are subject to some form of government regulation. The system of criminal law regulates our interactions with people and property. Local zoning laws regulate the ways in which the land that we own or occupy may be used. Regulatory commissions set rates for electricity, natural gas, local telephone service, and a host of other goods and services. Seat belts, brake lights, turn signals, air bags, internal door panels, bumpers, and catalytic converters are compulsory and regulated in quality—all in a single industry. The list goes on and on. A good case can be made that various governments in Canada have more effect on the economy through regulation than through taxing and spending.

The focus in this chapter is on a specific type of government regulation, one that has become increasingly important in recent years. In particular, we examine the negative externalities that lead to environmental degradation and the various government policies designed to address them. As we will see, policies intended to protect the environment do not always do so in an efficient manner. One of the central themes in this chapter is that the information available to the regulatory agencies, especially regarding firms' technologies for reducing pollution, is generally incomplete. This lack of good information leads to the result that *market-based* environmental regulations are usually more successful than methods based on the government's *direct control*.

The chapter concludes with a discussion of a specific environmental challenge that has become a crucial policy issue. We examine the issue of how greenhouse gas emissions are contributing to global climate change, the technical challenges associated with reducing these emissions, and policies designed to address this enormous challenge.

17.1 The Economic Rationale for Regulating Pollution

Pollution is a negative externality. As a consequence of producing or consuming goods and services, "bads" are produced as well. Steel plants produce smoke in addition to steel. Farms produce chemical runoff as well as food. Logging leads to soil erosion that contaminates fish breeding grounds. Cars, trucks, and factories, by burning carbon-rich fossil fuels, such as coal, oil, and natural gas, produce carbon dioxide and other greenhouse gases that contribute to global climate change. Households produce human waste and garbage as they consume goods and services. In all of these cases, the acts of production and consumption automatically generate pollution. Indeed, few human endeavours do not have negative pollution externalities.

For information about the *Canadian Environmental Protection Act,* see Environment Canada's website: www.ec.gc.ca.

Pollution as an Externality

Polluting firms that are profit maximizers do not regard a clean environment as a scarce resource and therefore fail to consider the full costs of using this resource when producing their product. When a paper mill produces newsprint for the world's newspapers, the production affects more than just the firm's suppliers, employees, and customers. Its water-discharged effluent damages natural ecosystems and imposes costs on all those who use the nearby water for drinking or swimming. The emissions from its smokestacks affect the cleanliness of the air and impose costs on all people or wildlife that rely on its purity. The profit-maximizing paper mill neglects these external effects of its actions because its profits are not directly affected by them.

As shown in Figure 17-1, allocative efficiency requires that the price (the value that consumers place on the marginal unit of output) be just equal to the marginal social cost (the value of the resources that society gives up to produce the marginal unit of output). When there are negative externalities, *social* marginal cost exceeds *private* marginal cost because the act of production generates costs for society that are not faced by the producer.

By producing where price equals private marginal cost and thereby ignoring the externality, the firms are maximizing profits but producing too much output. The price that consumers pay just covers the private marginal cost but does not pay for the external damage. The *social benefit* of the last unit of output (the market price) is less than the social cost (private marginal cost plus the extra cost to society from the externality). Reducing output would increase allocative efficiency and make society as a whole better off.

internalizing the externality
A process that results in a producer or consumer taking account of a previously external effect.

Making polluting firms bear the entire social cost of their production is called **internalizing the externality**. This leads them to produce a lower level of output, as shown in Figure 17-1. Indeed, at the optimal level of output, where the externality is completely internalized, consumer prices would just cover the *social* marginal cost of production. We would have the familiar condition for allocative efficiency that marginal benefits to consumers are just equal to the (social) marginal cost of producing these benefits.

> The socially optimal level of output is such that the social marginal cost equals the social marginal benefit.

In order to internalize the externality successfully, it is necessary to measure its size accurately. Looking at Figure 17-1, we must be able to measure the magnitude of the marginal external cost, *MEC*. In practice, however, external costs are quite difficult to measure. This measurement is especially difficult in the case of air pollution, where the damage is often spread over hundreds of thousands of square kilometres and can affect millions of people.

The Optimal Amount of Pollution Abatement

Notice from Figure 17-1 that the allocatively efficient outcome still has some pollution being generated. This is because the production of each unit of output in Figure 17-1 generates some pollution. It is simply impossible to produce goods and services without generating *some* environmental damage. The economic problem is then to determine how much environmental damage to allow or, equivalently, how much pollution abatement (reduction) to implement. In general, it is not optimal to eliminate all pollution.

> **Zero environmental damage is generally not allocatively efficient.**

The economics of determining how much pollution to prohibit, and therefore how much to allow, is summarized in Figure 17-2, which depicts

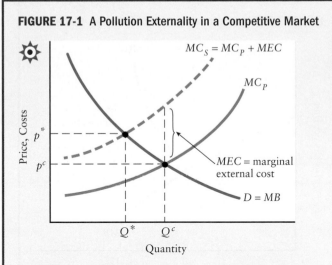

FIGURE 17-1 A Pollution Externality in a Competitive Market

A negative externality implies that a competitive free market will produce more output than the allocatively efficient level. If the externality can be internalized, allocative efficiency can be achieved. A competitive free market will produce where the demand and supply curves intersect—that is, at Q^c and p^c. If each unit of output of this good also generates an external cost of *MEC*, then social marginal cost is greater than private marginal cost by this amount. The allocatively efficient level of output is where marginal benefit equals social marginal cost—that is, at Q^*. The competitive free market therefore produces too much output.

If firms in this industry are now required to pay a tax of $$MEC$ per unit of output, the private marginal cost curve, MC_P, shifts up to MC_S. The externality will thus be internalized because firms will now be forced to pay the social marginal cost of their production. The new competitive equilibrium will be p^*, Q^*, and allocative efficiency will be achieved.

the social marginal benefits and social marginal costs of pollution abatement. The analysis might be thought of as applying, for example, to water pollution in a specific watershed. It is drawn from the perspective of a public authority whose mandate is to maximize social welfare.

Note that the figure is drawn in terms of the amount of pollution that is prevented (or abated) rather than in terms of the total amount of pollution produced. We do this because pollution abatement (rather than pollution itself) is a "good" of economic value, and we are more familiar with applying the concepts of supply and demand for goods with positive values. If no pollution is abated, the watershed will be subjected to the amount of pollution that would occur in an unregulated market. The greater the amount of pollution abated, the smaller the amount of pollution that remains. Thus, as we move to the right along the horizontal axis, there is more pollution abatement and therefore less remaining pollution. On the vertical axis, measured in dollars per unit, we show the marginal benefit and marginal cost of pollution abatement.

The marginal cost of abating pollution is often small at low levels of abatement but rises steeply after some point. This is the upward-sloping line shown in Figure 17-2. There are two reasons for believing that this shape is accurate. First is the familiar logic behind increasing marginal costs. Because some antipollution measures can be taken fairly easily, the first units of pollution abatement will be cheap relative to later units.

FIGURE 17-2 The Optimal Amount of Pollution Abatement

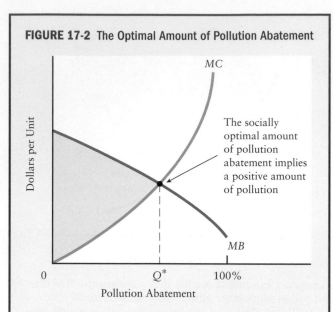

The optimal amount of pollution abatement occurs where the marginal cost of reducing pollution is just equal to the marginal benefits from doing so. *MB* represents the social marginal benefit of reducing pollution by one unit. *MC* represents the social marginal cost of reducing pollution by one unit. The optimal level of pollution abatement is Q^*, where $MB = MC$. Notice that not all pollution is eliminated. For each unit up to Q^*, the marginal benefit derived from pollution abatement exceeds the marginal cost. The total net benefit from the optimal amount of pollution abatement is given by the shaded area—the sum of the difference between marginal benefit and marginal cost at each level of abatement. Any further efforts to reduce pollution beyond Q^* would add more to social costs than to social benefits.

In addition, it is likely that pollution prevention of any degree will be easier for some firms than for others. New facilities are likely to run more cleanly than old ones, for example. Pollution abatement in a factory that was designed in the era of environmental concern may be much easier than obtaining similar abatement in an older factory. After some point, however, the easy fixes are exhausted, and the marginal cost of further pollution abatement rises steeply.

The downward-sloping curve in Figure 17-2 is the "demand" for pollution abatement and reflects the marginal benefit of pollution reduction. The curve slopes downward for much the same reason that the typical demand curve slopes downward. Starting at any level of pollution, people will derive some benefit from reducing the level of pollution, but the marginal benefit from a given amount of abatement will be lower, the lower the level of remaining pollution (or the higher the level of abatement). Put another way, in a very dirty environment, a little cleanliness will be much prized, but in a very clean environment, a little more cleanliness will be of only small additional value.

The optimal amount of pollution abatement occurs where the marginal benefit is equal to the marginal cost—where "supply" and "demand" in Figure 17-2 intersect. Since the optimal amount of abatement is usually not 100 percent, some pollution will likely exist at the optimal outcome. As we said earlier, zero pollution is generally not allocatively efficient.

In trying to reach this optimum, the pollution-control authority faces three serious problems. First, although Figure 17-2 looks like a supply–demand diagram, we have already seen that the private sector will not by itself create a market in pollution control. Hence, the government must intervene in private-sector markets if the optimal level of control shown in Figure 17-2 is to be attained.

The second problem is that the optimal level of pollution abatement is not easily known because the marginal benefit and the marginal cost curves shown in Figure 17-2 are not usually observable. In practice, the government can only estimate these curves, and accurate estimates are often difficult to obtain, especially when the technology of pollution abatement is changing and the health consequences and other costs associated with various pollutants are not known. An important example of our ignorance regarding the marginal costs and benefits of pollution abatement is related to the effects of greenhouse-gas emissions on global climate change. Though there is now a broad consensus among scientists (with some exceptions) that humankind's emissions of greenhouse gases are contributing to global climate change, the estimates of the *magnitude* of the effects of Earth's climate change, as well as the resulting costs, vary considerably.

The third problem is that the available techniques for regulating pollution are themselves imperfect. Even if the optimal level of pollution abatement were known with precision, there are both technical and legal impediments to achieving that level through regulation.

This brings us to a discussion of the various policies that governments can use to reduce pollution. As we will see, some policies are more effective than others.

17.2 Pollution-Control Policies

We examine three different types of policies designed to bring about the optimal amount of pollution abatement (or the optimal amount of pollution). These are *direct controls*, *emissions taxes*, and *tradable pollution permits*.

Pollution is an externality. Unless they are required by law to do so, most firms do not take the social costs of their pollution into account when they make their private profit-maximizing decisions.

Direct Controls

Direct control is the form of environmental regulation that is used most often in Canada and the United States, although it is often invisible to consumers. (Policies of direct control are sometimes referred to as *command-and-control* policies.) Automobile emissions standards are one example. The standards must be met by all new cars that are sold in Canada. They require that emissions per kilometre of a number of smog-producing pollutants be less than certain specified amounts, and the standards are the same no matter where the car is driven.

Another form of direct control is the simple prohibition of certain polluting behaviours. For example, many cities and towns prohibit the private burning of leaves and other trash because of the air pollution problem (as well as the fire dangers) that the burning would cause. A number of communities have banned the use of wood-burning stoves for the same reason. Some provinces outlaw the use of weed-control products because of the contamination they cause in the ground water. Similarly, the Canadian federal government gradually reduced the amount of lead allowed in leaded gasoline and then eliminated leaded gasoline altogether.

When the policy objective is to *eliminate* a specific type of pollution, direct pollution controls are probably the most practical policy instrument. In the case of weed-control products, for example, the costs imposed on homeowners by prohibiting their use of certain products are almost certainly smaller than the benefits from removing the contamination from the groundwater. In the case of leaded gasoline, the gradual reduction in the permissible lead content allowed producers and consumers to substitute toward unleaded gasoline at relatively low cost, while society gained the considerable benefits of the cleaner automobile emissions. In other situations, however, when the policy objective is to *reduce*, rather than eliminate a particular type of pollution, and when it may not be so clear to governments *how* the pollution can most effectively be reduced, direct pollution controls are far less effective.

Problems with Direct Controls In the terminology of Chapter 12, direct pollution controls are often not *productively efficient* because the total cost of achieving a given amount of pollution abatement is not minimized.

FIGURE 17-3 The Inefficiency of Direct Pollution Controls

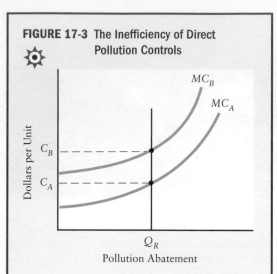

Requiring equal amounts of pollution abatement from different polluters is inefficient when the different polluters have different technologies of pollution abatement. Firm A is able to abate pollution according to the marginal cost curve MC_A. Firm B has a different abatement technology and has a higher marginal cost of abatement, MC_B. Suppose a regulatory authority requires that the two firms reduce pollution by the same amount, Q_R. Firm A will have a marginal cost of pollution abatement of C_A, whereas Firm B's marginal cost will be C_B, which is larger than C_A.

To see that this outcome is inefficient, consider what happens if Firm A increases its pollution abatement by one unit while Firm B decreases its abatement by one unit. Total pollution remains the same, but total costs fall.

Pollution is being abated efficiently when the marginal cost of pollution abatement is the same for all firms.

When firms are required to abide by the same direct pollution controls, however, the marginal cost of pollution abatement is usually *not* equated across firms. To see this, consider two firms that have different technologies and thus face different marginal costs of pollution abatement, as shown in Figure 17-3. These firms may be in the same industry, producing similar products, or they may be in different industries altogether. In either case, they are assumed to have different abilities to abate pollution. Suppose that, for any level of pollution abatement, Firm A's marginal costs of abatement are lower than those for Firm B.

In this situation, consider a system of direct pollution controls that requires Firm A and Firm B each to reduce pollution by a given amount, say Q_R. As shown in Figure 17-3, Firm A's marginal cost at Q_R (C_A) is less than Firm B's marginal cost (C_B). As long as C_A is less than C_B, it is possible to reduce the *total* cost of this amount of pollution abatement by reallocating it between the two firms. For example, suppose C_A is $10 and C_B is $18. If Firm A abated one more unit of pollution, its total costs would rise by $10; if Firm B abated one *less* unit of pollution, its total costs would fall by $18. By reallocating one unit of pollution abatement from Firm B to Firm A, total pollution abatement would be unaffected, but the total cost of the abatement would be reduced by $8. As long as the two firms' marginal costs of abatement are not equal, it is possible to reduce total costs further by further redistributing the abatement between the firms. Only when marginal costs are equal across the two firms is the given level of pollution abatement being achieved at the lowest possible cost.

Direct pollution controls are usually inefficient because they do not minimize the total cost of a given amount of pollution abatement.

Direct controls are also expensive to monitor and to enforce. The regulatory agency has to check—factory by factory, farm by farm—how many pollutants of what kinds are being emitted. It then also needs a mechanism for penalizing offenders. Accurate monitoring of all potential sources of pollution requires a considerable level of resources. Moreover, the system of fines and penalties needs to be harsh enough to induce potential polluters to obey the law. A potential polluter, required to limit emissions of a pollutant to so many kilograms or litres per day, will take into account the cost of meeting the standard, the probability of being caught, and the severity of the penalty before deciding how to behave. If the chances of being caught and the penalties are small, the direct controls may have little effect.

> Monitoring and enforcement of direct pollution controls are costly, and this costliness reduces the effectiveness of the controls.

As we will see, however, the considerable costs of monitoring and enforcement apply in a similar way to all kinds of pollution policies.

Emissions Taxes

An alternative method of pollution control is to levy a tax on emissions at the source. The advantage of imposing a tax on each unit of pollution that firms emit is that each individual polluting firm is forced to *internalize* the negative externality associated with the pollution it is producing. This can lead to *efficient* pollution abatement.

Again, suppose Firm A can reduce emissions cheaply, while it is more expensive for Firm B to reduce emissions. And further suppose that all firms are required to pay a tax equal to $t per unit of pollution emitted. Since firms must pay $t for every unit of pollution they produce, they will save $t for every unit of pollution they *do not produce*. It follows that the emissions tax of $t is each firm's marginal benefit of pollution abatement. The goal of profit maximization will then lead firms to reduce emissions to the point where the marginal cost of further reduction is just equal to $t. Such a situation is illustrated in Figure 17-4.

Note that when all firms facing an emissions tax are maximizing their profits, they will each abate pollution until their own marginal cost is equal to the tax. It follows that their marginal costs will be equated and thus the condition will be satisfied for *efficient* pollution abatement. This efficiency is the central appeal of emissions taxes, especially as compared to direct pollution controls.

The above analysis applies to any level of an emissions tax. But what is the level at which an emissions tax should be set to achieve allocative efficiency? If the regulatory agency is able to obtain a good estimate of the marginal cost generated by the pollution, it could set the tax rate just equal to that amount. In such a case, polluters would be forced by the tax to internalize the full pollution externality and allocative efficiency would be achieved. In terms of Figure 17-1, each firm's private marginal cost curve would shift up by the full amount of the tax (set to equal the marginal external cost, *MEC*) and thus the allocatively efficient level of output (and pollution) would be produced.

A second advantage of using emissions taxes is that regulators are not required to specify anything about *how* polluters should abate pollution and thus are not required to have expertise about the firms' technologies. Rather, polluters themselves can be left to find the most efficient abatement techniques. The profit motive will lead them to do so because they will want to avoid paying the tax.

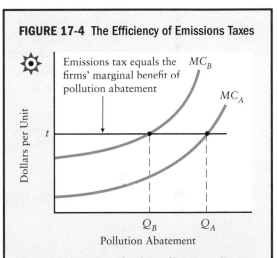

FIGURE 17-4 The Efficiency of Emissions Taxes

Emission taxes can lead to efficient pollution abatement. As in Figure 17-3, Firm A faces a lower marginal cost of pollution abatement than does Firm B. Suppose the regulatory authority imposes a tax of *t* dollars per unit of pollution emitted. Since each firm would then save *t* dollars for each unit of pollution it does not produce, *t* can be viewed as each firm's marginal benefit of pollution abatement.

Firm A chooses to reduce its pollution by Q_A. Up to this point, the tax saved (marginal benefit) from reducing pollution exceeds the marginal cost of reducing pollution. Firm B chooses to abate only a small amount of pollution, Q_B. Since the marginal cost of abatement is equated across firms, the total amount of pollution abatement ($Q_A + Q_B$) is achieved at minimum cost. This is efficient pollution abatement.

Emissions taxes lead profit-maximizing firms to abate pollution in a cost-minimizing manner. If the tax is set equal to the marginal external cost of the pollution, the externality will be fully internalized and the allocatively efficient amount of pollution abatement (and output) will be produced.

Problems with Emissions Taxes Emissions taxes can only be applied if it is possible for the government regulator to measure emissions with reasonable accuracy. For some kinds of pollution-creating activities, this does not pose much of a problem, but for many other types of pollution, good measuring devices that can be installed at reasonable cost do not exist. In these cases, emissions taxes cannot work, and direct controls are the only feasible approach (although appropriate enforcement may still be a problem).

Another problem with emissions taxes involves setting the tax rate. Ideally, the regulatory agency would obtain an estimate of the marginal external cost of each pollutant and set the tax equal to this amount. This ideal tax rate would perfectly internalize the pollution externality. However, the information that is needed to determine the marginal external cost (MEC) shown in Figure 17-1 is often difficult to obtain. If the regulatory agency sets the tax rate too high, too many resources will be devoted to pollution control. If the tax is set too low, there will be too little pollution abatement and thus too much pollution.

A disadvantage with emissions taxes is that information necessary to determine the optimal tax rate is often unavailable.

Tradable Pollution Permits: "Cap and Trade"

The third general policy approach to pollution reduction is often referred to as a system of "cap and trade." This system comprises two fundamental parts. First, the government mandates a limit (or "cap") on the total amount of pollution of some specific type. Second, the government distributes permits to firms (either by granting or auctioning) allowing the firms to emit a specified amount of pollution. These permits can be traded among the firms at prices determined in a free market. For example, the government might issue permits for a total of 10 000 megatonnes of annual sulphur dioxide emissions and distribute to each of 20 firms a permit for 500 megatonnes. In any given year, a firm is restricted to emitting an amount of sulphur dioxide no greater than the amount allowed by the permits it holds. Firms can then trade the permits freely among themselves and a market-determined price will be established. For obvious reasons, a cap-and-trade system is also referred to as a system of **tradable pollution permits**.

Like emissions taxes, tradable pollution permits can minimize the cost of a given amount of pollution abatement. To see this, consider starting from a situation similar to that with direct pollution controls. In Figure 17-5, both firms are abating pollution by Q^* units. (The inefficiency of this initial situation is reflected by the differential in marginal costs of the two firms.) Now suppose the government issues permits for a total amount of emissions consistent with the same total amount of pollution abatement (= $2 \times Q^*$ in the figure). What should each of the firms do? Should they abate more pollution, or less?

tradable pollution permits
Rights to emit specific amounts of specified pollutants that private firms may buy and sell among themselves. The total quantity of permits is set by government policy.

FIGURE 17-5 The Efficiency of Tradable Pollution Permits ("Cap and Trade")

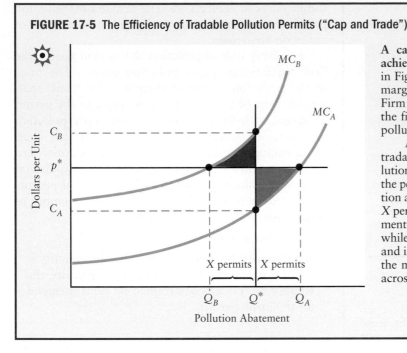

A cap-and-trade system is an efficient way to achieve a given amount of pollution abatement. As in Figure 17-3 and Figure 17-4, Firm A has lower marginal costs of pollution abatement than does Firm B. If each firm abates pollution by Q^* units, the firms' marginal costs are not equated and the pollution abatement is inefficient.

All firms can be better off if they are issued tradable pollution permits even though total pollution abatement remains unchanged. The price of the permits reflects firms' marginal benefit of pollution abatement. If the price is p^*, Firm A would sell X permits to Firm B. Firm B would reduce its abatement to Q_B and reduce its costs by the red area, while Firm A would increase its abatement to Q_A and increase its net earnings by the blue area. Since the marginal costs of abatement are then equated across firms, this is efficient pollution abatement.

Note that at Q^* units of pollution abatement, the marginal costs for Firm B exceed the marginal costs for Firm A—pollution abatement is more difficult for Firm B than for Firm A. Suppose the two firms could agree on a price p^* at which to buy and sell permits. Who would buy, and who would sell? Firm B, the high abatement-cost firm, would rather buy permits at p^* and avoid having to reduce pollution at high marginal costs. By buying X pollution permits from Firm A, Firm B ends up abating Q_B units of pollution and reduces its costs by the red-shaded area. Firm A, the low-abatement-cost firm, would rather sell its permits at p^* and abate more pollution at low marginal cost. By selling X permits to Firm B, Firm A ends up abating Q_A units of pollution and increases its profits by the blue-shaded area.

Therefore, with low-abatement-cost firms selling pollution permits to high-abatement-cost firms, both types of firms are better off than when they are subject to direct pollution controls even though the total amount of pollution abatement is unchanged. Since the marginal cost of abatement is now equal across firms, we know from our earlier discussion that the given amount of pollution abatement is being achieved at the lowest possible cost.

> With tradable pollution permits, profit-maximizing firms will reduce pollution until their marginal abatement costs equal the price of pollution permits. The costs of a given amount of pollution abatement will be minimized.

What determines the equilibrium market price for pollution permits? The total supply of pollution permits is determined by the government policy—the government-mandated "cap" on pollution. Let this amount be Q^S—it is represented by a vertical

FIGURE 17-6 The Market for Tradable Pollution Permits

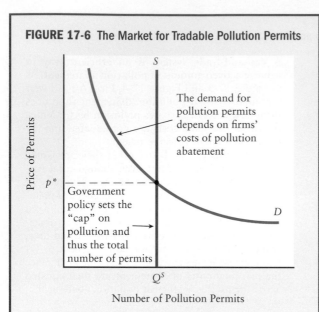

Number of Pollution Permits

The equilibrium price in the market for pollution permits is determined by government policy and by firms' technology of pollution abatement. The government sets the total quantity of pollution permits at Q^S. This is the vertical supply curve. At a lower price for permits (the marginal benefit of abatement) firms decide to abate less pollution and they therefore require more pollution permits. The demand curve for permits is therefore downward sloping. At the equilibrium price, the quantity of permits demanded by firms is equal to the number issued by the government.

supply curve in Figure 17-6. The demand for pollution permits comes from firms and depends on their costs of pollution abatement.

For every unit of pollution that a firm abates, the firm requires one fewer pollution permit. The price of the pollution permit is therefore the firms' marginal benefit of abatement. As the price of the permit increases, each firm decides to abate more pollution and therefore demand fewer pollution permits. Thus, the demand curve for pollution permits is downward sloping, as shown in Figure 17-6. At the equilibrium price for pollution permits, p^*, the number of permits demanded by firms will exactly equal the number of permits issued by the government.

> In the market for pollution permits, the quantity is set by government policy. Given that quantity, the equilibrium price is determined by firms' demand for pollution permits.

Technological Change One problem with direct pollution controls is that they tend, like much government regulation, to respond only slowly to changes in technology or market conditions. In contrast, tradable pollution permits, because they are a market-based method of pollution control, maintain their efficiency even in the midst of frequent and substantial changes in technology. As technological advances occur that reduce the marginal costs of pollution abatement, profit-maximizing firms will choose to abate more pollution at any given price for the pollution permits (see Figure 17-5). But this decision will imply a reduced overall demand for pollution permits and thus the equilibrium price for the permits will fall (see Figure 17-6). Whatever the market price for permits, profit-maximizing firms will equate the price to their marginal abatement costs, thus minimizing the total cost of a given amount of pollution abatement.

> Improvements in abatement technology will lead to a reduction in the demand for emissions permits and thus a reduction in their equilibrium price. The total cost of a given amount of pollution abatement will still be minimized.

Problems with Tradable Pollution Permits Tradable permits pose some problems of implementation. Some of these involve technical difficulties in measuring pollution and in designing mechanisms to ensure that firms and households comply with regulations (the same problems that exist for direct controls and emissions taxes). Furthermore, the potential efficiency gains arising from tradable permits cannot be realized if regulatory agencies are prone to change the rules under which trades may take place. Such changes have been a problem in the past, but they are a problem that can be corrected.

One problem with tradable permits is more political than economic, but it is certainly important in explaining why such policies are relatively rare. Opponents of tradable permits often argue that by providing permits, rather than simply outlawing pollution above some amount, the government is condoning crimes against society. Direct controls, according to this argument, have much greater normative force because they suggest that violating the standards is simply wrong. In contrast, emissions taxes and markets for pollution permits make violating the standards just one more element of cost for the firm to consider as it pursues its private goals.

Most economists find arguments of this kind unpersuasive. An absolute ban on pollution is impossible because any production of goods and services generates at least some pollution. In choosing how much pollution to allow, society must recognize the tradeoff between devoting resources toward pollution abatement and other valuable things. Economic analysis has a good deal to say about how a society might minimize the cost of *any* degree of pollution abatement. By taking the moral attitude that pollution is wrong and pollution permits should not be allowed, the result is that *less* pollution is abated for any given amount of society's scarce resources that are allocated toward this goal.

Uncertainty and the Choice Between Emissions Taxes and "Cap and Trade"

The analysis of Figures 17-4 and 17-5 on pages 423 and 425 suggests an important similarity between emissions taxes and a system of tradable emissions permits ("cap and trade"). Since both policies result in polluting firms having to pay the same price (either the tax or the price of a permit) whenever they pollute, both policies result in *efficiency* in pollution abatement.

This aspect of the two policies often leads economists to view emissions taxes as a close policy substitute for a system of tradable emissions permits. Comparison of Figures 17-4 and 17-5 suggests that for any emissions tax rate, t, the same amount of pollution abatement could be achieved by using a cap-and-trade system—as long as the cap on pollution is chosen so that the equilibrium price, p^*, equals t.

This close similarity, however, depends on the government or regulatory authority knowing the firms' technologies for pollution abatement and thus knowing the firms' MC curves. It is more realistic, however, that these MC curves are at best only approximately known. How does such *uncertainty* affect the practical choice between the two policies?

Let's begin with an emissions tax when the firms' MC of abatement is unknown. Part (i) of Figure 17-7 shows the economy's overall MC of pollution abatement, with the uncertainty about the MC curve shown by the range between the dashed MC curves. When an emissions tax of $\$t$ is imposed, individual firms respond in the way we described earlier, but the regulatory authorities do not know how much pollution will end up being abated. The uncertainty about firms' abatement technologies results in uncertainty about the *quantity* of overall pollution abatement.

When the government does not know firms' abatement technologies, emissions taxes impose a certain per unit cost on polluting firms but result in an uncertain amount of pollution abatement.

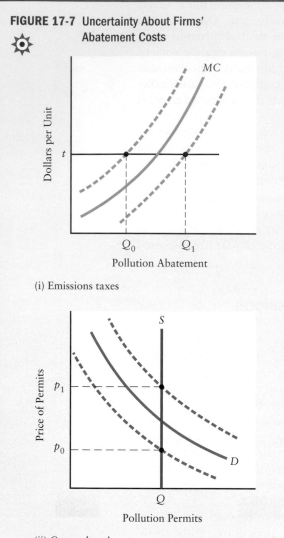

FIGURE 17-7 Uncertainty About Firms' Abatement Costs

(i) Emissions taxes

(ii) Cap and trade

When firms' abatement costs are uncertain, emissions taxes lead to an uncertain amount of pollution reduction, whereas a cap-and-trade system leads to an uncertain price for pollution permits. In part (i), a typical firm's MC of pollution abatement could be anywhere between the dashed lines. With an emissions tax of \$$t$ per unit of pollution, the amount of pollution abatement will be somewhere between Q_0 and Q_1. In part (ii), uncertainty over firms' abatement costs leads to uncertainty about their demand for pollution permits; the demand curve lies somewhere between the dashed lines. With a pollution cap of Q, the equilibrium permit price will be somewhere between p_0 and p_1.

Now consider a cap-and-trade system in the presence of the same uncertainty about firms' MC of abatement. Since firms' demand for pollution permits reflects their costs of pollution abatement, the government's uncertainty about their abatement costs results in uncertainty about firms' overall demand for pollution permits. Thus, in part (ii) of Figure 17-7 we see that the market demand for pollution permits could lie anywhere in the range between the dashed curves. If the government now introduces a cap on the number of pollution permits equal to Q, the market for pollution permits will clear at some price, and individual firms will respond in the manner described earlier. But before implementing such a policy, the government will be unable to know what the equilibrium price for permits will be. In this case, the uncertainty about firms' abatement costs results in uncertainty about the *price* firms will need to pay for pollution permits.

> **When the government does not know firms' abatement technologies, a cap-and-trade system ensures a certain quantity of pollution abatement but imposes an uncertain cost on polluting firms.**

In summary, uncertainty about firms' abatement costs results in an important practical difference between a policy of emissions taxes and a policy of tradable emissions permits (cap and trade). With a policy of emissions taxes, the government can be sure of how the tax will affect firms' costs, but it will then be unsure about the magnitude of the reduction in pollution. In contrast, with a cap-and-trade system, the government can be sure about the amount of pollution reduction but will be unsure about the magnitude of the costs imposed on individual firms.

This difference can have important implications for how the policies are communicated to the public and thus for the degree of political support they are able to garner. This difference was evident in the Canadian federal election of 2008. The Liberals proposed a tax on the use of carbon-based fuels, such as oil, natural gas, and coal. The Conservatives and NDP argued that the Liberal plan would impose high costs on firms and consumers without ensuring that there would be a significant reduction in greenhouse-gas emissions. The Conservatives and NDP instead advocated a cap-and-trade system, arguing that it would more effectively lead to meaningful emissions reductions. Neither the Conservatives nor the NDP chose to emphasize the point that their policies, if implemented, would also impose costs on firms and consumers. Firms would need to purchase permits in order to have any greenhouse-gas emissions; consumers would then be faced with higher prices for the goods and services produced by firms bearing these higher costs.

The Conservatives won the election of 2008 and continued to plan a cap-and-trade system. But the political winds then shifted, and the Conservatives decided to scrap the cap-and-trade system and in its place design a system of direct controls on large emitters of greenhouse gases—a system that would likely *not* achieve efficient pollution abatement. By 2013, after securing a majority government in the 2011 federal election, the Conservatives had still not implemented their policy, but many businesses and economists were then urging the government to return to the more efficient policies of either cap-and-trade or emissions taxes.

17.3 The Economic Challenge of Global Climate Change

So far in this chapter we have discussed the general case of environmental externalities and the types of policies that can be used to address them. We now go on to examine the particular case of global climate change, undoubtedly the most complex environmental externality the world has ever seen. Recall that a negative externality is an example of a market failure, where the private market fails to take account of the external cost associated with the production or use of a commodity. While some debate still exists, it is generally accepted in the scientific community that the burning of fossil fuels and the resulting emission of greenhouse gases is directly affecting the global climate and raising Earth's average temperature. Correcting this market failure will require coordinated actions by the world's 193 national governments. It is no surprise that global climate change has been described as the "mother of all externalities."

Former U.S. Vice-President Al Gore was a co-recipient of the 2007 Nobel Peace Prize for his efforts in urging individuals and governments to combat global warming by reducing the emission of greenhouse gases.

In this section we review the basic facts about the emission of greenhouse gases, their accumulation in the atmosphere, and the effects on Earth's climate. In addition, we examine the case for global collective action to reduce these emissions. Finally, we discuss the considerable technical challenges that must be overcome if emissions are to be reduced on a scale sufficient to stabilize Earth's climate. As will become clear, the issue of global climate change presents a complex combination of economic, political, and scientific challenges.

Greenhouse-Gas Emissions

Greenhouse gases include carbon dioxide, methane, and nitrous oxide, all of which are emitted through various industrial processes, especially the burning of fossil fuels, the production of cement, and the use of nitrogen-rich fertilizers in agriculture. Over the past decade, a clear consensus has emerged within the scientific community that these activities are responsible for the accumulation of greenhouse gases (GHGs) in the atmosphere, and that this rising atmospheric concentration is raising the Earth's average temperature. It is common to measure greenhouse gases in terms of their equivalent amount of carbon dioxide, referred to as CO_2e.

Flows Versus Stocks The world's total emissions of greenhouse gases in 2010 were approximately 50 billion tonnes of CO_2e, two-thirds of which were related to the production or consumption of energy—residential and commercial heating, transportation, electricity generation, and industrial processes. These emissions are a *flow* that occur annually and have been on a significant upward trend over the past century. Through the natural respiration of forests and absorption by the oceans, Earth can absorb only about 5 billion tonnes of GHGs every year. For each year that the total flow of GHG emissions exceed this natural absorptive level, the atmospheric concentration of greenhouse gases increases.

In the mid-1800s, before the Industrial Revolution began, current estimates suggest that the concentration of greenhouse gases in the atmosphere was roughly 280 parts per million (ppm) of CO_2e. But as the Industrial Revolution progressed, the burning of coal to operate steam engines and generate electricity became widespread, and later the burning of petroleum-based fuels was developed to fuel automobiles, diesel locomotives, ships, and airplanes. As the world's emissions of GHGs rose above Earth's absorptive capacity, the gases began to accumulate in the atmosphere. Today, a century and a half later, the atmospheric concentration of greenhouse gases has increased by over 50 percent to 430 ppm of CO_2e.

The Effect on Global Climate Why is the growing atmospheric concentration of greenhouse gases a problem? The accumulation of GHGs in the atmosphere acts like the walls and roof of a greenhouse to hold in the infrared radiation from Earth, thus raising Earth's temperature. If the atmospheric concentration increases to a level of 550 ppm of CO_2e, Earth's average temperature is predicted to rise above its pre-industrial level by 1.5 to 4.5°C. Even such an apparently modest increase in temperature is predicted to have potentially devastating effects, including

- melting of the world's glaciers, resulting in a loss of fresh-water supplies, especially in South Asia, China, and South America
- melting of the Greenland and Antarctic ice caps, resulting in rising sea levels and the likely displacement of tens of millions of people from their current homes (especially in the low island states of the developing world)
- a reduction of animal habitat and the extinction of some species, leading to a reduction in biodiversity
- reduced crop yields (especially in Africa and parts of Asia), resulting in reduced food supplies in regions already facing hunger problems
- rising intensity of storms and increasing volatility of weather patterns

The costs associated with these changes are easy to imagine but difficult to quantify precisely. Current estimates of the effects of climate change, expressed in terms of a permanent reduction in world GDP, range from 3 percent to 20 percent. The width of this range indicates just how much uncertainty and debate continues to exist about the effects of global climate change, but even the lower bound of this range—an annual global cost of U.S.$1.2 trillion forever—represents an enormous sum. Even worse, these costs will probably be unevenly distributed across the world's population; the developing world is likely to bear the lion's share of the burden of global climate change.

In summary, the atmospheric concentration of greenhouse gases is already 50 percent above its pre-industrial levels and some climate change is already occurring. But if the global climate is to be stabilized in the long run (albeit at a higher average temperature than today's), the atmospheric concentration of green-house gases must also be stabilized, at least eventually. Such stabilization will eventually require an enor-mous cut in the annual flow of GHG emissions from its current level of 50 billion tonnes of CO_2e to about 5 billion tonnes per year, the amount Earth can natur-ally absorb annually. Such a reduction in the annual flow of global GHG emissions is an enormous task and will take many years to accomplish.

One of the predicted effects of ongoing climate change is the increasing frequency and severity of extreme weather events.

The Case for Global Collective Action

The emission of greenhouse gases is a *negative externality*. Many production and con-sumption activities of individual firms and households emit greenhouse gases, and thereby impose costs on others. But because they are not required to incorporate these external costs into their own calculations, most firms and individuals act as if these external costs do not exist. As a result, they carry out too many of these polluting activ-ities relative to what is socially optimal; the market outcome is allocatively inefficient.

When such negative externalities occur within a community, bylaws can be enacted by local government to alter individuals' behaviour. We thus have bylaws in some cities pre-venting the use of wood-burning stoves. When negative externalities occur within larger regions, governments often step in to correct the market failure, and so we get provincial governments enforcing such laws as banning the dumping of toxic waste in waterways.

In the case of greenhouse-gas emissions, however, the negative externality is truly global. The GHG emissions that come from a coal-burning electricity plant in Canada or China rise into the atmosphere and disperse geographically. They both add to the atmospheric stock of existing GHGs and therefore contribute to the ongoing process of climate change. In both cases, the costs are imposed on people all over the world. As Professor Nicolas Stern says in his 2006 report written for the U.K. Treasury, "Climate change is the greatest market failure the world has ever seen"—its solution will require collective action on a global scale.

The Kyoto Protocol The global scale of the problem motivated the United Nations to spon-sor a set of conferences, beginning in the 1980s, aimed at discussing the emerging problem of climate change. In 1997, this process was further brought to the world's attention with a conference held in Kyoto, Japan, at which many countries signed an international agree-ment aimed at reducing GHG emissions. This agreement came to be called the *Kyoto Proto-col*, and by December 2006 had been ratified by the parliaments of 166 signatory countries.

The countries participating in the Kyoto Protocol agreed to an aggregate emis-sions-reduction target of 5 percent below the 1990 level of emissions by 2012. Each country also agreed to its own emissions-reduction target over the same period. Note,

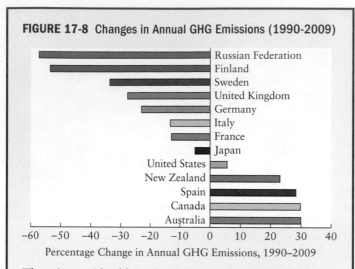

FIGURE 17-8 Changes in Annual GHG Emissions (1990-2009)

Percentage Change in Annual GHG Emissions, 1990–2009

There is considerable variation across countries in terms of the change in annual emissions of greenhouse gases since 1990. The data show the percentage change in annual GHG emissions between 1990 and 2009. Canada's and Australia's emissions increased by almost 30 percent; Sweden and Finland reduced their emissions by over 30 percent over the same period. All countries shown (except Australia and the United States) were signatories to the Kyoto Protocol.

(*Source:* United Nations Framework Convention on Climate Change. Data are GHG emissions including those due to land use, land-use change, and forestry (LULUCF); www.unfccc.int/ghg_data.)

however, that the countries that eventually adopted the Kyoto Protocol were responsible for only about one-third of global GHG emissions. Notably absent from the Kyoto signatories were the developed countries of the United States and Australia, and the large developing countries of China, India, and Indonesia.

Performance Figure 17-8 shows the change in annual GHG emissions for selected countries between 1990 and 2009. All of the countries shown in the figure were signatories to the Kyoto Protocol except Australia and the United States. Some countries, including Canada, have experienced significant *increases* in their annual emissions, despite their stated commitments to achieve modest reductions. On the other hand, many countries have been able to reduce their annual GHG emissions by 20 percent or more since 1990. In some cases, such as France, Sweden, and the United Kingdom, the emissions reductions were achieved despite continued growth in annual income (GDP) over the 20-year period. In other cases, however, notably the Russian Federation (and to a lesser extent Germany), a large part of the emissions reductions were associated with the steep economic declines that occurred as the former Eastern Bloc countries made the difficult transition from centrally planned to market economies.

One important lesson from Figure 17-8 is that the mere act of signing an international treaty and committing to a specific outcome does not guarantee the achievement of that outcome. Without effective policies being put in place, emissions reductions are unlikely to occur. We say more about specific policies below.

Beyond Kyoto Some countries achieved their Kyoto targets while many did not. By the time the Kyoto Protocol expired in 2012, however, it was increasingly clear to most countries that subsequent phases of international actions to reduce greenhouse-gas emissions needed to include participation by the world's largest emitters, including the United States, China, India, and Indonesia.

In Durban, South Africa, in 2011, a U.N.-sponsored conference achieved a notable success. All countries agreed to negotiate a legally binding emission-reduction agreement by 2015, to be implemented by 2020. Many observers hailed this as a major breakthrough because for the first time *all* countries would be taking part in emissions reductions, even though the details were yet to be determined. Critics pointed out that the "details" were crucial and that, in any event, delaying implementation until 2020 might prove to be too late to prevent an excessive increase in Earth's temperature.

There is no doubt that getting agreement on emissions reductions from a large number of countries is a complex and difficult task. But even apart from the politics and the diplomacy, there are enormous *technological* challenges involved in reducing greenhouse-gas emissions. We now turn to examine these challenges.

Energy Use, GDP, and Greenhouse-Gas Emissions

The data in Figure 17-8 suggest that it is not easy for a country to achieve significant reductions in greenhouse-gas emissions. If it were straightforward to achieve sizable reductions, then presumably emissions would not have *grown* in several large countries that claimed to be committed to achieving their stated emissions-reduction targets. Why are such reductions so difficult to achieve?

To organize our thoughts, it is useful to think about the following identity, which expresses GHG emissions in terms of three essential components.

$$\text{GHG} = \frac{\text{GHG}}{\text{Energy}} \times \frac{\text{Energy}}{\text{GDP}} \times \text{GDP} \qquad (17\text{-}1)$$

where "GHG" is the world's annual emissions of greenhouse gases, "Energy" is the amount of energy consumed globally per year, and "GDP" is the world's annual gross domestic product. It is obvious that Equation 17-1 is identically true since one could easily cancel out the "GDP" and "Energy" terms to get GHG = GHG.

The value of this identity is that it shows us three essential components of the world's annual emissions of greenhouse gases. Each time the annual rate of GHG emissions increases, at least one of the three components must have increased. There has been either an increase in GDP, an increase in the energy intensity of GDP (Energy/GDP), or an increase in the GHG intensity of energy (GHG/Energy). Conversely, if we are to reduce the world's annual GHG emissions, then at least one of these three components must fall. Let's consider these three components in turn and determine which specific route to reducing global GHG emissions appears to be most promising.

Reducing Global GDP For a given GHG intensity of energy, and for a given energy intensity of GDP, Equation 17-1 shows that more GDP means more greenhouse-gas emissions. This should not be surprising: The production of most goods and services requires the use of energy, which in turn tends to be associated with the release of greenhouse gases. Thus, other things being equal, we can expect GHG emissions to increase as world GDP rises.

For two reasons, it is unrealistic to consider a reduction in the world's GDP as a fruitful approach to reducing global GHG emissions. First, note that current population trends suggest that the world's population will rise from its current 7 billion people to approximately 10 billion over the next century. These 3 billion extra people will require more GDP just to be fed, clothed, and housed, not to mention to receive the various "extras" that most of us take for granted.

Second, even if we ignore the challenge of global population growth, it is likely that per capita GDP will continue to rise over time. It is probably inherent to human nature that individuals—in rich and poor countries alike—strive to do better and improve their quality of life. And this desire to increase per capita income will inevitably lead to increases in world GDP.

As a result, world GDP can be expected to *rise* over time, not fall. In the developed world, in countries like Canada, France, and the United States, the long-run annual growth rate of GDP is between 2 and 3 percent. But in the developing world, especially in the quickly emerging economies of China and India, GDP growth is closer to 8 or 9 percent per year. For the world as a whole, the average growth rate is usually between 4 and 5 percent per year. It follows that with unchanged "intensities" in Equation 17-1, the typical growth in world GDP will lead to growth in GHG emissions of between 4 and 5 percent per year. Note that even if the growth rate of world GDP were to fall by a few percentage points, world GDP would still be increasing and thus we would still have rising GHG emissions.

Reducing the Energy Intensity of GDP Now consider the second component in Equation 17-1, the energy intensity of GDP—the amount of energy that is used to produce one dollar's worth of real GDP. For a given GHG intensity of energy, and for a given level of world GDP, a reduction in the energy intensity of GDP will reduce the annual emissions of greenhouse gases.

Improvements in technology, driven in part by firms' efforts to economize on inputs that are becoming increasingly scarce and expensive, are one driver for reductions in the energy intensity of GDP. Another is that as the structure of the economy continues its gradual adjustment away from energy-intensive manufacturing and toward the less-energy-intensive service sector, less energy is used even if the same level of aggregate output is produced. In countries like Canada and the United States, the energy used per dollar of real GDP has fallen by about 35 percent since the mid-1970s—an annual rate of decline of about 1 percent. Similar declines have been observed in other developed economies.

Can we rely on reductions in energy intensity to achieve the necessary reductions in the world's greenhouse-gas emissions? The answer, again, is probably not. Reductions in energy intensity are ongoing, but are probably insufficient for the task at hand. With world GDP growing at 4 or 5 percent per year on average, even a 1.5 percent annual improvement in energy intensity (which is more than what we have observed over the past 35 years) means that the second two terms in Equation 17-1 are still likely to grow at a combined rate of about 3 percent per year.

Reducing the GHG Intensity of Energy We are thus left with only one remaining way to achieve sizable reductions in the annual flow of global GHG emissions: We must significantly cut the GHG intensity of our energy. In other words, we need to produce and consume energy in ways that release far fewer GHG emissions into the atmosphere.

Two general approaches are available for reducing the GHG intensity of the world's energy. The first is to switch, on a large scale, away from fossil fuel–based energy toward alternative forms of energy. Call this the *substitution* approach. The second is to continue using fossil fuels to generate energy, but to prevent the resulting greenhouse gases from being released into the atmosphere. Call this the *emissions-prevention* approach. Let's examine these two approaches in turn.

The Substitution Approach: Alternative Energy. The burning of fossil fuels is an extremely efficient and economical method of producing energy. The sun's heat and the weight of Earth's crust have combined over hundreds of millions of years to concentrate a tremendous amount of energy into every barrel of oil, bucket of coal, or cubic metre of natural gas. As a result, the burning of these fossil fuels is a very efficient way to produce energy. In addition, the costs (not including the negative externalities) of extracting and refining these fossil fuels are relatively low. The combination of these two factors results in a large economic advantage for fossil-fuel-based energy (sometimes called carbon-based energy) relative to non-carbon alternatives. It is therefore no wonder that roughly 85 percent of the world's energy is produced by burning fossil fuels.

The substitution approach to reducing GHG emissions is difficult because it requires making a substitution *away from* a low-cost and efficient energy source on an immense scale. In order to reduce the world's annual GHG emissions by 90 percent (even if we assumed that total energy consumption was held constant), it would be necessary to

This facility in Weyburn, Saskatchewan is designed to capture and store carbon dioxide. If it proves to be sufficiently effective and inexpensive, this procedure could be used to significantly reduce Canada's GHG emissions.

expand *by many times* the amount of energy currently being produced by hydroelectric dams, nuclear reactors, and renewable power sources like solar and wind. These alternative sources of energy have their own limitations, however, and in most cases it is unlikely that large-scale expansion can be readily achieved.[1]

The large-scale expansion of hydro power, for example, relies on being able to find enough new locations appropriate to the damming of large rivers, but such sites are already becoming quite scarce. Expansion of nuclear power is politically difficult for the simple reason that this method of power generation carries its own considerable environmental challenges—the safe storage of nuclear waste and the ongoing risk of nuclear accidents, such as what occurred in Fukushima, Japan, when a tsunami seriously damaged a nuclear plant in 2011. Wind power and solar power, though currently technically feasible and growing in use, both require large amounts of land, and this land often has a considerable opportunity cost. In addition, the capital costs for both types of renewable power are quite large, and without government subsidies, operators are currently unable to cover their costs if they must compete with cheaper, conventional carbon-based power. Another disadvantage of wind and solar power is their inherent intermittence; as the wind dies down or the sun moves behind the clouds, power generation naturally falls off. A major challenge for wind and solar power is therefore the development of efficient, large-capacity storage batteries. Finally, fuel cells are often regarded as the energy source of the future, and technically they are indeed promising; energy is created from hydrogen with zero emissions of harmful greenhouse gases. The production of hydrogen for fuel cells, however, is currently very costly and also very energy intensive, so considerably more technical progress is required before the fuel cell offers a credible alternative to carbon-based energy.

In summary, the large-scale substitution away from carbon-based energy and toward alternative, cleaner energy is not feasible in the short term. The various alternative energy sources have their own limitations, which probably explain why they are currently so rarely used as compared with carbon-based energy. Such a large-scale substitution, however, may prove to be possible over a much longer time frame. In the next section we will discuss several policies that may encourage a substitution toward alternative fuels.

The Emissions-Prevention Approach: Carbon Capture and Storage. The second approach to reducing the GHG intensity of energy—the emissions-prevention approach—is to continue reaping the enormous economic benefits that come from carbon-based energy production, but to actively try to minimize the associated environmental costs. In other words, we continue to burn fossil fuels to produce energy but prevent the harmful GHG emissions from escaping into the atmosphere. Instead, the GHGs could be "captured" and stored safely, either in secure manufactured storage containers or, perhaps more realistically, in the sedimentary layers from which the oil and natural gas were originally extracted. In principle, this is a very promising possibility, as the depleted oil and gas reservoirs at thousands of locations around the world could accommodate the pressurized greenhouse gases that the world will continue to produce.

The technology for *carbon capture and storage* (CCS) currently exists, and some small pilot projects are currently operating in Alberta, Saskatchewan, and elsewhere. But the process is quite expensive, and there remains considerable doubt regarding the extent to which the process can be scaled up to the degree necessary for CCS to play a large role in the reduction of global GHG emissions.

---

[1] For a discussion of these challenges, see. Green, C., Baksi, S., and Dilmaghani, M. (2007), "Challenges to a climate stabilizing energy future," *Energy Policy*, 35(1), 616–626.

Significant Policy Challenges

If climate change is the greatest market failure the world has ever seen, then it may also represent the largest scope for government intervention that has ever existed. It is one thing to suggest a role for government policy but quite another to design a set of policies that achieves the objectives in an effective manner. Our brief discussion of climate-change policy examines separately the international and the Canadian challenges.

International Negotiations As we said earlier, meeting through the UN-sponsored process, all countries have now agreed to design a legally binding emissions-reduction agreement by 2015, to be implemented by 2020. The details of this agreement are not yet determined, however, and importantly, it is not clear *who* will be responsible for *how much* emissions reduction. There is a powerful tension here between the developed and the developing nations.

The developed countries argue that in order for their domestic voters to accept stringent emissions-reductions policies, the developing countries must be seen to be equally committed to slowing and eventually reducing their own GHG emissions. The rich-country voters do not want the developing countries to be "free riding" on their costly actions.

The developing countries respond by pointing out that the vast majority of the greenhouse gases emitted over the past century have come from the developed countries and that it is unfair to expect developing countries to now slow their rate of economic advance. They argue that they should be allowed to continue their process of economic development while the rich countries take on the primary responsibility of reducing global GHG emissions. They also suggest that if the richer countries feel so strongly about reducing GHG emissions in the developing world, then the rich countries should be prepared to pay for it—by making large financial contributions to the developing countries to help finance the adoption of non-emitting technologies.

The developed countries respond in two ways. First, they point out that the structure of the world economy is changing dramatically, and that over the next 50 years, the lion's share of GHG emissions will come from the developing world, not the developed world. This is partly due to the higher rates of economic growth in the developing world and partly due to the greater reliance on energy-intensive production in those economies.

Second, and not surprisingly, the developed economies respond by suggesting that they have only limited public funds that can be transferred to the developing countries. This argument gained greater credibility with the onset of the major global recession of 2009 and the ongoing sovereign debt crisis and slow economic growth in Europe.

In short, the international climate-change negotiations contain a fascinating but complex set of challenges, including many details that have not been discussed here. But most economists agree that the global nature of the climate-change problem requires a global policy solution. It is therefore important that these negotiations continue and culminate in an effective international agreement.

Climate change is a global challenge. Complex negotiations between a large number of developed and developing countries are required to reach binding agreements regarding the reduction of global greenhouse-gas emissions.

Canadian Climate-Change Policy Whatever agreements are reached in the international negotiations, it is likely that individual countries will be responsible for designing and implementing their own domestic policies. The Canadian government is currently engaged in the development of new climate-change policies, unlikely to be implemented before 2014. It is too early to know even the broad outlines of these new policies.

Past Policy Failures. As was clear in Figure 17-8, Canada's greenhouse-gas emissions have increased by almost 30 percent since 1990. Why has Canada failed to reduce its emissions?

Professor Mark Jaccard from Simon Fraser University argues that Canada's past climate-change policy has been ineffective because it intentionally avoided forcing users of carbon-based fuels to pay a price incorporating the costs that their emissions impose on the rest of the world.[2] In the terminology that we used earlier in this chapter, the negative externality was not *internalized* for users with an appropriately designed tax. Instead, Canada's past climate-change policies amounted to little more than informing the public about the general problem and providing subsidies to homeowners to purchase energy-efficient appliances and to install better insulation in their homes. In addition, the government encouraged large industrial emitters to *voluntarily* reduce their GHG emissions.

Raising the public's awareness of the climate-change problem is important. But unless consumers are forced to recognize—by facing higher prices—that their choices impose significant costs on others, they are unlikely to change their consumption patterns. Most economists believe that a *necessary* part of any effective climate-change policy is that a high price be placed on any actions that result in the emission of greenhouse gases.

Government subsidies also have problems. Many individuals will simply ignore the subsidy programs because the benefits are small or perhaps the benefits are a hassle to receive. They can easily continue with the status quo, secure in the knowledge that they live in an economy with cheap and plentiful energy. Other individuals who were already in the process of re-insulating their homes may apply for and receive the subsidy, but in this case the re-insulation would have been done anyway and so the expenditure of public funds is not achieving any extra emissions reduction.

Finally, there are obvious problems with voluntary targets for large industrial emitters. Firms are in business to earn a profit from their activities. If they face no clear incentive to reduce their GHG emissions, it is difficult to understand why they would do so, especially if costs must be incurred along the way. Some firms will no doubt find that by reducing their emissions they can improve their reputation and thereby increase their appeal to consumers. In general, however, it is easy to be skeptical about the effectiveness of a climate-change policy based on voluntary action.

During the federal election campaign in the fall of 2008, an open letter was sent to the leaders of all federal political parties, arguing the need for a more coherent and effective policy to reduce Canada's greenhouse-gas emissions. The letter was signed by more than 230 Canadian economists and emphasized the need to go beyond the sort of public challenges, subsidies, and voluntary measures that characterized Canadian policy up to that point. The letter is reprinted in *Applying Economic Concepts 17-1*. Given the absence of any coherent federal policy aimed at reducing greenhouse-gas emissions, it remains as relevant today as it was in 2008.

Effective Future Policy? Any coherent and effective policy directed at reducing Canada's (or any other country's) greenhouse-gas emissions is likely to incorporate two central elements: a policy that, first, places a price on GHG emissions and that, second, provides strong public support for technological development. Both elements can work to reduce the GHG intensity of our energy.

---

[2] See Jaccard, M. (May 2006), "Burning Our Money to Warm the Planet," *C.D. Howe Institute Commentary*.

APPLYING ECONOMIC CONCEPTS 17-1

An Open Letter to the Leaders of Canada's Federal Political Parties (from more than 230 economists teaching in Canadian colleges and universities, October 7, 2008)

One of the few issues on which most economists agree is the need for public policy to protect the environment. . . . In the absence of policy, individuals generally don't take the environmental consequences of their actions into account, and the result is "market failure" and excessive levels of pollution. Environmental degradation diminishes the quality of life for all of us. And without a healthy environment, we can't sustain a healthy economy. We, the undersigned, have therefore joined together to express our shared views on effective policies to address climate change.

We are non-partisan and will undoubtedly be supporting different parties in this election. Our goal is not to criticize or praise one party or another, but rather to offer our collective views, as economists, to help inform public debate on these matters at a critical time—during a federal election campaign.

What Needs to Be Done

While Canada clearly cannot solve the climate-change problem on its own, we need to do our part, and this requires immediate and substantive action by our federal government. We make this statement fully acknowledging the importance of other issues to Canadian voters, such as the turmoil in financial markets and our military involvement in Afghanistan. But climate scientists state that we bear the costs of our lack of action on carbon reduction on a daily basis, and within a few decades the impacts of climate change could be truly catastrophic—unless we take action now. Even those who are not quite convinced by today's scientific evidence need to consider the costs of not acting now. If they turn out to be wrong, and we wait for complete certainty, it will be too late.

All the major political parties have stated that they understand the need to act on carbon emissions. The question then becomes what action to take. Any action (including inaction) will have substantial economic consequences and, thus, economics lies at the heart of the debate on climate change.

With this letter, we hope to help put the debate on a more solid economic foundation by offering the following set of principles upon which we believe climate-change policy should be founded.

1. **Canada needs to act on climate change now.**

2. **Any substantive action will involve economic costs.** Any effective carbon-reduction policy will necessarily entail changing the way we live and do business. All forms of regulation, taxes, or markets for the exchange of emission permits that have a significant impact on greenhouse-gas emissions will affect the prices of carbon-intensive goods.

3. **These economic impacts cannot be an excuse for inaction.** Climate scientists are clear on the costs of inaction, and that these costs will accumulate well beyond the current business cycle, possibly at an accelerating rate. Active and effective climate-change policy should be seen as an investment that will yield pay-offs for ourselves, our children and our grandchildren. Given the need to act, the question then becomes which policies would obtain the carbon-reduction goals we establish with the lowest cost and greatest level of fairness.

4. **Pricing carbon is the best approach from an economic perspective.** Approaches to reaching any particular climate-change goal that involve pricing carbon, such as carbon taxes and cap-and-trade systems, involve less economic damage to businesses and families than the alternatives. Carbon pricing is good for several reasons:

    a) Price mechanisms give everyone the incentive to reduce their carbon use, but to do so to the degree and in the way that is best for them. This is the main reason that pricing policies are the lowest-cost way to meet our climate-change goals.

    b) Pricing induces innovation. As the price of carbon increases, users of carbon-intensive goods will demand alternatives. This will induce innovations in the goods and services that are produced, how those goods and services are produced, and the way people live . . .

    c) Carbon is almost certainly under-priced right now. In a fully efficient price system, the price we pay for a product would reflect the full costs of producing and using it, including the costs to the environment. Prices do not currently reflect those environmental costs. When carbon is under-priced, consumers and businesses tend to use too much of it . . .

5. **Regulation tends to be the most expensive way to meet a given climate-change goal.** Under regulation,

businesses and consumers are mandated to take particular actions related to carbon use. . . . As a result, they are not given the choice of adjusting in the way that is best for them. Regulation therefore increases the costs of achieving carbon reduction compared to when pricing mechanisms such as a carbon tax or a cap-and-trade system are used. Furthermore, . . . those increased costs will be passed on to consumers due to normal market forces. There may be circumstances when regulation is the appropriate policy tool, but in most cases it is the most economically damaging.

6. **A carbon tax has the advantage of providing certainty in the price of carbon.** Under a carbon tax, a charge is added to the sale of all fuels according to the carbon emitted when they are used. With a well-designed carbon-tax strategy, the tax will be introduced gradually and increased in pre-announced increments until the environmental target is reached. This provides investors with a degree of certainty that is good for business, and allows consumers to make adjustments knowing what is coming. The exact impact of the price increase on the quantity of carbon emitted can be predicted, although with some margin of error. A carbon tax thus involves choosing price certainty but accepting some uncertainty in total carbon emissions.

7. **A cap-and-trade system provides certainty on the quantity of carbon emitted, but not on the price of carbon and can be a highly complex policy to implement.** In a cap-and-trade system, an upper limit (cap) is set on carbon emissions, usually for a particular industry. The government must then make a decision about whether to auction the permits (known as allowances), requiring each firm to buy enough allowances to cover its total emissions. Normal market forces then determine the price of these allowances such that supply equals demand. A cap-and-trade system with auctioned allowances then acts much like a carbon tax. The price cannot, however, be predicted in advance. . . . While a cap-and-trade system can in principle be equivalent to a carbon tax in terms of its ultimate impacts on the price and quantity of carbon, and will generally give more certainty in meeting environmental targets if the allowances are properly chosen, the price uncertainty in the cap-and-trade system generally implies a worse environment for long-range decision-making on the part of businesses and consumers.

8. **Policies that impose costs on producers (big or small) affect consumers.** Some voters seem to think that policies like cap and trade, which apply directly to producers, have less impact on the prices they face than carbon taxes, where the impact can be seen immediately. In fact, voters would do better to assume that all such policies would, ultimately, affect the prices they pay. Indeed, since the goal of these policies is to change what we buy, policies applied to producers must affect the prices faced by consumers if they are to meet environmental goals. The argument that a policy capable of reducing carbon emissions will only affect producers is without economic merit.

9. **Price mechanisms can be regressive and our policy should address this.** Like most taxes on goods and services that are widely consumed, carbon pricing will have a larger negative effect on lower-income Canadian families than others. . . . A complete policy should include some element of re-distribution to address the impacts it will have on the least well-off in our society. Not only will the costs to consumers ultimately be lower under a carbon tax or auctioned emission permits, these . . . policies also have the potential to bring revenue into the government that can be used to help offset any inordinate hardship experienced among the least well-off.

10. **A pricing mechanism can allow other taxes to be reduced and provide an opportunity to improve the tax system.** With the revenue brought in from a carbon tax or from auctioning the allowances in a cap-and-trade system, governments can provide general cuts in income and/or corporate taxes. Such systems can be "tax neutral," meaning the increased burden of the carbon taxes is exactly offset by tax reductions elsewhere. . . . Under such a plan, lighter carbon users will tend to pay lower taxes overall, while heavier polluters will pay more, corresponding to their greater negative effects on the environment. At the same time, all individuals will continue to have an incentive to reduce their carbon emissions when prices include the cost of their carbon usage. If the tax redesign is done thoughtfully, Canada could move toward an overall tax system which imposes fewer burdens on the economy and, as a result, leads to a more productive economy for all Canadians.

In closing, we ask you, the leaders of Canada's major political parties, to immediately begin a substantive public debate, grounded in the generally accepted economic principles outlined above, on the best ways to address climate change. Our collective future is truly in your hands.

As we saw earlier in this chapter, two policies would place a price on GHG emissions: an emissions tax and a cap-and-trade system. A tax on GHG emissions would directly increase the cost to polluters; a cap-and-trade system would force polluters to purchase costly permits in order to emit greenhouse gases.

Putting a price on GHG emissions would have three main advantages. First, by raising the price of carbon-based energy, users would be led to economize. Large cars would eventually be replaced by smaller vehicles, and carpooling and public transportation would become more attractive. The higher price of energy would also show up on electricity bills very quickly, thus providing people with a clear incentive to examine how best to reduce energy use within the home.

The second advantage of having a price on GHG emissions is that it would raise the relative price of carbon-based energy and thus make alternative, cleaner energy sources more competitive. For example, the current price of electricity in Ontario is roughly 7 cents per kilowatt hour, and much of Ontario's power is produced in coal-burning electricity plants. At this price, operators of wind turbines and solar panels cannot fully cover their costs, and thus very little of this alternative power is available. But suppose that a tax on emissions or a cap-and-trade system raises the price of electricity to 10 cents per kilowatt hour. At this higher price, wind and solar power may be able to cover their costs, even though there has been no change in their basic technology. By forcing the owners of carbon-based energy to sell their product at a price that includes the price on GHG emissions, thereby better reflecting the relevant external costs, the producers of cleaner, non-carbon energy would be able to enter the market and compete.

The third advantage is that by placing a price on the *emissions* of greenhouse gases rather than their *production*, an incentive would be created to actively capture and store the harmful GHGs. Owners of coal-burning electricity plants, for example, would be faced with significant costs if they released their GHGs into the atmosphere. They could avoid these costs if they captured the GHGs and stored them safely.

The second element of an effective climate-change policy is public support for the development of non-emitting technologies. We just argued that placing a price on GHG emissions would produce incentives for firms and consumers to switch from carbon-based energy systems to cleaner, non-emitting systems. But the *amount* of adoption of non-emitting technologies will depend crucially on the relevant elasticities of supply. Especially in the short run, however, these supplies are likely to be quite inelastic (unresponsive to price increases), and so even a substantial price on emissions may have only a modest effect on the adoption and development of non-emitting technologies.

A direct boost to the adoption of these cleaner technologies can be provided with carefully designed government policies to fund research. The government could even go so far as to sponsor a "technology race," not unlike the "space race" that the United States government entered in the late 1950s. In this case, the race would be to develop technologies that could increase the scale of alternative energy sources and overcome some of their existing technical challenges, and develop cost-effective methods of capturing and safely storing greenhouse gases.

Summary

It is essential that we recognize the likely impact of the ongoing process of climate change. It is just as important to realize that stabilizing Earth's climate, albeit at a temperature a few degrees above the current average, will require tremendous economic changes. Significant reductions in global greenhouse-gas emissions will not be achieved through a large number of small actions that are barely noticeable in our daily lives. Instead, bold but carefully designed government policies are needed to alter some of the prices that we face to better reflect the full social costs of our activities—both as consumers and as producers. Considerable resources will also have to be devoted to the development of new technologies. None of this will be simple, and real sacrifices will be involved. But these sacrifices today and in the near future may be far less than the long-term costs we will face if we do not take up the challenge now.

SUMMARY

17.1 The Economic Rationale for Regulating Pollution   LO 1

- Pollution is a negative externality. Polluting firms and households going about their daily business do harm to the environment and fail to take account of the costs that they impose on others.
- In a market that produces pollution as a byproduct, the external cost of the pollution implies that too much of the good is produced compared with what is allocatively efficient.

- The allocatively efficient level of pollution is generally not zero; it is the level at which the marginal cost of further pollution reduction is just equal to the marginal benefit of pollution reduction.
- If a firm or a household faces incentives that cause it to internalize fully the costs that pollution imposes, it will choose the allocatively efficient level of pollution.

17.2 Pollution-Control Policies   LO 2, 3

- Pollution can be regulated either directly or indirectly. Direct controls are used most often. They are often inefficient because they require that all polluters meet the same standard regardless of the benefits and costs of doing so.
- Efficient pollution abatement requires that the marginal cost of abatement is equated across firms. This can be achieved with market-based policies, such as emissions taxes or tradable pollution permits.
- Emission taxes work by requiring polluters to pay a tax per unit of pollution produced. The tax becomes the

marginal benefit of pollution abatement to the firms. Since all firms face the same tax per unit of pollution, their profit-maximizing behaviour will bring about efficiency in pollution abatement.
- Tradable pollution permits work by the government issuing permits to firms and then allowing those permits to be freely traded. The market price of the permit then represents firms' marginal benefit of pollution abatement. Efficiency in pollution abatement is achieved because firms' profit-maximizing behaviour leads their marginal abatement costs to be equated.

17.3 The Economic Challenge of Global Climate Change   LO 4

- There is a growing consensus that the burning of fossil fuels is adding to the atmospheric concentration of greenhouse gases (GHGs) and leading to increases in average global temperatures.
- Global emissions of GHGs can be reduced by reducing global GDP, by reducing the energy intensity of GDP, or by reducing the GHG intensity of the world's energy.

- Significant reductions in world GHG emissions will likely require dramatic reductions in the GHG intensity of energy.
- Most economists agree that an effective policy for reducing GHG emissions must involve placing a price on GHG emissions. Either an emissions tax or a cap-and-trade system could be effective.

KEY CONCEPTS

Negative pollution externalities
Marginal external cost
Costs and benefits of pollution
   abatement
The efficient level of pollution

Direct pollution controls
Emissions taxes
Tradable pollution permits
   (cap and trade)

Global climate change
Greenhouse-gas emissions
Kyoto Protocol

STUDY EXERCISES

MyEconLab   Make the grade with MyEconLab: Study Exercises marked in red can be found on MyEconLab. You can practise them as often as you want, and most feature step-by-step guided instructions to help you find the right answer.

1. Consider the following costs and benefits associated with cleaning up a polluted city lake.

Cleanliness of Water (%)	Marginal Cost ($)	Marginal Benefit ($)
0	50 000	550 000
20	100 000	400 000
40	160 000	300 000
60	230 000	230 000
80	350 000	180 000
100	infinite	150 000

a. Explain why the marginal cost of pollution reduction increases as the cleanliness of the water increases. Plot the MC curve in a diagram.
b. Explain why the marginal benefit of pollution reduction falls as the cleanliness of the water increases. Plot the MB curve in the same diagram.
c. What is the optimal level of water cleanliness?
d. Explain why the efficient level of pollution is greater than zero.

2. Fill in the blanks to make the following statements correct.

a. When there are pollution externalities associated with the production of steel, _____ marginal costs of steel production exceed _____ marginal costs of steel production.
b. By imposing a _____ on the production of steel, the externality can be _____.
c. If the tax is chosen to be exactly equal to the _____, the externality can be completely internalized. The result will be that private firms produce the _____ level of steel (and pollution).

3. Fill in the blanks to make the following statements correct.
a. Suppose the Canadian government announced that all homeowners must insulate their homes with R-40 insulation. As a pollution-control policy, this is an example of _____.

b. Suppose the Canadian government announced a tax of $2.50 per litre of home heating oil consumed. As a pollution-control policy, this is an example of _____.
c. Suppose the Canadian government distributed coupons to all homeowners allowing them to burn specified amounts of fossil fuels for home heating, and allowed homeowners to buy and sell these coupons. As a pollution-control policy, this is an example of _____. A _____ would develop for these coupons.

4. Consider the market for lumber, which we assume here to be perfectly competitive.

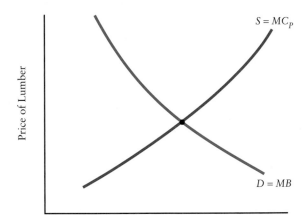

a. Suppose that for each unit of lumber produced, the firms also generate $10 of damage to the environment. Draw the social marginal cost curve in the diagram.
b. What is the allocatively efficient level of lumber output? Explain.
c. Describe and show the new market outcome if lumber producers are required to pay a tax of $10 per unit of lumber produced. Explain.
d. In part (c), does the equilibrium price of lumber rise by the full $10 of the tax? Explain.

5. The following diagram shows society's marginal benefit and marginal cost for abating a particular type of pollution—say greenhouse-gas emissions.

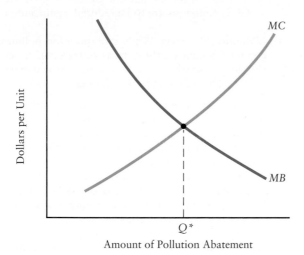

Amount of Pollution Abatement

a. Explain why the marginal cost curve is upward sloping.
b. Explain why the marginal benefit curve is downward sloping.
c. At Q^*, are all greenhouse-gas emissions eliminated? Explain.
d. Is there an "optimal" level of greenhouse-gas emissions? Explain.

6. Suppose there are only two firms—Softies Inc. and Cuddlies Inc.—producing disposable diapers. Both firms are releasing dioxins into the same river. To reduce the pollution, the regulatory agency must choose between using direct controls and emissions taxes. The following diagrams show each firm's marginal cost of pollution abatement.

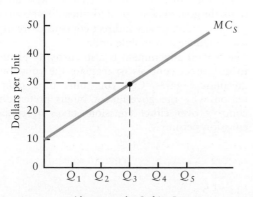

Abatement by Softies Inc.

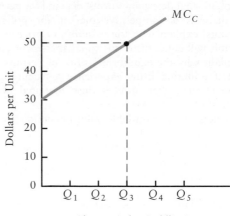

Abatement by Cuddlies Inc.

a. Suppose the regulatory agency requires that the two firms each abate Q_3 units of pollution. What is each firm's marginal abatement cost at Q_3?
b. Could the total cost of this amount of pollution abatement be reduced? Explain how.
c. Now suppose the regulatory agency instead imposes an emissions tax of \$40 per unit of emissions. Explain why this tax can be thought of as each firm's "marginal benefit of abatement."
d. In part (c), how much pollution will each firm choose to abate?
e. Is it possible to reduce the total cost of the amount of abatement being done in part (d)?

7. Suppose the government issues a fixed quantity, Q^*, of tradable pollution permits, each one permitting the emission of one tonne of sulphur dioxide. Use the accompanying figure to help answer the following questions.

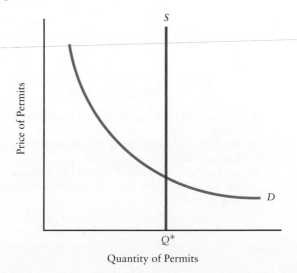

Quantity of Permits

a. Explain what determines firms' demand for permits.

b. If there is a competitive market for pollution permits, explain why the equilibrium price of the permit will equal firms' marginal abatement cost.

c. Explain why the equilibrium price of permits will fall if polluting firms experience a technological improvement that reduces their marginal abatement costs.

d. One advantage of tradable pollution permits is that they allow the public to express their preferences for pollution reduction through the market. What happens if Greenpeace decides to buy a large number of pollution permits and "retire" them?

8. Fill in the blanks to make the following statements correct.

a. The emission of greenhouse gases is a good example of a(n) _____ externality. Firms and individuals have not internalized the _____.

b. Geographically, the _____ externalities associated with greenhouse gas emissions are a(n) _____ problem, which was the motivation behind the _____ of 1997.

c. It is estimated that, in order to stabilize Earth's climate, the annual flow of global GHG emissions must fall by approximately _____ percent from its current level.

d. Canada's emissions of greenhouse gases increased by roughly _____ percent between 1990 and 2009.

e. Most economists believe that it is necessary to impose a(n) _____ on GHG emissions, which would force polluters to _____ the externality. Two market-based policy options to achieve this outcome are a(n) _____ and a(n) _____ system.

9. The following identity shows the three essential components of the world's annual emissions of greenhouse gases:

$$GHG = \frac{GHG}{Energy} \times \frac{Energy}{GDP} \times GDP$$

a. Explain the meaning of the first component, GHG/Energy.

b. Explain the meaning of the second component, Energy/GDP.

c. Explain why world GDP is likely to continue growing over time. How is this related to world population growth?

d. Explain why the second term is likely to fall over time but by less than the growth in world GDP.

e. Given your answers to parts (c) and (d), what is the implication for the path of GHG/Energy if overall GHG emissions are to be reduced significantly?

10. "Pollution is wrong. When a corporation pollutes, it commits assault on the citizens of the country, and it should be punished." Comment on this statement in light of the discussion in this chapter.

11. The European Union has a system for tradable permits for the emission of greenhouse gases. The authorities initially set the cap on emissions at a level that was expected to generate a permit price of about 20€ per tonne of emissions, and during the early 2000s the equilibrium price was close to 20€.

a. During the global recession of 2008–2009, many European firms reduced their output of goods and services. Why would this also reduce their demand for emission permits?

b. Could this explain why the market price for permits fell to as low as 7€ per tonne during this period? Explain.

c. Some commentators have argued that the observed price volatility within the European trading system shows that a cap-and-trade system does not work in practice, even though it has theoretical appeal. Does a properly functioning cap-and-trade system display constant permit prices? Why or why not?

d. Is there a particular problem associated with volatile permit prices in a cap-and-trade system? (Hint: Consider firms' incentives to make investments in either using or developing non-emitting technologies.)

12. The federal government has imposed many regulations aimed at reducing the pollution that is generated by driving. The more familiar regulations are direct—catalytic converters, fuel-efficiency standards, and the like.

a. Given the discussion in the chapter, why do you think the government opted for such direct controls?

b. Can you think of any indirect controls currently in use to reduce automobile pollution?

c. The federal government is also currently planning to use direct controls to regulate the emission of greenhouse gases. Can you think of a *political* reason why the government might prefer direct controls over either emissions taxes or tradable emission permits?

Taxation and Public Expenditure

CHAPTER OUTLINE

LEARNING OBJECTIVES (LO)

After studying this chapter you will be able to

1 describe the main taxes in use in Canada.

2 explain why a tax can lead to allocative inefficiency.
3 discuss the concept of fiscal federalism in Canada.

4 describe Canada's major social programs.

5 consider the costs and benefits of government intervention in the economy.

IN Chapter 16, we saw some of the reasons the scope of government is so extensive. Taxation is needed to raise money for public spending, and it can also play a policy role in its own right. Both taxes and government expenditure affect the distribution of income—some people are taxed more than others and some people benefit more from government programs than others. Moreover, taxation and public expenditure influence the allocation of resources. In some cases, government policy is carefully designed with such effects in mind; in other cases, the effects are unintended byproducts of policies pursued for other purposes.

In this chapter, we examine the various sources of government tax revenues and the various types of government expenditures. We examine the basis on which to evaluate a tax system, emphasizing the distinction between equity and efficiency. The types of public expenditures in Canada are examined along with the important concept of fiscal federalism. Finally, we briefly discuss Canada's main social programs, which account for approximately 65 percent of combined government spending.

18.1 Taxation in Canada

For detailed information about the Canadian tax system, go to the website of the independent Canadian Tax Foundation: www.ctf.ca.

There is a complex array of taxes in Canada. These are levied at the federal, provincial, and local levels. Some are highly visible, such as income taxes and the Goods and Services Tax (GST). Others are all but invisible because they do not show up on income-tax forms or on receipts for purchases. For example, there are special taxes levied on the sales of alcohol, cigarettes, and gasoline, but these taxes are levied directly on the producers (rather than on the consumers) of these goods. People and firms are taxed on what they earn, on what they spend, and on what they own. Not only are taxes numerous, but taken together they also raise a large amount of revenue. Table 18-1 shows, for the federal, provincial, and local governments combined, the amount of revenue raised by the different types of taxes in 2009.

At just over 40 percent of GDP, Canada lies roughly in the middle of other developed countries in terms of total government revenues as a share of GDP. Among the major industrialized countries, Denmark and Sweden collect over 55 percent of GDP in taxes and non-tax revenues. The lowest-tax industrialized countries are Japan and the United States, which each collect about 34 percent of GDP in government revenues.

Progressive Taxes

Before discussing details about the Canadian tax system, we examine the concept of *progressivity* of taxes.

When the government taxes one income group in society more heavily than it taxes another, it influences the distribution of income. The effect of taxes on the distribution of income can be summarized in terms of *progressivity*. A **progressive tax** takes a larger

progressive tax A tax that takes a larger percentage of income at higher levels of income.

TABLE 18-1 Tax Revenues of Canadian Governments, 2009

	Billions of Dollars	Percent of GDP
Income taxes	$248.7	15.9
Consumption taxes (GST, provincial sales taxes, and excise taxes)	107.2	6.9
Property and related taxes	54.9	3.5
Other taxes	21.8	1.4
Health and social insurance premiums	83.4	5.3
Total tax revenues	$516.0	33.0
Non-tax revenues (sales of goods and services, investment income)	117.8	7.5
Total government revenues	$633.8	40.5

Canadian governments (at all levels) collect over $630 billion in various taxes, over 40 percent of GDP. These data show total tax revenues for all levels of government combined. Notice that Canadian governments have considerable revenue, almost $120 billion in 2009, from non-tax sources.

(*Source:* Adapted from Statistics Canada, "Consolidated Government Revenue and Expenditures," www.statcan.gc.ca.)

percentage of income from high-income people than it does from low-income people. A **proportional tax** takes amounts of money from people in direct proportion to their incomes—for example, every individual might pay 10 percent of his or her income in taxes. A **regressive tax** takes a larger percentage of income from low-income people than it does from high-income people.

Note that the progressivity or regressivity of a tax is expressed in terms of *shares* of income rather than absolute dollar amounts. Thus, a tax that collects $1000 from each individual clearly collects the same dollar amount from everybody, though it collects a higher share of income from low-income people than from higher-income people. A tax of this type is therefore a regressive tax. It is often called a *lump-sum tax*, one that is the same at all levels of income.

The progressivity of a tax involves an important distinction between the average tax rate and the marginal tax rate. The **average tax rate** is the percentage of income that the individual pays in taxes. The **marginal tax rate** is the percentage *of the next dollar* earned that the individual pays in taxes. Progressivity of a tax requires an *average* tax rate that rises with income; we will see in this chapter that such progressivity can be achieved with either rising or constant marginal tax rates.

Progressive taxes play an important role in an overall tax and expenditure system designed to redistribute some income toward lower-income individuals. Since a progressive tax collects more from high-income individuals than it does from those with low incomes, a progressive tax system can achieve more redistribution than can proportional or regressive ones. Let's now go on to examine the various elements of the Canadian tax system.

The Canadian Tax System

Taxes are collected by the federal government, by each of the provinces, and by thousands of cities, townships, and villages. Here is a brief guide to the most important taxes.

Personal Income Taxes Personal income taxes are paid directly to the government by individuals. The amount of tax any individual pays is the result of a fairly complicated set of calculations. All types of income are included in what is called total income, although certain types of income qualify for total or partial exemption. Then a number of allowable deductions are subtracted from total income to determine taxable income. The most important deduction is called the "basic personal amount" and in 2012 was equal to $10 527. Once taxable income is calculated, the amount of tax payable is then computed by applying different tax rates to different levels of income. There are four federal personal income tax rates, each applying within what is called a tax bracket. In 2012, the four **tax brackets** and marginal tax rates within each bracket were as follows:

- $0–$42 707: marginal tax rate = 15 percent
- $42 708–$85 414: marginal tax rate = 22 percent
- $85 415–$132 406: marginal tax rate = 26 percent
- $132 407 and over: marginal tax rate = 29 percent

To see how to compute the amount of taxes payable with this system of tax brackets, consider Christine, who has a taxable income of $95 000. To the federal government she pays at a rate of 15 percent on the first $42 707 of taxable income ($6406), at a rate of 22 percent on her next $42 707 ($9396), and at a rate of 26 percent on her last 9586 (=$95 000−$85 414) of income ($2492). Since her taxable income is less than $132 407, she never enters the highest tax bracket and therefore does not face the

---

proportional tax A tax that takes a constant percentage of income at all levels of income.

regressive tax A tax that takes a lower percentage of income at higher levels of income.

average tax rate The ratio of total taxes paid to total income earned.

marginal tax rate The fraction of an additional dollar of income that is paid in taxes.

tax bracket A range of taxable income for which there is a constant marginal tax rate.

The Canada Revenue Agency, with headquarters in the Connaught Building in Ottawa, is the government department that collects all federal tax revenues in Canada.

29 percent tax rate. Christine's total tax payable is therefore $18 294. Recalling the definition of average and marginal tax rates, Christine's *average* tax rate is 18 294/95 000, or 19.3 percent. Her *marginal tax rate*—the rate on an additional dollar of income—is 26 percent.

The four federal personal income-tax rates do not represent the complete taxation of personal income in Canada because the provincial and territorial governments also tax personal income. Quebec operates its own income-tax system, whereas the other nine provinces simply use the federal tax base (and federally distributed tax forms) to calculate provincial income taxes according to their own legislated income-tax rates. In all provinces other than Quebec, taxpayers pay a single amount to the Canada Revenue Agency (CRA), which then distributes the total between the federal government and each province according to the amount collected from residents of that province.

The provincial taxation of income implies that Canada's highest marginal income-tax rate is not the highest *federal* rate, 29 percent. As of 2012, the highest combined (provincial plus federal) marginal tax rates varied from a low of 39 percent in Alberta to 50 percent in Nova Scotia.

EXTENSIONS IN THEORY 18-1

Who Really Pays the Corporate Income Tax?

As we saw in Chapter 7, there are two different measures of a firm's profit—*accounting* profit and *economic* profit. Accounting profit is the difference between the firm's revenues and its explicit costs, such as labour, materials, overhead, and depreciation. The same firm's economic profit would also take into account the opportunity costs of the owner's time and financial capital. Since there are additional costs included, economic profits are less than accounting profits. As it turns out, the burden of the corporate income tax depends crucially on which measure of profit is used as the basis for the tax.

Let's examine two alternative taxes: one that applies to economic profits and another that applies to accounting profits. To illustrate the two taxes, we consider an imaginary firm that produces hockey equipment—Canada Hockey Inc. (CHI), located in Brampton, Ontario. Suppose in 2013 CHI earns accounting profits of $1.5 million. Also suppose the opportunity cost of the owner's capital and time is $1.1 million. Once these opportunity costs are considered, CHI's economic profits are equal to $400 000.

A Tax on Economic Profits

Recall that *economic* profits are the return to the owner's capital over and above what could be earned elsewhere. Specifically, CHI's $400 000 of economic profits represents the firm's return to its capital in excess of what that capital

could earn in the (equally risky) next-best alternative investment. If CHI faces a 30 percent corporate tax that applies to its economic profits of $400 000, it will pay $120 000 in corporate taxes, and it will still have after-tax economic profits equal to $280 000. Since CHI is still earning positive economic profits—that is, it is still earning more than it could earn elsewhere—it has no incentive to leave this industry.

In fact, the firm has no incentive to do anything differently than it was doing previously—the tax on the firm's economic profit has *no effect* on the firm's output, prices, employment, or long-run investment choices. Before the tax, CHI was making output, employment, price, and investment decisions to maximize its (economic) profits. With the tax, some fraction of these economic profits must be paid to the government, but CHI still chooses to maximize its profits by doing whatever it was doing before the tax.

The implication is that if the corporate income tax applies to *economic* profits, firms and their owners bear the entire burden of the tax. But the tax will have no effect on the allocation of resources, and in this sense the tax would be efficient.

A Tax on Accounting Profits

Now consider the alternative case in which the corporate income tax applies not to economic profit but to *accounting* profit. CHI's *accounting* profits are $1.5 million, which are greater than (and include) its economic profits. If CHI

Corporate Income Taxes The federal corporate income tax is a flat-rate (proportional) tax on profits as defined by the taxing authorities. By 2012, following several years of reductions, the federal corporate income-tax rate for large businesses was 15 percent; provincial rates vary somewhat but the average is about 12 percent. Small businesses—those with business income below $500 000 per year—are taxed at lower rates by both the federal and (most) provincial governments.

Some corporate profits get distributed as dividends to shareholders. These dividends represent the shareholder's share of after-tax profits and would ordinarily be taxed along with his or her other income. To avoid double taxation on this income, however, individual shareholders get a personal income-tax credit for their share of the corporate tax already paid by the firm. In this way, the corporate and personal income-tax systems are said to be *integrated*.

When governments in Canada consider changes to income-tax rates, a debate usually occurs regarding which taxes should be changed: personal income taxes or corporate income taxes. Some people argue that corporate income-tax rates are already too low and that firms are not paying their "fair share" of the tax burden. Others argue that corporate taxes end up being paid partly by firms' customers and employees, and partly by the individuals who own shares in firms, which now include most individuals through some form of employer-sponsored or self-administered pension plan. In addition, they argue that corporate taxes, by reducing the rate of return on investment, impede the economy's long-run growth. *Extensions in Theory 18-1* discusses taxes on

For information about the Canadian tax system, see the website for the Canada Revenue Agency: www.cra-arc.gc.ca.

faces a 30 percent corporate tax on accounting profits of $1.5 million, it will pay $450 000 in corporate taxes. CHI's after-tax accounting profits will now be $1.05 million. But the presence of the corporate tax does not change the opportunity cost of the owner's capital and time; when including these costs ($1.1 million), CHI's economic profits are −$50 000. Negative economic profits indicate that the owner's capital is now earning less than what is available in the (equally risky) next-best alternative investment. In this situation, CHI may soon leave this industry.

Negative economic profits and the exit from the industry will obviously have implications for its output and employment decisions. In particular, as CHI scales down its operations, its workers will be laid off or have their wages reduced. And as supply in this industry falls, product prices will rise until the remaining firms earn enough profits to keep them in the industry.

The bottom line is that if the corporate income tax applies to accounting profits (and results in negative economic profits), some of the burden of the tax falls on consumers and workers. Only part of the burden of the tax falls on firms and their owners. Because the tax leads to changes in the allocation of resources, it also generates some inefficiency. We will see this idea in more detail later in this chapter when we discuss what economists call the "excess burden" of taxation.

A large body of economic research suggests that the biggest burden of the corporate income tax in this case is on the economy's long-run growth. By taxing accounting profits

rather than economic profits, investment in physical capital is made less attractive. The result will be lower investment in new machinery and equipment, and thus less adoption of many of the latest technologies that are usually embodied in such physical capital. The overall result for the economy is lower productivity growth and, eventually, slower growth in average living standards.

Which Tax Do We Use?

In Canada and other countries, corporations are taxed on the basis of their *accounting* profits, not their economic profits, despite the greater efficiency of the latter. Why do we use such a tax, given its inefficiency? The explanation comes down to simplicity: Accounting profits are easy to measure, whereas economic profits require an identification and measurement of the opportunity cost of the owner's time and capital. The precise identification of such opportunity costs, for each and every firm and group of owners, would be technically impossible for the tax authorities.

The end result is that the burden of the corporate tax in Canada is not borne only by firms and their owners—consumers and workers share the burden through higher product prices and lower wages. These effects are subtle but nonetheless important. Equally subtle, and probably more important, are the longer-term effects on the growth rate of the economy and Canadians' average standard of living.

corporate income and highlights the important difference between taxing *accounting* profits and *economic* profits—a distinction we first saw in Chapter 7.

Excise and Sales Taxes As we first saw in Chapter 4, an *excise tax* is a tax levied on a particular commodity. In many countries, such goods as tobacco, alcohol, and gasoline are singled out for high rates of excise taxation. Because these goods usually account for a much greater proportion of the expenditure of lower-income than higher-income groups, the excise taxes on them are regressive. A *sales tax* applies to the sale of all or most goods and services. All provinces except Alberta impose a retail sales tax. Such a tax is mildly regressive, because poorer families tend to spend a larger proportion of their incomes (and thus save a lower portion) than richer families. Both excise and sales taxes are often referred to as "indirect" taxes to contrast them with income taxes, which are levied directly on the income of individuals or firms.

In 1991, the federal government introduced the Goods and Services Tax (GST) which applies in all provinces to the sale of almost all goods and services.[1] With the notable exception of the United States, most developed economies levy a tax similar to our GST, referred to in Europe as a *value-added tax* and in some countries as a *consumption tax*. The main advantage of the GST (and other value added taxes) is that it taxes expenditure rather than income, and for this reason it generates no disincentive to save. In contrast, since income taxes apply to all sources of income, including interest income, they tend to discourage saving.

Consider an example to illustrate how taxes influence the incentive to save. Suppose you have after-tax earnings of $1000, all of which you would like to save. You put your $1000 in a bank account that pays 5 percent interest, and at the end of the year you receive $50 in interest income. But you must pay tax on this interest income. If the income-tax rate is 30 percent, you pay $0.3 \times 50 = 15$. You are left with only $35 in after-tax interest earnings on your original saving of $1000, which implies an after-tax rate of return of 3.5 percent. The income tax payable on your interest earnings has lowered your return from saving and thus reduced your incentive to save. As we saw in Chapter 15, any reduction in saving will imply less capital accumulation for the economy. In contrast, the GST only applies to the value of expenditure. Since the GST does not tax income (and therefore does not tax interest income) it does not discourage saving.

In practice, the GST works by taxing a firm on the gross value of its output and then allowing a tax credit equal to the taxes paid on the inputs that were produced by other firms. Thus, the GST taxes each firm's contribution to the value of final output—its value added. Figure 18-1 shows how the GST is calculated at each stage from the mining of iron ore to the final retail sale of a washing machine.

Like sales and excise taxes, the GST is applied to expenditure rather than income. The GST taken alone would therefore be mildly regressive, because the proportion of income saved, and hence not taxed, rises with income. This regressivity is reduced by exempting food and, more importantly, by giving low- and middle-income households a refundable tax credit. For the lowest-income households, the GST is a progressive tax because the refundable tax credit exceeds the value of GST that they would pay even if they spent all of their incomes on taxable commodities.

---

[1] In 2012 the GST rate was 5 percent. It has now been harmonized with the provincial sales taxes in several provinces. In these cases, the combined tax is referred to as a Harmonized Sales Tax (HST).

Property Taxes The property tax is the most important Canadian tax that is based on wealth and is an important source of revenue for municipalities. It is different from any other important tax because it is not related directly to a current transaction. In contrast, income taxes are levied on the current income received by owners of factors of production (land, labour, and capital), and sales taxes are levied on the value of a currently purchased good or service.

Taxing the value of existing property creates two problems. First, someone has to assess the current market value of the property that may not have changed hands in many years. Because the assessment is only an estimate, it is always subject to challenge. Second, sometimes owners of valuable real estate property have low *incomes* and thus have difficulty paying the tax from their available funds.

The progressivity of the property tax has been studied extensively. The rich typically live in more expensive houses than the poor and thus typically pay more in property taxes. This does not mean, however, that the rich pay more property taxes *as a fraction of their total income* than the poor. Thus, it is not readily apparent that property taxes are progressive. Indeed, most studies have shown that the property tax is mildly regressive.

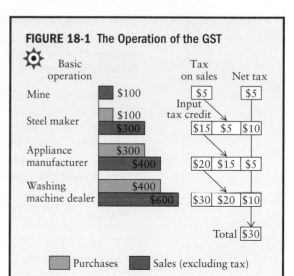

FIGURE 18-1 The Operation of the GST

| Purchases | Sales (excluding tax) |

A tax on value added is the same as a tax on the value of final goods with a credit allowed for the tax paid for purchased inputs. The example is for the stages involved as iron ore is mined and then sold to a steel maker, the steel then sold to an appliance manufacturer, and the washing machine sold to a retailer and then to a consumer. The example makes the simplifying assumption that no produced inputs are used in the mining operation (so that the value of the iron ore is all value added); at all further stages, however, the use of produced inputs makes the firm's value added less than the value of final output at that stage. The steel maker's value added is $200, and its tax is thus $10; $15 on the total value of its output less the $5 credit on the taxes already paid to the mine on the value of the iron ore. Total taxes paid equal $30, which is 5 percent of the $600 value of the final product; each firm pays 5 percent of its share in creating that $600 value.

18.2 Evaluating the Tax System

We have described several individual taxes in Canada, and in each case noted the tax's possible effects on behaviour as well as its progressivity. The overall tax *system*, however, is a complex combination of these various taxes. More important than evaluating each individual tax is evaluating the system as a whole. Economists focus on two key aspects of a tax system—efficiency and equity. Efficiency matters because governments strive to raise tax revenues in a manner that imposes the least overall cost on society. Equity matters because, as we saw in Chapter 16, governments often strive to redistribute income toward low-income people. A natural challenge when designing an overall tax system is to raise the revenue required to finance necessary public expenditures while at the same time improving equity and achieving as efficient a system as possible. We begin by exploring how taxation can affect equity.

Taxation and Equity

Debates about income distribution and tax policy usually involve the important but hard-to-define concept of *equity*.

What Do We Mean By Equity? *Equity* (or *fairness*) is a normative concept; what one group thinks is fair may seem outrageous to another. Two principles can be helpful in assessing equity in taxation: equity according to *ability to pay*, and equity according to *benefits received*.

The Ability-To-Pay Principle. Most people view an equitable tax system as being based on people's ability to pay taxes. In considering equity that is based on ability to pay, two concepts need to be distinguished.

Vertical equity concerns equity *across* income groups; it focuses on comparisons between individuals or families with different levels of income. The concept of vertical equity is central to discussions of the progressivity of taxation. Proponents of progressive taxation argue as follows. First, taxes should be based on ability to pay. Second, the greater one's income, the greater the percentage of income that is available for goods and services beyond the bare necessities. It follows, therefore, that the greater one's income, the greater the proportion of income that is available to pay taxes. Thus, an ability-to-pay standard of vertical equity requires progressive taxation.

Horizontal equity concerns equity *within* a given income group; it is concerned with establishing just who should be considered equal to whom in terms of ability to pay taxes. Two households with the same income may have different numbers of children to support. One of the households may have greater expenses for the care of an aging parent, leaving less for life's necessities and for taxes. One of the households may incur expenses that are necessary for earning income (e.g., requirements to buy uniforms or to pay union dues). There is no objective way to decide how much these and similar factors affect the ability to pay taxes. In practice, the income-tax law makes some allowance for factors that create differences in ability to pay by permitting taxpayers to exempt some of their income from tax. However, the corrections are rough at best.

The Benefit Principle. According to the benefit principle, taxes should be paid in proportion to the benefits that taxpayers derive from public expenditure. From this perspective, the ideal taxes are *user charges*, such as those that would be charged if private firms provided the government services.

The benefit principle is the basis for the excise tax on gasoline, since gasoline usage is closely related to the services obtained from using public roads. The benefit principle may also explain high taxes on cigarettes, since smokers tend to require more health-care services that, in Canada, are mostly provided by government. Although there are other examples, especially at the local level, the benefit principle has historically played only a minor role in the design of the Canadian tax system. But its use is growing in Canada and elsewhere as governments seek new ways to finance many of their expenditures. For example, two decades ago Statistics Canada supplied data for free to anybody who wanted it. Now, Statistics Canada charges on a "cost recovery basis" for any data other than the most general data, which it makes available on its website. So instead of covering the cost of producing the data from the general taxpayer, some costs are recovered from those who use it. The benefit principle can be easily applied to some government-provided goods and services. But it is difficult to see how the benefit principle could be applied to many of the most important categories of government spending. Who gets how much benefit from national defence, interest on the public debt, the judicial system, or environmental protection?

How Progressive Is the Canadian Tax System? For a modern government to raise sufficient funds, many taxes must be used. We have already discussed personal and corporate income taxes, excise and provincial sales taxes, the Canada-wide GST, and municipal property taxes. Not all of them are equally progressive in design and each one has its own loopholes and anomalies. So, how high-, middle-, and low-income households are taxed relative to each other depends on how the entire tax system impacts on each group.

Assessing how the entire tax system affects the distribution of income is complicated by two factors. First, the progressivity of the system depends on the mix of the different taxes. Federal taxes tend to be somewhat progressive; the progressivity of the income-tax system and the use of a low-income GST tax credit more than offset the regressivity of the federal GST. Provincial and municipal governments rely heavily on property and sales taxes and thus have tax systems that are probably slightly regressive.

Second, income from different sources is taxed at different rates. For example, in the federal personal income tax, income from royalties on oil wells is taxed less than income from royalties on books, and profits from sales of assets (capital gains) are taxed less than wages and salaries. To evaluate progressivity, therefore, one needs to know how different *levels* of income are related to different *sources* of income.

Many economists have concluded that the overall Canadian tax system is roughly proportional for middle-income classes and mildly progressive for low- and high-income persons.

Taxation and Efficiency

The tax system influences the allocation of resources by altering such things as the relative prices of various goods and factors and the relative profitability of various industries. Individual taxes shift consumption and production toward goods and services that are taxed relatively lightly and away from those that are taxed more heavily. This alteration of free-market outcomes often affects allocative efficiency.

Of course, if we were to live in a world without any taxes we would face other problems. For example, it would be impossible to pay for any government programs or public goods desired by society. In practice, then, the relevant objective for tax policy is to design a tax system that minimizes inefficiency, *holding constant the amount of revenue to be raised*. In designing such a tax system, a natural place to start would be with taxes that both raise revenue and enhance efficiency. An example of such a tax is the pollution emissions tax that we discussed in Chapter 17. Unfortunately, such taxes cannot raise nearly enough revenue to finance all of government expenditure.

In the following discussion we examine how taxes affect the economy's allocation of resources. We focus on the effects of excise taxes and income taxes since these are the main taxes used by Canadian governments to raise revenues.

The Two Burdens of Taxation A tax normally does two things. It takes money from the taxpayers, and it changes their behaviour. The money taken away from taxpayers is given to the government and is thus available to finance government policies of various

direct burden For an individual tax, the amount of money that is collected from taxpayers.

kinds. So, while the money taken from taxpayers, called the **direct burden** of the tax, is clearly a cost to taxpayers, it is *not* a cost to society overall; it is merely a transfer of resources within the economy.

When a tax changes behaviour, however, there are costs to taxpayers as well as to society overall. The cost that results from the induced changes in behaviour is called the **excess burden** and reflects the allocative inefficiency or *deadweight loss* of the tax.

excess burden The allocative inefficiency or deadweight loss generated by a tax.

The direct burden of a tax is the amount paid by taxpayers. The excess burden reflects the allocative inefficiency of the tax.

Figure 18-2 shows an example that illustrates this important distinction. Suppose your provincial government imposes a $2 excise tax on the purchase of compact discs. Suppose further that you are a serious music lover and that this tax does not change your quantity demanded of CDs—that is, your demand for them is perfectly inelastic and hence you continue to buy your usual five CDs per month. In this case, you pay $10 in excise taxes per month, and you therefore have to reduce your consumption of other goods (or your saving) by $10 per month.

The direct burden to you of this excise tax is $10 because that is what you pay to the government in taxes. There is no excess burden to you because the tax does not cause you to reduce your purchases of CDs. Thus, the total burden on you is equal to the direct burden, $10 a month; there is no excess burden of this tax. The absence of any excess burden from this tax is just another way of saying that there is no allocative

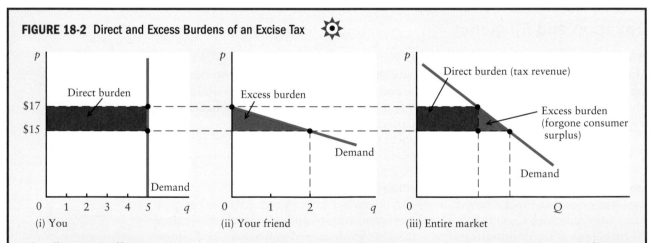

FIGURE 18-2 Direct and Excess Burdens of an Excise Tax ☀

The allocative inefficiency of a tax is measured by its excess burden. The excess burden is greater the more elastic is demand. Part (i) shows your demand for CDs. It is perfectly inelastic at five CDs per month. When the government imposes an excise tax of $2 per CD, the price rises from $15 to $17. Your quantity demanded is unchanged, so you pay $10 per month in taxes ($2 tax per CD × 5 CDs). The direct burden of the tax is $10; but because your quantity of CDs demanded is unchanged, there is no excess burden.

Part (ii) shows your friend's demand. Her quantity demanded falls from two CDs per month to zero as a result of the tax. Since she pays no tax (because she buys no CDs), she bears no direct burden of the tax. But because she has lost consumer surplus, she bears an excess burden from the tax.

Part (iii) shows the entire market demand. There is both a direct burden, the red shaded area, and an excess burden, the purple shaded area. The more elastic is the demand curve, the larger is the excess burden of the tax.

inefficiency; the cost of raising $10 a month for the province is just the $10 a month that you pay in taxes. In this case, the tax is *purely* a redistribution of resources from you to the government.

Now suppose a friend of yours is also a music lover but is not quite as dedicated—she has a downward-sloping demand curve for CDs. The tax leads her to cut back on her consumption of CDs from two per month to none. In this case, your friend pays no taxes and therefore experiences no reduction in her overall purchasing power. The direct burden of the tax is therefore zero. However, your friend is still worse off as a result of this tax. She is worse off by the amount of consumer surplus that she would have received had she made her usual purchases of two CDs per month. In this case, the direct burden is zero (because no tax is paid) but there *is* an excess burden. The excess burden is equal to her loss in consumer surplus from the two CDs per month that she no longer enjoys.

When an excise tax is imposed, some people behave like the music buff and do not change their consumption of the taxed good at all, others cease consuming the taxed good altogether, and most simply reduce their consumption. There will be an excess burden for those in the latter two groups. Thus, the revenue collected will *understate* the total cost to taxpayers of generating that revenue.

The same basic analysis applies to income taxes. Figure 18-3 shows the effect of levying a tax on workers' incomes. The income tax shifts the labour supply upward because workers will be prepared to supply any given amount of labour services only if the pre-tax wage is increased to offset the effect of the tax.

The income tax generates both a direct burden and an excess burden. The tax raises revenue by collecting some percentage of workers' wages. This is a cost borne by both workers and firms. By reducing the equilibrium level of employment and creating a deadweight loss, the income tax also creates an excess burden. As with the case of excise taxes, the revenue collected by the tax understates the total cost of the tax.

> **Excise taxes and income taxes impose costs in two ways. By taking resources from market participants (consumers, firms, workers), they impose a direct burden. By reducing the volume of specific market transactions, they also generate a deadweight loss—this is the excess burden of the tax.**

Recall that our exercise in judging the efficiency of a tax is to hold constant the amount of revenue raised, and therefore to hold constant the direct burden of the tax. This leads us to the following important conclusion:

> **An efficient tax system is one that minimizes the amount of excess burden (deadweight loss) for any given amount of tax revenue generated.**

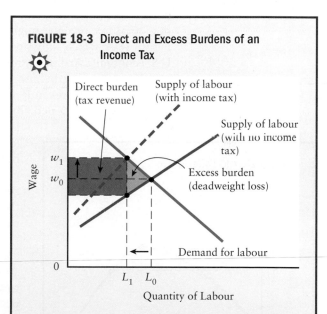

FIGURE 18-3 Direct and Excess Burdens of an Income Tax

An income tax generates both a direct and an excess burden. Without an income tax, the labour-market equilibrium has employment of L_0 and a wage of w_0. An income tax shifts the supply of labour curve upward. The result is an increase in the pre-tax wage to w_1 and a reduction in the level of employment to L_1. The tax revenue generated is the red area; this is the direct burden of the income tax. The tax also generates a deadweight loss, as shown by the purple area; this is the excess burden of the income tax. (As our discussion of tax incidence in Chapter 4 showed, the less elastic is labour demand and supply, the lower will be the deadweight loss of the tax.)

As Figure 18-2 shows, the excess burden of an excise tax is smaller when the demand for the product is less elastic. In the extreme case of a perfectly inelastic demand, the excess burden of an excise tax is zero; the tax raises revenue but leads to no reduction in consumption of the specific product. Unfortunately, because the demand for many of life's necessities (such as food) is very inelastic, a tax system that was based only on imposing excise taxes on goods with inelastic demands would prove to be very regressive.

Many economists argue that taxing income is more efficient *and* more equitable than imposing large numbers of excise taxes on products. The greater efficiency of the income tax comes from the fact that the supply of labour is relatively inelastic with respect to the real wage. Figure 18-3 shows that an income tax does generate an excess burden. But if the labour supply curve is very steep—as most empirical evidence suggests—the excess burden is small, and the income tax is therefore relatively efficient. The greater equity of the income tax comes from the fact that it can be designed to be either proportional or progressive, thus permitting some redistribution from high-income households to low-income households.

Disincentive Effects of Income Taxes Our discussion of income taxes, and the illustration in Figure 18-3, shows how an income tax affects workers' incentives. If an increase in the income-tax rate leads to a reduction in the amount of work effort, it is possible that total tax revenue might actually *fall* as a result. This possibility is illustrated in Figure 18-4, which shows what economists call a *Laffer curve*, named after well-known U.S. economist Arthur Laffer.

The reasoning behind the general shape of the Laffer curve is as follows. At a zero tax rate, no revenue would be collected. As rates are raised above zero, some revenue will be gained. But as rates continue to rise, revenue will eventually fall because the very high tax rates will lead people to work less and less. At a tax rate of 100 percent, they will not bother to work at all (because all of their income would go to the government) and so tax revenue will again be zero. It follows that there must be *some* tax rate, greater than zero and less than 100 percent, at which tax revenue reaches a maximum.

Figure 18-4 is drawn under the assumption that there is a steady increase in tax revenue as tax rates rise to t_0, and a steady decrease in tax revenues as tax rates continue to rise toward 100 percent. This particular shape—with a single peak in tax revenues—is not necessary. But the precise shape is beside the point. The key point is that there is *some* tax rate like t_0 that maximizes total tax revenue. And therefore tax rates above or below t_0 will generate less tax revenue than the amount raised at t_0.

In Canada and the United States, it is not uncommon to hear heated debates regarding the appropriate level of income-tax rates. In such debates, one side will often cite the logic of the Laffer curve, arguing that a reduction in tax rates will lead to such an increase in economic activity that total tax revenues will rise. This outcome is possible, but by no means guaranteed. Revenue will only increase if

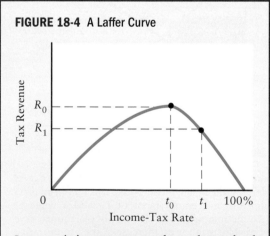

FIGURE 18-4 A Laffer Curve

Increases in income-tax rates beyond some level will decrease rather than increase tax revenues. The curve relates the government's tax revenue to the tax rate. As drawn, revenue reaches a maximum level of R_0 at the tax rate t_0. If the tax rate were t_1, then reducing it to t_0 would increase the government's tax revenue.

current tax rates are so high as to be above t_0 in Figure 18-4. The problem is that we do not know for sure where t_0 is, although some recent research in the United States suggests that t_0 may be as high as 80 percent, far above current tax rates.

18.3 Public Expenditure in Canada

In 2009 spending by the consolidated public sector—which includes federal, provincial, and municipal governments—was about 40 percent of Canadian GDP. Table 18-2 gives the distribution of consolidated government spending across a number of major *functions* for 2009. As can be seen, health care, education, and social services are very large items; collectively, they make up roughly 65 percent of the total spending of $631 billion. Interest on the public debt makes up about 7 percent of total spending. The remaining 28 percent covers everything else, from police protection and sanitation to general administration of government, environmental protection, and foreign aid.

Table 18-2 does not show which of the three levels of government actually do the spending. For example, of the $95.7 billion spent on education in 2009, the vast majority was spent by provincial and municipal governments. In contrast, expenditures on national defence and foreign aid are made exclusively by the federal government. Expenditures on social services are about equally divided between the federal and provincial governments, with only a small role played by the municipalities. Another thing that Table 18-2 does not show is the important distinction between the purchase of goods and services by government, and *transfers* that are made to individuals or firms.

Government Purchases and Transfers

The government spends to provide goods and services to the public, as when the government pays for physicians' services, highway repair, primary and secondary education, and so on. Included in this category of expenditures are the salaries that the government pays to its employees. Also included is the interest that governments pay on their outstanding stock of debt. A government's stock of debt is equal to the accumulation of its past budget deficits, where the deficit is the excess of spending over revenues.

TABLE 18-2 Expenditures by Canadian Governments, 2009

Category of Spending	Billions of Dollars	Percent of GDP
General government services	22.8	1.5
Protection of persons and property	50.8	3.2
Transportation and communication	32.2	2.1
Health	121.6	7.8
Social services	190.3	12.2
Education	95.7	6.1
Resource conservation, environment, and industrial development	36.9	2.4
Recreation and culture	16.3	1.0
Housing	6.1	0.4
Labour, employment, and immigration	2.4	0.2
Foreign affairs and international aid	6.5	0.4
Debt charges	43.6	2.8
Other expenditures	6.0	0.4
Total spending	631.3	40.3

Expenditures on health, social services, and education together make up almost 65 percent of total government expenditure. These data show the various categories of spending by all levels of government combined.

(*Source:* Adapted from Statistics Canada, "Consolidated Government Revenue and Expenditures," www.statcan.gc.ca.)

transfer payment A payment to an individual, a firm, or an organization that is not made in exchange for a good or service.

The government also makes **transfer payments**. These are payments to individuals, firms, organizations, or other levels of government that are *not* made in exchange for a good or a service. For example, when the federal government pays employment insurance benefits to an unemployed individual, the government is not getting any good or service in return. Similarly, when the federal government transfers money to the provincial governments, it is not getting any good or service in return. Table 18-3 shows total government transfers to individuals, which totalled $177 billion in 2009, about 30 percent of total government spending.

Canadian "Fiscal Federalism"

Canada is a federal state with governing powers divided between the central authority and the ten provinces and three territories. Municipalities provide a third level of government, whose powers are determined by the provincial legislatures. Understanding the fiscal interaction of the various levels of government is central to understanding the nature of government expenditure in Canada. In this section, we examine the concept of *fiscal federalism*; in the next section we examine how fiscal federalism affects the operation of Canada's social programs.

The Logic of Fiscal Federalism The essence of Canadian fiscal federalism is the recognition that Canada is a country with many different fiscal authorities (federal, provincial, and municipal governments) that need a certain amount of coordination to be responsive to the needs and desires of the citizens—who are free to move from one area to another. Four main considerations are important in understanding Canada's system of fiscal federalism.

1. Differences in Tax Bases. Canadian provinces vary considerably in terms of their average levels of prosperity. Alberta and Saskatchewan are currently well above the national average (as measured by per capita GDP) whereas Prince Edward Island and Nova Scotia are below the average. Ontario is just slightly below the national average of about $48 000 per person.

In order to provide services as varied as medical care, highways, and judicial systems, the provincial governments must levy various types of provincial taxes. Provinces that are more prosperous, and thus have larger tax bases, are able to provide a given amount of services while having relatively low tax rates. In contrast, less affluent provinces with smaller tax bases would only be able to provide the same amount of services if they had higher tax rates, but excessive tax rates create their own problems, as we saw earlier.

One of the guiding principles in Canada's system of fiscal federalism is that individuals, no matter where they live, should have approximately the same access to what is regarded as a reasonable level and quality of public services and should face approximately the same tax rates to finance those services. Since revenue sources do not always match revenue

TABLE 18-3 Government Transfer Payments to Individuals, 2009

	Billions of Dollars
Federal Government	**88.1**
Child Tax Benefit	9.7
War pensions and veterans' allowances	2.3
Employment Insurance benefits	18.8
Old Age Security payments	35.0
Grants to Aboriginal persons	6.5
GST tax credit	3.9
Other transfers	11.9
Provincial Governments	**45.0**
Income maintenance	8.2
Other social assistance	5.0
Workers' Compensation benefits	6.0
Grants to benevolent associations	12.9
Other transfers	12.9
Local Governments	**4.3**
Canada/Quebec Pension Plan	**39.2**
Total Transfers	**176.6**

(*Source:* Adapted from Statistics Canada, "Government Transfer Payments to Persons," www.statcan.gc.ca.)

needs at each level of government, some transfers *between* governments are necessary. We examine these transfers shortly.

2. Geographic Scope of Services. Because the government of a province or a municipality is unlikely to be responsive to the needs of citizens outside its jurisdiction, some public services may not be provided adequately unless responsibility for them is delegated to the level of government appropriate to the scope of the service provided. For example, national defence is normally delegated to the central government because it provides benefits to all residents of the country. At the other extreme is fire protection. If fire protection is to be effective, it is necessary to have fire stations serving small geographic areas. Accordingly, responsibility for fire stations lies with municipal governments.

3. Regional Differences in Preferences. The delegation of some functions to lower levels of government may provide a political process that is more responsive to regional differences in preferences for public versus private goods. Some people may prefer to live in communities with higher-quality schools and police protection, and they may be prepared to pay the high taxes required. Others may prefer lower taxes and lower levels of services. The differences in provincial tax rates that we noted earlier presumably reflect each provincial government's own view of the appropriate level of taxation.

4. Administrative Efficiency. Administrative efficiency requires that duplication of the services provided at different levels of government be minimized and that related programs be coordinated. For this reason, in all provinces except Quebec, income taxes are reported on a single form and paid to the federal government, which then remits the appropriate share of those taxes to the relevant provincial government. This coordination avoids the administrative burden that would exist if each province had its own tax-collection system.

Intergovernmental Transfers Canada's system of fiscal federalism requires transfers between various levels of government. For example, since all income taxes are paid directly to the federal government (except in Quebec) but spending on hospitals, education, and highways is undertaken by provincial governments, the federal government makes transfers every year to the various provincial governments. In addition, if some provinces have large tax bases, while others have much smaller tax bases, there is a role for transferring resources between provinces. Canada has two major programs in which cash is transferred from the federal to the provincial governments.

1. Canada Health and Social Transfers. The federal government makes two block grants to each provincial and territorial government every year—one to help finance expenditures on health care and the other to help finance expenditures on post-secondary education, social assistance, and early learning and childcare. Though the Canada Health Transfer (CHT) and the Canada Social Transfer (CST) are each described as being directed at these specific categories of expenditure, there is no practical way to prevent provincial governments from spending this money on whatever they deem to be appropriate. These block grants are financial support with "no strings attached."

The CHT and CST are allocated to provinces on an equal per capita basis so as to provide comparable treatment for all Canadians, regardless of where they live. The total CST payment is scheduled to grow annually at the rate of 3 percent, and in 2012–2013 the total amount to all provinces was $11.9 billion. The total CHT payment is scheduled to grow more quickly to accommodate the rapidly growing demands on Canada's public health-care system. In 2012–2013, the total CHT payment was $29 billion, and it was scheduled to grow at a 6 percent annual rate until 2017. After 2017, the CHT will grow at the rate of national income which is expected to be about 4.5 percent annually.

equalization payments Transfers of tax revenues from the federal government to the low-income provinces.

2. Equalization Payments. The Constitution of Canada, which was formally amended and repatriated (from the United Kingdom) in 1982, explicitly includes a provision for less prosperous provinces to receive **equalization payments** from the federal government. The Constitution states that "Parliament and the government of Canada are committed to the principle of making equalization payments to ensure that provincial governments have sufficient revenues to provide reasonably comparable levels of public services at reasonably comparable levels of taxation." Since the federal government collects revenues from economic activity generated in *all* provinces, and uses this revenue to support the lower-income ones, the equalization program is effectively a redistribution program from high-income to low-income provinces. Equalization payments are calculated by a complicated formula that involves five different revenue sources: personal income taxes, corporate income taxes, GST, property taxes, and natural resource taxes. From their inception in 1957, equalization payments have increased significantly. In the 2012–2013 fiscal year, total equalization payments were forecast to be $15.4 billion.

Canadian Social Programs

Table 18-2 on page 457 shows that government spending on health, education, and other social services represents roughly 65 percent of total government spending in Canada. Given their obvious fiscal importance, it is worth briefly reviewing Canada's major social programs.

demogrants Social benefits paid to anyone meeting only minimal requirements such as age or residence; in particular, not income-tested.

income-tested benefits Social benefits paid to recipients who qualify because their income is less than some critical level.

Some social programs are universal, in the sense that they pay benefits to anyone meeting only such minimal requirements as age or residence. These are referred to as **demogrants**. Other programs are selective, in the sense that they pay benefits only to people who qualify by meeting specific conditions, such as having young children, having very low income, or being unemployed. When these conditions are related to the individual's income, the term **income-tested benefits** is used. Some benefits are expenditure programs (including direct transfers to persons), while others are delivered through the tax system. Some programs are administered by the federal government, some by the provincial governments, and still others by the municipalities.

In this section we examine the five pillars of Canadian social policy: education, health care, income support, employment insurance, and retirement benefits. Each of these pillars, at various points in recent years, has been the focus of attention as financially strapped governments have explored new ways to provide these vital social services in a cost-effective manner.

Education Public education, one of the earliest types of social expenditure in Canada, remains one of the most important. It has been supplemented over the years by numerous other public programs aimed at developing human capital.

Basic Education. Primary and secondary schools are funded by provincial governments in Canada but are managed by local school boards. Basic education is publicly financed for both efficiency and equity reasons. In terms of efficiency, a literate and numerate population is necessary for an informed electorate that can participate in democratic society. Therefore, society as a whole is better off when all its citizens have at least a basic level of education. The equity argument is based on the fact that basic skills acquired in primary and secondary schools are usually necessary in order for individuals to secure careers that can provide reasonable incomes. If basic education were not financed by the government, many low-income households could not afford to send their children to school. The result in many cases would be a vicious circle of poverty in which children from low-income families would lack basic education and thus secure only poor jobs and earning only low incomes themselves.

Post-Secondary Education. Post-secondary education is a provincial responsibility in Canada. As discussed earlier in this chapter, however, the federal government makes large payments to the provinces to support post-secondary education as part of the Canada Social Transfer (CST).

For data on the financial position of Canadian universities, see Statistics Canada's website: www.statcan.gc.ca. *Browse by "Education" and then "Education Finance" and then choose "Summary Tables."*

In Canada, universities are public institutions, and university education is heavily subsidized by government. In 2009, total revenues for universities and colleges were $37.4 billion, with 55 percent coming from various levels of government. Only 20 percent came from student tuition fees and the remaining 25 percent comes from various other sources. In addition, many students receive student loans from commercial banks, with the loans guaranteed by the federal government. In cases when students default on their loans, the repayment by the government amounts to a subsidy to the student.

There is both an efficiency argument and an equity argument for subsidizing higher education. The efficiency argument is based on the claim that there are positive externalities from higher education—that is, that the country as a whole benefits when a student receives higher education. In many cases these externalities cannot be internalized by the students receiving the education, so, left to their own maximizing decisions, students who had to pay the full cost of their education would choose less than the socially optimal amount. The equity argument is that if students were forced to pay anything like the full cost of the services they receive, a university education would become prohibitively expensive to low- and even middle-income families. Government subsidies help provide education according to ability rather than according to income.

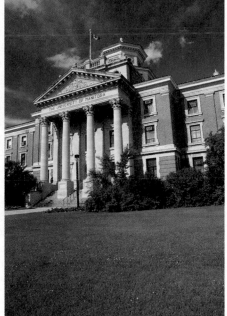

Roughly 55 percent of the operating revenues of Canadian universities comes from provincial governments. Only 20 percent of revenues comes from students' tuition fees. There is an active debate in Canada about how much students should be paying toward the full costs of their post-secondary education.

Arguments that rely on higher tuition fees to finance a larger fraction of the costs of running universities start with the observation that the value of many kinds of post-secondary education is internalized and recaptured in higher incomes earned by the recipients later in their life. This is particularly true of professional training in such fields as law, medicine, dentistry, management, and computer science. Yet students in these fields typically pay a smaller proportion of their real education costs than students in the arts, where the argument for externalities is greatest. Also, subsidized education does represent a significant income transfer from taxpayers to students, even though the average taxpayer may have a lower income than the average post-secondary student can expect to earn in the future.

Health Care In Canada, basic health care is financed mainly by the provincial governments, with significant transfers from the federal government under the Canada Health Transfer (CHT). In most provinces, residents pay nothing to receive medical attention—health care is free to users and is financed out of the government's general tax revenues. Though health care is publicly financed, physicians and private (for-profit) hospitals working on a "fee for service" basis form the core of Canada's health-care delivery system. Thus, the Canadian health-care system is based on public *financing* but private *delivery.*

Health care is financed by government for reasons of both efficiency and equity. The efficiency argument is much the same as for basic education—a healthy population is as important to the smooth functioning of a democratic country as is an educated one. The equity argument is even more powerful: Most people believe that basic health care is so important that denying it to people who cannot afford it would be unacceptable. But even when this equity argument is generally accepted, there is still a decision as to what and how much to provide for free.

Cost Containment. Taking federal and provincial payments into account, Canada's public health-care system is the country's single most expensive social program. In 2009, government expenditure on health care was $121.6 billion, over 19 percent of total government expenditure and 7.8 percent of GDP. Private spending on health care brought total spending up to almost 12 percent of GDP. In other words, more than one out of every nine dollars in income produced in the Canadian economy is spent on health care. This ratio is expected to rise as the baby-boom generation continues to age, thus increasing the average age in the Canadian population.

"Cost containment" in the health-care sector has become a priority for most provincial governments and the debate currently rages over what reforms would be practicable and acceptable. Most observers agree that some type of expenditure-controlling reform is urgently needed. Unfortunately, agreement stops there.

The Role of the Private Sector. Much of the debate over the reform of Canada's health-care system rests on the appropriate role of the private sector in what is a publicly financed system. Some provincial governments, notably Quebec and Alberta, have suggested that allowing a greater role for private, for-profit hospitals and clinics can reduce waiting lists and therefore improve the overall quality of health care that citizens receive.

The main concern with allowing a greater role for private clinics and hospitals is that private hospitals may begin "extra billing" their patients. In this case a "two-tiered" health-care system would develop in which individuals with higher incomes would have faster access to health care than would individuals with lower incomes. If extra billing becomes a feature of private hospitals and clinics, then only those individuals who can afford to pay the extra fees will be able to use them. Furthermore, it is argued that many nurses and doctors who are currently within the financially strapped public health-care system may move to the private facilities if salaries or working conditions are better there. The overall concern, therefore, is that the introduction of private hospitals and clinics into the existing public health-care system, while reducing waiting lists and providing more health-care services overall, may result in a high-quality system for the wealthy and a low-quality system for lower-income people. People who take this view argue that such a two-tiered health-care system would destroy the equity that the public system was initially designed to promote.

On the other hand, advocates of allowing a greater role for private hospitals and clinics argue that to a significant extent, Canada already has a two-tiered system. For example, for such services as laser eye surgery and diagnosis with MRIs, private clinics have existed for several years; people have a choice between waiting in line for service in the public

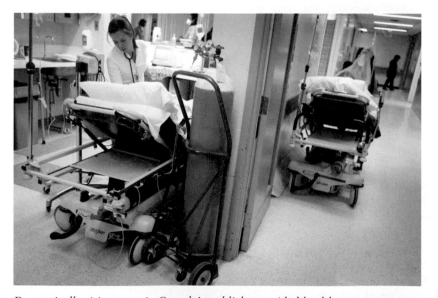

Dramatically rising costs in Canada's publicly provided health-care sector represent a serious challenge for Canadian governments.

hospitals, sometimes for many months, or going to a private clinic immediately and paying for the service. Even for more serious surgery, some Canadians, frustrated by the long waiting lists in the Canadian public health-care system, travel to the United States for medical treatment. Advocates of private for-profit hospitals also argue that the lack of public funding in the Canadian health-care system has already caused many doctors and nurses to leave Canada and move to the United States, and that the introduction of private hospitals would help stem the flow of nurses and doctors out of Canada, thereby *improving* Canada's overall health-care system. Furthermore, they argue that two-tier systems do not seem to lead to major health-care inequalities in the countries of the European Union, most of which operate some form of two-tier system.

Income-Support Programs Canada has various programs that provide assistance for people in dire financial need—these programs constitute what is often called the "social safety net." The overriding objectives of this safety net are to reduce poverty and increase individuals' sense of economic security. Though no longer the serious problem it was in Canada's past and still is in many other countries, poverty remains a matter of real concern to Canadian policymakers.

Statistics Canada defines the **poverty line** or *low-income cutoff* as the level of income below which the typical household spends more than 63 percent of its income on the three necessities of food, shelter, and clothing. (The average Canadian household spends only 43 percent of its income on these three necessities.) Not surprisingly, this poverty line varies depending on the size of the family and where it lives. In 2009, Statistics Canada's estimated poverty line for a family of four living in a major urban centre was $41 307. Thus, a family of four with pre-tax income less than this amount would be defined to be living in poverty. In 2009, 9.8 percent of people living in economic families had incomes below Statistics Canada's estimated poverty line. This percentage includes some of the working poor, whether stuck in low-paying jobs or doing their first job; some who were not working at all; and some whose incomes were only temporarily below the poverty line, such as students or other trainees.

There is considerable debate, however, about the methods used to estimate poverty. Central to this debate is whether poverty is best viewed as an *absolute* or a *relative* concept.

> **poverty line** An estimate of the annual family income that is required to maintain a minimum adequate standard of living.

If poverty is viewed as an absolute concept, then anybody without enough income to purchase a certain amount of food, shelter, and clothing is said to be in poverty. With such an absolute definition of poverty, sufficient growth in the economy could, at least in principle, eliminate poverty entirely as low-income households eventually see their income rise above the threshold level.

With a *relative* definition of poverty, however, there will *always* be some families defined as impoverished. For example, suppose households are defined as impoverished whenever their income is less than 50 percent of the economy's average household income. Since any realistic distribution of income will contain *some* households whose income is 50 percent of the average, there will always be some

Poverty and homelessness exist in Canada, though there is considerable disagreement about the scope of these problems.

poverty when it is defined this way. Advocates of a relative measure of poverty argue that poverty is more than just the absence of enough food and clothing—it is also the social exclusion from mainstream society that typically comes from having much lower income than most households.

Whatever the precise definition, all experts agree that many Canadians live in poverty. Canada has several income-support programs designed to address this important problem. They can be divided into three types. The first is designed to provide income assistance to those individuals whose incomes are deemed to be too low to provide an adequate standard of living. The second is designed to assist specifically those individuals who are in financial need because of temporary job loss—employment insurance. The third is designed to provide income assistance specifically to the elderly. In this subsection, we examine the first type. The next two subsections discuss employment insurance and elderly benefits, respectively.

Welfare. Social assistance for individuals below retirement age, usually called *welfare*, is mainly a provincial responsibility in Canada. The details of the programs vary considerably across the provinces even though they are partly financed by transfers received from the federal government under the Canada Social Transfer (CST).

poverty trap Occurs whenever individuals have little incentive to increase their pre-tax income because the resulting loss of benefits makes them worse off.

One important problem with welfare occurs with what are called *poverty traps*. **Poverty traps** occur whenever the tax-and-transfer system results in individuals having very little incentive to increase their pre-tax income (by accepting a job, for example) because such an increase in their pre-tax income would make them ineligible for some benefits (such as welfare) and might even make them worse off overall. Current research on the Canadian tax system shows that some Canadian families with incomes of approximately $20 000 are in this situation. The presence of such poverty traps reflects a tax-and-transfer system that has been modified in many small steps over many years, the result of which is a plethora of programs often working at cross-purposes. The elimination of poverty traps requires that the tax-and-transfer system be examined in its entirety rather than on a piecemeal basis. *Applying Economic Concepts 18-1* discusses one possible reform of the tax-and-transfer system that maintains progressivity of the system while eliminating poverty traps. This is the idea of the negative income tax.

Child Benefits. The Canada Child Tax Benefit is a federal non-taxable payment to parents according to the number of children in the family and varies according to family income. For families with net income below about $42 000, the benefit pays about $115 per month per child under the age of 18. There is an extra payment for third and additional children. For families with very low incomes (below $24 000 per year) there are additional child-support payments.

In addition to these income-tested programs, there is also a federal Universal Child Care Benefit which pays parents $100 per month for each child under the age of six. The payments are taxed in the hands of the lower-earning parent. Some provinces also have child benefits that are separate from and in addition to these federal programs.

Employment Insurance Employment insurance (EI) is a federal program designed to provide temporary income support to workers who lose their jobs. Employers and employees remit EI premiums to the government equal to a small percentage of wages and salaries. These premiums then finance the EI payments to unemployed workers who qualify for the benefits. In boom times, when there is little unemployment, the total amount of EI premiums collected exceeds the total amount dispersed as EI benefits; in times of high unemployment, the benefits exceed the premiums. As a result, the EI program is approximately self-financing over the duration of the average business cycle (six to seven years).

For details on Canada's Employment Insurance program, go to the website for Human Resources and Social Development Canada: www.hrsdc.gc.ca. *Then click on "Programs and Policies" and then "Employment Insurance."*

APPLYING ECONOMIC CONCEPTS 18-1

Poverty Traps and the Negative Income Tax

The underlying principle of the negative income tax (NIT) is that a family of a given size should be *guaranteed* a minimum annual income. The tax system must be designed, however, to guarantee this income without eliminating the household's incentive to be self-supporting.

As an example, consider a system in which each household is guaranteed a minimum annual income of $10 000 and the marginal tax rate on all earned income is 40 percent. Money can be thought of as flowing in two directions; the government gives every household $10 000, and then every household remits 40 percent of any *earned income* back to the government. The *break-even* level of earned income in this example is $25 000. All households earning less than $25 000 pay negative taxes overall; they receive more money from the government than they remit in taxes. Households earning exactly $25 000 pay no net taxes—their $10 000 from the government exactly equals the taxes they remit to the government on their earned income. All households earning more than $25 000 pay more than $10 000 in taxes so they are paying *positive* taxes overall.

The figure shows the operation of this scheme by relating earned income on the horizontal axis to after-tax income on the vertical axis. The red 45° line shows what after-tax income would be if there were no taxes.

The blue line shows after-tax income with an NIT. It starts at the guaranteed annual income of $10 000, rises by 60 cents for every one dollar increase in earned income, and crosses the 45° line at the break-even level of income, $25 000. The vertical distance between the two lines shows the net transfers between the household and the government.

Note that the NIT is a progressive tax, despite the *constant* marginal income-tax rate. To see this, note that a household's *average* tax rate is equal to the total taxes paid divided by total earned income. If I_E is earned income, then

$$\text{Average tax rate} = \frac{(0.40) \times I_E - 10\,000}{I_E}$$

$$= (0.40) - \frac{10\,000}{I_E}$$

The average tax rate for the household rises as earned income rises, but the average tax rate is *always less* than the marginal tax rate (40 percent). That the average tax rate rises with earned income means that higher-income households pay a larger fraction of their income in taxes than is paid by lower-income households—that is, the NIT is progressive.

Supporters of the NIT believe that it would be an effective tool for reducing poverty. The NIT provides a minimum level of income as a matter of right, not of charity, and it does so without removing the work incentives for people who are eligible for payments; every dollar earned adds to the after-tax income of the family. Poverty traps are avoided.

A step toward the NIT was taken in 2007 with the introduction of the Working Income Tax Benefit (WITB). The WITB is aimed at low-income working Canadians and is designed to reduce the marginal income-tax rate and thereby provide greater incentives for low-income people to increase their labour-force participation. The WITB works by offering a *refundable tax credit* for every dollar earned within a specific range. A *refundable* tax credit means that even if the individual pays no income tax, the credit would result in money being paid to (refunded to) the individual. The WITB is a small but important step toward the reduction of poverty traps in Canada.

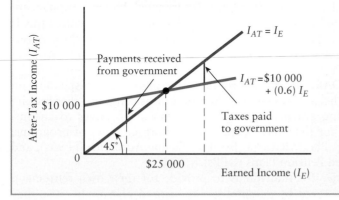

In its current form, the EI system provides workers with incentives to remain in seasonal jobs and in areas with poor employment prospects and to take EI-financed "holidays." That the EI system encourages behaviour that increases unemployment and reduces regional mobility does not mean that the unemployed themselves are responsible for the "abuses" of the system that lead to these results. The responsibility lies with the people who designed the incentives and those who strive to preserve them. They can alter the system to make it deliver the intended benefits with fewer incentives for undesired behaviour.

Retirement Benefits There are three components of the system of retirement benefits. These are the Canada Pension Plan (CPP), retirement income-support programs such as Old Age Security (OAS) and Guaranteed Income Supplement (GIS), and tax-assisted saving plans.

The Canada Pension Plan (CPP). The CPP provides a basic level of retirement income for all Canadians who have contributed to it over their working lives. A separate but similar scheme exists in Quebec—the Quebec Pension Plan or QPP. Unlike some private programs, the pension provided by the CPP is *portable*—changing jobs does not cause any loss of eligibility.

During the late 1990s, the challenges of an aging population led to significant reforms of the CPP. The system had initially been designed to finance retirees' benefits largely from the contributions of the working young. But the aging of the large baby-boom generation implied that the CPP would soon encounter financial difficulties as the number of retirees increased relative to the number of young workers. In 1998, the Canadian government reformed the CPP by increasing the required level of contributions by both employers and employees but leaving the pension benefits unchanged. The system is now deemed to be financially sound for the next 75 years.

Retirement Income-Support Programs. There are two parts to the existing public benefits system for the elderly. First, through a universal benefit called the Old Age Security (OAS) program, the government sends out monthly benefit cheques to each Canadian over the qualifying age of 65. OAS payments to higher-income individuals are recaptured by means of a tax "clawback." In 2012, the maximum annual OAS benefit was $6481 annually; the clawback began at net incomes above $69 562 and the OAS benefit was fully eliminated for individuals with annual incomes above $112 769. In 2012, the federal government announced that the OAS qualifying age would increase gradually so that by 2023 it would be 67 years of age.

Second, an income-tested program, called the Guaranteed Income Supplement (GIS), provides benefits targeted to the low-income elderly. (In some provinces this is supplemented by further targeted assistance.) The GIS provides for most of the progressivity that arises in the elderly benefits system.

Tax-Assisted Saving Plans. The OAS and GIS are programs that involve direct spending on the part of the government. The government also has important programs that require no direct government spending but instead rely on tax-based incentives to encourage individuals to save more for their retirement. There are three types of programs: Registered Retirement Savings Plans (RRSPs), Tax-Free Saving Accounts (TFSAs), and employer-sponsored Registered Pension Plans (RPPs).

RRSPs provide an incentive for individuals to provide for their own retirement, either because they are not covered by an employer-sponsored plan or because they want to supplement that plan. Funds contributed are deductible from taxable income (and accumulate year by year without any tax being paid) but they become fully taxable when they are withdrawn. It is thus a tax deferral plan, and as such it is more valuable the higher one's current taxable income and the lower one's expected future income.

Tax-Free Saving Accounts (TFSAs) were introduced in 2009 and permit individuals over 18 years of age to save up to $5000 per year in special accounts. The funds can be invested in any kind of assets (cash, stocks, or bonds) and any income earned on these funds (interest, dividends, or capital gains) is untaxed. By eliminating the tax on income earned inside these accounts, and thus increasing the after-tax rate of return, TFSAs increase individuals' incentive to save.

Individuals without RRSPs or TFSAs may still receive some tax assistance for saving if their employer has a Registered Pension Plan. In this case, contributions to the employer-sponsored pension plan (which are often mandatory and are withdrawn directly from the regular paycheque) are tax deductible in a manner similar to an RRSP contribution.

18.4 Evaluating the Role of Government

Earlier we pointed out that it is more informative to assess the progressivity of the overall tax system than any individual tax. It is even more informative to assess the progressivity of the combination of taxes and expenditures—that is, the entire tax-expenditure system. For example, a tax-expenditure system could be highly progressive even if all taxes were proportional, as long as government expenditures (including transfers) accounted for a higher portion of real incomes of the poor than of the rich. The evidence is that the overall Canadian tax-expenditure system is progressive and succeeds in successfully narrowing (but by no means eliminating) the inequalities of income generated by the market.

Even if there is widespread agreement that the Canadian tax-expenditure system is progressive and that it helps to produce a more desirable distribution of income, there is still considerable disagreement regarding the appropriate level of government activity in the economy.

Public Versus Private Sector

When the government raises money by taxation and spends it on an activity, it increases the spending of the public sector and decreases that of the private sector. Since the public sector and the private sector spend on different things, the government is changing the allocation of resources. Is this change good or bad? Should there be more schools and fewer houses or more houses and fewer schools?

For all goods that are produced and sold on the market, consumers' demand has a significant influence on the relative prices and quantities produced and thus on the allocation of the nation's resources. But no market provides relative prices for private houses versus public schools; thus, the choice between allowing money to be spent in the private sector and allowing it to be spent for public goods is a matter to be decided by Parliament and other legislative bodies.

John Kenneth Galbraith's 1958 bestseller, *The Affluent Society*, proclaimed that a correct assignment of marginal utilities would show them to be higher for an extra dollar's worth of public parks, clean water, and education than for an extra dollar's worth of

In his classic book The Affluent Society, *the late John Kenneth Galbraith argued that Western democracies often undervalue public goods and place too much value on private consumption. He lamented the resulting contrast between "private opulence" and "public squalor."*

television sets, shampoo, or automobiles. In Galbraith's view, the political process often fails to translate preferences for public goods into effective action; thus more resources are devoted to the private sector and fewer to the public sector than would be the case if the political mechanism were as effective as the market. He lamented the resulting "private opulence and public squalor." Many economists would argue that Galbraith's observations are even truer today, more than 50 years after he first published them.

An alternative view has many supporters who agree with Nobel Laureate James Buchanan that society has reached a point where the value of the *marginal* dollar spent by government is less than the value of that dollar left in the hands of households or firms. These people argue that because bureaucrats are spending other people's money, they care very little about a few million or billion dollars here or there. They have only a weak sense of the opportunity cost of public expenditure and, thus, tend to spend beyond the point at which marginal benefits equal marginal costs.

Scope of Government Activity

One of the most difficult problems for the student of the Canadian economic system is to maintain the appropriate perspective about the scope of government activity in the market economy. On the one hand, there are thousands of laws, regulations, and policies that affect firms and households. Many people believe that a general reduction in the role of government is both possible and desirable. On the other hand, private decision makers still have an enormous amount of discretion about what they do and how they do it.

One pitfall is to become so impressed (or obsessed) with the many ways in which government activity impinges on the individual that one fails to see that these make changes—sometimes large, but often small—only in market signals in a system that basically leaves individuals free to make their own decisions. It is in the private sector that most individuals choose their occupations, earn their living, spend their incomes, and live their lives. In this sector, too, firms are formed, choose products, live, grow, and sometimes die.

A different pitfall is to fail to see that a significant share of the taxes paid by the private sector is used to buy goods and services that add to the welfare of individuals. By and large, the public sector complements the private sector, doing things the private sector would leave undone or would do differently. For example, Canadians pay taxes that are used to finance expenditures on health and education. But certainly Canadians would continue to use hospitals and attend schools even if the various levels of government did not provide these goods and instead left more money in people's pockets. Thus, in many cases, the government is levying taxes to raise money to finance goods that people would have purchased anyway. To recognize that we often benefit directly from government spending, however, in no way denies that it is often wasteful, and sometimes worse.

Evolution of Policy

Public policies in operation at any time are not the result of a single master plan that specifies precisely where and how the public sector will seek to complement or interfere with the workings of the market mechanism. Rather, as individual problems arise, governments attempt to meet them by passing appropriate legislation to deal with the problem. These laws stay on the books, and some become obsolete and unenforceable. This pattern is generally true of systems of law.

Many anomalies exist in our economic policies; for example, laws designed to support the incomes of small farmers have created some agricultural millionaires, and commissions created to ensure competition between firms often end up creating and protecting monopolies. Neither individual policies nor whole programs are above criticism.

In a society that elects its policymakers at regular intervals, however, the majority view on the amount of government intervention that is desirable will have some considerable influence on the amount of intervention that actually occurs. Fundamentally, a free-market system is retained because it is valued for its lack of coercion and its ability to do much of the allocating of society's resources better than any known alternative. But we are not mesmerized by it; we feel free to intervene in pursuit of a better world in which to live. We also recognize, however, that sometimes government intervention has proved ineffective or even counterproductive.

SUMMARY

18.1 Taxation in Canada

LO 1

- Although the main purpose of the tax system is to raise revenue, tax policy is potentially a powerful device for income redistribution because the progressivity of different kinds of taxes varies greatly.
- The most important taxes in Canada are the personal income tax, the corporate income tax, excise and sales taxes (including the nationwide GST), and property taxes.

- The progressivity of a tax is determined by how the average tax rate (taxes paid divided by income) changes as income changes. If the average tax rate rises as income rises, the tax is progressive. If the average tax rate falls as income rises, the tax is regressive.

18.2 Evaluating the Tax System

LO 2, 3

- Evaluating the tax system involves evaluating the efficiency and progressivity of the entire system, rather than of individual taxes within the system. For a given amount of revenue to be raised, efficiency and progressivity can be altered by changing the mix of the various taxes used.
- The total Canadian tax structure is roughly proportional, except for very low-income and very high-income groups (where it is mildly progressive).
- Taxes often generate allocative inefficiency. The allocative inefficiency of a tax is measured by the excess

burden. Because of the excess burden, a tax is more costly than just the amount paid by the taxpayers (the direct burden).
- There are potentially important disincentive effects of taxation, as represented by a Laffer curve. A rise in the tax rate initially raises total tax revenue; after some point, however, further increases in the tax rate reduce the incentive to produce taxable income, and so total tax revenue falls. Thus, governments cannot always increase tax revenues by raising tax rates.

18.3 Public Expenditure in Canada

LO 4

- A large part of public expenditure is for the provision of goods and services. Other types of expenditures, including subsidies, transfer payments to individuals, and intergovernmental transfers, are also important.
- Fiscal federalism is the idea that the various fiscal authorities should be coordinated in their spending plans and should have a mechanism for transfers between the various levels of government. Understanding the relationship between the federal government and the various provincial governments is of utmost

importance in understanding many of Canada's most important government spending programs.
- The five pillars of Canadian social policy are

1. Education
2. Health care
3. Income support programs (welfare and child benefits)
4. Employment insurance
5. Retirement benefits (CPP, GIS, OAS, and tax-assisted saving plans)

18.4 Evaluating the Role of Government

- Government taxation and expenditure have a major effect on the allocation of resources. The government determines how much of society's total output is devoted to education, health care, highways, the armed forces, and so on.
- When evaluating the overall role of government in the economy, we should keep three basic issues in mind:
  1. What is the appropriate mix between public goods and private goods?
  2. Much government activity is directed to providing goods and services that add directly to the welfare of the private sector.
  3. We should continually re-evaluate existing programs; some that were needed in the past may no longer be needed; others may have unintended and undesirable side effects.

KEY CONCEPTS

Progressive, proportional, and regressive taxes

The benefit principle and the ability-to-pay principle

Vertical and horizontal equity

Direct and excess burdens of a tax

Disincentive effects of taxation

Transfer payments to individuals

Fiscal federalism

Intergovernmental transfers

Canadian social programs

STUDY EXERCISES

MyEconLab

Make the grade with MyEconLab: Study Exercises marked in red can be found on MyEconLab. You can practise them as often as you want, and most feature step-by-step guided instructions to help you find the right answer.

1. Fill in the blanks to make the following statements correct.
   a. Suppose you earn an annual income of $22 500 and you paid a total of $3600 in taxes. Your average tax rate is _____.
   b. Suppose you earn an annual income of $22 500 and each dollar earned is taxed at the same rate. Your marginal tax rate is the same as _____.
   c. Suppose the marginal tax rate on the first $25 000 of income is 20 percent, and on any income above that, the rate rises to 30 percent. If your annual income is $42 000, you will pay total income tax of _____.
   d. Lower-income groups typically spend a higher proportion of their income than do higher-income groups. For this reason, excise and sales taxes are considered to be somewhat _____.
   e. The most important source of revenue for municipalities is the _____ tax. Rather than being a tax on income or expenditure, it is a tax on _____.

2. Fill in the blanks to make the following statements correct.
   a. Evaluating a tax system requires consideration of the following two aspects of taxation: _____ and _____.
   b. Taxation usually causes allocative inefficiency because it distorts the equality between marginal _____ and marginal _____ of a given activity.
   c. Economists refer to the revenue collected as a result of a tax as the _____ burden of taxation. Economists refer to other costs imposed on society because of the tax as the _____ burden of taxation.
   d. An efficient tax system is one that collects a given amount of revenue while minimizing the amount of _____.
   e. The Laffer curve suggests that above some tax rate, further increases in the tax rate will _____ tax revenue.

3. Consider an income-tax system that has four tax brackets. The following table shows the marginal tax rate that applies to the income in each tax bracket.

Earned Income	Tax Rate in Bracket
Up to $20 000	0%
$20 001–$40 000	15%
$40 001–$80 000	30%
$80 001 and higher	35%

a. Compute the average income-tax rate at income levels $10 000, $20 000, and each increment of $10 000 up to $120 000.

b. Compute the marginal income-tax rate for each level of income in part (a).

c. On a graph with the tax rates on the vertical axis and income on the horizontal axis, plot the average and marginal tax rates for each level of income.

d. Is this tax system progressive? Explain.

4. The diagrams below show the market for gasoline in two countries, Midas and Neptune. In Midas, demand is perfectly inelastic; in Neptune, demand is relatively elastic. In both countries, supply is identical and upward sloping. The government in each country imposes an excise tax of $t per litre on the producers of gasoline. This tax shifts the supply curve up by $t.

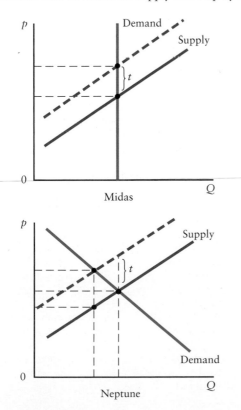

a. In each case, shade the area that is the direct burden of the tax.

b. In each case, shade the area that is the excess burden of the tax.

c. In which country does the tax cause the greater allocative inefficiency? Explain.

5. In Canada, capital gains—which occur when assets are sold at prices greater than their earlier purchase price—are taxed at half the rates applicable to other income.

a. Who are the likely beneficiaries of this policy?

b. What are the likely effects on the distribution of income and the allocation of resources?

c. Can you think of both equity and efficiency arguments supporting the special treatment of capital gains?

6. "Taxes on tobacco and alcohol are nearly perfect taxes. They raise lots of revenue and discourage smoking and drinking."

a. To what extent are the two effects inconsistent?

b. How is the burden of an excise tax related to the extent to which it discourages use of the product?

7. Rank the following taxes according to which has the highest excess burden relative to the direct burden. Start with the highest. Recall that the direct burden of the tax is equal to the revenue that the tax raises.

a. An excise tax on one brand of breakfast cereal

b. An excise tax on all breakfast cereals

c. An excise tax on all food

d. An excise tax on everything (which is basically what the GST is)

8. Classify each of the following government expenditures as either a transfer payment or a purchase of goods and services. Which ones clearly tend to decrease the inequality of income distribution?

a. Payments of wages and family living allowances to Canadian soldiers overseas

b. Employment insurance payments to unemployed workers

c. Payments to provinces for support of highway construction

d. Pensions of retired Supreme Court justices

e. Salaries paid to government workers

9. Governments in Canada, at all levels, make considerable transfer payments to individuals and to businesses. This question will show you how significant these transfer payments are. Go to Statistics Canada's

website (www.statcan.gc.ca), and answer the following questions.

a. For the years 2007–2009, what were the federal transfers for employment insurance benefits?

b. Were total government transfers to individuals growing faster or slower than GDP over these years?

c. For the years 2007–2009, what were total revenues for Canada's universities and colleges?

d. In part (c), how much of these revenues came as transfers from the federal and provincial governments?

10. The negative income tax has been proposed as a means of increasing both the efficiency and the equity of Canada's tax system (see *Applying Economic Concepts 18-1* on page 465). The most basic NIT can be described by two variables: the guaranteed annual income and the marginal tax rate. Suppose the guaranteed annual income is $8000 and the marginal tax rate on *every dollar earned* is 35 percent. With this NIT, after-tax income is given by

After-tax income =
$$8000 + (1 - 0.35) \times (\text{Earned income})$$

a. On a scale diagram with after-tax income on the vertical axis and earned income on the horizontal axis, draw the NIT relationship between earned income and after-tax income.

b. What is the level of income at which taxes paid on earned income exactly equal the guaranteed annual income?

c. The average tax rate is equal to total *net* taxes paid divided by earned income. Provide an algebraic expression for the average tax rate.

d. On a scale diagram with earned income on the horizontal axis and tax rates on the vertical axis, plot the average and marginal tax rates for the NIT. Is the NIT progressive?

11. Fill in the blanks to make the following statements correct.

a. Canada has different fiscal authorities, in the form of federal, provincial, territorial, and municipal governments. The coordination of the taxing and spending powers of these governments gives rise to our system of _____. One of the guiding principles of this system is that individuals, no matter where they live in Canada, should have access to a comparable level and quality of _____ and should face approximately the same _____.

b. The two major programs by which cash is transferred from Canada's federal government to provincial governments are _____ and _____.

c. What are the five pillars of Canada's social policy?
_____
_____
_____
_____
_____

d. Education and health care are primarily _____ responsibilities even though the _____ government makes large _____ to the provincial governments to help finance these programs.

e. Employment insurance is operated by the _____. It is designed to be approximately _____ over the course of the typical business cycle.

f. The government encourages households to save for their retirement by offering special tax treatment in _____ and _____.

12. It is common to read articles in the newspapers by people who think Canadians pay too much in taxes. One popular concept is "tax freedom day," the day in the year beyond which you get to keep your income rather than pay it to the government as taxes. For example, if the government collects 33 percent of GDP in taxes, then "tax freedom day" is the 122nd day of the year, May 2.

a. Does everyone in the economy have the same tax freedom day, no matter what his or her income?

b. How sensible is the concept of "tax freedom day" in a country where the government provides some goods and services to the people that they would otherwise purchase on their own, such as primary education and health-care services?

What Macroeconomics Is All About

CHAPTER OUTLINE	LEARNING OBJECTIVES (LO)
	After studying this chapter you will be able to
19.1 KEY MACROECONOMIC VARIABLES	1 define the key macroeconomic variables: national income, unemployment, inflation, interest rates, exchange rates, and net exports.
19.2 GROWTH VERSUS FLUCTUATIONS	2 understand that most macroeconomic issues are about either long-run trends or short-run fluctuations, and that government policy is relevant for both.

DURING the mid-2000s, the economies of Canada, the United States, Europe, and Asia were growing quickly, unemployment was low, and it appeared to many that there was nothing but smooth economic sailing ahead. Then in 2007, house prices in the United States, which had been rising quickly over the previous decade, began to fall—and sharply. Banks and other financial institutions that had invested heavily in mortgage-backed securities were in trouble, and some very large ones in Europe and the United States went bankrupt. The world economy entered its deepest recession in 70 years.

In the fall of 2008, government leaders of the world's largest economies, a group of countries known as the G20, met in Washington, D.C. They discussed large-scale policy interventions to prevent a repeat of the Great Depression, the massive decline in economic activity that occurred between 1929 and 1933 and that had enormous economic, political, and social consequences for years to come. The G20 leaders agreed to take many actions to stave off such an economic disaster, including increasing the level of government spending, reducing interest rates through aggressive central-bank actions, supporting their failing financial institutions, and avoiding the imposition of new tariffs and other protectionist measures.

Why did the U.S. housing collapse lead to serious problems for banks, and why did these problems lead to a global recession? How can various actions by governments help to dampen the scale of recession and what are the side effects of such large-scale policy interventions? These are central questions in macroeconomics, and the events of 2007–2010 show just how important these issues are. The next several chapters are devoted to understanding the essential elements of *macroeconomics*.

macroeconomics The study of the determination of economic aggregates, such as total output, total employment, the price level, and the rate of economic growth.

Macroeconomics is the study of how the economy behaves in broad outline without dwelling on much of the detail that occurs in markets for individual products. Macroeconomics is concerned with the behaviour of economic *aggregates* and *averages*, such as total output, total investment, total exports, and the price level, and with how they may be influenced by government policy. Their behaviour results from activities in many different markets and from the combined behaviour of millions of different decision makers.

An economy producing a lot of wheat and few computers is clearly different from one producing many computers but little wheat. An economy with cheap wheat and expensive computers is also different from one with cheap computers and expensive wheat. When we study aggregates and averages we ignore these important differences in order to focus our attention on some important issues for the economy as a whole.

In return for suppressing some valuable detail, studying macroeconomics allows us to view the big picture. When aggregate output rises, the output of many commodities and the incomes of many people rise with it. When the unemployment rate rises, many workers suffer reductions in their incomes. When significant disruptions occur in the credit markets, interest rates rise and borrowers find it more difficult to finance their desired purchases. Such movements in economic aggregates matter for most individuals because they influence the health of the industries in which they work. These are the reasons why macroeconomic issues get airtime on the evening news, and why we study macroeconomics.

It will become clear as we proceed through this chapter (and later ones) that macroeconomists consider two different aspects of the economy. They think about the *short-run* behaviour of macroeconomic variables, such as output, employment, and inflation, and about how government policy can influence these variables. This concerns, among other things, the study of *business cycles*. They also examine the long-run behaviour of the same variables, especially the long-run path of aggregate output. This is the study of *economic growth* and is concerned with explaining how investment and technological change affect our material living standards over long periods of time.

> A full understanding of macroeconomics requires understanding the nature of short-run fluctuations as well as the nature of long-run economic growth.

Before we examine some key macroeconomic variables, it is worth pointing out that there are two different streams of research in macroeconomics, even though the researchers in the two groups are generally interested in understanding the same macroeconomic phenomena. The first group of researchers takes an approach to macroeconomics that is based explicitly on *microeconomic foundations*. These economists build models of the economy that are populated by workers, consumers, and firms, all of whom are assumed to be *optimizers*—that is, individuals are assumed to maximize their utility and firms are assumed to maximize their profits. Having explicitly modelled these agents' optimization problems, and their resulting choices for work effort, consumption, and investment, the economists proceed to *aggregate* the choices of these agents to arrive at the model's values for aggregate employment, consumption, output, and so on.

The second group of researchers builds macroeconomic models based only implicitly on these same micro foundations. Although they often analyze the behaviour of individuals and firms, they do not formally aggregate their behaviour to derive the aggregate relationships in their models. Instead, these economists construct their models by using aggregate relationships for consumption, investment, and employment, each of which has been subjected to extensive empirical testing and is assumed to represent collectively the behaviour of the many firms and consumers in the economy.

A second difference between these two approaches relates to the assumptions regarding the flexibility of wages and prices. Economists using the first approach usually assume that wages and prices are perfectly flexible and thus adjust quickly to clear their respective markets. In contrast, economists using the second approach usually assume that because of the nature of well-established institutions in both labour and product markets, such as labour unions, long-term employment contracts, or costs associated with changing prices, wages and prices are slow to adjust, and thus markets can be in disequilibrium for longer periods of time.

This textbook follows the second approach to macroeconomic analysis. The macro model we begin building in Chapter 21 is not formally derived from the behaviour of optimizing firms and consumers, although the macro relationships we introduce are well motivated by microeconomic behaviour. Moreover, the model begins in its simplest version by assuming *no* wage and price flexibility. But as we gradually make the model more complicated and also more realistic, we introduce some wage and price flexibility. In later chapters we will see that the degree of wage and price flexibility is crucial in determining how the economy responds to shocks of various kinds, including changes in government policy. We will also see that our macroeconomic model is sufficiently versatile that we can use it to illustrate the case of perfect wage/price flexibility as a special case.

19.1 Key Macroeconomic Variables

In this chapter, we discuss several important macroeconomic variables, with an emphasis on what they mean and why they matter for our well-being. Here and in Chapter 20 we also explain how the key macroeconomic variables are measured. The remainder of this book is about the causes and consequences of changes in each of these variables, the many ways in which they interact, and the effects they have on our well-being.

Output and Income

The most comprehensive measure of a nation's overall level of economic activity is the value of its total production of goods and services, called *national product*, or sometimes just called *output*.

> One of the most important ideas in economics is that the production of goods and services generates income.

As a matter of convention, economists define their terms so that, for the nation as a whole, all of the economic value that is produced ultimately belongs to someone in the form of an income claim on that value. For example, if a firm produces $100 worth of ice cream, that $100 becomes income for the firm's workers, the firm's suppliers of material inputs, and the firm's owners. The value of national product is *by definition* equal to the value of national income.

There are several related measures of a nation's total output and total income. Their various definitions, and the relationships among them, are discussed in detail in the next chapter. In this chapter, we use the generic term *national income* to refer to both the value of total output and the value of the income claims generated by the production of that output.

National Income: Aggregation To measure national income we add up the *values* of the many different goods and services that are produced. We cannot add tonnes of steel to loaves of bread, but we can add the dollar value of steel production to the dollar value of bread production. We begin by multiplying the number of units of each good produced by the price at which each unit is sold. This yields a dollar value of production for each good. We then sum these values across all the different goods produced in the economy to give us the quantity of total output, or national income, *measured in dollars*. This is usually called **nominal national income**.

A change in nominal national income can be caused by a change in either the physical quantities or the prices on which it is based. To determine the extent to which any change is due to quantities or to prices, economists calculate **real national income**. This measures the value of individual outputs, not at current prices, but at a set of prices that prevailed in some base period.

Nominal national income is often referred to as *current-dollar national income*. Real national income is often called *constant-dollar national income*. Real national income tells us the value of current output measured at constant prices—the sum of the quantities valued at prices that prevailed in the base period. Since prices are held constant when computing real national income, changes in real national income from one year to another reflect *only* changes in quantities. Comparing real national incomes of different years therefore provides a measure of the change in real output that has occurred during the intervening period.

National Income: Recent History One of the most commonly used measures of national income is called *gross domestic product (GDP)*. GDP can be measured in either real or nominal terms; we focus here on real GDP. The details of its calculation will be discussed in Chapter 20.

Part (i) of Figure 19-1 shows real national income produced by the Canadian economy since 1965; part (ii) shows its annual percentage change for the same period. The GDP series in part (i) shows two kinds of movement. The major movement is a positive trend that increased real output by approximately four times since 1965. This is what economists refer to as *long-term economic growth*.

A second feature of the real GDP series is *short-term fluctuations* around the trend. Overall growth so dominates the real GDP series that the fluctuations are hardly visible in part (i) of Figure 19-1. However, as can be seen in part (ii), the growth of GDP has never been smooth. In most years, GDP increases, but in 1982, 1991, and 2009, GDP actually decreased, as shown by the negative rate of growth in the figure. Periods in which real GDP actually falls are called **recessions**.

The **business cycle** refers to this continual ebb and flow of business activity that occurs around the long-term trend. For example, a single cycle will usually include an interval of quickly growing output, followed by an interval of slowly growing or even falling output. The entire cycle may last for several years. No two business cycles are exactly the same—variations occur in duration and magnitude. Some expansions are long and drawn out. Others come to an end before high employment and industrial capacity are reached. Nonetheless, fluctuations are systematic enough that it is useful to identify common factors, as is done in *Applying Economic Concepts 19-1*.

---

nominal national income Total national income measured in current dollars. Also called *current-dollar national income.*

real national income National income measured in constant (base-period) dollars. It changes only when quantities change.

To see the most recent values for most of the macroeconomic variables discussed in this chapter, go to Statistics Canada's website: www.statcan.gc.ca *and search for "Latest Indicators."*

recession A fall in the level of real GDP. Often defined precisely as two consecutive quarters in which real GDP falls.

business cycle Fluctuations of national income around its trend value that follow a more or less wavelike pattern.

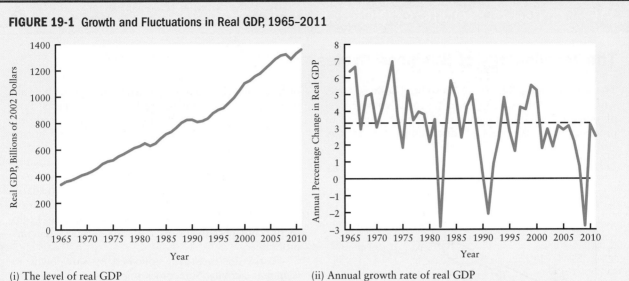

FIGURE 19-1 Growth and Fluctuations in Real GDP, 1965–2011

(i) The level of real GDP

(ii) Annual growth rate of real GDP

Real GDP measures the quantity of total output produced by the nation's economy over the period of a year. Real GDP is plotted in part (i). With only a few interruptions, it has risen steadily since 1965, demonstrating the long-term growth of the Canadian economy. Short-term fluctuations are obscured by the long-term trend in part (i) but are highlighted in part (ii). The growth rate fluctuates considerably from year to year. The long-term upward trend in part (i) reflects the positive average growth rate in part (ii), shown by the dashed line.

(*Source:* Adapted from Statistics Canada, CANSIM database, Table 380-0017, Gross Domestic Product. www.statcan. gc.ca. Search for "GDP.")

Potential Output and the Output Gap National output (or income) represents what the economy *actually* produces. An important related concept is the level of output the economy would produce if all resources—land, labour, and capital—were fully employed.[1] This concept is usually called **potential output**. The value of potential output must be estimated using statistical techniques whereas the value of actual output can be measured directly. For this reason, there is often disagreement among researchers regarding the level of potential output, owing to their different estimation approaches. In terms of notation, we use Y to denote the economy's actual output and Y^* to denote potential output.

The **output gap** measures the difference between potential output and actual output, and is computed as $Y - Y^*$. When actual output is less than potential output ($Y < Y^*$), the gap measures the market value of goods and services that are not produced because the economy's resources are not fully employed. When Y is less than Y^*, the output gap is called a **recessionary gap**. When actual output exceeds potential output ($Y > Y^*$), the gap measures the market value of production in excess of what the economy can produce on a sustained basis. Y can exceed Y^* because workers may work longer hours than normal or factories may operate an extra shift. When Y exceeds Y^* there is often upward pressure on prices, and thus we say the output gap is an **inflationary gap**.

potential output (Y^*) The real GDP that the economy would produce if its productive resources were fully employed. Also called *potential GDP*.

output gap Actual output minus potential output, $Y - Y^*$.

recessionary gap A situation in which actual output is less than potential output, $Y < Y^*$.

inflationary gap A situation in which actual output exceeds potential output, $Y > Y^*$.

---

[1] *Full employment* refers to a situation in which the factor markets display neither excess demand nor excess supply. We say more about full employment shortly.

The Terminology of Business Cycles

The accompanying figure shows a stylized business cycle, with real GDP fluctuating around a steadily rising level of potential GDP—the economy's normal capacity to produce output. We begin our discussion of terminology with a trough.

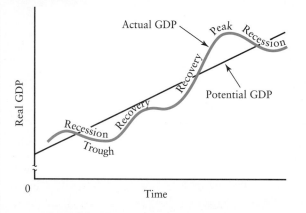

A *trough* is characterized by unemployed resources and a level of output that is low in relation to the economy's capacity to produce. There is a substantial amount of unused productive capacity. Business profits are low; for some individual companies, they are negative. Confidence about economic prospects in the immediate future is lacking, and, as a result, many firms are unwilling to risk making new investments.

The process of *recovery* moves the economy out of a trough. The characteristics of a recovery are many: rundown or obsolete equipment is replaced; employment, income, and consumer spending all begin to rise; and expectations become more favourable. Investments that once seemed risky may be undertaken as firms become more optimistic about future business prospects. Production can be increased with relative ease merely by re-employing the existing unused capacity and unemployed labour.

Eventually the recovery comes to a *peak* at the top of the cycle. At the peak, existing capacity is used to a high degree; labour shortages may develop, particularly in categories of key skills, and shortages of essential raw materials are likely. As shortages develop, costs begin to rise, but because prices rise also, business remains profitable.

Peaks are eventually followed by slowdowns in economic activity. Sometimes this is just a slowing of the rate of increase in income, while at other times the slowdown turns into a *recession*. A recession, or contraction, is a downturn in economic activity. Common usage defines a recession as a fall in real GDP for two successive quarters. As output falls, so do employment and households' incomes. Profits drop, and some firms encounter financial difficulties. Investments that looked profitable with the expectation of continually rising income now appear unprofitable. It may not even be worth replacing capital goods as they wear out because unused capacity is increasing steadily. In historical discussions, a recession that is deep and long lasting is often called a *depression*, such as the Great Depression in the early 1930s, during which aggregate output fell by 30 percent and the unemployment rate increased to 20 percent!

These terms are non-technical but descriptive: The entire falling half of the business cycle is often called a *slump*, and the entire rising half is often called a *boom*.

Figure 19-2 shows the path of potential GDP since 1985. The upward trend reflects the growth in the productive capacity of the Canadian economy over this period, caused by increases in the labour force, capital stock, and the level of technological knowledge. The figure also shows actual GDP (reproduced from Figure 19-1), which has kept approximately in step with potential GDP. The distance between the two, which is the output gap, is plotted in part (ii) of Figure 19-2. Fluctuations in economic activity are apparent from fluctuations in the size of the output gap.

Why National Income Matters National income is an important measure of economic performance. Short-run movements in the business cycle receive the most attention in politics and in the press, but most economists agree that long-term growth—as reflected by the growth of *potential GDP*—is in many ways the more important of the two.

FIGURE 19-2 Potential GDP and the Output Gap, 1985-2011

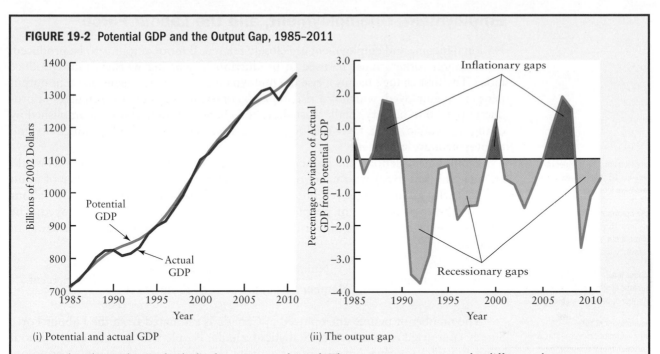

(i) Potential and actual GDP

(ii) The output gap

Potential and actual GDP both display an upward trend. The output gap measures the difference between an economy's potential output and its actual output; the gap is expressed here as a percentage of potential output. Since 1985, potential and actual GDP have almost doubled. The output gap in part (ii) shows clear fluctuations. Shaded areas show inflationary and recessionary gaps.

(*Source:* Real GDP: Statistics Canada, CANSIM database, Table 380-0017. Output gap: www.bankofcanada.ca. Potential output is based on author's calculations.)

Recessions are associated with unemployment and lost output. When actual GDP is below potential GDP, economic waste and human suffering result from the failure to fully employ the economy's resources. Booms, although associated with high employment and high output, can bring problems of their own. When actual GDP exceeds potential GDP, inflationary pressure usually ensues, causing concern for any government that is committed to keeping the inflation rate low.

The long-run trend in real per capita national income is an important determinant of improvements in a society's overall standard of living. When income per person grows, each generation can expect, on average, to be better off than preceding ones. For example, over the period shown in Figure 19-1, per capita income has grown at an average rate of about 1.5 percent per year. Even at such a modest growth rate, the average person's lifetime income will be about *twice* that of his or her grandparents.

Although economic growth makes people materially better off *on average*, it does not necessarily make *every* individual better off—the benefits of growth are never shared equally by all members of the population. For example, if growth involves significant changes in the structure of the economy, such as a shift away from agriculture and toward manufacturing (as happened in the first part of the twentieth century), or away from manufacturing toward some natural resources (as has been happening in recent years), then these changes will reduce some people's material living standards for extended periods of time.

Employment, Unemployment, and the Labour Force

National income and employment are closely related. If more output is to be produced, either more workers must be used in production or existing workers must produce more. The first change means a rise in employment; the second means a rise in output per person employed, which is a rise in *productivity*. In the short run, changes in productivity tend to be very small; most short-run changes in output are accomplished by changes in employment. Over the long run, however, changes in both productivity and employment are significant.

employment The number of persons 15 years of age or older who have jobs.

unemployment The number of persons 15 years of age or older who are not employed and are actively searching for a job.

labour force The number of persons employed plus the number of persons unemployed.

unemployment rate Unemployment expressed as a percentage of the labour force.

Employment denotes the number of adult workers (defined in Canada as workers aged 15 and over) who have jobs. **Unemployment** denotes the number of adult workers who are not employed but who are actively searching for a job. The **labour force** is the total number of people who are either employed or unemployed. The **unemployment rate** is the number of unemployed people expressed as a fraction of the labour force:

$$\text{Unemployment rate} = \frac{\text{Number of people unemployed}}{\text{Number of people in the labour force}} \times 100 \text{ percent}$$

The number of people unemployed in Canada is estimated from the Labour Force Survey conducted each month by Statistics Canada. People who are currently without a job but who say they have searched actively for one during the sample period are recorded as unemployed.

Frictional, Structural, and Cyclical Unemployment When the economy is at potential GDP, economists say there is *full employment*. But for two reasons there will still be some unemployment even when the economy is at potential GDP.

First, there is a constant turnover of individuals in given jobs and a constant change in job opportunities. New people enter the workforce; some people quit their jobs; others are fired. It may take some time for these people to find jobs. So at any point in time, there is unemployment caused by the normal turnover of labour. Such unemployment is called *frictional unemployment*.

Second, because the economy is constantly adapting to shocks of various kinds, at any moment there will always be some mismatch between the characteristics of the labour force and the characteristics of the available jobs. The mismatch may occur, for example, because labour does not currently have the skills that are in demand or because labour is not in the part of the country where the demand is located. This is a mismatch between the *structure* of the supplies of labour and the *structure* of the demands for labour. Such unemployment is therefore called *structural unemployment*.

Economists make the distinction between frictional, structural, and cyclical unemployment. This distinction is important for analyzing the economy but it matters little to the individual who has difficulty finding an appropriate job.

Even when the economy is at "full employment," some unemployment exists because of natural turnover in the labour market and mismatch between jobs and workers.

Full employment is said to occur when the *only* unemployment is frictional and structural, a situation that corresponds to actual GDP being equal to potential GDP. When actual GDP does not equal potential GDP, the economy is not at full employment. In these situations we say that there is some *cyclical* unemployment. Cyclical unemployment rises and falls with the ebb and flow of the business cycle. Unemployment also has *seasonal* fluctuations. For example, workers employed in the fishing industry often are unemployed during the winter, and ski instructors may be unemployed in the summer. Because these seasonal fluctuations are relatively regular and therefore easy to predict, Statistics Canada *seasonally adjusts* the unemployment statistics to remove these fluctuations, thereby revealing more clearly the cyclical and trend movements in the data. For example, suppose that, on average, the Canadian unemployment rate increases by 0.3 percentage points in December. Statistics Canada would then adjust the December unemployment rate so that it shows an increase only if the increase in the *unadjusted* rate exceeds 0.3 percentage points. In this way, the (seasonally adjusted) December unemployment rate is reported to increase only if unemployment rises by more than its normal seasonal increase. All the unemployment (and other macroeconomic) data shown in this book are seasonally adjusted.

Employment and Unemployment: Recent History Figure 19-3 shows the trends in the labour force, employment, and unemployment since 1960. Despite booms and slumps, employment has grown roughly in line with the growth in the labour force. Although the long-term trend dominates the employment data, the figure also shows that the short-term fluctuations in the unemployment rate have been substantial. The unemployment rate has been as low as 3.4 percent in 1966 and as high as 12 percent during the deep recession of 1982. Part (ii) of Figure 19-3 also shows that there has been a slight

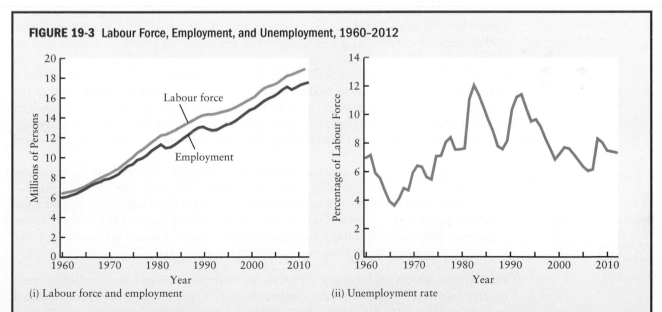

FIGURE 19-3 Labour Force, Employment, and Unemployment, 1960–2012

(i) Labour force and employment

(ii) Unemployment rate

The labour force and employment have grown since 1960 with only a few interruptions. The unemployment rate responds to the cyclical behaviour of the economy. The labour force and the level of employment in Canada have both almost tripled since 1960. Booms are associated with a low unemployment rate and slumps with a high unemployment rate.

(*Source:* These data are from Statistics Canada's CANSIM database, Table 282-002. Labour force: Series V2062810. Employment: Series V2062811. Unemployment rate is based on author's calculations. Current labour-force statistics are available on Statistics Canada's website at www.statcan.gc.ca by searching for "unemployment.")

upward trend in the unemployment rate over the past 50 years. In Chapter 31 we discuss how some structural changes in the economy can help explain this trend.

Why Unemployment Matters The social significance of unemployment is enormous because it involves economic waste and human suffering. Human effort is the least durable of economic commodities. If a fully employed economy has 18 million people who are willing to work, their services must either be used this year or wasted. When only 16 million people are actually employed, one year's potential output of 2 million workers is lost forever. In an economy in which there is not enough output to meet everyone's needs, such a waste of potential output is cause for concern.

The loss of income associated with unemployment is clearly harmful to individuals. In some cases, the loss of income pushes people into poverty. But this lost income does not capture the full cost of unemployment. A person's spirit can be broken by a long period of desiring work but being unable to find it. Research has shown that crime, mental illness, and general social unrest tend to be associated with long-term unemployment.

In the not-so-distant past, only personal savings, private charity, or help from friends and relatives stood between the unemployed and starvation. Today, employment insurance and social assistance ("welfare") have created a safety net, particularly when unemployment is for short periods, as is most often the case in Canada. However, when an economic slump lasts long enough, some unfortunate people exhaust their employment insurance and lose part of that safety net. Short-term unemployment can be a feasible though difficult adjustment for many; long-term unemployment can be a disaster.

Productivity

Figure 19-1 on page 477 shows that Canadian real GDP has increased relatively steadily for many years, reflecting steady growth in the country's productive capacity. This long-run growth has had three general sources. First, as shown in Figure 19-3, the level of employment has increased significantly. Rising employment generally results from a rising population, but at times is also explained by an increase in the proportion of the population that chooses to participate in the labour force. Second, Canada's stock of physical capital—the buildings, factories, and machines used to produce output—has increased more or less steadily over time. Third, *productivity* in Canada has increased in almost every year since 1960.

Productivity is a measure of the amount of output that the economy produces per unit of input. Since there are many inputs to production—land, labour, and capital—we can have several different measures of productivity. One commonly used measure is **labour productivity**, which is the amount of real GDP produced per unit of labour employed. The amount of labour employed can be measured either as the total number of employed workers or by the total number of hours worked.

labour productivity The level of real GDP divided by the level of employment (or total hours worked).

Productivity: Recent History Figure 19-4 shows two measures of Canadian labour productivity since 1976. The first is the amount of real GDP per employed worker (expressed in thousands of 2002 dollars). In 2011, real GDP per employed worker was $78 440. The second measure shows the amount of real GDP per *hour worked* (expressed in 2002 dollars). In 2011, real GDP per hour worked was $45.50.

The second measure is more accurate because the average number of hours worked per employed worker changes over time. In addition to fluctuating over the business cycle, it has shown a long-term decline, from just over 1850 hours per year in 1976 to just under 1700 hours per year in 2011. The second measure of productivity takes account of these changes in hours worked, whereas the first measure does not.

One pattern is immediately apparent for both measures of productivity. There has been a significant increase in labour productivity over the past three decades. Real GDP per employed worker increased by 39.4 percent from 1976 to 2011, an annual average growth rate of 0.95 percent. Real GDP per hour worked increased by 48.5 per cent over the same period, an annual average growth rate of 1.1 percent.

Why Productivity Matters Productivity growth is the single largest cause of rising material living standards over long periods of time. Over periods of a few years, changes in average real incomes have more to do with the ebb and flow of the business cycle than with changes in productivity; increases in employment during an economic recovery and reductions in employment during recessions explain much of the short-run movements in average real incomes. As is clear from Figure 19-1, however, these short-run fluctuations are dwarfed over the long term by the steady upward trend in real GDP—an upward trend that comes in large part from rising productivity.

Why is the real income for an average Canadian this year so much greater than it was for the average Canadian 50 or 100 years ago? Most of the answer lies in the fact that the Canadian worker today is vastly more productive than was his or her counterpart in the distant past. This greater productivity comes partly from the better physical capital with which Canadians now work and partly from their greater skills. The higher productivity for today's workers explains why their *real wages* (the purchasing power of their earnings) are so much higher than for workers in the past.

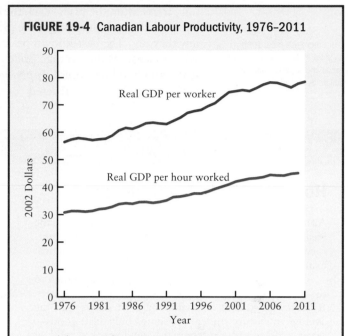

FIGURE 19-4 Canadian Labour Productivity, 1976–2011

Rising labour productivity is an important contributor to rising material living standards. The figure shows two measures of labour productivity: real GDP per employed worker and real GDP per hour worked. The first is expressed in *thousands* of 2002 dollars per worker and has increased at an average annual rate of 0.95 percent. The second is expressed in 2002 dollars per hour and has grown at the annual rate of 1.1 percent.

(*Source:* All data are based on author's calculations using Statistics Canada's CANSIM database. Real GDP: Table 380-0017. Total weekly hours worked: Table 282-0028. Employment: Table 282-0002.)

The close connection between productivity growth and rising material living standards explains the importance that is now placed on understanding the determinants of productivity growth. It is a very active area of economic research, but there are still many unanswered questions. In Chapter 26 we address the process of long-run growth in real GDP and explore the determinants of productivity growth.

Inflation and the Price Level

Inflation means that prices of goods and services are going up, *on average*. If you are a typical reader of this book, inflation has not been very noticeable during your lifetime. When your parents were your age, however, high inflation was a major economic problem. (Some countries have had their economies almost ruined by very high inflation, called *hyperinflation*. We will say more about this in Chapter 27.)

For studying inflation, there are two related but different concepts that are sometimes confused, and it is important to get them straight. The first is the **price level**, which refers to the average level of all prices in the economy and is given by the symbol P. The second is the rate of **inflation**, which is the rate at which the price level is rising.

price level The average level of all prices in the economy, expressed as an index number.

inflation A rise in the average level of all prices (the price level).

Consumer Price Index (CPI)
An index of the average prices of goods and services commonly bought by households.

To measure the price level, the economic statisticians at Statistics Canada construct a *price index*, which averages the prices of various commodities according to how important they are. The best-known price index in Canada is the **Consumer Price Index (CPI)**, which measures the average price of the goods and services that are bought by the typical Canadian household. *Applying Economic Concepts 19-2* shows how a price index such as the CPI is constructed.

APPLYING ECONOMIC CONCEPTS 19-2

How the CPI Is Constructed

Although the details are somewhat more complicated, the basic idea behind the Consumer Price Index is straightforward, as is illustrated by the following hypothetical example.

Suppose we want to discover what has happened to the overall cost of living for typical university students. A survey of student behaviour in 2003 shows that the average university student consumed only three goods—pizza, coffee, and photocopying—and spent a total of $200 a month on these items, as shown in Table 1.

TABLE 1 Expenditure Behaviour in 2003

Product	Price	Quantity per Month	Expenditure per Month
Photocopies	$0.10 per sheet	140 sheets	$14.00
Pizza	8.00 per pizza	15 pizzas	120.00
Coffee	0.75 per cup	88 cups	66.00
Total expenditure			$200.00

By 2013 in this example, the price of photocopying has fallen to 5 cents per copy, the price of pizza has increased to $9.00, and the price of coffee has increased to $1.00. What has happened to the cost of living over this 10-year period? In order to find out, we calculate the cost of purchasing the 2003 bundle of goods at the prices that prevailed in 2013, as shown in Table 2.

The total expenditure required to purchase the bundle of goods that cost $200.00 in 2003 has risen to $230.00. The increase in required expenditure is $30.00, which is a 15 percent increase over the original $200.00.

If we define 2003 as the base year for the "student price index" and assign an index value of 100 to the cost of the average student's expenditure in that year, the value of the index in 2013 is 115. Thus, goods and services that cost $100.00 in the base year cost $115.00 in 2013, exactly what is implied by Table 2.

TABLE 2 2003 Expenditure Behaviour at 2013 Prices

Product	Price	Quantity per Month	Expenditure per Month
Photocopies	$0.05 per sheet	140 sheets	$7.00
Pizza	9.00 per pizza	15 pizzas	135.00
Coffee	1.00 per cup	88 cups	88.00
Total expenditure			$230.00

The Consumer Price Index, as constructed by Statistics Canada, is built on exactly the same principles as the preceding example. In the case of the CPI, many thousands of consumers are surveyed, and the prices of thousands of products are monitored, but the basic method is the same:

1. Survey the consumption behaviour of consumers.
2. Calculate the cost of the goods and services purchased by the average consumer in the year in which the original survey was done. Define this as the base period of the index.
3. Calculate the cost of purchasing the same bundle of goods and services in other years.
4. Divide the result of Step 3 (in each year) by the result of Step 2, and multiply by 100. The result is the value of the CPI for each year.

The CPI is not a perfect measure of the cost of living because it does not automatically account for ongoing quality improvements or for changes in consumers' expenditure patterns. Changes of this type require the underlying survey of consumer expenditure to be updated from time to time to make sure that the expenditure patterns in the survey approximately match consumers' actual expenditure patterns.

As we saw in Chapter 2, a price index is a pure number—it does not have any units. Yet as we all know, prices in Canada are expressed in dollars. When we construct a price index, the units (dollars) are eliminated because the price index shows the price of a basket of goods at some specific time *relative to the price of the same basket of goods in some base period*. Currently, the base year for Statistics Canada's calculation of the CPI is 2002, which means that the price of the basket of goods is set to be 100 in 2002. If the CPI in 2013 is computed to be 123, the meaning is that the price of the basket of goods is 23 percent higher in 2013 than in 2002.

> Since the price level is measured with an index number, its value at any specific time has meaning only when it is compared with its value at some other time.

By allowing us to compare the general price level at different times, a price index, such as the CPI, also allows us to measure the rate of inflation. For example, the value of the CPI in April 2012 was 122.2 and in April 2011 it was 119.8. The *rate of inflation* during that one-year period, expressed in percentage terms, is equal to the change in the price level divided by the initial price level, times 100:

$$
\begin{aligned}
\text{Rate of inflation} \\
= \frac{122.2 - 119.8}{119.8} \times 100 \text{ percent} \\
= 2.0 \text{ percent}
\end{aligned}
$$

Inflation: Recent History The rate of inflation in Canada is currently around 2 percent per year and has been near that level since the early 1990s. But during the 1970s and 1980s inflation in Canada was both high and unpredictable from year to year. It was a serious macroeconomic problem.

Figure 19-5 shows the CPI and the inflation rate (measured by the annual rate of change in the CPI) from 1960 to 2012. What can we learn from this figure? First, we learn that the price level has not fallen at all since 1960 (in fact, the last time it fell was in 1953, and even then it fell only slightly). The cumulative effect of this sequence of repeated increases in the price level is quite dramatic: By 2012, the price level was more than six times as high as it was in 1960. In other words, you now pay more than $6 for what cost $1 in 1960. The second thing we learn is that, although the price level appears in the figure to be smoothly increasing, the rate of inflation is actually quite volatile. The increases in the inflation rate into double-digit levels in 1974 and 1979 were associated with major increases in the world prices of oil and foodstuffs and with loose monetary policy. The declines in inflation in the early 1980s and 1990s were delayed responses to major recessions, which were themselves brought about to a large extent by policy actions designed to reduce the existing inflation. (We will say much more about this in Chapters 29 and 30.)

Why Inflation Matters Money is the universal yardstick in our economy. This does not mean that we care only about money—it means simply that we measure *economic values* in terms of money, and we use money to conduct our economic affairs. Things as diverse as wages, share values in the stock market, the value of a house, and a university's financial endowment are all stated in terms of money. We value money, however, not for itself but for what we can purchase with it. The terms **purchasing power of money**

To compute the rate of inflation from any point in your lifetime to today, check out the "inflation calculator" at the Bank of Canada's website: www.bankofcanada.ca/en/rates/inflation_calc.htm.

purchasing power of money The amount of goods and services that can be purchased with a unit of money.

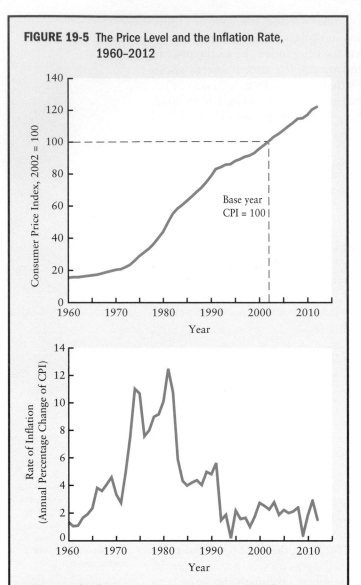

FIGURE 19-5 The Price Level and the Inflation Rate, 1960–2012

The rate of inflation measures the annual rate of increase in the price level. The trend in the price level has been upward over the past half-century. The rate of inflation has varied from almost 0 to more than 12 percent since 1960.

(*Source:* Based on author's calculations using data from Statistics Canada's CANSIM database: Series V41690973, monthly seasonally adjusted consumer price index. The figures shown are annual averages of the monthly data.)

and *real value of money* refer to the amount of goods and services that can be purchased with a given amount of money. The purchasing power of money is negatively related to the price level. For example, if the price level doubles, a dollar will buy only half as much, whereas if the price level halves, a dollar will buy twice as much. Inflation reduces the real value of anything whose *nominal value* is *fixed* in dollar terms. Thus, the real value of a $20 bill, a savings account, or the balance that is owed on a student loan is reduced by inflation.

> Inflation reduces the purchasing power of money. It also reduces the real value of any sum fixed in nominal (dollar) terms.

When analyzing the effects of inflation, economists usually make the distinction between *anticipated* and *unanticipated* inflation. If households and firms fully anticipate inflation over the coming year, they will be able to adjust many nominal prices and wages so as to maintain their real values. In this case, inflation will have fewer real effects on the economy than if it comes unexpectedly. For example, if both workers and firms expect 2 percent inflation over the coming year, they can agree to increase nominal wages by 2 percent, thus leaving wages constant in real terms.

Unanticipated inflation, on the other hand, generally leads to more changes in the real value of prices and wages. Suppose workers and firms expect 2 percent inflation and they increase nominal wages accordingly. If actual inflation ends up being 5 percent, real wages will be reduced and the quantities of labour demanded by firms and supplied by workers will change. As a result, the economy's allocation of resources will be affected more than when the inflation is anticipated.

> Anticipated inflation has a smaller effect on the economy than unanticipated inflation.

In reality, inflation is rarely fully anticipated or fully unanticipated. Usually there is some inflation that is expected but also some that comes as a surprise. As a result, some adjustments in wages and prices are made by firms, workers, and consumers, but not all the adjustments that would be required to leave the economy's allocation of resources unaffected. We will see later, in our discussions of monetary policy and inflation in Chapters 29 and 30, how the distinction between anticipated and unanticipated inflation helps us to understand the costs associated with *reducing* inflation.

Interest Rates

If a bank lends you money, it will charge you *interest* for the privilege of borrowing the money. If, for example, you borrow $1000 today, repayable in one year's time, you may also be asked to pay $6.67 per month in interest. This makes $80 in interest over the year, which can be expressed as an interest rate of 8 percent per annum.

The **interest rate** is the price that is paid to borrow money for a stated period of time. It is expressed as a percentage amount per year per dollar borrowed. For example, an interest rate of 8 percent per year means that the borrower must pay 8 cents per year for every dollar that is borrowed.

There are many interest rates. A bank will lend money to an industrial customer at a lower rate than it will lend money to you—there is a lower risk of not being repaid. The rate charged on a loan that is not to be repaid for a long time will usually differ from the rate on a loan that is to be repaid quickly.

When economists speak of "the" interest rate, they mean a rate that is typical of all the various interest rates in the economy. Dealing with only one interest rate suppresses much interesting detail. However, because interest rates usually rise and fall together, at least for major changes, following the movement of one rate allows us to consider changes in the general level of interest rates. The *prime interest rate*, the rate that banks charge to their best business customers, is noteworthy because when the prime rate changes, most other rates change in the same direction. Another high-profile interest rate is the *bank rate*, the interest rate that the Bank of Canada (Canada's central bank) charges on short-term loans to commercial banks such as the Royal Bank or the Bank of Montreal. The interest rate that the Canadian government pays on its short-term borrowing is also a rate that garners considerable attention.

Interest Rates and Inflation How does inflation affect interest rates? To begin developing an answer, imagine that your friend lends you $100 and that the loan is repayable in one year. The amount that you pay her for making this loan, measured in dollar terms, is determined by the **nominal interest rate**. If you pay her $108 in one year's time, $100 will be repayment of the amount of the loan (which is called the *principal*) and $8 will be payment of the interest. In this case, the nominal interest rate is 8 percent per year.

How much purchasing power has your friend gained or lost by making this loan? The answer depends on what happens to the price level during the year. The more the price level rises, the worse off your friend will be and the better the transaction will be for you. This result occurs because the more the price level rises, the less valuable are the dollars that you use to repay the loan. The **real interest rate** measures the return on a loan in terms of purchasing power.

If the price level remains constant over the year, the real rate of interest that your friend earns would also be 8 percent, because she can buy 8 percent more goods and services with the $108 that you repay her than with the $100 that she lent you.

interest rate The price paid per dollar borrowed per period of time, expressed either as a proportion (e.g., 0.06) or as a percentage (e.g., 6 percent).

nominal interest rate The price paid per dollar borrowed per period of time.

real interest rate The nominal rate of interest adjusted for the change in the purchasing power of money. Equal to the nominal interest rate minus the rate of inflation.

However, if the price level rises by 8 percent, the real rate of interest would be zero because the $108 that you repay her buys the same quantity of goods as the $100 that she originally gave up. If she is unlucky enough to lend money at 8 percent in a year in which prices rise by 10 percent, the real rate of interest that she earns is –2 percent. The repayment of $108 will purchase 2 percent fewer goods and services than the original loan of $100.

The burden of borrowing depends on the real, not the nominal, rate of interest.

For example, a nominal interest rate of 8 percent combined with a 2 percent rate of inflation (a real rate of 6 percent) is a much greater real burden on borrowers than a nominal rate of 16 percent combined with a 14 percent rate of inflation (a real rate of 2 percent). Figure 19-6 shows the nominal and real interest rates paid on short-term government borrowing since 1965.

Interest Rates and "Credit Flows" A loan represents a flow of credit between lenders and borrowers, with the interest rate representing the price of this credit. Credit is essential to the healthy functioning of a modern economy. Most firms require credit at some point—to finance the construction of a factory, to purchase inventories of intermediate inputs, or to continue paying their workers in a regular fashion even though their revenues may arrive at irregular intervals. Most households also require credit at various times—to finance the purchase of a home or car or to finance a child's university education.

Banks play a crucial role in the economy by *intermediating* between those households and firms that have available funds and those households and firms who require funds. In other words, banks play a key role in "making the credit market"—in channelling the funds from those who have them to those who need them.

During normal times, these credit markets function very smoothly and most of us notice little about them. While there are fluctuations in the price of credit (the interest rate), they tend to be relatively modest. In the fall of 2008, however, credit markets in the United States, Canada, and most other countries were thrown into turmoil by the sudden collapse of several large financial institutions, mainly in the United States and Europe. As a result, many banks became reluctant to lend to any but the safest borrowers, mostly out of fear that the borrowers would go bankrupt before they could repay the loan. The flows of credit slowed sharply and market interest rates spiked upward,

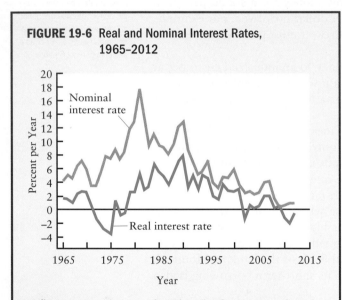

FIGURE 19-6 Real and Nominal Interest Rates, 1965–2012

Inflation over the past five decades has meant that the real interest rate has always been less than the nominal interest rate. The data for the nominal interest rate show the average rate on three-month Treasury bills in each year since 1965. The real interest rate is calculated as the nominal interest rate minus the actual rate of inflation over the same period. Through the early 1970s, the real interest rate was negative, indicating that the inflation rate exceeded the nominal interest rate. The 1980s saw real interest rates rise as high as 8 percent. Since then, real rates have declined again to levels that are closer to the long-term historical average. With the onset of the major global recession in 2008, both real and nominal interest rates fell below their long-term averages.

(*Source:* Nominal interest rate: 3-month Treasury bill rate, Statistics Canada, CANSIM database, Series V122541. Real interest rate is based on author's calculation of CPI inflation, using Series PCPISA from the Bank of Canada, www.bankofcanada.ca.)

reflecting the greater risk premium required by lenders. The reduction in the flow of credit was soon felt by firms who needed credit in order to finance material or labour inputs, and the effect was a reduction in production and employment. This *financial crisis*, by interrupting the vital flows of credit, was an important cause of the recession that enveloped the global economy in late 2008 and through 2009. We will discuss banking and the flow of credit in more detail in Chapter 27.

Why Interest Rates Matter Changes in real interest rates affect the standard of living of savers and borrowers. Many retirees, for example, rely on interest earnings from their stock of accumulated assets to provide much of their household income, and thus benefit when real interest rates rise. In contrast, borrowers are made better off with low real interest rates. This point was dramatically illustrated during the 1970s when homeowners who had long-term fixed-rate mortgages benefited tremendously from several years of high and largely unanticipated inflation, which resulted in *negative* real interest rates (see Figure 19-6).

Interest rates also matter for the economy as a whole. As we will see in Chapter 21, real interest rates are an important determinant of the level of investment by firms. Changes in real interest rates lead to changes in the cost of borrowing and thus to changes in firms' investment plans. Such changes in the level of desired investment have important consequences for the level of economic activity. We will see in Chapters 28 and 29 how the Bank of Canada influences interest rates as part of its objective of controlling inflation.

The International Economy

Two important variables reflecting the importance of the global economy to Canada are the *exchange rate* and *net exports*.

The Exchange Rate If you are going on a holiday to France, you will need euros to pay for your purchases. Many of the larger banks, as well as any foreign-exchange office, will make the necessary exchange of currencies for you; they will sell you euros in return for your Canadian dollars. If you get 0.77 euros for each dollar that you give up, the two currencies are trading at a rate of 1 dollar = 0.77 euros or, expressed another way, 1 euro = 1.30 dollars. This was, in fact, the actual rate of exchange between the Canadian dollar and the euro in June of 2012.

As our example shows, the exchange rate can be defined either as dollars per euro or euros per dollar. In this book we adopt the convention of defining the **exchange rate** between the Canadian dollar and any foreign currency as the number of Canadian dollars required to purchase one unit of foreign currency.

exchange rate The number of units of domestic currency required to purchase one unit of foreign currency.

> The exchange rate is the number of Canadian dollars required to purchase one unit of foreign currency.[2]

---

[2] The media often use a reverse definition of the exchange rate—the number of units of foreign currency that can be purchased with one Canadian dollar. It is up to the student, then, to examine carefully the definition that is being used by a particular writer or speaker. In this book the exchange rate is defined as the number of Canadian dollars required to purchase one unit of foreign currency because this measure emphasizes that foreign currency, like any other good or service, has a price in terms of Canadian dollars. In this case, the price has a special name—the exchange rate.

foreign exchange Foreign currencies that are traded on the foreign-exchange market.

foreign-exchange market The market in which different national currencies are traded.

depreciation A rise in the exchange rate—it takes more units of domestic currency to purchase one unit of foreign currency.

appreciation A fall in the exchange rate—it takes fewer units of domestic currency to purchase one unit of foreign currency.

The term **foreign exchange** refers to foreign currencies or claims on foreign currencies, such as bank deposits, cheques, and promissory notes, that are payable in foreign money. The **foreign-exchange market** is the market in which foreign exchange is traded—at a price expressed by the exchange rate.

Depreciation and Appreciation A rise in the exchange rate means that it takes *more* Canadian dollars to purchase one unit of foreign currency—this is a **depreciation** of the Canadian dollar. Conversely, a fall in the exchange rate means that it takes *fewer* Canadian dollars to purchase one unit of foreign currency—this is an **appreciation** of the dollar.

Figure 19-7 shows the path of the Canadian–U.S. exchange rate since 1970. Since more than 75 percent of Canada's trade is with the United States, this is the exchange rate most often discussed and analyzed in Canada. In countries with trade more evenly spread across several trading partners, more attention is paid to what is called a *trade-weighted exchange rate*—this is a weighted-average exchange rate between the home country and its trading partners, where the weights reflect each partner's share in the home country's total trade. In Canada, the path of such a trade-weighted exchange rate is virtually identical to the Canadian–U.S. exchange rate shown in Figure 19-7, reflecting the very large proportion of total Canadian trade with the United States.

As we will see in later chapters, both domestic policy and external events have important effects on the Canadian exchange rate. For example, most economists believe that the appreciation of the Canadian dollar between 1986 and 1992 was caused in part by the Bank of Canada's efforts to reduce the rate of inflation. The Bank's policy was controversial at the time, not least because of the effect it had on the exchange rate and the many export-oriented firms that were harmed by Canada's strong dollar. We examine the link between monetary policy and exchange rates in detail in Chapters 28 and 29.

The depreciation of the Canadian dollar in the late 1990s is thought by most economists to have resulted from a nearly 30 percent decline in the world prices of commodities, many of which are important Canadian exports. The appreciation of the Canadian dollar during the 2002–2012 period was associated with sharp increases in commodity prices. In both cases, the commodity prices were being driven by changes in global economic growth, illustrating the important point that events in faraway lands can have dramatic effects on the Canadian exchange rate. We examine the link between world commodity prices and the Canadian exchange rate in Chapter 35.

Exports and Imports Canada has long been a trading nation, buying many goods and

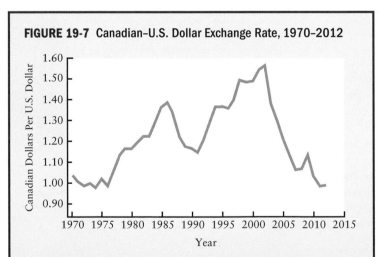

FIGURE 19-7 Canadian–U.S. Dollar Exchange Rate, 1970–2012

The Canadian–U.S. exchange rate has been quite volatile over the past 40 years. The Canadian-dollar price of one U.S. dollar increased from just over $1 in the early 1970s to over $1.55 in 2002, a long-term depreciation of the Canadian dollar. By 2012 the Canadian dollar had appreciated and it again cost about $1 to purchase one U.S. dollar.

(*Source:* Annual average of monthly data, Statistics Canada, CANSIM database, Series V37432.)

services from other countries—Canada's *imports*—and also selling many goods and services to other countries—Canada's *exports*. Figure 19-8 shows the dollar value of Canada's exports, imports, and *net exports* since 1970. Net exports are the difference between exports and imports and are often called the *trade balance*.

Canadian exports and imports have increased fairly closely in step with each other over the past 40 years. The trade balance has therefore fluctuated mildly over the years, but it has stayed relatively small, especially when viewed as a proportion of total GDP.

Also apparent in Figure 19-8 is that Canadian trade flows (both imports and exports) began to grow more quickly after 1990. The increased importance of international trade is largely due to the Canada–U.S. Free Trade Agreement, which began in 1989, and to the North American Free Trade Agreement (which added Mexico), which began in 1994. Note also the sharp decline in both exports and imports in 2009–2010, a result of the global economic recession that occurred at that time.

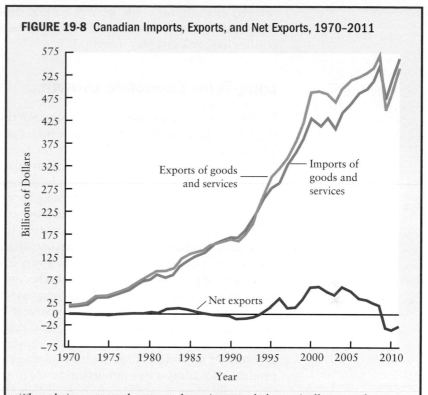

FIGURE 19-8 Canadian Imports, Exports, and Net Exports, 1970–2011

Though imports and exports have increased dramatically over the past 40 years, the trade balance has remained roughly in balance. The nominal values of imports and exports rose steadily over the past few decades because of both price increases and quantity increases. The growth of trade increased sharply after the early 1990s. The trade balance—net exports—is usually close to zero.

(*Source:* Statistics Canada, CANSIM database. Exports: Series V498103. Imports: Series V498106.)

19.2 Growth Versus Fluctuations

This chapter has provided a quick tour through macroeconomics and has introduced you to many important macroeconomic issues. If you take a few moments to flip again through the figures in this chapter, you will notice that most of the macroeconomic variables that we discussed are characterized by *long-run trends* and *short-run fluctuations*.

Figure 19-1 on page 477, which shows the path of real GDP, provides an excellent example of both characteristics. The figure shows that real GDP has increased by over four times since 1965—this is substantial *economic growth*. The figure also shows considerable year-to-year *fluctuations* in the growth rate of GDP.

An important theme in this book is that a full understanding of macroeconomics requires an understanding of both long-run growth and short-run fluctuations. As we proceed through this book, we will see that these two characteristics of modern economies have different sources and explanations. And the government's macroeconomic policies have roles to play in both.

Long-Term Economic Growth

Both total output and output per person have risen for many decades in most industrial countries. These long-term trends have meant rising average living standards. Although long-term growth gets less attention on the evening news than current economic developments, it has considerably more importance for a society's living standards from decade to decade and from generation to generation.

There is considerable debate regarding the ability of government policy to influence the economy's long-run rate of growth. Some economists believe that a policy designed to keep inflation low and stable will contribute to the economy's growth. Some, however, believe there are dangers from having inflation too low—that a moderate inflation rate is more conducive to growth than a very low inflation rate.

Many economists also believe that when governments spend less than they raise in tax revenue—and thus have a budget surplus—the reduced need for borrowing drives down interest rates and stimulates investment by the private sector. Such increases in investment imply a higher stock of physical capital available for future production and thus an increase in economic growth. Do government budget surpluses increase future growth? Or do budget surpluses have no effect at all on the economy's future ability to produce? We address this important debate in Chapter 32.

Finally, there is active debate regarding the appropriate role of the government in developing new technologies. Some economists believe that the private sector, left on its own, can produce a volume of inventions and innovation that will guarantee a satisfactory rate of long-term growth. Others point out that almost all of the major new technologies of the last 75 years were initially supported by public funds: The electronic computer was the creation of governments in the Second World War, miniaturized equipment came from the race to the moon, the Internet came from military communications research, the U.S. software industry was created by the U.S. Department of Defense, much of the early work on biotechnology came out of publicly funded research laboratories in universities and government institutions, and so on. The debate about the place of government in helping to foster inventions and innovations of truly fundamental technologies is an ongoing and highly important one.

Short-Term Fluctuations

Short-run fluctuations in economic activity, like the ones shown in part (ii) of Figure 19-1 (page 477), lead economists to wonder about the causes of *business cycles*. What caused the Great Depression in the 1930s, when almost one-fifth of the Canadian labour force was out of work and massive unemployment plagued all major industrial countries? Why did the Canadian economy begin a significant recession in 1990–1991, from which recovery was initially very gradual? What explains why, by 2007, the Canadian unemployment rate was lower than it had been in more than 30 years? What caused the deep worldwide recession that began in 2008?

Understanding business cycles requires an understanding of monetary policy—the Bank of Canada's policy with respect to the quantity of money that it makes available to the whole economy. Most economists agree that the increase in inflation in the 1970s and early 1980s was related to monetary policy, though they also agree that other events were partly responsible. When the Bank of Canada implemented a policy in the early 1990s designed to reduce inflation, was it merely a coincidence that a significant recession followed? Most economists think not, though they also think that the slowdown in the U.S. economy was an important contributor to Canada's recession. Chapters 28 and 29 focus on how the Bank of Canada uses its policy to influence the level of economic activity.

Government budget deficits and surpluses also enter the discussion of business cycles. Some economists think that, in recessionary years, the government ought to increase spending (and reduce taxes) in an effort to stimulate economic activity. Similarly, they believe that taxes should be raised to slow down a booming economy. Indeed, several government policies, from income taxation to employment insurance, are designed to mitigate the short-term fluctuations in national income. Other economists believe that the government cannot successfully "fine-tune" the economy by making frequent changes in spending and taxing because our knowledge of how the economy works is imperfect and because such policies tend to be imprecise. We address these issues in Chapters 22, 23, and 24.

What Lies Ahead?

There is much work to be done before any of these interesting policy debates can be discussed in more detail. Like firms that invest now to increase their production in the future, the next few chapters of this book will be an investment for you—an investment in understanding basic macro theory. The payoff will come when you are able to use a coherent model of the economy to analyze and debate some of the key macro issues of the day.

We begin in Chapter 20 by discussing the measurement of GDP. National income accounting is not exciting but is essential to a complete understanding of the chapters that follow. We then proceed to build a simple model of the economy to highlight some key macroeconomic relationships. As we proceed through the book, we modify the model, step by step, making it ever more realistic. With each step we take, more of today's controversial policy issues come within the grasp of our understanding. We hope that by the time you get to the end of the book, you will have developed some of the thrill for analyzing macroeconomic issues that we feel. Good luck, and enjoy the journey!

SUMMARY

19.1 Key Macroeconomic Variables

- The value of the total production of goods and services in a country is called its national product. Because production of output generates income in the form of claims on that output, the total is also referred to as national income. One of the most commonly used measures of national income is gross domestic product (GDP).
- Potential output is the level of output produced when factors of production are fully employed. The output

gap is the difference between actual and potential output.
- The unemployment rate is the percentage of the labour force not employed and actively searching for a job. The labour force and employment have both grown steadily for the past half-century. The unemployment rate fluctuates considerably from year to year. Unemployment imposes serious costs in the form of economic waste and human suffering.

- Labour productivity is measured as real GDP per employed worker (or per hour of work). It is an important determinant of material living standards.
- The price level is measured by a price index, which measures the cost of purchasing a set of goods in one year relative to the cost of the same goods in a base year. The inflation rate measures the rate of change of the price level. For almost 20 years, the annual inflation rate in Canada has been close to 2 percent.
- The interest rate is the price that is paid to borrow money for a stated period and is expressed as a percentage amount per dollar borrowed. The nominal interest rate is this price expressed in money terms; the real interest rate is this price expressed in terms of purchasing power.
- The flow of credit—borrowing and lending—is very important in a modern economy. Disruptions in the flow of credit can lead to increases in interest rates and reductions in economic activity.
- The exchange rate is the number of Canadian dollars needed to purchase one unit of foreign currency. A rise in the exchange rate is a depreciation of the Canadian dollar; a fall in the exchange rate is an appreciation of the Canadian dollar.

19.2 Growth Versus Fluctuations   LO 2

- Most macroeconomic variables have both long-run trends and short-run fluctuations. The sources of the two types of movements are different.
- Important questions for macroeconomics involve the role of policy in influencing long-run growth as well as short-run fluctuations.

KEY CONCEPTS

National product and national income
Real and nominal national income
Potential and actual output
The output gap
Employment, unemployment, and the labour force

Full employment
Frictional, structural, and cyclical unemployment
Labour productivity
The price level and the rate of inflation

Real and nominal interest rates
Interest rates and credit
The exchange rate
Depreciation and appreciation of the Canadian dollar
Exports, imports, and net exports

STUDY EXERCISES

MyEconLab   Make the grade with MyEconLab: Study Exercises marked in red can be found on MyEconLab. You can practise them as often as you want, and most feature step-by-step guided instructions to help you find the right answer.

1. Fill in the blanks to make the following statements correct.

   a. The value of total production of goods and services in Canada is called its _____. National _____ and national _____ are equal because all production generates a claim on its value in the form of income.

   b. In measuring Canada's total output, it would be meaningless to add together all goods and services produced during one year (i.e., 50 000 trucks plus 14 million dozen eggs plus 100 million haircuts, etc.). Instead, total output is measured in _____.

   c. The difference between nominal national income and real national income is that with the latter, _____ are held constant to enable us to see changes in _____.

   d. If all of Canada's resources—its land, labour, and capital—are "fully employed", then we say that Canada is producing its _____.

   e. The output gap measures the difference between _____ and _____. During booms, _____ is greater than _____; during recessions, _____ is less than _____.

2. Fill in the blanks to make the following statements correct.

   a. The labour force includes people who are _____ and people who are _____. The unemployment rate is expressed as the number of people who are _____ as a percentage of people in the _____.

   b. At any point in time, some people are unemployed because of the normal turnover of labour (new entrants to the labour force, job leavers, and job seekers). This unemployment is referred to as _____. Some people are said to be _____ unemployed because their skills do not match the skills necessary for the available jobs.

   c. Suppose 2002 is the base year in which the price of a basket of goods is set to be 100. If the price of the same basket of goods in 2013 is 137, then we can say that the price level is _____ and that the price of the basket of goods has increased by _____ percent between 2002 and 2013.

   d. Suppose Canada's CPI in May 2012 was 122.5 and in May 2013 was 125.1. The rate of inflation during that one-year period was _____ percent.

   e. The price that is paid to borrow money for a stated period of time is known as the _____.

   f. The real interest rate is equal to the nominal interest rate _____ the rate of inflation.

   g. The number of Canadian dollars required to purchase one unit of foreign currency is the _____ between the Canadian dollar and that foreign currency.

   h. A(n) _____ in the exchange rate reflects a depreciation of the Canadian dollar; a(n) _____ in the exchange rate reflects an appreciation of the Canadian dollar.

3. Consider the macroeconomic data shown below for a hypothetical country's economy.

Year	Real GDP Actual (billions of $)	Real GDP Potential (billions of $)	Output Gap (% of potential)	Unemployment Rate (% of labour force)
2005	1168	1188	—	11.1
2006	1184	1196	—	10.2
2007	1197	1205	—	9.1
2008	1211	1215	—	8.3
2009	1225	1225	—	7.6
2010	1240	1236	—	7.3
2011	1253	1247	—	7.1
2012	1262	1258	—	7.3
2013	1270	1270	—	7.6

   a. Compute the output gap for each year.
   b. Explain how GDP can exceed potential GDP.

   c. Does real GDP ever fall in the time period shown? What do economists call such periods?
   d. What is the unemployment rate when this economy is at "full employment"? What kind of unemployment exists at this time?

4. Consider the data shown below for the Canadian Consumer Price Index (CPI), drawn from the Bank of Canada's website.

Year	CPI (2002 = 100)	CPI Inflation (% change from previous year)
2000	95.4	2.7
2001	97.8	—
2002	—	2.3
2003	102.8	2.8
2004	104.7	—
2005	107.0	—
2006	—	2.0
2007	—	2.1
2008	114.1	2.4
2009	114.4	—
2010	—	1.8
2011	119.9	2.9

   a. Compute the missing data in the table.
   b. Do average prices ever fall in the time period shown? In which year do prices come closest to being stable?
   c. Across which two consecutive years is the rate of inflation closest to being stable?
   d. In a diagram with the price level on the vertical axis and time on the horizontal axis, illustrate the difference between a situation in which the price level is stable and a situation in which the rate of inflation is stable.

5. The data below show the nominal interest rate and the inflation rate for several developed economies as reported in The Economist in June 2012.

Country	Nominal Interest Rate (on 10-year government bonds)	Inflation Rate (% change in CPI from previous year)	Real Interest Rate
Australia	3.00	2.2	—
Canada	1.81	2.1*	—
Euro area	1.34	2.4	—
Japan	0.87	0.2	—
Switzerland	0.61	−0.3	—
U.K.	1.63	2.8	—
U.S.A.	1.65	2.2	—

a. Compute the real interest rate for each country, assuming that people expected the inflation rate at the time to persist.

b. If you were a lender, in which country would you have wanted to lend in June 2012? Explain.

c. If you were a borrower, in which country would you have wanted to borrow in June 2012? Explain.

6. Consider the following data drawn from *The Economist*. Recall that the Canadian exchange rate is the number of Canadian dollars needed to purchase one unit of some foreign currency.

Currency	Cdn Dollar Exchange Rate	
	June 2012	June 2011
U.S. dollar	1.03	0.98
Japanese yen	0.013	0.012
British pound	1.58	1.61
Swedish krona	0.14	0.16
Euro	1.29	1.44

a. Which currencies appreciated relative to the Canadian dollar from June 2011 to June 2012?

b. Which currencies depreciated relative to the Canadian dollar from June 2011 to June 2012?

c. Using the information provided in the table, can you tell whether the euro depreciated or appreciated *against the U.S. dollar* from June 2011 to June 2012? Explain.

7. As explained in the text, the unemployment rate is defined as:

Unemployment rate =
$$\frac{\text{Number of people unemployed}}{\text{Number of people in the labour force}} \times 100 \text{ percent}$$

a. Explain why people may decide to join the labour force during booms.

b. From part (a), explain why the unemployment rate might rise during a boom, even when the level of employment is also rising.

c. During a recession, suppose unemployed workers leave the labour force because they are discouraged about their inability to find a job. What happens to the unemployment rate?

d. "A declining unemployment rate is a clear positive sign for the economy." Comment.

8. Consider an imaginary 10-year period over which output per worker falls, but GDP increases. How can this happen? Do you think this is likely to be good for the economy?

9. When the Canadian dollar depreciates in foreign-exchange markets, many people view this as "good" for the Canadian economy. Who is likely to be harmed by and who is likely to benefit from a depreciation of the Canadian dollar?

The Measurement of National Income

CHAPTER OUTLINE

20.1 NATIONAL OUTPUT AND VALUE ADDED

20.2 NATIONAL INCOME ACCOUNTING: THE BASICS

20.3 NATIONAL INCOME ACCOUNTING: SOME FURTHER ISSUES

LEARNING OBJECTIVES (LO)

After studying this chapter you will be able to

1 see how the concept of value added solves the problem of "double counting" when measuring national income.

2 explain the income approach and the expenditure approach to measuring national income.

3 explain the difference between real and nominal GDP and understand the GDP deflator.

4 discuss the many important omissions from official measures of GDP.

5 understand why real per capita GDP is a good measure of average material living standards but an incomplete measure of overall well-being.

THIS chapter provides a detailed look at the measurement of national income. Once we know more precisely what is being measured and how it is measured, we will be ready to build a macroeconomic model to explain the determination of national income. Understanding how national income is measured is an important part of understanding how and why it changes. Indeed, this is a general rule of all economics and all science: Before using any data, it is essential to understand how those data are developed and what they measure.

20.1 National Output and Value Added

The central topic of macroeconomics is the overall level of economic activity—aggregate output and the income that is generated by its production. We start by asking: What do we mean by output?

This question may seem odd. Surely your local bakery knows what it produces. And if Air Canada or Imperial Oil or Bombardier does not know its own output, what does it know? If each firm knows the value of its total output, the national income statisticians simply have to add up each separate output value to get the nation's output—or is it really that simple?

Obtaining a total for the nation's output is not that simple because one firm's output is often another firm's input. The local baker uses flour that is the output of the flour milling company; the flour milling company, in turn, uses wheat that is the farmer's output. What is true for bread is true for most goods and services.

> Production occurs in stages: Some firms produce outputs that are used as inputs by other firms, and these other firms, in turn, produce outputs that are used as inputs by yet other firms.

If we merely added up the market values of all outputs of all firms, we would obtain a total greatly in excess of the value of the economy's actual output. Consider the example of wheat, flour, and bread. If we added the total value of the output of the wheat farmer, the flour mill, and the baker, we would be counting the value of the wheat three times, the value of the milled flour twice, and the value of the bread once.

The error that would arise in estimating the nation's output by adding all sales of all firms is called *double counting*. "Multiple counting" would actually be a better term because if we added up the values of all sales, the same output would be counted every time that it was sold by one firm to another. The problem of double counting could in principle be solved by distinguishing between two types of output. **Intermediate goods** are outputs of some firms that are used as inputs by other firms. **Final goods** are products that are not used as inputs by other firms, at least not in the period of time under consideration.

If the firms' sales could be easily disaggregated into sales of final goods and sales of intermediate goods, then measuring total output would be straightforward. It would simply be obtained by summing the value of all *final* goods produced by firms. However, when Stelco sells steel to the Ford Motor Company, it does not care, and usually does not know, whether the steel is for final use (say, construction of a warehouse that will not be sold by Ford) or for use as part of an automobile that will be sold again. Even in our earlier example of bread, a bakery cannot be sure that its sales are for final use, for the bread may be further "processed" by a restaurant prior to its final sale to a customer. In general, it is extremely difficult if not impossible to successfully distinguish final from intermediate goods. The problem of double counting must therefore be resolved in some other manner.

To avoid double counting, economists use the concept of **value added**, which is the amount of value that firms and workers add to their products over and above the costs of purchased intermediate goods. An individual firm's value added is

$$\text{Value added} = \text{Sales revenue} - \text{Cost of intermediate goods}$$

intermediate goods All outputs that are used as inputs by other producers in a further stage of production.

final goods Goods that are not used as inputs by other firms but are produced to be sold for consumption, investment, government, or export during the period under consideration.

value added The value of a firm's output minus the value of the inputs that it purchases from other firms.

Consider an example of a steel mill. A steel mill's value added is the revenue it earns from selling the steel it produces minus the cost of the ore that it buys from the mining company, the cost of the electricity and fuel oil that it uses, and the costs of all other inputs that it buys from other firms.

We have said that a firm's value added equals its sales revenue minus the cost of intermediate goods *purchased from other firms*. Payments made to factors of production, such as the wages paid to workers or the profits paid to owners, are not purchases from other firms and hence are not subtracted from the firm's revenue when computing value added. But since the firm's revenue must be fully exhausted by the cost of intermediate goods *plus* all payments to factors of production, it follows that value added is exactly equal to the sum of these factor payments.[1]

Value added = Payments owed to the firm's factors of production

> **Value added is the correct measure of each firm's contribution to total output—the amount of market value that is produced by that firm.**

The firm's value added is the *net value* of its output. It is this net value that is the firm's contribution to the nation's total output, representing the firm's own efforts that add to the value of what it takes in as inputs. The concept of value added is further illustrated in *Applying Economic Concepts 20-1*. In this simple example, as in all more

APPLYING ECONOMIC CONCEPTS 20-1

Value Added Through Stages of Production

Because the output of one firm often becomes the input of other firms, the total value of goods sold by all firms greatly exceeds the value of the output of final products. This general principle is illustrated by a simple example in which a mining company starts from scratch and produces iron ore valued at $1000; this firm's value added is $1000. The mining company then sells the iron ore to a different firm that produces steel valued at $1500. The steel producer's value added is $500 because the value of the goods is increased by $500 as a result of the firm's activities. Finally, the steel producer sells the steel to a metal fabricator who transforms the steel into folding chairs valued at $1800; the metal fabricator's value added is $300.

We find the value of the final goods, $1800, either by counting only the sales of the last firm or by taking the sum of the values added by each firm. This value is much smaller than the $4300 that we would obtain if we merely added up the market value of the output sold by each firm.

	Mining Company	Steel Producer	Metal Fabricator	All Firms	
Transactions at Three Different Stages of Production					
A. Purchases from other firms	$ 0	$1000	$1500	$2500	Total interfirm sales
B. Payments to factors of production	1000	500	300	1800	Total value added
A + B = value of product	$1000	$1500	$1800	$4300	Total value of all sales

---

[1] We are ignoring here the role of indirect taxes, such as provincial sales taxes or the Goods and Services Tax (GST). Such taxes are included in the market value of a firm's output, but these taxes are remitted to the government and do not represent a payment to factors of production.

complex cases, the value of the nation's total output is obtained by summing all the individual values added.

> The sum of all values added in an economy is a measure of the economy's total output.

20.2 National Income Accounting: The Basics

The measures of national income and national product that are used in Canada derive from an accounting system called the National Income and Expenditure Accounts (NIEA), which are produced by Statistics Canada. These accounts are not simply collections of economic data. They have a logical structure, based on the simple yet important idea of the circular flow of income, which you first saw in Chapter 1 and which is shown again in Figure 20-1. The figure shows the overall flows of national income and expenditure and also how government, the financial system, and foreign countries enter the flows. The key point from the circular flow is as follows:

> The value of domestic output is equal to the value of the expenditure on that output and is also equal to the total income claims generated by producing that output.

gross domestic product (GDP) The total value of goods and services produced in the economy during a given period.

The circular flow of income suggests three different ways of measuring national income. The first is simply to add up the value of all goods and services produced in the economy. This requires the concept of value added, which we discussed in the previous section. The remaining two approaches correspond to the two "halves" of the circular flow of income and are the ones most commonly used by Statistics Canada and other countries' national statistical agencies. One approach is to add up the total flow of *expenditure* on final domestic output; the other is to add up the total flow of *income* generated by the flow of domestic production. All three measures yield the same total, which is called **gross domestic product** (GDP). When GDP is calculated by adding up total expenditure for each of the main components of final output, the result is called *GDP on the expenditure side*. When GDP is calculated by adding up all the income claims generated by the act of production, it is called *GDP on the income side*.

The conventions of double-entry bookkeeping require that the value of all production must be accounted for by a claim that someone has to that value. Thus, the two values calculated from the income and the expenditure sides are identical conceptually and differ in practical measurements only because of errors of measurement. Any discrepancy arising from such errors is then reconciled so that one common total is given as *the* measure of GDP. Both calculations are of interest, however, because each gives a different and useful breakdown. Also, having these two independent ways of measuring the same quantity provides a useful check on statistical procedures and on errors in measurement.

FIGURE 20-1 The Circular Flow of Expenditure and Income ☀

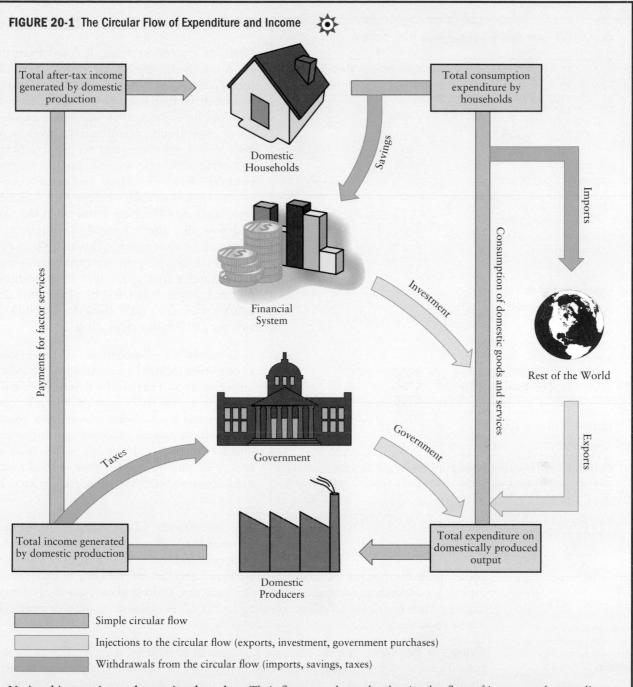

Simple circular flow

Injections to the circular flow (exports, investment, government purchases)

Withdrawals from the circular flow (imports, savings, taxes)

National income is equal to national product. Their flows are shown by the circular flow of income and expenditure. Consider first only the red lines. In this case, the flow would be a simple circle from households to producers and back to households. Now add the blue and green lines. The blue lines represent *injections* to the circular flow (exports, investment, and government purchases), while the green lines represent *withdrawals* from the circular flow (imports, saving, and taxes). Injections and withdrawals complicate the picture but do not change the basic relationship: Domestic production creates an income claim on the value of that production. When all the income claims are correctly added up, they must equal the total value of production.

TABLE 20-1 GDP from the Expenditure Side, 2011

Category	Billions of Dollars	Percent of GDP
Consumption		
Durable goods	113.7	
Semi-durable goods	72.6	
Non-durable goods	240.3	
Services	556.0	
	982.6	57.1
Investment		
Plant and equipment	201.9	
Residential structures	118.5	
Inventories	4.7	
	325.1	18.9
Government Purchases		
Current expenditure	367.6	
Investment	67.0	
	434.6	25.2
Net Exports		
Exports of goods and services	535.7	
Imports of goods and services	−556.7	
	−21.0	−1.2
Statistical Discrepancy	−0.5	0.0
Total GDP	1720.7	100.0

GDP measured from the expenditure side of the national accounts gives the size of the major components of aggregate expenditure.

(*Source:* Statistics Canada, "Gross Domestic Product, Expenditure-based, 2011," CANSIM database, Table 380-0017. Available at www.statcan.gc.ca.)

GDP from the Expenditure Side

GDP for a given year is calculated from the expenditure side by adding up the expenditures needed to purchase the final output produced in that year. Total expenditure on final output is the sum of four broad categories of expenditure: consumption, investment, government purchases, and net exports. In the following chapters, we will discuss in considerable detail the causes and consequences of movements in each of these four expenditure categories. Here we define what they are and how they are measured. Throughout, it is important to remember that these four categories of expenditure are exhaustive—they are *defined* in such a way that all expenditure on final output falls into one of the four categories. Canadian GDP from the expenditure side for 2011 is shown in Table 20-1.

1. Consumption Expenditure Consumption **expenditure** includes expenditure on all goods and services sold to their final users during the year. It includes services, such as haircuts, dental care, and legal advice; non-durable goods, such as fresh vegetables, clothing, cut flowers, and fresh meat; and durable goods, such as cars, TVs, and air conditioners. *Actual* measured consumption expenditure is denoted by the symbol C_a.

2. Investment Expenditure Investment **expenditure** is expenditure on goods not for present consumption, including inventories of goods made but not yet sold and of inputs purchased but not yet used in production; capital goods, such as factories, computers, machines, and warehouses; and residential housing. Such goods are called *investment goods.* Let's examine these three categories in a little more detail.

Changes in Inventories. Almost all firms hold stocks of their inputs and their own outputs. These stocks are called **inventories.** Inventories of inputs and unfinished materials allow firms to maintain a steady stream of production despite interruptions in the deliveries of inputs bought from other firms. Inventories of outputs allow firms to meet orders despite fluctuations in the rate of production.

The accumulation of inventories during any given year counts as positive investment for that year because it represents goods produced but not used for current consumption. These goods are included in the national income accounts at market value, which includes the wages and other costs that the firm incurred in producing them as well as the profit that the firm expects to make when they are sold in the future. The drawing down of inventories, often called *decumulation*, counts as disinvestment (negative

consumption expenditure
Household expenditure on all goods and services. Represented by the symbol *C*.

investment expenditure
Expenditure on the production of goods not for present consumption. Represented by the symbol *I*.

inventories Stocks of raw materials, goods in process, and finished goods held by firms to mitigate the effect of short-term fluctuations in production or sales.

investment) because it represents a reduction in the stock of finished goods that are available to be sold.

New Plant and Equipment. All production uses capital goods, which are manufactured aids to production, such as tools, machines, computers, vehicles, and factory buildings. The economy's total quantity of capital goods is called the **capital stock.** This is often called "plant and equipment," although the term refers to any manufactured aid to production used by firms. Creating new capital goods is an act of investment and is called *business fixed investment,* often shortened to **fixed investment.**

capital stock The aggregate quantity of capital goods.

fixed investment The creation of new plant and equipment.

New Residential Housing. A house or an apartment building is a durable asset that yields its utility over a long period of time. Because such an asset meets the definition of investment that we gave earlier, housing construction—the building of a *new* house—is counted as investment expenditure rather than as consumption expenditure. However, when an individual purchases an existing house from a builder or from another individual, the ownership of an existing asset is simply transferred, and the transaction is not part of national income. Only when a new house is built does it appear as residential investment in the national accounts.

Gross and Net Investment. The total investment that occurs in the economy is called *gross investment.* Gross investment is divided into two parts: replacement investment and net investment. Replacement investment is the amount of investment required to replace that part of the capital stock that loses its value through wear and tear; this loss in value is called **depreciation.** Net investment is equal to gross investment minus depreciation:

depreciation The amount by which the capital stock is depleted through the production process.

$$\text{Net investment} = \text{Gross investment} - \text{Depreciation}$$

When net investment is positive, the economy's capital stock is growing. If net investment is negative—which rarely happens—the economy's capital stock is shrinking.

All investment goods are part of the nation's total current output, and their production creates income whether the goods produced are a part of net investment or are merely replacement investment. Thus, all of gross investment is included in the calculation of national income. *Actual* total investment expenditure is denoted by the symbol I_a.

3. Government Purchases When governments provide goods and services that households want, such as street-cleaning and firefighting, they are adding to the sum total of valuable output in the economy. With other government activities, the case may not seem so clear. Should expenditures by the federal government to send soldiers overseas, or to pay a civil servant to refile papers from a now-defunct department, be regarded as contributions to national income?

government purchases All government expenditure on currently produced goods and services, exclusive of government transfer payments. Represented by the symbol *G*.

National income statisticians do not speculate about such matters. Instead they include all **government purchases** of goods and services as part of national income (some of which is government expenditure on investment goods). *Actual* government purchases of goods and services are denoted G_a.

Cost Versus Market Value. Government output is typically valued at cost rather than at market value. In many cases, there is really no choice. What, for example, is the market value of the law courts or of police protection or of the economic analysis done by economists at the

Unsold merchandise becomes part of firms' inventories. In national-income accounting, firms' expenditures on inventories are considered one part of investment expenditure.

Department of Finance? No one knows. But since we do know what it costs the government to provide these services, we value them at their cost of production.

Although valuing at cost is the only possible way to measure many government activities, it does have one curious consequence. If, because of an increase in productivity, one civil servant now does what two used to do, and the displaced worker shifts to the private sector, the government's measured contribution to national income will fall (but the private sector's contribution will rise). Conversely, if two workers now do what one worker used to do, the government's contribution will rise. Both changes could occur even though what the government actually produces has not changed. This is an inevitable but curious consequence of measuring the value of the government's output by the cost of producing it.

Government Purchases Versus Government Expenditure. Only government *purchases* of currently produced goods and services are included as part of GDP. As a result, a great deal of government spending does *not* count as part of GDP. For example, when the government makes payments to a retired person through the Canada Pension Plan, there is no market transaction involved as the government is not purchasing any currently produced goods or services from the retiree. The payment itself does not add to total output. The same is true of payments for employment insurance and welfare, and interest on the national debt (which transfers income from taxpayers to holders of government bonds). These are examples of **transfer payments**, which are government expenditures that are not made in return for currently produced goods and services. They are not a part of expenditure on the nation's total output and are therefore not included in GDP. (Of course, the recipients of transfer payments often choose to spend their money on consumption goods. Such expenditure then counts in the same way as any other consumption expenditure.)

transfer payments Payments to an individual or institution not made in exchange for a good or service.

4. Net Exports The fourth category of aggregate expenditure arises from foreign trade. How do imports and exports influence national income? **Imports** are domestic expenditure on foreign-produced goods and services, whereas **exports** are foreign expenditure on domestically produced goods and services.

imports The value of all domestically produced goods and services purchased from firms, households, or governments in other countries.

exports The value of all goods and services sold to firms, households, and governments in other countries.

Exports. If Canadian firms sell goods to German households, the goods are part of German consumption expenditure but constitute expenditure *on Canadian output*. Indeed, all goods and services that are produced in Canada and sold to foreigners must be counted as part of Canadian production and income; they are produced in Canada, and they create incomes for the Canadian residents who produce them. They are not purchased by Canadian residents, however, so they are not included as part of C_a, I_a, or G_a. Therefore, to arrive at the total value of expenditure *on Canadian output*, it is necessary to add in the value of Canadian exports of goods and services. The value of actual exports is denoted X_a.

Imports. If you buy a car that was made in Japan, only a small part of that value will represent expenditure on Canadian production. Some of it represents payment for the services of the Canadian dealers and for transportation; the rest is expenditure on Japanese products. If you take your next vacation in Italy, much of your expenditure will be on goods and services produced in Italy and thus will contribute to Italian GDP rather than to Canadian GDP.

Similarly, when a Canadian firm makes an investment expenditure on a machine that was made partly with imported raw materials, only part of the expenditure is on Canadian production; the rest is expenditure on foreign production. The same is true for government expenditure on such things as roads and dams; some of the expenditure is for imported materials, and only part of it is for domestically produced goods and services. The same is also true for exports, most of which use some imported inputs in their production process.

Consumption, investment, government purchases, and exports all have an import content. To arrive at total expenditure *on Canadian products*, we need to subtract from total Canadian expenditure the economy's total expenditure on imports. The value of actual imports is given the symbol IM_a.

It is customary to group actual imports and actual exports together as **net exports**. Net exports are defined as total exports minus total imports $(X_a - IM_a)$, which is also denoted NX_a. When the value of Canadian exports exceeds the value of Canadian imports, net exports are positive. When the value of imports exceeds the value of exports, net exports are negative.

net exports The value of total exports minus the value of total imports. Represented by the symbol *NX*.

Total Expenditures Gross domestic product measured from the expenditure side is equal to the sum of the four major expenditure categories that we have just discussed. In terms of a simple equation, we have

$$\text{GDP} = C_a + I_a + G_a + (X_a - IM_a)$$

These data are shown in Table 20-1 for Canada in 2011, including some data on the expenditure in the various subcategories.

> Measured from the expenditure side, GDP is equal to the total expenditure on domestically produced output. GDP is equal to $C_a + I_a + G_a + NX_a$.

GDP from the Income Side

As we said earlier, the conventions of national income accounting ensure that the production of a nation's output generates income *exactly* equal to the value of that production. Labour must be employed, land must be rented, and capital must be used. The calculation of GDP from the income side involves adding up factor incomes and other claims on the value of output until all of that value is accounted for.

1. Factor Incomes National income accountants distinguish three main components of factor incomes: wages and salaries, interest, and business profits (which includes rent received by property owners).

Wages and Salaries. Wages and salaries are the payment for the services of labour and they include all pre-tax labour earnings: take-home pay, income taxes withheld, employment-insurance contributions, pension-fund contributions, and other employee benefits. In total, wages and salaries represent the part of the value of production that is paid to labour.

Interest. Interest includes interest that is earned on bank deposits, interest that is earned on loans to firms, and miscellaneous other investment income (but excludes interest income earned from loans to Canadian governments).[2]

---

[2] The treatment of interest in the national accounts is a little odd. Interest paid by the government is considered a transfer payment, whereas interest paid by private households or firms is treated as expenditure (and its receipt is counted as a factor payment). This is only one example of arbitrary decisions in national income accounting. Others are discussed in *Extensions in Theory 20-1* on page 508.

Business Profits. Some profits are paid out as *dividends* to owners of firms; the rest are held by firms and are called *retained earnings*. Both dividends and retained earnings are included in the calculation of GDP. For accounting purposes, total profits include corporate profits, incomes of unincorporated businesses (mainly small businesses, farmers, partnerships, and professionals), rent paid on land and buildings, and profits of government business enterprises and Crown corporations (such as Canada Post and Export Development Canada).

Profits and interest together represent the payment for the use of capital—interest for borrowed capital and profits for capital contributed by the owners of firms.

Net Domestic Income. The sum of wages and salaries, interest, and profits is called *net domestic income at factor cost.* It is "net" because it excludes the value of output that is used as replacement investment. It is "domestic income" because it is the income accruing to domestic factors of production. It is "at factor cost" because it represents only that part of the value of final output that accrues to factors in the form of payments due to them for their services. As we will see next, some part of the value of final output does not accrue to the factors at all.

2. Non-factor Payments Every time a consumer spends $10 on some item, less than $10 is generated as income for factors of production. This shortfall is due to the presence of indirect taxes and depreciation.

Indirect Taxes and Subsidies. An important claim on the market value of output arises out of indirect taxes, which are taxes on the production and sale of goods and services. In Canada, the most important indirect taxes are provincial sales taxes, excise taxes on specific products, and the federal Goods and Services Tax (GST).

For example, if a good's market price of $10.00 includes 60 cents in provincial sales taxes and 50 cents in federal GST, only $8.90 is available as income to factors of production. Governments are claiming $1.10 of the $10.00 initial value of the good. Adding up income claims to determine GDP therefore necessitates including the portion of the total market value of output that is the governments' claims exercised through their taxes on goods and services.

Sometimes the government gives subsidies to firms, which act like negative taxes. When these occur, it is necessary to *subtract* their value, since they allow factor incomes to *exceed* the market value of output. Suppose a municipal bus company spends $150 000 providing bus rides and covers its costs by selling $140 000 in fares and obtaining a $10 000 subsidy from the local government. The total income that the company will generate from its production is $150 000, but the total market value of its output is only $140 000, with the difference made up by the subsidy. To get from total factor income to the market value of its total output, we must subtract the amount of the subsidy.

Depreciation. Another claim on the value of final output is depreciation. As we said earlier, depreciation is the loss in the value of physical capital generated by wear and tear during the production process. It is part of gross profits, but because it is needed to compensate for capital used up in the process of production, it is not part of net profits. Hence, depreciation is not income earned by any factor of production.

Total National Income The various components of the income side of the GDP in the Canadian economy in 2011 are shown in Table 20-2. Note that one of the terms in the table is called *statistical discrepancy*, a term that appears with equal magnitude but opposite sign in Table 20-1. This is a "fudge factor" to make sure that the independent measures of income and expenditure come to the same total. Statistical discrepancy is a clear indication that national income accounting is not error-free. Although national income and national expenditure are conceptually identical, in practice both are measured with slight error.

From the income side, GDP is the sum of factor incomes *plus* indirect taxes (net of subsidies) *plus* depreciation.

We have now seen the two commonly used methods for computing a country's national income. Both are correct and give us the same measure of GDP, but each gives us some different additional information. For some questions, such as what will be the likely future path of the nation's capital stock, it is useful to know the relative importance of consumption and investment. In this case, the expenditure approach for computing GDP provides some of the necessary information (Table 20-1 on page 502). For other questions, such as what is happening to the distribution of income between labour and capital, we need information about the composition of factor incomes. In this case, a useful starting point would be to examine GDP on the income side (Table 20-2).

Measuring national income is not problem-free. As in any accounting exercise, many arbitrary rules must be used. Some of them seem odd, but the important thing is that these rules be used consistently over time. Comparisons of GDP over time will then reflect genuine changes in economic activity, which is what we desire for the measure. *Extensions in Theory 20-1* discusses the issue of arbitrariness in national income accounting.

TABLE 20-2 GDP from the Income Side, 2011

Category	Billions of Dollars	Percent of GDP
Factor Incomes		
Wages, salaries, and supplementary income	889.5	51.7
Interest and miscellaneous investment income	73.8	4.3
Business profits (including rent and net income of farmers and unincorporated businesses)	336.7	19.5
Net Domestic Income at Factor Cost	1300.0	75.5
Non-factor Payments		
Depreciation	240.3	14.0
Indirect taxes less subsidies	178.0	10.5
Statistical Discrepancy	0.5	0.0
Total	1720.7	100.0

GDP measured from the income side of the national accounts gives the sizes of the major components of the income generated by producing the nation's output.

(*Source:* Statistics Canada, "Gross Domestic Product, Income-based, 2011," CANSIM database, Table 380-0001. Available at www.statcan.gc.ca.)

20.3 National Income Accounting: Some Further Issues

Now that we have examined the basics of national income accounting, we are ready to explore some more detailed issues. We discuss the distinction between GDP and the related concept of gross national product (GNP), the difference between real and nominal GDP, the major omissions from measured GDP, and the connection between GDP and "living standards."

EXTENSIONS IN THEORY 20-1

Arbitrary Decisions in National Income Accounting

National income accounting practices contain many arbitrary decisions. For example, goods that are finished and held in inventories are valued at market value, thereby anticipating their sale, even though the actual selling price may not be known. In the case of a Ford in a dealer's showroom, this practice may be justified because the *value* of this Ford is perhaps virtually the same as that of an identical Ford that has just been sold to a customer. However, what is the correct market value of a half-finished house or an unfinished novel? Accountants arbitrarily treat goods in process at cost (rather than at market value) if the goods are being made by firms. They ignore completely the value of the unfinished novel. The arbitrary nature of these decisions is inevitable: Because people must arrive at some practical compromise between consistent definitions and measurable magnitudes, any decision will be somewhat arbitrary.

Such arbitrary decisions surely affect the size of measured GDP. But does it matter? The surprising answer, for many purposes, is no. It is wrong to think that just because a statistical measure is imperfect (as all statistical measures are), it is useless. Simple measures often give estimates that are quite accurate, and substantial improvements in sophistication may make only trivial improvements in these estimates.

In 2011, for example, Canadian GDP was measured as $1720.7 billion. It is certain that the market value of all production in Canada in that year was neither $500 billion nor $2500 billion, but it might well have been $1600 billion or $1800 billion had different measures been defined with different arbitrary decisions built in. Similarly, Canadian per capita GDP is about three times the Mexican per capita GDP and is about 20 percent less than U.S. per capita GDP. Other measures might differ, but it is unlikely that any measure would reveal the Mexican per capita GDP to be higher than Canada's, or Canada's to be significantly above that of the United States.

GDP and GNP

gross national product (GNP) The value of total incomes earned by domestic residents.

A measure of national output closely related to GDP is **gross national product** (GNP). The difference between GDP and GNP is the difference between *income produced* and *income received*. GDP measures the value of total output *produced in Canada* and the total income generated as a result of that production. GNP measures the total amount of income *received by Canadian residents*, no matter where that income was generated. How can GDP differ from GNP? Let's consider two examples.

For the first example, consider a Toyota factory located in Cambridge, Ontario. Suppose in 2013 that the value added generated by that factory is $100 million. Canadian GDP is therefore higher by $100 million as a result of that production. But suppose $5 million of the profits (part of the value added) generated at that factory is remitted to foreign owners. Since only $95 million of the value added generates income *for Canadian residents*, Canadian GNP is higher by only $95 million.

The second example involves any Canadian-owned business located outside of Canada. The value added produced by that business contributes to the GDP in a foreign country but not in Canada. But if there are profits remitted to the Canadian owners, those profits will be part of the income of Canadian residents and thus part of Canadian GNP.

> GDP measures the value of all production located in Canada, no matter who receives the income from that production. GNP measures the income received by Canadian residents, no matter where the production occurred to generate that income.

The relative sizes of GDP and GNP depend on the balance between income earned by Canadian residents from Canadian investments located abroad, and income paid to foreign residents from foreign-owned investments located in Canada. For most of Canada's history, Canada has been a *net debtor* country. Thus, the value of foreign-located assets owned by Canadian residents has been less than the value of Canadian-located assets owned by foreigners. As a result, the foreign-generated income received by Canadian residents is less than the Canadian-generated income going to foreigners. This makes Canadian GNP less than Canadian GDP. But the difference is small. In most years, GNP is only 3 or 4 percent lower than GDP.

Toyota cars produced in Canada contribute to Canada's GDP. But the portion of profits that returns to foreign shareholders is not part of Canada's GNP.

Which Measure Is Better? Given the difference between GDP and GNP, we are naturally led to ask if one measure is better than the other. The answer depends on what we want to measure.

> GDP is superior to GNP as a measure of domestic economic activity. GNP is superior to GDP as a measure of the income of domestic residents.

If you want to know how easy it will be to find a job, or to determine whether factories are working double shifts or new buildings are going up, look to changes in the GDP. By its definition, it is the GDP that tells us how much is being produced within a nation's borders. To know how much income is available to the residents of a country, however, one should look at the GNP, which counts income earned abroad and subtracts income generated at home that accrues to residents of other nations. Thus, the GNP is a better measure of the income of a country's residents.

Disposable Personal Income Both GDP and GNP are important measures of overall economic activity and of national income. Most important to individual households, however, is **disposable personal income**, the part of national income that is available to households to spend or to save. The easiest way to calculate disposable personal income is to subtract from GNP the parts of the GNP that are not available to households. Hence, we must subtract all taxes (both income and sales taxes), depreciation, retained earnings, and interest paid to institutions. We then need to add in the transfer payments made to households. In recent years, disposable income has represented about 60 percent of GDP.

disposable personal income The part of national income that accrues to households and is available to spend or save.

Real and Nominal GDP

In Chapter 19, we distinguished between real and nominal measures of aggregate output. When we add up dollar values of outputs, expenditures, or incomes, we end up with what are called *nominal values*. Nominal GDP increased by 153.1 percent between 1990 and 2011. If we want to compare *real* GDP in 2011 to that in 1990, we need to determine how much of that nominal increase was due to increases in prices and how

TABLE 20-3 Nominal and Real GDP in Canada: Selected Years (billions of dollars)

Year	Nominal GDP (current prices)	Real GDP (2002 prices)	GDP Deflator
1985	485.7	716.1	67.8
1990	679.9	825.3	82.4
1995	810.4	898.8	90.2
2000	1076.6	1100.5	97.8
2002	1152.9	1152.9	100.0
2005	1373.8	1247.8	110.1
2010	1624.6	1325.0	122.6
2011	1720.7	1356.9	126.8

Nominal GDP tells us about the money value of output; real GDP tells us about the quantity of physical output. Nominal GDP gives the total value of output in any year, valued at the prices of that year. Real GDP gives the total value of output in any year, *valued at prices from some base year*, in this case 2002. The comparison of real and nominal GDP implicitly defines a price index, changes in which reveal changes in the (average) prices of goods produced domestically. Note that in 2002, nominal GDP equals real GDP (measured in 2002 prices), and thus the GDP deflator equals 100.

(*Source:* Statistics Canada, CANSIM database. Real GDP: Series V1992067. Nominal GDP: Series V1997757.)

much was due to increases in quantities produced. Although there are many possible ways of doing this, the underlying principle is always the same: The value of output in each period is computed by using a common set of *base-period prices*. When this is done, economists say that real output is measured in *constant dollars*.

> Total GDP valued at current prices is called *nominal* GDP. GDP valued at base-period prices is called *real* GDP.

Any change in nominal GDP reflects the combined effects of changes in quantities and changes in prices. However, when real income is measured over different periods by using a common set of base-period prices, changes in real income reflect only changes in quantities. Table 20-3 shows real and nominal GDP for selected years in Canada since 1985.

The GDP Deflator If nominal and real GDP change by different amounts over a given time period, then prices must have changed over that period. For example, if nominal GDP has increased by 6 percent and real GDP has increased by only 4 percent over the same period, we know that average prices must have increased by 2 percent. Comparing what has happened to nominal and real GDP over the same period implies the existence of a price index measuring the change in prices over that period—"implies" because no explicit price index is used in calculating either real or nominal GDP. However, an index can be inferred by comparing these two values. The *GDP deflator* is defined as follows:

$$\text{GDP deflator} = \frac{\text{GDP at current prices}}{\text{GDP at base-period prices}} \times 100 = \frac{\text{Nominal GDP}}{\text{Real GDP}} \times 100$$

GDP deflator An index number derived by dividing nominal GDP by real GDP. Its change measures the average change in price of all the items in the GDP.

The **GDP deflator** is the most comprehensive available index of the price level because it includes all the goods and services that are produced by the entire economy. It uses the current year's basket of production to compare the current year's prices with those prevailing in the base period. (Because it uses the current basket of goods and services, it does not run into the CPI's problem of sometimes being based on an out-of-date basket.) The GDP deflator was 26.8 percent higher in 2011 than in the base year 2002 (see Table 20-3). Thus, for those goods and services produced in 2011, their average price increased by 26.8 percent over the previous nine years. *Applying Economic Concepts 20-2* illustrates the calculation of real and nominal GDP and the GDP deflator for a simple hypothetical economy that produces only wheat and steel.

As we have said, a change in nominal GDP can be split into the change of prices and the change of quantities. For example, from the data in Table 20-3 we can calculate that in 2011, Canadian nominal GDP was 153.1 percent higher than in 1990. This increase was due to a 53.9 percent increase in prices (as calculated by the percentage change in the GDP deflator) and a 64.4 percent increase in real GDP.[3]

GDP Deflator Versus the CPI An important point about the GDP deflator is that it does not necessarily change in line with changes in the CPI. The two price indices are measuring different things. Movements in the CPI measure the change in the average price of consumer goods, whereas movements in the GDP deflator reflect the change in the average price of goods produced in Canada. So changes in the world price of coffee, for example, would have a larger effect on the CPI than on the GDP deflator, since Canadians drink a lot of coffee but no coffee is produced here. Conversely, a change in the world price of wheat is likely to have a bigger effect on the GDP deflator than on the CPI, since most of Canada's considerable production of wheat is exported to other countries, thus leaving a relatively small fraction to appear in the Canadian basket of consumer products.

> Changes in the GDP deflator and Consumer Price Index (CPI) similarly reflect overall inflationary trends. But changes in relative prices may lead the two price indices to move in different ways.

Omissions from GDP

National income as measured in the National Income and Expenditure Accounts provides an excellent measure of the flow of economic activity in organized markets in a given year. But much economic activity takes place outside the markets that the national income accountants survey. Although these activities are not typically included in the measure of GDP, they nevertheless use real resources.

Prostitution and other illegal activities involve genuine market transactions, but they are not included in official measures of national income.

Illegal Activities GDP does not measure illegal activities, even though many of them are ordinary business activities that produce goods and services sold in markets and that generate factor incomes. Many forms of illegal gambling, prostitution, and drug trade come into this category. To gain an accurate measure of the total demand for factors of production, of total marketable output, or of total incomes generated, we should include these activities, whether or not they are legal. The omission of illegal activities is no trivial matter: The drug trade alone is a multi-billion-dollar business.

Note that some illegal activities do get included in national income measures, although they are generally misclassified by industry. The income is included because people sometimes report their illegally earned income as part of their earnings from legal activities. They do this to avoid the fate of Al Capone, the famous Chicago gangster in the 1920s and 1930s, who, having avoided conviction on many more serious charges, was finally caught and imprisoned for income-tax evasion.

---

[3] For large percentage changes in price and quantity, the nominal percentage change is not exactly equal to the sum of the price and the quantity changes; generally, the relationship is multiplicative. In this case, prices and quantities are respectively 1.539 and 1.644 times their original values. Thus, nominal GDP is $(1.539) \times (1.644) = 2.531$ times its original value, which is an increase of 153.1 percent. For small percentage changes, the sum is a very good approximation of the multiplicative change. For example, if prices grow by 2 percent and quantities by 3 percent, the nominal change is $(1.02) \times (1.03) = 1.0506$, which is very close to 1.05, an increase of 5 percent.

APPLYING ECONOMIC CONCEPTS 20-2

Calculating Nominal and Real GDP

To see what is involved in calculating nominal GDP, real GDP, and the GDP deflator, an example may be helpful. Consider a simple hypothetical economy that produces only two commodities, wheat and steel.

Table 1 gives the basic data for output and prices in the economy for two years.

TABLE 1 Data for a Hypothetical Economy

	Quantity Produced		Prices	
	Wheat (bushels)	Steel (tonnes)	Wheat ($/bushel)	Steel ($/tonne)
Year 1	100	20	10	50
Year 2	110	16	12	55

Table 2 shows nominal GDP, calculated by adding the dollar values of wheat output and of steel output for each year. In year 1, the values of both wheat and steel production were $1000, so nominal GDP was $2000. In year 2, wheat output rose to $1320, and steel output fell to $880. Since the rise in the value of wheat was greater than the fall in the value of steel, nominal GDP rose by $200.

TABLE 2 Calculation of Nominal GDP

Year 1: $(100 \times \$10) + (20 \times \$50) = \$2000$

Year 2: $(110 \times \$12) + (16 \times \$55) = \$2200$

Table 3 shows real GDP, calculated by valuing output in each year *at year-2 prices*; that is, year 2 is used as the base year. In year 2, wheat output rose, but steel output fell. If we use year-2 prices, the fall in the value of steel output between years 1 and 2 exceeded the rise in the value of wheat output, and so real GDP fell.

TABLE 3 Calculation of Real GDP Using Year-2 Prices

Year 1: $(100 \times \$12) + (20 \times \$55) = \$2300$

Year 2: $(110 \times \$12) + (16 \times \$55) = \$2200$

In Table 4, the ratio of nominal to real GDP is calculated for each year and multiplied by 100. This ratio implicitly measures the change in prices over the period in question and is called the *GDP deflator*. The deflator shows that average prices increased by 15 percent between year 1 and year 2.

TABLE 4 Calculation of the GDP Deflator

Year 1: $(2000/2300) \times 100 = 86.96$

Year 2: $(2200/2200) \times 100 = 100.00$

Throughout this box we have used year 2 as the base year. But we could just as easily have used year 1. The changes we would have computed in real GDP and the deflator would have been very similar—but not identical—to the ones we did compute using year 2 as the base year. The choice of base year matters because of different *relative* prices in the different years (note that the price of steel relative to the price of wheat is lower in year 2 than in year 1). Put simply, with different relative prices in different years, the various output changes are weighted differently depending on which prices we use, and thus the *aggregate* measure of real GDP changes by different amounts. (If you want to understand this point in more detail, try doing Study Exercise #8 on page 517.)

How do we choose the "right" base year? As with many other elements of national income accounting, there is some arbitrariness in the choice. There is no "right" year. The important thing is not which year to use—the important thing is to be clear about which year you are using and then, for a given set of comparisons, to be sure that you are consistent in your choice. In recent years, Statistics Canada has avoided this problem by using "chain weighting," a technique that essentially uses an average over several measures, each one corresponding to a different base year.

The Underground Economy A significant omission from GDP is the so-called underground economy. The transactions that occur in the underground economy are perfectly legal in themselves; the only illegality involved is that such transactions are not reported for tax purposes. Because such transactions go unreported, they are omitted from GDP. One example of this is the carpenter who repairs a leak in your roof and takes payment in cash (and does not report it as income) to avoid taxation.

The growth of the underground economy is facilitated by the rising importance of services in the nation's total output. It is much easier for a carpenter to pass unnoticed by government authorities than it is for a manufacturing establishment. Estimates of the value of income earned in the underground economy run from 2 percent to 15 percent of GDP. In some countries, the figures are even higher. The Italian underground economy, for example, has been estimated at close to 25 percent of that country's GDP.

"Home Production" and Other Non-market Activities If a homeowner hires a firm to do some landscaping, the value of the landscaping enters into GDP (as long as the landscaper records the transaction and thus declares the income); if the homeowner does the landscaping herself, the value of the landscaping is omitted from GDP because there is no recorded market transaction. Such production of goods and services in the home is called *home production* and includes all of the "ordinary" work that is required to keep a household functioning, such as cooking, cleaning, shopping, and doing laundry. Other non-market activities include voluntary work, such as

The extraction, refining, and transportation of oil are all included as goods and services in measures of GDP. But the environmental damage inflicted by an oil spill—an economic "bad"—is not included in any measure of GDP.

canvassing for a political party or coaching a local hockey team. Both home production and volunteer activities clearly add to economic well-being, and both use economic resources. Yet neither is included in official measures of national income since they are non-market activities.

Another extremely important non-market activity is *leisure*. If a lawyer voluntarily chooses to reduce her time at work from 2400 hours to 2200 hours per year, measured national income will fall by the lawyer's wage rate times 200 hours. Yet the value to the lawyer of the 200 hours of new leisure enjoyed outside of the marketplace must exceed the lost wages (otherwise she would not have chosen to reduce her work effort by 200 hours), so total economic well-being has increased even though measured GDP has fallen. Over the years, one of the most important ways in which economic growth has benefited people is by permitting increased amounts of leisure. Because the leisure time is not marketed, its value does not show up in measures of national income.

Economic "Bads" When a coal-burning electric power plant sends sulphur dioxide into the atmosphere, leading to acid rain and environmental damage, the value of the electricity sold is included as part of GDP, but the value of the damage done by the acid rain is not deducted. Similarly, the gasoline that we use in our cars is part of national income when it is produced, but the environmental damage done by burning that gasoline is not deducted. To the extent that economic growth brings with it increases in pollution, congestion, and other disamenities of modern living, measurements of national income will overstate the improvement in living standards. Such measures capture the increased output of goods and services, but they fail to account for the increased output of "bads" that generally accompany economic growth.

Do the Omissions Matter? Should our current measure of GDP be modified to deal with these omissions? Changing the formal GDP measure to include illegal activities and home production would be extremely difficult, if not impossible. Not only would it be very costly to get accurate measurements of the level of these activities, but in the case of home production there are no prices associated with the "transactions."

Including economic "bads" in the measure of GDP would be possible but doing so would fundamentally change the nature of the measurement such that it would no longer give an accurate measure of the level of economic activity. Damage to the environment is certainly important, but addressing that problem does not require including it in a measure of economic activity.

The current approach to measuring GDP continues to be used for three reasons. First, as we have just said, correcting the major omissions in the measure would be difficult if not impossible. Second, even though the *level* of measured GDP in any given year may be inaccurate, the *change* in GDP from one year to the next is a good indication of the *changes* in economic activity (as long as the omissions are themselves not changing a lot from one year to the next).

The third reason is that policymakers need to measure the amount of market output in the economy in order to design policies to control inflation and set tax rates. To do so, they need to know the flow of money payments made to produce and purchase Canadian output. Modified measures that included non-market activities would distort these figures and likely lead to policy errors.

That the conventional measure of GDP continues to be used is not to say that economists and policymakers are not concerned about the imperfections and omissions. Statistics Canada is constantly striving to improve the measurement of GDP, while at the same time there is a recognition that some problems in measurement will probably always exist.

GDP and Living Standards

We have said that GDP does a good job of measuring the flow of economic activity during a given time period. But we have also said that many things are omitted from this measure, some of which represent beneficial economic activity and some of which represent economic "bads." These observations lead to the obvious question: To what extent does GDP provide even a rough measure of our living standards?

The answer depends on what we mean by "living standards." For many people, this term refers to our *purchasing power* or *real income*. When GDP rises, do we experience a rise in our average real incomes? The answer is not necessarily. As we will see in detail in Chapters 25 and 26, real GDP can rise for two general reasons. First, there may be an increase in the amounts of land, labour, and capital used as inputs to production. Second, these inputs may become more productive in the sense that there is an increase in the amount of output *per unit of input*. The *average* level of real income in the economy is best measured by real GDP *per person*, but this does not necessarily rise whenever real GDP rises. If real GDP rises because more people become employed, real GDP per person may not rise. However, if real GDP rises because the existing labour force becomes more productive, then average real incomes will also rise. This explains why most economists believe that productivity growth is such an important determinant of living standards.

To many people, however, the term "living standards" is much broader than simply real per capita income—it includes such important but intangible things as religious and political freedom, the quality of local community life, environmental sustainability, the distribution of income, and our ability to prevent and treat illness and disease. And since measures of real GDP omit many of these intangible things that contribute positively to our overall well-being, it is not even clear that changes in real per capita GDP accurately reflect changes in this broader concept of living standards. For example, greater productivity may lead to an increase in real per capita income and thus to a rise in our average *material* living standards, but if this change also leads to greater environmental damage or greater inequality in the distribution of income, some people may argue that while our material living standards have increased, our overall well-being has declined.

> **Changes in real per capita income are a good measure of average material living standards. But material living standards are only part of what most people consider their overall well-being.**

SUMMARY

20.1 National Output and Value Added

- Each firm's contribution to total output is equal to its value added, which is the value of the firm's output minus the values of all intermediate goods and services that it uses. The sum of all the values added produced in an economy is the economy's total output, which is called gross domestic product (GDP).

20.2 National Income Accounting: The Basics

- From the circular flow of income, there are two commonly used ways to compute national income. One is to add up total expenditure on domestic output. The other is to add up the total income generated by domestic production. By standard accounting conventions, these two aggregations define the same total.
- From the expenditure side of the national accounts,

$$GDP = C_a + I_a + G_a + (X_a - IM_a)$$

- C_a comprises consumption expenditures of households. I_a is investment in plant and equipment, residential construction, and inventory accumulation. G_a is government purchases of goods and services. $(X_a - IM_a)$ represents net exports of goods and services.
- GDP measured from the income side adds up all claims to the market value of production. Wages, interest, profits, depreciation, and indirect taxes (net of subsidies) are the major categories.

20.3 National Income Accounting: Some Further Issues

- GDP measures the value of all production located in Canada, no matter who receives the income from that production. GNP measures the income received by Canadian residents, no matter where the production occurred to generate that income.
- Real measures of national income reflect changes in real quantities. Nominal measures of national income reflect changes in both prices and quantities. Any change in nominal income can be split into a change in quantities and a change in prices.
- The comparison of nominal and real GDP yields the implicit GDP price deflator, an index of the average price of all goods and services produced in the economy.
- GDP and related measures of national income must be interpreted with their limitations in mind. GDP excludes

production resulting from activities that are illegal, that take place in the underground economy, or that do not pass through markets.
- Notwithstanding its limitations, GDP remains an important measure of the total economic activity that passes through the nation's markets. Recorded *changes* in GDP will generally do an accurate job of measuring *changes* in economic activity.
- Real per capita GDP is a good measure of average material living standards. But because GDP omits many intangible things that contribute positively to our quality of life, GDP-based measures miss important parts of our overall well-being.

KEY CONCEPTS

Intermediate and final goods
Value added
GDP as the sum of all values added
GDP from the expenditure side

GDP from the income side
GNP versus GDP
Disposable personal income
GDP deflator

Omissions from GDP
Per capita GDP and productivity
Living standards and GDP

STUDY EXERCISES

MyEconLab   Make the grade with MyEconLab: Study Exercises marked in red can be found on MyEconLab. You can practise them as often as you want, and most feature step-by-step guided instructions to help you find the right answer.

1. Fill in the blanks to make the following statements correct.

   a. If, when measuring Canada's national output, we add the market values of all firms' outputs in Canada, then we are committing the error of _____. Such an amount would greatly _____ the economy's actual output.

   b. Statisticians use the concept of _____ to avoid double counting in measuring national income. Each firm's _____ is the value of its output minus the costs of _____ that it purchases from other firms.

   c. If we measure GDP from the expenditure side, we are adding four broad categories of expenditure: _____, _____, _____, and _____. As an equation it is written as GDP = _____.

   d. If we measure GDP from the income side, we are adding three main components of factor incomes: _____, _____, and _____. To these items we must add non-factor payments of _____ and _____.

2. Fill in the blanks to make the following statements correct.

   a. Comparing GDP and GNP, if we want the best measure of Canada's domestic economic activity, we should look at _____; if we want the best measure of the income of Canada's residents, then we should look at _____.

   b. If nominal GDP increases by 35 percent over a 10-year period, then it is unclear how much of this increase is due to increases in _____ and how much is due to increases in _____. To overcome this problem, we look at GDP valued at _____

prices and we refer to this measure as _____ national income.

   c. GDP divided by total population gives us a measure of _____.

   d. GDP divided by the number of employed persons in Canada gives us a measure of labour _____.

3. In measuring GDP from the expenditure side (GDP = $C_a + I_a + G_a + NX_a$), which of the following expenditures are included and within which of the four categories?

   a. expenditures on automobiles by consumers
   b. expenditures on automobiles by firms
   c. expenditures on new machinery by Canadian-owned forest companies located in Canada
   d. expenditures on new machinery by Canadian-owned forest companies located in the United States
   e. expenditures on new machinery by U.S.-owned forest companies located in Canada
   f. reductions in business inventories
   g. purchases of second-hand cars and trucks
   h. the hiring of economic consultants by the Manitoba government
   i. the purchase of Canadian-produced software by a firm in Japan

4. The list below provides some national income figures for the country of Econoland. All figures are in millions of dollars.

Wages and salaries	5000
Interest income	200
Personal consumption	3900
Personal saving	1100

Personal income taxes	200
Business profits	465
Indirect taxes	175
Subsidies	30
Government purchases	1000
Exports	350
Imports	390
Net private investment	950
Depreciation	150

a. Using the expenditure approach, what is the value of GDP for Econoland?

b. Using the income approach, what is the value of GDP?

c. What is the value of net domestic income at factor cost?

5. The table below shows data for real and nominal GDP for a hypothetical economy over several years.

Year	Nominal GDP (billions of $)	Real GDP (billions of 2010 $)	GDP Deflator
2008	775.3	798.4	—
2009	814.1	838.6	—
2010	862.9	862.9	—
2011	901.5	882.5	—
2012	951.3	920.6	—
2013	998.8	950.5	—

a. Compute the GDP deflator for each year.

b. Compute the total percentage change in nominal GDP from 2008 to 2013. How much of this change was due to increases in prices and how much was due to changes in quantities?

6. Would inflation, as measured by the rate of change in the GDP deflator, ever be different from inflation as measured by the rate of change in the Consumer Price Index? Would it ever be the same? Explain.

7. For each of the following events, describe the likely effect on real GDP in Canada.

a. A major ice storm in Quebec damages homes and thus increases the demand for building materials.

b. A flood on the Red River destroys the annual barley crop on hundreds of thousands of acres of Manitoba farmland.

c. In a near-perfect growing season in 2012, Saskatchewan's wheat crop increases by 20 percent above normal levels.

d. A 30 percent increase in the world price of oil in 2011 causes Alberta-based oil producers to increase their oil production (measured in barrels) by 5 percent.

e. A large new hospital complex is built in Montreal in 2012.

f. The building of a larger arena in Toronto increases the demand for Maple Leafs tickets by Torontonians.

g. The building of a larger arena in Toronto increases the demand for Maple Leafs tickets by residents of Buffalo, New York.

8. Consider the following data for a hypothetical economy that produces two goods, milk and honey.

	Quantity Produced		Prices	
	Milk (litres)	Honey (kg)	Milk ($/litre)	Honey ($/kg)
Year 1	100	40	2	6
Year 2	120	25	3	6

a. Compute nominal GDP for each year in this economy.

b. Using year 1 as the base year, compute real GDP for each year. What is the percentage change in real GDP from year 1 to year 2?

c. Using year 1 as the base year, compute the GDP deflator for each year. What is the percentage change in the GDP deflator from year 1 to year 2?

d. Now compute the GDP deflator for each year, using year 2 as the base year.

e. Explain why the measures of real GDP growth (and growth in the deflator) depend on the choice of base year.

9. Residents of some Canadian cities have recently become concerned about the growing proportion of their local real estate that is being bought up by foreign residents. What is the effect of this transfer of ownership on Canadian GDP and GNP?

10. In 2011, the United Nations ranked Norway first on the Human Development Index—a ranking of the "quality of life" in many countries. Yet Norway was *not* ranked first in terms of real per capita GDP. Explain how the two rankings can be different.

11. A company's wages and salaries are part of its value added. Suppose, however, that the cleaning and machinery maintenance that its own employees used to do are now contracted out to specialist firms who come in to do the same work more cheaply.

a. What happens to the company's value added when it "contracts out" such work?

b. What happens to value added in the economy as a whole?

12. As we saw in the text, the expenditure approach to measuring GDP shows that

$$GDP = C_a + I_a + G_a + NX_a$$

a. Is this equation a *causal* relationship, suggesting that an increase in any one of the right-hand-side terms *causes* an increase in GDP?

b. It is common to hear commentators suggest that an increase in imports reduces Canadian GDP. Is this true?

The Simplest Short-Run Macro Model

CHAPTER OUTLINE	LEARNING OBJECTIVES (LO)
	After studying this chapter you will be able to
21.1 DESIRED AGGREGATE EXPENDITURE	1 explain the difference between desired and actual expenditure.
	2 identify the determinants of desired consumption and desired investment.
21.2 EQUILIBRIUM NATIONAL INCOME	3 understand the meaning of equilibrium national income.
21.3 CHANGES IN EQUILIBRIUM NATIONAL INCOME	4 explain how a change in desired expenditure affects equilibrium income through the "simple multiplier."

IN Chapters 19 and 20, we encountered a number of important macroeconomic variables. We considered how they are measured and how they have behaved over the past several decades. We now turn to a more detailed study of what *causes* these variables to behave as they do. In particular, we study the forces that determine real national income and the price level over short periods of time, say, up to a few years. We call this the *short run*.[1] In particular, in this chapter and the next two, we examine how the level of real GDP is determined and how it fluctuates around the level of potential GDP. For simplicity, we assume that potential GDP is constant; in later chapters we explore the long-run forces that explain the growth of potential GDP.

Real GDP and the price level are determined simultaneously. It is, however, easier to study them one at a time. So, in this chapter and the next, we simplify matters by seeing how real national income is determined *under the assumption that the price level is constant*. The simplified analysis is an important first step toward understanding how prices and GDP are determined together, which is the subject of Chapter 23.

Throughout this and later chapters, we will make many statements about what will happen as a result of some "shock" such as a change in household or firm behaviour or a change in government policy. In all such cases we are describing the predicted result in the model we are developing. Whether this predicted result also happens in reality depends on how well our model predicts real-world behaviour. This suggests two points. First, we would not waste time discussing our model of the economy if there was not ample reason to believe that it does to a significant extent predict the outcome of real-world events. Second, we must constantly keep in mind that our statements only apply formally to our model and that we need to be aware of the possibility that the model's ability to predict real-world behaviour may change over time.

Where do we begin? Our ability to explain the behaviour of real GDP depends on our understanding of what determines the amount that households and firms desire to spend. We therefore begin with an examination of their expenditure decisions.

---

[1] Readers who have studied microeconomics are familiar with a different concept of the short run. In microeconomics, the short run varies industry by industry and corresponds to the period of time for which there are one or more *fixed* factors of production. In macroeconomics, the short run refers to a period of time during which prices and wages have not fully adjusted to various shocks. We say much more about this adjustment process in later chapters.

21.1 Desired Aggregate Expenditure

In Chapter 20, we discussed how national income statisticians divide *actual* GDP into its expenditure components: consumption, investment, government purchases, and net exports. In this chapter and the next, we are concerned with a different concept. It is variously called *desired* or *planned* expenditure. Of course, most people would like to spend virtually unlimited amounts, if only they had the resources. Desired expenditure does not refer, however, to what people would like to do under imaginary circumstances; it refers to what people desire to spend out of the resources that they actually have. Recall from Chapter 20 that the *actual* values of the various categories of expenditure are indicated by C_a, I_a, G_a, and $(X_a - IM_a)$. Economists use the same letters without the subscript "*a*" to indicate the *desired* expenditure in the same categories: C, I, G, and $(X - IM)$.

Everyone makes expenditure decisions. Fortunately, it is unnecessary for our purposes to look at each of the millions of such individual decisions. Instead, it is sufficient to consider four main groups of decision makers: domestic households, firms, governments, and foreign purchasers of domestically produced commodities. The sum of their *desired* expenditures on domestically produced output is called **desired aggregate expenditure** (*AE*):

$$AE = C + I + G + (X - IM)$$

desired aggregate expenditure (*AE*) The sum of desired or planned spending on domestic output by households, firms, governments, and foreigners.

Desired expenditure need not equal actual expenditure, either in total or in any individual category. For example, firms might not plan to invest in inventory accumulation this year but might do so unintentionally if sales are unexpectedly low—the unsold goods that pile up on their shelves are undesired inventory accumulation. In this case, actual investment expenditure, I_a, will exceed desired investment expenditure, I.

> National income accounts measure *actual* expenditures in each of the four expenditure categories. Our model of the macro economy also deals with *desired* expenditures in each of these four categories.

You may be wondering why the distinction between desired and actual expenditure is so important. The answer will become clear in the next section, where we discuss the concept of *equilibrium* national income, which involves the relationship between desired and actual expenditure. For now, however, the remainder of this section examines more fully the various components of desired expenditure.

Autonomous Versus Induced Expenditure. In what follows, it will be useful to distinguish between *autonomous* and *induced* expenditure. Components of aggregate expenditure that do *not* depend on national income are called **autonomous expenditures**. Autonomous expenditures can and do change, but such changes do not occur systematically in response to changes in national income. Components of aggregate expenditure that *do* change systematically in response to changes in national income are called **induced expenditures**. As we will see, the induced response of desired aggregate expenditure to a change in national income plays a key role in the determination of equilibrium national income.

autonomous expenditure Elements of expenditure that do not change systematically with national income.

induced expenditure Any component of expenditure that is systematically related to national income.

Important Simplifications. Our goal in this chapter is to develop the simplest possible model of national-income determination. We begin by making three simplifying assumptions:

- there is no trade with other countries—that is, the economy we are studying is a **closed economy**
- there is no government—and hence no taxes
- the price level is constant.

closed economy An economy that has no foreign trade in goods, services, or assets.

These extreme assumptions serve a vital purpose. As we will soon see, the presence of government and foreign trade is *not* essential to understanding the basic principles of national-income determination. By simplifying the model as much as possible, we are better able to understand its structure and therefore how more complex versions of the model work. In following chapters we will complicate our simple macro model by adding a government and international trade and then by removing the assumption of a fixed price level. The result will be a more complete and useful model of the macro economy.

Desired Consumption Expenditure

Recall from Chapter 20 that *disposable income* is the amount of income households receive after deducting what they pay in taxes and adding what they receive in transfers. In our simple model with no government and no taxation, disposable income, Y_D, is equal to national income, Y. We define **saving** as all disposable income that is not spent on consumption.

saving All disposable income that is not spent on consumption.

> By definition, there are only two possible uses of disposable income—consumption and saving. When the household decides how much to put to one use, it has automatically decided how much to put to the other use.

Figure 21-1 shows the time series for real per capita consumption and disposable income in Canada since 1981. It is clear that the two variables tend to move together over time, although the relationship is not exact. The vertical distance between the two lines is the amount of saving done by households, and the figure shows that household saving as a share of disposable income has been declining over this period. In the early 1980s, household saving was roughly 25 percent of disposable income, whereas by 2010 it was about 7 percent. What determines the amount of their disposable income that households decide to consume and the amount they decide to save? The factors that influence this decision are summarized in the *consumption function* and the *saving function*.

The Consumption Function The **consumption function** relates the total desired consumption expenditures of all households to the several factors that determine it. The key factors influencing desired consumption are assumed to be

consumption function The relationship between desired consumption expenditure and all the variables that determine it. In the simplest case, the relationship between desired consumption expenditure and disposable income.

- disposable income
- wealth
- interest rates
- expectations about the future

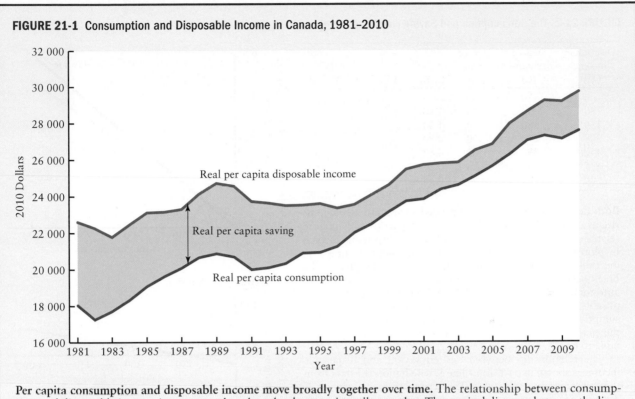

FIGURE 21-1 Consumption and Disposable Income in Canada, 1981–2010

Per capita consumption and disposable income move broadly together over time. The relationship between consumption and disposable income is not exact, but they clearly move broadly together. The vertical distance between the lines is household saving, which as a share of income has been declining since 1981.

(*Source:* Based on author's calculations using data from Statistics Canada, CANSIM database. Disposable income: Series V691566. Consumption expenditure: Series V691578. Population: Series V466668. Conversion from nominal to real values based on CPI: Series V41690973.)

In building our simple macro model, we emphasize the role of disposable income in influencing desired consumption; however, as we will see later, changes in the other variables are also important.

The assumption that desired consumption is related to disposable income is not surprising. As income rises, households naturally want to spend more, both now and in the future. For example, if a household's monthly disposable income permanently increases from $3000 to $3500, its monthly consumption will also increase, but probably by less than the full $500 increase. The remainder will be added to its monthly saving—assets that will accumulate and be available to finance future vacations, education, home purchases, or even retirement.

Holding constant other determinants of desired consumption, an increase in disposable income is assumed to lead to an increase in desired consumption.

The consumption function has an interesting history in economics. *Extensions in Theory 21-1* discusses consumption behaviour in two hypothetical households and

FIGURE 21-2 The Consumption and Saving Functions ✴

Disposable Income (Y_D)	Desired Consumption (C)	Desired Saving (S)	$APC = C/Y_D$	ΔY_D	ΔC	$MPC = \Delta C/\Delta Y_D$
0	30	−30	—			
30	54	−24	1.80	30	24	0.8
150	150	0	1.00	120	96	0.8
300	270	30	0.90	150	120	0.8
450	390	60	0.87	150	120	0.8
525	450	75	0.86	75	60	0.8
600	510	90	0.85	75	60	0.8

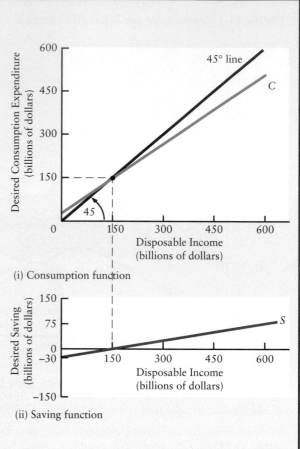

(i) Consumption function

(ii) Saving function

Both desired consumption and desired saving are assumed to rise as disposable income rises. Line C in part (i) of the figure relates desired consumption expenditure to disposable income by plotting the data from the second column of the accompanying table. The consumption function cuts the 45° line at the break-even level of disposable income. Note that the level of autonomous consumption is $30 billion; even with zero disposable income, consumers have this amount of desired consumption. The slope of the consumption function is equal to the marginal propensity to consume, which is shown in the table to be 0.8.

The relationship between desired saving and disposable income is shown in part (ii) by line S, which plots the data from the third column of the table. The vertical distance between C and the 45° line in part (i) is by definition the height of S in part (ii); that is, any given level of disposable income must be either consumed or saved. Note that the level of autonomous saving is −$30 billion.

illustrates a debate regarding the importance of *current* disposable income in determining consumption. As the discussion shows, however, our simple assumption that desired consumption is positively related to current disposable income is a good approximation of the behaviour of the *average* household and therefore is suitable for explaining aggregate behaviour.

Part (i) of Figure 21-2 illustrates a hypothetical consumption function. The first two columns of the table show the value of desired consumption (C) associated with each value of disposable income (Y_D). There is clearly a positive relationship. The figure plots these points and connects them with a smooth line. In this hypothetical economy, the equation of the consumption function is

$$C = 30 + 0.8Y_D$$

In words, this equation says that if disposable income is zero, desired aggregate consumption will be $30 billion, and that for every one-dollar increase in Y_D, desired consumption rises by 80 cents.

The $30 billion is said to be *autonomous* consumption because it is autonomous (or independent) of the level of income. Autonomous consumption is greater than zero because consumers are assumed to have some desired consumption even if there is no disposable income. The $0.8Y_D$ is called *induced* consumption because it is induced

EXTENSIONS IN THEORY 21-1

The Theory of the Consumption Function

Though it may seem natural to assume that a household's current consumption depends largely on its current disposable income, much debate and research has surrounded the issue of how to model consumption behaviour. To see what is involved, consider two quite different households.

The first household is short-sighted and spends everything it receives and puts nothing aside for the future. When some overtime work results in a large paycheque, the members of the household go out and spend it. When it is hard to find work, the household's paycheque is small and its members reduce their expenditures. This household's monthly expenditure is therefore exactly equal to its current monthly disposable income.

The second household is forward-looking. Its members think about the future as much as the present and make plans that stretch over their lifetimes. They put money aside for retirement and for the occasional rainy day when disposable income may fall temporarily. An unexpected windfall of income will be saved. An unexpected shortfall of income will be cushioned by spending some of the accumulated savings that were put aside for just such a rainy day. In short, this household's monthly expenditure will be closely related to the average monthly income it expects over its lifetime—the household's *permanent* income. Fluctuations in its current monthly income will have little effect on its current consumption expenditure. Economists refer to this behaviour as *consumption smoothing*.

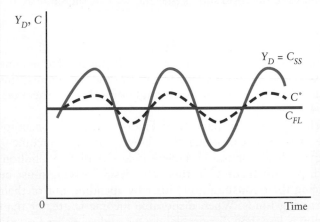

The figure shows the difference between our two sample households, short-sighted and forward-looking, and how their respective consumption expenditure is related to their current disposable income. We assume that disposable income, Y_D, fluctuates over time, as shown by the solid blue line. C_{SS} is the consumption path of the short-sighted household and is the same as the path of

disposable income. C_{FL} is the consumption path for the forward-looking household and is flat.

John Maynard Keynes (1883–1946), the famous English economist who developed much of the basic theory of macroeconomics, populated his theory with households whose current consumption expenditure depended mostly on their current income. But these households are not as extreme as the short-sighted households we just discussed. Keynes did not assume that households *never* saved. He simply assumed that their current level of expenditure and saving depended on their current level of income, as we do in this book. To this day, a consumption function based on this assumption is called a *Keynesian consumption function*.

In the 1950s, two U.S. economists, Franco Modigliani and Milton Friedman, both of whom were subsequently awarded Nobel Prizes in economics, analyzed the behaviour of forward-looking households. Their theories, which Modigliani called the *life-cycle theory* and Friedman called the *permanent-income theory*, explain some observed consumer behaviour that cannot be explained by the Keynesian consumption function.

The differences between the theories of Keynes, on the one hand, and Friedman and Modigliani on the other, are not as great as they might seem at first. To see why this is so, let us return to our two imaginary households.

Even the extremely short-sighted household may be able to do some consumption smoothing in the face of income fluctuations. Most households have some money in the bank and some ability to borrow, even if it is just from friends and relatives. As a result, every change in income need not be matched by an equal change in consumption expenditures.

In contrast, although the forward-looking household wants to smooth its pattern of consumption, it may not have the borrowing capacity to do so. Its bank may not be willing to lend money for consumption when the security consists of nothing more than the *expectation* that the household's income will be higher in later years. As a result, the household's consumption expenditure may fluctuate with its current income more than it would want.

The foregoing discussion suggests that the consumption expenditure of both types of households will fluctuate to some extent with their current disposable incomes and to some extent with their expectations of future disposable income. Moreover, in any economy there will be households of both types, and aggregate consumption will be determined by a mix of the two types. The consumption behaviour for the *average* household in such an economy is shown in the figure as the path C^*. Consumption fluctuates in response to changes in disposable income, rising when income rises and falling when income falls.

(or brought about) by a change in income. In part (i) of Figure 21-2, the autonomous part of desired consumption is the vertical intercept of the consumption function. The induced part of consumption occurs as disposable income changes and we move along the consumption function.

We now go on to examine the properties of the consumption function in more detail.

Average and Marginal Propensities to Consume. To discuss the consumption function concisely, economists use two technical expressions.

average propensity to consume (APC) Desired consumption divided by the level of disposable income.

The **average propensity to consume (*APC*)** is the proportion of disposable income that households want to consume. It is equal to desired consumption expenditure divided by disposable income:

$$APC = C/Y_D$$

The fourth column of the table in Figure 21-2 shows the *APC* calculated from the data in the table. Note that with this consumption function the *APC* falls as disposable income rises.

marginal propensity to consume (MPC) The change in desired consumption divided by the change in disposable income that brought it about.

The **marginal propensity to consume (*MPC*)** relates the *change* in desired consumption to the *change* in disposable income that brought it about. *MPC* is the change in desired consumption divided by the change in disposable income:

$$MPC = \Delta C/\Delta Y_D$$

where the Greek letter Δ, delta, means "a change in." The last column of the table in Figure 21-2 shows the *MPC* that corresponds to the data in the table. Note that in this simple example, the *MPC* is constant and equal to 0.8. [28]

The Slope of the Consumption Function. The consumption function shown in Figure 21-2 has a slope of $\Delta C/\Delta Y_D$, which is, by definition, the marginal propensity to consume. The positive slope of the consumption function shows that the *MPC* is positive; increases in disposable income lead to increases in desired consumption expenditure. The *constant* slope of the consumption function shows that the *MPC* is the same at any level of disposable income.

The 45° Line. Figure 21-2(i) contains a line that is constructed by connecting all points where desired consumption (measured on the vertical axis) equals disposable income (measured on the horizontal axis). Because both axes are given in the same units, this line has a positive slope equal to 1; that is, it forms an angle of 45° with the axes. The line is therefore called the *45° line.*

The 45° line is a useful reference line. In part (i) of Figure 21-2, the consumption function cuts the 45° line at what is called the "break-even" level of income—in this example, at $150 billion. When disposable income is less than $150 billion, desired consumption exceeds disposable income. In this case, desired saving must be negative; households are financing their consumption either by spending out of their accumulated saving or by borrowing funds. When disposable income is greater than $150 billion, desired consumption is less than disposable income and so desired saving is positive; households are paying back debt or accumulating assets. At the break-even level of disposable income, desired consumption exactly equals disposable income and so desired saving is zero.

The Saving Function Households decide how much to consume and how much to save. As we have said, this is only a single decision—how to divide disposable income between consumption and saving. Therefore, once we know the relationship between desired consumption and disposable income, we automatically know the relationship between desired saving and disposable income.

There are two saving concepts that are exactly parallel to the consumption concepts of *APC* and *MPC*. The **average propensity to save** (*APS*) is the proportion of disposable income that households want to save, computed by dividing desired saving by disposable income:

$$APS = S/Y_D$$

The **marginal propensity to save** (*MPS*) relates the change in desired saving to the change in disposable income that brought it about:

$$MPS = \Delta S/\Delta Y_D$$

There is a simple relationship between the saving and the consumption propensities. *APC* and *APS* must sum to 1, and *MPC* and *MPS* must also sum to 1. Because all disposable income is either spent or saved, it follows that the fractions of income consumed and saved must account for all income (*APC* + *APS* = 1). It also follows that the fractions of any *increment* to income consumed and saved must account for all of that increment (*MPC* + *MPS* = 1). [29]

Look back at the table in Figure 21-2 and calculate *APC* and *APS* for yourself by computing C/Y_D and S/Y_D for each row in the table. You will notice that the sum of *APC* and *APS* is *always* 1. Similarly, calculate *MPC* and *MPS* by computing $\Delta C/\Delta Y_D$ and $\Delta S/\Delta Y_D$ for each row in the table. You will also notice that *MPC* and *MPS always* sum to 1.

Part (ii) of Figure 21-2 shows the saving function in our simple model. Notice that it is positively sloped, indicating that increases in disposable income are assumed to lead to an increase in desired saving. Note also that the amount of desired saving is always equal to the vertical distance between the consumption function and the 45° line. When desired consumption exceeds income, desired saving is negative; when desired consumption is less than income, desired saving is positive.

Shifts of the Consumption Function Earlier we said that desired consumption is assumed to depend on four things—disposable income, wealth, interest rates, and households' expectations about the future. In Figure 21-2, we illustrate the most important relationship—between desired consumption and disposable income (when the other determinants are held constant). In this diagram, changes in disposable income lead to *movements along* the consumption function. Changes in the other three factors will lead to *shifts of* the consumption function. Let's see why.

A Change in Household Wealth. Household wealth is the value of all accumulated assets minus accumulated debts. The most common types of household assets are savings accounts, mutual funds, portfolios of stocks or bonds, Registered Retirement Savings Plans (RRSPs), and the ownership of homes and cars. The most common household debts are home mortgages, car loans, and outstanding lines of credit from banks (including credit-card debt).

What happens to desired consumption if household wealth increases even while disposable income is unchanged? Suppose, for example, that a rising stock market (often called a "bull" market) leads to an increase in aggregate household wealth. To the extent that this increase in wealth is expected to persist, less current income needs

average propensity to save (*APS*) Desired saving divided by disposable income.

marginal propensity to save (*MPS*) The change in desired saving divided by the change in disposable income that brought it about.

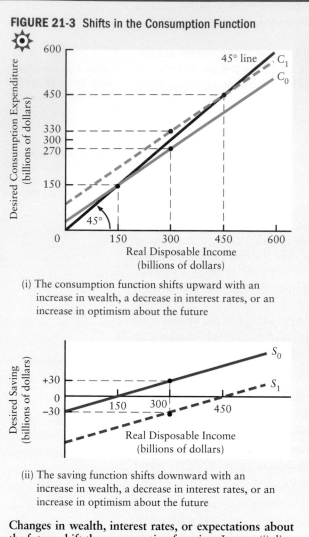

FIGURE 21-3 Shifts in the Consumption Function

(i) The consumption function shifts upward with an increase in wealth, a decrease in interest rates, or an increase in optimism about the future

(ii) The saving function shifts downward with an increase in wealth, a decrease in interest rates, or an increase in optimism about the future

Changes in wealth, interest rates, or expectations about the future shift the consumption function. In part (i), line C_0 reproduces the consumption function from part (i) of Figure 21-2. The consumption function then shifts up by $60 billion, so with disposable income of $300 billion, for example, desired consumption rises from $270 billion to $330 billion.

The saving function in part (ii) shifts down by $60 billion, from S_0 to S_1. At a disposable income of $300 billion, for example, desired saving falls from $30 billion to −$30 billion.

to be saved for the future, and households will therefore tend to spend a larger fraction of their current income. The consumption function will shift up, and the saving function down, as shown in Figure 21-3. Current estimates based on research from the International Monetary Fund suggest that an increase in aggregate Canadian wealth of $1 billion leads to an increase in desired aggregate consumption of approximately $50 million.

> An increase in household wealth shifts the consumption function up at any level of disposable income; a decrease in wealth shifts the consumption function down.

A Change in Interest Rates. Household consumption can be divided into consumption of *durable* and *non-durable* goods. Durable goods are goods that deliver benefits for several years, such as cars and household appliances. Non-durable goods are consumption goods that deliver benefits to households for only short periods of time, such as groceries, restaurant meals, and clothing. Since many durable goods are also expensive, many of them are purchased on credit—that is, households borrow in order to finance their purchases.

The cost of borrowing, as we discussed in Chapter 19, is the interest rate. A fall in the interest rate reduces the cost of borrowing and generally leads to an increase in desired consumption expenditure, especially of durable goods. That is, for any given level of disposable income, a fall in the interest rate leads to an increase in desired consumption; the consumption function shifts up and the saving function shifts down, as shown in Figure 21-3.[2]

> A fall in interest rates usually leads to an increase in desired consumption at any level of disposable income; the consumption function shifts up. A rise in interest rates shifts the consumption function down.

A Change in Expectations. Households' expectations about the future are important in determining their desired consumption. Suppose, for example, that large numbers of

---

[2] This is the *substitution* effect of a reduction in the interest rate, which induces all consumers to spend more when the interest rate falls (and less when it rises). The *income* effect of a change in the interest rate works in the opposite direction for creditors and debtors. Since these income effects tend to cancel out in the aggregate economy, they are ignored here.

households become pessimistic about the future state of the economy and about their own employment prospects. In many cases, these fears will lead households to increase their current desired saving in anticipation of rough economic times ahead. But increasing their current saving implies a reduction in current consumption at any given level of disposable income. The result will be a downward shift in the consumption function.

The reverse also tends to be true. Favourable expectations about the future state of the economy will lead many households to increase their current desired consumption and reduce their current desired saving. The result will be an upward shift in the consumption function and a downward shift in the saving function, as shown in Figure 21-3.

Expectations about the future state of the economy often influence desired consumption. Optimism leads to an upward shift in the consumption function; pessimism leads to a downward shift in the consumption function.

Summary It is useful to summarize what we have learned so far about the consumption function. As you will soon see, it will play a crucial role in our simple model of national income determination. The main points are as follows:

1. Desired consumption is assumed to be positively related to disposable income. In a graph, this relationship is shown by the positive slope of the consumption function, which is equal to the marginal propensity to consume (*MPC*).

2. There are both *autonomous* and *induced* components of desired consumption. A movement along the consumption function shows changes in consumption induced by changes in disposable income. A shift of the consumption function shows autonomous changes in consumption.

3. An increase in household wealth, a fall in interest rates, or greater optimism about the future are all assumed to lead to an increase in desired consumption and thus an upward shift of the consumption function.

4. All disposable income is either consumed or saved. Therefore, there is a saving function associated with the consumption function. Any event that causes the consumption function to shift must also cause the saving function to shift by an equal amount in the opposite direction.

Desired Investment Expenditure

Our simple macroeconomic model has only consumption and investment. Having spent considerable time discussing desired consumption expenditure, we are now ready to examine the determinants of desired investment. Recall from Chapter 20 the three categories of investment:

- inventory accumulation
- residential construction
- new plant and equipment

Investment expenditure is the most volatile component of GDP, and changes in investment are strongly associated with aggregate economic fluctuations. As shown in Figure 21-4, total investment in Canada fluctuates around an average of about 20 percent of GDP. In each of the last three recessions (1982, 1991, and 2009), investment as a share of GDP fell by between three and five percentage points. In contrast, consumption, government purchases, and net exports are much smoother over the business cycle, each typically changing by less than one percentage point. An important part of our understanding of business cycles will therefore rely on our understanding of the fluctuations in investment.

What explains such fluctuations in investment? Here we examine three important determinants of aggregate investment expenditure:

- the real interest rate
- changes in the level of sales
- business confidence

Let's now examine these in turn.

Desired Investment and the Real Interest Rate The real interest rate represents the real opportunity cost of using money (either borrowed money or retained earnings) for investment purposes. A rise in the real interest rate therefore reduces the amount of desired investment expenditure. This relationship is most easily understood if we separate investment into its three components: inventories, residential construction, and new plant and equipment.

Inventories. Changes in inventories represent only a small percentage of private investment in a typical year. As shown by the bottom line in Figure 21-4, inventory investment has been between –2 percent and 2 percent of GDP over the past 30 years. (Inventory investment of –2 percent in a year means that inventories *fall* by 2 percent of GDP.) But the average

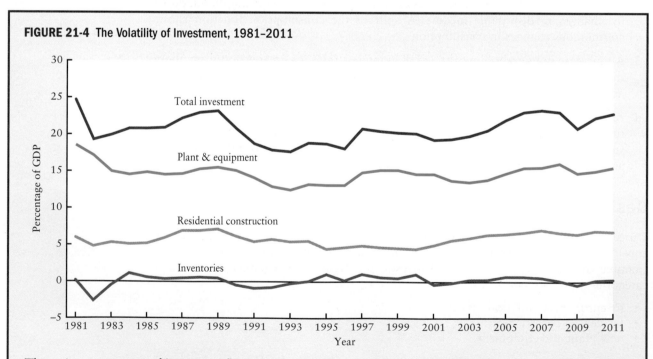

FIGURE 21-4 The Volatility of Investment, 1981–2011

The major components of investment fluctuate considerably as a share of GDP. The recessions of 1982, 1991, and 2009 are evident from the reductions in all components of investment.

(*Source:* Based on author's calculations using data from Statistics Canada's CANSIM database. Plant and Equipment: Table 380-0026. Residential Construction: Table 380-0025. Inventories: Table 380-0028. The measures are shown here as a fraction of current dollar GDP, Table 380-0017.)

amount of inventory investment is not an adequate measure of its importance. Since inventory investment is quite volatile, it has an important influence on fluctuations in investment expenditure.

When a firm ties up funds in inventories, those same funds cannot be used elsewhere to earn income. As an alternative to holding inventories, the firm could lend the money out at the going rate of interest. Hence, the higher the real rate of interest, the higher the opportunity cost of holding an inventory of a given size; the higher the opportunity cost, the smaller the inventories that will be desired.

Residential Construction. Expenditure on newly built residential housing is also volatile. Most houses are purchased with money that is borrowed by means of mortgages. Interest on the borrowed money typically accounts for more than one-half of the purchaser's annual mortgage payments; the remainder is repayment of the original loan, called the *principal*. Because interest payments are such a large part of mortgage payments, variations in interest rates exert a substantial effect on the demand for housing.

New Plant and Equipment. The real interest rate is also a major determinant of firms' investment in factories, equipment, and a whole range of durable capital goods that are used for production. When interest rates are high, it is expensive for firms to borrow funds that can be used to build new plants or purchase new capital equipment. Similarly, firms with cash on hand can earn high returns on interest-earning assets, again making investment in new capital a less attractive alternative. Thus, high real interest rates lead to a reduction in desired investment in capital equipment, whereas low real interest rates increase desired investment.

The largest part of investment by firms is in new plants and equipment, such as this expansion of a pulp mill in British Columbia.

> The real interest rate reflects the opportunity cost associated with investment, whether it is investment in inventories, residential construction, or new plant and equipment. The higher the real interest rate, the higher the opportunity cost of investment and thus the lower the amount of desired investment.

Desired Investment and Changes in Sales Firms hold inventories to meet unexpected changes in sales and production, and they usually have a target level of inventories that depends on their normal level of sales. Because the size of inventories is related to the level of sales, the *change* in inventories (which is part of current investment) is related to the *change* in the level of sales.

For example, suppose a firm wants to hold inventories equal to 10 percent of its monthly sales. If normal monthly sales are $100 000, it will want to hold inventories valued at $10 000. If monthly sales increase to $110 000, it will want to increase its inventories to $11 000. Over the period during which its stock of inventories is being increased, there will be a total of $1000 of new inventory investment.

> The higher the level of sales, the larger the desired stock of inventories. Changes in the rate of sales therefore cause temporary bouts of investment (or disinvestment) in inventories.

Changes in sales have similar effects on investment in plant and equipment. For example, if there is a general increase in consumers' demand for products that is expected to persist and that cannot be met by existing capacity, investment in new plant and equipment will be needed. Once the new plants have been built and put into operation, however, the rate of new investment will fall.

Desired Investment and Business Confidence Investment takes time. When a firm invests, it increases its future capacity to produce output. If it can sell the new output profitably, the investment will prove to be a good one. If the new output does not generate profits, the investment will have been a bad one. When it undertakes an investment, the firm does not know if it will turn out well or badly—it is betting on a favourable future that cannot be known with certainty.

When firms expect good times ahead, they will want to invest now so that they have a larger productive capacity in the future ready to satisfy the greater demand. When they expect bad times ahead, they will not invest because they expect no payoff from doing so.

The Conference Board of Canada publishes regular surveys of business and consumer confidence. Visit its website: www.conferenceboard.ca.

> **Investment depends on firms' expectations about the future state of the economy. Optimism about the future leads to more desired investment; pessimism leads to less desired investment.**

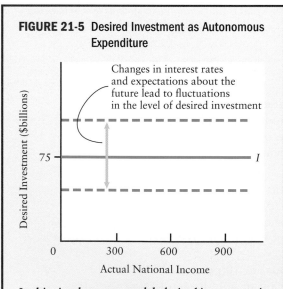

FIGURE 21-5 Desired Investment as Autonomous Expenditure

In this simple macro model, desired investment is assumed to be autonomous with respect to current national income. In this example, the level of desired investment is $75 billion. However, changes in interest rates or business confidence will lead to upward or downward shifts in the investment function.

Desired Investment as Autonomous Expenditure We have seen that desired investment is influenced by many things, and a complete discussion of the determination of national income is not possible without including all of these factors.

For the moment, however, our goal is to build the *simplest* model of the aggregate economy in which we can examine the interaction of actual national income and desired aggregate expenditure. To build this simple model, we begin by treating desired investment as *autonomous*—that is, we assume it to be unaffected by changes in national income. Figure 21-5 shows the investment function as a horizontal line.

It is important not to confuse the assumption that desired investment is *autonomous* with respect to national income (which we are making) with the assumption that it is *constant* (which we are not making). As we have said, investment is the most volatile component of aggregate expenditure, and it will therefore be important in our model that investment be able to change; shocks to firms' investment behaviour (upward or downward shifts in the investment function) will end up being an important explanation for fluctuations in national income. Our assumption that investment is autonomous with respect to national income (and hence the *I* function in Figure 21-5 is horizontal) is mainly a simplifying one. But the assumption does reflect the fact that investment is an act undertaken by firms for *future* benefit, and thus the *current* level of GDP is unlikely to have a significant effect on desired investment.

The Aggregate Expenditure Function

The **aggregate expenditure (AE) function** relates the level of desired aggregate expenditure to the level of actual national income. (In both cases we mean *real* as opposed to *nominal* variables.) In the simplified economy of this chapter without government and international trade, there is no G or $(X - IM)$ in our function. Desired aggregate expenditure is thus equal to desired consumption plus desired investment, $C + I$.

aggregate expenditure (AE) function The function that relates desired aggregate expenditure to actual national income.

$$AE = C + I$$

The table in Figure 21-6 shows how the AE function can be calculated, given the consumption function from Figure 21-2 on page 522 and the investment function from Figure 21-5 on page 530. The AE function is constructed by vertically summing the C function and the I function, thus showing desired total spending at each level of national income. In this specific case, all of desired investment expenditure is autonomous, as is the $30 billion of consumption that would be desired if national income were equal to zero. Total autonomous expenditure is therefore $105 billion—induced expenditure is just equal to induced consumption, which is equal to the MPC times disposable income ($0.8 \times Y_D$). Furthermore, since our simple model has no government and no taxes, disposable income, Y_D, is equal to national income, Y. Hence, desired aggregate expenditure can be written as

$$AE = \$105 \text{ billion} + (0.8)Y$$

The Marginal Propensity to Spend The fraction of any increment to national income that people spend on purchasing domestic output is called the economy's **marginal propensity to spend**. The marginal propensity to spend is measured by the change in desired aggregate expenditure divided by the change in national income that brings it about, or $\Delta AE / \Delta Y$. This is the slope of the aggregate expenditure function. In this book, the marginal propensity to spend is denoted by the symbol z, which is a number greater than zero and less than 1. For the example given in Figure 21-6, the marginal propensity to spend is 0.8. If national income increases by a dollar, 80 cents will go into increased desired (consumption) expenditure; 20 cents will go into increased desired saving. The marginal propensity to spend should not be confused with the marginal propensity to consume.

marginal propensity to spend The change in desired aggregate expenditure on domestic output divided by the change in national income that brought it about.

The marginal propensity to spend is the amount of extra total expenditure induced when national income rises by $1, whereas the marginal propensity to consume is the amount of extra consumption expenditure induced when households' disposable income rises by $1.

In the simple model of this chapter, however, the marginal propensity to spend is equal to the marginal propensity to consume because consumption is the only kind of expenditure that is assumed to vary with national income. In later chapters, when we add government and international trade to the model, the marginal propensity

FIGURE 21-6 The Aggregate Expenditure Function

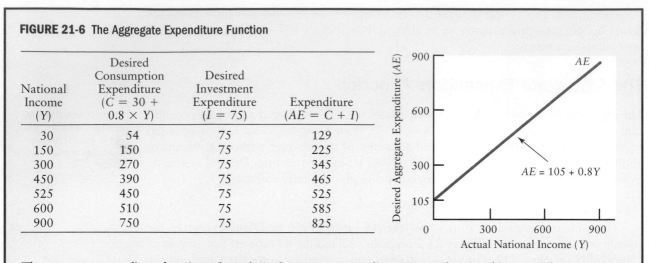

National Income (Y)	Desired Consumption Expenditure ($C = 30 + 0.8 \times Y$)	Desired Investment Expenditure ($I = 75$)	Expenditure ($AE = C + I$)
30	54	75	129
150	150	75	225
300	270	75	345
450	390	75	465
525	450	75	525
600	510	75	585
900	750	75	825

The aggregate expenditure function relates desired aggregate expenditure to actual national income. The curve *AE* in the figure plots the data from the first and last columns of the accompanying table. Its intercept, which in this case is $105 billion, shows the sum of autonomous consumption and autonomous investment. The slope of *AE* is equal to the marginal propensity to spend, which in this simple economy is just the marginal propensity to consume.

to spend will differ from the marginal propensity to consume. Both here and in later chapters, it is the more general measure—the marginal propensity to spend—that is important for determining equilibrium national income.

21.2 Equilibrium National Income

We have constructed an *AE* function that combines the spending plans of households and firms. The function shows, for any given level of *actual* national income, the level of *desired* aggregate spending. We are now ready to see what determines the *equilibrium* level of national income. When something is in equilibrium, there is no tendency for it to change. Any conditions that are required for something to be in equilibrium are called *equilibrium conditions*. We will see that the distinction between desired and actual expenditure is central to understanding the equilibrium conditions for national income.

In this chapter and the next, we make an important assumption that influences the nature of equilibrium. In particular, we assume that firms are able and willing to produce any amount of output that is demanded of them and that changes in their production levels do not require a change in their product prices. In this setting, we say that output is *demand determined*. This is an extreme assumption, and we will relax it in Chapter 23. Until then, however, it is a very useful assumption that allows us to more easily understand how our macro model works.

Table 21-1 illustrates the determination of equilibrium national income for our simple model economy. Suppose firms are producing a final output of $300 billion, and thus *actual* national income is $300 billion. According to the table, at this level of actual national income, *desired* aggregate expenditure is $345 billion. If firms persist in producing a current output of only $300 billion in the face of desired aggregate expenditure of $345 billion, one of two things will happen.

One possibility is that households and firms will be unable to spend the extra $45 billion that they would like to spend, so lines or waiting lists of unsatisfied customers will appear. These shortages will send a signal to firms that they could increase their sales if they increased their production. When the firms do increase their production, actual national income rises. Of course, the individual firms are interested only in their own sales and profits, but their individual actions have as their inevitable consequence an increase in GDP.

A more realistic possibility is that all spenders will spend everything that they wanted to spend and there will be no lineups of unsatisfied customers. Since desired expenditure exceeds the actual amount of output, this is possible only if some sales come from the producers' accumulated inventories. In our example, the fulfillment of plans to purchase $345 billion worth of goods in the face of a current output of only $300 billion will reduce inventories by $45 billion. As long as inventories last, more goods can be sold than are currently being produced. But since firms want to maintain a certain level of inventories, they will eventually increase their production. Once again, the consequence of each individual firm's decision to increase production is an increase in actual national income. Thus, the final response to an excess of desired aggregate expenditure over actual output is a rise in national income.

TABLE 21-1 Equilibrium National Income

Actual National Income (Y)	Desired Aggregate Expenditure ($AE = C + I$)	Effect
30	129 ⎫	Inventories are falling;
150	225 ⎪	firms increase output
300	345 ⎬	
450	465 ⎭	
525	525	Equilibrium income
600	585 ⎫	Inventories are rising;
900	825 ⎭	firms reduce output

National income is in equilibrium when desired aggregate expenditure equals actual national income. The data are from Figure 21-6.

> **For any level of national income at which desired aggregate expenditure exceeds actual income, there will be pressure for actual national income to rise.**

Next consider the $900 billion level of actual national income in Table 21-1. At this level of output, desired expenditure on domestically produced goods is only $825 billion. If firms persist in producing $900 billion worth of goods, $75 billion worth must remain unsold. Therefore, inventories must rise. However, firms will not allow inventories of unsold goods to rise indefinitely; sooner or later, they will reduce the level of output to the level of sales. When they reduce their level of output, national income will fall.

> **For any level of income at which desired aggregate expenditure is less than actual income, there will be pressure for national income to fall.**

Changes in firms' accumulated inventories often signal changes in desired aggregate expenditure and eventually induce firms to change their production decisions.

Finally, look at the national income level of $525 billion in Table 21-1. At this level, and only at this level, desired aggregate expenditure is equal to actual national income. Purchasers can fulfill their spending plans without causing inventories to change. There is no incentive for firms to alter output. Because everyone wants to purchase an amount equal to what is actually being produced, output and income will remain steady; they are in equilibrium.

> The equilibrium level of national income occurs where desired aggregate expenditure equals actual national income.

In other words, the *equilibrium condition* for our simple model of national income determination is

$$AE = Y$$

As we will now see, the combination of our *AE* function and this condition will determine the equilibrium level of national income.

Consider Figure 21-7. The line labelled *AE* graphs the specific aggregate expenditure function that we have been working with throughout this chapter. The 45° line ($AE = Y$) graphs the equilibrium condition that desired aggregate expenditure equals actual national income. Anywhere along the 45° line, the value of desired aggregate expenditure, which is measured on the vertical axis, is equal to the value of actual national income, which is measured on the horizontal axis.

Graphically, equilibrium occurs at the level of income at which the *AE* line intersects the 45° line. This is the level of income at which desired aggregate expenditure is just equal to actual national income. In Figure 21-7, the equilibrium level of national income (real GDP) is Y_0.

To understand how Figure 21-7 illustrates economic behaviour, consider some level of real GDP below Y_0. At this level of income, the *AE* curve lies above the 45° line, indicating that desired spending exceeds actual output. The vertical distance between *AE* and the 45° line reflects the size of this excess demand. As we said earlier, this excess demand will induce firms to increase their production. Conversely, at any level of GDP above Y_0, the *AE* curve is below the 45° line, indicating that desired spending is less than actual output. The vertical distance between the curves in this case shows the size of the excess supply, which will induce firms to reduce their production. Only when real GDP equals Y_0 is desired spending equal to actual output, thus providing firms with no incentive to change their production.

Now that we have explained the meaning of equilibrium national income, we will go on to examine the various forces that can *change* this equilibrium. We will then be well on our way to understanding some of the sources of short-run fluctuations in real GDP.

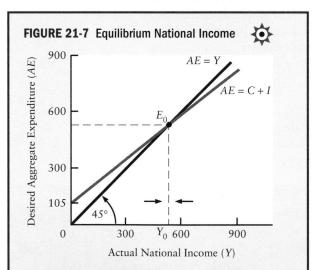

FIGURE 21-7 Equilibrium National Income

Equilibrium national income is that level of national income where desired aggregate expenditure equals actual national income. If actual national income is below Y_0, desired aggregate expenditure will exceed national income, and output will rise. If actual national income is above Y_0, desired aggregate expenditure will be less than national income, and production will fall. Only when national income is equal to Y_0 will the economy be in equilibrium, as shown at E_0.

21.3 Changes in Equilibrium National Income

Figure 21-7 shows that the equilibrium level of national income occurs where the *AE* function intersects the 45° line. Through the adjustment in firms' inventories and production levels, the level of actual national income will adjust until this equilibrium level is achieved. Because the *AE* function plays a central role in determining equilibrium national income, you should not be surprised to hear that *shifts* in the *AE* function are central to explaining why the equilibrium level of national income changes.

Shifts of the *AE* Function

The *AE* function shifts when one of its components shifts—that is, when there is a shift in the consumption function or in the investment function. As we have already mentioned, both the consumption function and the investment function will shift if there is a change in interest rates or expectations of the future state of the economy. A change in household wealth is an additional reason for the consumption function to shift. Let's now consider what happens when there is an upward shift in the *AE* function.

Upward Shifts in the *AE* Function Suppose households experience an increase in wealth and thus increase their desired consumption spending at each level of disposable income. Or suppose firms' expectations of higher future sales lead them to increase their planned investment. What is the effect of such events on national income?

Because any increase in autonomous expenditure shifts the entire *AE* function upward, the same analysis applies to each of the changes mentioned. Two types of shifts in *AE* can occur. First, if the same addition to expenditure occurs at all levels of income, the *AE* function shifts parallel to itself, as shown in part (i) of Figure 21-8. Second, if there is a change in the marginal propensity to spend, the slope of the *AE* function changes, as shown in part (ii) of Figure 21-8.

Figure 21-8 shows that an upward shift in the *AE* function increases equilibrium national income. After the shift in the *AE* curve, income is no longer in equilibrium at its original level because at that level desired aggregate expenditure exceeds actual national income. Given this excess demand, firms' inventories are being depleted and firms respond by increasing production. Equilibrium national income rises to the higher level indicated by the intersection of the *new AE* curve with the 45° line.

Downward Shifts in the *AE* Function What happens to national income if there is a decrease in the amount of consumption or investment expenditure desired at each level of income? These changes shift the *AE* function downward, as shown in Figure 21-8 by the movement from the dashed *AE* curve to the solid *AE* curve. An equal reduction in desired expenditure at all levels of income shifts *AE* parallel to itself. A fall in the marginal propensity to spend out of national income reduces the slope of the *AE* function. In both cases, the equilibrium level of national income decreases; the new equilibrium is found at the intersection of the 45° line and the *new AE* curve.

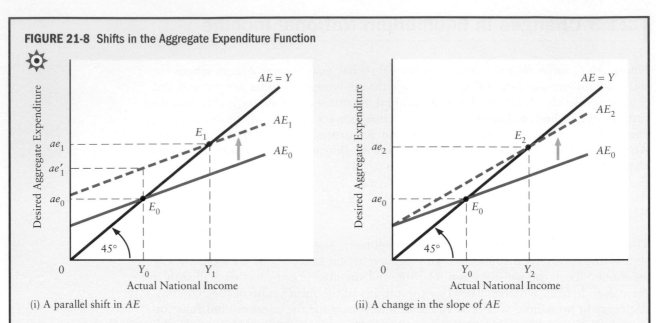

FIGURE 21-8 Shifts in the Aggregate Expenditure Function

(i) A parallel shift in AE

(ii) A change in the slope of AE

Upward shifts in the AE function increase equilibrium income; downward shifts decrease equilibrium income. In parts (i) and (ii), the AE function is initially AE_0 with equilibrium national income equal to Y_0.

In part (i), a parallel upward shift in the AE curve from AE_0 to AE_1 reflects an increase in desired expenditure at each level of national income. For example, at Y_0, desired expenditure rises from ae_0 to ae'_1 and therefore exceeds actual national income. Equilibrium is reached at E_1, where income is Y_1. The increase in desired expenditure from ae'_1 to ae_1, represented by a movement along AE_1, is an induced response to the increase in income from Y_0 to Y_1.

In part (ii), a non-parallel upward shift in the AE curve from AE_0 to AE_2 reflects an increase in the marginal propensity to spend. This leads to an increase in equilibrium national income. Equilibrium is reached at E_2, where national income is equal to Y_2.

Changes in household wealth, such as those created by large and persistent swings in stock-market values, are predicted to lead to changes in households' desired consumption expenditure, thus changing the equilibrium level of national income.

The Results Restated We have derived two important general propositions from our simple model of national income determination:

1. A rise in the amount of desired aggregate expenditure at each level of national income will shift the AE curve upward and increase equilibrium national income.

2. A fall in the amount of desired aggregate expenditure at each level of national income will shift the AE curve downward and reduce equilibrium national income.

In addition, part (ii) of Figure 21-8 suggests a third general proposition regarding the effect of a change in the *slope* of the AE function:

3. An increase in the marginal propensity to spend, z, steepens the AE curve and increases equilibrium national income. Conversely, a decrease in the marginal propensity to spend flattens the AE curve and decreases equilibrium national income.

The Multiplier

We have learned how specific changes in the AE function cause equilibrium national income to rise or fall. We would now like to understand what determines the *size* of these changes. A measure of the magnitude of such changes is provided by the *multiplier*. A change in autonomous expenditure increases equilibrium national income by a *multiple* of the initial change in autonomous expenditure. That is, the change in national income is *larger than* the initial change in desired expenditure.

> The multiplier is the change in equilibrium national income divided by the change in autonomous expenditure that brought it about. In the simple macro model, the multiplier is greater than 1.[3]

To see why the multiplier is greater than 1 in this model, consider a simple example. Imagine what would happen to national income if Kimberley-Clark decided to spend an additional $500 million per year on the construction of new paper mills. Initially, the construction of the paper mills would create $500 million worth of new national income and a corresponding amount of income for households and firms who produce the goods and services on which the initial $500 million is spent. But this is not the end of the story. The increase in national income of $500 million would cause an induced increase in desired consumption.

With our theory of the consumption function, electricians, masons, carpenters, and others—who gain new income directly from the building of the paper mills—will spend some of it on food, clothing, entertainment, cars, TVs, and other commodities. When output expands to meet this demand, new incomes will be created for workers and firms in the industries that produce these goods and services. When they, in turn, spend their newly earned incomes, output will rise further. More income will be created, and more expenditure will be induced. Indeed, at this stage, we might wonder whether the increases in income will ever come to an end. To deal with this concern, we need to consider the multiplier in somewhat more precise terms.

Let autonomous expenditure be denoted by A. Now consider an increase in autonomous expenditure of ΔA, which in our example is $500 million per year. Remember that ΔA stands for any increase in autonomous expenditure; this could be an increase

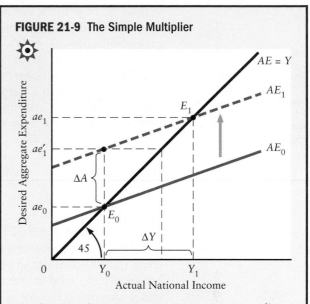

FIGURE 21-9 The Simple Multiplier

An increase in autonomous aggregate expenditure increases equilibrium national income by a multiple of the initial increase. The initial equilibrium is at E_0, where AE_0 intersects the 45° line. At this point, desired aggregate expenditure, ae_0, is equal to actual national income, Y_0. An increase in autonomous expenditure of ΔA then shifts the AE function upward to AE_1.

Equilibrium occurs when income rises to Y_1. Here desired expenditure, ae_1, equals national income, Y_1. The increase in desired expenditure from ae_1' to ae_1 represents the induced increase in expenditure that occurs as national income rises. Because ΔY is greater than ΔA, the simple multiplier is greater than 1 ($\Delta Y / \Delta A > 1$).

---

[3] In this chapter and the next, we assume that firms can readily change their output in response to changes in demand (perhaps because there is some unemployed labour and capital). This assumption of *demand-determined output* is central to the result of a multiplier being greater than 1. We relax this assumption in later chapters.

in investment or in the autonomous component of consumption. The *AE* function shifts upward by ΔA. National income is no longer in equilibrium because desired aggregate expenditure now exceeds actual national income. Equilibrium is restored by a *movement along* the new *AE* curve.

simple multiplier The ratio of the change in equilibrium national income to the change in autonomous expenditure that brought it about, calculated for a constant price level.

The **simple multiplier** measures the change in equilibrium national income that occurs in response to a change in autonomous expenditure when the price level is constant (reflecting the assumption that output is demand determined). We refer to it as "simple" because we have simplified the situation by assuming that the price level is fixed (an assumption we will remove in Chapter 23). Figure 21-9 illustrates the simple multiplier and makes clear that it is greater than 1. *Applying Economic Concepts 21-1* provides a numerical example.

The Size of the Simple Multiplier The size of the simple multiplier depends on the slope of the *AE* function—that is, on the marginal propensity to spend, z.

As shown in Figure 21-10, a high marginal propensity to spend means a steep *AE* curve. The expenditure induced by any initial increase in income is large, with the result that the final rise in income is correspondingly large. By contrast, a low marginal propensity to spend means a relatively flat *AE* curve. The expenditure induced by the initial increase in income is small, and the final rise in income is not much larger than the initial rise in autonomous expenditure that brought it about.

APPLYING ECONOMIC CONCEPTS 21-1

The Simple Multiplier: A Numerical Example

Consider an economy that has a marginal propensity to spend out of national income of 0.80. Suppose an increase in business confidence leads many firms to increase their investment in new capital equipment. Specifically, suppose desired investment increases by $1 billion per year. National income initially rises by $1 billion, but that is not the end of it. The factors of production that received the first $1 billion spend $800 million. This second round of spending generates $800 million of new production and income. This new income, in turn, induces $640 million of third-round spending, and so it continues, with each successive round of new production and income generating 80 percent as much in new expenditure. Each additional round of expenditure creates new production and income and yet another round of expenditure.

The table carries the process through 10 rounds. Students with sufficient patience (and no faith in mathematics) may compute as many rounds in the process as they want; they will find that the sum of the rounds of expenditures approaches a limit of $5 billion, which is five times the initial increase in expenditure. [30]

Notice that most of the total change in national income occurs in the first few rounds. Of the total change

of $5 billion, 68 percent ($3.4 billion) occurs after only five rounds of activity. By the end of the tenth round, 89 percent ($4.5 billion) of the total change has taken place.

Round of Spending	Increase in Expenditure (millions of dollars)	Cumulative Total (millions of dollars)
1 (initial increase)	1000.0	1000.0
2	800.0	1800.0
3	640.0	2440.0
4	512.0	2952.0
5	409.6	3361.6
6	327.7	3689.3
7	262.1	3951.4
8	209.7	4161.1
9	167.8	4328.9
10	134.2	4463.1
11 to 20 combined	479.3	4942.4
All others	57.6	5000.0

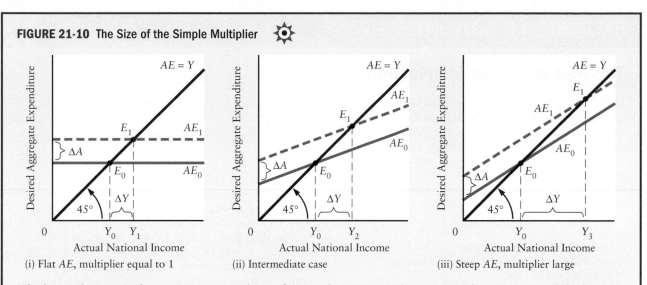

FIGURE 21-10 The Size of the Simple Multiplier

(i) Flat *AE*, multiplier equal to 1   (ii) Intermediate case   (iii) Steep *AE*, multiplier large

The larger the marginal propensity to spend out of national income (z), the steeper is the *AE* curve and the larger is the simple multiplier. In each part of the figure, the initial *AE* function is AE_0, equilibrium is at E_0, with income Y_0. The *AE* curve then shifts upward to AE_1 as a result of an increase in autonomous expenditure of ΔA. ΔA is the same in each part. The new equilibrium in each case is at E_1.

In part (i), the *AE* function is horizontal, indicating a marginal propensity to spend of zero ($z = 0$). The change in equilibrium income ΔY is only the increase in autonomous expenditure because there is no induced expenditure by the people who receive the initial increase in income. The simple multiplier is then equal to 1, its minimum possible value.

In part (ii), the *AE* curve slopes upward but is still relatively flat (z is low). The increase in equilibrium national income to Y_2 is only slightly greater than the increase in autonomous expenditure that brought it about. The simple multiplier is slightly greater than 1.

In part (iii), the *AE* function is quite steep (z is high). Now the increase in equilibrium income to Y_3 is much larger than the increase in autonomous expenditure that brought it about. The simple multiplier is much larger than 1.

The larger the marginal propensity to spend, the steeper the *AE* function and thus the larger the simple multiplier.

We can derive the precise value of the simple multiplier by using elementary algebra. (The formal derivation is given in *Extensions in Theory 21-2*.) The result is

$$\text{Simple multiplier} = \frac{\Delta Y}{\Delta A} = \frac{1}{1-z}$$

For the simple model we have developed in this chapter, $z = 0.8$ and so the simple multiplier $= 1/(1 - 0.8) = 1/0.2 = 5$. In this model, therefore, a \$1 billion increase in autonomous expenditure leads to a \$5 billion increase in equilibrium national income.

Recall that z is the marginal propensity to spend out of national income and is between zero and 1. The smallest simple multiplier occurs when z equals zero. In this case, $(1 - z)$ equals 1 and so the multiplier equals 1. On the other hand, if z is very close to 1, $(1 - z)$ is close to zero and so the multiplier becomes very large. The relationship between the slope of the *AE* function (z) and the size of the multiplier is shown in Figure 21-10.

EXTENSIONS IN THEORY 21-2

The Algebra of the Simple Multiplier

Basic algebra is all that is needed to derive the exact expression for the simple multiplier. First, we derive the equation for the *AE* curve. Desired aggregate expenditure comprises autonomous expenditure and induced expenditure. In the simple model of this chapter, autonomous expenditure is equal to investment plus autonomous consumption. Induced expenditure is equal to induced consumption. Hence, we can write

$$AE = zY + A \qquad [1]$$

where *A* is autonomous expenditure and zY is induced expenditure, *z* being the marginal propensity to spend out of national income.

Now we write the equation of the 45° line,

$$AE = Y \qquad [2]$$

which states the equilibrium condition that desired aggregate expenditure equals actual national income. Equation 1 and 2 are two equations with two unknowns, *AE* and *Y*. To solve them, we substitute Equation 1 into Equation 2 to obtain

$$Y = zY + A \qquad [3]$$

Equation 3 can be easily solved to get *Y* expressed in terms of *A* and *z*. The solution is

$$Y = \frac{A}{1 - z} \qquad [4]$$

Equation 4 tells us the equilibrium value of *Y* in terms of autonomous expenditures and the marginal propensity to spend out of national income. Now consider a $1 increase in *A*. The expression $Y = A/(1 - z)$ tells us that if *A* changes by one dollar, the resulting change in *Y* will be $1/(1 - z)$ dollars. Generally, for a change in autonomous spending of *A*, the resulting change in *Y* will be

$$\Delta Y = \frac{\Delta A}{1 - z} \qquad [5]$$

Dividing through by ΔA gives the value of the multiplier:

$$\text{Simple multiplier} = \frac{\Delta Y}{\Delta A} = \frac{1}{1 - z} \qquad [6]$$

Economic Fluctuations as Self-Fulfilling Prophecies

Expectations about the future play an important role in macroeconomics. We said earlier that households' and firms' expectations about the future state of the economy influence desired consumption and desired investment. But as we have just seen, changes in desired aggregate expenditure will, through the multiplier process, lead to changes in national income. This link between expectations and national income suggests that expectations about a healthy economy can actually produce a healthy economy—what economists call a *self-fulfilling prophecy*.

Imagine a situation in which many firms begin to feel optimistic about future economic prospects. This optimism may lead them to increase their desired investment, thus shifting up the economy's *AE* function. As we have seen, however, any upward shift in the *AE* function will lead to an increase in national income. Such "good" economic times will then be seen by firms to have justified their initial optimism. Many firms in such a situation may take pride in their ability to predict the future—but this would be misplaced pride. The truth of the matter is that if enough firms are optimistic and take actions based on that optimism, their actions will *create* the economic situation that they expected.

Now imagine the opposite situation, in which many firms begin to feel pessimistic about future economic conditions. This pessimism may lead them to scale down or cancel planned investment projects. Such a decline in planned investment would shift the *AE* function down and lead to a decrease in national income. The "bad" economic times will then be seen by the firms as justification for their initial pessimism, and many will take pride in their predictive powers. But again their pride would be misplaced; the truth is that sufficient pessimism on the part of firms will tend to *create* the conditions that they expected.

The aggregate consequences of pessimism on the part of both firms and consumers were an important contributing factor to the global recession that started in late 2008. In many countries, including Canada, the events surrounding the financial crisis of 2008–2009 led to a shattering of economic optimism. Measures of business and consumer confidence fell by more than had been observed in decades, and this decline in confidence partly explained the large declines in investment and household consumption that occurred at the time and lasted for more than a year. As we will see in later chapters, governments took actions to replace this drop in private-sector demand with increases in government spending.

SUMMARY

21.1 Desired Aggregate Expenditure

LO 1, 2

- Desired aggregate expenditure (*AE*) is equal to desired consumption plus desired investment plus desired government purchases plus desired net exports. It is the amount that economic agents want to spend on purchasing the national product.

$$AE = C + I + G + (X - IM)$$

- The relationship between disposable income and desired consumption is called the consumption function. The constant term in the consumption function is autonomous expenditure. The part of consumption that responds to income is called induced expenditure.
- A change in disposable income leads to a change in desired consumption and desired saving. The responsiveness of

these changes is measured by the marginal propensity to consume (*MPC*) and the marginal propensity to save (*MPS*), both of which are positive and sum to 1, indicating that all disposable income is either consumed or saved.

- Changes in wealth, interest rates, or expectations about the future lead to a change in autonomous consumption. As a result, the consumption function shifts.
- Firms' desired investment depends, among other things, on real interest rates, changes in sales, and business confidence. In our simplest model of the economy, investment is treated as autonomous with respect to changes in national income.

21.2 Equilibrium National Income

LO 3

- Equilibrium national income is defined as that level of national income at which desired aggregate expenditure equals actual national income. At incomes above equilibrium, desired expenditure is less than national income. In this case, inventories accumulate and firms will eventually reduce output. At incomes below equilibrium, desired expenditure exceeds national income. In

this case, inventories are depleted and firms will eventually increase output.

- Equilibrium national income is represented graphically by the point at which the aggregate expenditure (*AE*) curve cuts the 45° line—that is, where desired aggregate expenditure equals actual national income.

21.3 Changes in Equilibrium National Income   LO 4

- Equilibrium national income is increased by a rise in either autonomous consumption or autonomous investment expenditure. Equilibrium national income is reduced by a fall in these desired expenditures.
- The magnitude of the effect on national income of shifts in autonomous expenditure is given by the multiplier. It is defined as $\Delta Y/\Delta A$, where ΔA is the change in autonomous expenditure.
- The simple multiplier is the multiplier when the price level is constant. The simple multiplier $= \Delta Y/\Delta A = 1/(1 - z)$, where z is the marginal propensity to spend

out of national income. The larger is z, the larger is the simple multiplier.
- It is a basic prediction of our simple macro model that the simple multiplier is greater than 1.
- Expectations play an important role in the determination of national income. Optimism can lead households and firms to increase desired expenditure, which, through the multiplier process, leads to increases in national income. Pessimism can similarly lead to decreases in desired expenditure and national income.

KEY CONCEPTS

Desired versus actual expenditure
The consumption function
Average and marginal propensities to consume
Average and marginal propensities to save

The aggregate expenditure (AE) function
Marginal propensity to spend
Equilibrium national income
Effect on national income of shifts in the AE curve

The simple multiplier
The size of the multiplier and slope of the AE curve

STUDY EXERCISES

MyEconLab Make the grade with MyEconLab: Study Exercises marked in red can be found on MyEconLab. You can practise them as often as you want, and most feature step-by-step guided instructions to help you find the right answer.

1. Fill in the blanks to make the following statements correct.
    a. The equation for *actual* national income from the expenditure side is written as GDP = _____.
    b. The equation for *desired* aggregate expenditure is written as $AE =$ _____.
    c. National income accounts measure _____ expenditures in four broad categories. National income theory deals with _____ expenditure in the same four categories.
    d. The equation for a simple consumption function is written as $C = a + bY$. The letter a represents the _____ part of consumption. The letters bY represent the _____ part of consumption. When graphing a consumption function, the vertical intercept is given by the letter _____, and the slope of the function is given by the letter _____.

    e. In the simple macro model of this chapter, all investment is treated as _____ expenditure, meaning that it is unaffected by changes in national income.
    f. The aggregate expenditure function in the simple macro model of this chapter is written as $AE =$ _____ and is graphed with _____ on the vertical axis and _____ on the horizontal axis.
    g. An example of an aggregate expenditure function is $AE = \$47$ billion $+ 0.92Y$. Autonomous expenditure is _____ and the marginal propensity to spend out of national income is _____. In the simple model in this chapter, the marginal propensity to spend is the same as the marginal propensity to consume because _____.

2. Fill in the blanks to make the following statements correct.

   a. If actual national income is $200 billion and desired aggregate expenditure is $180 billion, inventories may begin to _____, firms will _____ the level of output, and national income will _____.

   b. If actual national income is $200 billion and desired aggregate expenditure is $214 billion, inventories may begin to _____, firms will _____ the level of output, and national income will _____.

   c. If households experience an increase in wealth that leads to an increase in desired consumption, the AE curve will shift _____. Equilibrium national income will _____ to the level indicated by the intersection of the AE curve with the _____ line.

   d. When autonomous desired expenditure increases by $10 billion, national income will increase by _____ than $10 billion. The magnitude of the change in national income is measured by the _____.

   e. The larger is the marginal propensity to spend, the _____ is the multiplier. Where z is the marginal propensity to spend, the multiplier is equal to _____.

3. Consider the following table showing aggregate consumption expenditures and disposable income. All values are expressed in billions of constant dollars.

Disposable Income (Y_D)	Desired Consumption (C)	$APC = C/Y_D$	$MPC = \Delta C/\Delta Y_D$
0	150	—	—
100	225	—	—
200	300	—	—
300	375	—	—
400	450	—	—
500	525	—	—
600	600	—	—
700	675	—	—
800	750	—	—

   a. Compute the average propensity to consume for each level of income and fill in the table.

   b. Compute the marginal propensity to consume for each successive change in income and fill in the table.

   c. Plot the consumption function on a scale diagram. What is its slope?

4. This question relates to desired saving, and is based on the table in Question 3.

   a. Compute desired saving at each level of disposable income. Plot the saving function on a scale diagram. What is its slope?

   b. Show that the average propensity to save plus the average propensity to consume must equal 1.

5. Relate the following newspaper headlines to shifts in the C, S, I, and AE functions and to changes in equilibrium national income.

   a. "Revival of consumer confidence leads to increased spending."

   b. "High mortgage rates discourage new house purchases."

   c. "Concern over future leads to a reduction in inventories."

   d. "Accelerated depreciation allowances in the new federal budget set off boom on equipment purchases."

   e. "Consumers spend as stock market soars."

6. In the chapter we explained at length the difference between *desired* expenditures and *actual* expenditures.

   a. Is national income accounting based on desired or actual expenditures? Explain.

   b. Suppose there were a sudden decrease in desired consumption expenditure. Explain why this would likely lead to an equally sudden increase in *actual* investment expenditure. Which type of investment would rise?

   c. Illustrate the event from part (b) in a 45°-line diagram.

7. Consider the following diagram of the AE function and the 45° line.

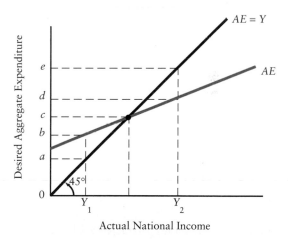

   a. Suppose the level of actual national income is Y_1. What is the level of desired aggregate expenditure? Is it greater or less than actual output? Are inventories being depleted or accumulated?

   b. If actual income is Y_1, explain the process by which national income changes toward equilibrium.

   c. Suppose the level of actual national income is Y_2. What is the level of desired aggregate expenditure? Is it greater or less than actual output? Are inventories being depleted or accumulated?

   d. If actual income is Y_2, explain the process by which national income changes toward equilibrium.

8. Consider a simple model like the one developed in this chapter. The following equations show the levels of desired consumption and investment:

$$C = 500 + 0.9Y$$
$$I = 100$$

Y	C	I	AE
0	—	—	—
2 000	—	—	—
4 000	—	—	—
6 000	—	—	—
8 000	—	—	—
10 000	—	—	—

   a. Complete the table above.
   b. What is the equilibrium level of national income in this model? Why?

9. Suppose you are given the following information for an economy without government spending, exports, or imports. C is desired consumption, I is desired investment, and Y is income. C and I are given by

$$C = 1400 + 0.8Y$$
$$I = 400$$

   a. What is the equation for the aggregate expenditure (AE) function?
   b. Applying the equilibrium condition that $Y = AE$, determine the level of equilibrium national income.
   c. Using your answer from part (b), determine the values of consumption, saving, and investment when the economy is in equilibrium.

10. For each of the following aggregate expenditure (AE) functions, identify the marginal propensity to spend and calculate the simple multiplier.
   a. $AE = 150 + 0.4Y$
   b. $AE = 900 + 0.62Y$
   c. $AE = 6250 + 0.92Y$
   d. $AE = 457 + 0.57Y$
   e. $AE = 500 + 0.2Y$
   f. $AE = 1000 + 0.35Y$

11. Consider an economy characterized by the following equations:

$$C = 500 + 0.75Y + 0.05W$$
$$I = 150$$

where C is desired consumption, I is desired investment, W is household wealth, and Y is national income.

   a. Suppose wealth is constant at $W = 10\ 000$. Draw the aggregate expenditure function on a scale diagram along with the 45° line. What is the equilibrium level of national income?
   b. What is the marginal propensity to spend in this economy?
   c. What is the value of the simple multiplier?
   d. Using your answer from part (c), what would be the change in equilibrium national income if desired investment increased to 250? Show this in your diagram.
   e. Begin with the new equilibrium level of national income from part (d). Now suppose household wealth increases from 10 000 to 15 000. What happens to the AE function and by how much does national income change?

12. The "Paradox of Thrift" is a famous idea in macroeconomics—one that we will discuss in later chapters. The basic idea is that if every household in the economy tries to increase its level of desired saving, the level of national income will fall and they will end up saving no more than they were initially. Use the model and diagrams of this chapter to show how an (autonomous) increase in desired saving would reduce equilibrium income and lead to no change in aggregate saving. (Though it is not essential, you may find it useful to see **Investment, Saving, and Equilibrium GDP** in the *Additional Topics* section of MyEconLab.)

13. In the simple model of this chapter, aggregate investment was assumed to be autonomous with respect to national income. The simple multiplier was $1/(1 - z)$, where z was the marginal propensity to spend. And with autonomous investment, the marginal propensity to spend is simply the marginal propensity to consume.

   But now suppose firms' investment is *not* completely autonomous. That is, suppose that $I = \bar{I} + \beta Y$, where $\bar{I}$ is autonomous investment and β is the "marginal propensity to invest" ($\beta > 0$). Explain how this modification to the simple model changes the simple multiplier, and why.

Adding Government and Trade to the Simple Macro Model

CHAPTER OUTLINE

22.1 INTRODUCING GOVERNMENT

22.2 INTRODUCING FOREIGN TRADE

22.3 EQUILIBRIUM NATIONAL INCOME

22.4 CHANGES IN EQUILIBRIUM NATIONAL INCOME

22.5 DEMAND-DETERMINED OUTPUT

LEARNING OBJECTIVES (LO)

After studying this chapter you will be able to

1 understand how government purchases and tax revenues relate to national income.

2 understand how exports and imports relate to national income.

3 distinguish between the marginal propensity to consume and the marginal propensity to spend.

4 explain why the introduction of government and foreign trade in the macro model reduces the value of the simple multiplier.

5 explain how government can use fiscal policy to influence the level of national income.

6 understand that output is demand determined in our simple macro model.

IN Chapter 21, we developed a simple short-run model of national income determination in a closed economy with fixed prices. In this chapter, we add a government and a foreign sector to that model. In Chapter 23, we will expand the model further to explain the determination of the price level.

Adding government to the model allows us to understand how the government's use of its taxing and spending powers can affect the level of national income. Adding foreign trade allows us to examine some ways in which external events affect the Canadian economy. Fortunately, the key elements of the previous chapter's theory of income determination are unchanged even after government and the foreign sector are incorporated.

| 22.1 Introducing Government

fiscal policy The use of the government's tax and spending policies to achieve government objectives.

A government's **fiscal policy** is defined by its plans for taxes and spending. Government spending and taxation influence national income in both the short and the long run. Our discussion of fiscal policy begins in this chapter; we go into more detail in Chapter 24 and again in Chapter 32.

Government Purchases

In Chapter 20, we distinguished between government *purchases of goods and services* and government *transfer payments*. The distinction bears repeating here. When the government hires a public servant, buys office supplies, purchases fuel for the Canadian Forces, or commissions a study by consultants, it is adding directly to the demands for the economy's current output of goods and services. Hence, desired government purchases, G, are part of aggregate desired expenditure.

The other part of government spending, transfer payments, also affects desired aggregate expenditure but only indirectly. Consider welfare or employment-insurance benefits, for example. These government expenditures place no direct demand on the nation's production of goods and services since they merely transfer funds to the recipients. The same is true of government transfers to firms, which often take the form of subsidies. However, when individuals or firms spend some of these payments on consumption or investment, their spending is part of aggregate expenditure. Thus, government transfer payments do affect aggregate expenditure but only through the effect these transfers have on households' and firms' spending.

In this chapter we make the simple assumption that the level of government purchases, G, is autonomous with respect to the level of national income. As GDP rises or falls, the level of the government's transfer payments will generally change, but we assume that G does not automatically change just because GDP changes. We then view any change in G as a result of a government policy decision.

Net Tax Revenues

Taxes reduce households' disposable income relative to national income. In contrast, transfer payments raise disposable income relative to national income. For the purpose of calculating the effect of government policy on desired consumption expenditure, it is the net effect of the two that matters.

net tax revenue Total tax revenue minus transfer payments, denoted T.

Net tax revenue is defined as total tax revenue received by the government minus total transfer payments made by the government, and it is denoted T. (For the remainder of this chapter, the term "taxes" means "net taxes" unless stated otherwise.) Because transfer payments are smaller than total tax revenues, net tax revenues are positive. In the model in this chapter, we assume that net tax revenues vary directly with the level of national income. As national income rises, a tax system with given tax rates will yield more revenue (net of transfers). For example, when income rises, people will pay more income tax in total even though the tax *rates* are unchanged. In addition, when income rises, the government generally reduces its transfers to households. We will use the following simple form for government net tax revenues, T:

$$T = tY$$

net tax rate The increase in net tax revenue generated when national income rises by one dollar.

where t is the **net tax rate**—the increase in net tax revenue generated when national income increases by \$1.

It may be tempting to think of t as the income-tax rate, but note that we are representing in a simple way what in reality is a complex tax and transfer structure that includes, in addition to several different types of financial transfers to households, the personal income tax, the corporate income tax, the GST, provincial sales tax, and property taxes. For that reason, t is not the rate on one specific type of tax. It is the amount by which total government tax revenues (less transfers) change when national income changes.

The Budget Balance

The *budget balance* is the difference between total government revenue and total government expenditure; equivalently, it equals net tax revenue minus government purchases, $T - G$. When net revenues exceed purchases, the government has a **budget surplus**. When purchases exceed net revenues, the government has a **budget deficit**. When the two amounts are equal, the government has a *balanced budget*.

> **budget surplus** Any excess of current revenue over current expenditure.

When the government runs a budget deficit, it must borrow the excess of spending over revenues. It does this by issuing additional *government debt* (bonds or Treasury bills). When the government runs a surplus, it uses the excess revenue to buy back outstanding government debt. Budget deficits and government debt are the principal topics of Chapter 32.

> **budget deficit** Any shortfall of current revenue below current expenditure.

Provincial and Municipal Governments

Many people are surprised to learn that the combined activities of the many Canadian provincial and municipal governments account for *more* purchases of goods and services than does the federal government. The federal government raises about the same amount of tax revenue as do the provincial and municipal governments combined, but it transfers a considerable amount of its revenue to the provinces.

> When measuring the overall contribution of government to desired aggregate expenditure, all levels of government must be included.

As we proceed through this chapter discussing the role of government in the determination of national income, think of "the government" as the combination of all levels of government—federal, provincial, territorial, and municipal.

The federal Department of Finance designs and implements Canada's fiscal policy. See its website: www.fin.gc.ca.

Summary

Before introducing foreign trade, let's summarize how the presence of government affects our simple model.

1. All levels of government add directly to desired aggregate expenditure through their purchases of goods and services, G. Later in this chapter when we are constructing the aggregate expenditure (AE) function for our model, we will include G and we will treat it as autonomous expenditure.

2. Governments also collect tax revenue and make transfer payments. Net tax revenues are denoted T and are positively related to national income. Since T does not represent any expenditure on goods and services, it is not included directly in

the *AE* function. *T* will enter the *AE* function *indirectly*, however, through its effect on disposable income (Y_D) and consumption. Recall that $Y_D = Y - T$ and that desired consumption is assumed to depend on Y_D.

22.2 Introducing Foreign Trade

Canada imports all kinds of goods and services, from French wine and Peruvian anchovies to Swiss financial and American architectural services. Canada also exports a variety of goods and services, including timber, nickel, automobiles, engineering services, computer software, flight simulators, and commuter jets. U.S.–Canadian trade is the largest two-way flow of trade between any two countries in the world today.

Of all the goods and services produced in Canada in a given year, roughly 35 percent are exported. A similar value of goods and services is imported into Canada every year. Thus, although *net* exports may contribute only a few percent to Canada's GDP in a typical year, foreign trade is tremendously important to Canada's economy.

Net Exports

Exports depend on spending decisions made by foreign households and firms that purchase Canadian products. Typically, exports will not change as a result of changes in Canadian national income. We therefore treat exports as autonomous expenditure.

Imports, however, depend on the spending decisions of Canadian households and firms. Almost all consumption goods have an import content. Canadian-made cars, for example, use large quantities of imported components in their manufacture. Canadian-made clothes most often use imported cotton or wool. And most restaurant meals contain some imported fruits, vegetables, or meats. Hence, as consumption rises, imports will also increase. Because consumption rises with national income, we also get a positive relationship between imports and national income. In this chapter, we use the following simple form for desired imports:

> **marginal propensity to import** The increase in import expenditures induced by a $1 increase in national income. Denoted by *m*.

$$IM = mY$$

where *m* is the **marginal propensity to import**, the amount that desired imports rise when national income rises by $1.

In our simple model, net exports can be described by the following simple equation:

$$NX = X - mY$$

Since exports are autonomous with respect to *Y* but imports are positively related to *Y*, we see that *net exports* are negatively related to national income. This negative relationship is called the *net export function*. Data for a hypothetical economy with autonomous exports and with imports that are 10 percent of national income ($m = 0.1$) are

International trade is very important for the Canadian economy. More than $2.5 billion worth of goods and services flows across the Canada–U.S. border every day, much of it in trucks like these.

illustrated in Figure 22-1. In this example, exports form the autonomous component and imports form the induced component of desired net exports.

Shifts in the Net Export Function

Any given net export function is drawn under the assumption that everything affecting net exports, except domestic national income, remains constant. The two major influences that are held constant when we draw the NX function are foreign national income and international relative prices. If either one changes, the NX function will shift. Notice that anything affecting Canadian exports will shift the NX function parallel to itself, upward if exports increase and downward if exports decrease. Also notice that anything affecting the *proportion of income* that Canadian consumers want to spend on imports will change the *slope* of the NX function. Let's now explore some of these changes in detail.

Changes in Foreign Income An increase in foreign income, other things being equal, will lead to an increase in the quantity of Canadian goods demanded by foreign countries—that is, to an increase in Canadian exports. This change causes the X curve in Figure 22-1 to shift upward and therefore the NX function also to shift upward, parallel to its original position. A fall in foreign income leads to a reduction in Canadian exports and thus to a parallel downward shift in the NX function.

Changes in International Relative Prices Any change in the prices of Canadian goods *relative* to those of foreign goods will cause both imports and exports to change. These changes will shift the NX function.

Consider what happens with a rise in Canadian prices relative to those in foreign countries. The increase in Canadian prices means that foreigners now see Canadian goods as more expensive relative both to goods produced in their own country and to goods imported from countries other than Canada.

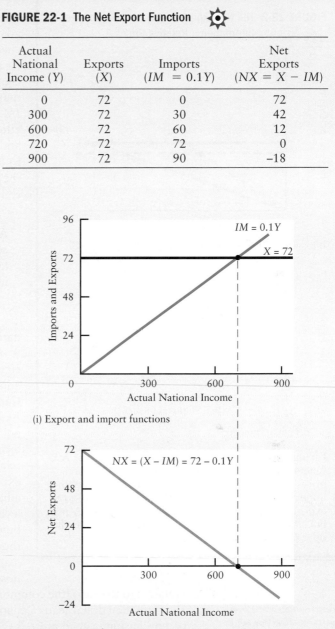

FIGURE 22-1 The Net Export Function ☀

Actual National Income (Y)	Exports (X)	Imports ($IM = 0.1Y$)	Net Exports ($NX = X - IM$)
0	72	0	72
300	72	30	42
600	72	60	12
720	72	72	0
900	72	90	−18

(i) Export and import functions

(ii) Net export function

Net exports fall as national income rises. The data are hypothetical. In part (i), exports are constant at $72 billion while imports rise with national income; the marginal propensity to import is assumed to be 0.10. Therefore, net exports, shown in part (ii), decline with national income. The slope of the import function in part (i) is equal to the marginal propensity to import. The slope of the net export function in part (ii) is the negative of the marginal propensity to import.

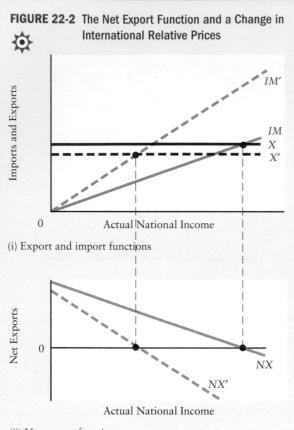

FIGURE 22-2 The Net Export Function and a Change in International Relative Prices

(i) Export and import functions

(ii) Net export function

Changes in international relative prices shift the NX function. A rise in Canadian prices relative to foreign prices lowers exports from X to X' and raises the import function from IM to IM'. This shifts the net export function downward from NX to NX'. A fall in Canadian prices (relative to foreign prices) has the opposite effect.

For lots of interesting information on Canada's international trade, go to the website for the Department of Foreign Affairs and International Trade: www.international.gc.ca.

As a result, the value of Canadian exports will fall.[1] The X curve shifts down in Figure 22-2. Similarly, Canadians will see imports from foreign countries become cheaper relative to the prices of Canadian-made goods. As a result, they will shift their expenditures toward foreign goods and away from Canadian goods. That is, the marginal propensity to import (m) will rise, and so the IM curve will rotate up. The combination of these two effects is that the net export function shifts downward and becomes steeper. A fall in Canadian prices relative to foreign prices would have the opposite effect, shifting the X function up and the IM function down, and thus shifting the NX function up.

> **A rise in Canadian prices relative to those in other countries reduces Canadian net exports at any level of national income. A fall in Canadian prices increases net exports at any level of national income.**

The most important cause of a change in international relative prices is a change in the exchange rate. A *depreciation* of the Canadian dollar means that foreigners must pay less of their money to buy one Canadian dollar, and Canadian residents must pay more Canadian dollars to buy a unit of any foreign currency. As a result, the price of foreign goods in terms of Canadian dollars rises, and the price of Canadian goods in terms of foreign currency falls. This reduction in the relative price of Canadian goods will cause a shift in expenditure away from foreign goods and toward Canadian goods. Canadian residents will import less at each level of Canadian national income, and foreigners will buy more Canadian exports. The net export function thus shifts upward.

An example may help to clarify the argument. Suppose something causes the Canadian dollar to depreciate relative to the euro (the common currency in the European Union). The depreciation of the Canadian dollar leads Canadians to switch away from French wines and German cars, purchasing instead more B.C. wine and Ontario-made cars. This reduction in the marginal propensity to import (m) is shown by a downward rotation of the IM curve. The depreciation of the Canadian dollar relative to the euro also stimulates Canadian exports. Quebec furniture and Maritime vacations now appear cheaper to Europeans than previously, and so their expenditure on such Canadian goods increases. This

---

[1] The rise in Canadian prices leads to a reduction in the quantity of Canadian goods demanded by foreigners. But in order for the *value* of Canadian exports to fall, the price elasticity of demand for Canadian exports must exceed 1 (so that the quantity reduction dominates the price increase). Throughout this book, we make this assumption.

increase in Canadian exports is shown by an upward shift in the X curve. The overall effect is that the net export function shifts up and becomes flatter.

One final word of caution is needed regarding prices, exchange rates, and net exports. It is important to keep in mind that the simple model in this chapter treats prices and exchange rates as *exogenous* variables. That is, though we can discuss what happens if they change, we do not yet *explain* where these changes come from. Of course, in the actual economy the price level and the exchange rate are key macroeconomic variables whose changes we want to understand. In the next chapter, the price level will be *endogenous* in our model and we can therefore consider why it changes. In Chapter 35, we explain in detail what causes the exchange rate to change. For now, however, keep in mind that the price level and the exchange rate are exogenous variables—we can explain what happens in our model *if* they change but we cannot use the current simple version of our model to explain *why* they change.

Summary

How does the presence of foreign trade modify our basic model? Let's summarize.

1. Foreign firms and households purchase Canadian-made goods. Changes in foreign income and international relative prices (including exchange rates) will affect Canadian exports (X), but we assume that X is autonomous with respect to Canadian national income. When we construct the economy's aggregate expenditure (AE) function, we will include X since it represents expenditure on domestically produced goods and services.

2. All components of domestic expenditure (C, I, and G) include some import content. Since C is positively related to national income, imports (IM) are also related positively to national income. When we construct the economy's AE function, which shows the desired aggregate expenditure on *domestic* products, we will *subtract IM* because these expenditures are on foreign products.

| 22.3 Equilibrium National Income

As in Chapter 21, equilibrium national income is the level of income at which desired aggregate expenditure equals actual national income. The addition of government and net exports changes the calculations that we must make but does not alter the equilibrium concept or the basic workings of the model.

Desired Consumption and National Income

Recall that disposable income is equal to national income minus net taxes, $Y_D = Y - T$. We take several steps to determine the relationship between consumption and national income in the presence of taxes.

1. First, assume that the net tax rate, t, is 10 percent, so that net tax revenues are 10 percent of national income:

$$T = (0.1)Y$$

2. Disposable income must therefore be 90 percent of national income:

$$Y_D = Y - T$$
$$= Y - (0.1)Y$$
$$= (0.9)Y$$

3. The consumption function we used last chapter is given as

$$C = 30 + (0.8)Y_D$$

which tells us that the *MPC* out of disposable income is 0.8.

4. We can now substitute $(0.9)Y$ for Y_D in the consumption function. By doing so, we get

$$C = 30 + (0.8)(0.9)Y$$
$$\Rightarrow C = 30 + (0.72)Y$$

So, we can express desired consumption as a function of Y_D or as a *different* function of Y. In this example, 0.72 is equal to the *MPC* times $(1 - t)$, where t is the net tax rate. Whereas 0.8 is the marginal propensity to consume out of *disposable* income, 0.72 is the marginal propensity to consume out of *national* income.

> **In the presence of taxes, the marginal propensity to consume out of national income is less than the marginal propensity to consume out of disposable income.**

The *AE* Function

In Chapter 21, the only components of desired aggregate expenditure were consumption and investment. We now add government purchases and net exports. The separate components in their general form are

$C = c + MPC \times Y_D$	consumption
I	autonomous investment
G	autonomous government purchases
$T = tY$	net tax revenues
X	autonomous exports
$IM = mY$	imports

Our first step in constructing the *AE* function is to express desired consumption in terms of national income. By using the four steps from above, we write desired consumption as

$$C = c + MPC(1 - t)Y$$

where c is autonomous consumption and *MPC* is the marginal propensity to consume. Now we sum the four components of desired aggregate expenditure:

$$AE = C + I + G + (X - IM)$$
$$= c + MPC(1 - t)Y + I + G + (X - mY)$$
$$AE = \underbrace{[c + I + G + X]}_{\substack{\text{Autonomous} \\ \text{expenditure}}} + \underbrace{[MPC(1 - t) - m]Y}_{\substack{\text{Induced} \\ \text{expenditure}}}$$

In this last equation, we can see the distinction between autonomous aggregate expenditure and induced aggregate expenditure. The first square bracket brings together all the autonomous parts of expenditure. The second square bracket brings together all the parts of expenditure that change when national income changes—the induced part of consumption and imports. The term in the second square bracket shows how much total desired spending on domestically produced output changes when national income changes by $1—the marginal propensity to spend out of national income.

Figure 22-3 graphs the AE function for our hypothetical economy in which we assume that desired investment is $75 billion and the level of government purchases is $51 billion. Notice that the slope of the AE function measures the change in desired aggregate expenditure (AE) that comes about from a $1 increase in national income (Y). This is the marginal propensity to spend out of national income and is equal to $MPC(1 - t) - m$.

Note that, unlike in Chapter 21, the marginal propensity to spend out of national income (z) is not simply equal to the marginal propensity to consume (MPC). To understand why, suppose the economy produces $1 of extra national income and that the

FIGURE 22-3 The Aggregate Expenditure Function

The aggregate expenditure function is the sum of desired consumption, investment, government purchases, and net export expenditures. The autonomous components of desired aggregate expenditure are desired investment, desired government purchases, desired export expenditures, and the autonomous part of desired consumption. These sum to $228 billion in the given example and this sum is the vertical intercept of the AE curve. The induced component is $[MPC(1 - t) - m]Y$, which in our example is equal to $(0.8(0.9) - 0.1)Y = 0.62Y$.

The equation for the AE function is $AE = 228 + 0.62Y$. The slope of the AE function, $\Delta AE/\Delta Y$, is 0.62, indicating that a $1 increase in Y leads to a 62-cent increase in desired expenditure. This is the marginal propensity to spend on domestic output. The equilibrium level of national income is $600 billion, the level of Y where the AE function intersects the 45° line.

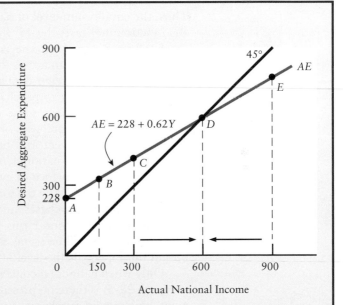

Point	Actual National Income (Y)	Desired Consumption Expenditure ($C = 30 + 0.72Y$)	Desired Investment Expenditure ($I = 75$)	Desired Government Expenditure ($G = 51$)	Desired Net Export Expenditure ($X - IM = 72 - 0.1Y$)	Desired Aggregate Expenditure ($AE = C + I + G + X - IM$)
A	0	30	75	51	72	228
B	150	138	75	51	57	321
C	300	246	75	51	42	414
D	600	462	75	51	12	600
E	900	678	75	51	−18	786

response to this is governed by the relationships in Figure 22-3. Because 10 cents is collected by the government as net taxes, 90 cents becomes disposable income, and 80 percent of this amount (72 cents) is spent on consumption. However, 10 cents of all expenditure goes to imports, so expenditure on *domestic* goods rises by only 62 cents (72 − 10). Hence, z, the marginal propensity to spend, is 0.62. In algebraic terms,

$$
\begin{aligned}
z &= MPC(1 - t) - m \\
&= (0.8)(1 - 0.1) - 0.1 \\
&= 0.72 - 0.1 \\
&= 0.62
\end{aligned}
$$

Equilibrium National Income

As in Chapter 21, we are assuming (for now) that firms are able and willing to produce whatever level of output is demanded of them at a constant price level. When output is *demand determined* in this way, the equilibrium level of national income is that level of national income where desired aggregate expenditure (along the *AE* function) equals the actual level of national income. As was also true in Chapter 21, the 45° line shows the *equilibrium condition*—the collection of points where $Y = AE$. Thus, the equilibrium level of national income in Figure 22-3 is at point D, where the *AE* function intersects the 45° line.

Suppose national income is less than its equilibrium amount. The forces leading back to equilibrium are exactly the same as those described in Chapter 21. When households, firms, foreign demanders, and governments try to spend at their desired amounts, they will try to purchase more goods and services than the economy is currently producing. Hence, some of the desired expenditure must either be frustrated or take the form of purchases of inventories of goods that were produced in the past. As firms see their inventories being depleted, they will increase production, thereby increasing the level of national income.

The opposite sequence of events occurs when national income is greater than its equilibrium amount. Now the total of desired household consumption, business investment, government purchases, and net foreign demand on the economy's production is less than national output. Firms will notice that they are unable to sell all their output. Their inventories will be rising, and sooner or later they will seek to reduce the level of output until it equals the level of sales. When they do, national income will fall.

Only when national income is equal to desired aggregate expenditure ($600 billion in Figure 22-3) is there no pressure for output to change. Desired consumption, investment, government purchases, and net exports just add up to national output.

| 22.4 Changes in Equilibrium National Income

Changes in any of the components of desired aggregate expenditure will cause changes in equilibrium national income. In Chapter 21, we investigated the consequences of shifts in the consumption function and in the investment function. Here we take a first look at fiscal policy—the effects of changes in government spending and taxation. We also consider shifts in the net export function. First, we explain why the simple multiplier is reduced by the presence of taxes and imports.

The Multiplier with Taxes and Imports

In Chapter 21, we saw that the *simple multiplier*, the amount by which equilibrium real GDP changes when autonomous expenditure changes by $1 was equal to $1/(1-z)$, where z is the marginal propensity to spend out of national income. In the simple model of Chapter 21, with no government and no international trade, z was simply the marginal propensity to consume out of disposable income. But in the more complex model of this chapter, which contains both government and foreign trade, we have seen that the marginal propensity to spend out of national income is slightly more complicated.

The presence of imports and taxes reduces the marginal propensity to spend out of national income and therefore reduces the value of the simple multiplier.

Let's be more specific. In Chapter 21, the marginal propensity to spend, z, was just equal to the marginal propensity to consume. Let ΔY be the change in equilibrium real GDP brought about by a change in autonomous spending, ΔA. We then have the following relationships:

Without Government and Foreign Trade:

$$z = MPC$$

$$\text{Simple multiplier} = \frac{\Delta Y}{\Delta A} = \frac{1}{1-z}$$

$$= \frac{1}{1-MPC}$$

In our example, the MPC was 0.8, and so the simple multiplier was equal to 5.

$$\text{Simple multiplier} = 1/(1-0.8) = 1/0.2 = 5$$

In our expanded model with government and foreign trade, the marginal propensity to spend out of national income must take account of the presence of net taxes and imports, both of which reduce the value of z.

With Government and Foreign Trade:

$$z = MPC(1-t) - m$$

$$\text{Simple multiplier} = \frac{\Delta Y}{\Delta A} = \frac{1}{1-z}$$

$$= \frac{1}{1-[MPC(1 \quad t) - m]}$$

In our example, $MPC = 0.8$, $t = 0.1$, and $m = 0.1$. This makes the simple multiplier equal to 2.63.

$$\text{Simple multiplier} = 1/\{1 - [0.8(1-0.1) - 0.1]\} = 1/[1-(0.72-0.1)]$$
$$= 1/(1-0.62) = 2.63$$

What is the central point here? When we introduce government and foreign trade to our model, the simple multiplier becomes smaller. Since some of any increase in national income goes to taxes and imports, the induced increase in desired expenditure on domestically produced goods is reduced. (The *AE* curve is flatter.) The result is that, in response to any change in autonomous expenditure, the overall change in equilibrium GDP is smaller.

> **The higher is the marginal propensity to import, the lower is the simple multiplier. The higher is the net tax rate, the lower is the simple multiplier.**

Applying Economic Concepts 22-1 examines what the size of the simple multiplier is likely to be in the Canadian economy. You may be surprised at the result!

APPLYING ECONOMIC CONCEPTS 22-1

How Large Is Canada's Simple Multiplier?

In our macro model, the "simple multiplier" expresses the overall change in equilibrium national income resulting from an increase in desired autonomous spending. To the extent that increases in output are only possible in the short run by increasing the level of employment, the multiplier can also tell us something about the total change in employment that will result from an initial increase in spending. And this is the way we usually hear about the effects of the multiplier in the popular press.

Imagine you hear a news story about a recent announcement by the government to increase its annual spending by $5 billion on the repairs of highways and bridges. Rather than claiming that the $5 billion increase in spending will lead to an overall increase in national income larger than $5 billion, the official making the announcement is likely to speak in terms of the number of jobs "created" in the economy as a result of the new government spending. For example, the official might claim that this new spending will *directly* create 5000 new jobs and that an additional 10 000 new jobs will be created *indirectly*. With such a claim, the government official appears to believe that the simple multiplier is equal to 3—the total increase in employment (and output) will be three times the direct increase. Is a simple multiplier of 3 a realistic estimate for Canada?

In the simple model we have developed in this chapter, we have used values for key parameters that are simple to work with but not necessarily realistic. In particular, we assumed values of *t* and *m* that are well below their actual values. To find a realistic estimate for the multiplier in Canada, we need to use more realistic values for the net tax rate (*t*) and the marginal propensity to import (*m*). In Canada a reasonable value for *t* is 0.25, the approximate share of combined government net taxation in GDP. Imports into Canada are close to 35 percent of GDP and so *m* = 0.35 is a reasonable value. If we use these more realistic values for *t* and *m*, and continue the reasonable assumption that the marginal propensity to consume out of disposable income is 0.8, the implied value of *z* is

$$z = MPC(1 - t) - m$$
$$= 0.8(1 - 0.25) - 0.35 = 0.25$$

and so the implied value of the simple multiplier is

$$\text{Simple multiplier} = 1/(1 - z) = 1/0.75 = 1.33$$

Two main lessons emerge from this analysis:

1. Net taxes and imports reduce the size of the simple multiplier.

2. Realistic values of *t* and *m* in Canada suggest a simple multiplier that is closer to 1 than to 2 and certainly far below the value of 5 that we used in the very simple model of Chapter 21.

So the next time you hear a government official make claims about how new spending plans are likely to have large effects on the level of employment and economic activity, think about what the implied value of the simple multiplier must be in order for the claims to be reasonable. The analysis here suggests that the simple multiplier in Canada is likely to be only moderately greater than 1.*

_____

* In the next two chapters we will see that once we allow for a price level that can adjust to changes in demand, the multiplier gets even smaller.

Net Exports

Earlier in this chapter, we discussed the determinants of net exports and of shifts in the net export function. As with the other elements of desired aggregate expenditure, if the net export function shifts upward, equilibrium national income will rise; if the net export function shifts downward, equilibrium national income will fall.

Generally, exports themselves are autonomous with respect to domestic national income. Foreign demand for Canadian products depends on foreign income, on foreign and Canadian prices, and on the exchange rate, but it does not depend on Canadian income. Export demand could also change because of a change in foreigners' preferences. Suppose foreign consumers develop a preference for Canadian-made furniture and desire to consume $1 billion more per year of these goods than they had in the past. The net export function (and the aggregate expenditure function) will shift up by $1 billion, and equilibrium national income will increase by $1 billion times the simple multiplier.

Fiscal Policy

In Chapter 19 we introduced the concept of potential GDP, the level of GDP that would exist if all factors of production were fully employed. Deviations of actual GDP (Y) from potential GDP (Y^*) usually create problems. When $Y < Y^*$, factor incomes are low and unemployment of factors is high; when $Y > Y^*$, rising costs create inflationary pressures. To reduce these problems, governments often try to *stabilize* the level of real GDP close to Y^*. Any attempt to use government policy in this manner is called **stabilization policy**, and here we focus on stabilization through fiscal policy. In Chapters 24 and 32, we examine some important details about fiscal policy, including why the real-world practice of fiscal policy is more complicated than our simple model suggests.

stabilization policy Any policy designed to reduce the economy's cyclical fluctuations and thereby stabilize national income.

The basic idea of fiscal stabilization policy follows from what we have already learned. A reduction in net tax rates or an increase in government purchases shifts the *AE* curve upward, setting in motion the multiplier process that tends to increase equilibrium national income. An increase in tax rates or a decrease in government purchases shifts the *AE* curve downward and tends to decrease equilibrium income.

Once we know the direction in which the government wants to change national income, the *directions* of the required changes in government purchases or taxation are easy to determine. But the *timing* and *magnitude* of the changes are more difficult issues. The issue of timing is difficult because it takes an uncertain amount of time before fiscal policies have an effect on real GDP. The issue of magnitude is difficult because the level of potential output can only be estimated imperfectly (and so the gap between actual and potential GDP is uncertain).

Let's now examine these two policy tools in more detail.

Changes in Government Purchases Suppose the government decides to reduce its purchases of all economic consulting services, thus eliminating $100 million per year in spending. Planned government purchases (G) would fall by $100 million, shifting *AE* downward by the same amount. How much would equilibrium income change? This amount can be calculated by using the simple multiplier. Government purchases are part of autonomous expenditure, so a *change* in government purchases of ΔG will lead to a *change* in equilibrium national income equal to the simple multiplier times ΔG. In this example, equilibrium income will fall by $100 million times the simple multiplier.

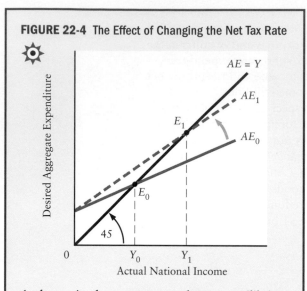

FIGURE 22-4 The Effect of Changing the Net Tax Rate

A change in the net tax rate changes equilibrium income by rotating the *AE* curve. A reduction in the net tax rate rotates the *AE* curve from AE_0 to AE_1. The new curve has a steeper slope because the lower net tax rate withdraws a smaller amount of national income from the desired consumption flow. Equilibrium income rises from Y_0 to Y_1. An increase in the net tax rate has the opposite effect.

Earlier we argued that a realistic value for the simple multiplier in Canada is about 1.3. Using this value in our example, the effect of the $100 million reduction in G is to reduce equilibrium national income by $130 million.

Increases in government purchases would have the opposite effect. If the government increases its spending by $1 billion on new highways, equilibrium national income will rise by $1 billion times the simple multiplier.

Changes in Tax Rates Recall that the slope of the *AE* function is z, the marginal propensity to spend on domestic output. As we saw earlier,

$$z = MPC(1 - t) - m$$

A change in the net tax rate will change z, rotate the *AE* function, and change the equilibrium level of national income.

Consider first a decrease in tax rates. If the government decreases its net tax rate so that it collects 5 cents less out of every dollar of national income, disposable income rises in relation to national income. Hence, desired consumption also rises at every level of national income. This increase in consumption results in an upward *rotation* of the *AE* curve—that is, an increase in the slope of the curve, as shown in Figure 22-4. The result of this shift will be an increase in equilibrium national income.

A rise in tax rates has the opposite effect. A rise in the net tax rate causes a decrease in disposable income, and hence desired consumption expenditure, at each level of national income. This results in a downward rotation of the *AE* curve and decreases the level of equilibrium national income.

Note that when the *AE* function rotates, as happens if anything causes z to change, the simple multiplier is *not* used to tell us about the resulting change in equilibrium national income. The simple multiplier is only used to tell us how much equilibrium national income changes in response to a change in *autonomous* desired spending—that is, in response to a *parallel shift* in the *AE* function.

22.5 Demand-Determined Output

In this and the preceding chapter, we have discussed the determination of the four categories of aggregate expenditure and have seen how they simultaneously determine equilibrium national income in the short run. An algebraic exposition of the complete model is presented in the appendix to this chapter.

Our macro model is based on three central concepts, and it is worth reviewing them.

Equilibrium National Income The equilibrium level of national income is that level at which *desired* aggregate expenditure equals *actual* national income ($AE = Y$). If actual national income exceeds desired expenditure, firms will eventually reduce production, causing national income to fall. If actual national income is less than desired expenditure, firms will eventually increase production, causing national income to rise.

The Simple Multiplier The simple multiplier measures the change in equilibrium national income that results from a change in the *autonomous* part of desired aggregate expenditure. The simple multiplier is equal to $1/(1 - z)$, where z is the marginal propensity to spend out of national income. In the model of Chapter 21, in which there is no government and no international trade, z is simply the marginal propensity to consume out of disposable income. In our expanded model that contains both government and foreign trade, z is reduced by the presence of net taxes and imports. To review:

$$\text{Simple multiplier } = 1/(1 - z)$$

$$\text{Closed economy with no government: } \quad z = MPC$$

$$\text{Open economy with government: } \quad z = MPC(1 - t) - m$$

Demand-Determined Output The model that we have examined is constructed *for a given price level*—that is, the price level is assumed to be constant. This assumption of a given price level is related to another assumption that we have been making. We have been assuming that firms are able and willing to produce any amount of output that is demanded without requiring any change in prices. When this is true, national income depends only on how much is demanded—that is, national income is *demand determined*. Things get more complicated if firms are either unable or unwilling to produce enough to meet all demands without requiring a change in prices. We deal with this possibility in Chapter 23 when we consider *supply-side* influences on national income.

There are two situations in which we might expect national income to be demand determined. First, when there are unemployed resources and firms have excess capacity, firms will often be prepared to provide whatever is demanded from them at unchanged prices. In contrast, if the economy's resources are fully employed and firms have no excess capacity, increases in output may be possible only with higher unit costs, and these cost increases may lead to price increases.

The second situation occurs when firms are *price setters*. Readers who have studied some microeconomics will recognize this term. It means that the firm has the ability to influence the price of its product, either because it is large relative to the market or, more usually, because it sells a product that is *differentiated* to some extent from the products of its competitors. Firms that are price setters often respond to changes in demand by altering their production and sales, at least initially, rather than by adjusting their prices. Only after some time has passed, and the change in demand has persisted, do such firms adjust their prices. This type of behaviour corresponds well to our short-run macro model in which changes in demand lead to changes in output (for a given price level).

> Our simple model of national income determination assumes a constant price level. In this model, national income is demand determined.

In the following chapters, we expand the model by making the price level an *endogenous* variable. In other words, movements in the price level are explained within the model. We do this by considering the *supply side* of the economy—that is, those things that influence the costs at which firms can produce, such as technology and factor prices. When we consider the demand side and the supply side of the economy simultaneously, we will see that changes in desired aggregate expenditure usually cause both prices and real GDP to change.

SUMMARY

22.1 Introducing Government

- Government desired purchases, G, are assumed to be part of autonomous aggregate expenditure. Taxes minus transfer payments are called net taxes and affect aggregate expenditure indirectly through households' disposable income. Taxes reduce disposable income, whereas transfers increase disposable income.

- The budget balance is defined as net tax revenues minus government purchases, $(T - G)$. When $(T - G)$ is positive, there is a budget surplus; when $(T - G)$ is negative, there is a budget deficit.

22.2 Introducing Foreign Trade

- Exports are foreign purchases of Canadian goods, and thus do not depend on Canadian national income. Desired imports are assumed to increase as national income increases. Hence, net exports decrease as national income increases.

- Changes in international relative prices lead to shifts in the net export function. A depreciation of the Canadian dollar implies that Canadian goods are now cheaper relative to foreign goods. This leads to a rise in exports and a fall in imports, shifting the net export function up. An appreciation of the Canadian dollar has the opposite effect.

22.3 Equilibrium National Income

- As in Chapter 21, national income is in equilibrium when desired aggregate expenditure equals actual national income. The equilibrium condition is

$$Y = AE, \text{ where } AE = C + I + G + (X - IM)$$

- The slope of the AE function in the model with government and foreign trade is $z = MPC(1 - t) - m$, where MPC is the marginal propensity to consume out of disposable income, t is the net tax rate, and m is the marginal propensity to import.

22.4 Changes in Equilibrium National Income

- The presence of taxes and net exports reduces the value of the simple multiplier. With taxes and imports, every increase in national income induces less new spending than in a model with no taxes or imports.

- An increase in government purchases shifts up the AE function and thus increases the equilibrium level of national income. A decrease in the net tax rate makes the AE function rotate upward and increases the equilibrium level of national income.

- An increase in exports can be caused by an increase in foreign demand for Canadian goods, a fall in the Canadian price level, or a depreciation of the Canadian dollar. An increase in exports shifts the AE function up and increases the equilibrium level of national income.

22.5 Demand-Determined Output

- Our simple model of national income determination is constructed for a given price level. That prices are assumed not to change in response to an increase in desired expenditure reflects a related assumption that output is demand determined.

- Output may be demand determined in two situations: if there are unemployed resources, or if firms are price setters.

KEY CONCEPTS

Taxes, transfers, and net taxes
The budget balance
The net export function

Calculation of the simple multiplier in
an open economy with government
Fiscal policy

Changes in government purchases
Changes in net tax rates
Demand-determined output

STUDY EXERCISES

MyEconLab Make the grade with MyEconLab: Study Exercises marked in red can be found on MyEconLab. You can practise them as often as you want, and most feature step-by-step guided instructions to help you find the right answer.

1. Consider the following table showing national income and government net tax revenues in billions of dollars. Assume that the level of government purchases is $155 billion.

Actual National Income (Y)	Net Tax Revenues (T)	Budget Balance ($T - G$)
100	45	—
200	70	—
300	95	—
400	120	—
500	145	—
600	170	—
700	195	—
800	220	—

a. Compute the government's budget balance for each level of national income and fill in the table.
b. Suppose that net taxes are given by T, where $T = t_0 + t_1 Y$. Using the data in the table, determine the values of t_0 and t_1.
c. What is the interpretation of t_0?
d. What is the interpretation of t_1?
e. Suppose the government decides to increase the level of its purchases of goods and services by $15 billion. What happens to the budget balance for any level of national income?

2. Consider the following table showing national income and imports in billions of dollars. Assume that the level of exports is $300 billion.

Actual National Income (Y)	Imports (IM)	Net Exports ($X - IM$)
100	85	—
200	120	—
300	155	—
400	190	—
500	225	—
600	260	—
700	295	—
800	330	—

a. Compute the level of net exports for each level of national income and fill in the table.
b. Plot the net export function on a scale diagram. Explain why it is downward sloping.
c. Suppose desired imports are given by $IM = m_0 + m_1 Y$. Using the data in the table, determine the values of m_0 and m_1.
d. What is the interpretation of m_0?
e. What is the interpretation of m_1?
f. Suppose that a major trading partner experiences a significant recession. Explain how this affects the net export function in your diagram.

3. Each of the following headlines describes an event that will have an effect on desired aggregate expenditure. What will be the effect on equilibrium national income? In each case, describe how the event would be illustrated in the 45°-line diagram.

a. "Minister takes an axe to the armed forces."
b. "Russia agrees to buy more Canadian wheat."

c. "High-tech firms to cut capital outlays."
d. "Finance minister pledges to cut income-tax rates."
e. "U.S. imposes import restrictions on Canadian lumber."
f. "Booming Chinese economy expands market for Canadian coal."
g. "Weak dollar spurs exports from Ontario manufacturers."
h. "Prime minister promises burst of infrastructure spending."

4. The following diagram shows desired aggregate expenditure for the economy of Sunset Island. The *AE* curve assumes a net tax rate (*t*) of 10 percent, autonomous exports of $25 billion, and a marginal propensity to import (*m*) of 15 percent.

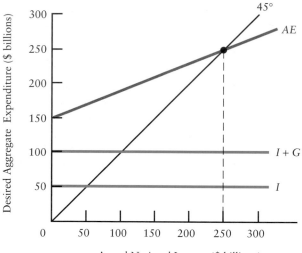

a. What is the level of desired investment expenditure (*I*)?
b. What is the level of government purchases (*G*)?
c. What is the autonomous portion of consumption?
d. What is total autonomous expenditure?
e. Starting from equilibrium national income of $250 billion, suppose government purchases decreased by $25 billion. Describe the effect on the *AE* curve and on equilibrium national income.
f. Starting from equilibrium national income of $250 billion, suppose the net tax rate increased from 10 percent to 30 percent of national income. Describe the effect on the *AE* curve and on equilibrium national income.
g. Starting from equilibrium national income of $250 billion, suppose investment increased by $50 billion. Describe the effect on the *AE* curve and on equilibrium national income.
h. Starting from equilibrium national income of $250 billion, suppose the marginal propensity to import fell from 15 percent to 5 percent of national

income. Describe the effect on the *AE* curve and on equilibrium national income.

5. The economy of Sunrise Island has the following features:
   - fixed price level
   - no foreign trade
   - autonomous desired investment (*I*) of $20 billion
   - autonomous government purchases (*G*) of $30 billion
   - autonomous desired consumption (*C*) of $15 billion
   - marginal propensity to consume out of disposable income of 0.75
   - net tax rate of 0.20 of national income

   a. Write an equation expressing consumption as a function of disposable income.
   b. Write an equation expressing net tax revenues as a function of national income.
   c. Write an equation expressing disposable income as a function of national income.
   d. Write an equation expressing consumption as a function of national income.
   e. What is the marginal propensity to spend out of national income?
   f. Calculate the simple multiplier for Sunrise Island.

6. The following table shows alternative hypothetical economies and the relevant values for the marginal propensity to consume out of disposable income (*MPC*), the net tax rate (*t*), and the marginal propensity to import, *m*.

Economy	MPC	t	m	z	Simple Multiplier $1/(1 - z)$
A	0.75	0.2	0.15	—	—
B	0.75	0.2	0.30	—	—
C	0.75	0.4	0.30	—	—
D	0.90	0.4	0.30	—	—

a. Recall that *z*, the marginal propensity to spend out of national income, is given by the simple expression $z = MPC(1 - t) - m$. By using this expression, compute *z* for each of the economies and fill in the table.
b. Compare Economies A and B (they differ only by the value of *m*). Which one has the larger multiplier? Explain why the size of the multiplier depends on *m*.
c. Compare Economies B and C (they differ only by the value of *t*). Which one has the larger multiplier? Explain why the size of the multiplier depends on *t*.
d. Compare Economies C and D (they differ only by the value of *MPC*). Which one has the larger multiplier? Explain why the size of the multiplier depends on *MPC*.

7. This question is based on the *Additional Topic* **The Saving-Investment Approach to Equilibrium in an Open Economy with Government,** which is found on this book's MyEconLab. Consider the diagram below that shows the national saving function and the national asset formation function.

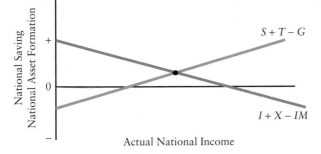

a. Explain why the national asset formation function is downward sloping. What determines its slope?
b. Explain why the national saving function is upward sloping. What determines its slope?
c. Suppose the government decided to increase its level of purchases. How would this policy change be illustrated in the diagram? What would happen to national income?
d. Suppose domestic firms decided to increase their desired investment. How would this change be illustrated in the diagram? What would happen to national income?
e. Suppose the Canadian government reduced net tax rates. How would this change be illustrated in the diagram? What would happen to national income?

8. This question requires you to solve a macro model algebraically. Reading the appendix to this chapter will help you to answer this question. But, just in case, we lead you through it step by step. The equations for the model are as follows:

i) $C = c + MPC \times Y_D$ consumption
ii) $I = I_0$ investment (autonomous)
iii) $G = G_0$ government purchases (autonomous)
iv) $T = tY$ net tax revenue
v) $X = X_0$ exports (autonomous)
vi) $IM = mY$ imports

a. Step 1: Recall that $Y_D = Y - T$. By using this fact, substitute the tax function into the consumption function and derive the relationship between desired consumption and national income.
b. Step 2: Sum the four components of desired aggregate expenditure (C, I, G, NX). This is the aggregate expenditure (AE) function. Collect the autonomous terms separately from the induced terms.
c. Step 3: Recall the equilibrium condition, $Y = AE$. Form the equation $Y = AE$, where AE is your expression for the AE function from part (b).

d. Step 4: Now collect terms and solve for Y. This is the equilibrium value of national income.
e. Step 5: Suppose the level of autonomous expenditure, which we could call A, rises by ΔA. What is the effect on the level of equilibrium national income?

9. This question repeats the exercise of Question 8, but for specific numerical values. The equations of the model are

$C = 50 + 0.7Y_D$ $T = (0.2)Y$
$I = 75$ $X = 50$
$G = 100$ $IM = (0.15)Y$

a. Compute the AE function and plot it in a diagram. What is total autonomous expenditure?
b. What is the slope of the AE function?
c. Compute the equilibrium level of national income.
d. Suppose X rises from 50 to 100. How does this affect the level of national income?
e. What is the simple multiplier in this model?

10. In the 2009 and 2010 Canadian federal budgets in the midst of a major global recession, the minister of finance presented a plan to stimulate the economy.

a. Describe the basic fiscal tools at his disposal.
b. Using the model from this chapter, explain the effect on GDP from an increase in G by $5 billion.
c. Using the model from this chapter, explain the effect on GDP from a tax rebate equal in value to $5 billion.
d. Can you offer one reason why the minister of finance chose to emphasize increases in government spending rather than tax reductions in his 2009 and 2010 federal budgets?

11. Classify each of the following government activities as either government purchases or transfers.

a. Welfare payments for the poor
b. Payments to teachers in public schools
c. Payments to teachers at a military college
d. Payments on account of hospital and medical care
e. Public vaccination programs

12. In Chapter 20 we examined how national income was *measured*. By using the expenditure approach, we showed that GDP is always equal to the sum of consumption, investment, government purchases, and net exports. In Chapters 21 and 22 we examined the *determination* of national income. We showed that equilibrium national income occurs when actual national income equals the sum of desired consumption, investment, government purchases, and net exports.

a. Does this mean that national income is always at its equilibrium level?
b. Explain the important difference between "actual" and "desired" expenditures.

We start with the definition of desired aggregate expenditure:

$$AE = C + I + G + (X - IM) \quad [1]$$

For each component of AE, we write down a behavioural function:

$$C = a + bY_D \text{ (consumption function)} \quad [2]$$

$$I = I_0 \text{ (autonomous investment)} \quad [3]$$

$$G = G_0 \text{ (autonomous government purchases)} \quad [4]$$

$$X = X_0 \text{ (autonomous exports)} \quad [5]$$

$$IM = mY \text{ (imports)} \quad [6]$$

where a is autonomous consumption spending, b is the marginal propensity to consume, and m is the marginal propensity to import. Obviously, the "behavioural" functions for investment, government purchases, and exports are very simple: These are all assumed to be independent of the level of national income.

Before deriving aggregate expenditure, we need to determine the relationship between national income (Y) and disposable income (Y_D), because it is Y_D that determines desired consumption expenditure. Y_D is defined as income after net taxes. In Chapter 22 we examined a very simple linear tax of the form

$$T = tY \quad [7]$$

Taxes must be subtracted from national income to obtain disposable income:

$$Y_D = Y - tY = Y(1 - t) \quad [8]$$

Substituting Equation 8 into the consumption function allows us to write consumption as a function of national income.

$$C = a + b(1 - t)Y \quad [9]$$

Now we can add up all the components of desired aggregate expenditure, substituting Equations 3, 4, 5, 6, and 7 into Equation 1:

$$AE = a + b(1 - t)Y + I_0 + G_0 + X_0 - mY \quad [10]$$

Equation 10 is the AE function, which shows desired aggregate expenditure as a function of actual national income.

In equilibrium, desired aggregate expenditure must equal actual national income:

$$AE = Y \quad [11]$$

Equation 11 is the equilibrium condition for our model. It is the equation of the 45° line in the figures in this chapter.

To solve for the equilibrium level of national income, we want to solve for the level of Y that satisfies both Equation 10 and 11. That is, solve for the level of Y that is determined by the intersection of the AE curve and the 45° line. Substitute Equation 11 into Equation 10:

$$Y = a + b(1 - t)Y + I_0 + G_0 + X_0 - mY \quad [12]$$

Group all the terms in Y on the right-hand side, and subtract them from both sides:

$$Y = Y[b(1 - t) - m] + a + I_0 + G_0 + X_0 \quad [13]$$

$$Y - Y[b(1 - t) - m] = a + I_0 + G_0 + X_0 \quad [14]$$

Notice that $[b(1 - t) - m]$ is exactly the marginal propensity to spend out of national income, defined earlier as z. When national income goes up by one dollar, only $1 - t$ dollars go into disposable income, and only b of that is spent on consumption. Additionally, m is spent on imports, which are not expenditures on domestic national income. Hence $[b(1 - t) - m]$ is spent on domestic output.

Substituting z for $[b(1 - t) - m]$ and solving Equation 14 for equilibrium Y yields

$$Y = \frac{a + I_0 + G_0 + X_0}{1 - z} \quad [15]$$

Notice that the numerator of Equation 15 is total autonomous expenditure, which we call A. Hence, Equation 15 can be rewritten as

$$Y = \frac{A}{1 - z} \quad [16]$$

Notice also that if autonomous expenditure rises by some amount ΔA, Y will rise by $\Delta A/(1 - z)$. So, the simple multiplier is $1/(1 - z)$.

The Algebra Illustrated

The numerical example that was carried through Chapters 21 and 22 can be used to illustrate the preceding exposition. In that example, the behavioural equations are:

$$C = 30 + 0.8Y_D \qquad [17]$$

$$I = 75 \qquad [18]$$

$$G = 51 \qquad [19]$$

$$X - IM = 72 - 0.1Y \qquad [20]$$

$$T = 0.1Y \qquad [21]$$

From Equation 8, disposable income is given by $Y(1 - t) = 0.9Y$. Substituting this into Equation 17 yields

$$C = 30 + 0.72Y$$

as in Equation 9.

Now, recalling that in equilibrium $AE = Y$, we add up all the components of AE and set the sum equal to Y, as in Equation 12:

$$Y = 30 + 0.72Y + 75 + 51 + 72 - 0.1Y \quad [22]$$

Collecting terms yields

$$Y = 228 + 0.62Y$$

Subtracting $0.62Y$ from both sides gives

$$0.38Y = 228$$

and dividing through by 0.38, we have

$$Y = \frac{228}{0.38} = 600$$

This can also be derived by using Equation 16. Autonomous expenditure is 228, and z, the marginal propensity to spend out of national income, is 0.62. Thus, from Equation 16, equilibrium income is $228/(1 - 0.62) = 600$, which is exactly the equilibrium we obtained in Figure 22-3 on page 553.

Output and Prices in the Short Run

LEARNING OBJECTIVES (LO)

After studying this chapter you will be able to

1. explain why an exogenous change in the price level shifts the *AE* curve and changes the equilibrium level of real GDP.
2. derive the aggregate demand (*AD*) curve and understand what causes it to shift.
3. describe the meaning of the aggregate supply (*AS*) curve and understand why it shifts when technology or factor prices change.
4. explain how *AD* and *AS* shocks affect equilibrium real GDP and the price level.

IN Chapters 21 and 22, we developed a simple model of national income determination. We saw that changes in wealth, interest rates, the government's fiscal policies, or expectations about the future lead to changes in desired aggregate expenditure. Through the multiplier process, such changes in desired expenditure cause equilibrium national income to change.

The simple model in Chapters 21 and 22 had a constant price level. We assumed that firms were prepared to provide more output when it was demanded without requiring an increase in prices. In this sense, we said that output was *demand determined*.

The actual economy, however, does not have a constant price level. Rather than assuming it is constant, we would like to understand what causes it to change. We therefore expand our model to make the price

level an *endogenous* variable—one whose changes are explained within the model.

We make the transition to a variable price level in three steps. First, we study the consequences for national income of *exogenous* changes in the price level—changes that happen for reasons that are not explained by our model of the economy. We ask how changes in the price level affect desired aggregate expenditure. That is, we examine the *demand side* of the economy. Second, we examine the *supply side* by exploring the relationship among the price level, the prices of factor inputs, and the level of output producers would like to supply. Finally, we examine the concept of *macroeconomic equilibrium* that combines both the demand and the supply sides to determine the price level and real GDP simultaneously.

23.1 The Demand Side of the Economy

Consider the macro model in Chapter 22 in which the price level is assumed to be constant. What would happen to equilibrium GDP in that model if there were a *different* price level? To find out, we need to understand how an exogenous change in the price level affects desired aggregate expenditure.

Exogenous Changes in the Price Level

The *AE* curve shifts in response to a change in the price level—a change, that is, in *all* the economy's prices. This shift occurs because a change in the price level affects desired consumption expenditures and desired net exports. These are the changes on which we will focus in this chapter. (In later chapters, we will see that changes in the price level will also change interest rates and thus shift the *AE* curve for an additional reason.)

Changes in Consumption You might think it is obvious that a fall in the price level leads to an increase in desired consumption for the simple reason that the demand curves for most individual products are negatively sloped. As we will see in a few pages, however, this logic is incorrect in the context of an aggregate model—our focus here is on the *aggregate* price level rather than on the prices of individual products. The relationship between the price level and desired consumption has to do with how changes in the price level lead to changes in household *wealth* and thus to changes in desired spending.

Much of the private sector's total wealth is held in the form of assets with a fixed nominal value. The most obvious example is money itself. We will discuss money in considerable detail in Chapters 27 and 28, but for now just note that most individuals and businesses hold money in their wallets, in their cash registers, or in their bank accounts. What this money can buy—its real value—depends on the price level. The higher the price level, the fewer goods and services a given amount of money can purchase. For this reason, a rise in the domestic price level lowers the real value of money holdings. Similarly, a reduction in the price level raises the real value of money holdings.

A rise in the price level lowers the real value of money held by the private sector. A fall in the price level raises the real value of money held by the private sector.

Changes in the price level cause changes in the real value of cash held by households and firms. This change in wealth leads to changes in the amount of desired consumption expenditure.

Other examples of assets that have fixed nominal values include government and corporate bonds. The bondholder has lent money to the issuer of the bond and receives a repayment from the issuer when the bond matures. What happens when there is a change in the price level in the intervening period? A rise in the price level means that the repayment to the bondholder is lower in real value than it otherwise would be. This is a decline in wealth for the bondholder. However, the issuer of the bond, having made a repayment of lower real value because of the increase in the price level, has experienced an increase in wealth. In dollar terms, the bondholder's reduction in wealth is exactly offset by the issuer's increase in wealth.

Changes in the price level change the wealth of bondholders and bond issuers, but because the changes offset each other, there is no change in aggregate wealth.[1]

In summary, a rise in the price level leads to a reduction in the real value of the private sector's wealth. And as we saw in Chapter 21, a reduction in wealth leads to a decrease in autonomous desired consumption and thus to a downward shift in the *AE* function. A fall in the domestic price level leads to a rise in wealth and desired consumption and thus to an upward shift in the *AE* curve.

Changes in Net Exports When the domestic price level rises (and the exchange rate remains unchanged), Canadian goods become more expensive relative to foreign goods. As we saw in Chapter 22, this change in international relative prices causes Canadian consumers to reduce their purchases of Canadian-made goods, which have now become relatively more expensive, and to increase their purchases of foreign goods, which have now become relatively less expensive. At the same time, consumers in other countries reduce their purchases of the now relatively more expensive Canadian-made goods. We saw in Chapter 22 that these changes cause a downward shift in the net export function.

A rise in the domestic price level (with a constant exchange rate) shifts the net export function downward, which causes a downward shift in the *AE* curve. A fall in the domestic price level shifts the net export function upward and hence the *AE* curve upward.

Changes in Equilibrium GDP

Because it causes downward shifts in both the net export function and the consumption function, an exogenous rise in the price level causes a downward shift in the *AE* curve, as shown in Figure 23-1. When the *AE* curve shifts downward, the equilibrium level of real GDP falls.

Conversely, with a fall in the price level, Canadian goods become relatively cheaper internationally, so net exports rise. Also, the purchasing power of nominal assets increases, so households spend more. The resulting increase in desired expenditure on Canadian goods causes the *AE* curve to shift upward. The equilibrium level of real GDP therefore rises.

A Change of Labels. In Chapters 21 and 22 the horizontal axis was labelled "Actual National Income" because we wanted to emphasize the important difference between *actual* income and *desired* expenditure. Notice in Figure 23-1, however, that we have labelled the horizontal axis "Real GDP." We use GDP rather than *national income*, but these have the same meaning. It is still *actual*, as opposed to *desired*, but we leave that

---

[1] If bonds are issued by domestic firms or governments but held by foreigners, the changes in domestic wealth caused by a change in the domestic price level will not completely offset each other. In particular, a rise in the domestic price level will lead to a transfer of wealth away from foreign bondholders and toward domestic bond issuers. This is why bondholders who expect future inflation usually demand higher returns in order to hold bonds. In Canada, most corporate and government bonds are held by Canadian firms or individuals and so we ignore this issue; in many other countries, where much debt is held abroad, the issue is of greater importance.

off, also for simplicity. Finally, we add *real* because from this chapter onward the price level will be changing and thus it is necessary to distinguish changes in nominal GDP from changes in real GDP.

The Aggregate Demand Curve

We have just seen, in the simple model from Chapters 21 and 22, that the price level and real equilibrium GDP are negatively related to each other. This negative relationship can be shown in an important new concept, the *aggregate demand curve*.

Recall that the *AE* curve is drawn with real GDP on the horizontal axis and desired aggregate expenditure on the vertical axis, and that it is plotted for a *given* price level. We are now going to let the price level vary and keep track of the various equilibrium points that occur as the *AE* function shifts. By doing so we can construct an **aggregate demand (AD) curve** that shows the relationship between the price level and the equilibrium level of real GDP. It will be plotted with the price level on the vertical axis and real GDP on the horizontal axis. Because the horizontal axes of both the *AE* and the *AD* curves measure real GDP, the two curves can be placed one above the other so that the levels of GDP on both can be compared directly. This is shown in Figure 23-2.

Now let us derive the *AD* curve. Given a value of the price level, P_0, equilibrium GDP is determined in part (i) of Figure 23-2 at the point where the AE_0 curve crosses the 45° line. The equilibrium level of real GDP is Y_0. Part (ii) of the figure shows the same equilibrium level of GDP, Y_0, plotted against the price level P_0. The equilibrium point in part (i), E_0, corresponds to point E_0 on the *AD* curve in part (ii).

As the price level rises to P_1, the *AE* curve shifts down to AE_1 and the equilibrium level of real GDP falls to Y_1. This determines a second point on the *AD* curve, E_1. By joining these points, we trace out the *AD* curve.

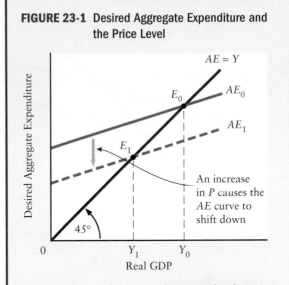

FIGURE 23-1 Desired Aggregate Expenditure and the Price Level

An exogenous change in the price level causes the *AE* curve to shift and equilibrium GDP to change. At the initial price level, the *AE* curve is given by AE_0, and hence equilibrium is at E_0 with real GDP equal to Y_0. An increase in the price level causes the *AE* curve to shift downward to the dashed line, AE_1. As a result, equilibrium changes to E_1 and equilibrium GDP falls to Y_1.

Recall from Chapter 22 that a change in the domestic price level also affects the marginal propensity to import (*m*) and thus the *slope* of the *AE* function. For simplicity, that effect is ignored in this chapter.

aggregate demand (AD) curve A curve showing combinations of real GDP and the price level that make desired aggregate expenditure equal to actual national income.

> For any given price level, the *AD* curve shows the level of real GDP for which desired aggregate expenditure equals actual GDP.

Note that because the *AD* curve relates equilibrium GDP to the price level, changes in the price level that cause *shifts in the AE* curve are simply *movements along* the *AD* curve. A movement along the *AD* curve thus traces out the response of equilibrium GDP to a change in the price level.[2]

---

[2] Our discussion of Figure 23-2 is for an economy open to international trade, and we emphasize the reduction of consumption and net exports that occurs in response to a rise in the domestic price level. In a *closed* economy, however, the second effect is absent, resulting in a steeper *AD* curve than what is shown in Figure 23-2.

FIGURE 23-2 Derivation of the AD Curve

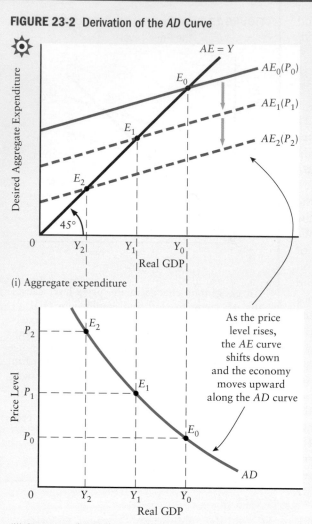

(i) Aggregate expenditure

(ii) Aggregate demand

As the price level rises, the AE curve shifts down and the economy moves upward along the AD curve

Equilibrium GDP is determined by the AE curve for each given price level; the level of equilibrium GDP and its associated price level are then plotted to yield a point on the AD curve. When the price level is P_0, the AE curve is AE_0, and hence equilibrium GDP is Y_0, as shown in part (i). Plotting Y_0 against P_0 yields the point E_0 on the AD curve in part (ii).

An increase in the price level to P_1 causes the AE curve to shift downward to AE_1 and causes equilibrium GDP to fall to Y_1. Plotting this new level of GDP against the higher price level yields a second point, E_1, on the AD curve. A further increase in the price level to P_2 causes the AE curve to shift downward to AE_2, and thus causes equilibrium GDP to fall to Y_2. Plotting P_2 and Y_2 yields a third point, E_2, on the AD curve.

A change in the price level causes a shift of the AE curve but a movement along the AD curve.

The AD Curve Is Not a Micro Demand Curve!

Figure 23-2 provides us with sufficient information to establish that the AD curve is negatively sloped.

1. A rise in the price level causes the AE curve to shift downward and hence leads to a movement upward and to the left along the AD curve, reflecting a fall in the equilibrium level of GDP.

2. A fall in the price level causes the AE curve to shift upward and hence leads to a movement downward and to the right along the AD curve, reflecting a rise in the equilibrium level of GDP.

In Chapter 3, we saw that demand curves for individual goods, such as coffee, T-shirts, and automobiles, are negatively sloped. However, the reasons for the negative slope of the AD curve are different from the reasons for the negative slope of individual demand curves used in microeconomics. Why is this the case?

A "micro" demand curve describes a situation in which the price of one commodity changes *while the prices of all other commodities and consumers' dollar incomes are constant.* Such an individual demand curve is negatively sloped for two reasons. First, as the price of the commodity falls, the purchasing power of each consumer's income will rise, and this rise in real income will lead to more units of the good being purchased. Second, as the price of the commodity falls, consumers buy more of that commodity and fewer of the now relatively more expensive substitutes.

The first reason does not apply to the AD curve because the dollar value of national income is not being held constant as the price level changes and we move along the AD curve. The second reason applies to the AD curve but only in a limited way. A change in the price level does not change the *relative* prices of domestic goods and thus does not cause consumers to substitute between them. However, a change in the domestic price level (for a given exchange rate) *does* lead to a change in *international* relative prices and thus to some substitution between domestic and foreign products; this is the link between the price level and net exports that we discussed earlier.

To summarize, the AD curve is negatively sloped for two reasons:

1. A fall in the price level leads to a rise in private-sector wealth, which increases desired consump-

tion and thus leads to an increase in equilibrium GDP.

2. A fall in the price level (for a given exchange rate) leads to a rise in net exports and thus leads to an increase in equilibrium GDP.

In later chapters, after we have discussed money, banking, and interest rates in detail, we will introduce a third reason for the negative slope of the AD curve.

Shifts in the AD Curve What can cause the AD curve to shift? For a given price level, any event that leads to a change in equilibrium GDP will cause the AD curve to shift. The event could be a change in government policy, such as the level of government purchases or taxation (or, as we will see later, a policy-induced change in interest rates). Or the event could be something beyond the government's control, such as a change in households' consumption expenditure, firms' investment behaviour, or foreigners' demand for Canadian exports.

Figure 23-3 shows a shift in the AD curve. Because the AD curve plots equilibrium GDP as a function of the price level, anything that alters equilibrium GDP *at a given price level* must shift the AD curve. In other words, any change—other than a change in the price level—that causes the AE curve to shift will also cause the AD curve to shift. Such a shift is called an **aggregate demand shock**.

For example, in the 2002–2008 period, strong economic growth in the world economy led to an increase in demand for Canadian-produced raw materials. This increase in demand caused an upward shift in Canada's net export function. This event, taken by itself, would shift Canada's AE function upward and thus would shift Canada's AD curve to the right.

Beginning in the fall of 2008, however, a dramatic slowdown in world economic growth, caused in large part by the collapse of the U.S. housing market and the resulting worldwide financial crisis, led to a reduction in foreign demand for Canadian products. There was also an associated reduction in both investment and consumption expenditure in Canada, driven partly by the pessimism that accompanied the crisis. The overall effect was a downward shift in the AE curve and thus a leftward shift of Canada's AD curve.

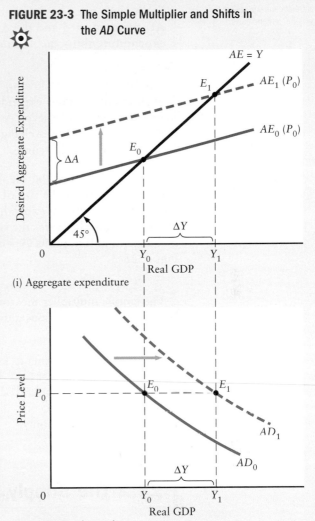

FIGURE 23-3 The Simple Multiplier and Shifts in the *AD* Curve

(i) Aggregate expenditure

(ii) Aggregate demand

A change in autonomous expenditure changes equilibrium GDP for any given price level. The simple multiplier measures the resulting horizontal shift in the *AD* curve. The original AE curve is AE_0 in part (i). Equilibrium is at E_0, with GDP of Y_0 at price level P_0. This yields point E_0 on the curve AD_0 in part (ii).

The AE curve in part (i) then shifts upward from AE_0 to AE_1 because of an increase in autonomous desired expenditure of ΔA. Equilibrium GDP now rises to Y_1, with the price level still constant at P_0. Thus, the AD curve in part (ii) shifts to the right to point E_1, indicating the higher equilibrium GDP of Y_1 associated with the same price level P_0. The size of the horizontal shift of the AD curve, ΔY, is equal to the simple multiplier times ΔA.

aggregate demand shock Any event that causes a shift in the aggregate demand curve.

For a given price level, an increase in autonomous aggregate expenditure shifts the *AE* curve upward and the *AD* curve to the right. A fall in autonomous aggregate expenditure shifts the *AE* curve downward and the *AD* curve to the left.

Remember the following important point: In order to shift the *AD* curve, the change in autonomous expenditure must be caused by something *other than* a change in the domestic price level. As we saw earlier in this chapter, a change in aggregate expenditure caused by a change in the domestic price level leads to a movement along (not a shift of) the *AD* curve.

The Simple Multiplier and the *AD* Curve We saw in Chapters 21 and 22 that the simple multiplier measures the size of the change in equilibrium national income caused by a change in autonomous expenditure *when the price level is held constant*. It follows that this same multiplier gives the size of the *horizontal shift* in the *AD* curve in response to a change in autonomous expenditure, as illustrated by the movement from E_0 to E_1 in Figure 23-3.

The simple multiplier measures the horizontal shift in the *AD* curve in response to a change in autonomous desired expenditure.

If the price level remains constant and producers are willing to supply everything that is demanded at that price level, the simple multiplier will also show the change in equilibrium income that will occur in response to a change in autonomous expenditure. This mention of producers' willingness to supply output brings us to a discussion of the *supply side* of the economy.

23.2 The Supply Side of the Economy

So far, we have explained how the equilibrium level of GDP is determined *when the price level is taken as given* and how that equilibrium changes as the price level is changed exogenously. We are now ready to take the important next step: adding an *explanation* for changes in the price level. To do this, we need to take account of the supply decisions of firms.

The Aggregate Supply Curve

aggregate supply (AS) curve A curve showing the relation between the price level and the quantity of aggregate output supplied, for given technology and factor prices.

Aggregate supply refers to the total output of goods and services that firms would like to produce and sell. The **aggregate supply (*AS*) curve** relates the price level to the quantity of output that firms would like to produce and sell under two assumptions:

- the state of technology is constant
- the prices of all factors of production are constant

What does the *AS* curve look like, and why?

The Positive Slope of the AS Curve Suppose firms want to increase their output above current levels. What will this do to their costs per unit of output—usually called their **unit costs**? The aggregate supply curve is drawn under the assumption that technology and the prices of all factors of production remain constant. This does not, however, mean that firms' unit costs will be constant. As output increases, less efficient standby plants may have to be used, and less efficient workers may have to be hired, while existing workers may have to be paid overtime rates for additional work. For these and other similar reasons, unit costs tend to rise as output rises, even when technology and input prices are constant. (Readers who have studied microeconomics will recognize the *law of diminishing returns* as one reason that costs may rise in the short run as firms squeeze more output out of a fixed quantity of capital equipment.)

This positive relationship between output and unit costs leads to the positive slope of the *AS* curve, as shown in Figure 23-4. Firms will not be prepared to produce and sell more output unless they are able to charge a higher price sufficient to cover their higher unit costs. This argument applies to *price-taking* firms who sell homogeneous products at market prices beyond their influence. It also applies to *price-setting* firms who sell differentiated products and have some ability to determine the price they charge. In both cases, the fact that unit costs generally rise with output means that firms generally increase their production only if they are able to receive higher prices.

> The actions of both price-taking and price-setting firms cause the price level and the supply of output to be positively related—the aggregate supply (*AS*) curve is positively sloped.

The Increasing Slope of the AS Curve In Figure 23-4 we see that at low levels of GDP the *AS* curve is relatively flat, but as GDP rises the *AS* curve gets progressively steeper. What explains this shape?

When output is low, firms typically have excess capacity—some plant and equipment are idle. When firms have excess capacity, only a small increase in the price of their output may be needed to induce them to expand production. Indeed, if firms have enough excess capacity, they may be willing to sell more at their existing prices when the demand for their product increases. In this case, output is truly demand determined up to the level at which costs begin to rise. Once output is pushed above normal capacity, however, unit costs tend to rise quite rapidly. Many higher-cost production methods may have to be adopted—such as standby capacity, overtime, and extra shifts. These higher-cost production methods will not be used unless the selling price of the output has risen enough to cover them. The more output is expanded beyond normal capacity, the more unit costs rise and hence the larger is the rise in price that is necessary to induce firms to increase output.

unit cost Cost per unit of output, equal to total cost divided by total output.

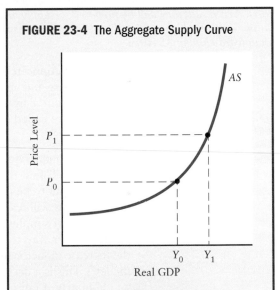

FIGURE 23-4 The Aggregate Supply Curve

The *AS* curve is positively sloped, indicating that firms will provide more aggregate output only at a higher price level. The *AS* curve is drawn for a given level of technology and factor prices. At price level P_0, firms are prepared to produce and supply output equal to Y_0. An expansion of their output to Y_1 leads to an increase in unit costs, and thus firms are prepared to supply Y_1 only at a higher price level, P_1.

The higher is the level of output, the faster unit costs tend to rise with each extra increment to output. This explains why the *AS* curve becomes steeper as output rises. At low levels of output, firms may have excess capacity and increases in output may not drive up unit costs. In these situations, the *AS* curve would be flat (horizontal).

For many firms, increases in output will drive up their unit costs. As a result, they will be prepared to supply more output only at a higher price. This behaviour gives rise to an upward-sloping AS curve.

As we will see later in this chapter, the shape of the *AS* curve is crucial for determining how the effect of an aggregate demand shock is divided between a change in the price level and a change in real GDP.

Shifts in the *AS* Curve

For a given level of output, anything that changes firms' production costs will cause the *AS* curve to shift. Two sources of such changes are of particular importance: changes in the prices of inputs and changes in firms' production technology. Input prices can, however, change for two different reasons. First, input prices may change because of things that are internal to our model. For example, if a rise in production increases the demand for labour and thus bids up wages, this will shift the *AS* curve upward and to the left. This shift is *endogenous* to our macro model, and we will discuss shifts of this type in Chapter 24. Second, input prices may change because of forces unconnected to our model—*exogenous* forces. For example, the world price of oil may rise and since this will raise the input prices of virtually all firms, it will also shift the *AS* curve upward and to the left. Shifts in the *AS* curve caused by such exogenous forces are called **aggregate supply shocks**. Let's now examine these shocks in more detail.

aggregate supply shock Any shift in the aggregate supply (*AS*) curve caused by an exogenous force.

Changes in Input Prices When factor prices change, the *AS* curve shifts. If factor prices rise, firms will find the profitability of their current production reduced. For any given level of output to be produced, an increase in the price level will be required. If prices do not rise, firms will react by decreasing production. For the economy as a whole, there will be less output supplied at each price level than before the increase in factor prices. Or, to put it another way, there will be a higher price level for each level of output than before the increase in factor prices. Thus, if factor prices rise, the *AS* curve shifts upward (and to the left). This is a decrease in aggregate supply and is shown in Figure 23-5.

Similarly, a fall in factor prices causes the *AS* curve to shift downward (and to the right). There will be more output supplied at each price level. Or, to put the same point differently, the same amount of output will be supplied at a lower price level. This is an increase in aggregate supply. A dramatic example of such a reduction in factor prices occurred in 1998 when the world prices of raw materials fell by an average of 30 percent. In the many countries that use raw materials as inputs in manufacturing, the *AS* curves shifted to the right. The opposite happened in 2002–2008 when energy and other commodity prices increased dramatically, thus shifting the *AS* curves to the left.

Changes in Technology Firms adopt new technologies in order to produce better versions of their products or to produce their existing products at lower costs (or both). For the purposes of our discussion, we define an *improvement* in technology as any change to production methods that reduces unit costs for any given level of output. Improvements in technology reduce unit costs and typically lead to lower prices as competing firms cut prices in attempts to raise their market share. Since the same output can now be sold at lower prices, the *AS* curve shifts downward and to the right. This is an increase in aggregate supply.

A *deterioration* in technology is any change in production methods that raises unit costs for any given level of output. Since firms are unlikely to intentionally adopt new methods that raise their costs, the latter occurrences are rare. However, in industries that rely on specific weather conditions for production—like agriculture—poor weather can be interpreted as a deterioration in technology. A deterioration in technology raises unit costs and causes the *AS* curve to shift upward and to the left, as shown in Figure 23-5.

> A change in either factor prices or technology will shift the *AS* curve, because any given output will be supplied at a different price level than previously. An increase in factor prices or a deterioration in technology shifts the *AS* curve to the left; a decrease in factor prices or an improvement in technology shifts the *AS* curve to the right.

▎23.3 Macroeconomic Equilibrium

We are now ready to see how both real GDP and the price level are simultaneously determined by the interaction of aggregate demand and aggregate supply. To begin, we assume that input prices and technology are constant.

The equilibrium values of real GDP and the price level occur at the intersection of the *AD* and *AS* curves, as shown by the pair Y_0 and P_0 that arises at point E_0 in Figure 23-6. The combination of real GDP and price level that is on both the *AD* and the *AS* curves is called a *macroeconomic equilibrium.*

To see why E_0 is the only macroeconomic equilibrium, consider what would occur at either a lower or a higher price level. First, consider the price level P_1. At this price level, total desired expenditure is Y_2 but the economy's firms are only prepared to produce and sell an output of Y_1; there is excess demand. Conversely, consider any price level above P_0. At these prices, the amount of output supplied by firms is greater than total desired expenditure; there is excess supply. Only at the price level P_0 is the desired production of output by firms consistent with aggregate expenditure decisions.

> Only at the combination of real GDP and price level given by the intersection of the *AS* and *AD* curves are demand behaviour and supply behaviour consistent.

Macroeconomic equilibrium thus requires that two conditions be satisfied. The first is familiar to us because it comes from Chapters 21 and 22. At the prevailing price level, desired aggregate expenditure must equal actual GDP. The *AD* curve is constructed in such a way that this condition holds everywhere along it. The second

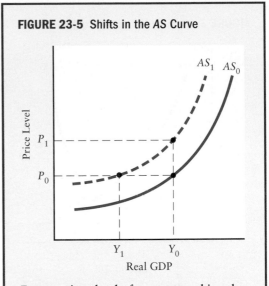

FIGURE 23-5 Shifts in the AS Curve

For any given level of output, anything that increases firms' costs will shift the *AS* curve upward (and to the left). Starting from (P_0, Y_0), a rise in input prices or a deterioration in technology would increase firms' unit costs. Firms would be prepared to continue supplying output of Y_0 only at the higher price level P_1. Or, at the initial price level P_0, firms would now be prepared to supply output of only Y_1. In either case, the *AS* curve has shifted up (or to the left) from AS_0 to AS_1. This is called a reduction in aggregate supply.

A fall in input prices or an improvement in technology would cause the *AS* curve to shift down (and to the right). This is an increase in aggregate supply.

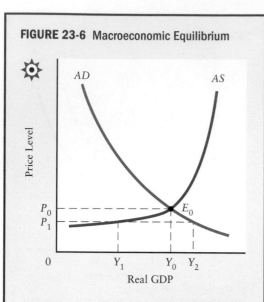

FIGURE 23-6 Macroeconomic Equilibrium

Macroeconomic equilibrium occurs at the intersection of the *AD* and *AS* curves and determines the equilibrium values for real GDP and the price level. Given the *AD* and *AS* curves in the figure, macroeconomic equilibrium occurs at E_0.

If the price level were equal to P_1, the desired output of firms would be Y_1. However, at P_1, the level of output that is consistent with expenditure decisions would be Y_2. Hence, when the price level is less than P_0, the desired output of firms will be less than the level of real GDP that is consistent with expenditure decisions. Conversely, for any price level above P_0, the desired output of firms exceeds the level of output that is consistent with expenditure decisions.

The only price level at which the supply decisions of firms are consistent with desired expenditure is P_0. At P_0, firms want to produce Y_0. When they do so, they generate a real GDP of Y_0; when real GDP is Y_0, decision makers want to spend exactly Y_0, thereby purchasing the nation's output. Hence, all decisions are consistent with each other.

requirement for macroeconomic equilibrium is introduced by consideration of aggregate supply. At the prevailing price level, firms must want to produce the prevailing level of GDP, no more and no less. This condition is fulfilled everywhere along the *AS* curve. Only where the two curves intersect are both conditions fulfilled simultaneously.

Changes in the Macroeconomic Equilibrium

The aggregate demand and aggregate supply curves can now be used to understand how various shocks to the economy change both real GDP and the price level.

As indicated earlier, a shift in the *AD* curve is called an aggregate demand shock. A rightward shift in the *AD* curve is an increase in aggregate demand; it means that at all price levels, expenditure decisions will now be consistent with a higher level of real GDP. This is called a *positive* shock. Similarly, a leftward shift in the *AD* curve is a decrease in aggregate demand—that is, at all price levels, expenditure decisions will now be consistent with a lower level of real GDP. This is called a *negative* shock.

Also as indicated earlier, a shift in the *AS* curve caused by an exogenous force is called an aggregate supply shock. A rightward shift in the *AS* curve is an increase in aggregate supply; at any given price level, more real GDP will be supplied. This is a *positive* shock. A leftward shift in the *AS* curve is a decrease in aggregate supply; at any given price level, less real GDP will be supplied. This is a *negative* shock.

> **Aggregate demand and supply shocks are labelled according to their effect on real GDP. Positive shocks increase equilibrium GDP; negative shocks reduce equilibrium GDP.**

Aggregate Demand Shocks

Figure 23-7 shows the effects of an increase in aggregate demand—a positive *AD* shock. This increase could have occurred because of, say, increased investment or government purchases, an increase in foreigners' demand for Canadian goods, or an increase in household consumption resulting from a reduction in personal income taxes or an increase in transfer payments. (Remember that each of these events causes the *AE* curve to shift up, and therefore the *AD* curve to shift to the right.) Whatever the cause, the increase in aggregate demand means that more domestic output is demanded at any given price level. As is shown in the figure, the increase in aggregate demand causes both the price level and real GDP to rise in the new macroeconomic equilibrium. Conversely, a decrease in demand causes both the price level and real GDP to fall.

> Aggregate demand shocks cause the price level and real GDP to change in the same direction; both rise with an increase in aggregate demand, and both fall with a decrease in aggregate demand.

Figure 23-7 shows how the macroeconomic equilibrium changes when there is an aggregate demand shock, but it does not show the complex adjustment going on "behind the scenes." We now examine this adjustment and see how the change in the price level alters the value of the multiplier.

The Multiplier When the Price Level Varies We saw earlier in this chapter that the simple multiplier gives the size of the horizontal shift in the AD curve in response to a change in autonomous expenditure. If the price level remains constant and firms supply all that is demanded at the existing price level (as would be the case with a horizontal AS curve), the simple multiplier gives the increase in equilibrium national income.

But what happens in the more usual case in which the AS curve slopes upward? As can be seen in Figure 23-7, when the AS curve is positively sloped, the change in real GDP caused by a change in autonomous expenditure is no longer equal to the size of the horizontal shift in the AD curve. Part of the expansionary impact of an increase in demand is dissipated by a rise in the price level, and only part is transmitted to a rise in real GDP. Of course, an increase in output does occur; thus, a multiplier may still be calculated, but its value is not the same as that of the *simple* multiplier.

Why is the multiplier smaller when the AS curve is positively sloped? The answer lies in the behaviour that is summarized by the AE curve. To understand this, it is useful to think of the final change in real GDP as occurring in two stages, as shown in Figure 23-8.

First, with a constant price level, an increase in autonomous expenditure shifts the AE curve upward (from AE_0 to AE_1'). This increase in autonomous expenditure is shown in part (ii) by a shift to the right of the AD curve. The movement marked ① is the horizontal shift of the AD curve and is equal to the simple multiplier times the change in autonomous expenditure. This is the end of the first stage, but is not the end of the whole story.

In the second stage we must take account of the rise in the price level that occurs because of the positive slope of the AS curve. As we saw earlier in this chapter, a rise in the price level, via its effect on net exports and desired consumption, leads to a downward shift in the AE curve (from AE_1' to AE_1). This second shift of the AE curve partly counteracts the initial rise in real GDP and so reduces the size of the multiplier. The second stage shows up as a downward shift of the AE curve in part (i)

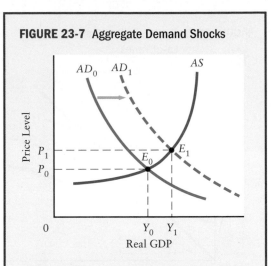

FIGURE 23-7 Aggregate Demand Shocks

Shifts in aggregate demand cause the price level and real GDP to move in the same direction. An increase in aggregate demand shifts the AD curve to the right, from AD_0 to AD_1. Macroeconomic equilibrium moves from E_0 to E_1. The price level rises from P_0 to P_1, and real GDP rises from Y_0 to Y_1, reflecting a movement along the AS curve.

FIGURE 23-8 The Multiplier When the Price Level Varies

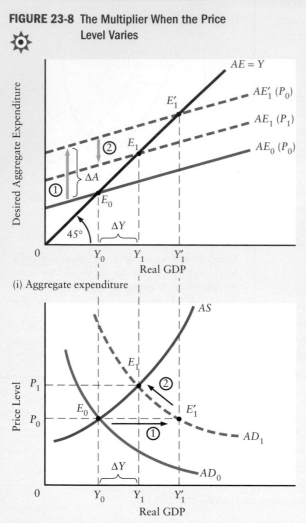

(i) Aggregate expenditure

(ii) Aggregate demand and supply

An increase in autonomous expenditure causes the AE curve to shift upward, but the rise in the price level causes it to shift part of the way down again. Hence, the multiplier is smaller than when the price level is constant. Originally, equilibrium is at point E_0 in both parts (i) and (ii). Desired aggregate expenditure then shifts by ΔA to AE_1', shifting the AD curve to AD_1. These shifts are shown by arrow ① in both parts. But the adjustment is not yet complete.

The shift in the AD curve raises the price level to P_1 because the AS curve is positively sloped. The rise in the price level shifts the AE curve down to AE_1, as shown by arrow ② in part (i). This is shown as a movement along the new AD curve, as indicated by arrow ② in part (ii). The new equilibrium is thus at E_1. The amount Y_0Y_1 is ΔY, the actual increase in real GDP. The multiplier, adjusted for the effect of the price increase, is the ratio $\Delta Y/\Delta A$.

of Figure 23-8 and a movement upward and to the left along the new AD curve, as shown by arrow ② in part (ii).

> If an aggregate demand shock leads to a change in the price level, the ultimate change in real GDP will be *less than* what is predicted by the simple multiplier. In other words, a variable price level reduces the value of the multiplier.

The Importance of the Shape of the AS Curve We have now seen that the shape of the AS curve has important implications for how the effects of an aggregate demand shock are divided between changes in real GDP and changes in the price level. Figure 23-9 highlights the price level and GDP effects of aggregate demand shocks by considering these shocks in the presence of an AS curve with three distinct ranges.

Over the *flat* range, any change in aggregate demand leads to no change in prices and, as seen earlier, a response of output equal to that predicted by the simple multiplier.

Over the *intermediate* range, along which the AS curve is positively sloped, a shift in the AD curve gives rise to appreciable changes in both real GDP and the price level. Because of the increase in the price level, the multiplier in this case is positive, but smaller than the simple multiplier.

Over the *steep* range, very little more can be produced, no matter how large the increase in demand. This range deals with an economy near its physical capacity constraints. Any change in aggregate demand leads to a sharp change in the price level and to little or no change in real GDP. The multiplier in this case is nearly zero.

> The effect of any given shift in aggregate demand will be divided between a change in real output and a change in the price level, depending on the conditions of aggregate supply. The steeper the AS curve, the greater the price effect and the smaller the output effect.

Extensions in Theory 23-1 deals with the case of a horizontal AS curve—sometimes called a *Keynesian AS* curve. In that case, the aggregate supply curve determines the price level, and the *AD* curve determines real GDP.

Reconciliation with Previous Analysis One of the central points of this chapter is that aggregate demand shocks typically lead to changes in *both* the price level and the level of real GDP. Furthermore, with a vertical *AS* curve, such aggregate demand shocks will result in no change in real GDP, but only a change in the price level. How do we reconcile this possibility with the analysis of Chapters 21 and 22, where shifts in *AE* *always* change real GDP? The answer is that each *AE* curve is drawn on the assumption that there is a constant price level. An upward shift in the *AE* curve shifts the *AD* curve to the right. However, a positively sloped *AS* curve means that the price level rises, and this rise shifts the *AE* curve back down, offsetting some of its initial rise. This process was explained in Figure 23-8.

It is instructive to consider an extreme version of Figure 23-8, one with a vertical *AS* curve. If you draw this diagram for yourself, you will note that an increase in autonomous expenditure shifts the *AE* curve upward, thus raising the amount demanded. However, a vertical *AS* curve means that output cannot be expanded to satisfy the increased demand. Instead, the extra demand merely forces prices up, and as prices rise, the *AE* curve shifts down again. The rise in prices continues until the *AE* curve is back to where it started. Thus, the rise in prices offsets the expansionary effect of the original shift and consequently leaves both real aggregate expenditure and equilibrium real GDP unchanged.

A vertical *AS* curve, however, is quite unrealistic. An *AS* curve shaped something like the one shown in Figure 23-9—that is, relatively flat for low levels of GDP and becoming steeper as GDP rises—is closer to reality.

We now complete our discussion of changes in the macroeconomic equilibrium by discussing supply shocks.

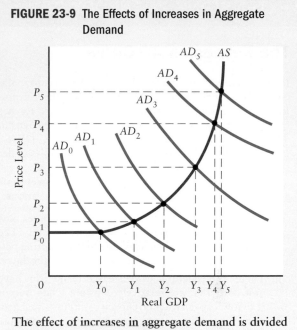

FIGURE 23-9 The Effects of Increases in Aggregate Demand

The effect of increases in aggregate demand is divided between increases in real GDP and increases in the price level, depending on the slope of the *AS* curve. Because of the increasing slope of the *AS* curve, increases in aggregate demand up to AD_0 have virtually no impact on the price level. Successive further increases bring larger price increases and relatively smaller output increases. By the time aggregate demand is at AD_4 or AD_5, virtually all of the effect is on the price level.

Aggregate Supply Shocks

A negative aggregate supply shock, shown by an upward (or leftward) shift in the *AS* curve, means that less real output will be supplied at any given price level. A positive aggregate supply shock, shown by a downward (or rightward) shift in the *AS* curve, means that more real output will be supplied at any given price level.

Figure 23-10 illustrates the effects on the price level and real GDP of a negative aggregate supply shock. This could have occurred because of, say, an increase in the world price of important inputs, such as oil, copper, or iron ore. As can be seen from the figure, following the decrease in aggregate supply, the price level rises and real GDP falls. Conversely, a positive aggregate supply shock leads to an increase in real GDP and a decrease in the price level.

EXTENSIONS IN THEORY 23-1

The Keynesian *AS* Curve

In this box, we consider an *AS* curve that is horizontal over some range of real GDP. It is called the *Keynesian aggregate supply curve*, after John Maynard Keynes (1883–1946), who, in his famous book *The General Theory of Employment, Interest and Money* (1936), pioneered the study of the behaviour of economies under conditions of high unemployment.

To see why the *AS* curve may be horizontal over some range of aggregate output, we make three observations:

1. Many firms operate their production facilities at a level of output below their "capacity" output. The excess capacity is then available to firms during periods of abnormally high demand for their products.

2. There is considerable evidence that many firms have unit costs that are relatively constant when output is below capacity. Once capacity output is reached, however, additional output can be produced only with rising unit costs.

3. For price-setting firms with output below capacity, short-run changes in demand are often met with changes in output but not changes in price. One explanation for this behaviour is that there are costs associated with changing prices.

The behaviour that gives rise to the Keynesian *AS* curve can then be described as follows. When real GDP is below potential GDP (the economy's "capacity" output), individual firms are operating with excess capacity. They then respond to changes in demand by altering output while keeping prices constant. In other words, they will supply whatever they can sell at their existing prices as long as they are producing below their normal capacity.

Under these circumstances, the economy has a horizontal *AS* curve, indicating that any output up to potential output will be supplied at the going price level. The amount that is actually produced is then determined by

John Maynard Keynes was the founder of much of modern macroeconomics, and emphasized the importance of aggregate demand in determining the level of economic activity.

the position of the *AD* curve. Thus, real GDP is said to be *demand determined*. If demand rises enough so that firms are trying to increase their output beyond capacity, their costs will rise and so will their prices. Hence, the horizontal Keynesian *AS* curve applies only to levels of GDP below potential GDP.

The case of a horizontal *AS* curve corresponds to the macro model that we developed in Chapters 21 and 22. Recall that in that simple model we assumed a constant price level. In other words, if the *AS* curve is horizontal, our macro model in this chapter is *exactly the same* as the simple version in Chapters 21 and 22. In this case, a change in autonomous expenditure, ΔA, will lead to increases in equilibrium GDP equal to ΔA times the simple multiplier.

Aggregate supply shocks cause the price level and real GDP to change in opposite directions. With an increase in supply, the price level falls and GDP rises; with a decrease in supply, the price level rises and GDP falls.

Oil-price increases have provided three major examples of negative aggregate supply shocks, the first two during the 1970s and the third between 2002 and 2008. The economy is especially responsive to changes in the price of oil because, in addition to being used to produce energy, oil is an input into plastics, chemicals, fertilizers, and many other materials that are widely used in industry. Massive increases in oil prices occurred during 1973–1974 and 1979–1980, caused by the successful efforts of the OPEC countries to form a cartel and restrict the output of oil. These increases in the price of oil caused leftward shifts in the *AS* curve in most countries. Real GDP fell while the price level rose, a combination commonly referred to as *stagflation*. (We will discuss shortly the more recent oil-price increases that occurred in the 2002–2008 period.)

Commodity prices have provided an important recent example of a positive aggregate supply shock. The Southeast Asian countries of Indonesia, Malaysia, Thailand, and South Korea are all significant users of raw materials. When their economies plunged into a major recession in 1997, the world demand for raw materials fell, and the prices of such goods fell as a result. From 1997 to 1998, the average price of raw materials fell by approximately 30 percent.

Though these were clearly bad economic times for much of Southeast Asia, the reduction in raw materials prices was a *positive* aggregate supply shock for countries that used raw materials as inputs for production. In countries like Canada, the United States, and most of Western Europe, the *AS* curves shifted to the right. The effect was to increase real GDP and reduce the price level.[3]

A Word of Warning

We have discussed the effects of aggregate demand and aggregate supply shocks on the economy's price level and real GDP. Students are sometimes puzzled, however, because some events would appear to be *both* demand and supply shocks. How do we analyze such complicated shocks? For example, when the world price of oil rises, as it did significantly between 2002 and 2008, this is a *negative supply shock* because oil is an important input to production for many firms. But for Canada, which produces and exports oil, doesn't the increase in the world price of oil also imply an increase in export revenue? And doesn't this imply a *positive demand shock*?

The answer to both questions is yes. An increase in world oil prices is indeed a negative aggregate supply shock to any country that uses oil as an input (which means most countries). But for those countries that also produce and

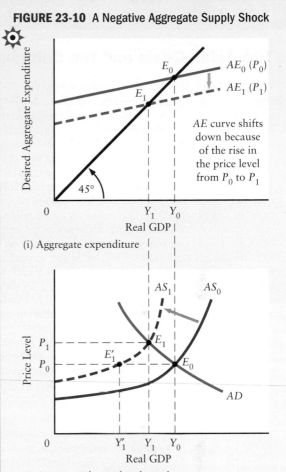

FIGURE 23-10 A Negative Aggregate Supply Shock

(i) Aggregate expenditure

(ii) Aggregate demand and supply

Aggregate supply shocks cause the price level and real GDP to move in opposite directions. The original equilibrium is at E_0, with GDP of Y_0 appearing in both parts of the figure. The price level is P_0 in part (ii), and at that price level, the desired aggregate expenditure curve is AE_0 in part (i).

A negative aggregate supply shock now shifts the *AS* curve in part (ii) to AS_1. At the original price level of P_0, firms are willing to supply only Y_1'. The fall in aggregate supply causes a rise in the price level. The new equilibrium is reached at E_1, where the *AD* curve intersects AS_1. At the new and higher equilibrium price level of P_1, the *AE* curve has shifted down to AE_1, as shown in part (i).

---

[3] Actually, it is more accurate to say that this shock reduced the price level *compared with what it otherwise would have been*. Because of ongoing inflation, the causes of which we will discuss in Chapters 29 and 30, the price level in Canada rarely falls. But we have been assuming throughout this chapter that there is no ongoing inflation, and in that setting a positive *AS* shock like the one described in the text would cause the price level to fall.

LESSONS FROM HISTORY 23-1

The Asian Crisis and the Canadian Economy

In the summer of 1997, the currencies of several countries in Southeast Asia plummeted (relative to the U.S. and Canadian dollars) as their central banks were no longer able to "peg" their exchange rates. In Chapter 35 we will discuss how such pegged exchange rates operate. For now, the important point is that, for various reasons, banks, firms, and households in these countries had accumulated a large stock of debt denominated in foreign currencies, especially U.S. dollars. The sudden depreciations of their currencies—in some cases by 70 percent in just a few days—led to dramatic increases in the amount of domestic income required to pay the interest on this debt. Financial institutions went bankrupt, manufacturing firms were unable to access credit, workers were laid off, and economic output fell sharply. By late in 1997, the economies of Malaysia, Indonesia, Thailand, South Korea, and the Philippines were suffering major recessions.

How did this Asian crisis affect Canada? It had offsetting positive and negative effects on the level of economic activity in Canada. The events in Asia generated both a *negative* aggregate demand shock and a *positive* aggregate supply shock for Canada.

To understand the demand side of the story, we must recognize that these Asian economies are important users of raw materials. When their economies went into recession, their demand for raw materials fell sharply. Indeed, average raw materials prices fell by roughly 30 percent between 1997 and 1998. And raw materials are an important export for Canada. The decline in the world's demand for raw materials implied a reduction in demand for Canadian goods. As a result, Canadian producers of copper, pork, newsprint, lumber, iron ore, and many other raw materials suffered significantly. In terms of our macroeconomic model, the Asian crisis caused a leftward shift of the Canadian AD curve.

The story does not end there. Also important to Canada is the fact that many Canadian firms use raw materials as inputs for their production of car parts, prefabricated houses and trailers, electrical equipment, and so on. A dramatic reduction in the prices of raw materials implies a reduction in costs for these firms. This is a positive aggregate supply shock, and is illustrated by a rightward shift of the Canadian AS curve.

What is the overall effect on the Canadian economy? The effect of each shock taken separately is to reduce the price level—so the overall effect is unambiguously a lower price level.* In contrast, the effect on real GDP would appear to be ambiguous since the AD shock reduces GDP whereas the AS shock increases it. But this is not quite right. Since Canada earns more from its sales of raw materials than it spends on them (that is, Canada is a net exporter of these products), it must experience a decrease in national income when these prices fall. In other words, the net effect of the negative demand shock and the positive supply shock is to reduce Canadian GDP. The figure is therefore drawn with the AD shock being larger than the AS shock and so the new equilibrium level of GDP, Y_1, is lower than in the initial equilibrium, Y_0.

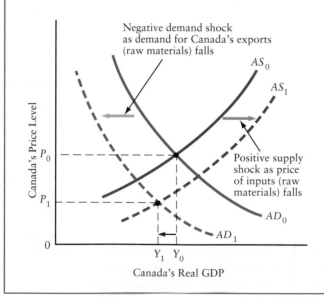

Negative demand shock as demand for Canada's exports (raw materials) falls

AS_0

AS_1

Positive supply shock as price of inputs (raw materials) falls

AD_0

AD_1

P_0

P_1

Y_1 Y_0

Canada's Price Level

Canada's Real GDP

---

*Recall footnote 3 on page 581. We are assuming in this analysis that there is no ongoing inflation, so a positive AS shock or a negative AD shock reduces the price level. A more accurate description for the Canadian economy in 1998, with some ongoing inflation, is that the price level fell below what it otherwise would have been. This appears as a reduction in the rate of inflation.

export oil—like Canada—a rise in the price of oil generates an increase in income to domestic oil producers and is thus a positive aggregate demand shock. It is no surprise that the economies of the oil-producing regions of Canada, especially Alberta, Saskatchewan, and Newfoundland and Labrador, were booming during the 2002–2008 period, when the price of oil increased from about U.S.$20 per barrel to more than U.S.$80 per barrel (and was very briefly at almost $U.S.150 per barrel during 2008).

A complete analysis of the macroeconomic effect of a rise in world oil prices must consider both a leftward shift of the *AS* curve and, for those countries that produce oil, a rightward shift of the *AD* curve. The equilibrium price level will certainly increase, but the overall effect on real GDP will depend on the relative importance of the demand-side and supply-side effects.

Our discussion here has been about the macroeconomic effects of oil-price increases, but the central message is more general:

For information on OPEC, see its website: www.opec.org.

> Many economic events—especially changes in the world prices of raw materials—cause both aggregate demand and aggregate supply shocks in the same economy. The overall effect on real GDP in that economy depends on the relative importance of the two separate effects.

This general principle should be kept in mind whenever our *AD/AS* macro model is used to analyze the macro economy. *Lessons from History 23-1* uses our model to interpret the effects of the 1997–1998 Asian economic crisis on the Canadian economy. As you will see in that discussion, the Asian crisis generated both *AD* and *AS* shocks for Canada.

SUMMARY

23.1 The Demand Side of the Economy

LO 1, 2

- The *AE* curve shows desired aggregate expenditure for each level of GDP at a particular price level. Its intersection with the 45° line determines equilibrium GDP for that price level. Equilibrium GDP thus occurs where desired aggregate expenditure equals actual GDP. A change in the price level causes a shift in the *AE* curve: upward when the price level falls and downward when the price level rises. This leads to a new equilibrium level of real GDP.

- The *AD* curve plots the equilibrium level of GDP that corresponds to each possible price level. A change in

equilibrium GDP following a change in the price level is shown by a movement along the *AD* curve.

- A rise in the price level lowers exports and lowers autonomous consumption expenditure. Both of these changes reduce equilibrium GDP and cause the *AD* curve to have a negative slope.

- The *AD* curve shifts horizontally when any element of autonomous expenditure changes, and the simple multiplier measures the size of the shift.

23.2 The Supply Side of the Economy

LO 3

- Any aggregate supply (*AS*) curve is drawn for given factor prices and given state of technology.

- The *AS* curve is usually drawn as an upward-sloping curve, reflecting the assumption that firms' unit costs tend to rise when their output rises.

- At levels of output below potential GDP, firms' excess capacity may result in a horizontal *AS* curve.

- An improvement in technology or a decrease in factor prices shifts the *AS* curve to the right. This is an increase in aggregate supply.

- A deterioration in technology or an increase in factor prices shifts the *AS* curve to the left. This is a decrease in aggregate supply.

23.3 Macroeconomic Equilibrium   LO 4

- Macroeconomic equilibrium refers to equilibrium values of real GDP and the price level, as determined by the intersection of the *AD* and *AS* curves. Shifts in the *AD* and *AS* curves, called aggregate demand and aggregate supply shocks, change the equilibrium values of real GDP and the price level.
- When the *AS* curve is positively sloped, an aggregate demand shock causes the price level and real GDP to move in the same direction. When the *AS* curve is flat, shifts in the *AD* curve primarily affect real GDP. When the *AS* curve is steep, shifts in the *AD* curve primarily affect the price level.
- With a positively sloped *AS* curve, a demand shock leads to a change in the price level. As a result, the

multiplier is smaller than the simple multiplier in Chapter 22.
- An aggregate supply shock moves equilibrium GDP along the *AD* curve, causing the price level and real GDP to move in opposite directions.
- Some events are both aggregate supply and aggregate demand shocks. Changes in the world prices of raw materials, for example, shift the *AS* curve. If the country (like Canada) is also a producer of such raw materials, there will also be a shift in the *AD* curve. The overall effect then depends on the relative sizes of the separate effects.

KEY CONCEPTS

Effects of an exogenous change in the price level
Relationship between the *AE* and *AD* curves

Negative slope of the *AD* curve
Positive slope of the *AS* curve
Macroeconomic equilibrium
Aggregate demand shocks

The multiplier when the price level varies
Aggregate supply shocks

STUDY EXERCISES

MyEconLab   Make the grade with MyEconLab: Study Exercises marked in red can be found on MyEconLab. You can practise them as often as you want, and most feature step-by-step guided instructions to help you find the right answer.

1. Fill in the blanks to make the following statements correct.

   a. In the simple macro model of the previous two chapters, the price level was _____. In the macro model of this chapter, the price level is _____.

   b. A change in the price level shifts the *AE* curve because the price level change affects desired _____ and desired _____.

   c. A rise in the price level causes a(n) _____ in households' wealth, which leads to a(n) _____ in desired consumption, which causes the *AE* curve to shift _____. A fall in the price level causes a(n) _____ in households' wealth, which leads to a(n) _____ in desired consumption, which causes the *AE* curve to shift _____.

   d. A rise in the domestic price level causes net exports to _____, which causes the *AE* curve to shift _____. A fall in the domestic price level causes net exports to _____, which causes the *AE* curve to shift _____.

   e. Equilibrium GDP is determined by the position of the *AE* function for each given price level. An equilibrium point for a particular price level corresponds to one point on the _____ curve.

   f. A rise in the price level causes a downward shift of the _____ curve and a movement upward along the _____ curve.

   g. An increase in autonomous expenditure, with no change in the price level, causes the *AE* curve to _____ and causes the *AD* curve to _____.

2. Fill in the blanks to make the following statements correct.

   a. The _____ curve relates the price level to the quantity of output that firms would like to produce and sell.
   b. Each aggregate supply curve is drawn under the assumption that _____ and _____ remain constant.
   c. The aggregate supply curve is upward sloping because firms will produce more output only if price _____ to offset higher unit costs.
   d. The aggregate supply curve is relatively flat when GDP is below potential output because firms typically have _____ and are able to expand production with little or no increase in unit costs.
   e. The aggregate supply curve is relatively steep when GDP is above potential output because firms are operating above _____ and _____ are rising rapidly.
   f. The aggregate supply curve shifts in response to changes in _____ and changes in _____. These are known as supply _____.

3. Fill in the blanks to make the following statements correct.

   a. Macroeconomic equilibrium occurs at the intersection of _____ and _____, and determines equilibrium levels of _____ and _____.
   b. If the *AS* curve is upward sloping, a positive *AD* shock will cause the price level to _____ and real GDP to _____. A negative *AD* shock will cause the price level to _____ and real GDP to _____.
   c. A positive *AS* shock will cause the price level to _____ and real GDP to _____. A negative *AS* shock will cause the price level to _____ and real GDP to _____.
   d. In previous chapters, the simple multiplier measured the change in real GDP in response to a change in autonomous expenditure when the price level was constant. When the price level varies, the multiplier is _____ than the simple multiplier.
   e. An increase in autonomous government spending is a(n) _____ *AD* shock, which will initially cause a(n) _____ shift of the *AE* curve and a(n) _____ shift of the *AD* curve. Given an upward-sloping aggregate supply curve, there will be a(n) _____ in the price level, which leads to a partial _____ shift of the *AE* curve.

4. Consider the effects of an exogenous increase in the domestic price level. For each of the assets listed, explain how the change in the price level would affect the wealth of the asset holder. Then explain the effect on *aggregate* (private sector) wealth. The footnote on page 568 will help to answer parts (d) and (e) of this question.

   a. Cash holdings
   b. Deposits in a bank account
   c. A household mortgage

d. A corporate bond that promises to pay the bondholder $10 000 on January 1, 2015
e. A government bond that promises to pay the holder $10 000 on January 1, 2015

5. Consider the following simplified *AE* function:

$$AE = 350 + 0.8Y + 0.1\,(M/P)$$

where *AE* is desired aggregate expenditure, *Y* is real GDP, *M* is the private sector's *nominal wealth*, and *P* is the price level. Suppose that *M* is constant and equal to 6000.

   a. Fill in the table below:

P	M/P	AE
1	6000	950 + 0.8Y
2	—	—
3	—	—
4	—	—
5	—	—
6	—	—

   b. Plot each of the *AE* functions—one for each price level—on the same-scale 45°-line diagram.
   c. Compute the level of equilibrium national income (*Y*) for each of the values of *P*. For example, when *P* = 1, *AE* = 950 + 0.8Y. Thus the equilibrium level of *Y* is such that *Y* = 950 + 0.8Y, which implies *Y* = 4750.
   d. Plot the pairs of price level and equilibrium national income on a scale diagram with *P* on the vertical axis and *Y* on the horizontal axis. What is this curve you have just constructed?
   e. Explain why the expression for *AE* above makes sense. Why do *M* and *P* enter the *AE* function?

6. Consider the following diagram showing the *AD* curves in two different economies. One economy is Autarkland—it does not trade with the rest of the world (*autarky* is a situation in which a country does not trade with other countries). The other economy is Openland—it exports to and imports from the rest of the world.

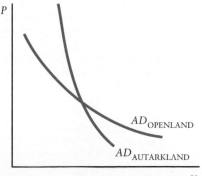

a. Explain why an increase in the domestic price level (for a given exchange rate) reduces net exports in Openland. How would you illustrate this with the *AE* curve in the 45°-line diagram?

b. Explain why the *AD* curve is steeper in Autarkland than in Openland.

c. If there are never any net exports in Autarkland, why isn't the *AD* curve vertical? Explain what other aspect of the economy generates a downward-sloping *AD* curve.

7. The economy of Neverland has the following *AD* and *AS* schedules. Denote Y_{AD} as the level of real GDP along the *AD* curve; let Y_{AS} be the level of real GDP along the *AS* curve. GDP is shown in billions of 2002 dollars.

Price Level	Y_{AD}	Y_{AS}
90	1100	750
100	1000	825
110	900	900
120	800	975
130	700	1050
140	600	1125

a. Plot the *AD* and *AS* curves on a scale diagram.

b. What is the price level and level of real GDP in Neverland's macroeconomic equilibrium?

c. Suppose the level of potential output in Neverland is $950 billion. Is the current equilibrium level of real GDP greater than or less than potential? How does one refer to this particular output gap?

8. Each of the following events caused a shift in the *AD* or *AS* curve in Canada. Identify which curve was affected and describe the effect on equilibrium real GDP and the price level.

a. OPEC's actions to restrict oil output significantly increased the world price of oil in 1979–1980.

b. World commodity prices increased sharply from 2002 to 2008. Many of these commodities are both produced in Canada and used as important inputs for Canadian firms.

c. The end of the Cold War led to large declines in defence spending in many countries (including Canada).

d. The federal government and (many) provincial governments reduced corporate income-tax rates between 2000 and 2011.

e. The federal government increased its level of government purchases (*G*) in 2009 and 2010, amidst a global recession.

f. The beginning of a recession in the United States in 2008 led to a large reduction in the demand for many Canadian exports.

9. The following diagrams show the *AD* and *AS* curves in two different economies.

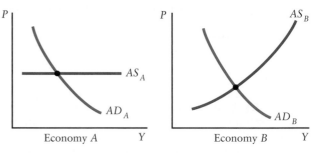

a. Explain what aspect of firms' behaviour might give rise to the horizontal *AS* curve in Economy *A*.

b. Explain what aspect of firms' behaviour gives rise to the upward-sloping *AS* curve in Economy *B*.

c. In which economy is output purely demand determined? Explain.

d. Consider the effects of an increase in autonomous expenditure. Which economy has the larger multiplier? Explain your reasoning.

10. This question involves algebraically solving the system of two equations given by the *AD* and *AS* curves. The equations for the curves are given by

$$AD: Y_{AD} = 710 - 30P + 5G$$

$$AS: Y_{AS} = 10 + 5P - 2P_{OIL}$$

where *Y* is real GDP, *P* is the price level, *G* is the level of government purchases, and P_{OIL} is the world price of oil.

a. Explain the various terms in the *AD* curve. Explain why *G* enters positively.

b. What is the value of the simple multiplier? (Hint: Refer back to the caption of Figure 23-3.)

c. Explain the various terms in the *AS* curve. Explain why the price of oil enters negatively.

d. Solve for the equilibrium value of real GDP and the price level.

e. Using your solution to part (d), what is the effect of a change in *G* on equilibrium *Y* and *P*? Explain.

f. Using your solution to part (d), what is the effect of a change in P_{OIL} on equilibrium *Y* and *P*? Explain.

From the Short Run to the Long Run: The Adjustment of Factor Prices

CHAPTER OUTLINE	LEARNING OBJECTIVES (LO)
	After studying this chapter you will be able to
24.1 THE ADJUSTMENT PROCESS	1 explain why output gaps cause wages and other factor prices to change.
	2 describe how induced changes in factor prices affect firms' costs and shift the AS curve.
24.2 AGGREGATE DEMAND AND SUPPLY SHOCKS	3 explain why real GDP gradually returns to potential output following an AD or AS shock.
24.3 FISCAL STABILIZATION POLICY	4 understand why lags and uncertainty place limitations on the use of fiscal stabilization policy.

IN the previous three chapters, we developed a model of the *short-run* determination of the equilibrium levels of real GDP and the price level. In this chapter, we discuss how this short-run macroeconomic equilibrium evolves, through an adjustment process in which wages and other factor prices change, into a *long-run* equilibrium, in which real GDP is equal to potential output, Y^*. In the next two chapters we examine theories explaining why Y^* increases over many years—what we call *long-run economic growth*. Before we proceed, however, we will define carefully our assumptions regarding the short run, the adjustment process, and the long run.

The Short Run

These are the defining assumptions of the *short run* in our macroeconomic model:

- Factor prices are assumed to be exogenous; they may change, but any change is not explained within the model.
- Technology and factor supplies are assumed to be constant (and therefore Y^* is constant).

With these assumptions, the short-run macroeconomic equilibrium is determined by the intersection of the *AD* and *AS* curves, both of which are subject to shocks of various kinds. These shocks cause the level of real GDP to fluctuate around a *constant* level of potential output, Y^*. This version of our macroeconomic model is convenient to use when analyzing the economy over short periods. Even though factor prices, technology, and factor supplies are rarely constant in reality, even over short periods of time, the simplifying assumption that they are constant in our short-run model allows us to focus on the important role of *AD* or *AS* shocks over this time span.

The Adjustment of Factor Prices

As we will see in detail in this chapter, our theory of the *adjustment process* that takes the economy from the short run to the long run is based on the following assumptions:

- Factor prices are assumed to adjust in response to output gaps.
- Technology and factor supplies are assumed to be constant (and therefore Y^* is constant).

This chapter will explain our model's assumption that deviations of real GDP from potential output cause wages and other factor prices to adjust. It will also explain how this adjustment is central to the economy's evolution from its short-run equilibrium to its long-run equilibrium. Note that, as in the short-run version of the model, the adjustment process is assumed to take place with a constant level of potential output.

Our theory of the macroeconomic adjustment process is useful for examining how the effects of shocks or policies differ in the short and long runs. As we will see, the assumption that potential output is constant leads to the prediction that *AD* or *AS* shocks have no long-run effect on real GDP; output eventually returns to Y^*.

In reality, neither technology nor factor supplies are constant over time; the level of potential output is continually changing. Our assumption throughout much of this chapter of a constant value for Y^* is a simplifying one, allowing us to focus on our theory of the *adjustment process* that brings the level of real GDP back to potential output.

The Long Run

In Chapters 25 and 26 we will examine the defining assumptions of the *long run* in our macro model. They are

- Factor prices are assumed to have fully adjusted to any output gap.
- Technology and factor supplies are assumed to be changing.

The first assumption tells us that, after factor prices have fully adjusted, real GDP will return to the level of potential output. The second assumption implies that the level of potential output is changing (and typically growing). Thus, in the long-run version of our macroeconomic model, our focus is not on the nature of short-run fluctuations in GDP but rather on the nature of *economic growth*—where technological change and the growth of factor supplies play key roles.

TABLE 24-1 Three Macroeconomic States

	The Short Run	The Adjustment Process	The Long Run
Key Assumptions	Factor prices are exogenous	Factor prices are flexible/endogenous	Factor prices are fully adjusted/endogenous
	Technology and factor supplies (and thus Y^*) are constant/exogenous	Technology and factor supplies (and thus Y^*) are constant/exogenous	Technology and factor supplies (and thus Y^*) are changing
What Happens	Real GDP (Y) is determined by aggregate demand and aggregate supply	Factor prices adjust to output gaps; real GDP eventually returns to Y^*	Potential GDP (Y^*) grows over the long run
Why We Study This State	To show the effects of *AD* and *AS* shocks on real GDP	To see how output gaps cause factor prices to change and why real GDP tends to return to Y^*	To understand the nature of long-run economic growth.

The economy is probably never "in" the long run in the sense that factor prices have fully adjusted to all *AD* and *AS* shocks. This is because such shocks are not isolated events but instead events that occur more or less continually. So, before the full adjustment to one shock is complete, another shock occurs and sets the adjustment process in motion again. Nonetheless, the long-run version of our model is very useful for examining some issues. For example, if we want to understand why our children's material standard of living will be significantly greater than our grandparents', we should not focus on short-run *AD* or *AS* shocks or the stabilization policies that may follow; the effects of particular shocks will disappear after a few years. Instead, we will gain more understanding if we abstract from short-run issues and focus on why Y^* increases dramatically over periods of several decades.

Summary

The three states of the economy central to macroeconomic analysis are summarized in Table 24-1. Note for each state the assumptions made regarding factor prices and the level of potential output and the causes of changes in real GDP. As we proceed through this chapter and the next two, you may find it useful to refer back to this table.

You already know from Chapter 23 how the short-run version of our macro model works. And now that you have a sketch of what is meant by the adjustment process and the long run, we are ready to fill in the details. In this chapter we will see how this adjustment process takes the economy from its short-run equilibrium to its long-run equilibrium. To repeat, we assume in this chapter that factor prices adjust in response to output gaps and that potential output (Y^*) is constant.

24.1 The Adjustment Process

We develop our theory of the adjustment process by examining the relationship among output gaps, factor markets, and factor prices. We begin by understanding the broad outline of how this process works. We then go on to discuss *how well* it works in greater detail.

Potential Output and the Output Gap

Recall that *potential output* is the total output that can be produced when all productive resources—land, labour, and capital—are fully employed. When a nation's actual output diverges from its potential output, the difference is called the output gap.

Although growth in potential output has powerful effects from one decade to the next, its change from one *year* to the next is small enough that we ignore it when studying the year-to-year behaviour of real GDP and the price level. In this chapter, therefore, we view variations in the output gap as determined solely by variations in *actual* GDP around a constant level of *potential* GDP. (In Chapter 26 we will examine why potential output grows over the long run.)

Figure 24-1 shows real GDP being determined in the short run by the intersection of the *AD* and *AS* curves. Potential output is assumed to be constant, and it is shown by identical vertical lines in the two parts of the figure. In part (i), the *AD* and *AS* curves intersect to produce an equilibrium real GDP less than potential output. The result, as we saw in Chapter 19, is called a *recessionary gap* because recessions are often characterized as having GDP below potential output. In part (ii), the *AD* and *AS* curves intersect to produce an equilibrium real GDP above potential output, resulting in what is called an *inflationary gap*. Why an inflationary output gap puts upward pressure on prices will become clear in the ensuing discussion.

Factor Prices and the Output Gap

We make two key assumptions in our macro model regarding factor prices and the output gap. First, when real GDP is above potential output, there will be pressure on factor prices to rise because of a higher than normal demand for factor inputs. Second,

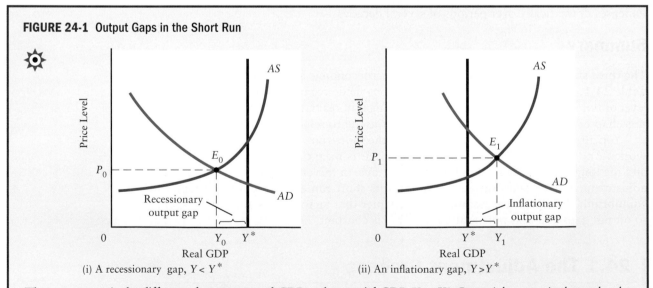

FIGURE 24-1 Output Gaps in the Short Run

(i) A recessionary gap, $Y < Y^*$

(ii) An inflationary gap, $Y > Y^*$

The output gap is the difference between actual GDP and potential GDP, $Y - Y^*$. Potential output is shown by the vertical line at Y^*. A recessionary gap, shown in part (i), occurs when actual output is less than potential GDP. An inflationary gap, shown in part (ii), occurs when actual output is greater than potential GDP.

when real GDP is below potential output, there will be pressure on factor prices to fall because of a lower than normal demand for factor inputs. These relationships are assumed to hold for the prices of all factors of production, including labour, land, and capital equipment.

Before we examine the detailed relationship between factor prices and output gaps, it is worth noting that even in the absence of an output gap, the presence of ongoing inflation influences factor prices, especially wages. Wage contracts often allow for changes in the price level that are expected to occur during the life of the contract. For the discussion in this chapter, however, we make the simplifying assumption that the price level is expected to be constant (and therefore inflation is expected to be zero); hence changes in nominal wages are also expected to be changes in real wages. We will discuss inflation in detail in Chapters 29 and 30.

Output Above Potential, $Y > Y^*$ Here is the reasoning behind our first assumption. Sometimes the *AD* and *AS* curves intersect where real GDP exceeds potential, as illustrated in part (ii) of Figure 24-1. Because firms are producing beyond their normal capacity output, there is an excess demand for all factor inputs, including labour. Labour shortages will emerge in some industries and among many groups of workers. Firms will try to bid workers away from other firms in order to maintain the high levels of output and sales made possible by the boom conditions.

As a result of this excess demand in factor markets, workers will find that they have considerable bargaining power with their employers, and they will put upward pressure on wages. Firms, recognizing that demand for their goods is strong, will be anxious to maintain a high level of output. To prevent their workers from either striking or quitting and moving to other employers, firms will be willing to accede to some of these upward pressures.

> The boom that is associated with an inflationary gap generates a set of conditions—high profits for firms and an excess demand for labour—that tends to cause wages (and other factor prices) to rise.

This increase in factor prices will increase firms' unit costs. As unit costs increase, firms will require higher prices in order to supply any given level of output, and the *AS* curve will therefore shift up. This shift has the effect of reducing equilibrium real GDP and raising the price level. Real GDP moves back toward potential and the inflationary gap begins to close.

In our model, factor prices are assumed to continue rising as long as some inflationary gap remains. In other words, they will continue rising until the *AS* curve shifts up to the point where the equilibrium level of GDP is equal to potential GDP. At this point, there is no longer an excess demand for factors, no more pressure for factor prices to rise, firms' costs are stable, and the *AS* curve stops shifting.

Output Below Potential, $Y < Y^*$ Here is the reasoning behind our second assumption regarding factor prices. Sometimes the *AD* and *AS* curves intersect where real GDP is less than potential, as illustrated in part (i) of Figure 24-1. Because firms are producing below their normal capacity output, there is an excess supply of all factor inputs, including labour. There will be labour surpluses in some industries and among some groups of workers. Firms will have below-normal sales and not only will resist upward pressures on wages but also may seek reductions in wages.

The slump that is associated with a recessionary gap generates a set of conditions—low profits for firms and an excess supply of labour—that tends to cause wages (and other factor prices) to fall.[1]

Such a reduction in factor prices will reduce firms' unit costs. As unit costs fall, firms require a lower price in order to supply any given level of output, and the *AS* curve therefore shifts down. This shift has the effect of increasing equilibrium real GDP and reducing the price level. Real GDP moves back toward potential and the recessionary gap begins to close.

In our model, wages and other factor prices are assumed to fall as long as some recessionary gap remains. As factor prices fall, the *AS* curve shifts down, and this process continues until the equilibrium level of GDP is equal to potential output. At this point, there is no longer an excess supply of factors, no more pressure for factor prices to fall, firms' unit costs are stable, and the *AS* curve stops shifting.

Downward Wage Stickiness At this stage, we encounter an important asymmetry in the economy's aggregate supply behaviour. Boom conditions (an inflationary gap), along with labour shortages, cause wages and unit costs to rise. The experience of many developed economies, however, suggests that the downward pressures on wages during slumps (recessionary gaps) often do not operate as strongly or as quickly as the upward pressures during booms. Even when wages do fall, they tend to fall more slowly than they would rise in an equally sized inflationary gap. This *downward wage stickiness* implies that the downward shift in the *AS* curve and the downward pressure on the price level are quite weak.[2]

Both upward and downward adjustments to wages and unit costs do occur, but there are differences in the speed at which they typically operate. Booms can cause wages to rise rapidly; recessions usually cause wages to fall only slowly.

The Phillips Curve The factor-price adjustment process that we have been discussing was explored many years ago in a famous study of wages and unemployment in the United Kingdom. Using data from the late nineteenth and early twentieth centuries, when wages were more flexible than they are now, A.W. Phillips observed that wages tended to fall in periods of high unemployment and rise in periods of low unemployment. The resulting negative relationship between unemployment and the rate of change in wages has been called the *Phillips* curve ever since. *Extensions in Theory 24-1* discusses the Phillips curve and its relationship to the aggregate supply curve.

---

[1] Because of ongoing inflation and productivity growth, nominal wages rarely fall, even when there is an excess supply of labour. But remember that in this chapter, to allow us to focus on the adjustment process, we are assuming that technology is constant and expected inflation is zero. Thus nominal (and real) wages and other factor prices are assumed to fall when real GDP is below potential output, although perhaps very slowly. With some ongoing inflation in our model, the assumption would be modified so that nominal wages rise less than prices, thus implying a slow reduction in real wages.

[2] This discussion is about the stickiness of aggregate nominal wages in response to cyclical changes in the demand for labour. Another kind of wage adjustment is much quicker, however. When one region or industry experiences an increase in demand, it is usual for nominal wages to rise there, even if nominal wages do not fall in the other regions or industries. The result is that we observe frequent changes in *relative* wages across different parts of the economy. So *relative* wages may be quite flexible even though aggregate nominal wages may be sticky downward.

Inflationary and Recessionary Gaps Now it should be clear why the output gaps are named as they are. When real GDP exceeds potential GDP in our model, there will normally be rising unit costs, and the *AS* curve will be shifting upward. This will in turn push the price level up and create temporary inflation. The larger the excess of real GDP over potential GDP, the greater the inflationary pressure. The term *inflationary gap* emphasizes this salient feature of the economy when $Y > Y^*$.

When actual output is less than potential output, as we have seen, there will be unemployment of labour and other productive resources. Unit costs will tend to fall slowly, leading to a slow downward shift in the *AS* curve. Hence, the price level will be falling only slowly so that *unemployment* will be the output gap's most obvious result. The term *recessionary gap* emphasizes this salient feature that high rates of unemployment occur when $Y < Y^*$.

Potential Output as an "Anchor"

According to our theory, there is pressure on wages and other factor prices to change when output is above or below potential. These changes in factor prices lead to changes in firms' unit costs that shift the *AS* curve and change the equilibrium level of GDP. Moreover, we assumed that this process of factor-price adjustment will continue as long as some output gap remains, coming to a halt only when the equilibrium level of GDP is equal to potential GDP, Y^*. This leads to an important prediction from our macroeconomic model:

Following an aggregate demand or supply shock, the short-run equilibrium level of output may be different from potential output. Any output gap is assumed to cause wages and other factor prices to adjust, eventually bringing the equilibrium level of output back to potential. In this model, therefore, the level of potential output acts like an "anchor" for the economy.

Potential output acts like an anchor for the level of real GDP. Following aggregate demand or supply shocks that push real GDP below or above potential, the adjustment of factor prices brings real GDP back to potential output.

We now go on to examine our theory of the factor-price adjustment process in greater detail, illustrating it for the cases of positive and negative shocks to aggregate demand and supply. We will also examine this factor-price adjustment process following changes in fiscal policy. The idea that Y^* acts as an "anchor" for the economy will become clear: Shocks of various kinds may cause output to rise above or fall below Y^* in the short run, but the adjustment of factor prices to output gaps ensures that output eventually returns to Y^*.

24.2 Aggregate Demand and Supply Shocks

We can now study the consequences of aggregate demand and aggregate supply shocks in our model, distinguishing between the immediate effects of *AD* and *AS* shocks and the longer-term effects, after factor prices have adjusted fully. It is necessary to examine expansionary and contractionary shocks separately because the adjustment of factor prices is not symmetrical for the two cases. Let's begin with demand shocks.

EXTENSIONS IN THEORY 24-1

The Phillips Curve and the Adjustment Process

In the 1950s, Professor A.W. Phillips of the London School of Economics was conducting pioneering research on macroeconomic policy. In his early models, he related the rate of inflation to the difference between actual and potential output. Later he investigated the empirical underpinnings of this equation by studying the relationship between the rate of increase of nominal wages and the level of unemployment. He studied these variables because unemployment data were available as far back as the mid-nineteenth century, whereas very few data on output gaps were available when he did his empirical work. In 1958, he reported that a stable relationship had existed between these two variables for 100 years in the United Kingdom. This relationship came to be known as the **Phillips curve**, which provided an explanation, rooted in empirical observation, of the speed with which wage changes shifted the AS curve by changing firms' unit costs.

In the form in which it became famous, the Phillips curve related wage changes to the level of unemployment, as shown in part (i) of the accompanying figure. But we can express the same information in a slightly different way. Note that unemployment and output gaps are negatively related—a recessionary gap is associated with high unemployment, and an inflationary gap is associated with low unemployment. We can therefore create another Phillips curve that plots wage changes against real GDP, as shown in part (ii). Both figures show the same information.

When output equals Y^* the corresponding unemployment rate is sometimes called the natural rate of unemployment, and is denoted U^*. Inflationary gaps (when $Y > Y^*$ and $U < U^*$) are associated with increases in

wages. Recessionary gaps (when $Y < Y^*$ and $U > U^*$) are associated with *decreases* in wages.[*] Thus, a Phillips curve that plots wage changes against real GDP is upward sloping, whereas a Phillips curve that plots wage changes against the unemployment rate is downward sloping. When output is at potential, there is neither upward nor downward pressure on wages (or other factor prices) because there is neither an excess demand nor an excess supply of labour. Hence, the Phillips curve cuts the horizontal axis at Y^* (and at U^*). This is how Phillips drew his original curve.

The Phillips curve is *not* the same as the AS curve. The AS curve has the *price level* on the vertical axis whereas the Phillips curve has the *rate of change of nominal wages* on the vertical axis. How are the two curves related? The economy's location on the Phillips curve indicates how the AS curve is shifting as a result of the existing output gap.

Part (iii) of the figure shows how the AD/AS diagram relates to the Phillips curve. For example, consider an economy that begins at point A in all three diagrams; there is no output gap and wages are stable. Now, suppose a positive aggregate demand shock causes real GDP to increase to Y_1 (and unemployment to fall to U_1) and thus produces an inflationary gap. The excess demand for labour puts upward pressure on wages and the economy moves along the Phillips curve to point B, where wages begin rising. The increase in wages increases unit costs and causes the AS curve to shift up. Thus, each point on the Phillips curve determines the rate at which the AS curve is shifting. To complete the example, note that as the AS curve shifts up, the level of GDP will fall back toward Y^* and the inflationary gap will begin to close. The economy moves back

Phillips curve Originally, a relationship between the unemployment rate and the rate of change of nominal wages. Now often drawn as a relationship between GDP and the rate of change of nominal wages.

Expansionary *AD* Shocks

Suppose the economy starts with a stable price level and real GDP equal to potential GDP, as shown by the initial equilibrium in part (i) of Figure 24-2. Now suppose this situation is disturbed by an increase in autonomous expenditure, perhaps caused by an upturn in business confidence and a resulting boom in investment spending. Figure 24-2(i) shows the effects of this aggregate demand shock in raising both the price level and real GDP. The AD curve shifts from AD_0 to AD_1, the economy moves along the AS curve, and real GDP rises above Y^*. An inflationary gap opens up.

We have assumed that an inflationary gap leads to increases in factor prices, which cause firms' unit costs to rise. The AS curve begins to shift up as firms respond by increasing their output prices. As seen in part (ii) of the figure, the upward shift of the AS curve causes a further rise in the price level, but this time the price rise is associated with a *fall* in output (along the AD_1 curve).

along the Phillips curve toward point *A*. Wages continue to rise, but the rate at which they are rising slows. When all adjustment is complete, the new equilibrium will be at point *C* in part (iii) of the figure, with output equal to Y^* and the price level and nominal wages higher than initially. On the Phillips curve, the economy will be back at point *A*, where real GDP equals Y^* and wages are stable (but at a higher level than before the demand shock occurred).

Note that the convex shape of the Phillips curve is not accidental—it reflects the adjustment asymmetry we mentioned in the text. The convexity of the Phillips curve implies that an inflationary gap of a given amount will lead to faster wage increases than an equally sized recessionary gap will lead to wage reductions. In other words, an inflationary gap will cause the *AS* curve to shift up more quickly than a recessionary gap will cause the *AS* curve to shift down.

Finally, you might be wondering what would happen if the Phillips curve were to shift. And what would cause such a shift? As we will see in Chapter 30 when we discuss the phenomenon of sustained inflation, an important cause of shifts of the Phillips curve is changes in firms' and households' *expectations* of future inflation. In this chapter, however, we have assumed expected inflation to be zero. Whether there is expected inflation or not, the Phillips curve embodies the factor-price adjustment process that is the focus of this chapter.

---

[*] Recall that we are assuming productivity to be constant so that changes in wages imply changes in unit labour costs. When productivity is growing, however, recessionary output gaps cause unit labour costs to fall. This requires only that wages are growing more slowly than productivity, not actually falling.

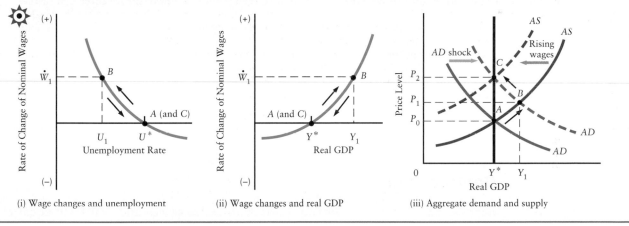

(i) Wage changes and unemployment

(ii) Wage changes and real GDP

(iii) Aggregate demand and supply

The increases in unit costs (and the consequent upward shifts of the *AS* curve) continue until the inflationary gap has been removed—that is, until in part (ii) real GDP returns to Y^*. Only then is there no excess demand for labour and other factors, and only then do factor prices and unit costs, and hence the *AS* curve, stabilize.

The adjustment in wages and other factor prices eventually eliminates any boom caused by a demand shock; real GDP returns to its potential level.

It is worth remembering here that a key assumption in our macro model is that the level of potential output, Y^*, is unaffected by the *AD* and *AS* shocks we are examining. This key assumption lies behind the strong result in our model that the adjustment process, once complete, fully reverses any shock's short-run effects on real GDP.

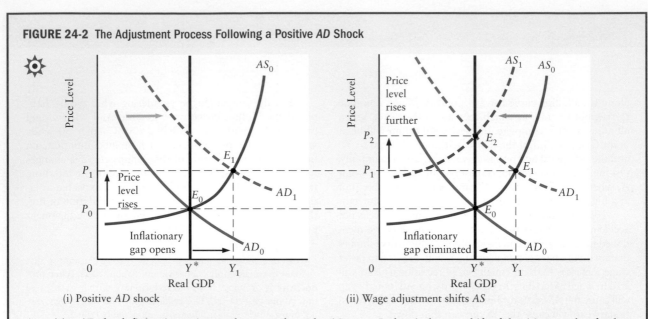

FIGURE 24-2 The Adjustment Process Following a Positive *AD* Shock

(i) Positive *AD* shock

(ii) Wage adjustment shifts *AS*

A positive *AD* shock first raises prices and output along the *AS* curve. It then induces a shift of the *AS* curve that further raises prices but lowers output along the new *AD* curve. In part (i), the economy is in equilibrium at E_0, at its level of potential output, Y^*, and price level P_0. The *AD* curve then shifts from AD_0 to AD_1. This moves equilibrium to E_1, with income Y_1 and price level P_1, and opens up an inflationary gap.

In part (ii), the inflationary gap results in an increase in wages and other factor prices, which drives up firms' unit costs and shifts the *AS* curve upward. As this happens, output falls and the price level rises along AD_1. Eventually, when the *AS* curve has shifted to AS_1, output is back to Y^* and the inflationary gap has been eliminated. However, the price level has risen to P_2. The eventual effect of the *AD* shock, after all adjustment has occurred, is to raise the price level but leave real GDP unchanged.

Contractionary *AD* Shocks

Suppose again that the economy starts with stable prices and real GDP equal to potential, as shown in part (i) of Figure 24-3. Now assume there is a *decline* in aggregate demand. This negative *AD* shock might be a reduction in investment expenditure, or perhaps a decline in the world demand for Canadian forest products or automobiles.

The first effects of the decline are a fall in output and some downward adjustment of prices, as shown in part (i) of the figure. As real GDP falls below potential, a recessionary gap is created, and unemployment rises. At this point we must analyze two separate cases. The first occurs when wages and other factor prices fall quickly in response to the excess supply of factors. The second occurs when factor prices fall only slowly.

Flexible Wages Suppose wages (and other factor prices) fell quickly in response to the recessionary gap. The *AS* curve would therefore shift quickly downward as the lower wages led to reduced unit costs.

As shown in part (ii) of Figure 24-3, the economy would move along the new *AD* curve, with falling prices and rising output, until real GDP was quickly restored to potential, Y^*. We conclude that if wages were to fall rapidly whenever there was unemployment, the resulting shift in the *AS* curve would quickly eliminate recessionary gaps.

FIGURE 24-3 The Adjustment Process Following a Negative *AD* Shock

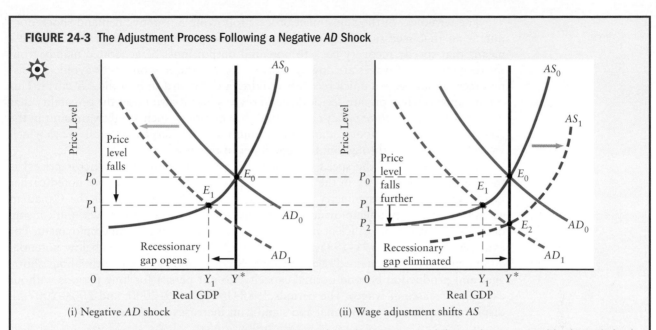

(i) Negative *AD* shock   (ii) Wage adjustment shifts *AS*

A negative *AD* shock first lowers the price level and GDP along the *AS* curve and then induces a (possibly slow) shift of the *AS* curve that further lowers prices but raises output along the new *AD* curve. In part (i), the economy is in equilibrium at E_0, at its level of potential output, Y^*, and price level P_0. The *AD* curve then shifts to AD_1, moving equilibrium to E_1, with income Y_1 and price level P_1, and opens up a recessionary gap.

Part (ii) shows the adjustment back to potential output that occurs from the supply side of the economy. The fall in wages and other factor prices shifts the *AS* curve downward. Real GDP rises, and the price level falls further along the new *AD* curve. Unless factor prices are completely rigid, the *AS* curve eventually reaches AS_1, with equilibrium at E_2. The eventual effect of the negative *AD* shock, after all adjustment has occurred, is to reduce the price level but leave real GDP unchanged.

Flexible wages that fall rapidly in the presence of a recessionary gap provide an automatic adjustment process that pushes the economy back quickly toward potential output.

Sticky Wages As we noted earlier, the experience of most economies suggests that wages typically do not fall rapidly in response to even large recessionary gaps. It is sometimes said that wages are "sticky" in the downward direction. This does not mean that wages never fall, only that they tend to fall much more slowly in a recessionary gap than they rise in an equally sized inflationary gap. When wages are sticky, the analysis is the same as when wages are flexible, and thus Figure 24-3 tells the correct story. The significant difference, however, is that the *AS* curve shifts more slowly when wages are sticky and thus the adjustment process may not close the recessionary gap for a long time.

If wages are downwardly sticky, the economy's adjustment process is sluggish and thus will not quickly eliminate a recessionary gap.[3]

---

[3] The causes of downward wage stickiness have been hotly debated among macroeconomists for years. We discuss several possible reasons in Chapter 31 when examining the causes of cyclical unemployment.

The weakness of the adjustment process following a negative demand shock does not mean that recessionary gaps must always be prolonged. Rather, this weakness means that speedy recovery back to potential output must be generated mainly from the demand side. If wages are downwardly sticky and the economy is to avoid a persistent recessionary gap, a quick recovery requires a rightward shift of the *AD* curve. This often happens when private-sector demand revives. But it also raises the possibility that government *stabilization policy* can be used to accomplish such a rightward shift in the *AD* curve. This is an important and contentious issue in macroeconomics, one to which we will return often throughout the remainder of this book.

The difference in the speed of adjustment of wages (and other factor prices) is the important asymmetry in the behaviour of aggregate supply that we noted earlier in this chapter. This asymmetry helps to explain two key facts about the Canadian economy. First, high unemployment can persist for quite long periods without causing decreases in wages of sufficient magnitude to quickly remove the unemployment. For example, during the 1991–1995 and 2009–2012 periods, output was below potential and unemployment remained relatively high. Second, booms, along with labour shortages and production beyond normal capacity, do not persist for long periods without causing increases in wages. The periods 1988–1990, 1999–2000, and 2004–2007 all displayed output above potential and significant increases in wages.

Aggregate Supply Shocks

We have discussed the economy's adjustment process that returns real GDP to Y^* following an aggregate demand shock. The same adjustment process operates following an aggregate supply shock.

Consider an economy that has a stable price level and real GDP at its potential level, as illustrated by point E_0 in part (i) of Figure 24-4. Suppose there is an increase in the world price of an important input, such as oil. An increase in the price of oil increases unit costs for firms and causes the *AS* curve to shift upward. Real GDP falls and the price level increases—a combination often called *stagflation*. The short-run equilibrium is at point E_1. With the opening of a recessionary gap, the economy's adjustment process comes into play, though sticky wages reduce the speed of this adjustment.

In our macro model, the recessionary gap caused by the negative supply shock causes some firms to shut down and some workers to be laid off. The excess supply of labour (and other factors) eventually pushes wages down and begins to reverse the initial increase in unit costs caused by the increase in the price of oil. This adjustment is shown in part (ii) of the figure. As wages fall, the *AS* curve shifts back toward its starting point, and real GDP rises back toward its potential level, Y^*. Since our model assumes that Y^* is constant, the reductions in factor prices eventually bring the economy back to its initial point, E_0. Note, however, that *relative* prices will have changed when the economy returns to E_0. The price level is back to P_0, its starting point, but real wages are lower while the relative price of oil is higher.

We leave it to the reader to analyze the adjustment process following a positive aggregate supply shock. The logic of the analysis is exactly the same as illustrated in Figure 24-4, except that the initial shift in the *AS* curve is to the right, creating an inflationary gap.

> Exogenous changes in input prices cause the *AS* curve to shift, creating an output gap. The adjustment process then reverses the initial *AS* shift and brings the economy back to potential output and the initial price level.

FIGURE 24-4 The Adjustment Process Following a Negative *AS* Shock

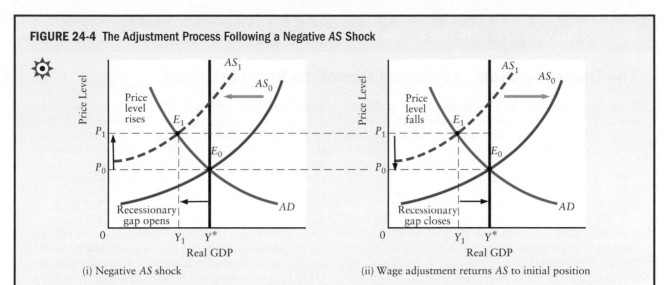

(i) Negative *AS* shock   (ii) Wage adjustment returns *AS* to initial position

A negative *AS* shock caused by an increase in input prices causes real GDP to fall and the price level to rise. The economy's adjustment process then reverses the *AS* shift and returns the economy to its starting point. The economy begins at point E_0 in part (i). The increase in the price of oil increases firms' unit costs and causes the *AS* curve to shift up to AS_1. Real GDP falls to Y_1 and the price level rises to P_1. A recessionary gap is created. In part (ii), the excess supply of factors associated with the recessionary gap causes wages and other factor prices to fall, possibly slowly. As factor prices fall, unit costs fall and so the *AS* curve shifts back down to AS_0. The eventual effect of the *AS* shock, after all adjustment has occurred, is to leave the price level and real GDP unchanged.

In this chapter we have emphasized the adjustment of factor prices to output gaps, and how this adjustment process returns real GDP to Y^* following *AD* or *AS* shocks. However, there are *additional* forces in the economy that also help to explain how real GDP changes over the business cycle; these additional forces also explain how recessionary gaps may be closed faster than if the only force at play was the (slow) reduction of factor prices. *Extensions in Theory 24-2* examines the dynamics of the business cycle in more detail.

Long-Run Equilibrium

Following any *AD* or *AS* shocks, we have assumed that the adjustment of factor prices continues until real GDP returns to Y^*. The economy is said to be in a *long-run equilibrium* when this adjustment process is complete, and there is no longer an output gap. In other words, the economy is in its long-run equilibrium when the intersection of the *AD* and *AS* curves occurs at Y^*.

We also assume in our macro model that the value of Y^* depends only on real variables, such as the labour force, capital stock, and the level of technology. We assume, in particular, that Y^* is independent of nominal variables, such as the price level. The level of output that firms will produce in the long run is thus independent of the price level. The vertical line at Y^* that we have seen in our diagrams is sometimes called a *long-run aggregate supply curve*—the relationship between the price level and the amount of output supplied by firms *after all factor prices have adjusted to output gaps*.

EXTENSIONS IN THEORY 24-2

The Business Cycle: Additional Pressures for Adjustment

In Chapter 19 we described the *business cycle* as the ebb and flow of economic activity that alternately tends to create recessionary and inflationary output gaps. In this chapter, we have seen that the factor-price adjustment process tends to eliminate such output gaps whenever they appear. The business cycle itself provides an *additional* set of pressures that reinforces the adjustment of factor prices and helps to return real GDP to Y^*.

During the expansionary phase of the business cycle, real GDP is growing; as the peak of the cycle is reached, real GDP is typically well above Y^* and unemployment is low. Expectations of rising sales and profits created during the economic expansion often lead to gains in stock-market prices that are not justified by current earnings; in addition, firms may undertake capital investments based on the assumption that the economic expansion will continue. As real GDP rises further above Y^*, however, bottlenecks and shortages eventually arise and restrict further expansion, thus slowing the growth rate of real GDP. When growth slows in this way, there is often a drastic revision in firms' expectations. A sell-off of stocks may cause their prices to tumble, thereby reducing consumers' wealth and confidence and hence causing them to curtail their consumption expenditures. The slowdown in growth, combined with the collapse of confidence, can lead firms to reduce their desired investment. These reductions in household consumption and business investment work, through the economy's multiplier process, to reduce real GDP. Thus, even in the absence of wage increases, an economic expansion usually contains the seeds of its own demise; real GDP tends to move back toward Y^*.

Once underway, the economic downturn tends to feed on itself as confidence wanes even further, leading to more cuts in investment and consumer spending. The downturn often overshoots Y^*, creating a recessionary gap. A trough is eventually reached, in which real GDP is well below Y^* and unemployment is high. At this point, the pace of economic activity begins to rise. Stocks of durable consumer goods, such as automobiles and home appliances, that were not replaced during the downturn eventually become depleted or obsolete enough that normal replacement expenditures recover, leading to an increase in the demand for such goods. Similarly, much of firms' replacement investment that has been put off during the economic downturn can be postponed no longer and investment expenditure recovers. The resulting recovery in both household and business spending can cause a revival of favourable expectations concerning the future, leading to further increases in spending. The increases in household consumption and business investment work, through the economy's multiplier process, to increase real GDP. Thus, even in the absence of falling wages, an economic downturn is usually followed by a recovery with real GDP rising back toward Y^*.

In summary, we should note two distinct forces that tend to return real GDP to Y^*. During an inflationary gap, both rising wages (which shift the *AS* curve to the left) and the intrinsic dynamics of the business cycle (which shift the *AD* curve to the left) are powerful forces. During a recessionary gap, however, wages are quite slow to adjust in the downward direction and so the business cycle dynamics typically play a much larger role than the wage-adjustment process in bringing real GDP back to Y^*. In this chapter, we have concentrated on understanding how the wage-adjustment process works. It must be remembered, however, that its strength is asymmetric, strong in removing an inflationary gap but much weaker in removing a recessionary one.

This vertical line is also sometimes called a *Classical aggregate supply curve* because the Classical economists were mainly concerned with the behaviour of the economy in long-run equilibrium.[4]

---

[4] The Classical school of economic thought began with Adam Smith (1723–1790) and was developed through the work of David Ricardo (1772–1823), Thomas Malthus (1766–1834), and John Stuart Mill (1806–1873). These economists emphasized the long-run behaviour of the economy. Beginning in the middle of the nineteenth century, Neoclassical economists devoted much time and effort to studying short-term fluctuations. *The General Theory of Employment, Interest and Money* (1936), written by John Maynard Keynes (1883–1946), was in a long tradition of the study of short-term fluctuations. Where Keynes differed from the Neoclassical economists was in approaching the issues from a macroeconomic perspective that emphasized fluctuations in aggregate expenditure. Each of the economists mentioned in this footnote, along with several others, is discussed in more detail in the timeline at the back of the book.

Figure 24-5 shows an *AD/AS* diagram without the usual upward-sloping *AS* curve. It is useful to omit this curve if our focus is on the state of the economy *after* all factor prices have fully adjusted and output has returned to Y^*. We can use this diagram to examine how shocks affect the economy's long-run equilibrium.

As shown in part (i) of Figure 24-5, any shift in the *AD* curve will cause a change in the price level in the long run but will not affect the level of potential output, Y^*. In our model, the only way that real GDP can change in the long run (*after* factor prices have fully adjusted) is for the level of Y^* to change, as in part (ii) of the figure.

> In the long run, real GDP is determined solely by Y^*; the role of aggregate demand is only to determine the price level.

This strong result—that changes in aggregate demand have no long-run effect on real GDP—follows from the assumption in our macro model that Y^* is independent of the price level and thus unaffected by *AD* shocks.[5]

We will discuss the long-run behaviour of the economy in detail in Chapters 25 and 26. There we develop theories explaining why Y^* grows over extended periods of time and why this growth is important for determining the ongoing increases in our material living standards.

24.3 Fiscal Stabilization Policy

In Chapter 22, we briefly examined fiscal policy in our macro model in which output was demand determined and the price level was assumed to be constant. Now that our model is more complete—and also more realistic—we can examine fiscal policy in more detail. We now consider taxation and government spending as tools of fiscal stabilization policy; in Chapter 32, we return to more advanced aspects of fiscal policy.

Fiscal stabilization policy is fundamentally a short-run policy. In response to various shocks that cause changes in real GDP, the government may use various fiscal tools in an attempt to push real GDP back towards potential output. The alternatives to using fiscal stabilization policy are to wait for the recovery of private-sector demand (a shift in the *AD* curve) or to wait for the economy's adjustment process (a shift in the *AS* curve)

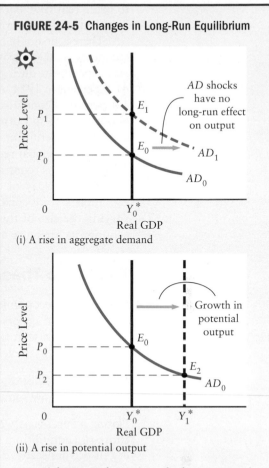

FIGURE 24-5 Changes in Long-Run Equilibrium

(i) A rise in aggregate demand

(ii) A rise in potential output

Potential output determines the long-run equilibrium value of real GDP. Given Y^*, aggregate demand determines the long-run equilibrium value of the price level. In both parts of the figure, the initial long-run equilibrium is at E_0, so the price level is P_0 and real GDP is Y_0^*.

In part (i), a shift in the *AD* curve from AD_0 to AD_1 moves the long-run equilibrium from E_0 to E_1. This raises the price level from P_0 to P_1 but leaves real GDP unchanged at Y_0^* in the long run.

In part (ii), an increase in potential output from Y_0^* to Y_1^* moves the long-run equilibrium from E_0 to E_2. This raises real GDP from Y_0^* to Y_1^* and lowers the price level from P_0 to P_2.

For information on the federal Department of Finance, the ministry in charge of fiscal policy, see www.fin.gc.ca.

---

[5] Whether short-run fluctuations in real GDP have an effect on the value of Y^* is an important area of research in macroeconomics. In Chapters 28 and 31 we discuss reasons why some short-run changes in real GDP may cause Y^* to change in the same direction.

to bring real GDP back to potential. The slower these processes are, the stronger is the justification for government to use its fiscal tools.

There is no doubt that the government can exert a major influence on real GDP. Prime examples are the massive increases in military spending during major wars. Canadian federal expenditure during the Second World War rose from 12.2 percent of GDP in 1939 to 41.8 percent in 1944. At the same time, the unemployment rate fell from 11.4 percent to 1.4 percent. Economists agree that the increase in government spending helped to bring about the rise in output and the associated fall in unemployment. More recently, the Canadian government dramatically increased spending in an effort to dampen the effects of the major global recession that began in late 2008. Most economists agree that this "fiscal stimulus" contributed significantly to real GDP growth in the 2009–2011 period.

In the heyday of "activist" fiscal policy, from about 1945 to about 1970, many economists were convinced that the economy could be stabilized adequately just by varying the size of the government's taxes and expenditures. That day is past. Today, economists are more aware of the many limitations of fiscal stabilization policy.

The Basic Theory of Fiscal Stabilization

In our macroeconomic model, a reduction in tax rates or an increase in government purchases or transfers will shift the AD curve to the right, causing an increase in real GDP. An increase in tax rates or a cut in government purchases or transfers will shift the AD curve to the left, causing a decrease in real GDP.

How Fiscal Stabilization Works A more detailed look at how fiscal stabilization works will help to show some of the complications that arise when implementing fiscal policy.

Closing a Recessionary Gap. A recessionary gap is shown in Figure 24-6; the economy's short-run equilibrium is at point E_0 with real GDP below Y^*. In the absence of a recovery in private-sector demand, such a recessionary gap can be closed in two ways. The first involves the economy's adjustment process. The excess supply of factors at E_0 will eventually cause wages and other factor prices to fall, shifting the AS curve downward and restoring output to Y^*, as shown in part (i) of the figure. However, because of the downward stickiness of wages, this process may take a long time. Policymakers may not be prepared to wait the time necessary for the recessionary gap to correct itself. The second way to close the recessionary gap involves an active policy choice. The government can use expansionary fiscal policy to shift the AD curve to the right. It would do this by reducing tax rates, increasing transfers, or increasing the level of government purchases.

The advantage of using fiscal policy rather than allowing the economy to recover naturally is that it may substantially shorten what might otherwise be a long recession. One disadvantage is that the use of fiscal policy may stimulate the economy just before private-sector spending recovers on its own. As a result, the economy may overshoot its potential output, and an inflationary gap may open up. In this case, fiscal policy that is intended to promote economic stability can actually cause instability.

Closing an Inflationary Gap. An inflationary gap is illustrated in Figure 24-7; the economy's short-run equilibrium is at point E_0, with real GDP above Y^*. In the absence of a downward adjustment of private-sector demand, there are two ways such an inflationary gap may be closed. The first involves the economy's adjustment process. Excess demand for factors will cause wages and other factor prices to rise, shifting the AS curve upward and gradually restoring output to Y^*. Alternatively, the government

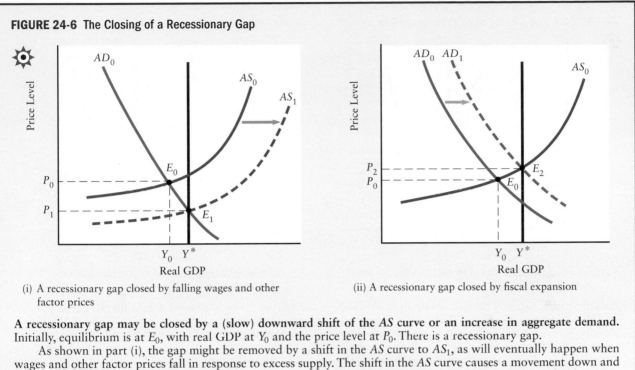

FIGURE 24-6 The Closing of a Recessionary Gap

(i) A recessionary gap closed by falling wages and other factor prices

(ii) A recessionary gap closed by fiscal expansion

A recessionary gap may be closed by a (slow) downward shift of the AS curve or an increase in aggregate demand. Initially, equilibrium is at E_0, with real GDP at Y_0 and the price level at P_0. There is a recessionary gap.

As shown in part (i), the gap might be removed by a shift in the AS curve to AS_1, as will eventually happen when wages and other factor prices fall in response to excess supply. The shift in the AS curve causes a movement down and to the right along AD_0 to a new equilibrium at E_1, achieving potential output Y^* and lowering the price level to P_1.

As shown in part (ii), the gap might also be removed by a shift of the AD curve to AD_1, caused by an expansionary fiscal policy (or a recovery of private-sector demand). The shift in the AD curve causes a movement up and to the right along AS_0. This movement shifts the equilibrium to E_2, raising output to Y^* and the price level to P_2.

can use a contractionary fiscal policy to shift the AD curve to the left and close the inflationary gap. The government would do this by increasing tax rates, reducing transfers, or reducing its level of purchases.

The advantage of using a contractionary fiscal policy to close the inflationary gap is that it avoids the inflation that would otherwise occur. One disadvantage is that if private-sector expenditures fall for some unrelated reason, the fiscal contraction may end up being too large and real GDP may be pushed below potential, thus opening up a recessionary gap.

This discussion leads to a key proposition:

When the economy's adjustment process is slow to operate, or produces undesirable side effects such as rising prices, there is a potential stabilization role for fiscal policy.

Fiscal Policy and the Paradox of Thrift Suppose you have a good job but you are sufficiently unsure about your economic future that you decide to increase the fraction of disposable income that you save. Your increased saving today would not influence your current income but these funds would accumulate and be useful in the future if your economic situation changed for the worse. Most people would agree that a decision to increase your saving in these circumstances would be prudent.

FIGURE 24-7 The Closing of an Inflationary Gap

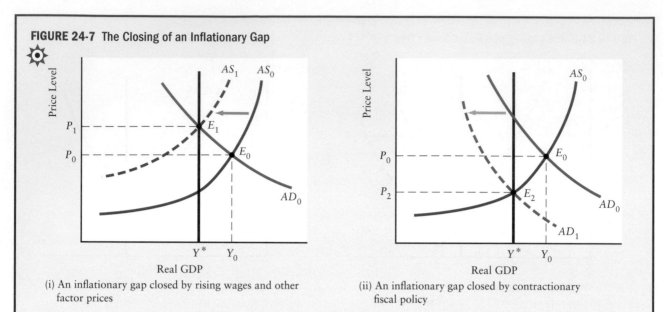

(i) An inflationary gap closed by rising wages and other factor prices

(ii) An inflationary gap closed by contractionary fiscal policy

An inflationary gap may be removed by an upward shift of the *AS* curve or by a leftward shift of the *AD* curve. Initially, equilibrium is at E_0, with real GDP at Y_0 and the price level at P_0. There is an inflationary gap.

As shown in part (i), the gap might be removed by a shift in the *AS* curve to AS_1, as will happen when wages and other factor prices rise in response to the excess demand. The shift in the *AS* curve causes a movement up and to the left along AD_0. This movement establishes a new equilibrium at E_1, reducing output to its potential level Y^* and raising the price level to P_1.

As shown in part (ii), the gap might also be removed by a shift in the *AD* curve to AD_1 caused by a contractionary fiscal policy (or by a reduction of private-sector demand). The shift in the *AD* curve causes a movement down and to the left along AS_0. This movement shifts the equilibrium to E_2, lowering income to Y^* and the price level to P_2.

But what would happen if *many people* did the same thing at the same time? In our macroeconomic model, an increase in the country's total desired saving would shift the *AD* curve to the left and *reduce* the equilibrium level of real GDP in the short run. Thus, frugality on the part of individuals, which may seem to be prudent behaviour for each individual taken separately, ends up reducing short-run real GDP. This phenomenon is known as the *paradox of thrift*—the paradox being that what may be good for any individual when viewed in isolation ends up being undesirable for the economy as a whole.

The policy implication of this phenomenon is that a major and persistent recession can be battled by encouraging governments, firms, and households to reduce their saving and therefore increase their spending. In times of unemployment and recession, a greater desire to save will only make things worse. This result goes directly against the idea that we should "tighten our belts" when times are tough. The notion that it is not only possible but even *desirable* to spend one's way out of a recession touches a sensitive point with people raised on the belief that success is based on hard work and frugality; as a result, the idea often arouses great hostility.

As is discussed in *Lessons from History 24-1*, the implications of the paradox of thrift were not generally understood during the Great Depression of the 1930s. Most governments, faced with depression-induced reductions in tax revenues, reduced their expenditures to balance their budgets. As a result, many economists argue that the fiscal policies at the time actually made things worse. When Nobel Prize–winning economist Milton Friedman (many years later) said, "We are all Keynesians now," he was referring to the general acceptance of the view that the government's budget is much more than just the revenue and expenditure statement of a very large organization. Whether we like it or not, the sheer size of the government's budget inevitably makes it a powerful tool for influencing the overall level of economic activity.

Knowledge of the fiscal policy mistakes during the Great Depression led most governments to avoid those same mistakes during the global financial crisis of 2008 and the recession that followed. In a decision that was coordinated across governments of the G20 countries, the Canadian government embarked on a program of fiscal stimulus in the 2009–2010 and 2010–2011 fiscal years. Over these two years, spending increased by approximately $40 billion, most of which was directed at public infrastructure projects. The provincial governments acted similarly, and the fiscal stimulus for all governments combined was about $52 billion, an average of 1.7 percent of GDP in each of the two years.

Short Run Versus Long Run The paradox of thrift applies to shifts in aggregate demand that have been caused by changes in saving (and hence spending) behaviour. That is why it applies only in the short run, when the *AD* curve plays an important role in the determination of real GDP.

The paradox of thrift does not apply after factor prices have fully adjusted and the economy has achieved its new long-run equilibrium with real GDP equal to Y^*. Remember from Figure 24-5 that in the long run, aggregate demand does not influence the level of real GDP—output is determined only by the level of potential output, Y^*. In the long run, the more people and government save, the larger is the supply of financial capital available for investment. As we will see in Chapter 26, this increase in the pool of financial capital will reduce interest rates and encourage more investment by firms. The greater rate of investment leads to a higher rate of growth of potential output.

> The paradox of thrift—the idea that an increase in saving reduces the level of real GDP—is true only in the short run. In the long run, the path of real GDP is determined by the path of potential output. The increase in saving has the long-run effect of increasing investment and therefore increasing potential output.

Automatic Fiscal Stabilizers

The fiscal policies that we have been discussing are referred to as *discretionary* because the government uses its discretion in changing its taxation or its spending in an attempt to change the level of real GDP. However, even if the government makes no active decisions regarding changes in spending or taxation, the mere existence of the government's tax-and-transfer system will act as an *automatic stabilizer* for the economy. Let's see how this works.

Consider a shock that shifts the *AD* curve to the right and thus increases the short-run level of real GDP. As real GDP increases, government tax revenues also increase. In addition, since there are fewer low-income households and unemployed persons requiring assistance, governments make fewer transfer payments to individuals. The rise in net tax revenues (taxes minus transfers) dampens the overall increase in real GDP caused by the initial shock. In other words, the tax-and-transfer system reduces the value of the multiplier and thus acts as an **automatic stabilizer** for the economy.

automatic stabilizers Elements of the tax-and-transfer system that reduce the responsiveness of real GDP to changes in autonomous expenditure.

Fiscal Policy in the Great Depression

The Great Depression, which is usually dated as beginning with the massive stock-market crash on October 29, 1929, was one of the most dramatic economic events of the twentieth century. As the accompanying figure shows, Canadian real GDP plummeted by almost 30 percent from its peak in 1929 to its low point in 1933. The price level fell beginning in 1930 and declined by about 20 percent over the next five years. The unemployment rate increased from 3 percent of the labour force in 1929 to an unparalleled 19.3 percent four years later. To put these numbers in perspective, by today's standards a very serious recession (like the most recent one in 2008 and 2009) sees real GDP fall by 2 to 3 percent, the unemployment rate rise to 8 to 10 percent, and prices continue rising but perhaps at a slower rate. The economic events of the 1930s certainly deserve to be called the Great Depression!

The Great Depression was not just a catastrophic event that happened exogenously—its depth and duration were made worse by some fundamental mistakes in policy. Failure to understand the implication of the paradox of thrift led many countries to adopt disastrous fiscal policies during the Great Depression. In addition, failure to understand the role of automatic stabilizers has led many observers to conclude, erroneously, that fiscal expansion was tried in the Great Depression but failed. Let us see how these two misperceptions are related.

The Paradox of Thrift in Action

In 1932, Canadian prime minister R.B. Bennett said, "We are now faced with the real crisis in the history of Canada. To maintain our credit we must practise the most rigid economy and not spend a single cent." His government that year—at the deepest point in the recession—brought down a budget based on the principle of trying to balance revenues and expenditures, and it included *increases* in tax rates.

In the same year, Franklin Roosevelt was elected U.S. president on a platform of fighting the Great Depression with government policies. In his inaugural address he urged, "Our great primary task is to put people to work. . . . [This task] can be helped by insistence that the federal, state, and local governments act forthwith on the demand that their costs be drastically reduced. . . ."

Across the Atlantic, King George V told the British House of Commons in 1931, "The present condition of the national finances, in the opinion of His Majesty's ministers, calls for the imposition of additional taxation and for the effecting of economies in public expenditure."

As the paradox of thrift predicts, these policies tended to worsen, rather than cure, the Great Depression.

Interpreting the Deficits in the 1930s

In general, governments can have a budget deficit for two different reasons. First, a government might increase its level of purchases without increasing its tax revenues. Such a *deficit-financed* increase in government spending represents an expansion in aggregate demand. Second, a government might leave its purchases unchanged but have lower tax revenues. If the lower tax revenues are caused by a policy decision to reduce *tax rates*, then this policy also represents an expansion in aggregate demand. But if the decline in tax revenues is caused by a fall in real GDP

As we saw in Chapter 22, in the absence of the tax-and-transfer system, the multiplier would be larger and thus any given positive shock would lead to a larger shift in the *AD* curve and thus to a larger increase in real GDP.

The same is true in the presence of a negative *AD* shock. As real GDP declines in response to the shock, the reduction in government net tax revenues dampens the overall decline in real GDP.

> Even in the absence of discretionary fiscal stabilization policy, the government's tax-and-transfer system provides the economy with an automatic stabilizer.

At the end of Chapter 22 we argued that realistic Canadian values for our model's key parameters are as follows:

- marginal propensity to consume (*MPC*) = 0.8
- net tax rate (*t*) = 0.25
- marginal propensity to import (*m*) = 0.35

with unchanged tax rates, the existing budget deficit *does not* represent an expansion in aggregate demand. These distinctions are central to interpreting the budget deficits of the 1930s.

Government budget deficits did increase in the 1930s, but they were not the result of an increase in government expenditures or reductions in tax rates. Rather, they were the result of the fall in tax revenues, brought about by the fall in real GDP as the economy sank into depression. The various governments did not advocate programs of massive deficit-financed spending to shift the *AD* curve to the right. Instead, they hoped that a small amount of government spending in addition to numerous policies designed to stabilize prices and to restore confidence would lead to a recovery of private investment expenditure that would substantially shift the *AD* curve. To have expected a massive revival of private investment expenditure as a result of the puny increase in aggregate demand that was instituted by the federal government now seems hopelessly naïve.

When we judge these policies from the viewpoint of modern macro theory, their failure is no mystery. Indeed, Professor E. Cary Brown of MIT, after a careful study for the United States, concluded, "Fiscal policy seems to have been an unsuccessful recovery device in the thirties—not because it did not work, but because it was not tried." Once the massive, war-geared expenditure of the 1940s began, output responded sharply and unemployment all but evaporated. A similar pattern occurred in Canada, as seen clearly in the figure.

The performance of the Canadian and U.S. economies from 1930 to 1945 is well explained by the macroeconomic theory that we have developed in the last few chapters. The governments did not effectively use fiscal policy to stabilize their economies. War brought the Depression to an end because war demands made acceptable a level of government expenditure sufficient to remove the recessionary gap. Had the Canadian and American administrations been able to do the same in the early 1930s, it might have ended the waste of the Great Depression many years sooner.

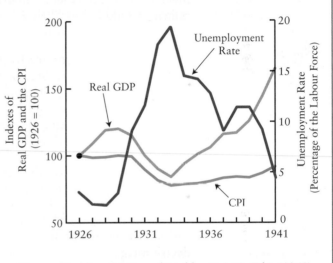

(*Source:* Urquhart, M.C., and Buckley, K.A.H. (Ed.). (1965). *Historical Statistics of Canada.* Toronto: Macmillan.)

The implied value of *z*, the marginal propensity to spend on national income, is therefore

$$z = MPC(1 - t) - m$$
$$= (0.8)(0.75) - 0.35 = 0.25$$

As a result, a realistic value for the simple multiplier in Canada is

$$\text{Simple multiplier} = 1/(1 - z) = 1/0.75 = 1.33$$

The lower is the net tax rate, the larger is the simple multiplier and thus the less stable is real GDP in response to shocks to autonomous spending. For example, if the net tax rate were reduced to 20 percent ($t = 0.20$), the value of *z* would rise to 0.29 and the simple multiplier would rise to $1/(1 - 0.29) = 1/0.71 = 1.41$. The larger multiplier implies that a shock to autonomous expenditure would result in a larger shift in the *AD* curve and thus a larger total change in GDP—that is, the economy would be less stable. Therefore, whatever benefits might arise from a reduction in the net tax rate (and we will see later that lower rates on some specific taxes may tend to increase the economy's long-run growth rate), one drawback is that the tax reduction would lead to the economy being less stable following shocks to autonomous expenditure.[6]

The great advantage of automatic fiscal stabilizers is that they are "automatic." As long as the tax-and-transfer system is in place (and there is no sign of its imminent disappearance!), some stability is provided without anyone having to make active decisions about fiscal policy. As we see next, the sorts of decisions required for successful *discretionary* fiscal policy are not simple, and some attempts to provide stability through discretionary fiscal policy may actually reduce the stability of the economy.

Practical Limitations of Discretionary Fiscal Policy

According to our earlier discussion of fiscal stabilization policy, returning the economy to potential output would appear to be a simple matter of changing taxes and government spending, in some combination. Why do so many economists believe that such policies would be "as likely to harm as help"? Part of the answer is that the practical use of discretionary fiscal policy is anything but simple.

Decision and Execution Lags To change fiscal policy requires making changes in taxes and government expenditures. The changes must be agreed on by the Cabinet and passed by Parliament. The political stakes in such changes are generally very large; taxes and spending are called "bread-and-butter issues" precisely because they affect the economic well-being of almost everyone. Even if economists agreed that the economy would be helped by, say, a tax cut, politicians would likely spend a good deal of time debating *whose* taxes should be cut and by *how much*. If the assessment by economists was that an increase in government spending was desirable, the lengthy political debate would then be about what *type* of spending should increase and whether it should focus on particular industries or regions. The delay between the initial recognition of a recessionary or inflationary gap and the enactment of legislation to change fiscal policy, which may be several months long, is called a **decision lag**.

decision lag The period of time between perceiving some problem and reaching a decision on what to do about it.

Once policy changes are agreed on, there is still an **execution lag**, adding time between the enactment of the legislation and the implementation of the policy action. Furthermore, once the new policies are in place, it will usually take still more time for their economic consequences to be felt. Because of these lags, it is quite possible that by the time a given policy decision has any impact on the economy, circumstances will have changed such that the policy is no longer appropriate.

execution lag The time that it takes to put policies in place after a decision has been made.

The decision lag applies more or less equally to both tax and expenditure policies. The execution lag, however, tends to be considerably longer for expenditure than tax policies. Once Parliament agrees to specific tax changes, the effects can be realized quite soon by individual or corporate taxpayers. For an increase in expenditure, however, new programs may need to be created or infrastructure projects planned and designed before the bulk of the new spending can occur. Even for planned reductions in expenditure, it often takes time to scale down or cancel existing spending programs and to identify the public servants who will be laid off.

---

[6] We have said that automatic stabilizers reduce the multiplier so that a given change in autonomous expenditures leads to a smaller horizontal shift in the *AD* curve than would otherwise be the case. It is also true that the same automatic stabilizers lead to a *steeper AD* curve; the result is that real GDP is more stable in the presence of *AS* shocks.

Temporary Versus Permanent Tax Changes Changes in taxation that are known to be temporary are generally less effective than measures that are expected to be permanent. For example, if households know that an announced tax cut will last only a year, they may recognize that the effect on their long-run consumption possibilities is small and may choose to save rather than spend their increase in disposable income. If so, the effect of the tax cut on aggregate demand will be nil.

In other cases, however, temporary changes in taxes may be quite effective at changing aggregate demand. If the government temporarily increases employment-insurance (EI) benefits to the long-term unemployed, for example, it is quite likely that they will spend a large fraction of the increased benefits and that aggregate demand will increase as a result.

For most tax changes, the following general principle is a useful guide for policy: The more closely household consumption expenditure is related to *lifetime* income rather than to *current* income, the smaller will be the effects on current consumption of tax changes that are known to be of short duration. Or, to use the language that we used when introducing the consumption function in Chapter 21, the more forward-looking households are, the smaller will be the effects of what are perceived to be temporary changes in taxes.

The Role of Discretionary Fiscal Policy Attempts to use discretionary fiscal policy to "fine tune" the economy are thus fraught with difficulties. **Fine tuning** refers to the use of fiscal (and monetary) policy to offset virtually all fluctuations in private-sector spending so as to keep real GDP at or near its potential level. However, neither economics nor political science has yet advanced far enough to allow policymakers to undo the consequences of every aggregate demand or supply shock. Nevertheless, many economists still argue that when a recessionary gap is large enough and persists for long enough, *gross tuning* may be appropriate. **Gross tuning** refers to the use of fiscal and monetary policy to remove large and persistent output gaps. Other economists believe that fiscal policy should not be used for economic stabilization under any circumstances. Rather, they would argue, tax and spending behaviour should be the outcome of public choices regarding the long-term size and financing of the public sector and should not be altered for short-term considerations. We return to these debates in Chapter 32.

fine tuning The attempt to maintain output at its potential level by means of frequent changes in fiscal or monetary policy.

gross tuning The use of macroeconomic policy to stabilize the economy such that large deviations from potential output do not persist for extended periods of time.

Fiscal Policy and Growth

Fiscal policy has both short-run and long-run effects on the economy. Its short-run effects, which we have discussed in this chapter, are reflected by shifts in the AD curve and changes in the level of GDP. However, the theory presented in this chapter predicts that the adjustment of factor prices will eventually bring real GDP back to Y^* so that the long-run effects of any given fiscal policy will depend on the policy's effects on Y^*. In both of the following examples, to highlight the difference between the short-run and long-run effects of the policies, we imagine starting in a macroeconomic equilibrium with real GDP equal to Y^*.

Increases in Government Purchases A fiscal expansion created by an increase in government purchases (G) will shift the AD curve to the right and increase real GDP in the short run. As factor prices rise in response to the inflationary output gap, output will return back to Y^* but at a higher price level. At this point, let's consider two possibilities. In the first, the level of Y^* is unaffected by the increase in G; in the second, for reasons that we will see shortly, the increase in G causes Y^* to rise.

The Increase in G Leaves Y* Unchanged. As we will see in later chapters, even though the adjustment of factor prices will bring real GDP back to the initial Y^*, the *composition* of output will be altered. From the national-income accounting we saw in Chapter 20, we know that $Y = C_a + I_a + G_a + NX_a$, where the "$a$" subscripts denote the actual components of aggregate expenditure. If real GDP returns to Y^* after factor prices have fully adjusted, then the *rise* in G_a must be equal to the *fall* in $C_a + I_a + NX_a$. In this case we say that the increase in government purchases has "crowded out" private expenditures. Of particular concern is the possibility that private investment in plant and equipment will be reduced. If private investment is crowded out, there will be a slower rate of accumulation of physical capital, and this will likely lead to a reduction in the future growth rate of potential output.[7]

> Even if an increase in government purchases leaves the *current level* of potential output unchanged, the crowding out of private investment may reduce the *future growth rate* of potential output.

The Increase in G Causes Y* to Rise. We have assumed throughout this chapter that short-run AD shocks leave Y^* unchanged. Though this is a useful simplifying assumption in our model, it may not be true in the real world. Suppose, in particular, that the increase in G is spent on public infrastructure that increases the productivity of private-sector production. Improved highways, bridges, ports, or public-health networks may all have such an effect. In this case, the rise in G will still cause an inflationary gap and set in place the economy's adjustment process. As factor prices rise, firms' unit costs will increase; the AS curve will shift to the left, thus returning real GDP back toward Y^*. But if Y^* has now increased as a result of the productivity-enhancing increase in G, the extent of crowding out of private expenditures will be less than in the previous case (where Y^* was constant). The result is that the negative effect on the economy's long-run growth rate may be reduced or even eliminated.

> If an increase in government purchases leads to an increase in potential output (or its growth rate), the negative effects from the crowding out of private investment will be reduced.

Beginning When Y < Y*. The analysis is slightly different, however, if the fiscal expansion is undertaken when real GDP is initially well below Y^*. In an ideal situation, the increase in government purchases is just enough to increase real GDP back to Y^*; government purchases are then reduced as private consumption and investment recover. In this case, the fiscal policy has put to work resources that would otherwise have been idle and it has no crowding out effect because it is reduced as private expenditure recovers. There is then a short-term gain from raising real GDP above what it would otherwise have been. There may even be some long-term gain to growth if the increased government expenditure was on productive assets, such as infrastructure. Of course, this is an ideal situation. If the government expenditure does not fall as private expenditure recovers, the situation becomes the first case with

---

[7] Since some of the rise in G_a may be government investment in such things as roads or power plants or other productivity-enhancing infrastructure, the overall effect on the path of Y^* depends on the productivity of the new public investment compared with that of the private investment that was crowded out.

an expansionary fiscal policy combined with an economy already at Y^*. In this case, the short-run simulative benefits of the fiscal expansion need to be weighed against the long-run costs.

Reductions in Taxes Now consider a fiscal expansion created by a reduction in tax rates, and suppose that we begin the analysis with real GDP equal to Y^*. The short-run demand-side effects are straightforward. Reductions in the GST rate or in the corporate or personal income-tax rates that are thought to be long-lasting will increase both investment and consumption spending and shift the *AD* curve to the right. The level of real GDP will rise in the short run. As wages and other factor prices increase, however, the level of output will gradually return to Y^*.

Will the level of Y^* or its growth rate be affected by the reduction in taxes? It depends to a large extent on which taxes are cut, and by how much. Reductions in GST rates and personal income-tax rates may provide an incentive for individuals to increase their work effort, thus increasing overall labour supply and the level of Y^*. Reductions in corporate income-tax rates are likely to increase the economy's rate of investment and, through this channel, increase the future growth rate of Y^*.

Reductions in tax rates generate a short-run demand stimulus and may also generate a longer-run increase in the level and growth rate of potential output.

Reductions in tax rates *may* lead to increases in the economy's potential growth rate. But this is not a certain outcome. In the event that growth is increased, however, there would appear to be no clear tradeoff between the short-run and long-run effects of the fiscal expansion. The economy benefits in the short run from the increase in economic activity and in the long run from the increase in the growth rate. The absence of a tradeoff may, however, be illusory. Even though the growth rate of potential output is higher, the reduced tax revenues lead to fewer resources under the command of government. This means less public spending on many of the things that citizens value, such as national parks, public education, health care, roads, bridges, airports, other infrastructure, and research and development. The essential tradeoff then becomes one between having more resources in the hands of the private sector or more resources in the hands of the public sector. This choice is a crucial one—and often a contentious one—for all economies.

Another extreme possibility is that the reduction in tax rates leads to such a significant increase in potential output that the government's tax revenues actually increase. In this case, the tax reduction unleashes such a flood of investment and work effort that the increase in national income is sufficient to more than offset the reduction in tax rates, thus leaving the government able to fund more worthwhile public spending than before. This idea is central to what is often called "supply side" economics, as popularized during the early 1980s by advisors to U.S. president Ronald Reagan and British prime minister Margaret Thatcher. More recently, the central idea that tax reductions may significantly stimulate economic activity and growth played an important role in the policies of former premiers Ralph Klein of Alberta and Mike Harris of Ontario, as well as in the tax cuts implemented in 2004 by former U.S. president George W. Bush. In these cases, there is ample evidence that the tax cuts helped to generate significant increases in economic activity; there is little or no evidence, however, that they led to *increases* in government tax revenue.

SUMMARY

24.1 The Adjustment Process

- Potential output, Y^*, is the level of real GDP at which all factors of production are fully employed.
- The output gap is the difference between potential output and the actual level of real GDP, the latter determined by the intersection of the AD and AS curves.
- An inflationary gap means that Y is greater than Y^*, and hence there is excess demand in factor markets. As a result, wages and other factor prices rise, causing firms' unit costs to rise. The AS curve shifts upward, and the price level rises.

- A recessionary gap means that Y is less than Y^*, and hence there is excess supply in factor markets. Wages and other factor prices fall but perhaps very slowly. As firms' unit costs fall, the AS curve gradually shifts downward, eventually returning output to potential.
- In our macro model, the level of potential output, Y^*, acts as an "anchor" for the economy. Given the short-run equilibrium as determined by the AD and AS curves, wages and other factor prices will adjust, shifting the AS curve, until output returns to Y^*.

24.2 Aggregate Demand and Supply Shocks

- Beginning from a position of potential output, an expansionary demand shock creates an inflationary gap, causing wages and other factor prices to rise. Firms' unit costs rise, shifting the AS curve upward and bringing output back toward Y^*.
- Beginning from a position of potential output, a contractionary demand shock creates a recessionary gap. Because factor prices tend to be sticky downward, the adjustment process tends to be slow, and a recessionary gap tends to persist for some time.
- Aggregate supply shocks, such as those caused by changes in the prices of inputs, lead the AS curve to shift, changing real GDP and the price level. But the

economy's adjustment process reverses the shift in AS, tending eventually to bring the economy back to its initial level of output and prices.
- In the short run, macroeconomic equilibrium is determined by the intersection of the AD and AS curves. In the long run, the economy is in equilibrium only when real GDP is equal to potential output. In the long run, the price level is determined by the intersection of the AD curve and the vertical Y^* curve.
- Shocks to the AD or AS curves can change real GDP in the short run. For a shock to have long-run effects, the value of Y^* must be altered.

24.3 Fiscal Stabilization Policy

- In our macro model, fiscal policy can be used to stabilize output at Y^*. To remove a recessionary gap, governments can shift AD to the right by cutting taxes or increasing spending. To remove an inflationary gap, governments can adopt the opposite policies.
- In the short run, increases in desired saving on the part of firms, households, and governments lead to reductions in real GDP. This phenomenon is called the paradox of thrift. In the long run, the paradox of thrift does not apply, and increased saving will lead to increased investment and economic growth.
- Because government tax and transfer programs tend to reduce the size of the multiplier, they act as automatic stabilizers.

- Discretionary fiscal policy is subject to decision lags and execution lags that limit its ability to take effect quickly.
- Fiscal policy has different effects in the short and long run. In the short run, a fiscal expansion created by an increase in government purchases (G) will increase real GDP. In the long run, the rise in G may "crowd out" private spending. If private investment is crowded out, the growth rate of potential output may be reduced.
- A fiscal expansion created by a reduction in taxes increases real GDP in the short run. In the long run, if the tax reduction leads to more investment and work effort, there will be a positive effect on the level and growth rate of potential output.

KEY CONCEPTS

The output gap and factor prices
Inflationary and recessionary gaps
Asymmetry of wage adjustment: flex-
   ible and sticky wages
The Phillips curve

Potential output as an "anchor" for
   the economy
Short-run versus long-run effects of
   AD and *AS* shocks
Fiscal stabilization policy

The paradox of thrift
Decision lags and execution lags
Automatic stabilizers
Fine tuning and gross tuning

STUDY EXERCISES

MyEconLab

Make the grade with MyEconLab: Study Exercises marked in red can be found on
MyEconLab. You can practise them as often as you want, and most feature step-by-step
guided instructions to help you find the right answer.

1. Fill in the blanks to make the following statements
   correct.

   a. In our short-run macro model, it is assumed that
      factor prices are _____ and the level of potential
      output is _____. Changes in real GDP are caused
      by fluctuations in _____ and _____.

   b. During the adjustment process highlighted in this
      chapter, the central assumption is that factor prices
      are _____ and responding to _____. Potential
      output is assumed to be _____, and acts as a(n)
      _____ for real GDP following *AD* or *AS* shocks.

2. Fill in the blanks to make the following statements
   correct.

   a. When actual GDP is higher than potential GDP, we
      say that there is a(n) _____ gap. When actual
      GDP is less than potential GDP we say there is a(n)
      _____ gap.

   b. An inflationary gap leads to excess demand for
      labour, which causes wages and thus _____ costs
      to rise. Firms require higher _____ in order to
      supply any level of output, and so the *AS* curve
      shifts _____.

   c. A recessionary gap leads to excess supply of
      labour, which tends to cause wages and thus
      _____ costs to fall. Firms reduce _____ for
      any level of output supplied, and so the *AS* curve
      shifts _____.

   d. The downward adjustment of wages in response
      to a recessionary gap is much _____ than the
      upward adjustment of wages in response to a(n)

      _____ gap. Economists refer to this phenomenon
      as _____.

3. Fill in the blanks to make the following statements
   correct.

   a. Beginning with output equal to potential, suppose
      there is a sudden increase in demand for Canadian
      exports. This is a(n) _____ shock to the Cana-
      dian economy, which will result in the _____
      curve shifting to the _____ and the opening
      of a(n) _____ gap. Firms' unit costs will start
      to _____ and the _____ curve will shift
      _____. Long-run equilibrium will be restored at
      _____ output and _____ price level.

   b. Beginning with output equal to potential, sup-
      pose there is a drop in business confidence and
      investment falls. This is a(n) _____ shock to
      the Canadian economy, which shifts the _____
      curve to the left and creates a(n) _____ gap.
      Unit costs will start to _____ and the _____
      curve will shift _____. Long-run equilibrium
      will (slowly) be restored at _____ output and
      _____ price level.

   c. Beginning with output equal to potential, suppose
      there is a large and sudden increase in the price of
      electricity. This is a(n) _____ shock to the Cana-
      dian economy, which will result in the _____
      curve shifting _____ and the opening of a(n)
      _____ gap. If wages are downwardly sticky the
      economy's _____ process could be very slow and
      the _____ will persist for a long time.

d. Beginning with output equal to potential, suppose there is a large and sudden decrease in the price of electricity. This is a(n) _____ shock to the Canadian economy, which will result in the _____ curve shifting _____ and the opening of a(n) _____ gap. Unit costs will start to _____ and the _____ curve will shift _____, restoring equilibrium at _____ output and _____ price level.

4. Fill in the blanks to make the following statements correct.

   a. In the long run, total output is determined only by _____. In the long run, aggregate demand determines the _____.
   b. Permanent increases in real GDP are possible only if _____ is increasing.
   c. Suppose illiteracy in Canada were eliminated, and the school dropout rate were reduced to zero. The effect would be a permanent _____ in productivity and a(n) _____ in potential output.
   d. A reduction in corporate income tax is likely to make _____ more attractive and thus shift the _____ curve to the right. The result is a(n) _____ in the short-run level of real GDP. In the long run, the greater rate of _____ by firms will lead to a greater rate of growth of _____.

5. The following diagram shows two economies, A and B. Each are in short-run equilibrium at point E, where the AD and AS curves intersect.

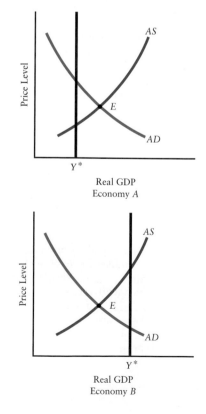

Real GDP
Economy A

Real GDP
Economy B

a. Explain why in Economy A wages and other factor prices will begin to rise, and why this will increase firms' unit costs.
b. Following your answer in part (a), show the effect on the AS curve. Explain what happens to real GDP and the price level.
c. Explain why in Economy B wages and other factor prices will begin to fall, and why this will decrease firms' unit costs.
d. Following your answer in part (c), show the effect on the AS curve. Explain what happens to real GDP and the price level.

6. The table shows several possible situations for the economy in terms of output gaps and the rate of change of wages. Real GDP is measured in billions of dollars. Assume that potential output is $800 billion.

Situation	Real GDP	Output Gap	Rate of Wage Change	Shift of AS Curve
A	775	—	−2.0%	—
B	785	—	−1.2%	—
C	795	—	−0.2%	—
D	800	—	0.0%	—
E	805	—	1.0%	—
F	815	—	2.4%	—
G	825	—	4.0%	—
H	835	—	5.8%	—

a. Compute the output gap $(Y − Y^*)$ for each situation and fill in the table.
b. Explain why wages rise when output is greater than potential but fall when output is less than potential.
c. For each situation, explain whether the economy's AS curve is shifting up, shifting down, or stationary. Fill in the table.
d. Plot the Phillips curve on a scale diagram for this economy, with the rate of change of nominal wages on the vertical axis and the level of GDP on the horizontal axis. (See *Extensions in Theory 24-1* on pages 594–595 for a review of the Phillips curve.)

7. Consider an economy that is in equilibrium with output equal to Y^*. There is then a significant reduction in the world's demand for this country's goods.
a. Illustrate the initial equilibrium in a diagram.
b. What kind of shock occurred—aggregate demand or aggregate supply? Show the effects of the shock in your diagram.
c. Explain the process by which the economy will adjust back toward Y^* in the long run. Show this in your diagram.
d. Explain why policymakers may want to use a fiscal expansion to restore output back to Y^* rather than wait for the process you described in part (c). What

role does downward wage stickiness play in the policymakers' thinking?

8. Consider an economy that is in equilibrium with output equal to Y^*. There is then a significant reduction in the world price of an important raw material, such as iron ore.

a. Illustrate the initial equilibrium in a diagram.

b. What kind of shock occurred—aggregate demand or aggregate supply? Show the effects of the shock in your diagram.

c. Explain the process by which the economy will adjust back toward Y^* in the long run. Show this in your diagram.

d. Is there a strong case for using a fiscal contraction to return output to Y^*? Explain why or why not.

9. The table below shows hypothetical data for five economies. Real GDP is measured in millions of dollars.

	Real GDP	Potential GDP (Y^*)	Output Gap (% of Y^*)	Rate of Wage Change
Economy 1	10 050	9 100	—	+2.0%
Economy 2	70 000	77 000	—	−0.3%
Economy 3	115 000	130 000	—	−0.5%
Economy 4	4 000	3 700	—	+1.0%
Economy 5	50 000	50 000	—	0.0%

a. Fill in the missing data. Which economies have an inflationary gap? Which have a recessionary gap?

b. Which economies likely have the most unused capacity? Explain.

c. In which economies are labour and other factors of production in excess demand?

d. Explain why the rate of change of nominal wages is high in Economies 1 and 4, and low in Economies 2 and 3.

e. Assuming that labour productivity is constant, in which economies are unit costs rising? In which are they falling? Explain.

10. In our discussion of automatic fiscal stabilizers, we argued that income taxes and transfers increased the stability of real GDP in the face of AD and AS shocks. Recall from Chapter 22 that the simple multiplier is given by $1/[1 - MPC(1 - t) - m]$.

a. Explain how the size of the simple multiplier is related to the *slope* of the AD curve. (You may want to review the relationship between the AE curve and the AD curve, as discussed in Chapter 23.)

b. Explain how the slope of the AD curve affects the stability of real GDP in the presence of AS shocks.

c. Now explain how the size of the simple multiplier is related to the size of the *shift* in the AD curve for any given change in autonomous expenditure.

d. For any given AS curve, show how the size of the AD shift affects the stability of real GDP.

e. Finally, explain how the economy's automatic stabilizers depend on the sizes of MPC, t, and m.

11. Which of the following would be automatic stabilizers? Explain why.

a. Employment-insurance payments

b. Cost-of-living escalators in government contracts and pensions

c. Income taxes

d. Free university tuition for unemployed workers after six months of unemployment, provided that they are under 30 years old and have had five or more years of full-time work experience since high school

12. The following diagram shows the AD, AS, and Y^* curves for an economy. Suppose the economy begins at point A. Then the government increases its level of purchases (G).

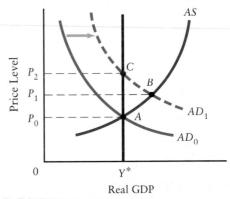

a. Describe the short-run effects of this fiscal expansion.

b. Describe the adjustment process, and the new long-run equilibrium for the economy.

c. Explain how the *composition* of real GDP has changed from the initial to the new long-run equilibrium.

d. Repeat parts (a), (b), and (c) for a fiscal expansion generated by a reduction in the net tax rate.

13. Between 2006 and 2012, the Canadian government reduced both personal and corporate income taxes. Is this a demand-side or a supply-side policy? Explain.

The Difference Between Short-Run and Long-Run Macroeconomics

LEARNING OBJECTIVES (LO)

After studying this chapter you will be able to

1 see the importance of distinguishing between the short run and the long run when analyzing macroeconomics.

2 understand how any change in real GDP can be decomposed into changes in factor supply, the utilization rate of factors, and productivity.

3 understand that short-run changes in GDP are mostly caused by changes in factor utilization, whereas long-run changes in GDP are mostly caused by changes in factor supplies and productivity.

4 explain why macroeconomic policies will only have a long-run effect on output if they influence the level of potential output.

IN Chapters 21, 22, and 23, we developed a model of the economy in the short run. In Chapter 24, we showed how this model evolves, through a process of factor-price adjustment, from its short-run equilibrium to its long-run equilibrium. There we saw how the level of potential output, Y^*, acts as an "anchor" for the economy. Aggregate demand or supply shocks can lead to short-run deviations of real GDP from Y^*, but the economy's adjustment process tends to bring real GDP back to Y^* in the long run. We are now set to examine why Y^* grows over periods of many years—a process that we call *long-run economic growth*.

In this chapter, we focus on the distinction between the short run and the long run in macroeconomics. This distinction becomes especially important when policy-makers try to evaluate the effects of various policies.

Different economists will sometimes use different time frames for the evaluation of any given policy. For example, one economist may say that a fiscal expansion is desirable because it will provide stimulus to an economy with high unemployment; another economist may claim that it will have negative effects on the economy's long-run growth. Both views might be correct (as we saw at the end of the previous chapter), but the listener is left confused because it is not clear in the debate whether the discussion is about the short-run or the long-run effects of the policy.

In this chapter, we seek to clarify the distinction between short-run GDP fluctuations and long-run GDP growth. With this distinction firmly in place, we will be ready for the detailed discussion of long-run economic growth in the next chapter.

25.1 Two Examples from Recent History

We begin with two examples of the difference between short-run and long-run macroeconomic relationships. Though the specific examples date from the 1990s, the principles involved apply more generally.

Inflation and Interest Rates in Canada

In the early 1990s, Canada's central bank (the Bank of Canada) embarked on a policy designed to reduce the rate of inflation. For reasons that we will see in detail in Chapters 29 and 30, the Bank's policy was controversial. The governor of the Bank, however, was committed to explaining the policy to an often-skeptical public. As we will see, the explanation relies crucially on making the distinction between short-run and long-run macroeconomic relationships.

In April 1995, Bank of Canada Governor Gordon Thiessen was interviewed on CBC Radio. Thiessen was asked about the Bank's policy of reducing inflation, from about 6 percent a few years earlier, and maintaining it at a lower rate of about 2 percent. Thiessen argued that the high nominal interest rates of the past were caused mostly by high inflation. The main reason for this connection between inflation and nominal interest rates is that inflation erodes the value of money. Lenders need to be compensated for the inflation-induced fall in the real value of their money between the time they lend it and the time they are repaid. This requires charging a nominal interest rate high enough to cover the effects of inflation and deliver a positive return to the lender. Thus, higher inflation pushes up interest rates; lower inflation pushes them down.

At this point, the interviewer had no problem with Thiessen's line of argument, as he easily recalled the time back in 1981 when inflation was at an all-time high of 12 percent and mortgage rates at Canada's banks were an astounding 20 percent! In contrast, by 1995, the rate of inflation was down to just over 2 percent and mortgage rates were only 8 percent. So periods of high inflation did indeed appear to coincide with periods of high interest rates.

Thiessen then started the next part of his argument. He stated that in order to reduce the rate of inflation the Bank of Canada had to tighten up credit-market conditions and push up interest rates. Understandably confused at this point, the interviewer asked the inevitable question: How can a policy that raises interest rates be a necessary part of a policy designed to *reduce* both inflation and interest rates?

Thiessen understood the apparent contradiction and was ready with his answer. He stressed that the key to answering the question is to understand the different short-run and long-run effects of monetary policy. Thiessen argued that, in the short run, the Bank's policies to raise interest rates will lead firms to reduce their investment and lead households to reduce their spending on big-ticket items. Such reductions in expenditure will lead, through the multiplier process that we have seen in earlier chapters, to a reduction in real GDP. In short, the Bank of Canada's policy shifts the *AD* curve to the left and generates a recession. When we examine the detailed workings of monetary policy in later chapters, we will see that a monetary policy designed to reduce inflation is usually effective precisely because *it creates a temporary recession.*

So much for the short-run effects of the Bank's policy. What happens as wages and other factor prices adjust and the economy therefore starts to approach its new long-run equilibrium? As we saw in Chapter 24, the excess supply of factors that is a key part of the recession puts downward pressure on factor prices. In other words, wages start to increase at a slower rate than before and maybe even begin to fall. As wage growth declines, the pressure on prices to rise also declines. That is, the rate of inflation falls. As inflation falls, nominal interest rates will also fall. In the new long-run equilibrium, both inflation and nominal interest rates will be lower than before the policy was initiated. As Gordon Thiessen said in the interview, "The best way to get low interest rates is to get low inflation."

The details of monetary policy will be discussed in Chapters 28 and 29, and this argument will be repeated in considerable detail. At that time, we will more clearly see the difference between the short-run and long-run effects of monetary policy.

Saving and Growth in Japan

For the entire decade of the 1990s, the Japanese economy showed very little growth. This period is often referred to as Japan's "Lost Decade." Many economists argued that an important part of the solution to Japan's economic malaise was for its firms and consumers to spend more. One problem with Japan, they argued, was that its firms and consumers saved "too much." On the other hand, many of these same economists acknowledged that Japan's remarkable economic success in the 40 years following the Second World War—high growth rates of real GDP and low unemployment—was to a significant extent due to its high saving rate. But if "too much" saving was an important reason for Japan's economic slump during the 1990s, how could high saving also have been a primary reason for its remarkable economic success over four decades? How can both of these views be correct?

Once again, the key to understanding this apparent contradiction is to recognize that the short-run effect of saving is different from its long-run effect. We saw this distinction in Chapter 24 when we discussed the "paradox of thrift," but it is worth repeating. In the short run, with factor prices and technology more or less constant, an increase in households' desire to save, perhaps caused by some uncertainty about future economic events, implies a reduction in expenditure. Uncertainty leads firms to spend less on investment goods; households spend less on all sorts of consumer goods. This reduction in desired expenditure leads, through the usual multiplier process, to a reduction in output. In terms of our macro model, the *AD* curve shifts to the left and real GDP falls. Increased saving in the short run, therefore, can be one reason why an economy, such as Japan's, enters or remains in an economic slump.

If an increase in firms' and households' saving can cause a recession, how can a high saving rate also help to explain Japan's many years of healthy economic growth? The answer is that in the long run, after wages and factor prices adjust to the recessionary gap, greater saving leads to a larger pool of financial capital. This larger pool of available funds drives down the price of credit—the interest rate—and makes firms' investment projects more profitable. More investment in research and development to develop new products as well as more investment in factories, machines, and warehouses leads to a higher level of potential output, and it is to this higher level of potential output that the economy converges in the long run. Once this long-run mechanism is

The high private saving rate in Japan is one reason that the Japanese economic recovery in the 1990s was so slow.

understood, we can see that Japan's high saving rate over many years may indeed be a contributor to its high-growth experience.

This long-run relationship among saving, investment, and growth explains the striking correlation that we will see in the next chapter: over long periods, countries with high saving and investment rates tend to be countries with high rates of per capita GDP growth.

A Need to Think Differently

These two examples from recent history suggest that a complete understanding of macroeconomics requires an understanding of both the short run and the long run. Such an understanding, in turn, requires us to think differently about short-run and long-run behaviour. It is one thing to say that macroeconomic variables behave differently over the short run than over the long run; it is quite another to understand *why* this is the case.

In this chapter, we emphasize the distinction between viewing short-run changes in GDP as deviations of output from potential, and long-run changes in GDP as changes in the level of potential output. We introduce a simple method of GDP accounting that clarifies this distinction and also shows us the various sources of short-run and long-run changes in GDP.[1]

25.2 Accounting for Changes in GDP

The simplest illustration of the distinction between short-run and long-run changes in economic activity is the behaviour of real GDP over time, as shown in Figure 25-1. The figure shows the paths of Canadian real GDP and potential GDP, beginning from 1985. Actual GDP is measured by Statistics Canada. Potential GDP is the level of output that the economy produces when all factors of production are "fully employed." But Statistics Canada can't tell us the value of potential GDP because it is not an observed variable—it must be estimated. The value of potential GDP is estimated by combining three pieces of information: the amounts of available factors of production (such as the labour force and the capital stock); an estimate of these factors' rates of utilization when they are fully employed; and an estimate of each factor's productivity.

Figure 25-1 shows two different types of changes in GDP. First, some changes involve departures of actual GDP from potential GDP. For example, notice that actual GDP is equal to potential GDP at point *A* in 1990. As the Canadian economy then entered a major recession, actual GDP dropped below potential GDP to point *B* in 1992. An economic recovery then took place, eventually taking actual GDP back to potential GDP at point *C* in 1999. Real GDP again dropped significantly below potential GDP when a global recession began in 2008; by early in 2013, however, GDP had not yet

---

[1] It is worth emphasizing the different use of the terms "short run" and "long run" in macroeconomics and in microeconomics. In microeconomics, the short run for a firm or industry is the span of time during which the amount of physical capital is constant; the long run is the period of time during which firms are able to adjust their capital stock. In macroeconomics, however, the key distinction relates to whether wages and other factor prices have fully adjusted to excess demand or supply (the output gap) in the aggregate economy. Economists take wages and other factor prices to be given in the short run but fully adjusted to the output gap in the long run.

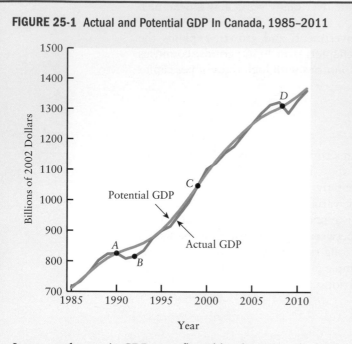

FIGURE 25-1 Actual and Potential GDP In Canada, 1985–2011

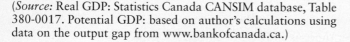

Long-run changes in GDP are reflected by changes in the level of potential GDP. Short-run changes in GDP are shown mostly by changes in the output gap.

(*Source:* Real GDP: Statistics Canada CANSIM database, Table 380-0017. Potential GDP: based on author's calculations using data on the output gap from www.bankofcanada.ca.)

returned to potential. Such changes in GDP are what economists call short-run changes in GDP—they involve primarily the opening and then closing of an output gap.

The second type of change in GDP involves changes in potential GDP, with little or no change in the output gap. For example, the change in actual GDP from point *A* in 1990 to point *D* in 2008 represents entirely a change in potential GDP. We know this because the output gap in both years was zero (that is, in both 1990 and 2008 GDP was equal to potential GDP). Such changes in GDP are what economists call long-run changes in GDP—they involve a change in potential GDP, with little or no change in the output gap.

> When studying long-run trends in GDP, economists focus on the change in potential output. When studying short-run fluctuations, economists focus on the change in the output gap.

Figure 25-1 may make us wonder whether short-run changes in GDP have a different cause than long-run changes. In our macro model this is certainly the case; output is determined in the short run by the *AD* and *AS* curves but in the long run by the level of *Y** (which is usually assumed to be unaffected by the *AD* or *AS* shocks). To explore the different causes of changes in GDP, we turn to a very simple accounting framework that applies to *all* changes in GDP.

GDP Accounting: The Basic Principle

Suppose we could break down any change in GDP into its component parts. By understanding how each component changes, we can then gain some insights into how short-run changes differ from long-run changes. To break up GDP into the parts we want to study, we do the following obvious but useful things. First, we write

$$GDP = GDP$$

This is obviously true! Next, we multiply the right-hand side of the equation by F/F, where F is the economy's total available stock of factors, such as land, labour, and capital. This gives

$$GDP = F \times (GDP/F)$$

Next, we multiply the right-hand side by F_E/F_E, where F_E is the number of the economy's factors that are employed. After reordering the terms, we have

$$GDP = F \times (F_E/F) \times (GDP/F_E) \tag{25-1}$$

It may seem like we have done nothing useful since we have simply twice multiplied the right-hand side of an obviously true equation by one. But, in fact, Equation 25-1 is very useful when thinking about the different sources of GDP changes.

First, however, note that Equation 25-1 implies that we have added together units of labour, land, and capital to get a meaningful number for the economy's "available factors," F. This is not actually possible since different factors are measured in different units. For example, we can't add together six workers and five machines and two hectares of land to get a total of 13 factors. In the next section, we will focus on a single factor of production (labour) to avoid this problem. For now, however, our point is simplified by thinking about the economy's total available factors, F, and the number of those factors that are employed, F_E.

To make the discussion less cumbersome, let's name the three components of Equation 25-1.

1. F is the economy's *factor supply*; it is the total amount of all factors of production that the economy currently possesses.

2. F_E/F is the *factor utilization rate*; it is the fraction of the total supply of factors that is actually employed at any time.

3. GDP/F_E is a simple measure of *productivity* because it shows the amount of output (GDP) per unit of input employed (F_E).

Note that Equation 25-1 does nothing more than separate any change in GDP into a change in one or more of the three components, F, F_E/F, or GDP/F_E. For example, Canadian GDP increased dramatically in the 50 years between 1950 and 2000. Also, Canadian GDP increased by only a few percentage points between 2008 and 2012. In both cases, the increase in GDP can be attributed to changes in one or more of the three components—either the factor supply (F) increased, the factor utilization rate (F_E/F) increased, or the level of productivity (GDP/F_E) increased.

Any change in GDP can be decomposed conceptually into a change in factor supply, a change in factor utilization, and a change in productivity.

The usefulness of this accounting exercise becomes clear when we recognize that two of these components, factor supply and productivity, change mostly over long periods of time, whereas the third component, factor utilization, changes mostly over shorter periods. This points us toward a better understanding of the difference between short-run and long-run changes in GDP. We discuss each component in turn.

The Long Run: Factor Supply Two main factors of production—labour and capital—account for most of the change in the economy's supply of factors.

Labour. The economy's supply of labour can increase for two main reasons. First, population can increase. An increase in population can be caused, in turn, by greater immigration, an increase in birth rates, or a decrease in the mortality rate. The second way to increase the economy's supply of labour is to increase the fraction of the population that chooses to seek employment. This fraction is called the *labour-force participation rate*. In Canada, the labour-force participation rate is currently about 66 percent. It has increased steadily from the 1960s, mostly because of the increase in the participation rate of married women.

No matter how the economy's supply of labour increases, the important point for our purposes is that such changes are mostly *long-run changes*. Population growth, through whatever means, is a very gradual process. Large changes in labour-force participation also tend to take place gradually (although there are some fluctuations over the course of the business cycle as people enter or leave the labour force depending on their assessment of being able to find a job). As a result, the economy's supply of labour does not usually change significantly from year to year. Over a period of many years, however, the increase in the supply of labour can be very substantial.

Capital. The economy's supply of physical capital—computers, machines, factories, and warehouses—increases for one reason. Firms that choose to purchase or build such investment goods today are accumulating physical capital that will be used to produce output in the future. Thus, today's flow of investment expenditure adds to the economy's stock of physical capital.[2]

As is the case for labour, the economy's stock of physical capital changes very gradually. This is not to be confused with the very dramatic swings in investment that are often observed over the course of the business cycle. The difference is that investment is the *flow* that contributes to the *stock* of capital. But the economy's capital stock is so large compared with the annual flow of investment expenditure that even dramatic swings in the annual flow of investment generate almost imperceptible changes in the stock of capital.

> **Changes in the economy's supply of labour and capital occur gradually, but over periods of many years their growth is considerable. As a result, changes in factor supply are important for explaining long-run changes in output but relatively unimportant for explaining short-run changes.**

The Long Run: Productivity The economy's level of productivity (GDP/F_E) is a measure of the average amount of output that is produced per unit of input. In practice, there are several possible measures of productivity, each one measuring something slightly different. Although there is more than one measure of productivity, Equation 25-1 uses the concept of output per employed factor, GDP/F_E. An increase in productivity is called *productivity growth*. Productivity growth is an important source of long-term increases in per capita income and thus in rising living standards, and we will say much more about it in Chapter 26.

The economy's level of productivity changes only slowly over time. For example, labour productivity in Canada—measured as real GDP per hour of work—has grown at an average rate of 1.3 percent per year since 1975. Such low growth rates do not lead to significant changes in GDP or living standards over short periods of time but can generate huge improvements in living conditions over many years. For example, you would barely notice a 1.3 percent increase in your income from one year to the next, but if this growth were sustained over 55 years your income would double. [31]

---

[2] The part of investment that represents a change in inventories does not add to the economy's capital stock, but this component of investment is typically quite small (though volatile).

> The economy's level of productivity grows only gradually from year to year but increases substantially over periods of many years. As a result, productivity growth is very important for explaining long-run changes in output and living standards but less important for explaining short-run changes.

Many people find productivity an abstract concept that is difficult to comprehend, and cannot easily see how productivity grows over time. *Applying Economic Concepts 25-1* provides some examples of productivity-enhancing developments in various occupational settings.

The Short Run: Factor Utilization In Chapters 21, 22, and 23 we examined in detail the behaviour of the economy in the short run. Here we review some of these now-familiar concepts but express them in a way that helps us to understand our central equation decomposing the changes in real GDP.

The factor utilization rate (F_E/F) is the last remaining component from our equation. Recall that it is simply the fraction of the economy's total supply of factors that is employed. An immediate question comes to mind: Why would firms ever use fewer factors than are available to them? The answer has to do with how firms respond to changes in the demand for their product. When a firm's sales start dropping off, it must make a choice. It can continue producing at the current rate and let its inventories build up. Or it can reduce its rate of production. For a firm that is interested in maximizing profits, there is a limit to the amount of costly inventories it will be prepared to accumulate. Eventually, a reduction in demand for its product leads the firm to reduce its output and reduce its employment of factors. Workers are laid off and equipment and other physical capital are used less intensively, thus lowering the value of F_E/F for the economy.

Similarly, a firm that is faced with a sudden increase in demand for its product has two alternatives. It can continue with its previous rate of production and satisfy the increased demand by letting its inventories run down. Or it can increase its rate of production by hiring more available workers and machines. Since profit-maximizing firms do not want to miss an opportunity to make a profitable sale, as would happen if the stockpile of inventories were to get fully depleted, eventually the increase in demand leads them to increase production and hire more factors. Extra workers are hired, existing workers work overtime, and machines and other physical capital are used more intensively, thus increasing F_E/F for the economy.

These responses by firms to changes in demand are only the firms' short-run responses. A low factor utilization rate describes *excess supply* in the factor markets. As we saw in Chapter 24, such a situation of excess supply typically causes some downward pressure on wages and other factor prices. This reduction of factor prices, in turn, reduces firms' costs, shifts the *AS* curve downward, and puts downward pressure on product prices. Similarly, in the case of the increase in demand, the situation of a high factor utilization rate describes *excess demand* in factor markets. Such excess demand causes upward pressure on wages and other factor prices. As factor prices rise, firms' costs increase, the *AS* curve shifts upward, and there is upward pressure on the price level. This process of factor-price adjustment continues in our model until output returns to potential, at which point all factors of production are said to be fully employed.

APPLYING ECONOMIC CONCEPTS 25-1

What Does Productivity Growth Really Look Like?

The most commonly used measure of productivity is *labour productivity*, defined as the amount of output produced per hour of work, and it can be measured for the aggregate economy or for a particular firm or industry. For the aggregate economy, the appropriate measure of output is real GDP, and labour productivity is then measured as real GDP divided by the total number of hours worked. In 2012, Canadian labour productivity was about $46 per hour (expressed in 2002 dollars); it has been rising at an average annual rate of 1.3 percent since the mid-1970s.

How does labour productivity grow over time? Any new production process or technique that raises output proportionally more than it raises labour input will increase labour productivity. Often the introduction of new physical capital or new techniques allow firms to increase output while *reducing* their use of labour. In this case, labour productivity for the firm might increase significantly. Here are some examples from various industries and occupations:

- Accountants who prepare income-tax forms for their clients have experienced an enormous increase in labour productivity with the use of software packages designed specifically for the task. The software allows a given number of accountants to complete more tax returns per hour of work, thus increasing labour productivity.

- Residential landscaping companies move large amounts of soil, sand, and rock. In recent years, the development of small and inexpensive bulldozers has vastly increased the amount of work that can be done with a crew of two or three workers, thus dramatically raising labour productivity.

- In modern, high-tech lumber mills, a computer "reads" each log in three dimensions and then computes how the log can most efficiently be cut into the various regular sizes of cut lumber. Fewer workers are needed to sort the logs and more marketable lumber is produced from a given number of logs because the amount of waste is reduced. Labour productivity rises as a result.

- Doctors who specialize in eye surgery have been greatly aided by the recent development of precise medical lasers. The equipment is expensive, but allows

a single doctor to perform more surgical procedures per day than was possible only a decade ago, thus increasing labour productivity.

In each of these examples, the use of new and better capital equipment allows the enterprise in question to produce more output with a given number of workers, or perhaps the same amount of output with a reduced number of workers. Both are an increase in measured labour productivity.

How do we get from these specific micro examples back to macroeconomics and the change in real GDP and aggregate labour productivity? If in each example the amount of work is unchanged but output rises, real GDP and aggregate labour productivity will both be higher as a result. If instead each specific output is unchanged but the amount of work is reduced, then we need to recognize that the workers released from these activities are now available to move to other firms and industries. When they begin working elsewhere in the economy, their new production will constitute an increase in real GDP. In this case, total work effort will be back to its original level but real GDP will be higher—an increase in aggregate labour productivity.

Small digging machines like this have replaced the difficult work of individuals with shovels and have significantly increased labor productivity.

The factor utilization rate fluctuates in response to aggregate demand and aggregate supply shocks. Over time, however, the adjustment of factor prices tends to return the factor-utilization rate to the level consistent with full employment.

When the economy's factors are fully employed (and thus real GDP equals Y^*), the value of F_E/F will be slightly less than one, indicating that some labour is normally unemployed and some capital is normally idle. There is thus some "normal" rate of factor utilization that corresponds to full employment.

What do we mean by a "normal" factor utilization rate? In Chapter 19 we briefly discussed the fact that even when the economy is at potential output, some unemployment still exists because of regular turnover in the labour market and new entrants seeking a first job. The rate of unemployment when real GDP is equal to potential output is often called the *natural rate of unemployment*. This "natural" or "normal" rate of unemployment is the rate of unemployment against which we compare the actual unemployment rate to judge whether the labour market has excess supply or excess demand. That is, if unemployment is above the natural rate, there is an excess supply of labour; if unemployment is below the natural rate, there is an excess demand for labour. For physical capital, the utilization rate is called the *capacity utilization rate* because the amount of physical capital largely determines the productive *capacity* of a given plant or factory. As with labour, so too is there a "natural" or "normal" capacity utilization rate for capital.

> Changes in the factor utilization rate are important for explaining short-run changes in GDP. But after factor prices have fully adjusted, the factor utilization rate returns to its "normal" level. As a result, changes in the factor utilization rate are not important for explaining long-run changes in GDP.

GDP Accounting: An Application

We made some strong statements in the previous section regarding the relative importance of short-run versus long-run changes in productivity, factor supplies, and factor utilization. Are these statements supported by the evidence? In this section, we apply the accounting exercise from Equation 25-1 to Canadian GDP data to illustrate the basic arguments. Unfortunately, we cannot use *exactly* the same equation because, as we noted then, it is not possible to add units of labour together with units of physical capital and units of land. By using exactly the same intuition as earlier, however, we can express the GDP accounting equation in terms of a single factor of production—labour. Letting L be the labour force and E be the number of individuals employed, the new equation is[3]

$$GDP = L \times (E/L) \times (GDP/E) \qquad (25\text{-}2)$$

The basic interpretation of Equation 25-2 is the same as for Equation 25-1, except now the discussion relates only to labour. The labour force (L) is the supply of labour. The employment rate (E/L) is the fraction of the labour force actually employed (which is equal to one minus the unemployment rate). And the measure of productivity—in this case, labour productivity—is GDP/E.[4]

Figure 25-2 shows the behaviour of these three components for Canada beginning in 1960. Each variable is expressed as an index number, with the value in 1960 set

---

[3] We get this equation by beginning with GDP = GDP. We then multiply the right-hand side by E/E and then by L/L.

[4] For reasons of data availability over long periods of time, our denominator for the measure of labour productivity is the number of workers employed rather than total hours worked. This choice makes little difference for the purposes of Figure 25-2.

FIGURE 25-2 Three Sources of Changes in GDP

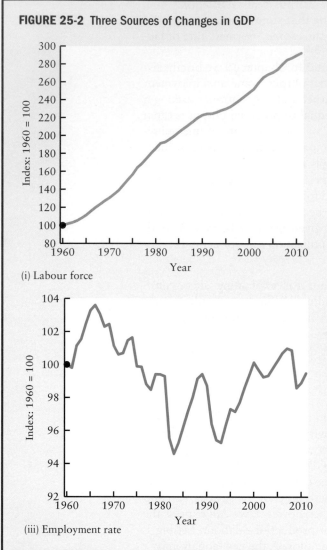

(i) Labour force

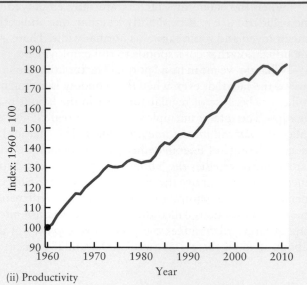

(ii) Productivity

(iii) Employment rate

The sources of long-run changes in GDP differ from the sources of short-run changes in GDP. Panel (i) shows the upward trend in the Canadian labour force. Panel (ii) shows the upward trend in productivity, measured as GDP per worker. Both show substantial growth over the long run, but relatively small short-run fluctuations. Panel (iii) shows the employment rate, the fraction of the labour force that is employed. It shows almost no long-run trend but considerable short-run fluctuations.

(*Source:* All data for figures are author's calculations using data from Statistics Canada CANSIM database. Labour force: Table 282-0002. Employment: Table 282-0087. Real GDP: Table 380-0017.)

equal to 100. Expressing each variable in this way makes it easy to see each variable's percentage change over the five decades. Note that the vertical scale is different for each of the three variables. We do this intentionally so that we can see whatever trend and volatility exist for each variable separately. If we used the same vertical scale for graphing employment that we use for graphing the labour force and productivity, we would barely notice the large fluctuations that do exist in employment.

Part (i) of the figure shows the growth of the Canadian labour force. From 1960 to 2011, the index number increased from 100 to 292, an increase of 192 percent. It is clear from the graph that any short-run fluctuations in the Canadian labour force are dwarfed in importance by the long-run upward trend.

Now look at the second panel, showing the growth of Canadian labour productivity. The level of GDP per person employed, expressed as an index number, increases from 100 in 1960 to 182 in 2011, an increase of 82 percent. Like the labour force, the level of labour productivity has its short-run fluctuations, but it is clear that the overriding change—the upward trend—takes place over many years.

Finally, consider part (iii), showing the Canadian employment rate—the utilization rate of labour. Compared with the other two variables graphed in Figure 25-2, the employment rate shows much more short-run volatility and much less long-run change. The employment rate (expressed as an index number) is almost the same in 2011 as it was in 1960. There is very little change over the long run, but considerable changes are occurring over shorter periods of time.

Summing Up

To summarize, we can decompose *any* change in GDP into changes in factor supply, the factor utilization rate, and productivity. But these three components typically contribute to GDP changes over different spans of time. In particular, factor supply and productivity typically change only gradually and hence are important for explaining long-run changes in GDP but are not usually helpful in explaining short-run changes in GDP. In contrast, the factor utilization rate is quite volatile over short periods of time but returns to its normal level over several years. Thus, changes in the factor utilization rate are important for explaining short-run changes in GDP but are not of much importance for explaining long-run changes.

25.3 Policy Implications

Economists think differently about short-run and long-run macroeconomic relationships. When thinking about short-run fluctuations, economists focus on understanding why actual GDP deviates from potential GDP. As we have seen in previous chapters, such changes in real GDP are caused by aggregate demand and aggregate supply shocks. When thinking about long-run growth, however, economists focus on understanding why potential GDP changes over time. As we have said, such long-run growth has its source in the growth of factor supplies and productivity. Thus, in understanding long-run growth, economists focus on what causes factor supplies and productivity to change.

> When studying short-run fluctuations, economists focus on the deviations of actual output from potential output. When studying long-run growth, economists focus on changes in potential output.

Through the development of our macro model in the previous four chapters, we have a better understanding of what causes the *AD* and *AS* curves to shift, and thus a better understanding of the causes of short-run fluctuations in real GDP. Our picture of the short run will be more fully developed after we discuss monetary policy and interest rates in Chapters 27 and 28 and exchange rates and international trade in Chapter 35.

What we have not yet done, however, is discuss in detail why potential output grows substantially over long periods of time, thereby improving average living standards from one generation to the next. In the next chapter we explore the issue of long-run economic growth, focusing on the importance of capital accumulation and technological change.

Before we do that, however, it is worth returning to a point that we raised at the beginning of this chapter—that the distinction between the short run and the long run has an important implication for the role and effectiveness of various macroeconomic policies.

We have discussed in this chapter how shocks to aggregate demand may cause actual GDP to depart from potential GDP. For example, firms may feel optimistic about the future and increase their investment expenditure, thereby increasing the overall level of demand. Or the government may increase its purchases of goods and services, thus adding to demand. Or foreigners may decide to increase their demand for Canadian goods, thus adding to the overall demand for goods produced by Canadian firms. All of these changes would increase the overall level of demand in the economy and, in the short run, would lead actual GDP to rise above potential GDP. Conversely, any decrease in the demand for goods would, in the short run, cause actual GDP to fall below potential GDP.

In the long run, however, the economy has an adjustment process that tends to return the factor utilization rate to its "normal" level. As we saw in Chapter 24, when actual GDP is above potential GDP, there is an excess demand for factors. This causes factor prices to rise and thus the *AS* curve to shift upward, bringing actual GDP back to potential. Conversely, when actual GDP is less than potential GDP, there is an excess supply of factors. This tends to cause factor prices to fall (though perhaps slowly) and thus the *AS* curve to shift downward, thereby bringing actual GDP back to potential.

This adjustment process that brings the economy back to the level of potential output in the long run implies a stark result regarding the effects of macroeconomic policy:

> Fiscal and monetary policies affect the short-run level of GDP because they alter the level of demand and thus the position of the *AD* curve. But unless they are able to affect the level of *potential* output, Y^*, they will have no long-run effect on GDP.

As we saw in the previous chapter, fiscal policy can have important effects on the level of potential output—both through changes in government purchases and investment and through changes in personal and corporate taxes. In Chapters 28 and 29 we will explore monetary policy in detail and will see that it has few if any effects on the level of potential output.

Looking Ahead

The discussion in this chapter has focused on one topic—the difference between the short run and the long run in macroeconomics. We have shown that short-run movements in GDP are mostly accounted for by changes in the factor utilization rate. For example, as economic events cause the *AD* or *AS* curves to shift, output will deviate from Y^* and the factor utilization rate will change. In contrast, long-run changes in GDP are mostly accounted for by growth in factor supplies and productivity, which lead to increases in Y^*. This difference forces economists to think differently about macroeconomic relationships that exist over a few months as compared to those that exist over several years.

In the previous four chapters we examined in detail the behaviour of the economy in the short run, and the adjustment process that tends to bring real GDP back to Y^*. We are now ready to take the next step and examine why Y^* increases over time—the process of long-run growth.

SUMMARY

25.1 Two Examples from Recent History LO 1

- Macroeconomic variables behave differently over the short run and over the long run. One example: A monetary policy designed to reduce inflation and nominal interest rates in the long run requires an *increase* in interest rates in the short run. Another example: An increase in households' or firms' saving rates will reduce the level of output in the short run, but it will increase output in the long run.

- In the short run, there is some adjustment of output and employment but little adjustment of wages and prices. In the long run, full adjustment of wages and prices is assumed to take place.

25.2 Accounting for Changes in GDP LO 2, 3

- Changes in GDP can be accounted for by changes in one or more of the following three variables:
    1. Supply of factors
    2. Factor utilization rates
    3. Factor productivity
- Long-run changes in GDP are caused mostly by changes in factor supplies and factor productivity; the utilization rate of factors does not change significantly over the long run.

- Short-run changes in GDP are caused mostly by changes in the factor utilization rate; factor supplies and productivity have relatively minor short-run fluctuations.

25.3 Policy Implications LO 4

- When studying short-run fluctuations, economists focus on changes in the output gap and tend to ignore changes in potential output. When studying long-run growth, economists focus on changes in potential output and ignore changes in the output gap.

- Fiscal and monetary policies affect GDP in the short run because they affect the level of demand, and thus the position of the *AD* curve. Any long-run effect on real GDP must come through their effect on *potential* GDP.

KEY CONCEPTS

Short-run fluctuations
Long-run trends
Changes in the output gap

Changes in potential output
Accounting for changes in GDP
Factor supplies

Factor utilization rates
Productivity

STUDY EXERCISES

MyEconLab Make the grade with MyEconLab: Study Exercises marked in red can be found on MyEconLab. You can practise them as often as you want, and most feature step-by-step guided instructions to help you find the right answer.

1. Fill in the blanks to make the following statements correct.

   a. Short-run changes in real GDP are caused by _____ and _____ shocks, with little or no change in _____. In the short run, _____ prices and the level of _____ are assumed to be constant.

   b. Long-run trends in GDP involve changes in _____ output. Short-run fluctuations in GDP involve changes in the output gap with little or no change in _____.

c. Any change in GDP is caused by changes in at least one of the following three component parts: _____, _____, and _____.

d. Long-run changes in GDP are caused mainly by changes in _____ and _____. Short-run changes in GDP are caused mainly by changes in _____.

e. The economy's adjustment process returns the _____ rate to its "normal" level in the long run.

f. Fiscal and monetary policies alter the level of output in the short run by causing the _____ curve to shift. There will be a long-run effect on output only if _____ changes.

2. Consider Economies A, B, and C for which you are given data for the factor supply (F), the numbers of factors employed (F_E), and the GDP, for two different time periods.

Economy	Time Period	F	F_E	GDP	F_E/F	GDP/F_E
A	Period 1	1000	800	$100 000	____	____
	Period 2	1300	1040	$155 000	____	____
B	Period 1	2000	1800	$225 000	____	____
	Period 2	2000	1500	$187 500	____	____
C	Period 1	6500	6175	$399 000	____	____
	Period 2	6500	6175	$665 000	____	____

a. For each economy and each period, calculate the factor utilization rate (F_E/F) and a measure of productivity (GDP/F_E). Fill in the table.

b. For each economy and each period, use the numbers from the table to substitute into Equation 25-1 (GDP = F × F_E/F × GDP/F_E).

c. For each economy, describe whether you think the economy has experienced a short-run or a long-run change in GDP from Period 1 to Period 2. Explain.

d. Do you detect an important difference between Economies A and C? Explain.

3. Using the basic equation of GDP accounting that we developed in this chapter (GDP = F × F_E/F × GDP/F_E), calculate the economy's GDP in each of the following cases.

a. Factor supply is 4 million units, the factor utilization rate is 0.85, and the GDP per unit of input employed is $150.

b. Factor supply is 1.25 million units, the factor utilization rate is 0.9, and the GDP per unit of input employed is $110.

c. Factor supply is 250 million units, the factor utilization rate is 0.92, and the GDP per unit of input employed is $185.

4. Consider the data below for a hypothetical country.

a. Using the definitions in the chapter, compute the employment rate (E/L) and the level of productivity (GDP/E) for each year.

b. For each five-year period, compute the percentage change in the labour force, the employment rate, and the level of productivity.

c. Using Equation 25-2, the percentage change in real GDP for any relatively short period is approximately equal to the sum of the three percentage changes you computed in part (b). Using this approximation, compute the percentage change in real GDP for each five-year period.

Year	Real GDP	L	E	E/L	GDP/E	%ΔL	%Δ(E/L)	%ΔGDP
1960	100	1.5	1.4	—	—			
1965	130	1.6	1.45	—	—	—	—	—
1970	175	1.75	1.55	—	—	—	—	—
1975	250	1.95	1.65	—	—	—	—	—
1980	230	2.15	1.85	—	—	—	—	—
1985	265	2.40	2.0	—	—	—	—	—
1990	300	2.70	2.2	—	—	—	—	—
1995	340	3.0	2.8	—	—	—	—	—
2000	375	3.3	3.05	—	—	—	—	—
2005	410	3.6	3.4	—	—	—	—	—
2010	450	3.95	3.7	—	—	—	—	—

Real GDP: billions of constant dollars
L: labour force (millions of people)
E: employment (millions of people)

d. For each five-year period, what fraction of the percentage change in GDP is accounted for by the change in the employment rate?

e. Now compute the percentage change of real GDP over the entire 50-year period. Do the same for the employment rate. How much of the long-term change in GDP is accounted for by the change in the employment rate? Explain what you find based on the discussion in this chapter.

5. Go to the Bank of Canada's website (www.bankofcanada. ca) and look for data on capacity utilization rates in Canadian industries. The capacity utilization rate is the fraction of the capital stock that is utilized or employed. How has this variable changed over the past several decades? Contrast the short-run versus the long-run movements.

6. At the beginning of the chapter we discussed the short-run and long-run effects of an increase in desired saving (as applied to Japan's economy). Based on what you learned in Chapter 24 regarding the economy's adjustment process, use the *AD/AS* model to do the following:

a. Show the short-run effects of an increase in desired saving (assuming that the economy is initially in a long-run equilibrium with $Y = Y^*$).

b. Describe the adjustment process that brings the economy to its new long-run equilibrium.

c. Compare the initial and the new long-run equilibrium. What is the long-run effect of the increase in desired saving?

7. Figure 25-1 on page 620 shows the path of actual GDP and the path of potential GDP.

a. Describe the economy's adjustment process that brings GDP back to potential, and how it relates to the concept of market-clearing.

b. Suppose that, following the implementation of some policy, actual GDP eventually returns to potential GDP. Does this mean that policy can have no long-run effect on GDP?

c. Based on our discussion of fiscal policy in Chapter 24, explain why an increase in government purchases (G) could have a *positive* effect on Y^*.

d. Now provide an example of an increase in G that could have a *negative* effect on Y^*.

e. Explain how a politician might sacrifice the long-run behaviour of the economy in order to generate an outcome that is deemed to be desirable in the short run.

Long-Run Economic Growth

CHAPTER OUTLINE	LEARNING OBJECTIVES (LO)
	After studying this chapter you will be able to
26.1 THE NATURE OF ECONOMIC GROWTH	1 discuss the costs and benefits of economic growth.
	2 list four important determinants of growth in real GDP.
26.2 ESTABLISHED THEORIES OF ECONOMIC GROWTH	3 explain the main elements of Neoclassical growth theory in which technological change is exogenous.
26.3 NEWER GROWTH THEORIES	4 discuss alternative growth theories based on endogenous technical change.
26.4 ARE THERE LIMITS TO GROWTH?	5 explain why resource exhaustion and environmental degradation may create serious challenges for public policy directed at sustaining economic growth.

ECONOMIC growth is the single most powerful engine for generating long-term increases in living standards. What happens to our material living standards over time depends largely on the growth in real GDP in relation to the growth in population—that is, it depends on the growth of real per capita GDP. Such growth does not necessarily make *everybody* in Canada materially better off in the short term. But it does increase the *average* standard of living over the short term and virtually everyone's in the long term.

What determines the long-run growth rate of per capita GDP in Canada? Is this something that is beyond our control, or are there some government policies that can stimulate economic growth and others that can slow it down? What are the costs and benefits of each type of policy?

In this chapter we examine this important issue of economic growth, beginning with some basic concepts and then moving on to explore the costs and benefits of growth. In the remainder of the chapter we consider various theories of economic growth and then go on to examine the idea that there may be *limits to growth* imposed by resource exhaustion and environmental degradation.

26.1 The Nature of Economic Growth

Economic growth is sought after in the rich, developed economies of Canada, France, and Australia as well as in the much poorer, developing countries of Haiti, South Africa, and Vietnam. Governments in all countries view economic growth as an important objective. While the *urgency* for growth is clearly higher in poorer countries than it is in richer ones, the fundamental nature of growth—its causes and consequences—is strikingly similar across all countries. We begin our discussion by examining some Canadian data.

The Centre for the Study of Living Standards is an Ottawa-based research institute that studies the determinants of economic growth. Visit its website at www.csls.ca.

Figure 26-1 shows the paths of three variables in the Canadian economy since 1960, each of which relates to long-run economic growth. Each variable is expressed as an index number, which takes a value of 100 in 1960. The first is real GDP, which shows an overall growth from 1960 to 2011 of 429 percent, an average annual growth rate of 3.3 percent. Though real GDP is an accepted measure of the amount of annual economic activity that passes through markets, it does not tell us about changes in average material living standards because it does not take into account the growth in the population—more income is not necessarily better if more people have to share it. The second variable shown is the index of real *per capita* GDP. It shows an overall growth of 175 percent between 1960 and 2011, an annual average growth rate of 2.0 percent.

As we will see in this chapter, one of the most important reasons that per capita GDP increases over many years is growth in *productivity*. The third variable provides one measure of productivity; it is an index of real GDP *per employed worker*. Its overall

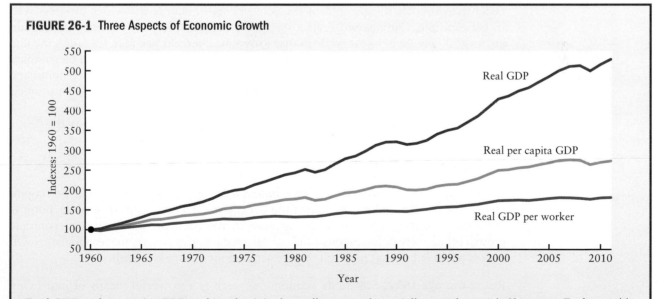

FIGURE 26-1 Three Aspects of Economic Growth

Real GDP, real per capita GDP, and productivity have all grown substantially over the past half-century. Each variable shown is an index number with 1960 = 100. Real GDP has grown faster than real per capita GDP because the population has grown. Real per capita GDP has grown faster than real GDP per worker because the level of employment has grown faster than the population.

(*Source:* All variables are based on author's calculations, using data from Statistics Canada, CANSIM database. Real GDP: Series V1992067. Employment: Series V2091072. Population: Series V2062809.)

TABLE 26-1 The Cumulative Effect of Economic Growth

	Annual Growth Rate				
Year	1%	2%	3%	5%	7%
0	100	100	100	100	100
10	111	122	135	165	201
30	135	182	246	448	817
50	165	272	448	1 218	3 312
70	201	406	817	3 312	13 429
100	272	739	2 009	14 841	109 660

Small differences in income growth rates make enormous differences in levels of income over a few decades. Let income be 100 in year 0. At a growth rate of 3 percent per year, it will be 135 in 10 years, 448 after 50 years, and more than 2000 in a century. Notice the difference between 2 percent and 3 percent growth—even small differences in growth rates make big differences in future income levels.

economic growth Sustained, long-run increases in the level of real GDP.

growth from 1960 to 2011 is 83 percent, an average annual growth rate of 1.2 percent; the average Canadian worker produced 83 percent more in 2011 than in 1960.

The three variables in Figure 26-1 show different aspects of **economic growth**, a term that economists usually reserve for describing sustained or long-run increases in real GDP. This chapter will discuss each of these three aspects of economic growth—real GDP, real per capita GDP, and productivity.

The average annual growth rates shown in Figure 26-1 may seem small, especially those for the measure of productivity. It is important to realize, however, that because these growth rates are sustained for many years, they have a profound influence on material living standards from one generation to the next. Table 26-1 illustrates the cumulative effect of what appear to be very small differences in growth rates.

When thinking about the long-run cumulative effect of annual growth rates, it is useful to know the "rule of 72." For any variable that grows at an annual rate of X percent, that variable will double in approximately 72/X years. [31] For example, if your income grows at 2 percent per year, it will double in 36 years; at an annual rate of 3 percent, it will take only 24 years to double. Another application of the rule of 72 is to determine the *gap* in living standards between countries with different growth rates. If one country grows faster than another, the gap in their respective living standards will widen progressively. If, for example, Canada and France start from the same level of income but Canada grows at 3 percent per year while France grows at 2 percent per year, Canada's income will be twice France's in 72 years. The central lesson from Table 26-1 can be summed up as follows: The longer your time horizon is, the more you should care about the economy's long-run growth rate. Small differences in annual growth rates, if sustained for many years, lead to large differences in income levels.

We now examine in more detail the benefits and costs of economic growth.

Benefits of Economic Growth

Economists typically measure average *material* living standards with real per capita GDP.[1] The benefits of long-run growth in per capita GDP may appear obvious. But it is important to distinguish between the increases in average living standards that economic growth brings more or less automatically and the reduction in poverty that economic growth makes possible but that may still require active policy to make a reality.

Rising Average Living Standards Economic growth is a powerful means of improving average material living standards. The average Canadian family today earns about $70 000 per year before taxes. With 2 percent annual growth in its *real* income, that

---

[1] As we noted in Chapter 20, per capita GDP is a good measure of average *material* living standards because it shows the average person's command over resources. But it is not necessarily a good measure of *well-being*, which is a broader and more subjective measure including such things as income distribution, political and religious freedom, environmental quality, and other things that are not captured by measures of GDP.

same family will earn \$85 300 (in constant dollars) in ten years' time, an increase in its purchasing power of almost 22 percent. If the annual growth rate is instead 3 percent, its income will rise to \$94 100 in ten years, an increase of over 34 percent.

A family often finds that an increase in its income can lead to changes in the pattern of its consumption—extra money buys important amenities of life and also allows more saving for the future. Similarly, economic growth that raises average income tends to change the whole society's consumption patterns, shifting away from tangible goods such as TVs and furniture and cars and toward services such as vacations, restaurant meals, and financial services. In Canada and other rich, developed countries, services account for roughly 70 percent of aggregate consumption, whereas this ratio is significantly lower in poorer, developing countries.

Another example of how economic growth can improve living standards involves environmental protection. In developing countries, most resources are devoted to providing basic requirements of life, such as food, shelter, and clothing. These countries typically do not have the "luxury" of being concerned about environmental degradation. Some people in richer societies may consider this a short-sighted view, but the fact is that the concerns associated with hunger *today* are much more urgent than the concerns associated with *future* environmental problems. In contrast, richer countries are wealthy enough that they can more easily afford to provide the basic requirements of life *and* devote significant resources to environmental protection. Economic growth provides the higher incomes that often lead to a demand for a cleaner environment, thus leading to higher average living standards that are not directly captured by measures of per capita GDP.

One recent example of this phenomenon can be seen in China, whose government paid almost no attention to environmental protection when the country was very poor. As average income in China has risen in the past 30 years, where it is now well above a subsistence level, concern within China has been growing over the extent of environmental degradation, which in some cases is causing serious human health problems. The Chinese government has been responding with policies to address some of these concerns, and will likely do much more as Chinese prosperity continues to rise.

Addressing Poverty and Income Inequality Not everyone benefits equally from economic growth, and some may not benefit at all. Many of the poorest members of the population are not in the labour force and do not receive the higher wages and profits that are the primary means by which the gains from growth are distributed. Others, although they *are* in the labour force, may experience wage gains that are far smaller than the average.

In recent years, growing attention has been paid to the fact that the majority of aggregate income growth in many countries, including Canada, has been accruing to the top earners in the income distribution. The result is that, while average per capita incomes have been rising (as shown in Figure 26-1), there has also been a rise in income inequality and also a relative stagnation of incomes for those at or below the middle of the income distribution. Both poverty and income inequality are important challenges for public policy.

A rapid growth rate makes the alleviation of poverty and the reduction of income inequality easier to achieve politically. If existing income is to be redistributed through the government's tax or spending policies, someone's standard of living will actually have to be lowered. However, when there is economic growth and when some of the *increment* in income is redistributed (through active government policy), it is possible to reduce income inequalities while simultaneously allowing all incomes to rise. It is much easier for a rapidly growing economy to be generous toward its less fortunate citizens—or neighbours—than it is for a static economy.

Costs of Economic Growth

Economic growth comes with real costs, some of which may be more obvious than others. For example, the simple act of producing goods and services necessarily uses resources and causes environmental damage. While these effects may be very small for some products, for others they are significant. As a logical matter, we cannot deny that economic production has negative consequences. Indeed, many of those who advocate *against* continued economic growth do so on the grounds that it depletes our natural resources and leads to environmental degradation.

This debate is important, and continues to gain prominence among academic and government economists. *Applying Economic Concepts 26-1* presents a case against continued economic growth, especially in the developed countries. We take up some of these ideas in this chapter's final section where we examine the extent to which there are *limits to growth*. Here, we address two other costs associated with economic growth: the cost of forgone consumption, and the social costs of the disruption that typically accompanies growth.

APPLYING ECONOMIC CONCEPTS 26-1

A Case Against Economic Growth

Economists have long recognized that economic growth comes with real costs. In recent years, however, many economists have been arguing that the benefits of further growth are outweighed by the costs now being imposed on the earth and its inhabitants. While these arguments are not the mainstream view within the profession, they are increasingly receiving serious attention. This box presents some of their main arguments against continued economic growth.[*]

Growth Is Not Sustainable

There is overwhelming evidence that the effects on the biosphere of the world's growing economies and population are not sustainable over the long term. Expanding production and consumption of goods and services is causing biodiversity losses, land degradation, scarcities of fresh water, ocean acidification, climate change, and the disruption of the earth's nutrient cycles. This environmental damage will eventually reduce our capacity to continue producing and consuming at current rates.

In addition, the low-cost supplies of fossil fuels on which economic growth has depended for over a century are rapidly being depleted. As supplies diminish, there is a need to introduce new technologies to obtain resources from less accessible locations. Extraction of oil sands, hydraulic fracturing for natural gas, and deep-sea drilling for oil and gas are examples of new technologies that

bring increased environmental impact and risks. This extraction of less accessible and higher-cost fossil fuels highlights the conflict between the need for new supplies of resources to sustain economic growth and the need to reduce our overall burden on the environment.

The ongoing degradation of the planet in pursuit of economic growth also runs counter to the interests of other species that inhabit Earth. Mainstream economics is not well equipped to address this important ethical issue, but it should not be ignored.

Growth May Not Increase Overall Well-Being

Quite apart from whether current growth rates are sustainable, the benefits from continued growth, especially in developed countries, are questionable. Economists have long understood that GDP is a reasonable measure of the level of economic activity and income but that it is not an accurate measure of overall *well-being*. Other measures that include a range of environmental and social factors suggest that income growth in the developed economies is no longer closely related

---

[*]The author thanks Peter Victor for providing material on which this box is based. For a thorough discussion of the case against economic growth, see Peter Victor, *Managing Without Growth: Slower by Design,* Edward Elgar, 2008.

Forgone Consumption In a world of scarcity, almost nothing is free, including economic growth. As we will soon see, increases in real per capita GDP typically result from investment in capital goods, as well as in such activities as education and scientific research. Often these investments yield no immediate return in terms of goods and services for consumption; thus, they imply that sacrifices are being made by the current generation of consumers.

Economic growth, which promises more goods and services tomorrow, is achieved by consuming fewer goods today. This sacrifice of current consumption is an important cost of growth.

For example, suppose an economy's annual growth rate could be permanently increased by 1 percentage point if investment as a share of GDP increased permanently by 4 percentage points (and consumption's share fell by 4 percentage points). If such a reallocation of resources were made, consumption would be lower for several years along the new growth path, and the payoff from faster growth—higher future consumption—would not occur for several years. Lower consumption now and in the near future would be the cost of obtaining higher consumption in the more distant future.

with greater well-being. People typically attach far more significance to their income in relation to others' incomes than to its absolute level, and it is simply not possible for economic growth to raise everyone's relative income.

In addition, the growing evidence on income and wealth inequality in the developed economies suggests that over the past few decades the lion's share of total income growth has been captured by the highest income earners. The resulting increase in income and wealth inequality has actually led to rising discontent among large parts of the population. So growth in national income, given its current distribution, may actually be causing a reduction rather than an increase in overall well-being.

The Weakness of the Technological Defence

Economists who argue in favour of further economic growth typically note the possibility of increasing GDP even while reducing resource use and environmental damage. They argue that by producing and consuming fewer goods and more services, employing more efficient and improved technologies, and more compact forms of land use, economic growth can continue indefinitely.

Those who argue against further growth see a serious problem with this argument. While it is true that the amount of resources used per dollar of GDP continues to shrink gradually in the developed countries, it is also

true that the absolute resource use and absolute environmental damage continue to grow.

Looking to the future, if the world economy grows at a rate of 3 percent per year, after a century the economy will have increased in size by nearly 20 times. To prevent any absolute increase in resource and energy use would require an ambitious twenty-fold improvement in resource and environmental efficiency—a far greater improvement than we have witnessed over the past century.

So the belief that ongoing technological improvement can be consistent with continued economic growth and a reduced impact on Earth's resources and environment is a belief that must be based on extreme—and probably unrealistic—optimism.

Not So Gloomy

These economists are quick to emphasize that their message is not so gloomy. The good news is that further economic growth in the developed economies isn't necessary for continued prosperity. The benefits of ongoing productivity growth can be taken in the form of reduced work and production, and also by directing effort at reducing our absolute resource use and environmental damage. Making these adjustments will surely require a significant change in most peoples' way of thinking, but there is no reason why they can't be made. Prosperity can continue without economic growth.

Social Costs A growing economy is also a changing economy. Part of growth is accounted for by existing firms expanding and producing more output, hiring more workers, and using more equipment and intermediate goods. But another aspect of growth is that existing firms are overtaken and made obsolete by new firms, old products are made obsolete by new products, and existing skills are made obsolete by new skills.

> **The process of economic growth renders some machines obsolete and also leaves the skills of some workers obsolete.**

No matter how well trained workers are at age 25, in another 25 years many will find that their skills are at least partly obsolete. A high growth rate usually requires rapid adjustments in the labour force, which can cause much upset and misery to some of the people affected by it.

It is often argued that costs of this kind are a small price to pay for the great benefits that growth can bring. Even if this is true in the aggregate, these personal costs are borne very unevenly. Indeed, many of the people for whom growth is most costly (in terms of lost jobs or lowered incomes) share least in the fruits that growth brings.

Sources of Economic Growth

Four major determinants of growth are

1. *Growth in the labour force.* Growth in population or increases in the fraction of the population that chooses to participate in the labour force cause the labour force to grow.

2. *Growth in human capital.* **Human capital** is the term economists use to refer to the set of skills that workers have; it can increase either through formal education or on-the-job training. Human capital can be thought of as the *quality* of the labour force.

3. *Growth in physical capital.* The stock of physical capital (such as factories, machines, electronic equipment, and transportation and communications facilities) grows only through the process of investment. We include here improvements in the *quality* of the physical capital.

4. *Technological improvement.* This is brought about by innovation that introduces new products, new ways of producing existing products, and new forms of organizing economic activity.

The various theories of economic growth that we explore next emphasize these different sources of economic growth. For example, some theories emphasize the role of increases in physical capital in explaining growth; others emphasize the role of increases in human capital; and still others emphasize the importance of technological improvements.

human capital The set of skills workers acquire through formal education and on-the-job training.

| 26.2 Established Theories of Economic Growth

In this section we discuss some of the theories of economic growth that have been used by economists for many years. These long-established theories remain relevant because they contain important insights about the growth process. Learning them provides a basis for examining the more recent theories in the next section. We begin by studying the relationship among saving, investment, and economic growth. We then examine the precise predictions of what economists call the Neoclassical growth theory. For simplicity, we assume that the economy is closed—there is no trade in goods, services, or assets with the rest of the world.

A Long-Run Analysis

Though our discussion of economic growth will focus on the long-run behaviour of the economy, we can use some of the insights we developed in the short-run version of our macro model. Think back to Chapter 21 when we were building the simplest short-run macro model (with no government or foreign trade). The equilibrium level of real GDP in that model was such that real GDP equals desired consumption plus desired investment:

$$Y = C + I$$

We can rearrange this equilibrium condition to get

$$Y - C = I$$

or

$$S = I$$

which says that at the equilibrium level of real GDP, desired saving equals desired investment. This is just an alternative way to think about exactly the same equilibrium.

Recall also that in Chapter 21 we took the real interest rate as given, or *exogenous*. Taking the interest rate (and several other variables) as exogenous, we then determined the equilibrium level of real GDP. We will now extend that same model to help us consider the long-run behaviour of the economy by making the interest rate an *endogenous* variable—that is, a variable whose value is explained within the model. Fortunately, the equilibrium condition from the simple short-run model also applies in its long-run version. In the long run, with real GDP equal to Y^*, we can use the saving/investment equilibrium condition by turning it "on its head." To do so, we make two assumptions. First, we assume that real GDP is equal to Y^*, which means that all factor-price adjustments discussed in Chapter 24 are complete. Second, we assume that Y^* is constant during the period under consideration (although in reality it is gradually changing through time). With these two assumptions, we take Y^* as given and use the condition that desired saving equals desired investment to determine the equilibrium real interest rate.

In the short-run macro model, real GDP varies to determine equilibrium, in which desired saving equals desired investment. In the model's long-run version, real GDP is equal to Y^* and the interest rate varies to determine equilibrium.

This long-run perspective of our model will tell us a great deal about the relationship among saving, investment, and economic growth—and the interest rate will play an important role.

A Theory of Investment, Saving, and Growth

We now complicate our model slightly by adding a government sector that purchases goods and services (G) and collects taxes net of transfers (T). National saving is the sum of private saving and public (government) saving. Desired private saving is the difference between disposable income and desired consumption. With real GDP equal to Y^* in the long run, desired private saving is equal to

$$\text{Private saving} = Y^* - T - C$$

Public saving is equal to the combined budget surpluses of the federal, provincial, and municipal governments:

$$\text{Public saving} = T - G$$

National saving is therefore equal to

$$\text{National saving} = NS = (Y^* - T - C) + (T - G)$$
$$\Rightarrow NS = Y^* - C - G$$

For a given level of real GDP in the long run (Y^*), an increase in household consumption or government purchases must imply a reduction in national saving.[2]

Figure 26-2 shows the supply of national saving as a function of the real interest rate. The horizontal axis measures the quantity of national saving, measured in dollars. The real interest rate is shown on the vertical axis. The national saving (NS) curve is upward sloping because, as we first saw in Chapter 21, an increase in the interest rate is assumed to lead households to reduce their current consumption, especially on big-ticket items and durable goods, such as cars, furniture, and appliances, that are often purchased on credit. Note also that the NS curve is quite steep, in keeping with empirical evidence suggesting that household consumption responds only modestly to changes in the real interest rate.

Figure 26-2 also shows a downward-sloping investment demand curve, I. As we first saw in Chapter 21, all components of desired investment (plant and equipment, inventories, and residential investment) are negatively related to the real interest rate because, whether the investment is financed by borrowing or by using the firm's retained earnings, the real interest rate reflects the opportunity cost of using these funds.

The supply curve for national saving (NS) and the investment demand curve (I) make up the economy's market for financial capital. The NS curve shows the

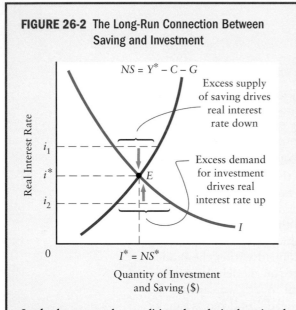

FIGURE 26-2 The Long-Run Connection Between Saving and Investment

In the long run, the condition that desired national saving equals desired investment determines the equilibrium real interest rate. Investment demand by firms is negatively related to the real interest rate. The supply of national (private plus public) saving is positively related to the real interest rate, since increases in the interest rate lead to a decline in desired consumption (C). Since the analysis applies to the long run, we have assumed that real GDP is equal to Y^*. In the long run, the equilibrium real interest rate is i^*. At this real interest rate, the amount of investment is I^*, which equals the amount of national saving, NS^*.

---

[2] It appears in our NS equation that changes in taxes have no effect on the level of national saving, but this is misleading. Changes in T may affect national saving through an *indirect* effect on C. For example, as we saw at the end of Chapter 24, a reduction in taxes is likely to lead to an increase in consumption spending and therefore to a reduction in national saving (for given values of Y^* and G).

supply of financial capital that comes from households and governments. The I curve shows the demand for financial capital derived from firms' desired investment in plant, equipment, and residential construction. The interest rate that clears this market for financial capital determines the amount of investment and saving that occur in the economy's long-run equilibrium, when real GDP is equal to Y^*.[3]

With Figure 26-2 in place, our long-run model of saving and investment is complete. In the short-run model in Chapter 21, the economy is in equilibrium when desired saving equals desired investment. We have now modified that setting in two ways. First, we have added government. Second, because we are holding real GDP constant at Y^*, we let the condition that desired saving equals desired investment determine the equilibrium real interest rate.

> In the long-run version of our macro model, with real GDP equal to Y^*, the equilibrium interest rate is determined where desired national saving equals desired investment.

In Figure 26-2, equilibrium occurs at interest rate i^* where $NS = I$. Imagine what would happen if the real interest rate were above i^* at i_1. At this high interest rate, the amount of desired saving exceeds the amount of desired investment, and this excess supply of financial capital pushes down the price of credit—the real interest rate. Conversely, if the interest rate is below i^* at i_2, the quantity of desired investment exceeds the quantity of desired saving, and this excess demand for financial capital pushes up the real interest rate. Only at point E is the economy in equilibrium, with the real interest rate equal to i^* and desired investment equal to desired saving.

Let's now see how changes in the supply of saving or investment demand lead to changes in the real interest rate and what these changes imply for the economy's long-run economic growth.

An Increase in the Supply of National Saving Suppose the supply of national saving increases, so that the NS curve shifts to the right, as shown in part (i) of Figure 26-3. This increase in the supply of national saving could happen either because household consumption (C) falls or because government purchases (G) fall (or because T rises, which reduces C). A decline in either C or G means that national saving rises at any real interest rate, and so the NS curve shifts to the right.

The increase in the supply of national saving leads to an excess supply of financial capital and thus to a decline in the real interest rate. As the interest rate falls, firms decide to undertake more investment projects and the economy moves from the initial equilibrium E_0 to the new equilibrium E_1. At the new equilibrium, more of the economy's resources are devoted to investment than before, and thus the country's stock of physical capital is rising at a faster rate. The higher rate of investment therefore leads to a higher future growth rate of potential output.

> In the long run, an increase in the supply of national saving reduces the real interest rate and encourages more investment. The higher rate of investment leads to a higher future growth rate of potential output.

---

[3] In Chapters 28 and 29, when we introduce money, banking, and monetary policy, we will see that in the short run, when Y can differ from Y^*, the interest rate is heavily influenced by the policies of the Bank of Canada. In the long-run version of our model, however, this influence is assumed to be negligible.

FIGURE 26-3 Increases in Investment Demand and the Supply of National Saving

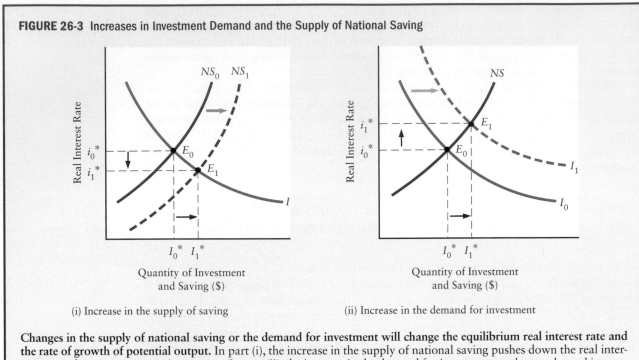

(i) Increase in the supply of saving   (ii) Increase in the demand for investment

Changes in the supply of national saving or the demand for investment will change the equilibrium real interest rate and the rate of growth of potential output. In part (i), the increase in the supply of national saving pushes down the real interest rate and encourages more investment. In part (ii), the increase in the demand for investment pushes up the real interest rate and encourages more saving. In both cases, there is an increase in the equilibrium amount of investment (and saving) and the economy moves from E_0 to E_1; this higher rate of capital accumulation leads to an increase in the economy's long-run rate of growth.

An Increase in Investment Demand Now suppose firms' demand for investment increases so that the I curve shifts to the right, as shown in part (ii) of Figure 26-3. The increase in desired investment might be caused by technological improvements that increase the productivity of investment goods or by a government tax incentive aimed at encouraging investment. Whatever its cause, the increase in investment demand creates an excess demand for financial capital and therefore leads to a rise in the real interest rate. The rise in the interest rate encourages households to reduce their current consumption and increase their desired saving. At the new equilibrium, E_1, both the real interest rate and the amount of investment are higher than at the initial equilibrium. The greater investment means faster growth in the economy's capital stock and therefore a higher future rate of growth of potential output.

> In the long run, an increase in the demand for investment pushes up the real interest rate and encourages more saving by households. The higher rate of saving (and investment) leads to a higher future growth rate of potential output.

Summary In our macro model, which we have now extended to enable us to determine the real interest rate in long-run equilibrium, there is a close relationship among saving, investment, and the rate of economic growth. We can see this relationship most clearly when studying the market for financial capital. Let's summarize our results.

1. In long-run equilibrium, with $Y = Y^*$, the condition that desired national saving equals desired investment determines the equilibrium interest rate in the market for financial capital. This equilibrium also determines the economy's flows of investment and saving.

2. An increase in the supply of national saving will lead to a fall in the real interest rate and thus to an increase in the amount of investment. This is a shift of the *NS* curve and a movement along the *I* curve.

3. An increase in the demand for investment will lead to a rise in the real interest rate and thus to an increase in the amount of national saving. This is a shift of the *I* curve and a movement along the *NS* curve.

4. A shift in either the *NS* or the *I* curve will lead to a change in the equilibrium real interest rate and thus to a change in the amount of the economy's resources devoted to investment. An increase in the equilibrium amount of investment implies a greater growth rate of the capital stock and thus a higher future growth rate of potential output.

Investment and Growth in Industrialized Countries Our model predicts that countries with high rates of investment are also countries with high rates of real GDP growth. To provide evidence in support of this prediction, Figure 26-4 shows data from the most industrialized countries between 1950 and 2009. Each point in the figure corresponds to a single country and shows that country's annual average investment rate (as a percentage of GDP) plotted against the annual average growth rate in real per capita GDP. What is clear from the figure is a positive relationship between investment rates and growth rates, as predicted by our model.

Neoclassical Growth Theory

Recall the four sources of economic growth that we discussed at the beginning of this section. Much of the *Neoclassical growth theory* is based on the idea that these four forces of economic growth can be connected by what is called the **aggregate production function**. This is an expression for the relationship between the total amounts of labour (L) and physical capital (K) employed, the quality of labour's human capital (H), the state of technology (T), and the nation's total level of output (GDP). The aggregate production function can be expressed as

aggregate production function The relationship between the total amount of each factor of production employed in the nation and the nation's total GDP.

$$\text{GDP} = F_T(L, K, H)$$

It is an *aggregate* production function because it relates the economy's *total* output to the *total* amount of the factors that are used to produce that output.[4] (Those who have studied microeconomics will recall that a micro production function, such as is discussed in Chapters 7 and 8, relates the output of *one firm* to the factors of production employed by *that firm*.)

The production function above—indicated by F_T—tells us how much GDP will be produced for given amounts of labour and physical capital employed, given levels of human capital, and a given state of technology. Using the notation F_T is a simple way of indicating that the function relating L, K, and H to GDP depends on the state of

---

[4] Natural resources (including land, forests, mineral deposits, etc.) are also important inputs to the production process. We leave them out of this discussion only for simplicity.

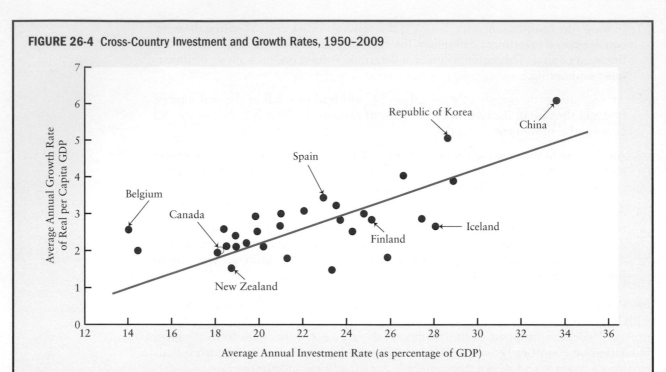

FIGURE 26-4 Cross-Country Investment and Growth Rates, 1950–2009

There is a positive relationship between a country's investment rate (as a percentage of GDP) and its growth rate of real per capita GDP. For each of the countries, the annual averages for investment rates and per capita GDP growth rates are computed between 1950 and 2009. Each point represents the average values of these variables for a single country over this 59-year period. The straight line is the "line of best fit" between the growth rates and the investment rates. Countries with high investment rates tend to be countries with high rates of economic growth.

(*Source:* Based on author's calculations by using data from the Penn World Tables 7.0. The data for Greece starts in 1951, China in 1952, South Korea in 1953, Romania in 1960, and Germany, Hungary, and Poland in 1970. Alan Heston, Robert Summers, and Bettina Aten, Penn World Table Version 7.0, Center for International Comparisons of Production, Income and Prices at the University of Pennsylvania, September 2011.)

technology. For a given state of technology (*T*), changes in either *L*, *K*, or *H* will lead to changes in GDP. Similarly, for given values of *L*, *K*, and *H*, changes in *T* will lead to changes in GDP. [32]

Recall that we are assuming throughout this chapter that real GDP is equal to *Y** because we are examining the economy's long-run behaviour. Let's now examine the properties of the aggregate production function and the predictions that follow.

Properties of the Aggregate Production Function The key assumptions of the Neoclassical theory are that the aggregate production function displays diminishing marginal returns when any one of the factors is increased on its own and constant returns to scale when all factors are increased together (and in the same proportion). To explain the meaning of these concepts more clearly, we will assume for simplicity that human capital and physical capital can be combined into a single variable called capital and that technology is held constant; this allows us to focus on the effects of changes in *K* and *L*.

1. Diminishing Marginal Returns. To begin, suppose that the labour force grows while the stock of capital remains constant. More and more people go to work using a fixed quantity of capital. The amount that each new worker adds to total output is called labour's *marginal product*. The **law of diminishing marginal returns** tells us that the employment of additional workers (or hours of work) will eventually add less to total output than the previous worker did. A simple production function is shown in Figure 26-5 and the law of diminishing marginal returns is illustrated.

> **law of diminishing marginal returns** The hypothesis that if increasing quantities of a variable factor are applied to a given quantity of fixed factors, the marginal product of the variable factor will eventually decrease.

The law of diminishing returns applies to any factor that is varied while the other factors are held constant. Hence, successive amounts of capital added to a fixed supply of labour will also eventually add less and less to GDP.

FIGURE 26-5 The Aggregate Production Function and Diminishing Marginal Returns

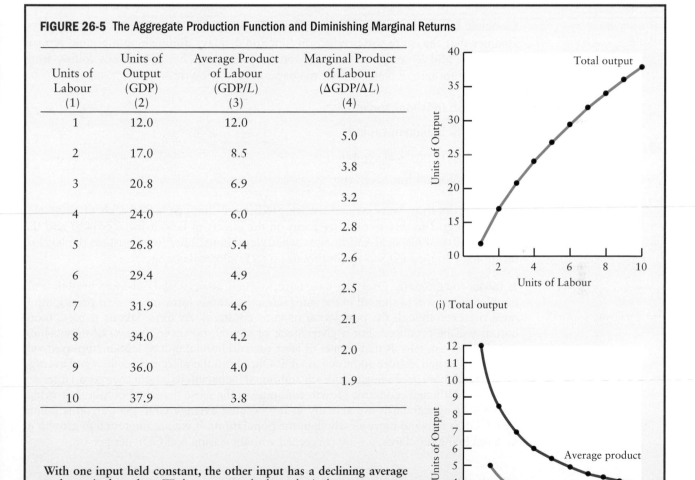

Units of Labour (1)	Units of Output (GDP) (2)	Average Product of Labour (GDP/L) (3)	Marginal Product of Labour (ΔGDP/ΔL) (4)
1	12.0	12.0	
			5.0
2	17.0	8.5	
			3.8
3	20.8	6.9	
			3.2
4	24.0	6.0	
			2.8
5	26.8	5.4	
			2.6
6	29.4	4.9	
			2.5
7	31.9	4.6	
			2.1
8	34.0	4.2	
			2.0
9	36.0	4.0	
			1.9
10	37.9	3.8	

(i) Total output

(ii) Marginal and average product of labour

With one input held constant, the other input has a declining average and marginal product. We have assumed a hypothetical aggregate production function given by GDP = $4\sqrt{KL}$; we have also assumed that K is constant and equal to 9. Column 2 shows total output as more of the variable factor, labour, is used with a fixed amount of capital. Total output is plotted in part (i) of the figure. Both the average product of labour and the marginal product of labour decline continuously. They are plotted in part (ii) of the figure.

According to the law of diminishing marginal returns, whenever equal increases of one factor of production are combined with a fixed amount of another factor, the *increment* to total production will eventually decline.

constant returns to scale A situation in which output increases in proportion to the change in all inputs as the scale of production is increased.

2. Constant Returns to Scale. The other main assumption concerning the Neoclassical aggregate production function is that it displays **constant returns to scale**. Remember that we are assuming for simplicity that labour and capital are the only two inputs. With constant returns to scale, if L and K both change in an equal proportion, total output will change by that same proportion. For example, if L and K both increase by 10 percent, GDP will also increase by 10 percent. [33]

Economic Growth in the Neoclassical Model To recap: The Neoclassical growth theory assumes that the aggregate production function displays diminishing marginal returns (in both L and K) and also constant returns to scale. What predictions follow from these assumptions? Recall the four major sources of growth:

1. Growth in labour force

2. Growth in human capital

3. Growth in physical capital

4. Technological improvement

What does the Neoclassical theory predict will happen when each of these elements changes? In this section, we focus on the effects of labour-force growth and the accumulation of physical and human capital (combined), holding constant the level of technology. In the next section, we focus on technological change.

1. Labour-Force Growth. Over the long term, we can associate labour-force growth with population growth (although in the short term, the labour force can grow if participation rates rise even though the population remains constant). As more labour is used, more output will be produced. For a given stock of capital, however, the law of diminishing marginal returns tells us that sooner or later, each additional unit of labour employed will cause smaller and smaller additions to GDP. Once both the marginal product and average product of labour are falling (with each additional increment to labour), we get an interesting result. Although economic growth continues in the sense that total output is growing, material living standards are actually *falling* because average GDP *per person* is falling (real GDP is growing more slowly than the population). If we are interested in growth in material living standards, we are concerned with increasing real GDP per person.

In the Neoclassical growth model with diminishing marginal returns, increases in population (with a fixed stock of capital) lead to increases in GDP but an eventual decline in material living standards.

2. Physical and Human Capital Accumulation. Consider the accumulation of both physical and human capital. Growth in physical capital occurs whenever there is positive (net) investment in the economy. For example, if Canadian firms produce $300 billion of capital goods this year, and only $40 billion is for the replacement of old, worn-out equipment, then Canada's capital stock increases by $260 billion.

How does human capital accumulate? Human capital has several aspects. One involves improvements in the health and longevity of the population. Of course, these are desired as ends in themselves, but they also have consequences for both the size and the productivity of the labour force. There is no doubt that improvements in the health of workers tend to increase productivity per worker-hour by cutting down on illness, accidents, and absenteeism. A second aspect of human capital concerns specific training and education—from learning to operate a machine or software program to learning how to be a scientist. Sometimes this increase in human capital occurs through on-the-job training; sometimes it occurs through formal educational programs. Advances in knowledge allow us not only to build more productive physical capital but also to create more effective human capital. Also, the longer a person has been educated, the more adaptable and, hence, the more productive in the long run that person is in the face of new and changing challenges.

Increases in the amount and quality of physical capital lead to improvements in the productivity of labour. These productivity improvements raise material living standards, as measured by real per capita GDP.

The accumulation of capital—either physical or human—affects GDP in a manner similar to population growth. The law of diminishing marginal returns implies that, eventually, each successive unit of capital will add less to total output than each previous unit of capital.

There is, however, a major contrast with the case of labour-force growth because it is output *per person* that determines material living standards, not output per unit of capital. Thus, for a constant population, increases in the stock of physical or human capital *always* lead to increases in living standards because output *per person* increases. However, because the increases in capital are subject to diminishing marginal returns, successive additions to the economy's capital stock bring smaller and smaller increases in per capita output.

> In the Neoclassical model, capital accumulation leads to improvements in material living standards, but because of the law of diminishing marginal returns, these improvements become smaller with each additional increment of capital.

3. Balanced Growth with Constant Technology. Now consider what happens if labour and capital (both human and physical capital) grow at the same rate. This is what economists call "balanced" growth. In this case, the Neoclassical assumption of constant returns to scale means that GDP grows in proportion to the increases in inputs. For example, if capital and labour both increase by 2 percent per year, then GDP also increases by 2 percent per year. As a result, per capita output (GDP/L) remains constant. Thus, balanced growth in labour and capital leads to growth in total GDP but unchanged per capita GDP.

This balanced growth is not, however, the kind of growth that concerns people interested in explaining rising material living standards. Since increases in living standards are determined by *increases* in per capita output, it is clear that balanced growth is unable to explain *rising* living standards.

> If capital and labour grow at the same rate, GDP will increase. But in the Neoclassical growth model with constant returns to scale, such balanced growth will not lead to increases in per capita output and therefore will not generate improvements in material living standards.

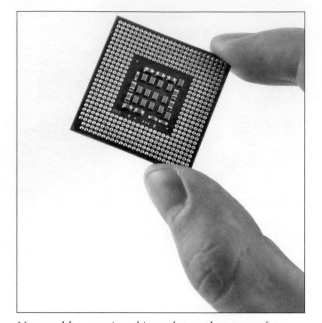

New and better microchips enhance the range of capabilities of countless types of physical capital. But such improvements in technology are embodied in the capital stock, making it difficult to estimate the change in technology independently from the change in the capital stock.

The Neoclassical growth theory predicts that growth in the labour force alone leads to declining per capita income, while capital accumulation alone leads to positive but ever-diminishing growth rates of per capita income. Increases in labour and capital together cause an increase in real GDP but leave per capita income unchanged. What we observe in many countries around the world, however, is sustained growth in real per capita incomes. How does the Neoclassical theory explain this observation, if not through growth in labour or capital? The answer is technological change, to which we now turn.

The Importance of Technological Change In Neoclassical growth theory, technological change is assumed to be exogenous—that is, it is not explained by the theory itself. This is an important weakness of the theory because it means that the theory is unable to explain what is undoubtedly the most important determinant of long-run improvements in living standards. For now we focus on the importance of technological change itself and on how it might be measured. In the next section we move beyond Neoclassical growth theory and see some more modern theories designed to explain the sources of technological change.

New knowledge and inventions can contribute markedly to the growth of potential output, even without capital accumulation or labour-force growth. To illustrate this point, suppose the proportion of a society's resources devoted to the production of capital goods is just sufficient to replace capital as it wears out. If the old capital is merely replaced in the same form, the capital stock will be constant, and there will be no increase in the capacity to produce. However, if there is a growth of knowledge so that as old equipment wears out it is replaced by more productive equipment, then productive capacity will be growing.

embodied technical change
Technical change that is intrinsic to the particular capital goods in use.

The increase in productive capacity created by installing new and better capital goods is called **embodied technical change**. This term reflects the idea that technological improvements are contained in the new capital goods. Thus, even if the *quantity* of capital may be unchanged, improvements in its *quality* lead to increases in the economy's productive capacity. Embodied technical change has been enormously important through history and continues to be important today. Consider how the invention of propeller and then jet airplanes has revolutionized transportation over the past 50 years, or how the invention of the electronic computer and satellite transmission has revolutionized communications over an even shorter period. Indeed, once you start thinking about embodied technical change, you see many examples of it around you on a daily basis.

Less obvious but nonetheless important are technical changes that are embodied in *human* capital. These are changes that result from a better-educated, more experienced labour force; better management practices and techniques; improved design, marketing, and organization of business activities; and feedback from user experience leading to product improvement.

> **Many innovations are embodied in either physical or human capital. These innovations cause continual changes in the techniques of production and in the nature of what is produced. Embodied technical change leads to increases in potential output even if the amounts of labour and capital are held constant.**

We have been discussing the benefits of technological change in terms of raising overall living standards. Ever since the Industrial Revolution, however, some workers have feared the effects of technological change. After all, changes in technology are often responsible for workers losing their jobs as employers replace less efficient labour with more efficient equipment. *Lessons from History 26-1* examines the relationship between technological progress and changes in employment.

LESSONS FROM HISTORY 26-1

Should Workers Be Afraid of Technological Change?

For centuries people have observed that technological change destroys particular jobs and have worried that it will destroy jobs in general. Should they worry?

Technological change *does* destroy particular jobs. When water wheels were used to automate the production of cloth in twelfth-century Europe, there were riots and protests among the workers who lost their jobs. A century ago, 50 percent of the labour force in North America and Europe was required to produce the required food. Today, less than 5 percent of the labour force is needed in the high-income countries to feed all their citizens. In other words, out of every 100 jobs that existed in 1900, 50 were in agriculture and 45 of those were destroyed by technological progress over the course of the twentieth century.

Individual workers are therefore right to fear that technological changes may destroy particular jobs. This process of job destruction has been going on for centuries and will undoubtedly continue in the future. Those individuals who cannot retrain for jobs in other industries or regions may suffer reduced wages or employment prospects. This concern is especially acute for older workers who may find retraining difficult or who may find it difficult to convince potential new employers to hire them.

What about the overall level of employment? Do workers need to worry that technological changes will cause widespread unemployment? Just as technological change destroys some jobs, it also creates many new jobs. The displaced agricultural workers did not join the ranks of the permanently unemployed—although some of the older ones may have, their children did not. Instead they, and their children, took jobs in the expanding manufacturing and service industries and helped to produce the mass of new goods and services—such as automobiles,

refrigerators, computers, and foreign travel—that have raised living standards over the century.

Worries that technological change will cause general unemployment have been recorded for centuries, but, so far at least, there is no sign that those displaced by technological change (or their children) are being forced into the ranks of the permanently unemployed. Over all of recorded history, technological change has created more jobs than it has destroyed.

How about today? Aren't there good reasons to be more afraid of technological change now than in the past? Modern technologies have two aspects that worry some observers. First, they tend to be *knowledge intensive*. A fairly high degree of literacy and numeracy, as well as familiarity with computers, is needed to work with many of these new technologies. Second, through the process of globalization, unskilled workers in advanced countries have come into competition with unskilled workers everywhere in the world. Both of these forces are decreasing the relative demand for unskilled workers in developed countries and have led to falling relative wages for unskilled workers in countries like Canada. If labour markets are insufficiently flexible, this change in relative demand may also lead to some structural unemployment.

For these reasons, some people blame the high unemployment rates in Europe (and to a lesser extent, in Canada) on the new technologies. This is hard to reconcile, however, with the fact that the lowest unemployment rates in the industrialized countries have (until very recently) been recorded in the United States, the most technologically dynamic of all countries. This suggests that the cause of high European unemployment rates may be not enough technological change and too much inflexibility in labour markets rather than too much technological change.

Can We Measure Technological Change? Technological change is obviously important. You need only look around you at the current products and production methods that did not exist a generation ago, or even a few years ago, to realize how the advance of technology changes our lives. But *how much* does technology change? Unfortunately, technology is not something that is easily measured and so it is very difficult to know just how important it is to the process of economic growth.

In 1957, Robert Solow, an economist at MIT who was awarded the Nobel Prize 30 years later for his research on economic growth, attempted to measure the amount of technical change in the United States. He devised a way to infer from the data (under some assumptions about the aggregate production function) how much of the observed growth in real GDP was due to the growth in labour and capital and how much was due to technical change. His method led to the creation of what is now called the "Solow residual." The Solow residual is the amount of growth in GDP that cannot be accounted for by growth in the labour force or by growth in the capital stock. Since Solow was thinking about changes in GDP as having only three possible sources—changes in capital, changes in labour, and changes in technology—the "residual" was naturally interpreted as a measure of technical change.

Today, economists do not view the Solow residual as a precise estimate of the amount of technical change. One reason is that much technical change is known to be embodied in new physical and human capital, as we discussed earlier. Thus, capital accumulation and technological change are inherently connected. For example, imagine a firm that adds to its stock of capital by purchasing two new computers. These new computers embody the latest technology and are more productive than the firm's existing computers. In this case, there has been an increase in the capital stock but there has also been an increase—though not easily measured—in the level of technology. Solow's method would attribute much of the change in (embodied) technology to the change in the capital stock, even though we know that a technological change has also taken place. Thus, in the presence of embodied technical change that gets measured as increases in capital, the Solow residual is, at best, an underestimate of the true amount of technological change.

Despite these problems, the Solow residual is still used by many economists in universities and government, and it often goes by another name—the rate of growth of *total factor productivity* (TFP).

26.3 Newer Growth Theories

Some newer theories of economic growth go beyond the Neoclassical theory. Economic growth is an active area of research in which there is considerable debate over whether new theories are necessary, or whether the established theories do an adequate job of explaining the process of long-term economic growth.

In this section, we give a brief discussion of two strands of this new research—models that emphasize *endogenous technological change* and models based on *increasing marginal returns*.

Endogenous Technological Change

In Neoclassical growth theory, innovation increases the amount of output producible from a given level of factor inputs. But this innovation is itself unexplained. The Neoclassical model thus views technological change as *exogenous*. It has profound effects on economic variables but it is not itself influenced by economic causes. It just happens.

Yet research by many scholars has established that technological change is responsive to such economic signals as prices and profits; in other words, it is *endogenous* to the economic system. Though much of the earliest work on this issue was done in Europe, the most influential overall single study was by an American, Nathan Rosenberg, whose trailblazing 1982 book *Inside the Black Box: Technology and Economics* argued this case in great detail.

Technological change stems from research and development and from innovating activities that put the results of R&D into practice. These are costly and highly risky activities, undertaken largely by firms and usually in pursuit of profit. It is not surprising, therefore, that these activities respond to economic incentives. If the price of some particular input, such as petroleum or skilled labour, goes up, R&D and innovating activities may be directed to altering the production function to economize on these expensive inputs. This process is not simply a substitution of less expensive inputs for more expensive ones within the confines of known technologies; rather, it is the *development of new technologies* in response to changes in relative prices.

There are several important implications of this new understanding that, to a great extent, growth is achieved through costly, risky, innovative activity that often occurs in response to economic signals.

Learning by Doing The pioneering theorist of innovation, Joseph Schumpeter (1883–1950), developed a model in which innovation flowed in one direction from a pure discovery "upstream," to more applied R&D, then to working machines, and finally to output "downstream."

In contrast, modern research shows that innovation involves a large amount of "learning by doing" at all of its stages. (We discuss this kind of learning in more detail in Chapter 33.) What is learned downstream then modifies what must be done upstream. The best innovation-managing systems encourage such "feedback" from the more applied steps to the purer researchers and from users to designers.

This interaction is illustrated, for example, by the differences that existed for many years between the Japanese automobile manufacturers and their North American competitors in the design and production of new models. North American design was traditionally centralized: design production teams developed the overall design and then instructed their production sections and asked for bids from parts manufacturers to produce according to specified blueprints. As a result, defects in the original design were often not discovered until production was underway, causing many costly delays and rejection of parts already supplied. In contrast, Japanese firms involved their design and production departments and their parts manufacturers in all stages of the design process. Parts manufacturers were not given specific blueprints for production; instead, they were given general specifications and asked to develop their own detailed designs. As they did so, they learned. They then fed information about the problems they were encountering back to the main designers while the general outlines of the new model were not yet finalized. As a result, the Japanese were able to design a new product faster, at less cost, and with far fewer problems than were the North American firms. Since that time, however, the North American automotive firms have adopted many of these Japanese design and production methods.

Knowledge Transfer The diffusion of technological knowledge from those who have it to those who want it is not costless (as it was assumed to be in Schumpeter's model). We often think that once a production process is developed, it can easily be copied by others. In practice, however, the diffusion of new technological knowledge is not so simple. Firms need research capacity just to adopt the technologies developed by others. Some of the knowledge needed to use a new technology can be learned only through experience by plant managers, technicians, and operators.

For example, research has shown that most industrial technologies require technology-specific organizational skills that cannot be "embodied" in the machines themselves, instruction books, or blueprints. The needed knowledge is *tacit* in the sense that it cannot be taught through books and can be acquired only by experience—much like driving a car or playing a video game. Acquiring tacit knowledge requires a deliberate process of building up new skills, work practices, knowledge, and experience.

The fact that diffusion is a costly and time-consuming process explains why new technologies take considerable time to diffuse, first through the economy of the originating country and then through the rest of the world. If diffusion were simple and virtually costless, the puzzle would be why technological knowledge and best industrial practices did not diffuse very quickly. As it is, decades can pass before a new technological process is diffused everywhere that it could be employed.

Market Structure and Innovation Because it is highly risky, innovation is encouraged by strong rivalry among firms and discouraged by monopoly practices. Competition among three or four large firms often produces much innovation, but a single firm, especially if it serves a secure home market protected by trade barriers, often seems much less inclined to innovate. The reduction in trade barriers over the past several decades and the increasing globalization of markets as a result of falling transportation and communication costs have increased international competition. Whereas one firm in a national market might have had substantial monopoly power three or four decades ago, today it is more likely to be in intense competition with firms based in other countries. This greater international competition generally leads to more innovation.

An important implication of this idea is that policies that make firms more competitive—either by lowering protective tariffs or by reducing domestic regulations that hamper competition—are likely to have a positive effect on the amount of innovation and thus on an economy's rate of growth of productivity. This is a central conclusion in William Lewis's *The Power of Productivity*, an influential book published in 2004.

Shocks and Innovation One interesting consequence of endogenous technical change is that shocks that would be unambiguously adverse to an economy operating with fixed technology can sometimes provide a spur to innovation that proves a blessing in disguise. A sharp rise in the price of one input can raise costs and lower the value of output per person for some time. But it may lead to a wave of innovations that reduce the need for this expensive input and, as a side effect, greatly raise productivity. One example is the ongoing development of fuel-efficient jet engines in response to large increases in the world price of oil.

Sometimes individual firms will respond differently to the same economic signal. Sometimes those that respond by altering technology will do better than those that concentrate their efforts on substituting within the confines of known technology. For example, several years ago when the consumer electronics industry was beset with high costs in both Japan and the United States, some U.S. firms moved their operations abroad to avoid high, rigid labour costs. They continued to use their existing technology and went where labour costs were low enough to make that technology pay. Their Japanese competitors, however, stayed at home. They innovated away most of their labour costs and then built factories in the United States to replace the factories of U.S. firms that had gone abroad!

Increasing Marginal Returns

We saw earlier that Neoclassical theories of economic growth assume that investment in capital is subject to diminishing marginal returns. Some research suggests, however, the possibility of *increasing returns* that remain for considerable periods of time: As investment in some new geographic area, new product, or new production technology proceeds through time, new increments of investment are often *more* productive than previous increments. The sources of such increasing returns fall under the two general categories of *market-development costs* and *knowledge*.

Market-Development Costs There are at least three reasons why there may be important costs associated with the initial development of a market. These costs result in increasing marginal returns to investment.

1. Investment in the early stages of development of a country, province, or town may create new skills and attitudes in the workforce that are then available to all subsequent firms, whose costs are therefore lower than those encountered by the initial firms.

2. Each new firm may find the environment more and more favourable to its investment because of the physical infrastructure that has been created by those who came before.

3. The first investment in a new product will encounter countless production problems that, once overcome, cause fewer problems to subsequent investors.

In each of these examples, the returns to later investment are greater than the returns to the same investment made earlier for the simple reason that the economic environment becomes more fully developed over time. Early firms must incur costs in order to develop various aspects of the market, but some benefits of this development are then reaped by later firms that need not incur these costs. As a result, the investment returns for "followers" can be substantially greater than the investment returns for "pioneers." In short, doing something really new is difficult, whereas making further variations on an accepted and developed new idea becomes progressively easier over time. (For those who have studied microeconomics, the early firms are conferring a positive *externality* on those who follow them, as described in Chapter 16.)

Another important issue concerns the behaviour of customers. When a new product is developed, customers will often resist adopting it, both because they may be conservative and because they know that new products often experience "growing pains." Customers also need time to learn how best to use the new product—they need to do what is called "learning by using." And it may take time and "using experience" before producers get all the bugs out of the design of new products.

The development of the electric car has been expensive for those companies involved at early stages. As a result, there may be significant advantages to other firms who follow the pioneers.

A computer is a private good because if I own it then you cannot also own it. But the knowledge required to build the computer is a public good. And knowledge, unlike traditional factors of production, is not necessarily subject to the law of diminishing returns.

Slow acceptance of new products by customers is not necessarily unreasonable. When a sophisticated new product comes on the market, no one is sure if it will be a success, and the first customers to buy it take the risk that the product may subsequently turn out to be a failure. They also incur the costs of learning how to use it effectively. Many potential users take the reasonable approach of letting others try a new product, following only after the product's success has been demonstrated. This makes the early stages of innovation especially costly and risky.

> **Successive increments of investment associated with an innovation often yield a range of increasing marginal returns as costs that are incurred in earlier investment expenditure provide publicly available knowledge and experience and as customer attitudes and abilities become more receptive to new products.**

Knowledge Many of the newer growth theories shift the emphasis from the economics of goods to the economics of *ideas*. Physical goods, such as factories and machines, exist in one place at one time. This has two consequences. First, when physical goods are used by someone, they cannot be used by someone else. Second, if a given labour force is provided with more and more physical objects to use in production, sooner or later diminishing marginal returns will be encountered.

Ideas have different characteristics. Once someone develops an idea, it is available for use by everyone. For example, if one firm uses a truck, another firm cannot use it at the same time; but one firm's use of a revolutionary design for a new suspension system on a truck does not prevent other firms from using that design as well. (For those who have studied microeconomics, some knowledge has aspects that make it a *public good*, as we discussed in Chapter 16.)

Ideas are also not necessarily subject to diminishing marginal returns. As our knowledge increases, each increment of new knowledge does not inevitably add less to our productive ability than each previous increment. Indeed, the reverse is often the case: one new idea may spawn several additional ideas that build on or extend it in some ways. For example, the discovery of genes and the subsequent work on gene technology has spawned entire biotechnology industries that are revolutionizing aspects of medicine, agriculture, and environmental control.

Ideas produce what is called *knowledge-driven growth*. New knowledge provides the input that allows investment to produce increasing rather than diminishing marginal returns. Because there are no practical limits to human knowledge, there need be no immediate boundaries to finding new ways to produce more output by using less of all inputs.

> **Neoclassical growth theories gave economics the name "the dismal science" by emphasizing diminishing marginal returns under conditions of given technology. Newer growth theories are more optimistic because they emphasize the unlimited potential of knowledge-driven technological change.**

Probably the most important contrast between these ideas-based theories and the Neoclassical theory concerns investment and income. In the Neoclassical model, diminishing marginal returns to investment imply a limit to the possible increase of per capita GDP. In the newer theories, investment alone can hold an economy on a "sustained growth path" in which per capita GDP increases without limit, provided that the investment embodies the results of continual advances in technological knowledge.

26.4 Are There Limits to Growth?

Many opponents of growth argue that sustained growth of the world economy is undesirable; some argue that it is impossible. The idea that economic growth is limited by nature is not new. In the early 1970s, a group called the "Club of Rome" published a book entitled *The Limits to Growth*, which focused on the limits to growth arising from the finite supply of natural resources. Extrapolating from the oil shortages and price increases caused by the OPEC cartel, the Club of Rome concluded that industrialized countries faced an imminent absolute limit to growth. Do such limits really exist? We now discuss the two issues of resource exhaustion and environmental degradation.

See the United Nations' website for international data on economic development: www. un.org. *Click on "Development" and then go to "Statistics."*

Resource Exhaustion

The years since the Second World War have seen a rapid acceleration in the consumption of the world's resources, particularly fossil fuels and basic minerals. World population has increased from fewer than 2.5 billion to more than 7 billion in that period; this increase alone has intensified the demand for the world's resources. Furthermore, as people attain higher incomes, they generally consume more resources. Thus, not only are there more people in the world, but many of those people are consuming increasing quantities of resources.

Most everyone in the world today would like to achieve a standard of living equal to that of the average Canadian family. Unfortunately, the world's current resources and its present capacity to cope with pollution and environmental degradation are insufficient to accomplish this rise in global living standards with present technology.

Most economists, however, agree that absolute limits to growth, based on the assumptions of constant technology and fixed resources, are not relevant. As emphasized by the growth theories we discussed in the previous section, technology changes continually, as do the available stocks of resources. For example, 75 years ago, few would have thought that the world could produce enough food to feed its present population of 7 billion people, let alone the 10 billion at which the population is projected to stabilize sometime later this century. Yet significant advances in agricultural methods make this task now seem feasible. Further, while existing resources are being depleted, new ones are constantly being discovered or developed. One example is the development of the Alberta oil sands. In the early 1970s, this resource appeared to be far too expensive to develop and therefore an unlikely source of economical oil. Four decades later, after considerable technological improvement, the oil sands now rank among the world's largest reserves of economical petroleum.

Another consideration relates to both resource use and technological progress. Along with advances in technological knowledge typically comes an increase in the economy's *resource efficiency*—a reduction in the amount of resources needed to produce one unit of output. In Canada, for example, an average dollar of real GDP is currently produced with nearly 40 percent less energy than was the case in 1978, and if we focus just on petroleum use, the reduction is almost 50 percent. More generally, every dollar's worth of real GDP produced in the world has used steadily fewer resources over the past century. Part of this reduction is due to an improvement in the efficiency with which resources are used; part is due to the gradual shift toward the production of services (and away from the production of goods) in world GDP. Improvements in resource efficiency do not eliminate the concerns about resource exhaustion, but they do underline the importance of recognizing the role of technological change when considering limits to economic growth.

> **Technology is constantly advancing, and many things that seemed impossible a generation ago will be commonplace a generation from now. Such technological advance makes any absolute limits to economic growth less likely.**

Yet there is surely cause for concern. Although many barriers can be overcome by technological advances, such achievements are not instantaneous and are certainly not automatic. There is a critical problem of timing: How soon can we discover and put into practice the knowledge required to solve the problems that are made ever more imminent by the growth in the population, the affluence of the rich nations, and the aspirations of the billions who now live in poverty? There is no guarantee that a whole generation will not be caught in transition between technologies, with enormous social and political consequences.

A final point worth noting is that the extent of resource depletion is not something that "just happens." Since natural resources are typically owned by the public, government policy can be used to influence the rate of resource extraction if that objective is deemed to be appropriate. If we fail to protect some key natural resources, it will not be because we lacked the ability or the technology to do so, only that we lacked the political will to make contentious and difficult decisions—decisions that may nonetheless be in our long-run interests.

The development of the Alberta oil sands has significantly increased Canada's oil-production capacity. At the same time, it has raised concerns regarding environmental degradation, including substantial emissions of greenhouse gases.

Environmental Degradation

A much more important problem associated with economic growth is the generation of pollution and the degradation of our natural environment. Air, water, and soil are polluted by a variety of natural activities, and, for billions of years, the environment has coped with them. The Earth's natural processes had little trouble coping with the pollution generated by its 1 billion inhabitants in 1800. But the 7 billion people who now exist put such extreme demands on Earth's ecosystems that there are now legitimate concerns about environmental sustainability. Smoke, sewage, chemical waste, hydrocarbon and greenhouse-gas emissions, spent nuclear fuel, and a host of other pollutants threaten to overwhelm Earth's natural regenerative processes.

> Conscious management of pollution was unnecessary when the world's population was 1 billion people, but such management has now become a pressing matter.

Reducing the extent of environmental degradation, however, is different from advocating an "anti-growth" position. To put it differently, there is nothing inconsistent about an economy displaying *both* high rates of economic growth and active environmental protection. As students of microeconomics will recognize, an important part of a policy designed to reduce the extent of environmental degradation is to get polluters (firms or households) to face the full cost of their polluting activities—especially the external costs that their activities impose on society. This often involves levying some form of tax on polluters for every unit of pollution emitted. Although such policies, if stringently enforced, will lead to output reductions in specific industries, they need not lead to reductions in the *overall* level of economic activity. And long-run economic growth is related to growth in the overall level of economic activity, not to the growth of specific industries.

Furthermore, many technological advances reduce the amount of pollution per unit of output and also reduce the costs of dealing with whatever pollution remains. Rich, advanced economies, such as Canada, the United States, and the European Union, create less pollution per dollar of GDP and find it easier to bear the cost of pollution clean-up than do poorer, less technologically advanced economies.

None of this implies that environmental issues are not serious. It is possible that our management of these issues will be sufficiently inadequate that growth will be impaired and our living standards will suffer by significant amounts. If this happens, it will probably *not* be because we lacked the technology or know-how to solve these problems once they were recognized. If we do create environmental disasters, more likely it will be because we failed to respond quickly enough (if at all) to the growing dangers as they were occurring.

Most climate scientists believe, for example, that we may already be too late to reverse the forces leading to global climate change and that significant increases in sea level are now a virtual certainty over the next few decades. However, most agree that there is still time to take actions that could stabilize Earth's climate over the course of this century. Concerted global actions and considerable political will in many countries must be part of the solution. *Applying Economic Concepts 26-2* explores in more detail the problem of climate change caused by greenhouse-gas emissions associated with the burning of fossil fuels.

Conclusion

The world faces many problems. Starvation and poverty are the common lot of citizens in many countries and are not unknown even in such countries as Canada and the United States, where average living standards are very high. Growth has raised the average citizens of advanced countries from poverty to plenty in the course of two centuries—a short time in terms of human history. Further growth is needed if people in developing countries are to escape material poverty, and further growth would also help advanced countries to deal with many of their pressing economic problems.

Rising population and consumption, however, put pressure on the world's natural ecosystems, especially through the many forms of pollution. Further growth can only occur if it is *sustainable* growth, that is in turn based on knowledge-driven technological change. Past experience suggests that new technologies will use less of all resources per unit of output. But if they are to dramatically reduce the demands placed on the Earth's

APPLYING ECONOMIC CONCEPTS 26-2

Climate Change and Economic Growth

There is no doubt that Earth's average surface temperature has been rising over the past century, and that the increase has been unevenly distributed, from less than 1°C near the equator to over 5°C near the poles. As a result of this global warming, the polar ice caps have been melting significantly, the world's deserts have been gradually increasing in size, and extreme weather events are becoming more frequent and severe. The melting of the Antarctic and Greenland ice caps is predicted to cause a significant increase in sea level, with potentially catastrophic effects for the many highly populated island and coastal regions of Asia and Africa. The creeping desertification and changing rainfall patterns are predicted to cause significant reductions in agricultural productivity, especially in the developing countries. The effects of climate change will be felt by people in many countries, but the most dramatic effects are likely to be experienced in the lowest-income countries least prepared to shoulder the burden.

Although the underlying cause of the rising global temperatures is still debated, the bulk of the scientific evidence points to a clear causal link. The burning of fossil fuels leads to the emission of carbon dioxide and other "greenhouse gases," which accumulate in the atmosphere and remain there for many years. This rising atmospheric concentration of gases acts like a greenhouse to lock in the sun's warmth, thus increasing average global temperature.

The world's annual emissions of greenhouse gases have been increasing steadily, broadly in line with the growth of the world economy. In the absence of policies aimed at reducing these emissions, they are predicted to approximately double between today and 2050. Yet the weight of scientific evidence suggests that in order to stabilize the atmospheric concentration of greenhouse gases (at a level well above today's), and thus to stabilize Earth's average temperature (at a level 1° to 2°C above today's average temperature), annual emissions will need to fall by 80 to 90 percent from *current* levels by 2050. Achieving such reductions will certainly affect the world's economic growth.

What is the connection between global warming and economic growth? First, modern economic growth is a significant cause of global warming. Since energy is an important input to production for most goods and services, and since the burning of fossil fuels is currently one of the most efficient ways to produce energy, it is not surprising that a close relationship exists between the growth of real GDP and the growth of greenhouse-gas emissions. But reducing emissions by reducing world GDP is probably both unrealistic and undesirable. As the world's population continues to grow, and the people of the developing world strive to increase their per capita incomes to levels closer to ours, there will inevitably be a rise in global GDP.

A more realistic way to reduce greenhouse-gas emissions is to reduce our reliance on energy and, in particular, our reliance on those forms of energy that release greenhouse gases into the atmosphere. Most economists argue that the most effective policy to reduce the world's emissions of greenhouse gases involves placing a price on the emission of greenhouse gases, either through a direct tax (such as a "carbon tax") or by directly restricting the amount of total emissions and then allowing the distribution of emissions among firms to be determined through the trading of emissions permits (a "cap-and-trade" system). Either policy approach will increase the cost associated with emitting greenhouse gases and thus will create incentives for firms and households to use non-emitting forms of energy. Incentives will also be created for the further development of non-emitting energy sources such as solar, wind, nuclear, and hydroelectricity.

Since these policies will be effective only by imposing costs on firms and households, their use will highlight a second connection between economic growth and global warming. These higher costs will eventually lead to the adoption of cleaner energy systems and thus a reduction of greenhouse-gas emissions, but they will probably also lead to a reduction in the growth rate of real GDP, at least for several years. Current estimates suggest that reducing Canadian greenhouse-gas emissions by approximately 20 percent from current levels by 2020 would lead to a reduction in real GDP by between 4 and 8 percent from the level that would otherwise exist in 2020. This implies a reduction in the growth rate of real GDP over this period of approximately 0.5 percent per year. Over the long term, however, once the economy adjusts to the new and possibly more efficient fuel sources, it is possible that the rate of economic growth would increase.

Policymakers are thus faced with difficult choices. If their objective was to make such choices sensibly, they would first need to estimate the costs to the economy of taking the "business as usual" approach and thus experiencing the predicted changes in the world climate over the next several decades. Then they would need to estimate the costs associated with taking aggressive policy actions designed to dramatically reduce the emission of greenhouse gases. Finally, they would need to choose a policy approach, appropriately weighing the costs of inaction against the costs of action. These would be very difficult decisions to make, partly because of the uncertainty surrounding the impact of any policies and partly because of the considerable political pressures generated by advocates on both sides of the debate.

ecosystems, price and policy incentives will be needed to direct technological change in more environmentally sustainable ways. Just as present technologies are much less polluting than the technologies of a century ago, the technologies of the future need to be made much less polluting than today's.

There is no guarantee that the world will solve the problems of sustainable growth in the time available, but there is nothing in modern growth theory and existing evidence to suggest that such an achievement is impossible.

SUMMARY

26.1 The Nature of Economic Growth   LO 1, 2

- Long-term economic growth refers to sustained increases in potential GDP.
- The cumulative effects of even small differences in growth rates become very large over periods of a decade or more.
- The most important benefit of growth lies in its contribution to raising average material living standards.
- Growth also facilitates the redistribution of income among people.

- The opportunity cost of growth is the reduction of consumption as resources are used instead for investment in capital goods.
- An additional cost of growth is the personal losses to those whose skills are made obsolete by the economic disruption caused by growth.
- There are four major determinants of growth: increases in the labour force; increases in physical capital; increases in human capital; and improvements in technology.

26.2 Established Theories of Economic Growth   LO 3

- The long-run relationship among saving, investment, and economic growth is most easily observed in the market for financial capital, in which the interest rate is determined by the equality of desired investment and desired national saving.
- Increases in the supply of national saving will reduce the interest rate and encourage more investment by firms, thus increasing the rate of growth of potential output.
- Increases in the demand for investment will increase the interest rate and encourage an increase in household saving. The higher saving (and investment) in equilibrium leads to a higher growth rate of potential output.
- Neoclassical growth theory assumes an aggregate production function that displays diminishing marginal returns (when one factor is changed in isolation) and

constant returns to scale (when all factors are changed in equal proportions).
- In a balanced growth path, the quantity of labour, the quantity of capital, and real GDP all increase at a constant rate. But since per capita output is constant, material living standards are not rising.
- Changes in output that cannot be accounted for by changes in the levels of physical and human capital and in the size of the labour force are called growth in total factor productivity (TFP).
- In the Neoclassical growth model, technological change is assumed to be exogenous—unaffected by the size of the labour force, the size of the capital stock, or the level of economic activity.

26.3 Newer Growth Theories   LO 4

- Unlike the Neoclassical growth theory, newer growth theories emphasize endogenous technological change that responds to market signals, such as prices and profits. In addition, shocks that would be adverse in a setting of fixed technology may provide a spur to innovation and result in technological improvements.
- These growth theories also suggest that investment embodying new technologies may be subject to *increasing* rather than diminishing marginal returns. Investment

that embodies a continuing flow of new technologies can explain ongoing growth in per capita incomes caused by capital accumulation—a phenomenon difficult to explain with the Neoclassical growth model.
- New knowledge is an important input to the growth process and, because it is a public good that can be used simultaneously by many, it is not subject to diminishing marginal returns.

26.4 Are There Limits to Growth?

- The critical importance of increasing knowledge and new technology to the goal of sustaining growth is highlighted by the great drain on existing natural resources that has resulted from the explosive growth of population and output in recent decades.
- Without ongoing technological change, world living standards could not be raised to those currently existing in the developed nations.
- Rising population and rising real incomes place pressure on resources. Technological improvements, however, lead to less resource use per unit of output produced and also to the discovery and development of new resources.

- Earth's environment could cope naturally with much of human pollution 200 years ago, but the present population and level of output is so large that pollution has outstripped many of nature's coping mechanisms.
- Although problems associated with environmental degradation have been surmounted in the past, there is no guarantee that the ones now being encountered, such as the effects of global warming, will be effectively addressed by policies before the effects can be reversed.

KEY CONCEPTS

The cumulative nature of growth
Benefits and costs of growth
The market for financial capital and the equilibrium interest rate
Saving, investment, and growth

Neoclassical growth theory
The aggregate production function
Diminishing marginal returns
Constant returns to scale
Balanced growth

Endogenous technical change
Increasing marginal returns to investment
Resource depletion
Environmental degradation

STUDY EXERCISES

MyEconLab Make the grade with MyEconLab: Study Exercises marked in red can be found on MyEconLab. You can practise them as often as you want, and most feature step-by-step guided instructions to help you find the right answer.

1. Fill in the blanks to make the following statements correct.

   a. Long-run, sustained increases in potential output are called _____.
   b. Increases in material living standards occur with increases in real _____.
   c. An important cost of economic growth is the sacrifice of current _____ in exchange for investment that raises future _____.
   d. Four major determinants of growth examined in this chapter are
      - _____
      - _____
      - _____
      - _____

2. In this chapter, we developed a theory of the market for financial capital. Using that theory, fill in the blanks to make the following statements correct.

   a. An increase in the real interest rate leads to a(n) _____ in the amount of national saving as households reduce their _____.
   b. An increase in the interest rate leads firms to _____ their amount of desired investment.
   c. In the long run, with output equal to potential, equilibrium in the market for financial capital determines the interest rate as well as the amount of _____ and _____ in the economy.
   d. Following a shift in either the supply of national saving or the demand for investment, there will be a change in both the equilibrium _____ and the amount of _____ in the economy.

e. An increase in the amount of the economy's resources devoted to _____ leads to an increase in the growth rate of _____.

3. Fill in the blanks to make the following statements correct.

   a. An important aspect of Neoclassical growth theory is that increases in the supply of one factor, all else held constant, imply eventually _____ marginal returns to that factor.

   b. In Neoclassical growth theory, an increase in the labour force alone _____ total output and _____ the level of per capita output.

   c. When a new and better harvesting machine replaces an old harvesting machine on a farm and is more productive than the old one, we say there has been _____ technical change.

   d. Some newer growth theories are based on the assumption that technological change is _____ to the economic system; others are based on the possibility that there are _____ marginal returns to investment.

   e. Neoclassical growth theories are pessimistic because they emphasize _____ returns with a given state of _____. Modern growth theories are more optimistic because they emphasize the unlimited potential of _____.

4. In the text we said that, over many years, small differences in growth rates can have large effects on the level of income. This question will help you understand this important point. Consider an initial value of real GDP equal to Y_0. If real GDP grows at a rate of g percent annually, after N years real GDP will equal $Y_0(1 + g)^N$. Now consider the following table. Let the initial level of GDP in all cases be 100.

	Real GDP with Alternative Growth Rates					
	1%	1.5%	2%	2.5%	3%	3.5%
Year	(1)	(2)	(3)	(4)	(5)	(6)
0	100	100	100	100	100	100
1	—	—	—	—	—	—
3	—	—	—	—	—	—
5	—	—	—	—	—	—
10	—	—	—	—	—	—
20	—	—	—	—	—	—
30	—	—	—	—	—	—
50	—	—	—	—	—	—

   a. By using the formula provided above, compute the level of real GDP in column 1 for each year. For example, in Year 1, real GDP will equal $100(1.01)^1 = 101$. For each year, compute the GDP to two decimal places.

   b. Now do the same for the rest of the columns.

   c. In Year 20, how much larger (in percentage terms) is real GDP in the 3 percent growth case compared with the 1.5 percent growth case?

   d. In Year 50, how much larger (in percentage terms) is real GDP in the 3 percent growth case compared with the 1.5 percent growth case?

5. The diagram below shows two paths for aggregate consumption. One grows at a rate of 3 percent per year; the other grows at 4 percent per year but begins at a lower level.

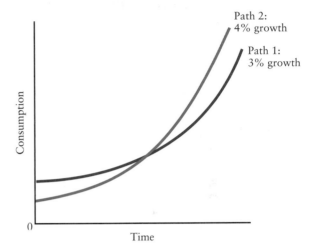

   a. Suppose the economy jumps from Path 1 to Path 2 in Year 0 because its rate of capital accumulation increases. What is the opportunity cost in this economy for this increase in capital accumulation?

   b. Suppose the economy jumps from Path 1 to Path 2 in Year 0 because its rate of R&D (research and development) expenditures increases. The greater R&D leads to technological improvements that generate the higher growth rate. What is the opportunity cost to this economy for the increase in R&D expenditures?

   c. Given the two paths in the diagram, can you offer a way to identify the "break-even" point for making the jump from Path 1 to Path 2? Explain.

6. Consider an economy in the long run with real GDP equal to the level of potential output, Y^*.

   a. Draw the diagram of the market for financial capital. Explain the slopes of the investment demand curve and the national saving curve.

   b. Suppose the government pursued a fiscal contraction by reducing the level of government purchases. Explain what would happen to the equilibrium interest rate, the amount of investment in the economy, and the long-run growth rate.

   c. Now suppose the fiscal contraction occurs by increasing taxes. Explain what effect this would have on the interest rate, investment, and long-run growth rate. (Hint: An increase in taxes is likely to reduce disposable income and thus reduce aggregate consumption.)

7. The Neoclassical growth theory is based on the existence of an aggregate production function—showing the relationship between labour (*L*), capital (*K*), technology (*T*), and real GDP (*Y*). The table below shows various values for *L*, *K*, and *T*. In all cases, the aggregate production function is assumed to take the following form:

$$Y = T \times \sqrt{KL}$$

Labour (*L*)	Capital (*K*)	Technology (*T*)	Real GDP (*Y*)
10	20	1	—
15	20	1	—
20	20	1	—
25	20	1	—
10	20	1	—
15	30	1	—
20	40	1	—
25	50	1	—
20	20	1	—
20	20	3	—
20	20	4	—
20	20	5	—

a. Compute real GDP for each case and complete the table.

b. In the first part of the table, capital is constant but labour is increasing. What property of the production function is displayed? Explain.

c. In the second part of the table, capital and labour are increasing by the same proportion. What property of the production function is displayed? Explain.

d. What type of growth is being shown in the third part of the table?

8. In this chapter we discussed four major determinants of growth in real output: increases in the labour force, increases in the stock of physical capital, increases in human capital, and improvements in technology.

a. For each of the four determinants, give an example of a government policy that is likely to increase growth.

b. Discuss the likely cost associated with each policy.

c. Does one of your proposed policies appear better (in a cost–benefit sense) than the others? Explain.

9. Consider the market for financial capital and the relationship among saving, investment, and the interest rate. In what follows, assume that the economy is in a long-run equilibrium with $Y = Y^*$.

a. Suppose the government wants to encourage national saving. How could it do this, and what would be the effects of such a policy? Illustrate in a diagram.

b. Suppose instead that the government wants to encourage investment. How might this be accomplished, and what would be the effects? Illustrate in a diagram.

c. It is often heard in public debate that "high interest rates are bad for investment and growth." Is this true? Can you come up with a simple rule of thumb to describe the relationship between interest rates, investment, and growth?

10. In the early 1970s the Club of Rome, extrapolating from the rates of resource use at the time, predicted that the supply of natural resources (especially oil) would be used up within a few decades. Subsequent events appear to have proven them wrong.

a. What is predicted to happen to the price of oil (and other natural resources) as population and per capita incomes rise?

b. Given your answer to part (a), what is the likely response by firms and consumers who use such resources?

c. Explain why resource exhaustion should, through the workings of the price system, lead to technological developments that reduce the use of the resource.

11. Dr. David Suzuki, an opponent of further economic growth, has argued that despite the fact that "in the twentieth century the list of scientific and technological achievements has been absolutely dazzling, the costs of such progress are so large that negative economic growth may be right for the future." Policies to achieve this include "rigorous reduction of waste, a questioning and distrustful attitude toward technological progress, and braking demands on the globe's resources." Identify some of the benefits and costs of economic growth, and evaluate Suzuki's position. What government policies would be needed to achieve his ends?

12. This question is based on the MyEconLab *Additional Topic* **Investment and Saving in Globalized Financial Markets.** Consider the market for financial capital and the long-run relationship among saving, investment, and economic growth.

a. For a closed economy, if the government wants a higher long-run growth rate, explain why it can directly promote saving *or* investment.

b. For an open economy, explain why the amount of investment (and growth rate of output) is unlikely to be affected by a policy that encourages national saving.

c. If desired saving need not be equal to desired investment in an open economy, what accounts for the difference?

Money and Banking

IN the next three chapters, we look at the role of money and monetary policy. The role of money may seem obvious to most readers: money is what people use to buy things. Yet as we will see, increasing the amount of money circulating in Canada may not make the average Canadian better off in the long run. Although money allows those who have it to buy someone else's output, the total amount of goods and services available for everyone to buy depends on the total output produced, and thus may be unaffected by the total amount of money circulating in the economy. In other words, an increase in the quantity of money may not increase the level of potential real GDP. However, most economists agree that changes in the amount of

money have important short-run effects on national income. A complete understanding of money's role in the economy requires that we recognize the distinction between the short run and the long run.

We begin by talking in detail about what money is and how it evolved over the centuries to its current form. We then examine the Canadian banking system, which includes a central bank (the Bank of Canada) and many commercial banks. Finally, we explain the process whereby commercial banks "create" money, seemingly out of thin air. This money creation process will play a central role in our discussion of how money influences the level of economic activity, a topic we begin in the next chapter.

| 27.1 The Nature of Money

What exactly is money? In this section, we describe the functions of money and briefly outline its history.

What Is Money?

medium of exchange Anything that is generally accepted in return for goods and services sold.

Money is any generally accepted **medium of exchange**, which means anything widely accepted in a society in exchange for goods and services. Although its medium-of-exchange role is perhaps its most important one, money also acts as a *store of value* and as a *unit of account*. Different kinds of money vary in their abilities to fulfill these functions. As we will see, the *money supply* is measured by using different definitions for different purposes.

barter A system in which goods and services are traded directly for other goods and services.

Money as a Medium of Exchange If there were no money, goods would have to be exchanged by barter. **Barter** is the system whereby goods and services are exchanged directly with each other. The major difficulty with barter is that each transaction requires a *double coincidence of wants*: Anyone who specialized in producing one commodity would have to spend a great deal of time searching for satisfactory transactions. For example, the barber who needs his sink repaired would have to find a plumber who wants a haircut. In a world of many different goods and many different people, the effort required to make all transactions by barter would be extreme. The use of money as a medium of exchange solves this problem. People can sell their output for money and then, in separate transactions, use the money to buy what they want from others.

> The double coincidence of wants is unnecessary when a medium of exchange is used.

By facilitating transactions, money makes possible the benefits of specialization and the division of labour, two concepts we first discussed in Chapter 1. As a result, money greatly contributes to the efficiency of the economic system. Not surprisingly, money has been called one of the great inventions contributing to human freedom and well-being.

To serve as an efficient medium of exchange, money must have a number of characteristics. It must be both easily recognizable and readily acceptable. It must have a high value relative to its weight (otherwise it would be a nuisance to carry around). It must be divisible, because money that comes only in large denominations is useless for transactions having only a small value. It must be reasonably durable (notice that Canadian paper money can easily survive several trips through a washing machine!). Finally, it must be difficult, if not impossible, to counterfeit.

Money as a Store of Value Money is a convenient means of storing purchasing power; goods may be sold today for money and the money may then be stored until it is needed for some future purchase. To be a satisfactory store of value, however, money must have a relatively stable value. Recall from the beginning of Chapter 23 that a rise in the price level causes a decrease in the purchasing power of money. When the price level is stable, the purchasing power of a given sum of money is also stable; when the price level is highly variable, so is the purchasing power of money, and the usefulness of money as a store of value is undermined.

Between the early 1970s and the early 1990s, inflation in Canada was high enough and sufficiently variable to diminish money's usefulness as a store of value. Since 1992, however, inflation has been low and relatively stable, thus increasing money's effectiveness as a store of value. Even Canada's high-inflation experience, however, is very modest compared with that in some other countries, such as Chile in the mid-1970s, Bolivia in the mid-1980s, Argentina, Romania, and Brazil in the early 1990s, and Zimbabwe in the mid-2000s. One of the most infamous experiences of very high inflation—*hyperinflation*—comes from Germany in the early 1920s. This case is discussed in *Lessons from History 27-1*.

Canadian bank notes are money. They serve the function of a medium of exchange and a unit of account. And if the rate of inflation is low, they also serve as a reasonable store of value.

Money as a Unit of Account Money is also used for accounting, and its use for such purpose does not rely on its physical existence. Canadian businesses, governments, charities, and households all record their financial accounts, whether in paper ledgers or electronic spreadsheets, in terms of dollars. Expenditures and receipts and deficits and surpluses are computed in dollar terms even without the immediate presence of physical money.

Indeed, money can be used for accounting purposes even if it has *no* physical existence whatsoever. For instance, a government store in a communist society might say that everyone was allocated so many "dollars" to use each month. Goods could then be assigned prices and each consumer's purchases recorded, the consumer being allowed to buy until the allocated supply of dollars was exhausted. These dollars need have no existence other than as entries in the store's books, yet they would serve as a perfectly satisfactory unit of account. Whether they could also serve as a medium of exchange between individuals depends on whether the store would agree to transfer dollar credits from one customer to another at the customer's request. Canadian banks transfer dollars credited to deposits in this way each time you make a purchase with your ATM or debit card. Thus, a bank deposit can serve as both a unit of account and a medium of exchange. Notice that the use of *dollars* in this context suggests a further sense in which money is a unit of account. People think about values in terms of the monetary unit with which they are familiar.

The Origins of Money

The origins of money go far back in antiquity. Most primitive societies are known to have made some use of it.

Metallic Money All sorts of commodities have been used as money at one time or another, but gold and silver proved to have great advantages. They were precious because their supplies were relatively limited, and they were in constant demand by the wealthy for ornament and decoration. Further, they were easily recognized, they were divisible into extremely small units, and they did not easily wear out. For these reasons, precious metals came to circulate as money and to be used in many transactions.

Before the invention of coins, it was necessary to carry the metals in bulk. When a purchase was made, the requisite quantity of the metal was carefully weighed on

LESSONS FROM HISTORY 27-1

Hyperinflation and the Value of Money

Hyperinflation is generally defined as inflation that exceeds 50 percent per month. At this rate of inflation, a chocolate bar that costs $1 on January 1 would cost $129.74 by December 31 of the same year. When prices are rising at such rapid rates, is it possible for money to maintain its usefulness as a medium of exchange or as a store of value? Several examples from history have allowed economists to study the role of money during hyperinflation. This historical record is not very reassuring. In a number of instances, prices were rising so quickly that the nation's money ceased to be a satisfactory store of value, even for short periods.

A spectacular example of hyperinflation is the experience of Germany in the period after the First World War. The price index in the accompanying table shows that a good purchased for one 100-mark note in July 1923 would cost *10 million* 100-mark notes only four months later! Germany had experienced substantial inflation during the First World War, averaging more than 30 percent per year, but the immediate postwar years of 1920 and 1921 gave no sign of explosive inflation. By the summer of 1922, however, the rate of inflation was extremely high and by November 1923 the German mark was officially repudiated, its value wholly destroyed. How could such a dramatic increase in prices happen?

The main cause was the German government's inability to finance its rising expenditures with tax revenues and its resort to printing new money on a massive scale. As more and more physical money was being spent to purchase the same volume of real goods and services, the rate of inflation soared.

When inflation becomes so high that people lose confidence in the purchasing power of their currency, they rush to spend it. People who have goods become increasingly reluctant to accept the rapidly depreciating money in exchange. The rush to spend money accelerates the increase in prices until people finally become unwilling to accept money on any terms. What was once money ceases to be money. The price system can then be restored only by repudiation of the old monetary unit and its replacement by a new unit.

About a dozen hyperinflations in world history have been documented, among them the collapse of the continental during the American Revolution in 1776, the ruble during the Russian Revolution in 1917, the drachma during and after the German occupation of Greece in the Second World War, the pengö in Hungary in 1945–1946, the Chinese national currency from 1946 to 1948, the Bolivian peso in 1984–1985, and the Argentinian peso in the early 1990s. Between 2004 and 2009, there was a massive hyperinflation in Zimbabwe—the

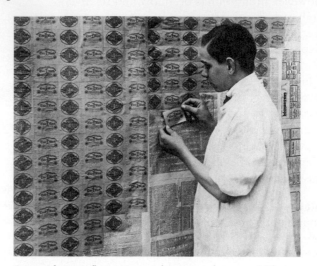

During hyperinflation money loses its value so quickly that people cease to accept it as a means of payment. At that point, money may as well be used for wallpaper.

largest in recorded history. At the height of the hyperinflation in 2008, the *annual* inflation rate was estimated at over 230 million percent!

Every one of these hyperinflations was accompanied by great increases in the money supply; new money was printed to give governments purchasing power that they could not or would not obtain by taxation. Further, every hyperinflation occurred in the midst of a major political upheaval in which serious doubts existed about the stability and the future of the government itself.

Is hyperinflation likely in the absence of civil war, revolution, or collapse of the government? Most economists think not. Further, it is clear that high inflation rates over a period of time do not mean the inevitable or even likely onset of hyperinflation.

Date	German Wholesale Price Index (1913 = 1)
January 1913	1
January 1920	13
January 1921	14
January 1922	37
July 1922	101
January 1923	2 785
July 1923	74 800
August 1923	944 000
September 1923	23 900 000
October 1923	7 096 000 000

a scale. The invention of coinage eliminated the need to weigh the metal at each transaction, but it created an important role for an authority, usually a king or queen, who made the coins and affixed his or her seal, guaranteeing the amount of precious metal that the coin contained. This was clearly a great convenience, as long as traders knew that they could accept the coin at its "face value." The face value was nothing more than a statement that a certain weight of the precious metal was contained therein.

However, coins often could not be taken at their face value. The practice of clipping a thin slice off the edge of the coin and keeping the valuable metal became common. This, of course, served to undermine the acceptability of coins, even if they were stamped. To get around this problem, the idea arose of minting the coins with a rough edge. The absence of the rough edge would immediately indicate that the coin had been clipped. This practice, called *milling*, survives on Canadian dimes, quarters, and two-dollar coins as an interesting anachronism to remind us that there were days when the market value of the metal in the coin was equal to the face value of the coin.

Canadian quarters are intentionally produced with rough or bumpy edges. Such milling of coins is now unnecessary, but many decades ago when coins were made from precious metals, it was useful in preventing individuals from clipping the coins.

Not to be outdone by the cunning of their subjects, some rulers were quick to seize the chance of getting something for nothing. The power to mint coins placed rulers in a position to work a very profitable fraud. They often used some suitable occasion—a marriage, an anniversary, an alliance—to remint the coinage. Subjects would be ordered to bring their coins in to the mint to be melted down and coined afresh with a new stamp. Between the melting down and the recoining, however, the rulers had only to toss some further inexpensive base metal in with the melted coins. This *debasing* of the coinage allowed the ruler to earn a handsome profit by minting more new coins than the number of old ones collected and putting the extras in the royal vault. Through debasement, the amount of money in the economy (but not the amount of gold) had increased.

The eventual result of such debasement was inflation. The subjects had the same number of coins as before and hence could demand the same quantity of goods. When rulers paid their bills, however, the recipients of the extra coins could be expected to spend them. This caused a net increase in demand, which in turn bid up prices. Thus, increasing the money supply by debasing the coinage was a common cause of inflation.

Gresham's Law. The early experience of currency debasement led to the observation known as **Gresham's Law**, after Sir Thomas Gresham (1519–1579), an advisor to the Elizabethan court, who coined the phrase "bad money drives out good."

When Queen Elizabeth I came to the throne of England in the middle of the sixteenth century, the coinage had been severely debased. Seeking to help trade, Elizabeth minted new coins that contained their full face value of gold. However, as fast as she fed these new coins into circulation, they disappeared. Why?

Suppose you possessed one of these new coins and one of the old ones, each with the same face value, and had to make a purchase. What would you do? You would use the debased coin to make the purchase and keep the undebased one; you part with less gold that way. Suppose you wanted to obtain a certain amount of gold bullion by melting

Gresham's Law The theory that "bad," or debased, money drives "good," or undebased, money out of circulation.

down the gold coins (as was frequently done). Which coins would you use? You would use new, undebased coins because it would take more of the debased coins than the new coins to get a given amount of gold bullion. The debased coins (bad money) would thus remain in circulation, and the undebased coins (good money) would disappear into peoples' private hoards—the "bad" money would drive out the "good" money.

> Gresham's Law predicts that when two types of money are used side by side, the one with the greater intrinsic value will be driven out of circulation.

Gresham's insights have proven helpful in explaining the experience of a number of modern high-inflation economies. For example, in the 1970s, inflation in Chile raised the value of the metallic content in coins above their face value. Coins quickly disappeared from circulation as the coins were melted down for their metal. Only paper currency remained in circulation and was used even for tiny transactions, such as purchasing a pack of matches. Gresham's law is one reason that modern coins, unlike their historical counterparts, are merely tokens that contain a metallic value that is only a small fraction of their face value.

The development of paper money, such as this bank note issued by The Montreal Bank more than a century ago, was an important step in the evolution of modern, fractional-reserve banking systems. Paper money allowed individuals to avoid the cumbersome transportation of gold when making their daily transactions.

Paper Money The next important step in the history of money was the evolution of paper currency. Artisans who worked with gold required secure safes, and the public began to deposit gold with these goldsmiths for safekeeping. Goldsmiths would give their depositors receipts promising to return the gold on demand. When a depositor wanted to make a large purchase, he could go to his goldsmith, reclaim some of his gold, and pay it to the seller of the goods. If the seller had no immediate need for the gold, he would carry it back to the goldsmith for safekeeping.

If people knew the goldsmith to be reliable, there was no need to go through the cumbersome and risky business of physically transferring the gold. The buyer needed only to transfer the goldsmith's receipt to the seller, who would accept it as long as he was confident that the goldsmith would pay over the gold whenever it was needed. This transferring of paper receipts rather than gold was essentially the invention of paper money.[1]

When it first came into being, paper money represented a promise to pay so much gold on demand. In this case, the promise was made first by goldsmiths and later by banks. Such paper money was *backed* by precious metal and was *convertible on demand* into this metal. In the nineteenth century, private banks commonly issued paper money, called **bank notes**, nominally convertible into gold. As with the goldsmiths, each bank issued its own notes, and these notes were convertible into gold at the issuing bank. Thus, in the nineteenth century, bank notes from many different banks circulated side by side, each of them being backed by gold at the bank that issued them.

bank notes Paper money issued by commercial banks.

---

[1] Paper money dates back as far as the T'ang dynasty in China (A.D. 618–907) but first appeared in Europe much later, in the 1660s in Sweden. For a very readable history of the development of money, see Jack Weatherford, *The History of Money*, Three Rivers Press, 1997.

Fractionally Backed Paper Money. Early on, many goldsmiths and banks discovered that it was not necessary to keep one ounce of gold in the vaults for every claim to one ounce circulating as paper money. At any one time, some of the bank's customers would be withdrawing gold, others would be depositing it, and most would be using the bank's paper notes without any need or desire to convert those notes into gold. As a result, the bank was able to issue more paper money redeemable in gold than the amount of gold that it held in its vaults. This was good business because the extra paper money could be invested profitably in interest-earning loans to households and firms. To this day, banks have many more claims outstanding against them than they actually have in reserves available to pay those claims. We say that such a currency is *fractionally backed* by the reserves.

The major problem with a fractionally backed currency was maintaining its convertibility into the precious metal behind it. The imprudent bank that issued too much paper money would find itself unable to redeem its currency in gold when the demand for gold was even slightly higher than usual. It would then have to suspend payments, and all holders of its notes would suddenly find that the notes were worthless. The prudent bank that kept a reasonable relationship between its note issues and its gold reserves would find that it could meet a normal range of demand for gold without any trouble.

If, for whatever reason, the public lost confidence in the banks and demanded redemption of its currency *en masse*, even the most prudent bank would be unable to honour its promises. The history of nineteenth- and early-twentieth-century banking on both sides of the Atlantic is full of examples of banks that were ruined by "panics," or sudden runs on their gold reserves. When these happened, the banks' depositors and the holders of their notes would find themselves with worthless pieces of paper.

Paper money used to be backed by the value of gold—meaning that it was redeemable for gold. But now money is not redeemable for anything except itself—people hold it because they know that others will accept it as payment for goods and services.

Fiat Money As time went on, currency (notes and coins) issued by private banks became less common, and central banks took control of issuing currency. In time, *only* central banks were permitted by law to issue currency. Originally, the central banks issued currency that was fully convertible into gold. In those days, gold would be brought to the central bank, which would issue currency in the form of "gold certificates" that asserted that the gold was available on demand. The reserves of gold thus set an upper limit on the amount of currency that could circulate in the economy. This practice of backing the currency with gold is known as a **gold standard**.

However, central banks, like private banks before them, could issue more currency than they had in gold because in normal circumstances only a small fraction of the outstanding currency would be presented for payment at any one time. Thus, even though the need to maintain convertibility into gold put some upper limit on note issuance, central banks had substantial discretionary control over the quantity of currency outstanding. For example, if the central bank decided to hold gold reserves equal to at least 20 percent of its outstanding currency, the total amount of currency would be limited to five times the gold reserves. But the central bank would nonetheless have complete discretion in choosing this fraction; the smaller the fraction held in reserves, the larger the supply of paper currency that could be supported with a given stock of gold.

During the period between the First and Second World Wars (1919–1939), almost all the countries of the world abandoned the gold standard; their currencies were thus

gold standard A currency standard whereby a country's currency is convertible into gold at a fixed rate of exchange.

no longer convertible into gold. Money that is not convertible by law into anything tangible derives its value from its acceptability in exchange. Such **fiat money** is widely acceptable because it is declared by government order, or *fiat*, to be legal tender. *Legal tender* is anything that by law must be accepted when offered either for the purchase of goods or services or to repay a debt.

fiat money Paper money or coinage that is neither backed by nor convertible into anything else but is decreed by the government to be legal tender.

Today, no country allows its currency to be converted into gold on demand. Gold backing for Canadian currency was eliminated in 1940, although note issues continued to carry the traditional statement "will pay to the bearer on demand" until 1954. Today's Bank of Canada notes simply say, "This note is legal tender." It is, in other words, fiat money pure and simple.[2]

> If fiat money is generally acceptable, it is a medium of exchange. If its purchasing power remains stable, it is a satisfactory store of value. If both of these things are true, it serves as a satisfactory unit of account. Today, almost all currency is fiat money.

Many people are disturbed to learn that present-day paper money is neither backed by nor convertible into anything more valuable—that it consists of nothing but pieces of paper whose value derives from common acceptance and from confidence that it will continue to be accepted in the future. Many people believe that their money should be more "substantial" than this. Yet money is, in fact, nothing more than generally acceptable pieces of paper.

Modern Money: Deposit Money

Today's bank customers deposit coins and paper money with the banks for safekeeping, just as in former times they deposited gold. Such a deposit is recorded as a credit to the customer's account, and is a liability (a promise to pay) for the commercial bank.

When the customer wants to purchase goods or services, or wants to settle a debt, three options are available. First, the customer can withdraw cash from the bank account and use it to make a transaction. Second, the customer can write a *cheque* to the recipient, who then deposits the cheque in their own bank account. A cheque is simply an order for a *transfer* of funds from the customer's account to the recipient's account, possibly at a different bank. The development of automatic teller machines (ATMs) in the past 30 years has made the cash option more convenient than it was before ATMs existed, and the cheque-writing option was common until quite recently, but is now much less so.

The customer's third option involves an electronic transfer of funds. Like a cheque, although must faster, a purchase using a bank card or debit card leads to a transfer of funds from the bank account of the purchaser to the bank account of the seller. Other electronic transfers of funds are also commonly used, such as direct-deposit payments by employers to employees and online payments that individuals can make from their bank accounts to firms for the provision of various services, such as Internet service, credit cards, and telephone service.

deposit money Money held by the public in the form of deposits with commercial banks.

Deposits contained inside bank accounts can easily be used to facilitate transactions, even though they exist only as electronic entries; they are referred to as **deposit money**.

---

[2] See *A History of the Canadian Dollar* (written by James Powell and published by the Bank of Canada) for a detailed and very readable discussion of the evolution of Canadian money.

As we will see later in this chapter, the value of deposit money in a modern economy far exceeds the value of coins and paper currency. As in much earlier times, modern banks create more promises to pay (deposit money) than they hold as cash in reserve.

> Bank deposits are money. Today, just as in the past, banks create money by issuing more promises to pay (deposits) than they have cash reserves available to pay out.

27.2 The Canadian Banking System

Several types of institutions make up a modern banking system, such as exists in Canada today. The **central bank** is the government-owned and government-operated institution that is the sole money-issuing authority and serves to control the banking system. Through it, the government's monetary policy is conducted. In Canada, the central bank is the Bank of Canada, often called just the Bank.

Financial intermediaries are privately owned institutions that serve the general public. They are called *intermediaries* because they stand between savers, from whom they accept deposits, and borrowers, to whom they make loans. For many years, government regulations created sharp distinctions among the various types of financial intermediaries by limiting the types of transactions in which each could engage. The past three decades have seen a sweeping deregulation of the financial system so that many of these traditional distinctions no longer apply. In this book, we use the term *commercial banks* to extend to all financial intermediaries that accept deposits and create deposit money, including chartered banks, trust companies, credit unions, and caisses populaires.

central bank A bank that acts as banker to the commercial banking system and often to the government as well. Usually a government-owned institution that is the sole money-issuing authority.

The Bank of Canada

Many of the world's early central banks were initially private, profit-making institutions that provided services to ordinary banks. Their importance, however, caused them to develop close ties with government. Central banks soon became instruments of the government, though not all of them were publicly owned. The Bank of England, one of the world's oldest and most famous central banks, began to operate as the central bank of England in the seventeenth century, but it was not formally taken over by the government until 1947.

The similarities in the functions performed and the tools used by the world's central banks are much more important than the differences in their organization. Although we give our attention to the operations of the Bank of Canada, its basic functions are similar to those of the Bank of England, the Federal Reserve System in the United States, or the European Central Bank (the sole issuer of the euro).

Organization of the Bank of Canada The Bank of Canada commenced operations on March 11, 1935. It is a publicly owned corporation; all profits it earns are remitted to the Government of Canada. The responsibility for the Bank's affairs rests with a board of directors composed of the governor, the senior deputy governor, the deputy minister of finance, and 12 directors.

The European Central Bank's website is www.ecb.int.

The Bank of Canada is located on Wellington Street in Ottawa, across the street from the Parliament Buildings.

The governor is appointed by the directors, with the approval of the federal cabinet, for a seven-year term.

The organization of the Bank of Canada is designed to keep the operation of monetary policy free from day-to-day political influence. The Bank is not responsible to Parliament for its day-to-day behaviour in the way that the department of finance is for the operation of fiscal policy. In this sense, the Bank of Canada has considerable autonomy in the way it carries out monetary policy. But the Bank is not completely independent. The *ultimate* responsibility for the Bank's actions rests with the government, since it is the government that must answer to Parliament. This system is known as "joint responsibility," and it dates back to 1967.

Under the system of joint responsibility, the governor of the Bank and the minister of finance consult regularly. In the case of fundamental disagreement over monetary policy, the minister of finance has the option of issuing an explicit *directive* to the governor and announcing this decision publicly. In such a case (which has not happened since the inception of joint responsibility), the governor would simply carry out the minister's directive or ignore the directive and resign. In the absence of such a directive, however, responsibility for monetary policy rests with the governor of the Bank.

For information on the Bank of Canada, see its website: www.bankofcanada.ca.

> The system of joint responsibility keeps the conduct of monetary policy free from day-to-day political influence while ensuring that the government retains ultimate responsibility for monetary policy.[3]

Basic Functions of the Bank of Canada A central bank serves four main functions: as a banker for private banks, as a bank for the government, as the regulator of the nation's money supply, and as a supporter of financial markets. The first three functions are reflected in Table 27-1, which shows the balance sheet of the Bank of Canada as of December 2011.

Banker to the Commercial Banks. The central bank accepts deposits from commercial banks and will, on order, transfer them to the account of another bank. In this way, the central bank provides the commercial banks with the means of settling debts to other banks. The deposits of the commercial banks with the Bank of Canada—part of their *reserves*—appear in Table 27-1. In December 2011 the banks had $107 million on reserve at the Bank of Canada. Notice that the cash reserves of the commercial banks deposited with the central bank are liabilities of the central bank, because it promises to pay them on demand.

Historically, one of the earliest services provided by central banks was that of "lender of last resort" to the banking system. Central banks would lend money to private banks that had sound investments (such as government securities) but were in urgent need of cash. If such banks could not obtain ready cash, they might be forced into insolvency, because they could not meet the demands of their depositors, in spite of

---

[3] This system was motivated by the "Coyne Affair" in 1961, during the Progressive Conservative government of John Diefenbaker. James Coyne, then governor of the Bank of Canada, disagreed with the minister of finance, Donald Fleming, over the conduct of monetary policy and was eventually forced to resign. Louis Rasminsky then accepted the position as governor of the Bank on the condition that the *Bank of Canada Act* be modified to incorporate the idea of joint responsibility. The *Bank of Canada Act* was so amended in 1967. For a discussion of the early history of the Bank of Canada, see George Watts, *The Bank of Canada: Origins and Early History*, Carleton University Press, 1993.

TABLE 27-1 Assets and Liabilities of the Bank of Canada, December 2011 (millions of dollars)

Assets		Liabilities	
Government of Canada securities	62 098.9	Notes in circulation	61 028.8
Advances to commercial banks	81.5	Government of Canada deposits	1 512.5
Net foreign-currency assets	11.7	Deposits of commercial banks (reserves)	106.7
Other assets	2 055.1	Other liabilities and capital	1 599.2
Total	64 247.2	Total	64 247.2

The balance sheet of the Bank of Canada shows that it serves as banker to the commercial banks and to the government of Canada, and as issuer of our currency; it also suggests the Bank's role as regulator of money markets and the money supply. The principal liabilities of the Bank are the basis of the money supply. Bank of Canada notes are currency, and the deposits of the commercial banks give them the reserves they need to create deposit money. The Bank's holdings of Government of Canada securities arise from its operations designed to regulate the money supply and financial markets.

(*Source:* Bank of Canada, *Annual Report 2011.* www.bankofcanada.ca.)

their being basically sound. Today's central banks continue to be lenders of last resort. Table 27-1 shows that in December 2011 the Bank of Canada had $81.5 million in outstanding loans to commercial banks.

Banker to the Federal Government. Governments, too, need to hold their funds in an account into which they can make deposits and on which they can write cheques. The Government of Canada keeps some of its chequing deposits at the Bank of Canada. In December 2011, the federal government had $1.5 billion in deposits at the Bank of Canada.

When the government requires more money than it collects in taxes, it needs to borrow, and it does so by issuing government securities (short-term Treasury bills or longer-term bonds). Most are sold directly to financial institutions and large institutional investors, but in most years the Bank of Canada buys some and credits the government's account with a deposit for the amount of the purchase. In December 2011, the Bank of Canada held $62.1 billion in Government of Canada securities. These securities are the Bank of Canada's primary asset, usually representing over 95 percent of the Bank's total assets. It is largely by earning interest on these securities that the Bank of Canada earns a profit every year—a profit that is eventually remitted to the government.

Regulator of the Money Supply. One of the most important functions of a central bank is to regulate the *money supply*. Though we have not yet defined the money supply precisely—and there are several different definitions of the money supply that we will encounter—we will see that most measures of the money supply include currency in circulation plus deposits held at commercial banks. Table 27-1 shows that the vast majority of the Bank of Canada's liabilities (its promises to pay) are the currency in

When the Government of Canada borrows money to finance some of its expenditures, it issues bonds like these. The Bank of Canada is the Government's "fiscal agent" and manages its outstanding debt.

circulation (held by the public) or the reserves of the commercial banks.[4] These reserves, in turn, underlie the deposits of households and firms—in exactly the same way that in much earlier times the goldsmith's holdings of gold underlay its issue of notes.

By changing its liabilities (currency plus reserves), the Bank of Canada can change the money supply. The Bank can change the levels of its assets and liabilities in many ways and, as its liabilities rise and fall, so does the money supply. In Chapter 29, we will explore in detail how this happens and how it is related to the Bank's decisions regarding monetary policy. At that point we will see how the Bank's holdings of government securities (its largest asset) are closely related to the value of notes in circulation (its largest liability).

Supporter of Financial Markets. Various institutions—including commercial banks, credit unions, trust companies, and caisses populaires—are in the business of accepting deposits from customers and then using these funds to extend long-term loans to borrowers. Large, unanticipated increases in interest rates tend to squeeze these institutions. The average rate they earn on their portfolio of loans rises only slowly as old contracts mature and new ones are made, but they must either pay higher rates to hold on to their deposits or accept wide-scale withdrawals that could easily bring about insolvency. Such dramatic events are relatively rare in the Canadian banking sector, though Canadian banks have failed in the past and it is possible, though unlikely, that more may fail in the future.

As we have already mentioned, during the global financial crisis of 2008 the Bank of Canada played a much more active role than usual in supporting financial markets. At that time, commercial banks around the world dramatically reduced their interbank lending after the failure of some large U.S. and U.K. financial institutions. The reduction in lending reflected heightened uncertainty regarding the credit-worthiness of *all* commercial banks. In response, the Bank of Canada took unprecedented actions designed to keep credit flowing as normally as possible in Canada, including the significant provision of short-term loans to Canadian financial institutions.

Commercial Banks in Canada

commercial bank A privately owned, profit-seeking institution that provides a variety of financial services, such as accepting deposits from customers and making loans and other investments.

All Canadian banks owned in the private sector are referred to as **commercial banks**. Commercial banks have common attributes: they hold deposits for their customers; they permit certain deposits to be transferred electronically or by cheque from an individual account to other accounts in the same or other banks; they invest in government

---

[4] Currency is a liability for the central bank because holders of currency can take it back to the central bank and redeem it for . . . currency! In the days of the gold standard, currency was redeemable for gold. Today, it is just redeemable for itself.

securities (short-term Treasury bills and longer-term bonds); they make loans to households and firms; and they often divide these loans into small pieces and re-package them into securities, each of which contains a diversified collection of many pieces from the original loans—a process called *securitization*.

Banks are not the only financial institutions in the country. Many other privately owned, profit-seeking institutions, such as trust companies and credit unions, accept deposits and grant loans for specific purposes. Many retail stores and credit-card companies also extend credit so that purchases can be made on a buy-now, pay-later basis.

The Provision of Credit From the perspective of the overall economy, the most important role played by commercial banks and other financial institutions is that of *financial intermediary*. Banks borrow (accept deposits) from households and firms that have money that they do not currently need, and they lend (provide credit) to those households and firms that need credit to achieve their objectives. They therefore act as essential *intermediaries* in the credit market.

Credit can be viewed as the "lifeblood" of a modern economy. Households often require credit to make large purchases, such as home appliances and cars, and they almost always use credit (a mortgage) when they buy a house. Without easy access to credit, most of these household purchases would either be delayed by many years or impossible altogether. Firms require credit to finance several aspects of their operations. For example, payments for workers and for material inputs often must be made well before revenue from the associated production is received. In addition, firms often finance their capital investments—purchases of equipment or the construction of facilities—with the use of borrowed money. Without easy access to credit, many firms would be unable to conduct their normal business operations and, as a result, the level of economic activity would decline.

This crucial function of banks and other financial institutions—the provision of credit—is easy to overlook when credit markets are functioning smoothly. Like the flow of electricity, we usually take it for granted in our daily activities, only to be reminded of its importance when the next power failure occurs. Similarly, when the credit markets cease to function well, as they did during the global financial crisis of 2008, their importance to the economy becomes clear to all. Indeed, the economic recession that began in the United States in 2008 and quickly spread around the world originated in the failure of some large U.S. and U.K. banks, which in turn led to a reduction in the flow of credit and a rise in interest rates (the price of credit) in most countries. The effect on economic activity was quick and significant. A central part of the policy response, in Canada and elsewhere, involved taking actions to ensure that banks and other financial institutions were in a position to extend credit in a normal manner.

Interbank Activities Commercial banks have a number of interbank cooperative relationships. For example, banks often share loans. Even the biggest bank cannot meet all the credit needs of a giant corporation, and often a group of banks will offer a "pool loan," agreeing on common terms and dividing the loan up into manageable segments. Another form of interbank cooperation is the bank credit card. Visa and MasterCard are the two most widely used credit cards, and each is operated by a group of banks.

Probably the most important form of interbank cooperation is cheque clearing and collection, including the clearing of electronic transfers through debit cards and online banking activities. Bank deposits are an effective medium of exchange only because banks accept each other's cheques and allow funds to be transferred electronically when purchases are made with debit cards and other forms of electronic transfer. If a depositor in the Bank of Montreal writes a cheque to someone who deposits it in an account at CIBC, the Bank of Montreal now owes money to CIBC. This creates a need for the banks to present cheques to each other for payment. The same is true for transactions made electronically.

Millions of such transactions take place in the course of a day, and they result in an enormous sorting and bookkeeping job. Multibank systems make use of a **clearing house** where interbank debts are settled. At the end of the day, all the transfers (cheque and electronic) from the Bank of Montreal's customers for deposit to CIBC are totalled and set against the total of all the transfers from CIBC's customers for deposit to the Bank of Montreal. It is necessary only to settle the difference between the two sums. Electronic transfers take place immediately whereas cheques are passed through the clearing house back to the bank on which they were drawn. Both banks are then able to adjust the individual accounts by a set of book entries. An overall transfer between banks is necessary only when there is a net transfer from the customers of one bank to those of another. This is accomplished by a daily transfer of deposits held by the commercial banks with the Bank of Canada.

Banks as Profit Seekers Banks are private firms that seek to make profits. A commercial bank provides a variety of services to its customers: the convenience of deposits that can be transferred by personal cheque, debit card, or online transaction; a safe and convenient place to earn a modest but guaranteed return on savings; and financial advice and wealth-management services.

Table 27-2 is the combined balance sheet of the chartered banks in Canada. The bulk of any bank's liabilities are deposits owed to its depositors. The principal assets of a bank are the *securities* it owns (including government bonds), which pay interest or dividends, and the interest-earning *loans* it makes to individuals and to businesses, both in Canada and abroad (which may be denominated in foreign currencies). A bank loan is a liability to the borrower (who must pay it back) but an asset to the bank.

Commercial banks attract deposits by paying interest to depositors and by providing them with services, such as clearing cheques, automated teller machines, debit cards, and online banking. Banks earn profits by lending and investing money deposited with them for more than they pay their depositors in terms of interest and other services provided. They also earn profits through the wealth-management and investment services they provide to their customers.

Competition for deposits is active among commercial banks and between banks and other financial institutions. Interest paid on deposits, special high-interest certificates of deposit (CDs), advertising, personal solicitation of accounts, giveaway programs for new deposits to existing accounts, and improved services are all forms of competition for funds.

Commercial Banks' Reserves

Commercial banks keep sufficient cash on hand to be able to meet depositors' day-to-day requirements for cash (plus they keep deposits at the central bank which can be readily converted into cash). However, just as the goldsmiths of long ago discovered that only a fraction of the gold they held was ever withdrawn at any given time, and just as banks of long ago discovered that only a small fraction of convertible bank notes were actually converted, so too do modern bankers know that only a small fraction of their deposits will be withdrawn in cash at any one time.

clearing house An institution in which interbank indebtedness, arising from the transfer of cheques between banks, is computed and offset and net amounts owing are calculated.

TABLE 27-2 Consolidated Balance Sheet of the Canadian Chartered Banks, February 2012 (millions of dollars)

Assets		Liabilities	
Reserves (including deposits with Bank of Canada)	9 049	Demand and notice deposits	723 451
Government securities	241 348		
Mortgage and non-mortgage loans	1 606 225	Term deposits	563 401
Canadian corporate securities	186 737	Government deposits	10 667
		Foreign-currency liabilities	1 246 952
Foreign-currency assets	1 193 498	Shareholders' equity	194 626
Other assets	425 870	Other liabilities	923 630
Total	3 662 727	Total	3 662 727

Reserves are only a tiny fraction of deposit liabilities. If all the chartered banks' customers who held demand and notice deposits tried to withdraw them in cash, the banks could not meet this demand without liquidating over $700 billion of other assets. This would be impossible without assistance from the Bank of Canada.

(*Source:* Adapted from Bank of Canada, *Banking and Financial Statistics,* May 2012, Tables C3 and C4.)

The reserves needed to ensure that depositors can withdraw their deposits on demand will normally be quite small.

In abnormal times, however, nothing short of 100 percent would do the job if the commercial banking system had to stand alone. If a major bank were to fail, it would probably cause a general loss of confidence in the ability of other banks to redeem their deposits. The results would then be devastating. Such an event—or even the rumour of it—could lead to a **bank run** as depositors rushed to withdraw their money. Faced with such a panic, banks would have to close until either they had borrowed enough funds or sold enough assets to meet the demand, or the demand subsided. However, banks could not instantly turn their loans into cash because the borrowers would have the money tied up in such things as real estate or business enterprises. Neither could the banks obtain cash by selling their securities to the public because payments would be made by cheques, which would not provide cash to pay off depositors.

The difficulty of providing sufficient reserves to meet abnormal situations is alleviated by the central bank, which can provide all the reserves that are needed to meet any abnormal situation. It can do this in two ways. First, it can lend reserves directly to commercial banks on the security of assets that are sound but not easy to liquidate quickly, such as interest-earning residential or commercial mortgages. Second, it can enter the open market and buy all the government securities that commercial banks need to sell in order to increase their available cash reserves. Once the public finds that deposits can be turned into cash at their request, any panic would usually subside and any further drain of cash out of banks would cease.

The possibility of a bank run in Canada has been all but eliminated by the provision of deposit insurance by the Canada Deposit Insurance Corporation (CDIC), a federal

bank run A situation in which many depositors rush to withdraw their money, possibly leading to a bank's financial collapse.

The late Jimmy Stewart plays George Bailey in It's a Wonderful Life. *In this scene, Bailey, the owner of a small commercial bank, explains to his panicking customers why they can't all take their money out at the same time. It is a great illustration of the workings of a fractional-reserve banking system.*

Crown corporation. The CDIC guarantees that, in the unlikely event of a bank failure, depositors will get their money back, up to a limit of $100 000 per eligible deposit (there are seven different types of deposit that are eligible for CDIC insurance). Most depositors will not rush to withdraw all of their money as long as they are certain they can get it when they need it.

Target and Excess Reserves Canada's banks hold reserves against their deposit liabilities for the simple reason that they want to avoid situations in which they cannot satisfy their depositors' demands for cash, and it is costly for them to borrow from other banks or from the Bank of Canada when they run short of reserves. Look again at Table 27-2. Notice that the chartered banks' reserves of just over $9 billion are less than 1 percent of their *deposit* liabilities of more than $1.25 trillion.

Thus, if the holders of even 1 percent of deposits demanded cash, the banks would be unable to meet the demand without outside help. Reserves can be as low as they are because, first, banks know that it is very unlikely that even 1 percent of their total deposits will be withdrawn at any given time and, second, the banks know that the Bank of Canada will help them out in time of temporary need. The Canadian banking system is thus a **fractional-reserve system**, with commercial banks holding reserves—either as cash or as deposits at the Bank of Canada—of just a small fraction of their total deposits.

A bank's **reserve ratio** is the fraction of its deposits that it *actually* holds as reserves at any point in time, either as cash or as deposits with the Bank of Canada. A bank's **target reserve ratio** is the fraction of its deposits it would *ideally* like to hold as reserves. This target reserve ratio will generally not be constant over time. During holiday seasons, for example, banks may choose to hold more reserves because they know, based on past experience, that there will be heavy demands for cash.

At any given time, any commercial bank will probably not be exactly at its target level of reserves. Reserves may be slightly above or slightly below the target, but the commercial bank will take actions to gradually restore its actual reserves toward its target level. Any reserves in excess of the target level are called **excess reserves**. As we will see next, a bank can expand or contract its portfolio of loans to adjust its actual reserves toward its target level. Understanding this process is the key to understanding the "creation" of deposit money.

fractional-reserve system A banking system in which commercial banks keep only a fraction of their deposits in cash or on deposit with the central bank.

reserve ratio The fraction of its deposits that a commercial bank actually holds as reserves in the form of cash or deposits with the central bank.

target reserve ratio The fraction of its deposits that a commercial bank wants to hold as reserves.

excess reserves Reserves held by a commercial bank in excess of its target reserves.

| 27.3 Money Creation by the Banking System

We noted before that the *money supply* includes both currency and deposits at commercial banks. The fractional-reserve system provides the means to permit commercial banks to create new deposits and thus to create new money. The process is important, so it is worth examining in some detail.

Some Simplifying Assumptions

To focus on the essential aspects of how banks create money, suppose that banks can invest in only one kind of asset—loans—and they have only one kind of deposit. Two other assumptions are provisional and will be relaxed after we have developed some basic ideas about the creation of money:

1. *Fixed target reserve ratio.* We assume that all banks have the same target reserve ratio, which does not change. In our numerical illustration, we will assume that the target reserve ratio is 20 percent (0.20); that is, for every $5 of deposits, the banks want to hold $1 in reserves, investing the rest in new loans.

2. *No cash drain from the banking system.* We also assume that the public holds a fixed absolute amount of the currency in circulation. In particular, we assume that the amount of currency held by the public is *not* a constant ratio of their bank deposits. (Later on we will assume that the amount of currency held by the public grows as total bank deposits grow. This is called a *cash drain*.)

The Creation of Deposit Money

A hypothetical balance sheet, with assets and liabilities, is shown for TD Bank (TD) in Table 27-3. TD has assets of $200 of reserves, held partly as cash on hand and partly as deposits with the central bank, and $900 of loans outstanding to its customers. Its liabilities are $100 to investors (owners) who contributed financial capital to start the bank and $1000 to current depositors. The bank's ratio of reserves to deposits is 0.20 (200/1000), exactly equal to its target reserve ratio.

What Is a New Deposit? In what follows, we are interested in knowing how the commercial banking system can "create money" when confronted with a new deposit. But what do we mean by a new deposit? By "new," we mean a deposit of cash that is new to the *commercial banking system*. There are three examples.

- First, an individual might immigrate to Canada and bring cash. When that cash is deposited into a commercial bank, it constitutes a new deposit to the Canadian banking system.
- Second, an individual who had some cash stashed under his bed (or in a safety deposit box) has now decided to deposit it into an account at a commercial bank.
- Third is the most interesting but also the most complicated example. If the Bank of Canada were to purchase a government security from an individual or from a firm, it would purchase that asset with a cheque drawn on the Bank of Canada. When the individual or firm deposits the cheque with a commercial bank, it would be a new deposit to the commercial banking system.

The important point to keep in mind here is that the *source* of the new deposit is irrelevant to the process of money creation by the commercial banks. In the

TABLE 27-3 The Initial Balance Sheet of TD

Assets ($)		Liabilities ($)	
Reserves (cash and deposits with the central bank)	200	Deposits	1 000
Loans	900	Capital	100
	1 100		1 100

TD has reserves equal to 20 percent of its deposit liabilities. The commercial bank earns profits by finding profitable investments for much of the money deposited with it. In this balance sheet, loans are its income-earning assets.

TABLE 27-4 TD's Balance Sheet Immediately After a New Deposit of $100

Assets ($)		Liabilities ($)	
Reserves	300	Deposits	1 100
Loans	900	Capital	100
	1 200		1 200

The new deposit raises liabilities and assets by the same amount. Because both reserves and deposits rise by $100, the bank's actual reserve ratio, formerly 0.20, increases to 0.27. The bank now has excess reserves of $80.

TABLE 27-5 TD's Balance Sheet After Making a New Loan of $80

Assets ($)		Liabilities ($)	
Reserves	220	Deposits	1 100
Loans	980	Capital	100
	1 200		1 200

TD converts its excess cash reserves into new loans. The bank keeps $20 as a reserve against the initial new deposit of $100. It lends the remaining $80 to a customer, who writes a cheque to someone who deals with another bank. Comparing Table 27-3 and 27-5 shows that the bank has increased its deposit liabilities by the $100 initially deposited and has increased its assets by $20 of cash reserves and $80 of new loans. It has also restored its target reserve ratio of 0.20.

TABLE 27-6 Changes in the Balance Sheets of Second-Round Banks

Assets ($)		Liabilities ($)	
Reserves	+16	Deposits	+80
Loans	+64		
	+80		+80

Second-round banks receive cash deposits and expand loans. The second-round banks gain new deposits of $80 as a result of the loan granted by TD. These banks keep 20 percent of the cash that they acquire as their reserve against the new deposit, and they can make new loans using the other 80 percent.

discussion that follows, we use the example of the Bank of Canada buying government securities from firms or households as a way of generating a new deposit. But this is not crucial. We use this example because, as we will see in Chapter 29, this is how the Bank of Canada directly alters the level of reserves in the banking system when it chooses to do so. But the general process of money creation we are about to describe applies to *any* new deposit, whatever its source.

The Expansion of Money from a Single New Deposit Suppose the Bank of Canada enters the open market and buys $100 worth of Government of Canada bonds from John Smith. The Bank issues a cheque to Smith, who then deposits the $100 cheque into his account at TD. This $100 is a wholly new deposit for the commercial bank, and it results in a revised balance sheet (Table 27-4). As a result of the new deposit, TD's reserve assets and deposit liabilities have both increased by $100. More important, TD's ratio of reserves to deposits has increased from 0.20 to 0.27 (300/1100). The bank now has $80 in excess reserves; with $1100 in deposits, its target reserves are only $220.

TD can now lend the $80 in excess reserves that it is holding. As it lends the $80, it increases its loan portfolio by $80 but reduces its reserves by the same amount. Table 27-5 shows TD's balance sheet after this new loan is made. Notice that TD has restored its reserve ratio to 20 percent, its target reserve ratio.

So far, of the $100 initial deposited at TD, $20 is held by TD as reserves against the deposit and $80 has been lent out in the system. As a result, other banks have received new deposits of $80 stemming from the loans made by TD; persons receiving payment from those who borrowed the $80 from TD will have deposited those payments in their own banks.

The banks that receive deposits from the proceeds of TD's loan are called second-round banks, third-round banks, and so on. In this case, the second-round banks receive new deposits of $80, and when the cheques clear, they have new reserves of $80. Because they desire to hold only $16 in additional reserves to support the new deposits, they have $64 of excess reserves. They now increase their loans by $64. After this money has been spent by the borrowers and has been deposited in other, third-round banks, the balance sheets of the second-round banks will have changed, as in Table 27-6.

The third-round banks now find themselves with $64 of new deposits. Against these they want to hold only $12.80 as reserves, so they have excess reserves of $51.20 that they can immediately lend out. Thus, there begins a long sequence of new deposits, new loans, new deposits, and new loans. These stages are shown in Table 27-7.

The new deposit of $100 to the banking system has led, through the banks' desire to lend their excess reserves, to the creation of new money. After the completion of the process depicted in Table 27-7, the total change in the combined balance sheets of the entire banking system is shown in Table 27-8.

> If v is the target reserve ratio, a new deposit to the banking system will increase the total amount of deposits by $1/v$ times the new deposit. [34]

In our example, where $v = 0.2$ and the new deposit equals $100, total deposits in the banking system will eventually increase by $(1/0.2)$ times $100—that is, by $500. In our example in which there was an initial new deposit of $100, this $100 was also the amount by which reserves increased in the banking system as a whole. This is because the entire amount of new cash eventually ends up in reserves held against a much larger volume of new deposits. Identifying a new deposit as the change in reserves in the banking system permits us to state our central result slightly differently.

> With no cash drain from the banking system, a banking system with a target reserve ratio of v can change its deposits by $1/v$ times any change in reserves.

TABLE 27-7 The Sequence of Loans and Deposits After a Single New Deposit of $100

Bank	New Deposits	New Loans	Addition to Reserves
TD	100.00	80.00	20.00
2nd-round bank	80.00	64.00	16.00
3rd-round bank	64.00	51.20	12.80
4th-round bank	51.20	40.96	10.24
5th-round bank	40.96	32.77	8.19
6th-round bank	32.77	26.22	6.55
7th-round bank	26.22	20.98	5.24
8th-round bank	20.98	16.78	4.20
9th-round bank	16.78	13.42	3.36
10th-round bank	13.42	10.74	2.68
Total for first 10 rounds	446.33	357.07	89.26
All remaining rounds	53.67	42.93	10.74
Total for banking system	500.00	400.00	100.00

The banking system as a whole can create deposit money whenever it receives new deposits. The table shows the process of the creation of deposit money on the assumptions that all the loans made by one set of banks end up as deposits in another set of banks (the next-round banks), that the target reserve ratio (v) is 0.20, and that banks always lend out any excess reserves. With no cash drain to the public, the banking system as a whole eventually increases deposits by $1/v$, which, in this example, is five times the amount of any increase in reserves that it obtains.

Recalling that the Greek letter delta (Δ) means "the change in," we can express this result in a simple equation:

$$\Delta \text{ Deposits} = \frac{\text{New cash deposits}}{v} = \frac{\Delta \text{ Reserves}}{v}$$

The "multiple expansion of deposits" that we have just described applies in reverse to a withdrawal of funds. Deposits of the banking system will fall by $1/v$ times the amount withdrawn from the banking system creating a "multiple contraction of deposits."

Excess Reserves and Cash Drains

The two simplifying assumptions that were made earlier can now be relaxed.

TABLE 27-8 Change in the Combined Balance Sheets of All the Banks in the System Following the Multiple Expansion of Deposits

Assets ($)		Liabilities ($)	
Reserves	+100	Deposits	+500
Loans	+400		
	+500		+500

The reserve ratio is returned to 0.20. The entire initial deposit of $100 ends up as additional reserves of the banking system. Therefore, deposits rise by $(1/0.2)$ times the initial deposit—that is, by $500.

Excess Reserves If banks do not choose to lend their excess reserves, the multiple expansion that we discussed will not occur. Go back to Table 27-4. If TD had been content to hold 27 percent of its deposits in reserves, it would have done nothing more. Other things being equal, banks will choose to lend their excess reserves because of the profit motive, but there may be times when they believe that the risk is too great. It is one thing to be offered a good rate of interest on a loan, but if the borrower defaults on the payment of interest and principal, the bank will be the loser. Similarly, if the bank expects interest rates to rise in the future, it may hold off making loans now so that it will have reserves available to make more profitable loans after the interest rate has risen.

Deposit creation does not happen automatically; it depends on the decisions of bankers. If commercial banks do not choose to lend their excess reserves, there will not be a multiple expansion of deposits.

Recall that we have said that the money supply includes both currency and bank deposits. What we have just seen is that the behaviour of commercial banks is crucial to the process of deposit creation. It follows that the money supply is partly determined by the commercial banks—in response, for example, to changes in national income, interest rates, and expectations of future business conditions.

Cash Drain Until now, we have been assuming that the public holds a fixed amount of cash, so that when deposits were multiplying in the economy, there was no change in the amount of cash held by the public. But now suppose that instead of holding a fixed *number* of dollars, people decide to hold an amount of cash equal to a fixed *fraction* of their bank deposits. An extra $100 that now gets injected into the banking system as a new cash deposit will not all stay in the banking system. As the amount of deposits multiplies, some fraction of that $100 will be added to the cash held by the public. In such a situation, any multiple expansion of bank deposits will be accompanied by what is called a *cash drain* to the public. This cash drain will reduce the multiple expansion of bank deposits in exactly the same way that taxes and imports reduced the value of the simple multiplier in Chapter 22.

In the case of a cash drain, the relationship between the eventual change in deposits and a new injection of cash into the banking system is slightly more complicated. If new cash is injected into the system, it will ultimately show up either as reserves or as cash held by the public. If c is the ratio of cash to deposits that people want to maintain, the final change in deposits will be given by

$$\Delta \text{ Deposits} = \frac{\text{New cash deposit}}{c + v}$$

For example, suppose the Bank of Canada were to purchase $100 of government securities from some current bondholders. As the bondholders deposit their $100 into their bank accounts, there is an injection of $100 into the banking system. If commercial banks' target reserve ratio is 20 percent and there is *no* cash drain, the eventual expansion of deposits will be $500 ($\Delta$ Deposits = $100/0.20). But if there is a cash drain of 10 percent, the eventual expansion of deposits will only be $333.33 ($\Delta$ Deposits = $100/(0.10 + 0.20)). [35]

> The larger is the cash drain from the banking system, the smaller will be the total expansion of deposits created by a new cash deposit.

Realistic Expansion of Deposits So far we have explained the expansion of deposits in the banking system by using reserve-deposit and cash-deposit ratios that are easy to work with but unrealistic for Canada. In particular, we have been assuming a reserve-deposit ratio (v) equal to 20 percent, whereas Table 27-2 on page 677 shows that Canadian commercial banks hold reserves equal to *less than 1 percent* of their deposit liabilities. A realistic value for the cash-deposit ratio in Canada is roughly 5 percent—indicating that firms and households hold cash outside the banks equal to 5 percent of the value of their bank deposits. Putting these more realistic values for v and c into our equation, we see that a $100 cash injection (new deposit) to the banking system will eventually lead to a total change in deposits equal to $100/(c + v) = \$100/(0.01 + 0.05) = \$100/(0.06) = \$1666.67$. Therefore, small changes in the amount of cash can lead, through the commercial banks' process of deposit creation, to very large changes in the total level of deposits. Commercial banks really do create a lot of (deposit) money out of thin air!

27.4 The Money Supply

Several times in this chapter we have mentioned the *money supply* without ever defining it precisely. But now that you are familiar with the balance sheets of the Bank of Canada and the commercial banking system, and are comfortable with the idea of deposit creation by the commercial banks, we are ready to be more precise about what we mean by the money supply.

The total stock of money in the economy at any moment is called the **money supply** or the *supply of money*. Economists use several alternative definitions for the money supply. Each definition includes the amount of currency in circulation *plus* some types of deposit liabilities of the financial institutions.

money supply The total quantity of money in an economy at a point in time. Also called the *supply of money*.

Money supply = Currency + Bank deposits

The different definitions vary only by which deposit liabilities are included. We begin by looking at the different kinds of deposits.

Kinds of Deposits

Over the past 30 years or so, banks have evolved a bewildering array of deposit options. From our point of view, the most important distinction is between deposits that can be readily transferred by cheque, Internet banking, phone, or debit card, and those that cannot be so easily transferred. The first type of deposits are media of exchange; the second type are not.

For many years, the distinction lay between *demand deposits*, which earned little or no interest but were transferable on demand (by cheque), and *savings deposits*, which earned a higher interest return but were not easily transferable. Today, however, it is so easy to transfer funds between almost all accounts that the distinction becomes quite

term deposit An interest-earning bank deposit, subject to notice before withdrawal. Also called a *notice deposit*.

blurred. The deposit that is genuinely tied up for a period of time now takes the form of a **term deposit**, which has a specified withdrawal date a minimum of 30 days into the future, and which pays a much reduced interest rate in the event of early withdrawal. Term and other "notice" deposits pay significantly higher interest rates than do regular demand deposits.

Non-bank financial institutions, such as asset-management firms, now offer *money market mutual funds* and *money market deposit accounts*. These accounts earn higher interest and are chequable, although some are subject to minimum withdrawal restrictions and others to prior notice of withdrawal.

> The long-standing distinction between money and other highly liquid assets used to be that, narrowly defined, money was a medium of exchange that did not earn interest, whereas other liquid assets earned interest but were not media of exchange. Today, this distinction has almost completely disappeared.

Definitions of the Money Supply

M2 Currency plus demand and notice deposits at the chartered banks.

M2+ M2 plus similar deposits at other financial institutions.

Different definitions of the money supply include different types of deposits. Until recently, a common definition of the money supply used by the Bank of Canada was called M1, which included currency in circulation plus demand (chequable) deposits held at the chartered banks. But M1 did not include similar deposits at other financial institutions or any non-chequable term or notice deposits. With the changing nature of deposits, it is now more common to use broader measures of the money supply. Two commonly used measures in Canada today are M2 and M2+. **M2** includes currency in circulation plus demand and notice deposits at the chartered banks; **M2+** includes M2 plus similar deposits at other financial institutions (trust and mortgage-loan companies, credit unions and caisses populaires) and holdings of money-market mutual funds. Table 27-9 shows the composition of M2 and M2+ in Canada as of March 2012.

The Bank of Canada computes other measures of the money supply even broader than M2+. These are referred to as M2++, M3, and so on, where each measure is broader than the previous one, meaning that it includes more types of financial assets. For example, M2++ includes M2+ plus holdings of Canada Savings Bonds and non-money-market funds. In general, the broader the measure of the money supply, the more the concept of money being measured includes assets that do not serve as a direct medium of exchange but do serve the store-of-value function and can be converted into a medium of exchange.

Near Money and Money Substitutes

near money Liquid assets that are easily convertible into money without risk of significant loss of value. They can be used as short-term stores of value but are not themselves media of exchange.

Recall our early discussion of money as a medium of exchange and as a store of value. In arriving at empirical measures of money, we must consider some assets that do not perform one or both of these roles perfectly. This brings us to the concepts of *near money* and *money substitutes*.

Assets that adequately fulfill the store-of-value function and are readily converted into a medium of exchange but are not themselves a medium of exchange are sometimes called **near money**. Term deposits are a good example of near money. When you have a term deposit, you know exactly how much purchasing power you hold (at current prices), and, given modern banking practices, you can turn your deposit into a medium of exchange—cash or a demand deposit—at a moment's notice (though you may pay a penalty in the form of reduced interest if you withdraw the funds before the end of the specified term).

Why then does everybody not keep his or her money in such deposits instead of in demand deposits or currency? The answer is that the inconvenience of continually shifting money back and forth may outweigh the interest that can be earned. One week's interest on $100 (at 5 percent per year) is only about 10 cents, not enough to cover bus fare to the bank, the time spent going to an ATM, or perhaps even the time spent making an online transfer. For money that will be needed soon, it would hardly pay to shift it to a term deposit.

Things that serve as media of exchange but are not a store of value are sometimes called **money substitutes**. Credit cards are a prime example. With a credit card, many transactions can be made without either cash, a debit card, or a cheque. The credit card serves the short-run function of a medium of exchange by allowing you to make purchases, even though you have no cash or bank deposit currently in your possession. But this is only temporary; money remains the final medium of exchange for these transactions when the credit-card bill is paid.

TABLE 27-9 M2 and M2 + in Canada, March 2012 (millions of dollars)	
Currency	58 528
Demand Deposits (chequable)	
Personal	223 494
Non-personal	271 097
Notice Deposits (non-chequable)	
Personal	496 575
Non-personal	25 771
Adjustment	−3 507
M2	**1 071 958**
Deposits at:	
Trust and mortgage-loan companies	28 459
Credit unions and caisses populaires	235 328
Money-market mutual funds	32 819
Other	58 456
M2+	**1 427 020**

M2 and M2+ are two commonly used measures of the money supply in Canada. M2 includes demand (chequable) and notice (non-chequable) deposits at the chartered banks; M2+ adds similar deposits at other financial institutions. These deposits all serve the medium-of-exchange function of money. Still broader measures (like M2++ and M3) include financial assets that best serve the store-of-value function but can readily be converted into a medium of exchange.

(*Source*: Adapted from Bank of Canada, *Weekly Financial Statistics*, June 15, 2012.)

The Role of the Bank of Canada

In this chapter, we have seen that the commercial banking system, when confronted with a new deposit, can create a multiple expansion of bank deposits. This shows how the reserves of the banking system are systematically related to the money supply. In Chapter 29 we will see the details of how the Bank of Canada conducts its monetary policy and how its actions influence the total amount of reserves in the banking system. At that point we will have a more complete picture of the connection among the Bank's monetary policy, reserves in the banking system, and the overall money supply.

Recall that in the previous chapter we examined how in the long run, with real GDP equal to Y^*, the real interest rate was determined by desired saving and desired investment. In the next chapter, we return to the short-run version of our macro model (in which Y is no longer assumed to equal Y^*) but add money to that model explicitly. There we will see how the interaction of money demand and money supply determines the equilibrium interest rate in the short run. We will also see how changes in the money market lead to changes in desired aggregate expenditure and real GDP. In Chapter 29 we examine the details of the Bank of Canada's monetary policy, with an emphasis on its current policy regime of *inflation targeting*.

money substitute Something that serves as a medium of exchange but is not a store of value.

SUMMARY

27.1 The Nature of Money

- Money is anything that serves as a medium of exchange, a store of value, and a unit of account.
- Money arose because of the inconvenience of barter, and it developed in stages: from precious metal to metal coinage, to paper money convertible to precious metals, to token coinage and paper money fractionally backed by precious metals, to fiat money, and to deposit money.

27.2 The Canadian Banking System

- The banking system in Canada consists of two main elements: the Bank of Canada (the central bank) and the commercial banks.
- The Bank of Canada is a government-owned corporation that is responsible for the day-to-day conduct of monetary policy. Though the Bank has considerable autonomy in its policy decisions, ultimate responsibility for monetary policy resides with the government.
- Commercial banks and other financial institutions play a key role as intermediaries in the credit market.

Significant interruptions in the flow of credit usually lead to increases in interest rates and reductions in the level of economic activity.

- Commercial banks are profit-seeking institutions that allow their customers to transfer deposits from one bank to another by means of cheques or electronic transfer. They create deposit money as a byproduct of their commercial operations of making loans and other investments.

27.3 Money Creation by the Banking System

- Because most customers are content to pay by cheque or debit card rather than with cash, banks need only small reserves to back their deposit liabilities. It is this *fractional-reserve aspect* of the banking system that enables commercial banks to create deposit money.
- When the banking system receives a new cash deposit, it can create new deposits equal to some multiple of this amount. For a target reserve ratio of v and a cash-deposit ratio of c, the total change in deposits following a new cash deposit is

$$\Delta \text{ Deposits} = \frac{\text{New cash deposit}}{c + v}$$

27.4 The Money Supply

- The money supply—the stock of money in an economy at a specific moment—can be defined in various ways. M2 includes currency plus demand and notice deposits at the chartered banks. M2+ includes M2 plus deposits at non-bank financial institutions and money-market mutual funds.

- Near money includes interest-earning assets that are convertible into money on a dollar-for-dollar basis but that are not currently a medium of exchange. Money substitutes are things such as credit cards that serve as a medium of exchange but are not money.

KEY CONCEPTS

Medium of exchange, store of value, and unit of account
Fully backed, fractionally backed, and fiat money

The banking system and the Bank of Canada
Target reserve ratio and excess reserves

The creation of deposit money
Demand and term deposits
The money supply
Near money and money substitutes

STUDY EXERCISES

MyEconLab Make the grade with MyEconLab: Study Exercises marked in red can be found on MyEconLab. You can practise them as often as you want, and most feature step-by-step guided instructions to help you find the right answer.

1. Fill in the blanks to make the following statements correct.

   a. Money serves three functions: _____, _____, and _____.

   b. Suppose children at a summer camp are each given a credit of $20 at the snack shop, where purchases are recorded but no cash is exchanged. This is an example of money as a(n) _____ and a(n) _____.

   c. Paper money and coins that are not convertible into anything with intrinsic value, but are declared by the government to be legal tender, are known as _____.

   d. The Bank of Canada has four main functions in the Canadian economy:
   • _____
   • _____
   • _____
   • _____

   e. Canada has a(n) _____ reserve banking system, in which commercial banks keep only a fraction of their total deposits in reserves. A commercial bank has a(n) _____ ratio that governs what it attempts to keep as reserves.

2. Fill in the blanks to make the following statements correct. Answer these questions in the sequence given.

   a. Suppose the Bank of Canada purchases a $1000 bond from Bob's Financial Firm, and Bob's deposits its cheque at the CIBC. This is a(n) _____ deposit to the banking system and will allow the commercial banks to _____.

   b. Continuing on from part (a), if the CIBC has a target reserve ratio of 5 percent, it will keep _____ dollars as reserves and will lend _____ dollars.

   c. Assuming there is no cash drain from the banking system, the ultimate effect is a(n) _____ in deposits in the banking system of _____ × $1000 = _____.

   d. Suppose the Bank of Canada sells a $1000 bond to Bob's Financial Firm, and Bob's pays for that bond with a cheque drawn on its account at the CIBC. This is a(n) _____ of funds from the banking

system and will cause the commercial banks to _____.

   e. If the CIBC pays the $1000 from its reserves, its reserve ratio will then be _____ its target rate of 5 percent. If the CIBC keeps its reserves at the new level, its loans must fall by _____ to restore the 5-percent target reserve ratio.

3. Which of the following items can be considered money in the Canadian economy? Explain your answers by discussing the three functions of money—medium of exchange, store of value, and unit of account.

   a. A Canadian $100 bill
   b. A Visa credit card
   c. A well-known painting by Robert Bateman
   d. The balance in an interest-earning savings account
   e. A U.S. Treasury bill payable in three months
   f. A share of Tim Hortons stock
   g. A $1 bill of Canadian Tire money

4. The table below shows the balance sheet for the Regal Bank, a hypothetical commercial bank. Assume that the Regal Bank has achieved its target reserve ratio.

Balance Sheet: Regal Bank			
Assets		Liabilities	
Reserves	$ 200	Deposits	$4000
Loans	$4200	Capital	$ 400

   a. What is the Regal Bank's target reserve ratio?
   b. What is the value of the owners' investment in the bank?
   c. Suppose someone makes a new deposit to the Regal Bank of $100. Draw a new balance sheet showing the *immediate* effect of the new deposit. What is the Regal Bank's new reserve ratio?
   d. Suppose instead that someone *withdraws* $100 cash from the Regal Bank. Show the new balance sheet and the new reserve ratio.

5. Consider a new deposit to the Canadian banking system of $1000. Suppose that all commercial banks have a target reserve ratio of 10 percent and there is no cash drain. The following table shows how deposits,

reserves, and loans change as the new deposit permits the banks to "create" money.

Round	Δ Deposits	Δ Reserves	Δ Loans
First	$1000	$100	$900
Second	___	___	___
Third	___	___	___
Fourth	___	___	___
Fifth	___	___	___

a. The first round has been completed in the table. Now, recalling that the new loans in the first round become the new deposits in the second round, complete the second round in the table.

b. By using the same approach, complete the entire table.

c. You have now completed the first five rounds of the deposit-creation process. What is the total change in deposits *so far* as a result of the single new deposit of $1000?

d. This deposit-creation process could go on forever, but it would still have a *finite* sum. In the text, we showed that the eventual total change in deposits is equal to $1/v$ times the new deposit, where v is the target reserve ratio. What is the eventual total change in deposits in this case?

e. What is the eventual total change in reserves? What is the eventual change in loans?

6. Consider a withdrawal of $5000 from the Canadian banking system. Suppose all commercial banks have a target reserve ratio of 8 percent and there is no cash drain.

a. Using a table like that shown in the previous question, show the change in deposits, reserves, and loans for the first three "rounds" of activity.

b. Compute the eventual total change in deposits, reserves, and loans.

7. Consider an individual who immigrates to Canada and deposits $3000 in Canadian currency into the Canadian banking system. Suppose all commercial banks have a target reserve ratio of 10 percent and individuals choose to hold cash equal to 10 percent of their bank deposits.

a. In the text, we showed that the eventual total change in deposits is equal to $1/(v + c)$ times the new deposit, where v is the target reserve ratio and c is the ratio of cash to deposits. What is the eventual total change in deposits in this case?

b. What is the eventual total change in reserves?

c. What is the eventual total change in loans?

8. Consider an individual who moves to Canada and brings with him $40 000 in Canadian currency, which he deposits in a Canadian bank. For each of the cases below, compute the overall change in deposits and reserves in the Canadian banking system as a result of this new deposit.

a. 10 percent target reserve ratio, no cash drain, no excess reserves

b. 10 percent target reserve ratio, 5 percent cash drain, no excess reserves

c. 10 percent target reserve ratio, 5 percent cash drain, 5 percent excess reserves

9. This question is intended to illustrate the similarity between the simple income-expenditure multiplier from Chapters 21 and 22 and the deposit multiplier that we examined in this chapter.

a. Recalling the macro model of Chapters 21 and 22, suppose the marginal propensity to spend out of GDP, z, is 0.6. If autonomous spending increases by $1000, fill in the table below.

Round	Δ AE	Δ Y
First	$1000	$1000
Second	___	___
Third	___	___
Fourth	___	___
Fifth	___	___

b. The sum of the values in the third column should be

$$\Delta Y = \$1000 + z \,\$1000 + z^2 \,\$1000 + z^3 \,\$1000 + \ldots$$

What is the total change in GDP?

c. Now consider the process of deposit creation from this chapter. Consider a new deposit of $1000 and a target reserve ratio, v, of 0.25 (with no cash drain). Fill in the following table:

Round	Δ Deposits	Δ Reserves	Δ Loans
First	$1000	$250	$750
Second	___	___	___
Third	___	___	___
Fourth	___	___	___
Fifth	___	___	___

d. The sum of the values in the first column should be

$$\Delta \text{Deposits} = \$1000 + (1 - v)\$1000 + (1 - v)^2 \,\$1000 + (1 - v)^3 \,\$1000 + \ldots$$

What is the total change in deposits?

e. Explain why taxes and imports for the simple multiplier in Chapter 21 are similar to a reserve ratio for the deposit multiplier in this chapter.

10. Suppose that on January 1, 2011, a household had $300 000, which it wanted to hold for use one year later. Calculate, by using resources available online or in your university library, which of the following

would have been the best store of value over that period. Will the best store of value over that period necessarily be the best over the next 24 months?

a. The (Canadian) dollar
b. Stocks whose prices moved with the Toronto Stock Exchange (S&P/TSX) index
c. A Government of Canada 5.75 percent bond coming due in 2029
d. Gold

e. A house whose value changed with the average house price in Canada

11. During the 2008 global financial crisis, the governor of the Bank of Canada expressed concern that the commercial banks were "hoarding" cash rather than extending a more appropriate volume of loans. Why might the banks do this, and what is the implication for the money supply?

Money, Interest Rates, and Economic Activity

LEARNING OBJECTIVES (LO)

After studying this chapter you will be able to

1 explain why the price of a bond is inversely related to the market interest rate.

2 describe how the demand for money depends on the interest rate, the price level, and real GDP.

3 explain how monetary equilibrium determines the interest rate in the short run.

4 describe the transmission mechanism of monetary policy.

5 understand the difference between the short-run and long-run effects of monetary policy.

6 describe under what conditions monetary policy is most effective in the short run.

IN Chapter 27, we learned how the commercial banking system multiplies a given amount of reserves into deposit money and thus influences the nation's money supply. We also learned that because the Bank of Canada can set the amount of commercial-bank reserves, it too has an influence on the money supply. What we have not yet discussed, however, is *how* the Bank influences the amount of reserves. We will leave that discussion until the next chapter, when we examine Canadian monetary policy. For now, just think of the nation's money supply as being determined jointly by the actions of the Bank of Canada and the commercial banking system.

In this chapter, we develop a theory to explain how money affects the economy. Understanding the role of money, however, requires an understanding of the interaction of money supply and money demand. To examine the nature of money demand, we begin by examining how households decide to divide their total holdings of assets between money and interest-earning assets (which here are called "bonds"). Once that is done, we put money supply and money demand together to examine *monetary equilibrium*. Only then can we ask how changes in the supply of money or in the demand for money affect the economy in the short term—interest rates, real GDP, and the price level. We begin with a discussion of the relationship between bond prices and interest rates.

28.1 Understanding Bonds

At any moment, households have a stock of financial wealth that they hold in several forms. Some of it is money in the bank or in the wallet. Some may be in *Treasury bills* and *bonds*, which are IOUs issued by the government or corporations. Some may be in *equity*, meaning ownership shares of a company.

To simplify our discussion, we will group financial wealth into just two categories, which we call "money" and "bonds." By money we mean all assets that serve as a medium of exchange—that is, paper money, coins, and bank deposits that can be transferred on demand by cheque or electronic means. By bonds we mean all other forms of financial wealth; this includes interest-earning financial assets and claims on real capital (equity). This simplification is useful because it emphasizes the important distinction between interest-earning and non–interest-earning assets, a distinction that is central for understanding the demand for money.

Before discussing how individuals decide to divide their assets between money and bonds, we need to make sure we understand what bonds are and how they are priced. This requires an understanding of *present value*.

Economists often simplify the analysis of financial assets by considering only two types of assets— non–interest-bearing "money" and interest-bearing "bonds."

Present Value and the Interest Rate

A bond is a financial asset that promises to make one or more specified payments at specified dates in the future. The **present value (PV)** of any asset refers to the value now of the future payments that the asset offers. Present value depends on the market interest rate because when we calculate present value, the interest rate is used to *discount* the value of the future payments to obtain their *present* value. Let's consider two examples to illustrate the concept of present value.

present value (PV) The value now of one or more payments or receipts made in the future; often referred to as *discounted present value.*

A Single Payment One Year Hence We start with the simplest case. What is the value *now* of a bond that will return a single payment of $100 in one year's time?

Suppose the market interest rate is 5 percent. Now ask how much you would have to lend out at that interest rate today in order to have $100 a year from now. If we use PV to stand for this unknown amount, we can write $PV \times (1.05) = \$100$. Thus, $PV = \$100/1.05 = \$95.24$.[1] This tells us that the present value of $100 receivable in one year's time is $95.24; if you lend out $95.24 for one year at 5 percent interest you will get back the original $95.24 that you lent (the principal) plus $4.76 in interest, which makes $100.

We can generalize this relationship with a simple equation. If R_1 is the amount we receive one year from now and i is the annual interest rate, the present value of R_1 is

$$PV = \frac{R_1}{1 + i}$$

If the interest rate is 7 percent ($i = 0.07$) and the bond pays $100 in one year ($R_1 = \$100$), the present value of that bond is $PV = \$100/1.07 = \$93.46$. Notice

---

[1] Notice that in this type of formula, the interest rate is expressed as a decimal fraction where, for example, 5 percent is expressed as 0.05, so $1 + i = 1.05$.

that, when compared with the previous numerical example, the higher market interest rate leads to a lower present value. The future payment of $100 gets discounted at a higher rate and so is worth less at the present time.

A Sequence of Future Payments Now consider a more complicated case, but one that is actually more typical. Many bonds promise to make "coupon" payments every year and then return the face value of the bond at the end of the term of the loan. For example, imagine a three-year bond that promises to repay the face value of $1000 in three years, but will also pay a 10 percent coupon payment of $100 at the end of each of the three years that the bond is held. How much is this bond worth now? We can compute the present value of this bond by adding together the present values of each of the payments. If the market interest rate is 7 percent, the present value of this bond is

$$PV = \frac{\$100}{1.07} + \frac{\$100}{(1.07)^2} + \frac{\$1100}{(1.07)^3}$$

The first term is the value today of receiving $100 one year from now. The second term is the value today of receiving the second $100 payment two years from now. Note that we discount this second payment twice—once from Year 2 to Year 1, and once again from Year 1 to now—and thus the denominator shows an interest rate of 7 percent *compounded* for two years. Finally, the third term shows the value today of the $1100 repayment ($1000 of face value plus $100 of coupon payment) three years from now. The present value of this bond is

$$PV = \$93.46 + \$87.34 + \$897.93$$
$$= \$1078.73$$

In general, any asset that promises to make a sequence of payments for T periods into the future of $R_1, R_2, \ldots$, and so on, up to R_T has a present value given by

$$PV = \frac{R_1}{1 + i} + \frac{R_2}{(1 + i)^2} + \cdots + \frac{R_T}{(1 + i)^T}$$

It is useful to try another example. Let's continue with the case in which the bond repays its face value of $1000 three years from now and makes three $100 coupon payments at the end of each year the bond is held. But this time we assume the market interest rate is 9 percent. In this case, the present value of the bond is

$$PV = \frac{\$100}{1.09} + \frac{\$100}{(1.09)^2} + \frac{\$1100}{(1.09)^3}$$
$$= \$91.74 + \$84.17 + \$849.40$$
$$= \$1025.31$$

Notice that when the market interest rate is 9 percent, the present value of the bond is lower than the present value of the same bond when the market interest rate is 7 percent. The higher interest rate implies that any future payments are discounted at a higher rate and thus have a lower present value.

A General Relationship There are many types of bonds. Some make no coupon payments and only a single payment (the "face value") at some point in the future. This is the case for short-term government bonds called *Treasury bills*. Other bonds, typically longer-term government or corporate bonds, make regular coupon payments as well as a final payment of the bond's face value. Though there are many types of bonds, they all have one thing in common: They promise to make some payment or sequence of payments in the future. Because bonds make payments in the future, their present value is negatively related to the market interest rate.

> The present value of any bond that promises a future payment or sequence of future payments is negatively related to the market interest rate.

Present Value and Market Price

Most bonds are bought and sold in financial markets in which there are large numbers of both buyers and sellers. The present value of a bond is important because it establishes the price at which a bond will be exchanged in the financial markets.

> The present value of a bond is the most someone would be willing to pay now to own the bond's future stream of payments.[2]

To understand this concept, let us return to our example of a bond that promises to pay $100 one year from now. When the interest rate is 5 percent, the present value of this bond is $95.24. To see why this is the maximum that anyone would pay for this bond, suppose that some sellers offer to sell the bond at some other price, say, $98. If, instead of paying this amount for the bond, a potential buyer lends $98 out at 5 percent interest, he or she would have at the end of one year more than the $100 that the bond will produce. (At 5 percent interest, $98 yields $4.90 in interest, which when added to the principal makes $102.90.) Clearly, no well-informed individual would pay $98—or, by the same reasoning, any sum in excess of $95.24—for the bond. Thus, at any price above the bond's present value, the lack of demand will cause the price to fall.

Now suppose the bond is offered for sale at a price less than $95.24, say, $90. A potential buyer could borrow $90 to buy the bond and would pay $4.50 in interest on the loan. At the end of the year, the bond yields $100. When this is used to repay the $90 loan and the $4.50 in interest, $5.50 is left as profit. Clearly, it would be worthwhile for someone to buy the bond at the price of $90 or, by the same argument, at any price less than $95.24. Thus, at any price below the bond's present value, the abundance of demand will cause the price to rise.

This discussion should make clear that the present value of an asset determines its equilibrium market price. If the market price of any asset is greater than the present value of its income stream, no one will want to buy it, and the resulting excess supply will push down the market price. If the market price is below its present value, there will be a rush to buy it, and the resulting excess demand will push up the market price. When the bond's market price is exactly equal to its present value, there is no pressure for the price to change.

---

[2] We ignore for now the possibility that the issuer of the bond will *default* and thereby fail to make some or all of the future payments. If such a risk does exist, it will reduce the *expected* present value of the bond and thus reduce the price that buyers will be prepared to pay. We address bond riskiness shortly.

> The equilibrium market price of any bond is the present value of the income stream that it produces.

Interest Rates, Bond Prices, and Bond Yields

We now have two relationships that can be put together to tell us about the link between the market interest rate and bond prices. Let's restate these two relationships.

1. The present value of any given bond is negatively related to the market interest rate.

2. A bond's equilibrium market price will be equal to its present value.

Putting these two relationships together, we come to a key relationship:

> An increase in the market interest rate leads to a fall in the price of any given bond. A decrease in the market interest rate leads to an increase in the price of any given bond.

Remember that a bond is a financial investment for the purchaser. The cost of the investment is the price of the bond, and the return on the investment is the sequence of future payments. Thus, for a given sequence of future payments, a lower bond price implies a higher rate of return on the bond, or a higher *bond yield*.

To illustrate the yield on a bond, consider a simple example of a bond that promises to pay $1000 two years from now. If you purchase this bond for $857.34, your return on your investment will be 8 percent per year because $857.34 compounded for two years at 8 percent will yield $1000 in two years.

$$\$857.34 \times (1.08)^2 = \$1000$$

In other words, your yield on the bond will be 8 percent per year.

Notice that we are making a distinction between the concept of the *yield* on a bond and the *market interest rate*. The bond yield is a function of the sequence of payments and the bond price. The market interest rate is the rate at which you can borrow or lend money in the credit market.

Although they are logically distinct from each other, there is a close relationship between the market interest rate and bond yields. A rise in the market interest rate will lead to a decline in the present value of any bond and thus to a decline in its equilibrium price. As the bond price falls, its yield naturally rises. Thus, we see that market interest rates and bond yields tend to move in the same direction.

> An increase in the market interest rate will reduce bond prices and increase bond yields. A reduction in the market interest rate will increase bond prices and reduce bond yields. Therefore, market interest rates and bond yields tend to move together.

Because of this close relationship between bond yields and market interest rates, economists discussing the role of money in the macroeconomy typically refer to "the" interest rate—or perhaps to "interest rates" in general—rather than to any specific interest rate among the many different rates corresponding to the many different financial assets. Since these rates all tend to rise or fall together, it is a very useful simplification to refer only to "the" interest rate, meaning the rate of return that can be earned by holding interest-earning assets rather than money.

Bond Riskiness

We have been discussing present values and bond prices under the assumption that the bond is *risk free*—that is, that the coupon payments and the repayment of principal are absolutely certain. In reality, however, there is some chance that bond issuers will be unable to make some or all of these payments. In the face of this possibility, purchasers of bonds reduce the price they are prepared to pay by an amount that reflects the likelihood of non-repayment.

Beginning in early 2010, very high levels of Greek government debt led many to expect the government to default on some or all of its bonds. This fear led to a sharp fall in Greek bond prices and thus a sharp increase in bond yields.

It follows that not all changes in bond yields are caused by changes in market interest rates. Sometimes the yields on specific bonds change because of a change in their perceived *riskiness*. For example, if some event increases the likelihood that a specific corporate bond issuer will soon go bankrupt, bond purchasers will revise downward the *expected* present value of the issuer's bonds. As a result, the demand for the bond will fall and its equilibrium price will decline. As the price falls, the bond's yield will rise—the higher bond yield now reflecting the greater riskiness of the bond.

> An increase in the riskiness of any bond leads to a decline in its *expected* present value and thus to a decline in the bond's price. The lower bond price implies a higher bond yield.

It is rare in Canada that government bonds are perceived as risky, but in recent years some bonds issued by some southern European countries have been viewed as high-risk assets, and this riskiness has been reflected in high bond yields. In general, however, since governments have the power to collect revenue through taxation, it is unusual for a government bond to be viewed as a risky asset. More usual at any given time is specific corporations that are believed to be in precarious financial situations and thus their bonds are perceived to be risky assets. As a result, there are often very high yields (low bond prices) on specific corporate bonds. *Applying Economic Concepts 28-1* discusses the relationship among bond prices, bond yields, riskiness, and *term to maturity* of government and corporate bonds.

28.2 The Theory of Money Demand

Our discussion of bonds, bond prices, and interest rates leads us to a theory that explains how individuals allocate their current stock of financial wealth between "bonds" and "money." An individual's decision to hold more bonds is at the same time a decision to hold less money, and the decision to hold fewer bonds is a decision to hold more money.

APPLYING ECONOMIC CONCEPTS 28-1

Understanding Bond Prices and Bond Yields

Various kinds of bonds are traded every day, and they differ in terms of the issuer, price, yield, riskiness, and term to maturity. We focus here on how to understand these bond characteristics.

How to Read the Bond Tables

The accompanying table shows seven bond listings just as they appeared on www.globeinvestor.com on June 22, 2012. The five columns are as follows:

1. **Issuer.** This is the issuer of the bond—that is, the borrower of the money. The first five bonds shown are issued by the Government of Canada. The last two are issued by large private-sector firms.

2. **Coupon.** This is the coupon rate—the annual rate of interest that the bond pays before it matures. For example, a 6 percent coupon rate means that the bondholder (the lender) will receive 6 percent of the face value of the bond every year until the bond matures.

3. **Maturity.** This is when the bond matures and the face value is repaid to the bondholder. All debt obligations are then fulfilled.

4. **Price.** This is the market price of the bond (on June 22, 2012), expressed as the price per $100 of face value. For example, a price of $103.93 means that for every $100 of face value, the purchaser must pay $103.93. When the price is greater than $100, we say there is a *premium*; when the price is less than $100, we say the bond is selling at a *discount*.

5. **Yield.** This is the rate of return earned by the bondholder if the bond is bought at the *current* price and held to maturity, earning all regular coupon payments.

Issuer	Coupon (%)	Maturity	Price ($)	Yield (%)
1. Canada	5.25	June 1, 2013	103.93	1.01
2. Canada	2.50	Sept 1, 2013	101.73	1.03
3. Canada	4.00	June 1, 2016	110.62	1.22
4. Canada	9.75	June 1, 2021	167.57	1.60
5. Canada	8.00	June 1, 2027	175.92	2.06
6. Gaz Metro	5.45	July 12, 2021	120.06	2.91
7. Bell Canada	8.88	April 17, 2026	135.52	5.48

Bond Prices and Yields

Three general patterns can be seen in the table. First, for a given issuer and maturity, there is a positive relationship between the bond price and the coupon rate. Rows 1 and 2,

for example, show two bonds, both issued by the Government of Canada and maturing at (almost) the same date in 2013. The common issuer suggests a common risk of non-repayment (in this case a very low risk). The first bond has a 5.25 percent coupon whereas the second has a 2.50 percent coupon. Not surprisingly, the higher coupon payments make the first bond a more attractive asset and thus its market price is higher—$103.93 as compared with $101.73. Note, however, that the implied yield on the two bonds is almost identical. If this weren't the case, demand would shift toward the high-yield (low-price) bond, driving down the yield (increasing the price) until the two yields were the same.

Second, for a given bond issuer, there is a positive relationship between the bond yield and the term to maturity. This is shown in the first five rows, as yields rise from just over 1 percent on bonds maturing in one year's time (from the date of the listing) to 2.06 percent on bonds maturing in 15 years' time. This positive relationship is often referred to as the *yield curve* or the *term structure of interest rates*. The higher yields on longer-term bonds reflect what is often called a *term premium*—the higher yield that bondholders must be paid in order to induce them to have their money tied up for longer periods of time.

Third, for a given term to maturity, there is a positive relationship between the bond yield and the perceived riskiness of the bond issuer. Compare rows 4 and 6, for example. Both bonds have almost identical maturity dates in 2021, but one is issued by the Government of Canada while the other is issued by Gaz Metro Inc. Though it is almost impossible for the Government of Canada to go bankrupt and almost inconceivable that it would default on its debt, it is certainly possible for Gaz Metro to do so. This difference explains the difference in yields. The same is true between rows 5 and 7, where the more than three-percentage-point yield difference is attributable to the higher likelihood of default by Bell Canada than by the Canadian government.

If you run your eyes down the bond tables, you will easily see those corporations viewed by the market as being risky borrowers because the yields on their bonds will be higher—often dramatically so—than the yields on similar-maturity government bonds. For example, in the summer of 2012, when some European banks were experiencing great difficulty, the bonds issued by the Royal Bank of Scotland were selling at such a discount that the implied annual yield was more than 20 percent. Such high yields represent a great investment opportunity only if you are prepared to take the associated risk. Beware!

We can therefore build our theory by considering the desire to hold bonds or by considering the desire to hold money. We follow the tradition among economists by focusing on the desire to hold money. The amount of money that everyone (collectively) wants to hold at any time is called the **demand for money**.

demand for money The total amount of money balances that the public wants to hold for all purposes.

Three Reasons for Holding Money

Why do firms and households hold money? Our theory offers three reasons. First, households and firms hold money in order to carry out transactions. Economists call this the *transactions demand* for money. You carry money in your pocket or keep it in a chequing account in order to have it readily available for your upcoming transactions; it would be very inconvenient to have to sell bonds or withdraw money from your GIC (guaranteed investment certificate) every time you wanted to spend. Similarly, firms are continually making expenditures on intermediate inputs and payments to labour, and they keep money available in their chequing accounts to pay these expenses.

A second and related reason firms and households hold money is that they are uncertain about when some expenditures will be necessary, and they hold money as a precaution to avoid the problems associated with missing a transaction. This is referred to as the *precautionary demand* for money. For example, you might hold some cash because of the possibility that you might need to take an unplanned taxi ride during a rainstorm; a small business may hold cash because of the possibility that it might need the emergency services of a tradesperson, such as a plumber or an electrician. In the days before the invention of ATMs, the precautionary demand for money was quite large, since to be caught on a weekend or away from home without sufficient cash could be a serious matter. Today, this motive for holding money is less important.

The third assumed reason for holding money applies more to large businesses and to professional money managers than to individuals because it involves *speculating* about how interest rates are likely to change in the future. Economists call this the *speculative demand* for money. To understand this reason for holding money, recall what we said earlier about the negative relationship between market interest rates and bond prices. If interest rates are expected to rise in the future, bond prices will be expected to fall. Whenever bond prices fall, bondholders experience a decline in the value of their bond holdings. The expectation of increases in *future* interest rates will therefore lead to the holding of more money (and fewer bonds) *now* as financial managers adjust their portfolios in order to preserve their values.

A related motive for holding money relates to *uncertainty*. Commercial banks that are uncertain about their borrowers' ability to repay loans, or about the riskiness of potential new borrowers, may decide to sacrifice an uncertain rate of return for the safety that comes from holding more cash reserves than normal. Other firms that regularly borrow to finance their operations may choose to hold large cash balances if they are uncertain about whether they will continue to have sufficient access to credit. Both of these reasons for holding large cash balances were evident in the immediate aftermath of the 2008 global financial crisis and recession, and continue today during a slow economic recovery.

The Determinants of Money Demand

We have just seen several reasons why firms and households hold money. We now want to examine which key macroeconomic variables affect the *amount* of money that is demanded in our macro model. We focus on three: the interest rate, the level of real GDP, and the price level.

FIGURE 28-1 Money Demand as a Function of the Interest Rate, Real GDP, and the Price Level

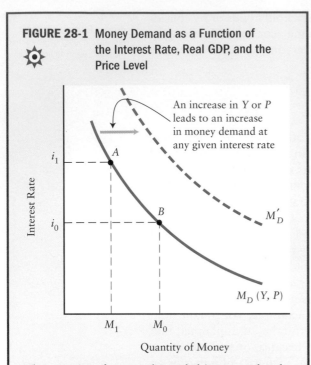

The quantity of money demanded is assumed to be negatively related to the interest rate and positively related to real GDP and the price level. The negative slope of the M_D curve comes from the choice between holding money and holding bonds. A fall in the interest rate from i_1 to i_0 reduces the opportunity cost of holding money because the rate of return on bonds declines. Thus, the decision to hold more money (the movement from A to B as the interest rate falls) is the "flip side" of the decision to hold fewer bonds.

We show the initial money demand curve as M_D (Y, P), indicating that the curve is drawn for given values of Y and P. Increases in Y or P shift the M_D curve to the right; decreases in Y or P shift the M_D curve to the left.

The Interest Rate No matter what benefits households or firms receive from holding money, there is also a cost. The cost of holding money is the income that *could have been earned* if that wealth were instead held in the form of interest-earning bonds. This is the *opportunity cost* of holding money. In our macro model, we assume that an increase in the interest rate leads firms and households to reduce their desired money holdings. Conversely, a reduction in the interest rate means that holding money is less costly, and so firms and households are assumed to increase their desired money holdings.

> Other things being equal, the demand for money is assumed to be negatively related to the interest rate.[3]

This negative relationship between interest rates and desired money holdings is shown in Figure 28-1 and is drawn as the money demand (M_D) curve. Remember that the decision to hold money is also the decision *not* to hold bonds, and so movements along the M_D curve imply the substitution of assets between money and bonds. For example, as interest rates decline, bonds become a less attractive asset and money becomes more attractive, so firms and households substitute away from bonds and toward money.

Real GDP As we said earlier, an important reason for holding money is to make transactions. Not surprisingly, the number of transactions that firms and households want to make is positively related to the level of income and production in the economy—that is, to the level of real GDP. This positive relationship between real GDP and desired money holdings is shown in Figure 28-1 by a rightward shift of the M_D curve to M'_D. At any given interest rate, an increase in Y is assumed to generate more transactions and thus greater desired money holdings.

> Other things being equal, the demand for money is assumed to be positively related to real GDP.

The Price Level An increase in the price level leads to an increase in the *dollar* value of transactions even if there is no change in the *real* value of transactions. That is, as P rises, households and firms will need to hold more money in order to carry out an

---

[3] The opportunity cost of holding money is the interest that could have been earned on bonds—this is the *nominal* interest rate. In the presence of expected inflation, we must distinguish between the *nominal* and real interest rates. In this chapter we assume, however, that expected inflation is zero, and so we simply speak of "the" interest rate. We discuss inflation in detail in Chapter 30.

unchanged real value of transactions. This positive relationship between the price level and desired money holdings is also shown in Figure 28-1 as a rightward shift of the M_D curve to M'_D.

> Other things being equal, the demand for money is assumed to be positively related to the price level.

We can be more precise than just saying that there is a positive relationship between P and desired money holdings. Suppose, for example, that Y and i are constant but that all prices in the economy increase by 10 percent. Since Y is unchanged, the *real* value of desired transactions should also be unchanged. Furthermore, since i is unchanged, the opportunity cost of holding money is constant. Therefore, in order to make the same transactions as before, households and firms must not just hold more money than before—they must hold precisely 10 percent more. In other words, we assume that if real GDP and the interest rate are constant, the demand for money is *proportional* to the price level.

Money Demand: Summing Up

We have discussed the theory of why firms and households hold money, and we have examined the relationship between desired money holding and three macroeconomic variables. Since the demand for money reflects firms' and households' preference to hold wealth in the form of a *liquid* asset (money) rather than a less liquid asset (bonds), economists sometimes refer to the money demand function as a *liquidity preference* function. We can summarize our assumptions regarding money demand with the following algebraic statement:

$$M_D = M_D(\overset{-}{i}, \overset{+}{Y}, \overset{+}{P})$$

This equation says that the amount of money firms and households want to hold at any given time depends on (is a function of) three variables; the sign above each variable indicates whether that variable positively or negatively affects desired money holding. Our central assumptions are as follows:

1. An increase in the interest rate increases the opportunity cost of holding money and leads to a reduction in the quantity of money demanded.

2. An increase in real GDP increases the volume of transactions and leads to an increase in the quantity of money demanded.

3. An increase in the price level increases the dollar value of a given volume of transactions and leads to an increase in the quantity of money demanded.

Remember that money demand is also related to bond demand. Firms and households must decide at any time how to divide their financial assets between money and bonds. Therefore, our statements here about money demand apply in reverse to the demand for bonds. For example, in Figure 28-1, a movement down the M_D curve from point A to point B indicates that firms and households are deciding to hold more money and fewer bonds as the interest rate falls. In other words, the movement from A to B involves a substitution away from holding bonds and toward holding money.

28.3 Monetary Equilibrium and National Income

So far, this chapter has been devoted to understanding bonds and how they relate to the demand for money. In the previous chapter we examined the supply of money. We are now ready to put these two sides of the money market together to develop a theory of how interest rates are determined in the short run. You may recall, however, that we already developed in Chapter 26 a theory of how interest rates are determined. But remember that Chapter 26 was a discussion of long-run economic growth, and real GDP was assumed to be equal to Y^* throughout that discussion. What we do in this chapter and the next is return to the short-run version of our macro model but make it more complete by adding money and interest rates explicitly. We will see how changes in the money market can cause real GDP and interest rates to diverge for short periods of time from their long-run values.

We begin by examining the concept of *monetary equilibrium*—the theory of how interest rates are determined in the short run by the interaction of money demand and money supply. We then explore what economists call the *monetary transmission mechanism*—the chain of events that takes us from changes in the interest rate, through to changes in desired aggregate expenditure, to changes in the level of real GDP and the price level.

Monetary Equilibrium

monetary equilibrium The situation in which the quantity of money demanded equals the quantity of money supplied.

Figure 28-2 illustrates the money market. The money supply (M_S) curve is vertical, indicating that it is assumed to be independent of the interest rate. The money supply increases (M_S shifts to the right) if the central bank increases reserves in the banking system or if the commercial banks decide to lend out a larger fraction of those reserves. The money supply decreases (M_S shifts to the left) if the central bank decreases reserves in the banking system or if the commercial banks decide to reduce lending. The money demand (M_D) curve is downward sloping, indicating that firms and households decide to hold more money (and fewer bonds) when the interest rate falls.

Monetary equilibrium occurs when the quantity of money demanded equals the quantity of money supplied. In Chapter 3, we saw that in a competitive market for some commodity, the price will adjust to establish equilibrium. In the market for money, the interest rate is that "price" that adjusts to bring about equilibrium. Let's see how this equilibrium is achieved.

When a single household or firm finds that it is holding a smaller fraction of its wealth in money than it wants, it can sell some bonds and add the cash proceeds to its money holdings. Such behaviour by an individual firm or a household will have a negligible effect on the economy.

But what happens when *all* the firms and households try to add to their money balances? They all try to sell bonds to obtain the extra money they desire. But what one person can do in this case, all persons cannot do simultaneously. At any moment, the economy's total supply of money and bonds is fixed. Thus, as everyone tries to sell bonds, an excess supply of bonds develops. But since people are simply trying to switch between a given amount of bonds and money, the excess supply of bonds implies an excess demand for money, as shown at interest rate i_1 in Figure 28-2.

What happens when there is an excess supply of bonds? Like any other good or service, an excess supply causes a fall in the market price. As we saw earlier in the chapter, a fall in the price of bonds implies an increase in the interest rate. As the interest rate rises, people economize on money balances because the opportunity cost of holding such balances is rising. Eventually, the interest rate will rise enough that people will no longer be trying to add to their money balances by selling bonds. At that point, there is no longer an excess supply of bonds (or an excess demand for money), and the interest rate will stop rising. The monetary equilibrium will have been achieved, as at point E in Figure 28-2.

Suppose now there is more money than firms and households want to hold. That is, there is an excess supply of money, as at interest rate i_2 in Figure 28-2. The excess supply of money implies an excess demand for bonds—people are trying to "get rid of" their excess money balances by acquiring bonds. But when all households try to buy bonds, they bid up the price of bonds, and the interest rate falls. As the interest rate falls, households and firms become willing to hold larger quantities of money. The interest rate falls until firms and households stop trying to convert bonds into money. In other words, it continues until everyone is content to hold the existing supply of money and bonds, as at point E in Figure 28-2.

> **Monetary equilibrium occurs when the interest rate is such that the quantity of money demanded equals the quantity of money supplied.**

The theory of interest-rate determination depicted in Figure 28-2 is often called the *liquidity preference theory of interest*. This name reflects the fact that when there are only two financial assets, a demand to hold money (rather than bonds) is a demand for the more liquid of the two assets—a preference for liquidity. The theory determines how the interest rate fluctuates in the short term as people seek to achieve *portfolio balance*, given fixed supplies of both money and bonds.

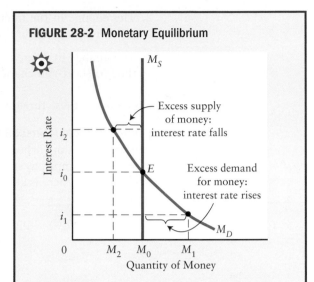

FIGURE 28-2 Monetary Equilibrium

The interest rate rises when there is an excess demand for money and falls when there is an excess supply of money. The fixed quantity of money M_0 is shown by the vertical supply curve M_S. The money supply is determined by the behaviour of the central bank as well as the commercial banks (as we saw in Chapter 27). The demand for money is given by M_D; its negative slope indicates that a fall in the rate of interest causes the quantity of money demanded to increase. Monetary equilibrium is at E, with a rate of interest of i_0.

If the interest rate is i_1, there will be an excess demand for money of M_0M_1. Bonds will be offered for sale in an attempt to increase money holdings. This will force the rate of interest up to i_0 (the price of bonds falls), at which point the quantity of money demanded is equal to the fixed available quantity of M_0. If the interest rate is i_2, there will be an excess supply of money M_2M_0. Bonds will be demanded in return for excess money balances. This will force the rate of interest down to i_0 (the price of bonds rises), at which point the quantity of money demanded is equal to the fixed supply of M_0.

The Monetary Transmission Mechanism

The connection between changes in the demand for and supply of money and the level of aggregate demand is called the **monetary transmission mechanism**. It operates in three stages:

1. Changes in the demand for money or the supply of money cause a change in the equilibrium interest rate in the short run.

monetary transmission mechanism The channels by which a change in the demand for or supply of money leads to a shift of the aggregate demand curve.

2. The change in the interest rate leads to a change in desired investment and consumption expenditure (and net exports in an open economy).

3. The change in desired aggregate expenditure leads to a shift in the *AD* curve and thus to short-run changes in real GDP and the price level.

Let's examine these three stages in more detail.

1. Changes in the Interest Rate   The interest rate will change if the equilibrium depicted in Figure 28-2 is disturbed by a change in either the supply of money or the demand for money. For example, as shown in part (i) of Figure 28-3, we see the following sequence of events when there is an increase in the supply of money but no change in the money demand curve:

$\uparrow$ money supply $\Rightarrow$ excess supply of money at initial interest rate

$\Rightarrow$ firms and households buy bonds

$\Rightarrow \uparrow$ bond prices

$\Rightarrow \downarrow$ equilibrium interest rate

Note that the original increase in the supply of money could be caused either by the central bank increasing the reserves in the banking system or by the commercial banks lending out a higher fraction of their existing reserves.

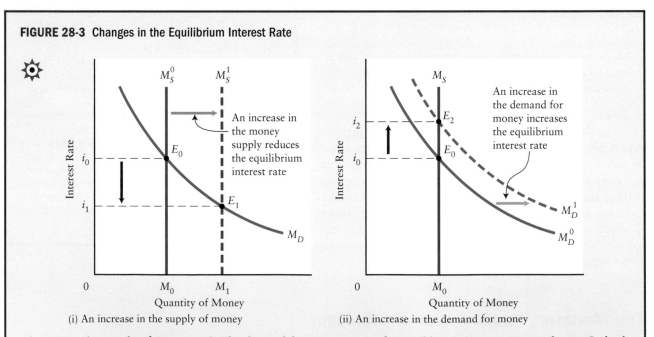

FIGURE 28-3   Changes in the Equilibrium Interest Rate

(i) An increase in the supply of money

(ii) An increase in the demand for money

Changes in the supply of money or in the demand for money cause the equilibrium interest rate to change. In both parts of the figure, the money supply is shown by the vertical curve M_S, and the demand for money is shown by the negatively sloped curve M_D. The initial monetary equilibrium is at E_0, with corresponding interest rate i_0. In part (i), an increase in the money supply causes M_S^0 to shift to M_S^1. The new equilibrium is at E_1, where the equilibrium interest rate has fallen to i_1. In part (ii), an increase in the demand for money shifts M_D^0 to M_D^1. The new monetary equilibrium occurs at E_2, and the equilibrium interest rate increases to i_2.

As shown in part (ii) of Figure 28-3, an increase in the demand for money, with an unchanged supply of money, leads to the following sequence of events:

↑ money demand ⇒ excess demand for money at initial interest rate

⇒ firms and households sell bonds

⇒ ↓ bond prices

⇒ ↑ equilibrium interest rate

The original increase in the demand for money could be caused by an increase in real GDP or by an increase in the price level. It could also be caused by an increased preference to hold money rather than bonds, as would happen if there were an increase in the perceived riskiness of bonds.

> **Changes in either the demand for or the supply of money cause changes in the short-run equilibrium interest rate.**

2. Changes in Desired Investment and Consumption The second link in the monetary transmission mechanism relates interest rates to desired investment and consumption expenditure. We saw in Chapter 21 that desired investment, which includes expenditure on inventory accumulation, residential construction, and business fixed investment, responds to changes in the interest rate. Other things being equal, a decrease in the interest rate reduces the opportunity cost of borrowing or using retained earnings for investment purposes. As a result, the lower interest rate leads to an increase in desired investment expenditure. We also saw that consumption expenditures, especially on big-ticket durable items such as cars and furniture, which are often purchased on credit, are negatively related to the interest rate. In Figure 28-4, this negative relationship

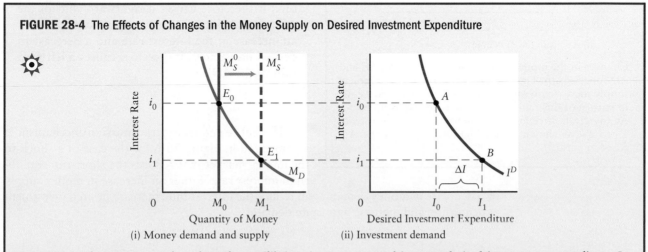

FIGURE 28-4 The Effects of Changes in the Money Supply on Desired Investment Expenditure

(i) Money demand and supply

(ii) Investment demand

Increases in the money supply reduce the equilibrium interest rate and increase desired investment expenditure. In part (i), monetary equilibrium is at E_0, with a quantity of money of M_0 and an interest rate of i_0. The corresponding level of desired investment is I_0 (point A) in part (ii). An increase in the money supply to M_1 reduces the equilibrium interest rate to i_1 and increases investment expenditure by ΔI to I_1 (point B).

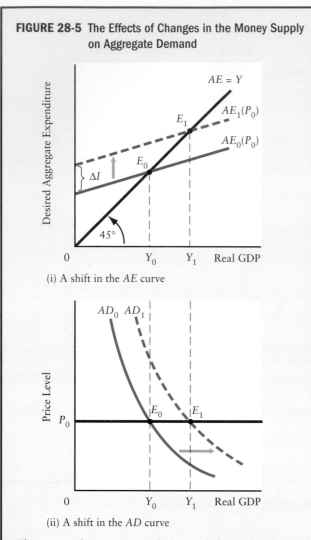

FIGURE 28-5 The Effects of Changes in the Money Supply on Aggregate Demand

(i) A shift in the *AE* curve

(ii) A shift in the *AD* curve

Changes in the money supply cause shifts in the *AE* and *AD* functions. In Figure 28-4, an increase in the money supply increased desired investment expenditure by ΔI. In part (i) of this figure, the *AE* function shifts up by ΔI. At any given price level P_0, equilibrium GDP rises from Y_0 to Y_1, as shown by the rightward shift in the *AD* curve in part (ii).

between desired expenditure and the interest rate is labelled I^D for investment demand, reflecting the fact that investment is the *most* interest-sensitive part of expenditure.

The first two links in the monetary transmission mechanism are shown in Figure 28-4.[4] Although the analysis in Figure 28-4 illustrates a change in the money supply, remember that the transmission mechanism can also be set in motion by a change in the demand for money. In part (i), we see that an increase in the money supply reduces the short-run equilibrium interest rate. In part (ii), we see that a fall in the interest rate leads to an increase in desired investment (and consumption) expenditure.

3. Changes in Aggregate Demand The third link in our theory of the monetary transmission mechanism is from changes in desired expenditure to shifts in the *AE* function and in the *AD* curve. This is familiar ground. In Chapter 23, we saw that a shift in the aggregate expenditure curve (caused by something *other than* a change in the price level) leads to a shift in the *AD* curve. This situation is shown again in Figure 28-5.

> An increase in the money supply causes a reduction in the interest rate and an increase in desired investment and other interest-sensitive expenditure; it therefore causes a rightward shift of the *AD* curve. A decrease in the money supply causes an increase in the interest rate and a decrease in desired investment; it therefore causes a leftward shift of the *AD* curve.

The entire monetary transmission mechanism is summarized in Figure 28-6 for the case of a shock to the money market that reduces the short-run equilibrium interest rate. Either an increase in money supply or a decrease in money demand will reduce the interest rate, increase desired investment expenditure, and increase aggregate demand.

---

[4] In part (i) of Figure 28-4, it is the *nominal* interest rate—the rate of return on bonds—that affects money demand. In part (ii), however, it is the *real* interest rate that influences desired investment expenditure. It is therefore worth emphasizing that we are continuing with the assumption that inflation is expected to be zero, and thus the nominal and real interest rates are the same. This assumption allows us to use the same vertical axis in the two parts of the figure.

An Open-Economy Modification

So far, the emphasis in our discussion of the monetary transmission mechanism has been on the effect that a change in the interest rate has on desired investment and desired consumption. In an open economy, however, where financial capital flows easily across borders, the monetary transmission mechanism is a little more complex.

Financial capital is very mobile across international boundaries. Bondholders, either in Canada or abroad, are able to substitute among Canadian bonds, U.S. bonds, German bonds, and bonds from almost any country you can think of. Bonds from different countries are generally not *perfect* substitutes for each other because the varying amounts of political and economic instability imply that different levels of *risk* are associated with different bonds. But bonds from similar countries—Canada and the United States, for example—are often viewed as very close substitutes.

The ability of bondholders to substitute easily between bonds from different countries implies that monetary disturbances that cause changes in interest rates often lead to international flows of financial capital, which in turn cause changes in exchange rates and changes in exports and imports.

To understand how capital mobility adds a second channel to the monetary transmission mechanism, consider an example. Suppose the Bank of Canada decides to increase the money supply. As shown in part (i) of Figure 28-4, the increase in money supply reduces the interest rate and increases desired investment expenditure. This is the first channel of the monetary transmission mechanism. But the story does not end there.

The reduction in Canadian interest rates also makes Canadian bonds less attractive relative to foreign bonds. Canadian and foreign investors alike will sell some of their Canadian bonds and buy more of the high-return foreign bonds. But to buy foreign bonds, it is necessary first to exchange Canadian dollars for foreign currency. The desire to sell Canadian dollars and purchase foreign currency causes the Canadian dollar to depreciate relative to other currencies.

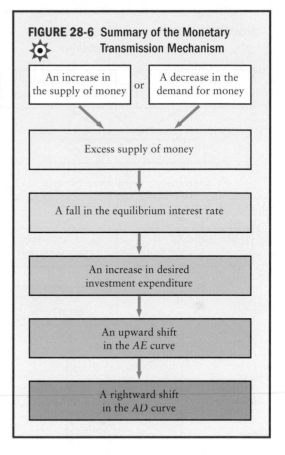

FIGURE 28-6 Summary of the Monetary Transmission Mechanism

An increase in the supply of money or A decrease in the demand for money

Excess supply of money

A fall in the equilibrium interest rate

An increase in desired investment expenditure

An upward shift in the *AE* curve

A rightward shift in the *AD* curve

An increase in the Canadian money supply reduces Canadian interest rates and leads to an outflow of financial capital. This capital outflow causes the Canadian dollar to depreciate.

As the Canadian dollar depreciates, however, Canadian goods and services become less expensive relative to those from other countries. As we first saw in Chapter 22, this change in international relative prices causes households and firms—both in Canada and abroad—to substitute away from foreign goods and toward Canadian goods. Imports fall and exports rise.

So the overall effect of the increase in the Canadian money supply is not just a fall in Canadian interest rates and an increase in investment. Because of the international

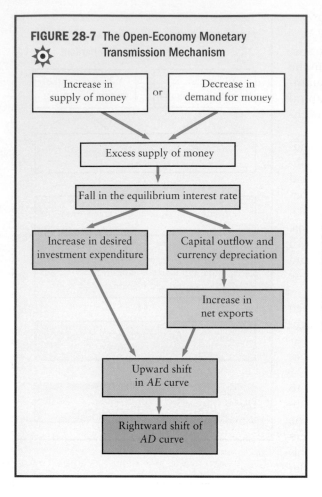

FIGURE 28-7 The Open-Economy Monetary Transmission Mechanism

mobility of financial capital, the low Canadian interest rates also lead to a capital outflow, a depreciation of the Canadian dollar, and an increase in Canadian net exports. This increase in net exports, of course, *strengthens* the positive effect on aggregate demand already coming from the increase in desired investment.

This complete open-economy monetary transmission mechanism is shown in Figure 28-7. This figure is based on Figure 28-6, but simply adds the second channel of the transmission mechanism that works through capital mobility, exchange rates, and net exports.

> In an open economy with capital mobility, an increase in the money supply is predicted to cause an increase in aggregate demand for two reasons. First, the reduction in interest rates causes an increase in investment. Second, the lower interest rate causes a capital outflow, a currency depreciation, and a rise in net exports.

Our example has been that of a monetary expansion. A monetary contraction has the opposite effect, but the logic of the mechanism is the same. A reduction in the Canadian money supply raises Canadian interest rates and reduces desired investment expenditure. The higher Canadian interest rates attract foreign financial capital as bondholders sell low-return foreign bonds and purchase high-return Canadian bonds. This action increases the demand for Canadian dollars in the foreign-exchange market and thus causes the Canadian dollar to appreciate. Finally, the appreciation of the Canadian dollar increases Canadians' imports of foreign goods and reduces Canadian exports to other countries. Canadian net exports fall.

The Slope of the *AD* Curve

We can now use our theory of the monetary transmission mechanism to add to the explanation of the negative slope of the *AD* curve. In Chapter 23, we mentioned two reasons for its negative slope: the change in wealth and the substitution between domestic and foreign goods, both of which occur when the domestic price level changes. A third effect operates through interest rates, and works as follows. A rise in the price level raises the money value of transactions and thus leads to an increase in the demand for money. For a given supply of money (a vertical M_S curve), the increase in money demand means that the M_D curve shifts to the right, raising the equilibrium interest rate. The higher interest rate then leads to a reduction in desired investment expenditure. We therefore have a third reason that the price level and the level of aggregate demand are negatively related. This third reason for the negative slope of the *AD* curve is important because, empirically, the interest rate is the most important link between monetary factors and real expenditure flows.

28.4 The Strength of Monetary Forces

In the previous section we saw that a change in the money supply leads to a change in interest rates. The change in interest rates, in turn, leads to changes in investment and, through international capital flows and changes in the exchange rate, to changes in net exports. A change in the money supply therefore leads to a change in desired aggregate expenditure and to a shift in the AD curve. From our analysis in Chapter 24, we know that a shift in the AD curve will lead to different effects in the short run and in the long run. It is in the long run that factor prices tend to fully adjust to excess demands or excess supplies, and output tends to return to the level of potential output, Y^*. Let's begin by examining the long-run effects of increases in the money supply, and then turn to a long-standing debate about the strength of monetary forces in the short run.

The Neutrality of Money

Starting from a long-run equilibrium in our macro model with real GDP equal to Y^*, any AD or AS shock that creates an output gap sets in place an adjustment process that will eventually close that gap and return real GDP to Y^*. The operation of this adjustment process following an increase in the money supply is illustrated in Figure 28-8. In the figure, the only long-run effect of the shift in the AD curve is a change in the price level; there is no long-run effect on real GDP or any other real economic variable. This result is referred to as **long-run money neutrality**. The long-run neutrality of money requires that Y^* be unaffected by changes in the supply of money.

The Classical Dichotomy Many eighteenth- and nineteenth-century economists developed theories of the economy's long-run equilibrium and emphasized the neutrality of money. They argued that the "monetary side" of the economy was independent from the "real side" in the long run. This belief came to be referred to as the *Classical dichotomy*. In the long run, relative prices, real GDP, employment, investment, and all other real economic variables were assumed to be determined by real factors,

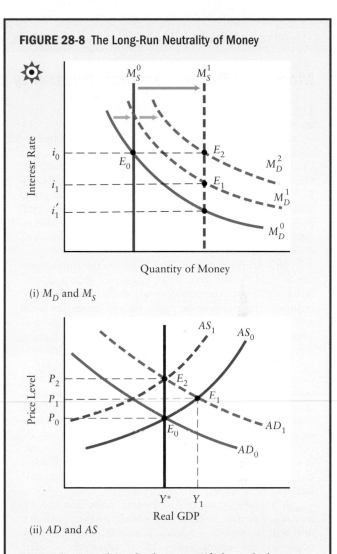

FIGURE 28-8 The Long-Run Neutrality of Money

(i) M_D and M_S

(ii) AD and AS

Money is neutral in the long run if the only long-run effect of an increase in the money supply is a higher price level. The economy begins in long-run equilibrium at E_0 in both diagrams, with real GDP equal to Y^* and the price level equal to P_0. An increase in the money supply from M_S^0 to M_S^1 reduces interest rates immediately to i_1' and stimulates aggregate demand, thus shifting the aggregate demand curve from AD_0 to AD_1. As real GDP and the price level increase, the demand for money increases to M_D^1, thus pushing i_1' up to i_1. The point E_1 in part (i) therefore corresponds to E_1 in part (ii). Since real GDP is now above Y^*, wages and other factor prices start to increase, thus shifting the AS curve upward. The adjustment process continues until Y is back to Y^* and the price level has increased to P_2. In the new long-run equilibrium, the higher price level (with unchanged Y^*) has increased money demand to M_D^2, thus restoring the interest rate to its initial level, i_0.

APPLYING ECONOMIC CONCEPTS 28-2

Monetary Reform and the Neutrality of Money

The least controversial proposition regarding the neutrality of money is that altering the number of zeros on the monetary unit, and on everything else stated in those units, will have no economic consequences. For example, if an extra zero were added to all Bank of Canada notes—so that all $5 bills became $50 bills, all $10 bills became $100 bills, and so on—and the same adjustment was made to all nominal wages, prices, and contracts in the economy, there would be no effects on real GDP, real wages, relative prices, and other real economic variables.*

This proposition has been tested many times since the Second World War, when countries that had suffered major inflations undertook *monetary reform* by reducing the number of zeros on the monetary unit and everything else that was specified in money terms. The evidence is clear that no significant or lasting effects followed from these reforms. That such money neutrality is a testable theory, rather than merely a definitional statement, is shown by the observable possibility that for a short time after the monetary reforms some people may be so ill informed, and others such creatures of habit, that they make mistakes based on assuming that the new money is the same as the old. Although some such behaviour probably occurred, it was not significant enough to show up as a sudden change in any of the economic data that have been collected in these cases.

A slightly stronger proposition regarding money neutrality is that altering the nature of the monetary unit will have no real economic effects. Such a change occurred, for example, in 1971, when the United Kingdom changed from a system in which the basic monetary unit, the pound sterling, was composed of 240 pence to a system in which it contained 100 pence. Another example is Ireland's 1999 conversion from the punt, which contained 240 pence, to the euro, which contained 100 cents. In these cases there were some alterations in real behaviour immediately after the change was made, as many people were confused by the new units. Once again, however, these changes were neither important enough nor long-lasting enough to show up in the macroeconomic data.

These two propositions regarding the neutrality of money are important because they emphasize the nominal nature of money and the important distinction between nominal and real values. It would be unusual indeed if multiplying all nominal values in the economy by the same scalar had any real effect other than some temporary confusion. For this reason, these two propositions are accepted by virtually all economists and central bankers.

The stronger and more controversial proposition regarding money neutrality is the one discussed in the text—that the economy's level of potential output is unaffected by changes in the supply of money. This assumption is common in many macroeconomic models but, as we argue in the text, there are good reasons to think that monetary policy may have effects on Y^* and thus have long-run effects on real GDP.

---

*Of course, there would be *some* real effects from such an adjustment, including the level of inconvenience associated with using paper money with larger denominations (which would be enormous if we added many zeros rather than just one to all existing bills and prices).

---

long-run money neutrality The idea that a change in the supply of money has no long-run effect on any real variables; it affects only the price level.

such as firms' technologies and consumers' preferences. The absolute level of money prices was then determined by the monetary side of the economy, where the quantity of money determined the price level. In macro models that contain this dichotomy, the long-run effect of a change in the money supply is a change in the price level, with no changes to any real economic variables.

The concept of money neutrality is interpreted differently by different people. Our definition above, which emphasizes the independence of Y^* from the country's money supply, is probably the most commonly used definition today, but there are others as well. *Applying Economic Concepts 28-2* examines the concept of money neutrality as it relates to changes in the denominations of a country's paper currency.

> Money is neutral in the long run if a change in the money supply has no long-run effect on real GDP or any other real variables. Much empirical evidence is consistent with long-run money neutrality, although the proposition is often debated.

Hysteresis Effects The proposition of long-run money neutrality is debatable. Though it is a common assumption in many macroeconomic models, there are good reasons to think that changes in a country's money supply may have effects on Y^* and thus have long-run effects on real GDP. Here we examine what is called *hysteresis*—the possibility that the level or growth rate of Y^* may be affected by the short-run path of real GDP.

Investment and Technology. Theories that assume long-run money neutrality typically omit some key economic behaviour that blurs the division between the real and monetary sectors of the economy. Credit plays a key role in linking these two sectors. Most firms use credit to finance aspects of their regular operations as well as their investments in research and development and the expansion of their production facilities. In short, credit can be viewed as an important input to firms' production and investment activities.

Now consider the effects of a change in the country's money supply. As we have seen in this chapter, the likely short-run effects are changes in interest rates and the level of real GDP. But if the change in firms' access to credit—associated with the change in interest rates—also leads firms to alter their capital investment and expenditures on research and development, there may be a permanent effect on the economy's capital stock and state of technology. If so, there will be a permanent effect on the level of potential output.

A dramatic example of the important role of credit occurred with the global financial crisis that began in 2008. As several large U.S. and European banks failed, the flows of credit to non-financial firms dropped sharply in many countries. The reduced access to credit led to reductions in investment, employment, and output, and contributed to the largest global recession in over half a century.

> Long-run money neutrality is called into question by the possibility that a change in the money supply, through its effect on the interest rate, can affect the course of investment and technological change and hence the path of potential output.

Human Capital. Another reason for hysteresis is the effect on human capital that often accompanies prolonged unemployment. Consider a negative shock that reduces real GDP and increases the unemployment rate. If wages and other factor prices are slow to adjust, some individuals will experience long spells of unemployment. Prolonged lack of work for even experienced workers may cause their skills to deteriorate. The effect can be even stronger with first entrants to the labour force. If young people are denied the experience of early jobs that teach them the disciplines and basic skills required of all members of the labour force, it may be difficult or even impossible for them to learn these skills later when jobs do become available. If the recession lasts long enough, both groups may eventually become "unemployable," even after the aggregate economy recovers. In this case, the fall in the level of real GDP, if prolonged, leads through hysteresis effects to a fall in the level of Y^*.

The major global recession that began in 2008 again provides an example to illustrate these effects. Even three years into a slow economic recovery, the amount of long-term unemployment among both experienced and young workers was higher in the United States than at any time in the recent past. In Europe, the situation was even worse, with long-term youth unemployment running from 20 to over 40 percent in the more depressed economies such as Greece and Spain. There is little doubt that the stock of productive human capital that will exist when these countries eventually return to something like full employment will be permanently below what it would have been if the prolonged recession had not occurred.

> If a long period of unemployment associated with a prolonged recessionary gap causes workers to lose human capital, or accumulate less than they otherwise would, both the level and rate of growth of Y^* may be reduced when the recessionary gap is eventually closed.

Money and Inflation

Whether or not money is neutral in the long run, it is certainly closely related to the price level. As we observed in Chapter 27 (in *Applying Economic Concepts 27-1*), there have been many examples throughout history of countries experiencing dramatic increases in the money supply and equally dramatic increases in the price level.

The close connection between money growth and inflation does not hold just in the dramatic examples; it is a connection that applies in the long run to most if not all economies. Figure 28-9 shows a scatter plot of inflation and money growth for a large sample of countries between 1978 and 2010. The vertical axis measures each country's average annual inflation rate. The horizontal axis measures each country's average annual growth rate of the money supply. Each point in the figure represents the rates of inflation and money supply growth for one country averaged over the sample period. As is clear in the figure, there is a strong positive correlation between the growth rate of the money supply and the rate of inflation, as reflected by the tight bunching of points around the upward-sloping line. This line is the statistical "line of best fit" between money supply growth and inflation. Its slope is 0.97, indicating that two countries that differ in their money growth rates by 10 percent will, on average, differ in their inflation rates by 9.7 percent.

> Across many countries over long periods of time, the rate of inflation and the growth rate of the money supply are highly correlated.

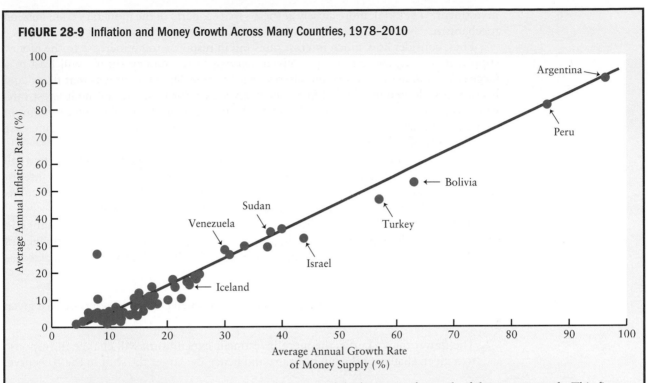

FIGURE 28-9 Inflation and Money Growth Across Many Countries, 1978–2010

Countries with higher inflation rates tend to be countries with higher rates of growth of the money supply. This figure plots long-run data for many countries. Each point shows the average annual inflation rate and the average annual growth rate of the money supply for a specific country for the 1978–2010 period. For all countries, the inflation data refer to the rate of change of the Consumer Price Index; the money supply data refer to the growth rate of M2. The positive relationship between inflation and money supply growth (with a slope of the best-fit line very close to 1) is consistent with the proposition of long-run money neutrality.

(*Source:* Based on author's calculations using data from the World Bank. Go to www.worldbank.org and look for "world development indicators and global development finance.")

The Short-Run Effects of Monetary Shocks

In our macro model, money is clearly not neutral in the short run. We have seen that a change in the money supply shifts the *AD* curve and hence alters the short-run equilibrium level of real GDP. For a given *AS* curve, the short-run effect of a change in the money supply on real GDP and the price level is determined by the extent of the shift of the *AD* curve.

How Effective Is Monetary Policy? How much the *AD* curve shifts in response to an increase in the money supply depends on the amount of investment expenditure that is stimulated. The increase in investment expenditure in turn depends on the strength of two of the linkages that make up the monetary transmission mechanism: the link between money supply and interest rates, and the link between interest rates and investment.[5] Let's look more closely at these separate parts of the monetary transmission mechanism.

First, consider how much interest rates fall in response to an increase in the money supply. If the M_D curve is steep, a given increase in the money supply will lead to a large reduction in the equilibrium interest rate. A steep M_D curve means that firms' and households' desired money holding is not very sensitive to changes in the interest rate, so interest rates have to fall a lot to get people to be content to hold a larger amount of money. The flatter the M_D curve, the less interest rates will fall for any given increase in the supply of money.

Second, consider how much investment expenditure increases in response to a fall in interest rates. If the I^D curve is relatively flat, then any given reduction in interest rates will lead to a large increase in firms' desired investment. The steeper the I^D curve, the less investment will increase for any given reduction in interest rates.

It follows that the size of the shift of the AD curve in response to a change in the money supply depends on the shapes of the M_D and I^D curves. The influence of the shapes of the two curves is shown in Figure 28-10 and can be summarized as follows:

1. The steeper the M_D curve, the more interest rates will change in response to a given change in the money supply.

2. The flatter the I^D curve, the more investment expenditure will change in response to a given change in the interest rate, and hence the larger the shift in the AD curve.

The combination that produces the largest shift in the AD curve for a given change in the money supply is a steep M_D curve and a flat I^D curve. This combination is illustrated in part (i) of Figure 28-10. It makes monetary policy relatively effective as a means of influencing real GDP in the short run. The combination that produces the smallest shift in the AD curve is a flat M_D curve and a steep I^D curve. This combination is illustrated in part (ii) of Figure 28-10. It makes monetary policy relatively ineffective in the short run.

> The effectiveness of monetary policy in inducing short-run changes in real GDP depends on the slopes of the M_D and I^D curves. The steeper is the M_D curve, and the flatter is the I^D curve, the more effective is monetary policy.

Keynesians Versus Monetarists Figure 28-10 illustrates a famous debate among economists that occurred in the three decades following the Second World War. Some economists, following the ideas of John Maynard Keynes, argued that changes in the money supply led to relatively small changes in interest rates, and that investment was relatively insensitive to changes in the interest rate. These *Keynesian* economists concluded that monetary policy was not a very effective method of stimulating aggregate demand—they therefore emphasized the value of using fiscal policy (as Keynes himself had argued during the Great Depression). Another group of economists, led by Milton Friedman, argued that changes in the money supply caused sharp changes

---

[5] As we saw earlier in the chapter, the consumption of durable goods is also sensitive to changes in the interest rate. In this section, however, we simplify by focusing only on the behaviour of desired investment.

FIGURE 28-10 Two Views on the Strength of Monetary Changes

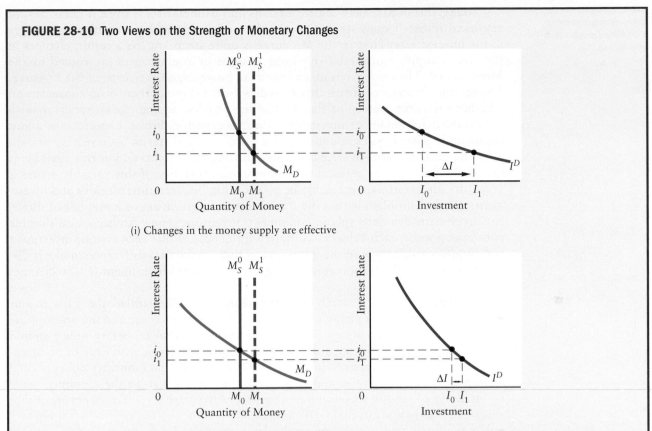

(i) Changes in the money supply are effective

(ii) Changes in the money supply are ineffective

The effect of a change in the money supply on aggregate demand depends on the slopes of the M_D and I^D curves. Initially, in parts (i) and (ii), the money supply is M_S^0, and the economy has an interest rate of i_0 and investment expenditure of I_0. The central bank then expands the money supply from M_S^0 to M_S^1. The rate of interest thus falls from i_0 to i_1, as shown in each of the left panels. This causes an increase in investment expenditure of ΔI, from I_0 to I_1, as shown in each of the right panels.

In part (i), the demand for money is insensitive to the interest rate, so the increase in the money supply leads to a large fall in the interest rate. Further, desired investment expenditure is highly interest sensitive, so the large fall in interest rates also leads to a large increase in investment expenditure. In this case, the change in the money supply will be very effective in stimulating aggregate demand.

In part (ii), the demand for money is more sensitive to the interest rate, so the increase in the money supply leads to only a small fall in the interest rate. Further, desired investment expenditure is much less sensitive to the interest rate, and so the small fall in interest rates leads to only a small increase in investment expenditure. In this case, the change in the money supply will be less effective in stimulating aggregate demand.

in interest rates, which, in turn, led to significant changes in investment expenditure. These *Monetarist* economists concluded that monetary policy was a very effective tool for stimulating aggregate demand.[6]

---

[6] Monetarists argued that monetary policy was very effective for stimulating aggregate demand but they *did not* advocate an "activist" monetary policy. One of their concerns was that monetary forces were so strong that an activist monetary policy would potentially destabilize the economy. We address these issues in Chapter 29.

For brief descriptions of the contributions to economics of the Nobel laureates, go to www.nobel.se/economics/laureates/.

Today, this debate between Keynesians and Monetarists is over. A great deal of empirical research suggests that money demand is relatively insensitive to changes in the interest rate. That is, the M_D curve is quite steep and, as a result, changes in the money supply cause relatively large changes in interest rates (as argued by the Monetarists). The evidence is much less clear, however, on the slope of the I^D curve. Though the evidence confirms that I^D is downward sloping, there is no consensus on whether the curve is steep or flat. Part of the problem facing researchers is that an important determinant of investment is not observable. Firms' expectations about the future—what Keynes famously called firms' "animal spirits"—have a significant effect on their investment decisions (thus shifting the I^D curve), but this variable is not easily measured by researchers. The non-observability of this variable makes it very difficult to estimate precisely the relationship between interest rates and investment. Another problem is that the I^D curve is an aggregation of a number of different investment demands (plant, equipment, inventories, new housing, and durable consumer goods), each subject to different influences. While each type of investment is responsive to changes in the interest rate, their individual differences make it difficult to estimate the responsiveness of *aggregate* desired investment (I^D) to changes in the interest rate.

Though empirical research over the years has largely filled the gaps in our knowledge, there is still plenty of debate about the effectiveness and the appropriate objectives of monetary policy. Some economists argue that monetary policy should be directed only to achieving a desired path of the price level, with little or no attention being paid to fluctuations in real GDP. Others argue that monetary policy should attempt to offset the largest and most persistent shocks that hit the economy, while maintaining a long-run focus on the behaviour of the price level. Yet others argue that short-run fluctuations in real GDP and employment are so important that monetary policy ought to place much less emphasis on the price level and instead be actively engaged in reducing the economy's fluctuations in the face of all but the smallest and most transient shocks.

In the next chapter we examine the details of how monetary policy is conducted in Canada. For several reasons, the real-world practice of monetary policy is more complex than it appears in this chapter. But as we will see, the Bank of Canada's system of *inflation targeting* can be viewed as a means of providing both short-run stabilization and a long-run focus on the behaviour of the price level.

SUMMARY

28.1 Understanding Bonds   LO 1

- The present value of any bond that promises to pay some sequence of payments in the future is negatively related to the market interest rate. A bond's present value determines its market price. Thus, there is a negative relationship between the market interest rate and the price of a bond.
- The yield on a bond is the rate of return the bondholder receives, having bought the bond at its

purchase price and then receiving the entire stream of future payments the bond offers. For a given stream of future payments, a lower purchase price implies a higher bond yield.
- An increase in the perceived riskiness of bonds leads to a reduction in bond prices and thus an increase in bond yields.

28.2 The Theory of Money Demand

- In our macro model, households and firms are assumed to divide their financial assets between interest-bearing "bonds" and non–interest-bearing "money." They hold money to facilitate both expected and unexpected transactions, and also to protect against the possibility of a decline in bond prices (a rise in interest rates).
- The opportunity cost of holding money is the interest that would have been earned if bonds had been held instead.
- Households' and firms' desired money holdings are assumed to be influenced by three key macroeconomic variables:

1. Increases in the interest rate reduce desired money holdings.
2. Increases in real GDP increase desired money holdings.
3. Increases in the price level increase desired money holdings.

- These relationships are captured in the M_D curve, which is drawn as a negative relationship between interest rates (i) and desired money holding (M_D). Increases in real GDP (Y) or the price level (P) lead to a rightward shift of this M_D curve.

28.3 Monetary Equilibrium and National Income

- In the short run, the interest rate is determined by the interaction of money supply and money demand. Monetary equilibrium is established when the interest rate is such that the quantity of money supplied is equal to the quantity of money demanded.
- A change in the money supply (coming from the central bank or the commercial banking system) or in the demand for money (coming from a change in Y or P) will lead to a change in the equilibrium interest rate. This is the first stage of the monetary transmission mechanism.

- The second stage of the monetary transmission mechanism is that any change in the interest rate leads to a change in desired investment and consumption expenditure. In an open economy with capital mobility, the change in the interest rate leads to capital flows, changes in the exchange rate, and changes in net exports.
- The third stage of the monetary transmission mechanism is that any change in desired investment, consumption, or net exports leads to a shift in the aggregate demand (AD) curve, and thus to a change in real GDP and the price level.

28.4 The Strength of Monetary Forces

- Changes in the money supply have different effects on the economy in the short run and in the long run.
- Money is said to be neutral in the long run if a change in the money supply leads to no changes in the long-run level of real GDP (or other real variables).
- In the long run, after wages and other factor prices have fully adjusted to any output gaps, real GDP returns to potential output, Y^*. If Y^* is unaffected by the change in the money supply, there will be no long-run effect from the monetary shock.
- If there is *hysteresis*, short-run changes in real GDP will lead to changes in Y^*. In these cases, monetary shocks will have long-run effects on real GDP.

- There is a strong positive correlation between the rate of money growth and the rate of inflation across countries when viewed over the long run.
- In the short run, the effects of a change in the money supply depend on the shape of the M_D and I^D curves in our macro model. The steeper the M_D curve and the flatter the I^D curve, the more effective changes in the money supply will be in causing short-run changes in real GDP.

KEY CONCEPTS

The interest rate and present value
Interest rates, bond prices, and bond yields
Reasons for holding money
The money demand (M_D) function

Monetary equilibrium
The monetary transmission mechanism
The investment demand (I^D) function

Effects of changes in the money supply
Neutrality and non-neutrality of money
Hysteresis

STUDY EXERCISES

MyEconLab   Make the grade with MyEconLab: Study Exercises marked in red can be found on MyEconLab. You can practise them as often as you want, and most feature step-by-step guided instructions to help you find the right answer.

---

1. Fill in the blanks to make the following statements correctly reflect the theory developed in this chapter.

   a. Monetary equilibrium occurs when the quantity of _____ equals the quantity of _____. Monetary equilibrium determines the _____.

   b. When there is an excess supply of money, households and firms will attempt to _____ bonds. This action will cause the price of bonds to _____ and the interest rate to _____.

   c. When there is an excess demand for money, households and firms will attempt to _____ bonds. This action will cause the price of bonds to _____ and the interest rate to _____.

   d. The _____ _____ _____ refers to the three stages that link the money market to aggregate demand. The first link is between monetary equilibrium and the _____; the second link is between the _____ and desired _____; the third link is between desired _____ and _____.

   e. Suppose the economy is in equilibrium and then the Bank of Canada increases the money supply. The first effect will be an excess _____ of/for money, which will then lead to a(n) _____ in the interest rate, which will in turn lead to a(n) _____ in desired investment.

   f. Suppose the economy is in equilibrium and the Bank of Canada decreases the money supply. The first effect will be an excess _____ of/for money, which will lead to a _____ in the interest rate, which will in turn lead to a(n) _____ in desired investment.

   g. Through the monetary transmission mechanism, a rightward shift of the AD curve can be caused by a(n) _____ in the money supply; a leftward shift of the AD curve can be caused by a(n) _____ in the money supply.

   h. In an open economy with capital mobility, an increase in the money supply causes interest rates to _____, which leads to a capital outflow. This causes a(n) _____ of the Canadian dollar and thus to a(n) _____ in net exports, which leads the AD curve to shift _____.

2. Fill in the blanks to make the following statements correctly reflect the theory developed in this chapter.

   a. If money is neutral in the long run, then changes in the money supply have no effect on _____ in the long run.

   b. If the demand for money is not very sensitive to changes in the interest rate, then the M_D curve will be relatively _____. An increase in the money supply will lead to a(n) _____ reduction in the interest rate.

   c. If the demand for money is very sensitive to changes in the interest rate, then the M_D curve will be relatively _____. An increase in the money supply will lead to a(n) _____ reduction in the interest rate.

   d. A relatively flat investment demand curve means that a change in the interest rate will have a(n) _____ effect on _____, which leads to a relatively large shift in the _____ curve.

   e. A relatively steep investment demand curve means that a change in the interest rate will have a(n) _____ effect on _____, which leads to a relatively small shift in the _____ curve.

   f. Changes in the money supply will have the largest effect on the position of the AD curve when the M_D curve is relatively _____ and the I^D curve is relatively _____.

3. The following table shows the stream of income produced by several different assets. In each case, P_1, P_2, and P_3 are the payments made by the asset in Years 1, 2, and 3.

Asset	Market Interest Rate (i)	P_1	P_2	P_3	Present Value
Treasury Bill	4%	$1000	$0	$0	—
Bond	3%	$0	$0	$5000	—
Bond	5%	$200	$200	$200	—
Stock	6%	$50	$40	$60	—

a. For each asset, compute the asset's present value. (Note that the market interest rate, i, is not the same in each situation.)

b. Explain why the market price for each asset is expected to be the asset's present value.

4. The table below provides information for six different bonds: current market price (P), the face value of the bond (V), and the number of years before the bond matures (N).

Bond Number	Market Price (P)	Face Value (V)	Years to Maturity (N)
1a	$926	$1000	1
1b	$850	$1000	1
2a	$1270	$2000	5
2b	$838	$2000	5
3a	$1760	$5000	10
3b	$684	$5000	10

a. In each case, compute the bond's yield, assuming that you buy the bond at its current market price and hold the bond until it matures. There are no coupons. If x is the bond's yield, then $P(1 + x)^N = V$.

b. Suppose bonds 1a, 2a, and 3a are all issued by the same borrower. Can you offer an explanation for the relationship between the bond yields and the terms to maturity?

c. Suppose bonds 1b, 2b, and 3b are all issued by the same borrower. What can you conclude about the riskiness of the "a" borrower versus that of the "b" borrower? Explain.

d. Notice that the market interest rate is not shown in the table. Explain why knowledge of the market interest rate is unnecessary in order to compute a bond's yield, once you already know the bond's market price. What aspect of the bond does the market interest rate influence, if anything?

5. Consider a bond that promises to make coupon payments of $100 one year from now and $100 two years from now, and to repay the principal of $1000 three years from now. Suppose also that the market interest rate is 8 percent per year, and that no perceived risk is associated with the bond.

a. Compute the present value of this bond.

b. Suppose the bond is being offered for $995. Would you buy the bond at that price? What do you expect to happen to the bond price in the very near future?

c. Suppose the bond is instead being offered at a price of $950. Would you buy the bond at that price? Do you expect the bond price to change in the near future?

d. If the price of the bond is equal to its computed present value from part (a), what is the implied bond yield?

e. Explain why bond yields and the market interest rate tend to move together so that economists can then sensibly speak about "the" interest rate.

6. What motives for holding money—transactions, precautionary, or speculative—do you think explain the following holdings? Explain.

a. Currency in the cash register of the local grocery store at the start of each working day.

b. Money to meet Queen's University's biweekly payroll deposited in the local bank.

c. A household tries to keep a "buffer" of $1000 in its savings account.

d. An investor sells bonds for cash, which she then deposits in a low-return bank account.

e. You carry $20 in your pocket even though you have no planned expenditures.

7. The diagram below shows the demand for money and the supply of money.

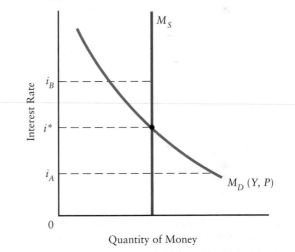

a. Explain why the M_D function is downward sloping.

b. Suppose the interest rate is at i_A. Explain how firms and households attempt to satisfy their excess demand for money. What is the effect of their actions?

c. Suppose the interest rate is at i_B. Explain how firms and households attempt to dispose of their excess supply of money. What is the effect of their actions?

d. Now suppose there is an increase in the transactions demand for money (perhaps because of growth in real GDP). Beginning at i^*, explain what happens in the money market. How is this shown in the diagram?

8. The following diagrams show the determination of monetary equilibrium and the demand for investment. The economy begins with money supply M_S, money demand M_D, and investment demand I^D. The interest rate is i_0 and desired investment is I_0.

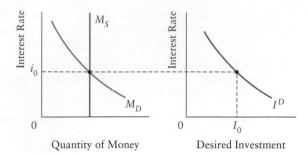

a. Beginning at the initial equilibrium, suppose the Bank of Canada increases the money supply. What happens in the money market, and what happens to desired investment expenditure?

b. Beginning in the initial equilibrium, suppose there is a reduction in the demand for money (caused, perhaps, by bonds becoming more attractive to firms and households). What happens in the money market, and what happens to desired investment expenditure?

c. Explain why an increase in money supply can have the same effects on desired investment expenditure as a reduction in money demand.

9. In the text we discussed why, in an open economy with international capital mobility, there is a second part to the monetary transmission mechanism. (It may be useful to review Figure 28-7 on page 706 when answering this question.)

   a. Explain why an increase in Canada's money supply makes investors shift their portfolios away from Canadian bonds and toward foreign bonds.

   b. Explain why this portfolio adjustment leads to a depreciation of the Canadian dollar.

   c. Why would such a depreciation of the Canadian dollar lead to an increase in Canada's net exports?

   d. Now suppose that the Bank of Canada does not change its policy at all, but the Federal Reserve (the U.S. central bank) increases the U.S. money supply. What is the likely effect on Canada? Explain.

10. In the text we discussed the historical debate between Keynesians and Monetarists regarding the effectiveness of monetary policy in changing real GDP (see Figure 28-10 on page 713 to review). Using the same sort of diagram, discuss two conditions in which a change in the money supply would have *no* short-run effect on real GDP.

11. In 2008, stock markets in Canada and other developed countries experienced very large declines, largely in response to the failure of several large U.S. and European banks and the resulting disruption in global financial markets.

    a. Explain how such stock-market declines affect wealth and thus are likely to affect the *AD* curve.

    b. If the central banks attempt to keep output close to Y^*, what will they likely do in response? Explain.

    c. Did the Bank of Canada act as predicted in part (b)? Explain how you know.

12. Consider the effects of events in the U.S. economy on the Canadian economy and on Canadian monetary policy.

    a. If a serious recession begins in the United States, what is the likely effect on Canadian aggregate demand? Explain.

    b. If Canadian real GDP was equal to Y^* before the U.S. recession began, what would be the likely response by the Bank of Canada?

    c. Given the mobility of financial capital across international boundaries, what is the likely effect on Canadian aggregate demand from a policy by the U.S. Federal Reserve that reduces U.S. interest rates?

    d. Given your answer to part (c), explain why Canadian monetary policy might sometimes appear to "mirror" U.S. monetary policy even though the Bank of Canada is wholly independent from the U.S. Federal Reserve.

Monetary Policy in Canada

IN the previous two chapters we encountered many details about money and its importance for the economy. In Chapter 27 we saw how commercial banks, through their activities of accepting deposits and extending loans, create deposit money. These bank deposits, together with the currency in circulation, make up the nation's money supply. In Chapter 28 we examined the variables that influence households' and firms' money demand. We then put money demand together with money supply to examine how interest rates are determined in the short run in monetary equilibrium. Finally, we examined the monetary transmission mechanism—the chain of cause-and-effect events describing how changes in money demand or supply lead to changes in interest rates, aggregate demand, real GDP, and the price level.

Chapters 27 and 28 presented a general view of the role of money in the economy. What is still missing is a detailed account of how the Bank of Canada conducts its monetary policy. We begin this chapter by describing some technical details about how the Bank influences the monetary equilibrium and thereby sets in motion the monetary transmission mechanism. We then discuss the Bank's current system of inflation targeting and how this system helps to stabilize the economy. Finally, we discuss some limitations for monetary policy and some of the Bank's major policy challenges over the past 30 years.

29.1 How the Bank of Canada Implements Monetary Policy

The monetary transmission mechanism describes how changes in the demand for or supply of money cause changes in the interest rate, which then lead to changes in aggregate demand, real GDP, and the price level. But how does the Bank of Canada influence the money market and thereby implement its monetary policy?

As we saw in Chapter 27, the money supply is the sum of currency in circulation and total bank deposits, and commercial banks play a key role in influencing the level of these deposits. As a result, the Bank of Canada cannot directly *set* the money supply. As we will soon see, the Bank of Canada is also unable to directly *set* interest rates. In what follows, therefore, we speak of the Bank "targeting" the money supply or interest rates rather than "setting" them directly.

Money Supply Versus the Interest Rate

In general, any central bank has two alternative approaches for implementing its monetary policy—it can choose to target the money supply or it can choose to target the interest rate. These two approaches are illustrated in Figure 29-1, which shows money demand, money supply, and the equilibrium interest rate. For any given M_D curve, the central bank must choose one approach or the other; it cannot target *both* the money supply and the

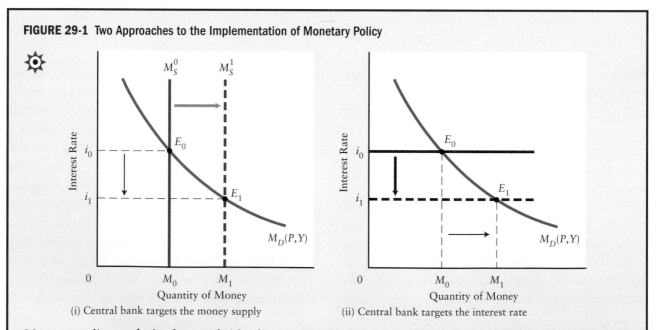

FIGURE 29-1 Two Approaches to the Implementation of Monetary Policy

(i) Central bank targets the money supply

(ii) Central bank targets the interest rate

Monetary policy can be implemented either by targeting the money supply directly or by targeting the interest rate directly—but not both. In part (i), the Bank of Canada could attempt to shift the M_S curve directly and thereby change the equilibrium interest rate. But because the Bank cannot directly control the money supply, and because the slope and position of the M_D curve are uncertain, this is an ineffective way to conduct monetary policy. The Bank's chosen method is illustrated in part (ii), in which it targets the interest rate directly. It then accommodates the resulting change in money demand through its open-market operations.

interest rate independently. If it chooses to target the money supply, monetary equilibrium will determine the interest rate. Alternatively, if the central bank targets the interest rate, the money supply must adjust to accommodate the movement along the M_D curve.

> **In principle, monetary policy can be implemented either by targeting the money supply or by targeting the interest rate. But for a given M_D curve, both cannot be targeted independently.**

Part (i) of Figure 29-1 shows how the Bank of Canada could attempt to shift the M_S curve directly, by changing the amount of currency in circulation in the economy. It could do this by buying or selling government securities in the financial markets—transactions called *open-market operations*. For example, by using currency to buy $100 000 of government bonds from a willing seller, the Bank of Canada would increase the amount of cash reserves in the banking system by $100 000. As we saw in Chapter 27, commercial banks would then be able to lend out these new reserves and thereby increase the amount of deposit money in the economy. The combined effect of the new reserves and the new deposit money would be an increase in the money supply and thus a shift of the M_S curve to the right. For a given M_D curve, this increase in money supply would lead to a reduction in the equilibrium interest rate and, through the various parts of the transmission mechanism, to an eventual increase in aggregate demand.

The Bank of Canada does not implement its monetary policy in this way, for three reasons. First, while the Bank of Canada *can* control the amount of cash reserves in the banking system (through open-market operations) it *cannot* control the process of deposit expansion carried out by the commercial banks. And since the money supply is the sum of currency and deposits, it follows that the Bank can influence the money supply but cannot *control* it. For example, if the Bank increased the amount of cash reserves in the system, the commercial banks might choose not to expand their lending, and as a result the overall increase in the money supply would be far smaller than the Bank initially intended.

The second reason the Bank does not try to target the money supply directly is the uncertainty regarding the slope of the M_D curve. Even if the Bank had perfect control over the money supply (which it does not), it would be unsure about the change in the interest rate that would result from any given change in the supply of money. Since it is the change in the interest rate that ultimately determines the subsequent changes in aggregate demand, this uncertainty would make the conduct of monetary policy very difficult.

Finally, in addition to being uncertain about the *slope* of the M_D curve, the Bank is also unable to predict accurately the *position* of the M_D curve at any given time. Changes in both real GDP and the price level cause changes in money demand that the Bank can only approximate. Even more difficult to predict are the changes in money demand that occur as a result of innovations in the financial sector. During the late 1970s and early 1980s, for example, the creation of new types of bank deposits led to unprecedented and unpredicted changes in money demand, as people transferred funds between bank accounts of different types. Unpredictable fluctuations in the demand for money make a monetary policy based on the direct control of the money supply difficult to implement.

In summary, the disadvantages of conducting monetary policy by targeting the money supply are as follows:

1. The Bank of Canada cannot control the process of deposit creation.

2. There is uncertainty regarding the slope of the M_D curve.

3. There is uncertainty regarding the position of the M_D curve.

If the Bank of Canada chose to target the money supply, it would have little control over the resulting interest rate. It therefore chooses *not* to implement its monetary policy in this way.

The alternative approach to implementing monetary policy is to target the interest rate directly. This is the approach used by most central banks, including the Bank of Canada. As part (ii) of Figure 29-1 shows, if the Bank can directly change the interest rate, the result will be a change in the quantity of money demanded. In order for this new interest rate to be consistent with monetary equilibrium, the Bank must *accommodate* the change in the amount of money demanded—that is, it must alter the supply of money in order to satisfy the change in desired money holdings by firms and households (we will see shortly how this occurs).

Why does the Bank of Canada choose to implement its monetary policy in this manner? Let's consider the advantages. First, while the Bank cannot control the money supply for the reasons we have just discussed, it *is* able to almost completely control a particular interest rate. (We will see shortly which rate it targets and how it does so.) Second, the Bank's uncertainty about the slope and position of the M_D curve is not a problem when the Bank chooses instead to target the interest rate directly. If the Bank ascertains that a lower interest rate is necessary in order to achieve its policy objectives, it can act directly to reduce the interest rate. Any uncertainty about the M_D curve then implies uncertainty about the ultimate change in the quantity of money, but it is the interest rate that matters, through the transmission mechanism, for determining the level of aggregate demand.

Finally, the Bank can more easily *communicate* its policy actions to the public by targeting the interest rate than by targeting the level of reserves in the banking system. Changes in the interest rate are more meaningful to firms and households than changes in the level of reserves or the money supply. For example, if we hear that the interest rate just decreased by one percentage point, most people can readily assess what this means for their plans to buy a new house financed by a mortgage. In contrast, if we were to hear that the level of reserves in the banking system had just increased by $1 billion, it would not be clear to most people what this means, or that it would have any effect on the interest rate, or by how much. Even the Bank itself might be uncertain about the magnitude of these effects.

In summary, these are the advantages of conducting monetary policy by targeting the interest rate:

1. The Bank of Canada is able to control a particular interest rate.

2. Uncertainty about the slope and position of the M_D curve does not prevent the Bank of Canada from establishing its desired interest rate.

3. The Bank of Canada can easily communicate its interest-rate policy to the public.

The Bank of Canada and the Overnight Interest Rate

We have just explained why the Bank of Canada chooses to implement its monetary policy by targeting the interest rate rather than by targeting the money supply directly. But *how* does the Bank do this, and *which* interest rate (among many) does it target?

As we discussed in Chapter 28, there are many interest rates in the Canadian economy. Commercial banks pay different rates to depositors on each of several different types of bank deposits. They also lend at different rates for different kinds of loans—home mortgages, small business loans, personal lines of credit, and car loans, to name just a few. In addition, government securities trade at different yields (interest rates) depending on the term to maturity. Economists refer to the overall pattern of interest rates corresponding to government securities of different maturities as the *term structure of interest rates*. Since inflation and other risks generally lead bondholders to require a higher rate of return in order to lend their funds for a longer period of time, yields on government securities generally increase as the term to maturity increases. At any given time, the yield on 90-day Treasury bills is usually less than that on 5-year government bonds, which in turn is less than the yield on 30-year bonds. Furthermore, because these various assets are viewed as close substitutes by bondholders, the different interest rates tend to rise and fall together.

The interest rate corresponding to the shortest period of borrowing or lending is called the **overnight interest rate,** which is the interest rate that commercial banks charge one another for overnight loans. Commercial banks that need cash because they have run short of reserves can borrow in the *overnight market* from banks that have excess reserves available. The overnight interest rate is a market-determined interest rate that fluctuates daily as the cash requirements of commercial banks change.

overnight interest rate The interest rate that commercial banks charge one another for overnight loans.

The Bank of Canada exercises enormous influence over the overnight interest rate. As this rate rises or falls, the other interest rates in the economy—from short-term lines of credit to longer-term home mortgages and government securities—tend to rise or fall as well.

> By influencing the overnight interest rate, the Bank of Canada also influences the longer-term interest rates that are more relevant for determining aggregate consumption and investment expenditure.

To see how the Bank of Canada influences the overnight interest rate, we need to make an important distinction between the Bank's target and the instrument that it uses to achieve that target. The Bank establishes a target for the overnight rate and announces this target eight times per year at pre-specified dates called *fixed announcement dates*, or FADs.

The Bank's instrument for achieving its target is its lending and borrowing activities with the commercial banking system. When the Bank announces its target for the overnight rate, it also announces the **bank rate,** an interest rate 0.25 percentage points above the target rate. The Bank promises to lend at this bank rate any amount that commercial banks want to borrow. At the same time, the Bank offers to borrow (accept deposits) in unlimited amounts from commercial banks and pay them an interest rate 0.25 percentage points below the target rate. With these promises by the Bank, the actual overnight interest rate stays within the 0.5-percentage-point range centred around the target rate, and is usually very close to the target rate itself.

bank rate The interest rate the Bank of Canada charges commercial banks for loans.

Consider an example that illustrates the Bank's control over the overnight interest rate. We begin by assuming that the Bank's announced target for the overnight interest rate is 3 percent. The Bank is then willing to lend to commercial banks at the bank rate, 3.25 percent. The Bank is also willing to pay 2.75 percent on any deposits it receives from commercial banks. In this case, what will be the *actual* overnight interest rate? Without knowing more details about commercial banks' demands and supplies for overnight funds, we cannot know exactly what the rate will be, but we can be sure that it will be within the Bank's target range—that is, *between* 2.75 percent and 3.25 percent. It will not be above 3.25 percent because any borrower would rather borrow from the Bank of Canada at 3.25 percent than at a higher rate from any commercial lender. Similarly, it will not be below 2.75 percent because any lender would rather lend to the Bank of Canada at 2.75 percent than accept a lower rate from any commercial borrower. Thus, the Bank can ensure that the actual overnight interest rate remains within its target range.[1]

> The Bank of Canada establishes a target for the overnight interest rate. Its instrument for achieving this target is its borrowing and lending activities with commercial banks. By raising or lowering its target rate, the Bank affects the actual overnight interest rate. Changes in the overnight rate then lead to changes in other, longer-term, interest rates.

Figure 29-2 shows the path of the actual overnight interest rate and the Bank's target rate since 2000. It is almost impossible to tell the difference between the two lines in the figure, which shows the considerable influence that the Bank of Canada's actions have on the actual overnight interest rate.

FIGURE 29-2 The Overnight Interest Rate: Target and Actual

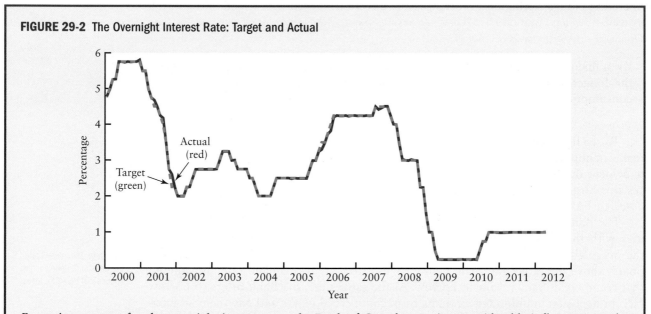

By setting a target for the overnight interest rate, the Bank of Canada exercises considerable influence over the actual overnight interest rate. By establishing an upper lending rate (the bank rate) and a lower borrowing rate, the Bank can ensure that the actual overnight interest rate remains within the Bank's target range. Since 2000, there have been only negligible differences between the actual overnight interest rate, the solid red line, and the Bank's target for the overnight rate, the green dashed line.

(*Source:* All data are from the Bank of Canada: www.bankofcanada.ca. Overnight interest rate: Series V122514. Bank rate: Series V122530. The Bank's target rate is the bank rate minus 0.25 percentage points.)

---

[1] The actual overnight rate is usually indistinguishable from the Bank's target rate, but it occasionally deviates by as much as 10 basis points (0.1 percentage point). When this occurs, typically only a few days per month, the Bank of Canada initiates further temporary lending and borrowing transactions with the commercial banks in order to push the overnight rate back toward the Bank's target rate.

The Money Supply Is Endogenous

When the Bank of Canada changes its target for the overnight rate, the change in the actual overnight rate happens almost instantly. Changes in other market interest rates, from home mortgage rates and the prime interest rate to the yields on short- and long-term government securities, also happen very quickly, usually within a day or two. As these rates adjust, firms and households begin to adjust their borrowing behaviour, but these changes take considerably longer to occur. For example, if the Bank of Canada lowered its target for the overnight rate by 25 basis points (0.25 percentage points), commercial banks might follow immediately by reducing the rate on home mortgages. But individuals will not respond to this rate reduction by immediately increasing their demand for home mortgages. Usually such changes take a while to occur, as borrowers consider how interest-rate changes affect their own economic situations, the affordability of a possible house purchase, or, in the case of firms, the profitability of a potential investment.

As the demand for new loans gradually adjusts to changes in interest rates, commercial banks often find themselves in need of more cash reserves with which to make new loans. When this occurs, banks can sell some of their government securities to the Bank of Canada in exchange for cash (or electronic reserves) and then use this cash to extend new loans. By buying government securities with cash in such an **open-market operation**, the Bank of Canada increases the amount of currency in circulation in the economy. This new currency arrives at the commercial banks as cash reserves, which can then be loaned out to firms or households. As we saw in Chapter 27, this process of making loans results in an expansion in deposit money and thus an expansion of the money supply.

open-market operation The purchase and sale of government securities on the open market by the central bank.

> Through its open-market operations, the Bank of Canada changes the amount of currency in circulation. These operations, however, are not initiated by the Bank; it conducts them to accommodate the changing demand for cash reserves by the commercial banks.

Economists often say that the amount of currency in circulation (and also the money supply) is *endogenous*. It is not directly controlled by the Bank of Canada, but instead is determined by the economic decisions of households, firms, and commercial banks. The Bank of Canada is *passive* in its decisions regarding the money supply; it conducts its open-market operations to accommodate the changing demand for currency coming from the commercial banks. *Applying Economic Concepts 29-1* discusses in more detail how the Bank of Canada conducts open-market operations in response to this changing demand.

Expansionary and Contractionary Monetary Policies

We can now clarify the meaning of a *contractionary* or an *expansionary* monetary policy. As we saw earlier, unpredictable shifts in the money demand curve imply that there is no clear relationship between changes in the interest rate and changes in the quantity of money in circulation. And since what matters for the monetary transmission mechanism is the change in interest rates, economists label a monetary-policy action as being expansionary or contractionary depending on how the policy affects interest rates, rather than on how it affects the overall amount of money.

If the Bank of Canada wants to stimulate aggregate demand, it will reduce its target for the overnight interest rate, and the effect will soon be felt on longer-term market

APPLYING ECONOMIC CONCEPTS 29-1

What Determines the Amount of Currency in Circulation?

The Bank of Canada uses its target for the overnight interest rate to influence the money market and implement its monetary policy. A reduction in the Bank's target for the overnight rate will reduce market interest rates and lead to a greater demand for borrowing and hence spending by firms and households. In contrast, an increase in the Bank's target for the overnight rate will tend to raise market interest rates and reduce the demand for borrowing and spending by firms and households.

In response to these changes in the demand for loans, commercial banks may find themselves either with too few cash reserves with which to make new loans or with too many cash reserves for the amount of loans they want to make. What happens in each case?

If Banks Need More Cash

Suppose that at the current market interest rates and level of economic activity, commercial banks are facing a growing demand for loans. If banks have excess reserves, these loans can be made easily. But once banks reach their target reserve ratio, they will be unable to extend new loans without increasing their cash reserves. Banks can increase their cash reserves by selling some of their government bonds to the Bank of Canada. In this case, the Bank of Canada is *purchasing* government bonds from the commercial banks. This transaction is called an *open-market purchase*.

Suppose a commercial bank wants to sell a $10 000 bond to the Bank of Canada. As the accompanying balance sheets show, this transaction does not change the total assets or liabilities for the commercial bank, although it changes the *form* of its assets. With more cash reserves (and fewer bonds), the commercial bank can now make more loans. For the Bank of Canada, however, there *is* a change in the level of assets and liabilities. Its holdings of bonds (assets) have increased and the amount of currency in circulation (liabilities) has also increased. Open-market purchases by the Bank of Canada are the means by which the amount of currency in the economy increases.

If Banks Have Excess Reserves

Now suppose that at the current market interest rates and level of economic activity the commercial banks cannot find enough suitable borrowers to whom they can lend their excess cash reserves. The commercial banks can reduce their excess cash reserves by using the cash to purchase government bonds from the Bank of Canada. In this case, the Bank of Canada is *selling* government bonds to the commercial banks. This transaction is called an *open-market sale*.

The changes are the opposite of those shown in the accompanying balance sheets. The commercial bank now has less cash and more (interest-earning) bonds, but its total assets and liabilities are unchanged. The Bank of Canada now has fewer bonds and there is also less currency in circulation in the economy.

An Open-Market Purchase of Bonds from a Commercial Bank

Commercial Bank Balance Sheet

Assets		Liabilities
Bonds	−$10 000	No change
Cash Reserves	+$10 000	

Bank of Canada Balance Sheet

Assets		Liabilities	
Bonds	+ $10 000	Currency in Circulation	+ $10 000

Currency in a Growing Economy

If you look at the Bank of Canada's balance sheets (like the one we showed in Chapter 27) over several years, you will notice that the amount of currency in circulation rarely (if ever) falls. In an economy where real GDP is steadily growing, the demand for loans by firms and households is also usually growing, as is the demand for currency by commercial banks. In some years, the demand for currency is growing very quickly, in which case the Bank of Canada has many open-market purchases. In other years, the demand for currency grows only slowly, in which case the Bank has fewer (or smaller) open-market purchases. In a typical year, however, the amount of currency in circulation increases by about 5 percent, which in 2012 represented about $3 billion. Thus, in a typical week, the Bank of Canada purchases about $55 million of government bonds in the open market.

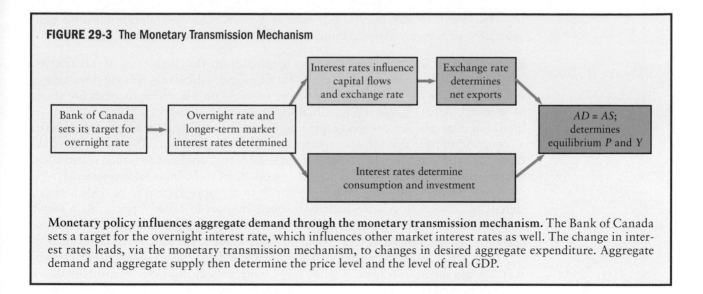

FIGURE 29-3 The Monetary Transmission Mechanism

Monetary policy influences aggregate demand through the monetary transmission mechanism. The Bank of Canada sets a target for the overnight interest rate, which influences other market interest rates as well. The change in interest rates leads, via the monetary transmission mechanism, to changes in desired aggregate expenditure. Aggregate demand and aggregate supply then determine the price level and the level of real GDP.

interest rates. Reducing the interest rate is an *expansionary* monetary policy because it leads to an expansion of aggregate demand. If the Bank instead wants to reduce aggregate demand (or its growth rate), it will increase its target for the overnight interest rate, and longer-term market interest rates will soon rise as a result. Increasing the interest rate is a *contractionary* monetary policy because it leads to a contraction (or a reduction in the growth rate) of aggregate demand.

As the longer-term market interest rates change, the various steps in the monetary transmission mechanism come into play. As we saw in Chapter 28, in an open economy like Canada's there are two separate channels in this transmission mechanism. First, desired investment and consumption expenditure will begin to change. At the same time, international capital flows in response to changes in interest rates will cause the exchange rate to change, which, in turn, causes net exports to change. Taken together, the total changes in aggregate expenditure lead to shifts in the *AD* curve, which then lead to changes in real GDP and the price level. The monetary transmission mechanism is reviewed in Figure 29-3.

29.2 Inflation Targeting

In the previous section we examined the technical details of how the Bank of Canada implements its monetary policy. In this section we examine the Bank's current policy objectives and how it conducts its monetary policy to achieve those objectives. Our emphasis is on the Bank's policy of *inflation targeting*.

Why Target Inflation?

Some people wonder why many central banks have established formal targets for the rate of inflation rather than for other important economic variables such as the rate of growth of real GDP or the unemployment rate. Central banks' focus on inflation comes from two fundamental observations regarding macroeconomic relationships: the costs associated with high inflation, and the ultimate cause of sustained inflation.

High Inflation Is Costly Economists have long accepted that high rates of inflation are damaging to the economy and are costly for firms and individuals. Among other things, inflation reduces the real purchasing power of those people whose incomes are stated in nominal (dollar) terms and insufficiently *indexed* to adjust for changes in the price level. For example, seniors whose pension incomes are not indexed to inflation suffer a reduction in their real incomes whenever inflation occurs. Similarly, those who have made loans or purchased bonds with interest rates that are fixed in nominal terms lose because inflation erodes the real purchasing power of their financial investments.

High inflation also undermines the ability of the price system to provide accurate signals of changes in relative scarcity through changes in relative prices. As a result, both producers and consumers may make mistakes regarding their own production and consumption decisions that they would not have made in the absence of high inflation.

Finally, the *uncertainty* generated by inflation is damaging to the economy in many ways. When inflation is high, it tends to be quite volatile, and this volatility makes it difficult to predict the future course of prices. As a result, periods of high inflation are often characterized as having much *unexpected* inflation. The risk of unexpected inflation makes it difficult for firms to make long-range plans, and such plans are crucial when firms undertake costly investment and R&D activities in order to expand their production facilities or to invent and innovate new products and new production processes. High and volatile inflation is thus likely to be harmful to economic growth.

> High and uncertain inflation leads to arbitrary income redistributions and also hampers the ability of the price system both to allocate resources efficiently and to produce satisfactory rates of economic growth.

Monetary Policy Is the Cause of Sustained Inflation Until recent decades there was uncertainty about the causes of inflation. During the 1970s, many policymakers blamed inflation on the "cost push" exerted on wages by powerful unions and on prices by oligopolistic firms. In response, many governments adopted formal wage-and-price controls in an attempt to contain the inflations that they assumed were being generated from the cost (supply) side of the economy rather than from the demand side.

These attempts to control inflation proved to be costly failures as high inflation continued to plague many Western economies well into the 1980s. As a result of such failures, most economists soon came to adopt the argument that Nobel laureate Milton Friedman had been making for many years, that inflation was mainly a monetary phenomenon. It was already recognized that shocks unrelated to monetary policy cause shifts in the *AD* and *AS* curves and thus cause temporary changes in the rate of inflation as the economy responds to these shocks. The change in view, however, was that *sustained* inflation was not caused by such shocks—instead, sustained inflation appeared to occur only in those situations in which monetary policy was allowing continual and rapid growth in the money supply. In other words, economists came to recognize that sustained inflation must ultimately be caused by monetary policy.

With the acceptance of this view that sustained inflation is ultimately the result of monetary policy, central banks came to be seen as the main actors in the anti-inflation drama. If high and variable inflation rates were harmful to the economy and if central bank validation was a necessary condition for an inflation to be sustained, the central bank could prevent sustained inflation by adopting an appropriate monetary policy. In response to this belief, central banks around most of the developed world were given as their main responsibility the control of the price level and instructed to do this by adopting policies that targeted the rate of inflation.

> **Most economists and central bankers accept that monetary policy is the most important determinant of a country's long-run rate of inflation.**

The Adoption of Inflation Targeting In 1990, New Zealand became the first country to adopt a formal system of *inflation targeting*. Canada was second, in 1991, followed soon by Israel, the United Kingdom, Australia, Finland, Spain, and Sweden. Since the mid-1990s, the list has grown to include Chile, Brazil, Colombia, Mexico, the Czech Republic, Poland, South Africa, Thailand, and others. The U.S. Federal Reserve has *not* yet adopted a formal inflation target, although its current chairman, Ben Bernanke, has indicated that he would like the Federal Reserve to do so.

When the Bank of Canada first adopted its formal inflation targets in 1991 the annual rate of inflation was almost 6 percent. The targets were expressed as the midpoint of a 2-percentage-point band, in recognition of the fact that it is unrealistic to expect the Bank to keep the inflation rate at a single, precise value in the face of the many shocks that influence it in the short term. Beginning in 1992, the Bank of Canada's target range for inflation was 3 to 5 percent, with the range falling to 2 to 4 percent by 1993 and to 1 to 3 percent by the end of 1995. The Bank's formal inflation targets were renewed every five years between 1991 and 2011, with the current targets in place until 2016. (The Bank now emphasizes its 2 percent inflation target and places much less emphasis on the 1 to 3 percent range.) Figure 29-4 shows quarterly data for Canadian inflation since 1992.

Inflation Targeting and the Output Gap

The control of inflation is the Bank of Canada's stated policy objective. Keeping inflation close to its formal 2 percent target, however, requires the Bank to monitor the output gap and the associated pressures that may be pushing inflation above or below the target.

The Bank recognizes that because monetary policy has the potential to influence real GDP, it simultaneously has the potential to alter the size of the current output gap, from which comes the pressure for inflation to rise or fall. Faced with a persistent recessionary gap ($Y < Y^*$), which eventually tends to reduce inflation below the Bank's 2-percent target, the Bank can pursue an expansionary monetary policy in an attempt to increase real GDP and reduce the recessionary gap. Such a policy would be pursued until the output gap is eliminated and inflationary pressures threaten to move the inflation rate above the 2-percent target. Faced with a persistent inflationary gap ($Y > Y^*$) and the associated tendency for inflation to rise above the 2-percent target, the Bank can pursue a contractionary policy in an attempt to bring real GDP back toward Y^* and the inflation rate closer to 2 percent.

> **Persistent output gaps generally create pressure for the rate of inflation to change. To keep the rate of inflation close to the 2-percent target, the Bank of Canada closely monitors real GDP in the short run and designs its policy to keep real GDP close to potential output.**

FIGURE 29-4 Canadian CPI and Core Inflation, 1992–2012

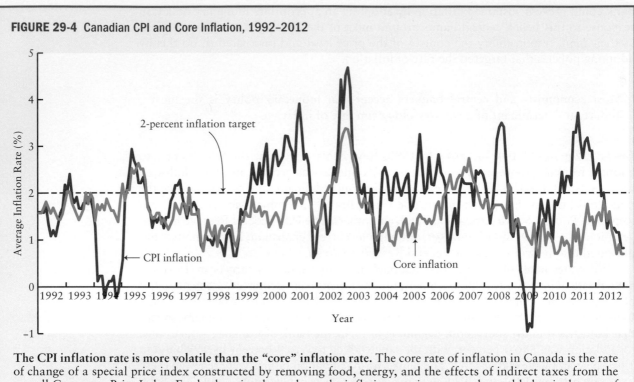

The CPI inflation rate is more volatile than the "core" inflation rate. The core rate of inflation in Canada is the rate of change of a special price index constructed by removing food, energy, and the effects of indirect taxes from the overall Consumer Price Index. For both series shown here, the inflation rate is computed monthly but is the rate of change in the price index from 12 months earlier.

(*Source:* Based on author's calculations using data from Statistics Canada, CANSIM database. CPI: Table 326-0020. Core: Table 176-0003.)

Inflation Targeting as a Stabilizing Policy

If the Bank of Canada is committed to keeping the rate of inflation near 2 percent, positive shocks to the economy that create an inflationary gap and threaten to increase the rate of inflation will be met by a contractionary monetary policy. The Bank will increase interest rates and shift the *AD* curve to the left. This policy will reduce the size of the output gap and push the rate of inflation back toward 2 percent. Similarly, if a negative shock to the economy creates a persistent recessionary gap, the Bank will respond with an expansionary monetary policy, reducing interest rates and shifting the *AD* curve to the right.

The short-run effects of the Bank's actions suggest that its policy of inflation targeting can be seen as an "automatic" stabilizer. But this is an exaggeration, as we can see by recalling our discussion in Chapter 24 of automatic fiscal stabilizers, which are caused by taxes and transfers that vary with the level of national income. Automatic fiscal stabilizers are truly "automatic" in the sense that no group of policymakers has to actively adjust policy—the stabilizers are built right into the tax-and-transfer system. With inflation targeting, however, there must be an active policy decision to keep inflation close to its target rate, and only then will the Bank's policy adjustments work to stabilize the economy in the face of shocks that create inflationary or recessionary output gaps.

Inflation targets are not as "automatic" a stabilizer as the fiscal stabilizers built into the tax-and-transfer system. However, as long as the central bank is committed to achieving its inflation target, its policy adjustments will act to stabilize real GDP.

Complications in Inflation Targeting

So far, our discussion of inflation targeting makes the conduct of monetary policy seem relatively straightforward. But there are several details that complicate the task considerably. In this section we discuss two complications for the conduct of monetary policy, and in the next section we address a more general difficulty.

Volatile Food and Energy Prices Sometimes the rate of inflation increases for reasons unrelated to a change in the output gap. For example, many commodities whose prices are included in the Consumer Price Index (CPI) are internationally traded goods and their prices are determined in world markets. Oil is an obvious example, as are many raw materials and fruits and vegetables. When these prices rise suddenly, perhaps because of political instability in the Middle East (oil) or because of poor crop conditions in tropical countries (fruits and vegetables), the measured rate of inflation of the Canadian CPI also rises. Yet these price increases have little or nothing to do with the size of the output gap in Canada and thus have little implication for what policy should be followed by the Bank of Canada. By focusing exclusively on the rate of inflation of the CPI, the Bank would be misled about the extent of inflationary pressures coming from excess demand in Canada.

For this reason, the Bank of Canada also monitors closely what is called the "core" rate of inflation. This is the rate of growth of a special price index, one that is constructed by extracting food, energy, and the effects of indirect taxes (such as the GST or excise taxes) from the Consumer Price Index. Figure 29-4 shows the paths of core and CPI inflation since 1992. As is clear from the figure, even though the two measures of inflation move broadly together, core inflation is much less volatile than is CPI inflation.

Because the volatility of food and energy prices is often unrelated to the level of the output gap in Canada, the Bank of Canada closely monitors the rate of "core" inflation even though its formal target of 2 percent applies to the rate of CPI inflation. Changes in core inflation are a better indicator of *domestic* inflationary pressures than are changes in CPI inflation.

Note the sharp divergence between the two inflation rates in 1994. At that time, there were substantial decreases in the excise taxes on cigarettes. Since the resulting sharp decline in CPI inflation was caused by a reduction in taxes rather than by domestic excess supply, it would have been inappropriate for the Bank of Canada to respond to this decline in inflation by implementing an expansionary monetary policy. Instead, the Bank focused on the core inflation rate that excludes the effect of changes in indirect taxes. The core inflation rate in 1994 was relatively stable and close to the Bank's 2 percent target, indicating no need for a change in monetary policy.

Note also the volatility of the CPI inflation rate during 2008 and 2009. Energy and commodity prices had been rising for the previous few years, but they increased especially rapidly in the early part of 2008. This helped to push the CPI inflation rate well above 3 percent. But then the worst part of the global financial crisis occurred in the autumn of that year, energy and commodity prices plunged, and the CPI inflation rate fell quickly and was *negative* for a period of a few months in 2009. In contrast, the core rate of inflation was much less volatile during these events and remained much closer to 2 percent.

The Exchange Rate and Monetary Policy Given the large amount of trade that Canadian firms and households do with the rest of the world, it is not surprising that the Bank of Canada pays close attention to movements in the exchange rate, the Canadian-dollar price of one unit of foreign currency. However, because changes in the exchange rate can have several different causes, care must be taken when drawing inferences about the desired change in monetary policy resulting from changes in the exchange rate. As we will see, there is no simple "rule of thumb" for how the Bank should react to a change in the exchange rate.

We consider two illustrative examples. In the first, an appreciation of the Canadian dollar leads the Bank to tighten its monetary policy by raising its target for the overnight interest rate. In the second example, an appreciation of the Canadian dollar leads the Bank to loosen its monetary policy by reducing its target for the overnight interest rate. In both cases, the Bank's actions are consistent with its objective of keeping the inflation rate near the Bank's 2 percent target.

For the first example, suppose that the economies of Canada's trading partners are booming and thus demanding more Canadian exports. Foreigners' heightened demand for Canadian goods creates an increase in demand for the Canadian dollar in foreign-exchange markets. The Canadian dollar therefore appreciates. But the increase in demand for Canadian goods has added directly to Canadian aggregate demand. If this shock persists, it will eventually add to domestic inflationary pressures. In this case, if the Bank notes the appreciation of the dollar (and correctly determines its cause), it can take action to offset the positive demand shock by tightening monetary policy, which it does by raising its target for the overnight interest rate.

The second example involves an increase in demand for Canadian *assets* rather than Canadian goods and has quite different implications from the first example. Suppose that investors, because of events happening elsewhere in the world, decide to liquidate some of their foreign assets and purchase more Canadian assets instead. In this case, the increase in demand for Canadian assets leads to an increase in demand for the Canadian dollar in foreign-exchange markets. This causes an appreciation of the Canadian dollar. As the dollar appreciates, however, Canadian exports become more expensive to foreigners. There will be a reduction in Canadian net exports and thus a reduction in Canadian aggregate demand. If this shock persists, it will eventually create a recessionary gap in Canada. In this case, if the Bank notes the appreciation of the dollar (and correctly determines its cause), it can take action to offset the negative demand shock by loosening monetary policy which it does by reducing its target for the overnight interest rate.

Notice in both examples that the Canadian dollar appreciated as a result of the external shock, but the causes of the appreciation were different. In the first case, there was a positive demand shock to net exports, which then caused the appreciation, which in turn dampened the initial increase in net exports. But the overall effect on the demand for Canadian goods was positive. In the second case, there was a positive shock to the *asset* market, which then caused the appreciation, which in turn reduced the demand for net exports. The overall effect on the demand for Canadian goods was negative. In the first case, the appropriate response for monetary policy was contractionary, whereas in the second case the appropriate response for monetary policy was expansionary.

> Changes in the exchange rate can signal the need for changes in the stance of monetary policy. However, the Bank needs to determine the cause of the exchange-rate change before it can design a policy response appropriate for keeping real GDP close to potential and inflation close to the 2 percent target.

29.3 Long and Variable Lags

In Chapter 28 we encountered a debate that was prominent from the 1950s to the early 1980s. *Monetarists* argued that monetary policy was potentially very powerful in the sense that a given change in the money supply would lead to a substantial change in aggregate demand, whereas *Keynesians* argued that monetary policy was much less powerful.

This debate had some of its roots in differing interpretations of the causes of the Great Depression. One interesting part of the debate is why Canada and the United Kingdom had collapses in economic activity similar in magnitude to that in the United States even though they did not suffer the widespread bank failures that featured in the U.S. experience. *Lessons from History 29-1* provides a brief summary of this interesting debate and applies some of the lessons about monetary policy we have learned in the past two chapters.

The debate between Monetarists and Keynesians was about more than just the *effectiveness* of monetary policy. The debate sometimes also focused on the question of whether active use of monetary policy in an attempt to stabilize output and the price level was likely to be successful or whether it would instead lead to an increase in fluctuations in those variables. This debate is as important today as it was then, and at its centre is the role of *lags*.

What Are the Lags in Monetary Policy?

Experience has shown that lags in the operation of policy can sometimes cause stabilization policy to be destabilizing. In Chapter 24, we discussed how decision and implementation lags might limit the extent to which active use of fiscal policy can be relied upon to stabilize the economy. Although both of these sources of lags are less relevant for monetary policy, the full effects of monetary policy nevertheless occur only after quite long time lags. There are two reasons that a change in monetary policy does not affect the economy instantly.

Changes in Expenditure Take Time When the Bank of Canada changes its target for the overnight interest rate, the actual overnight rate changes almost instantly. Other, longer-term interest rates also change quickly, usually within a day or two. However, it takes more time before households and firms adjust their spending and borrowing plans in response to the change in interest rates. Consumers may respond relatively quickly and alter their plans for purchasing durable goods like cars and appliances. But it takes longer for firms to modify their investment plans and then put them into effect.

LESSONS FROM HISTORY 29-1

Two Views on the Role of Money in the Great Depression

In most people's minds, the Great Depression began with the stock market crash of October 1929. In the United States, Canada, and Europe, the decline in economic activity over the next four years was massive. From 1929 to 1933, real output fell by roughly 25 percent, one-quarter of the labour force was unemployed by 1933, the price level fell by more than 25 percent, and businesses failed on a massive scale. In the more than seven decades that have followed, no recession has come close to the Great Depression in terms of reduced economic activity, business failures, or unemployment.

The Great Depression has naturally attracted the attention of economists and, especially in the United States, these few years of experience have served as a kind of "retrospective laboratory" in which they have tried to test their theories.

The Basic Facts

The stock market crash of 1929, and other factors associated with a moderate downswing in business activity during the late 1920s, caused U.S. firms and households to want to hold more cash and fewer demand deposits. The banking system, however, could not meet this increased demand for liquidity (cash) without help from the Federal Reserve System (the U.S. central bank). As we saw in Chapter 27, because of the fractional-reserve banking system, commercial banks are never able to satisfy from their own reserves a large and sudden demand for cash—their reserves are always only a small fraction of total deposits.

The Federal Reserve had been set up to provide just such emergency assistance to commercial banks that were basically sound but were unable to meet sudden demands

by depositors to withdraw cash. However, the Federal Reserve refused to extend the necessary help, and successive waves of bank failures followed as a direct result. During each wave, hundreds of banks failed, ruining many depositors, reducing the flow of credit, and worsening an already severe depression. In the second half of 1931, almost 2000 U.S. banks were forced to suspend operations. One consequence of these failures was a sharp drop in the money supply; by 1933, M2 was 33 percent lower than it had been in 1929.

Competing Explanations

After the Great Depression was over, economists were able to examine the data and construct explanations for these dramatic events. To Monetarists, the basic facts seem decisive: to them, the fall in the money supply was clearly the major *cause* of the fall in output and employment that occurred during the Great Depression. Monetarists see the Great Depression as perhaps the single best piece of evidence of the strength of monetary forces and the single best lesson of the importance of monetary policy. In their view, the increased cash drain that led to the massive monetary contraction could have been prevented had the Federal Reserve quickly increased the level of cash reserves in the commercial banking system. In this case, the rise in cash reserves would have offset the increase in the cash drain, so that the money supply (currency plus bank deposits) could be maintained.

Keynesians argued that the fundamental cause of the Great Depression was a reduction in autonomous expenditure. They cite a large decline in housing construction (in response to a glut of housing), a decline in automobile

It may take a year or more before the full increase in investment expenditure occurs in response to a fall in interest rates.

In an open economy such as Canada's, the change in the interest rate also leads to flows of financial capital and a change in the exchange rate. These changes occur very quickly. But the effect on net exports takes more time while purchasers of internationally traded goods and services switch to lower-cost suppliers.

The Multiplier Process Takes Time Changes in consumption, investment, and net export expenditures brought about by a change in monetary policy set off the multiplier process that increases national income. This process, too, takes some time to work through. Furthermore, although the end result is fairly predictable, the speed with which the entire expansionary or contractionary process works itself out can vary in ways that are hard to predict. Thus, though the overall effects of monetary policy might be reasonably straightforward to predict, the timing of those effects is difficult to predict.

purchases (as most first-time buying was done and only replacement demand remained), and a reduction in consumption driven largely by pessimism caused by the stock market crash. Although Keynesians accept the argument that the Federal Reserve's behaviour was perverse and exacerbated an already bad situation, they do not attribute a pivotal role to the Federal Reserve or to the money supply. Instead, they see the fall in the money supply as a *result* of the decline in economic activity (through a reduced demand for loans and thus reduced bank lending) rather than as its cause.

Lessons from Canada's Experience

Canada had broadly the same magnitude of economic collapse as did the United States during the Great Depression, but had *no* bank failures. Unfortunately, Canada's experience is not able to resolve the disagreement—both sides of the debate can offer explanations of the Canadian experience consistent with their central arguments.

Keynesians look to Canada's experience to support their view that money was not central to the cause of the economic collapse in the United States. They point out that since Canada did not escape the Great Depression but *did* escape the banking crisis and the associated collapse in the money supply, money was unlikely to have been the central cause of the U.S. economic collapse.

Monetarists accept the point that Canada did not have a massive reduction in the money supply, but they argue that the economic contraction in the United States (which *was* caused by the collapse in the money supply) spilled over into Canada, largely through a dramatic reduction in demand for Canadian goods. This spillover implies a large decline in export expenditure for Canada, and thus a decline in Canadian national income. Thus, Monetarists essentially argue that money in the United States was an important contributor to the economic decline in Canada.

During the Great Depression, bank failures were widespread in the United States but did not occur at all in Canada. This difference in experience can be used to test hypotheses regarding the causes of the Great Depression. But considerable disagreement still remains.

For a discussion of these two views, and some attempts to discriminate between them, see Peter Temin, *Did Monetary Forces Cause the Great Depression?*, Norton, 1976.

Monetary policy is capable of exerting expansionary and contractionary forces on the economy, but it operates with a time lag that is long and difficult to predict.

Economists at the Bank of Canada estimate that it normally takes between 9 and 12 months for a change in monetary policy to have its main effect on real GDP, and a further 9 to 12 months for the policy to have its main effect on the price level (or the rate of inflation).

Destabilizing Policy?

The fact that monetary-policy actions taken today will not affect output and inflation until one to two years in the future means that the Bank of Canada must design its policy for what *is expected* to occur in the future rather than what *has already been observed.* To see why a monetary policy guided only by past and current events may be destabilizing, consider the following simple example. Suppose that on January 1 the Bank observes that real GDP is less than potential output and concludes that an expansionary monetary policy is appropriate. It can reduce its target for the overnight rate at the next fixed announcement date (FAD), typically within a few weeks. By early February, the overnight interest rate will be reduced, as will the longer-term interest rates in the economy. The effects on aggregate demand, however, will not be felt in any significant way until late summer or early fall of that same year.

This policy action may turn out to be destabilizing, however. Some of the cyclical forces in the economy, unrelated to the Bank's actions, may have reversed since January, and by fall there may be an inflationary output gap. However, since the effects of the monetary expansion that was initiated nine months earlier are just beginning to be felt, an expansionary monetary stimulus is adding to the existing inflationary gap.

If the Bank now applies the monetary brakes by raising its target for the overnight interest rate, the output effects of this policy reversal will not be felt for another year or so. By that time, a contraction may have already set in because of the natural cyclical forces of the economy. Thus, the delayed effects of the monetary policy may turn a minor downturn into a major recession.

> The long time lags in the effectiveness of monetary policy increase the difficulty of stabilizing the economy; monetary policy may have a destabilizing effect.

The Bank of Canada recognizes the possibility that if it responds to every shock that influences real GDP, the overall effect of its policy may be to destabilize the economy rather than stabilize it. As a result, it is careful to assess the causes of the shocks that buffet the Canadian economy. It tries to avoid situations in which it responds to shocks that are believed to be short-lived and then must reverse its policy in the near future when the shocks disappear. In general, the Bank responds only to those shocks that are significant in magnitude and are expected to persist for several months or more. For example, the global recession that began in 2008 was both large and long-lasting, and the Bank's expansionary policies had ample time to operate in the appropriate direction even after the expected lags in their effectiveness.

Political Difficulties

Long lags in the workings of monetary policy also lead to some political criticism for the central bank.

Figure 29-5 shows a situation in which the current inflation rate is well below the 2 percent target but the expectation of future events suggests that inflation will soon rise and exceed the target. This situation is often faced by the Bank when the economy is in the early stages of an economic recovery, as occurred in late 2012. At that time, monetary policy had been expansionary for over three years in an effort to stimulate the economy and offset the effects of a global economic recession. But as real GDP began to grow and the existing recessionary gap began to narrow, the Bank needed to judge the appropriate time to begin tightening its policy in an attempt to keep inflation from rising above the 2 percent target.

What is the political problem? Remember that because of the time lags involved, any policy change that occurs today has no effect on real GDP for roughly 9 months and the full effect on the price level (or the rate of inflation) does not occur for 18 to 24 months. If the economy is at point *A* in Figure 29-5, and inflation is expected to rise in the near future, then monetary policy must be changed *now* in order to counteract this future inflation. But this action could generate some criticism because the *current* inflation rate is low. In such situations, the Bank finds itself in the awkward position of advocating a tightening of monetary policy, in order to fight the expectation of future inflation, at a time when the *current* inflation rate suggests no need for tightening. But if the goal is to keep inflation close to the 2 percent target, such *pre-emptive* monetary policy is necessary because of the unavoidable time lags.

> Time lags in monetary policy require that decisions regarding a loosening or tightening of monetary policy be forward-looking. This often leads to criticism of monetary policy, especially by those who do not recognize the long time lags.

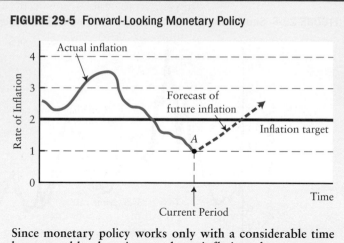

FIGURE 29-5 Forward-Looking Monetary Policy

Since monetary policy works only with a considerable time lag, central-bank actions to keep inflation close to target must be taken in advance of expected future events. Suppose the economy is currently at point *A* with inflation well below the target. If events in the near future are expected to cause inflation to rise and exceed the target, then monetary policy must be tightened, even though *current* inflation is low.

29.4 Thirty Years of Canadian Monetary Policy

This section describes a few key episodes in recent Canadian monetary history. This is not done to teach history for its own sake, but because the lessons of past experience and past policy mistakes, interpreted through the filter of economic theory, provide our best hope for improving our policy performance in the future.

The OPEC oil-price shocks of 1973 and 1979–1980 led to reductions in GDP growth rates and increases in inflation in Canada—what came to be known as *stagflation*. At that time, the role of aggregate-supply shocks and their effect on macroeconomic equilibrium was not as well understood as it is today. The Bank of Canada's policy response involved considerable monetary expansion, and by 1980 the rate of inflation in Canada was more than 12 percent.

The Bank of Canada (and the U.S. Federal Reserve) then embarked on policies designed to reduce the growth rate of the money supply and eventually reduce the inflation rate. Unfortunately, at the same time innovations in the financial sector led to unexpected increases in the demand for money. The result was a much sharper increase in interest rates (see Figure 29-6) than was intended by the Bank of Canada and the most serious recession since the 1930s. But the rate of inflation *did* fall, from more than 12 percent in 1980 to about 4 percent in 1984. This experience taught the Bank two important lessons:

1. Monetary policy can be *very* effective in reducing inflation.

2. Because of unexpected changes in money demand, monetary policy should focus more on interest rates than on the money supply.

As we saw earlier in this chapter, this second lesson is an important reason why the Bank now implements its policy by targeting the interest rate rather than by directly targeting the money supply.

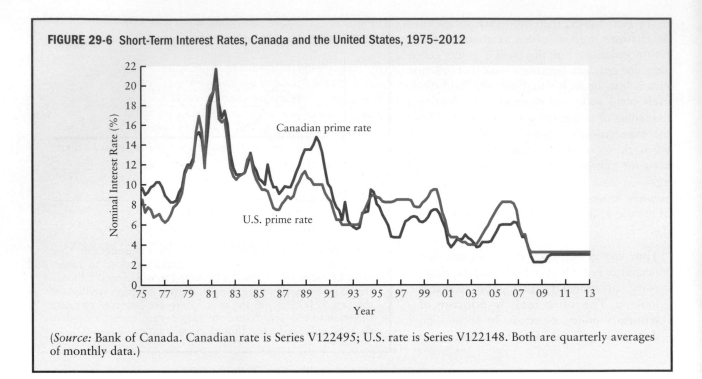

FIGURE 29-6 Short-Term Interest Rates, Canada and the United States, 1975–2012

(*Source:* Bank of Canada. Canadian rate is Series V122495; U.S. rate is Series V122148. Both are quarterly averages of monthly data.)

Economic Recovery: 1983–1987

In early 1983, a sustained recovery began, and by mid-1987, real GDP had moved back toward potential. Much of the growth was centred in the export-oriented manufacturing industries in Ontario and Quebec. The first four years of the recovery saw cumulative real GDP growth of 15.7 percent.

> The main challenge for monetary policy in this period was to create sufficient liquidity to accommodate the recovery without triggering a return to the high inflation rates that prevailed at the start of the decade.

In other words, the Bank of Canada had to increase the money supply to *accommodate* the recovery-induced increase in money demand *without* increasing the money supply so much that it refuelled inflationary pressures.

In spite of much debate and uncertainty, the Bank handled this "re-entry" problem quite well. The Bank allowed a short but rapid burst of growth in the nominal money supply, thus generating the desired increase in real money balances. Once the new level of real balances was achieved, money growth was cut back to a rate consistent with low inflation (and for the underlying rate of growth in real income). The trick with this policy was that to avoid triggering expectations of renewed inflation, the Bank had to generate a one-shot increase in the *level* of the money supply without creating the impression that it was raising the long-term *rate of growth* of the money supply.

In late 1983 and early 1984, when growth in the money supply first started to surge, many voiced the fear that the Bank was being overly expansionary and was risking a return to higher inflation. As the re-entry problem came to be more widely understood and as inflationary pressures failed to re-emerge, these criticisms subsided, and the consensus appeared to be that the Bank had done a commendable job of handling the re-entry problem.

Rising Inflation: 1987–1990

By mid-1987, many observers began to worry that Canadian policymakers were too complacent in accepting the 4 percent range into which Canadian inflation had settled. Further, there was concern that inflationary pressures were starting to build—the money supply was growing quickly, real output growth was strong, unemployment was falling, and an inflationary gap was opening.

> In 1987, many economists argued that if monetary policy was not tightened, Canada would experience gradually increasing inflation until once again a severe monetary restriction would be required to reduce the rate of inflation.

Inflation slowly crept upward. A monetary restriction designed to reduce inflation would obviously impose costs in the form of lower output and higher unemployment. Was the Bank prepared to inflict such costs, especially given that Canada had emerged from a deep recession only five years earlier?

In January 1988, Bank of Canada Governor John Crow announced that monetary policy would henceforth be guided less by short-term stabilization issues and more by the goal of long-term "price stability." Specifically, he said that "monetary policy should be conducted so as to achieve a pace of monetary expansion that promotes stability in the value of money. This means pursuing a policy aimed at achieving and maintaining stable prices."[2]

Disinflation: 1990–1992

This explicit adoption of price stability as the Bank's only target set off a heated debate about the appropriate stance for monetary policy. The debate was fuelled by Crow's decision to give a high profile to his policy by repeatedly articulating and defending it in speeches and public appearances. He believed that this was necessary because expectations of continuing inflation had become entrenched. In his view, until the public believed that the Bank was serious about controlling inflation, whatever the short-term consequences, inflation could not be reduced. Some critics said that price stability was unobtainable. Others said the costs of reaching it would be too large in terms of several years of recessionary gaps. Supporters said that the long-term gains from having a stable price level would exceed the costs of getting there.

John Crow was the governor of the Bank of Canada from 1987 to 1994. In 1988 he announced that "price stability" would thenceforth be the Bank of Canada's objective.

> Despite the Bank's explicit policy of "price stability," the actual inflation rate increased slightly in the years immediately following John Crow's policy announcement, from about 4 percent in 1987 to just over 5 percent in 1990.

---

[2] John W. Crow, "The Work of Canadian Monetary Policy," speech given at the University of Alberta, January 18, 1988; reprinted in *Bank of Canada Review*, February 1988.

The controversy reached new heights when in 1990 the country (and much of the world) entered a sustained recession. Maintaining a tight monetary policy with high interest rates (see Figure 29-6) seemed perverse to many when the economy was already suffering from too little aggregate demand to sustain potential output.

Furthermore, the high Canadian interest rates attracted foreign financial capital. Foreigners who wanted to buy Canadian bonds needed Canadian dollars, and their demands led to an appreciation of the Canadian dollar. This increased the price of Canadian exports while reducing the price of Canadian imports, putting Canadian export and import-competing industries at a competitive disadvantage and further increasing the unemployment that had been generated by the worldwide recession.

Inflation Targeting I: 1991–2000

In spite of heavy political pressure to lower interest rates, and of criticism from some economists who might have supported a move toward price stability in less depressed times, the Bank stood by its tight monetary policy. Indeed, in 1991, it formally announced *inflation-control targets* for the next several years. Beginning in 1992, inflation was to lie within the 3 to 5 percent range, with the range falling to 2 to 4 percent by 1993 and to 1 to 3 percent by the end of 1995.

As a result of the tight monetary policy, the inflation rate fell sharply, from about 5 percent in 1990 to less than 2 percent in 1992. For 1993 and 1994, inflation hovered around 2 percent. Furthermore, short-term nominal interest rates fell from a high of about 13 percent in 1990 to about 6 percent by the end of 1993. Recall that the nominal interest rate is equal to the real interest rate plus the rate of inflation. So this decline in nominal interest rates was the eventual result of the tight monetary policy that reduced inflation.

The Bank had succeeded in coming close to its target of price stability. Controversy continued, however, on two issues. First, was the result worth the price of a deeper, possibly more prolonged recession than might have occurred if the Bank had been willing to accept 3 to 4 percent inflation? Second, would the low inflation rate be sustainable once the recovery took the economy back toward potential output? If the inflation rate were to rise to 4 percent during the post-1993 recovery, then the verdict might well be that the cost of temporarily reducing the rate to below 2 percent was not worth the transitory gains.

Gordon Thiessen became the governor of the Bank of Canada in 1994 after inflation had hovered around 2 percent for about two years.

The debate over the Bank's emphasis on maintaining low inflation became centred on Governor John Crow, especially during the federal election campaign of 1993. Some called for the non-renewal of Crow's term as governor (which was scheduled to end in 1994) and his replacement with someone perceived to care more about the costs of fighting inflation. Others argued that the Bank's policy of "price stability" under Crow's stewardship was the right policy for the times and that the long-run benefits of maintaining low inflation would be worth the costs required to achieve it.

In 1994, the minister of finance appointed Gordon Thiessen, the former senior deputy governor of the Bank, to be the new governor. With some irony, the minister of finance, whose party had been severe critics of Crow's policy while they were in opposition, affirmed the previous monetary policy of the Bank and urged the new governor to maintain the hard-won low inflation rate. The new governor agreed and extended the formal inflation target of 2 percent until 2001.

For the next three years, the rate of inflation continued to hover between 1 and 2 percent. The main challenge for the Bank in the next few years was to keep inflation low while at the same time encouraging the economy to progress through what was viewed as a fragile recovery. Excessive stimulation of the economy would lead to the rise of inflation, which would sacrifice the hard-won gains achieved only a few years earlier. On the other hand, insufficient stimulation would itself be an obstacle to economic recovery.

Beginning in the summer of 1997, the economies of Thailand, Malaysia, Indonesia, and South Korea fell into serious recessions, thus beginning what is now known as the Asian Economic Crisis.[3] Since these countries are major importers of raw materials, their recessions led to a large decline in the world's demand for raw materials. As a result, the world price of raw materials fell by an average of about 30 percent in the subsequent year. Since Canada is a major producer and exporter of raw materials, this decline in the demand for raw materials was a negative aggregate demand shock for Canada. Working in the opposite direction, however, was the expansionary supply-side effect of lower raw materials prices for the many Canadian manufacturing firms that use raw materials as inputs. This positive supply shock was especially important for the United States, a major importer and user of raw materials. The impact of the Asian Crisis on the U.S. economy produced a third effect on Canada as the quickly growing U.S. economy increased its demand for Canadian goods and services.

In the spring of 1997, before the Asian Crisis had begun, the Canadian economy was growing and steadily reducing its recessionary gap. The combination of forces created by the Asian Economic Crisis presented problems for the Bank of Canada and for the appropriate direction for monetary policy. Especially difficult was judging the relative strengths of the three separate effects. As it turned out, Canada's recessionary gap continued to shrink as the economy grew steadily. By 1999, the Asian economies were on their way to a healthy recovery.

Changes in stock-market values also created some challenges for the Bank of Canada in the 1990s. From 1994 through 1999, U.S. and Canadian stocks enjoyed unprecedented bull markets. The Dow Jones Industrial Average (an index of U.S. stock prices) increased from about 3500 in mid-1994 to about 11 000 in late 1999, an average annual increase of 26 percent. The Toronto Stock Exchange Index (now called the S&P/TSX), increased from roughly 4000 to 8000 over the same period, an average annual increase of 14 percent.

The concern for the Bank of Canada during this time was that the increase in wealth generated by these stock-market gains would stimulate consumption expenditures in what was already a steadily growing economy, thus increasing inflationary pressures. In December 1996, the chairman of the U.S. Federal Reserve, Alan Greenspan, warned market participants about their "irrational exuberance," a phrase that is now often quoted. Bank of Canada Governor Gordon Thiessen made similar remarks in Canada. Both central bankers were trying to dampen expectations in the stock market so that the stock-market gains, and thus the increases in wealth-induced spending, would not significantly contribute to inflationary pressures. But they had to be careful not to have their comments create a "crash" in the market that would have even more dramatic effects in the opposite direction.

As it turned out, the crash happened anyway. In both the United States and Canada, the stock markets had reached such levels that many commentators said it was only a matter of time before participants realized that stock prices no longer reflected the

---

[3] An important part of the cause of these recessions was the sudden collapse of their currencies, which were previously pegged in value to the U.S. dollar. We examine fixed and flexible exchange rates in detail in Chapter 35.

David Dodge was the governor of the Bank of Canada from 2001 to early 2008. He needed to steer monetary policy during a time of a strong appreciation of the Canadian dollar, driven partly by rising world commodity prices.

underlying values of the companies, at which point there would be massive selling and an inevitable crash. From the fall of 2000 to the spring of 2001, the major Canadian stock-market indexes fell by roughly 40 percent, driven to a large extent by huge reductions in the stock prices of high-tech firms. This stock-market decline is often referred to as the "dot-com" crash.

Inflation Targeting II: 2001–2007

David Dodge became the new governor of the Bank of Canada in the spring of 2001. During his tenure as governor, the Bank faced several significant policy challenges.

When the terrorist attacks in New York and Washington occurred on September 11, 2001, the stock markets took another dramatic plunge. By late in 2003, stock markets were still far below their pre-crash levels. The main challenge for monetary policy was to provide enough liquidity to the banking systems to prevent the economy from entering a recession. In both Canada and the United States, the central banks dramatically lowered their key interest rates over a period of several months.

From 2002 to 2005, the Bank of Canada's target for the overnight interest rate was 3 percentage points below its level from the summer of 2000. During this period, two external forces on the Canadian economy became apparent and presented a further challenge for the Bank of Canada. First, strong world economic growth, especially in China and India, contributed to a substantial increase in the world prices of oil and other raw materials. Given Canada's position as a major producer and exporter of these products, these price increases represented a significant positive external shock to aggregate demand. They also contributed to a substantial appreciation of the Canadian dollar, by more than 40 percent from 2002 to 2005. Taken by itself, this positive shock to Canadian aggregate demand created a justification for the Bank of Canada to tighten its monetary policy.

Working in the opposite direction was a second external shock, also contributing to an appreciation of the Canadian dollar. During the 2002–2005 period, partly in response to a large and growing U.S. current account deficit, the U.S. dollar was depreciating against the pound sterling and the euro. This "realignment" of the U.S. dollar also involved Canada and explained some part of the Canadian dollar's appreciation during that period. These exchange-rate changes, which were not themselves being caused by changes in the demand for Canadian goods and services, nonetheless tended to reduce Canadian net exports and aggregate demand, thus providing some justification for a loosening of Canadian monetary policy.

The problem for the Bank of Canada during this period was to determine the *relative* strength of these opposing forces and thus the appropriate *overall* direction for monetary policy. During the early part of this period, when Canadian real GDP was below potential, the Bank resisted tightening its policy, choosing instead to allow the commodity-price-driven expansion to close the existing output gap. By the summer of 2005, however, when the output gap appeared to be all but closed, the Bank began a series of increases in the target for the overnight interest rate, and by the summer of 2006 it had increased its target by two percentage points.

Throughout 2006 and 2007, world commodity prices continued their steep ascent and the effect on the Canadian economy was dramatic. Employment grew rapidly, real

GDP grew above the level of potential output, and serious concerns about inflation began to mount. During this period, the Bank of Canada continued to gradually raise its policy interest rate.

A related challenge for the Bank during this period involved regional and sectoral differences in economic performance within Canada. The strong growth in the prices of oil and raw materials naturally led to boom conditions in these sectors, which tend to be located in both Western and Atlantic Canada. However, these price increases harmed the profitability of many central Canadian manufacturing firms who used these products as important inputs. In addition, the appreciation of the Canadian dollar further challenged these firms, as foreign buyers reduced their demand for more expensive Canadian-made products.

Regional and sectoral differences highlight an inherent difficulty with monetary policy in a country as economically diverse as Canada. Because there must be a single monetary policy for the nation as a whole (as long as all parts of Canada continue to use the same currency), policy must be guided by the *average* level of economic activity in order to keep the *average* rate of inflation close to its target. But significant differences in economic activity across regions and/or sectors mean that many people will feel that monetary policy is being conducted inappropriately because economic activity in their specific region or sector is not the same as the national average.

Financial Crisis, Recession, and Recovery: 2007–Present

The next significant phase of Canadian monetary policy was determined largely by events taking place in other countries. From 2002 to 2006, U.S. housing prices had been rising unusually rapidly, but they began to slow their ascent in the middle of 2006. In 2007, these prices reached their peak and then collapsed, falling by more than 30 percent in many parts of the country. On a large scale, U.S. homeowners began "walking away" from their houses, whose market values had fallen below the total amount owing on the associated mortgages. In these situations, the financial institution holding the mortgage no longer receives regular mortgage payments from the homeowner and instead takes ownership of the vacated house.

For the many financial institutions that held the mortgages—or the securities backed by the mortgages—the housing collapse led to a significant decline in the value of their assets. It soon became clear that millions of U.S. mortgages and mortgage-backed securities had been bought by financial institutions all over the world, and thus many large financial institutions in many countries were soon on the edge of insolvency and bankruptcy. What began as a collapse of U.S. housing prices soon became a global financial crisis.

Mark Carney became the new governor of the Bank of Canada in February 2008, just as the financial crisis was entering its most serious phase. With the collapse of major U.S. and U.K. financial institutions only a few months later, panic spread throughout the world's financial sector. It was unclear which institutions held large amounts of these "toxic" mortgage-backed securities and thus which institutions were in danger of going under. In this setting, the widespread fear in financial markets led to a virtual disappearance of short-term interbank

Mark Carney became the Bank of Canada's governor in early 2008, amid a global financial crisis and the beginning of a significant economic recession.

lending. The flow of credit declined, and most lending that did take place was transacted at much higher interest rates. Given the importance of credit in a market economy, restoring the flow of credit was essential to maintaining the level of economic activity.

In Canada, it soon became clear that Canadian banks were far less exposed to these "toxic" mortgage-backed securities than were the banks in the United States and much of Europe. As a result, there was no significant danger of a Canadian bank becoming insolvent during this episode. However, the globalized nature of financial markets implies that short-term credit markets in Canada are highly integrated with those in other countries, with the result that Canada also experienced a decline in interbank lending and a rise in short-term interest rates. The Bank of Canada took two sets of actions during 2007–2008. First, it reduced its target for the overnight rate by more than 3.5 percentage points between the fall of 2007 and the end of 2008. Second, it eased the terms with which it was prepared to make short-term loans to financial institutions. Both sets of actions were designed to restore the flow of credit and reduce interest rates, thus helping to maintain the level of economic activity.

By late in 2008, however, it was clear that Canada would not be shielded from the global recession that was then beginning. The global financial crisis had a dramatic effect on the level of economic activity in the United States, the European Union, and many countries in Asia. With these economies experiencing recessions, there was a sharp decline in demand for Canada's exports. Canadian real GDP slowed sharply in late 2008 and began to fall in early 2009. The Bank of Canada's objective at this time was to provide as much monetary stimulus as was possible, complementing the large fiscal stimulus implemented by the Canadian government in its budget of 2009.

The Canadian economy experienced a significant recession through most of 2009, but returned to positive growth in real GDP in 2010. Despite the fact that the Bank was still holding its target for the overnight rate at historically very low levels, a significant recessionary gap persisted. Two external forces played an important role in dampening the growth of real GDP. First, the U.S. economy, though technically out of recession, was experiencing only a slow and gradual recovery; the low U.S. growth implied low demand for that economy's traditional imports of Canadian goods and services. Second, the global financial crisis of 2008 had eventually led to a "sovereign debt crisis" in Europe, in which government (sovereign) debt had increased dramatically in response to the recession and the provision of financial support to failing banks. By 2011 and 2012, it was unclear whether the high debts, and the unwillingness of bondholders to renew their lending, would force governments to abandon their fiscal policies or even force some governments to exit the European common currency (the euro). The considerable uncertainty in the world's financial markets worked to delay investment activities and dampen already fragile recoveries in many countries.

By early 2013, the Bank of Canada was trying to choose a policy path that balanced the emerging economic strengths and inflationary forces within Canada with the weakness and uncertainty that was originating mostly outside of Canada's borders.

SUMMARY

29.1 How the Bank of Canada Implements Monetary Policy

- Monetary policy can be conducted either by setting the money supply or by setting the interest rate. But for a given negatively sloped M_D curve, both cannot be set independently.
- Because of its incomplete control over the money supply, as well as the uncertainty regarding both the slope and the position of the M_D curve, the Bank chooses to implement its policy by setting the interest rate.
- The Bank establishes a target for the overnight interest rate. By offering to lend funds at a rate 25 basis points above this target (the bank rate) and to accept deposits

- on which it pays interest at 25 basis points below the target, the Bank of Canada can control the actual overnight interest rate.
- Changes in the Bank's target for the overnight rate lead to changes in the actual overnight rate and also to changes in longer-term interest rates. The various steps in the monetary transmission mechanism then come into play.
- The Bank of Canada conducts an expansionary monetary policy by reducing its target for the overnight interest rate. It conducts a contractionary monetary policy by raising its target for the overnight interest rate.

29.2 Inflation Targeting

- It has long been understood that high inflation is damaging to economies and costly for individuals and firms.
- Experience with attempts to control inflation has led to the understanding that sustained inflation is ultimately determined by monetary policy.
- For these two reasons, many central banks now focus their attention on maintaining a low and stable rate of inflation.
- The Bank of Canada's formal inflation target is the rate of CPI inflation. It seeks to keep the annual inflation rate close to 2 percent.

- In the short run, the Bank closely monitors the output gap. By tightening its policy during an inflationary gap (and loosening it during a recessionary gap), the Bank can keep the rate of inflation near 2 percent.
- The policy of inflation targeting helps to stabilize the economy. The Bank responds to positive shocks with a contractionary policy and responds to negative shocks with an expansionary policy.
- Two technical issues complicate the conduct of monetary policy:
  1. Volatile food and energy prices
  2. Changes in the exchange rate

29.3 Long and Variable Lags

- Though the Bank of Canada can change interest rates very quickly, it takes time for firms and households to change their expenditure. Even once those new plans are carried out, it takes time for the multiplier process to work its way through the economy, eventually increasing equilibrium national income.

- Long and variable lags in monetary policy lead many economists to argue that the Bank should not try to "fine-tune" the economy by responding to economic shocks. Instead, it should respond only to shocks that are significant in size and persistent in duration.

29.4 Thirty Years of Canadian Monetary Policy

- In the early 1980s, the Bank of Canada embarked on a policy of tight money to reduce inflation. This policy contributed to the severity of the recession.
- A sustained economic recovery occurred from 1983 to 1987. The main challenge for monetary policy during this time was to create sufficient liquidity to accommodate the recovery without triggering a return to the high inflation rates that prevailed at the start of the decade.
- In 1988, when inflation was between 4 and 5 percent, the Bank of Canada announced that monetary policy

- would henceforth be guided by the long-term goal of "price stability." By 1992, the Bank's tight money policy had reduced inflation to below 2 percent.
- Controversy concerned two issues. First, was the cost in terms of lost output and heavy unemployment worth the benefits of lower inflation? Second, could the low inflation rate be sustained?
- This controversy was partly responsible for the 1994 change in the Bank of Canada's governor, from John Crow to Gordon Thiessen. Despite this administrative

change, the stated policy of price stability continued. By 2000, the rate of inflation had been around 2 percent for about seven years.

- Following the stock-market declines in 2000–2001 and the terrorist attacks in the United States in September 2001, the Bank of Canada and the U.S. Federal Reserve dramatically reduced their policy interest rates in an attempt to prevent a recession.
- In the 2002–2005 period, the main challenges for the Bank involved determining the relative strength of the two different forces leading to a substantial appreciation of the Canadian dollar. By summer of 2006, the

Bank had increased its target for the overnight interest rate by two percentage points, to a level still below its previous peak in the summer of 2000.

- The onset of the global financial crisis in 2008 led the Bank of Canada to implement policies designed to restore the flow of credit and also to reduce interest rates.
- By 2012, three years into a modest recovery, the Bank of Canada still had a historically low target for the overnight interest rate. The weakness of the U.S. and European economies at that time were offsetting the stronger economic performance within Canada.

KEY CONCEPTS

Money supply vs. the interest rate
Overnight interest rate
The target overnight interest rate
The bank rate

Endogenous money supply
Open-market operations
Inflation targeting
CPI inflation vs. core inflation

The exchange rate and monetary policy
Lags in the effect of monetary policy

STUDY EXERCISES

MyEconLab Make the grade with MyEconLab: Study Exercises marked in red can be found on MyEconLab. You can practise them as often as you want, and most feature step-by-step guided instructions to help you find the right answer.

1. Fill in the blanks to make the following statements correct.

   a. In general, there are two approaches to implementing monetary policy. The central bank can attempt to influence _____ directly or to influence _____ directly.

   b. The Bank of Canada chooses to implement its monetary policy by influencing the _____ directly. The Bank then uses _____ to accommodate the resulting change in money demand.

   c. The Bank of Canada does not try to influence the money supply directly because (1) the Bank cannot control the process of _____ carried out by the commercial banks; (2) the Bank is unsure about the change in _____ that would result from a change in the money supply; and (3) the Bank is unsure of the position of the _____ curve at any given time.

2. Fill in the blanks to make the following statements correct.

   a. The interest rate that commercial banks charge each other for overnight loans is called the _____.

   b. The bank rate is _____ points above the target overnight interest rate. At this interest rate, the Bank stands ready to _____ to commercial banks. At a rate _____ points below the target, the Bank stands ready to _____ from commercial banks (and pay that rate as interest).

   c. The Bank of Canada can change the amount of currency in circulation through _____. The Bank conducts these transactions to accommodate the changing demand for _____ by the commercial banks.

   d. An expansionary monetary policy is one where the Bank of Canada _____ its target for the overnight interest rate. A contractionary monetary policy is one in which the Bank _____ its target for the overnight interest rate.

   e. If the Bank of Canada wants to stimulate aggregate demand it can implement a(n) _____ monetary policy by _____ its target for the overnight interest rate. If the Bank wants to dampen aggregate demand it can implement a(n) _____ monetary policy by _____ its target for the overnight interest rate.

3. Fill in the blanks to make the following statements correct.

   a. The long-run policy target for the Bank of Canada is the _____. The current target is to keep the inflation rate at _____ percent.

   b. In the short run, the Bank of Canada closely monitors the _____.

   c. The Bank of Canada conducts its monetary policy by announcing a change in the _____. It then conducts the necessary _____ in order to make this rate an equilibrium in the money market.

   d. The conduct of monetary policy is made more difficult because of lags. Two reasons for these time lags are

   - _____

   - _____

   e. Economists have estimated that a change in monetary policy has an effect on real GDP after a period of _____ months and an effect on the price level after a period of _____ months.

   f. Because of the long time lags involved in the execution of monetary policy, it is very possible that the policy may in fact have a(n) _____ effect on the economy.

4. Read *Applying Economic Concepts 29-1* (page 726), which discusses the Bank of Canada's open-market operations and how these influence the amount of currency in circulation in the Canadian economy. Using simplified balance sheets like the ones shown below, suppose that a commercial bank uses $100 000 of excess cash reserves to purchase a government bond from the Bank of Canada.

   a. What are the immediate effects on assets and liabilities for the commercial bank? Fill in the left-hand table.

   b. What are the changes for the Bank of Canada? Fill in the right-hand table.

   c. Explain what has happened to the amount of currency in circulation.

Commercial Bank		Bank of Canada	
Assets	Liabilities	Assets	Liabilities
Reserves	Deposits	Bonds	Commercial bank deposits
Bonds			Currency

5. In the text we stated that the Bank of Canada's long-run policy target is the rate of inflation.

   a. What experiences have led many central banks to choose this long-run policy target?

   b. The Bank of Canada closely monitors the level of real GDP and the output gap in the short run. How does it use this information in pursuit of its long-run policy of targeting the rate of inflation at 2 percent?

6. The diagram below shows the demand for money and the supply of money.

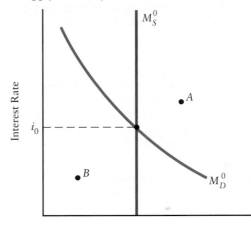

Quantity of Money

   a. Given the position of the M_D curve, explain why it is not possible for the Bank of Canada to set the money supply and the interest rate at point A or at point B.

   b. In the diagram, draw a new money demand curve, M_D^1, to the right of M_D^0. Suppose the M_D curve is shifting in unpredictable ways between M_D^0 and M_D^1. Why is a monetary policy that sets the interest rate more stable (and therefore preferable) to one that sets the money supply?

   c. The Bank of Canada implements its monetary policy by setting the target for the overnight interest rate. If the Bank reduces its target, explain what happens to the amount of money in the economy. What is the role of open-market operations in the Bank's policy?

7. Milton Friedman was for many years a professor of economics at the University of Chicago and was the most influential Monetarist of his generation. He was known for accusing the Federal Reserve (the U.S. central bank) of following "an unstable monetary policy," arguing that although the Federal Reserve "has given lip service to controlling the quantity of money ... it has given its heart to controlling interest rates."

   a. Explain why if the M_D function were approximately stable, targeting the growth rate in the money supply would produce a "stable" monetary policy. Show this in a diagram.

   b. Explain why if the M_D function moves suddenly and in unpredictable ways, targeting the money supply produces an "unstable" monetary policy. Show this in a diagram.

c. The Bank of Canada conducts its policy by setting short-term interest rates. What is the implication for this policy of an "unstable" M_D function?

8. Suppose it is mid-2007 and the stock market has been growing rapidly for the past five years. Some economists argue that the stock market has become "overvalued" and thus a "crash" is imminent.

a. How does a rising stock market affect aggregate demand? Show this in an *AD/AS* diagram.

b. For a central bank that is trying to keep real GDP close to potential, explain what challenges are posed by a rapidly rising stock market.

c. Suppose the stock market "crashes," falling suddenly by approximately 35 percent as it did in the fall of 2008. How does this affect aggregate demand? Show this in an *AD/AS* diagram.

9. Consider the relationship among exchange-rate changes, aggregate demand, and monetary policy. Assume we begin in a situation with real GDP equal to Y^*.

a. Suppose the world price for raw materials rises because of growing demand for these products. Given that Canada is a net exporter of raw materials, what is the likely effect on Canadian aggregate demand? Show this in an *AD/AS* diagram (assuming no change in the exchange rate).

b. Suppose instead that there is an increase in the demand by foreigners for Canadian financial assets such as government bonds. What is the direct effect on Canadian aggregate demand? Show this in an *AD/AS* diagram (assuming again no change in the exchange rate).

c. Both of the shocks described above are likely to cause an appreciation of the Canadian dollar on foreign-exchange markets. As the Canadian dollar appreciates, what are the effects on aggregate demand in part (a) and in part (b)? Show these "secondary" effects in your diagram and explain.

d. Given your answers to parts (a), (b), and (c), explain why the appropriate monetary policy response to a change in the exchange rate depends crucially on the *cause* of the exchange-rate change. What are the appropriate responses to each of the shocks (assuming they occur separately)?

10. In the last few years, the path of CPI inflation has deviated from the path of core inflation several times (see Figure 29-4 on page 730).

a. Why is core inflation less volatile than CPI inflation?

b. Why might the Bank focus more on core inflation during some periods?

11. During the financial crisis of 2007–2008, the Bank of Canada took extraordinary actions to inject liquidity into the banking system. As a result, the amount of reserves in the banking system increased significantly.

a. Why might the Bank choose to increase reserves in the banking system in such an economic environment?

b. Despite the large increase in reserves, there was not a large increase in the Canadian money supply. Can you provide an explanation?

c. Given your answer to part (b), would you predict that the Bank's actions would lead to more inflation? Explain why or why not.

Inflation and Disinflation

LEARNING OBJECTIVES (LO)

After studying this chapter you will be able to

1 understand why wages tend to change in response to both output gaps and inflation expectations.
2 describe how a constant rate of inflation can be incorporated into the basic macroeconomic model.

3 explain how *AD* and *AS* shocks affect inflation and real GDP.
4 explain what happens when the Bank of Canada validates demand and supply shocks.

5 understand the three phases of a disinflation.
6 explain how the cost of disinflation can be measured by the sacrifice ratio.

IF you are a typical reader of this book, you were born in the mid-1990s. By the time you were old enough to notice some economic developments going on around you, it was the mid-2000s. By that time, the rate of inflation in Canada was about 2 percent per year and had been at that level for over a decade. Thus, unless you are older than the typical student taking a course in introductory economics, or you have come to Canada recently from a high-inflation country, inflation has not been a significant phenomenon in your life. It was not so long ago, however, that inflation was considered to be a serious problem in Canada (and many other countries as well). Even though high inflation in Canada is no longer a "headline" issue, understanding the process of inflation, and how it can be reduced, is central to understanding why the Bank of Canada is so committed to keeping inflation low.

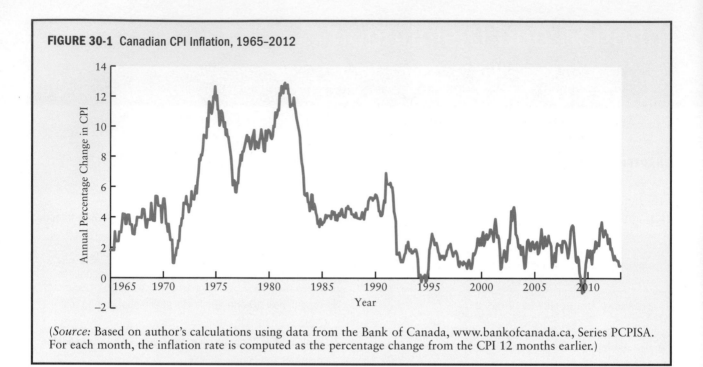

FIGURE 30-1 Canadian CPI Inflation, 1965–2012

(*Source:* Based on author's calculations using data from the Bank of Canada, www.bankofcanada.ca, Series PCPISA. For each month, the inflation rate is computed as the percentage change from the CPI 12 months earlier.)

inflation A rise in the average level of all prices. Usually expressed as the annual percentage change in the Consumer Price Index.

Recall that **inflation** is a rise in the average level of prices—that is, a rise in the price level. Figure 30-1 shows the rate of CPI inflation in Canada since 1965 and shows what is sometimes called the "twin peaks" of inflation. Rising from the mid-1960s, inflation peaked in 1974 at more than 12 percent, fell and then peaked again in 1981 at almost 13 percent, and then started its long but bumpy decline to its current level at around 2 percent, the Bank of Canada's current target rate of inflation.

This bumpy path for the rate of inflation nicely illustrates one of the reasons that inflation is a problem for the economy. As we mentioned in Chapter 19, economists make the distinction between *anticipated* and *unanticipated* inflation, and we showed why unanticipated inflation is the more serious problem. If firms and workers have difficulty predicting what inflation will be, they have problems determining how wages and prices should be set. The result will be unexpected changes in real wages and relative prices as inflation ends up being different from what was expected. These inflation-induced changes in real wages and relative prices cause redistributions of income and may lead to inefficient changes in the economy. As you can imagine by looking at Figure 30-1, many of the changes in inflation between 1965 and 2012 were sudden and thus difficult to predict. To avoid this uncertainty in the economy, the Bank of Canada now strives to keep inflation both *low* and *stable*, near the official target of 2 percent. The result is an environment in which firms, workers, and households can more easily make plans for the future, secure in the knowledge that real wages, real interest rates, and relative prices will not be significantly affected by a volatile inflation rate.

To compute the total inflation since the day of your birth to today, check out the "Inflation Calculator" at the Bank of Canada's website: www. bankofcanada.ca. Click on "Monetary Policy" and then "Inflation."

What causes inflation? How can it be eliminated? And why have policies designed to reduce inflation been so controversial? These are the central topics of this chapter.

30.1 Adding Inflation to the Model

In the previous several chapters we examined the effects of shocks to aggregate demand and aggregate supply. In our macroeconomic model, *AD* and *AS* shocks influenced the values of both real GDP and the price level. Following these shocks, the economy's adjustment process tended to push the economy back toward the potential level of real GDP with a stable price level. In other words, any inflation that we have so far seen in our macroeconomic model was temporary—it existed only while the economy was adjusting toward its long-run equilibrium.

In this chapter we modify our model to explain how a *sustained* and *constant* inflation can exist. After all, even though Canadian inflation is very low by recent historical standards, over the past two decades it has been sustained and relatively stable at an average rate of 2 percent.

As we will soon see, one of the keys to understanding sustained inflation is to understand the role of *inflation expectations*. When combined with excess demand or excess supply, as reflected by the economy's output gap, such expectations give us a more complete explanation of why costs and prices change. Let's begin our analysis by examining in more detail why wages change.

Why Wages Change

Readers who have studied microeconomics will have examined why wages in *particular* firms and industries change relative to wages in other firms and industries. Movements in these *relative* wages are explained by many factors, including the power of industrial labour unions, firms' market power, the nature of work in specific industries, the skills of the workers, and much else. Here we ignore this microeconomic detail and focus instead on the *general* level of wages in the economy. Our emphasis is on the role played by broad macroeconomic forces.

In Chapter 24, when we examined the economy's adjustment process, we saw that increases in wages led to increases in unit costs—because we maintained the assumption that technology (and thus productivity) was held constant. We continue with that assumption in this chapter. Thus, as wages and other factor prices rise, unit costs increase and the *AS* curve shifts up. Conversely, when wages and other factor prices fall, unit costs fall and the *AS* curve shifts down.

What are the macroeconomic forces that cause the overall level of nominal wages to change? The two main forces that we consider are the output gap and expectations of future inflation. Much of what we discuss in the case of the output gap was first seen in Chapter 24, but the points are important enough to bear repeating.

Wages and the Output Gap In Chapter 24, we encountered three propositions about how changes in nominal (or money) wages were influenced by the output gap:

1. The excess demand for labour that is associated with an inflationary gap ($Y > Y^*$) puts upward pressure on nominal wages.

2. The excess supply of labour associated with a recessionary gap ($Y < Y^*$) puts downward pressure on nominal wages, though the adjustment may be quite slow.

3. The absence of either an inflationary or a recessionary gap ($Y = Y^*$) implies that demand forces are not exerting any pressure on nominal wages.

When real GDP is equal to Y^*, the unemployment rate is said to be equal to the NAIRU, which stands for the *non-accelerating inflation rate of unemployment* and is designated by U^*. The use of this particular name will be explained later in this chapter. Another name sometimes used in place of NAIRU is the *natural rate of unemployment*.

The NAIRU is not zero. Instead, even when $Y = Y^*$, there may be a substantial amount of *frictional* and *structural* unemployment caused, for example, by the movement of people between jobs or between regions. When real GDP exceeds potential GDP ($Y > Y^*$), the unemployment rate will be less than the NAIRU ($U < U^*$). When real GDP is less than potential GDP ($Y < Y^*$), the unemployment rate will exceed the NAIRU ($U > U^*$).

We have assumed that nominal wages tend to react to various pressures of demand. These demand pressures can be stated either in terms of the relationship between actual and potential GDP or in terms of the relationship between the actual unemployment rate and the NAIRU. When $Y > Y^*$ (or $U < U^*$), there is an inflationary gap characterized by excess demand for labour, and wages are assumed to rise. Conversely, when $Y < Y^*$ (or $U > U^*$), there is a recessionary gap characterized by excess supply of labour, and wages are assumed to fall.

This assumed relationship between the excess demand or supply of labour and the rate of change of nominal wages is represented by the Phillips curve, which we first discussed in Chapter 24.

Wages and Expected Inflation A second force that can influence nominal wages is *expectations* of future inflation. Suppose both employers and employees expect 2 percent inflation next year. Workers will tend to start negotiations from a base of a 2 percent increase in nominal wages, which would hold their *real wages* constant. Firms will also be inclined to begin bargaining from a base of a 2 percent increase in nominal wages because they expect that the prices at which they sell their products will rise by 2 percent. Starting from that base, workers may attempt to obtain some desired increase in their real wages while firms may attempt to reduce real wages. At this point, such factors as profits and bargaining power become important.

> **The expectation of some specific inflation rate creates pressure for nominal wages to rise by that rate.**

The key point is that nominal wages can be rising even if no inflationary gap is present. As long as people *expect* prices to rise, their behaviour will put upward pressure on nominal wages. Indeed, in every year since the Second World War, average nominal wages have increased in Canada, even though in some years there were notable recessionary gaps when nominal wages increased by less than prices. The reason is that in every year the price level was expected to increase (and did, in fact, increase). Clarifying the distinction between these two separate forces on nominal wages—excess demand and inflation expectations—is an important objective of this chapter.

The central role for the *expectations* of future inflation suggests the importance of examining how firms and workers *form* their expectations. *Applying Economic Concepts 30-1* discusses the formation of expectations and explains the important difference between *backward-looking* and *forward-looking* expectations.

rational expectations The theory that people understand how the economy works and learn quickly from their mistakes, so that even though random errors may be made, systematic and persistent errors are not.

APPLYING ECONOMIC CONCEPTS 30-1

How Do People Form Their Expectations?

How firms and workers form their expectations about future inflation may have an important effect on that inflation. Generally, we can distinguish two main patterns: One is to look backward at past experience; the other is to look at current circumstances for a clue as to what may happen in the near future.

The first type of expectations are called *backward-looking*. People look at the past in order to predict what will happen in the future. The simplest possible form of such expectations is to expect the past to be repeated in the future. According to this view, if inflation has been 5 percent over the past few years, people will expect it to be 5 percent next year. This expectation, however, is quite naïve. Everyone knows that the inflation rate sometimes changes, and therefore the past cannot be a perfectly accurate guide to the future.

A less naïve version has people revising their expectations in light of the mistakes that they made in estimating inflation in the past. For example, if you thought that this year's inflation rate was going to be 5 percent but it turned out to be only 3 percent, you might revise your estimate of next year's rate down somewhat from 5 percent.

Backward-looking expectations tend to change slowly because some time must pass before a change in the actual rate of inflation provides enough past experience to cause expectations to adjust.

The second main type of expectations are those that look to current economic conditions to estimate what is likely to happen in the future. One version of this type assumes that people look to the government's current macroeconomic policy to form their expectations of future inflation. They are assumed to understand how the economy works, and they form their expectations by predicting the outcome of the policies now being followed. In an obvious sense, such expectations are *forward-looking*.

A strong version of forward-looking expectations is called **rational expectations**. Rational expectations are not necessarily always correct; rather, the *rational expectations hypothesis* assumes that people make the best possible use of all the information available to them. One implication is that they will not continue to make persistent, systematic errors when forming their expectations. Thus, if the economic system about which they are forming expectations remains stable, their expectations

will be correct *on average*. Sometimes next year's inflation rate will turn out to be above what people expected it to be; at other times, it will turn out to be below what people expected it to be. On average over many years, however, the actual rate will not, according to the rational expectations theory, be consistently under- or overestimated.

Forward-looking expectations can adjust quickly to changes in events. Instead of being based on past inflation rates, expected inflation is based on expected economic conditions and government policies.

Assuming that expectations are solely backward-looking seems overly naïve. People do look ahead and assess future possibilities rather than just blindly reacting to what has gone before. Yet the assumption of "fully rational" forward-looking expectations requires workers and firms to have a degree of understanding of the economy that few economists would claim to have. The actual process of wage setting probably combines forward-looking behaviour with expectations based on the experience of the recent past. Depending on the circumstances, expectations will sometimes tend to rely more on past experience and at other times more on present events whose effects are expected to influence the future.

A third type of expectations formation, which combines the other two, fits the current Canadian situation quite well. It assumes that the central bank is committed to maintaining a low and stable inflation rate and has established its credibility by being willing to implement whatever policies are necessary to maintain such a rate. For example, since 1991 the Bank of Canada has taken whatever policy decisions were necessary in the face of various economic shocks to achieve its formal inflation target; since that time, inflation has varied slightly but its annual average over more than 20 years has been almost exactly 2 percent. Once the Bank's credibility is established, expectations will be for the 2 percent rate to continue. Both forward-looking and backward-looking theories would predict that the Bank's target rate would become the expected rate. Even if expectations are formed in some other manner, all that is needed is that the public believes that the Bank is determined and able to maintain its inflation target. This appears to have been the case in Canada since the early 1990s.

Overall Effect on Wages We can now think of changes in average nominal wages as resulting from two different forces:[1]

$$\text{Change in} \atop \text{nominal wages} = {\text{Output-gap} \atop \text{effect}} + {\text{Expectational} \atop \text{effect}}$$

What happens to wages is the *net* effect of the two forces. Consider two examples. First, suppose both labour and management expect 2 percent inflation next year and are therefore willing to allow nominal wages to increase by 2 percent. Doing so would leave *real* wages unchanged. Suppose as well that there is a significant inflationary gap with an associated labour shortage and that the excess demand for labour causes wages to rise by an additional 1 percentage point. The final outcome is that nominal wages rise by 3 percent, the net effect of a 2 percent increase caused by expected inflation and a 1 percent increase caused by the excess demand for labour when $Y > Y^*$.

For the second example, assume again that expected inflation is 2 percent, but this time there is a large recessionary gap. The associated high unemployment represents an excess supply of labour that exerts downward pressure on wage bargains. Hence, the output-gap effect now works to dampen wage increases, say, to the extent of 1 percentage point. Nominal wages therefore rise only by 1 percent, the net effect of a 2 percent increase caused by expected inflation and a 1 percent *decrease* caused by the excess supply of labour when $Y < Y^*$.

From Wages to Prices

We saw in Chapters 23 and 24 that shifts in the *AS* curve depend on what happens to wages and other factor prices. We have just seen that output gaps and expectations of future inflation put pressure on wages to change and hence cause the *AS* curve to shift.

> The net effect of the two macro forces acting on wages—output gaps and inflation expectations—determines what happens to the *AS* curve.

If the net effect of the output-gap effect and the expectational effect is to raise wages, then the *AS* curve will shift up. This shift will cause the price level to rise—that is, the forces pushing up wages will be *inflationary*. On the other hand, if the net effect of the output-gap effect and the expectational effect is to reduce wages, the *AS* curve will shift down—the forces reducing wages will be *deflationary*.[2]

Since anything that leads to higher nominal wages will shift the *AS* curve up and lead to higher prices, we can decompose inflation caused by wage increases into two component parts: *output-gap inflation* and *expected inflation*. But because the *AS* curve can also shift for reasons unrelated to changes in wages, we must add a third element. Specifically, we must consider the effect of non-wage supply shocks on the *AS* curve and

---

[1] Average nominal wages may also be affected by things unrelated to output gaps and expected inflation, such as government guidelines and union power. Such factors may be regarded as random shocks and analyzed separately from the two principal macro forces that we examine here.

[2] This is a good time to remind the reader that we are assuming constant productivity throughout this chapter. With ongoing productivity growth, the *AS* curve would shift upward when wages rise *faster than productivity* and shift downward when wages *rise slower than productivity*. But with constant productivity, any increase in nominal wages causes *AS* to shift up and any decrease in nominal wages causes *AS* to shift down.

thus on the price level. The best example of a non-wage supply shock is a change in the prices of imported raw materials. We can then decompose actual inflation into its three systematic components:

$$\underset{\text{inflation}}{\text{Actual}} = \underset{\text{inflation}}{\text{Output-gap}} + \underset{\text{inflation}}{\text{Expected}} + \underset{\text{inflation}}{\text{Supply-shock}}$$

As an example, consider an economy that begins with real GDP equal to Y^* and expectations of inflation at zero. In this case, the first two terms on the right-hand side are zero. But if an adverse supply shock then occurs, such as a significant increase in the price of imported raw materials, the *AS* curve shifts up and the price level rises. Actual inflation will be positive. As we will see later in the chapter, such supply shocks are not uncommon, and they generate challenges for the Bank of Canada in its attempt to maintain low inflation.

Having discussed these components of inflation, we are now in a position to see how constant inflation can be included in our macroeconomic model.

Constant Inflation

Suppose the inflation rate is 2 percent per year and has been 2 percent for several years. This is what we mean by a *constant* inflation. In such a setting, people with backward-looking expectations about inflation will expect the actual rate to continue into the future. Furthermore, in the absence of any announcements that the central bank will be altering its monetary policy, people with forward-looking expectations will expect the actual inflation rate to continue. Thus, for the economy as a whole, the expected rate of inflation will equal the actual rate of inflation.

The Conference Board of Canada conducts a regular survey about people's expectations about inflation. See its website at www.conferenceboard.ca.

> If inflation and monetary policy have been constant for several years, the expected rate of inflation will tend to equal the actual rate of inflation.

Suppose there are no supply shocks (we address these later in the chapter). Since actual inflation equals expected inflation, it follows from the equation above that there can be *no* output gap—real GDP must equal its potential level, Y^*.

> In the absence of supply shocks, if expected inflation equals actual inflation, real GDP must be equal to potential GDP.[3]

Figure 30-2 shows a constant inflation in the *AD/AS* diagram. What is causing this inflation? As we will see, such a constant inflation requires both the *expectations* of inflation (which shift the *AS* curve) and the continuing expansion of the money supply by the central bank (which shifts the *AD* curve). Let's see how this works.

Suppose workers and employers expect 2 percent inflation over the coming years and employers are prepared to increase nominal wages by 2 percent per year. As wages rise by 2 percent, the *AS* curve shifts up by that amount. But in order for 2 percent

---

[3] Another realistic possibility is that real GDP is below Y^* but there is only weak downward pressure on wages, and so relatively constant inflation. Recall our discussion from Chapter 24 that large and persistent recessionary gaps may be necessary to generate even small wage reductions. For simplicity, in this chapter we maintain the assumption that wages *do* fall when $Y < Y^*$, although we recognize that these forces may be both weak and slow.

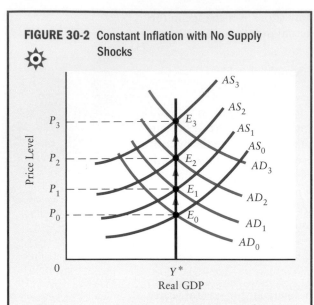

FIGURE 30-2 Constant Inflation with No Supply Shocks

Price Level (vertical axis) · Real GDP (horizontal axis)

AS_3, AS_2, AS_1, AS_0
AD_3, AD_2, AD_1, AD_0
E_3, E_2, E_1, E_0
P_3, P_2, P_1, P_0
Y^*

In the AD/AS model with no supply shocks, constant inflation occurs when $Y = Y^*$. Expectations of a constant rate of inflation cause wages and thus the AS curve to shift upward at a uniform rate from AS_0 to AS_1 to AS_2. Monetary validation is causing the AD curve to shift upward at the same time from AD_0 to AD_1 to AD_2. As a result, real GDP remains at Y^* as the economy moves from equilibrium E_0 to E_1 to E_2 and so on. The constant inflation rate takes the price level from P_0 to P_1 to P_2. Wage costs are rising because of expectations of inflation, and these expectations are being validated by the central bank.

to be the *actual* rate of inflation, the intersection of the AS and AD curves must be shifting up at the rate of 2 percent. This requires the AD curve to be shifting up at the same 2 percent rate—this AD shift is caused by the growth of the money supply. So in this case there is no output-gap inflation ($Y - Y^*$), and actual and expected inflation are equal. When the central bank increases the money supply at such a rate that the expectations of inflation end up being correct, it is said to be *validating* the expectations.

> Constant inflation with $Y = Y^*$ occurs when the rate of monetary growth, the rate of wage increase, and the expected rate of inflation are all consistent with the actual inflation rate.

The key point about constant inflation in our macro model is that there is no output-gap effect operating on wages: either there is no output gap at all or whatever gap exists is not large enough to create wage adjustments. As a result, nominal wages rise exactly at the expected rate of inflation. Expansions of the money supply validate those expectations.

Note that in this constant-inflation equilibrium, interest rates are being kept stable by two equal but offsetting forces. The central bank is increasing the money supply, which tends to push interest rates down. But at the same time, rising prices are increasing the demand for money and pushing interest rates up. In equilibrium, the monetary policy is just expansionary enough to accommodate the growing money demand, thus leaving interest rates unchanged. As we will see later in this chapter, in order to *reduce* the rate of inflation, the central bank must implement a contractionary monetary policy—by reducing the growth rate of the money supply sufficiently to raise interest rates.

Figure 30-2 can be used to analyze any constant (and positive) rate of inflation. It could also be used to analyze the case of deflation, a situation in which the price level is falling so that the inflation rate is negative. In this case, the AD and AS curves would be shifting down at a constant rate, keeping $Y = Y^*$. *Applying Economic Concepts 30-2* discusses deflation, the reasons that some people seem to fear its effect on the economy, and why these fears may be misplaced.

30.2 Shocks and Policy Responses

A constant rate of inflation is a special case in our macroeconomic model because the rising price level is not caused by an inflationary output gap. In many cases of inflation, however, inflationary pressure is initially created by an aggregate demand or aggregate supply shock. In this section we examine the effects of AS and AD shocks and the subsequent effects of the policy responses chosen by the central bank.

APPLYING ECONOMIC CONCEPTS 30-2

Is Deflation a Problem?

We have discussed how inflation can be incorporated into our basic macroeconomic model. The model can also be used to discuss *deflation*, a situation in which the price level experiences an ongoing decline. For example, a deflation of 2 percent per year means that the price level is falling annually by 2 percent; in other words, deflation means a negative inflation rate.

Sustained deflation is very rare; it has been experienced only a few times in the last century. During the Great Depression, the price level in Canada fell by approximately 25 percent between 1930 and 1933; when the Japanese economy was growing very slowly in the early 2000s, the price level declined by about 1 percent per year.

In recent years, especially during the 2009 recession, it was common to hear media discussion of the dangers of deflation and the need for central banks to take whatever actions were necessary to prevent it. The fear of deflation appears to stem from the belief that deflation causes a decline in economic activity, and this argument is usually based on the evidence drawn from the Great Depression, when real GDP fell by about 30 percent from 1929 to 1933.

How could deflation cause a decline in economic activity? A commonly heard argument is that when prices are falling, firms and consumers delay their spending because they know that prices will be lower in the future. The delay in spending leads to a leftward shift in the *AD* curve and, other things being equal, causes a decline in real GDP.

Economists who reject this line of argument usually make two observations, one about the historical evidence and the other about the proposed link from deflation to recession. First, while it is certainly true that there was significant deflation during the Great Depression, it was probably a *result* rather than a *cause* of the economic events. In this view, a combination of the 1929 stock-market crash, widespread bank failures, inappropriate monetary and fiscal policies, and a significant rise in protectionist trade policies caused a major decline in aggregate demand. This decline in turn caused a leftward shift of the *AD* curve, resulting in *both* a decline in real GDP and a decline in the price level (deflation).

The second point relates to the possibility that buyers delay their purchases because of deflation, and that this delay can cause a recession. How important can this effect be? If the rate of deflation were 25 percent per year, it is easy to imagine that many firms and consumers would delay some purchases—after all, a saving of 25 percent provides a significant incentive to wait. But this effect is almost absent when deflation is only 1 or 2 percent per year, as it was in Japan during the early 2000s. And if this effect is absent, there is no fundamental danger associated with a small deflation.

Consider the opposite situation, that of prices rising by 1 or 2 percent annually. In this situation, do we expect firms and consumers to rush to purchase their products before prices rise, thereby pushing real GDP well above the economy's potential? The answer is no. When inflation is low and relatively stable, firms and consumers build it into their expectations, central banks build it into their policy decisions, and the economy can operate with real GDP equal to potential output, as we have shown in this chapter. The same would likely be true of a constant and anticipated deflation of 1 or 2 percent per year.

In this analysis, we make a central assumption in our macro model—that *AD* and *AS* shocks do not influence the level of potential output, Y^*. With this assumption in place, we know that a central prediction of our model is that the long-run effect of *AD* and *AS* shocks involves no change in real GDP because the economy's adjustment process brings real GDP back to (the unchanged) Y^*. As we explained in Chapter 28, however, this assumption is often debated; there are good reasons to believe that Y^* may be influenced by the short-run path of real GDP. For the remainder of this chapter, however, we maintain the strong assumption that Y^* is unaffected by the various *AD* and *AS* shocks that we consider.

Demand Shocks

Any rightward shift in the *AD* curve that creates an inflationary output gap also creates what is called **demand inflation**. The shift in the *AD* curve could have been caused by a reduction in tax rates, by an increase in such autonomous expenditure items as investment, government, and net exports, or by an expansionary monetary policy.

demand inflation Inflation arising from an inflationary output gap caused, in turn, by a positive *AD* shock.

Major demand-shock inflations occurred in Canada during and after the First and Second World Wars. In these cases, large increases in government expenditure without fully offsetting increases in taxes led to general excess demand ($Y > Y^*$). More generally, demand inflation sometimes occurs at the end of a strong upswing, as rising output causes excess demand to develop simultaneously in the markets for labour, intermediate goods, and final output. Demand inflation of this type occurred in Canada in 1989–1990 and to a lesser extent in 2003–2006.

To begin our study of demand inflation, we make some simplifying assumptions. First, we continue to assume that Y^* is constant. Second, we assume that initially there is no ongoing inflation. These two assumptions imply that our starting point is a stable long-run equilibrium, with constant real GDP and price level, rather than the long-run equilibrium with constant inflation as shown in Figure 30-2. We then suppose that this long-run equilibrium is disturbed by a rightward shift in the AD curve. This shift causes the price level and output to rise. It is important next to distinguish between the case in which the Bank of Canada validates the demand shock and the case in which it does not.

No Monetary Validation Because the initial rise in AD takes output above potential, an inflationary gap opens up. The pressure of excess demand soon causes nominal wages to rise, shifting the AS curve upward as shown in Figure 30-3. As long as the Bank of Canada holds the money supply constant, the rise in the price level moves the economy upward and to the left along the new AD curve, reducing the inflationary gap. Eventually, the gap is eliminated, and equilibrium is established at a higher but stable price level, with output at Y^*. In this case, the initial period of inflation is followed by further inflation that lasts only until the new long-run equilibrium is reached.

Monetary Validation Suppose that after the demand shock created an inflationary gap, the Bank of Canada chose to attempt to sustain these "good economic times." It would then validate the demand shock through an expansionary monetary policy. We illustrate this situation in Figure 30-4.

Two forces are now brought into play. Spurred by the inflationary gap, the increase in nominal wages causes the AS curve to shift upward. Fuelled by the expansionary monetary policy, however, the AD curve shifts further to the right. As a result of both of these shifts, the price level rises, but real GDP remains above Y^*. Indeed, if the shift in the AD curve *exactly* offsets the shift in the AS curve, real GDP and the inflationary gap will remain constant.

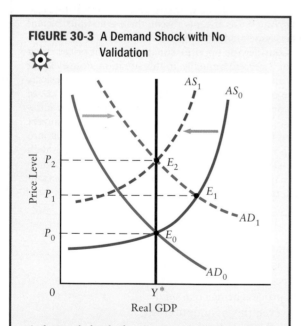

FIGURE 30-3 A Demand Shock with No Validation

A demand shock that is not validated produces temporary inflation, but the economy's adjustment process eventually restores potential GDP and stable prices. The initial long-run equilibrium is at P_0 and Y^*. A positive demand shock shifts AD_0 to AD_1, generating an inflationary gap. The excess demand puts upward pressure on wages, thus shifting AS_0 to AS_1. There is inflation as the economy moves from E_0 to E_1 to E_2, but at E_2 the price level is again stable.

> Continued validation of a demand shock turns what would have been transitory inflation into sustained inflation fuelled by monetary expansion.

In other words, the Bank of Canada could indeed choose to sustain the "good economic times" characterized by high output and low unemployment. But the result of this choice would be sustained inflation (and as we will soon see, the inflation rate would continually increase).

Supply Shocks

Any leftward shift in the *AS* curve that is *not* caused by excess demand in the markets for factors of production creates what is called **supply inflation**.

An example of a supply shock is a rise in the costs of imported raw materials. Another is a rise in domestic wages not due to excess demand in the labour market. The rise in wages might occur, as we saw earlier, because of generally held expectations of future inflation. If employers and employees expect inflation, nominal wages are likely to rise in anticipation of that inflation. These shocks cause the *AS* curve to shift upward.[4]

The initial effects of any negative supply shock are that the price level rises while output falls, as shown in Figure 30-5. As with the case of a demand shock, what happens next depends on how the Bank of Canada reacts. If the Bank allows the money supply to increase, it validates the supply shock; if it holds the money supply constant, the shock is not validated.

No Monetary Validation The upward shift in the *AS* curve in Figure 30-5 causes the price level to rise and pushes output below Y^*, opening up a recessionary gap. Pressure mounts for nominal wages and other factor prices to fall. As wages and other factor prices fall, unit costs will fall. Consequently, the *AS* curve shifts down, increasing output while reducing the price level. The *AS* curve will continue to shift slowly downward, stopping only when real GDP is returned to Y^* and the price level is returned to its initial value of P_0. Thus, the period of inflation accompanying the original supply shock is eventually reversed until the initial long-run equilibrium is re-established.

A major concern in this case is the speed of wage adjustment. If wages do not fall rapidly in the face of excess supply in the labour market, the adjustment back to potential output can take a long time. For example, suppose the original shock raised firms' costs by 6 percent. To reverse this shock and return real GDP to Y^*, firms' costs must fall by 6 percent. If nominal wages fell by only 1 percent per year, it would take six years to complete the adjustment.[5]

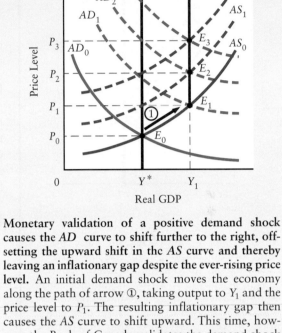

FIGURE 30-4 A Demand Shock with Validation

Monetary validation of a positive demand shock causes the *AD* curve to shift further to the right, offsetting the upward shift in the *AS* curve and thereby leaving an inflationary gap despite the ever-rising price level. An initial demand shock moves the economy along the path of arrow ①, taking output to Y_1 and the price level to P_1. The resulting inflationary gap then causes the *AS* curve to shift upward. This time, however, the Bank of Canada validates the demand shock with a monetary expansion that shifts the *AD* curve to the right. By the time the aggregate supply curve has reached AS_1, the aggregate demand curve has reached AD_2. The new equilibrium is at E_2. Output remains constant at Y_1, leaving the inflationary gap constant while the price level rises to P_2.

The persistent inflationary gap continues to push the *AS* curve upward, while the continued monetary validation continues to push the *AD* curve to the right. As long as this monetary validation continues, the economy moves along the vertical path of arrow ②.

supply inflation Inflation arising from a negative AS shock that is not the result of excess demand in the domestic markets for factors of production.

---

[4] Recall our discussion in Chapter 23 of how some shocks affect *both* the *AD* and the *AS* curves. A rise in the world price of oil is one example. Since Canada both uses and produces oil, a rise in the price of oil causes both the *AD* and *AS* curves to shift upward. In this discussion we confine ourselves to the effect of the *AS* shift.

[5] Nominal wages rarely fall because there is ongoing productivity growth that offsets the effect on wages of excess supply. But in this chapter we are holding productivity (and thus Y^*) constant so we can focus on the causes and consequences of inflation.

FIGURE 30-5 A Supply Shock with and without Validation

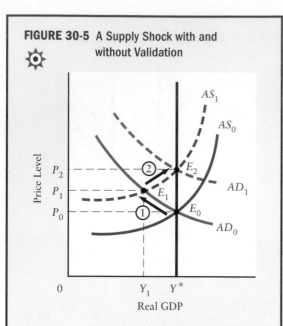

Adverse supply shocks initially raise prices while lowering output. An adverse supply shock causes the AS curve to shift upward from AS_0 to AS_1, as shown by arrow ①. Equilibrium is established at E_1. If there is no monetary validation, the reduction in wages and other factor prices makes the AS curve shift slowly back down to AS_0. If there is monetary validation, the AD curve shifts from AD_0 to AD_1, as shown by arrow ②. Equilibrium is re-established at E_2 with output equal to potential output but with a higher price level, P_2.

Whenever wages and other factor prices fall only slowly in the face of excess supply, the recovery to potential output after a non-validated negative supply shock will take a long time.

Concern that such a lengthy adjustment will occur is often the motivation for the Bank of Canada to validate negative supply shocks.

Monetary Validation What happens if the Bank of Canada responds to the negative supply shock by lowering interest rates and so allowing the money supply to increase, thus *validating* the shock? The monetary validation shifts the AD curve to the right and closes the output gap. As the recessionary gap is eliminated, the price level rises further, rather than falling back to its original value as it did when the supply shock was not validated. These effects are also illustrated in Figure 30-5.

Monetary validation of a negative supply shock causes the initial rise in the price level to be followed by a further rise, resulting in a higher price level but a much faster return to potential output than would occur if the recessionary gap were relied on to reduce wages and other factor prices.

The most dramatic example of a supply-shock inflation came in the wake of the first OPEC oil-price shock. In 1974, the member countries of the Organization of the Petroleum Exporting Countries (OPEC) agreed to restrict output. Their action caused a threefold increase in the price of oil and dramatic increases in the prices of many petroleum-related products, such as fertilizer and chemicals. The resulting increase in industrial costs shifted AS curves upward in all industrial countries. At this time, the Bank of Canada validated the supply shock with large increases in the money supply, whereas the Federal Reserve (the U.S. central bank) did not. As the theory predicts, Canada experienced a large increase in its price level but almost no recession, while the United States experienced a much smaller increase in its price level but a deeper recession.

Is Monetary Validation of Supply Shocks Desirable? Suppose the Bank of Canada were to validate a negative supply shock and thus prevent what could otherwise be a protracted recession. Expressed in this way, monetary validation sounds like a good policy. Unfortunately, however, there is also a possible cost associated with this policy. The effect of the monetary validation is to extend the period of inflation. If this inflation leads firms and workers to expect *further* inflation, then point E_2 in Figure 30-5 will not be the end of the story. As expectations for further inflation develop, the AS curve will continue to shift upward. But if the Bank continues its policy of validation, then the AD curve will also continue to shift upward. It may not take long before the economy is in a *wage–price spiral*.

Once started, a wage–price spiral can be halted only if the Bank of Canada stops validating the expectational inflation initially caused by the supply shock. But the longer it waits to do so, the more firmly held will be the *expectations* that it will continue its policy of validating the shocks. These entrenched expectations may cause wages to continue rising even after validation has ceased. Because employers expect prices to rise, they go on granting wage increases. If expectations are entrenched firmly enough, the wage push can continue for quite some time, in spite of whatever downward pressure on wages is caused by the high unemployment associated with the recessionary gap.

Because of this possibility, some economists argue that the wage–price spiral should not be allowed to begin. One way to ensure that it does not begin is to refuse to validate any supply shock and accept whatever recessionary gap the shock creates, as the United States did after the OPEC oil-price shock in the early 1970s. The choice between a deeper recession with less expected inflation and a less severe recession with the possibility of higher entrenched inflation expectations involves an important value judgement and is not a matter that can be settled solely by economic analysis.

For information on OPEC, see its website: www.opec.org.

Accelerating Inflation

Consider a situation in which a demand or supply shock increases real GDP above Y^*. For example, a booming U.S. economy may lead to an increase in demand for Canadian goods, thus shifting Canada's *AD* curve to the right. Or a reduction in the world price of raw materials may reduce firms' costs and shift the Canadian *AS* curve downward. In both cases, the effect in Canada would be to increase real GDP above Y^*—unemployment is low and businesses are booming. As we saw in Chapter 29, as real GDP rises above Y^*, the Bank of Canada would normally begin to tighten its monetary policy in order to prevent inflation from rising above its target. Some people, however, might argue that the Bank of Canada should not "spoil the party" and instead should allow these boom conditions to continue. What would be the result if the Bank acted to maintain output above Y^*?

A contract settlement that raises wages for a large number of workers will increase firms' costs and shift the AS curve upward, thus tending to reduce real GDP and raise the price level.

What happens to the rate of inflation is predicted by the **acceleration hypothesis**, which says that when the central bank conducts its policy to hold the inflationary gap constant, the actual inflation rate will *accelerate*. The Bank of Canada may start by validating 2 percent inflation, but soon 2 percent will become expected, and given the demand pressure the inflation rate will rise to 3 percent and, if the Bank insists on validating 3 percent, the rate will become 4 percent, and so on, without limit. The process will end only when the Bank ends its policy of validation. Avoiding this possibility of gradually increasing inflation is one important reason that the Bank has adopted a formal (and unchanging) inflation target of 2 percent.

acceleration hypothesis The hypothesis that when real GDP is held above potential, the persistent inflationary gap will cause inflation to accelerate.

To see the argument in detail, recall our earlier discussion in this chapter about how actual inflation has three separate components: output gaps, expectations, and non-wage supply shocks. It is restated here:

$$\begin{matrix} \text{Actual} \\ \text{inflation} \end{matrix} = \begin{matrix} \text{Output-gap} \\ \text{inflation} \end{matrix} + \begin{matrix} \text{Expected} \\ \text{inflation} \end{matrix} + \begin{matrix} \text{Supply-shock} \\ \text{inflation} \end{matrix}$$

EXTENSIONS IN THEORY 30-1

The Phillips Curve and Accelerating Inflation

As we first saw in Chapter 24, the Phillips curve describes the relationship between unemployment (or output) and the rate of change of wages. The Phillips curve was born in 1958 when Professor A.W. Phillips from the London School of Economics noted a relationship between unemployment and the rate of change of wages over a period of 100 years in the United Kingdom. Phillips was interested in studying the short-run behaviour of an economy subjected to cyclical fluctuations. In the years following Phillips's study,

however, some economists treated the Phillips curve as establishing a long-term tradeoff between inflation and unemployment.

Suppose the government stabilizes output at Y_1 (and hence the unemployment rate at U_1), as shown by points A in the accompanying figures. To do this, it must validate the ensuing wage inflation, which is indicated by $\dot{W}_1$ in the figures. The government thus *appears* to be able to choose among particular combinations of (wage) inflation and

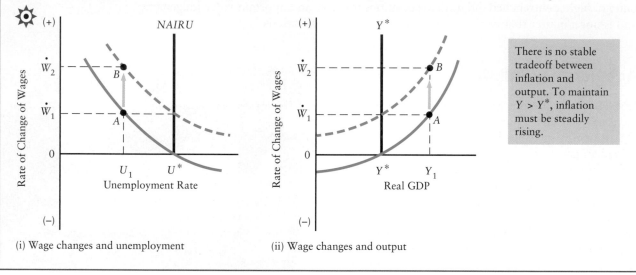

There is no stable tradeoff between inflation and output. To maintain $Y > Y^*$, inflation must be steadily rising.

(i) Wage changes and unemployment

(ii) Wage changes and output

To illustrate the importance of expectations in accelerating inflation, suppose the inflationary output gap creates sufficient excess demand to push up wages by 2 percent per year. As a result, the *AS* curve will also tend to be shifting upward at 2 percent per year.

When inflation has persisted for some time, however, people will likely come to expect that the inflation will continue. The expectation of 2 percent inflation will tend to push up wages by that amount *in addition to* the demand pressure. As the output-gap effect on wages is augmented by the expectational effect, the *AS* curve will begin to shift upward more rapidly (look back to Figure 30-4). When expectations are for a 2 percent inflation and demand pressure is also pushing wages up by 2 percent, the overall effect will be a 4 percent increase in wages. Sooner or later, however, 4 percent inflation will come to be expected, and the expectational effect will rise to 4 percent. This new expectational component of 4 percent, when added to the output-gap component, will create an inflation rate of 6 percent. And so this cycle will go on. As long as there is excess demand arising from an inflationary output gap, the inflation rate cannot stay constant because expectations will always be revised upward toward the actual inflation rate.

Now we see the reason for the name NAIRU. If real GDP is held above Y^* (and thus the unemployment rate is below the NAIRU), the inflation rate tends to accelerate.

unemployment, in which lower levels of unemployment are attained at the cost of higher rates of inflation.

In the 1960s, Phillips curves were fitted to the data for many countries, and governments made decisions about where they wanted to be on the tradeoff between inflation and unemployment. Then, in the late 1960s, in country after country, the rate of wage and price inflation associated with any given level of unemployment began to rise. Instead of being stable, the Phillips curves began to shift upward. The explanation lay primarily in the rise of inflation expectations.

It was gradually understood that the original Phillips curve concerned only the influence of the output gap and left out inflationary expectations. This was not unreasonable for Phillips's original curve, which was fitted mainly to nineteenth-century data where the price level was relatively constant. But in the inflationary period following the Second World War, this omission proved important and unfortunate. An increase in expected inflation shows up as an upward shift in the original Phillips curve that was drawn in Chapter 24. The importance of expectations can be shown by drawing what is called an **expectations-augmented Phillips curve**, as shown by the dashed Phillips curves here. The height of the Phillips curves above the axis at Y^* and at U^* show the expected inflation rate. These distances represent the amount that wages will rise even when $Y = Y^*$ (or $U = U^*$) and there is neither excess demand nor supply in labour markets. The actual wage increase is shown by the augmented (dashed) curve, with the increase in wages exceeding expected inflation whenever $Y > Y^*(U < U^*)$ and falling short of expected inflation whenever $Y < Y^*(U > U^*)$.

Now we can see what was wrong with the idea of a stable inflation–unemployment tradeoff. Maintaining a particular output Y_1 or unemployment U_1 in the figures requires some inflation $\dot{W}_1$. And once this rate of inflation comes to be expected, people will demand that much just to hold their own. The Phillips curve will then shift upward to the position shown in the figures and the economy will be at point B. Now there is inflation $\dot{W}_2$ because of the combined effects of expectations and excess demand. However, this higher rate is above the expected rate $\dot{W}_1$. Once this higher rate comes to be expected, the Phillips curve will shift upward once again.

As a result of the combination of output-gap inflation and expectational inflation, the inflation rate associated with any given positive output gap ($Y > Y^*$ or $U < U^*$) rises over time. This is the phenomenon of accelerating inflation that we discussed in the text.

The shifts in the Phillips curve are such that most economists agree that in the long run, when inflationary expectations have fully adjusted to actual inflation, there is no tradeoff between inflation and unemployment. In other words, the long-run Phillips curve is a vertical line above U^* (or Y^*).

The NAIRU is therefore the lowest level of sustained unemployment consistent with a *non-accelerating* rate of inflation.

expectations-augmented Phillips curve The relationship between unemployment and the rate of increase of nominal wages that arises when the output-gap and expectations components of inflation are combined.

> According to the acceleration hypothesis, as long as an inflationary output gap persists, expectations of inflation will be rising, which will lead to increases in the actual rate of inflation.

The tendency for inflation to accelerate is discussed further in *Extensions in Theory 30-1*, which examines how expected inflation affects the position of the Phillips curve.

Inflation as a Monetary Phenomenon

For many years, a debate among economists concerned the extent to which inflation is a monetary phenomenon. Does it have purely monetary causes—changes in the demand or the supply of money? Does it have purely monetary consequences—only the price level is affected? One slogan that states an extreme position on this issue was popularized many years ago by the late Milton Friedman: "Inflation is *everywhere* and *always* a monetary phenomenon." To consider these issues, let us summarize what we have learned already. First, look at the various *causes* of inflation:

- Anything that shifts the *AD* curve to the right will cause the price level to rise (demand inflation).
- Anything that shifts the *AS* curve upward will cause the price level to rise (supply inflation).
- Increases in the price level caused by *AD* and *AS* shocks will eventually come to a halt unless they are continually validated by monetary policy.

The first two points tell us that a temporary burst of inflation need not be a monetary phenomenon. It need not have monetary causes, and it need not be accompanied by monetary expansion. The third point tells us that *sustained* inflation *must* be a monetary phenomenon. If a rise in prices is to continue indefinitely, it *must* be accompanied by a monetary policy that allows the money supply to continually increase. This is true regardless of the cause that set the inflation in motion.

Now, let us summarize the macroeconomic changes that accompany inflation, assuming that real GDP was initially at its potential level.

- In the short run, demand inflation tends to be accompanied by an *increase* in real GDP above its potential level.
- In the short run, supply inflation tends to be accompanied by a *decrease* in real GDP below its potential level.
- When all costs and prices are adjusted *fully* and real GDP has returned to its potential level, the only long-run effect of *AD* or *AS* shocks is a change in the price level.

The first two points tell us that inflation is not, in the short run, a purely monetary phenomenon. The third point tells us that inflation is a monetary phenomenon from the point of view of long-run equilibrium. There is still plenty of room for debate, however, on how long the short run will last. Most economists believe that the short run can be long enough for inflation to have major real effects on important economic variables, such as the distribution of wealth (which partly explains why most economists believe that keeping inflation low is desirable).

We have now reached three important conclusions:

- Without monetary validation, positive demand shocks cause inflationary output gaps and a temporary burst of inflation. The gaps are removed as rising factor prices push the *AS* curve upward, returning real GDP to its potential level but at a higher price level.
- Without monetary validation, negative supply shocks cause recessionary output gaps and a temporary burst of inflation. The gaps are eventually removed when factor prices fall sufficiently to restore real GDP to its potential and the price level to its initial level.
- Only with continuing monetary validation can inflation initiated by either supply or demand shocks continue indefinitely.

To put these conclusions differently, we can modify Friedman's statement slightly to represent the causes of inflation more accurately. While *AD* and *AS* shocks may lead to temporary inflation even in the absence of any actions by the central bank, *sustained* inflation can occur only if there is continual monetary validation by the central bank.

Sustained inflation is everywhere and always caused by sustained monetary expansion.

We have been assuming in our macro model that wages rise when unemployment is less than the NAIRU ($Y > Y^*$) and that wages fall when unemployment exceeds the NAIRU ($Y < Y^*$). This assumption leads to the stark prediction that inflation can only be stable when unemployment exactly equals the NAIRU ($Y = Y^*$). In recent years, however, some economists have come to question this theory, believing instead that the NAIRU is best viewed as a range rather than a unique, precise value. In this case, stable inflation would be consistent with a range of unemployment rates. *Extensions in Theory 30-2* explores this issue in greater detail.

30.3 Reducing Inflation

Suppose an economy has had a sustained and constant rate of inflation for several years. What must the central bank do to reduce the rate of inflation? What are the costs involved in doing so?

The Process of Disinflation

Disinflation means a reduction in the rate of inflation. Canada has had two notable periods of disinflation—in 1981–1982, when inflation fell from more than 12 percent to 4 percent, and in 1990–1992, when inflation fell from 6 percent to less than 2 percent.

disinflation A reduction in the rate of inflation.

The process of reducing sustained inflation can be divided into three phases. In the first phase, the monetary validation is stopped and any inflationary gap is eliminated. In the second phase, the economy still suffers from declining output and rising prices—*stagflation*. In the final phase, the economy experiences both increasing output and increasing prices, but the inflation then comes to an end. We now examine these three phases in detail.

The starting point for our analysis is an economy with an inflationary gap ($Y > Y^*$) and rising inflation.[6]

Phase 1: Removing Monetary Validation The first phase consists of tightening monetary policy by raising interest rates and thus reducing the growth rate of the money supply. This policy action slows the rate at which the *AD* curve is shifting upward. An extreme case of monetary tightening in this setting is one where the Bank of Canada adopts a "cold-turkey approach:" interest rates are increased so much that the growth rate of the money supply is reduced to zero and the upward shift of the *AD* curve is halted abruptly. This extreme case is shown in part (i) of Figure 30-6.

The Bank's tight-money policy stops the *AD* curve from shifting. But under the combined influence of the present inflationary gap and expectations of continued inflation, wages continue to rise. Hence, the *AS* curve continues to shift upward. Eventually, the inflationary gap will be removed, as real GDP falls back toward Y^*.

If the excess demand from the inflationary output gap were the only influence on nominal wages, the story would be ended. At $Y = Y^*$, there would be no upward demand pressure on wages and other factor prices. The *AS* curve would be stabilized, and real GDP would remain at Y^*. But it is usually not so simple.

---

[6] In the simpler case in which the economy begins with $Y = Y^*$ and constant inflation, only the second and third phases are relevant.

EXTENSIONS IN THEORY 30-2

Is the NAIRU Like a Razor's Edge?

We have described the standard theory of inflation in which the only stable position for the economy is one in which unemployment is equal to the NAIRU and real GDP is equal to potential GDP, Y^*. According to this theory, the labour market is poised on a "razor's edge"; wages rise when unemployment is less than the NAIRU and wages fall when unemployment exceeds the NAIRU.

In recent years, however, this view has come under some criticism. For example, Canadian economist Lars Osberg and his colleagues from Dalhousie University were unable to find any unique value for the NAIRU in a careful empirical study of Canada's unemployment and inflation experience. Depending on the precise specification of the empirical model used and the number of years included in the statistical sample, they found that the estimated value for the NAIRU could lie within a range of several percentage points. When unemployment usually varies between a low of 6 percent and a high of 11 percent, a possible range of *several percentage points* indicates a very low degree of precision in the estimated NAIRU.

A glance at the accompanying figure for Canadian inflation and unemployment since 1984 shows no clear tendency for inflation to increase when unemployment is below some critical rate, nor to decrease when unemployment is above such a critical rate. If anything, there appear to be two distinct periods in the data. From 1984 to 1991, the unemployment rate varied between a high of 11.5 percent and a low of 7.5 percent, all while the rate of inflation varied between 4 percent and 6 percent per year. Over the next 20 years, from 1992 until 2012, the unemployment rate fluctuated over a wider range, but inflation was generally less variable around a 2 percent average.

Several possible explanations for these data have been advanced, each of which may contribute something to the full explanation. First, when the public has confidence in the Bank of Canada's commitment to maintaining inflation at some given level, these expectations tend to remain relatively constant as unemployment changes. Thus the influence of inflationary expectations on wages will be relatively insensitive to changes in the unemployment rate. In this case, we say that inflation expectations are "well anchored" because changes in the economic environment do not lead to significant changes in expectations. According to this view, for about a decade starting in 1984 the public had confidence in the Bank of Canada's commitment to keeping inflation in the 4 to 6 percent range. Then from 1992 onward, after the Bank of Canada had adopted its formal inflation target of 2 percent, the public once again believed that the Bank would carry out its stated objective. Thus the influence of inflation expectations on the path of wages was relatively invariant to large variations in the actual level of unemployment and real GDP; as a result, large swings in the unemployment rate were consistent with a relatively stable rate of inflation, as the figure shows.

A second explanation emphasizes the fact that most labour markets are not *auction markets* in which wages continually adjust to equate the demand and supply for labour. If employers have a reduced demand for workers, they usually respond by laying some workers off rather than by driving down wages. Instead of responding quickly to changes in excess demand or supplies in the labour market, wages tend to be set with longer-term conditions in mind. (We will say more about such long-term employment relationships in the next chapter.)

A third explanation is that the willingness of workers to push for higher wages (and in some situations to risk strikes) may depend on the nature of technological change. When technological change is creating good middle-wage jobs faster than it is destroying them, workers may be willing to push for higher wages whenever the labour market becomes relatively tight. This is a good description of the type of technological change that occurred between 1945

Phase 2: Stagflation As we explained earlier, wages depend not only on current excess demand but also on inflation expectations. Once inflation expectations have been established, it is not always easy to get people to revise them downward, even in the face of announced changes in monetary policies. Hence, the *AS* curve continues to shift upward, causing the price level to continue to rise and output to fall. A recessionary gap is created. The combination of increased inflation and a reduction in output (or its growth rate) is called **stagflation**. This is phase 2, shown in part (ii) of Figure 30-6.

The ease with which the Bank of Canada can end such an inflation depends on how easy it is to change these expectations of continued inflation. This change is more difficult to the extent that expectations are backward-looking and easier to the extent that expectations are forward-looking.

stagflation The simultaneous increase in inflation and reduction in output (or its growth rate) that is caused by an upward shift of the *AS* curve.

and the early 1970s, when factory jobs flourished, providing good wages for workers who did not have to be highly skilled. This may explain the appearance during this period of a well-defined Phillips curve with a razor's edge NAIRU. In contrast, the past four decades have seen technological change that destroys middle-wage manufacturing jobs while at the same time creating many high-wage jobs for highly trained and educated persons, as well as many low-wage jobs for the unskilled and uneducated. In this situation, workers who remain in manufacturing jobs may be reluctant to press for wage increases lest they be the next ones to lose their increasingly scarce, good jobs. In such

an environment, even tight labour markets may not lead to substantial wage increases and hence there may not be a well-defined Phillips curve with its razor's edge NAIRU.

In summary, the description in our macro model of the wage-adjustment process has a certain compelling and valuable logic: wages tend to rise when labour markets are tight and they tend to fall (although more slowly) when labour markets have excess supply. However, this relationship should be viewed as a general tendency rather than a strict, formulaic rule; there is unlikely to be a unique value of the NAIRU that acts as a "razor's edge" to determine wage adjustments.

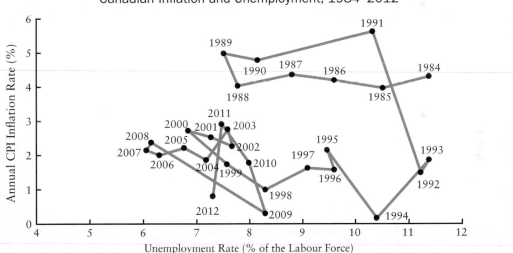

Canadian Inflation and Unemployment, 1984–2012

(*Source*: Author's calculations based on data from Statistics Canada. Consumer Price Index: CANSIM V41690973. Unemployment: CANSIM V2062815. The figure uses annual averages of monthly data.)

If most people are backward-looking when forming their expectations, inflation will remain high even well after the Bank of Canada has implemented its tight monetary policy. In this case, the *AS* curve will continue shifting upward and the stagflation will endure. However, if most people are forward-looking, the change in the Bank's policy will be widely acknowledged and expected inflation will fall relatively quickly. In this case, the upward shifts of the *AS* curve will soon come to an end.

> **How long inflation persists after the inflationary gap has been removed, and the depth of the associated recessionary gap during the stagflationary phase, depend on how quickly inflation expectations are revised downward.**

FIGURE 30-6 Eliminating a Sustained Inflation

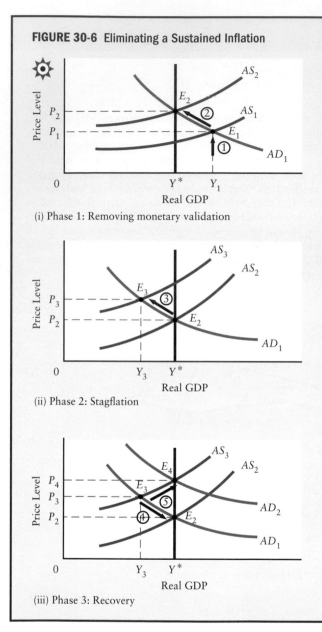

(i) Phase 1: Removing monetary validation

(ii) Phase 2: Stagflation

(iii) Phase 3: Recovery

(i) Phase 1: The elimination of a sustained inflation begins with a monetary tightening to remove the inflationary gap. The initial position is one where fully validated inflation is taking the economy along the path shown by arrow ①. When the curves reach AS_1 and AD_1, the central bank adopts a tight monetary policy, which halts the growth of the money supply, thus stabilizing aggregate demand at AD_1. Due to the output gap and inflation expectations, wages continue to rise, taking the AS curve leftward. The economy moves along arrow ②, with output falling and the price level rising. When aggregate supply reaches AS_2, the inflationary gap is is removed, output is Y^*, and the price level is P_2.

(ii) Phase 2: Expectations and wage momentum lead to stagflation, with falling output and continuing inflation. The economy moves along the path shown by arrow ③. The driving force is now the AS curve, which continues to shift because inflation expectations cause wages to continue rising. The recessionary gap grows as output falls. Inflation continues, but at a diminishing rate. If wages stop rising when output has reached Y_3 and the price level has reached P_3, the stagflation phase is over, with equilibrium at E_3.

(iii) Phase 3: After expectations are reversed, recovery takes output to Y^* and the price level is stabilized. There are two possible scenarios for recovery. In the first, the recessionary gap causes wages to fall (slowly), taking the AS curve back to AS_2 (slowly), as shown by arrow ④. The economy retraces the path originally followed in part (ii) back to E_2. In the second scenario, the central bank increases the money supply sufficiently to shift the AD curve to AD_2. The economy then moves along the path shown by arrow ⑤. This restores output to potential at the cost of further temporary inflation that takes the price level to P_4. Potential output and a stable price level are now achieved.

The importance of expectations explains why the Bank of Canada and other central banks emphasize their precise objectives in their many public speeches. In 1990–1991, the Bank's governor, John Crow, gave many speeches in an effort to convince the public that the Bank would stick to its newly adopted inflation target. This communications strategy was an attempt to reduce inflationary expectations and thus slow the upward shift of Canada's AS curve. And today, the governor of the Bank of Canada regularly speaks publicly about the Bank's 2 percent inflation target and about the importance of achieving it. Such public communications help to "anchor" inflation expectations at the 2 percent target.

Phase 3: Recovery The final phase is the return to potential output. When the economy comes to rest at the end of the stagflation, the situation is exactly the same as when the economy is hit by a negative supply shock. The move back to potential output can be accomplished in either of two ways. First, the recessionary gap may reduce factor prices, thereby shifting the *AS* curve downward, reducing prices but increasing real GDP. Second, an expansionary monetary policy can shift the *AD* curve upward, increasing both prices and real GDP. These two possibilities are illustrated in part (iii) of Figure 30-6.

Many economists worry about relying on the *AS* curve to shift downward to return the economy to potential output. Their concern is that it will take too long for wages to fall sufficiently to shift the *AS* curve—though output will eventually return to potential, the long adjustment period will be characterized by high unemployment.

Other economists worry about a temporary monetary expansion because they fear that expectations of inflation may be rekindled when the Bank's monetary expansion shifts the *AD* curve to the right. And if inflationary expectations *are* revived, the Bank will then be faced with a tough decision—either it must let another recession develop to break these new inflation expectations or it must validate the inflation to reduce unemployment. In the latter case, the Bank is back where it started, with validated inflation on its hands—and diminished credibility.

The Cost of Disinflation

As the foregoing discussion suggests, disinflation is a classic example of a policy that brings short-term pain for long-term gain. The long-term gain is the reduced costs to individuals and firms associated with the lower rate of inflation; the short-term pain is the temporary loss in economic activity and rise in unemployment that occurs during the process of disinflation.

> The cost of disinflation is the loss of output that is generated in the process.

As we said earlier, the size and duration of the recession depends to a large extent on how quickly inflation expectations are revised downward as the disinflation continues. If expectations are mainly backward-looking and thus slow to adjust to the changes in policy, the recession will be deep and protracted. Conversely, if expectations are mainly forward-looking and thus quick to adjust to changes in policy, the recession may be mild and of short duration.

But *how costly* is the process of disinflation? Economists have derived a simple measure of the cost of disinflation based on the depth and length of the recession and on the amount of disinflation. This measure is called the **sacrifice ratio** and is defined as the cumulative loss of real GDP caused by a given disinflation (expressed as a percentage of potential GDP) divided by the number of percentage points by which inflation has fallen. For example, the 1990–1992 disinflation in Canada reduced inflation by roughly 4 percentage points. Suppose the cumulative loss of real GDP caused by that disinflation was equal to $80 billion and that potential GDP at the time was equal to $800 billion. The cumulative loss of output would then have been 10 percent of potential output. The sacrifice ratio would therefore have been $10/4 = 2.5$. The interpretation of this number is that it "costs" 2.5 percent of real GDP for each percentage point of inflation that is reduced.

The numbers in the previous example are hypothetical, but typical estimates of the sacrifice ratio for many developed countries range between 2 and 4. Figure 30-7

sacrifice ratio The cumulative loss in real GDP, expressed as a percentage of potential output, divided by the percentage-point reduction in the rate of inflation.

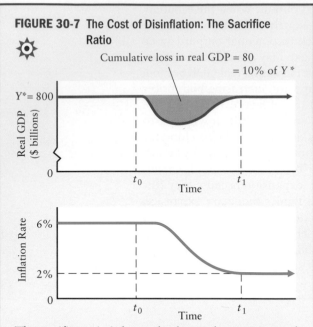

FIGURE 30-7 The Cost of Disinflation: The Sacrifice Ratio

The sacrifice ratio is larger the deeper the recession and the longer it takes real GDP to return to potential. In this example, the economy begins with $Y = Y^*$ and inflation of 6 percent. At t_0, a tightening of monetary policy initiates a disinflation. A recessionary gap opens up and inflation falls only slowly. By t_1, real GDP has returned to Y^* and inflation has been reduced by four percentage points. In this figure, the cumulative loss of real GDP is 10 percent of Y^* and inflation has fallen by four percentage points. The sacrifice ratio is therefore $10/4 = 2.5$, indicating that it costs 2.5 percent of GDP to reduce inflation by one percentage point.

illustrates the time paths of real GDP and inflation following a disinflation and shows how to compute the sacrifice ratio. Note an important assumption that is implicit whenever measuring the sacrifice ratio in this way: that all changes in the path of real GDP are *caused by* the disinflation.

Conclusion

Throughout the history of economics, inflation has been recognized as a harmful phenomenon. The high inflation rates that Canada experienced in the 1970s and early 1980s (see Figure 30-1 on page 750) were also experienced in many developed countries. In the past 40 years these countries have learned much about the causes of inflation, the policies required to reduce it, and the costs associated with doing so.

In particular, Canada and several other countries have adopted formal inflation-targeting regimes, which have been successful at keeping inflation low and stable. An important aspect of inflation targeting is to keep the *expectations* of inflation low. As we have seen in this chapter, keeping inflation expectations low is crucial to keeping actual inflation low.

In recent years, some commentators have argued that the dangers of inflation have been eliminated, that inflation is now "dead." Central to these arguments is the view that greater international competition through the process of globalization will keep inflationary pressures at bay. Yet, whatever forces globalization might bring, it remains true that *sustained* inflation is ultimately caused by monetary policy. Unless central banks remain committed to keeping inflation low and stable, damaging inflation could return as a potential threat to the economy.

SUMMARY

30.1 Adding Inflation to the Model   LO 1, 2

- Sustained price inflation will be accompanied by closely related growth in wages and other factor prices such that the AS curve is shifting upward. Factors that influence wages can be divided into two main components: output gaps and expectations.
- Inflationary output gaps tend to cause wages to rise; recessionary output gaps tend to cause wages to fall, but only slowly.
- Expectations of inflation tend to cause wage increases equal to the expected price-level increases. Expectations

can be backward-looking, forward-looking, or some combination of the two.
- With a constant rate of inflation and no supply shocks, expected inflation will eventually come to equal actual inflation. This implies that there is no output-gap effect on inflation.
- With real GDP equal to Y^*, a constant inflation can occur with the AD and AS curves shifting upward at the same rate.

30.2 Shocks and Policy Responses

- The initial effects of a single positive demand shock are a rise in the price level and a rise in real GDP. If the shock is unvalidated, output tends to return to its potential level while the price level rises further (as the *AS* curve shifts upward). Monetary validation allows demand inflation to proceed without reducing the inflationary gap (*AD* curve continues to shift upward).
- The initial effects of a single negative supply shock are a rise in the price level and a fall in real GDP. If inflation is unvalidated, output will slowly move back to its potential level as the price level slowly falls to its

pre-shock level (*AS* curve slowly shifts down). Monetary validation allows supply inflation to continue in spite of a persistent recessionary gap (*AD* curve shifts up with monetary validation).
- If the Bank of Canada tries to keep real GDP constant at some level above Y^*, the actual inflation rate will eventually accelerate.
- Aggregate demand and supply shocks have temporary effects on inflation. But sustained inflation is caused by sustained monetary expansion.

30.3 Reducing Inflation

- The process of ending a sustained inflation can be divided into three phases.
  1. Phase 1 consists of ending monetary validation and allowing the upward shift in the *AS* curve to remove any inflationary gap that does exist.
  2. In Phase 2, a recessionary gap develops as expectations of further inflation cause the *AS* curve to continue to shift upward even after the inflationary gap is removed.

  3. In Phase 3, the economy returns to potential output, sometimes aided by a one-time monetary expansion that raises the *AD* curve to the level consistent with potential output.
- The cost of disinflation is the recession (output loss) that is created in the process. The sacrifice ratio is a measure of this cost and is calculated as the cumulative loss in real GDP (expressed as a percentage of Y^*) divided by the reduction in inflation.

KEY CONCEPTS

Temporary and sustained inflation
The NAIRU
Forward-looking and backward-looking expectations

Expectational, output-gap, and supply-shock pressures on inflation
Monetary validation of demand and supply shocks

Expectations-augmented Phillips curve
Accelerating inflation
Disinflation
Sacrifice ratio

STUDY EXERCISES

1. Fill in the blanks to make the following statements correct.
   a. The term NAIRU stands for the _____.
   b. Unemployment is said to be equal to the NAIRU when GDP is equal to _____.

   c. Changes in nominal wages result from two effects: the _____ effect and the _____ effect. Both of these effects cause the _____ curve to shift.
   d. The *AS* curve shifts up when nominal wages _____ and also shifts up with a negative _____ shock.

e. Actual inflation can come from any of its three component parts. They are _____, _____, and _____.

f. If the rate of inflation is constant at 6 percent and actual GDP equals potential GDP, then we can say that the central bank is _____ inflation expectations. That is, the central bank is permitting a(n) _____ in the money supply such that the expected and actual inflation rates are equal at _____ percent.

2. Fill in the blanks to make the following statements correct.

a. Suppose the economy is initially at potential GDP (Y^*) and then there is a sudden increase in the demand for Canadian exports. The AD curve shifts to the _____ and opens a(n) _____ gap.

b. With an inflationary gap, the economy is operating where GDP is above _____. In an effort to maintain the output gap, the Bank of Canada may choose to validate the inflation by _____ the interest rate and allowing the money supply to _____. The actual inflation rate will _____.

c. The alternative policy response to an inflationary gap is to not validate the inflation. The _____ curve stops shifting upward. The _____ curve shifts upward due to rising wages caused by _____. Real GDP eventually returns to _____ at a higher _____.

d. Sustained inflation can be said to be a(n) _____ phenomenon.

e. Reducing a sustained inflation requires that monetary _____ be stopped. Inflation will persist, however, until _____ of continued inflation are revised downward.

f. The cost of disinflation is the cost of the _____ that is generated in the process.

3. The table below shows several macroeconomic situations, each with a given amount of excess demand (or supply) for labour and a level of inflation expectations. Both are expressed in percentage per year. For example, in Case A excess demand for labour is pushing wages up by 4 percent per year, and expected inflation is pushing wages up by 3 percent per year.

Case	Excess Demand	Inflation Expectations	Total Wage Change	AS Shift
A	+4	+3	___	___
B	+4	0	___	___
C	0	+3	___	___
D	−3	0	___	___
E	−3	+4	___	___

a. For each case, identify whether there is an inflationary or a recessionary output gap.

b. For each case, what is the total effect on nominal wages? Fill in the third column.

c. For each case, in which direction is the AS curve shifting (up or down)? Fill in the last column.

4. This exercise requires you to compute inflationary expectations based on a simple formula, and it will help you to understand why backward-looking expectations adjust slowly to changes in economic events. Suppose that the *actual* inflation rate in year t is denoted Π_t. *Expected* inflation for year $t + 1$ is denoted Π_{t+1}^e. Now, suppose that workers and firms form their expectations according to

$$\Pi_{t+1}^e = \theta \Pi^T + (1 - \theta)\Pi_t \quad \text{(with } 0 < \theta < 1)$$

where Π^T is the central bank's announced *inflation target*. This simple equation says that people's expectations for inflation at $t + 1$ are a weighted average of last year's actual inflation rate and the central bank's currently announced target. We will use this equation to see how the size of θ determines the extent to which expectations are backward-looking. Consider the table below, which shows the data for a reduction in actual inflation from 10 percent to 2 percent.

Year (t)	Π^T	Π_t	$\theta = 0.1$ Π_{t+1}^e	$\theta = 0.9$ Π_{t+1}^e
1	2	10	___	___
2	2	9	___	___
3	2	6	___	___
4	2	3	___	___
5	2	2	___	___
6	2	2	___	___
7	2	2	___	___
8	2	2	___	___

a. Assume that θ is equal to 0.1. Compute expected inflation for each year and fill in the table.

b. On a scale diagram, plot the time path of actual inflation, expected inflation, and the inflation target.

c. Now assume that θ equals 0.9. Repeat parts (a) and (b).

d. Which value of θ corresponds to more backward-looking expectations? Explain.

e. Given the different speed of adjustment of inflationary expectations, predict which disinflation is more costly in terms of lost output—the one with $\theta = 0.1$ or with $\theta = 0.9$. Explain.

5. In the *AD/AS* diagram here, the economy is in long-run equilibrium with real GDP equal to Y^*; the price level is stable at P_0.

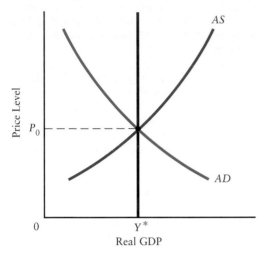

a. Suppose the central bank announces that it will implement an expansionary monetary policy that will shift the *AD* curve up by 5 percent. Show the likely effect of this announcement on the *AS* curve.

b. Does the shift of the *AS* curve in part (a) depend on whether workers and firms believe the central bank's announcement? Explain.

c. In a new *AD/AS* diagram, show how a sustained and constant inflation of 5 percent is represented (with $Y = Y^*$).

d. In the absence of any supply shocks, explain why a constant inflation is only possible when real GDP is equal to Y^*.

6. Consider the following *AD/AS* diagram. Suppose the economy experiences a positive aggregate demand shock—say, an increase in the demand for Canada's exports. This increases real GDP to Y_1.

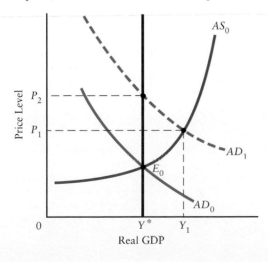

a. Explain what happens if the Bank of Canada does not react to the shock. Show this in the diagram.

b. Now suppose the Bank decides to maintain real GDP at Y_1—that is, it decides to validate the shock. Explain how this is possible, and show it in a diagram.

c. What is the effect on inflation from the policy in part (b)? Is inflation constant or is it rising? Explain.

7. What sources of inflation are suggested by each of the following quotations?

a. A newspaper editorial in Manchester, England: "If American unions were as strong as those in Britain, America's inflationary experience would have been as disastrous as Britain's."

b. An article in *The Economist*: "Oil price collapse will reduce inflation."

c. A Canadian newspaper article in June 2012: "Tensions in Iran fuel an oil-driven inflation."

d. A newspaper headline in October 2008: "Bank's fast growth of money will spur inflation."

e. A newspaper headline in July 2012: "Bumper crops across the West will dampen consumer inflation."

8. Consider the following *AD/AS* diagram. Suppose the economy experiences a negative aggregate supply shock—say, an increase in wages driven by a major union settlement. This reduces real GDP to Y_1.

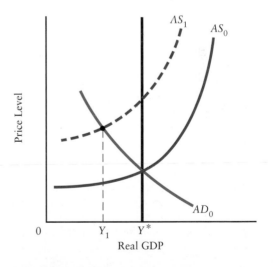

a. Explain what happens if the Bank of Canada does not react to the shock. Show this in the diagram.

b. Now suppose the Bank decides to offset the shock's effect on real GDP—that is, it validates the shock. Explain how this is possible, and show it in a diagram.

c. What danger do many economists see in validating such supply shocks? What is the alternative?

9. The table that follows shows some data on various dis-inflations. In each case, assume that potential GDP is equal to $900 billion.

Case	Inflation Reduction (percentage points)	Cumulative GDP Loss ($ billion)	Sacrifice Ratio
A	5	100	___
B	2	30	___
C	6	60	___
D	8	80	___

a. In each case, compute the sacrifice ratio.
b. Explain why the sacrifice ratio can be expected to be smaller when expectations are more forward-looking.
c. Explain why the sacrifice ratio can be expected to be smaller when central-bank announcements are more credible.

10. What is the relationship between the sacrifice ratio and the central bank's credibility?
a. Explain why a more credible policy of disinflation reduces the costs of disinflation.
b. Explain how you think the Bank of Canada might be able to make its disinflation policy more credible.
c. Can the Bank's policy responses to negative supply shocks influence the credibility it is likely to have when trying to end a sustained inflation? Explain.

11. In the summer of 2006, a time when U.S. inflation was rising and output was above potential, a story in *The Globe and Mail* reported that the release of strong employment-growth data for the United States led to a plunge in prices on the U.S. stock market.
a. Explain why high employment growth would lead people to expect the U.S. central bank to tighten its monetary policy.
b. Explain why higher U.S. interest rates would lead to lower prices of U.S. stocks.
c. How would you expect this announcement to affect Canada?

Unemployment Fluctuations and the NAIRU

WHEN the level of economic activity changes, so do the levels of employment and unemployment. When real GDP increases in the short run, employment usually rises and unemployment usually falls. Conversely, when real GDP falls in the short run, employment falls and unemployment rises. Figure 31-1 shows the course of the unemployment rate in Canada over the past few decades. Recall from Chapter 19 that the unemployment rate is the percentage of the labour force that is not working but actively searching for a job. It is clear that the unemployment rate has followed a cyclical path, rising during the recessions of 1981–1982, 1991–1992, and 2009, and falling during the expansions of the late 1980s, late 1990s and mid-2000s. In this chapter we examine theories designed to explain these short-run fluctuations.

In addition to examining short-run fluctuations in the unemployment rate, economists also study the concept of the NAIRU—the rate of unemployment that exists when real GDP is equal to potential output, Y^*. At points A, B, C, and D in Figure 31-1, real GDP was approximately equal to potential output, and thus the unemployment rates then were approximately equal to the NAIRU. We will see in this chapter several reasons why the NAIRU might change over time and thus offer some explanations for the gradual decline in the NAIRU apparent in the figure, from about 8 percent in 1977 (point A) to approximately 6 percent in 2007 (point D).

We begin by examining some basic facts about employment and unemployment.

31.1 Employment and Unemployment

Look back at Figure 19-3 on page 481, which shows the path of employment and the labour force in Canada since 1960. The most striking feature of part (i) of the figure is that both employment and the labour force have tripled over the past half-century, with only relatively minor fluctuations. Also notice in part (ii) of Figure 19-3, and again in Figure 31-1, that the unemployment rate displays considerable short-run fluctuations but no significant long-term trend. These two characteristics of the labour force—long-term growth in employment but short-term fluctuations in the unemployment rate—are common to most developed countries.

> Over the span of many years, increases in the labour force are more or less matched by increases in employment. Over the short term, however, the unemployment rate fluctuates considerably because changes in the labour force are not exactly matched by changes in employment.

Changes in Employment

The amount of employment in Canada has increased dramatically over the past few decades. In 1959, there were approximately 5 million employed Canadians. By 2012, total employment was 17.5 million. The actual amount of employment, of course, is determined both by the demand for labour and by the supply of labour. How have the two "sides" of the Canadian labour market been changing?

On the supply side, the labour force has grown virtually every year since the end of the Second World War. The causes have included a rising population, which boosts entry into the labour force of people born 15 to 25 years previously; increased labour

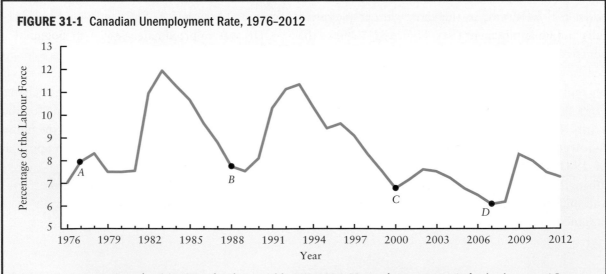

FIGURE 31-1 Canadian Unemployment Rate, 1976–2012

(*Source:* Statistics Canada, CANSIM database, Table 282-0087. Unemployment rate is for both sexes, 15 years and over, seasonally adjusted.)

force participation by various groups, especially women; and net immigration of working-age persons.

On the demand side, many existing jobs are eliminated every year, and many new jobs are created. The technological improvements that drive economic growth often cause great disruptions in an economy. Some sectors of the economy decline while others expand. Jobs are lost in the sectors that are contracting and created in sectors that are expanding. Furthermore, even in relatively stable industries, many firms disappear and many new ones are set up. The net increase in employment is the difference between all the jobs that are created and all those that are lost.

> In most years, enough new jobs are created both to offset the number of jobs that have been eliminated and also to provide jobs for the growing labour force. The result is a net increase in employment in most years.

In 2012, Canadian employment was just over 17.5 million workers. In a typical year employment increases by about 230 000 workers, an annual growth rate of roughly 1.3 percent.

Changes in Unemployment

In the early 1980s, worldwide unemployment rose to high levels. The unemployment rate remained high in many advanced industrial countries and only began to fall, and even then very slowly, during the latter half of the decade. Canadian experience reflected these international developments rather closely. From a high of more than 12 percent in 1983, the Canadian unemployment rate fell to 7.5 percent in 1988, a point that many economists at the time thought was close to the Canadian NAIRU (see point *B* in Figure 31-1).

With the onset of another recession in the early 1990s, the unemployment rate then rose through 1990 and 1991, reaching 11.3 percent by 1992. During the next few years, the unemployment rate fell only slowly as the Canadian recovery was weak; by early 1994 the unemployment rate was still more than 10 percent. But the speed of the Canadian recovery quickened and unemployment began to drop. By early 2000, after five years of steady economic recovery, the unemployment rate was 6.8 percent.

Following the large stock-market decline in late 2000, together with the decline in confidence associated with the 2001 terrorist attacks in New York and Washington, the Canadian and U.S. economies slowed, and unemployment increased. Recovery was rapid, however, and by the summer of 2007 Canadian real GDP was at or above its potential, and the unemployment rate had fallen to just below 6 percent, the lowest it had been in more than 30 years.

With the onset of the 2008 global financial crisis, and the worldwide recession that immediately followed, unemployment increased again. The Canadian economy fared much better than others, however, and unemployment increased only to 8.7 percent at the depth of the recession in mid-2009 (whereas it was considerably higher in the United States and most of Europe). After three years of modest economic recovery, the Canadian unemployment rate was just above 7 percent by early in 2013.

> During periods of rapid economic growth, the unemployment rate usually falls. During recessions or periods of slow growth, the unemployment rate usually rises.

Flows in the Labour Market

As we have just observed, many existing jobs are eliminated every year as existing firms adopt new technologies that require different types of workers, some industries shrink, and some firms disappear altogether. Similarly, new jobs are continually being created, as other industries expand and new firms are born. The public's and the media's focus on the labour market, however, tends to be on the overall level of employment and unemployment rather than on the amount of *job creation* and *job destruction*. This focus can often lead us to the conclusion that few changes are occurring in the labour market when in fact the truth is quite the opposite.

For data on current employment and unemployment in Canada, see Statistics Canada's website: www.statcan.gc.ca. Search for "unemployment rate" and follow the suggested links.

For example, the Canadian unemployment rate was roughly constant at 7.3 percent from 2011 to 2012. Does this mean no jobs were created during the year? Or that the Canadian labour market was stagnant during this period? No. In fact, workers were finding jobs at the rate of roughly 400 000 *per month*. At the same time, however, other workers were leaving jobs or entering the labour force at roughly the same rate. These large flows *out of unemployment* were being approximately matched by the large flows *into unemployment*. The net result was that total unemployment changed only slightly.

> The amount of activity in the labour market is better reflected by the flows into and out of unemployment than by the overall unemployment rate.

By looking at the *gross flows* in the labour market, we are able to see economic activity that is hidden when we look just at changes in the overall amount of employment and unemployment (which is determined by *net* flows). Indeed, the gross flows are typically so large that they dwarf the net flows. See *Applying Economic Concepts 31-1* for more discussion of the gross flows in the Canadian labour market, and how these gross-flows data can be used to compute the average length of unemployment spells.

Measurement Problems

The official labour-market data produced and reported by Statistics Canada understate the full effects of recessions on unemployment. The unemployment data refer to those individuals who are not currently working and who are actively searching for a job. As a recession continues, many workers who have been unable to find a job become discouraged and give up the search. Statistically, these *discouraged workers* are no longer included in the labour force; they are therefore not classified as unemployed, even though they would still accept a job if one were offered. In addition, this pool of discouraged workers becomes larger as the recession continues, which means that the official data become a larger understatement of the amount of "true" unemployment.

A second problem with the official measure of unemployment is that it fails to take account of situations where an individual is *underemployed*. Many workers who have lost their job and are still searching for a suitable replacement may temporarily take a part-time job or a job that requires much lower qualifications than their previous one. These workers prefer a part-time or low-paying job to the alternative of being totally unemployed, and they are appropriately represented in the data as being employed. It is also true, however, that they usually continue to search for a job that is more suited to their experience and qualifications.[1]

Care must therefore be taken when assessing the state of the labour market from the official unemployment data. A fall in the unemployment rate is sometimes caused by discouraged workers giving up the search and leaving the labour force. And just because individuals are recorded as being employed does not mean that they are not still searching for jobs that better match their skills and experience.

Consequences of Unemployment

To most people, unemployment is seen as a social "bad," just as output is seen as a social "good." But this does not mean *all* unemployment is bad, just as we know that not all output—such as noise or air pollution—is good. Indeed, we will see later in this chapter that some unemployment is socially desirable as it reflects the necessary time spent searching to make appropriate matches between firms who are seeking new employees and workers who are seeking new jobs.

We examine two costs of unemployment. The first is the associated loss in output. The second is the harm done to the individuals who are unemployed.

Lost Output Every person counted as unemployed is willing and able to work and is seeking a job but has yet to find one. Hence, unemployed individuals are valuable resources who are currently not producing output. The output that is not produced, but potentially could be, is a loss for society. Once an unemployed person regains employment, however, output rises again and this loss no longer occurs. But nothing makes up for the *past* loss that existed while the person was unemployed. In other words, the loss of output that accompanies unemployment is lost forever. In a world of scarcity with many unsatisfied desires, this loss represents a serious waste of resources.

Personal Costs For the typical Canadian worker, being unemployed for long periods of time is unusual. Most spells of unemployment are short. In 2008, *before* the onset of a major recession, the OECD estimated that only 7.1 percent of Canadian unemployment spells lasted 12 months or longer; this number increased to 12 percent by 2010. In other words, the vast majority of unemployed workers find new jobs in just a few months. Moreover, many workers experiencing temporary unemployment have access to the employment insurance program that provides some income during their spell of unemployment.

This does not mean, however, there are no problems associated with unemployment, especially for those relatively few workers who are unemployed for long periods of time. The effects of long-term unemployment, in terms of the disillusioned who have given up trying to make it within the system and who contribute to social unrest, is a serious social problem. The loss of self-esteem and the dislocation of families that often result from situations of prolonged unemployment are genuine tragedies.

---

[1] The problem of under-employment in Canada is particularly acute among some groups of immigrants, whose foreign credentials for specific, technical occupations are not fully recognized in Canada. This problem is getting increased attention among Canadian policymakers.

APPLYING ECONOMIC CONCEPTS 31-1

Stocks and Flows in the Canadian Labour Market

In most reports about changes in unemployment, both in Canada and abroad, emphasis is typically on the changes in the *stock* of unemployment—that is, on the number of people who are unemployed at a particular point in time. But as we said in the text, the focus on the stock of unemployment can often hide much activity in the labour market, activity that is revealed by looking at *gross flows*.

What Are Labour-Market Flows?

The first figure in this box shows the difference between stocks and flows in the labour market. The blue circles represent the number of individuals at the end of each month (the *stocks*) in each possible "state"—employment (*E*), unemployment (*U*), and *not* in the labour force (*N*). The six red arrows represent the monthly *flows* of individuals among the various states. For example, arrow ① shows the monthly flow of individuals from *E* to *U*. These individuals begin the month in *E*(employed), leave their jobs sometime during the month, and end the month as unemployed individuals, in *U*. Arrow ③ shows the flow from *N* to *U*—these individuals are new entrants to the labour force during the month and begin their labour-force experience as unemployed individuals.

In the second figure, three series of data are shown for Canada from 1976 to 2003—a period that includes the

major recessions of 1981 and 1991. (Unfortunately, Statistics Canada has stopped publishing these data, so more recent data are not available.) The top line is the stock of unemployment—the actual *number* of people unemployed at a specific point in time. During the severe recession of the early 1980s, unemployment peaked at approximately 1.7 million people and then fell during the recovery until 1989. With the onset of the next recession in 1990–1991, unemployment rose again, reaching nearly 1.8 million in 1992.

The two lower lines show *gross flows* in the labour market. (These flows data are not available for 1997 and 1998, which explains the break in the lines at that point.) The orange line shows the monthly flow into unemployment, corresponding to the sum of the flows in arrows ① and ③ in the first figure. This flow into unemployment represents

- workers losing jobs through layoffs or plant closure
- workers quitting jobs to search for different jobs
- new entrants to the labour force searching for jobs

The monthly flow into unemployment varies between approximately 300 000 and 500 000 individuals *per month*.

The green line shows the monthly flow out of unemployment, corresponding to the sum of the flows in arrows ② and ④ in the first figure. This outflow represents

- unemployed individuals finding new jobs
- unemployed individuals becoming discouraged and leaving the labour force

The monthly flow out of unemployment is roughly the same size as the monthly inflow, 300 000 to 500 000 individuals per month.

What is the connection between the flows and the stocks in the labour market? Whenever the flows into unemployment exceed the flows out of unemployment, the stock of unemployment rises. Conversely, whenever the flows out of unemployment exceed the flows into unemployment, the stock of unemployment falls.

Using Flows Data

For two reasons data on flows can be very useful when thinking about the labour market. First, they show the tremendous amount of activity in the labour market even

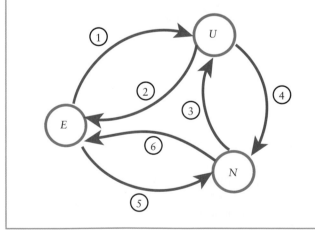

In the United States, as in Canada, the amount of long-term unemployment has historically not been large. For example, in the depths of the recessions of 1982 and 1991, the fraction of total unemployed workers who were unemployed for six months or more was just under 25 percent. In the most recent recession of 2009–2010, however,

though the stock of unemployment may not be changing significantly. For example, between 1991 and 1992 the stock of unemployment in Canada varied between 1.4 million and 1.6 million persons. But during that two-year period, roughly 400 000 persons *per month* either became unemployed or ceased being unemployed. This number reflects the massive amount of regular turnover that exists in the Canadian labour market—turnover that is the essence of what economists call *frictional unemployment*.

The second reason flows data are useful is that the relationship between the flows and the stock can tell us something about the amount of time the average unemployed person spends unemployed. If U_s is the stock of unemployment, and U_o is the monthly outflow from unemployment, then one simple estimate of the average length of an unemployment spell is

$$\text{Average duration of unemployment spell} = \frac{U_s}{U_o}$$

Consider the situation in 1999, at the peak of the business cycle (a low point for unemployment). At that time, the stock of unemployment was approximately 1 million people and the outflow from unemployment was approximately 400 000 persons per month. Thus, the average unemployed person in 1999 could expect to leave unemployment in about 2.5 months (1000 000 people/400 000 people per month = 2.5 months). In contrast, in 1992, at the depth of the previous recession (and thus a high point for unemployment), the expected duration of an unemployment spell was 3.6 months (1600000/450000 = 3.6).

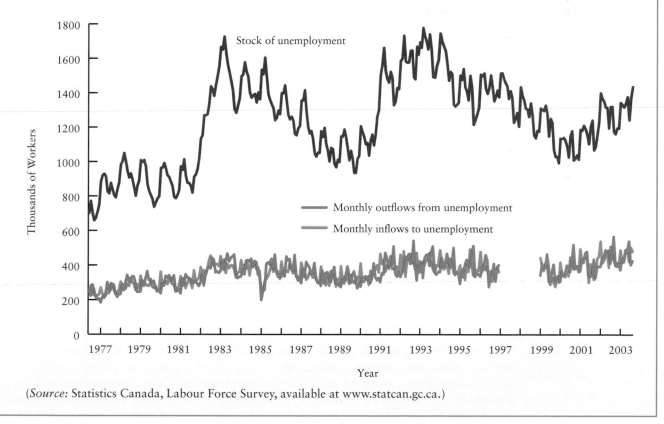

(*Source:* Statistics Canada, Labour Force Survey, available at www.statcan.gc.ca.)

long-term unemployment in the United States became a more serious problem. Even by mid-2012, more than two years into a modest economic recovery, 45 percent of all unemployed U.S. workers had been out of work for over six months. As we will describe later in this chapter, extensive long-term unemployment can be an important force behind increases in the economy's NAIRU. The general case for concern about high unemployment has been eloquently put by Princeton economist Alan Blinder:

> *A high-pressure economy provides opportunities, facilitates structural change, encourages inventiveness and innovation, and opens doors for society's under-dogs. . . . All these promote the social cohesion and economic progress that make democratic mixed capitalism such a wonderful system when it works well. A low-pressure economy slams the doors shut, breeds a bunker mentality that resists change, stifles productivity growth, and fosters both inequality and mean-spirited public policy. All this makes reducing high unemployment a political, economic, and moral challenge of the highest order.*[2]

31.2 Unemployment Fluctuations

It is clear from Figure 31-1 on page 776 that the unemployment rate fluctuates considerably over relatively short periods of time. Over the years, economists have debated the sources of these fluctuations, and many different theories have been developed to try to explain them. One set of theories emphasizes the distinction between the unemployment that exists when real GDP is equal to Y^*, and unemployment that is due to deviations of real GDP from Y^*. The former, as we saw in Chapter 19, is called the NAIRU, and is made up of frictional and structural unemployment. The latter is often called **cyclical unemployment**, which falls (or rises) as real GDP rises above (or falls below) Y^*. As we will soon see, this first set of theories suggests that cyclical unemployment exists because real wages do not quickly adjust to clear labour markets in response to shocks of various kinds. We refer to these as "non-market-clearing" theories of the labour market.

The second set of theories contains a very different view of labour markets. In these theories, real wages adjust instantly to clear the labour market after any AD or AS shock occurs, and as a result real GDP is always equal to Y^*. (As we saw in Chapter 24, if the economy's adjustment process works quickly, real GDP returns to Y^* very soon after any AD or AS shock.) In this perspective, the unemployment rate still fluctuates, but only due to changes in frictional or structural unemployment. In these "market-clearing" theories, there is no cyclical unemployment whatsoever.

cyclical unemployment
Unemployment not due to frictional or structural factors; it is due to deviations of GDP from Y^*.

Market-Clearing Theories

Two major characteristics of modern market-clearing theories of the labour market are that firms and workers continuously optimize and markets continuously clear. In such models, there can be no *involuntary* unemployment. These theories then seek to explain unemployment as the outcome of voluntary decisions made by individuals who are choosing to do what they do, including spending some time out of employment.

Market-clearing theories explain fluctuations in employment and real wages as having one of two causes. First, as shown in part (i) of Figure 31-2, changes in technology that affect the *marginal product* of labour will lead to changes in the demand for labour. If these technological shocks are sometimes positive and sometimes negative,

---

[2] Blinder, A.S., "The challenge of high unemployment," *American Economic Review*, 1988.

they will lead to fluctuations in the level of employment and real wages. Second, as shown in part (ii) of Figure 31-2, changes in the willingness of individuals to work will lead to changes in the supply of labour and thus to fluctuations in the level of employment and real wages. In both cases, however, note that the flexibility of real wages results in a *clearing* of the labour market. In this setting, whatever unemployment exists cannot be involuntary and must be caused by either frictional or structural causes, the two components of the NAIRU.

> **Market-clearing theories of the labour market assume that real wages always adjust to clear the labour market. People who are not working are assumed to have voluntarily withdrawn from the labour market for one reason or another. There is no involuntary unemployment.**

There are two major problems with this theory of labour markets. First, empirical observation is not consistent with the fluctuations in real wages predicted by the theory. In Canada and other developed economies, employment tends to be quite volatile over the business cycle, whereas real wages tend to be relatively stable—they do *not* show the cyclical variation predicted in Figure 31-2. The second problem is that the market-clearing theories predict no involuntary unemployment whatsoever, a prediction that many economists argue is unsupported by empirical observation. In Canada and other countries, a large fraction of unemployed workers are eligible for and collect

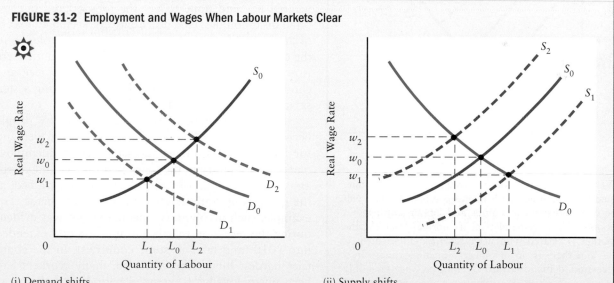

FIGURE 31-2 Employment and Wages When Labour Markets Clear

(i) Demand shifts

(ii) Supply shifts

In a market-clearing theory of the labour market, there is no involuntary unemployment. The figure shows a perfectly competitive market for one type of labour. In part (i), the demand curves D_1, D_0, and D_2 are the demands for this market corresponding to low, medium, and high values for the marginal product of labour. As demand rises from D_1 to D_0 to D_2, real wages rise from w_1 to w_0 to w_2, and employment rises from L_1 to L_0 to L_2. In part (ii), changes in workers' willingness to work causes the supply of labour to fluctuate from S_1 to S_0 to S_2, and wages to fluctuate from w_1 to w_0 to w_2. In both parts, the labour market always clears and there is no involuntary unemployment.

employment insurance. In order to collect the insurance benefits, they are required to state that they are actively searching for a job. For those who are truly engaged in an active job search, it is difficult to describe them as *voluntarily* unemployed. We will say more about the distinction between voluntary and involuntary unemployment later in the chapter.

Non-Market-Clearing Theories

The many economists who reject the market-clearing theories of unemployment fluctuations emphasize that labour markets do not operate in the extreme manner shown in Figure 31-2. Just as the prices of TVs, cars, blue jeans, sushi, and cell phones do not change daily, or even monthly, to equate current demand with current supply, so the wages paid to various types of labour, such as factory workers, schoolteachers, professors, architects, fast-food workers, train engineers, TV commentators, and product designers, do not change frequently to equate current demands with current supplies. These economists use non-market-clearing theories of the labour market in which "wage stickiness" plays a central role in explaining unemployment fluctuations.

When unemployed workers are looking for jobs during a recession, they do not knock on employers' doors and offer to work at lower wages than are being paid to current workers; instead, they answer help-wanted ads and hope to get the jobs offered but are often disappointed. Nor do employers, seeing an excess of applicants for the few jobs that are available, go to the current workers and reduce their wages until there is no one left looking for a job; instead, they pick and choose until they fill their needs and then hang a sign saying "No Help Wanted."

As a result of this wage stickiness, many people become involuntarily unemployed when the demand for labour falls during a recession. Their unemployment is involuntary in the sense that they would accept an offer of work in jobs for which they are trained, at the going wage rate, if such an offer were made. For example, such involuntary unemployment was evident during the recession that began in 2008 and extended into 2010 (and later in some countries). In the countries hardest hit by the recession, many workers had been unemployed for extended periods and their loss of income caused them to lose their homes and other possessions. In the European Union, where youth unemployment approached 50 percent in some countries, it was obvious that labour markets were not clearing to eliminate involuntary unemployment and that many unemployed workers would have gladly accepted work if it had been available. The cyclical behaviour of involuntary unemployment when wages are sticky is illustrated in Figure 31-3.

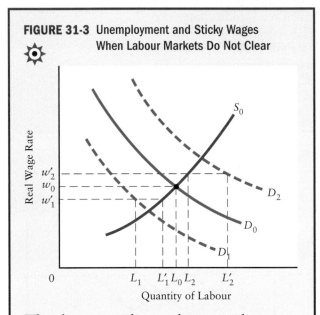

FIGURE 31-3 Unemployment and Sticky Wages When Labour Markets Do Not Clear

When the wage rate does not change enough to equate quantity demanded with quantity supplied, there will be unemployment in slumps and labour shortages in booms. When demand is at its normal level D_0, the market is cleared with wage rate w_0, employment is L_0, and there is no involuntary unemployment. In a recession, demand falls to D_1, but the wage falls only to w_1'. As a result, L_1 of labour is demanded and L_1' is supplied. Employment is determined by the quantity demanded at L_1. The remainder of the supply for which there is no demand, L_1L_1', is involuntarily unemployed. In a boom, demand rises to D_2, but the wage rate rises only to w_2'. As a result, the quantity demanded is L_2', whereas only L_2 is supplied. Employment rises to L_2, which is the amount supplied. The rest of the demand cannot be satisfied, making excess demand for labour of L_2L_2'.

The main challenge for these non-market-clearing theories is to explain *why* wages do not quickly adjust to eliminate involuntary unemployment. This issue has been debated among economists for years, and several plausible reasons have been presented.

Long-Term Employment Relationships The most obvious reason for wage stickiness over the business cycle is that many workers and their employers have long-term relationships in which the wages and conditions of work are determined for extended periods of time, often for one or more years. This situation applies to most groups of workers such as schoolteachers, professors, hospital technicians, office workers, supervisors, middle managers, and skilled construction workers. Such long-term relationships between employers and employees are actually the norm in modern, developed economies. The only kind of worker whose wage *does* fluctuate more or less continually with the conditions of current demand and supply are the relatively few casual daily workers who show up at hiring points each day hoping to be offered a job for that day.

Wage stickiness is obvious from even the most casual observation of the conditions under which most people work. The problem for economists is then to explain why such behaviour occurs. Why are the wages of workers not set for short periods of time that could then fluctuate with changes in demand and supply?

To explore this issue, imagine a worker being faced with a choice between two employment arrangements:

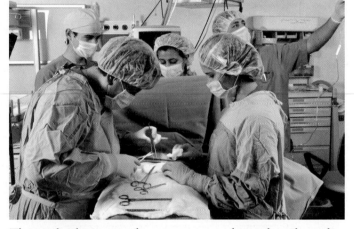

1. A high average wage but one that fluctuates over the business cycle, and the chance of job loss during a recession.

2. A somewhat lower wage that is stable over the business cycle, and a reduced chance of job loss during a recession.

Most workers would prefer the second employment arrangement. Most employees value the relative employment (and thus income) security offered by the second arrangement because it allows the individual to make long-term financial

The quick adjustment of wages to excess demands and supplies is not a characteristic of labour markets in which employees and firms have long-term relationships, such as in the health-care sector.

plans. The ability to use a mortgage to purchase a home or consumer debt to buy big-ticket items such as cars, furniture, and appliances is more manageable with a relatively secure job and income. The lower wage in the second employment arrangement can be seen as the price the worker pays for greater employment and income security.

Why do employers also prefer such long-term employment arrangements? Employers want to retain workers who have the knowledge required for a particular job—knowledge of the firm's organization, production techniques, operating procedures, and marketing plans. If all workers were identical, an employer would not mind laying off one individual from a particular job during a recession and then hiring a different worker for that job when demand recovers. But, of course, workers are not all the same, even in fairly routine jobs and even among workers having the same formal qualifications. What the worker learns through on-the-job experience is valuable to the firm and makes each individual a unique asset. If a firm laid off one worker and then later hired another worker for the same job, it would lose all the knowledge that the first worker had acquired on the job and would lose efficiency until the new worker acquired similar experience. In today's knowledge-intensive world, this loss can be quite substantial and typically applies for a wide range of workers.

For these and other similar reasons, wages tend to be insensitive to fluctuations in current economic conditions. Wages are often, in effect, regular payments to workers over an extended employment relationship rather than a device for fine-tuning the current supplies of and demands for labour. Employers tend to "smooth" the income of employees by paying a steady wage and letting profits and employment fluctuate to absorb the effects of temporary changes in demand. It is these fluctuations in employment over the business cycle that cause the fluctuations in involuntary unemployment.

A number of labour-market institutions sustain such long-term relationships between employees and employers. For example, many long-term labour contracts provide for a schedule of wages over a period of several years. Similarly, employee benefits, such as pensions and supplementary health insurance, tend to bind workers to particular employers. Salaries or pension benefits that rise with years of service also help to bind the employee to the company, whereas seniority rules for layoffs bind the employer to the long-term worker.

> **Long-term relationships between firms and workers are important in most labour markets, and wages in such labour markets do not adjust frequently to eliminate involuntary unemployment.**

Economic Climate Versus Economic Weather Two additional observations are important to this discussion. First, despite the fact that wages are *generally* insensitive to short-run changes in labour demand and labour supply, there are exceptional circumstances. For example, wages sometimes fall during a severe recession. Occasionally, management calls the workers together and offers them a stark choice between the firm going out of business or the workers accepting a cut in their wages. The result is some cyclical variation in wages, especially when a recession is deep and long lasting. But the headlines generated by such occurrences speak to their relative infrequency.

The second observation relates to longer-run considerations. As we discussed in Chapter 24, wages do tend to respond to persistent situations of excess demand or excess supply in the labour market. For example, sustained and large recessionary gaps will tend to reduce the rate of growth of wages and, in extreme situations, may even lead to reductions in overall wage levels. Similarly, sustained inflation gaps will tend to cause wages to grow faster than they otherwise would.

The conclusion is that changes in the conditions of labour demand and labour supply, if sustained, are important for determining variations in real wages. But short-run changes in labour-market conditions may cause little or no change in wages because of the widespread long-term relationships between firms and workers.

> **Variations in real wages tend to be determined by the long-term economic climate rather than by the short-term economic weather.**

We have emphasized the importance of long-term employment relationships as an explanation for wage stickiness and the existence of involuntary unemployment. *Extensions in Theory 31-1* provides some additional explanations.

EXTENSIONS IN THEORY 31-1

Wage Stickiness and Involuntary Unemployment

Economists have developed many labour-market theories in which real wages do not fluctuate continuously to equate labour demand with labour supply. In the text we emphasized the importance of long-term employment relationships. Three additional theories are briefly described here.

Menu Costs

A typical large firm sells dozens of differentiated products and employs many different types of labour. Changing prices and wages in response to every fluctuation in demand is a costly and time-consuming activity. Many firms therefore find it optimal to keep their price lists (*menus*) constant for significant periods of time. Since large firms are often operating in imperfectly competitive markets, they have discretion over the prices of their products. Hence, firms often react to changes in demand by holding prices constant and responding with changes in output and employment.

If firms did alter their prices dramatically over the business cycle, they would be more or less forced to alter wages correspondingly or else suffer losses that could threaten their existence during recessions. As it is, the presence of relatively sticky prices allows firms to keep wages relatively sticky over the cycle for all of the reasons discussed in the text.

Efficiency Wages

Employers may find that they get more output per dollar of wages paid—that is, a more efficient workforce—when they pay labour somewhat more than the minimum amount that would induce people to work for them.

Suppose it is costly for employers to monitor workers' performance on the job so that some workers will be able to shirk duties with a low probability of being caught. Given prevailing labour-market institutions, it is generally impossible for employers to levy fines on employees for shirking on the job since the employees could just leave their jobs rather than pay the fines. So firms may instead choose to pay a wage premium—an *efficiency wage*—to the workers, in excess of the wage that the workers could get elsewhere in the labour market. With such a wage premium, workers will be reluctant to shirk because if they get caught and laid off, they will then lose this high wage.

Such high wages are rational responses of firms to the conditions they face and imply that firms will not alter wages in the face of temporary reductions in demand.

Union Bargaining

In many employment situations, those already working ("insiders") have more say in wage bargaining than those currently not employed ("outsiders"). Employed workers are often represented by a union, which negotiates the wage rate with firms. The union will generally represent the interests of the insiders but will not necessarily reflect the interests of the outsiders. Insiders will naturally want to bid up wages even though to do so will harm the employment prospects of the outsiders. Hence, this theory generates an outcome to the bargaining process between firms and unions in which the wage is set higher than the market-clearing level, just as with efficiency wages.

31.3 What Determines the NAIRU?

When the unemployment rate is equal to the NAIRU, there is only frictional and structural unemployment. Our interest here is in why the NAIRU changes over time and in the extent to which economic policy can affect it.

Frictional Unemployment

As we saw in Chapter 19, **frictional unemployment** results from the normal turnover of labour. One source of frictional unemployment is young people who enter the labour force and look for jobs. Another source is people who leave their jobs. Some may quit because they are dissatisfied with the type of work or their working conditions; others

frictional unemployment
Unemployment that results from the turnover in the labour market as workers move between jobs.

may be fired because of incompetence or laid off because their employers go out of business. Yet others may lose their jobs because the jobs themselves are eliminated by the introduction of new technologies. Whatever the reason, they must search for new jobs, which takes time. People who are unemployed while searching for jobs are said to be frictionally unemployed or in *search unemployment*.

> **The normal turnover of labour causes frictional unemployment to persist, even if the economy is at potential output.**

How "voluntary" is frictional unemployment? Some of it is clearly voluntary. For example, a worker may know of an available job but may not accept it so she can search for a better one, or one for which she is more appropriately trained. Some of it is also involuntary, such as when a worker gets laid off and cannot find *any* job offer for a period of weeks, even though he may be actively searching. *Applying Economic Concepts 31-2* shows that the distinction between voluntary and involuntary unemployment is not always as clear as it might at first seem.

Structural Unemployment

structural unemployment
Unemployment caused by a mismatch in skills, industry, or location between available jobs and unemployed workers.

Structural unemployment is defined as a mismatch between the current structure of the labour force—in terms of skills, occupations, industries, or geographical locations—and the current structure of firms' demand for labour. Since changes in the structure of the demand for labour are occurring continually in any modern economy, and since it takes time for workers to adjust, some amount of structural unemployment always exists.

Natural Causes Changes that accompany economic growth shift the structure of the demand for labour. Demand might rise in such expanding areas as British Columbia's Lower Mainland or northern Alberta and might fall in parts of Ontario and Quebec. Demand rises for workers with certain skills, such as computer programming and electronics engineering, and falls for workers with other skills, such as stenography, assembly line work, and middle management. To meet changing demands, the structure of the labour force must change. Some existing workers can retrain and some new entrants can acquire fresh skills, but the transition is often difficult, especially for older workers whose skills become economically obsolete.

Increases in international competition can also cause structural unemployment. As the geographical distribution of world production changes, so does the composition of production and of labour demand in any one country. Labour adapts to such shifts by changing jobs, skills, and locations, but until the transition is complete, structural unemployment exists.

> **Structural unemployment will increase if there is either an increase in the pace at which the structure of the demand for labour is changing or a decrease in the pace at which labour is adapting to these changes.**

Following the Canada–U.S. Free Trade Agreement in 1989 and the North American Free Trade Agreement (NAFTA) in 1994, there were significant shifts of economic activity within Canada. For example, the textiles industry, much of which was located in

APPLYING ECONOMIC CONCEPTS 31-2

Voluntary Versus Involuntary Unemployment

Frictional unemployment is *involuntary* if the job seeker has not yet found a job for which his or her training and experience are suitable, whether or not such jobs exist somewhere in the economy. Frictional unemployment is *voluntary* if the unemployed person is aware of available jobs for which he or she is suited but is searching for better options. But how should we classify an unemployed person who refuses to accept a job at a lower skill level than the one for which she is qualified? What if she turns down a job for which she is trained because she hopes to get a higher wage offer for a similar job from another employer?

In one sense, people in search unemployment are voluntarily unemployed because they could almost always find *some* job, no matter how poorly paid or inappropriate to their training. In another sense, they are involuntarily unemployed because they have not yet succeeded in finding the job that they believe exists and for which they feel they are suited at a rate of pay that they believe is attainable.

Workers do not have perfect knowledge of all available jobs and rates of pay, and they may be able to gain information only by searching the labour market. Facing this uncertainty, they may find it sensible to refuse a first job offer, for the offer may prove to be a poor one in light of further market information. But too much search—for example, holding off while being supported by others in the hope of finding a job better than a job for which one is really suited—is an economic waste. Thus, search unemployment is a grey area: Some of it is useful and some of it is wasteful.

Some search unemployment is desirable because it gives unemployed people time to find an available job that makes the best use of their skills.

How long it pays for people to remain in search unemployment depends on the economic costs of being unemployed. By lowering the costs of being unemployed, employment insurance tends to increase the incentives for more search unemployment. This may or may not increase economic efficiency, depending on whether or not it induces people to search beyond the point at which they acquire new and valuable information about the labour market.

Quebec, contracted; at the same time there was an expansion of the high-tech industry, much of which was located in the Ottawa Valley. The types of workers released from the textiles industry, however, were not exactly what were required in the expanding high-tech industry. This type of mismatch in skills and locations contributed to structural unemployment during the 1990s.

Structural unemployment also increased during the 2002–2008 period in response to the five-fold increase in the world price of oil. The demand for labour increased sharply in the petroleum-producing regions of Alberta, Saskatchewan, and Newfoundland. At the same time, many jobs were lost in the manufacturing heartland of Ontario and Quebec because the rising price of oil significantly increased firms' costs. Some of the displaced workers could find jobs relatively quickly in expanding firms in other regions or sectors, but for most workers this transition was slow. Structural unemployment was the result.

Policy Causes Government policies can influence the speed with which labour markets adapt to changes. Some countries, including Canada, have adopted policies that *discourage* movement among regions, industries, and occupations. These policies (which may be desirable for other reasons) tend to reduce the rate at which unemployed workers are matched with vacant jobs, and thus tend to raise the amount of structural unemployment.

For two related reasons, the employment-insurance (EI) program contributes to structural unemployment. First, the Canadian EI system ties workers' benefits to the regional unemployment rate in such a way that unemployed workers can collect EI benefits for more weeks in regions where unemployment is high than where it is low.

For information on Canada's Employment Insurance program, see the website for Human Resources and Skills Development Canada:
www.hrsdc.gc.ca.

Increases in the world price of oil between 2002 and 2008 led to a reduction in manufacturing activity in Central Canada and economic expansions in oil-producing regions of the country, such as the Alberta oil sands shown here. Structural unemployment was created until workers could move from Eastern and Central Canada to Alberta.

The EI system therefore encourages unemployed workers to remain in high-unemployment regions rather than encouraging them to move to regions where employment prospects are more favourable. Second, workers are eligible for employment insurance only if they have worked for a given number of weeks in the previous year—this is known as the *entrance requirement*. In some cases, however, these entrance requirements are very low and thus seasonal workers may be encouraged to work for a few months and then collect employment insurance and wait for the next season, rather than finding other jobs during the off season.[3]

Finally, labour-market policies that make it difficult or costly for firms to fire workers also make employers more reluctant to hire workers in the first place. Such policies, which are very common in the European Union, reduce the amount of turnover in the labour market and are believed to be an important contributor to the amount of long-term unemployment in those countries. In Germany, Italy, and Belgium, for example, the labour laws impose very high costs on firms whenever workers are laid off. In those countries, even when their economies are growing moderately, approximately 50 percent of all unemployment spells last for *longer* than 12 months.

The Frictional–Structural Distinction

As with many distinctions, the one between frictional and structural unemployment is not precise. In a sense, structural unemployment is really long-term frictional unemployment. Consider, for example, what would happen if there were an increase in world demand for Canadian-made car parts but at the same time a decline in world demand for Canadian-assembled cars. This change would require labour to move from one sector (the car-assembly sector) to another (the car-parts manufacturing sector). If the reallocation were to occur quickly, we would call the unemployment *frictional*; if the reallocation were to occur slowly, we would call the unemployment *structural*.

In practice, structural and frictional unemployment cannot be separated. But the two of them, taken together, *can* be separated from cyclical unemployment. Specifically, when real GDP is at its potential level, the *only* unemployment (by definition) is the NAIRU, which comprises frictional and structural unemployment. For example, real GDP in Canada was approximately equal to potential GDP in 2007. (See Figure 31-1.) At that time, the unemployment rate was 6 percent, and thus the NAIRU was approximately 6 percent. In contrast, two years later in 2009, in the midst of the most recent recession, the unemployment rate was about 8.5 percent. If the underlying frictions and structural change in the economy were unaltered over those two years, we could conclude that in 2009, 2.5 percentage points of the actual unemployment rate was due to cyclical factors and the rest was due to frictional and structural factors.

---

[3] That the EI system contributes to the amount of structural unemployment is not to deny the significant benefits from the system. First, EI encourages unemployed workers to search for jobs appropriate to their desires and skills. Second, EI provides a financial cushion that reduces the personal suffering which often accompanies periods of unemployment and low income.

Why Does the NAIRU Change?

In general, the NAIRU can rise for two reasons. First, the economy may be subjected to *more* shocks requiring an adjustment of the labour force between sectors or regions. Second, the *ability* of the labour force to adjust to any given shock may decline. In either case, the amount of frictional or structural unemployment will rise, and the NAIRU will therefore increase. We now examine several specific causes of changes in the NAIRU.

Young workers have higher unemployment rates than do older workers. As the share of younger workers in the labour force changes, so will the economy's NAIRU.

Demographic Shifts Because young people usually try several jobs before settling into one for a longer period of time, young workers have more labour-market turnover and therefore higher unemployment rates than older, more experienced workers. The proportion of young workers in the labour force rose significantly as the baby-boom generation of the 1950s entered the labour force in the 1970s and 1980s. This trend had the effect of increasing the NAIRU during the 1970s and 1980s. But as the baby-boom generation aged, and the fraction of young workers in the labour force declined in the late 1990s and early 2000s, the opposite effect was observed and tended to reduce the NAIRU.

A second demographic trend relates to the labour-force participation of women. During the 1960s and 1970s women tended to have higher unemployment rates than men. Since this was true at all points of the business cycle, the higher unemployment was higher frictional and structural unemployment. Thus, when female labour-force participation rates increased dramatically in the 1960s and 1970s, the NAIRU naturally increased. In recent years, however, female unemployment rates have dropped below the rates for men, and so further increases in female participation will, if anything, tend to decrease the NAIRU.

> Greater labour-force participation by groups with high unemployment rates increases the NAIRU.

See Figure 31-4 for Canadian unemployment rates for various demographic groups in 2012. Notice especially the significantly higher unemployment rates for youth of both sexes. These data form the basis for the often-heard view that while overall unemployment may be at acceptable levels, high youth unemployment may be a serious problem.

Hysteresis We saw in Chapter 28 that short-run changes in real GDP sometimes cause changes in the level of potential output, Y^*. One possible reason that we examined was due to the operation of labour markets, whereby the NAIRU can be influenced by the current rate of unemployment. Such models get their name from the Greek word *hysteresis*, meaning "lagged effect."

One mechanism that can lead to hysteresis arises from the importance of experience and on-the-job training. Suppose a recession causes a significant group of new entrants to the labour force to encounter unusual difficulty obtaining their first jobs. As a result, this unlucky group will be slow to acquire the important skills that workers generally learn in their first jobs. When demand increases again, this group of workers will be at a disadvantage relative to workers with normal histories of experience, and

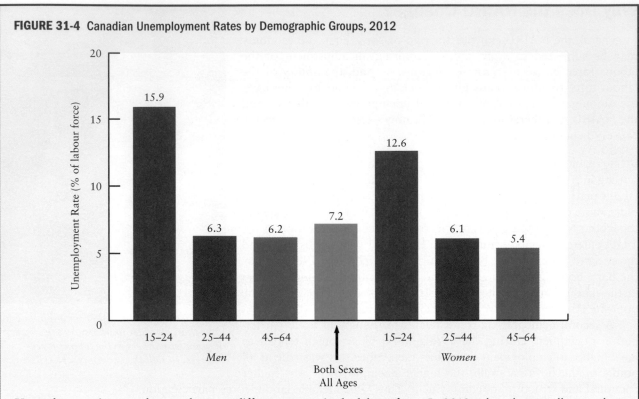

FIGURE 31-4 Canadian Unemployment Rates by Demographic Groups, 2012

Unemployment is unevenly spread among different groups in the labour force. In 2012, when the overall unemployment rate was 7.2 percent, the unemployment rates for youths (of both sexes) were considerably higher.

(*Source:* These data are available on Statistics Canada's website, www.statcan.gc.ca, by searching for "Labour force" and then "Labour force characteristics by age and sex.")

the unlucky group may take longer to find jobs and thus have unemployment rates that will be higher than average. Hence, the NAIRU will be higher than it would have been had there been no recession.

Another force that can cause hysteresis is emphasized by commentators in the European Union, which has a more heavily unionized labour force than does either Canada or the United States. In times of high unemployment, people who are currently employed ("insiders") may use their bargaining power to ensure that their own status is maintained and prevent new entrants to the labour force ("outsiders") from competing effectively. For this reason, high unemployment—whatever its initial cause—will tend to become "locked in." If outsiders are denied access to the labour market, their unemployment will fail to exert downward pressure on wages, and the NAIRU will tend to rise.

Globalization and Structural Change The ongoing process of globalization, especially since the mid-1970s, has increased the rate at which labour is being reallocated across regions and sectors in the Canadian economy.[4] While most economists argue that the

---

[4] Recall from Chapter 1 that we use the term *globalization* to refer to the significant declines in transportation and communication costs that have been taking place over the past two centuries (especially rapidly over the past 40 years) and which have led to an increased volume of world trade in goods, services, and assets.

growing integration of Canada in the global economy generates net benefits for Canada, they also recognize a downside. One unfortunate consequence is that Canadian labour markets are increasingly affected by changes in demand and supply conditions elsewhere in the world. As Canadian labour markets require more frequent and larger adjustments to economic events occurring in other parts of the world, the NAIRU will tend to increase.

Policy and Labour-Market Flexibility We mentioned earlier how policies such as employment insurance can increase structural unemployment and thereby increase the NAIRU. This is one example of a policy reducing the *flexibility* of the labour market.

Such inflexibility is an important cause of unemployment. If wages are inflexible, shocks to labour demand or supply can cause unemployment. If workers are unable or unwilling to move between regions or between industries, changes in the structure of the economy can cause unemployment. If it is costly for firms to hire workers, firms will find other ways of increasing output (such as switching to more capital-intensive methods of production). In general, since the economy is always being buffeted by shocks of one sort or another, the less flexible is the labour market, the higher structural unemployment will be.

> **Any government policy that reduces labour-market flexibility is likely to increase the NAIRU.**

Another example of a policy that reduces labour-market flexibility is mandated job security for workers. In most Western European countries, firms cannot lay off workers without showing cause, which can lead to costly delays and even litigation. When firms do lay workers off, they are required either to give several months' notice before doing so or, in lieu of such notice, are required to make severance payments equal to several months' worth of pay. In Italy, for example, a worker who has been with the firm for 10 years is guaranteed either 20 months' notice before termination or a severance payment equal to 20 months' worth of pay.

Such job-security provisions greatly reduce the flexibility of firms. But this inflexibility on the part of the firms is passed on to workers. Any policy that forces the firm to incur large costs for laying off workers is likely to lead the same firm to be very hesitant about hiring workers in the first place. Given this reduction in labour-market flexibility, such policies are likely to increase the NAIRU.

Such mandated job security is relatively rare in Canada and the United States. Its rarity contributes to the general belief among economists that North American labour markets are much more flexible than those in Europe. Many economists see this as the most important explanation for why unemployment rates in Canada and the United States are below the unemployment rates in Europe and have been for more than two decades.

31.4 Reducing Unemployment

In the remainder of this chapter we briefly examine what can be done to reduce unemployment. Other things being equal, all governments would like to reduce unemployment. The questions are "Can it be done?" and "If so, at what cost?"

Cyclical Unemployment

We do not need to say much more about cyclical unemployment because its control is the subject of stabilization policy, which we have studied in several earlier chapters. A major recession that occurs because of negative *AD* or *AS* shocks can be countered by monetary and fiscal policies to reduce cyclical unemployment.

There is room for debate, however, about *how much* the government can and should do in this respect. Advocates of stabilization policy call for expansionary fiscal and monetary policies to reduce cyclical unemployment (and increase output) during recessionary gaps, at least when they last for sustained periods of time. Advocates of a hands-off approach say that normal market adjustments can be relied on to remove recessionary gaps and that government policy, no matter how well intentioned, will only make things worse. They call for setting simple rules for monetary and fiscal policy that would make discretionary stabilization policy impossible.

Whatever may be argued in principle, however, policymakers have not yet agreed to abandon stabilization measures in practice. In the recession that began in most countries in 2008, for example, governments were quite aggressive in their implementation of expansionary fiscal and monetary policies in an attempt to dampen the recession's effects on falling output and rising unemployment. Today, most economists look back to these decisions and agree that governments' aggressive policy actions helped to reduce what would have otherwise been a much deeper recession.

Frictional Unemployment

The turnover in the labour market that causes frictional unemployment is an inevitable part of the functioning of the economy. Some frictional unemployment is a natural part of the learning process for young workers. As we observed earlier, new entrants to the labour force (many of whom are young) have to try several jobs to see which is most suitable, and this leads to a high turnover rate among the young and hence high frictional unemployment.

Employment insurance is one method of helping people cope with unemployment. It has reduced significantly the human costs of the bouts with unemployment that are inevitable in a changing society. Nothing, however, is without cost. Although employment insurance alleviates the suffering caused by some kinds of unemployment, it also contributes to search unemployment, as we have already observed. As with any policy, a rational assessment of the value of employment insurance requires an evaluation of its costs and benefits. Many Canadians believe that when this calculation is made, the benefits greatly exceed the costs, although many also recognize the scope for reform of certain aspects of the program.

For two of the most widely used job-match websites, go to www.monster.ca or www.workopolis.ca.

Many provisions have been added over the years to the employment insurance scheme to focus it more on people in general need and to reduce its effect of raising the unemployment rate. For example, workers must be actively seeking employment in order to be eligible for EI. Also, workers who voluntarily quit their jobs (without cause) are not eligible to collect EI. In recent years, the benefits received by eligible unemployed workers have been reduced, thus decreasing the likelihood that job seekers will reject early job offers. These changes have contributed to a decline in the amount of frictional unemployment.

Structural Unemployment

The reallocation of labour among occupations, industries, skill categories, and regions that gives rise to structural unemployment is an inevitable part of a market economy. Much of this required reallocation is driven by technological change, which occurs in different ways and at different paces in various parts of the economy. Ever since the beginning of the Industrial Revolution in the late eighteenth century, workers have resisted the introduction of new techniques that replace the older techniques at which they were skilled. Such resistance is understandable. New techniques often destroy the value of the knowledge and experience of workers skilled in the displaced techniques. Older workers may not even get a chance to start over with the new technique. Employers may prefer to hire younger persons who will learn the new skills faster than older workers who are set in their ways of thinking. From society's point of view, new techniques are beneficial because they are a major source of economic growth. From the point of view of the workers they displace, however, new techniques can be an unmitigated disaster.

There are two basic approaches to reducing structural unemployment: try to resist the changes that the economy experiences or accept the changes and try to assist the necessary adjustments. Throughout history, both approaches have been tried.

Resisting Change Over the long term, policies aimed at maintaining employment levels in declining industries run into increasing difficulties. Agreements to hire unneeded workers raise costs and can hasten the decline of an industry threatened by competitive products. An industry that is declining because of economic change becomes an increasingly large burden on the public purse as economic forces become less and less favourable to its success. Sooner or later, public support is withdrawn, and it is followed by a precipitous decline.

As we assess these remedies for structural unemployment, it is important to realize that although they are not viable in the long run for the entire economy, they may be the best alternatives for the affected workers during their lifetimes.

There is often a genuine conflict between the private interest of workers threatened by structural unemployment, whose interests lie in preserving existing jobs, and the social interest served by reallocating resources to where they are most valuable.

Assisting Adjustment A second general approach to dealing with structural change is to accept the decline of specific industries and the loss of specific jobs that go with them and to try to reduce the cost of adjustment for the workers affected. A number of policies have been introduced in Canada to ease the adjustment to changing economic conditions.

One such policy is publicly subsidized education and retraining schemes. The public involvement is motivated partly by positive externalities to education and partly by imperfections in capital markets that make it difficult for workers to borrow funds for education, training, or retraining. A major component of labour-market policies is a system of loans and subsidies for higher education.

Another policy is motivated by the difficulty in obtaining good information about current and future job prospects. In recent years, the development of the Internet has greatly improved the flow of this type of information. Human Resources and Skills

To learn more about the national Job Bank, go to Service Canada's website: www.jobbank. gc.ca.

Development Canada (HRSDC), for example, operates an Internet-based service to speed up and improve the quality of matches between firms and workers. This national Job Bank allows firms (or workers) to specify certain characteristics and skills and then match these characteristics with workers (or firms) on the "other side" of the labour market.

> **Policies to increase retraining and to improve the flow of labour-market information will tend to reduce the amount of structural unemployment.**

The choice between designing policies to "resist change" or "assist adjustment" was apparent early in 2009 when the Canadian, Ontario, and U.S. governments were faced with the probable collapse of Chrysler and General Motors. The desperate financial position of these storied auto companies was partly due to the deep global recession, but it was also partly due to business practices that over several decades had proven to be unsuccessful. If the governments did nothing to help the auto companies, their collapse would likely lead to thousands of job losses in the auto and auto-parts sectors. If instead the governments decided to provide financial assistance to the troubled companies, there was a real possibility that the assistance would only delay the companies' inevitable collapse, but at great cost to taxpayers.

In the end, the three governments coordinated their actions and made large financial contributions to the firms in exchange for partial ownership. In addition, both companies were required to restructure their businesses and provide credible plans for how their firms would compete effectively against their domestic and foreign rivals. By 2013, both companies were doing well amid a modestly growing world economy.

Conclusion

Over the years, unemployment has been regarded in many different ways. Harsh critics see it as proof that the market system is badly flawed. Moderates regard it as a necessary evil of the market system and a suitable object for government policy to reduce its incidence and its harmful effects. More extreme observers see it as overblown in importance and believe that it does not reflect any real inability of workers to obtain jobs if they really want to work.

Most government policy follows a middle route. Fiscal and monetary policies generally seek to reduce at least the most persistent of recessionary gaps, and a host of labour-market policies are designed to reduce frictional and structural unemployment. Such social policies as employment insurance seek to reduce the sting of unemployment for the many who suffer from it for reasons beyond their control.

As global economic competition becomes more intense and as new knowledge-driven methods of production spread, the ability to adjust to economic change will become increasingly important. Countries that succeed in the global marketplace, while also managing to maintain humane social welfare systems, will be those that best learn how to deal with changes in the economic landscape. This will mean avoiding economic policies that inhibit change while adopting social policies that reduce the human cost of adjusting to change. This is an enormous challenge for future Canadian economic and social policies.

SUMMARY

31.1 Employment and Unemployment

- Canadian employment and the Canadian labour force increased along a strong upward trend throughout the twentieth century. The unemployment rate fluctuates significantly over the course of the business cycle.
- Looking only at the level of employment or unemployment misses a tremendous amount of activity in the labour market as individuals flow from unemployment to employment or from employment to unemployment. Such gross flows reflect the turnover that is a normal part of any labour market.
- It is useful to distinguish among several types of unemployment: cyclical unemployment, which is associated with output gaps; frictional unemployment, which is a result of normal labour-market turnover; and structural unemployment, which is caused by the need to reallocate resources among occupations, regions, and industries as the structure of demand and supply changes.
- Together, frictional unemployment and structural unemployment make up the NAIRU. The actual unemployment rate is equal to the NAIRU when real GDP is equal to Y^*.

31.2 Unemployment Fluctuations

- There is a long-standing debate among economists regarding the causes of unemployment fluctuations.
- Market-clearing theories look to explanations that allow the labour market to be cleared continuously by perfectly flexible wages and prices. Such theories can explain cyclical variations in employment but predict no involuntary unemployment.
- Empirical evidence suggests that wages are relatively stable over the business cycle, in contrast to what is predicted by market-clearing theories of the labour market.
- Non-market-clearing theories of the labour market provide an explanation for involuntary unemployment based on wage stickiness; real wages do not adjust frequently in response to all shocks to labour demand and supply.
- To explain wage stickiness, non-market-clearing theories have focused on the long-term nature of employer–worker relationships in which wages tend to respond only a little, and employment tends to respond a lot, to changes in the demand and supply of labour.

31.3 What Determines the NAIRU?

- The NAIRU will always be positive because it takes time for labour to move between jobs both in normal turnover (frictional unemployment) and in response to changes in the structure of the demand for labour (structural unemployment).
- Because different workers have different sets of skills and because different firms require workers with different sets of skills, some unemployment—resulting from workers searching for appropriate job matches with employers—is socially desirable.
- Anything that increases the rate of turnover in the labour market, or the pace of structural change in the economy, will likely increase the NAIRU.
- Employment insurance also increases the NAIRU by encouraging workers to continue searching for an appropriate job. Policies that mandate job security increase the costs to firms of laying off workers. This makes them reluctant to hire workers in the first place and may increase the NAIRU.

31.4 Reducing Unemployment

- Cyclical unemployment can be reduced by using monetary or fiscal policies to close recessionary gaps.
- Frictional and structural unemployment can be reduced by making it easier to move between jobs and by raising the cost of staying unemployed (e.g., by reducing employment insurance benefits).
- In a growing, changing economy populated by people who want to change jobs for many reasons, it is neither possible nor desirable to reduce unemployment to zero.
- Policies that assist workers in retraining and in moving between jobs, regions, or industries may be the most effective way to deal with the various shocks that buffet the economy.

KEY CONCEPTS

Gross flows in the labour market
Cyclical, frictional, and structural
  unemployment
Market-clearing theories of the labour
  market

Non-market-clearing theories of the
  labour market
Long-term employment relationships
Frictional and structural
  unemployment

Determinants of the NAIRU
Hysteresis
Policies to reduce the NAIRU
Labour-market flexibility

STUDY EXERCISES

MyEconLab   Make the grade with MyEconLab: Study Exercises marked in red can be found on
MyEconLab. You can practise them as often as you want, and most feature step-by-step
guided instructions to help you find the right answer.

1. Fill in the blanks to make the following statements
   correct.

   a. The overall unemployment rate in Canada is not a
      good indicator of the level of *activity* in the labour
      market because _____.
   b. *Gross* flows in the labour market are much
      _____ than net flows in the labour market.
   c. In a typical month in Canada, _____ workers
      flow in each direction between unemployment and
      employment.
   d. Cyclical unemployment exists when real GDP is
      _____ than potential GDP. When real GDP is
      equal to potential GDP, then all unemployment is
      either _____ or _____.
   e. Market-clearing theories assume that the labour
      market always _____ with flexible _____
      and that any unemployment that does exist is
      _____.
   f. Non-market-clearing theories assume that wages do
      not instantly _____ to clear the market. A reces-
      sionary gap can persist and result in unemployment
      that is _____.

2. Fill in the blanks to make the following statements
   correct.

   a. The NAIRU is composed of _____ unemploy-
      ment and _____ unemployment. The NAIRU is
      always _____ than zero.
   b. If there are 1000 loggers in British Columbia who
      are unemployed, and 1000 vacant positions for
      call-centre operators in New Brunswick, we say
      that this unemployment is _____.
   c. Suppose the NAIRU in June 2009 was 6.0 percent.
      If the actual unemployment rate was 8.2 percent,

   we can conclude that _____ percentage points
   are due to _____ factors and the remaining
   _____ percentage points are due to _____
   and _____ factors.
   d. Suppose the government increased the number of
      weeks that an unemployed worker can collect EI
      benefits from 12 weeks to 16 weeks. The NAIRU
      is likely to _____ because of an increase in the
      amount of _____ unemployment.
   e. Countries with greater labour-market flexibility are
      likely to have _____ unemployment rates than
      countries in which policies inhibit flexibility.
   f. Cyclical unemployment can be reduced by closing
      a(n) _____ gap by using _____ and _____
      policies.

3. The following table shows the pattern of real GDP,
   potential GDP, and the unemployment rate for several
   years in Cycleland.

Year	Real GDP (billions of $)	Potential GDP (billions of $)	Unemployment Rate (%)
2006	790	740	6.3
2007	800	760	6.5
2008	780	780	6.8
2009	750	800	8.2
2010	765	810	8.4
2011	790	830	8.4
2012	815	850	8.0
2013	845	870	7.5
2014	875	890	7.2
2015	900	900	6.8
2016	930	920	6.7

a. On a scale diagram, draw the path of real GDP and potential GDP (with time on the horizontal axis).
b. On a separate diagram (below the first one) show the path of the unemployment rate.
c. For which years is it possible to determine the value of the NAIRU?
d. Does the NAIRU change over the 10-year period? Provide one reason that the NAIRU could increase.

4. Interpret the following statements from newspapers in terms of types of unemployment.
    a. "Recession hits local factory; 1800 workers laid off."
    b. "Of course, I could take a job as a dishwasher, but I'm trying to find something that makes use of my high school education," says a local teenager in our survey of the unemployed.
    c. "Retraining is the best reaction to the increased use of robots."
    d. "Uneven growth: Alberta booms while Ontario sputters."

5. The diagram below shows a simple AD/AS diagram. The economy begins in long-run equilibrium at E_0 with real GDP equal to Y^*.

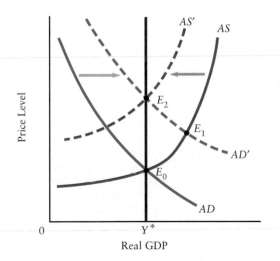

a. At E_0, the unemployment rate is 8 percent. What type of unemployment is this?
b. A positive aggregate demand shock now shifts the AD curve to AD'. At E_1 the unemployment rate is only 6.5 percent. Is there cyclical unemployment at E_1?
c. Describe the economy's adjustment process to E_2.
d. What is the unemployment rate at E_2? What kind of unemployment exists at E_2?

6. The diagram below shows a simple AD/AS diagram. The economy begins in long-run equilibrium at E_0 with real GDP equal to Y^*.

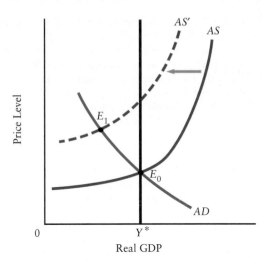

a. At E_0, the unemployment rate is 6 percent. What type of unemployment is this?
b. A negative aggregate supply shock now shifts the AS curve to AS'. At E_1 the unemployment rate is 7.5 percent. Is there cyclical unemployment at E_1? How much?
c. If monetary and fiscal policy do not react to the shock, describe the economy's adjustment process to its new long-run equilibrium.
d. What is the unemployment rate at the economy's new long-run equilibrium? What kind of unemployment exists there? Explain.

7. The diagram below shows a perfectly competitive labour market. The initial equilibrium is with wage w^* and employment L^*.

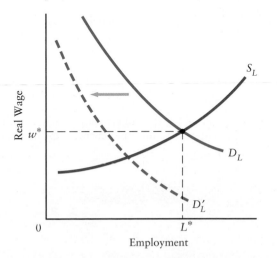

a. Suppose the demand for labour decreases to D_L'. If wages are perfectly flexible, what is the effect on wages and employment? Show this in the diagram.

b. Is there any involuntary unemployment in part (a) after the shock?

c. Now suppose wages can only adjust half as much as in part (a)—that is, wages are sticky. What is the effect on wages and employment in this case? Show this in the diagram.

d. Is there any involuntary unemployment in part (c) after the shock? How much?

8. Consider two hypothetical countries. In Country A, 20 percent of the labour force is unemployed for half the year and employed for the other half; the remaining 80 percent of the labour force is never unemployed. In Country B, 100 percent of the labour force is unemployed for 10 percent of the year and employed for the other 90 percent of the year. Note that both countries have an overall unemployment rate of 10 percent. Which of these countries seems to have the more serious unemployment problem, and why?

9. In 2012, the Canadian government announced its plan to modify the employment insurance (EI) program, and this generated a great deal of debate over the appropriate level of generosity for EI.

a. Explain what problem can be caused by having an EI system that is too generous.

b. Explain what problem can be caused by having an EI system that is not generous enough.

c. If EI generosity were reduced and the NAIRU declined as a result, is this necessarily a desirable outcome?

10. Consider an economy that begins with real GDP equal to potential. There is then a sudden increase in the prices of raw materials, which shifts the *AS* curve upward.

a. Draw the initial long-run equilibrium in an *AD/AS* diagram.

b. Now show the immediate effect of the supply shock in your diagram.

c. Suppose wages and prices in this economy adjust instantly to shocks. Describe what happens to unemployment in this economy. Explain.

d. If wages and prices adjust only slowly to shocks, what happens to unemployment? Explain.

11. The table below shows the percentage of the labour force accounted for by youths (15 to 24 years old) and older workers (25 years and older) over several years. Suppose that because of their lower skills and greater turnover, youths have a higher unemployment rate than older workers (see Figure 31-4 on page 792).

Year	Percentage of Labour Force	
	Youths	Older Workers
1	20	80
2	21	79
3	22	78
4	23	77
5	25	75
6	27	73
7	29	71
8	31	69

a. Suppose that in Year 1 real GDP is equal to potential GDP, and the unemployment rate among older workers is 6 percent but is 14 percent among youths. What is the economy's NAIRU?

b. Now suppose that for the next eight years real GDP remains equal to potential and that the unemployment rates for each group remain the same. Compute the value of the NAIRU for each year.

c. Explain why the NAIRU rises even though output is always equal to potential.

12. In its 2009 and 2010 budgets, the Canadian government significantly increased its planned spending on infrastructure projects in order to fight the existing recession and protect jobs.

a. Explain why such a policy may "create" jobs.

b. Is such a policy equally likely to create jobs during a recession as when the economy is already operating at potential output? Explain.

Government Debt and Deficits

UNTIL the mid-1990s, no single measure associated with the Canadian federal government was the focus of more attention and controversy than the size of the government's annual budget deficit and its accumulated level of debt. Some people argued that the debt was an economic time bomb, waiting to explode and cause serious harm to our living standards. Others argued that the only real danger posed by debt was from the dramatic policy changes proposed to reduce it.

By 2002, after two decades of debate about debt and deficits, the focus shifted to what the governments—federal and provincial—should do with their actual and projected budget surpluses. Just as earlier debates raged over the harmful effects of high government budget deficits, debates raged then about whether governments facing budget surpluses should increase spending, reduce taxes, or use the surpluses to reduce the outstanding stock of government debt.

By 2009, with the onset of a global economic recession, the federal government then announced a return to significant budget deficits, in part caused by the recession-induced decline in tax revenues and in part caused by an intentional increase in spending designed to stimulate the struggling economy. Debate then turned to the most appropriate set of fiscal policies for the government to implement.

The global recession of 2008–2009 drove up government debt in many countries. As this book went to press in early 2013, news stories around the world were describing the very high government debts in Greece, Spain, Ireland, and other European countries. There was active debate about whether these countries should implement "fiscal austerity" in order to reduce existing debt, or whether they needed "fiscal stimulus" in order to prevent a return to recession.

In this chapter, we examine various issues surrounding government debt, deficits, and surpluses. We begin by considering the simple arithmetic of government budgets. This tells us how the deficit or surplus in any given year is related to the outstanding stock of debt. We then explore why deficits and debt matter for the performance of the economy—as well as what changes we can expect over the near future if Canadian governments are successful in returning to either balanced budgets or budget surpluses.

| 32.1 Facts and Definitions

There is a simple relationship between the government's expenditures, its tax revenues, and its borrowing. This relationship is summarized in what economists call the government's *budget constraint*.

The Government's Budget Constraint

As is true for any individual's expenditures, government expenditures must be financed either by income or by borrowing. The difference between individuals and governments, however, is that governments typically do not earn income by selling products or labour services; instead, they earn income by levying taxes. Thus, all government expenditure must be financed either by tax revenues or by borrowing. This point is illustrated by the following simple equation, which is called the government's *budget constraint*:

$$\text{Government expenditure} = \text{Tax revenue} + \text{Borrowing}$$

debt-service payments
Payments that represent the interest owed on a current stock of debt.

We divide government expenditure into two categories. The first is purchases of goods and services, G. The second is the interest payments on the outstanding stock of debt; this is referred to as **debt-service payments** and is denoted $i \times D$, where i is the interest rate and D is the stock of government debt (which has accumulated over time from the government's past borrowing). A third category of government spending is *transfers* to individuals and firms (such as employment-insurance benefits, public pensions, and industrial subsidies) but, as we did in earlier chapters, we include transfers as part of T, which is the government's *net tax revenue* (tax revenue minus transfers). The government's budget constraint can therefore be rewritten as

$$G + i \times D = T + \text{Borrowing}$$

or, subtracting T from both sides,

$$(G + i \times D) - T = \text{Borrowing}$$

This equation simply says that any excess of total government spending over net tax revenues must be financed by government borrowing.[1]

budget deficit Any shortfall of current revenue below current expenditure.

government debt The outstanding stock of financial liabilities for the government, equal to the accumulation of past budget deficits.

Debt and Deficits The government's annual **budget deficit** is the excess of government expenditure over tax revenues in a given year. From the budget constraint just given, this annual deficit is exactly the same as the amount borrowed by the government during the year. Since the government borrows by issuing bonds and selling them to lenders, borrowing by the government increases the stock of **government debt**. Since D is the outstanding stock of government debt, ΔD is the *change* in the stock of debt during the course of the year. The budget deficit can therefore be written as

$$\text{Budget deficit} = \Delta D = (G + i \times D) - T$$

---

[1] A small amount of the Canadian government's annual borrowing (roughly $1 to $3 billion) represents bonds sold to the Bank of Canada as part of its regular operations of increasing the money supply. This process is called *monetizing the debt* and we will discuss it later in the chapter. Our emphasis here is on the vast majority of government borrowing, which is from individuals and private institutions in Canada and elsewhere.

> The government's annual budget deficit is the excess of expenditure over tax revenues in a given year. It is also equal to the change in the stock of government debt during the year.

Notice two points about budget deficits. First, a change in the size of the deficit requires a change in expenditures *relative* to tax revenues. For given tax revenues, a smaller deficit can come about only through a reduction in government expenditures; conversely, for given expenditures, a smaller deficit requires an increase in tax revenues. Second, since the budget deficit is equal to the amount of new government borrowing, the stock of government debt will rise whenever the budget deficit is positive. Even a drastic reduction in the size of the annual budget deficit is therefore not sufficient to reduce the outstanding stock of government debt; the stock of debt will fall only if the budget deficit becomes *negative*. In this case, there is said to be a **budget surplus**.

budget surplus Any excess of current revenue over current expenditure.

> A budget deficit increases the stock of government debt; a budget surplus reduces it.

The Primary Budget Deficit One component of government expenditure is debt-service payments ($i \times D$). Since at any point in time the outstanding stock of government debt—determined by *past* government borrowing—cannot be influenced by current government policy, the debt-service component of total expenditures is beyond the immediate control of the government. In contrast, the other components of the government's budget (G and T) are determined by the current set of spending programs and tax policies, all of which can be adjusted if the government chooses to do so. To capture the part of the budget deficit that is attributable to current spending and tax policies, we can compute the **primary budget deficit**, defined to be the difference between government purchases and net tax revenues:

primary budget deficit The difference between the government's overall budget deficit and its debt-service payments.

$$\text{Primary budget deficit} = G - T$$

The government's primary budget deficit shows the extent to which current tax revenues are sufficient to finance expenditure on current government programs.

Because of the need to make debt-service payments, there are often large differences between the government's overall budget deficit (or surplus) and its primary budget deficit (or surplus). In the 2005–2006 fiscal year, for example, the Canadian government had an overall budget surplus of $8 billion. Since the debt-service payments in that year were $34 billion, we see that the government actually had a primary surplus that year of $42 billion. In other words, total tax revenues in 2005–2006 were $42 billion more than the *program* spending, but only $8 billion more than *total* spending.

By the 2009–2010 fiscal year, however, the onset of the global recession had changed the budget situation considerably. Tax revenues dropped sharply and program spending increased, and the overall budget deficit was then $56 billion. Debt-service payments that year were $31 billion, so the government's primary deficit was $25 billion. In other words, tax revenues were $25 billion below program spending in 2009–2010, and fully $56 billion below total spending.

For the most recent federal budget forecasts, see the website for the Department of Finance: www.fin.gc.ca.

> The primary budget surplus or deficit shows the extent to which current tax revenues can cover the government's current program spending; it is equal to the overall budget deficit minus debt-service payments.

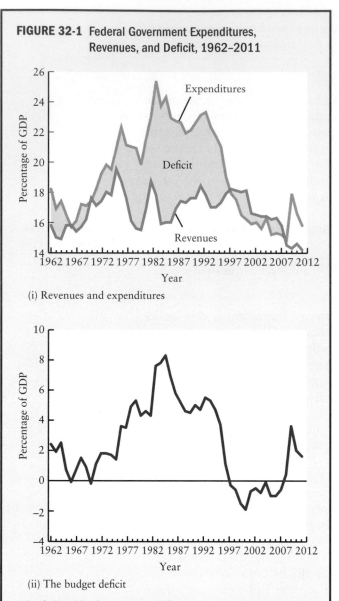

FIGURE 32-1 Federal Government Expenditures, Revenues, and Deficit, 1962–2011

(i) Revenues and expenditures

(ii) The budget deficit

The federal budget was in deficit every year between 1971 and 1997. From 1998 to 2008 there were budget surpluses. The budget returned to deficit in 2009 but is forecast to be back in balance by about 2016. Part (i) shows revenues and expenditures as a percentage of GDP. Part (ii) shows the budget deficit (or surplus) as a percentage of GDP.

(*Source:* Based on data from the Department of Finance, *Fiscal Reference Tables*, October 2012, Tables 4 and 8.)

Deficits and Debt in Canada

In a growing economy, many macroeconomic variables, such as the levels of government expenditure and tax revenue, also tend to grow. As a result, rather than looking at the absolute size of the government deficit or debt, economists focus on government debt and deficits in relation to the overall size of the economy. Some budget deficits that would be unmanageable in a small country like New Zealand might be quite acceptable for a larger country like Canada, and trivial for a huge economy like the United States. Similarly, a government budget deficit that seemed crushing in Canada in 1913 might appear trivial in 2013 because the size of the Canadian economy is many times larger now than it was then.

Federal Government The path of federal budget deficits since 1962 is shown in Figure 32-1. The top panel shows total federal spending and total federal tax revenues as percentages of GDP.[2] The bottom panel shows the total federal budget deficit as a percentage of GDP. Large and persistent budget deficits began in the mid-1970s. Throughout the 1980s and early 1990s, the average budget deficit was over 5 percent of GDP. In the mid-1990s, the federal government embarked on a successful policy of deficit reduction and by 1998 reported its first budget surplus in almost 20 years. The federal budget was then continually in surplus until the 2008–2009 fiscal year, at which point the budget returned to a deficit for several years, mostly as a result of a major recession.

As we saw in the previous section, a deficit implies that the stock of government debt is rising. Thus, the persistent deficits that began in the 1970s have their counterpart in a steadily rising stock of government debt. Figure 32-2 shows the path of Canadian federal government debt since 1940. At the beginning of the Second World War, the stock of federal debt was equal to about 45 percent of GDP. The enormous increase in the debt-to-GDP ratio over the next five years reflects wartime borrowing used to finance military expenditures. From 1946 to 1974, however, there was a continual decline in the debt-to-GDP ratio. The economy was growing quickly during this period, but equally important was that the federal government in the post-war

---

[2] In Figure 32-1 government expenditures include purchases, transfer payments, and debt-service payments. Tax revenues are not net of transfers.

years typically ran significant budget surpluses. These two factors explain the dramatic decline in the debt-to-GDP ratio between 1946 and 1974.

By 1974 the federal debt was only 14 percent of GDP. The large and persistent budget deficits beginning in the mid-1970s, however, along with a general slowdown in the rate of economic growth, led to a significant upward trend in the debt-to-GDP ratio. The ratio climbed steadily from 1979 to 1996, when it peaked at more than 69 percent of GDP. Then, with the significant reductions in the budget deficit beginning in 1996, the debt-to-GDP ratio began to fall. By 2008, the federal government's net debt was just above 30 percent of GDP, the lowest it had been since the early 1980s. The debt ratio then increased during the 2008–2009 recession, but by 2012 was again on a downward path and was forecast to be about 30 percent by 2015.

Provincial Governments Canadian provincial governments are responsible for a significant fraction of total government revenues and expenditures. In many countries, sizable regional governments either do not exist, as in the United Kingdom and New Zealand, or are often legally required to run balanced budgets, as is the case for about two-thirds of the 50 states in the United States. In contrast, the size of Canadian provincial governments—measured by their spending and taxing powers relative to that of the federal government—means that an examination of government debt and deficits in Canada would not be complete without paying attention to the provincial governments' fiscal positions.

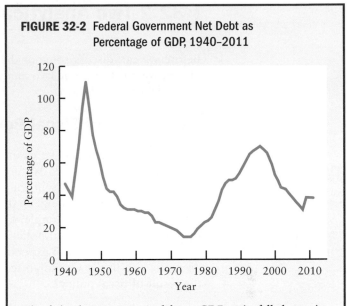

FIGURE 32-2 Federal Government Net Debt as Percentage of GDP, 1940–2011

The federal government's debt-to-GDP ratio fell dramatically after the Second World War and continued falling until 1975. It then increased markedly for the next two decades. In the late 1990s when government deficits were reduced and the economy was in a healthy recovery, the debt-to-GDP ratio began to fall.

(*Source:* Based on author's calculations using data from Statistics Canada, CANSIM database. Nominal GDP; Table 380-0017. Net financial debt; Series V151548. Most recent data from the Department of Finance's *Fiscal Reference Tables 2012.*)

When examining the size and effects of budget deficits or surpluses, it is important to consider all levels of government—federal, provincial, territorial, and municipal.

During the 1970s, the provincial governments were running budget deficits and so the stock of provincial government debt was increasing. But the deficits were small enough for the debt not to be growing relative to GDP. During the 1980s and early 1990s, however, provincial deficits grew dramatically. Total provincial debt grew from roughly 4 percent of GDP in 1980 to 25 percent in 1998. In the subsequent decade, most provincial governments eliminated their deficits and some had budget surpluses. By 2009, however, economic recession had driven them back into deficit. The total provincial and territorial debt at that time was about 15 percent of GDP and rising.

The Canadian government ran very large budget deficits to finance Canada's participation in the Second World War. As a result, Canadian federal debt increased to 110 percent of GDP by 1946.

32.2 Two Analytical Issues

Before we can discuss some of the macroeconomic effects of budget deficits and surpluses, we must examine two analytical issues: the stance of fiscal policy and changes in the debt-to-GDP ratio.

The Stance of Fiscal Policy

For macroeconomic data that are comparable across countries, see the OECD's website: www.oecd.org.

In Chapters 22 and 24 we examined *fiscal policy*, which is the use of government spending and tax policies. We noted there that changes in expenditure and taxation normally lead to changes in the government's budget deficit or surplus. Thus, it is tempting to view any change in the government's budget deficit as reflecting a change in its fiscal policy. For example, we could interpret an increase in the deficit as indicating an expansionary fiscal policy, since the rise in the deficit is associated with either an increase in government expenditures or a decrease in tax revenue (or both). Was the dramatic rise in the Canadian federal budget deficit between 2008 and 2010 *purely* the result of fiscal policy?

No. In general, only some changes in the budget deficit are due to changes in the government's policies regarding expenditure or taxation. Other changes have nothing to do with explicit changes in policy, but instead are the result of changes in the level of economic activity which nonetheless have an impact on the budget. If our goal is to judge the stance of fiscal policy, however, it is only the changes in the deficit *caused by changes in policy* that are relevant.

The Budget Deficit Function To see why the budget deficit can rise or fall even when there is no change in fiscal policy, recall the equation defining the government's budget deficit.

$$\text{Budget deficit} = (G + i \times D) - T$$

As we first discussed in Chapter 22, the level of net tax revenues typically depends on the level of national income, even with unchanged policy. For example, as national income rises the level of tax revenues also rises. In addition, as income rises there are typically fewer transfers (such as welfare or employment insurance) made to the private sector. Thus, net tax revenues, T, increase when national income increases. In contrast, the level of government purchases and debt-service payments can be viewed as more or less independent of the level of national income, at least over short periods of time. Thus, with no changes in the government's fiscal policies, the budget deficit will tend to increase in recessions

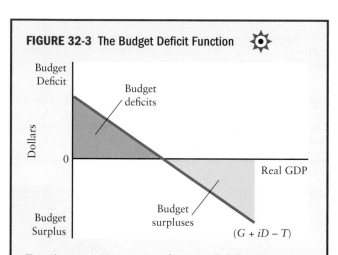

FIGURE 32-3 The Budget Deficit Function ☀

For given government purchases and debt-service payments, there is a negative relationship between real GDP and the government budget deficit. G and iD are assumed to be independent of the level of real GDP. In contrast, a rise in real GDP leads to higher tax revenues and lower transfers, and thus to higher net tax revenue, T. Thus, the budget deficit falls as real GDP increases. Therefore, even with unchanged fiscal policies, changes in real GDP will lead to changes in the budget deficit.

A more expansionary fiscal policy implies an increase in spending or a reduction in net taxes at *any level of real GDP* and thus an upward shift of the budget deficit function. A more contractionary fiscal policy shifts the budget deficit function down.

and fall in booms. That is, there is a negative relationship between real GDP and the government's budget deficit.

> **For a given set of expenditure and taxation policies, the budget deficit rises as real GDP falls, and falls as real GDP rises.**

Figure 32-3 plots this basic relationship, which is called the **budget deficit function**. When the government determines its expenditure and taxation polices, it determines the *position* of the budget deficit function. A more expansionary fiscal policy shifts the budget deficit function up. A more contractionary fiscal policy shifts the budget deficit function down. In contrast, a change in the level of real GDP in the absence of any policy change will represent a *movement along* the budget deficit function. Thus, for a given set of fiscal policies, the budget deficit will decrease when Y rises and increase when Y falls.

budget deficit function A relationship that plots, for a given fiscal policy, the government's budget deficit as a function of the level of real GDP.

cyclically adjusted deficit (CAD) An estimate of what the government budget deficit would be if real GDP were equal to Y^*; sometimes called a *structural deficit*.

> **Fiscal policy determines the position of the budget deficit function. Changes in real GDP lead to movements along a given budget deficit function.**

The Cyclically Adjusted Deficit We have said that a more expansionary fiscal policy will shift the budget deficit function up, whereas a more contractionary policy will shift it down. Therefore, *if we could hold real GDP constant*, an increase in the observed budget deficit would reveal a fiscal expansion, whereas a decrease in the deficit would reveal a fiscal contraction. While we cannot actually hold GDP constant in practice, we can accomplish the same thing by estimating what the budget deficit would be at a specific level of GDP. The **cyclically adjusted deficit (CAD)** does just this; it estimates the deficit as if real GDP were equal to Y^*. Changes in the CAD then reveal changes in the stance of fiscal policy, as illustrated in Figure 32-4. The cyclically adjusted deficit is sometimes called the *structural deficit* because its emphasis is on the *structure* of fiscal policy, separate from the current *cyclical* position of the economy.

> **An expansionary change in fiscal policy increases the cyclically adjusted deficit; a contractionary change in fiscal policy reduces the cyclically adjusted deficit.**

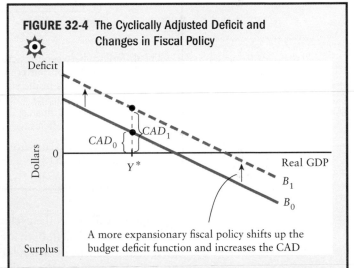

FIGURE 32-4 The Cyclically Adjusted Deficit and Changes in Fiscal Policy

A more expansionary fiscal policy shifts up the budget deficit function and increases the CAD

A more expansionary fiscal policy increases the cyclically adjusted deficit; a more contractionary fiscal policy reduces it. Initially, fiscal policy gives rise to the budget deficit function B_0. The actual budget deficit will depend on the actual level of real GDP, which is not shown in the figure. The CAD is the deficit that would exist if real GDP were equal to Y^*. With the budget deficit function B_0, the cyclically adjusted deficit is CAD_0.

Now suppose that fiscal policy becomes more expansionary because of greater spending or a reduction in tax rates. The budget deficit function shifts upward to B_1 and the cyclically adjusted deficit rises to CAD_1. The increase in the CAD reveals the expansionary change in fiscal policy. Conversely, a more contractionary fiscal policy would shift the budget deficit function down and reduce the CAD.

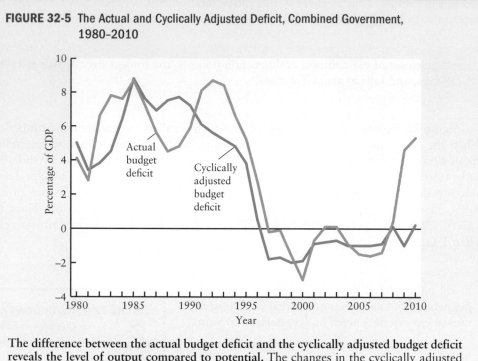

FIGURE 32-5 The Actual and Cyclically Adjusted Deficit, Combined Government, 1980–2010

The difference between the actual budget deficit and the cyclically adjusted budget deficit reveals the level of output compared to potential. The changes in the cyclically adjusted deficit show changes in the stance of fiscal policy. The actual budget deficit is above the cyclically adjusted budget deficit when output is below potential; the actual deficit is less than the cyclically adjusted deficit when output is above potential. An increase in the cyclically adjusted deficit reveals a fiscal expansion; a decrease reveals a fiscal contraction.

(*Source:* Based on data from the Department of Finance, *Fiscal Reference Tables*, September 2011, p. 51.)

Figure 32-5 shows the cyclically adjusted deficit in Canada and plots it together with the actual budget deficit. Both are expressed as percentages of GDP and represent the combined budget deficits of all levels of government. Unlike the actual budget deficit, which can be precisely measured, the cyclically adjusted deficit can only be estimated. The reason is that its value depends on the value of potential GDP, Y^*, which itself is not directly observable and hence must be estimated. Note from Figure 32-5 that the actual deficit is larger than the cyclically adjusted deficit during times of recessionary gaps, such as 1981–1985, 1991–1995, and 2009–2011. This relationship reflects the fact that during these periods actual GDP is less than potential GDP, and thus actual tax revenues are less than they would be if output were equal to potential. Conversely, the actual budget deficit is less than the cyclically adjusted deficit during periods of inflationary gaps, such as 1986–1990, 2000, and 2004–2007, reflecting the fact that during these periods actual GDP is greater than potential and thus tax revenues are greater than they would be if output were equal to potential. In years where the actual deficit is approximately equal to the cyclically adjusted deficit, such as 1985, 1990, and 1999, real GDP is approximately equal to potential.

Changes in the expansionary or contractionary stance of fiscal policy are shown by the *changes* in the cyclically adjusted deficit. For example, the dramatic rise in Canada's cyclically adjusted deficit from 1982 to 1986 reveals a considerable fiscal expansion; the more gradual decline from 1986 to 1996 reveals a moderate fiscal contraction. From 1996 to 2000, the substantial fiscal contraction, at both federal and provincial levels, led to the sharp decline in the cyclically adjusted deficit. Between 2000 and 2008, the combined government sector had an actual and a cyclically adjusted budget surplus of about 1 percent of GDP, and the stance of fiscal policy did not change markedly. Beginning in 2009, there is then a substantial increase in the actual budget deficit to approximately 5 percent of GDP. Most of this rise in the deficit resulted from a decline in real GDP as the economy went into recession. But Canadian governments also increased their spending and reduced some taxes so that the cyclically adjusted deficit also increased but only by about 1 percentage point of GDP.

Debt Dynamics

As we have already observed, in order to gauge the importance of government deficits and debt, they should be considered relative to the size of the economy. This is why economists often discuss the federal government's debt-to-GDP ratio rather than the absolute amount of government debt. Here we examine the link between the overall budget deficit, the primary budget deficit, and changes in the debt-to-GDP ratio.

With a little algebra, it is possible to write a simple expression that relates the government's primary budget deficit to the change in the debt-to-GDP ratio. Economists often use this relationship for analyzing the dynamics of government debt. The equation is

$$\Delta d = x + (r - g) \times d$$

where d is the debt-to-GDP ratio, x is the government's primary budget deficit as a percentage of GDP, r is the real interest rate on government bonds, g is the growth rate of real GDP, and Δd is the *change* in the debt-to-GDP ratio. We will not spend the time necessary to derive this equation here, but readers who are interested in doing so can refer to the math note. [36]

This simple equation shows two separate forces, each of which tends to increase the debt-to-GDP ratio. First, if the real interest rate exceeds the growth rate of real GDP (if r exceeds g), the debt-to-GDP ratio will rise for the simple reason that the debt accumulates at a faster rate than GDP grows. Second, if the government has a *primary* budget deficit (if x is positive), the debt-to-GDP ratio will rise because the government is incurring new debt to finance its program spending.

Let's use some recent numbers for Canada to illustrate the use of this equation. The global financial crisis that began in 2008 was followed immediately by a worldwide recession and, like most of the G20 countries, Canada embarked on a major fiscal expansion to offset its effects. At the beginning of 2009, the federal debt-to-GDP ratio was 29 percent ($d = 0.29$). During that year, revenues fell sharply, expenditures increased, and the government ran a primary budget deficit of 1.7 percent of GDP ($x = 0.017$). The average real interest rate on government bonds in 2009 was 5.3 percent ($r = 0.053$) while real GDP *fell* in that year by 2.8 percent ($g = -0.028$).

Using all of these data, our equation for the change in the federal debt-to-GDP ratio over the course of 2009 becomes:

$$\Delta d = 0.017 + (0.053 - (-0.028)) \times (0.29)$$
$$= 0.017 + (0.081) \times (0.29)$$
$$= 0.017 + 0.023$$
$$= 0.04$$

which means that the government's debt-to-GDP ratio increased during 2009 by four percentage points, from 29 percent to 33 percent. Note also that the *decline* in real GDP during 2009 ($g = -0.028$) substantially contributed to the increase in the debt ratio. In a typical year in which real GDP grows by 2 percent or more, a primary budget deficit of 1.7 percent of GDP would not generate such a large increase in the debt-to-GDP ratio.

Since 2011, the Canadian government has announced its goal of further reducing the debt-to-GDP ratio. What will be necessary for this objective to be met? First, primary budget surpluses will be helpful. Second, a real interest rate that is less than the growth rate of real GDP will be helpful. If both of these occur, the debt ratio will definitely fall; if only one of these two occurs, the overall effect on the debt ratio will depend on the relative size of the two effects. By early 2013, the federal government had a primary surplus and the gap between r and g had fallen. As a result, the debt-to-GDP ratio was on a downward path and was forecast to fall below 30 percent by 2015.

> If the real interest rate on government debt is approximately equal to the growth rate of real GDP, reductions in the debt-to-GDP ratio require the government to run primary budget surpluses.

APPLYING ECONOMIC CONCEPTS 32-1

The Continuing Greek Tragedy of Debt Dynamics

By 2011, the Greek economy had been in recession for three years, the unemployment rate was over 20 percent, and the government was implementing deep cuts in its spending programs in an effort to reduce its overall budget deficit of 9.2 percent of GDP. This toxic mixture of deep recession and large cutbacks in public services brought hundreds of thousands of Greek citizens into the streets—protesting the government's policies and demanding improvements in their country's economic situation.

Why was the Greek government cutting spending if the economy was in a deep recession? And how were these cuts related to the existing level of Greek government debt? We can use the debt-dynamics equation discussed in the text to shed light on these issues. Specifically, we can use the equation to determine how much fiscal adjustment would have been necessary to *stabilize* Greece's debt-to-GDP ratio at its 2011 level.*

Stabilizing the Debt-to-GDP Ratio

Consider the data for Greece as published by the International Monetary Fund (IMF). At the beginning of 2011, Greece's public debt was 143 percent of its GDP ($d = 1.43$). The average nominal interest rate on its government debt was 4.3 percent and inflation was 3.1 percent; the real interest rate, r, was therefore 1.2 percent ($r = 0.012$). The Greek economy was then in its fourth continuous year of recession, and real GDP growth in 2011 was *negative* 6.9 percent ($g = -0.069$).

Using these data, we can compute the value of the primary budget balance that would have been necessary to stabilize the Greek debt-to-GDP ratio during 2011. Recall the equation that describes the change in the debt-to GDP ratio:

$$\Delta d = x + (r - g)d$$

If d is to be held constant ($\Delta d = 0$), the necessary value for x, which we call x^*, is

$$x^* = -(r - g)d$$

Using the data for Greece in 2011 we see that x^* is

$$x^* = -(0.012 - (-0.069)) \times (1.43)$$
$$= -(0.081) \times (1.43)$$
$$= -0.116$$

The interpretation of this number is that Greece would have needed a primary budget *surplus* of 11.6 percent of GDP in 2011 in order to stabilize its debt-to-GDP ratio that year. Its actual primary balance that year was a *deficit* of 2.3 percent. Thus, to stabilize d would have required a reduction in government expenditures and/or an increase in tax revenues of roughly 14 percent of GDP—an enormous fiscal adjustment for any government to make over several years, let alone in a single year.

An Impending Default?

By late in 2011 it was clear to most holders of Greek government bonds that any realistic fiscal adjustment by the Greek government would be insufficient to stabilize the debt-to-GDP ratio in the near future. Instead, the debt ratio would almost certainly continue to rise

As a result of the 2008 global financial crisis and the recession that followed, many highly indebted European governments experienced significant further increases in their public debts. Some of this new debt was incurred as governments provided assistance to failing financial institutions; some was incurred through more conventional fiscal stabilization policies such as those we examined in Chapter 24. By 2011, the public debts in Greece, Portugal, Spain, and some other countries were so high that bondholders came to believe that these governments were effectively bankrupt and would be unable to repay or even service their existing debts. Fear of *debt defaults* by these governments led to massive increases in bond yields and created great uncertainty within the European Union. By early 2013, what became known as Europe's "sovereign debt crisis" had not yet been resolved. *Applying Economic Concepts 32-1* examines how our simple debt-dynamics equation can be used to understand Greece's extremely difficult fiscal situation in 2011.

for several years. Bondholders then wondered how the Greek government would ever repay the existing bonds. Once these concerns became entrenched, the demand for Greek bonds plummeted and the bond yields increased sharply to reflect the risk of default by the Greek government. In 2011, the yields on Greek 10-year bonds were 34 percent—as compared to approximately 2 percent on 10-year bonds issued by the German government.

The increase in yields on Greek bonds exacerbated the fiscal situation of the Greek government and threatened the creation of a vicious cycle. The high bond yields made it more costly to finance its large overall budget deficit (9.2 percent of GDP in 2011) and also more costly to finance the regular "rollover" of existing bonds that occurs regularly in any modern economy. These greater financing costs increased the need for fiscal contraction as a means of reducing the existing budget deficit, but fiscal contraction would reduce aggregate demand and reduce real GDP growth even further. In addition, any further decline in real GDP growth would, as is clear from the debt-dynamics equation, cause an even larger increase in the debt-to-GDP ratio and thus cause further fears of default, thus driving up bond yields even further.

To break this vicious cycle, the Greek government turned to the IMF and other members of the European Union for substantial loans that would permit Greece to finance its budget deficit and bond rollovers at reasonable rates for a few years while Greece implemented its necessary fiscal adjustments and tried to restore its fiscal credibility in the eyes of global bondholders.

Resolution

By early in 2013, the Greek fiscal situation had yet to be resolved. Even after a partial debt default equal to roughly 70 percent of the value of its outstanding debt, and large loans from both the IMF and other members of the European Union, the Greek government could not agree on a set of fiscal policies that would satisfy Greek voters and at the same time satisfy the conditions set forth by the European countries that had become Greece's most important creditors.

A further complication is that Greece shares a currency (the euro) with 16 other members of the European Union. As Greece's fiscal situation worsened, and its resolution was appearing less and less likely, the possibility of Greece leaving the euro zone and re-introducing its own currency became more likely. As this book went to press in January 2013, it was extremely difficult to predict the most likely outcome.

---

*The economic situation in Greece was determined by a complex set of factors, including various problems encountered within a group of countries using a common currency. In this box, we focus only on the *fiscal* situation in Greece. Readers interested in a thorough discussion of the various aspects of the European debt crisis are referred to "The future of the euro: An economic perspective on the Eurozone crisis," McKinsey and Company, January 2012.

32.3 The Effects of Government Debt and Deficits

Let's now examine why we should care about the size of the government deficit (or surplus) and its debt. We begin with the important idea that deficits may *crowd out* private-sector activity and thereby may harm future generations by reducing the economy's long-run growth rate. The opposite idea is equally important—that budget surpluses may *crowd in* private-sector activity and be beneficial to future generations by increasing the economy's long-run growth rate.

Before beginning our analysis, we must be clear about one of our assumptions in the macro model that we have developed in previous chapters. As we saw earlier in this chapter, when the government increases its budget deficit, it necessarily increases its borrowing. This increase in borrowing is a reduction in the government's saving. In our model, we make the assumption that any reduction in the government's saving has only small effects on the amount of saving by the private sector—with the result that *national* saving falls along with government saving. Thus, we assume in our model that an increase in the government's budget deficit leads to a reduction in national saving. We make this assumption because it is consistent with the bulk of empirical evidence on this issue.

> In our macro model, we assume that an increase in the government's budget deficit leads to a decrease in national saving.

Do Deficits Crowd Out Private Activity?

It is useful to make the distinction between an economy that is *closed* to international trade in goods, service, and assets and one that is *open* to such trade. We consider the two cases separately.

Investment in Closed Economies Recall from Chapter 26 the close long-run relationship between desired investment and desired national saving in a closed economy. In the long-run version of our macro model, with real GDP equal to Y^*, the real interest rate is determined by the equality of desired investment and desired national saving. What is the effect in this model of an increase in the government's budget deficit, caused either by an increase in government spending or a reduction in taxes? An increase in the budget deficit is assumed to cause a reduction in the supply of national saving. As we saw in Chapter 26, a reduction in the supply of national saving will increase the equilibrium real interest rate and reduce the amount of investment in the economy. This **crowding out** of investment by the expansionary fiscal policy is shown in Figure 32-6.

Note in the figure the different short-run and long-run effects of the fiscal expansion. In the short run, the fiscal expansion shifts the *AD* curve to the right and increases real GDP. In the long run, however, after wages and other factor prices have fully adjusted to the output gap, real GDP returns to Y^* at an increased equilibrium real interest rate. So the amount of investment in the new long-run equilibrium is less than it was prior to the increase in the budget deficit.

> The long-run effect of a fiscal expansion in our macro model is to drive up the real interest rate and crowd out private investment.

crowding out The offsetting reduction in private expenditure caused by the rise in interest rates that follows an expansionary fiscal policy.

Net Exports in Open Economies There is a second effect in an open economy when financial capital is internationally mobile. Consider once again the possibility that the Canadian government increases its budget deficit either by increasing spending or by reducing taxes. What is the effect of the reduction in national saving in an open economy, like Canada's?

As real interest rates rise in Canada, foreigners are attracted to the higher-yield Canadian assets and thus foreign financial capital flows into Canada. But since Canadian dollars are required in order to buy Canadian interest-earning assets, this capital inflow increases the demand for Canadian dollars in the foreign-exchange market and leads to an appreciation of the Canadian dollar. If the currency appreciation is sustained over several months or longer, it will cause a reduction in Canada's exports and an increase in Canada's imports; Canadian net exports, NX, will fall.

> In an open economy, the government budget deficit attracts foreign financial capital and appreciates the domestic currency. The long-run result is a crowding out of net exports.

How Much Crowding Out? We have argued that the long-run effect of an increase in the government's budget deficit is to crowd out private investment and net exports. We have said nothing, however, about *how much* crowding out takes place. For example, does a \$10 billion increase in the budget deficit reduce private expenditure by the full \$10 billion, or by less, or by more?

To examine this issue, recall an equation of national income accounting from Chapter 20:

$$Y = C_a + I_a + G_a + NX_a$$

where the a subscripts denote actual (as opposed to desired) quantities. By definition, the sum of the four expenditure components is always exactly equal to real GDP. Now think about the change in these expenditure components as we follow the effects of a fiscal expansion in Figure 32-6. Suppose that we begin in a long-run equilibrium with $Y = Y^*$ and then the government increases its purchases of goods and services. In the short run in our macro model, this fiscal expansion leads to an increase in Y above Y^* and also causes an increase in consumption (which rises as Y rises). In the long run, however, after Y has returned

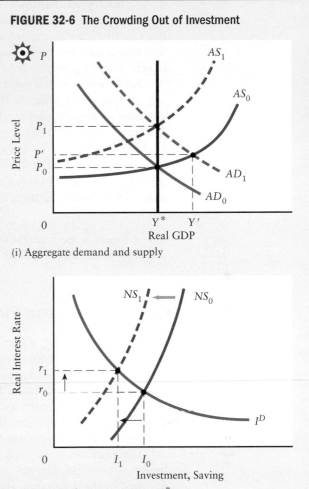

FIGURE 32-6 The Crowding Out of Investment

(i) Aggregate demand and supply

(ii) Saving and investment ($Y = Y^*$)

For a closed economy, the long-run effects of an increase in the budget deficit will be a higher real interest rate and a reduction in private investment. Consider a closed economy that is in long-run equilibrium at Y^* and P_0 in part (i). Suppose the government increases its spending or reduces its taxes, thus increasing the budget deficit. Either policy raises aggregate demand and shifts AD_0 to AD_1. The new short-run equilibrium is at Y' and P', but the adjustment process will then cause factor prices to rise, shifting the AS curve from AS_0 to AS_1. The new long-run equilibrium will be at Y^* and P_1.

The long-run effect of this change on saving and investment can be seen in part (ii), which shows the market for financial capital in the long run, with real GDP equal to Y^*. The increase in the government's budget deficit reduces national saving and shifts NS_0 to NS_1. The equilibrium real interest rate rises and the amount of investment falls from I_0 to I_1.

to Y^*, the higher-than-initial value of government purchases implies that the sum of the three private expenditure components must be lower than it was at the initial long-run equilibrium. We cannot say precisely how the reduction in private spending is distributed across the three components, but in the long run in our model total private expenditure $(C_a + I_a + NX_a)$ has been *fully* crowded out by the fiscal expansion.

Note, however, that full crowding out does *not* occur if the level of potential output, Y^*, increases as a result of the fiscal expansion. For example, suppose the government increases its spending on productivity-enhancing infrastructure projects or improvements in education or health-care programs. These kinds of expenditures are likely to increase the level of Y^*. If Y^* rises, then the long-run adjustment in Figure 32-6 brings the economy back to a *higher* level of Y^*, in which case the fiscal expansion does *not* fully crowd out private expenditure. In other words, the extent of crowding out depends crucially on the change in Y^* which, in turn, depends on the nature of the increased government spending.

> The larger is the increase in potential output caused by a fiscal expansion, the less private expenditure will be crowded out.

Do Deficits Harm Future Generations?

In a closed economy, a rise in the government deficit pushes up interest rates and crowds out domestic investment. In an open economy, a rise in the government deficit also appreciates the currency and crowds out net exports. In both cases, there may be a cost to future generations. Economists call this cost the *long-term burden of government debt*. Such a burden will be present if the private expenditure that is crowded out would have added more to the economy's productive capacity than what is added by the government's expenditure financed by the budget deficit.

The previous paragraph suggests that whether government budget deficits harm future generations depends on the nature of the government goods and services being financed by the deficit (and also on the nature of the private expenditure that gets crowded out). At one extreme, the government borrowing may finance a project that generates a substantial return to future generations, and thus the future generations may be made better off by today's budget deficit. An example might be the government's financing of long-term medical research projects that generate a return in the distant future. Another example is the government's financing of a new highway that reduces transport times for people and products for many years. At the other extreme, the government deficit may finance some government program that benefits mainly the current generation. An example might be the government's financing of cultural or sporting events that benefit the current generation but produce little or no benefits for future generations.

The concern that budget deficits may be inappropriately placing a burden on future generations has led some economists to advocate the idea of *capital budgeting* by the government. Under this scheme, the government would essentially classify each of its expenditures as either consumption or investment; the former would be spending that mostly benefits the current generation while the latter would be spending that mostly benefits future generations.

With capital budgeting, government deficits could be used to minimize the undesirable redistributions of income between generations. For example, the government might be committed to borrowing no more in any given year than the expenditures classified as investments. In this way, future generations would receive benefits from current government spending that are at least equal to the future taxes they will pay.

> Government budget deficits represent taxes that must be paid by future generations. Whether these future generations are harmed by the current budget deficit depends to a large extent on the nature of the government spending financed by the deficit.

Does Government Debt Hamper Economic Policy?

The costs imposed on future generations by government debt are real, though they are often ignored because they occur in the very distant future. But other problems associated with the presence of government debt are more immediately apparent. In particular, high levels of government debt may make the conduct of monetary and fiscal policy more difficult.

Monetary Policy To see how a large stock of government debt can hamper the conduct of monetary policy, consider a country that has a high debt-to-GDP ratio and that has a real interest rate above the growth rate of GDP. As we saw previously, the debt-to-GDP ratio will continue to grow in this situation unless the government starts running significant primary budget *surpluses*. But such primary surpluses require either increases in taxation or reductions in program spending, both of which may be politically unpopular. If such primary surpluses look unlikely to be achieved in the near future, both foreign and domestic bondholders may come to expect the government to put pressure on the central bank to purchase—or *monetize*—an increasing portion of its deficit. Such monetization means that the money supply is increasing and will eventually cause inflation. Any ensuing inflation would erode the real value of the bonds held by creditors.

Budget deficits used to finance investment projects may not harm future generations because the future generations will benefit from the investment.

Fears of future debt monetization will likely lead to expectations of future inflation and put upward pressure on nominal interest rates and on some prices and wages. Thus, even in the absence of any *current* actions by the central bank to increase the rate of growth of the money supply, a large government debt may lead to the *expectation* of future inflation, thus hampering the task of the central bank in keeping inflation and inflationary expectations low.

Fiscal Policy In Chapter 22 we saw that fiscal policy could potentially be used to stabilize aggregate demand and thereby stabilize real GDP. For example, in a booming economy, the government might reduce spending or increase tax rates to reduce inflationary pressures. Or during a recession, the government might reduce tax rates and increase spending in an attempt to stimulate aggregate demand, as it did in 2009 and 2010 during a major global recession. Having cyclically adjusted budget deficits during recessions and cyclically adjusted budget surpluses during booms is one way of implementing *counter-cyclical fiscal policy*.

How does the presence of government debt affect the government's ability to conduct such counter-cyclical fiscal policy? Perhaps the easiest way to answer this question is to recall the equation that describes the change in the debt-to-GDP ratio:

$$\Delta d = x + (r - g) \times d$$

This equation shows that the *change* in the debt-to-GDP ratio (Δd) depends on the *level* of the debt-to-GDP ratio (d). For example, if the real interest rate exceeds the growth rate of real GDP, so that $r - g$ is positive, the increase in the debt-to-GDP ratio (Δd) will be higher if d is already high than if it is low (for any given value of x). We examine the case where $r - g$ is positive because this is the typical situation in a developed economy such as Canada's.

With this relationship in mind, consider the problem faced during a recession by a government that is considering an expansionary fiscal policy. Such a policy would increase the primary budget deficit and therefore increase x. On the one hand, there would be short-run benefits from the higher level of real GDP; on the other hand, the government may be wary of taking actions that lead to large increases in the debt-to-GDP ratio.

If the stock of outstanding government debt is small relative to the size of the economy, the government has a great deal of flexibility in conducting counter-cyclical fiscal policy. The small value of d implies that d will be rising only slowly in the absence of a primary deficit. Thus, the government may be able to increase the primary deficit—either by increasing program spending or by reducing tax rates—without generating a large increase in the debt-to-GDP ratio. But the government has significantly less flexibility if the stock of outstanding government debt is already very large. In this case, and with our assumption that r is greater than g, the high value of d means that even in the absence of a primary budget deficit, d will be increasing quickly. Thus, any increase in the primary deficit brought about by the counter-cyclical fiscal policy runs the danger of generating increases in the debt-to-GDP ratio that may be viewed by creditors as unsustainable. Such perceptions of unsustainability may lead to an increase in the real interest rate on government debt, which exacerbates the problem by driving d up even faster.

The idea that a large and rising stock of government debt could "tie the hands" of the government in times when it would otherwise want to conduct counter-cyclical fiscal policy was brought to the fore of Canadian economic policy by the late Douglas Purvis of Queen's University (and a co-author of this textbook for many years). Purvis argued in the mid-1980s that Canadian government deficits must be brought under control quickly so that the debt would not accumulate to the point where the government would have no room left for fiscal stabilization policy. These warnings were not heeded. By the onset of the next recession in 1991, the federal government had added roughly $200 billion to the stock of debt and the debt-to-GDP ratio was just less than 70 percent. Predictably, the government felt unable to use discretionary fiscal policy to reduce some of the effects of the recession.

However, by 2008, the federal debt-to-GDP ratio had fallen to less than 30 percent as a result of more than a decade of fiscal restraint and rapid economic growth. When the Canadian economy entered recession late in 2008, the Conservative government recognized that Canada's past fiscal prudence gave it the needed flexibility to design an aggressively counter-cyclical fiscal policy. The federal budgets of 2009 and 2010 announced large spending increases and tax reductions that were predicted to result in budget deficits that would increase the debt-to-GDP ratio by roughly 4 percentage points over the next two years. The government was careful, however, to indicate clearly its intentions of

With the arrival of the global economic recession in 2008, Finance Minister Jim Flaherty implemented a significant fiscal expansion that contributed to a large increase in the federal budget deficit. The federal budget is now projected to return to balance by about 2016.

returning the debt-to-GDP ratio to its previously announced target of 25 percent. The need for short-term fiscal stimulus was tempered by the recognition of the importance of long-term fiscal prudence.

32.4 Formal Fiscal Rules

After more than two decades of persistent budget deficits in Canada, and then several years of budget surpluses, the nature of political debate about fiscal policy shifted considerably. Whereas during the mid-1980s there was active political debate about whether deficits were a problem, and what costs would be involved in reducing them, by 2007 all major political parties in Canada stressed the importance of avoiding budget deficits. But the onset of the global recession in 2008 changed the debate again. As the severity of the recession became clearer, all political parties argued the need for fiscal measures to stimulate the economy, but at the same time accepted the goal of returning to a balanced budget (or surplus) as soon as the economy showed signs of a solid recovery.

In some quarters, there is support for the idea that legislation should be amended to impose restrictions on the size of budget deficits. Would such legislation be desirable? We examine three different proposals.

Annually Balanced Budgets

It would be extremely difficult to balance the budget on an annual basis. The reason is that a significant portion of the government budget is beyond its short-term control, and a further large amount is hard to change quickly. For example, the entire debt-service component of government expenditures is determined by past borrowing and thus cannot be altered by the current government. Also, many spending programs such as equalization and public pensions are set in current legislation and cannot be changed without the lengthy process of legislative reform. In addition, as we saw in our discussion of the cyclically adjusted deficit, changes in real GDP that are beyond the control of the government lead to significant changes in tax revenues (and transfer payments) and thus generate significant changes in the budget deficit or surplus.

Even if it were possible for the government to control its spending and revenues perfectly on a year-to-year basis, it would probably be *undesirable* to balance the budget every year. Recall that tax revenues rise in booms and fall in recessions; and many expenditures on transfers fall in booms and rise in recessions. As we first saw in Chapter 22, this property of the tax-and-transfer system implies that fiscal policy contains a built-in stabilizer. In recessions, the increase in the budget deficit stimulates aggregate demand whereas in booms the budget surplus reduces aggregate demand.

But things would be very different with an annually balanced budget. With a balanced budget, government expenditures would be *forced* to adjust to the changing level of tax revenues. In a recession, when tax revenues naturally decline, a balanced budget would require either a *reduction* in government expenditures or an *increase* in tax rates, thus generating a major *destabilizing* force on real GDP. Similarly, as tax revenues naturally rise in an economic boom, a balanced budget would require either an increase in government expenditures or a reduction in taxes, thus stimulating aggregate demand when an inflationary gap may already exist.

For some forecasts and analysis of the government's fiscal options, see the Royal Bank's website: www.rbc.com. *Go to "economics."*

An annually balanced budget would eliminate the automatic fiscal stabilizers and accentuate the swings in real GDP.

Cyclically Balanced Budgets

One alternative to the extreme policy of requiring an annually balanced budget is to require that the government budget be balanced over the course of a full economic cycle. Budget deficits would be permitted in recessions as long as they were matched by surpluses in booms. In this way, the built-in stabilizers could still perform their important role, but there would be no persistent build-up of government debt. In principle, this is a desirable treatment of the tradeoff between the short-run benefits of deficits and the long-run costs of debt.

Despite its appeal, the idea of cyclically balanced budgets has its problems as well. Perhaps the most important problem with a cyclically balanced budget is an operational one. In order to have a law that requires the budget to be balanced over the business cycle, it is necessary to be able to *define* the cycle precisely. But there will always be disagreement about what stage of the cycle the economy is currently in, and thus there will be disagreement as to whether the current government should be increasing or reducing its deficit. Compounding this problem is the fact that politicians will have a stake in the identification of the cycle. Those who favour increased deficits will argue that this year is an unusually bad year and thus an increase in the deficit is justified; deficit "hawks," in contrast, will always tend to find this year to be unusually good and thus a time to run budget surpluses.

A second problem is largely political. Suppose one government runs large deficits for a few years during a recession and then gets replaced in an election. Would the succeeding government then be bound to run budget surpluses after the recovery? What one government commits itself to in one year does not necessarily restrict what it (or its successor) does in the next year.

Balancing the budget over the course of the business cycle is in principle a desirable means of reconciling short-term stabilization with long-term fiscal prudence. The difficulty in precisely defining the business cycle, however, suggests that governments could best follow this as an approximate guide rather than as a formal rule.

Maintaining a Prudent Debt-to-GDP Ratio

A further problem with any policy that requires a balanced budget—whether over one year or over the business cycle—is that the emphasis is naturally on the overall budget deficit. But, as we saw earlier in this chapter, what determines the change in the debt-to-GDP ratio is the growth of the debt *relative* to the growth of the economy. With a growing economy, it is possible to have positive overall budget deficits—and thus a growing debt—and still have a falling debt-to-GDP ratio. Thus, to the extent that the debt-to-GDP ratio is the relevant gauge of a country's debt problem, focus should be placed on the debt-to-GDP ratio rather than on the budget deficit itself.

Some economists view a low and relatively stable debt-to-GDP ratio as the appropriate indicator of fiscal prudence. Their view permits a budget deficit such that the stock of debt grows no faster than GDP.

This view recognizes that not all government debt represents a problem. As we argued earlier in this chapter, government expenditure on items that deliver benefits for many years can sensibly be financed by borrowing so that the future generations who benefit from the spending also bear some the burden of repayment. However, admitting that some government debt may be appropriate is not to deny that genuine problems do exist when the government's debt-to-GDP ratio is very high. The challenge is then to permit government budget deficits necessary to finance worthwhile public investment while at the same time ensuring that the debt-to-GDP ratio does not become excessive. Such an approach to fiscal policy would be considered prudent by many economists.

By this standard, the Canadian federal budgets of the last several years have been prudent because they have led to a growth rate in the stock of debt smaller than the growth rate of real GDP, and thus a reduction in the debt-to-GDP ratio. For example, in 1996, the debt-to-GDP ratio reached its recent maximum of 70 percent. Significant fiscal contractions, combined with strong economic growth, led to a decline in the debt-to-GDP ratio to 50 percent by 2001, less than 40 percent by 2005, and less than 30 percent by 2008. The arrival of the 2008 global recession then led to substantial federal (and provincial) budget deficits, partly because of the recession-induced decline in net tax revenues and partly because of policy actions taken to stimulate the economy. The federal debt-to-GDP ratio increased to 38 percent by 2010. By 2012, however, after two years of modest recovery, the federal budget deficit was declining and the debt-to-GDP ratio was projected to fall below 30 percent by 2015.

SUMMARY

32.1 Facts and Definitions

LO 1

- The government's budget deficit is equal to total government expenditure minus total government revenue. Since the government must borrow to finance any shortfall in its revenues, the annual deficit is equal to the annual increase in the stock of government debt. Whenever the deficit is positive, the stock of government debt is growing.
- The primary budget deficit is equal to the excess of the government's program spending over total tax revenues.

- Large and persistent budget deficits beginning in the 1970s increased the stock of debt so that by 1996 the federal government net debt was equal to 70 percent of GDP. By 2008, after several years of fiscal contraction, the federal debt-to-GDP ratio was approximately 30 percent.
- The 2008–2009 recession increased the federal debt-to-GDP ratio to 38 percent, but it was projected to fall back down to 30 percent by 2015.

32.2 Two Analytical Issues

LO 2

- Since tax revenues tend to rise when real GDP rises, the overall budget deficit tends to rise during recessions and fall during booms. This tendency makes the budget deficit a poor measure of the stance of fiscal policy.
- The cyclically adjusted deficit is the budget deficit that would exist with the current set of fiscal policies if real GDP were equal to potential GDP. Changes in the cyclically adjusted deficit reflect changes in the stance of fiscal policy.

- The change in the debt-to-GDP ratio from one year to the next is given by

$$\Delta d = x + (r - g) \times d$$

where d is the debt-to-GDP ratio, x is the primary deficit as a percentage of GDP, r is the real interest rate on government bonds, and g is the growth rate of real GDP.

32.2 The Effects of Government Debt and Deficits

LO 3, 4

- In a closed economy, the long-run effect of an increase in the budget deficit is to reduce national saving and increase real interest rates. This increase in interest rates reduces the amount of investment.
- In an open economy, the long-run effect of an increase in the budget deficit is to push up interest rates and attract foreign financial capital. This leads to a currency appreciation and a reduction in net exports.
- Unless government debt is incurred to finance worthwhile public investments, the long-term burden of the debt is a redistribution of resources away from future generations and toward current generations.
- A large debt-to-GDP ratio may lead creditors to expect increases in inflation, as the government attempts to finance deficits through the creation of money. Such increases in inflationary expectations hamper the conduct of monetary policy.
- The higher is the debt-to-GDP ratio, the more constrained is the government in conducting counter-cyclical fiscal policy.

32.4 Formal Fiscal Rules

LO 5

- Since tax revenues (net of transfers) naturally rise as real GDP increases, legislation requiring an annually balanced budget forces either expenditures to rise or tax rates to fall during booms. This produces destabilizing fiscal policy.
- Cyclically balanced budgets, in principle, permit the short-run benefits of deficits to be realized without incurring the long-run costs of debt accumulation. Implementation of this policy is difficult, however, since the precise identification of the business cycle is controversial.
- Budget deficits need not lead to increases in the debt-to-GDP ratio if the economy is growing.
- Prudent fiscal policy can permit budget deficits during recessions and allow the financing of worthwhile public investments, while ensuring that the debt-to-GDP ratio does not become excessive.

KEY CONCEPTS

Government's budget constraint	Debt-service payments	Long-term burden of the debt
Primary budget deficit	Debt-to-GDP ratio	Annually balanced budget
The relationship between deficits and the national debt	Crowding out of investment	Cyclically balanced budget
	Crowding out of net exports	

STUDY EXERCISES

MyEconLab Make the grade with MyEconLab: Study Exercises marked in red can be found on MyEconLab. You can practise them as often as you want, and most feature step-by-step guided instructions to help you find the right answer.

1. Fill in the blanks to make the following statements correct.

   a. The government's budget constraint shows that government expenditures must be equal to the sum of _____ and _____.

   b. The government's annual budget deficit is the excess of total _____ over total _____ in a given year.

   c. If the government's total budget deficit is $20 billion and its debt-service payments are $18 billion, then its _____ is $2 billion. If the total budget deficit is $20 billion and its debt-service payments are $26 billion, then its _____ is $6 billion.

2. Fill in the blanks to make the following statements correct.

   a. When there is no change in the government's fiscal policy it is still possible for the budget deficit to fall because _____.

b. For a given set of fiscal policies, the budget deficit _____ as real GDP rises and _____ as real GDP falls.

c. The cyclically adjusted deficit is the budget deficit that would exist if real GDP equalled _____ and the government's _____ were at their current levels.

d. Suppose the real interest rate is 2 percent and the growth rate of real GDP is 1.5 percent. If the government wants to stabilize the debt-to-GDP ratio, then it is necessary to have a(n) _____.

3. Fill in the blanks to make the following statements correct.

a. In a closed economy, when the government borrows to finance the deficit, interest rates will _____ and some private investment will be _____.

b. In an open economy, when the government borrows to finance the deficit, interest rates will _____, the Canadian dollar will _____, and net exports will _____.

c. Suppose a law was passed that required the government to balance its budget each year. Fiscal policy would then have a(n) _____ effect.

d. A cyclically balanced budget is difficult to implement because it is difficult to identify the _____.

4. The table below shows government spending data over eight years in Debtland. All figures are in billions of dollars. The symbols used are as defined in the text.

Year	G (1)	T (2)	iD (3)	Budget Deficit (4)	Primary Budget Deficit (5)	Stock of Debt (6)
2006	175	175	25	—	—	—
2007	180	180	26	—	—	—
2008	185	185	27	—	—	—
2009	188	190	26	—	—	—
2010	185	195	25	—	—	—
2011	185	200	24	—	—	—
2012	180	205	23	—	—	—
2013	175	210	22	—	—	—

a. Compute Debtland's budget deficit in each year and complete column 4 in the table. (Since we are computing the deficit, a negative number indicates a surplus.)

b. Compute Debtland's primary budget deficit in each year and complete column 5 in the table.

c. Suppose the initial stock of debt (in 2005) was $400 billion. Noting that the deficit in 2006 adds to the existing stock of debt, what is the stock of debt by the end of 2006?

d. Compute the stock of debt for each year and complete column 6 in the table.

e. Suppose you know that Debtland's debt-to-GDP ratio was the same in 2013 as in 2005. By what percentage did GDP grow between 2005 and 2013?

5. The figure below shows the budget deficit function for a country.

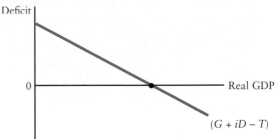

a. Explain why the budget deficit function is downward sloping.

b. If the government increases its level of purchases (G), what happens to the budget deficit at any level of real GDP? Show this in the diagram.

c. If the government increases the net tax rate, what happens to the deficit at any level of real GDP? Show this in the diagram.

d. Explain why a rise in the actual budget deficit does not necessarily reflect a change in fiscal policy.

e. How would a fiscal expansion appear in the diagram? A fiscal contraction?

6. In the late 1990s, the U.S. government was slightly ahead of the Canadian government in reducing its budget deficit. The following table shows the actual budget deficit and the cyclically adjusted deficit (both as a percentage of GDP) for the United States from 1989 to 1997.

Year	Actual Deficit	CAD
1989	2.8	2.9
1990	3.9	3.2
1991	4.6	3.4
1992	4.7	3.7
1993	3.9	3.7
1994	3.0	2.8
1995	2.3	2.6
1996	1.4	1.6
1997	0.3	1.0

a. On a scale diagram (with the year on the horizontal axis), graph the actual deficit and the cyclically adjusted deficit.

b. From 1990 to 1994, the actual budget deficit is above the CAD. Explain why.

c. From 1995 to 1997, the actual budget deficit is below the CAD. Explain why.

d. Identify the periods when U.S. fiscal policy was expansionary.

e. Identify the periods when U.S. fiscal policy was contractionary.

f. Look back at Figure 32-5 on page 808. How does the stance of U.S. fiscal policy over this period compare with Canada's?

7. The following table shows hypothetical data from 2007 to 2013 that can be used to compute the change in the debt-to-GDP ratio. The symbols used are as defined in the text.

Year	x (1)	r (2)	g (3)	d (4)	Δd (5)
2007	0.03	0.045	0.025	0.70	___
2008	0.02	0.04	0.025	___	___
2009	0.01	0.035	0.025	___	___
2010	0.00	0.035	0.025	___	___
2011	−0.01	0.03	0.025	___	___
2012	−0.02	0.03	0.025	___	___
2013	−0.03	0.025	0.025	___	___

a. Remember from the text that the change in the debt-to-GDP ratio (Δd) during a year is given by $\Delta d = x + (r - g)d$. Compute Δd for 2007.
b. Note that d at the beginning of 2008 is equal to d at the beginning of 2007 plus Δd during 2007. Compute d in 2008.
c. Using the same method, compute d and Δd for each year, and complete columns 4 and 5.
d. Plot d in a scale diagram with the year on the horizontal axis. What discretionary variable was most responsible for the observed decline in d?
e. Note that as the primary deficit (x) falls between 2007 and 2013, there is also a downward trend in the real interest rate. Can you offer an explanation for this?

8. The diagram below shows an AD/AS diagram. The economy begins at E_0 with output equal to Y^*. Suppose the government in this closed economy increases G and finances it by running a deficit (borrowing). The AD curve shifts to the right.

a. How does the interest rate at E_1 compare with that at E_0? Explain.
b. Given your answer to part (a), how does investment at E_1 compare with investment at E_0?
c. Explain the economy's adjustment toward E_2. What happens to the interest rate and investment?
d. What is the likely long-run effect for the economy from the fiscal expansion? Explain.

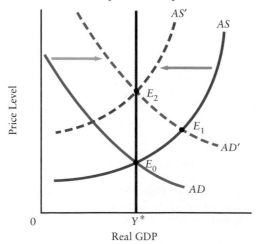

9. The diagram below shows an AD/AS diagram. The economy begins at E_0 with output equal to Y^*. Suppose the government in this closed economy decreases its budget deficit by increasing T (and keeping G unchanged), thus causing the AD curve to shift to the left.

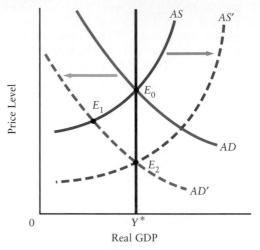

a. How does the interest rate at E_1 compare with that at E_0? Explain.
b. Given your answer to part (a), how does investment at E_1 compare with investment at E_0?
c. Explain the economy's adjustment toward E_2. What happens to the interest rate and investment?
d. What is the long-run effect of the government deficit on the growth rate of Y^*?
e. Comparing the short-run and the long-run effects of this policy, what dilemma does the government face in reducing its deficit?

10. A Member of Parliament recently exclaimed, "The prime minister's policies are working! Lower interest rates combined with staunch fiscal policy have reduced the deficit significantly." What do interest rates have to do with government spending and taxes when it comes to deficit management?

11. The Canadian federal budget moved from a surplus of $9.6 billion in the 2007–2008 fiscal year to a deficit of $5.8 billion the next year, and a large deficit of $55.6 billion in 2009–2010.

a. Suppose real GDP was at potential in each of the first two years. What can you conclude about the cause of the change in the budget deficit? Show this change in a diagram of the budget deficit function.
b. Suppose from 2008–2009 to 2009–2010, two things happened: real GDP fell and the government implemented an expansionary fiscal policy. Show these two separate events in a diagram of the budget deficit function.

The Gains from International Trade

LEARNING OBJECTIVES (LO)

After studying this chapter you will be able to

1 explain why the gains from trade depend on the pattern of comparative advantage.
2 understand how factor endowments and climate can influence a country's comparative advantage.

3 describe the law of one price.
4 explain why countries export some goods and import others.

TRADE between peoples and nations has been going on throughout human history, and humans have gone to great lengths and endured severe hardship in order to reap the benefits of trade. Centuries ago, for example, the inhabitants of remote islands in Southeast Polynesia travelled the open ocean in canoes for days at a time to trade oyster shells, volcanic glass, basalt, and food items with inhabitants of other, distant islands.

Today, the required activities for trade may be far less demanding, but the transactions themselves are no less important. Canadian consumers buy cars from Germany, Germans take holidays in Italy, Italians buy spices from Africa, Africans import oil from Kuwait, Kuwaitis buy Japanese cameras, and the Japanese buy Canadian lumber. *International trade* refers to the exchange of goods and services that takes place across international boundaries.

The founders of modern economics were concerned with foreign trade problems. The great eighteenth-century British philosopher and economist David Hume (1711–1776), one of the first to work out the theory of the price system, developed his concepts mainly in terms of prices in foreign trade. Adam Smith (1723–1790), in *The Wealth of Nations*, attacked government restriction of international trade. David Ricardo (1772–1823) developed the basic theory of the gains from trade that is studied in this chapter. The 1846 repeal of the Corn Laws—tariffs on the importation of corn and other grains into the United Kingdom—and the transformation of that country during the nineteenth century from a country of high tariffs to one of complete free trade were to some extent the result of arguments by economists whose theories of the gains from international trade led them to condemn tariffs.

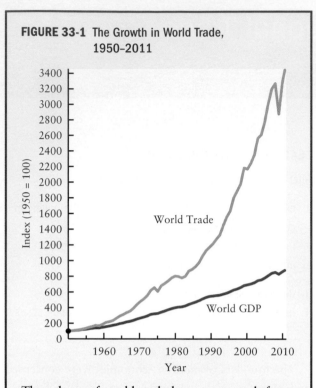

FIGURE 33-1 The Growth in World Trade, 1950–2011

The volume of world trade has grown much faster than world GDP over the past six decades. The figure shows the growth of real GDP and the volume of trade since 1950. Both are expressed as index numbers, set equal to 100 in 1950. Real world GDP has increased more than seven times since 1950; world trade volume has increased by over 33 times. The major global recession in 2009 is clearly evident with the sharp decline in the flow of trade in that year.

(*Source:* World Trade Organization, *International Trade Statistics 2012*, Table A1. www.wto.org.)

International trade is becoming increasingly important, not just for Canada but for the world as a whole. As Figure 33-1 shows, the volume of world trade has grown much faster than world real GDP over the past six decades. Since 1950, the world's real GDP has increased by more than seven times, an average annual growth rate of 3.7 percent. Over the same period, however, the volume of world trade has increased by more than 30 times, an average annual growth rate of 6.1 percent.

Figure 33-2 shows some data for Canadian trade in 2011. The figure shows the value of Canadian exports and imports of goods in several broad industry groupings. There are three important points to note from the figure. First, international trade is very important for Canada. In 2011, Canada exported $458 billion and imported $456 billion in goods—if we added trade in services, each of these values would be higher by about $80 billion; each flow (exports and imports) amounts to about 32 percent of GDP. Second, exports and imports are roughly the same size, so that the *volume* of trade is much larger than the *balance* of trade—the value of exports minus the value of imports. Third, in most of the industry groupings there are significant amounts of both imports and exports. Such *intra-industry trade* will be discussed later in the chapter. Canada does not just export resource products and import manufactured goods; it also imports many resource products and exports many manufactured goods.

In this chapter, we examine the increases in living standards that result from international trade. We find that the source of the gains from trade lies in differing cost conditions among geographical regions. World income would be vastly lower if countries did not specialize in the products in which they have the lowest opportunity costs of production. These costs are partly determined by natural endowments (geographical and climatic conditions), partly by public policy, and partly by historical accident.

For information on world trade, see the World Trade Organization's website: www.wto.org.

33.1 The Gains from Trade

open economy An economy that engages in international trade.

closed economy An economy that has no foreign trade.

An economy that engages in international trade is called an **open economy**; one that does not is called a **closed economy**. A situation in which a country does no foreign trade is called one of *autarky*.

Although politicians often regard foreign trade differently from domestic trade, economists from Adam Smith on have argued that the causes and consequences of international trade are simply an extension of the principles governing trade between domestic firms and individuals. What are the benefits of trade among individuals, among groups, among regions, or among countries?

Interpersonal, Interregional, and International Trade

To begin, consider trade among individuals. Without trade, each person would have to be self-sufficient: Each would have to produce all the food, clothing, shelter, medical services, entertainment, and luxuries that he or she consumed. Because no individual could effectively produce such a large range of products, a world of individual self-sufficiency would be a world with extremely low living standards: individuals would work very hard but not be able to produce or consume very much.

Trade among individuals allows people to specialize in activities they can do well and to buy from others the goods and services they cannot easily produce. A good doctor who is a bad carpenter can provide medical services not only for her own family but also for a good carpenter without the training or the ability to practise medicine. Trade and specialization are intimately connected.

> **Without trade, everyone must be self-sufficient; with trade, people can specialize in what they do well and satisfy other needs by trading.**

The same principle applies to regions. Without interregional trade, each region would be forced to be self-sufficient. With trade, each region can specialize in producing products for which it has some natural or acquired advantage.

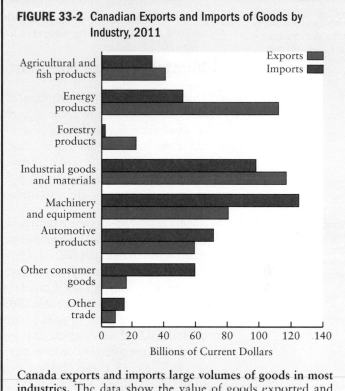

FIGURE 33-2 Canadian Exports and Imports of Goods by Industry, 2011

Billions of Current Dollars

Canada exports and imports large volumes of goods in most industries. The data show the value of goods exported and imported by industry in 2011 (trade in services is not shown). The total value of goods exported was $458 billion; the total value of goods imported was $456 billion.

(*Source:* These data are available on Statistics Canada's website: www.statcan.gc.ca. Search for "International trade" and then "Canada's merchandise exports.")

Prairie regions can specialize in growing grain, mountain regions in mining and forest products, and regions with abundant power can specialize in manufacturing. Cool regions can produce wheat and other crops that thrive in temperate climates, and hot regions can grow such tropical crops as bananas, sugarcane, and coffee. The living standards of the inhabitants of all regions will be higher when each region specializes in products in which it has some natural or acquired advantage and obtains other products by trade than when all regions seek to be self-sufficient.

This same principle also applies to countries. A national boundary is a political invention and rarely delimits an area that is naturally self-sufficient. Countries, like regions and individuals, can gain from specialization. More of some goods are produced domestically than residents want to consume, while residents would like to consume larger quantities of other goods than are produced domestically. International trade is necessary to achieve the gains that international specialization makes possible.

> **With trade, each individual, region, or country is able to concentrate on producing goods and services that it produces efficiently while trading to obtain goods and services that it does not produce efficiently.**

gains from trade The increased output attributable to the specialization according to comparative advantage that is made possible by trade.

Specialization and trade go hand in hand because there is no incentive to achieve the gains from specialization without being able to trade the goods produced for goods desired. Economists use the term **gains from trade** to embrace the results of both.

Illustrating the Gains from Trade

Our discussion so far has emphasized the *differences* that exist between individuals, regions, and countries, and how these differences lie behind the benefits derived from trade. In order to show these benefits more precisely, we will focus on trade between two countries. We make the important assumption that within each country the average cost of production of any good is independent of *how much* of that good is produced. That is, we are making the assumption of *constant costs*. Our example involves two countries and two products, but the general principles apply to the case of many countries and many products.

absolute advantage The situation that exists when one country can produce some commodity at lower absolute cost than another country.

Absolute Advantage One region is said to have an **absolute advantage** over another in the production of good X when an equal quantity of resources can produce more X in the first region than in the second. Or, to put it differently, if it takes fewer resources to produce one unit of good X there than in another country. Table 33-1 shows an example. The two "countries" are Canada and the European Union (EU), and the two goods are wheat and cloth. The table shows the *absolute cost* of producing one unit of wheat and one unit of cloth in each country. The absolute cost is the dollar cost of the labour, capital, and other resources required to produce the goods. Thus, the country that can produce a specific good with fewer resources can produce it at a lower absolute cost.

In Table 33-1, the absolute cost for both wheat and cloth is less in Canada than in the EU. Canada is therefore said to have an *absolute advantage* over the EU in the production of both wheat and cloth because it is a more efficient producer—it takes less labour and other resources to produce the goods in Canada than in the EU.

The situation in Table 33-1 is hypothetical, but it is encountered often in the real world. Some countries, because they have access to cheap natural resources or better-trained workers or more sophisticated capital equipment, are low-cost producers for a wide range of products. Does this mean that high-cost countries stand no chance of being successful producers in a globalized world of international trade? Will the low-cost countries produce everything, leaving nothing to be done by high-cost countries? The answer is no. As we will see immediately, the gains from international trade do *not* depend on the pattern of absolute advantage.

comparative advantage The situation that exists when a country can produce a good with less forgone output of other goods than can another country.

Comparative Advantage The great English economist David Ricardo (1772–1823) was the first to provide an explanation of the pattern of international trade in a world in which countries had different costs. His theory of *comparative advantage* is still accepted by economists as a valid statement of one of the major sources of the gains from international trade. A country is said to have a **comparative advantage** in the production of good X if the cost of producing X *in terms of forgone output of other goods* is lower in that country than in another. Thus, the pattern of comparative advantage is based on *opportunity costs* rather than absolute costs. Table 33-2 illustrates the pattern of comparative advantage in the Canada–EU example. The opportunity cost in Canada for one kilogram of wheat is computed by determining how much

---

TABLE 33-1 Absolute Costs and Absolute Advantage

	Wheat (kilograms)	Cloth (metres)
Canada	$1 per kilogram	$5 per metre
EU	$3 per kilogram	$6 per metre

Absolute advantage reflects the differences in absolute costs of producing goods between countries. The numbers show the dollar cost of the total amount of resources necessary for producing wheat and cloth in Canada and the EU. Note that Canada is a lower-cost producer than the EU for both wheat and cloth. Canada is therefore said to have an absolute advantage in the production of both goods.

cloth must be given up in Canada in order to produce an additional kilogram of wheat. From Table 33-1, the absolute costs of wheat and cloth were $1 per kilogram and $5 per metre, respectively. Thus, in order to produce one extra kilogram of wheat, Canada must use resources that could have produced one-fifth of a metre of cloth. So the opportunity cost of one kilogram of wheat is 0.2 metres of cloth. By exactly the same reasoning, the opportunity cost of one metre of cloth in Canada is 5.0 kilograms of wheat. These opportunity costs are shown in Table 33-2.

Even though a country may have an absolute advantage in all goods (as Canada does in Table 33-1), it *cannot* have a comparative advantage in all goods. Similarly, even though a country may be inefficient in absolute terms and thus have an absolute disadvantage in all goods (as is the case for the EU in Table 33-1) it *cannot* have a comparative disadvantage in all goods. In Table 33-2, Canada has a comparative advantage in the production of wheat because Canada must give up less cloth to produce one kilogram of wheat than must be given up in the EU. Similarly, the EU has a comparative advantage in the production of cloth because the EU must give up less wheat in order to produce one metre of cloth than must be given up in Canada.

TABLE 33-2 Opportunity Costs and Comparative Advantage	
Canada:	opportunity cost of 1 kg of wheat = 0.2 m cloth
EU:	opportunity cost of 1 kg of wheat = 0.5 m cloth
Canada:	opportunity cost of 1 m of cloth = 5 kg wheat
EU:	opportunity cost of 1 m of cloth = 2 kg wheat

Comparative advantages reflect opportunity costs that differ between countries. The opportunity costs are computed using the data provided in Table 33-1. For example, for Canada to produce one additional kilogram of wheat, it must use resources that could have been used to produce 0.2 metres of cloth; the opportunity cost of 1 kg of wheat in Canada is therefore 0.2 metres of cloth. The comparative advantages for each country are shown by the shaded rows. Canada has a comparative advantage in wheat production because it has a lower opportunity cost for wheat than does the EU. The EU has a comparative advantage in cloth because its opportunity cost for cloth is lower than that in Canada.

> The gains from specialization and trade depend on the pattern of comparative, not absolute, advantage.

In our example, total world wheat production can be increased if Canada devotes more resources to the production of wheat and fewer resources to the production of cloth. Similarly, total world cloth production can be increased if the EU devotes more resources to the production of cloth and fewer to wheat. In the extreme case, Canada could *specialize* by producing *only* wheat and the EU could specialize by producing only cloth. Such reallocations of resources increase total world output because each country is specializing in the production of the good in which it has the lowest opportunity cost. The gains from specialization along the lines of comparative advantage are shown in Table 33-3.

> World output increases if countries specialize in the production of the goods in which they have a comparative advantage.

Not *every possible* pattern of specialization, however, is beneficial for the world. In our example, if Canada were to specialize in cloth and the EU in wheat, total world output would *fall*. To see this, note that in order to produce one extra metre of cloth in Canada,

TABLE 33-3 The Gains from Specialization		
Changes from each country producing more units of the product in which it has the lower opportunity cost		
	Wheat (kilograms)	Cloth (metres)
Canada	+5.0	−1.0
EU	−4.0	+2.0
Total	+1.0	+1.0

Whenever opportunity costs differ between countries, specialization can increase the world's production of both products. These calculations show that there are gains from specialization given the opportunity costs of Table 33-2. To produce five more kilograms of wheat, Canada must sacrifice 1.0 m of cloth. To produce two more metres of cloth, the EU must sacrifice 4.0 kg of wheat. This combination of changes increases world production of both wheat and cloth.

five kilograms of wheat must be sacrificed (see Table 33-2). Similarly, in order to produce four extra kilograms of wheat in the EU, two metres of cloth must be sacrificed. Thus, if each country produced these additional units of the "wrong" good, total world output of wheat would fall by one kilogram and total output of cloth would fall by one metre.

> **Specialization of production *against* the pattern of comparative advantage leads to a decline in total world output.**

We have discussed comparative advantage in terms of opportunity costs. We can also illustrate it by considering the two countries' production possibilities boundaries. Recall from Chapter 1 the connection between a country's production possibilities boundary and the opportunity costs of production. The slope of the production possibilities boundary indicates the opportunity costs. The existence of different opportunity costs across countries implies comparative advantages that can lead to gains from trade. Figure 33-3 illustrates how two countries can both gain from trade when they have different

FIGURE 33-3 The Gains from Trade with Constant Opportunity Costs

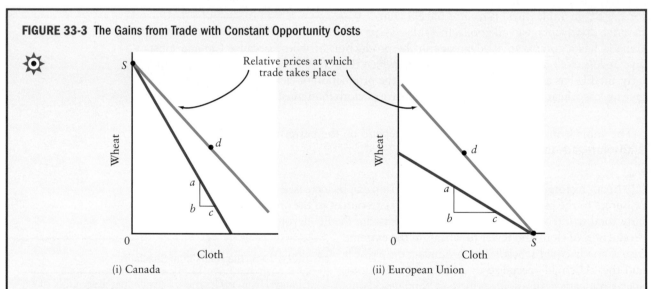

(i) Canada

(ii) European Union

International trade leads to specialization in production and increased consumption possibilities. The purple lines in parts (i) and (ii) represent the production possibilities boundaries for Canada and the EU, respectively. In the absence of any international trade, these also represent each country's consumption possibilities.

The difference in the slopes of the production possibilities boundaries reflects differences in comparative advantage, as shown in Table 33-2. In each part the opportunity cost of increasing production of wheat by the same amount (measured by the distance *ba*) is the amount by which the production of cloth must be reduced (measured by the distance *bc*). The relatively steep production possibilities boundary for Canada thus indicates that the opportunity cost of producing wheat in Canada is less than that in the EU.

If trade is possible at some relative prices between the two countries' opportunity costs of production, each country will specialize in the production of the good in which it has a comparative advantage. In each part of the figure, the slope of the green line shows the relative prices at which trade takes place. Production occurs in each country at point *S* (for specialization); Canada produces only wheat, and the EU produces only cloth.

Consumption possibilities for each country are now given by the green line that passes through point *S*. Consumption possibilities are increased in both countries; consumption may occur at some point, such as *d*, that involves a combination of wheat and cloth that was not attainable in the absence of trade.

opportunity costs in production and those opportunity costs are independent of the level of production. An alternative diagrammatic illustration of the gains from trade appears in *Extensions in Theory 33-1*, where the production possibilities boundary is concave (which means that the opportunity cost for each good is higher when more of that good is being produced).

The conclusions about the gains from trade arising from international differences in opportunity costs are summarized below.

1. The opportunity cost of producing X is the amount of output of other products that must be sacrificed in order to increase the output of X by one unit.

2. Country A has a comparative advantage over Country B in producing a product when the opportunity cost of production in Country A is lower. This implies, however, that it has a comparative *dis*advantage in some other product(s).

3. When opportunity costs for all products are the same in all countries, there is no comparative advantage and there is no possibility of gains from specialization and trade.

4. When opportunity costs differ in any two countries and both countries are producing both products, it is always possible to increase production of both products by a suitable reallocation of resources within each country.

Though the concepts of comparative advantage and specialization are relatively straightforward, it is helpful to work through numerical examples to solidify your understanding. *Applying Economic Concepts 33-1* provides two examples and works through the computations of absolute and comparative advantage.

The Gains from Trade with Variable Costs

So far, we have assumed that opportunity costs are the same whatever the scale of output, and we have seen that there are gains from specialization and trade as long as there are differences in opportunity costs across countries. If costs vary with the level of output, or as experience is acquired via specialization, *additional* gains are possible.

Economies of Scale In many industries, production costs fall as the scale of output increases. The larger the scale of operations, the more efficiently large-scale machinery can be used and the more a detailed division of tasks among workers is possible. Small countries (such as Switzerland, Belgium, and Israel) whose domestic markets are not large enough to exploit economies of scale would find it prohibitively expensive to become self-sufficient by producing a little bit of everything at very high cost.

One of the important lessons learned from patterns of world trade since the Second World War has concerned imperfect competition and product differentiation. Virtually all of today's manufactured consumer goods are produced in a vast array of differentiated product lines. In some industries, many firms produce different items in this array; in others, only a few firms produce the entire array. In either case, they may not exhaust all available economies of scale. Thus, an increase in the size of the market, even in a large economy, may allow the exploitation of some previously unexploited scale economies in individual product lines.

These possibilities were first dramatically illustrated when the European Common Market (now known as the European Union) was set up in the late 1950s.

EXTENSIONS IN THEORY 33-1

The Gains from Trade More Generally

Examining the gains from trade is relatively easy in the case where each country's production possibilities boundary is a straight line. What happens in the more realistic case where the production possibilities boundary is concave? As this box shows, the same basic principles of the gains from trade apply to this more complex case.

International trade leads to an expansion of the set of goods that can be consumed in the economy in two ways:

1. By allowing the bundle of goods consumed to differ from the bundle produced

2. By permitting a profitable change in the pattern of production

Without international trade, the bundle of goods produced must be the same as the bundle consumed. With international trade, the consumption and production bundles can be altered independently to reflect the relative values placed on goods by international markets.

Fixed Production

In each part of the figure, the purple curve is the economy's production possibilities boundary. In the absence of international trade, the economy must consume the same bundle of goods that it produces. Thus, the production possibilities boundary is also the consumption possibilities boundary. Suppose the economy produces and consumes at point a, with x_1 of good X and y_1 of good Y, as in part (i) of the figure.

Next suppose that production remains at point a but we now allow good Y to be traded for good X internationally. The consumption possibilities are now shown by the line tt drawn through point a. The slope of tt indicates the quantity of Y that exchanges for a unit of X on the international market—that is, the relative price of X in terms of Y.

Although production is fixed at point a, consumption can now be anywhere on the line tt. For example, the

consumption point could be at b. This could be achieved by exporting y_2y_1 units of Y and importing x_1x_2 units of X. Because point b (and all others on line tt to the right of a) lies outside the production possibilities boundary, there are potential gains from trade. Consumers are no longer limited by their own country's production possibilities. Let us suppose that they prefer point b to point a. They have achieved a gain from trade by being allowed to exchange some of their production of good Y for some quantity of good X and thus to consume more of good X than is produced at home.

Variable Production

In general, however, openness to trade with other countries will change the pattern of domestic production, and this will create *further* gains from trade. The country can now produce the bundle of goods that is most valuable in world markets. That is represented by the bundle d in part (ii). The consumption possibilities boundary is shifted to the line $t't'$ by changing production from a to d and thereby increasing the country's degree of specialization in good Y. For every point on the original consumption possibilities boundary tt, there are points on the new boundary $t't'$ that allow more consumption of both goods—for example, compare points b and f. Notice also that, except at the zero-trade point d, the new consumption possibilities boundary lies *everywhere above the production possibilities boundary*.

The benefits of moving from a no-trade position, such as point a, to a trading position, such as points b or f, are the *gains from trade* to the country. When the production of good Y is increased and the production of good X decreased, the country is able to move to a point, such as f, by producing more of good Y, in which the country has a comparative advantage, and trading the additional production for good X.

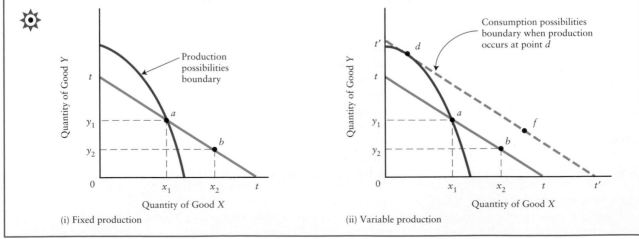

(i) Fixed production

(ii) Variable production

APPLYING ECONOMIC CONCEPTS 33-1

Two Examples of Absolute and Comparative Advantage

Example #1

Argentina and Brazil can both produce fish and leather. The table shows the total resource cost, in dollars, of producing one kilogram of each good in both countries.

	Fish (kg)	Leather (kg)
Argentina	$2	$5
Brazil	$3	$4

Absolute Advantage Argentina is the more efficient producer of fish since its total resource cost ($2) is less than Brazil's ($3), and so it has the absolute advantage in producing fish. Brazil has the absolute advantage in producing leather.

Comparative Advantage To know the pattern of comparative advantage, we must compute the *opportunity costs of production*. In Argentina, producing one more kilogram of leather requires using $5 of resources—the amount that could have been used to produce 2.5 kg of fish. Thus, producing 1 kg of leather involves giving up 2.5 kg of fish. In Brazil, however, one extra kilogram of leather only requires a sacrifice of 1.33 kg of fish. Since Brazil has the lower opportunity cost for leather (it gives up the least fish), it has the comparative advantage in leather production.

The opportunity cost for fish production *must* be the inverse of that for leather. In Argentina, one extra kilogram of fish "costs" 0.4 kg of leather. In Brazil, one extra kilogram of fish "costs" 0.75 kg of leather. Since Argentina has the lower opportunity cost of fish, it has the comparative advantage in fish production.

Specialization If Argentina and Brazil were to trade with each other, total production would be increased if each country specialized in the production of the good in which it has the comparative advantage. Argentina should produce fish and buy its leather from Brazil; Brazil should produce leather and buy its fish from Argentina.

Example #2

Switzerland and Austria can both produce glass and chocolate. Each country has 1000 units of identical resources, which we will call "labour." The table shows the maximum amount of each good that each country could produce if it devoted all of its labour to the production of that good.

	Glass (tonnes)	Chocolate (kg)
Austria	5 000	400 000
Switzerland	4 000	200 000

Absolute Advantage Each unit of labour in Austria can produce 5 tonnes of glass or 400 kg of chocolate. The identical unit of labour in Switzerland can produce only 4 tonnes of glass or 200 kg of chocolate. Switzerland is less efficient than Austria in the production of both goods; Austria therefore has the absolute advantage in *both* goods.

Comparative Advantage Once again, we need to know the opportunity costs of production. In Austria, producing one extra tonne of glass requires giving up 80 kg (= 400 000/5000) of chocolate. In Switzerland, producing one extra tonne of glass "costs" 50 kg (= 200 000/4000) of chocolate. Switzerland has the lower opportunity cost for glass and thus has the comparative advantage in glass production. It follows that Austria *must* have the comparative advantage in the production of chocolate. Austria's opportunity cost of 1 kg of chocolate is 1/80 tonne of glass, whereas Switzerland's opportunity cost of 1 kg of chocolate is 1/50 tonne of glass.

Specialization If the two countries engaged in international trade, total output would be maximized if Austria specialized in the production of chocolate and Switzerland specialized in the production of glass.

Economists had expected that specialization would occur according to the theory of comparative advantage, with one country specializing in cars, another in refrigerators, another in fashion and clothing, another in shoes, and so on. This is not the way it worked out. Instead, much of the vast growth of trade was in *intra-industry* trade—that is, trade of goods or services within the same broad industry. Today, one can buy French, English, Italian, and German fashion goods, cars, shoes, appliances, and a host of other products in Paris, London, Rome, and Berlin. Ships loaded with Swedish furniture bound for London pass ships loaded with English furniture bound for Stockholm, and so on.

Wine is a good example of an industry in which there is much intra-industry trade. Canada, for example, imports wine from many countries but also exports Canadian-made wine to the same countries.

The same increase in intra-industry trade happened with Canada–U.S. trade over successive rounds of tariff cuts that were negotiated after the Second World War, the most recent being those associated with the 1989 Canada–U.S. Free Trade Agreement, and its 1994 expansion into the North American Free Trade Agreement (NAFTA), which included Mexico. In several broad industrial groups, including automotive products, machinery, textiles, and forestry products, both imports and exports increased in each country. What free trade in Europe and North America did was to allow a proliferation of differentiated products, with different countries each specializing in different subproduct lines. Consumers have shown by their expenditures that they value this enormous increase in the range of choice among differentiated products, and producers have gained economies by being able to operate at a larger scale.

In industries with significant scale economies, small countries that do not trade will have low levels of output and therefore high costs. With international trade, however, small countries can produce for the large global market and thus produce at lower costs. International trade therefore allows small countries to reap the benefits of scale economies.

Learning by Doing The discussion so far has assumed that costs vary with the *level* of output. But they may also vary with the *accumulated experience* in producing a product over time.

learning by doing The reduction in unit costs that often results as workers learn through repeatedly performing the same tasks. It causes a downward shift in the average cost curve.

Early economists placed great importance on a concept that is now called **learning by doing.** They believed that as countries gained experience in particular tasks, workers and managers would become more efficient in performing them. As people acquire expertise, costs tend to fall. There is substantial evidence that such learning by doing does occur. It is particularly important in many of today's knowledge-intensive high-tech industries. The distinction between this phenomenon and economies of scale is illustrated in Figure 33-4. It is one more example of the difference between a movement along a curve and a shift of the curve.

The opportunity for learning by doing has an important implication: Policymakers need not accept current comparative advantages as given. Through such means as education and tax incentives, they can seek to develop new comparative advantages. Moreover, countries cannot complacently assume that their existing comparative advantages will persist. Misguided education policies, the wrong tax incentives, or policies that discourage risk taking can lead to the rapid erosion of a country's comparative advantage in particular products and industries.

Sources of Comparative Advantage

David Ricardo's analysis taught us that the gains from trade arise from the pattern of comparative advantage. However, his analysis did not explain the *sources* of a country's comparative advantage. Why do comparative advantages exist? Since a country's comparative advantage depends on its opportunity costs, we could also ask: Why do different countries have different opportunity costs?

Different Factor Endowments One answer to this question was offered early in the twentieth century by two Swedish economists, Eli Heckscher and Bertil Ohlin. Ohlin was subsequently awarded the Nobel Prize in economics for his work in the theory of international trade. According to their theory, the international cost differences that form the basis for comparative advantage arise because factor endowments differ across countries. This is often called the *factor endowment theory of comparative advantage.*

To see how this theory works, consider the prices for various types of goods in countries *in the absence of trade.* A country that is well endowed with fertile land but has a small population will find that land is cheap but labour is expensive. It will therefore produce land-intensive agricultural goods cheaply and labour-intensive goods, such as machine tools, only at high cost. The reverse will be true for a second country that is small in size but possesses abundant and efficient labour. As a result, the first country will have a comparative advantage in agricultural production and the second in goods that use much labour and little land.

> According to the Heckscher-Ohlin theory, countries have comparative advantages in the production of goods that use intensively the factors of production with which they are abundantly endowed.

For example, Canada is abundantly endowed with forests relative to most other countries. According to the Heckscher-Ohlin theory, Canada has a comparative advantage in goods that use forest products intensively, such as paper, framing materials, raw lumber, and wooden furniture. In contrast, relative to most other countries, Canada is sparsely endowed with labour. Thus, Canada has a comparative disadvantage in goods that use labour intensively, such as cotton or many other textile products.

Different Climates The factor endowment theory provides only part of the entire explanation for the sources of comparative advantage. Another important influence comes from all those natural factors that can be called *climate* in the broadest sense. If you combine land, labour, and capital in the same way in Nicaragua and in Iceland, you will not get the same output of most agricultural goods. Sunshine, rainfall, and average temperature also matter. You can, of course, artificially create any climate you want in a greenhouse, but it costs money to create what is freely provided elsewhere.

> A country's comparative advantage is influenced by various aspects of its climate.

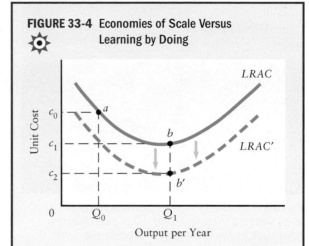

FIGURE 33-4 Economies of Scale Versus Learning by Doing

Specialization may lead to gains from trade through scale economies, learning by doing, or both. Consider a country that wants to consume the quantity Q_0. Suppose it can produce that quantity at an average cost per unit of c_0. Suppose further that the country has a comparative advantage in producing this product and can export the quantity Q_0Q_1 if it produces Q_1. This may lead to cost savings in two ways.

First, the increased level of production of Q_1 compared with Q_0 permits it to move along its long-run cost curve from a to b, thereby reducing costs per unit to c_1. This is an economy of scale.

Second, as workers and management become more experienced, they may be able to produce at lower costs. This is learning by doing and it shifts the cost curve from $LRAC$ to $LRAC'$. At output Q_1, costs per unit fall to c_2. The movement from a to b' incorporates both economies of scale and learning by doing.

Canada is extremely well endowed with forests. It is no surprise, therefore, that it has a comparative advantage in a whole range of forestry products.

Of course, if we consider "warm weather" a factor of production, then we could simply say that countries like Nicaragua are better endowed with that factor than countries like Iceland. In this sense, explanations of comparative advantage based on different climates are really just a special case of explanations based on factor endowments.

Human Capital Acquired skills, what economists call *human capital*, matter greatly in determining comparative advantage. Beginning in the late nineteenth century, Germany had an excellent set of trade schools that were attended by virtually every male who did not go on to higher academic education. As a result, Germany developed, and still maintains, a strong comparative advantage in many consumer goods that require significant skills to produce, such as electric razors, cake mixers, and blenders. The people of Persia (now Iran) produced carpets of high quality over the centuries, and from childhood their workers developed skills in carpet making that few others could match. So they had a comparative advantage in high-quality carpets and some related commodities.

Early on, Americans developed the skills necessary to mass-produce goods of reasonable quality made from standardized parts. So the United States developed a comparative advantage in many products made with mass-production techniques. One early set of products made in this way was firearms. Rifles and pistols were mass-produced and assembled from standardized parts. This allowed U.S. firms to produce their firearms at much lower costs than in other countries where similar weapons were made one at a time by craftsmen. One of these, the Colt six-shooter, blazed its way into fame in the nineteenth century in the American "Wild West."

Acquired Comparative Advantage The example of human capital makes it clear that many comparative advantages are *acquired*. Further, they can change. Thus, comparative advantage should be viewed as being *dynamic* rather than static. Many of today's industries depend more on human capital than on fixed physical capital or natural resources. The skills of a computer designer, a video game programmer, or a sound mix technician are acquired by education and on-the-job training. Natural endowments of energy and raw materials cannot account for Silicon Valley's leadership in computer technology, for Canada's prominence in communications technology, for Taiwan's excellence in electronics, or for Switzerland's prominence in private banking.

If comparative advantage can be acquired, it can also be *lost*. If firms within one country fail to innovate and adopt the latest technologies available in their industry, but competing firms in other countries are aggressively innovating and reducing their production costs, the first country will eventually lose whatever comparative advantage it once had in that industry. In recent years, for example, pulp and paper mills in Canada have been closing, driven out of the industry by Scandinavian firms that more aggressively pursue improvements in productivity.

With today's growing international competition and rapidly changing technologies, no country's comparative advantages are secure unless its firms innovate and keep up with their foreign competitors and its education system produces workers, managers, and innovators with the requisite skills.

Contrasting Views? The view that a country's comparative advantages change over time and can be influenced by education, innovation, and government policy is a relatively modern one. It contrasts sharply with the traditional view that a country's natural endowments of land, labour, and natural resources are the prime determinants of its comparative advantage. The traditional view suggested that a government interested in maximizing its citizens' material standard of living should encourage specialization of production in goods for which it *currently* had a comparative advantage. If all countries followed this advice, each would have been specialized in a relatively narrow range of distinct products. The British would have produced engineering products, Canadians would have produced resource-based primary products, Americans would have been farmers and factory workers, Central Americans would have been banana and coffee growers, the Chinese would have produced rice and cheap toys, and so on.

There are surely elements of truth in both views. It would be unwise to neglect resource endowments, climate, culture, social patterns, and institutional arrangements. But it would also be unwise to assume that all advantages are innate and immutable.

33.2 The Determination of Trade Patterns

Comparative advantage has been the central concept in our discussion about the gains from trade. If Canada has a comparative advantage in lumber and Italy has a comparative advantage in shoes, then the total output of lumber and shoes can be increased if Canada specializes in the production of lumber and Italy specializes in the production of shoes. With such patterns of specialization, Canada will naturally export lumber to Italy and Italy will export shoes to Canada.

For data on Canadian trade by industry and by country, go to Statistics Canada's website at www.statcan.gc.ca. and search for "trade."

It is one thing to discuss the *potential* gains from trade if countries specialized in the production of particular goods and exported these to other countries. But do *actual* trade patterns occur along the lines of comparative advantage? In this section of the chapter we use a simple demand-and-supply model to examine why Canada exports some products and imports others. We will see that comparative advantage, whether natural or acquired, plays a central role in determining actual trade patterns.

There are some products, such as coffee and mangoes, that Canada does not produce (and will probably never produce). Any domestic consumption of these products must therefore be satisfied by imports from other countries. At the other extreme, there are some products, such as nickel and potash, of which Canada is one of the world's major suppliers, and demand in the rest of the world must be satisfied partly by exports from Canada. Finally, there are some products, such as houses and crushed stone, that are so expensive to transport that every country produces approximately what it consumes.

Our interest in this section is with the vast number of intermediate cases in which Canada is only one of many producers of an internationally traded product, as with beef, oil, copper, wheat, lumber, and newsprint. Will Canada be an exporter or an importer of such products? And what is the role played by comparative advantage?

The Law of One Price

Whether Canada imports or exports a product for which it is only one of many producers depends to a great extent on the product's price. This brings us to what economists call the *law of one price*.

The law of one price states that when a product is traded throughout the entire world, the prices in various countries (net of any specific taxes or tariffs) will differ by no more than the cost of transporting the product between countries. Aside from differences caused by these transport costs, there is a single world price.

Many basic products—such as copper wire, steel pipe, iron ore, and computer RAM chips—fall within this category. The world price for each good is the price that equates the quantity demanded worldwide with the quantity supplied worldwide. The world price of an internationally traded product may be influenced greatly, or only slightly, by the demand and supply coming from any one country. The extent of one country's influence will depend on how important its quantities demanded and supplied are in relation to the worldwide totals.

The simplest case for us to study arises when the country, which we will take to be Canada, accounts for only a small part of the total worldwide demand and supply. In this case, Canada does not itself produce enough to influence the world price significantly. Similarly, Canadian purchases are too small a proportion of worldwide demand to affect the world price in any significant way. Producers and consumers in Canada thus face a world price that they cannot influence by their own actions.

In this case, the price that rules in the Canadian market must be the world price (adjusted for the exchange rate between the Canadian dollar and the foreign currency). The law of one price says that this must be so. What would happen if the Canadian domestic price diverged from the world price? If the Canadian price were below the world price, no supplier would sell in the Canadian market because higher profits could be made by selling abroad. The absence of supply to the Canadian market would thus drive up the Canadian price. Conversely, if the Canadian domestic price were above the worldwide price, no buyer would buy from a Canadian seller because lower prices are available by buying abroad. The absence of demand on the Canadian market would thus drive down the Canadian price.

The Pattern of Foreign Trade

Let us now see what determines the pattern of international trade in such circumstances.

An Exported Product To determine the pattern of Canadian trade, we first show the Canadian domestic demand and supply curves for some product, say, lumber. This is done in Figure 33-5. The intersection of these two curves tells us what the price and quantity would be in Canada *if there were no foreign trade.* Now compare this no-trade price with the world price of that product.[1] If the world price is higher, the actual price in Canada will exceed the no-trade

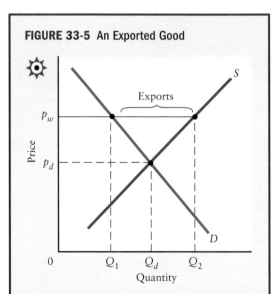

FIGURE 33-5 An Exported Good

Exports occur whenever there is excess supply domestically at the world price. The domestic demand and supply curves are D and S, respectively. The domestic price in the absence of foreign trade is p_d, with Q_d produced and consumed domestically. The world price of p_w is higher than p_d. At p_w, Q_1 is demanded while Q_2 is supplied domestically. The excess of the domestic supply over the domestic demand is exported.

---

[1] If the world price is stated in terms of some foreign currency (as it often is), the price must be converted into Canadian dollars by using the current exchange rate between the foreign currency and Canadian dollars.

price. In this situation there will be an excess of Canadian supply over Canadian demand. Domestic producers want to sell Q_2 units of lumber but domestic consumers want to buy only Q_1 units. If Canada were a closed economy, such excess supply would drive the price down to p_d. But in an open economy with a world price of p_w, this excess supply is exported to Canada's trading partners.

What is the role of comparative advantage in this analysis? We have said that Canada will export lumber if the world price exceeds Canada's no-trade price. Note that in a competitive market the price of the product reflects the product's marginal cost, which in turn reflects the opportunity cost of producing the product. That Canada's no-trade price for lumber is lower than the world price reflects the fact that the opportunity cost of producing lumber in Canada is less than the opportunity cost of producing it in the rest of the world. Thus, by exporting goods that have a low no-trade price, Canada is exporting the goods for which it has a comparative advantage.

> **Countries export the goods for which they are low-cost producers. That is, they export goods for which they have a comparative advantage.**

An Imported Product Now consider some other product—for example, computer RAM chips. Once again, look first at the domestic demand and supply curves, shown this time in Figure 33-6. The intersection of these curves determines the price that would exist in Canada if there were no foreign trade. The world price of RAM chips is below the Canadian no-trade price so that, at the price ruling in Canada, domestic demand is larger and domestic supply is smaller than if the no-trade price had ruled. The excess of domestic demand over domestic supply is met by imports.

Again, this analysis can be restated in terms of comparative advantage. The high Canadian no-trade price of RAM chips reflects the fact that the production of RAM chips has a higher opportunity cost in Canada than elsewhere in the world. This high cost means that Canada has a comparative disadvantage in RAM chips. So Canada imports goods for which it has a comparative disadvantage.

> **Countries import the goods for which they are high-cost producers. That is, they import goods for which they have a comparative disadvantage.**

Is Comparative Advantage Obsolete?

It is sometimes said that the theory of comparative advantage is nearly 200 years old, and things have changed so much since then that the theory must surely be obsolete.

Contrary to such assertions, comparative advantage remains an important economic concept. At any one time—because comparative advantage is reflected in international relative prices, and these relative prices determine what goods a country will import

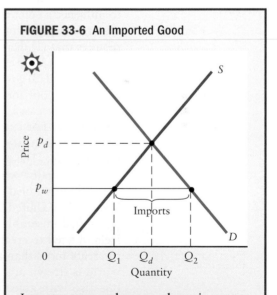

FIGURE 33-6 An Imported Good

Imports occur whenever there is excess demand domestically at the world price. The domestic demand and supply curves are D and S, respectively. The domestic price in the absence of foreign trade is p_d, with Q_d produced and consumed domestically. The world price of p_w is less than p_d. At the world price Q_2 is demanded, whereas Q_1 is supplied domestically. The excess of domestic demand over domestic supply is satisfied through imports.

and what it will export—the operation of the price system will result in trade that follows the current pattern of comparative advantage. For example, if Canadian costs of producing steel are particularly low relative to other Canadian costs, Canada will export steel at international prices (which it does). If Canada's costs of producing textiles are particularly high relative to other Canadian costs, Canada will import textiles at international prices (which it does). Thus, there is no reason to change the view that David Ricardo long ago expounded: *Current comparative advantage is a major determinant of trade under free-market conditions.*

What has changed, however, is economists' views about the *determinants* of comparative advantage. It is now clear that current comparative advantage is more open to change by private entrepreneurial activities and by government policy than used to be thought. Thus, what is obsolete is the belief that a country's current pattern of comparative advantage, and hence its current pattern of imports and exports, must be accepted as given and unchangeable.

> **The theory that comparative advantage is a major influence on trade flows is not obsolete, but the theory that comparative advantage is completely determined by forces beyond the reach of decisions made by private firms and by public policy has been discredited.**

One caveat should be noted. It is one thing to observe that it is *possible* for governments to influence a country's pattern of comparative advantage. It is quite another to conclude that it is *advisable* for them to try. The case in support of a specific government intervention requires that (1) there is scope for governments to improve on the results achieved by the free market, (2) the costs of the intervention be less than the value of the improvement to be achieved, and (3) governments will actually be able to carry out the required interventionist policies (without, for example, being sidetracked by considerations of electoral advantage).

In many cases, governments have succeeded in creating important comparative advantages. For example, the Taiwanese government virtually created that nation's electronics industry and then passed it over to private hands in which it became a world leader. The government of Singapore created a computer-parts industry that became a major world supplier. However, there are also many examples in which governments failed in their attempts to create comparative advantage. The government of the United Kingdom tried to create a comparative advantage in computers and failed miserably, wasting much public money in the process. The government of Ireland tried to create a comparative advantage in automobile production and failed to create more than a modest, unprofitable industry that eventually disappeared. The world is strewn not only with spectacular successes, which show that it can be done, but also with abject failures, which show that the attempt to do so is fraught with many dangers.

One other comment needs to be made regarding the relevance of the concept of comparative advantage. For understanding international trade in copper wire, lumber, oil, bananas, coffee, textiles, and many other relatively simple products, the concept of comparative advantage is very useful. In some manufacturing industries, however, where products have dozens or perhaps hundreds of components, the determinants of trade flows are more complex than the theory of comparative advantage suggests. For example, it is difficult to see why Canada might have a comparative advantage in the production of automobile transmissions but not in automobile brake systems or air-conditioning systems. Yet, the automobile sector is perhaps the best example of an industry in which a firm's "supply chain" includes products made by several other firms in several countries. *Applying Economic Concepts 33-2* discusses how the forces of globalization and economies of scale have led to the development of complex global supply chains.

The Terms of Trade

We have seen that world production can be increased when countries specialize in the production of the goods for which they have a comparative advantage and then trade with one another. We now ask: How will these gains from specialization and trade be shared among countries? The division of the gain depends on what is called the **terms of trade**, which relate to the quantity of imported goods that can be obtained per unit of goods exported. The terms of trade are measured by the ratio of the price of exports to the price of imports.

terms of trade The ratio of the average price of a country's exports to the average price of its imports.

A rise in the price of imported goods, with the price of exports unchanged, indicates a *fall in the terms of trade*; it will now take more exports to buy the same quantity of imports. Similarly, a rise in the price of exported goods, with the price of imports unchanged, indicates a *rise in the terms of trade*; it will now take fewer exports to buy the same quantity of imports. Thus, the ratio of these prices measures the amount of imports that can be obtained per unit of goods exported.

The terms of trade can be illustrated with a country's production possibilities boundary, as shown in Figure 33-7. The figure shows the hypothetical case in which Canada can produce only wheat and cloth. As we saw earlier, the slope of Canada's production possibilities boundary shows the relative opportunity costs of producing the two goods in Canada. A steep production possibilities boundary indicates that only a small amount of cloth must be given up to get more wheat; thus cloth is relatively costly and wheat is relatively cheap. A flatter production possibilities boundary indicates that a larger amount of cloth must be given up to get more wheat; thus cloth is relatively cheap and wheat is relatively expensive. Thus, the slope of the production possibilities boundary in Figure 33-7 shows the relative price of cloth (in terms of wheat) that Canada faces in the absence of international trade.

If, through international trade, Canada has access to different relative prices, Canada will be led to specialize in the production of one good or the other. In Figure 33-7, we show a case in which the world relative price of cloth is lower than the relative price Canada would have if it did not trade. (This lower *world* relative price of cloth reflects the fact that other countries can produce cloth more cheaply than Canada.) Faced with a lower relative price of cloth, Canada ends up specializing in the production of the relatively high-priced product (wheat), and importing the relatively low-priced product (cloth). This point of specialization is point S in Figure 33-7.

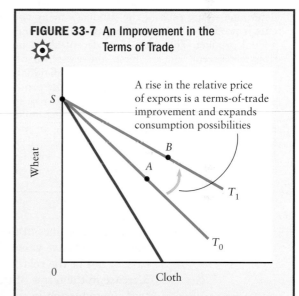

FIGURE 33-7 An Improvement in the Terms of Trade

A rise in the relative price of exports is a terms-of-trade improvement and expands consumption possibilities

Changes in the terms of trade lead to changes in a country's consumption possibilities. The hypothetical production possibilities boundary is shown for Canada. With international trade at relative prices T_0, Canada specializes in the production of wheat, producing at point S, but is able to consume at a point like A. It pays for its imports of cloth with its exports of wheat.

If the price of wheat rises relative to the price of cloth, production remains at S but the line T_1 shows Canada's new consumption possibilities. Consumption can now take place at a point like B where consumption of both wheat and cloth has increased. The increase in the terms of trade makes Canada better off because of the increase in consumption possibilities.

APPLYING ECONOMIC CONCEPTS 33-2

Comparative Advantage and Global Supply Chains

The discussion of comparative advantage developed in this chapter applies easily to many products with one or even a few components. One can sensibly speak of national comparative advantages for whole products, such as Costa Rica for bananas, Canada for sawn logs, Chile for copper, Korea for steel, and Saudi Arabia for oil.

For many manufactured products, however, and even for some resource-based products and service industries, production is carried out in complex and integrated "global supply chains," with a product's several different components being produced in different countries and often by different firms. In this world of "integrative trade," it is no longer clear where some products are "made," even though one could easily determine where each of the product's many components is produced and where they are all assembled into a final product. This method of decentralized production has several causes. First, the existence of scale economies provides an incentive for individual firms to reduce their costs by concentrating the production of each individual component in a different specialized large factory. Second, differences in national wage rates for various types of labour provide an incentive for these production facilities to be located in different countries. Third, the current very low costs of communication and transportation make it possible to

coordinate supply chains globally and ship parts and final products anywhere at low cost. (If fuel becomes expensive enough to make transport costs a significant part of total costs, it will become economic to do much more production closer to final markets than it has been over the last several decades.)

Consider three examples. The famous iPod sold by Apple clearly says "Made in China" on the box, but most of the value from its design occurs in the United States, many electronic components come from Korea and Japan, and only the iPod's final assembly occurs in China. Apple chooses to locate assembly in China, using components manufactured elsewhere, because by doing so it can maximize its product quality and minimize costs.

Bombardier jet aircraft designed and assembled in Canada also involve global supply chains. Fuselage parts come from Japan, the wings are produced in Northern Ireland, engines are imported from the United States, and the avionics are engineered in the United States but sourced from Asian suppliers. Bombardier adopts this business model because costs can be reduced and quality maximized by using specialty suppliers at each link in the global supply chain.

Such global supply chains even exist for some products that appear to have few "components," such as fish. For example, a Canadian firm may hire a Chilean trawler to fish in the Indian Ocean, land its catch in Malaysia where it is

The *green* lines in the figure show alternative values of the world relative prices—that is, alternative values for Canada's terms of trade. A rise in the terms of trade indicates a fall in the relative price of cloth (or a rise in the relative price of wheat). This increase in the terms of trade is shown as an upward rotation of the green line from T_0 to T_1. A reduction in the terms of trade is shown as a downward rotation in the green line, from T_1 to T_0.

It should be clear from Figure 33-7 why changes in the terms of trade are important. Suppose the international relative prices are initially given by T_0. Canada specializes in the production of wheat (point S) but consumes at some point like A, where it finances its imports of cloth with exports of wheat. Now suppose there is a shift in world demand toward wheat and away from cloth, and this leads to an increase in the relative price of wheat. The terms of trade increase to T_1 and, with unchanged production at point S, Canada can now afford to consume at a point like B where consumption of both wheat and cloth has increased.

A rise in a country's terms of trade is beneficial because it expands the country's consumption possibilities.

frozen, and then send it to China for further processing before it is finally sold to Japanese wholesalers. This supply chain can operate in two different ways. First, the Canadian firm can manage the entire process but leave ownership to the individual firms at each stage of the supply chain. In this case, the Canadian firm is providing management expertise and earns a return that in the data appears as a Canadian export of services. Alternatively, the Canadian firm can own the product but merely hire the services of the required firms at each stage of the supply chain. In this case, the return to the Canadian firm will be significantly higher because of the need to manage the various risks involved in production, such as unexpected swings in prices, natural disasters, and human error.

There are three implications for how we think about international trade in the presence of integrated global supply chains. First, we should not view countries as having comparative advantages in entire products but rather in the specific productive activities that take place along the global supply chain. China may not have a comparative advantage in "producing" consumer electronics but may have one in assembling them. Canada may not have a comparative advantage in "producing" jet aircraft but may have one in designing them.

Second, these comparative advantages may not be long-lasting because they are sensitive to changes in the economic environment and in technology. For example, significant changes in national corporate tax rates, exchange rates, and wages for factory workers will generally change the optimal location for the production of a product's various components. Also, newly developed technologies for producing existing products and creating new ones can alter the patterns of comparative advantage significantly and quickly.

Third, traditional data on international trade does not capture the extent of integration in global supply chains. The iPod assembled in China and exported to the United States appears simply as a Chinese export; but the significant value generated by the U.S.-based design team may appear in no trade statistics whatsoever. It follows that the measured flow of a country's exports of some products does not necessarily correspond closely with the level of local economic activity (production and employment) actually generated by those products. Even in Canada's resource sector, the domestic content of exports is not 100 percent, although it is typically more than 75 percent, meaning that up to one-quarter of the value of the final exported product comes from imported inputs. In most manufacturing industries, however, the domestic content of exports is 50 percent or lower, and in the automobile industry it is only 35 percent.

The presence of such highly integrated global supply chains indicates the importance of two-way trade in the Canadian economy: Access to low-price and high-quality imports is as crucial to the Canadian economy as is our access to world markets where we can sell our intermediate and final products.

Conversely, a reduction in the price of a country's exports (relative to the price of its imports) is harmful for a country. In Figure 33-7, this is shown as a change of the terms of trade from T_1 to T_0. Even though production may remain unchanged, the range of goods available to be consumed falls, and this reduction in consumption possibilities leads to an overall loss of welfare.

How do we measure the terms of trade in real economies? Because international trade involves many countries and many products, we cannot use the simple ratio of the prices of two goods as in Figure 33-7. The basic principle, however, is the same. A country's terms of trade are computed as an index number:

$$\text{Terms of trade} = \frac{\text{Index of export prices}}{\text{Index of import prices}} \times 100$$

A rise in the index is referred to as a *favourable* change in a country's terms of trade (sometimes called a terms of trade *improvement*). A decrease in the index of the terms of trade is called an *unfavourable* change (or a terms of trade *deterioration*). For example, the sharp rise in oil prices in the 1970s led to large unfavourable shifts in the terms of trade of oil-importing countries. When oil prices fell sharply in the mid-1980s, the terms of trade of oil-importing countries changed favourably. The converse was true for oil-exporting countries.

FIGURE 33-8 Canada's Terms of Trade, 1961–2012

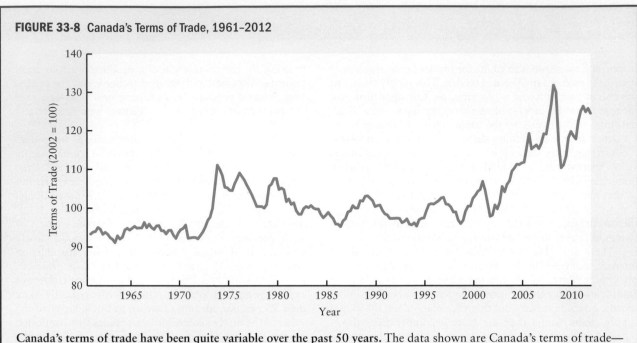

Canada's terms of trade have been quite variable over the past 50 years. The data shown are Canada's terms of trade—the ratio of an index of Canadian export prices to an index of Canadian import prices. As the relative prices of lumber, oil, wheat, electronic equipment, textiles, fruit, and other products change, the terms of trade naturally change.

(*Source:* Author's calculations using data from Statistics Canada, CANSIM database, Table 380-0003.)

Canada's terms of trade since 1961 are shown in Figure 33-8. As is clear, the terms of trade are quite variable, reflecting frequent changes in the relative prices of different products. Note the dramatic increase (improvement) in Canada's terms of trade in the early 1970s, reflecting the large increase in oil prices caused by OPEC's output restrictions. Since Canada is a net exporter of oil, its terms of trade improve when the price of oil increases. An even larger increase occurred in the 2002–2008 period, when the world prices of most commodities, especially energy-related commodities, increased sharply.

SUMMARY

33.1 The Gains from Trade

- Country A has an *absolute* advantage over Country B in the production of a specific product when the absolute cost of the product is less in Country A than in Country B.
- Country A has a *comparative* advantage over Country B in the production of a specific good if the forgone output of other goods is less in Country A than in Country B.
- Comparative advantage occurs whenever countries have different opportunity costs of producing particular goods. World production of all products can be increased if each country transfers resources into the production of the products for which it has a comparative advantage.
- Trade allows all countries to obtain the goods for which they do not have a comparative advantage at a lower

opportunity cost than they would face if they were to produce all products for themselves; specialization and trade therefore allow all countries to have more of all products than they could have if they tried to be self-sufficient.
- A nation that engages in trade and specialization may also realize the benefits of economies of large-scale production and of learning by doing.
- Traditional theories regarded comparative advantage as largely determined by natural resource endowments that are difficult to change. Economists now know that some comparative advantages can be acquired and consequently can be changed. A country may, in this view, influence its role in world production and trade.

33.2 The Determination of Trade Patterns

- The law of one price says that the national prices of tradable goods (net of taxes and tariffs) must differ by no more than the costs of transporting these goods between countries. After accounting for these transport costs, there is a single world price.
- Countries will export a good when the world price exceeds the price that would exist in the country if there were no trade. The low no-trade price reflects a low opportunity cost and thus a comparative advantage in that good. Thus, countries export goods for which they have a comparative advantage.
- Countries will import a good when the world price is less than the price that would exist in the country if

there were no trade. The high no-trade price reflects a high opportunity cost and thus a comparative disadvantage in that good. Thus, countries import goods for which they have a comparative disadvantage.
- The terms of trade refer to the ratio of the prices of goods exported to the prices of those imported. The terms of trade determine the quantity of imports that can be obtained per unit of exports.
- A favourable change in the terms of trade—a rise in export prices relative to import prices—is beneficial for a country because it expands its consumption possibilities.

KEY CONCEPTS

Interpersonal, interregional, and international specialization
Absolute advantage and comparative advantage
Opportunity cost and comparative advantage

The gains from trade: specialization, scale economies, and learning by doing
The sources of comparative advantage
Factor endowments

Acquired comparative advantage
The law of one price
The terms of trade

STUDY EXERCISES

MyEconLab   Make the grade with MyEconLab: Study Exercises marked in red can be found on MyEconLab. You can practise them as often as you want, and most feature step-by-step guided instructions to help you find the right answer.

1. Fill in the blanks to make the following statements correct.

   a. The "gains from trade" refers to the increased _____ caused by specialization and trade.
   b. Suppose Argentina can produce one kilogram of beef for $2.50 and Brazil can produce one kilogram of beef for $2.90. Argentina is said to have a(n) _____ in beef production over Brazil. The gains from trade do *not* depend on _____.
   c. Comparative advantage is based on _____ rather than absolute costs.
   d. It is possible for a country to have a comparative advantage in some good and a(n) _____ in none.
   e. If all countries specialize in the production of goods for which they have a comparative advantage, then world output will _____.
   f. If opportunity costs are the same in all countries, there is no _____ and no possibility of _____.

2. Fill in the blanks to make the following statements correct.

   a. Such a product as coffee beans is cheaply transported and is traded around the world. The law of _____ tells us that it will tend to have _____ worldwide price.
   b. If the domestic price of copper wire in Canada (in the absence of trade) is $20 per unit and the world price is $24 per unit, then Canada will have an excess _____, which it will then _____. The opportunity cost of producing copper wire in Canada is _____ than the opportunity cost of producing it in the rest of the world.
   c. Canada will import goods for which it has an excess _____ at the world price. In the absence of trade, the _____ price of these goods would be less than the _____ price.
   d. A rise in Canada's terms of trade means that the average price of Canada's _____ has risen compared with the average price of Canada's _____. This change is referred to as a terms of trade _____.
   e. The terms of trade determine the quantity of _____ that can be obtained per unit of _____.

3. The following diagram shows the production possibilities boundary for Arcticland, a country that produces only two goods, ice and fish. Labour is the only factor of production. Recall that a linear production possibilities boundary reflects *constant* opportunity costs for both products.

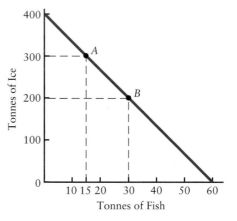

   a. Beginning at any point on Arcticland's production possibilities boundary, what is the opportunity cost of producing 10 more tonnes of fish?
   b. Beginning at any point on Arcticland's production possibilities boundary, what is the opportunity cost of producing 100 more tonnes of ice?

4. The following table shows the production of wheat and corn in Brazil and Mexico. Assume that both countries have one million acres of arable land.

	Brazil	Mexico
Wheat	90 bushels per acre	50 bushels per acre
Corn	30 bushels per acre	20 bushels per acre

   a. Which country has the absolute advantage in wheat? In corn? Explain.
   b. What is the opportunity cost of producing an extra bushel of wheat in Brazil? In Mexico? Which country has the comparative advantage in wheat production? Explain.

c. Which country has the comparative advantage in corn production? Explain.

d. Explain why one country can have an absolute advantage in both goods but cannot have a comparative advantage in both goods.

e. On a scale diagram with wheat on the horizontal axis and corn on the vertical axis, draw each country's production possibilities boundary.

f. What is shown by the slope of each country's production possibilities boundary? Be as precise as possible.

5. The following diagrams show the production possibilities boundaries for Canada and France, both of which produce only two goods, wine and lumber.

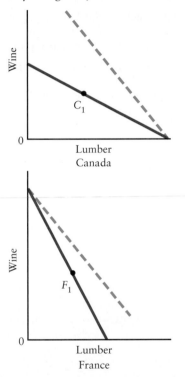

a. Which country has the comparative advantage in lumber? Explain.

b. Which country has the comparative advantage in wine? Explain.

c. Suppose Canada and France are initially not trading with each other and are producing at points C_1 and F_1, respectively. Suppose when trade is introduced, the free-trade relative prices are shown by the slope of the dashed line. Show in the diagrams which combination of goods each country will now produce.

d. In this case, what will be the pattern of trade for each country?

6. The following diagrams show the Canadian markets for newsprint and machinery, which we assume to be competitive.

a. Suppose there is no international trade. What would be the equilibrium price and quantity in the Canadian newsprint and machinery markets?

b. Now suppose Canada is open to trade with the rest of the world and the world price of newsprint is higher than the price of newsprint from part (a). Show in the diagram the quantities of domestic consumption and production and the quantity of newsprint that is either exported or imported.

c. Similarly, suppose the world price of machinery is lower than the price of machinery from part (a). Show in the diagram the quantity of domestic consumption and production and the quantity of machinery that is either exported or imported.

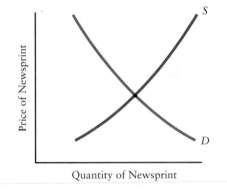

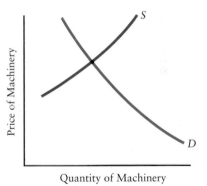

7. The table below shows indexes for the prices of imports and exports over several years for a hypothetical country.

Year	Import Prices	Export Prices	Terms of Trade
2008	90	110	____
2009	95	87	____
2010	98	83	____
2011	100	100	____
2012	102	105	____
2013	100	112	____
2014	103	118	____

a. Compute the terms of trade in each year for this country and fill in the table.

b. In which years do the terms of trade improve?

c. In which years do the terms of trade deteriorate?

d. Explain why a terms of trade "improvement" is good for the country.

8. For each of the following events, explain the likely effect on Canada's terms of trade. Your existing knowledge of Canada's imports and exports should be adequate to answer this question.

a. A hurricane damages much of Brazil's coffee crop.

b. OPEC countries succeed in significantly restricting the world supply of oil.

c. Several new large copper mines come into production in Chile.

d. A major recession in Southeast Asia reduces the world demand for pork.

e. Russia, a large producer of wheat, experiences a massive drought that reduces its wheat crop by more than 30 percent.

f. Three major potash-producing firms form a cartel and restrict the world's output of potash.

9. When the North American Free Trade Agreement (NAFTA) was being negotiated in the early 1990s, there was a great deal of debate. One critic argued that "it can't be in our interest to sign this deal; Mexico gains too much from it." What does the theory of the gains from trade have to say about that criticism?

10. Adam Smith saw a close connection between a nation's wealth and its ability and willingness "freely to engage" in trade with other countries.

a. Based on what you have learned in this chapter, what is the connection?

b. Explain why trading with countries that are "most different" from our own is likely to generate the most benefits. Which differences are of central importance?

c. Under what circumstances are there *no* benefits from a country specializing and trading with other countries?

d. Illustrate the argument from part (c) in a simple diagram of a country's production possibilities boundary.

11. Predict what each of the following events would do to the terms of trade of the importing country and the exporting country, other things being equal.

a. A blight destroys a large part of the coffee beans produced in the world.

b. Korean producers cut the price of the steel they sell to Canada.

c. General inflation of 4 percent occurs around the world.

d. Violation of OPEC output quotas leads to a sharp fall in the price of oil.

Trade Policy

CONDUCTING business in a foreign country is not always easy. Differences in language, in local laws and customs, and in currency often complicate transactions. Our concern in this chapter, however, is not with these complications but with government policy toward international trade, which is called *trade policy*. At one extreme is a policy of free trade—that is, an absence of any form of government interference with the free flow of international trade. Any departure from free trade designed to protect domestic industries from foreign competition is called *protectionism*.

We begin by briefly restating the case for free trade and then go on to examine various valid and invalid arguments that are commonly advanced for some degree of protection. We then explore some of the methods commonly used to restrict trade, such as tariffs and quotas. Finally, we examine the many modern institutions designed to foster freer trade on either a global or a regional basis. In particular, we discuss the North American Free Trade Agreement (NAFTA) and the World Trade Organization (WTO).

34.1 Free Trade or Protection?

Today, most governments accept the proposition that a relatively free flow of international trade is desirable for the health of their individual economies. But heated debates still occur over trade policy. Should a country permit the *completely* free flow of international trade, or should it use policies to restrict the flow of trade and thereby protect its local producers from foreign competition? If some protection is desired, should it be achieved by tariffs or by non-tariff barriers? **Tariffs** are taxes designed to raise the price of imported goods. **Non-tariff barriers (NTBs)** are policies other than tariffs designed to reduce the flow of imports; examples are import quotas and customs procedures that are deliberately more cumbersome than necessary.

tariff A tax applied on imports of goods or services.

non-tariff barriers (NTBs) Restrictions other than tariffs designed to reduce imports.

The Case for Free Trade

The gains from trade were presented in Chapter 33. Comparative advantages arise whenever countries have different opportunity costs. Free trade encourages all countries to specialize in producing products in which they have a comparative advantage. This pattern of specialization maximizes world production and hence maximizes average world living standards (as measured by the world's per capita GDP).

However, free trade does not necessarily make *everyone* better off than they would be in its absence. For example, reducing an existing tariff often results in individual groups receiving a smaller share of a larger world output so that they lose even though the average person gains. If we ask whether it is *possible* for free trade to improve everyone's living standards, the answer is yes because the larger total value of output that free trade generates could, at least in principle, be divided up in such a way that every individual is better off. If we ask whether free trade always does so in practice, however, the answer is, not necessarily.

> Free trade makes the country as a whole better off, even though it may not make every individual in the country better off.

In today's world, a country's products must stand up to international competition if they are to survive. Over even as short a period as a few years, firms that do not develop new products and new production methods fall seriously behind their foreign competitors. If one country protects its domestic firms by imposing a tariff, those firms are likely to become complacent about the need to adopt new technologies, and over time they will become less competitive in international markets. As the technology gap between domestic and foreign firms widens, the tariff wall will provide less and less protection. Eventually, the domestic firms will succumb to foreign competition. Meanwhile, domestic living standards will fall relative to foreign ones.

Given that any country can be better off by specializing in those goods in which it has a comparative advantage, one might wonder why most countries of the world continue in some way to restrict the flow of trade. Why do tariffs and other barriers to trade continue to exist two centuries after Adam Smith and David Ricardo argued the case for free trade? Is there a valid case for some protection?

The Case for Protection

A country engages in trade **protection** whenever it uses policies that restrict the flow of trade in a way that favours domestic firms over their foreign competitors. There are several valid arguments for protection, including

- promoting diversification
- protecting specific groups
- improving the terms of trade
- protecting infant industries
- earning economic profits in foreign markets

We will discuss each of these arguments briefly. Note that the first two arguments generally involve achieving some worthy objective at the cost of a *reduction* in national income. The last three arguments are reasons for protection as a means of *increasing* a country's national income.

Countries whose economies are based on the production of only a few goods face risks from fluctuations in world prices. For this reason, protection to promote diversification may be viewed as desirable.

protection Any government policy that interferes with free trade in order to protect domestic firms and workers from foreign competition.

Promoting Diversification For a very small country, specializing in the production of only a few products—though dictated by comparative advantage—might involve risks that the country does not want to take. One such risk is that technological advances may render its basic product obsolete. Another risk, especially for countries specialized in producing a small range of agricultural products, is that swings in world prices lead to large swings in national income. By using protectionist policies, the government can encourage the creation of some domestic industries that may otherwise not exist. The cost is the loss of national income associated with devoting resources to production in industries in which there is no domestic comparative advantage. The benefit is that overall national income and employment become less volatile.

Protecting Specific Groups Although specialization according to comparative advantage will maximize *average* per capita GDP, some specific groups may have higher incomes under protection than under free trade. Of particular interest in Canada and the United States has been the effect that greater international trade has on the incomes of unskilled workers.

Consider the ratio of skilled workers to unskilled workers. There are plenty of both types throughout the world. Compared with much of the rest of the world, however, Canada has more skilled and fewer unskilled people. When trade is expanded because of a reduction in tariffs, Canada will tend to export goods made by its abundant skilled workers and import goods made by unskilled workers. (This is the basic prediction of the *factor endowment theory* of comparative advantage that we discussed in Chapter 33.) Because Canada is now exporting more goods made by skilled labour, the domestic demand for such labour rises. Because Canada is now importing more goods made by unskilled labour, the domestic demand for such labour falls. This specialization according to comparative advantage raises average Canadian living standards, but it will also tend to raise the wages and employment prospects of skilled Canadian workers relative to the wages of unskilled Canadian workers.

If increasing trade has these effects, then reducing trade by erecting protectionist trade barriers can have the opposite effects. Protectionist policies may raise the incomes of unskilled Canadian workers, giving them a larger share of a smaller total GDP. The conclusion is that trade restrictions can improve the earnings of one group whenever the restrictions increase the demand for that group's services. This is done, however, at the expense of a reduction in *overall* national income and hence the country's average living standards.

This analysis is important because it reveals both the grain of truth and the dangers that lie behind the resistance to policies that promote free trade on the part of some labour groups and some organizations whose main concern is with the poor.

> Social and distributional concerns may lead to the rational adoption of protectionist policies. But the cost of such protection is a reduction in the country's *average* living standards.

Improving the Terms of Trade Tariffs can be used to change the terms of trade in favour of a country that makes up a large fraction of the world demand for some product that it imports. By restricting its demand for that product through a tariff, it can force down the price that foreign exporters receive for that product. The price paid by domestic consumers will probably rise but as long as the increase is less than the tariff, foreign suppliers will receive less per unit. For example, a 20 percent U.S. tariff on the import of Canadian softwood lumber might raise the price paid by U.S. consumers by 12 percent and lower the price received by Canadian suppliers by 8 percent (the difference between the two prices being received by the U.S. Treasury). This reduction in the price received by the Canadian suppliers of a U.S. import is a terms-of-trade improvement for the United States (and a terms-of-trade deterioration for Canada).

Note that not all countries can improve their terms of trade by levying tariffs on imported goods. A *necessary* condition is that the importing country has *market power*—in other words, that its imports represent a large proportion of total world demand for the good in question, so that its restrictive trade policies lead to a decline in the world price of its imports. Small countries, like Canada, are not large enough importers of any good to have a significant effect on world prices. For small countries, therefore, tariffs cannot improve their terms of trade.

> Large countries can sometimes improve their terms of trade (and thus increase their national income) by levying tariffs on some imported goods; small countries cannot.

infant industry argument The argument that new domestic industries with potential for economies of scale or learning by doing need to be protected from competition from established, low-cost foreign producers so that they can grow large enough to achieve costs as low as those of foreign producers.

Protecting Infant Industries The oldest valid arguments for protection as a means of raising living standards concern economies of scale or learning by doing. It is usually called the **infant industry argument**. An infant industry is nothing more than a new, small industry. If such an industry has large economies of scale or the scope for learning by doing, costs will be high when the industry is small but will fall as the industry grows. In such industries, the country that first enters the field has a tremendous advantage. A developing country may find that in the early stages of development, its industries are unable to compete with established foreign rivals. A trade restriction may protect these industries from foreign competition while they "grow up." When they are large enough, they will be able to produce as cheaply as their larger foreign rivals and thus be able to compete without protection.

Most of the now industrialized countries developed their industries initially under quite heavy tariff protection. (In Canada's case, the National Policy of 1876 established a high tariff wall behind which many Canadian industries developed and thrived for many years.) Once the industrial sector was well developed, these countries reduced their levels of protection, thus moving a long way toward free trade. Electronics in Taiwan, automobiles in Japan, commercial aircraft in Europe (specifically the consortium of European governments that created Airbus), and shipbuilding in South Korea are all examples in which protection of infant industries was successful. In each case, the national industry, protected by its home government, developed into a major player in the global marketplace.

One practical problem with this argument for protection is that some infants "never grow up." Once the young firm gets used to operating in a protected environment, it may resist having that protection disappear, even though all economies of scale may have been achieved. This is as much a political problem as an economic one. Political leaders must therefore be careful before offering protection to infant industries because they must recognize the political difficulties involved in removing that protection in the future. The countries that were most successful in having their protected industries eventually grow up and succeed in fierce international competition were those, such as Taiwan and South Korea, that ruthlessly withdrew support from unsuccessful infants within a specified time period.

Earning Economic Profits in Foreign Markets Another argument for protectionist policies is to help create an advantage in producing or marketing some product that is expected to generate economic profits through its sales to foreign consumers. If protection of the domestic market, which might include subsidizing domestic firms, can increase the chance that one of the domestic firms will become established and thus earn high profits, the protection may pay off. The economic profits earned in foreign markets may exceed the cost to domestic taxpayers of the protection. This is the general idea of *strategic trade policy*.

Opponents of strategic trade policy argue that it is nothing more than a modern version of age-old and faulty justifications for tariff protection. Once all countries try to be strategic, they will all waste vast sums trying to break into industries in which there is no room for most of them. Domestic consumers would benefit most, they say, if their governments let other countries engage in this game. Consumers could then buy the cheap, subsidized foreign products and export traditional non-subsidized products in return. The opponents of strategic trade policy also argue that democratic governments that enter the game of picking and backing winners are likely to make more bad choices than good ones. One bad choice, with all of its massive development costs written off, would require that many good choices also be made in order to make the equivalent in profits that would allow taxpayers to break even overall.

For many years, Canada and Brazil have been in a trade dispute centred on each country's alleged support of aerospace manufacturers. Canada's Bombardier and Brazil's Embraer both receive considerable financial assistance from their respective federal governments. Taxpayers in each country foot the bill.

An ongoing dispute between Canada and Brazil illustrates how strategic trade policy is often difficult to distinguish from pure protection. The world's two major producers of regional jets are Bombardier, based in Montreal, and Embraer SA, based in Brazil. For several years, each company has accused its competitor's government of using illegal subsidies to help the domestic company sell jets in world markets. Brazil's Pro-Ex program provides Embraer's customers with low-interest loans with which to purchase Embraer's jets. Export Development Canada (EDC) provides similar loans to Bombardier's customers. In addition, the Canadian government's Technology Partnerships program (which recently expired) subsidized research and development activities in high-tech aerospace and defence companies. As the leading Canadian aerospace company, Bombardier benefited significantly from this program.

Between 1996 and 2002 there were several complaints brought to the World Trade Organization (WTO) by both the Canadian and Brazilian governments. In various rulings the WTO determined that both governments were using illegal subsidy programs to support their aerospace firms. Both countries, however, naturally view their respective programs as necessary responses to the other country's subsidization. Many economists believe that an agreement to eliminate both programs would leave a "level playing field," while saving Brazilian and Canadian taxpayers a considerable amount of money. As of 2012, however, both countries continue to support their respective aerospace firms and both sets of taxpayers continue to foot the bill.

For a list and discussion of many ongoing trade disputes, see the WTO's website: www. wto.org.

> A country can potentially increase its national income by protecting infant industries and by subsidizing "strategic" firms. Unless carefully applied, however, such policies can end up being redistributions from consumers and taxpayers to domestic firms, without any benefit to overall living standards.

Invalid Arguments for Protection

We have seen that free trade is generally beneficial for a country overall even though it does not necessarily make every person better off. We have also seen that there are some situations in which there are valid arguments for restricting trade. For every valid argument, however, there are many invalid arguments—many of these are based, directly or indirectly, on the misconception that in every transaction there is a winner and a loser. Here we review a few arguments that are frequently heard in political debates concerning international trade.

Keep the Money at Home This argument says that if I buy a foreign good, I have the good and the foreigner has the money, whereas if I buy the same good locally, I have the good and our country has the money, too. This argument is based on a common misconception. It assumes that domestic money actually goes abroad physically when imports are purchased and that trade flows only in one direction. But when Canadian importers purchase Japanese goods, they do not send dollars abroad. They (or their financial agents) buy Japanese yen and use them to pay the Japanese manufacturers. They purchase the yen on the foreign-exchange market by giving up dollars to someone who wants to use them for expenditure in Canada. Even if the money did go abroad physically—that is, if a Japanese firm accepted a bunch of Canadian $100 bills—it would be because that firm (or someone to whom it could sell the dollars) wanted them to spend in the only country where they are legal tender—Canada.

Canadian currency ultimately does no one any good except as purchasing power in Canada. It would be miraculous if Canadian money could be exported in return for real goods. After all, the Bank of Canada has the power to create as much new Canadian money as it wants (at almost zero direct cost). It is only because Canadian money can buy Canadian products and Canadian assets that others want it.

Protect Against Low-Wage Foreign Labour This argument says that the products of low-wage countries will drive Canadian products from the market, and the high Canadian standard of living will be dragged down to that of its poorer trading partners. For example, if Canada imports cotton shirts from India, higher-cost Canadian textile firms may go out of business and Canadian workers may be laid off. This argument says that Canada is worse off *overall* by trading with India. Is this really true?

As a prelude to considering this argument, think what the argument would imply if taken out of the context of countries and applied instead to individuals, where the same principles govern the gains from trade. Is it impossible for a rich person to gain by trading with a poor person? Would Bill Gates and Warren Buffett really be better off if they did all their own typing, gardening, cooking and cleaning? No one believes that a rich person gains nothing by trading with those who are less rich.

Why, then, must a rich group of people lose when they trade with a poor group? "Well," some may say, "the poor group will price its goods too cheaply." Consumers gain, however, when they can buy the same goods at a lower price. If Chinese, Mexican, or Indian workers earn low wages and the goods they produce are sold at low prices, Canadians will gain by obtaining imports at a low cost in terms of the goods that must be exported in return. The cheaper our imports are, the better off we are in terms of the goods and services available for domestic consumption.

As we said earlier in this chapter, *some* Canadians may be better off if Canada places high tariffs on the import of goods from China or India or other developing nations. In particular, if the goods produced in these countries compete with goods made by unskilled Canadian workers, then those unskilled workers will be better off if a Canadian tariff protects their firms and thus their jobs. But Canadian income overall—that is, average per capita real income—will be higher when there is free trade.

Exports Are Good; Imports Are Bad Exports create domestic income; imports create income for foreigners. Surely, then, it is desirable to encourage exports by subsidizing them and to discourage imports by taxing them. This is an appealing argument, but it is incorrect.

Exports raise GDP by adding to the value of domestic output and income, but they do not add to the value of domestic consumption. The standard of living in a country depends on the level of consumption, not on the level of income. In other words, income is not of much use except that it provides the means for consumption.

If exports really were "good" and imports really were "bad," then a fully employed economy that managed to increase exports without a corresponding increase in imports ought to be better off. Such a change, however, would result in a reduction in current standards of living because when more goods are sent abroad but no more are brought in from abroad, the total goods available for domestic consumption must fall.

The living standards of a country depend on the goods and services consumed in that country. The importance of exports is that they provide the resources required to purchase imports, either now or in the future.

Create Domestic Jobs It is sometimes said that an economy with substantial unemployment, such as Canada during and immediately after the 2009 recession, provides an exception to the case for freer trade. Suppose tariffs or import quotas reduce the imports of Japanese cars, Indian textiles, German kitchen equipment, and Polish vodka. Surely, the argument goes, these polices will create more employment in Canadian industries producing similar products. This may be true but it will also *reduce* employment in other industries.

The Japanese, Indians, Germans, and Poles can buy products from Canada only if they earn Canadian dollars by selling their domestically produced goods and services to

LESSONS FROM HISTORY 34-1

Trade Protection and Recession

With the onset of the Great Depression in 1929, governments in many countries responded to internal political pressures to protect domestic jobs. In the United States, Congress passed the Smoot-Hawley Tariff Act in June 1930, legislation that raised tariffs on hundreds of different imported products. At the time, a petition against the legislation was signed by 1028 economists who argued that such tariffs would be costly for America and would initiate a "tariff war" between the United States and its trading partners, thereby worsening the economic situation.

In retrospect, the economists were clearly correct. Dozens of countries protested the increase in U.S. tariffs but then retaliated by increasing their own tariffs. Here in Canada, Liberal Prime Minister Mackenzie King raised tariffs on imported U.S. products and lowered them on imports from the rest of the British Empire. Confident that he would earn the public's support for his aggressive actions, he promptly called a federal election. But the Conservatives under R.B. Bennett argued that the Liberal actions were far too timid, and the voters apparently agreed. The Liberals were soundly defeated, Bennett became prime minister, and Canadian tariffs on U.S. products were raised even further.

Economists today agree that the widespread increase in tariffs in the 1930s contributed significantly to a reduction in global trade and made the economic situation worse. In January of 1929, before the onset of the Depression, the volume of world trade was $5.3 billion. Four years later, at the depth of the Depression, world trade had collapsed to $1.8 billion, a reduction of 66 percent. The net effect, instead of increasing employment in any country, was to shift jobs from efficient export industries to inefficient domestic industries, supplying local markets in place of imports.

When the most recent worldwide recession began in the wake of the 2008 global financial crisis, world leaders were mindful of this important lesson from the Great Depression. When meeting in Washington, D.C., to coordinate their policy responses, the leaders of the world's largest developed and developing countries (the G20 group of countries) publicly committed to not raising any tariffs for at least one year.

Despite this commitment, however, protectionist measures soon emerged. In the United States, the fiscal stimulus package passed by Congress included a "buy American"

Canada (or by borrowing dollars from Canada).[1] The decline in their sales of cars, textiles, kitchen equipment, and vodka will decrease their purchases of Canadian lumber, software, banking services, and holidays. Jobs will be lost in Canadian export industries and gained in industries that formerly faced competition from imports. The major long-term effect is that the same amount of total employment in Canada will merely be redistributed among industries. In the process, average living standards will be reduced because employment expands in inefficient import-competing industries and contracts in efficient exporting industries.

A country that imposes tariffs in an attempt to create domestic jobs risks starting a "tariff war" with its trading partners. Such a trade war can easily leave every country worse off, as world output (and thus income) falls significantly. An income-reducing trade war followed the onset of the Great Depression in 1929 as many countries increased tariffs to protect their domestic industries in an attempt to stimulate domestic production and employment. Most economists agree that this trade war made the Great Depression worse than it otherwise would have been. *Lessons from History 34-1* discusses this relationship between tariffs and recession and how it resurfaced during the major recession that followed the 2008 global financial crisis.

---

[1] They can also get dollars by selling to other countries and then using their currencies to buy Canadian dollars. But this intermediate step only complicates the transaction; it does not change its fundamental nature. Other countries must have earned the dollars by selling goods to Canada or borrowing from Canada.

clause requiring that any funds from the package not be spent on imported construction materials. Similar kinds of protection were built in to the fiscal stimulus packages in China and some European countries. Canada and other major trading nations were understandably concerned by these actions and soon began threatening their own retaliatory measures. The Canadian government went to great lengths to argue that U.S. trade protection would not only hurt Canada but would also hurt the United States by raising prices for American consumers, thus making economic recovery more difficult.

While the lessons from history were being forgotten by some political leaders, a few prominent voices were arguing the dangers of increased trade protection. The World Bank issued a report in March 2009 indicating that in the previous four months world leaders had proposed or implemented 78 different protectionist measures. The president of the World Bank urged leaders to rethink these policies: "Leaders must not heed the siren-song of protectionist fixes, whether for trade, stimulus packages or bailouts. . . . Economic isolationism can lead to a negative spiral of events such as those we saw in the 1930s, which made a bad situation much, much worse."

Canadian Prime Ministers Bennett (left) and Mackenzie King (right) both learned in the 1930s that protectionist policies often make better politics than economics.

34.2 Methods of Protection

We now go on to explore the effects of two specific protectionist policies. Both cause the price of the imported good to rise and the quantity demanded by domestic consumers to fall. They differ, however, in how they achieve these results.

Tariffs

A tariff, also called an *import duty*, is a tax on imported goods. For example, consider a Canadian firm that wants to import cotton T-shirts from India at $5 per shirt. If the Canadian government levies a 20 percent tariff on imported cotton shirts, the Canadian firm pays $5 to the Indian exporter *plus* $1 (20 percent of $5) in import duties to the Canada Revenue Agency. The immediate effect of a tariff is therefore to increase the domestic price of the T-shirt to $6. This price increase has important implications for domestic consumers as well as domestic producers. The effect of a tariff is shown in Figure 34-1.

The initial effect of the tariff is to raise the domestic price of the imported product above its world price by the amount of the tariff. Imports fall. The price received on domestically produced units rises, as does the quantity produced domestically. On both counts, domestic producers earn more. However, the cost of producing the extra production at

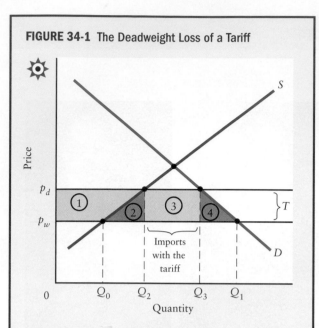

FIGURE 34-1 The Deadweight Loss of a Tariff

A tariff imposes a deadweight loss for the importing country. Before the tariff, the price in the domestic economy is the world price, p_w. Imports are $Q_0 Q_1$. With a tariff of $\$T$ per unit, the domestic price rises to p_d. Domestic consumption falls to Q_3, and consumer surplus falls by areas ① + ② + ③ + ④. Domestic production rises to Q_2 and producer surplus increases by area ①. Imports fall to $Q_2 Q_3$, and the government collects tariff revenue equal to area ③. The sum of areas ② and ④ represents the deadweight loss of the tariff.

home exceeds the price at which it could be purchased on the world market. Thus, the benefit to domestic producers comes at the expense of domestic consumers. Indeed, domestic consumers lose on two counts: First, they consume less of the product because its price rises, and second, they pay a higher price for the amount that they do consume. This extra spending ends up in two places: The extra that is paid on all units produced at home goes to domestic producers, and the extra that is paid on units still imported goes to the government as tariff revenue.

The overall loss to the domestic economy from levying a tariff is best seen in terms of the changes in consumer and producer surplus. Before the tariff, consumer surplus was equal to the entire area below the demand curve and above the price line at p_w.

After the tariff, the price increase leads to less consumption and less consumer surplus. The loss of consumer surplus is the sum of the areas ①, ②, ③, and ④ in Figure 34-1. As domestic producers respond to the higher domestic price by increasing their production and sales, they earn more producer surplus, equal to area ①. Finally, the taxpayers gain the tariff revenue equal to area ③. This is simply a redistribution of surplus away from consumers toward taxpayers. In summary:

Loss of consumer surplus = ① + ② + ③ + ④
Gain of producer surplus = ①
Gain of tariff revenue   = ③
_____
Net loss in surplus   = ② + ④

The overall effect of the tariff is therefore to create a deadweight loss to the domestic economy equal to areas ② plus ④. Domestic consumers are worse off, while domestic firms and taxpayers are better off. But the net effect is a loss of surplus for the economy as a whole. This is the overall cost of levying a tariff.

A tariff imposes costs on domestic consumers, generates benefits for domestic producers, and generates revenue for the government. But the overall net effect is negative; a tariff generates a deadweight loss for the economy.

Quotas and Voluntary Export Restrictions (VERs)

import quota A limit set on the quantity of a foreign commodity that may be imported in a given time period.

voluntary export restriction (VER) An agreement by an exporting country to limit the amount of a good exported to another country.

The second type of protectionist policy directly restricts the quantity of imports of a specific product. A common example is the **import quota**, by which the importing country sets a maximum quantity of some product that may be imported each year. Another measure is the **voluntary export restriction (VER)**, an agreement by an exporting country to limit the amount of a product that it sells to the importing country.

Figure 34-2 shows that a quantity restriction and a tariff have similar effects on domestic consumers and producers—they both raise domestic prices, increase domestic production, and reduce domestic consumption. But a direct quantity restriction is actually *worse* than a tariff for the importing country because the effect of the quantity restriction is to raise the price received by the foreign suppliers of the good. In contrast, a tariff leaves the foreign suppliers' price unchanged and instead generates tariff revenue for the government of the importing country.

> Import quotas and voluntary export restrictions (VERs) impose larger deadweight losses on the importing country than do tariffs that lead to the same level of imports.

Canada, the United States, and the European Union have used VERs extensively, and the EU makes frequent use of import quotas. Japan has been pressured into negotiating several VERs with Canada, the United States, and the EU in order to limit sales of some of the Japanese goods that have had the most success in international competition. For example, in 1983, the United States and Canada negotiated VERs whereby the Japanese government agreed to restrict total sales of Japanese cars to these two countries for three years. When the agreements ran out in 1986, the Japanese continued to restrict their automobile sales by unilateral voluntary action. Japan's readiness to restrict its exports to North America reflects the high profits that Japanese automobile producers were making under the system of VERs, as explained in Figure 34-2. In recent years, such VERs have become less important because Japan's major automobile producers have established manufacturing plants in Canada.

Tariffs Versus Quotas: An Application

The dispute that raged for several years between Canada and the United States over the exports of Canadian softwood lumber (spruce, pine, fir, cedar) exports illustrates an important distinction between tariffs and quotas. The United States protected its softwood lumber industry in two ways:

- by imposing tariffs on U.S. imports of Canadian softwood lumber
- by pressuring Canadian governments to place quotas on Canadian exports to the United States

Analysis of Figure 34-1 and 34-2 reveals that the choice between tariffs and quotas matters greatly for Canadian producers.

In the case of a U.S. tariff on imported Canadian softwood lumber, Figure 34-1 illustrates the U.S. market. An import tariff raises the domestic price for U.S. lumber users and also increases the profits of U.S. lumber producers. Canadian lumber producers are harmed because there is less demand for their product at the unchanged world

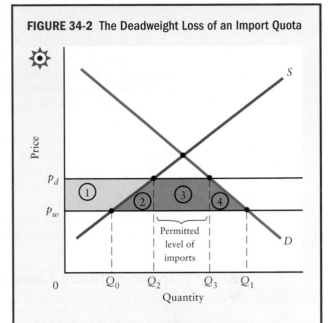

FIGURE 34-2 The Deadweight Loss of an Import Quota

An import quota drives up the domestic price and imposes a deadweight loss on the importing country. With free trade, the domestic price is the world price, p_w. Imports are Q_0Q_1. If imports are restricted to only Q_2Q_3 (through either quotas or VERs), the domestic price must rise to the point where the restricted level of imports just satisfies the domestic excess demand—this occurs only at P_d. The rise in price and reduction in consumption reduces consumer surplus by areas ① + ② + ③ + ④. Domestic producers increase their output as the domestic price rises, and producer surplus increases by area ①. Area ③ does not accrue to the domestic economy; instead this area represents extra producer surplus for the foreign firms that export their product to this country. The net effect of the quota or VER is a deadweight loss for the importing country of areas ② + ③ + ④. Import quotas are therefore worse than tariffs for the importing country.

price. Area ③ in the figure represents U.S. tariff revenue collected on the imports of Canadian lumber—revenue that accrues to the United States government.

Figure 34-2 illustrates the U.S. market for softwood lumber when a quota is placed on the level of Canadian exports (U.S. imports). As with the tariff, the restricted supply of Canadian lumber to the U.S. market drives up the price to U.S. users and also raises profits for U.S. producers. But with a quota there is an important difference: The higher price in the U.S. market is received by the Canadian lumber producers, as shown by area ③ in the figure.

While a tariff and quota may lead to the same reduced volume of exports, the tariff permits some surplus to be captured by the importing country, whereas the quota allows some surplus to be captured by the exporting country (area ③ in both cases). In the U.S.–Canadian softwood lumber dispute, both tariffs and quotas were used. And while both systems were to be preferred *overall* by a system of free trade, Canada had an interest in imposing quotas on Canadian lumber exporters rather than having the same export reduction accomplished by a U.S. tariff.

Trade-Remedy Laws and Non-tariff Barriers

As tariffs in many countries were lowered over the years since the Second World War, countries that wanted to protect domestic industries began using, and often abusing, a series of trade restrictions that came to be known as *non-tariff barriers* (NTBs). The original purpose of some of these barriers was to remedy certain legitimate problems that arise in international trade and, for this reason, they are often called *trade-remedy laws*. All too often, however, such laws are misused and over time become powerful means of simple protection.

dumping The practice of selling a commodity at a lower price in the export market than in the domestic market for reasons unrelated to differences in costs of servicing the two markets.

Dumping Selling a product in a foreign country at a lower price than in the domestic market is known as **dumping**. For example, if U.S.-made cars were sold for less in Canada than in the United States, the U.S. automobile firms would be said to be *dumping*. Dumping is a form of price discrimination studied in the theory of monopoly (see Chapter 10). Most governments have antidumping duties designed to protect their own industries against what is viewed as unfair foreign pricing practices.

> Dumping, if it lasts indefinitely, can be a gift to the receiving country. Its consumers get goods from abroad at lower prices than they otherwise would.

Dumping is more often a temporary measure, designed to get rid of unwanted surpluses, or a predatory attempt to drive competitors out of business. In either case, domestic producers complain about unfair foreign competition. In both cases, it is accepted international practice to levy *antidumping duties* on foreign imports. These duties are designed to eliminate the discriminatory elements in their prices.

Unfortunately, antidumping laws have been evolving over the past three decades in ways that allow antidumping duties to become barriers to trade and competition rather than to provide redress for genuinely unfair trading practices.

Several features of the antidumping system that is now in place in many countries make it highly protectionist. First, any price discrimination between national markets is classified as dumping and is subject to penalties. Thus, prices in the producer's domestic market become, in effect, minimum prices below which no sales can be made in foreign markets, whatever the nature of demand in the domestic and foreign markets. Second, many countries' laws calculate the "margin of dumping" as the difference between the price that is charged in that country's market and the foreign producer's average cost. Thus, when there is a global slump in some industry so that the profit-maximizing price for all producers is below average cost, foreign producers can be convicted of dumping. This gives domestic producers enormous protection whenever the market price falls temporarily below average cost. Third, law in the United States (but not in all other countries) places the onus of proof on the accused. Facing a charge of dumping, a foreign producer must prove that the charge is unfounded. Fourth, U.S. antidumping duties are imposed with no time limit, so they often persist long after foreign firms have altered the prices that gave rise to them.

> Antidumping laws were first designed to permit countries to respond to predatory pricing by foreign firms. More recently, they have been used to protect domestic firms against any foreign competition.

Countervailing Duties A **countervailing duty** is a tariff imposed by one country designed to offset the effects of specific subsidies provided by foreign governments to their exporting firms. For example, if the German government provided subsidies to its firms that produce and export machine tools, the Canadian government might respond by imposing a countervailing duty—a tariff—on the imports of German machine tools designed to "level the playing field" between German and Canadian firms in that industry. Countervailing duties, which are commonly used by the U.S. government but much less so elsewhere, provide another case in which a trade-remedy law can become a covert method of protection.

> **countervailing duty** A tariff imposed by one country designed to offset the effects of specific subsidies provided by foreign governments.

There is no doubt that countervailing duties have sometimes been used to counteract the effects of foreign subsidies. Many governments complain, however, that countervailing duties are often used as thinly disguised protection. At the early stages of the development of countervailing duties, only subsidies whose prime effect was to distort trade were possible objects of countervailing duties. Even then, however, the existence of equivalent domestic subsidies was not taken into account when decisions were made to put countervailing duties on subsidized imports. Thus, the United States levies some countervailing duties against foreign goods even though the foreign subsidy is less than the domestic (U.S.) subsidy. This does not create a level playing field.

Over time, the type of subsidy that is subject to countervailing duties has evolved until almost any government program that affects industry now risks becoming the object of a countervailing duty. Because all governments, including most U.S. state governments, have programs that provide direct or indirect assistance to industry, the potential for the use of countervailing duties as thinly disguised trade barriers is enormous.

Softwood lumber (spruce, pine, and fir) is used extensively in North America for the framing of houses and small buildings. For many years, the United States levied countervailing duties on Canadian softwood lumber exports, alleging that Canadian provinces unfairly subsidized production. In 2006, the Canadian and U.S. governments reached an agreement to end the dispute.

> Countervailing duties can be used to offset the effects of foreign export subsidies, but often they are nothing more than thinly disguised protection.

The best-known example in Canada of a U.S. countervailing duty is the 27 percent duty imposed on U.S. imports of Canadian softwood lumber between 2001 and 2005. The U.S. government's claim was that Canadian provincial governments provided a subsidy to domestic lumber producers by charging artificially low *stumpage fees*—the fees paid by the companies to cut trees on Crown land. In 2006, the U.S. government agreed to eliminate the countervailing duty but only if restrictions were placed on Canadian lumber exports. Thus, a tariff was replaced by a combination of an export quota and an export tax.

| 34.3 Current Trade Policy

In the remainder of the chapter, we discuss trade policy in practice. We start with the many international agreements that govern current trade policies and then look in a little more detail at the NAFTA.

Before 1947, in the absence of any international agreement, any country was free to impose tariffs on its imports. However, when one country increased its tariffs, the action often triggered retaliatory actions by its trading partners. During the Great Depression in the 1930s, widespread increases in protection occurred as many countries sought to raise their employment and output by raising its tariffs. The end result was lowered efficiency, less trade, and a deeper economic decline. Since the end of the Second World War, much effort has been devoted to reducing tariff barriers, both on a multilateral and on a regional basis.

The GATT and the WTO

One of the most notable achievements of the post–Second World War era was the creation in 1947 of the General Agreement on Tariffs and Trade (GATT). The principle of the GATT was that each member country agreed not to make unilateral tariff increases. This prevented the outbreak of "tariff wars" in which countries raised tariffs to protect particular domestic industries and to retaliate against other countries' tariff increases. The GATT has since been replaced by the World Trade Organization (WTO), which continues the work of the GATT.

The Uruguay Round The Uruguay Round—the final round of trade agreements under the GATT—was completed in 1994 after years of negotiations. It reduced world tariffs by about 40 percent. A significant failure of these negotiations was the absence of an agreement to liberalize trade in agricultural goods. The European Union and Canada both resisted an agreement in this area. The EU's Common Agricultural Policy (CAP) provides general support for most of its agricultural products, many of which are exported. Canada, which has free trade in many agricultural commodities, was concerned about maintaining its "supply management" over a number of industries including poultry, eggs, and dairy products. These schemes restrict domestic production and push domestic prices well above world levels. The Canadian government made (and continues to make) such high domestic prices possible by imposing very high tariffs on the import of foreign products. In the case of imported milk and cheese, for example, the Canadian tariffs are *well over 200 percent*.

Despite the failure to achieve free trade in agricultural products, the Uruguay Round was generally viewed as a success. Perhaps its most significant achievement was the creation of the World Trade Organization (WTO) to replace the GATT. An important part of the WTO is its formal dispute-settlement mechanism. This mechanism allows countries to take cases of alleged trade violations—such as illegal subsidies or tariffs—to the WTO for a formal ruling, and obliges member countries to follow the ruling. The WTO's dispute-settlement mechanism is thus a significant step toward a "rules-based" global trading system.

The Doha Round Agriculture also plays a central role in the ongoing round of trade negotiations, which began in Doha, Qatar, in 2000. Many issues were discussed and negotiated over the next several years, ranging from competition policy to antidumping and from environmental policies to electronic commerce. But one of the most contentious issues is agriculture. The WTO member governments claim to be committed to reducing export subsidies and other forms of government support to agriculture. Movements in this direction will naturally cause political friction within the developed economies that currently protect and support their agricultural producers. A failure to reduce agricultural support in the developed countries, however, will increase the political frictions that already exist between developed and developing nations. For the many developing countries that have natural comparative advantages in agricultural products and that cannot afford to compete in a "subsidy war" with the developed countries, the liberalization of trade in agricultural products is crucial. They see the Doha round as central to their economic development.

International trade negotiations sometimes generate considerable grass-roots opposition. There is some opposition to the reduction of tariffs in developed countries and some controversy regarding the appropriate way to address the concerns of developing countries.

Opposition to the WTO Despite the WTO's successes in recent years, the organization has many critics. One common criticism is that the WTO's process of negotiating trade agreements pays insufficient attention to environmental and labour standards, especially as they exist in the developing countries. Another criticism is that the presence of the WTO does not prevent some rich and powerful countries from ruthlessly pursuing their own interests, often to the detriment of economic conditions in weaker countries. *Applying Economic Concepts 34-1* addresses some of the often-heard criticisms of the WTO and argues that, as imperfect as the institution may be, it holds out much promise for continued progress in trade liberalization.

For more information on the WTO, see its website at www. wto.org.

Regional Trade Agreements

Regional agreements seek to liberalize trade over a much smaller group of countries than the WTO membership. Three standard forms of regional trade-liberalizing agreements are *free trade areas, customs unions*, and *common markets*.

A **free trade area (FTA)** is the least comprehensive of the three. It allows for tariff-free trade among the member countries, but it leaves each member free to establish its own trade policy with respect to other countries. As a result, members are required to maintain customs points at their common borders to make sure that imports into the free trade area do not all enter through the member that is levying the lowest tariff on each item. They must also agree on *rules of origin* to establish when a good is made in a member country and hence is able to pass tariff-free across their borders, and when it

free trade area (FTA) An agreement among two or more countries to abolish tariffs on trade among themselves while each remains free to set its own tariffs against other countries.

APPLYING ECONOMIC CONCEPTS 34-1

Does the WTO Do More Harm Than Good?

There are many critics of the World Trade Organization. Extremists argue that all institutions supporting globalization should be abolished. Other critics admit that globalization is inevitable but say that the WTO is so faulty in providing a rules-based system that it does more harm than good.

Supporters of the WTO argue that it is the best hope for poor countries that would be most oppressed in a lawless world in which rich countries, particularly the United States and members of the European Union, could behave as they wanted. Rather than allowing the poorer countries to flounder in a lawless world, the WTO provides a rules-based regime and has a dispute-settlement function that has heard more than 300 cases. Even if the rich countries do exert undue power over the negotiations, at least the WTO meetings provide a forum for poor nations to speak out and broker alliances. The alternative—no voice in a no-rules system—would be much worse.

Critics often respond that while the existence of the dispute-settlement mechanism may be beneficial, the enforcement of those settlements is undermined by disparities in economic power. Nations with large economies can use trade sanctions against small nations, but the small nation that attempts the same often inflicts the most harm on its own economy. Supporters of the WTO agree that this *is* a major defect, but the dispute-settlement mechanism has accomplished much, and to discard it because of imperfect enforcement would be a great loss. What is needed is *reform*—with larger economies agreeing to graduated enforcement mechanisms, including stiffer penalties for themselves.

Critics also claim that the WTO is a failure because it does not permit the imposition of trade sanctions against countries that pollute their own environments or exploit their own workers. But the poorest countries, many of whom are strong WTO supporters, fear that advanced countries would use environmental and labour standards written into the body of trade agreements as disguised non-tariff barriers. To the poorer countries it would be "policy imperialism" to argue that they should be forced to accept the standards of environmental and labour protection that the rich countries can only now afford. Nonetheless, environmental and labour protections are being written into some new trade agreements, and it remains to be seen if they will work beneficially or harmfully—or not at all.

Critics also complain that the WTO is undemocratic. In response, supporters point out that it is representatives of sovereign nations, usually elected ones, who conduct the negotiations, and that any agreements must be ratified by respective national parliaments before they come into effect. It is unlikely that any organization able to achieve agreement among 155 member-country governments could be any more democratic while still being effective.

Finally, some critics claim that the WTO is simply a tool for those who advocate a doctrinaire form of laissez-faire capitalism. It is true that some WTO supporters believe that unfettered free markets can meet all social requirements. A far larger number of supporters, however, believe that the market system needs government involvement if it is to meet societal needs for social justice and growth. The vast majority of supporters agree that most, if not all, trade restrictions are harmful and that the WTO, with its mission of continued trade liberalization, can create significant benefits to rich and poor countries alike.

---

is imported from outside the FTA and hence is subject to tariffs when it crosses borders within the FTA. The three countries in North America formed a free-trade area when they created the NAFTA in 1994.

In recent years, Canada has signed bilateral free-trade agreements with Israel, Chile, Costa Rica, Peru, Colombia, and Jordan and is currently negotiating with Japan and the European Union. In 2012, Canada gained admission to the Trans-Pacific Partnership (TPP), a new proposed free-trade agreement between several Pacific-rim countries, including Australia, New Zealand, the United States, Chile, Singapore, Vietnam, and others. The details of the agreement are currently being negotiated. Canada's ongoing efforts to negotiate free-trade agreements with many countries reveal a desire on the part of the Canadian government to diversify Canada's pattern of trade. See *Applying Economic Concepts 34-2* for more on this important topic.

A **customs union** is a free trade area in which the member countries agree to establish a common trade policy with the rest of the world. Because they have a common trade policy,

customs union A group of countries that agree to have free trade among themselves and a common set of barriers against imports from the rest of the world.

the members need neither customs controls on goods moving among themselves nor rules of origin. Once a good has entered any member country it has met the common rules and regulations and paid the common tariff and so it may henceforth be treated the same as a good that is produced within the union. An example of a customs union is Mercosur, an agreement linking Argentina, Brazil, Paraguay, and Uruguay. A **common market** is a customs union that also has free movement of labour and capital among its members. The European Union is by far the most successful example of a common market.

common market A customs union with the added provision that labour and capital can move freely among the members.

Trade Creation and Trade Diversion

A major effect of regional trade liberalization is to alter the pattern of production and trade as countries reallocate their resources toward the production of goods in which they have a comparative advantage. Economists divide the effects on trade into two categories: *trade creation* and *trade diversion*. These concepts were first developed by Jacob Viner, a Canadian-born economist who taught at the University of Chicago and Princeton University in the first half of the twentieth century.

Trade creation occurs when producers in one member country find that they can export products to another member country that previously were produced there because of tariff protection. For example, when the North American Free Trade Agreement (NAFTA) eliminated most cross-border tariffs among Mexico, Canada, and the United States, some U.S. firms found that they could undersell their Canadian competitors in some product lines, and some Canadian firms found that they could undersell their U.S. competitors in other product lines. As a result, specialization occurred, and new international trade developed among the three countries.

trade creation A consequence of reduced trade barriers among a set of countries whereby trade within the group is increased and trade with the rest of the world remains roughly constant.

Trade creation represents efficient specialization according to comparative advantage.

Trade diversion occurs when exporters in one member country *replace* foreign exporters as suppliers to another member country. For example, trade diversion occurs when U.S. firms find that they can undersell competitors from the rest of the world in the Canadian market, not because they are the cheapest source of supply, but because their tariff-free prices under NAFTA are lower than the tariff-burdened prices of imports from other countries. This effect is a gain to U.S. firms and Canadian consumers of the product. U.S. firms get new business and therefore they clearly gain. Canadian consumers buy the product at a lower, tariff-free price from the U.S. producer than they used to pay to the third-country producer (with a tariff), and so they are also better off. But Canada as a whole is worse off as a result of the trade diversion. Canada is now buying the product from a U.S. producer at a higher price with no tariff. Before the agreement, it was buying from a third-country producer at a lower price (and collecting tariff revenue).

trade diversion A consequence of reduced trade barriers among a set of countries whereby trade within the group replaces trade that used to take place with countries outside the group.

From the global perspective, trade diversion represents an inefficient use of resources.

The main argument *against* regional trade agreements is that the costs of trade diversion may outweigh the benefits of trade creation. While recognizing this possibility, many economists believe that regional agreements, especially among only a few countries, are much easier to negotiate than multilateral agreements through the WTO. In addition, regional agreements may represent effective *incremental* progress in what is a very lengthy process of achieving global free trade.

APPLYING ECONOMIC CONCEPTS 34-2

The Transformation of Canada's International Trade

Look at Canada's location on a world map and you will immediately see why the vast majority of Canada's international trade has long been (and likely will always be) with the United States. In 2011, for example, trade with the United States accounted for 72 percent of Canadian merchandise exports and 61 percent of merchandise imports.*

Many economists argue that Canada would benefit by increasing the share of its total trade that occurs with countries other than the United States. With greater diversification in its trade, Canada would be less vulnerable to downturns in the U.S. economy. This concern increased during the 2008–2009 global recession, which hit the U.S. economy especially hard and from which the United States was still slowly recovering five years later. Other economists acknowledge the benefits of greater diversification but argue that the more important goal should be to increase the *overall volume* of Canadian trade. According to the theory of comparative advantage that we reviewed in Chapter 33, a greater volume of trade suggests greater gains from trade, with implications for growth in average material living standards.

Greater trade between Canada and the "emerging" markets of Asia, South America, and parts of Africa may help Canada achieve both outcomes—greater trade diversification and an expansion of overall trade flows.

Events in the United States

Canada's trade with the United States declined significantly during the 2008–2009 global recession.

*A country's "merchandise" trade is the trade in goods, excluding the trade in services. In a typical year in Canada, roughly three-quarters of total trade is merchandise trade.

For more on Canada's export performance and some of the challenges faced by Canadian exporting firms, see *EDC Global Export Forecast*, published annually by Export Development Canada, www.edc.ca.

Merchandise exports to the United States fell from $370 billion in 2008 to $331 billion in 2011, while merchandise imports fell and then recovered to their 2008 level of $281 billion. But Canadian exports to the United States had been declining well before the recession. The collapse in the high-tech sector in 2000–2001, the heightened security concerns in the aftermath of the 2001 terrorist attacks in New York and Washington, and the dramatic appreciation of the Canadian dollar from 2004 through 2008 (driven mostly by rising commodity prices) all put immense strains on Canadian exports to the United States. For many Canadian exporting firms, the decade of the 2000s presented severe challenges.

How did Canada's exporters respond to these challenges? Unable to compete, thousands of businesses closed their doors, and others relocated to other countries. Many survivors, however, met the challenges through an extraordinary transformation. Faced with little or no growth in traditional markets, many Canadian exporters launched into riskier emerging markets and discovered their potential for growth. Canadian merchandise exports to the emerging markets grew from just 4 percent of total merchandise exports in 2000 to 11 percent by 2011. Although still a small share of Canada's total trade, Canadian trade with the emerging world accounted for the majority of the *growth* of total merchandise exports over this period. Having tasted success in these markets, there is good reason to expect Canadian firms to continue this expansion.

Canadian Trade Policy

The ongoing transformation in Canadian trade is also driven by changes in government policy. After the creation of the Canada–U.S. Free Trade Agreement in 1989, its expansion into NAFTA to include Mexico in 1994,

The North American Free Trade Agreement

The NAFTA dates from 1994 and is an extension of the 1989 Canada–U.S. Free Trade Agreement (FTA). It established a free trade area, as opposed to a customs union; each member country retains its own external trade policy, and rules of origin are needed to determine when a good is made within North America and thus allowed to move freely among the members.

National Treatment The fundamental principle that guides the NAFTA is that of *national treatment*. The principle of national treatment is that individual countries are free to establish any laws they want, with the sole proviso that these laws must not

and the Canada–Chile free-trade agreement in 1997, Canadian trade negotiations virtually ceased for a decade. Adding to the inactivity was the glacial pace of discussions within WTO's Doha Round. As a result, Canada's trade pattern across various countries was relatively stable.

In 2007, however, Canadian trade negotiators began a flurry of activity. Between 2007 and 2011, five bilateral free-trade agreements were finalized by the Canadian government, and discussions on a number of others were initiated. Ongoing negotiations with the European Union, India, China, Japan, and the members of the new Trans-Pacific Partnership could potentially lead to enormous changes in Canada's trade opportunities over the near future.

Projections

Canada's trade landscape is likely to be quite different in just a few years. The accompanying figure shows the change in Canada's merchandise trade (exports plus imports) as a share of GDP with the United States, the combined emerging economies, and all other countries, since 2000. The actual increase in the relative importance of trade with the emerging economies between 2000 and 2011 is clear. Though not shown in the figure, the projections for the future are equally striking: Export Development Canada projects that if current trends continue, emerging markets will account for over 30 percent of Canada's total trade by 2025.

Greater trade with the emerging world will have the effect of increasing Canada's overall trade volumes and also of diversifying Canada's trade away from the United States. The first will lead to greater gains from trade; the second will reduce our dependence on the U.S. economy and increase our trade linkages with countries projected to have higher rates of future economic growth. Canada stands to gain on both fronts.

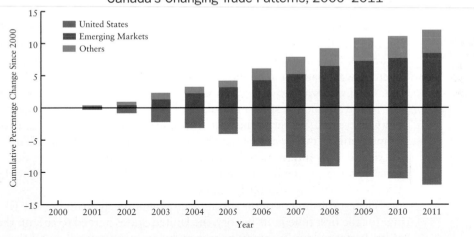

Canada's Changing Trade Patterns, 2000–2011

discriminate on the basis of nationality. For example, Canada can choose to have stringent laws against dumping pollutants in waterways or against the emission of noxious gases into the atmosphere. The principle of national treatment requires that the Canadian government enforce these laws equally on all firms located in Canada, independent of their ownership or nationality. It is against the NAFTA conditions to apply more stringent laws to foreign-owned firms than to domestic firms, or vice versa. Canada can also choose to impose strict product standards related to the chemical content of paint or the nutritional content of foods, but again the NAFTA condition requires that such laws be applied to products independent of where they are produced. For example, it would be against the NAFTA conditions to require a specific level of fuel efficiency on imported cars but not on those cars produced and sold in Canada.

The principle of national treatment allows each member country a maximum of policy independence while preventing national policies from being used as trade barriers. In the absence of national treatment, Canada could impose stringent environmental or product standards on the products of *foreign* firms only and thereby offer effective protection to its domestic firms who need only satisfy less stringent standards.

Other Major Provisions There are several other major provisions in the NAFTA.

1. All tariffs on trade between Canada, the United States, and Mexico were eliminated as of 2010.

2. The principle of national treatment (described above) applies to foreign investment once it enters a country, but each country can screen foreign investment before it enters.

3. Some restrictions on trade and investment are not eliminated by the agreement. In Canada's case, the main examples are supply-managed agricultural products and cultural industries such as magazine and book publishing.

4. Trade in most non-agricultural service industries is liberalized and subject to the principle of national treatment.

5. A significant amount of government procurement is open to cross-border bidding, though a large part is still exempt from NAFTA.

For information about the NAFTA, go to the website for the NAFTA Secretariat: www.nafta-sec-alena.org.

Dispute Settlement From Canada's point of view, by far the biggest setback in the negotiations for the Canada–U.S. FTA was the failure to obtain agreement on a common regime for countervailing and antidumping duties. In view of that failure, no significant attempt was made to deal with this issue in the subsequent NAFTA negotiations. The U.S. Congress was unwilling to abandon the unilateral use of these powerful weapons.

In the absence of such a multilateral regime, a NAFTA dispute-settlement mechanism was created. Under it, the justifications required for the levying of antidumping and countervailing duties are subject to review by a panel of Canadians, Americans, and Mexicans. This international review replaces appeal through the domestic courts. The panel has the power to suspend any duties until it is satisfied that the domestic laws have been correctly and fairly applied.

The establishment of the dispute-settlement mechanism in NAFTA was path breaking: for the first time in its history, the United States agreed to submit the administration of its domestic laws to *binding* scrutiny by an international panel that often contains a majority of foreigners.

Results The Canada–U.S. FTA aroused a great debate in Canada. Indeed, the Canadian federal election of 1988 was fought almost entirely on the issue of free trade. Supporters looked for major increases in the security of existing trade from U.S. protectionist attacks and for a growth of new trade. Detractors predicted a flight of firms to the United States, the loss of many Canadian jobs, and even the demise of Canada's political independence.

By and large, however, both the Canada–U.S. FTA and the NAFTA agreements worked out just about as expected by their supporters. Industry restructured in the direction of greater export orientation in all three countries, and trade creation occurred. The flow of trade among the three countries increased markedly, but especially so between Canada and the United States. As the theory of trade predicts, specialization

APPLYING ECONOMIC CONCEPTS 34-3

Canadian Wine: A Free-Trade Success Story

Before the Canada–U.S. FTA was signed in 1989, great fears were expressed over the fate of the Canadian wine industry, located mainly in Ontario and British Columbia. It was heavily tariff protected and, with a few notable exceptions, produced mainly cheap, low-quality products. Contrary to most people's expectations, rather than being decimated, the industry now produces a wide variety of high-quality products, some of which win international competitions.

The nature of the pre-FTA protection largely explains the dramatic turnaround of the Canadian wine industry once the FTA took effect. First, Canadian wine producers had been protected by high tariffs on imported wine but were at the same time required by law to produce wine by using only domestically grown grapes. The domestic grape growers, however, produced varieties of grapes not conducive to the production of high-quality wines, and with a captive domestic market, they had little incentive to change their behaviour. Thus, Canadian wine producers concentrated their efforts on "hiding" the attributes of poor-quality grapes rather than enhancing the attributes of high-quality grapes. The result was low-quality wine.

The second important aspect of the protection was that the high Canadian tariff was levied on a per unit rather than on an *ad valorem* basis. For example, the tariff was expressed as so many dollars per litre rather than as a specific percentage of the price. Charging a tariff by the litre gave most protection to the low-quality wines with low value per litre. The higher the per litre value of the wine, the lower the percentage tariff protection. For example, a $5-per-litre tariff would have the following effects. A low-quality imported wine valued at $5 per

litre would have its price raised to $10, a 100 percent increase in price, whereas a higher-quality imported wine valued at $25 per litre would have its price increased to $30, only a 20 percent increase in price.

Responding to these incentives, the Canadian industry concentrated on producing low-quality wines. The market for these wines was protected by the nearly prohibitive tariffs on competing low-quality imports and by the high prices charged for high-quality imports. In addition, protection was provided by many hidden charges that the various provincial governments' liquor monopolies levied in order to protect local producers.

When the tariff was removed under the FTA, the incentives were to move up-market, producing much more value per hectare of land. Fortunately, much of the Canadian wine-growing land in the Okanagan Valley in B.C. and the Niagara Peninsula in Ontario is well suited for growing the grapes required for good wines. Within a very few years, and with some government assistance to grape growers to make the transition from low-quality to high-quality grapes, Canadian wines were competing effectively with imported products in the medium-quality range. B.C. and Ontario wines do not yet reach the quality of major French wines in the $50 to $70 (per bottle) range, but they compete very effectively in quality with wines in the $15 to $25 range and sometimes even higher up the quality scale.

The success of the wine industry is a good example of how tariffs can distort incentives and push an industry into a structure that makes it dependent on the tariff. Looking at the pre-FTA industry, very few people suspected that it would be able to survive, let alone become a world-class industry.

---

occurred in many areas, resulting in more U.S. imports of some product lines from Canada and more U.S. exports of other goods to Canada. In 1988, before the Canada–U.S. FTA took effect, Canada exported $85 billion in goods to the United States and imported $74 billion from the United States. By 2011, the value of Canada–U.S. trade had almost quadrupled—Canadian exports of goods to the United States had increased to $331 billion and imports from the United States had increased to $281 billion. (Note that these figures exclude trade in services; with services included, the increase in Canada–U.S. trade between 1988 and 2011 would be even larger.)[2]

---

[2] These data are in nominal dollars, which naturally grow over time along with real GDP and the price level. As a share of GDP, however, Canadian trade with the United States has also grown substantially. In 1988, exports and imports of goods (excluding services) with the United States were each roughly 13 percent of Canadian GDP; by 2011, they were each almost 18 percent of Canadian GDP.

It is hard to say how much trade diversion there has been and will be in the future. The greatest potential for trade diversion is with Mexico, which competes in the Canadian and U.S. markets with a large number of products produced in other low-wage countries. Southeast Asian exporters to the United States and Canada have been worried that Mexico would capture some of their markets by virtue of having tariff-free access denied to their goods. Most estimates predict, however, that trade creation will dominate over trade diversion.

Most transitional difficulties were initially felt in each country's import-competing industries, just as theory predicts. Such an agreement as the NAFTA brings its advantages by encouraging a movement of resources out of protected but inefficient import-competing industries, which decline, and into efficient export industries, which expand because they have better access to the markets of other member countries. Southern Ontario and parts of Quebec had difficulties as some traditional exports fell and labour and capital were shifting to sectors where trade was expanding. By the late 1990s, however, Southern Ontario was booming again and its most profitable sectors were those that exported to the United States.

There were also some pleasant surprises resulting from free trade. Two Canadian industries that many economists expected to suffer from the FTA and the NAFTA were winemaking and textiles. Yet both of these industries prospered as Canadian firms improved quality, productivity, and benefited from increased access to the huge U.S. market. *Applying Economic Concepts 34-3* discusses the success of the Canadian wine industry after the tariffs on wine were eliminated.

Finally, the dispute-settlement mechanism seems to have worked well. A large number of disputes have arisen and have been referred to panels. (Interested readers can read updated accounts of settled and ongoing disputes on the website for the Department of Foreign Affairs and International Trade at **www.international.gc.ca**.) Panel members have usually reacted as professionals rather than as nationals. Most cases have been decided on their merits; allegations that decisions were reached on national rather than professional grounds have been rare.

SUMMARY

34.1 Free Trade or Protection?
LO 1, 2

- The case for free trade is that world output of all products can be higher under free trade than when protectionism restricts regional specialization.
- Trade protection may be advocated to promote economic diversification or to provide protection for specific groups. The cost of such protection is lower average living standards.
- Protection can also be urged on the grounds that it may lead to higher living standards for the protectionist country than would a policy of free trade. Such a result might come about by using market power to influence the terms of trade or by developing a dynamic comparative advantage by allowing inexperienced or uneconomically small industries to become efficient enough to compete with foreign industries.
- Some invalid protectionist arguments are that (a) mutually advantageous trade is impossible because one trader's gain must always be the other's loss; (b) buying abroad sends our money abroad, while buying at home keeps our money at home; (c) our high-paid workers must be protected against the competition from low-paid foreign workers; and (d) imports are to be discouraged because they reduce national income and cause unemployment.

34.2 Methods of Protection   LO 3, 4

- A tariff raises the domestic price of the imported product and leads to a reduction in the level of imports. Domestic consumers lose and domestic producers gain. The overall effect of a tariff is a deadweight loss for the importing country.
- A quota (or voluntary export restriction) restricts the amount of imports and thus drives up the domestic price of the good. Domestic consumers lose and domestic

producers gain. The overall effect is a *larger* deadweight loss than with a tariff because, rather than the importing country collecting tariff revenue, foreign producers benefit from a higher price.
- Antidumping and countervailing duties, although providing legitimate restraints on unfair trading practices, are often used as serious barriers to trade.

34.3 Current Trade Policy   LO 5, 6

- The General Agreement on Tariffs and Trade (GATT), under which countries agreed to reduce trade barriers through multilateral negotiations and not to raise them unilaterally, has greatly reduced world tariffs since its inception in 1947.
- The World Trade Organization (WTO) was created in 1995 as the successor to GATT. It has 155 member countries and contains a formal dispute-settlement mechanism.
- Regional trade-liberalizing agreements, such as free trade areas and common markets, bring efficiency gains

through trade creation and efficiency losses through trade diversion.
- The North American Free Trade Agreement (NAFTA) is the world's largest and most successful free trade area, and the European Union is the world's largest and most successful common market.
- NAFTA is based on the principle of "national treatment." This allows Canada, the United States, and Mexico to implement whatever social, economic, or environmental policies they choose providing that such policies treat foreign and domestic firms (and their products) equally.

KEY CONCEPTS

Free trade and protection
Tariffs and import quotas
Voluntary export restrictions (VERs)
Countervailing and antidumping
  duties

The General Agreement on Tariffs and
  Trade (GATT)
The World Trade Organization (WTO)
Common markets, customs unions,
  and free-trade areas

Trade creation and trade diversion
Non-tariff barriers
The North American Free Trade
  Agreement (NAFTA)

STUDY EXERCISES

MyEconLab Make the grade with MyEconLab: Study Exercises marked in red can be found on MyEconLab. You can practise them as often as you want, and most feature step-by-step guided instructions to help you find the right answer.

1. Fill in the blanks to make the following statements correct.

   a. The _____ argument provided the rationale for Canada's National Policy of 1876. A high tariff wall allowed many Canadian industries to develop where they may not have been able to compete otherwise.
   b. Advertisements that encourage us to "buy Canadian" are promoting a(n) _____ argument

for protection. The reason is that money spent on imported goods must ultimately be spent on _____ goods and services anyway.
   c. Invalid arguments for protection usually come from a misunderstanding of the gains from _____ or from the misbelief that protection can increase total _____.

2. Fill in the blanks to make the following statements correct.

   a. A tariff imposed on the import of leather shoes will cause a(n) _____ in the domestic price. Total quantity of leather shoes sold in Canada will _____. Domestic (Canadian) production of leather shoes will _____ and the quantity of shoes imported will _____.

   b. The beneficiaries of the tariff described above are _____ because they receive a higher price for the same good and _____ because they receive tariff revenue. The parties that are clearly worse off are _____ because they now pay a higher price for the same good, and _____ because they sell less in the Canadian market.

   c. The overall effect of a tariff on the importing country is a(n) _____ in welfare. The tariff creates a(n) _____ loss for the economy.

   d. Suppose an import quota restricted the import of leather shoes into Canada to 20 000 pairs per year when the free trade imported amount was 40 000 pairs. The domestic price will _____, total quantity sold in Canada will _____, and domestic production will _____.

   e. The beneficiaries of the quota described above are _____ and _____ because they both receive a higher price in the Canadian market. The party that is clearly worse off is _____ because they are now paying a higher price.

   f. The overall effect of an import quota on the importing country is a(n) _____ in welfare. The quota imposes a(n) _____ loss for the economy.

3. Fill in the blanks to make the following statements correct.

   a. A regional trade agreement, such as the NAFTA, or a common market, such as the European Union, allows for _____, whereby trade within the group of member countries is increased.

   b. A regional trade agreement, such as the NAFTA, or a common market, such as the European Union, also results in _____, whereby trade within the group of member countries replaces trade previously done with other _____.

   c. The fundamental principle that guides the NAFTA is the principle of _____, which means that any member country can implement the policies of its choosing, as long as _____ and _____ firms are treated equally.

4. Canada produces steel domestically and also imports it from abroad. Assume that the world market for steel is competitive and that Canada is a small producer, unable to affect the world price. Since Canada imports steel, we know that in the absence of trade, the Canadian equilibrium price would exceed the world price.

   a. Draw a diagram showing the Canadian market for steel, with imports at the world price.

   b. Explain why the imposition of a tariff on imported steel will increase the price of steel in Canada.

   c. Who benefits and who is harmed by such a tariff? Show these effects in your diagram.

5. The diagram below shows the Canadian market for leather shoes, which we assume to be competitive. The world price is p_w. If the Canadian government imposes a tariff of t dollars per unit, the domestic price then rises to $p_w + t$

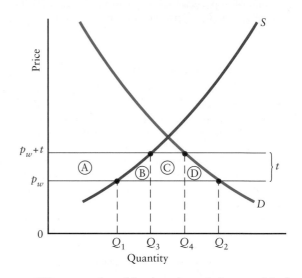

   a. What quantity of leather shoes is imported before the tariff is imposed? After the tariff?

   b. What is the effect of the tariff on the Canadian production of shoes? Which areas in the diagram show the increase in domestic producer surplus?

   c. Which areas in the diagram show the reduction in domestic consumer surplus as a result of the higher Canadian price?

   d. The Canadian government earns tariff revenue on the imported shoes. Which area in the diagram shows this tariff revenue?

   e. What is the overall effect of this tariff on the economy? Which area in the diagram shows the deadweight loss?

6. Use the diagram from Question 5 to analyze the effects of imposing an import quota instead of a tariff to protect domestic shoe producers. Draw the diagram as in Question 5 and answer the following questions.

   a. Explain why an import quota of $Q_3 Q_4$ raises the domestic price to $p_w + t$.

   b. With import quotas, the Canadian government earns no tariff revenue. Who gets this money now?

   c. Is the import quota better or worse than the tariff for Canada as a whole? Explain.

7. Under pressure from the Canadian and U.S. governments in the early 1980s, Japanese automobile producers agreed to restrict their exports to the North American market. After the formal agreement ended,

the Japanese producers decided unilaterally to continue restricting their exports. Carefully review Figure 34-2 on page 857 and then answer the following questions.

a. Explain why the Japanese producers would voluntarily continue these restrictions.
b. Explain why an agreement to export only 100 000 cars to North America is better for the Japanese producers than a North American tariff that results in the same volume of Japanese exports.
c. Who is paying for these benefits to the Japanese producers?

8. Go to Statistics Canada's website: **www.statcan.gc.ca**. Search for "exports and imports," and answer the following questions related to imports and exports of *goods* (trade data for *services* are generally harder to obtain).

a. For the most recent year shown, what was the value of Canada's exports to the United States? To the European Union?
b. For the same year, what was the value of Canada's imports from the United States? From the European Union?
c. Compute what economists call the "volume of trade" (the sum of exports and imports) between Canada and the United States. How has the volume of trade grown over the past five years? Has trade grown faster than national income?

9. The table below shows the prices *in Canada* of cotton towels produced in the United States, Canada, and Malaysia. Assume that all cotton towels are identical.

Producing Country	Canadian Price ($) Without Tariff	Canadian Price ($) With 20% Tariff
Canada	4.75	4.75
United States	4.50	5.40
Malaysia	4.00	4.80

a. Suppose Canada imposes a 20 percent tariff on imported towels from any country. Assuming that Canadians purchase only the lowest-price towels, from which country will Canada buy its towels?
b. Now suppose Canada eliminates tariffs on towels from all countries. Which towels will Canada now buy?
c. Canada and the United States now negotiate a free-trade agreement that eliminates all tariffs between the two countries, but Canada maintains the 20 percent tariff on other countries. Which towels now get imported into Canada?
d. Which of the situations described above is called trade creation and which is called trade diversion?

10. In the past few years, trade between Canada and China has been growing quickly (though from a very low level). Many observers are concerned that Canadian firms are not able to compete with Chinese ones and that Canada may therefore be harmed by trading more with China. Comment on the following points in relation to the above worries:

a. "Chinese are the most expensive cheap labour I have ever encountered." Statement by the owner of a Canadian firm that is moving back to Canada from China.
b. The theory of the gains from trade says that a high-productivity, high-wage country can gain from trading with a low-wage, low-productivity country.
c. Technological change is rapidly reducing labour costs as a proportion of total costs in many products; in many industries that use high-tech production methods this proportion is already well below 20 percent.

11. Import quotas and voluntary export restrictions are often used instead of tariffs.

a. What real difference, if any, is there among quotas, voluntary export restrictions (VERs), and tariffs?
b. Explain why lobbyists for some import-competing industries (such as cheese, milk, shoes) support import quotas while lobbyists for others (such as pizza manufacturers, soft drink manufacturers, retail stores) oppose them.
c. Would you expect labour unions to support or oppose import quotas? Why?

12. Consider a mythical country called Forestland, which exports a large amount of lumber to a nearby country called Houseland. The lumber industry in Houseland has convinced its federal government that it is being harmed by the low prices being charged by the lumber producers in Forestland. You are an advisor to the government in Forestland. Explain who gains and who loses from each of the following policies.

a. Houseland imposes a tariff on lumber imports from Forestland.
b. Forestland imposes a tax on each unit of lumber exported to Houseland.
c. Forestland agrees to restrict its exports of lumber to Houseland.
d. Which policy is likely to garner the most political support in Houseland? In Forestland?

13. Canada has recently imposed antidumping duties of up to 43 percent on hot-rolled steel imports from France, Russia, Slovakia, and Romania. The allegation is that these countries were dumping steel into the Canadian market.

a. Who benefits from such alleged dumping? Who is harmed?
b. Who benefits from the imposition of the antidumping duties? Who is harmed?
c. Is Canada as a whole made better off by the imposition of the duties? Explain.

Exchange Rates and the Balance of Payments

CHAPTER OUTLINE

LEARNING OBJECTIVES (LO)

After studying this chapter you will be able to

1 list the components of Canada's balance of payments and explain why the balance of payments must always balance.

2 describe the demand for and supply of foreign exchange.

3 discuss various factors that cause fluctuations in exchange rates.

4 discuss why a current account deficit is not necessarily undesirable.

5 understand the theory of purchasing power parity (PPP) and its limitations.

6 explain how flexible exchange rates can dampen the effects of external shocks.

CANADIANS import products from other countries and take vacations abroad. For both reasons, they care about the exchange rate between the Canadian dollar and foreign currencies. When the Canadian dollar depreciates, it costs more to purchase imported products, and foreign vacations become more expensive. On the other hand, Canadian firms that export their products to other countries usually benefit from a depreciation of the Canadian dollar because foreigners are induced to buy more Canadian products. In some way or another, most Canadians are affected by changes in the exchange rate.

In this chapter we examine what determines the exchange rate, why it changes, and the effects these changes have on the economy. The discussion will bring together material on three topics studied elsewhere in this book: the theory of supply and demand (Chapter 3), monetary policy and inflation (Chapters 29 and 30), and international trade (Chapter 33).

We begin by examining a country's balance of payments—the record of transactions in goods, services, and assets with the rest of the world. After introducing terms, we see why the balance of payments is defined in such a way that it *always* balances.

35.1 The Balance of Payments

Statistics Canada documents transactions between Canada and the rest of the world. The record of such transactions is made in the **balance of payments accounts**. Each transaction, such as the exports or imports of goods, or the international purchase or sales of assets, is classified according to whether the transaction generates a *payment* or a *receipt* for Canada.

Table 35-1 shows the major items in the Canadian balance of payments accounts for 2011. Transactions that represent a receipt for Canada, such as the sale of a product or asset to foreigners, are recorded in the balance of payments accounts as a *credit* item. Transactions that represent a payment for Canada, such as the purchase of a product or asset from foreigners, are recorded as a *debit* item.

There are two main categories to the balance of payments: the *current account* and the *capital account*. We examine each account in turn.

> **balance of payments accounts** A summary record of a country's transactions with the rest of the world, including the buying and selling of goods, services, and assets.

The Current Account

The **current account** records transactions arising from trade in goods and services. It also includes net investment income earned from foreign asset holdings. The current account is divided into two main sections.

The first section, called the **trade account**, records payments and receipts arising from the import and export of goods, such as computers and cars, and services, such as legal or architectural services. (Tourism constitutes a large part of the trade in services.) Canadian imports of goods and services require a payment to foreigners and thus are entered as debit items on the trade account; Canadian exports of goods and services generate a receipt to Canada and thus are recorded as credit items.

The second section, called the **capital-service account**, records the payments and receipts that represent income on assets. When a firm located in Canada, for example, pays dividends to foreign owners, the payments to foreigners are a debit item in Canada's balance of payments. In contrast, when Canadians earn income from their foreign-located investments, these receipts for Canada are recorded as credit items.

As shown in Table 35-1, Canadian exports of goods and services in 2011 were $534 billion, while imports of goods and services were slightly larger at $556 billion. The trade account therefore had a deficit of just over $22 billion—meaning that Canada purchased $22 billion more in goods and services from the rest of the world than it sold to the world. The capital-service account that year was also in deficit—Canadians paid $26 billion more to foreigners as investment income (plus transfers) than they received from foreigners. The overall current account balance in 2011 (the sum of the trade and capital-service accounts) had a deficit of $48.4 billion.

> **current account** The part of the balance of payments accounts that records payments and receipts arising from trade in goods and services and from interest and dividends that are earned on assets owned in one country and invested in another.

> **trade account** In the balance of payments, this account records the value of exports and imports of goods and services.

> **capital-service account** In the balance of payments, this account records the payments and receipts that represent income on assets (such as interest and dividends).

The Capital Account

The **capital account** records international transactions in assets, including bonds, shares of companies, real estate, and factories. When a Canadian purchases a foreign asset, the transaction is treated just like the purchase of foreign goods. Since purchasing a foreign asset requires a payment from Canadians to foreigners, it is entered as a debit item in the Canadian capital account. Note that when Canadians purchase foreign assets, financial capital is leaving Canada and going abroad, and so this is called a *capital outflow*.

> **capital account** The part of the balance of payments accounts that records payments and receipts arising from the purchase and sale of assets.

TABLE 35-1 Canadian Balance of Payments, 2011 (billions of dollars)

CURRENT ACCOUNT	
Trade Account	
Merchandise exports	+458.2
Service exports	+75.3
Merchandise imports	−455.9
Service imports	−100.0
Trade balance	−22.4
Capital-Service Account	
Net investment income (including unilateral transfers)	−26.0
Current Account Balance	**−48.4**
CAPITAL ACCOUNT	
Net change in Canadian investments abroad [capital outflow (−)]	−103.1
Net change in foreign investments in Canada [capital inflow (+)]	+167.0
Official Financing Account	
Changes in official international reserves [increases (−)]	−8.1
Capital Account Balance	**+55.8**
Statistical Discrepancy	**−7.4**
Balance of Payments	**0.0**

The overall balance of payments always balances, but the individual components do not have to. In 2011, Canada had an overall trade deficit (including trade in goods and services) of $22.4 billion. There was also a deficit of $26.0 billion on the capital-service account. There was thus a $48.4 billion deficit on the current account. There was a surplus on the capital account of $55.8 billion because the trading of assets internationally resulted in a net inflow of capital. The statistical discrepancy entry of −$7.4 billion compensates for the inability to measure some items accurately. The current account plus the capital account (plus the statistical discrepancy) is equal to the balance of payments—which is always zero.

(*Source:* Statistics Canada, www.statcan.gc.ca. Search for "balance of payments, 2011.")

When a foreigner purchases a Canadian asset, the transaction is treated just like the sale of Canadian goods. It generates a receipt for Canada and thus is entered as a credit item in the Canadian capital account. When Canadians sell assets to foreigners, financial capital is entering Canada from abroad, and so this is called a *capital inflow.*

As shown in Table 35-1, in 2011, Canadians increased their holdings of assets abroad by $103.1 billion, resulting in a capital outflow of that amount. At the same time, foreigners increased their holdings of assets in Canada by $167 billion, resulting in a capital inflow of that amount. Though not shown in the table, the capital account distinguishes between *direct investment* and *portfolio investment*. The former involves the purchase or sale of assets that alter the legal control of those assets, such as when a controlling interest of a company is purchased. The latter involves transactions in assets that do not alter the legal control of the assets, such as when a minority of a company's shares is purchased.

One part of the capital account shows the government's transactions in its official foreign-exchange reserves. This *official financing account* is included as part of the capital account because official reserves are *assets* rather than goods or services. If the government increases its reserves, it does so by purchasing foreign-currency assets, and this is recorded as a debit item in the official financing account. If the government instead reduces its reserves, it sells some foreign-currency assets, and this transaction would be recorded as a credit item in the official financing account. In 2011, the Government of Canada increased its official reserves by $8.1 billion.

In 2011, the overall capital account had a surplus of $55.8 billion, meaning that there was a net capital inflow of this amount to Canada from the rest of the world. In other words, foreign households, firms and governments increased their net holdings of Canadian assets by $55.8 billion in 2011.

The Balance of Payments Must Balance

The current account balance represents the difference between the payments and receipts from international transactions in goods and services. The capital account balance is the difference between payments and receipts from international transactions in assets. The balance of payments is the sum of current account and capital account balances. In any given period (usually a year) the *current account plus the capital account must equal zero*. In other words, the balance of payments is always equal to zero. In algebraic terms, we can write

$$\text{Balance of payments} = CA + KA = 0$$

where CA is the current account balance and KA is the capital account balance. Note that this is an *identity*—the accounting system used for the balance of payments defines transactions in such a way that $CA + KA = 0$. But this accounting system is based on some economic logic. Let's consider an example that illustrates the logical connection between the current and capital accounts.

Consider a year in which Canadian households, firms, and governments, taken together, purchase $100 billion in goods and services from the rest of the world. During the same year, Canadians sell $150 billion of goods and services to the rest of the world. Exports are $150 billion and imports are $100 billion, so Canada has a current account surplus of $50 billion, $CA = \$50$ billion. (We suppose for simplicity that the capital-service account is zero.) The meaning of this $50 billion surplus is that Canadians now have claims on foreigners equal to $50 billion—that is, foreigners owe Canadians $50 billion. What does Canada do with these claims?

Consider two possibilities.

1. Canadians purchase $50 billion more of goods and services from the rest of the world. In this case, Canada's imports rise to $150 billion and the current account is now in balance ($CA = 0$). Since there have been no transactions in assets, the capital account is also in balance ($KA = 0$). It is clear now that $CA + KA = 0$.

2. Canadians purchase $50 billion more of assets from foreigners—a capital outflow from Canada. They could purchase land, bonds, corporate shares, or factories. But whatever they purchase, the capital account will now be in deficit by $50 billion ($KA = -\$50$ billion). In this case, the current account surplus of $50 billion is exactly offset by the capital account deficit of $50 billion. Once again we have $CA + KA = 0$.

Of course, Canadians could do a combination of these two options—buy some more imports and some assets as well, with a total value of $50 billion. In this case, we would still have $CA + KA = 0$.

Some readers may wonder why Canadians couldn't simply leave their purchases of goods and services unchanged *and* decide not to purchase any additional assets. For example, couldn't we have the CA surplus of $50 billion but not make any transactions in the capital account (so that $KA = 0$)? With such a CA surplus, however, Canadians are holding an "IOU" from foreigners of $50 billion which is an asset for Canada as a whole. That asset can be held in many forms (stocks, bonds, bank balances, etc.), any of which will appear in the balance of payments as a capital account deficit. Balance of payments accounting ensures that any CA balance is matched by an increase of some assets in the capital account so that $CA + KA = 0$.

> Any surplus on the current account must be matched by an equal deficit on the capital account. A current account surplus thus implies a capital outflow. The balance of payments is always zero.

Notice that the opposite situation is also possible and that the balance of payments again sums to zero. Suppose Canadians purchase $75 billion more in goods and services from the rest of the world than they sell—so Canada has a current account deficit of $75 billion, $CA = -\$75$ billion. (We continue to assume that the capital-service account is zero.) The rest of the world now has claims of this amount on Canadians, meaning that Canadians owe $75 billion to foreigners. Foreigners can either purchase more Canadian goods and services or more Canadian assets. If foreigners purchase $75 billion in additional Canadian goods and services, Canada's current account is balanced ($CA = 0$) and we again have $CA + KA = 0$. If foreigners choose instead to purchase $75 billion in Canadian assets, then Canada's capital account will be in surplus by $75 billion—a capital inflow. In this case, the current account will be in deficit ($CA = -\$75$billion) and the capital account will be in surplus ($KA = \$75$ billion), but again we see that $CA + KA = 0$.

For balance of payments statistics for many countries, see the IMF's website: www.imf.org.

Any deficit in the current account must be matched by an equal surplus in the capital account. A current-account deficit thus implies a capital inflow. The balance of payments is always zero.

Let's go back and review the actual numbers from Table 35-1. In 2011, Canada had a current account deficit of $48.4 billion. In order to purchase these net imports of goods and services, Canadian firms and households had to sell the same value (aside from the statistical discrepancy) of assets to foreigners in that year, so there was a capital inflow, or capital account surplus. The balance of payments, as always, was in balance. That the balance of payments always sums to zero is important. This result is not based on assumptions about behaviour or any other theoretical reasoning—it is an *accounting identity.* Many people nonetheless find balance of payments accounting confusing. *Applying Economic Concepts 35-1* discusses an individual student's balance of payments with the rest of the world and illustrates why an individual's balance of payments must always balance.

No Such Thing as a Balance of Payments Deficit!

Unless further qualified, the term "balance of payments deficit" does not make sense since the balance of payments must always balance. But such a term is nonetheless often used in the press and even by some economists. What does this mean? Most often the term is used carelessly—a balance of payments deficit is mentioned when what is actually meant is a current account deficit.

There are also occasions when people speak of a country as having a balance of payments deficit or surplus when they are actually referring to the balance of all accounts *excluding* the official financing account. In other words, they are referring to the combined balance on current and capital accounts, *excluding* the changes in the government's foreign-currency reserves. For example, consider a year in which the Government of Canada sells $5 billion of its foreign-currency reserves. This transaction is a credit item in the official financing account (part of Canada's capital account). It must be the case that *all other* items in the current and capital accounts *combined* sum to an overall deficit. In this case, some people might say that Canada's balance of payments "deficit" is being financed by the government's sale of foreign-currency reserves. But when we use the terms properly, we know that Canada's balance of payments, as always, is balanced.

APPLYING ECONOMIC CONCEPTS 35-1

A Student's Balance of Payments with the Rest of the World

Many students find a country's balance of payments confusing, especially the idea that the balance of payments *must always* balance. Why, they often ask, can't Canada export more goods and services to the world than it imports and at the same time have a net sale of assets to the rest of the world? The connection between the current-account transactions and the capital-account transactions is not always obvious.

Perhaps the easiest way to see this connection is to consider an individual's "balance of payments" with the rest of the world. Of course, most individuals would not normally compute their balance of payments, but by doing so we can recognize the everyday concepts involved and also see the necessary connection between any individual's "current account" and "capital account." The reason that Canada's balance of payments must always balance is exactly the same reason that an individual's balance of payments must always balance.

The table shows the balance of payments for Stefan, a university student. Stefan is fortunate in several respects. First, his parents are able to provide some of the funds needed to finance his education. Second, he has a summer job that pays well. Third, he was given some Canada Savings Bonds when he was born that provide him with some interest income every year.

Stefan's Balance of Payments

Current Account (Income and Expenditure)	
Labour income ("exports")	+$10 000
Purchase of goods and services ("imports")	−$17 000
Interest income	+$ 500
Transfers (from his parents)	+$10 000
Current Account Balance	+$3 500

Capital Account (Changes in Assets) (− denotes an increase in assets, or a "capital outflow")	
Purchase of mutual funds	−$1 500
Increase in savings account deposits	−$2 000
Capital Account Balance	−$3 500
BALANCE OF PAYMENTS	$0

The top part of the table shows Stefan's income and expenditures for a single year. This is his current account. The bottom part shows the *change* in Stefan's assets over the same year. This is his capital account. (Note that for Stefan as well as for any country, the capital account does not show the overall stock of assets—it only shows the *changes* in the stock of assets during the year.)

Let's begin with his current account. Stefan has a good summer job that earns him $10 000 after taxes. This $10 000 represents Stefan's "exports" to the rest of the world—he earns this income by selling his labour services to a tree-planting company. Over the year, however, he spends $17 000 on tuition, books, clothes, groceries, and other goods and services. These are Stefan's "imports" from the rest of the world. Stefan clearly has a "trade deficit" equal to $7000—he "imports" more than he "exports."

There are two other sources of income shown in Stefan's current account. First, he earns $500 in interest income. Second, his parents give him $10 000 to help pay for his education—a *transfer* in the terminology of balance of payments accounting. The interest income and transfer together make up Stefan's "capital-service account"—Stefan has a surplus of $10 500.

Stefan's overall current account shows a surplus of $3500. This means he receives $3500 more than he spends on goods and services. But where does this $3500 go?

Now let's consider Stefan's capital account, the bottom part of the table. The $3500 surplus on current account *must* end up as increases in Stefan's assets. He invests $1500 in a mutual fund and he also increases his savings-account deposits by $2000. In both cases he is purchasing assets—he buys units in a mutual fund and he also "buys" a bank deposit. Since Stefan must make a payment to purchase these assets, each appears as a debit item in his capital account. Stefan's capital account balance is a deficit of $3500; in other words, there is a "capital outflow" of $3500.

Finally, note that Stefan's current account and capital account *must* sum to zero. There is no way around this. Any surplus of income over expenditures (on current account) must show up as an increase in his assets (or a decrease in his debts) on his capital account. Conversely, any excess of expenditures over income must be financed by reducing his assets (or by increasing his debts). Stefan's balance of payments *must* balance.

What is true for Stefan is true for any individual and also true for any accounting unit you choose to consider. Saskatoon's balance of payments with the rest of the world must balance. Saskatchewan's balance of payments with the rest of the world must balance. Western Canada's balance of payments with the rest of the world must balance. And so must Canada's, and any other country's.

Strictly speaking, a balance of payments deficit or surplus cannot exist. When the terms are used, a "balance of payments deficit" probably refers to a situation in which the government is selling official foreign-currency reserves. A "balance of payments surplus" probably refers to a situation in which the government is buying official foreign-currency reserves. In both cases, as always, the balance of payments is actually in balance.

Summary

This brings us to the end of our discussion of the balance of payments. Keep in mind that this is just an exercise in accounting. Though at times you may find it difficult to keep the various credits and debits in the various accounts straight in your mind, remember that the structure of the accounting system is quite simple. Here is a brief review:

1. The current account shows all transactions in goods and services between Canada and the rest of the world (including investment income and transfers).

2. The capital account shows all transactions in assets between Canada and the rest of the world. Part of the capital account shows the change in the government's holding of foreign-currency reserves.

3. All transactions involving a payment from Canada appear as debit items. All transactions involving a receipt to Canada appear as credit items.

4. The balance of payments—the sum of the current account and the capital account—must, by definition, always be zero.

We now go on to explore how exchange rates are determined in the foreign-exchange market. We will see that a knowledge of the various categories in the balance of payments will help in our understanding of why changes in exchange rates occur.

35.2 The Foreign-Exchange Market

Money is vital in any sophisticated economy that relies on specialization and trade. Yet money as we know it is a *national* matter. If you live in Argentina, you earn pesos and spend pesos; if you operate a business in Austria, you borrow euros and pay your workers in euros. The currency of a country is acceptable within the border of that country, but usually it will not be accepted by firms and households in another country. Just try buying your next pair of jeans in Canada with British pounds sterling or Japanese yen.

Trade between countries normally requires the exchange of the currency of one country for that of another.

exchange rate The number of units of domestic currency required to purchase one unit of foreign currency.

The exchange of one currency for another is called a *foreign-exchange transaction*. The **exchange rate** is the rate at which one currency exchanges for another. In Canada's case, the exchange rate is the Canadian-dollar price of one unit of foreign currency. For example, in July 2012, the price of one U.S. dollar was 1.03 Canadian dollars. Thus, the Canada–U.S. exchange rate was 1.03.

Note that in the Canadian news media the exchange rate is usually expressed in the opposite way—as the number of U.S. dollars that it takes to buy one Canadian dollar. So instead of reporting that the Canadian–U.S. exchange rate in July 2012 was 1.03, the press would say that the Canadian dollar was "worth" 97 U.S. cents (1/1.03 = 0.97).

We can choose to define the Canada–U.S. exchange rate either way: as the Canadian-dollar price of one U.S. dollar (Cdn$/U.S.$) or as the U.S.-dollar price of one Canadian dollar (U.S.$/Cdn$). But we must choose one method and stick to it; otherwise, our discussions will quickly become very confusing. In this book we *always* define the exchange rate in the way Canadian economists usually do—as the Canadian-dollar price of one unit of foreign currency. This definition makes it clear that foreign currency, like any good or service, has a price expressed in Canadian dollars. In this case, the price has a special name—the exchange rate.

An **appreciation** of the Canadian dollar means that the Canadian dollar has become more valuable so that it takes fewer Canadian dollars to purchase one unit of foreign currency. For example, if the Canadian dollar appreciates against the U.S. dollar from 1.03 to 0.97, it takes 6 fewer Canadian cents to purchase one U.S. dollar. Thus, an appreciation of the Canadian dollar implies a *fall* in the exchange rate. Conversely, a **depreciation** of the Canadian dollar means that the Canadian dollar has become less valuable so that it takes more Canadian dollars to purchase one unit of foreign currency. Thus, a depreciation of the Canadian dollar means a *rise* in the exchange rate.

> **appreciation** A fall in the exchange rate—the domestic currency has become more valuable so that it takes fewer units of domestic currency to purchase one unit of foreign currency.

> **depreciation** A rise in the exchange rate—the domestic currency has become less valuable so that it takes more units of domestic currency to purchase one unit of foreign currency.

> An appreciation of the Canadian dollar is a fall in the exchange rate; a depreciation of the Canadian dollar is a rise in the exchange rate.

We now go on to build a simple theory of the foreign-exchange market. This will allow us to analyze the determinants of the exchange rate. To keep things simple, we use an example involving trade between Canada and Europe, and thus we examine the determination of the exchange rate between the two currencies: the Canadian dollar and the euro. In this example, think of Europe as a shorthand for "the rest of the world" and the euro as a shorthand for "all other currencies."

> Because Canadian dollars are traded for euros in the foreign-exchange market, it follows that a demand for euros implies a supply of Canadian dollars and that a supply of euros implies a demand for Canadian dollars.

For this reason, a theory of the exchange rate between dollars and euros can deal *either* with the demand and supply of dollars *or* with the demand and supply of euros; both need not be considered. We will concentrate on the demand, supply, and price of euros. Thus, the market we will be considering (in general terms) is the

Trade between countries that use different currencies requires that currencies also be exchanged; this takes place in foreign-exchange markets where exchange rates—the price of one currency in terms of another—are determined.

foreign-exchange market—the "product" is foreign exchange (euros in our case) and the "price" is the exchange rate (the Canadian-dollar price of euros).

We develop our example in terms of the demand and supply analysis first encountered in Chapter 3. To do so, we need only recall that in the market for foreign exchange, transactions that generate a receipt for Canada in its balance of payments represent a *supply* of foreign exchange. Foreign exchange is being supplied by the foreigners who need Canadian funds to purchase Canadian goods or assets. Conversely, transactions that are a payment from Canada in the balance of payments represent a *demand* for foreign exchange. Foreign exchange is being demanded by the Canadians who are purchasing foreign goods or assets. In what follows we make the (realistic) assumption that the Bank of Canada makes no transactions in the foreign-exchange market. Later we discuss the role of central-bank transactions.

The Supply of Foreign Exchange

Whenever foreigners purchase Canadian goods, services, or assets, they supply foreign currency to the foreign-exchange market and demand, in return, Canadian dollars with which to pay for their purchases. Thus, the supply of foreign exchange (and the associated demand for Canadian dollars) arises from Canada's sales of goods, services, and assets to the rest of the world.

Canadian Exports One important source of supply of foreign exchange is foreigners who wish to buy Canadian-made goods and services. A French importer of lumber is such a purchaser; an Austrian couple planning a vacation in Canada is another; the Hungarian government seeking to buy Canadian engineering services is a third. All are sources of supply of foreign exchange, arising out of international trade. Each potential buyer wants to sell its own currency in exchange for Canadian dollars that it can then use to purchase Canadian goods and services.

Asset Sales: Capital Inflows A second source of supply of foreign exchange comes from foreigners who want to purchase Canadian assets, such as government or corporate bonds, real estate, or shares in a Canadian firm. To buy Canadian assets, holders of foreign currencies must first sell their foreign currency and buy Canadian dollars. As we saw earlier in the chapter, when Canadians sell assets to foreigners, we say there is a *capital inflow* to Canada.

Reserve Currency Firms, banks, and governments often accumulate and hold foreign-exchange reserves, just as individuals maintain savings accounts. These reserves may be in several different currencies. For example, the government of Poland may decide to increase its reserve holdings of Canadian dollars and reduce its reserve holdings of euros; if it does so, it will be a supplier of euros (and a demander of Canadian dollars) in foreign-exchange markets.

The Total Supply of Foreign Exchange The supply of foreign exchange (or the demand for Canadian dollars) is the sum of the supplies for all the purposes just discussed—for purchases of Canadian exports, for capital inflow to Canada, and for the purchase of Canadian dollars to add to currency reserves.

Furthermore, because people, firms, and governments in all countries purchase goods and assets from many other countries, the demand for any one currency will be the aggregate demand of individuals, firms, and governments in a number of different countries. Thus, the total supply of foreign exchange (or the demand for Canadian dollars) may include Germans who are offering euros, Japanese who are offering yen, Argentinians who are offering pesos, and so on. For simplicity, however, we go back to our two-country example and use only Canada and Europe.

The Supply Curve for Foreign Exchange The supply of foreign exchange on the foreign-exchange market is represented by a positively sloped curve, such as the one shown in Figure 35-1. This figure plots the Canadian-dollar price of euros (the exchange rate) on the vertical axis and the quantity of euros on the horizontal axis. Moving up the vertical axis, more dollars are needed to purchase one euro—the Canadian dollar is depreciating. Moving down the vertical axis, fewer dollars are needed to purchase one euro—the dollar is appreciating.

Why is the supply curve for foreign exchange positively sloped? Let's consider what happens when Europeans are buying Canadian exports. If the Canadian dollar is depreciating (moving up the vertical axis), the euro prices of the Canadian exports are falling and so Europeans will want to buy more. To make these additional purchases, they increase their supply of euros to the foreign-exchange market in order to acquire the Canadian dollars they need to pay for the Canadian products. In the opposite case, when the dollar appreciates (moving down the vertical axis), the euro price of Canadian exports rises. European consumers will buy fewer Canadian goods and thus supply less foreign exchange.[1]

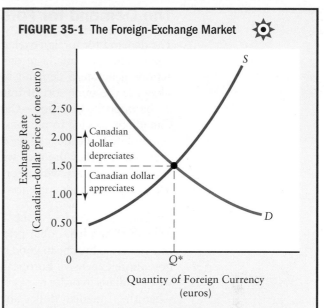

FIGURE 35-1 The Foreign-Exchange Market

The demand for foreign exchange is negatively sloped, and the supply of foreign exchange is positively sloped, when plotted against the exchange rate, measured as the Canadian-dollar price of one unit of foreign currency. The demand for foreign exchange is given by the blue line *D*. It represents the sum of transactions on both current and capital accounts that require payments to foreigners. The supply of foreign exchange is given by the red line *S*. It represents the sum of transactions on both current and capital accounts that represent receipts from foreigners.

In this example, the equilibrium value of the exchange rate is 1.50—it takes 1.50 Canadian dollars to purchase one euro.

Similar considerations affect other sources of supply of foreign exchange. When the Canadian dollar depreciates (a higher exchange rate), Canadian securities and other assets become more attractive purchases, and the quantity purchased by foreigners will rise. With this rise, the amount of foreign exchange supplied to pay for the purchases will increase.

> The supply curve for foreign exchange is positively sloped when it is plotted against the exchange rate; a depreciation of the Canadian dollar (a rise in the exchange rate) increases the quantity of foreign exchange supplied.

---

[1] We have assumed here that the foreign price elasticity of demand for Canadian exports is greater than 1, so that a price change leads to a proportionately larger change in quantity demanded. This is a common assumption in the analysis of international trade.

The Demand for Foreign Exchange

The demand for foreign exchange arises from all international transactions that represent a payment for Canada in our balance of payments. What sorts of international transactions generate a demand for foreign exchange (and a supply of Canadian dollars)? They are the same sort of transactions we just discussed, but this time they are moving in the opposite direction—Canadians, rather than foreigners, are doing the purchasing. Canadians seeking to purchase foreign products will be supplying Canadian dollars and demanding foreign exchange for this purpose. Canadians may also seek to purchase foreign assets. If they do, they will supply Canadian dollars and demand foreign exchange. Similarly, a country with reserves of Canadian dollars may decide to sell them in order to demand some other currency.

The Demand Curve for Foreign Exchange When the Canadian dollar depreciates against the euro, the Canadian-dollar price of European goods rises. Because it takes more dollars to buy the same European good at an unchanged euro price, Canadians will buy fewer of the now more expensive European goods. The amount of foreign exchange being demanded by Canadians in order to pay for imported European goods will fall.[2] In the opposite case, when the Canadian dollar appreciates, European goods become cheaper, more are sold, and more dollars are spent on them. Thus, more foreign exchange will be demanded to pay for the extra imports. This same argument applies in exactly the same way to the purchases of foreign assets. Figure 35-1 shows the demand curve for foreign exchange.

> The demand curve for foreign exchange is negatively sloped when it is plotted against the exchange rate; an appreciation of the Canadian dollar (a fall in the exchange rate) increases the quantity of foreign exchange demanded.

| 35.3 The Determination of Exchange Rates

flexible exchange rate An exchange rate that is left free to be determined by the forces of demand and supply on the free market, with no intervention by central banks.

fixed exchange rate An exchange rate that is maintained within a small range around its publicly stated par value by the intervention in the foreign-exchange market by a country's central bank.

The demand and supply curves in Figure 35-1 do not include official financing transactions (the demands for or supplies of foreign exchange by the Bank of Canada). To complete our analysis, we must incorporate the role of official financing transactions. We need to consider three important cases:

1. When the central bank makes no transactions in the foreign-exchange market, there is said to be a purely *floating* or **flexible exchange rate**.

2. When the central bank intervenes in the foreign-exchange market to "fix" or "peg" the exchange rate at a particular value, there is said to be a **fixed exchange rate** or *pegged exchange rate*.

---

[2] As long as the price elasticity of demand for imports is greater than 1, the fall in the volume of imports will exceed the rise in price, and hence fewer dollars will be spent on them. This condition (and the one in the previous footnote on page 881) is related to a famous long-standing issue in international economics, called the *Marshall-Lerner condition*. In what follows, we take the standard approach of assuming that both the price elasticity of demand for imports and the price elasticity of the demand for Canadian exports exceeds 1. This guarantees that the slopes of the curves are as shown in Figure 35-1.

3. Between these two "pure" systems is a variety of possible intermediate cases, including the *adjustable peg* and the *managed float*. In the adjustable peg system, central banks fix specific values for their exchange rates, but they explicitly recognize that circumstances may arise in which they will change that value. In a managed float, the central bank seeks to have some stabilizing influence on the exchange rate but does not try to fix it at some publicly announced value.

Most industrialized countries today operate a mostly flexible exchange rate. It is mostly market determined but the central bank sometimes intervenes to offset short-run fluctuations. The countries of the European Union (EU) had a system of fixed exchange rates (relative to one another's currencies) between 1979 and 1999. In 1999 most of the countries of the EU adopted a common currency—the euro (an important exception being the United Kingdom). Within what is now called the *euro zone*, the countries have no exchange rates for national currencies but the single common currency has a flexible exchange rate relative to countries outside the euro zone. The United States, Japan, the United Kingdom, Australia, and most other major industrialized countries have flexible exchange rates with relatively small amounts of foreign-exchange intervention by their central banks.

Canada alternated between a system of fixed exchange rates and flexible exchange rates (with limited intervention) throughout most of the period between the Second World War and 1970. In contrast, most other countries pegged their currencies to the U.S. dollar under the Bretton Woods system. Canada has had a flexible exchange rate since 1970. Later in the chapter we examine the issues involved in choosing between a flexible and fixed exchange-rate system. For now, let's explore how the various systems operate.

Flexible Exchange Rates

We begin with an exchange rate that is set in a freely competitive market, with no intervention by the central bank. Like any competitive price, the exchange rate fluctuates as the conditions of demand and supply change.

Suppose the current exchange rate is so high (say, e_1 in Figure 35-2) that the quantity of foreign exchange supplied exceeds the quantity demanded. There is thus an excess supply of foreign exchange (and an excess demand of Canadian dollars). This excess supply of foreign exchange, just as in our analysis in Chapter 3, will cause the price of foreign exchange (the exchange rate) to fall. As the exchange rate falls—an appreciation of the Canadian dollar—the euro price of Canadian goods rises, and this leads to a

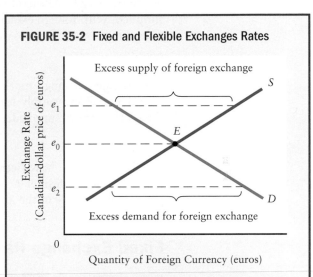

FIGURE 35-2 Fixed and Flexible Exchanges Rates

In the absence of central-bank intervention, the exchange rate adjusts to clear the foreign-exchange market. The demand for and supply of foreign exchange are as in Figure 35-1 on page 881. If official financing is zero, there is a purely flexible exchange rate. It will adjust to equate the demand and supply of foreign exchange; this occurs at E with an exchange rate of e_0.

If the exchange rate is higher than that, say at e_1, the supply of foreign exchange will exceed the demand. The exchange rate will fall (the dollar will appreciate) until it reaches e_0, where balance is achieved at E. If the exchange rate is below e_0, say at e_2, the demand for foreign exchange will exceed the supply. The exchange rate will rise (the dollar will depreciate) until it reaches e_0, where balance is achieved at E.

In the case of a fixed exchange rate, the central bank uses its official financing transactions to meet the excess demands or supplies that arise at the fixed value of the exchange rate. For example, if it chooses to fix the exchange rate at e_1, there will be an excess supply of foreign exchange. The central bank will purchase foreign exchange (and sell dollars) to meet the excess supply and keep the exchange rate constant. Alternatively, if the central bank chooses to fix the exchange rate at e_2, there will be an excess demand for foreign exchange. The central bank will sell foreign exchange (and buy dollars) to meet the excess demand and keep the exchange rate constant.

reduction in the quantity of foreign exchange supplied. Also, as the exchange rate falls, the Canadian-dollar price of European goods falls, and this fall leads to an increase in the quantity of foreign exchange demanded. Thus, the excess supply of foreign exchange leads to a fall in the exchange rate, which in turn reduces the amount of excess supply. Where the two curves intersect, quantity demanded equals quantity supplied, and the exchange rate is at its equilibrium or market-clearing value.

What happens when the exchange rate is below its equilibrium value, such as at e_2 in Figure 35-2? The quantity of foreign exchange demanded will exceed the quantity supplied. With foreign exchange in excess demand, its price will naturally rise, and as it does the amount of excess demand will be reduced until equilibrium is re-established.

> **A foreign-exchange market is like other competitive markets in that the forces of demand and supply lead to an equilibrium price at which quantity demanded equals quantity supplied.**

Recall that we have been assuming that there is no official financing by the central bank. We now consider a system of fixed exchange rates in which official financing plays a central role in the analysis.

Fixed Exchange Rates

If the central bank chooses to fix the exchange rate at a particular value, its official financing transactions must offset any excess demand or supply of foreign exchange that arises at that exchange rate. These transactions are described in Figure 35-2.

The gold standard that operated for much of the nineteenth century and the early part of the twentieth century was a fixed exchange-rate system. The Bretton Woods system, established by international agreement in 1944 and operated until the early 1970s, was a fixed exchange-rate system that provided for circumstances under which exchange rates could be adjusted. It was thus an adjustable peg system; the International Monetary Fund (IMF) has its origins in the Bretton Woods system, and one of its principal tasks was approving and monitoring exchange-rate changes. The European Exchange Rate Mechanism (ERM), which existed from 1979 to 1999, was also a fixed exchange-rate system for the countries in the European Union; their exchange rates were fixed to one another but floated as a block against the U.S. dollar and other currencies. As mentioned earlier, this system of separate currencies with fixed exchange rates was replaced in 1999 when most of the countries of the EU adopted a common currency—the euro.

Applying Economic Concepts 35-2 examines how a fixed exchange-rate system operates. It shows why a central bank that chooses to fix its exchange rate must give up some control of its foreign-exchange reserves as occurred in Thailand in 1997 and is occurring in China today. We now go on to study the workings of a flexible exchange-rate system, the system used in Canada and most industrialized countries.

In 1999, 11 countries of the European Union adopted a common currency—the euro. By 2012, when 17 countries were in the euro zone, the price of one euro was 1.35 Canadian dollars.

Changes in Flexible Exchange Rates

What causes exchange rates to vary? The simplest answer to this question is changes in demand or supply in the foreign-exchange market. Anything that shifts the demand curve for foreign exchange to the right or the supply curve for foreign exchange to the left leads to a rise in the exchange rate—a depreciation of the Canadian dollar. Conversely, anything that shifts the demand curve for foreign exchange to the left or the supply curve for foreign exchange to the right leads to a fall in the exchange rate—an appreciation of the Canadian dollar. These points are nothing more than a restatement of the laws of supply and demand, applied now to the market for foreign exchange; they are illustrated in Figure 35-3.

What causes the shifts in demand and supply that lead to changes in exchange rates? There are many causes, some transitory and some persistent. Let's look at several of the most important ones.

For information on the European Central Bank, see its website: www.ecb.int.

A Rise in the World Price of Exports Suppose there is an increase in the world price of a major Canadian export, such as wheat, oil, copper, or nickel. For almost all of Canada's major exports, Canada's production is small relative to the world market and so no event in Canada is likely to cause a change in the world price. The higher world price, whether caused by an increase in world demand or by a reduction in supply from

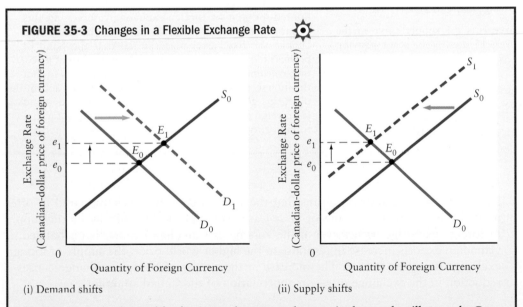

FIGURE 35-3 Changes in a Flexible Exchange Rate

(i) Demand shifts

(ii) Supply shifts

An increase in the demand for foreign exchange or a decrease in the supply will cause the Canadian dollar to depreciate (the exchange rate to rise); a decrease in the demand or an increase in supply will cause the dollar to appreciate (the exchange rate to fall). The initial demand and supply curves are D_0 and S_0. Equilibrium is at E_0 with an exchange rate of e_0. An increase in the demand for foreign exchange from D_0 to D_1 in part (i), or a decrease in the supply of foreign exchange from S_0 to S_1 in part (ii), will cause the dollar to depreciate. In both parts, the new equilibrium is at E_1, and the dollar depreciation is shown by the rise in the exchange rate from e_0 to e_1. Conversely, a decrease in the demand for foreign exchange or an increase in the supply of foreign exchange will cause the dollar to appreciate and the equilibrium exchange rate to fall.

APPLYING ECONOMIC CONCEPTS 35-2

Managing Fixed Exchange Rates

This box provides some details on how a central bank operates a regime of fixed exchange rates. Though Canada has a flexible exchange rate (with very rare foreign-exchange intervention by the Bank of Canada), we will imagine a situation in which the Bank of Canada pegs the Canadian–U.S. exchange rate. The accompanying figure shows the *monthly* demand for and supply of foreign exchange (U.S. dollars).

Suppose the Bank of Canada fixed the exchange rate between the narrow limits of, say, C$0.95 to C$1.05 to the U.S. dollar. The Bank then stabilizes the exchange rate in the face of seasonal, cyclical, and other fluctuations in demand and supply, entering the market to prevent the rate from going outside the permitted band. At the price of $0.95, the Bank offers to buy any amount of U.S. dollars; at the price of $1.05, the Bank offers to sell any amount of U.S. dollars. When the Bank buys U.S. dollars, its foreign-exchange reserves rise; when it sells U.S. dollars, its foreign-exchange reserves fall.

We make the following observations:

1. If the demand curve cuts the supply curve in the range 0.95 to 1.05, as D_0 does in the accompanying figure, the Bank need not intervene in the market.

2. If the demand curve shifts to D_1, there is an excess demand for U.S. dollars that the Bank must satisfy. The Bank sells U.S. dollars from its reserves to the extent of Q_4Q_1 per month in order to prevent the exchange rate from rising above 1.05.

3. If the demand curve shifts to D_2, there is an excess supply of U.S. dollars that the Bank must satisfy. The Bank buys U.S. dollars to the extent of Q_2Q_3 per month in order to prevent the exchange rate from falling below 0.95.

If, on average, the demand and supply curves intersect in the range 0.95 to 1.05, the Bank's foreign-exchange reserves will be relatively stable, with the Bank buying U.S. dollars when the demand is abnormally low and selling them when the demand is abnormally high. Over a long period, however, the average level of reserves will be fairly stable.

If conditions change, the Bank's foreign-exchange reserves will rise or fall more or less continuously. For example, suppose the average level of demand becomes D_1, with fluctuations on either side of this level. The average drain on the Bank's foreign-exchange reserves will then be Q_4Q_1 *per month*. But this situation cannot continue indefinitely because the Bank has only a limited amount of foreign-exchange reserves. In this situation, there are two alternatives: the Bank can change the fixed exchange rate so that the band of permissible prices straddles the new equilibrium price, or government policy can try to shift the curves so that the intersection is in the band 0.95 to 1.05. To accomplish this goal, the government must restrict demand for foreign exchange: it can impose import quotas and foreign-travel restrictions, or it can seek to increase

larger producing countries, means that the world's consumers are prepared to offer more foreign currency per unit of these Canadian exports. The increase in the supply of foreign exchange occurs even if the volume of Canadian exports is unchanged; if Canadian exports increase in response to the higher world price, the supply of foreign exchange increases further. The increase in the supply of foreign exchange causes a reduction in the exchange rate—an appreciation of the Canadian dollar.

A Rise in the Foreign Price of Imports Suppose the euro price of European automobiles increases sharply. Suppose also that Canadian consumers have an elastic demand for European cars because they can easily switch to Canadian-made substitutes. Consequently, they spend fewer euros for European automobiles than they did before and hence demand less foreign exchange. The demand curve for foreign exchange shifts to the left, and the Canadian dollar will appreciate. If the demand for European cars were inelastic, total spending on them would rise, and the demand for foreign exchange would shift to the right, leading to a depreciation of the Canadian dollar. For many products, demand will be relatively inelastic in the short run and so the short-run effect

the supply of U.S. dollars by encouraging Canadian exports.

Thailand in 1997 provides an example of an exchange rate fixed at a level that led to a persistent excess demand for foreign exchange. Thailand's central bank had fixed the value of its currency, the baht, to the U.S. dollar. When an excess demand for foreign currency developed in Thailand, the central bank began to deplete its stock of foreign-exchange reserves as it purchased the baht in an attempt to support its external value. By July of 1997, however, the central bank's stock of foreign-exchange reserves had been depleted to such an extent that it could no longer fix the exchange rate. With an excess demand for foreign exchange and a central bank that could no longer fix the exchange rate, depreciation was the natural result. The baht depreciated dramatically and Thailand then moved away from a fixed exchange-rate system.

For most of the past decade, China has operated an adjustable peg exchange-rate system for its currency, the yuan (sometimes called the renminbi). In 2005 the exchange rate was 8.3 yuan to the U.S. dollar but today it has appreciated to be about 6.2 yuan to the U.S. dollar. Throughout this period, the Chinese central bank has held the exchange rate above the free-market equilibrium level; in other words, the yuan has been undervalued relative to what would have been observed with a purely flexible exchange

rate. As a result, there has been a persistent excess supply of foreign currency offered in exchange for Chinese yuan (and thus an excess demand for the Chinese yuan). To reduce the amount of appreciation of the yuan, the Chinese central bank purchases foreign-exchange reserves every month. In recent years, these purchases have led to an enormous accumulation of foreign-exchange reserves in China.

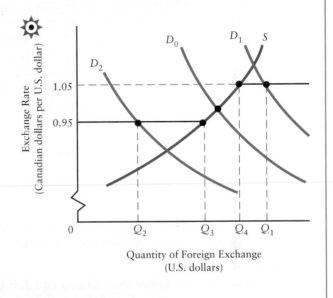

of a rise in foreign prices will be a depreciation of the Canadian dollar. This is illustrated in part (i) of Figure 35-3.

> Exchange rates often respond to changes in the prices of major exports and imports. A rise in the world price of Canadian exports causes the Canadian dollar to appreciate. If demand for foreign products is inelastic, a rise in the price of Canadian imports causes the Canadian dollar to depreciate.

Changes in Overall Price Levels Suppose that instead of a change in the price of a specific product there is a change in *all* prices because of general inflation. We consider separate cases, each corresponding to a different pattern of Canadian inflation relative to foreign inflation.

Equal Inflation in Both Countries. Suppose inflation is running at 5 percent in both Canada and Europe. In this case, the euro prices of European goods and the dollar prices of Canadian goods both rise by 5 percent. At the *existing* exchange rate, the dollar prices of European goods and the euro prices of Canadian goods will each rise by 5 percent, and hence the relative prices of imports and domestically produced goods will be unchanged in both countries. Since there is no reason to expect a change in either country's demand for imports at the original exchange rate, the inflation in the two countries leaves the equilibrium exchange rate unchanged.

Inflation in Only One Country. What will happen if there is inflation in Canada while the price level remains stable in Europe? The dollar price of Canadian goods will rise, and they will become more expensive in Europe. This increase will cause the quantity of Canadian exports, and therefore the amount of foreign exchange supplied by European importers, to decrease. Thus, the supply curve for foreign exchange shifts to the left.

At the same time, European goods in Canada will have an unchanged Canadian-dollar price, while the price of Canadian goods sold in Canada will increase because of the inflation. Thus, European goods will be more attractive compared with Canadian goods (because they have become relatively cheaper), and thus more European goods will be bought in Canada. At any exchange rate, the amount of foreign exchange demanded to purchase imports will rise. Thus, the demand curve for foreign exchange shifts to the right.

Canadian inflation that is unmatched in Europe will therefore cause the supply curve for foreign exchange to shift to the left and the demand curve for foreign exchange to shift to the right. As a result, the equilibrium exchange rate *must* rise—there is a depreciation of the Canadian dollar relative to the euro.

Inflation at Unequal Rates. The two foregoing examples are, of course, just limiting cases of a more general situation in which the rate of inflation is different in the two countries. The arguments can readily be extended when we realize that it is the *relative* inflation in two countries that determines whether home goods or foreign goods look more or less attractive. If country A's inflation rate is higher than country B's, country A's exports are becoming relatively expensive in B's markets while imports from B are becoming relatively cheap in A's markets. This causes A's currency to depreciate relative to B's.

> Other things being equal, if Canada has higher inflation than other countries, the Canadian dollar will be depreciating relative to other currencies. If Canada has lower inflation than other countries, the Canadian dollar will be appreciating.

An increase in the world price of a major Canadian export, such as forestry products, generally leads to an appreciation of the Canadian dollar.

Capital Movements Flows of financial capital can exert strong influences on exchange rates. For example, an increased desire by Canadians to purchase European assets (a capital outflow from Canada) will shift the demand curve for foreign exchange to the right, and the dollar will depreciate. In contrast, a desire by foreigners to increase their holdings of Canadian assets will shift the supply curve for foreign currency to the right and cause the Canadian dollar to appreciate.

Short-Term Capital Movements. An important motive for short-term capital flows is a change in interest rates. International traders hold transaction balances just as do domestic traders. These balances are often lent out on a short-term basis rather than being left idle. Naturally, the holders of these balances will tend to lend them, other things being equal, in markets in which interest rates are highest. This is often referred to as the *carry trade*. If one country's short-term interest rate rises above the rates in other countries (say, because that country undertakes a contractionary monetary policy), there will tend to be a large inflow of short-term capital into that country in an effort to take advantage of the high rate. This inflow of financial capital will increase the demand for the domestic currency and cause it to appreciate. If the short-term interest rate should fall in one country (say, because of a monetary expansion in that country), there will tend to be a shift of financial capital away from that country, and its currency will tend to depreciate. We saw this basic relationship between interest rates, capital flows, and the exchange rate in Chapter 28 when we discussed the monetary transmission mechanism in an open economy.

Changes in monetary policy lead to changes in interest rates and thus to international flows of financial capital. A contractionary monetary policy in Canada will lead to a rise in Canadian interest rates, a capital inflow, and an appreciation of the Canadian dollar. An expansionary monetary policy in Canada will lead to a reduction in Canadian interest rates, a capital outflow, and a depreciation of the Canadian dollar.

A second motive for short-term capital movements is speculation about the *future value* of a country's exchange rate. If foreigners expect the Canadian dollar to appreciate in the near future, they will be induced to buy assets that pay off in Canadian dollars, such as Canadian stocks or bonds; if they expect the Canadian dollar to depreciate in the near future, they will be reluctant to buy or to hold Canadian securities.

Long-Term Capital Movements. Long-term capital movements are largely influenced by long-term expectations about another country's profit opportunities and the long-run value of its currency. A French firm would be more willing to purchase a Canadian factory if it expected that the dollar profits would buy more euros in future years than the profits from investment in a French factory. This could happen if the Canadian firm earned greater profits than the French firm, with exchange rates remaining unchanged. It could also happen if the profits were the same but the French firm expected the Canadian dollar to appreciate relative to the euro.

Structural Changes

An economy can undergo structural changes that alter the equilibrium exchange rate. *Structural change* is an all-purpose term for a change in cost structures, the invention of new products, changes in preferences between products, or anything else that affects the pattern of comparative advantage. Consider two examples.

Suppose the reluctance of firms in one country to adopt technological innovations results in that country's products not improving as rapidly as those produced in other countries. Consumers' demand will shift slowly away from the first country's products and toward those of its foreign competitors. This shift will cause a gradual depreciation in the first country's currency because fewer people want to buy that country's goods and thus fewer people want to buy that country's currency. For this reason, a country with faster productivity growth than other countries tends to experience an appreciation of its currency.

A second example relates to the discovery of valuable mineral resources. Prominent examples are the development of natural gas in the Netherlands in the early 1960s, the development of North Sea oil in the United Kingdom in the 1970s, and the recent discovery of large diamond deposits in the Northwest Territories. If firms in one country make such a discovery and begin selling these resources to the rest of the world, the foreign purchasers must supply their foreign currency in order to purchase the currency of the exporting country. The result is an appreciation of the currency of the exporting country.

> Anything that leads to changes in the pattern of trade, such as changes in costs or changes in demand, will generally lead to changes in exchange rates.

The Volatility of Exchange Rates

We have discussed several variables that can lead to changes in the exchange rate, including changes in relative prices, changes in interest rates, and changes in the pattern of trade. Since these variables are changing at different times by different amounts and often in different directions, it should not be surprising that exchange rates are constantly changing. Indeed, exchange rates are one of the most volatile of all macroeconomic variables. One reason for this volatility that we have not yet discussed is that foreign-exchange traders, when they are deciding whether to buy or sell foreign currency, respond to all sorts of "news" that they think will influence economic conditions, both currently and in the future. Since such news is constantly becoming available, the exchange rate is continuously changing as this new information leads traders to change their demand and supply decisions. *Applying Economic Concepts 35-3* discusses in more detail how news affects the volatility of exchange rates.

| 35.4 Three Policy Issues

This chapter has so far explained how the balance of payments accounts are constructed and how exchange rates are determined. It is now time to use this knowledge to explore some important policy issues. We examine three issues commonly discussed in the media. As we will see, these media discussions are not always as well informed as they could be. We pose the three policy issues as questions:

1. Is a current account deficit "bad" and a surplus "good"?

2. Is there a "correct" value for the Canadian dollar?

3. Should Canada fix its exchange rate with the U.S. dollar?

Current Account Deficits and Surpluses

Figure 35-4 shows the path of Canada's current account balance (as a percentage of GDP) since 1961. In most years, Canada has a significant trade surplus since it exports more goods and services to the world than it imports. But because it makes more investment payments (both interest and dividends) to foreigners than it receives from foreigners, it has a deficit on the capital-service portion of the current account. During most of the 1960–1995 period, Canada had an overall current account deficit of between 2 and 4 percent of GDP. From the late 1990s to 2007, however, Canada's trade surplus increased by more than the capital-service deficit, and the result was a significant

APPLYING ECONOMIC CONCEPTS 35-3

News and the Exchange Rate

Foreign-exchange markets are different from markets for consumer goods in that the vast bulk of trading takes place between professional foreign-exchange traders working for banks, mutual-fund companies, and pension funds. These traders do not meet one another face to face. Rather, they do their transactions over the telephone or the computer, and the other party to the transaction could be anywhere in the world. The structure of this market has one interesting implication: exchange rates respond to news. Let's see why this is and what this means.

Deals done by professional traders are all on a large scale, typically involving sums no smaller than $1 million and often very much larger. Each trader tends to specialize in trades between a small number of currencies, say the Canadian and the U.S. dollars, or the U.S. dollar and the Japanese yen. But the traders for all currencies for each bank sit close together in a trading room so they can hear what is going on in the other markets. When a big news event breaks, anywhere in the world, this will be shouted out simultaneously to all traders in the room.

Each trader is also faced with several computer screens and many buttons that connect him or her quickly by telephone to other traders. Speed of transaction can be very important if you are dealing with large amounts of money in a market that is continuously changing the prices quoted. The most recent price quotes from around the world appear on the screens. However, contracts are agreed over the telephone (and are recorded in case of a disagreement) and the paperwork follows within two days.

As exchange rates are closely related to expectations and to interest rates, the foreign-exchange traders have to keep an eye on all major news events affecting the economic environment. Since all the players in the foreign-exchange markets are professionals, they are well informed, not just about what has happened but also about forecasts of what is likely to happen. Accordingly, the exchange rate at any point in time reflects not just history but also current expectations of future events.

As soon as some future event comes to be expected—such as the central bank's plans to tighten monetary policy—it will be reflected in the current exchange rate. Events expected to happen soon will be given more weight than those events expected to happen in the more distant future. The fact that expectations of future events are incorporated quickly into the exchange rate has an interesting implication: the only component in today's news that will cause the exchange rate to change is what was *not expected* to happen. Economists attribute the unforecastable component of news to a random error. It is random in the sense that it has no detectable pattern and it is unrelated to the information available before it happened.

Some events are clearly unforecastable, like an earthquake or a head of state having a heart attack. Others are the production of economic statistics for which forecasts have generally been published. In the latter case it is the deviation of announced figures from their forecast value that tends to move exchange rates.

Exchange rates are therefore moved by news. And since much news is random and unpredictable, many changes in exchange rates will tend to be random. Some people, observing the volatility of exchange rates, conclude that foreign-exchange markets are inefficient. However, with well-informed professional traders who have forward-looking expectations, new information is rapidly transmitted into prices. The volatility of exchange rates, therefore, largely reflects the volatility of relevant, but unexpected, events around the world.

Current news events, the announcements made by public officials, and the expectation of future events play a large role in determining whether currency traders decide to buy or sell foreign exchange. The frequency and randomness of news releases partly explain why exchange rates tend to be so volatile.

turnaround in the current account balance. But with the arrival of the global recession in 2008, Canada's exports fell far more than its imports and the result was a return to current account deficits.

As we have learned, Canada's balance of payments are defined in such a way that they must always balance, so during the 1960–1995 period the current account

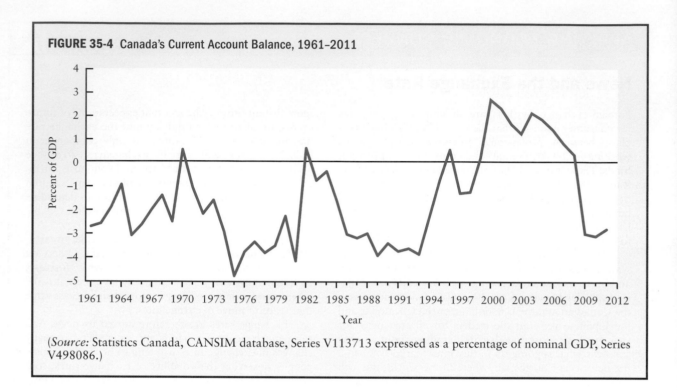

FIGURE 35-4 Canada's Current Account Balance, 1961–2011

(*Source:* Statistics Canada, CANSIM database, Series V113713 expressed as a percentage of nominal GDP, Series V498086.)

deficits were matched by capital account surpluses of the same size. During these years, Canada was selling more assets to the rest of the world—both bonds and equity—than it was buying from the rest of the world. Similarly, the current account surpluses from 1998 to 2007 were matched by capital account deficits, meaning that in recent years Canada was buying more assets from foreigners than we were selling to foreigners.

It is common for TV anchors to report negatively on an increase in the current account deficit and positively on its decline. But are current account deficits really a problem? Should we be celebrating Canada's current account surpluses when they occur? We address this issue in three parts.

Mercantilism Many people argue that a current account deficit is undesirable because it means that Canada is buying more goods and services from the world than it is selling to the world. Central to this view is the belief that exports are "good" and imports are "bad." We discussed this belief, and argued why it was incorrect, in Chapter 34 when we explored some of the invalid arguments for trade protection.

As a carryover from a long-discredited eighteenth-century doctrine called *mercantilism*, a current account surplus is sometimes called a "favourable balance," and a current account deficit is sometimes called an "unfavourable balance." Mercantilists, both ancient and modern, believe that a country's gains from trade arise only from having a "favourable" balance of trade—that is, by exporting more goods and services than it imports. But this belief misses the central point of comparative advantage that we explored in Chapter 33—that countries gain from trade because trade allows each country to specialize in the production of those products in which its opportunity costs are low. The gains from trade have *nothing* to do with whether there is a trade deficit or a trade surplus.

Lessons from History 35-1 discusses the doctrine of mercantilism. The lesson to be learned is that the gains from trade depend on the *volume* of trade (exports plus imports) rather than the *balance* of trade (exports minus imports). There is nothing inherently bad about having a current account deficit and nothing inherently good about having a current account surplus.

International Borrowing If Canada has a current account deficit, it also has a capital account surplus. It is a net seller of assets to the rest of the world. These assets are either bonds, in which case Canadians are borrowing from foreigners, or they are shares in firms (equities), in which case Canadians are selling their capital stock to foreigners.

It follows that the question "Should Canada have a current account deficit?" is the same as the question "Should Canadians be net sellers of assets to foreigners?" It is not immediately clear that the answer to this question should be no. It is true that by selling bonds to foreigners, Canadians increase their indebtedness to foreigners and will eventually have to redeem the bonds and pay interest. And by selling income-earning equities to foreigners, Canadians give up a stream of income that they would otherwise have. But, in both cases, they get a lump sum of funds that can be used for any type of consumption or investment. Is it obviously "better" to have a lower debt or a higher

---

LESSONS FROM HISTORY 35-1

Mercantilism, Then and Now

Media commentators, politicians, and much of the general public often appear to believe that a country should export more than it imports and thereby secure a current account surplus. They appear to believe that the benefits derived from international trade are measured by the size of that surplus.

This view is related to the *exploitation doctrine* of international trade: one country's surplus is another country's deficit. Hence, one country's gain, judged by its surplus, must be another country's loss, judged by its deficit.

People who hold such views today are echoing an ancient economic doctrine called *mercantilism*. The mercantilists were a group of economists who preceded Adam Smith. They judged the success of trade by the size of the trade balance. In many cases, this doctrine made sense in terms of their objective, which was to use international trade as a means of building up the political and military power of the state, rather than as a means of raising the living standards of its citizens. A current account surplus allowed the country (then and now) to acquire assets. (In those days, the assets took the form of gold. Today, they are mostly claims on the currencies of other countries.) These assets could then be used to pay armies, to purchase weapons from abroad, and to finance colonial expansions.

If the objective is to promote the welfare and living standards of ordinary citizens, however, the mercantilist focus on the balance of trade makes no sense. The principle of comparative advantage shows that average living standards are maximized by having individuals, regions, and countries specialize in the things they produce comparatively best and then trading to obtain the things they produce comparatively worst. With specialization, domestic consumers get access to products they want at the lowest possible prices, while domestic firms are able to sell their products at higher prices than would otherwise be possible. The more specialization takes place, the more trade occurs and thus the more average living standards increase.

For the country as a whole, therefore, the gains from trade are to be judged by the *volume* of trade rather than by the *balance* of trade. A situation in which there is a large volume of trade even though each country has a zero balance of trade is thus entirely satisfactory. Furthermore, a change in policy that results in an equal increase in both exports and imports will generate gains because it allows for specialization according to comparative advantage, even though it causes no change in either country's trade balance.

future income stream than to have a lump sum of funds right now? If it were obviously better, no family would ever borrow money to buy a house or a car, and no firm would ever borrow money to build a factory.

> A country that has a current account deficit is either borrowing from the rest of the world or selling some of its capital assets to the rest of the world. This is not necessarily undesirable.

To argue that it is undesirable for Canada to have a current account deficit is to argue that Canadians as a whole should not borrow from (or sell assets to) the rest of the world. But surely the wisdom of borrowing depends on *why* Canadians are borrowing. It is therefore important to know *why* there is a current account deficit.

Causes of Current Account Deficits There are several possible causes of a current account deficit. This can be seen most clearly by recalling some national-income accounting from Chapter 20. Recall that GDP is equal to the sum of actual consumption, investment, government purchases, and net exports,

$$\text{GDP} = C_a + I_a + G_a + NX_a$$

where the subscript "*a*" denotes *actual* expenditure rather than desired expenditure. Next, recall from Chapter 20 the difference between GDP and GNP where the latter is the total income that accrues to Canadian residents. GNP is equal to GDP plus the net investment income received from abroad, which we call R.

$$\text{GNP} = \text{GDP} + R = C_a + I_a + G_a + NX_a + R$$

Note that the current account balance is simply the trade balance, NX_a, plus the net investment income, R. We denote the actual current account balance CA_a. If CA_a is positive, there is a current account surplus; if CA_a is negative, there is a current account deficit. The equation now becomes

$$\text{GNP} = C_a + I_a + G_a + CA_a \tag{35-1}$$

Now consider how the income accruing to Canadian households (GNP) can be spent. There are only three ways to dispose of income. It can be consumed, saved, or paid in taxes. That is,

$$\text{GNP} = C_a + S_a + T_a \tag{35-2}$$

By equating Equations 35-1 and 35-2, and by omitting the "*a*" subscripts for simplicity, we derive an interesting relationship among national saving, investment, and the current account balance:

$$C + I + G + CA = C + S + T$$

$$\Rightarrow CA = S + (T - G) - I$$

This last equation says that the current account balance in any year is exactly equal to the excess of national saving, $S + (T - G)$, over domestic investment I. If Canadians (and their governments) decide to save more than is needed to finance the amount of domestic investment, where do the excess funds go? They are used to acquire foreign assets, and thus Canada has a current account surplus ($CA > 0$). In contrast, if Canadians do not save enough to finance the amount of domestic investment, the balance must be financed by foreign funds. Thus, Canada has a current account deficit ($CA < 0$). Finally, we can re-arrange this equation very slightly to get

$$CA = (S - I) + (T - G) \qquad (35\text{-}3)$$

which says that the current account balance is equal to the excess of private saving over investment plus the government budget surplus.

Equation 35-3 shows three separate reasons for any given increase in the current account deficit (a fall in CA). First, a reduction in private saving, other things being equal, will lead to a rise in the current account deficit. Second, a rise in domestic investment, other things being equal, will increase the current account deficit. Finally, other things being equal, a rise in the government's budget deficit (a smaller value of $T - G$) will raise the current account deficit. This third case is often referred to as a situation of *twin deficits*. That is, a rise in the government's budget deficit will also have the effect (if S and I remain constant) of increasing the current account deficit.

> **An increase in the level of investment, a decrease in the level of private saving, and an increase in the government's budget deficit are all possible causes of an increase in a country's current account deficit.**

It makes little sense to discuss the desirability of a change in the current account deficit without first knowing the *cause* of the change. Knowing the cause is crucial to knowing whether the change in the current account deficit is undesirable. The following two examples illustrate this important point.

First, suppose business opportunities in Canada are very promising and, as a result, there is an increase in the level of private-sector investment. Most people would consider such an investment boom desirable because it would increase current output and employment and, by increasing the country's capital stock, it would also increase the level of potential output in the future. But as is clear from Equation 35-3, other things being equal, the effect of the rise in Canadian investment is an increase in the Canadian current account deficit. The current account deficit increases because, in the absence of increased domestic saving, the increase in domestic investment can only take place if it is financed by a capital inflow from other countries. This capital inflow represents a rise in Canada's current account deficit (or capital account surplus). In this case, however, it would be difficult to argue that the increase in Canada's current account deficit is undesirable as it simply reflects a boom in domestic business opportunities.

For a second example, suppose the domestic economy begins to slow and households and firms become pessimistic about the future. In such a situation, we expect households to increase their saving and firms to reduce their investment, thus increasing the value of $(S - I)$. As the economy slows we would also expect the government's net tax revenues to fall, thus decreasing the value of $(T - G)$. But it is possible that the first effect dominates the second effect, thus leading to an increase in the current account surplus. Is the increase in Canada's current account surplus desirable? Most people would probably agree that the onset of a recession as just described is surely undesirable, involving a loss of output and employment.

An increase in domestic investment, other things being equal, will lead to an increase in the current account deficit. But there is little that is undesirable about this situation.

A country's current account deficit can increase for a number of reasons. Whether the rise in the current account deficit is desirable depends on its underlying cause. A rise in the current account deficit may reflect a positive economic development; a decline in the current account deficit may reflect a negative economic development.

Is There a "Correct" Value for the Canadian Dollar?

From the summer of 1997 to the end of 1999, the external value of the Canadian dollar fell from about 72 to 65 U.S. cents. (The exchange rate increased from 1.39 to 1.54.) It was common to hear financial commentators discuss how the Canadian dollar was "undervalued." Retailers selling imported products and firms using imported supplies complained that the weak Canadian dollar was undermining their business. Opposite statements were heard between 2002 and 2008 when, as a result of high world prices for raw materials, the Canadian dollar appreciated enormously. At the time, some financial commentators argued that the Canadian dollar was "overvalued." Canadian firms in the tourist-oriented hospitality industry and those exporting manufactured products complained that the strong Canadian dollar was damaging their business. In both cases, the observers appeared to believe that there was some "correct" value for the Canadian dollar. Is there?

As we saw in the previous section, a country that chooses to use a flexible exchange rate has its exchange rate determined by competitive forces in the foreign-exchange market. In Canada, and other countries as well, fluctuations in exchange rates have many causes. Some changes may be good for Canada, such as a worldwide shortage of wheat that drives up the world price of wheat, a major Canadian export. Others may be bad for Canada, such as the discovery of new copper deposits in Chile that drives down the price of copper, also a major Canadian export. But the various supply and demand forces are coming together in the foreign-exchange market to determine the equilibrium value of the exchange rate. Changes in this value may reflect positive or negative events for Canada, but it is difficult to think of this equilibrium value as being either "too high" or "too low."

With a flexible exchange rate, the market determines the value of the exchange rate. With respect to the forces of demand and supply, the equilibrium exchange rate is the "correct" exchange rate.

Saying that the current equilibrium exchange rate is the "correct" rate in no way suggests that this "correct" rate is constant. Indeed, foreign-exchange markets are so large, with so many participants in so many countries, each responding to a slightly different set of events and expectations, that the equilibrium exchange rate is constantly changing. In other words, as various forces lead to frequent changes in the demand for and supply of the Canadian dollar in foreign-exchange markets, the "correct" value of the Canadian exchange rate is constantly changing.

Some economists accept that the current exchange rate, as determined by the foreign-exchange market, is indeed the correct rate, but they make a distinction between the current value of the exchange rate and its long-run value. These economists argue that, whereas various shocks may cause the exchange rate to rise or fall in the short run, there nonetheless exists some "fundamental" level to which it will eventually return. This brings us to the theory of *purchasing power parity*.

Purchasing Power Parity The theory of **purchasing power parity** (PPP) holds that, over the long term, the value of the exchange rate between two currencies depends on the two currencies' relative purchasing power. The theory holds that a currency will tend to have the same purchasing power when it is spent in its home country as it would have if it were converted to foreign exchange and spent in the foreign country. Another way to say the same thing is that the price of *identical baskets of goods* should be the same in the two countries when the price is expressed in the same currency. If we let P_C and P_E be the price levels in Canada and Europe, respectively, and let e be the Canadian-dollar price of euros (the exchange rate), then the theory of purchasing power parity predicts the following equality in the long run:

$$P_C = e \times P_E \qquad (35\text{-}4)$$

This equation simply says that if a basket of goods costs 1000 euros in Europe and the exchange rate is 1.3 (that is, 1.3 Canadian dollars per euro), then that same basket of goods should cost 1300 dollars in Canada ($1.3 \times 1000 = 1300$).

> According to the theory of purchasing power parity, the exchange rate between two countries' currencies is determined by the relative price levels in the two countries.

The idea behind PPP is a simple one. Suppose that Equation 35-4 did *not* hold—specifically, suppose that P_C was greater than $e \times P_E$, so that Canadian-dollar prices in Canada exceeded the Canadian-dollar prices of the same goods in Europe. In this case, people would eventually increase their purchases of the cheaper European goods and reduce their purchases of the expensive Canadian goods. These actions would have the effect of depreciating the Canadian dollar (a rise in e); this depreciation would continue until the equality was re-established.

The *PPP exchange rate* is the value of the exchange rate that makes Equation 35-4 hold. That is, the PPP exchange rate (between the Canadian dollar and the euro) is defined to be

$$e^{PPP} \equiv P_C/P_E \qquad (35\text{-}5)$$

Note that the PPP exchange rate is itself not constant. If inflation is higher in Canada than in Europe, for example, P_C will be rising faster than P_E and so the PPP exchange rate will be rising. Conversely, if inflation is lower in Canada than in Europe, P_C will be rising more slowly than P_E and the PPP exchange rate will be falling.[3]

A Caveat About PPP Should we expect the *actual* exchange rate to equal the PPP exchange rate? The theory of purchasing power parity predicts that if the actual exchange rate (e) does not equal the PPP exchange rate (e^{PPP}), then demands and supplies of Canadian and European goods will change until the equality holds. Thus, the theory of PPP predicts that the actual exchange rate will eventually equal the PPP exchange rate.

purchasing power parity (PPP) The theory that, over the long term, the exchange rate between two currencies adjusts to reflect relative price levels.

For The Economist's *Big Mac Index, which uses the idea of PPP, see its website:* www.economist.com.

---

[3] For a very readable review of the PPP theory and its empirical testing, see R. Lafrance and L. Schembri, "Purchasing Power Parity: Definitions, Measurement, and Interpretation," *Bank of Canada Review*, Autumn, 2002.

Figure 35-5 shows the path of the actual Canadian–U.S. exchange rate and the PPP exchange rate since 1981. It is clear from the figure that there are long periods over which the actual exchange rate deviates significantly from the PPP exchange rate. Why is this the case? Is there something wrong with the theory of purchasing power parity?

Recall from Equation 35-4 that P_C and P_E were defined as the prices of *identical baskets of goods* in Canada and Europe, respectively. Given that the goods are the same, the argument that the prices should (eventually) be equated across the two countries is sensible—if the prices are not equated across the two countries, there would be an incentive to purchase in the cheaper country rather than in the more expensive country, and this would lead to changes in the exchange rate until Equation 35-4 *did* hold.

One problem, however, when we apply the theory of purchasing power parity to *national price indices*, such as the Consumer Price Index or the implicit GDP deflator, is that the two baskets of goods are typically *not* the same—for two reasons.

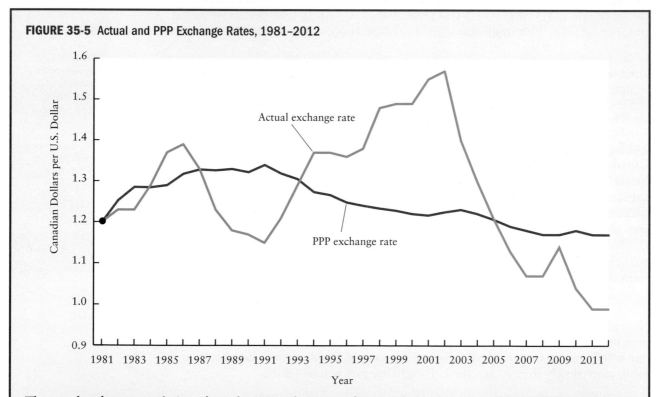

FIGURE 35-5 Actual and PPP Exchange Rates, 1981–2012

The actual exchange rate deviates from the PPP exchange rate for extended periods. The Canada–U.S. PPP exchange rate is the ratio of Canadian to U.S. price indices. This PPP exchange rate increased during the 1980s when Canadian inflation was above that in the United States; it declined over the next 20 years when Canadian inflation was lower than in the United States. The actual Canada–U.S. exchange rate has fluctuated more dramatically and shows little tendency to track the PPP exchange rate. (The PPP exchange rate is a ratio of two price indexes; it has been constructed to be equal to the actual exchange rate in 1981, the first year of the sample period.)

(*Source:* Canadian CPI is from the Bank of Canada, Series PCPISA, annual average. U.S. CPI is from U.S. Bureau of Labor Statistics: www.bls.gov. Exchange rate is from Statistics Canada, CANSIM database, Series V37432, annual average.)

Different Countries Produce Different Goods. Suppose we apply the theory of PPP to the Canada–Europe exchange rate and we use the GDP deflators from the two countries as the measures of prices. Recall from Chapter 20 that the GDP deflator is an index of prices of goods *produced within the country*. But Canada and Europe clearly produce very different goods. The price of forest products will have a large weight in the Canadian GDP deflator but less weight in the European GDP deflator; in contrast, the price of wine will have a much larger weight in the European GDP deflator than in the Canadian GDP deflator.

The implication of these differences for the theory of PPP is important. As long as changes in the *relative* prices of goods occur, such as a change in the price of forest products relative to wine, then P_C (the Canadian GDP deflator) will change relative to P_E (the European GDP deflator) *even though the prices of individual goods might be equated across the two countries*. Thus, differences in the structure of the price indices between two countries mean that using a PPP exchange rate computed on the basis of Equation 35-5 will be misleading. In other words, in the presence of changing relative prices, there is no reason to expect the actual exchange rate to equal the PPP exchange rate.

Non-Traded Goods Are Important. The previous discussion emphasized that the *baskets* of goods across two countries might differ even though the products in the baskets were the same. But even if Canada and Europe produced exactly the same range of goods, so that the various weights in the GDP deflators were the same, there is another reason why the basket of goods in Canada differs from the basket of goods in Europe. Many products in any country are *not traded internationally*, such as haircuts, restaurant meals, dry cleaning, car-repair and landscaping services, and tickets to theatres or sporting events. But, since such products cannot be traded across international boundaries, there is nothing that will force their prices to be equal across the two countries. If haircuts are more expensive in Paris than in Toronto (as they are), we do not expect people to shift their consumption of haircuts away from Paris toward Toronto, and thus we should not expect the actual exchange rate to move to make Equation 35-4 hold.

The conclusion of this discussion is that we must be very careful in selecting the price indices we use when we apply the theory of purchasing power parity. We know that countries have different patterns of production and thus have different structures to their national price indices. Thus, in the presence of changes in relative prices of various products, the national price indices can change in ways that will not lead to changes in the exchange rate. Similarly, the presence of non-traded goods implies that some differences in prices across countries will not lead to changes in the location of demand and thus changes in the exchange rate.

> **Changes in relative prices and the presence of non-traded goods imply that purchasing power parity need not hold—not even in the long run.**

Should Canada Have a Fixed Exchange Rate?

In recent years, some economists have suggested that Canada peg the value of its currency to the U.S. dollar. Advocates of a fixed Canadian exchange rate see this policy as a means of avoiding the significant fluctuations in the Canadian–U.S. dollar exchange rate that would otherwise occur—fluctuations such as the 10 percent depreciation that occurred between 1997 and 1999 and the 60 percent appreciation that occurred between 2002 and 2008. They argue that exchange-rate fluctuations generate uncertainty for importers and exporters and thus increase the costs associated with trade.

Others have gone further in suggesting that Canada actually abandon its currency altogether and simply adopt the U.S. dollar. They point to the European Union, which introduced the euro as its common currency in 1999. If a common currency is acceptable to most of Europe, why should Canada and the United States be any different?[4]

These are contentious suggestions that have attracted a great deal of public attention in recent years. We examine this issue by comparing the main benefits of flexible and fixed exchange rates. Whereas flexible exchange rates dampen the effects on output and employment from external shocks to the economy, fixed exchange rates reduce the uncertainty faced by importers and exporters.

Flexible Exchange Rates as "Shock Absorbers" For most of the years following the Second World War, Canada has used a flexible exchange rate. Even when most other major countries chose to peg the value of their currencies to the U.S. dollar (and to gold) under the Bretton Woods system, Canada usually chose a flexible exchange rate (there were a few short periods in which Canada fixed its exchange rate). For all of its history Canada's economy has been heavily reliant on the export of resource-based products, the prices of which are determined in world markets and are often highly variable from year to year. Changes in these prices constitute changes in Canada's terms of trade and, as we saw earlier in this chapter, changes in a country's terms of trade are an important reason why exchange rates are so variable.

That the exchange rate adjusts in response to shocks is actually the main advantage of a flexible (rather than fixed) exchange rate. A flexible exchange rate acts as a "shock absorber," dampening the effects on the country's output and employment from external shocks. To understand how this happens, consider a simple example.

Suppose a reduction in world demand leads to a reduction in the world prices of raw materials, which are major Canadian exports. When world demand for raw materials declines, there is a reduction in demand for Canadian exports and an accompanying reduction in demand for Canadian dollars (or a reduction in the supply of foreign exchange) in the foreign-exchange market. The effect on Canadian real GDP is shown in part (ii) of Figure 35-6 by the leftward shift of the AD curve. The effect in the foreign-exchange market is shown in part (i) by the leftward shift of the supply curve for foreign exchange. Consider the effect of this shock in two different situations. In the first, the Bank of Canada maintains a fixed exchange rate; in the second, the Bank of Canada allows the exchange rate to be freely determined by demand and supply.

If the Bank of Canada fixes the exchange rate at e_0, the reduction in the supply of foreign exchange from S_0 to S_1 leads to an excess demand for foreign currency. To keep the exchange rate fixed at e_0, the Bank must sell sufficient foreign-exchange reserves to satisfy the excess demand. But the negative shock to aggregate demand still occurs and thus output and employment in Canada fall, as shown in part (ii) of Figure 35-6. If this shock is large and persistent enough, Canadian wages will eventually fall and the AS curve will eventually shift downward, returning real GDP to the level of potential output. But the closing of the recessionary gap may be slow and painful.

If Canada instead has a flexible exchange rate, the reduction in the world prices of raw materials will lead to a reduction in the supply of foreign exchange and thus to a

---

[4] After over a decade of apparent success with the euro, by late 2012 Europe's adoption of a common currency was viewed by many economists as a failure. A major problem within the euro zone is the absence of independent monetary policies and flexible exchange rates between the various member countries. Individual countries within the euro zone therefore lack the macroeconomic "shock absorbers" discussed in this section.

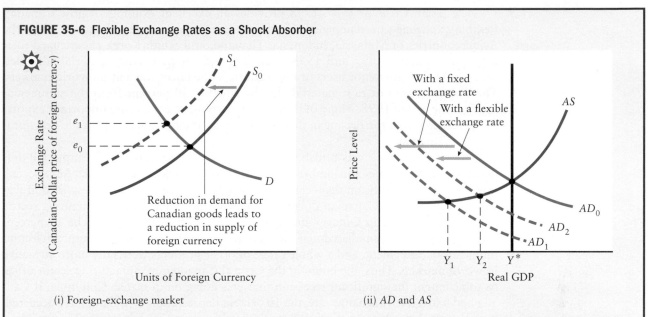

FIGURE 35-6 Flexible Exchange Rates as a Shock Absorber

(i) Foreign-exchange market

(ii) *AD* and *AS*

Flexible exchange rates adjust to terms of trade shocks and thus dampen the effect on output and employment. The economy begins with the exchange rate equal to e_0 in part (i) and GDP equal to Y^* in part (ii). A reduction in the world's demand for Canadian exports causes a reduction in the supply of foreign exchange, shifting S_0 to S_1 in part (i).

With a fixed exchange rate, the Bank of Canada maintains the exchange rate at e_0, satisfying the excess demand for foreign exchange by selling its foreign-currency reserves. The reduction in the demand for Canada's exports is a negative aggregate demand shock. AD_0 shifts to the left to AD_1 in part (ii), causing GDP to fall to Y_1. The recessionary gap eventually pushes wages down, the *AS* curve shifts downward over time, and the economy moves along AD_1 to Y^*. The adjustment, however, may be very slow.

With a flexible exchange rate, the Bank of Canada allows the Canadian dollar to depreciate. The exchange rate rises to e_1 in part (i). The reduction in demand for Canadian exports still causes the *AD* curve to shift to the left in part (ii), but the shift is dampened by the depreciation of the dollar, which makes Canadian exports more attractive in world markets. The *AD* curve shifts only to AD_2 and so GDP falls only to Y_2. There is still a recession, but smaller than in the case with a fixed exchange rate.

depreciation of the Canadian dollar. The exchange rate will increase from e_0 to e_1. The *AD* curve will shift to the left, reducing Canada's GDP, just as in the fixed-exchange-rate case, but it will not shift as far. The sectors of the Canadian economy producing raw materials will still be in recession, for there has been a reduction in demand for these products. But the overall Canadian downturn will be dampened by the depreciation of the Canadian dollar. Other exporting sectors of the Canadian economy will actually *expand* as a result of the depreciation because their products are now less expensive in world markets. Thus, as shown in part (ii) of Figure 35-6, the leftward shift of the *AD* curve will not be as large as in the case of the fixed exchange rate. The overall result is that, with a flexible exchange rate, the decline in world demand for Canadian goods leads to a less severe Canadian recession than if Canada had a fixed exchange rate.

One of the advantages of flexible exchange rates is that, in response to shocks to the terms of trade, the exchange rate can act as a shock absorber, dampening the effects of the shock on output and employment.

The Asian Crisis of 1997–1998 provides an excellent example of how Canada's flexible exchange rate dampened the effects of a negative external shock. When the Asian countries of Malaysia, Indonesia, Thailand, and South Korea experienced their large recessions in 1997 and 1998, their demand for many raw materials declined sharply. As they are major users of raw materials, the effect was felt on world markets. The average prices of raw materials fell by roughly 30 percent from the summer of 1997 to the end of 1998. Many of these raw materials, of course, are important exports for Canada, and so the decline in their world prices implied a terms-of-trade deterioration for Canada.

Especially hard hit was British Columbia's forestry sector, in which output fell dramatically in many paper and lumber mills because of the lack of sales in Asia. As expected, there was also a significant depreciation of the Canadian dollar, just as described in Figure 35-6. But as the Canadian dollar depreciated, the Canadian manufacturing sector, concentrated mainly in Ontario and Quebec, was given a large boost. The 10 percent depreciation of the Canadian dollar meant that Canadian machinery, furniture, telecommunications equipment, and a whole range of other products were now more attractive in world markets. Thus, the boom in the Central Canadian manufacturing sector offset to some extent the significant recession that was going on in British Columbia. If Canada had had a fixed exchange rate, the 10 percent depreciation would not have occurred. But the initial shock from the Asian Crisis would still have taken place. The net result would have been lower output and higher unemployment than actually occurred.

A few years later, between 2002 and 2008, the opposite forces were at work, and once again Canada's flexible exchange rate acted as a shock absorber. Because of strong global economic growth, especially in China and India, world prices for energy and other raw materials increased significantly. This was a positive shock to Canadian aggregate demand, and the price increase caused an improvement in Canada's terms of trade and an appreciation of the Canadian dollar by more than 60 percent. During this period the energy and commodity-producing sectors of the Canadian economy were booming. At the same time, however, the appreciation of the Canadian dollar tended to reduce activity in the central Canadian manufacturing sector, thus dampening the overall effect of the positive shock on the Canadian economy.

Note that having a fixed exchange rate does not prevent a country from being subjected to shocks from the rest of the world. Some advocates of fixed exchange rates seem to think that by fixing the value of a country's currency, the country is shielding itself from undesirable fluctuations. But shocks to a country's terms of trade will always occur. As long as there are changes in the demand for and supply of various products around the world, there will also be changes in a country's terms of trade. What Figure 35-6 shows, however, is that by fixing the exchange rate and thus avoiding the fluctuations in the value of the currency, the effects of the shock merely show up as increased volatility in output and employment.

> A country will always experience shocks in its terms of trade. A flexible exchange rate absorbs some of the shock, reducing the effect on output and employment. A fixed exchange rate simply redistributes the effect of the shock—the exchange rate is smoother but output and employment are more volatile.

Trade, Transaction Costs, and Uncertainty Despite the benefits of international trade, there are costs involved in exporting and importing goods and services. The *transaction costs* of international trade involve the costs associated with converting one currency to another, as must be done either by the importer or by the exporter of the product that is traded. For example, if you have an import–export business in Canada and want to import some bicycles from Japan, you will probably have to purchase Japanese yen at a bank or foreign-exchange dealer and, with those yen, pay the Japanese seller for the bicycles. Even if the Japanese seller accepts Canadian dollars for the bicycles, and this often is the case, he will be required to convert those Canadian dollars into yen before he can use that money in Japan to pay his workers or pay for other costs of production.

The greater is the volume of trade between two countries, the higher are the aggregate transaction costs associated with international trade.

Such transaction costs exist even if trade takes place between two countries with fixed exchange rates. For example, if the Bank of Canada pegged the value of the Canadian dollar to the U.S. dollar, any trade between the two countries would still require the costly conversion of one currency to the other. Thus, the existence of transaction costs cannot be used as an argument in favour of fixed exchange rates and against flexible exchange rates. As long as there are two currencies, the transaction costs must be borne by one party or the other. These transaction costs could be avoided only if the two countries shared a common currency.

Many economists believe, however, that the volatility of flexible exchange rates generates another type of cost for importers and exporters. Specifically, the unpredictability of the exchange rate leads to *uncertainty* about the profitability of any specific international transaction. Such uncertainty, given risk-averse firms, can be expected to lead to a smaller volume of international trade and thus to fewer benefits from such trade.

For example, suppose a Canadian appliance manufacturer enters into a contract to purchase a specified amount of steel from a Japanese producer for a specified yen price in one year's time. In this case, the Japanese producer bears no *foreign-exchange risk* because the price is specified in yen. But the Canadian appliance manufacturer bears considerable risk. If the yen depreciates relative to the dollar over the coming year, fewer Canadian dollars will be required to pay for the steel. But if the yen appreciates relative to the dollar over the coming year, more Canadian dollars will be required to pay for the steel. The Canadian buyer therefore faces a risk in terms of the Canadian-dollar cost of the steel. If the firm is *risk averse*, meaning simply that it would be prepared to pay a cost to avoid the risk, the presence of the risk may lead to fewer international transactions of this type. Perhaps to avoid the foreign-exchange risk, the Canadian buyer will decide instead to buy Canadian-made steel, even though it may be slightly more expensive or not quite the right type that is needed.

If the presence of foreign-exchange risk leads to less international trade, there will be a reduction in the gains from trade.

Many of the people who advocate Canada's move to a fixed exchange rate point to the avoidance of this foreign-exchange risk as the main benefit. They argue that if the Canadian dollar were pegged in value to the U.S. dollar, both importers and exporters would face less uncertainty on the most important part of their trade—that between Canada and the United States. With the greater certainty, they argue, would come greater trade flows and thus an increase in the overall gains from trade.

But many economists disagree. While accepting the basic argument regarding the risks created by flexible (and volatile) exchange rates, they note that importers and exporters already have the means to avoid this uncertainty. In particular, traders can participate in *forward markets* in which they can buy or sell foreign exchange *in the future* at prices specified today. For example, the Canadian appliance manufacturer could enter into a contract to purchase the required amount of yen in one year's time at a price specified today. In this case, no matter what happened to the yen–dollar exchange rate in the intervening year, the uncertainty regarding the Canadian-dollar price of the steel would be entirely eliminated.

Limitations for Monetary Policy One final point should be noted about the choice between flexible and fixed exchange rates. If the Bank of Canada chooses to allow the exchange rate to fluctuate in response to shocks, it can focus its monetary policy on the control of inflation. In other words, it can adjust its monetary policy—sometimes tightening and other times loosening—to keep inflation close to the stated 2 percent target. But if the Bank chooses instead to fix the exchange rate, it is not *also* able to control inflation.

As we saw in Chapter 29, the Bank of Canada conducts its monetary policy by establishing a target for the overnight interest rate and maintaining that rate through its lending and borrowing activities with the commercial banks. If the Bank chooses to intervene in the foreign-exchange market to keep the exchange rate fixed—sometimes buying foreign exchange and other times selling it—these transactions will influence the Canadian money supply directly and thus influence Canadian interest rates. But these changes in interest rates may not be consistent with the Bank's policy objective of keeping inflation close to the 2 percent target.

> Efforts by the Bank of Canada to maintain a fixed exchange rate are likely to be inconsistent with its efforts to keep inflation close to the 2 percent target.

Summing Up So, should Canada give up its flexible exchange rate and instead peg the value of the Canadian dollar to the U.S. dollar? Advocates of this policy emphasize the foreign-exchange risk faced by importers, exporters, and investors, and the gains from increased trade that would result from a fixed exchange rate. Opponents to the policy emphasize the shock-absorption benefits from a flexible exchange rate.

This debate will surely continue, partly because it is difficult to quantify the costs and benefits of a flexible exchange rate. Economists on both sides of the debate understand and accept the logic of the arguments from the other side. But researchers have so far been unable to determine how much of a shock is absorbed by a flexible exchange rate, and thus to estimate how much more volatile output and employment would be with a fixed exchange rate. Similarly, it is very difficult to estimate just how much more trade would take place if the foreign-exchange risk faced by traders were eliminated by means of a fixed exchange rate. Without convincing empirical evidence supporting the move to a fixed exchange rate, however, the status quo will probably remain. It is probably safe to assume that Canada will continue to have a flexible exchange rate, at least for the next several years.

SUMMARY

35.1 The Balance of Payments

- Actual transactions among Canadian firms, households, and governments and those in the rest of the world are reported in the balance of payments accounts. In these accounts, any transaction that represents a receipt for Canada (Canadians sell goods or assets to foreigners) is recorded as a credit item. Any transaction that represents a payment from Canada (Canadians purchase goods or assets from foreigners) is recorded as a debit item.
- Categories in the balance of payments accounts are the trade account, the capital-service account, the current account (which is equal to the trade account plus the capital-service account), and the capital account (which includes the official financing account).
- If all transactions are recorded in the balance of payments, the sum of all credit items necessarily equals the sum of all debit items. Thus, the balance of payments must always balance.
- A country with a current account deficit must also have a capital inflow—a capital account surplus. A country with a current account surplus must also have a capital outflow—a capital account deficit.

35.2 The Foreign-Exchange Market

- The exchange rate between the Canadian dollar and some foreign currency is defined as the number of Canadian dollars required to purchase one unit of the foreign currency. A rise in the exchange rate is a depreciation of the Canadian dollar; a fall in the exchange rate is an appreciation of the Canadian dollar.
- The supply of foreign exchange (or the demand for Canadian dollars) arises from Canadian exports of goods and services, capital flows into Canada, and the desire of foreign banks, firms, and governments to use Canadian dollars as part of their reserves.
- The demand for foreign exchange (or the supply of Canadian dollars to purchase foreign currencies) arises from Canadian imports of goods and services, capital flows from Canada, and the desire of holders of Canadian dollars to decrease the size of their holdings.
- A depreciation of the Canadian dollar lowers the foreign price of Canadian exports and increases the amount of foreign exchange supplied (to purchase Canadian exports). Thus, the supply curve for foreign exchange is positively sloped when plotted against the exchange rate.
- A depreciation of the Canadian dollar raises the dollar price of imports from abroad and hence lowers the amount of foreign exchange demanded to purchase foreign goods. Thus, the demand curve for foreign exchange is negatively sloped when plotted against the exchange rate.

35.3 The Determination of Exchange Rates

- When the central bank does not intervene in the foreign exchange market, there is a purely flexible exchange rate. Under fixed exchange rates, the central bank intervenes in the foreign-exchange market to maintain the exchange rate at an announced value. To do this, the central bank must hold sufficient stocks of foreign-exchange reserves.
- Under a flexible, or floating, exchange rate, the exchange rate is determined by supply of and demand for the currency.
- The Canadian dollar will appreciate in foreign-exchange markets if there is an increase in the supply of foreign exchange (an increase in the demand for Canadian dollars) or if there is a reduction in the demand for foreign exchange (a reduction in the supply of Canadian dollars). The opposite changes will lead to a depreciation of the Canadian dollar.
- Changes in the exchange rate are caused by changes in such things as changes in world prices, the rate of inflation in different countries, capital flows, structural conditions, and expectations about the future exchange rate.

35.4 Three Policy Issues

- The view that current account deficits are undesirable is usually based on the mercantilist notion that exports are "good" and imports are "bad." But the gains from trade have nothing to do with the balance of trade—they depend on the volume of trade.
- From national income accounting, the current account balance is given by

$$CA = (S - I) + (T - G)$$

- An increase in investment, a decrease in saving, and an increase in the government budget deficit can each be the cause of a rise in the current account deficit.
- With a flexible exchange rate, supply and demand in the foreign-exchange market determine the "correct" value of the exchange rate. But this "correct" value is constantly changing as market conditions vary.
- The theory of purchasing power parity (PPP) predicts that exchange rates will adjust so that the purchasing power of

a given currency is the same in different countries. That is, the prices of identical baskets of goods will be equated in different countries (when expressed in the same currency).
- If price indices from different countries are used as the basis for computing the PPP exchange rate, differences in the structure of price indices across countries, together with the presence of non-traded goods, can be responsible for persistent deviations of the actual exchange rate from this measure of the PPP exchange rate.
- An important benefit of a flexible exchange rate is that it acts as a shock absorber, dampening the effects on output and employment from shocks to a country's terms of trade.
- An important benefit of fixed exchange rates is that they reduce transaction costs and foreign-exchange risk faced by importers and exporters.

KEY CONCEPTS

Balance of payments
Current and capital accounts
Changes in official reserves
Foreign exchange and exchange rates
Appreciation and depreciation

Sources of the demand for and supply of foreign exchange
Fixed and flexible exchange rates
Mercantilism
Purchasing power parity

PPP exchange rate
Flexible exchange rates as shock absorbers
Foreign-exchange risk

STUDY EXERCISES

MyEconLab   Make the grade with MyEconLab: Study Exercises marked in red can be found on MyEconLab. You can practise them as often as you want, and most feature step-by-step guided instructions to help you find the right answer.

1. Fill in the blanks to make the following statements correct.

   a. If a wine shop in Alberta buys a case of wine from Chile, the transaction is recorded as a(n) _____ in the _____ account, which is a subsection of the _____ account.

   b. If a Canadian receives dividend payments from a firm in Britain, the transaction is recorded as a(n) _____ in the _____ account, which is a subsection of the _____ account.

   c. If a German pension-fund manager purchases a B.C. Hydro bond, the transaction is recorded as a(n) _____ in the _____ account. If a

Canadian sells her ownership stake in a newspaper chain to an American, the transaction is recorded as a(n) _____ in the _____ account.

   d. The sum of the current account and the capital account is known as the _____ and must *always* equal _____.

2. Fill in the blanks to make the following statements correct.

   a. A depreciation of the Canadian dollar means that it takes _____ Canadian dollars to purchase one unit of foreign currency, and there has been a(n) _____ in the exchange rate. An appreciation of the Canadian dollar means that it takes _____ Canadian dollars to purchase one unit of foreign currency, and there has been a(n) _____ in the exchange rate.

b. Suppose a newscaster tells us that the Canadian dollar is valued at 89.6 U.S. cents. Using the definition from this chapter, we say the Canadian–U.S. exchange rate is _____, meaning that it takes _____ Canadian dollars to buy one U.S. dollar.

c. The exchange rate is determined at the intersection of the _____ curve for foreign exchange and the _____ curve for foreign exchange. An exchange rate above this level means an excess _____ foreign exchange, which is also an excess _____ Canadian dollars. The exchange rate will _____ and the Canadian dollar will _____.

d. If there is a rise in foreign GDP, and foreign demand for Canadian goods increases, there will be a(n) _____ in supply of foreign currency. The Canadian dollar will _____.

e. An increase in Canadian prices relative to foreign prices will cause a(n) _____ in the demand for foreign exchange, and a(n) _____ in the supply of foreign exchange. The exchange rate will _____ and the Canadian dollar will therefore _____.

3. Fill in the blanks to make the following statements correct.

a. If the exchange rate is determined by the equality of supply and demand for foreign exchange and the central bank makes no foreign-exchange transactions, we say there is a(n) _____ exchange rate.

b. If the central bank buys and sells foreign exchange in an effort to maintain the exchange rate at a specific value, we say we have a(n) _____ exchange rate.

c. If the central bank pegs the exchange rate above its free-market equilibrium level, there will be a(n) _____ foreign exchange and the central bank will _____ foreign currency.

d. If the central bank pegs the exchange rate below its free-market equilibrium level, there will be a(n) _____ foreign exchange and the central bank will _____ foreign currency.

4. The table below shows Scott's financial details for 2013. Answer the following questions about his "balance of payments."

Scott's Financial Details, 2013	
Income from lifeguarding	$2 500
Income from lawn mowing	3 500
Gift from grandparents	1 000
Interest from bank deposits	150
Expenditure on coffee and pastry	1 000
Expenditure on tuition	3 500
Purchase of mutual funds	1 200
Bank balance at end of year	3 500
Increase in bank balance during the year	1 450

a. What is Scott's "trade balance"? Explain.

b. What is Scott's overall current account balance? Explain.

c. What is Scott's capital account balance? Explain.

d. There is one (and only one) piece of information shown above that is not needed to compute Scott's balance of payments. What is it? Explain why it is not needed.

5. The diagram below shows the demand for foreign currency (the supply of Canadian dollars) and the supply of foreign currency (the demand for Canadian dollars). The equilibrium exchange rate is e^*. Assume that Canada has a purely flexible exchange rate.

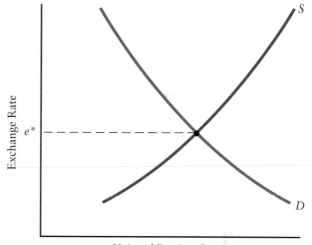

a. Show in the diagram the effect of a general inflation in Canada (when there is no inflation in the rest of the world). Explain.

b. Show what happens to the exchange rate if there is a large increase in foreign demand for Canadian telecommunications equipment. Explain.

c. Show the effect of an increase in Canadian investors' demand for Japanese government bonds. Explain.

6. What is the probable effect of each of the following on the exchange rate of a country, other things being equal?

a. The quantity of oil imports is greatly decreased, but the expenditure on imported oil is higher because of price increases.

b. The country's inflation rate falls much lower than that of its trading partners.

c. Rising labour costs of the country's manufacturers lead to a worsening ability to compete in world markets.

d. The government greatly expands its gifts of food and machinery to developing countries.

e. A major boom occurs with rising employment.

f. The central bank raises interest rates sharply.

g. More domestic oil is discovered and developed.

7. Many commentators are perplexed when they observe a depreciation of the Canadian dollar but not a reduction in the Canadian current account deficit. Explain why there is not a precise relationship between the value of the dollar and the current account balance. Give one example of an event that would give rise to each of the following:

   a. Appreciation of the Canadian dollar and a fall in Canada's current account surplus

   b. Depreciation of the Canadian dollar and a fall in Canada's current account surplus

8. The diagram below shows the demand for foreign currency (the supply of Canadian dollars) and the supply of foreign currency (the demand for Canadian dollars). The equilibrium exchange rate is e^*.

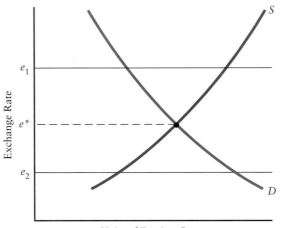

a. Suppose the Bank of Canada decides to fix the exchange rate at e_1. What must the Bank do to accomplish its goal? How do the Bank's actions show up in the balance of payments accounts?

b. In part (a), explain why some people would call this a "a balance of payments surplus" even though the balance of payments is in balance.

c. Now suppose the Bank of Canada decides to fix the exchange rate at e_2. What must the Bank do to accomplish this goal? How do the Bank's actions show up in the balance of payments accounts?

d. With the exchange rate fixed at e_2, explain why some people would call this a "balance of payments deficit" even though the balance of payments is in balance.

9. Suppose that Canadian real GDP is equal to potential output, the price level is stable, and the exchange rate is equal to e_0, its market-clearing value. There is then an upturn in the world demand for construction materials, especially lumber.

a. Draw a diagram of the foreign-exchange market. Assuming that Canada has a flexible exchange rate, show the likely effect on Canada's exchange rate of the increase in world demand for construction materials.

b. Explain the Bank of Canada's participation in the foreign-exchange market if Canada's exchange rate is fixed at e_0.

c. Now draw an *AD/AS* diagram for the Canadian economy. What is the likely effect of the shock on Canadian GDP under the conditions in part (a)?

d. On the same *AD/AS* diagram from part (c), show the effect of the shock on Canadian GDP under the conditions of part (b).

e. Explain how a flexible exchange rate acts as a shock absorber, insulating the economy from both positive and negative shocks.

10. Every few months, *The Economist* publishes its "Big Mac Index." Using the current exchange rates, it compares the U.S.-dollar price of Big Macs in several countries. It then concludes that countries in which the Big Mac is cheaper (in U.S. dollars) than in the United States have "undervalued" currencies. Similarly, countries with Big Macs more expensive than in the United States have "overvalued" currencies. The table below shows data from July 2012. (Data from **www.economist.com**.) It shows the domestic-currency prices of Big Macs in various countries. It also shows the exchange rate, expressed as the number of units of domestic currency needed to purchase one U.S. dollar.

Country	Domestic Currency Price	Exchange Rate	U.S. Dollar Price
Canada	$3.89 (Cdn.)	1.02	$___
Australia	$4.56 (Aus.)	0.97	$___
U.S.A.	$4.33	1.00	$___
Japan	320 yen	78.22	$___
Euro area	3.58 euros	0.83	$___
U.K.	2.69 pounds	0.65	$___

a. For each country, use the exchange rate provided to convert the domestic-currency price to the U.S.-dollar price. The price in terms of the currency for any country i is $P_i = e \times P_{U.S.}$.

b. By the logic used in *The Economist*, which currencies are overvalued and which are undervalued relative to the U.S. dollar?

c. Are Big Macs traded goods? If not, does this present a problem for *The Economist*? Explain.

d. Which of the following goods do you think would be a better candidate for this exercise? Explain your choice.
(**i**) cement
(**ii**) diamonds
(**iii**) fresh fruit
(**iv**) computer RAM chips

11. A former Canadian prime minister once suggested that Canada should try to have balanced trade, industry by industry.

   a. Do you think this makes sense? Explain.
   b. How about the idea of balanced trade, country by country? Explain whether this makes sense.

12. In 2007, after the Canadian dollar had appreciated significantly over the previous few years, a letter to *The Globe and Mail* said that "the economy of this once wonderful country is in the sewer and the politicians keep on tinkering, not knowing how to fix it." The letter proposed a 20 percent depreciation of the Canadian dollar and argued that the immediate effects would be (among other things)

   • a dramatic rise in exports
   • a dramatic fall in imports
   • a large net inflow of new foreign investment

   a. What could the Bank of Canada do to generate a 20 percent depreciation of the Canadian dollar?
   b. Would the action necessary in part (a) be consistent with the Bank's stated commitment to keeping inflation close to the 2 percent target? Explain.
   c. However such a depreciation of the Canadian dollar might occur, is it possible to have the three effects claimed by the author of the letter? Explain.

MyEconLab   Additional Chapter Online

The chapter **Challenges Facing the Developing Countries** can be found on the MyEconLab. www.myeconlab.com

Mathematical Notes

1. Because one cannot divide by zero, the ratio $\Delta Y/\Delta X$ cannot be evaluated when $\Delta X = 0$. However, as ΔX *approaches* zero, the ratio $\Delta Y/\Delta X$ increases without limit:

$$\lim_{\Delta X \to 0} \frac{\Delta Y}{\Delta X} = \infty$$

Therefore, we say that the slope of a vertical line (when $\Delta X = 0$ for any ΔY) is equal to infinity. (p. 46)

2. Many variables affect the quantity demanded. Using functional notation, the argument of the next several pages of the text can be anticipated. Let Q^D represent the quantity of a commodity demanded and

$$T, \overline{Y}, N, \hat{Y}, p, p_j$$

represent, respectively, tastes, average household income, population, income distribution, the commodity's own price, and the price of the jth other commodity.

The demand function is

$$Q^D = D(T, \overline{Y}, N, \hat{Y}, p, p_j), \qquad j = 1, 2, \ldots, n$$

The demand schedule or curve is given by

$$Q^D = d(p)\Big|_{T, \overline{Y}, N, \hat{Y}, p_j}$$

where the notation means that the variables to the right of the vertical line are held constant.

This function is correctly described as the demand function with respect to price, all other variables being held constant. This function, often written concisely as $Q^D = d(p)$, shifts in response to changes in other variables. Consider average income: if, as is usually hypothesized, $\partial Q^D/\partial \overline{Y} > 0$, then increases in average income shift $Q^D = d(p)$ rightward and decreases in average income shift $Q^D = d(p)$ leftward. Changes in other variables likewise shift this function in the direction implied by the relationship of that variable to the quantity demanded. (p. 56)

3. Quantity demanded is a simple and straightforward but frequently misunderstood concept in everyday use, but it has a clear mathematical meaning. It refers to the dependent variable in the demand function from note 2:

$$Q^D = D(T, \overline{Y}, N, \hat{Y}, p, p_j)$$

It takes on a specific value whenever a specific value is assigned to each of the independent variables. The value of Q^D changes whenever the value of any independent variable is changed. Q^D could change, for example, as a result of a change in any one price, in average income, in the distribution of income, in tastes, or in population. It could also change as a result of the net effect of changes in all of the independent variables occurring at once.

Some textbooks reserve the term *change in quantity demanded* for a movement along a demand curve, that is, a change in Q^D as a result *only* of a change in p. They then use other words for a change in Q^D caused by a change in the other variables in the demand function. This usage is potentially confusing because it gives the single variable Q^D more than one name.

Our usage, which corresponds to that in more advanced treatments, avoids this confusion. We call Q^D *quantity demanded* and refer to any change in Q^D as a *change in quantity demanded*. In this usage it is correct to say that a movement along a demand curve is a change in quantity demanded, but it is incorrect to say that a change in quantity demanded can occur *only because of* a movement along a demand curve (because Q^D can change for other reasons, for example, a *ceteris paribus* change in average household income). (p. 63)

4. Similar to the way we treated quantity demanded in note 2, let Q^S represent the quantity of a commodity supplied and

$$C, X, p, w_i$$

represent, respectively, producers' goals, technology, the product's price, and the price of the ith input.

The supply function is

$$Q^S = S(C, X, p, w_i), \qquad i = 1, 2, \ldots, m$$

The supply schedule or curve is given by

$$Q^S = s(p)\Big|_{C,\,X,\,w_i}$$

This is the supply function with respect to price, all other variables being held constant. This function, often written concisely as $Q^S = s(p)$, shifts in response to changes in other variables. (p. 64)

5. Equilibrium occurs where $Q^D = Q^S$. For *specified values of all other variables,* this requires that

$$d(p) = s(p) \qquad [5.1]$$

Equation 5.1 defines an equilibrium value of p; hence, although p is an *independent* or *exogenous* variable in each of the supply and demand functions, it is an *endogenous* variable in the economic model that imposes the equilibrium condition expressed in Equation 5.1. Price is endogenous because it is assumed to adjust to bring about equality between quantity demanded and quantity supplied. Equilibrium quantity, also an endogenous variable, is determined by substituting the equilibrium price into either $d(p)$ or $s(p)$.

Graphically, Equation 5.1 is satisfied only at the point where the demand and supply curves intersect. Thus, supply and demand curves are said to determine the equilibrium values of the endogenous variables, price and quantity. A shift in any of the independent variables held constant in the d and s functions will shift the demand or supply curves and lead to different equilibrium values for price and quantity. (p. 70)

6. The axis reversal arose in the following way. Alfred Marshall (1842–1924) theorized in terms of "demand price" and "supply price," which were the prices that would lead to a given quantity being demanded or supplied. Thus,

$$p^D = d(Q) \qquad [6.1]$$

$$p^S = s(Q) \qquad [6.2]$$

and the condition of equilibrium is

$$d(Q) = s(Q)$$

When graphing the behavioural relationships expressed in Equations 6.1 and 6.2, Marshall naturally put the independent variable, Q, on the horizontal axis.

Leon Walras (1834–1910), whose formulation of the working of a competitive market has become the accepted one, focused on quantity demanded and quantity supplied *at a given price.* Thus,

$$Q^D = d(p)$$

$$Q^S = s(p)$$

and the condition of equilibrium is

$$d(p) = s(p)$$

Walras did not use graphical representation. Had he done so, he would surely have placed p (his independent variable) on the horizontal axis.

Marshall's work influenced later generations of economists, in particular because he was the great popularizer of graphical analysis in economics. Today, we use his graphs, even for Walras's analysis. The axis reversal is thus one of those historical accidents that seem odd to people who did not live through the "perfectly natural" sequence of steps that produced it. (p. 71)

7. The definition in the text uses finite changes and is called *arc elasticity.* The parallel definition using derivatives is

$$\eta = \frac{dQ}{dp} \cdot \frac{p}{Q}$$

and is called *point elasticity.* Further discussion appears in the *Additional Topic* "Some Further Details About Demand Elasticity." (p. 85)

8. The propositions in the text are proved as follows. Letting *TE* stand for total expenditure, we can write

$$TE = p \cdot Q$$

It follows that the change in total expenditure is

$$dTE = Q \cdot dp + p \cdot dQ \qquad [8.1]$$

Multiplying and dividing both terms on the right-hand side of Equation 8.1 by $p \cdot Q$ yields

$$dTE = \left[\frac{dp}{p} + \frac{dQ}{Q}\right] \cdot (p \cdot Q)$$

Because dp and dQ are opposite in sign as we move along the demand curve, dTE will have the same sign as the term in brackets on the right-hand side that dominates—that is, on which percentage change is largest.

A second way of arranging Equation 8.1 is to divide both sides by dp to get

$$\frac{dTE}{dp} = Q + p \cdot \frac{dQ}{dp} \qquad [8.2]$$

From the definition of point elasticity in note 7, however,

$$Q \cdot \eta = p \cdot \frac{dQ}{dp} \qquad [8.3]$$

which we can substitute into Equation 8.1 to obtain

$$\frac{dTE}{dp} = Q + Q \cdot \eta = Q \cdot (1 + \eta) \qquad [8.4]$$

Because η is a negative number, the sign of the right-hand side of Equation 8.4 is negative if the absolute value of η exceeds unity (elastic demand) and positive if it is less than unity (inelastic demand).

Total expenditure is maximized when dTE/dp is equal to zero. As can be seen from Equation 8.4, this occurs when elasticity is equal to -1. (p. 89)

9. The distinction made between an incremental change and a marginal change is the distinction for the function $Y = Y(X)$ between $\Delta Y/\Delta X$ and the derivative dY/dX. The latter is the limit of the former as ΔX approaches zero. We shall meet this distinction repeatedly—in this chapter in reference to marginal and incremental *utility* and in later chapters with respect to such concepts as marginal and incremental *product, cost,* and *revenue.* Where Y is a function of more than one variable—for example, $Y = f(X,Z)$—the marginal relationship between Y and X is the partial derivative $\partial Y/\partial X$ rather than the total derivative dY/dX. (p. 125)

10. The hypothesis of diminishing marginal utility requires that we can measure utility of consumption by a function

$$U = U(X_1, X_2, \ldots, X_n)$$

where $X_1, \ldots, X_n$ are quantities of the n goods consumed by a household. It really embodies two utility hypotheses: first,

$$\partial U/\partial X_i > 0$$

which says that the consumer can get more utility by increasing consumption of the commodity; second,

$$\partial^2 U/\partial X_i^2 < 0$$

which says that the utility of *additional* consumption of some good declines as the amount of that good consumed increases. (p. 126)

11. Because the slope of the indifference curve is negative, it is the absolute value of the slope that declines as one moves downward to the right along the curve. The algebraic value, of course, increases. The phrase *diminishing marginal rate of substitution* thus refers to the absolute, not the algebraic, value of the slope. (p. 145)

12. The relationship between the slope of the budget line and relative prices can be seen as follows. In the two-good example with prices held constant, a change in expenditure (ΔE) is given by the equation

$$\Delta E = p_C \cdot \Delta C + p_F \cdot \Delta F \qquad [12.1]$$

Expenditure is constant for all combinations of F and C that lie on the same budget line. Thus, along such a line we have $\Delta E = 0$. This implies

$$p_C \cdot \Delta C + p_F \cdot \Delta F = 0 \qquad [12.2]$$

and thus

$$\Delta C/\Delta F = -p_F/p_C \qquad [12.3]$$

The ratio $\Delta C/\Delta F$ is the slope of the budget line. It is negative because, with a fixed budget, one must consume less C in order to consume more F. In other words, Equation 12.3 says that the negative of the slope of the budget line is the ratio of the absolute prices (i.e., the relative price). Although prices do not show directly in Figure 6A-3, they are implicit in the budget line: Its slope depends solely on the relative price, while its position, given a fixed money income, depends on the absolute prices of the two goods. (p. 147)

13. *Marginal product,* as defined in the text, is really *incremental* product. More advanced treatments distinguish between this notion and marginal product as the limit of the ratio as ΔL approaches

zero. Marginal product thus measures the rate at which total product is changing as one factor is varied and is the partial derivative of the total product with respect to the variable factor. In symbols,

$$MP = \frac{\partial TP}{\partial L}$$

(p. 164)

14. We have referred specifically both to diminishing *marginal* product and to diminishing *average* product. In most cases, eventually diminishing marginal product implies eventually diminishing average product. This is, however, not necessary, as the accompanying figure shows.

   In this case, marginal product diminishes after v units of the variable factor are employed. Because marginal product falls toward, but never quite reaches, a value of m, average product rises continually toward, but never quite reaches, the same value. (p. 166)

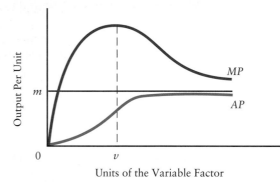

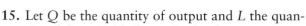

Units of the Variable Factor

15. Let Q be the quantity of output and L the quantity of the variable factor. In the short run,

$$TP = Q = f(L) \qquad [15.1]$$

We now define

$$AP = \frac{Q}{L} = \frac{f(L)}{L} \qquad [15.2]$$

$$MP = \frac{dQ}{dL} \qquad [15.3]$$

We are concerned with the relationship between AP and MP. Where average product is rising, at a maximum, or falling is determined by its derivative with respect to L:

$$\frac{d(Q/L)}{dL} = \frac{L \cdot (dQ/dL) - Q}{L^2} \qquad [15.4]$$

This may be rewritten

$$\frac{1}{L} \cdot \left[\frac{dQ}{dL} - \frac{Q}{L} \right] = \frac{1}{L} \cdot (MP - AP) \qquad [15.5]$$

Clearly, when MP is greater than AP, the expression in Equation 15.5 is positive and thus AP is rising. When MP is less than AP, AP is falling. When they are equal, AP is neither rising nor falling. (p. 166)

16. The text defines *incremental cost*. Strictly, marginal cost is the rate of change of total cost with respect to output, Q. Thus,

$$MC = \frac{dTC}{dQ}$$

From the definitions, $TC = TFC + TVC$. Fixed costs are not a function of output. Thus, we may write $TC = Z + f(Q)$, where $f(Q)$ is total variable costs and Z is a constant. From this we see that $MC = df(Q)/dQ$. MC is thus independent of the size of the fixed costs. (p. 167)

17. This point is easily seen if a little algebra is used:

$$AVC = \frac{TVC}{Q}$$

but note that $TVC = L \cdot w$ and $Q = AP \cdot L$, where L is the quantity of the variable factor used and w is its cost per unit. Therefore,

$$AVC = \frac{L \cdot w}{AP \cdot L} = \frac{w}{AP}$$

Because w is a constant, it follows that AVC and AP vary inversely with each other, and when AP is at its maximum value, AVC must be at its minimum value. (p. 170)

18. A little elementary calculus will prove the point:

$$MC = \frac{dTC}{dQ} = \frac{dTVC}{dQ} = \frac{d(L \cdot w)}{dQ}$$

If w does not vary with output,

$$MC = \frac{dL}{dQ} \cdot w$$

However, referring to note 15 (Equation 15.3), we see that

$$\frac{dL}{dQ} = \frac{1}{MP}$$

Thus,

$$MC = \frac{w}{MP}$$

Because w is fixed, MC varies negatively with MP. When MP is at a maximum, MC is at a minimum. (p. 170)

19. Strictly speaking, the marginal rate of substitution refers to the slope of the tangent to the isoquant at a particular point, whereas the calculations in Table 8A-1 refer to the average rate of substitution between two distinct points on the isoquant. Assume a production function

$$Q = Q(K,L) \qquad [19.1]$$

Isoquants are given by the function

$$K = I(L, \overline{Q}) \qquad [19.2]$$

derived from Equation 19.1 by expressing K as an explicit function of L and Q. A single isoquant relates to a particular level of output, $\overline{Q}$. Define Q_K and Q_L as an alternative, more compact notation for $\partial Q/\partial K$ and $\partial Q/\partial L$, the marginal products of capital and labour. Also, let Q_{KK} and Q_{LL} stand for $\partial^2 Q/\partial K^2$ and $\partial^2 Q/\partial L^2$, respectively. To obtain the slope of the isoquant, totally differentiate Equation 19.1 to obtain

$$dQ = Q_K.dK + Q_L \cdot dL$$

Then, because we are moving along a single isoquant, set $dQ = 0$ to obtain

$$\frac{dK}{dL} = -\frac{Q_L}{Q_K} = MRS$$

Diminishing marginal productivity implies $Q_{LL} < 0$ and $Q_{KK} < 0$, and hence, as we move down the isoquant of Figure 8A-1, Q_K is rising and Q_L is falling, so the absolute value of MRS is diminishing. This is called the *hypothesis of a diminishing marginal rate of substitution*. (p. 195)

20. Formally, the problem is to choose K and L in order to maximize

$$Q = Q(K, L)$$

subject to the constraint

$$p_K \cdot K + p_L \cdot L = C$$

To do this, form the Lagrangean,

$$\mathscr{L} = Q(K,L) - \lambda(p_K \cdot K + p_L \cdot L - C)$$

where λ is called the Lagrange multiplier.

The first-order conditions for this maximization problem are

$$Q_K = \lambda \cdot p_K \qquad [20.1]$$

$$Q_L = \lambda \cdot p_L \qquad [20.2]$$

$$p_K \cdot K + p_L \cdot L = C \qquad [20.3]$$

Dividing Equation 20.1 by Equation 20.2 yields

$$\frac{Q_K}{Q_L} = \frac{p_K}{p_L}$$

That is, the ratio of the marginal products, which is -1 times the MRS, is equal to the ratio of the factor prices, which is -1 times the slope of the isocost line. (p. 197)

21. Marginal revenue is mathematically the derivative of total revenue with respect to output, dTR/dQ. Incremental revenue is $\Delta TR/\Delta Q$. However, the term *marginal revenue* is used loosely to refer to both concepts. (p. 205)

22. For notes 22 through 24, it is helpful first to define some terms. Let

$$\pi_n = TR_n - TC_n$$

where π_n is the profit when Q_n units are sold.

If the firm is maximizing its profits by producing Q_n units, its profits must be at least as large as the profits at output zero.

That is,

$$\pi_n \geq \pi_0 \qquad [22.1]$$

This condition says that profits from producing must be greater than profits from not producing. Condition 22.1 can be rewritten as

$$TR_n - TVC_n - TFC_n$$
$$\geq TR_0 - TVC_0 - TFC_0 \qquad [22.2]$$

However, note that by definition

$$TR_0 = 0 \qquad [22.3]$$

$$TVC_0 = 0 \qquad [22.4]$$

$$TFC_n = TFC_0 = Z \qquad [22.5]$$

where Z is a constant. By substituting Equations 22.3, 22.4, and Equation 22.5 into Condition 22.2, we get

$$TR_n - TVC_n \geq 0$$

from which we obtain

$$TR_n \geq TVC_n$$

This proves Rule 1.

On a per-unit basis, it becomes

$$\frac{TR_n}{Q_n} \geq \frac{TVC_n}{Q_n} \qquad [22.6]$$

where Q_n is the number of units produced.

Because $TR_n = Q_n \times p_n$, where p_n is the price when n units are sold, Condition 22.6 may be rewritten as

$$p_n \geq AVC_n$$

(p. 207)

23. Using elementary calculus, we may prove Rule 2.

$$\pi_n = TR_n - TC_n$$

each of which is a function of output Q. To maximize π, it is necessary that

$$\frac{d\pi}{dQ} = 0 \qquad [23.1]$$

and that

$$\frac{d^2\pi}{dQ^2} < 0 \qquad [23.2]$$

From the definitions,

$$\frac{d\pi}{dQ} = \frac{dTR}{dQ} - \frac{dTC}{dQ} = MR - MC \quad [23.3]$$

From Equations 23.1 and 23.3, a necessary condition for attaining maximum π is $MR - MC = 0$, or $MR = MC$, as is required by Rule 2. (p. 208)

24. To prove that for a negatively sloped demand curve, marginal revenue is less than price, let $p = p(Q)$. Then

$$TR = p \cdot Q = p(Q) \cdot Q$$

$$MR = \frac{dTR}{dQ} = Q \cdot \frac{dp}{dQ} + p$$

For a negatively sloped demand curve, dp/dQ is negative, and thus MR is less than price for positive values of Q. (p. 229)

25. The equation for a downward-sloping straight-line demand curve with price on the vertical axis is

$$p = a - b \cdot Q$$

where a is the vertical intercept (when $Q=0$) and $-b$ is the slope of the demand curve. Total revenue is price times quantity:

$$TR = p \cdot Q = a \cdot Q - b \cdot Q^2$$

Marginal revenue is

$$MR = \frac{dTR}{dQ} = a - 2 \cdot b \cdot Q$$

Thus, the MR curve and the demand curve are both straight lines, they have the same vertical intercept (a), and the (absolute value of the) slope of the MR curve ($2b$) is twice that of the demand curve (b). (p. 230)

26. The marginal revenue produced by the factor involves two elements: first, the additional output that an extra unit of the factor produces and, second, the change in price of the product that the extra output causes. Let Q be output, R revenue, and L the number of units of the variable factor hired. The contribution to revenue of additional labour is $\partial R / \partial L$. This, in turn, depends on the contribution of the extra labour to output $\partial Q / \partial L$ (the marginal product of the factor) and $\partial R / \partial Q$ (the firm's marginal revenue from the extra output). Thus,

$$\frac{\partial R}{\partial L} = \frac{\partial Q}{\partial L} \cdot \frac{\partial R}{\partial Q}$$

We define the left-hand side as marginal revenue product, MRP. Thus,

$$MRP = MP \cdot MR$$

(p. 311)

27. The proposition that the marginal labour cost is above the average labour cost when the average is rising is essentially the same mathematical proposition proved in note 15. Nevertheless, let us do it again, using elementary calculus.

The quantity of labour supplied depends on the wage rate: $L^s = f(w)$. Total labour cost along the supply curve is $w \cdot L^s$. The average cost of labour is $(w \cdot L^s)/L^s = w$. The marginal cost of labour is

$$\frac{d(w \cdot L^s)}{dL^s} = w + L^s \cdot \frac{dw}{dL^s}$$

Rewrite this as

$$MC = AC + L^s \cdot \frac{dw}{dL^s}$$

As long as the supply curve slopes upward, $dw/dL^s > 0$; therefore, $MC > AC$. (p. 345)

28. In the text, we define MPC as an incremental ratio. For mathematical treatment, it is sometimes convenient to define all marginal concepts as derivatives: $MPC = dC/dY_D$, $MPS = dS/dY_D$, and so on. (p. 524)

29. The basic relationship is

$$Y_D = C + S$$

Dividing through by Y_D yields

$$\frac{Y_D}{Y_D} = \frac{C}{Y_D} + \frac{S}{Y_D}$$

and thus

$$1 = APC + APS$$

Next, take the first difference of the basic relationship to get

$$\Delta Y_D = \Delta C + \Delta S$$

Dividing through by ΔY_D gives

$$\frac{\Delta Y_D}{\Delta Y_D} = \frac{\Delta C}{\Delta Y_D} + \frac{\Delta S}{\Delta Y_D}$$

and thus

$$1 = MPC + MPS$$

(p. 525)

30. The total expenditure over all rounds is the sum of an infinite series. If we let A stand for autonomous expenditure and z for the marginal propensity to spend, the change in autonomous expenditure is ΔA in the first round, $z \cdot \Delta A$ in the second, $z^2 \cdot \Delta A$ in the third, and so on. This can be written as

$$\Delta A \cdot (1 + z + z^2 + \ldots + z^n)$$

If z is less than 1, the series in parentheses converges to $1/(1 - z)$ as n approaches infinity. The total change in expenditure is thus $\Delta A/(1 - z)$. In the example in the box, $z = 0.80$; therefore, the change in total expenditure is

$$\frac{\Delta A}{1 - z} = \frac{\Delta A}{0.2} = 5 \cdot \Delta A$$

(p. 538)

31. The "rule of 72" says that any sum growing at the rate of X percent per year will double in approximately $72/X$ years. For two sums growing at the rates of X percent and Y percent per year, the *difference* between the two sums will double in approximately $72/(X - Y)$ years. The rule of 72 is only an approximation, but at low annual rates of growth it is extremely accurate. (pp. 622, 634)

32. A simple example of a production function is $GDP = z(LK)^{1/2}$. This equation says that to find the amount of GDP produced, multiply the amount of labour by the amount of capital, take the square root, and multiply the result by the constant z. This production function has positive but diminishing marginal returns to either factor. This can be seen by evaluating the first and second partial derivatives and showing the first derivatives to be positive and the second derivatives to be negative.

For example,

$$\frac{\partial GDP}{\partial K} = \frac{z \cdot L^{1/2}}{2 \cdot K^{1/2}} > 0$$

and

$$\frac{\partial^2 GDP}{\partial K^2} = -\frac{z \cdot L^{1/2}}{4 \cdot K^{3/2}} < 0$$

(p. 644)

33. The production function $GDP = z(LK)^{1/2}$ displays constant returns to scale. To see this, multiply both L and K by the same constant, θ, and see that this multiplies the whole value of GDP by θ:

$$z(\theta L \cdot \theta K)^{1/2} = z(\theta^2 \cdot LK)^{1/2} = \theta z(LK)^{1/2} = \theta \cdot GDP$$

(p. 646)

34. This is easily proved. The banking system wants sufficient deposits (D) to establish the target ratio

(v) of deposits to reserves (R). This gives $R/D = v$. Any change in D of size ΔD has to be accompanied by a change in R of ΔR of sufficient size to restore v. Thus, $\Delta R/\Delta D = v$, so $\Delta D = \Delta R/v$ and $\Delta D/\Delta R = 1/v$. This can be shown also in terms of the deposits created by the sequence in Table 27-7. Let v be the reserve ratio and $e = 1 - v$ be the excess reserves per dollar of new deposits. If X dollars are initially deposited in the system, the successive rounds of new deposits will be X, eX, e^2X, e^3X, ... The series

$$X + eX + e^2X + e^3X + \ldots$$
$$= X \cdot [1 + e + e^2 + e^3 + \ldots]$$

has a limit of $X \cdot \dfrac{1}{1 - e}$

$$= X \cdot \frac{1}{1 - (1 - v)} = \frac{X}{v}$$

This is the total new deposits created by an injection of \$$X$ of new reserves into the banking system. For example, when $v = 0.20$, an injection of \$100 into the system will lead to an overall increase in deposits of \$500. (p. 681)

35. Suppose that the public wants to hold a fraction, c, of deposits in cash, C. Now suppose that X dollars are injected into the system. Ultimately, this money will be held either as reserves by the banking system or as cash by the public. Thus, we have

$$\Delta C + \Delta R = X$$

From the banking system's reserve behaviour, we have $\Delta R = v \cdot \Delta D$, and from the public's cash behaviour, we have $\Delta C = c \cdot \Delta D$. Substituting into the above equation, we get the result that

$$\Delta D = \frac{X}{v + c}$$

From this we can also relate the change in reserves and the change in cash holdings to the initial injection:

$$\Delta R = \frac{v}{v + c} \cdot X$$
$$\Delta C = \frac{c}{v + c} \cdot X$$

For example, when $v = 0.20$ and $c = 0.05$, an injection of \$100 will lead to an increase in reserves of \$80, an increase in cash in the hands of the public of \$20, and an increase in deposits of \$400. (p. 682)

36. Let d be the government's debt-to-GDP ratio and let Δd be the annual change in d. The percentage change in d over the year is therefore $\Delta d/d$, which for small percentage changes is very closely approximated by

$$\Delta d/d = \Delta D/D - \Delta \text{GDP}/\text{GDP}$$

where ΔD is the budget deficit and is equal to $G - T + iD$. The second term is the percentage change in *nominal* GDP, which is approximately equal to $g + n$, where g is the growth rate of real GDP and π is the rate of inflation. We therefore rewrite the expression as

$$\Delta d/d = (G - T + iD)/D - (g + \pi)$$

Now, multiply both sides by d to get:

$$\Delta d = (G - T + iD)/\text{GDP} - (g + \pi)d$$

We can now let x be the primary budget deficit ($G - T$) as a share of GDP. The equation then becomes

$$\Delta d = x + (i - \pi - g)d$$

Finally, note that the real interest rate on government bonds is $r = i - \pi$, and so our final equation becomes

$$\Delta d = x + (r - g)d$$

(p. 809)

Photo Credits

Timeline of Great Economists

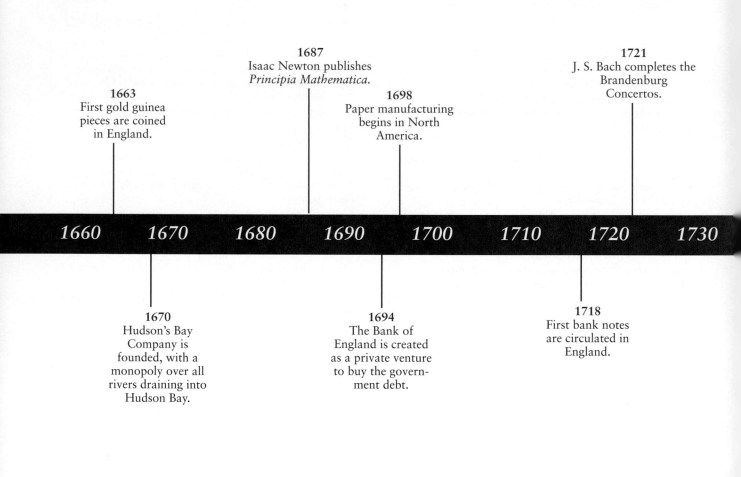

1687
Isaac Newton publishes
Principia Mathematica.

1721
J. S. Bach completes the
Brandenburg
Concertos.

1663
First gold guinea
pieces are coined
in England.

1698
Paper manufacturing
begins in North
America.

1660   1670   1680   1690   1700   1710   1720   1730

1670
Hudson's Bay
Company is
founded, with a
monopoly over all
rivers draining into
Hudson Bay.

1694
The Bank of
England is created
as a private venture
to buy the govern-
ment debt.

1718
First bank notes
are circulated in
England.

ADAM SMITH   *(1723–1790)*

Adam Smith was born in 1723 in the small Scottish town of Kirkcaldy. He is perhaps the single most influential figure in the development of modern economics, and even those who have never studied economics know of his most famous work, *The Wealth of Nations,* and are familiar with the terms *laissez-faire* and the *invisible hand,* both attributable to Smith. He described the workings of the capitalist market economy, the division of labour in production, the role of money, free trade, and the nature of economic growth. Even today, the breadth of his scholarship is considered astounding.

Smith was raised by his mother, as his father had died before his birth. His intellectual promise was discovered early, and at age 14 Smith was sent to study at Glasgow and then at Oxford. He returned to an appointment as professor of moral philosophy at University of Glasgow, where he became one of the leading philosophers of his day. He lectured on natural theology, ethics, jurisprudence, and political economy to students who travelled from as far away as Russia to hear his lectures.

In 1759, Smith published *The Theory of Moral Sentiments,* in which he attempted to identify the origins of moral judgment. In this early work, Smith writes of the motivation of self-interest and of the morality that keeps it in check. After its publication, Smith left his post at the University of Glasgow to embark on a European tour as the tutor to a young aristocrat, the Duke of Buccleuch, with whom he travelled for two years. In exchange for this assignment Smith was provided with a salary for the remainder of his life. He returned to the small town of his birth and spent the next 10 years alone, writing his most famous work.

An Inquiry into the Nature and Causes of the Wealth of Nations was published in 1776. His contributions in this book (generally known as *The Wealth of Nations*) were revolutionary, and the text became the foundation for much of modern economics. It continues to be reprinted today. Smith rejected the notion that a country's supply of gold and silver was the measure of its wealth—rather, it was the real incomes of the people that determined national wealth. Growth in the real incomes of the country's citizens—that is, economic growth—would result from specialization in production, the division of labour, and the use of money to facilitate trade. Smith provided a framework for analyzing the questions of income growth, value, and distribution.

Smith's work marked the beginning of what is called the Classical period in economic thought, which continued for the next 75 years. This school of thought was centred on the principles of natural liberty (laissez-faire) and the importance of economic growth as a means of bettering the conditions of human existence.

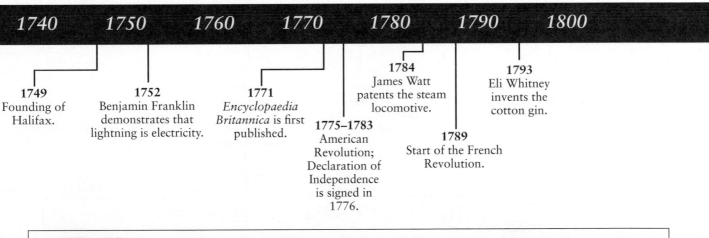

| 1740 | 1750 | 1760 | 1770 | 1780 | 1790 | 1800 |

1784
James Watt patents the steam locomotive.

1793
Eli Whitney invents the cotton gin.

1749
Founding of Halifax.

1752
Benjamin Franklin demonstrates that lightning is electricity.

1771
Encyclopaedia Britannica is first published.

1775–1783
American Revolution; Declaration of Independence is signed in 1776.

1789
Start of the French Revolution.

THOMAS MALTHUS   *(1766–1834)*

Thomas Malthus was born into a reasonably well-to-do English family. He was educated at Cambridge, and from 1805 until his death he held the first British professorship of political economy in the East India Company's college at Haileybury. In 1798 he published *An Essay on the Principle of Population as It Affects the Future Improvement of Society,* which was revised many times in subsequent years until finally he published *A Summary View of the Principle of Population* in 1830.

It is these essays on population for which Malthus is best known. His first proposition was that population, when unchecked, would increase in a geometric progression such that the population would double every 25 years. His second proposition was that the means of subsistence (i.e., the food supply) cannot possibly increase faster than in arithmetic progression (increasing by a given number of units every year). The result would be population growth eventually outstripping food production, and thus abject poverty and suffering for the majority of people in every society.

Malthus's population theory had tremendous intellectual influence at the time and became an integral part of the Classical theory of income distribution. However, it is no longer taken as a good description of current or past trends.

DAVID RICARDO   *(1772–1823)*

David Ricardo was born in London to parents who had emigrated from the Netherlands. Ricardo's father was very successful in money markets, and Ricardo himself was very wealthy before he was 30 by earning money on the stock exchange. He had little formal education, but after reading Adam Smith's *The Wealth of Nations* in 1799, he chose to divide his time between studying and writing about political economy and increasing his own personal wealth.

Ricardo's place in the history of economics was assured by his achievement in constructing an abstract model of how capitalism worked. He built an analytic "system" using deductive reasoning that characterizes economic theorizing to the present day. The three critical principles in Ricardo's system were (1) the theory of rent, (2) Thomas Malthus's population principle, and (3) the wages-fund doctrine. Ricardo published *The Principles of Political Economy and Taxation* in 1817, and the work dominated Classical economics for the following half-century.

Ricardo also contributed the concept of comparative advantage to the study of international trade. Ricardo's theories regarding the gains from trade had some influence on the repeal of the British Corn Laws in 1846—tariffs on the importation of grains into Great Britain—and the subsequent transformation of that country during the nineteenth century from a country of high tariffs to one of completely free trade.

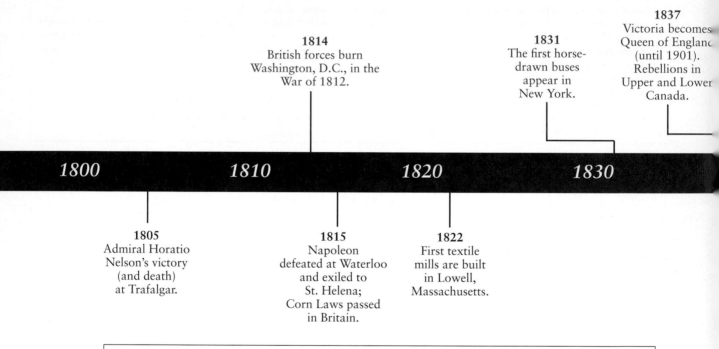

1814
British forces burn
Washington, D.C., in the
War of 1812.

1831
The first horse-
drawn buses
appear in
New York.

1837
Victoria becomes
Queen of England
(until 1901).
Rebellions in
Upper and Lower
Canada.

1800   1810   1820   1830

1805
Admiral Horatio
Nelson's victory
(and death)
at Trafalgar.

1815
Napoleon
defeated at Waterloo
and exiled to
St. Helena;
Corn Laws passed
in Britain.

1822
First textile
mills are built
in Lowell,
Massachusetts.

JOHN STUART MILL   *(1806–1873)*

John Stuart Mill, born in London, was the son of James Mill, a prominent British historian, economist, and philosopher. By age 12 he was acquainted with the major economics works of the day, and at 13 he was correcting the proofs of his father's book, *Elements of Political Economy*. J. S. Mill spent most of his life working at the East India Company—his extraordinarily prolific writing career was conducted entirely as an aside. In 1848 he published his *Principles of Political Economy,* which updated the principles found in Adam Smith's *The Wealth of Nations* and which remained the basic textbook for students of economics until the end of the nineteenth century. In *Principles,* Mill made an important contribution to the economics discipline by distinguishing between the economics of production and of distribution. He pointed out that economic laws had nothing to do with the distribution of wealth, which was a societal matter, but had everything to do with production.

Previous to Mill's *Principles* was his *System of Logic* (1843), which was the century's most influential text on logic and the theory of knowledge. His essays on ethics, contemporary culture, and freedom of speech, such as *Utilitarianism* and *On Liberty,* are still widely studied today.

KARL MARX *(1818–1883)*

Karl Marx was born in Trier, Germany (then part of Prussia), and studied law, history, and philosophy at the universities of Bonn, Berlin, and Jena. Marx travelled between Prussia, Paris, and Brussels, working at various jobs until finally settling in London in 1849, where he lived the remainder of his life. Most of his time was spent in the mainly unpaid pursuits of writing and studying economics in the library of the British Museum. Marx's contributions to economics are intricately bound to his views of history and society. *The Communist Manifesto* was published with Friedrich Engels in 1848, his *Critique of Political Economy* was published in 1859, and in 1867 the first volume of *Das Kapital* was completed. (The remaining volumes, edited by Engels, were published after Marx's death.)

For Marx, capitalism was a stage in an evolutionary process from a primitive agricultural economy toward an inevitable elimination of private property and the class structure. Marx's "labour theory of value," whereby the quantity of labour used in the manufacture of a product determined its value, held the central place in his economic thought. He believed that the worker provided "surplus value" to the capitalist. The capitalist would then use the profit arising from this surplus value to reinvest in plant and machinery. Through time, more would be spent for plant and machinery than for wages, which would lead to lower profits (since profits arose only from the surplus value from labour) and a resulting squeeze in the real income of workers. Marx believed that in the capitalists' effort to maintain profits in this unstable system, there would emerge a "reserve army of the unemployed." The resulting class conflict would become increasingly acute until revolution by the workers would overthrow capitalism.

1859
Charles Darwin publishes *On the Origin of Species*.

1846
Britain repeals the Corn Laws.

1867
British North America Act establishes the Dominion of Canada. Alfred Nobel invents dynamite.

1840   1850   1860   1870

1844
Electric telegraph opens between Washington and Baltimore.

1861–1865
The U.S. Civil War; Abraham Lincoln is assassinated in 1865.

1869
Opening of the Suez Canal.

1840
Act of Union unites Upper and Lower Canada.

LEON WALRAS *(1834–1910)*

Leon Walras was born in France, the son of an economist. After being trained inauspiciously in engineering and performing poorly in mathematics, Walras spent some time pursuing other endeavours, such as novel writing and working for the railway. Eventually he promised his father he would study economics, and by 1870 he was given a professorship in economics in the Faculty of Law at the University of Lausanne in Switzerland. Once there, Walras began the feverish activity that eventually led to his important contributions to economic theory.

In the 1870s, Walras was one of three economists to put forward the marginal utility theory of value (simultaneously with William Stanley Jevons of England and Carl Menger of Austria). Further, he constructed a mathematical model of general equilibrium using a system of simultaneous equations that he used to argue that equilibrium prices and quantities are uniquely determined. Central to general equilibrium analysis is the notion that the prices and quantities of all commodities are determined simultaneously because the whole system is interdependent. Walras's most important work was *Elements of Pure Economics*, published in 1874. In addition to all of Walras's other accomplishments in economics (and despite his early poor performance in mathematics!), we today regard him as the founder of mathematical economics.

Leon Walras and Alfred Marshall are regarded by many economists as the two most important economic theorists who ever lived. Much of the framework of economic theory studied today is either Walrasian or Marshallian in character.

CARL MENGER   *(1840–1921)*

Carl Menger was born in Galicia (then part of Austria), and he came from a family of Austrian civil servants and army officers. After studying law in Prague and Vienna, he turned to economics and in 1871 published *Grundsatze der Volkswirtschaftslehre* (translated as *Principles of Economics*), for which he became famous. He held a professorship at the University of Vienna until 1903. Menger was the founder of a school of thought known as the "Austrian School," which effectively displaced the German historical method on the continent and which survives today as an alternative to mainstream Neoclassical economics.

Menger was one of three economists in the 1870s who independently put forward a theory of value based on marginal utility. Prior to what economists now call the "marginal revolution," value was thought to be derived solely from the inputs of labour and capital. Menger developed the marginal utility theory of value, in which the value of any good is determined by individuals' subjective evaluations of that good. According to Menger, a good has some value if it has the ability to satisfy some human want or desire, and *utility* is the capacity of the good to do so. Menger went on to develop the idea that the individual will maximize total utility at the point where the last unit of each good consumed provides equal utility—that is, where marginal utilities are equal.

Menger's emphasis on the marginal utility theory of value led him to focus on consumption rather than production as the determinant of price. Menger focused only on the demand for goods and largely ignored the supply. It would remain for Alfred Marshall and Leon Walras to combine demand and supply for a more complete picture of price determination.

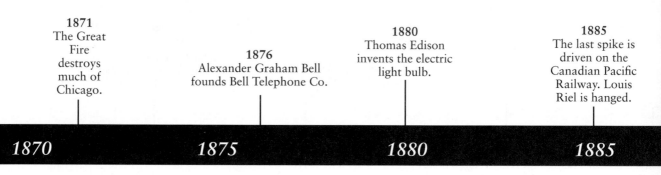

1871
The Great Fire destroys much of Chicago.

1876
Alexander Graham Bell founds Bell Telephone Co.

1880
Thomas Edison invents the electric light bulb.

1885
The last spike is driven on the Canadian Pacific Railway. Louis Riel is hanged.

1870   *1875*   *1880*   *1885*

ALFRED MARSHALL   *(1842–1924)*

Alfred Marshall was born in Clapham, England, the son of a bank cashier, and was descended from a long line of clerics. Marshall's father, despite intense effort, was unable to steer the young Marshall into the church. Instead, Marshall followed his passion for mathematics at Cambridge and chose economics as a field of study after reading J. S. Mill's *Principles of Political Economy*. His career was then spent mainly at Cambridge, where he taught economics to John Maynard Keynes, Arthur Pigou, Joan Robinson, and countless other British theorists in the "Cambridge tradition." His *Principles of Economics,* published in 1890, replaced Mill's *Principles* as the dominant economics textbook of English-speaking universities.

Marshall institutionalized modern marginal analysis, the basic concepts of supply and demand, and perhaps most importantly the notion of economic equilibrium resulting from the interaction of supply and demand. He also pioneered partial equilibrium analysis—examining the forces of supply and demand in a particular market provided that all other influences can be excluded, *ceteris paribus*.

Although many of the ideas had been put forward by earlier writers, Marshall was able to synthesize the previous analyses of utility and cost and present a thorough and complete statement of the laws of demand and supply. Marshall refined and developed microeconomic theory to such a degree that much of what he wrote would be familiar to students of this textbook today.

It is also interesting to note that although Alfred Marshall and Leon Walras were simultaneously expanding the frontiers of economic theory, there was almost no communication between the two men. Though Marshall chose partial equilibrium analysis as the appropriate method for dealing with selected markets in a complex world, he did acknowledge the correctness of Walras's general equilibrium system. Walras, on the other hand, was adamant (and sometimes rude) in his opposition to the methods that Marshall was putting forward. History has shown that both the partial and the general equilibrium approaches to economic analysis are required for understanding the functioning of the economy.

THORSTEIN VEBLEN (1857–1929)

Thorstein Veblen was born on a farm in Wisconsin to Norwegian parents. He received his Ph.D. in philosophy from Yale University, after which he returned to his father's farm because he was unable to secure an academic position. For seven years he remained there, reading voraciously on economics and other social sciences. Eventually, he took academic positions at the University of Chicago, Stanford University, the University of Missouri, and the New School for Social Research (in New York). Veblen was the founder of "institutional economics," the only uniquely North American school of economic thought.

In 1899, Veblen published *The Theory of the Leisure Class,* in which he sought to apply Charles Darwin's evolutionism to the study of modern economic life. He examined problems in the social institutions of the day, and savagely criticized Classical and Neoclassical economic analysis. Although Veblen failed to shift the path of mainstream economic analysis, he did contribute the idea of the importance of long-run institutional studies as a useful complement to short-run price theory analysis. He also reminded the profession that economics is a *social* science, and not merely a branch of mathematics.

Veblen remains most famous today for his idea of "conspicuous consumption." He observed that some commodities were consumed not for their intrinsic qualities but because they carried snob appeal. He suggested that the more expensive such a commodity became, the greater might be its ability to confer status on its purchaser.

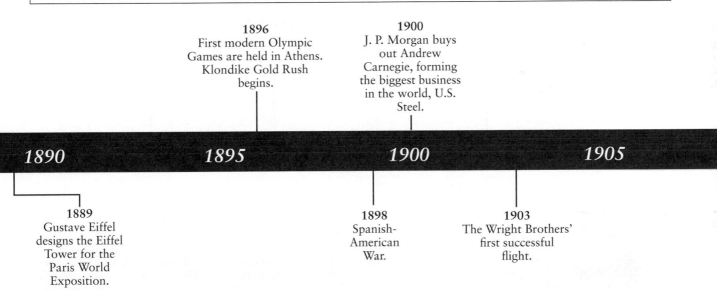

1896
First modern Olympic Games are held in Athens. Klondike Gold Rush begins.

1900
J. P. Morgan buys out Andrew Carnegie, forming the biggest business in the world, U.S. Steel.

1890   1895   1900   1905

1889
Gustave Eiffel designs the Eiffel Tower for the Paris World Exposition.

1898
Spanish-American War.

1903
The Wright Brothers' first successful flight.

VILFREDO PARETO (1848–1923)

Vilfredo Pareto was an Italian, born in Paris, and was trained to be an engineer. Though he actually practised as an engineer, he would later succeed Leon Walras to the Chair of Economics in the Faculty of Law at the University of Lausanne.

Pareto built on the system of general equilibrium that Walras had developed. In his *Cours d'économie politique* (1897) and his *Manuel d'économie politique* (1906), Pareto set forth the foundations of modern welfare economics. He showed that theories of consumer behaviour and exchange could be constructed on assumptions of ordinal utility, rather than cardinal utility, eliminating the need to compare one person's utility with another's. Using the indifference curve analysis developed by F. Y. Edgeworth, Pareto was able to demonstrate that total welfare could be increased by an exchange if one person could be made better off without anyone else becoming worse off. Pareto applied this analysis to consumption and exchange as well as to production. Pareto's contributions in this area are remembered in economists' references to *Pareto optimality* and *Pareto efficiency.*

JOSEPH SCHUMPETER   *(1883–1950)*

Joseph Schumpeter was born in Triesch, Moravia (now in the Czech Republic). He was a university professor and later a minister of finance in Austria. In 1932, he emigrated to the United States to avoid the rise to power of Adolf Hitler. He spent his remaining years at Harvard University.

Schumpeter, a pioneering theorist of innovation, emphasized the role of the entrepreneur in economic development. The existence of the entrepreneur meant continuous innovation and waves of adaptation to changing technology. He is best known for his theory of "creative destruction," where the prospect of monopoly profits provides owners the incentive to finance inventions and innovations. One monopoly can replace another with superior technology or a superior product, thereby circumventing the entry barriers of a monopolized industry. He criticized mainstream economists for emphasizing the static (allocative) efficiency of perfect competition—a market structure that would, if it could ever be achieved, retard technological change and economic growth.

Schumpeter's best known works are *The Theory of Economic Development* (1911), *Business Cycles* (1939), and *Capitalism, Socialism and Democracy* (1943).

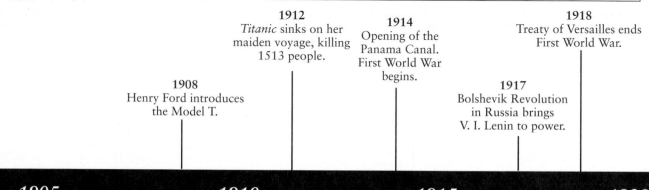

1912
Titanic sinks on her maiden voyage, killing 1513 people.

1914
Opening of the Panama Canal. First World War begins.

1918
Treaty of Versailles ends First World War.

1908
Henry Ford introduces the Model T.

1917
Bolshevik Revolution in Russia brings V. I. Lenin to power.

1905   **1910**   **1915**   **1920**

JOHN MAYNARD KEYNES   *(1883–1946)*

John Maynard Keynes was born in Cambridge, England. His parents were both intellectuals, and his father, John Neville Keynes, was a famous logician and writer on economic methodology. The young Keynes was educated at Eton and then at Kings College, Cambridge, where he was a student of Alfred Marshall and Arthur Pigou. His career included appointments to the Treasury in Britain during both world wars, a leading role in the establishment of the International Monetary Fund (through discussions at Bretton Woods, New Hampshire, in 1944), and editorship of the *Economic Journal* from 1911 to 1945, all in addition to his academic position at Kings College.

Keynes published extensively during his life, but his most influential work, *The General Theory of Employment, Interest, and Money,* appeared in 1936. This book was published in the midst of the Great Depression when the output of goods and services had fallen drastically, unemployment was intolerably high, and it had become clear to many that the market would not self-adjust to achieve potential output within an acceptable period of time. Fluctuations in economic activity were familiar at this point, but the failure of the economy to recover rapidly from this depression was unprecedented. Neoclassical economists held that during a downturn both wages and the interest rate would fall low enough to induce investment and employment and bring about a recovery. They believed that the persistent unemployment during the 1930s was caused by inflexible wages and they recommended that workers be convinced to accept wage cuts.

Keynes believed that this policy, though perhaps correct for a single industry, was not correct for the entire economy. Widespread wage cuts would reduce the consumption portion of aggregate demand, which would offset any increase in employment. Keynes argued that unemployment could be cured only by manipulating aggregate demand, whereby increased demand (through government expenditure) would increase the price level, reduce real wages, and thereby stimulate employment.

Keynes's views found acceptance after the publication of his *General Theory* and had a profound effect on government policy around the world, particularly in the 1940s, 1950s, and 1960s. As we know from this textbook, Keynes's name is associated with much of macroeconomics, from its basic theory to the Keynesian short-run aggregate supply curve and the Keynesian consumption function. His contributions to economics go well beyond what can be mentioned in a few paragraphs—in effect, he laid the foundations for modern macroeconomics.

EDWARD CHAMBERLIN *(1899–1967)*

Edward Chamberlin was born in La Conner, Washington, and received his Ph.D. from Harvard University in 1927. He became a full professor at Harvard in 1937 and stayed there until his retirement in 1966. He published *The Theory of Monopolistic Competition* in 1933.

Before Chamberlin's book (which appeared more or less simultaneously with Joan Robinson's *The Economics of Imperfect Competition*), the models of perfect competition and monopoly had been fairly well worked out. Though economists were aware of a middle ground between these two market structures and some analysis of duopoly (two sellers) had been presented, it was Chamberlin and Robinson who closely examined this problem of imperfect markets.

Chamberlin's main contribution was explaining the importance of product differentiation for firms in market structures between perfect competition and monopoly. Chamberlin saw that though there may be a large number of firms in the market (the competitive element), each firm created for itself a unique product or advantage that gave it some control over price (the monopoly element). Specifically, he identified items such as copyrights, trademarks, brand names, and location as monopoly elements behind a product. Though Alfred Marshall regarded price as the only variable in question, Chamberlin saw both price and the product itself as variables under control of the firm in monopolistically competitive markets.

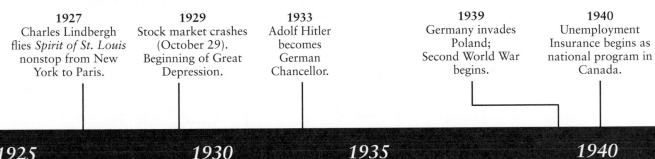

1927
Charles Lindbergh flies *Spirit of St. Louis* nonstop from New York to Paris.

1929
Stock market crashes (October 29). Beginning of Great Depression.

1933
Adolf Hitler becomes German Chancellor.

1939
Germany invades Poland; Second World War begins.

1940
Unemployment Insurance begins as national program in Canada.

1925   1930   1935   1940

1922
The Soviet Union is formed; Joseph Stalin named Secretary General of the Communist Party.

FRIEDRICH AUGUST VON HAYEK *(1899–1992)*

Friedrich von Hayek was born in Vienna and studied at the University of Vienna, where he was trained in the Austrian tradition of economics (a school of thought originating with Carl Menger). He held academic positions at the London School of Economics and the University of Chicago. He returned to Europe in 1962 to the University of Freiburg in what was then West Germany and the University of Salzburg in Austria. He was awarded the Nobel Prize in Economics in 1974.

Hayek contributed new ideas and theories in many different areas of economics, but he is perhaps best known for his general conception of economics as a "coordination problem." His observation of market economies suggested that the relative prices determined in free markets provided the signals that allowed the actions of all decision makers to mesh—even though there was no formal planning taking place to coordinate these actions. He emphasized this "spontaneous order" at work in the economy as the subject matter for economics. The role of knowledge and information in the market process became central to Hayek, an idea that has grown in importance to the economics profession over the years.

Hayek's theory of business cycles provided an example of the breakdown of this coordination. A monetary disturbance (e.g., an increase in the money supply) would distort the signals (relative prices) by artificially raising the return to certain types of economic activity. When the disturbance disappeared, the boom caused by these distorted signals would be followed by a slump. Although Hayek's business-cycle theory was eclipsed by the Keynesian revolution, his emphasis on economics as a coordination problem has had a major influence on contemporary economic thought.

Hayek was also prominent in advocating the virtues of free markets as contributing to human freedom in the broad sense as well as to economic efficiency in the narrow sense. His *The Road to Serfdom* (1944) sounded an alarm about the political and economic implications of the then-growing belief in the virtues of central planning. His *Constitution of Liberty* (1960) is a much deeper philosophical analysis of the forces, economic and otherwise, that contribute to the liberty of the individual.

MILTON FRIEDMAN   *(1912–2006)*

Milton Friedman completed graduate studies in economics at the University of Chicago and at Columbia University, where he received his Ph.D. in 1946. Most of Friedman's academic career was spent as a professor at the University of Chicago, and after retiring in 1977 he was a senior research fellow at the Hoover Institution at Stanford University. Friedman is best known as one of the leading proponents of Monetarism and for his belief in the power of free markets. His work greatly influenced modern macroeconomics.

Friedman made his first significant mark on the profession with the publication of *The Theory of the Consumption Function* in 1957. There he developed the permanent income hypothesis and argued that consumption depends on long-run average income rather than current disposable income, as it does in Keynesian analysis. This was an early example of a macroeconomic theory that emphasized the importance of forward-looking consumers. In 1963, he co-authored with Anna Schwartz his most influential book, *A Monetary History of the United States, 1867–1960,* where they presented evidence in support of the Monetarist view that changes in the supply of money can cause dramatic fluctuations in the level of economic activity. Although this view was seriously challenged by subsequent research, Friedman helped the profession to understand the power of and the limitations of monetary policy.

Capitalism and Freedom (1962) and *Free to Choose* (1980), the latter co-written with his wife, Rose Friedman, are part of Friedman's attempts to communicate his ideas about economics and, in particular, the power of the free market, to a mass audience of noneconomists. Both books became international bestsellers, and these books, in addition to his writing for newspapers and magazines, made Milton Friedman one of the most famous modern economists. He was awarded the Nobel Prize in Economics in 1976.

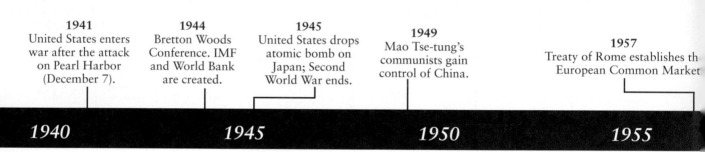

| **1941** | **1944** | **1945** | **1949** | **1957** |
| United States enters war after the attack on Pearl Harbor (December 7). | Bretton Woods Conference. IMF and World Bank are created. | United States drops atomic bomb on Japan; Second World War ends. | Mao Tse-tung's communists gain control of China. | Treaty of Rome establishes th European Common Market |

1940   **1945**   **1950**   **1955**

JOHN KENNETH GALBRAITH   *(1908–2006)*

John Kenneth Galbraith was born on a farm in southeastern Ontario, to a family of Scottish-Canadian farmers. He began his undergraduate education at the Ontario Agricultural College in Guelph in 1926, where he studied agricultural economics and animal husbandry. He moved to California to study at the University of California at Berkeley and completed a Ph.D. in agricultural economics in 1934. Galbraith was hired by Harvard University in 1934 and, aside from his government and diplomatic postings, remained on staff there until his death.

Galbraith was heavily influenced by the ideas of John Maynard Keynes, Thorstein Veblen, and the "institutional" school of economics. He rejected the technical and mathematical approach of Neoclassical economics. Instead he emphasized the interplay of economics, politics, culture, and tradition, a combination that does not lend itself well to mathematical modelling. He was much more of a "political economist" in the style of the nineteenth century than a theoretical economist of the late twentieth century.

His most famous book was *The Affluent Society* (1958), where he argued that the United States had become obsessed with overproducing consumer goods and instead should be making large public investments in highways, education, and other public services. His expression "private opulence and public squalor" became well known, and many would agree is even more relevant today than it was when he wrote the words more than 50 years ago. In a later book, *The New Industrial State* (1967), Galbraith argued that very few U.S. industries fit economists' model of perfect competition, and that the economy was dominated by large, powerful firms. In general, Galbraith continued to write about topics that he believed the economics profession had neglected—topics such as advertising, the separation of corporate ownership and management, oligopoly, and government and military spending.

Because of Galbraith's desire to focus on the interplay of economics, politics, and society, he was often criticized (or ignored) by mainstream economists. But he was undeterred. And while many economists disagreed with his approach and some of his political views, he was widely recognized as a gifted and insightful writer and speaker.

KENNETH ARROW *(b. 1921)*

Kenneth Arrow was born and educated in New York City. He began graduate work at Columbia University and received an M.A. in mathematics in 1941. Over the following 10 years, after Arrow had completed his Ph.D. course work, he served in the U.S. Army Air Corps during World War II and held various research jobs while searching for a dissertation topic. His dissertation, which earned him his Ph.D. from Columbia in 1951, subsequently became a classic in economics, *Social Choice and Individual Values* (1951). Kenneth Arrow is currently professor emeritus at Stanford University.

In his 1951 book, Arrow presented his "Impossibility Theorem," in which he shows that it is not possible to construct a set of voting rules for making public choices that is simultaneously democratic and efficient. This theorem led to decades of work by economists, philosophers, and political scientists in the field of social choice theory.

Arrow also made significant contributions in other areas of economics. In 1954 (with Gerard Debreu) he constructed a mathematical model of an economy with many individual, interrelated markets and proved the existence of a theoretical general market-clearing equilibrium. Arrow's work in the economics of uncertainty was also a major contribution. In *Essays in the Theory of Risk-Bearing* (1971), he introduced the concepts of moral hazard and adverse selection (among other ideas about risk), which we encounter in Chapter 16 of this book. Arrow was one of the first economists to develop the idea of "learning by doing," which has played an important role in modern theories of economic growth.

Arrow was awarded the Nobel Prize in 1972 (jointly with British economist John Hicks) and in 2004 was awarded the National Medal of Science, the United States' highest scientific honour.

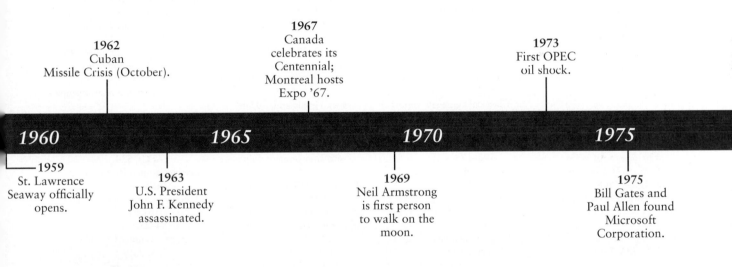

1962
Cuban
Missile Crisis (October).

1967
Canada
celebrates its
Centennial;
Montreal hosts
Expo '67.

1973
First OPEC
oil shock.

1960   **1965**   **1970**   **1975**

1959
St. Lawrence
Seaway officially
opens.

1963
U.S. President
John F. Kennedy
assassinated.

1969
Neil Armstrong
is first person
to walk on the
moon.

1975
Bill Gates and
Paul Allen found
Microsoft
Corporation.

PAUL SAMUELSON *(1915–2009)*

Paul Samuelson was born in Gary, Indiana, the son of a drugstore owner. He received his PhD in economics in 1941 from Harvard University and spent his academic career at the Massachusetts Institute of Technology (MIT).

Samuelson is generally regarded as one of the greatest economic theorists of the twentieth century. While still a graduate student at Harvard, Samuelson wrote most of *Foundations of Economic Analysis* (1947), which was path-breaking at the time and used mathematical analysis and constrained optimization techniques to shed insight into economic behaviour. He systematized economic theory into a more rigorous mathematical discipline, which has had enormous effects on the way economics is studied today.

Though Samuelson made major contributions to many branches of economics, three are particularly notable. First, he showed how the central predictions of demand theory could be tested using the "revealed preferences" of consumers from observed market behaviour. Second, in international trade theory, he made important contributions in the analysis of the gains from trade and the effects of tariff protection on the distribution of income. Third, most familiar to readers of this book, he is credited with introducing the 45°-line model of short-run national income determination. This diagram, encountered throughout Chapters 21 and 22 of this book, has become the standard tool for teaching the Keynesian theory of national-income determination in the short run. Samuelson's work also provided valuable insights in other areas of economics, including government taxation and expenditure, capital theory, and theories of economic growth.

Samuelson was also well known for his famous introductory economics textbook, *Economics*, first published in 1948, which provided a systematic treatment of both micro- and macroeconomics in a way that had not been presented before. In general, he is credited with raising the level of scientific and mathematical analysis in economics. Samuelson was awarded the Nobel Prize in Economics in 1970, and was the first American scholar to receive this honour.

Index

Key terms and their page references are in boldface.

The Growth in World Trade, 1950–2010

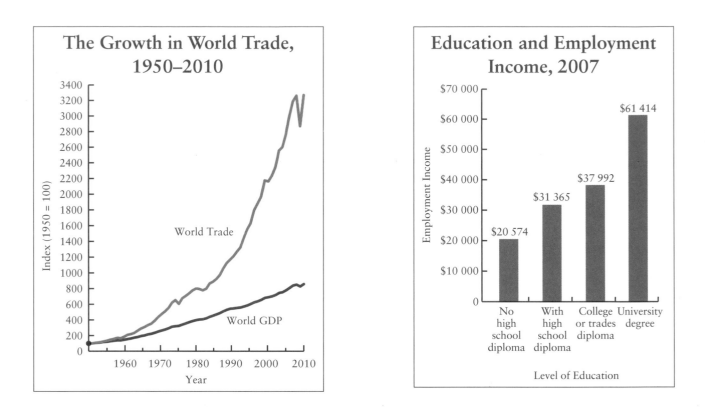

Education and Employment Income, 2007

Inflation and Money Growth Across Many Countries, 1978–2010

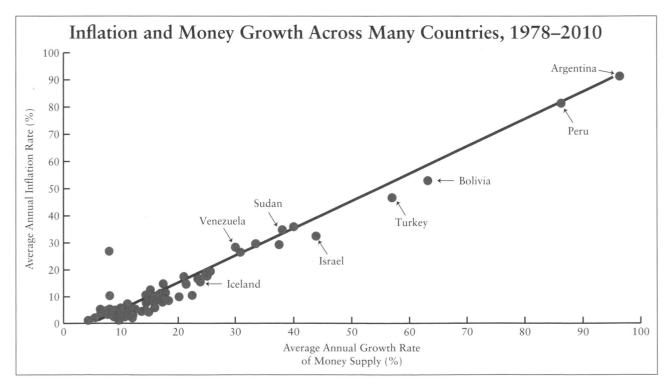